Poetry and Criticism
of the
Romantic Movement

Poetry and Criticism

of the

Romantic Movement

Editors

OSCAR JAMES CAMPBELL

Columbia University

J. F. A. PYRE

Late of the University of Wisconsin

BENNETT WEAVER

University of Michigan

APPLETON-CENTURY-CROFTS, INC.

NEW YORK   LONDON

COPYRIGHT RENEWED, 1960, BY
OSCAR JAMES CAMPBELL, AUGUSTIN PYRE,
JACKMAN PYRE, & BENNETT WEAVER

6106-14

PREFACE

This book purposes to put into the hands of the teacher and the student those materials most useful for the understanding of the literature of the early Nineteenth Century. As valuable as former anthologies have been, they have presented largely the poetry of the period. Not doubting that a peculiar feature of the first quarter of the last century is the crowding together of great poets, we have nevertheless come to feel that a full comprehension of the significance of the era cannot be reached without a study of the prose criticism of the time. Practical experience in the classroom has led us to believe that the presenting of the poetry of Wordsworth or of his contemporaries can be aided distinctly not only by a study of certain documents in which they forwarded their theories of poetry, but also by observing the criticisms which other men passed alike upon their theories and their work. That there is an intrinsic value in the prose criticism of a Coleridge or of a Hazlitt needs no urging.

It is especially in bringing together selected materials from the critical reviews of the time that we hope to add a new usefulness to this book. Few things can make more alive and more real to the mind of the student the literary, the social, the political issues which obtained from 1800 to 1830, than the comparison of the articles written in the *Examiner,* the *Quarterly,* the *Edinburgh,* or the *Blackwood's.* Instead of making reference to the article that, supposedly, snuffed out the life of John Keats, we present Croker's work entire. Instead of accepting in an unqualified way the tradition that the Lyrical Ballads were hailed only with adverse criticism, we print early reviews which give evidence of appreciation as well as those which do not. In this book we hope that the teacher and the student will find materials for that kind of comparative criticism which will make possible a scholarly and satisfying knowledge of the Romantic Movement.

The new emphasis which this volume gives to prose has not kept us from presenting almost all of the best known compositions of the greater poets of the period. Complete poems have been presented, except in the case of works obviously too long. Of this latter sort the editors have included passages extended and representative enough to give a fair impression of the character and scope of the entire work. The introductory essays have been written not with the idea of their forming a history of the development of English poetry during the Nineteenth Century, but to enable the student to place the work of each writer in its proper intellectual environment. The advantages in the use of a collection of this sort instead of a separate volume for each poet are obvious, and in the minds of many teachers outweigh the equally obvious disadvantages.

It is the hope of the editors that this collection will reveal to students the beauties of the individual poets represented; that it will assist them in understanding the critical vitality of these same men and of their contemporaries; and that, by bringing together the work of both poets and prose writers, it may finally aid students in gaining a fuller comprehension of the literature of a significant creative era.

CONTENTS

SIR WALTER SCOTT (1771–1832)

LORD BYRON (1788–1824)

MAJOR CRITICS OF THE ROMANTIC MOVEMENT

WILLIAM HAZLITT (1778–1830)

MAJOR POETS
OF THE
ROMANTIC MOVEMENT

SAMUEL TAYLOR COLERIDGE

THE BEGINNINGS OF THE ROMANTIC MOVEMENT

This collection of poetry begins with the work of the English Romantic Poets, of whom Coleridge and Wordsworth were the first to appear. Coleridge's initial collection was published in 1796 and Wordsworth's first distinctive work appeared in 1798. Their poetry was the fruit of a long period of growth and was different in all its essentials from that of the great classicists of the mid-eighteenth century, such as Alexander Pope. Instead of the polished monotony of the closed couplet, the poets wrote in blank verse, and all sorts of free stanzaic forms. Their subjects were drawn not from the closed and ordered life of man in society, but from a limitless world in which all things were possible to the spirit and will of the individual. In temper the literature was no longer judicial and objective; it was enthusiastic and expressive of the inmost soul of the poet. Indeed the indispensable sign of romanticism is the presence of the author persistently haunting the work of his imagination.

The movement which produced these results began slowly and almost imperceptibly. For a number of years after Pope's death, poets continued to write in his metre, either didactic or satiric verse. The massive Doctor Johnson composed two poems of this general sort: London (1738), and The Vanity of Human Wishes (1749). The first is a specific imitation of Juvenal's satire on the vices of Rome, the equivalent of which he found in London. The second is also pervaded by Juvenal's spirit, but contrives to be a much freer expression of Johnson's severe moral temper. In Blair's The Grave (1743), and Young's Night Thoughts (1742-5), this didacticism was transformed into gloomy moralizing about life, immortality and death—particularly death. These authors, and others like them, are called graveyard poets, because they seek to awaken the emotion appropriate to their solemnity by filling their poems with properties of cemeteries as seen at midnight, such as screech-owls, coffins, epitaphs and worms. Both The Grave and Night Thoughts were written in stately blank-verse. In the work of Gray and Collins, this gloom is lightened. In Gray's Ode on a Distant Prospect of Eton College, (1747) in his Elegy Written in a Country Churchyard, (1751) in Collins's Ode to Evening, and in his Ode on the Passions, (1747) the reflections are interwoven with natural scenery, particularly with the objects to be apprehended on a quiet English evening. The diction of these poets never rises above the formalism of the eighteenth century conventions. Gray's work was marked not so much by an absence of feeling, as by an unfamiliar emotional lucidity, and Collins's odes were distinguished by a sweep and fervor of both imagery and form. Out of didacticism had come revery and half-inarticulate personal feeling.

However, before subjective emotions could become again the heart of poetry, new life had to sweep through it. This began to develop with the appearance of fresh subjects of poetic interest. Poets became aware of the life of a remote and primitive past. Gray translated a song of the Fatal Sisters of Norse mythology and presented the prophetic curse of a frantic Welsh bard. This interest in medieval life was stimulated by the old ballads which appeared in Bishop Percy's Reliques of Ancient English Poetry (1765). These simple narratives invigorated both the style and content of poetry. Chatterton, the marvellous boy poet, who committed suicide in a London garret in 1770 at the age of seventeen, by an act of imagination created a medieval world of his own. He pretended that he had found in a cathedral at Bristol, a number of poems written by Thomas Rowley, a forgotten author of the fifteenth century. These works, ballads of a kind, Chatterton himself composed in a language fabricated to resemble Middle English. In them, the youth displayed great power and versatility in his use of new metrical forms. His genius, mysteriously God-given, his neglect by the cold world and his early lonely death, made him, to the later romanticists, a symbol of the career of the true poet.

Other men than the social creatures living in an urban environment, began to be considered worthy of poetic treatment. Simple persons in a simple world were regarded with tender and pitiful emotion. Goldsmith, in his Deserted Village (1770), described the inhabitants of an Irish town which he used to know, as seen through the mist of his sentimental memory. Shenstone devoted a number of Spenserian stanzas to a half humorous, half affectionate description of a village Schoolmistress (1742). Burns and Crabbe found in peasants the principal source of their poetic power. Crabbe, in The Village (1783) and a number of later works, illustrated with savage realism the wretched and sordid life of the poor folk of a decayed fishing village. Burns was a Scottish peasant himself and in a volume published in 1786, composed largely of poems in the Scotch dialect, presented the life

3

he knew in both grave and hilarious mood. In the *Jolly Beggars* and *Tam O'Shanter*, he reflects the grotesque and ribald in humble Scottish lives; in the *Cotter's Saturday Night*, the idyllic and sturdy. Permeating all this work is his bold spirit, asserting the dignity of the most lowly of mankind. In spite of all distinctions of rank, "a man's a man for a' that." His verse is also hospitable to all sorts of animals from the fields and woods that he knew. His sympathy and pity for them and their hardships becomes often sentimental. Perhaps the most important service which Burns did English poetry was to re-open the vein of lyricism which for years had been unworked. His songs express all the feelings of his own passionate heart in forms as natural and inevitable as the emotions which were poured into them.

The mystic poet, William Blake, in his *Songs of Innocence* (1789) and *Songs of Experience* (1794), wrote similarly of simple things, particularly of animals and of children, in a language and form of almost mannered naïveté. However, he contrived to fill them with poetic passion, in its own way as intense as that of Burns.

Finally these pre-romantic poets began to discover in Nature an inexhaustible source of inspiration. James Thomson, in *The Seasons* (1726–1730), catalogued the various phenomena that appeared in her majestic annual cycle. He wrote in blank-verse, but retained the traditional poetic diction of his time. John Dyer, in his *Fleece* (1757), dwells upon the familiar sights and sounds of the English countryside. William Cowper, in *The Task*, (1785) devoted hundreds of blank-verse lines to chronicling his quiet observation of the objects which he beheld as he looked from his window or walked through the fields and woods which lay near his house. Thomson's observation had been general and an occasion for repeated moralizing; Cowper's was minute, affectionate and justified for its own sake. Dyer also wrote *Grongar Hill* (1725), a description of a journey which he took in Wales. Men of taste began to travel to remote and wild spots and to discover beauty in them. Gray delighted in the Alps and in the Lake district of England, but expressed his joy only in his letters and journals. Gradually, however, the belief grew that lonely communication with natural objects was the surest way to authentic poetic inspiration. James Beattie in his *Minstrel* (1771) represents a poet thus gaining his essential education. In these ways man was being securely placed in Nature, where he was to discover not only the durable satisfactions of his life, but also its essential dignity and meaning.

All of these movements, vital and reformative as they were, could not by themselves have developed the abounding spirit of great romantic poetry. That came only after the stream of English life had been driven to turbulence by the ideas and events of the French Revolution. From France came the notion that the central fact of existence was the individual man and his rights. He was essentially good. The evils of his life and of his situation were due to the perversion of his natural virtue by pestilent social institutions. Accordingly, humanity was to be completely liberated and allowed to remake the world into a fit home for its perfectible nature. Every man was to meet all his fellows as brothers. The boundaries of rank, of social class, even of nation, were to be razed. Indeed, all old restraints were to be hacked down, if necessary, by violence. Then man, using his own feelings as a guide and guardian of his nature, would attain new, undreamed-of felicity. This revolutionary spirit had been faintly suggested in the range of Cowper's social sympathy and in his hatred of oppression of all sorts, and more clearly prefigured in Burns's fierce spirit of individual assertion. It became in later poets, the vital current of their minds and carried them, with all their new interests, into regions of thought and feeling before unexplored and unrealized.

SAMUEL TAYLOR COLERIDGE

1772–1834

Samuel Taylor Coleridge was born on October 21, 1772, at the vicarage of a small village in Devonshire. He was the youngest of the nine sons of Rev. John Coleridge, vicar and head-master of a private boarding-school for boys, and the latest born of his father's thirteen children. From him the poet inherited his absentmindedness and his tendency to vague, unpractical dreams. Coleridge, by his own account, was a precocious and imaginative child. To one of his friends in later life he described his childhood as follows: "Sensibility, imagination, vanity, sloth, and understanding were even then prominent and manifest." He devoured tales of wonder, such as the *Arabian Nights' Entertainment* and lived constantly in a world of fantasy and enchantment. Though this preoccupation with dreams cut him off from normal association with other boys and divorced him almost completely from real experience, Coleridge used to justify it on the ground that it early habituated his mind to the Vast, and taught him to love the Great and the Whole.

When he was just nine years' old, his father died suddenly and a friend obtained him a place in Christ's Hospital School in London. The building had been a monastery and had been transformed into a school, originally for orphan boys, by the orphan King, Edward VI. The boys—there were about seven hundred of them—continued to wear a kind of equivalent of a monk's costume, which made them picturesque figures about the London streets. Coleridge, "the poor friendless boy," there met Charles Lamb and the two established an intimate and lasting friendship "pent mid cloisters dim."

The school was an excellent one, for its day. The Headmaster, the Rev. T. Boyer, though he used to flog the boys incessantly, was a good teacher. In his narrow way, he gave Coleridge training in both scholarship and verse-making of a sensible, pedestrian sort. The master's distaste for flights of the imagination, did not dispel the boy's imperious dreams. It simply deprived them of direction and expression. Coleridge left school neither on leave-days nor during vacations, and the deserted buildings at such times used to emphasize this isolation and drive him as a refuge more deeply into his world of fantasy.

In his wide reading he encountered the Neo-Platonists and became enraptured with their doctrines. Their Christian version of Plato which united God and Beauty in a mystical harmony, kindled his imagination until he reuttered their philosophy to all the boys who would listen, in floods of precocious eloquence. Lamb describes his "deep and sweet intonations" as he unfolded the mysteries of some of the Neo-Platon philosophers until "the walls of the old Grey Friars re-echoed to the accents of the inspired charity boy." This gift of improvisation was to the end of his life a marvel to all who heard. Hazlitt wrote of it enthusiastically: "He talked on forever and you wished him to talk on forever. His genius had . . . angelic wings and fed upon manna." Philosophic and poetic talk remained always the most complete expression of his volatile and ranging mind.

From its first manifestations, Coleridge gave the French Revolution his enthusiastic approval. He wrote an *Ode on the Destruction of the Bastille,* celebrating joyously not only the freedom which this event was to usher into the world of politics, but also into every aspect of life, Poetic, philosophic and even religious thought henceforward was to be utterly free from the restraints of dogma and tradition.

In February, 1791, the poet entered Jesus College at Cambridge. We know little of his career there except that the undergraduates flocked to hear his torrents of talk. Particularly exciting was his ability to repeat whole passages verbatim from radical political pamphlets of the moment. Gradually his interest in his college tasks became desultory, and in a mood of discouragement he suddenly left Cambridge to enlist as a dragoon under the name of Silas Tomkyn Comberbacke. Nothing could have been more unpractical. He could not even curry his mount, much less stick on its back. He was almost immediately appalled at what he had done, revealed his whereabouts to some of his friends, and, with the aid of his brother, procured his discharge and his re-admission to the University.

In June of this year, 1794, he visited Oxford, where he met Southey, then just twenty years old. The two young men found their radical beliefs so much alike that they lost no time in swearing eternal friendship. The idealism of the two was so impatient for immediate practical results that they forthwith decided to establish an ideal co-operative society in America on the banks of the Susquehanna (what poet could resist the spell of this name?) to be called a "Pantisocracy." Twelve gentlemen of education and liberal principles were to embark with their wives the next April to a trans-Atlantic Paradise. One of the first requirements for the execution of the plan was the acquisition of wives. Southey and another enthusiast named Lovell were engaged to sisters named Fricker. What more natural and convenient than that Coleridge should marry a third sister, Sara? He confessed later that at first his addresses to her "were paid from principle and not feelings." She was a woman of no culture and little intelligence, a most unsuitable companion for Coleridge. His intention soon to leave England forever did not prevent him from attacking political and social abuses there. His *Religious Musings,* written at this time, is a scornful answer, in terms of his Neo-Platonic religion of love, to the English political fiction that the war against France had to be prosecuted for the sake of Christianity. He spent more than a year in polishing and revising this poem; but though he occasionally attains in it the "highest sublimity," the general effect of the work is turgid.

In October, 1795, Coleridge married Sara Fricker. His honeymoon he spent at Clevedon on the seashore in a cottage, the kitchen of which he had completely neglected to furnish. From the perfect peace and contentment which he enjoyed there came two or three of his most exquisite poems. One of these was *The Æolian Harp,* which Coleridge pronounced "the most perfect poem I ever wrote."

While the poet was dreaming here, Southey gave up the project of the Pantisocracy, and Coleridge, faced by the prospect of making a living in England, left his bride and went to Bristol to found and edit a liberal newspaper to be called *The Watchman.* In spite of unwonted energy, he gradually alienated most of his one thousand subscribers by delays in publishing and by his indiscriminate attacks on every sort of sanctity. The tenth issue was the last. Fortunately "the bread and cheese question at home" was solved for Coleridge by a wealthy bachelor, Thomas Poole. He invited the poet to live near him in Nether Stowey and in return for his intellectual companionship agreed to subsidize him.

While Coleridge was here at Nether Stowey, his friendship with Wordsworth was founded and eternally cemented. To be near their friend, Dorothy and William moved to Alfoxden. The first result of Wordsworth's influence on Coleridge was to banish from his work some of its turgidity both in form and in content. Coleridge's *Ode to France,* in which he recounts the rise and fall of the hopes of all liberal young Englishmen with the various stages of progress of the French Revolution, shows the clarifying, chastening influence of Wordsworth. The greatest result of this association was *The Lyrical Ballads,* the inception and growth of which is later described. Coleridge's principal contribution to the first edition was *The Ancient Mariner,* his greatest and most characteristic work. It revives in modern minds the ready belief and the sense of wonder and awe which primitive man felt in the presence of the supernatural. Professor Lowes has recently shown the extent of Coleridge's reading in books of travel to strange inaccessible parts of the world before he wrote his poem. As he says, at this time Coleridge's imagination was "playing about the remote horizons of the world." Thence he brought numerous ideas and images which, dropped in the deep well of his subconscious mind, made new and vivid associations there. When the Ancient Mariner's ship sailed forth on desolate seas, these images came forth and gave the vessel and its course an atmosphere of magic and poetic wonder unique in English poetry.

Christabel, begun in the same year 1798 and never finished, is a tale of the bewitching of a lady by a fiend disguised as a damsel in distress. It evokes the mystery and romance of the forest almost as potently as *The Ancient Mariner* does that of the Sea.

Coleridge began taking opium as a cure for rheumatism. He contracted the habit by following bad medical advice. A dose of opium induced in him a deep sleep which lasted two or three hours. In it he was visited by dreams both delicious and tormenting. *Kubla Khan* was a product of these opium visions and the store-house of gorgeous images which formed the fabric of *The Ancient Mariner.* After reading an account of a palace belonging to the medieval Tartar Kubla Khan, he fell asleep. Then the images from the book and those spun from his half-forgotten reading in the marvellous all became engulfed in the supernatural sweetness of his opium dream. When he awoke, he began to write; but when he had completed but fifty-four lines of his poem, a person from Porlock interrupted him; and when he left, the vision splendid had faded completely. The work therefore remains a fragment,—the inchoate stuff of poetry. For this reason, many regard it as Coleridge's most characteristic achievement.

The publication of *The Lyrical Ballads* marks the end of an epoch in Coleridge's life. Never did he produce supreme poetry after the termination of his happy association with Wordsworth at Stowey. He accompanied his friend and his sister Dorothy to Germany, but left them so that he might participate enthusiastically in German life. He associated with every sort of German person, read German ballads, the German poets and the German philosophers. The chief poetic result of this sojourn was a translation of the last two parts of Schiller's dramatic trilogy *Wallenstein.*

In 1800 Coleridge took a house at Keswick, a town in the Lake District about twelve miles from Grasmere. At first he was very happy there, but his rheumatism returned and with it his addiction to opium. He became incapable of steady work. All his activity became abnormally desultory and dawdling. Estrangement from his uncongenial wife developed. Worst of all, his creative imagination suffered total eclipse. In his *Dejection: an Ode* he voices the bitter distress over his realization that this, the most prized of his spiritual possessions, had disappeared. About the same time in *The Pains of Sleep,* he writes

a despairing equivalent of *Kubla Khan.* In it he describes the horror that his opium dreams had become.

Coleridge had long believed that a sojourn in some warm climate would perhaps cure his rheumatism. In April 1804, therefore, he sailed for Malta, where he stayed for a year. But he failed to accomplish the great object of his visit. The English colony, composed largely of consumptives, was very depressing. Nothing that he heard or saw aroused in him the slightest impulse toward poetry. His return to England by way of Italy did yield some excitement. When Napoleon learned that he was in Rome, he ordered his arrest as punishment for some violent articles against him which Coleridge had contributed to *The Morning Post* years before. He escaped on an American vessel, disguised as a steward. He reached home in August, 1806, very little improved in body or in spirit. Lamb whimsically described his appearance as that of "an archangel, a little damaged."

He naturally went to visit Wordsworth almost immediately. On this occasion his friend read or recited to him *The Prelude,* a poem written for Coleridge and addressed to him. The latter was so much moved by the work and its power that he wrote a touching poetic response called *To William Wordsworth.* The presence of his friend and the inspiration of his poetry were at this time the only forces which could reawaken Coleridge's artistic powers.

For a number of years after this date, 1806, his life was hopelessly futile and aimless. He seemed devoid of mental or moral responsibility. Finally in 1810 a certain John Morgan and his wife took the poet to live with them in London. They threw away his opiates, invited his old friends to visit him and provided him with stimulating books. Under this treatment he gradually recovered his self-respect and his intellectual energy. In 1816 the Morgans' finances became so much reduced that they could not afford to have Coleridge with them longer. Then his physician induced Dr. Gillman and his wife to take him in, and with these cultivated charming people he spent the last eighteen years of his life. He died in 1834.

The work produced in his later years was almost exclusively philosophy and criticism. It appeared in his second magazine *The Friend,* 1809–1810, in his lectures on Shakespeare and on the *Principles of Poetry* and in his *Biographia Literaria.* This last book was a kind of prose equivalent of Wordsworth's *Prelude.* It is a history of the development not of Coleridge's poetical powers, but of his critical principles and critical intelligence. The final works in which his point of view was expressed were his *Lay Sermons* and his *Aids to Reflection.*

In these works he applied principles of subjectivity and intuition to literature and to religion. A separate faculty, a kind of transcendental insight which acquaints a critic with invisible and spiritual realities, became the central fact in all his criticism. In liberating this faculty he carried romantic thinking into areas of life as yet unfamiliar to it. His influence was strong far into the nineteenth century, during which he continued to be in many aspects of thought the emancipator of the imagination.

SELECTED BIBLIOGRAPHY

TEXTS

The Poetical Works, Globe Edition, ed. with a biography by J. Dykes Campbell. 1 Vol., 1909.
The standard one Volume edition.
Letters, ed. by Hartley Coleridge, 2 Vols. 1895.
Biographia Libraria, ed. with an introduction by H. N. Coleridge and his wife Sara Coleridge, 2 Vols., 1847.

CRITICAL WORKS

Campbell, J. Dykes, *Samuel Taylor Coleridge,* a narrative of the events of his life, 1896.
A sound and authoritative book.
Fausset, Hugh I'Anson, *Samuel Taylor Coleridge,* 1926.
An interesting attempt to interpret the poems in the light of the author's disturbed inner life.
Lowes, John Livingston, *The Road to Xanadu,* a study in the ways of the imagination, 1927.
A fascinating study of the manner in which Coleridge's reading became transmuted into poetry.

TO THE AUTHOR OF 'THE ROBBERS'

SCHILLER! that hour I would have wish'd to die.
If through the shuddering midnight I had sent
From the dark dungeon of the Tower timerent
That fearful voice, a famish'd Father's cry—
Lest in some after moment aught more mean
Might stamp me mortal! A triumphant shout
Black Horror scream'd, and all her *goblin* rout
Diminish'd shrunk from the more withering scene!
Ah! Bard tremendous in sublimity!
Could I behold thee in thy loftier mood   10
Wandering at eve with finely-frenzied eye
Beneath some vast old tempest-swinging wood!
Awhile with mute awe gazing I would brood:
Then weep aloud in a wild ecstasy!

TO A YOUNG ASS

ITS MOTHER BEING TETHERED NEAR IT

POOR little Foal of an oppressèd race!
I love the languid patience of thy face:
And oft with gentle hand I give thee bread,
And clap thy ragged coat, and pat thy head.
But what thy dulléd spirits hath dismay'd,
That never thou dost sport along the glade?

And (most unlike the nature of things young)
That earthward still thy moveless head is hung?
Do thy prophetic fears anticipate,
Meek Child of Misery! thy future fate?   10
The starving meal, and all the thousand aches
'Which patient Merit of the Unworthy takes'?
Or is thy sad heart thrill'd with filial pain

To see thy wretched mother's shorten'd chain?
And truly, very piteous is *her* lot—
Chain'd to a log within a narrow spot,
Where the close-eaten grass is scarcely seen,
While sweet around her waves the tempting green!

Poor Ass! thy master should have learnt to show
Pity—best taught by fellowship of Woe!   20
For much I fear me that *He* lives like thee,
Half famish'd in a land of Luxury!
How *askingly* its footsteps hither bend?
It seems to say, 'And have I then *one* friend?'
Innocent foal! thou poor despis'd forlorn!
I hail thee *Brother*—spite of the fool's scorn!
And fain would take thee with me, in the Dell
Of Peace and mild Equality to dwell,
Where Toil shall call the charmer Health his bride,
And Laughter tickle Plenty's ribless side!   30

How thou wouldst toss thy heels in gamesome play,
And frisk about, as lamb or kitten gay!
Yea! and more musically sweet to me
Thy dissonant harsh bray of joy would be,
Than warbled melodies that soothe to rest
The aching of pale Fashion's vacant breast!

THE EOLIAN HARP

COMPOSED AT CLEVEDON, SOMERSETSHIRE

MY pensive Sara! thy soft cheek reclined
Thus on mine arm, most soothing sweet it is
To sit beside our Cot, our Cot o'ergrown

With white-flower'd Jasmin, and broad-leav'd
   Myrtle,
(Meet emblems they of Innocence and Love!)
And watch the clouds, that late were rich
   with light,
Slow saddening round, and mark the star of
   eve
Serenely brilliant (such should Wisdom be)
Shine opposite! How exquisite the scents
Snatch'd from yon bean-field! and the world
   so hush'd!   10
The stilly murmur of the distant Sea
Tells us of silence.
              And that simplest Lute,
Placed length-ways in the clasping casement,
   hark!

How by the desultory breeze caress'd,
Like some coy maid half yielding to her lover,
It pours such sweet upbraiding, as must needs
Tempt to repeat the wrong! And now, its
   strings
Boldlier swept, the long sequacious notes
Over delicious surges sink and rise,
Such a soft floating witchery of sound   20
As twilight Elfins make, when they at eve
Voyage on gentle gales from Fairy-Land,
Where Melodies round honey-dropping flowers,
Footless and wild, like birds of Paradise,
Nor pause, nor perch, hovering on untam'd
   wing!
O! the one Life within us and abroad,
Which meets all motion and becomes its soul,
A light in sound, a sound-like power in light,
Rhythm in all thought, and joyance every
   where—
Methinks, it should have been impossible   30
Not to love all things in a world so fill'd;
Where the breeze warbles, and the mute still
   air
Is Music slumbering on her instrument.

And thus, my Love! as on the midway slope
Of yonder hill I stretch my limbs at noon,
Whilst through my half-clos'd eye-lids I be-
   hold
The sunbeams dance, like diamonds, on the
   main,
And tranquil muse upon tranquillity;
Full many a thought uncall'd and undetain'd,
And many idle flitting phantasies,   40
Traverse my indolent and passive brain,
As wild and various as the random gales

That swell and flutter on this subject Lute!
And what if all of animated nature
Be but organic Harps diversely fram'd,
That tremble into thought, as o'er them
   sweeps
Plastic and vast, one intellectual breeze,
At once the Soul of each, and God of all?
But thy more serious eye a mild reproof
Darts, O belovéd Woman! nor such thoughts 50
Dim and unhallow'd dost thou not reject,
And biddest me walk humbly with my God.
Meek Daughter in the family of Christ!
Well hast thou said and holily disprais'd
These shapings of the unregenerate mind;
Bubbles that glitter as they rise and break
On vain Philosophy's aye-babbling spring.
For never guiltless may I speak of him,
The Incomprehensible! save when with awe
I praise him, and with Faith that only
   feels;   60
Who with his saving mercies healéd me,
A sinful and most miserable man,
Wilder'd and dark, and gave me to possess
Peace, and this Cot, and thee, heart-honour'd
   Maid!

REFLECTIONS ON HAVING LEFT
A PLACE OF RETIREMENT

Sermoni propriora.—HOR.

Low was our pretty Cot: our tallest Rose
Peep'd at the chamber-window. We could
   hear
At silent noon, and eve, and early morn,
The Sea's faint murmur. In the open air
Our Myrtles blossom'd; and across the porch
Thick Jasmins twined: the little landscape
   round
Was green and woody, and refresh'd the eye.
It was a spot which you might aptly call
The Valley of Seclusion! Once I saw
(Hallowing his Sabbath-day by quietness) 10
A wealthy son of Commerce saunter by,
Bristowa's citizen: methought, it calm'd
His thirst of idle gold, and made him muse
With wiser feelings: for he paus'd, and look'd
With a pleas'd sadness, and gaz'd all around,
Then eyed our Cottage, and gaz'd round again,
And sigh'd, and said, it was a Blesséd Place.
And we *were* bless'd. Oft with patient ear
Long-listening to the viewless sky-lark's note
(Viewless, or haply for a moment seen   20
Gleaming on sunny wings) in whisper'd tones

I've said to my Belovéd, 'Such, sweet Girl!
The inobtrusive song of Happiness,
Unearthly minstrelsy! then only heard
When the Soul seeks to hear; when all is
 hush'd,
And the Heart listens!'

        But the time, when first
From that low Dell, steep up the stony Mount
I climb'd with perilous toil and reach'd the top,
Oh! what a goodly scene! *Here* the bleak
 mount,
The bare bleak mountain speckled thin with
 sheep;   30
Grey clouds, that shadowing spot the sunny
 fields;
And river, now with bushy rocks o'er-brow'd,
Now winding bright and full, with naked
 banks;
And seats, and lawns, the Abbey and the
 wood,
And cots, and hamlets, and faint city-spire;
The Channel *there,* the Islands and white sails,
Dim coasts, and cloud-like hills, and shoreless
 Ocean—
It seem'd like Omnipresence! God, methought,
Had built him there a Temple: the whole
 World
Seem'd *imag'd* in its vast circumference: 40
No *wish* profan'd my overwhelméd heart.

Blest hour! It was a luxury,—to be!
Ah! quiet Dell! dear Cot, and Mount sub-
 lime!
I was constrain'd to quit you. Was it right,
While my unnumber'd brethren toil'd and bled,
That I should dream away the entrusted hours
On rose-leaf beds, pampering the coward heart
With feelings all too delicate for use?
Sweet is the tear that from some Howard's
 eye
Drops on the cheek of one he lifts from
 earth: 50
And he that works me good with unmov'd
 face,
Does it but half: he chills me while he aids,
My benefactor, not my brother man!
Yet even this, this cold beneficence
Praise, praise it, O my Soul! oft as thou
 scann'st
The sluggard Pity's vision-weaving tribe!
Who sigh for Wretchedness, yet shun the
 Wretched,
Nursing in some delicious solitude

Their slothful loves and dainty sympathies!
I therefore go, and join head, heart, and
 hand,   60
Active and firm, to fight the bloodless fight
Of Science, Freedom, and the Truth in Christ.

Yet oft when after honourable toil
Rests the tir'd mind, and waking loves **to**
 dream,
My spirit shall revisit thee, dear Cot!
Thy Jasmin and thy window-peeping Rose,
And Myrtles fearless of the mild sea-air.
And I shall sigh fond wishes—sweet Abode!
Ah!—had none greater! And that all had
 such!
It might be so—but the time is not yet 70
Speed it, O Father! Let thy Kingdom come!

ODE TO THE DEPARTING YEAR

           Ἰοὺ ἰού, ὢ ὢ κακά.
Ὑπ' αὖ με δεινὸς ὀρθομαντείας πόνος
Στροβεῖ, ταράσσων φροιμίοις δυσφροιμίοις.
  ·   ·   ·   ·
Τὸ μέλλον ἥξει. Καὶ σύ μ' ἐν τάχει παρὼν
Ἄγαν ἀληθόμαντιν οἰκτείρας ἐρεῖς
    Aeschyl. *Agam.* 1773–75; 1199–1200.

ARGUMENT

    The Ode commences with an address to the Divine
Providence that regulates into one vast harmony all the
events of time, however calamitous some of them may
appear to mortals. The second Strophe calls on men
to suspend their private joys and sorrows, and devote them for a while to the cause of human nature
in general. The first Epode speaks of the Empress of
Russia, who died of an apoplexy on the 17th of November 1796; having just concluded a subsidiary
treaty with the Kings combined against France. The
first and second Antistrophe describe the Image of
the Departing Year, etc., as in a vision. The second
Epode prophesies, in anguish of spirit, the downfall
of this country.

I

SPIRIT who sweepest the wild Harp of Time!
  It is most hard, with an untroubled ear
  Thy dark inwoven harmonies to hear!
Yet, mine eye fix'd on Heaven's unchanging
 clime
Long had I listen'd, free from mortal fear,
  With inward stillness, and a bowéd mind;
  When lo! its folds far waving on the wind,
I saw the train of the Departing Year!
  Starting from my silent sadness
  Then with no unholy madness, 10
Ere yet the enter'd cloud foreclos'd my sight,
I rais'd the impetuous song, and solemnis'd
 his flight.

II

Hither, from the recent tomb,
From the prison's direr gloom,
From Distemper's midnight anguish;
And thence, where Poverty doth waste and
languish;
Or where, his two bright torches blending,
Love illumine Manhood's maze;
Or where o'er cradled infants bending,
Hope has fix'd her wishful gaze;   20
Hither, in perplexéd dance,
Ye Woes! ye young-eyed Joys! advance!
By Times's wild harp, and by the hand
Whose indefatigable sweep
Raises its fateful strings from sleep,
I bid you haste, a mix'd tumultuous band!
From every private bower,
And each domestic hearth,
Haste for one solemn hour;
And with a loud and yet a louder voice, 30
O'er Nature struggling in portentous birth,
Weep and rejoice!
Still echoes the dread Name that o'er the
earth
Let slip the storm, and woke the brood of
Hell:
And now advance in saintly Jubilee
Justice and Truth! They too have heard thy
Spell,
They too obey thy name, divinest
Liberty!

III

I mark'd Ambition in his war-array!
I heard the mailéd Monarch's troublous
cry—
'Ah! wherefore does the Northern Conqueress
stay!   40
Groans not her chariot on its onward way?'
Fly, mailéd Monarch, fly!
Stunn'd by Death's twice mortal mace,
No more on Murder's lurid face
The insatiate Hag shall gloat with drunken
eye!
Manes of the unnumber'd slain!
Ye that gasp'd on Warsaw's plain!
Ye that erst at Ismail's tower,
When human ruin choked the streams,
Fell in Conquest's glutted hour,   50
Mid women's shrieks and infants' screams!
Spirits of the uncoffin'd slain,

Sudden blasts of triumph swelling,
Oft, at night, in misty train,
Rush around her narrow dwelling!
The exterminating Fiend is fled—
(Foul her life, and dark her doom)
Mighty armies of the dead
Dance, like death-fires, round her tomb!
Then with prophetic song relate,   60
Each some Tyrant-Murderer's fate!

IV

Departing Year! 'twas on no earthly shore
My soul beheld thy Vision! Where alone,
Voiceless and stern, before the cloudy
throne,
Aye Memory sits: thy robe inscrib'd with
gore,
With many an unimaginable groan
Thou storied'st thy sad hours! Silence en-
sued,
Deep silence o'er the ethereal multitude,
Whose locks with wreaths, whose wreaths with
glories shone.
Then, his eye wild ardours glancing,   70
From the choiréd gods advancing,
The Spirit of the Earth made reverence meet,
And stood up, beautiful, before the cloudy
seat.

V

Throughout the blissful throng,
Hush'd were harp and song:
Till wheeling round the throne the Lampads
seven,
(The mystic Words of Heaven)
Permissive signal make:
The fervent Spirit bow'd, then spread his
wings and spake!
'Thou in stormy blackness throning   80
Love and uncreated Light,
By the Earth's unsolaced groaning,
Seize thy terrors, Arm of might!
By Peace with proffer'd insult scared,
Masked Hate and envying Scorn!
By years of Havoc yet unborn!
And Hunger's bosom to the frost-winds bared!
But chief by Afric's wrongs,
Strange, horrible, and foul!
By what deep guilt belongs   90
To the deaf Synod, 'full of gifts and lies!'

By Wealth's insensate laugh! by Torture's
    howl!
        Avenger, rise!
For ever shall the thankless Island scowl,
  Her quiver full, and with unbroken bow?
Speak! from thy storm-black Heaven O speak
    aloud!
      And on the darkling foe
Open thine eye of fire from some uncertain
    cloud!
  O dart the flash! O rise and deal the blow!
The Past to thee, to thee the Future cries! 100
  Hark! how wide Nature joins her groans
    below!
    Rise, God of Nature! rise.'

VI

The voice had ceas'd, the Vision fled;
Yet still I gasp'd and reel'd with dread.
And ever, when the dream of night
Renews the phantom to my sight,
Cold sweat-drops gather on my limbs,
  My ears throb hot; my eye-balls start;
My brain with horrid tumult swims;
  Wild is the tempest of my heart;   110
And my thick and struggling breath
Imitates the toil of death!
No stranger agony confounds
  The Soldier on the war-field spread,
When all foredone with toil and wounds,
  Death-like he dozes among heaps of dead!
(The strife is o'er, the day-light fled,
  And the night-wind clamours hoarse!
See! the starting wretch's head
  Lies pillow'd on a brother's corse!)   120

VII

Not yet enslaved, not wholly vile,
O Albion! O my mother Isle!
Thy valleys, fair as Eden's bowers
Glitter green with sunny showers;
Thy grassy uplands' gentle swells
  Echo to the bleat of flocks;
(Those grassy hills, those glittering dells
  Proudly ramparted with rocks)
And Ocean mid his uproar wild
  Speaks safety to his Island-child!   130
  Hence for many a fearless age
  Has social Quiet lov'd thy shore;
  Nor ever proud Invader's rage
Or sack'd thy towers, or stain'd thy fields with
  gore.

VIII

Abandon'd of Heaven! mad Avarice thy
    guide,
At cowardly distance, yet kindling with
    pride—
Mid thy herds and thy corn-fields secure thou
    hast stood,
And join'd the wild yelling of Famine and
    Blood!
The nations curse thee! They with eager won-
    dering
  Shall hear Destruction, like a vulture,
    scream!   140
  Strange-eyed Destruction! who with many
    a dream
Of central fires through nether seas up-thun-
    dering
Soothes her fierce solitude; yet as she lies
  By livid fount, or red volcanic stream,
  If ever to her lidless dragon-eyes,
  O Albion! thy predestin'd ruins rise,
The fiend-hag on her perilous couch doth
    leap,
Muttering distemper'd triumph in her charméd
    sleep.

IX

    Away, my soul, away!
  In vain, in vain the Birds of warning
    sing—   150
And hark! I hear the famish'd brood of prey
Flap their lank pennons on the groaning wind!
    Away, my soul, away!
I unpartaking of the evil thing,
  With daily prayer and daily toil
  Soliciting for food my scanty soil,
  Have wail'd my country with a loud
    Lament.
Now I recentre my immortal mind
  In the deep Sabbath of meek self-content;
Cleans'd from the vaporous passions that be-
    dim   160
God's Image, sister of the Seraphim.

THIS LIME-TREE BOWER MY PRISON

ADDRESSED TO CHARLES LAMB, OF THE
INDIA HOUSE, LONDON

In the June of 1797 some long-expected friends
paid a visit to the author's cottage; and on the
morning of their arrival, he met with an accident,

which disabled him from walking during the whole time of their stay. One evening, when they had left him for a few hours, he composed the following lines in the garden-bower.

WELL, they are gone, and here must I remain,
This lime-tree bower my prison! I have lost
Beauties and feelings, such as would have been
Most sweet to my remembrance even when age
Had dimm'd mine eyes to blindness! They, meanwhile,
Friends, whom I never more may meet again,
On springy heath, along the hill-top edge,
Wander in gladness, and wind down, perchance,
To that still roaring dell, of which I told;
The roaring dell, o'erwooded, narrow, deep, 10
And only speckled by the mid-day sun;
Where its slim trunk the ash from rock to rock
Flings arching like a bridge;—that branchless ash,
Unsunn'd and damp, whose few poor yellow leaves
Ne'er tremble in the gale, yet tremble still,
Fann'd by the water-fall! and there my friends
Behold the dark green file of long lank weeds,
That all at once (a most fantastic sight!)
Still nod and drip beneath the dripping edge
Of the blue clay-stone.
                    Now, my friends emerge 20
Beneath the wide wide Heaven—and view again
The many-steepled tract magnificent
Of hilly fields and meadows, and the sea,
With some fair bark, perhaps, whose sails light up
The slip of smooth clear blue betwixt two Isles
Of purple shadow! Yes! they wander on
In gladness all; but thou, methinks, most glad,
My gentle-hearted Charles! for thou hast pined
And hunger'd after Nature, many a year,
In the great City pent, winning thy way 30
With sad yet patient soul, through evil and pain
And strange calamity! Ah! slowly sink
Behind the western ridge, thou glorious Sun!
Shine in the slant beams of the sinking orb,
Ye purple heath-flowers! richlier burn, ye clouds!
Live in the yellow light, ye distant groves!
And kindle, thou blue Ocean! So my friend

Struck with deep joy may stand, as I have stood,
Silent with swimming sense; yea, gazing round
On the wide landscape, gaze till all doth seem 40
Less gross than bodily; and of such hues
As veil the Almighty Spirit, when yet he makes
Spirits perceive his presence.

                              A delight
Comes sudden on my heart, and I am glad
As I myself were there! Nor in this bower,
This little lime-tree bower, have I not mark'd
Much that has sooth'd me. Pale beneath the blaze
Hung the transparent foliage; and I watch'd
Some broad and sunny leaf, and lov'd to see
The shadow of the leaf and stem above 50
Dappling its sunshine! And that walnut-tree
Was richly ting'd, and a deep radiance lay
Full on the ancient ivy, which usurps
Those fronting elms, and now, with blackest mass
Makes their dark branches gleam a lighter hue
Through the late twilight: and though now the bat
Wheels silent by, and not a swallow twitters,
Yet still the solitary humble-bee
Sings in the bean-flower! Henceforth I shall know
That Nature ne'er deserts the wise and pure; 60
No plot so narrow, be but Nature there,
No waste so vacant, but may well employ
Each faculty of sense, and keep the heart
Awake to Love and Beauty! and sometimes
'Tis well to be bereft of promis'd good,
That we may lift the soul, and contemplate
With lively joy the joys we cannot share.
My gentle-hearted Charles! when the last rook
Beat its straight path along the dusky air
Homewards, I blest it! deeming its black wing 70
(Now a dim speck, now vanishing in light)
Had cross'd the mighty Orb's dilated glory,
While thou stood'st gazing; or, when all was still,
Flew creeking o'er thy head, and had a charm
For thee, my gentle-hearted Charles, to whom
No sound is dissonant which tells of Life.

THE RIME OF THE ANCIENT MARINER

IN SEVEN PARTS

Facile credo, plures esse Naturas invisibles quam
visibiles in rerum universitate. Sed horum omnium
familiam quis nobis enarrabit?? et gradus et cogna-
tiones et discrimina et singulorum munera? Quid
agunt? quae loca habitant? Harum rerum notitiam
semper ambivit ingenium humanum, nunquam attigit.
Juvat, interea, non diffiteor, quandoque in animo,
tanquam in tabula, majoris et melioris mundi
imaginem contemplari: ne mens assuefacta hodiernae
vitae minutiis se contrahat nimis, et tota subsidat
in pusillas cogitationes. Sed veritati interea in
vigilandum est, modusque servandus, ut certa ab in-
certis, diem a nocte, distinguamus—T. Burnet,
Archaeol. Phil. P. 68.

ARGUMENT

How a Ship having passed the Line was driven by
storms to the cold Country towards the South Pole;
and how from thence she made her course to the
tropical Latitude of the Great Pacific Ocean; and of
the strange things that befell; and in what manner
the Ancyent Marinere came back to his own
Country. [*L. B.* 1798.]

PART I

It is an ancient Mariner,
And he stoppeth one of three.
'By thy long grey beard and glittering eye,
Now wherefore stopp'st thou me?

The Bridegroom's doors are opened wide,
And I am next of kin;
The guests are met, the feast is set:
May'st hear the merry din.'

He holds him with his skinny hand,
'There was a ship,' quoth he.   10
'Hold off! unhand me, grey-beard loon!'
Eftsoons his hand dropt he.

He holds him with his glittering eye—
The Wedding-Guest stood still,
And listens like a three years' child:
The Mariner hath his will.

The Wedding-Guest sat on a stone:
He cannot choose but hear;
And thus spake on that ancient man,
The bright-eyed Mariner.   20

'The ship was cheered, the harbour cleared,
Merrily did we drop
Below the kirk, below the hill,
Below the lighthouse top.

The Sun came up upon the left,
Out of the sea came he!
And he shone bright, and on the right
Went down into the sea.

Higher and higher every day,
Till over the mast at noon—'   30
The Wedding-Guest here beat his breast,
For he heard the loud bassoon.

The bride hath paced into the hall,
Red as a rose is she;
Nodding their heads before her goes
The merry minstrelsy.

The Wedding-Guest he beat his breast,
Yet he cannot choose but hear;
And thus spake on that ancient man,
The bright-eyed Mariner.   40

'And now the STORM-BLAST came, and he
Was tyrannous and strong:
He struck with his o'ertaking wings,
And chased us south along.

With sloping masts and dipping prow,
As who pursued with yell and blow
Still treads the shadow of his foe,
And forward bends his head,
The ship drove fast, loud roared the blast,
And southward aye we fled.   50

And now there came both mist and snow,
And it grew wondrous cold:
And ice, mast-high, came floating by,
As green as emerald.

And through the drifts the snowy clifts
Did send a dismal sheen:
Nor shapes of men nor beasts we ken—
The ice was all between.

The ice was here, the ice was there,
The ice was all around: 60
It cracked and growled, and roared and
howled,
Like noises in a swound!

At length did cross an Albatross,
Through the fog it came;
As if it had been a Christian soul,
We hailed it in God's name.

It ate the food it ne'er had eat,
And round and round it flew.
The ice did split with a thunder-fit;
The helmsman steered us through!   70

And a good south wind sprung up behind;
The Albatross did follow,
And every day, for food or play,
Came to the mariner's hollo!

In mist or cloud, on mast or shroud,
It perched for vespers nine;
Whiles all the night, through fog-smoke white,
Glimmered the white Moon-shine.'

'God save thee, ancient Mariner!
From the fiends, that plague thee thus!— 80
Why look'st thou so?'—With my cross-bow
I shot the ALBATROSS.

PART II

The Sun now rose upon the right:
Out of the sea came he,
Still hid in mist, and on the left
Went down into the sea.

And the good south wind still blew behind,
But no sweet bird did follow,
Nor any day for food or play
Came to the mariners' hollo!   90

And I had done a hellish thing,
And it would work 'em woe:
For all averred, I had killed the bird
That made the breeze to blow.
Ah wretch! said they, the bird to slay,
That made the breeze to blow!

Nor dim nor red, like God's own head,
The glorious Sun uprist:
Then all averred, I had killed the bird
That brought the fog and mist.   100
'Twas right, said they, such birds to slay.
That bring the fog and mist.

The fair breeze blew, the white foam flew,
The furrow followed free;
We were the first that ever burst
Into that silent sea.

Down dropt the breeze, the sails dropt down,
'Twas sad as sad could be;
And we did speak only to break
The silence of the sea!   110

All in a hot and copper sky,
The bloody Sun, at noon,
Right up above the mast did stand,
No bigger than the Moon.

Day after day, day after day,
We stuck, nor breath nor motion;
As idle as a painted ship
Upon a painted ocean.

Water, water, every where,
And all the boards did shrink;   120
Water, water every where,
Nor any drop to drink.

The very deep did rot: O Christ!
That ever this should be!
Yea, slimy things did crawl with legs
Upon the slimy sea.

About, about, in reel and rout
The death-fires danced at night;
The water, like a witch's oils,
Burnt green, and blue and white.   130

And some in dreams assuréd were
Of the Spirit that plagued us so;
Nine fathom deep he had followed us
From the land of mist and snow.

And every tongue, through utter drought,
Was withered at the root;
We could not speak, no more than if
We had been choked with soot.

Ah! well a-day! what evil looks
Had I from old and young!   140
Instead of the cross, the Albatross
About my neck was hung.

PART III

There passed a weary time. Each throat
Was parched, and glazed each eye.
A weary time! a weary time!
How glazed each weary eye,
When looking westward, I beheld
A something in the sky.

At first it seemed a little speck,
And then it seemed a mist;   150
It moved and moved, and took at last
A certain shape, I wist.

A speck, a mist, a shape, I wist!
And still it neared and neared:
As if it dodged a water-sprite,
It plunged and tacked and veered.

With throats unslaked, with black lips baked,
We could nor laugh nor wail;
Through utter drought all dumb we stood!
I bit my arm, I sucked the blood,   160
And cried, A sail! a sail!

With throats unslaked, with black lips baked,
Agape they heard me call:
Gramercy! they for joy did grin,
And all at once their breath drew in,
As they were drinking all.

See! see! (I cried) she tacks no more!
Hither to work us weal;
Without a breeze, without a tide,
She steadies with upright keel!   170

The western wave was all a-flame.
The day was well nigh done!
Almost upon the western wave
Rested the broad bright Sun;
When that strange shape drove suddenly
Betwixt us and the Sun.

And straight the Sun was flecked with bars,
(Heaven's Mother send us grace!)
As if through a dungeon-grate he peered
With broad and burning face.   180

Alas! (thought I, and my heart beat loud)
How fast she nears and nears!
Are those *her* sails that glance in the Sun,
Like restless gossameres?

Are those *her* ribs through which the Sun
Did peer, as through a grate?
And is that Woman all her crew?
Is that a DEATH? and are there two?
Is DEATH that woman's mate?

Her lips were red, *her* looks were free,   190
Her locks were yellow as gold:
Her skin was as white as leprosy,
The Night-mare LIFE-IN-DEATH was she,
Who thicks man's blood with cold.

The naked hulk alongside came,
And the twain were casting dice;
'The game is done! I've won! I've won!'
Quoth she, and whistles thrice.

The Sun's rim dips; the stars rush out:
At one stride comes the dark;   200
With far-heard whisper, o'er the sea,
Off shot the spectre-bark.

We listened and looked sideways up!
Fear at my heart, as at a cup,
My life-blood seemed to sip!
The stars were dim, and thick the night,
The steersman's face by his lamp gleamed
     white;

From the sails the dew did drip—
Till clomb above the eastern bar
The hornéd Moon, with one bright star   210
Within the nether tip.

One after one, by the star-dogged Moon,
Too quick for groan or sigh,
Each turned his face with a ghastly pang,
And cursed me with his eye.

Four times fifty living men,
(And I heard nor sigh nor groan)
With heavy thump, a lifeless lump,
They dropped down one by one.

The souls did from their bodies fly,—   220
They fled to bliss or woe!
And every soul, it passed me by,
Like the whizz of my cross-bow!

PART IV

'I fear thee, ancient Mariner!
I fear thy skinny hand!
And thou art long, and lank, and brown,
As is the ribbed sea-sand.

I fear thee and thy glittering eye,
And thy skinny hand, so brown.'—
Fear not, fear not, thou Wedding-Guest!   230
This body dropt not down.

Alone, alone, all, all alone,
Alone on a wide wide sea!
And never a saint took pity on
My soul in agony.

The many men, so beautiful!
And they all dead did lie:
And a thousand thousand slimy things
Lived on; and so did I.

I looked upon the rotting sea,   240
And drew my eyes away;
I looked upon the rotting deck,
And there the dead men lay.

I looked to heaven, and tried to pray;
But or ever a prayer had gusht,
A wicked whisper came, and made
My heart as dry as dust.

I closed my lids, and kept them close,
And the balls like pulses beat;
For the sky and the sea, and the sea and the
    sky   250
Lay like a load on my weary eye,
And the dead were at my feet.

The cold sweat melted from their limbs,
Nor rot nor reek did they:
The look with which they looked on me
Had never passed away.

An orphan's curse would drag to hell
A spirit from on high;
But oh! more horrible than that
Is the curse in a dead man's eye!   260
Seven days, seven nights, I saw that curse,
And yet I could not die.

The moving Moon went up the sky,
And no where did abide:
Softly she was going up,
And a star or two beside—

And a star was going up,
Her beams bemocked the sultry main,
Like April hoar-frost spread;
But where the ship's huge shadow lay,   270
The charméd water burnt alway
A still and awful red.

Beyond the shadow of the ship,
I watched the water-snakes:
They moved in tracks of shining white,
And when they reared, the elfish light
Fell off in hoary flakes.

Within the shadow of the ship
I watched their rich attire:
Blue, glossy green, and velvet black,   280
They coiled and swam; and every track
Was a flash of golden fire.

O happy living things! no tongue
Their beauty might declare:
A spring of love gushed from my heart,
And I blessed them unaware:
Sure my kind saint took pity on me,
And I blessed them unaware.

The self-same moment I could pray;
And from my neck so free   290
The Albatross fell off, and sank
Like lead into the sea.

PART V

Oh sleep! it is a gentle thing,
Beloved from pole to pole!
To Mary Queen the praise be given!
She sent the gentle sleep from Heaven,
That slid into my soul.

The silly buckets on the deck,
That had so long remained,
I dreamt that they were filled with dew;   300
And when I awoke, it rained.

My lips were wet, my throat was cold,
My garments all were dank;
Sure I had drunken in my dreams,
And still my body drank.

I moved, and could not feel my limbs:
I was so light—almost
I thought that I had died in sleep,
And was a blesséd ghost.

And soon I heard a roaring wind: 310
It did not come anear;
But with its sound it shook the sails,
That were so thin and sere.

The upper air burst into life!
And a hundred fire-flags sheen,
To and fro they were hurried about!
And to and fro, and in and out,
The wan stars danced between.

And the coming wind did roar more loud,
And the sails did sigh like sedge;   320
And the rain poured down from one black
    cloud;
The Moon was at its edge.

The thick black cloud was cleft, and still
The Moon was at its side:
Like waters shot from some high crag,
The lightning fell with never a jag,
A river steep and wide.

The loud wind never reached the ship,
Yet now the ship moved on!
Beneath the lightning and the Moon   330
The dead men gave a groan.

They groaned, they stirred, they all uprose,
Nor spake, nor moved their eyes;
It had been strange, even in a dream,
To have seen those dead men rise.

The helmsman steered, the ship moved on;
Yet never a breeze up-blew;
The mariners all 'gan work the ropes,
Where they were wont to do;
They raised their limbs like lifeless tools— 340
We were a ghastly crew.

The body of my brother's son
Stood by me, knee to knee:
The body and I pulled at one rope,
But he said nought to me.

'I fear thee, ancient Mariner!'
Be calm, thou Wedding-Guest!
'Twas not those souls that fled in pain,
Which to their corses came again,
But a troop of spirits blest: 350

For when it dawned—they dropped their arms,
And clustered round the mast;
Sweet sounds rose slowly through their
    mouths,
And from their bodies passed.

Around, around, flew each sweet sound,
Then darted to the Sun;
Slowly the sounds came back again,
Now mixed, now one by one.

Sometimes a-dropping from the sky
I heard the sky-lark sing;   360
Sometimes all little birds that are,
How they seemed to fill the sea and air
With their sweet jargoning!

And now 'twas like all instruments,
Now like a lonely flute;
And now it is an angel's song,
That makes the heavens be mute.

It ceased; yet still the sails made on
A pleasant noise till noon,
A noise like of a hidden brook   370
In the leafy month of June,
That to the sleeping woods all night
Singeth a quiet tune.

Till noon we quietly sailed on,
Yet never a breeze did breathe:
Slowly and smoothly went the ship,
Moved onward from beneath.

Under the keel nine fathom deep,
From the land of mist and snow,
The spirit slid: and it was he   380
That made the ship to go.
The sails at noon left off their tune,
And the ship stood still also.

The Sun, right up above the mast,
Had fixed her to the ocean:
But in a minute she 'gan stir,
With a short uneasy motion—
Backwards and forwards half her length
With a short uneasy motion.

Then like a pawing horse let go,   390
She made a sudden bound:
It flung the blood into my head,
And I fell down in a swound.

How long in that same fit I lay,
I have not to declare;
But ere my living life returned,
I heard and in my soul discerned
Two voices in the air.

'Is it he?' quoth one, 'Is this the man?
By him who died on cross,   400
With his cruel bow he laid full low
The harmless Albatross.

The spirit who bideth by himself
In the land of mist and snow ,
He loved the bird that loved the man
Who shot him with his bow.'

The other was a softer voice,
As soft as honey-dew:
Quoth he, 'The man hath penance done,
And penance more will do.'   410

PART VI

FIRST VOICE

'But tell me, tell me! speak again,
Thy soft response renewing—
What makes that ship drive on so fast?
What is the ocean doing?'

SECOND VOICE

'Still as a slave before his lord,
The ocean hath no blast;
His great bright eye most silently
Up to the Moon is cast—

If he may know which way to go;
For she guides him smooth or grim.   420
See, brother, see! how graciously
She looketh down on him.'

FIRST VOICE

'But why drives on that ship so fast,
Without or wave or wind?'

SECOND VOICE

'The air is cut away before,
And closes from behind.

Fly, brother, fly! more high, more high!
Or we shall be belated:
For slow and slow that ship will go,
When the Mariner's trance is abated.'   430

I woke, and we were sailing on
As in a gentle weather:
'Twas night, calm night, the moon was high;
The dead men stood together.

All stood together on the deck,
For a charnel-dungeon fitter:
All fixed on me their stony eyes,
That in the Moon did glitter.

The pang, the curse, with which they died,
Had never passed away: 440
I could not draw my eyes from theirs,
Nor turn them up to pray.

And now this spell was snapt: once more
I viewed the ocean green,
And looked far forth, yet little saw
Of what had else been seen—

Like one, that on a lonesome road
Doth walk in fear and dread,
And having once turned round walks on,
And turns no more his head;   450
Because he knows, a frightful fiend
Doth close behind him tread.

But soon there breathed a wind on me,
Nor sound nor motion made:
Its path was not upon the sea,
In ripple or in shade.

It raised my hair, it fanned my cheek
Like a meadow-gale of spring—
It mingled strangely with my fears,
Yet it felt like a welcoming.   460

Swiftly, swiftly flew the ship,
Yet she sailed softly too:
Sweetly, sweetly blew the breeze—
On me alone it blew.

Oh! dream of joy! is this indeed
The light-house top I see?
Is this the hill? is this the kirk?
Is this mine own countree?

We drifted o'er the harbour-bar,
And I with sobs did pray—   470
O let me be awake, my God!
Or let me sleep alway.

The harbour-bay was clear as glass,
So smoothly it was strewn!
And on the bay the moonlight lay,
And the shadow of the Moon.

The rock shone bright, the kirk no less,
That stands above the rock:
The moonlight steeped in silentness
The steady weathercock.   480

And the bay was white with silent light,
Till rising from the same,
Full many shapes, that shadows were,
In crimson colours came.

A little distance from the prow
Those crimson shadows were:
I turned my eyes upon the deck—
Oh, Christ! what saw I there!

Each corse lay flat, lifeless and flat,
And, by the holy rood!   490
A man all light, a seraph-man,
On every corse there stood.

This seraph-band, each waved his hand:
It was a heavenly sight!
They stood as signals to the land,
Each one a lovely light;

This seraph-band, each waved his hand,
No voice did they impart—
No voice; but oh! the silence sank
Like music on my heart.   500

But soon I heard the dash of oars,
I heard the Pilot's cheer;
My head was turned perforce away
And I saw a boat appear.

The Pilot and the Pilot's boy,
I heard them coming fast:
Dear Lord in Heaven! it was a joy
The dead men could not blast.

I saw a third—I heard his voice:
It is the Hermit good!   510
He singeth loud his godly hymns
That he makes in the wood.
He'll shrieve my soul, he'll wash away
The Albatross's blood.

PART VII

This Hermit good lives in that wood
Which slopes down to the sea.
How loudly his sweet voice he rears!
He loves to talk with mariners
That come from a far countree.

He kneels at morn, and noon, and eve—   520
He hath a cushion plump:
It is the moss that wholly hides
The rotted old oak-stump.

The skiff-boat neared: I heard them talk,
'Why, this is strange, I trow!
Where are those lights so many and fair,
That signal made but now?'

'Strange by my faith!' the Hermit said—
'And they answered not our cheer!
The planks looked warped! and see those
        sails,   530
How thin they are and sere!
I never saw aught like to them,
Unless perchance it were

Brown skeletons of leaves that lag
My forest-brook along;
When the ivy-tod is heavy with snow,
And the owlet whoops to the wolf below,
That eats the she-wolf's young.'

'Dear Lord! it hath a fiendish look—
(The Pilot made reply)   540
I am a-feared'—'Push on, push on!'
Said the Hermit cheerily.

The boat came closer to the ship,
But I nor spake nor stirred;
The boat came close beneath the ship,
And straight a sound was heard.

Under the water it rumbled on,
Still louder and more dread:
It reached the ship, it split the bay;
The ship went down like lead.   550

Stunned by that loud and dreadful sound
Which sky and ocean smote,
Like one that hath been seven days drowned
My body lay afloat;
But swift as dreams, myself I found
Within the Pilot's boat.

Upon the whirl, where sank the ship,
The boat spun round and round;
And all was still, save that the hill
Was telling of the sound.   560

I moved my lips—the Pilot shrieked
And fell down in a fit;
The holy Hermit raised his eyes,
And prayed where he did sit.

I took the oars: the Pilot's boy,
Who now doth crazy go,
Laughed loud and long, and all the while
His eyes went to and fro.
'Ha! ha!' quoth he, 'full plain I see,
The Devil knows how to row.'   570

And now, all in my own countree,
I stood on the firm land!
The Hermit stepped forth from the boat,
And scarcely he could stand.

'O shrieve me, shrieve me, holy man!'
The Hermit crossed his brow.
'Say quick,' quoth he, 'I bid thee say—
What manner of man art thou?'

Forthwith this frame of mine was wrenched
With a woful agony,   580
Which forced me to begin my tale;
And then it left me free.

Since then, at an uncertain hour,
That agony returns:
And till my ghastly tale is told,
This heart within me burns.

I pass, like night, from land to land;
I have strange power of speech;
That moment that his face I see,
I know the man that must hear me: 590
To him my tale I teach.

What loud uproar bursts from that door!
The wedding-guests are there:
But in the garden-bower the bride
And bride-maids singing are:
And hark the little vesper bell,
Which biddeth me to prayer!

O Wedding-Guest! this soul hath been
Alone on a wide wide sea:
So lonely 'twas, that God himself   600
Scarce seeméd there to be.

O sweeter than the marriage-feast,
'Tis sweeter far to me,
To walk together to the kirk
With a goodly company!—

To walk together to the kirk,
And all together pray,
While each to his great Father bends,
Old men, and babes, and loving friends
And youths and maidens gay!   610

Farewell, farewell! but this I tell
To thee, thou Wedding-Guest!
He prayeth well, who loveth well
Both man and bird and beast.

He prayeth best, who loveth best
All things both great and small;
For the dear God who loveth us,
He made and loveth all.

The Mariner, whose eye is bright,
Whose beard with age is hoar,   620
Is gone: and now the Wedding-Guest
Turned from the bridegroom's door.

He went like one that hath been stunned,
And is of sense forlorn:
A sadder and a wiser man,
He rose the morrow morn.

CHRISTABEL

PREFACE

The first part of the following poem was written in the year 1797, at Stowey, in the country of Somerset. The second part, after my return from Germany, in the year 1800, at Keswick, Cumberland. It is probable that if the poem had been finished at either of the former periods, or if even the first and second part had been published in the year 1800, the impression of its originality would have been much greater than I dare at present expect. But for this I have only my own indolence to blame. The dates are mentioned for the exclusive purpose of precluding charges of plagiarism or servile imitation from myself. For there is amongst us a set of critics, who seem to hold, that every possible thought and image is traditional; who have no notion that there are such things as fountains in the world, small as well as great; and who would therefore charitably derive every rill they behold flowing, from a perforation made in some other man's tank. I am confident, however, that as far as the present poem is concerned, the celebrated poets whose writings I might be suspected of having imitated, either in particular passages, or in the tone and the spirit of the whole, would be among the first to vindicate me from the charge, and who, on any striking coincidence, would permit me to address them in this doggerel version of two monkish Latin hexameters.

> 'Tis mine and it is likewise yours;
> But an if this will not do;
> Let it be mine, good friend! for I
> Am the poorer of the two.

I have only to add that the meter of Christabel is not, properly speaking, irregular, though it may seem so from its being founded on a new principle: namely, that of counting in each line the accents, not the syllables. Though the latter may vary from seven to twelve, yet in each line the accents will be found to be only four. Nevertheless, this occasional variation in number of syllables is not introduced wantonly, or for the mere ends of convenience, but in correspondence with some transition in the nature of the imagery or passion.

PART I

'TIS the middle of night by the castle clock,
And the owls have awakened the crowing
    cock;
Tu—whit!——Tu—whoo!
And hark, again! the crowing cock,
How drowsily it crew.

Sir Leoline, the Baron rich,
Hath a toothless mastiff bitch;
From her kennel beneath the rock
She maketh answer to the clock,
Four for the quarters, and twelve for the
    hour;   10
Ever and aye, by shine and shower,
Sixteen short howls, not over loud;
Some say, she sees my lady's shroud.

Is the night chilly and dark?
The night is chilly, but not dark,

The thin gray cloud is spread on high,
It covers but not hides the sky.
The moon is behind, and at the full;
And yet she looks both small and dull.
The night is chill, the cloud is gray: 20
'Tis a month before the month of May,
And the Spring comes slowly up this way.

The lovely lady, Christabel,
Whom her father loves so well,
What makes her in the wood so late,
A furlong from the castle gate?
She had dreams all yesternight
Of her own betrothéd knight;
And she in the midnight wood will pray
For the weal of her lover that's far away.   30

She stole along, she nothing spoke,
The sighs she heaved were soft and low,
And naught was green upon the oak
But moss and rarest mistletoe:
She kneels beneath the huge oak tree,
And in silence prayeth she.

The lady sprang up suddenly,
The lovely lady, Christabel!
It moaned as near, as near can be,
But what it is she cannot tell.—   40
On the other side it seems to be,
Of the huge, broad-breasted, old oak tree.

The night is chill; the forest bare;
Is it the wind that moaneth bleak?
There is not wind enough in the air
To move away the ringlet curl
From the lovely lady's cheek—
There is not wind enough to twirl
The one red leaf, the last of its clan,
That dances as often as dance it can,   50
Hanging so light, and hanging so high,
On the topmost twig that looks up at the sky.

Hush, beating heart of Christabel!
Jesu, Maria, shield her well!
She folded her arms beneath her cloak,
And stole to the other side of the oak.
        What sees she there?

There she sees a damsel bright,
Drest in a silken robe of white,
That shadowy in the moonlight shone: 60
The neck that made that white robe wan,
Her stately neck, and arms were bare;
Her blue-veined feet unsandal'd were,
And wildly glittered here and there

The gems entangled in her hair.
I guess, 'twas frightful there to see
A lady so richly clad as she—
Beautiful exceedingly!

Mary Mother, save me now!
(Said Christabel,) And who art thou?   70

The lady strange made answer meet,
And her voice was faint and sweet:—
Have pity on my sore distress,
I scarce can speak for weariness:
Stretch forth thy hand, and have no fear!
Said Christabel, How camest thou here?
And the lady, whose voice was faint and sweet,
Did thus pursue her answer meet:—

My sire is of a noble line,
And my name is Geraldine: 80
Five warriors seized me yestermorn,
Me, even me, a maid forlorn:
They choked my cries with force and fright,
And tied me on a palfrey white.
The palfrey was as fleet as wind,
And they rode furiously behind.

They spurred amain, their steeds were white:
And once we crossed the shade of night.
As sure as Heaven shall rescue me,
I have no thought what men they be;   90
Nor do I know how long it is
(For I have lain entranced I wis)
Since one, the tallest of the five,
Took me from the palfrey's back,
A weary woman, scarce alive.
Some muttered words his comrades spoke:
He placed me underneath this oak;
He swore they would return with haste;
Whither they went I cannot tell—
I thought I heard, some minutes past,   100
Sounds as of a castle bell.
Stretch forth thy hand (thus ended she),
And help a wretched maid to flee.

Then Christabel stretched forth her hand,
And comforted fair Geraldine:
O well, bright dame! may you command
The service of Sir Leoline;
And gladly our stout chivalry
Will he send forth and friends withal
To guide and guard you safe and free   110
Home to your noble father's hall.

She rose: and forth with steps they passed
That strove to be, and were not, fast.

Her gracious stars the lady blest,
And thus spake on sweet Christabel:
All our household are at rest,
The hall as silent as the cell;
Sir Leoline is weak in health,
And may not well awakened be,
But we will move as if in stealth,   120
And I beseech your courtesy,
This night, to share your couch with me.

They crossed the moat, and Christabel
Took the key that fitted well;
A little door she opened straight,
All in the middle of the gate;
The gate that was ironed within and without,
Where an army in battle array had marched
    out.
The lady sank, belike through pain,
And Christabel with might and main   130
Lifted her up, a weary weight,
Over the threshold of the gate:
Then the lady rose again,
And moved, as she were not in pain.

So free from danger, free from fear,
They crossed the court: right glad they were,
And Christabel devoutly cried
To the lady by her side,
Praise we the Virgin all divine
Who hath rescued thee from thy distress!   140
Alas, alas! said Geraldine,
I cannot speak for weariness.
So free from danger, free from fear,
They crossed the court: right glad they were.

Outside her kennel, the mastiff old
Lay fast asleep, in moonshine cold.
The mastiff old did not awake,
Yet she an angry moan did make!
And what can ail the mastiff bitch?
Never till now she uttered yell   150
Beneath the eye of Christabel.
Perhaps it is the owlet's scritch:
For what can ail the mastiff bitch?

They passed the hall, that echoes still,
Pass as lightly as you will!
The brands were flat, the brands were dying,
Amid their own white ashes lying;
But when the lady passed, there came
A tongue of light, a fit of flame;
And Christabel saw the lady's eye,   160
And nothing else saw she thereby,
Save the boss of the shield of Sir Leoline tall,

Which hung in a murky old niche in the wall.
O softly tread, said Christabel,
My father seldom sleepeth well.

Sweet Christabel her feet doth bare,
And jealous of the listening air
They steal their way from stair to stair,
Now in glimmer, and now in gloom,
And now they pass the Baron's room,   170
As still as death, with stifled breath!
And now have reached her chamber door;
And now doth Geraldine press down
The rushes of the chamber floor.

The moon shines dim in the open air,
And not a moonbeam enters here.
But they without its light can see
The chamber carved so curiously,
Carved with figures strange and sweet,
All made out of the carver's brain,   180
For a lady's chamber meet:
The lamp with twofold silver chain
Is fastened to an angel's feet.

The silver lamp burns dead and dim;
But Christabel the lamp will trim.
She trimmed the lamp, and made it bright,
And left it swinging to and fro,
While Geraldine, in wretched plight,
Sank down upon the floor below.

O weary lady, Geraldine,   190
I pray you, drink this cordial wine!
It is a wine of virtuous powers;
My mother made it of wild flowers.

And will your mother pity me,
Who am a maiden most forlorn?
Christabel answered—Woe is me!
She died the hour that I was born.
I have heard the grey-haired friar tell
How on her death-bed she did say,
That she should hear the castle-bell   200
Strike twelve upon my wedding-day.
O mother dear! that thou wert here!
I would, said Geraldine, she were!

But soon with altered voice, said she—
'Off, wandering mother! Peak and pine!
I have power to bid thee flee.'
Alas! what ails poor Geraldine?
Why stares she with unsettled eye?
Can she the bodiless dead espy?
And why with hollow voice cries she,   210

'Off, woman, off! this hour is mine—
Though thou her guardian spirit be,
Off, woman, off! 'tis given to me.'

Then Christabel knelt by the lady's side,
And raised to heaven her eyes so blue—
Alas! said she, this ghastly ride—
Dear lady! it hath wildered you!
The lady wiped her moist cold brow,
And faintly said, ' 'tis over now!'

Again the wild-flower wine she drank: 220
Her fair large eyes 'gan glitter bright,
And from the floor whereon she sank,
The lofty lady stood upright:
She was most beautiful to see,
Like a lady of a far countrée.

And thus the lofty lady spake—
'All they who live in the upper sky,
Do love you, holy Christabel!
And you love them, and for their sake
And for the good which me befel,   230
Even I in my degree will try,
Fair maiden, to requite you well.
But now unrobe yourself; for I
Must pray, ere yet in bed I lie.'

Quoth Christabel, So let it be!
And as the lady bade, did she.
Her gentle limbs did she undress,
And lay down in her loveliness.
But through her brain of weal and woe
So many thoughts moved to and fro,   240
That vain it were her lids to close;
So half-way from the bed she rose,
And on her elbow did recline
To look at the lady Geraldine.

Beneath the lamp the lady bowed,
And slowly rolled her eyes around;
Then drawing in her breath aloud,
Like one that shuddered, she unbound
The cincture from beneath her breast:
Her silken robe, and inner vest,   250
Dropt to her feet, and full in view,
Behold! her bosom and half her side—
A sight to dream of, not to tell!
O shield her! shield sweet Christabel!

Yet Geraldine nor speaks nor stirs;
Ah! what a stricken look was hers!
Deep from within she seems half-way
To lift some weight with sick assay,

And eyes the maid and seeks delay;
Then suddenly, as one defied,   260
Collects herself in scorn and pride,
And lay down by the Maiden's side!—
And in her arms the maid she took,
          Ah wel-a-day!
And with low voice and doleful look
These words did say:
'In the touch of this bosom there worketh a
          spell,
Which is lord of thy utterance, Christabel!
Thou knowest to-night, and wilt know to-
          morrow,
This mark of my shame, this seal of my sor-
          row;   270
          But vainly thou warrest,
          For this is alone in
          Thy power to declare,
          That in the dim forest,
          Thou heard'st a low moaning,
And found'st a bright lady, surpassingly fair;
And didst bring her home with thee in love
          and in charity,
To shield her and shelter her from the damp
          air.'

THE CONCLUSION TO PART I

It was a lovely sight to see
The lady Christabel, when she   280
Was praying at the old oak tree.
          Amid the jaggéd shadows
          Of mossy leafless boughs,
          Kneeling in the moonlight,
          To make her gentle vows;
Her slender palms together prest,
Heaving sometimes on her breast;
Her face resigned to bliss or bale—
Her face, oh call it fair not pale,
And both blue eyes more bright than clear, 290
Each about to have a tear.

With open eyes (ah woe is me!)
Asleep, and dreaming fearfully,
Fearfully dreaming, yet, I wis,
Dreaming that alone, which is—
O sorrow and shame! Can this be she,
The lady, who knelt at the old oak tree?
And lo! the worker of these harms,
That holds the maiden in her arms,
Seems to slumber still and mild,   300
As a mother with her child.

A star hath set, a star hath risen,
O Geraldine! since arms of thine
Have been the lovely lady's prison.
O Geraldine! one hour was thine—
Thou'st had thy will! By tairn and rill,
The night-birds all that hour were still.
But now they are jubilant anew.
From cliff and tower, tu—whoo! tu—whoo!
Tu—whoo! tu—whoo! from wood and fell! 310

And see! the lady Christabel
Gathers herself from out her trance;
Her limbs relax, her countenance
Grows sad and soft; the smooth thin lids
Close o'er her eyes; and tears she sheds—
Large tears that leave the lashes bright!
And oft the while she seems to smile
As infants at a sudden light!

Yea, she doth smile, and she doth weep,
Like a youthful hermitess,   320
Beauteous in a wilderness,
Who, praying always, prays in sleep.
And, if she move unquietly,
Perchance, 'tis but the blood so free
Comes back and tingles in her feet.
No doubt, she hath a vision sweet.
What if her guardian spirit 'twere,
What if she knew her mother near?
But this she knows, in joys and woes,
That saints will aid if men will call: 330
For the blue sky bends over all!

PART II

Each matin bell, the Baron saith,
Knells us back to a world of death.
These words Sir Leoline first said,
When he rose and found his lady dead:
These words Sir Leoline will say
Many a morn to his dying day!

And hence the custom and law began
That still at dawn the sacristan,
Who duly pulls the heavy bell,   340
Five and forty beads must tell
Between each stroke—a warning knell,
Which not a soul can choose but hear
From Bratha Head to Wyndermere.

Saith Bracy the bard, So let it knell!
And let the drowsy sacristan
Still count as slowly as he can!

There is no lack of such, I ween,
As well fill up the space between.
In Langdale Pike and Witch's Lair,   350
And Dungeon-ghyll so foully rent,
With ropes of rock and bells of air
Three sinful sextons' ghosts are pent,
Who all give back, one after t'other,
The death-note to their living brother;
And oft too, by the knell offended,
Just as their one! two! three! is ended,
The devil mocks the doleful tale
With a merry peal from Borodale.

The air is still! through mist and cloud   360
That merry peal comes ringing loud;
And Geraldine shakes off her dread,
And rises lightly from the bed;
Puts on her silken vestments white,
And tricks her hair in lovely plight,

And nothing doubting of her spell
Awakens the lady Christabel.
'Sleep you, sweet lady Christabel?
I trust that you have rested well.'

And Christabel awoke and spied   370
The same who lay down by her side—
O rather say, the same whom she
Raised up beneath the old oak tree!
Nay, fairer yet! and yet more fair
For she belike hath drunken deep
Of all the blessedness of sleep!
And while she spake, her looks, her air
Such gentle thankfulness declare,
That (so it seemed) her girded vests
Grew tight beneath her heaving breasts.   380
'Sure I have sinn'd!' said Christabel,
'Now heaven be praised if all be well!'
And in low faltering tones, yet sweet,
Did she the lofty lady greet
With such perplexity of mind
As dreams too lively leave behind.

So quickly she rose, and quickly arrayed
Her maiden limbs, and having prayed
That He, who on the cross did groan,
Might wash away her sins unknown,   390
She forthwith led fair Geraldine
To meet her sire, Sir Leoline.

The lovely maid and the lady tall
Are pacing both into the hall,
And pacing on through page and groom,
Enter the Baron's presence-room.

The Baron rose, and while he prest
His gentle daughter to his breast,
With cheerful wonder in his eyes
The lady Geraldine espies,⁣ 400
And gave such welcome to the same,
As might beseem so bright a dame!

But when he heard the lady's tale,
And when she told her father's name,
Why waxed Sir Leoline so pale,
Murmuring o'er the name again,
Lord Roland de Vaux of Tryermaine?

Alas! they had been friends in youth;
But whispering tongues can poison truth;
And constancy lives in realms above; 410
And life is thorny; and youth is vain;
And to be wroth with one we love
Doth work like madness in the brain.
And thus it chanced, as I divine,
With Roland and Sir Leoline.
Each spake words of high disdain
And insult to his heart's best brother:
They parted—ne'er to meet again!
But never either found another
To free the hollow heart from paining— 420
They stood aloof, the scars remaining,
Like cliffs which had been rent asunder;
A dreary sea now flows between;—
But neither heat, nor frost, nor thunder,
Shall wholly do away, I ween,
The marks of that which once hath been.

Sir Leoline, a moment's space,
Stood gazing on the damsel's face:
And the youthful Lord of Tryermaine
Came back upon his heart again. 430

O then the Baron forgot his age,
His noble heart swelled high with rage;
He swore by the wounds in Jesu's side
He would proclaim it far and wide,
With trump and solemn heraldry,
That they, who thus had wronged the dame,
Were base as spotted infamy!
'And if they dare deny the same.
My herald shall appoint a week,
And let the recreant traitors seek, 440
My tourney court—that there and then
I may dislodge their reptile souls
From the bodies and forms of men!'
He spake: his eye in lightning rolls!
For the lady was ruthlessly seized; and he
  kenned

In the beautiful lady the child of his friend!
And now the tears were on his face,
And fondly in his arms he took
Fair Geraldine, who met the embrace,
Prolonging it with joyous look.⁣ 450
Which when she viewed, a vision fell
Upon the soul of Christabel,
The vision of fear, the touch and pain!
She shrunk and shuddered, and saw again—
(Ah, woe is me! Was it for thee,
Thou gentle maid! such sights to see?)

Again she saw that bosom old,
Again she felt that bosom cold,
And drew in her breath with a hissing sound:
Whereat the Knight turned wildly round, 460
And nothing saw, but his own sweet maid
With eyes upraised, as one that prayed.

The touch, the sight, had passed away,
And in its stead that vision blest,
Which comforted her after-rest
While in the lady's arms she lay,
Had put a rapture in her breast,
And on her lips and o'er her eyes
Spread smiles like light!
⁣   With new surprise,
'What ails then my belovéd child?' 470
The Baron said—His daughter mild
Made answer, 'All will yet be well!'
I ween, she had no power to tell
Aught else: so mighty was the spell.
Yet he, who saw this Geraldine,
Had deemed her sure a thing divine:
Such sorrow with such grace she blended,
As if she feared she had offended
Sweet Christabel, that gentle maid!
And with such lowly tones she prayed 480
She might be sent without delay
Home to her father's mansion.
⁣   'Nay!

Nay, by my soul!' said Leoline.
'Ho! Bracy the bard, the charge be thine!
Go thou, with music sweet and loud,
And take two steeds with trappings proud,
And take the youth whom thou lov'st best
To bear thy harp, and learn thy song,
And clothe you both in solemn vest,
And over the mountains haste along, 490
Lest wandering folk, that are abroad,
Detain you on the valley road.

'And when he has crossed the Irthing flood,
My merry bard! he hastes, he hastes

Up Knorren Moor, through Halegarth Wood,
And reaches soon that castle good
Which stands and threatens Scotland's wastes.

'Bard Bracy! bard Bracy! your horses are
    fleet,
Ye must ride up the hall, your music so sweet,
More loud than your horses' echoing feet!   500
And loud and loud to Lord Roland call,
Thy daughter is safe in Langdale hall!
Thy beautiful daughter is safe and free—
Sir Leoline greets thee thus through me!
He bids thee come without delay
With all thy numerous array
And take thy lovely daughter home:
And he will meet thee on the way
With all his numerous array
White with their panting palfreys' foam: 510
And, by mine honour! I will say,
That I repent me of the day
When I spake words of fierce disdain
To Roland de Vaux of Tryermaine!—
—For since that evil hour hath flown,
Many a summer's sun hath shone;
Yet ne'er found I a friend again
Like Roland de Vaux of Tryermaine.

The lady fell, and clasped his knees,
Her face upraised, her eyes o'erflowing;   520
And Bracy replied, with faltering voice,
His gracious Hail on all bestowing!—

'Thy words, thou sire of Christabel,
Are sweeter than my harp can tell;
Yet might I gain a boon of thee,
This day my journey should not be,
So strange a dream hath come to me,
That I had vowed with music loud
To clear yon wood from thing unblest,
Warned by a vision in my rest!   530
For in my sleep I saw that dove,
That gentle bird, whom thou dost love,
And call'st by thy own daughter's name—
Sir Leoline! I saw the same
Fluttering, and uttering fearful moan,
Among the green herbs in the forest alone.
Which when I saw and when I heard,
I wonder'd what might ail the bird;
For nothing near it could I see,
Save the grass and green herbs underneath the
    old tree.

'And in my dream methought I went   540
To search out what might there be found;

And what the sweet bird's trouble meant,
That thus lay fluttering on the ground.
I went and peered, and could descry
No cause for her distressful cry;
But yet for her dear lady's sake
I stooped, methought, the dove to take,
When lo! I saw a bright green snake
Coiled around its wings and neck.   550
Green as the herbs on which it couched,
Close by the dove's its head it crouched;
And with the dove it heaves and stirs,
Swelling its neck as she swelled hers!
I woke; it was the midnight hour,
The clock was echoing in the tower;
But though my slumber was gone by,
This dream it would not pass away—
It seems to live upon my eye!
And thence I vowed this self-same day   560
With music strong and saintly song
To wander through the forest bare,
Lest aught unholy loiter there.'

Thus Bracy said: the Baron, the while,
Half-listening heard him with a smile;
Then turned to Lady Geraldine,
His eyes made up of wonder and love;
And said in courtly accents fine,
'Sweet maid, Lord Roland's beauteous dove,
With arms more strong than harp or song,   570
Thy sire and I will crush the snake!'
He kissed her forehead as he spake,
And Geraldine in maiden wise
Casting down her large bright eyes,
With blushing cheek and courtesy fine
She turned her from Sir Leoline;
Softly gathering up her train,
That o'er her right arm fell again;
And folded her arms across her chest,
And couched her head upon her breast,   580
And looked askance at Christabel—
Jesu, Maria, shield her well!

A snake's small eye blinks dull and shy;
And the lady's eyes they shrunk in her head,
Each shrunk up to a serpent's eye,
And with somewhat of malice, and more of
    dread,
At Christabel she looked askance!—
One moment—and the sight was fled!
But Christabel in dizzy trance
Stumbling on the unsteady ground   590
Shuddered aloud, with a hissing sound;
And Geraldine again turned round,
And like a thing, that sought relief,

Full of wonder and full of grief,
She rolled her large bright eyes divine
Wildly on Sir Leoline.

The maid, alas! her thoughts are gone,
She nothing sees—no sight but one!
The maid, devoid of guile and sin,
I know not how, in fearful wise,   600
So deeply had she drunken in
That look, those shrunken serpent eyes,
That all her features were resigned
To this sole image in her mind:
And passively did imitate
That look of dull and treacherous hate!
And thus she stood, in dizzy trance,
Still picturing that look askance
With forced unconscious sympathy
Full before her father's view—   610
As far as such a look could be
In eyes so innocent and blue!

And when the trance was o'er, the maid
Paused awhile, and inly prayed:
Then falling at the Baron's feet,
'By my mother's soul do I entreat
That thou this woman send away!'
She said; and more she could not say:
For what she knew she could not tell,
O'er-mastered by the mighty spell.   620

Why is thy cheek so wan and wild,
Sir Leoline? Thy only child
Lies at thy feet, thy joy, thy pride,
So fair, so innocent, so mild;
The same, for whom thy lady died!
O by the pangs of her dear mother
Think thou no evil of thy child!
For her, and thee, and for no other,
She prayed the moment ere she died:
Prayed that the babe for whom she died, 630
Might prove her dear lord's joy and pride!
   That prayer her deadly pangs beguiled,
      Sir Leoline!
   And wouldst thou wrong thy only child,
      Her child and thine?

Within the Baron's heart and brain
If thoughts, like these, had any share,
They only swelled his rage and pain,
And did but work confusion there.
His heart was cleft with pain and rage, 640
His cheeks they quivered, his eyes were wild,

Dishonoured thus in his old age;
Dishonoured by his only child,

And all his hospitality
To the wronged daughter of his friend
By more than woman's jealousy
Brought thus to a disgraceful end—
   He rolled his eye with stern regard
Upon the gentle minstrel bard,
And said in tones abrupt, austere—   650
'Why Bracy! dost thou loiter here?
I bade thee hence!' The bard obeyed;
And turning from his own sweet maid,
The agéd knight, Sir Leoline,
Led forth the lady Geraldine!

THE CONCLUSION TO PART II

A little child, a limber elf,
Singing, dancing to itself,
A fairy thing with red round cheeks,
That always finds, and never seeks,
Makes such a vision to the sight   660
As fills a father's eyes with light;
And pleasures flow in so thick and fast
Upon his heart, that he at last
Must needs express his love's excess
With words of unmeant bitterness.
Perhaps 'tis pretty to force together
Thoughts so all unlike each other;
To mutter and mock a broken charm,
To dally with wrong that does no harm.
Perhaps 'tis tender too and pretty   670
At each wild word to feel within
A sweet recoil of love and pity.
And what, if in a world of sin
(O sorrow and shame should this be true!)
Such giddiness of heart and brain
Comes seldom save from rage and pain,
So talks as it's most used to do.

FROST AT MIDNIGHT

THE Frost performs its secret ministry,
Unhelped by any wind. The owlet's cry
Came loud—and hark, again! loud as before.
The inmates of my cottage, all at rest,
Have left me to that solitude, which suits
Abstruser musings: save that at my side
My cradled infant slumbers peacefully.
'Tis calm indeed! so calm, that it disturbs
And vexes meditation with its strange
And extreme silentness. Sea, hill, and wood, 10
This populous village! Sea, and hill, and wood,
With all the numberless goings-on of life,

Inaudible as dreams! the thin blue flame
Lies on my low-burnt fire, and quivers not;
Only that film, which fluttered on the grate,
Still flutters there, the sole unquiet thing.
Methinks, its motion in this hush of nature
Gives it dim sympathies with me who live,
Making it a companionable form,
Whose puny flaps and freaks the idling
    Spirit   20
By its own moods interprets, every where
Echo or mirror seeking of itself,
And makes a toy of Thought.

                But O! how oft,
How oft, at school, with most believing mind,
Presageful, have I gazed upon the bars,
To watch that fluttering *stranger!* and as oft
With unclosed lids, already had I dreamt
Of my sweet birth-place, and the old church-
    tower,
Whose bells, the poor man's only music, rang
From morn to evening, all the hot Fair-day, 30
So sweetly, that they stirred and haunted me
With a wild pleasure, falling on mine ear
Most like articulate sounds of things to come!
So gazed I, till the soothing things, I dreamt,
Lulled me to sleep, and sleep prolonged my
    dreams!
And so I brooded all the following morn,
Awed by the stern preceptor's face, mine eye
Fixed with mock study on my swimming book:
Save if the door half opened, and I snatched
A hasty glance, and still my heart leaped up, 40
For still I hoped to see the *stranger's* face,
Townsman, or aunt, or sister more beloved,
My play-mate when we both were clothed
    alike!

    Dear Babe, that sleepest cradled by my
    side,
Whose gentle breathings, heard in this deep
    calm,
Fill up the interspersèd vacancies
And momentary pauses of the thought!
My babe so beautiful! it thrills my heart
With tender gladness, thus to look at thee,
And think that thou shalt learn far other
    lore,   50
And in far other scenes! For I was reared
In the great city, pent 'mid cloisters dim,
And saw nought lovely but the sky and stars.
But *thou,* my babe! shalt wander like a breeze
By lakes and sandy shores, beneath the crags
Of ancient mountain, and beneath the clouds,

Which image in their bulk both lakes and
    shores
And mountain crags: so shalt thou see and
    hear
The lovely shapes and sounds intelligible
Of that eternal language, which thy God   60
Utters, who from eternity doth teach
Himself in all, and all things in himself.
Great universal Teacher! he shall mould
Thy spirit, and by giving make it ask.

    Therefore all seasons shall be sweet to thee,
Whether the summer clothe the general earth
With greenness, or the redbreast sit and sing
Betwixt the tufts of snow on the bare branch
Of mossy apple-tree, while the nigh thatch
Smokes in the sun-thaw; whether the eave-
    drops fall   70
Heard only in the trances of the blast,
Or if the secret ministry of frost
Shall hang them up in silent icicles,
Quietly shining to the quiet Moon.

FRANCE: AN ODE

I

Yẽ Clouds! that far above me float and pause,
    Whose pathless march no mortal may con-
        trol!
    Ye Ocean-Waves! that, wheresoe'er ye roll,
Yield homage only to eternal laws!
Ye Woods! that listen to the night-birds sing-
    ing,
    Midway the smooth and perilous slope re-
        clined,
Save when your own imperious branches
    swinging,
Have made a solemn music of the wind!
Where, like a man beloved of God,
Through glooms, which never woodman trod 10
    How oft, pursuing fancies holy,
My moonlight way o'er flowering weeds I
    wound,
    Inspired, beyond the guess of folly,
By each rude shape and wild unconquerable
    sound!
O ye loud Waves! and O ye Forests high!
    And O ye Clouds that far above me soared!
Thou rising Sun! thou blue rejoicing Sky!
    Yea, every thing that is and will be free!
Bear witness for me, wheresoe'er ye be,

With what deep worship I have still
  adored   20
 The spirit of divinest Liberty.

II

When France in wrath her giant-limbs up-
  reared,
 And with that oath, which smote air, earth,
  and sea,
 Stamped her strong foot and said she would
  be free,
Bear witness for me, how I hoped and feared!
With what a joy my lofty gratulation
 Unawed I sang, amid a slavish band:
And when to whelm the disenchanted nation,
 Like fiends embattled by a wizard's wand,
  The Monarchs marched in evil day, 30
  And Britain joined the dire array;
 Though dear her shores and circling ocean,
Though many friendships, many youthful
  loves
 Had swoln the patriot emotion
And flung a magic light o'er all her hills and
  groves;
Yet still my voice, unaltered, sang defeat
 To all that braved the tyrant-quelling lance,
And shame too long delayed and vain retreat!
For ne'er, O Liberty! with partial aim
I dimmed thy light or damped thy holy
  flame;   40
But blessed the pæans of delivered France,
 And hung my head and wept at Britain's
  name.

III

'And what,' I said, 'though Blasphemy's loud
  scream
 With that sweet music of deliverance
  strove!
Though all the fierce and drunken passions
  wove
A dance more wild than e'er was maniac's
  dream!
 Ye storms, that round the dawning East
  assembled,
The Sun was rising, though ye hid his light!'
 And when, to soothe my soul, that hoped
  and trembled,
The dissonance ceased, and all seemed calm
  and bright: 50

When France her front deep-scarr'd and
  gory
 Concealed with clustering wreaths of glory;
  When, insupportably advancing,
 Her arm made mockery of the warrior's
  ramp;
  While timid looks of fury glancing,
 Domestic treason, crushed beneath her fatal
  stamp,
Writhed like a wounded dragon in his gore;
 Then I reproached my fears that would not
  flee;
'And soon,' I said, 'shall Wisdom teach her
  lore
In the low huts of them that toil and groan! 60
And, conquering by her happiness alone,
 Shall France compel the nations to be free,
Till Love and Joy look round, and call the
  Earth their own.'

IV

Forgive me, Freedom! O forgive those
  dreams!
I hear thy voice, I hear thy loud lament,
 From bleak Helvetia's icy caverns sent—
I hear thy groans upon her blood-stained
  streams!
 Heroes, that for your peaceful country per-
  ished,
And ye that, fleeing, spot your mountain-
  snows
 With bleeding wounds; forgive me, that I
  cherished   70
One thought that ever blessed your cruel foes!
 To scatter rage, and traitorous guilt,
 Where Peace her jealous home had built;
  A patriot-race to disinherit
Of all that made their stormy wilds so dear;
  And with inexpiable spirit
To taint the bloodless freedom of the moun-
  taineer—
O France, that mockest Heaven, adulterous,
  blind,
 And patriot only in pernicious toils!
Are these thy boasts, Champion of human
  kind?   80
 To mix with Kings in the low lust of sway,
Yell in the hunt, and share the murderous
  prey;
To insult the shrine of Liberty with spoils
 From freemen torn; to tempt and to be-
  tray?

V

The Sensual and the Dark rebel in vain,
Slaves by their own compulsion! In mad game
They burst their manacles and wear the name
Of Freedom, graven on a heavier chain!
O Liberty! with profitless endeavour
Have I pursued thee, many a weary hour; 90
But thou nor swell'st the victor's strain, nor ever
Didst breathe thy soul in forms of human power.
Alike from all, howe'er they praise thee,
(Nor prayer, nor boastful name delays thee)
Alike from Priestcraft's harpy minions,
And factious Blasphemy's obscener slaves,
Thou speedest on thy subtle pinions,
The guide of homeless winds, and playmate of the waves!
And there I felt thee!—on that sea-cliff's verge,
Whose pines, scarce travelled by the breeze above, 100
Had made one murmur with the distant surge!
Yes, while I stood and gazed, my temples bare,
And shot my being through earth, sea, and air,
Possessing all things with intensest love,
O Liberty! my spirit felt thee there.

LEWTI

OR THE CIRCASSIAN LOVE-CHAUNT

At midnight by the stream I roved,
To forget the form I loved.
Image of Lewti! from my mind
Depart; for Lewti is not kind.

The Moon was high, the moonlight gleam
And the shadow of a star
Heaved upon Tamaha's stream;
But the rock shone brighter far,
The rock half sheltered from my view
By pendent boughs of tressy yew.— 10
So shines my Lewti's forehead fair,
Gleaming through her sable hair,
Image of Lewti! from my mind
Depart; for Lewti is not kind.

I saw a cloud of palest hue,
Onward to the moon it passed;

Still brighter and more bright it grew,
With floating colours not a few,
Till it reached the moon at last:
Then the cloud was wholly bright, 20
With a rich and amber light!
And so with many a hope I seek,
And with such joy I find my Lewti;
And even so my pale wan cheek
Drinks in as deep a flush of beauty!
Nay, treacherous image! leave my mind,
If Lewti never will be kind.

The little cloud—it floats away,
Away it goes; away so soon!
Alas! it has no power to stay: 30
Its hues are dim, its hues are grey—
Away it passes from the moon!
How mournfully it seems to fly,
Ever fading more and more,
To joyless regions of the sky—
And now 'tis whiter than before!
As white as my poor cheek will be,
When, Lewti! on my couch I lie,
A dying man for love of thee.
Nay, treacherous image! leave my mind— 40
And yet, thou didst not look unkind.

I saw a vapour in the sky,
Thin, and white, and very high;
I ne'er beheld so thin a cloud:
Perhaps the breezes that can fly
Now below and now above,
Have snatched aloft the lawny shroud
Of Lady fair—that died for love.
For maids, as well as youths, have perished
From fruitless love too fondly cherished. 50
Nay, treacherous image! leave my mind—
For Lewti never will be kind.

Hush! my heedless feet from under
Slip the crumbling banks for ever:
Like echoes to a distant thunder,
They plunge into the gentle river.
The river-swans have heard my tread,
And startle from their reedy bed.
O beauteous birds! methinks ye measure
Your movements to some heavenly tune! 60
O beauteous birds! 'tis such a pleasure
To see you move beneath the moon,
I would it were your true delight
To sleep by day and wake all night.

I know the place where Lewti lies,
When silent night has closed her eyes:

It is a breezy jasmine-bower,
The nightingale sings o'er her head:
  Voice of the Night! had I the power
That leafy labyrinth to thread,   70
And creep, like thee, with soundless tread,
I then might view her bosom white
Heaving lovely to my sight,
  As these two swans together heave
On the gently-swelling wave.

Oh! that she saw me in a dream,
  And dreamt that I had died for care;
All pale and wasted I would seem,
  Yet fair withal, as spirits are!
I'd die indeed, if I might see   80
Her bosom heave, and heave for me!
Soothe, gentle image! soothe my mind!
To-morrow Lewti may be kind.

FEARS IN SOLITUDE

WRITTEN IN APRIL 1798, DURING THE ALARM
OF AN INVASION

A GREEN and silent spot, amid the hills,
A small and silent dell! O'er stiller place
No singing sky-lark ever poised himself.
The hills are heathy, save that swelling slope,
Which hath a gay and gorgeous covering on,
All golden with the never-bloomless furze,
Which now blooms most profusely: but the
    dell,
Bathed by the mist, is fresh and delicate
As vernal corn-field, or the unripe flax,
When, through its half-transparent stalks, at
    eve,   10
The level sunshine glimmers with green light.
Oh! 'tis a quiet spirit-healing nook!
Which all, methinks, would love; but chiefly
    he,
The humble man, who, in his youthful years,
Knew just so much of folly, as had made
His early manhood more securely wise!
Here he might lie on fern or withered heath,
While from the singing lark (that sings un-
    seen
The minstrelsy that solitude loves best),
And from the sun, and from the breezy air, 20
Sweet influences trembled o'er his frame;
And he, with many feelings, many thoughts,
Made up a meditative joy, and found
Religious meanings in the forms of Nature!
And so, his senses gradually wrapt

In a half sleep, he dreams of better worlds,
And dreaming hears thee still, O singing lark,
That singest like an angel in the clouds!

My God! it is a melancholy thing
For such a man, who would full fain pre-
    serve   30
His soul in calmness, yet perforce must feel
For all his human brethren—O my God!
It weighs upon the heart, that he must think
What uproar and what strife may now be
    stirring
This way or that way o'er these silent hills—
Invasion, and the thunder and the shout,
And all the crash of onset; fear and rage,
And undetermined conflict—even now,
Even now, perchance, and in his native isle:
Carnage and groans beneath this blessed
    sun!   40
We have offended, Oh! my countrymen!
We have offended very grievously,
And been most tyrannous. From east to west
A groan of accusation pierces Heaven!
The wretched plead against us; multitudes
Countless and vehement, the sons of God,
Our brethren! Like a cloud that travels on,
Steamed up from Cairo's swamps of pesti-
    lence,
Even so, my countrymen! have we gone forth
And borne to distant tribes slavery and
    pangs,   50
And, deadlier far, our vices, whose deep taint
With slow perdition murders the whole man,
His body and his soul! Meanwhile, at home,
All individual dignity and power
Engulfed in Courts, Committees, Institutions,
Associations and Societies,
A vain, speech-mouthing, speech-reporting
    Guild,
One Benefit-Club for mutual flattery,
We have drunk up, demure as at a grace,
Pollutions from the brimming cup of wealth; 60
Contemptuous of all honourable rule,
Yet bartering freedom and the poor man's life
For gold, as at a market! The sweet words
Of Christian promise, words that even yet
Might stem destruction, were they wisely
    preached,
Are muttered o'er by men, whose tones pro-
    claim
How flat and wearisome they feel their trade:
Rank scoffers some, but most too indolent
To deem them falsehoods or to know their
    truth.

Oh! blasphemous! the Book of Life is made 70
A superstitous instrument, on which
We gabble o'er the oaths we mean to break;
For all must swear—all and in every place,
College and wharf, council and justice-court;
All, all must swear, the briber and the bribed,
Merchant and lawyer, senator and priest,
The rich, the poor, the old man and the young;
All, all make up one scheme of perjury,
That faith doth reel; the very name of God
Sounds like a juggler's charm; and, bold with
   joy, 80
Forth from his dark and lonely hiding-place,
(Portentous sight!) the owlet Atheism,
Sailing on obscene wings athwart the noon,
Drops his blue-fringéd lids, and holds them
   close,
And hooting at the glorious sun in Heaven,
Cries out, 'Where is it?'

               Thankless too for peace,
(Peace long preserved by fleets and perilous
   seas)
Secure from acutal warfare, we have loved
To swell the war-whoop, passionate for war!
Alas! for ages ignorant of all 90
Its ghastlier workings, (famine or blue plague,
Battle, or siege, or flight through wintry
   snows,)
We, this whole people, have been clamorous
For war and bloodshed; animating sports,
The which we pay for as a thing to talk of,
Spectators and not combatants! No guess
Anticipative of a wrong unfelt,
No speculation on contingency,
However dim and vague, too vague and dim
To yield a justifying cause; and forth, 100
(Stuffed out with big preamble, holy names,
And adjurations of the God in Heaven,)
We send our mandates for the certain death
Of thousands and ten thousands! Boys and
   girls,
And women, that would groan to see a child
Pull off an insect's leg, all read of war,
The best amusement for our morning meal!
The poor wretch, who has learnt his only
   prayers
From curses, who knows scarcely words
   enough
To ask a blessing from his Heavenly Father, 110
Becomes a fluent phraseman, absolute
And technical in victories and defeats,
And all our dainty terms for fratricide;

Terms which we trundle smoothly o'er our
   tongues
Like mere abstractions, empty sounds to which
We join no feeling and attach no form!
As if the soldier died without a wound;
As if the fibres of this godlike frame
Were gored without a pang; as if the wretch,
Who fell in battle, doing bloody deeds, 120
Passed off to Heaven, translated and not
   killed;
As though he had no wife to pine for him,
No God to judge him! Therefore, evil days
Are coming on us, O my countrymen!
And what if all-avenging Providence,
Strong and retributive, should make us know
The meaning of our words, force us to feel
The desolation and the agony
Of our fierce doings?

               Spare us yet awhile,
Father and God! O! spare us yet awhile! 130
Oh! let not English women drag their flight
Fainting beneath the burthen of their babes,
Of the sweet infants, that but yesterday
Laughed at the breast! Sons, brothers, hus-
   bands, all
Who ever gazed with fondness on the forms
Which grew up with you round the same fire-
   side,
And all who ever heard the sabbath-bells
Without the infidel's scorn, make yourselves
   pure!
Stand forth! be men! repel an impious foe,
Impious and false, a light yet cruel race, 140
Who laugh away all virtue, mingling mirth
With deeds of murder; and still promising
Freedom, themselves too sensual to be free,
Poison life's amities, and cheat the heart
Of faith and quiet hope, and all that soothes,
And all that lifts the spirit! Stand we forth;
Render them back upon the insulted ocean,
And let them toss as idly on its waves
As the vile sea-weed, which some mountain-
   blast
Swept from our shores! and Oh! may we re-
   turn 150
Not with a drunken triumph, but with fear,
Repenting of the wrongs with which we stung
So fierce a foe to frenzy!

               I have told,
O Britons! O my brethren! I have told
Most bitter truth, but without bitterness.
Nor deem my zeal or factious or mistimed;

For never can true courage dwell with them,
Who, playing tricks with conscience, dare not
   look
At their own vices. We have been too long
Dupes of a deep delusion! Some, belike, 160
Groaning with restless enmity, expect
All change from change of constituted power;
As if a Government had been a robe,
On which our vice and wretchedness were
   tagged
Like fancy-points and fringes, with the robe
Pulled off at pleasure. Fondly these attach
A radical causation to a few
Poor drudges of chastising Providence,
Who borrow all their hues and qualities
From our own folly and rank wickedness, 170
Which gave them birth and nursed them.
   Others, meanwhile,
Dote with a mad idolatry; and all
Who will not fall before their images,
And yield them worship, they are enemies
Even of their country!

       Such have I been deemed—
But, O dear Britain! O my Mother Isle!
Needs must thou prove a name most dear and
   holy
To me, a son, a brother, and a friend,
A husband, and a father! who revere
All bonds of natural love, and find them all 180
Within the limits of thy rocky shores.
O native Britain! O my Mother Isle!
How shouldst thou prove aught else but dear
   and holy
To me, who from thy lakes and mountain-
   hills,
Thy clouds, thy quiet dales, thy rocks and
   seas,
Have drunk in all my intellectual life,
All sweet sensations, all ennobling thoughts,
All adoration of the God in nature,
All lovely and all honourable things,
Whatever makes this mortal spirit feel 190
The joy and greatness of its future being?
There lives nor form nor feeling in my soul
Unborrowed from my country! O divine
And beauteous island! thou hast been my sole
And most magnificent temple, in the which
I walk with awe, and sing my stately songs,
Loving the God that made me!—

       May my fears,
My filial fears, be vain! and may the vaunts
And menace of the vengeful enemy

Pass like the gust, that roared and died
   away   200
In the distant tree: which heard, and only
   heard
In this low dell, bowed not the delicate grass.

But now the gentle dew-fall sends abroad
The fruit-like perfume of the golden furze:
The light has left the summit of the hill,
Though still a sunny gleam lies beautiful,
Aslant the ivied beacon. Now farewell,
Farewell, awhile, O soft and silent spot!
On the green sheep-track, up the heathy hill,
Homeward I wind my way; and lo! recalled 210
From bodings that have well-nigh wearied me,
I find myself upon the brow, and pause
Startled! And after lonely sojourning
In such a quiet and surrounded nook,
This burst of prospect, here the shadowy
   main,
Dim-tinted, there the mighty majesty
Of that huge amphitheatre of rich
And elmy fields, seems like society—
Conversing with the mind, and giving it
A livelier impulse and a dance of thought! 220
And now, beloved Stowey! I behold
Thy church-tower, and, methinks, the four
   huge elms
Clustering, which mark the mansion of my
   friend;
And close behind them, hidden from my view,
Is my own lowly cottage, where my babe
And my babe's mother dwell in peace! With
   light
And quickened footsteps thitherward I tend,
Remembering thee, O green and silent dell!
And grateful, that by nature's quietness
And solitary musings, all my heart   230
Is softened, and made worthy to indulge
Love, and the thoughts that yearn for human
   kind.

THE NIGHTINGALE

A CONVERSATION POEM, APRIL, 1798

No cloud, no relique of the sunken day
Distinguishes the West, no long thin slip
Of sullen light, no obscure trembling hues.
Come, we will rest on this old mossy bridge!
You see the glimmer of the stream beneath,
But hear no murmuring: it flows silently,
O'er its soft bed of verdure. All is still,

A balmy night! and though the stars be dim,
Yet let us think upon the vernal showers
That gladden the green earth, and we shall
    find   10
A pleasure in the dimness of the stars.
And hark! the Nightingale begins its song,
'Most musical, most melancholy' bird!
A melancholy bird? Oh! idle thought!
In Nature there is nothing melancholy.
But some night-wandering man whose heart
    was pierced
With the remembrance of a grievous wrong,
Or slow distemper, or neglected love,
(And so, poor wretch! filled all things with
    himself,
And made all gentle sounds tell back the
    tale   20
Of his own sorrow) he, and such as he,
First named these notes a melancholy strain.
And many a poet echoes the conceit;
Poet who hath been building up the rhyme
When he had better far have stretched his
    limbs
Beside a brook in mossy forest-dell,
By sun or moon-light, to the influxes
Of shapes and sounds and shifting elements
Surrendering his whole spirit, of his song
And of his fame forgetful! so his fame   30
Should share in Nature's immortality,
A venerable thing! and so his song
Should make all Nature lovelier, and itself
Be loved like Nature! But 'twill not be so;
And youths and maidens most poetical,
Who lose the deepening twilights of the spring
In ball-rooms and hot theatres, they still
Full of meek sympathy must heave their sighs
O'er Philomela's pity-pleading strains.

My Friend, and thou, our Sister! we have
    learnt   40
A different lore: we may not thus profane
Nature's sweet voices, always full of love
And joyance! 'Tis the merry Nightingale
That crowds, and hurries, and precipitates
With fast thick warble his delicious notes,
As he were fearful that an April night
Would be too short, for him to utter forth
His love-chant, and disburthen his full soul
Of all its music!
                    And I know a grove
Of large extent, hard by a castle huge,   50
Which the great lord inhabits not; and so
This grove is wild with tangling underwood,
And the trim walks are broken up, and grass,

Thin grass and king-cups grow within the
    paths.
But never elsewhere in one place I knew
So many nightingales; and far and near,
In wood and thicket, over the wide grove,
They answer and provoke each other's song,
With skirmish and capricious passagings
And murmurs musical and swift jug jug,   60
And one low piping sound more sweet than
    all—
Stirring the air with such a harmony,
That should you close your eyes, you might
    almost
Forget it was not day! On moonlight bushes,
Whose dewy leaflets are but half-disclosed,
You may perchance behold them on the twigs,
Their bright, bright eyes, their eyes both
    bright and full,
Glistening, while many a glow-worm in the
    shade
Lights up her love-torch.

                        A most gentle Maid,
Who dwelleth in her hospitable home   70
Hard by the castle, and at latest eve
(Even like a Lady vowed and dedicate
To something more than Nature in the grove)
Glides through the pathways; she knows all
    their notes,
That gentle Maid! and oft, a moment's space,
What time the moon was lost behind a cloud,
Hath heard a pause of silence; till the moon
Emerging, hath awakened earth and sky
With one sensation, and those wakeful birds
Have all burst forth in choral minstrelsy,   80
As if some sudden gale had swept at once
A hundred airy harps! And she hath watched
Many a nightingale perch giddily
On blossomy twig still swinging from the
    breeze,
And to that motion tune his wanton song
Like tipsy Joy that reels with tossing head.

Farewell, O Warbler! till to-morrow eve,
And you, my friends! farewell, a short fare-
    well!
We have been loitering long and pleasantly,
And now for our dear homes—That strain
    again!   90
Full fain it would delay me! My dear babe,
Who, capable of no articulate sound,
Mars all things with his imitative lisp,
How he would place his hand beside his ear,
His little hand, the small forefinger up,

And bid us listen! And I deem it wise
To make him Nature's play-mate. He knows
    well
The evening-star; and once, when he awoke
In most distressful mood (some inward pain
Had made up that strange thing, an infant's
    dream—)   100
I hurried with him to our orchard-plot,
And he beheld the moon, and, hushed at once,
Suspends his sobs, and laughs most silently,
While his fair eyes, that swam with undropped
    tears,
Did glitter in the yellow moon-beam! Well!—
It is a father's tale: But if that Heaven
Should give me life, his childhood shall grow
    up
Familiar with these songs, that with the night
He may associate joy.—Once more, farewell,
Sweet Nightingale! once more, my friends!
    farewell.   110

THE BALLAD OF THE DARK LADIE

A FRAGMENT

BENEATH yon birch with silver bark,
And boughs so pendulous and fair,
The brook falls scatter'd down the rock:
    And all is mossy there!

And there upon the moss she sits,
The Dark Ladié in silent pain;
The heavy tear is in her eye,
    And drops and swells again.

Three times she sends her little page
Up the castled mountain's breast,   10
If he might find the Knight that wears
    The Griffin for his crest.

The sun was sloping down the sky,
And she had linger'd there all day,
Counting moments, dreaming fears—
    Oh wherefore can he stay?

She hears a rustling o'er the brook,
She sees far off a swinging bough!
'Tis He! 'Tis my betrothéd Knight!
    Lord Falkland, it is thou!   20

She springs, she clasps him round the neck,
She sobs a thousand hopes and fears,

Her kisses glowing on his cheeks
    She quenches with her tears.

      *   *   *

'My friends with rude ungentle words
They scoff and bid me fly to thee!
O give me shelter in thy breast!
    O shield and shelter me!

'My Henry, I have given thee much,
I gave what I can ne'er recall,   30
I gave my heart, I gave my peace,
    O Heaven! I gave thee all.'

The Knight made answer to the Maid,
While to his heart he held her hand,
'Nine castles hath my noble-sire,
    None statelier in the land.

'The fairest one shall be my love's,
The fairest castle of the nine!
Wait only till the stars peep out,
    The fairest shall be thine: 40

'Wait only till the hand of eve
Hath wholly closed yon western bars,
And through the dark we two will steal
    Beneath the twinkling stars!'—

'The dark? the dark? No! not the dark?
The twinkling stars? How, Henry? How?'
O God! 'twas in the eye of noon
    He pledged his sacred vow!

And in the eye of noon my love
Shall lead me from my mother's door,   50
Sweet boys and girls all clothed in white
    Strewing flowers before:

But first the nodding minstrels go
With music meet for lordly bowers,
The children next in snow-white vests.
    Strewing buds and flowers!

And then my love and I shall pace,
My jet black hair in pearly braids,
Between our comely bachelors
    And blushing bridal maids.   60

      *   *   *

KUBLA KHAN

IN Xanadu did Kubla Khan
A stately pleasure-dome decree:

Where Alph, the sacred river, ran
Through caverns measureless to man
  Down to a sunless sea.
So twice five miles of fertile ground
With walls and towers were girdled round:
And there were gardens bright with sinuous
    rills,
Where blossomed many an incense-bearing
    tree;
And here were forests ancient as the hills, 10
Enfolding sunny spots of greenery.

But oh! that deep romantic chasm which
    slanted
Down the green hill athwart a cedarn cover!
A savage place! as holy and enchanted
As e'er beneath a waning moon was haunted
By woman wailing for her demon-lover!
And from this chasm, with ceaseless turmoil
    seething,
As if this earth in fast thick pants were
    breathing,
A mighty fountain momently was forced:
Amid whose swift half-intermitted burst   20
Huge fragments vaulted like rebounding hail,
Or chaffy grain beneath the thresher's flail,
And 'mid these dancing rocks at once and
    ever
It flung up momently the sacred river.
Five miles meandering with a mazy motion
Through wood and dale the sacred river ran,
Then reached the caverns measureless to man,
And sank in tumult to a lifeless ocean:
And 'mid this tumult Kubla heard from far
Ancestral voices prophesying war!   30

  The shadow of the dome of pleasure
  Floated midway on the waves;
  Where was heard the mingled measure
  From the fountain and the caves.
It was a miracle of rare device,
A sunny pleasure-dome with caves of ice!

  A damsel with a dulcimer
  In a vision once I saw:
  It was an Abyssinian maid,
  And on her dulcimer she played,   40
  Singing of Mount Abora.
  Could I revive within me
  Her symphony and song,
  To such a deep delight 'twould win me,
That with music loud and long,
I would build that dome in air,
That sunny dome! those caves of ice!

And all who heard should see them there,
And all should cry, Beware! Beware!
His flashing eyes, his floating hair!   50
Weave a circle round him thrice,
And close your eyes with holy dread,
For he on honey-dew hath fed,
And drunk the milk of Paradise.

ON A CATARACT

FROM A CAVERN NEAR THE SUMMIT OF A MOUNTAIN PRECIPICE

STROPHE

UNPERISHING youth!
Thou leapest from forth
The cell of thy hidden nativity;
Never mortal saw
The cradle of the strong one;
Never mortal heard
The gathering of his voices;
The deep-murmured charm of the son of the
    rock,
That is lisp'd evermore at his slumberless foun-
    tain.
There's a cloud at the portal, a spray-woven
    veil   10
At the shrine of his ceaseless renewing;
It embosoms the roses of dawn,
It entangles the shafts of the noon,
And into the bed of its stillness
The moonshine sinks down as in slumber,
That the son of the rock, that the nursling of
    heaven
May be born in a holy twilight!

ANTISTROPHE

The wild goat in awe
Looks up and beholds
Above thee the cliff inaccessible;—   20
Thou at once full-born
Madd'nest in thy joyance,
Whirlest, shatter'st, splitt'st,
Life invulnerable.

THE DEVIL'S THOUGHTS

I

FROM his brimstone bed at break of day
A walking the Devil is gone,
To visit his snug little farm the earth,
And see how his stock goes on.

II

Over the hill and over the dale,
And he went over the plain,
And backward and forward he switched his
    long tail
As a gentleman switches his cane.

III

And how then was the Devil drest?
Oh! he was in his Sunday's best: 10
His jacket was red and his breeches were blue,
And there was a hole where the tail came
    through.

IV

He saw a Lawyer killing a Viper
On a dunghill hard by his own stable;
And the Devil smiled, for it put him in mind
Of Cain and his brother, Abel.

V

He saw an Apothecary on a white horse
Ride by on his vocations,
And the Devil thought of his old Friend
Death in the Revelations.   20

VI

He saw a cottage with a double coach-house,
A cottage of gentility;
And the Devil did grin, for his darling sin
Is pride that apes humility.

VII

He peep'd into a rich bookseller's shop,
Quoth he! we are both of one college!
For I sate myself, like a cormorant, once
Hard by the tree of knowledge.

VIII

Down the river did glide, with wind and tide,
A pig with vast celerity;   30
And the Devil look'd wise as he saw how the
    while,
It cut its own throat. 'There!' quoth he with a
    smile,
'Goes "England's commercial prosperity." '

IX

As he went through Cold-Bath Fields he saw
    A solitary cell;
And the Devil was pleased, for it gave him a
    hint
    For improving his prisons in Hell.

X

He saw a Turnkey in a trice
    Fetter a troublesome blade;
'Nimbly,' quoth he, 'do the fingers move   40
    If a man be but used to his trade.'

XI

He saw the same Turnkey unfetter a man,
    With but little expedition,
Which put him in mind of the long debate
    On the Slave-trade abolition.

XII

He saw an old acquaintance
    As he passed by a Methodist meeting;—
She holds a consecrated key,
    And the devil nods her a greeting.

XIII

She turned up her nose, and said,   50
    'Avaunt! my name's Religion,'
And she looked to Mr. ——
    And leered like a love-sick pigeon.

XIV

He saw a certain minister
    (A minister to his mind)
Go up into a certain House,
    With a majority, behind.

XV

The Devil quoted Genesis
    Like a very learnéd clerk,
How 'Noah and his creeping things   60
    Went up into the Ark.'

XVI

He took from the poor,
    And he gave to the rich,
And he shook hands with a Scotchman,
    For he was not afraid of the ——

XVII

General —————'s burning face
    He saw with consternation,
And back to hell his way did he take,
For the Devil thought by a slight mistake
    It was general conflagration.   70

LOVE

ALL thoughts, all passions, all delights,
Whatever stirs this mortal frame,
All are but ministers of Love,
    And feed his sacred flame.

Oft in my waking dreams do I
Live o'er again that happy hour,
When midway on the mount I lay,
    Beside the ruined tower.

The moonshine, stealing o'er the scene
Had blended with the lights of eve;   10
And she was there, my hope, my joy,
    My own dear Genevieve!

She leant against the arméd man,
The statue of the arméd knight;
She stood and listened to my lay,
    Amid the lingering light.

Few sorrows hath she of her own,
My hope! my joy! my Genevieve!
She loves me best, whene'er I sing
    The songs that make her grieve.   20

I played a soft and doleful air,
I sang an old and moving story—
And old rude song, that suited well
    That ruin wild and hoary.

She listened with a flitting blush,
With downcast eyes and modest grace;
For well she knew, I could not choose
    But gaze upon her face.

I told her of the Knight that wore
Upon his shield a burning brand;   30
And that for ten long years he wooed
    The lady of the Land.

I told her how he pined: and ah!
The deep, the low, the pleading tone
With which I sang another's love,
    Interpreted my own.

She listened with a flitting blush,
With downcast eyes, and modest grace;
And she forgave me, that I gazed
    Too fondly on her face.   40

But when I told the cruel scorn
That crazed that bold and lovely Knight,
And that he crossed the mountain-woods,
    Nor rested day nor night;

That sometimes from the savage den,
And sometimes from the darksome shade,
And sometimes starting up at once
    In green and sunny glade,—

There came and looked him in the face
An angel beautiful and bright;   50
And that he knew it was a Fiend,
    This miserable Knight!

And that unknowing what he did,
He leaped amid a murderous band,
And saved from outrage worse than death
    The Lady of the Land!

And how she wept, and clasped his knees;
And how she tended him in vain—
And ever strove to expiate
    The scorn that crazed his brain;—   60

And that she nursed him in a cave;
And how his madness went away,
When on the yellow forest-leaves
    A dying man he lay;—

His dying words—but when I reached
That tenderest strain of all the ditty,
My faltering voice and pausing harp
    Disturbed her soul with pity!

All impulses of soul and sense
Had thrilled my guileless Genevieve;   70
The music and the doleful tale,
    The rich and balmy eve;

And hopes, and fears that kindle hope,
An undistinguishable throng,
And gentle wishes long subdued,
    Subdued and cherished long!

She wept with pity and delight,
She blushed with love, and virgin-shame;
And like the murmur of a dream,
    I heard her breathe my name.   80

Her bosom heaved—she stepped aside,
As conscious of my look she stepped—
Then suddenly, with timorous eye
    She fled to me and wept.

She half enclosed me with her arms,
She pressed me with a meek embrace;
And bending back her head, looked up,
    And gazed upon my face.

'Twas partly love, and partly fear,
And partly 'twas a bashful art,   90
That I might rather feel, than see,
    The swelling of her heart.

I calmed her fears, and she was calm,
And told her love with virgin pride;
And so I won my Genevieve,
    My bright and Beauteous Bride.

DEJECTION: AN ODE

(WRITTEN APRIL 4, 1802)

Late, late yestreen I saw the new Moon,
With the old Moon in her arms;
And I fear, I fear, my Master dear!
We shall have a deadly storm.
Ballad of Sir Patrick Spence.

I

WELL! If the Bard was weather-wise, who
    made
  The grand old ballad of Sir Patrick Spence,
  This night, so tranquil now, will not go
    hence
Unroused by winds, that ply a busier trade
Than those which mould yon cloud in lazy
    flakes,
Or the dull sobbing draft, that moans and
    rakes
  Upon the strings of this Æolian lute,
  Which better far were mute.
For lo! the New-moon winter-bright!
And overspread with phantom light,   10
(With swimming phantom light o'erspread
But rimmed and circled by a silver thread)
I see the old Moon in her lap, foretelling
  The coming-on of rain and squally blast.
And oh! that even now the gust were swelling,
  And the slant night-shower driving loud and
    fast!
Those sounds which oft have raised me, whilst
    they awed,
  And sent my soul abroad,

Might now perhaps their wonted impulse give,
Might startle this dull pain, and make it move
    and live!   20

II

A grief without a pang, void, dark, and drear,
  A stifled, drowsy, unimpassioned grief,
  Which finds no natural outlet, no relief,
    In word, or sigh, or tear—
O Lady! in this wan and heartless mood,
To other thoughts by yonder throstle woo'd,
  All this long eve, so balmy and serene,
Have I been gazing on the western sky,
  And its peculiar tint of yellow green:
And still I gaze—and with how blank an
    eye!   30
And those thin clouds above, in flakes and
    bars,
That give away their motion to the stars;
Those stars, that glide behind them or be-
    tween,
Now sparkling, now bedimmed, but always
    seen:
Yon crescent Moon, as fixed as if it grew
In its own cloudless, starless lake of blue:
I see them all so excellently fair,
I see, not feel, how beautiful they are!

III

  My genial spirits fail;
  And what can these avail   40
To lift the smothering weight from off my
    breast?
  It were a vain endeavour,
  Though I should gaze for ever
On that green light that lingers in the west:
I may not hope from outward forms to win
The passion and the life, whose fountains are
    within.

IV

O Lady! we receive but what we give,
And in our life alone does Nature live:
Ours is her wedding garment, ours her shroud!
  And would we aught behold, of higher
    worth,   50
Than that inanimate cold world allowed
To the poor loveless ever-anxious crowd,
  Ah! from the soul itself must issue forth
A light, a glory, a fair luminous cloud
    Enveloping the Earth—

And from the soul itself must there be sent
  A sweet and potent voice, of its own birth,
Of all sweet sounds the life and element!

V

O pure of heart! thou need'st not ask of me
What this strong music in the soul may be! 60
What, and wherein it doth exist,
This light, this glory, this fair luminous mist,
This beautiful and beauty-making power.
  Joy, virtuous Lady! Joy that ne'er was
    given,
Save to the pure, and in their purest hour,
Life, and Life's effluence, cloud at once and
    shower,
Joy, Lady! is the spirit and the power,
Which wedding Nature to us gives in dower
  A new Earth and new Heaven,
Undreamt of by the sensual and the proud— 70
Joy is the sweet voice, Joy the luminous
    cloud—
  We in ourselves rejoice!
And thence flows all that charms or ear or
    sight,
  All melodies the echoes of that voice,
All colours a suffusion from that light.

VI

There was a time when, though my path was
    rough,
  This joy within me dallied with distress,
And all misfortunes were but as the stuff
  Whence Fancy made me dreams of happi-
    ness:
For hope grew round me, like the twining
    vine, 80
And fruits, and foliage, not my own, seemed
    mine.
But now afflictions bow me down to earth:
Nor care I that they rob me of my mirth;
  But oh! each visitation
Suspends what nature gave me at my birth,
  My shaping spirit of Imagination.
For not to think of what I needs must feel,
  But to be still and patient, all I can;
And haply by abstruse research to steal
  From my own nature all the natural man— 90
  This was my sole resource, my only plan:
Till that which suits a part infects the whole,
And now is almost grown the habit of my
    soul.

VII

Hence, viper thoughts, that coil around my
    mind,
  Reality's dark dream!
I turn from you, and listen to the wind,
  Which long has raved unnoticed. What a
    scream
Of agony by torture lengthened out
That lute sent forth! Thou Wind, that rav'st
    without,
  Bare crag, or mountain-tairn, or blasted
    tree, 100
Or pine-grove whither woodman never clomb,
Or lonely house, long held the witches' home,
  Methinks were fitter instruments for thee,
Mad Lutanist! who in this month of showers,
Of dark-brown gardens, and of peeping
    flowers,
Mak'st Devils' yule, with worse than wintry
    song,
The blossoms, buds, and timorous leaves
    among.
  Thou Actor, perfect in all tragic sounds!
Thou mighty Poet, e'en to frenzy bold!
    What tell'st thou now about? 110
  'Tis of the rushing of an host in rout,
  With groans, of trampled men, with smart-
    ing wounds—
At once they groan with pain, and shudder
    with the cold!
But hush! there is a pause of deepest silence!
  And all that noise, as of a rushing crowd,
With groans, and tremulous shudderings—all
    is over—
  It tells another tale, with sounds less deep
    and loud!
  A tale of less affright,
  And tempered with delight,
As Otway's self had framed the tender
    lay,— 120
  'Tis of a little child
  Upon a lonesome wild,
Not far from home, but she hath lost her way:
And now moans low in bitter grief and fear,
And now screams loud, and hopes to make her
    mother hear.

VIII

'Tis midnight, but small thoughts have I of
    sleep:
Full seldom may my friend such vigils keep!
Visit her, gentle Sleep! with wings of healing,

And may this storm be but a mountain-
　　birth,
May all the stars hang bright above her dwell-
　　ing,　　　　　　　　　　　　　　130
Silent as though they watched the sleeping
　　Earth!
　　With light heart may she rise,
　　Gay fancy, cheerful eyes,
Joy lift her spirit, joy attune her voice;
To her may all things live, from pole to pole,
Their life the eddying of her living soul!
O simple spirit, guided from above,
Dear Lady! friend devoutest of my choice,
Thus mayest thou ever, evermore rejoice.

HYMN BEFORE SUNRISE, IN THE VALE OF CHAMOUNI

HAST thou a charm to stay the morning-star
In his steep course? So long he seems to
　　pause
On thy bald awful head, O sovran Blanc,
The Arve and Arveiron at thy base
Rave ceaselessly; but thou, most awful Form!
Risest from forth thy silent sea of pines,
How silently! Around thee and above
Deep is the air and dark, substantial, black,
An ebon mass: methinks thou piercest it,
As with a wedge! But when I look again,　10
It is thine own calm home, thy crystal shrine,
Thy habitation from eternity!
O dread and silent Mount! I gazed upon thee,
Till thou, still present to the bodily sense,
Didst vanish from my thought: entranced in
　　prayer
I worshipped the Invisible alone.

Yet, like some sweet beguiling melody,
So sweet, we know not we are listening to it,
Thou, the meanwhile, wast blending with my
　　Thought,
Yea, with my Life and Life's own secret
　　joy:　　　　　　　　　　　　　　20
Till the dilating Soul, enrapt, transfused,
Into the mighty vision passing—there
As in her natural form swelled vast to Heaven!

Awake, my soul! not only passive praise
Thou owest! not alone these swelling tears,
Mute thanks and secret ecstasy! Awake,
Voice of sweet song! Awake, my heart, awake!
Green vales and icy cliffs, all join my Hymn.

Thou first and chief, sole sovereign of the
　　Vale!
O struggling with the darkness all the night, 30
And visited all night by troops of stars,
Or when they climb the sky or when they
　　sink:
Companion of the morning-star at dawn,
Thyself Earth's rosy star, and of the dawn
Co-herald: wake, O wake, and utter praise!
Who sank thy sunless pillars deep in Earth?
Who filled thy countenance with rosy light?
Who made thee parent of perpetual streams?

And you, ye five wild torrents fiercely glad!
Who called you forth from night and utter
　　death,　　　　　　　　　　　　　40
From dark and icy caverns called you forth,
Down those precipitous, black, jaggéd rocks,
For ever shattered and the same for ever?
Who gave you your invulnerable life,
Your strength, your speed, your fury, and
　　your joy,
Unceasing thunder and eternal foam?
And who commanded (and the silence came),
Here let the billows stiffen, and have rest?

Ye Ice-falls! ye that from the mountain's
　　brow
Adown enormous ravines slope amain—　50
Torrents, methinks, that heard a mighty voice,
And stopped at once amid their maddest
　　plunge!
Motionless torrents! silent cataracts!
Who made you glorious as the Gates of
　　Heaven
Beneath the keen full moon? Who bade the
　　sun
Clothe you with rainbows? Who, with living
　　flowers
Of loveliest blue, spread garlands at your
　　feet?—
God! let the torrents, like a shout of nations,
Answer! and let the ice-plains echo, God!
God! sing ye meadow-streams with gladsome
　　voice!　　　　　　　　　　　　　60
Ye pine-groves, with your soft and soul-like
　　sounds!
And they too have a voice, yon piles of snow,
And in their perilous fall shall thunder, God!

Ye living flowers that skirt the eternal frost!
Ye wild goats sporting round the eagle's nest!
Ye eagles, play-mates of the mountain-storm!
Ye lightnings, the dread arrows of the clouds!

Ye signs and wonders of the element!
Utter forth God, and fill the hills with praise!

Thou too, hoar Mount! with thy sky-point-
   ing peaks,   70
Oft from whose feet the avalanche, unheard
Shoots downward, glittering through the pure
   serene
Into the depth of clouds, that veil thy
   breast—
Thou too again, stupendous Mountain! thou
That as I raise my head, awhile bowed low
In adoration, upward from thy base
Slow travelling with dim eyes suffused with
   tears,
Solemnly seemest, like a vapoury cloud,
To rise before me—Rise, O ever rise,
Rise like a cloud of incense from the Earth! 80
Thou kingly Spirit throned among the hills,
Thou dread ambassador from Earth to
   Heaven,
Great Hierarch! tell thou the silent sky,
And tell the stars, and tell yon rising sun
Earth, with her thousand voices, praises God.

THE PAINS OF SLEEP

ERE on my bed my limbs I lay,
It hath not been my use to pray
With moving lips or bended knees;
But silently, by slow degrees,
My spirit I to Love compose,
In humble trust mine eye-lids close,
With reverential resignation,
No wish conceived, no thought exprest,
Only a sense of supplication;
A sense o'er all my soul imprest   10
That I am weak, yet not unblest,
Since in me, round me, every where
Eternal Strength and Wisdom are.

But yester-night I prayed aloud
In anguish and in agony,
Up-starting from the fiendish crowd
Of shapes and thoughts that tortured me:
A lurid light, a trampling throng,
Sense of intolerable wrong,
And whom I scorned, those only strong!   20
Thirst of revenge, the powerless will
Still baffled, and yet burning still!
Desire with loathing strangely mixed
On wild or hateful objects fixed.
Fantastic passions! maddening brawl!

And shame and terror over all!
Deeds to be hid which were not hid,
Which all confused I could not know
Whether I suffered, or I did:
For all seemed guilt, remorse or woe,   30
My own or others still the same
Life-stifling fear, soul-stifling shame.

So two nights passed: the night's dismay
Saddened and stunned the coming day.
Sleep, the wide blessing, seemed to me
Distemper's worst calamity.
The third night, when my own loud scream
Had waked me from the fiendish dream,
O'ercome with sufferings strange and wild,
I wept as I had been a child;   40
And having thus by tears subdued
My anguish to a milder mood,
Such punishments, I said, were due
To natures deepliest stained with sin,—
For aye entempesting anew
The unfathomable hell within,
The horror of their deeds to view,
To know and loathe, yet wish and do!

Such griefs with such men well agree,
But wherefore, wherefore fall on me?   50
To be beloved is all I need,
And whom I love, I love indeed.

TO WILLIAM WORDSWORTH

COMPOSED ON THE NIGHT AFTER HIS RECITATION
OF A POEM ON THE GROWTH
OF AN INDIVIDUAL MIND

FRIEND of the Wise! and Teacher of the Good!
Into my heart have I received that Lay
More than historic, that prophetic Lay
Wherein (high theme by thee first sung aright)
Of the foundations and the building up
Of a Human Spirit thou hast dared to tell
What may be told, to the understanding mind
Revealable; and what within the mind
By vital breathings secret as the soul
Of vernal growth, oft quickens in the heart 10
Thoughts all too deep for words!—

                Theme hard as high!
Of smiles spontaneous, and mysterious fears
(The first-born they of Reason and twin-
   birth),
Of tides obedient to external force,

And currents self-determined, as might seem,
Or by some inner Power; of moments awful,
Now in thy inner life, and now abroad,
When power streamed from thee, and thy
    soul received
The light reflected, as a light bestowed—
Of fancies fair, and milder hours of youth, 20
Hyblean murmurs of poetic thought
Industrious in its joys, in vales and glens
Native or outland, lakes and famous hills!
Or on the lonely high-road, when the stars
Were rising; or by secret mountain-streams,
The guides and the companions of thy way!

Of more than Fancy, of the Social Sense
Distending wide, and man beloved as man,
Where France in all her towns lay vibrating
Like some becalméd bark beneath the burst 30
Of Heaven's immediate thunder, when no
    cloud
Is visible, or shadow on the main.
For thou wert there, thine own brows gar-
    landed,
Amid the tremor of a realm aglow,
Amid a mighty nation jubilant,
When from the general heart of human kind
Hope sprang forth like a full-born Deity!
——Of that dear Hope afflicted and struck
    down,
So summoned homeward, thenceforth calm and
    sure
From the dread watch-tower of man's absolute
    self,   40
With light unwaning on her eyes, to look
Far on—herself a glory to behold,
The Angel of the vision! Then (last strain)
Of Duty, chosen Laws controlling choice,
Action and joy!—An Orphic song indeed,
A song divine of high and passionate thoughts
To their own music chaunted!

                           O great Bard!
Ere yet that last strain dying awed the air,
With stedfast eye I viewed thee in the choir
Of ever-enduring men. The truly great   50
Have all one age, and from one visible space
Shed influence! They, both in power and act,
Are permanent, and Time is not with them,
Save as it worketh for them, they in it.
Nor less a sacred Roll, than those of old,
And to be placed, as they, with gradual fame
Among the archives of mankind, thy work
Makes audible a linkéd lay of Truth,
Of Truth profound a sweet continuous lay,

Not learnt, but native, her own natural
    notes!   60
Ah! as I listened with a heart forlorn,
The pulses of my being beat anew:
And even as Life returns upon the drowned,
Life's joy rekindling roused a throng of
    pains—
Keen pangs of Love, awakening as a babe
Turbulent, with an outcry in the heart;
And fears self-willed, that shunned the eye
    of Hope;
And Hope that scarce would know itself from
    Fear;
Sense of past Youth, and Manhood come in
    vain,
And Genius given, and Knowledge won in
    vain;   70
And all which I had culled in wood-walks wild,
And all which patient toil had reared, and all,
Commune with thee had opened out—but
    flowers
Strewed on my corse, and borne upon my
    bier
In the same coffin, for the self-same grave!

That way no more! and ill beseems it me,
Who came a welcomer in herald's guise,
Singing of Glory, and Futurity,
To wander back on such unhealthful road,
Plucking the poisons of self-harm! And ill 80
Such intertwine beseems triumphal wreaths
Strew'd before thy advancing!

                           Nor do thou,
Sage Bard! impair the memory of that hour
Of thy communion with my nobler mind
By pity or grief, already felt too long!
Nor let my words import more blame than
    needs.
The tumult rose and ceased: for Peace is nigh
Where Wisdom's voice has found a listening
    heart.
Amid the howl of more than wintry storms,
The Halcyon hears the voice of vernal hours 90
Already on the wing.

                           Eve following eve,
Dear tranquil time, when the sweet sense of
    Home
Is sweetest! moments for their own sake
    hailed
And more desired, more precious, for thy
    song,
In silence listening, like a devout child,

My soul lay passive, by thy various strain
Driven as in surges now beneath the stars,
With momentary stars of my own birth,
Fair constellated foam, still darting off
Into the darkness; now a tranquil sea,   100
Outspread and bright, yet swelling to the
      moon.

And when—O Friend! my comforter and
      guide!
Strong in thyself, and powerful to give
      strength!—
Thy long sustainéd Song finally closed,
And thy deep voice had ceased—yet thou
      thyself
Wert still before my eyes, and round us both
That happy vision of belovéd faces—
Scarce conscious, and yet conscious of its close
I sate, my being blended in one thought
(Thought was it? or aspiration? or re-
      solve?)   110
Absorbed, yet hanging still upon the sound—
And when I rose, I found myself in prayer.

A TOMBLESS EPITAPH

'Tis true, Idoloclastes Satyrane!
(So call him, for so mingling blame with
      praise,
And smiles with anxious looks, his earliest
      friends,
Masking his birth-name, wont to character
His wild-wood fancy, and impetuous zeal,)
'Tis true that, passionate for ancient truths,
And honouring with religious love the Great
Of elder times, he hated to excess,
With an unquiet and intolerant scorn,
The hollow puppets of a hollow Age,   10
Ever idolatrous, and changing ever
Its worthless Idols! Learning, Power and
      Time,
(Too much of all) thus wasting in vain war
Of fervid colloquy. Sickness, 'tis true,
Whole years of weary days, besieged him
      close,
Even to the gates and inlets of his life!
But it is true, no less, that strenuous, firm,
And with a natural gladness, he maintained
The citadel unconquered, and in joy
Was strong to follow the delightful Muse. 20
For not a hidden path, that to the shades
Of the beloved Parnassian forest leads,
Lurked undiscovered by him; not a rill

There issues from the fount of Hippocrene,
But he had traced it upward to its source,
Through open glade, dark glen, and secret dell,
Knew the gay wild flowers on its banks, and
      culled
Its med'cinable herbs. Yea, oft alone,
Piercing the long-neglected holy cave,
The haunt obscure of old Philosophy,   30
He bade with lifted torch its starry walls
Sparkle, as erst they sparkled to the flame
Of odorous lamps tended by Saint and Sage.
O framed for calmer times and nobler hearts!
O studious Poet, eloquent for truth!
Philosopher! contemning wealth and death,
Yet docile, childlike, full of Life and Love!
Here, rather than on monumental stone,
This record of thy worth thy Friend inscribes,
Thoughtful, with quiet tears upon his cheek. 40

TIME, REAL AND IMAGINARY

AN ALLEGORY

ON the wide level of a mountain's head,
(I knew not where, but 'twas some faery
      place)
Their pinions, ostrich-like, for sails out-spread,
Two lovely children run an endless race,
      A sister and a brother!
      This far outstripp'd the other;
Yet ever runs she with reverted face,
      And looks and listens for the boy behind:
      For he, alas! is blind!
O'er rough and smooth with even step he
      passed,   10
And knows not whether he be first or last.

YOUTH AND AGE

VERSE, a breeze mid blossoms straying,
Where Hope clung feeding, like a bee—
Both were mine! Life went a-maying
            With Nature, Hope and Poesy,
                  When I was young!

When I was young?—Ah, woful When!
Ah! for the change 'twixt Now and Then!
This breathing house not built with hands,
This body that does me grievous wrong,
O'er aery cliffs and glittering sands,   10
How lightly then it flashed along:—
Like those trim skiffs, unknown of yore,

On winding lakes and rivers wide,
That ask no aid of sail or oar,
That fear no spite of wind or tide!

Nought cared this body for wind or weather
When Youth and I lived in't together.

Flowers are lovely; Love is flower-like;
Friendship is a sheltering tree;
O! the joys, that came down shower-like,   20
Of Friendship, Love, and Liberty,
                                    Ere I was old!

Ere I was old? Ah woful Ere,
Which tells me, Youth's no longer here!
O Youth! for years so many and sweet,
'Tis known, that Thou and I were one,
I'll think it but a fond conceit—
It cannot be that Thou art gone!
Thy vesper-bell hath not yet toll'd:—
And thou wert aye a masker bold!   30

What strange disguise hast now put on,
To make believe, that thou art gone?
I see these locks in silvery slips,
This drooping gait, this altered size:
But Spring-tide blossoms on thy lips,
And tears take sunshine from thine eyes!
Life is but thought: so think I will
That Youth and I are house-mates still.

Dew-drops are the gems of morning,
But the tears of mournful eve!   40
Where no hope is, life's a warning
That only serves to make us grieve,
                        When we are old:
That only serves to make us grieve
With oft and tedious taking-leave,
Like some poor nigh-related guest,
That may not rudely be dismist;
Yet hath outstay'd his welcome while,
And tells the jest without the smile.

SELECTIONS FROM THE BIOGRAPHIA LITERARIA
1817

CHAPTER IV

The Lyrical Ballads with the Preface—Mr. Wordsworth's earlier poems—On fancy and imagination—The investigation of the distinction important to the Fine Arts.

I have wandered far from the object in
view, but as I fancied to myself readers who
would respect the feelings that had tempted
me from the main road; so I dare calculate
on not a few, who will warmly sympathize with
them. At present it will be sufficient for my
purpose, if I have proved, that Mr. Southey's
writings no more than my own furnished the
original occasion to this fiction of a new school
of poetry, and to the clamours against its supposed founders and proselytes.

As little do I believe that Mr. Wordsworth's
Lyrical Ballads were in themselves the cause.
I speak exclusively of the two volumes so entitled. A careful and repeated examination of
these confirms me in the belief, that the omission of less than a hundred lines would have
precluded nine-tenths of the criticism on this
work. I hazard this declaration, however, on
the supposition, that the reader has taken it
up, as he would have done any other collection
of poems purporting to derive their subjects

or interests from the incidents of domestic or
ordinary life, intermingled with higher strains
of meditation which the poet utters in his
own person and character; with the proviso,
that these poems were perused without knowledge of, or reference to, the author's peculiar
opinions, and that the reader had not had his
attention previously directed to those peculiarities. In that case, as actually happened
with Mr. Southey's earlier works, the lines
and passages which might have offended the
general taste, would have been considered as
mere inequalities, and attributed to inattention, not to perversity of judgment. The men
of business who had passed their lives chiefly
in cities, and who might therefore be expected
to derive the highest pleasure from acute notices of men and manners conveyed in easy,
yet correct and pointed language; and all those
who, reading but little poetry, are most stimulated with that species of it, which seems
most distant from prose, would probably have
passed by the volumes altogether. Others more
catholic in their taste, and yet habituated to
be most pleased when most excited, would
have contented themselves with deciding, that
the author had been successful in proportion
to the elevation of his style and subject. Not a

few, perhaps, might, by their admiration of the "Lines written near Tintern Abbey," on revisiting the Wye, those "Left upon a Yew Tree Seat," "The Old Cumberland Beggar," and "Ruth," have been gradually led to peruse with kindred feeling "The Brothers," the "Hart-leap Well," and whatever other poems in that collection may be described as holding a middle place between those written in the highest and those in the humblest style; as for instance between the "Tintern Abbey," and "The Thorn," or "Simon Lee." Should their taste submit to no further change, and still remain unreconciled to the colloquial phrases, or the imitations of them, that are, more or less, scattered through the class last mentioned; yet even from the small number of the latter, they would have deemed them but an inconsiderable subtraction from the merit of the whole work; or, what is sometimes not unpleasing in the publication of a new writer, as serving to ascertain the natural tendency, and consequently the proper direction of the author's genius.

In the critical remarks, therefore, prefixed and annexed to the *Lyrical Ballads,* I believe, we may safely rest, as the true origin of the unexampled opposition which Mr. Wordsworth's writings have been since doomed to encounter. The humbler passages in the poems themselves were dwelt on and cited to justify the rejection of the theory. What in and for themselves would have been either forgotten or forgiven as imperfections, or at least comparative failures, provoked direct hostility when announced as intentional, as the result of choice after full deliberation. Thus the poems, admitted by all as excellent, joined with those which had pleased the far greater number, though they formed two-thirds of the whole work, instead of being deemed (as in all right they should have been, even if we take for granted that the reader judged aright) an atonement for the few exceptions, gave wind and fuel to the animosity against both the poems and the poet. In all perplexity there is a portion of fear, which predisposes the mind to anger. Not able to deny that the author possessed both genius and a powerful intellect, they felt *very positive,*—but yet were not *quite certain* that he might not be in the right, and they themselves in the wrong; an unquiet state of mind, which seeks alleviation by quarrelling with the occasion of it, and by

wondering at the perverseness of the man, who had written a long and argumentative essay to persuade them, that

Fair is foul, and foul is fair;

in other words, that they had been all their lives admiring without judgment, and were now about to censure without reason.

That this conjecture is not wide from the mark, I am induced to believe from the noticeable fact, which I can state on my own knowledge, that the same general censure has been grounded by almost every different person on some different poem. Among those, whose candour and judgment I estimate highly, I distinctly remember six who expressed their objections to the *Lyrical Ballads* almost in the same words, and altogether to the same purport, at the same time admitting, that several of the poems had given them great pleasure; and, strange as it might seem, the composition which one cited as execrable, another quoted as his favourite. I am indeed convinced in my own mind, that could the same experiment have been tried with these volumes, as was made in the well known story of the picture, the result would have been the same; the parts which had been covered by black spots on the one day, would be found equally *albo lapide notatæ* on the succeeding.

However this may be, it was assuredly hard and unjust to fix the attention on a few separate and insulated poems with as much aversion, as if they had been so many plague-spots on the whole work, instead of passing them over in silence, as so much blank paper, or leaves of a bookseller's catalogue; especially, as no one pretended to have found in them any immorality or indelicacy; and the poems, therefore, at the worst, could only be regarded as so many light or inferior coins in a rouleau of gold, not as so much alloy in a weight of bullion. A friend whose talents I hold in the highest respect, but whose judgment and strong sound sense I have had almost continued occasion to revere, making the usual complaints to me concerning both the style and subjects of Mr. Wordsworth's minor poems; I admitted that there were some few of the tales and incidents, in which I could not myself find a sufficient cause for their having been recorded in metre. I mentioned "Alice Fell" as an instance; "Nay," replied my friend with more than usual quickness of manner, "I cannot agree with you there!—that, I own, does seem to me a remarkably pleasing poem." In the *Lyrical Ballads,* (for my experience does not enable me to extend the remark equally unqualified to the two subsequent volumes,) I have heard at different times, and from different individuals, every single poem extolled and reprobated, with the exception of those of loftier kind, which as was before observed, seem to have won universal praise. This fact of itself would have made me diffident in my censures, had not a still stronger ground been furnished by the strange contrast of the heat and long continuance of the opposition, with the nature of the faults stated as justifying it. The seductive faults, the *dulcia vitia* of Cowley, Marini, or Darwin might reasonably be thought capable of corrupting the public judgment for half a century, and require a twenty years war, campaign after campaign, in order to dethrone the usurper and re-establish the legitimate taste. But that a downright simpleness, under the affectation of simplicity, prosaic words in feeble metre, silly thoughts in childish phrases, and a preference of mean, degrading, or at best trivial associations and characters, should succeed in forming a school of imitators, a company of almost religious admirers, and this too among young men of ardent minds, liberal education, and not

——with academic laurels unbestowed;

and that this bare and bald counterfeit of poetry, which is characterized as below criticism, should for nearly twenty years have well-nigh engrossed criticism, as the main, if not the only, butt of review, magazine, pamphlet, poem, and paragraph; this is indeed matter of wonder. . . .

During the last year of my residence at Cambridge, 1794, I became acquainted with Mr. Wordsworth's first publication entitled *Descriptive Sketches;* and seldom, if ever, was the emergence of an original poetic genius above the literary horizon more evidently announced. In the form, style, and manner of the whole poem, and in the structure of the particular lines and periods, there is a harshness and acerbity connected and combined with words and images all a-glow, which might recall those products of the vegetable world, where gorgeous blossoms rise out of a hard and thorny rind and shell, within which the rich fruit is elaborating. The language is not only peculiar and strong, but at times knotty and contorted, as by its own impatient strength; while the novelty and struggling crowd of images, acting in conjunction with the difficulties of the style, demands always a greater closeness of attention, than poetry,—at all events, than descriptive poetry—has a right to claim. It not seldom therefore justified the complaint of obscurity. In the following extract I have sometimes fancied, that I saw an emblem of the poem itself, and of the author's genius as it was then displayed.—

'Tis storm; and hid in mist from hour to hour,
All day the floods a deepening murmur pour;
The sky is veiled, and every cheerful sight:
Dark is the region as with coming night;
Yet what a sudden burst of overpowering light!
Triumphant on the bosom of the storm,
Glances the fire-clad eagle's wheeling form;
Eastward, in long perspective glittering, shine
The wood-crowned cliffs that o'er the lake recline;
Those Eastern cliffs a hundred streams unfold,
At once to pillars turned that flame with gold;
Behind his sail the peasant strives to shun
The *west,* that burns like one dilated sun,
Where in a mighty crucible expire
The mountains, glowing hot, like coals of fire.

The poetic Psyche, in its process to full development, undergoes as many changes as its Greek namesake, the butterfly. And it is remarkable how soon genius clears and purifies itself from the faults and errors of its earliest products; faults which, in its earliest compositions, are the more obtrusive and confluent, because as heterogeneous elements, which had only a temporary use, they constitute the very ferment, by which themselves are carried off. Or we may compare them to some diseases, which must work on the humours, and be thrown out on the surface, in order to secure the patient from their future recurrence. I was in my twenty-fourth year, when I had the happiness of knowing Mr. Wordsworth personally, and while memory lasts, I shall hardly forget the sudden effect produced on my mind, by his recitation of a manuscript poem, which still remains unpublished, but of which the stanza and tone of style were the same as those of "The Female Vagrant," as originally printed in the first volume of the *Lyrical Ballads.* There was here no mark of strained thought, or forced diction, no crowd or turbulence of imagery; and, as the poet hath himself well described in his Lines on revisiting the Wye, manly reflection and human associations had given both variety, and an additional interest to natural objects, which, in the passion and appetite of the first love, they had seemed to him neither to need nor permit. The occasional obscurities, which had risen from an imperfect control over the resources of his native language, had almost wholly disappeared, together with that worse defect of arbitrary and illogical phrases, at once hackneyed and fantastic, which hold so distinguished a place in the *technique* of ordinary poetry, and will, more or less, alloy the earlier poems of the truest genius, unless the attention has been specially directed to their worthlessness and incongruity.[1] I did not perceive anything particular in the mere style of the poem alluded to during its recitation, except indeed such difference as was not separable from the thought and manner; and the Spenserian stanza, which always, more or less, recalls to the reader's mind Spenser's own style, would doubtless have authorized, in my then opinion, a more frequent descent to the phrases of ordinary life, than could without an ill effect have been hazarded in the heroic couplet. It was not however the freedom from false taste, whether as to common defects, or to those more properly his own, which made so unusual an impression on my feelings immediately, and subsequently on my judgment. It was the union of deep feeling with profound thought; the fine balance of truth in observing, with the imaginative faculty in modifying, the objects observed; and above all the original gift of spreading the tone, the atmosphere, and with it the depth and

---

[1] Mr. Wordsworth, even in his two earliest poems, "The Evening Walk" and the "Descriptive Sketches," is more free from this latter defect than most of the young poets his contemporaries. It may however be exemplified, together with the harsh and obscure construction, in which he more often offended, in the following lines:—

" 'Mid stormy vapours ever driving by,
Where ospreys, cormorants, and herons cry;
Where hardly given the hopeless waste to cheer,
Denied the bread of life the foodful ear,
Dwindles the pear on autumn's latest spray,
And *apple sickens* pale in summer's ray;
*Ev'n here content has fixed her smiling reign
With independence, child of high disdain.*"

I hope, I need not say, that I have quoted these lines for no other purpose than to make my meaning fully understood. It is to be regretted that Mr. Wordsworth has not republished these two poems entire.

height of the ideal world around forms, incidents, and situations, of which, for the common view, custom had bedimmed all the lustre, had dried up the sparkle and the dew drops.

This excellence, which in all Mr. Wordsworth's writings is more or less predominant, and which constitutes the character of his mind, I no sooner felt, than I sought to understand. Repeated meditations led me first to suspect,—(and a more intimate analysis of the human faculties, their appropriate marks, functions, and effects matured my conjecture into full conviction,)—that Fancy and Imagination were two distinct and widely different faculties, instead of being, according to the general belief, either two names with one meaning, or, at furthest, the lower and higher degree of one and the same power. It is not, I own, easy to conceive a more apposite translation of the Greek φαντασία than the Latin *imaginatio;* but it is equally true that in all societies there exists an instinct of growth, a certain collective, unconscious good sense working progressively to desynonymize those words originally of the same meaning, which the conflux of dialects supplied to the more homogeneous languages, as the Greek and German: and which the same cause, joined with accidents of translation from original works of different countries, occasion in mixed languages like our own. The first and most important point to be proved is, that two conceptions perfectly distinct are confused under one and the same word, and—this done—to appropriate that word exclusively to the one meaning, and the synonyme, should there be one, to the other. But if,—(as will be often the case in the arts and sciences,)—no synonyme exists, we must either invent or borrow a word. In the present instance the appropriation has already begun, and been legitimated in the derivative adjective: Milton had a highly *imaginative,* Cowley a very *fanciful* mind. If therefore I should succeed in establishing the actual existence of two faculties generally different, the nomenclature would be at once determined. To the faculty by which I had characterized Milton, we should confine the term 'imagination;' while the other would be contra-distinguished as 'fancy.' Now were it once fully ascertained, that this division is no less grounded in nature than that of *delirium* from *mania,* or Otway's

Lutes, laurels, seas of milk, and ships of amber,

from Shakespeare's

What! have his daughters brought him to this
    pass?

or from the preceding apostrophe to the elements; the theory of the fine arts, and of
poetry in particular, could not but derive some
additional and important light. It would in
its immediate effects furnish a torch of guidance to the philosophical critic; and ultimately
to the poet himself. In energetic minds, truth
soon changes by domestication into power;
and from directing in the discrimination and
appraisal of the product, becomes influencive
in the production. To admire on principle, is
the only way to imitate without loss of originality.

It has been already hinted, that metaphysics
and psychology have long been my hobby-
horse. But to have a hobby-horse, and to be
vain of it, are so commonly found together,
that they pass almost for the same. I trust
therefore, that there will be more good humour
than contempt, in the smile with which the
reader chastises my self-complacency, if I confess myself uncertain, whether the satisfaction
from the perception of a truth new to myself
may not have been rendered more poignant by
the conceit, that it would be equally so to the
public. There was a time, certainly, in which
I took some little credit to myself, in the
belief that I had been the first of my countrymen, who had pointed out the diverse meaning
of which the two terms were capable, and
analyzed the faculties to which they should
be appropriated. Mr. W. Taylor's recent volume of synonymes I have not yet seen; but
his specification of the terms in question has
been clearly shown to be both insufficient and
erroneous by Mr. Wordsworth in the Preface
added to the late collection of his *Poems*. The
explanation which Mr. Wordsworth has himself given, will be found to differ from mine,
chiefly, perhaps as our objects are different.
It could scarcely indeed happen otherwise,
from the advantage I have enjoyed of frequent
conversation with him on a subject to which
a poem of his own first directed my attention,
and my conclusions concerning which he had
made more lucid to myself by many happy instances drawn from the operation of natural
objects on the mind. But it was Mr. Wordsworth's purpose to consider the influences of
fancy and imagination as they are manifested
in poetry, and from the different effects to
conclude their diversity in kind; while it is
my object to investigate the seminal principle, and then from the kind to deduce the degree. My friend has drawn a masterly sketch
of the branches with their poetic fruitage. I
wish to add the trunk, and even the roots as
far as they lift themselves above ground, and
are visible to the naked eye of our common
consciousness.

Yet even in this attempt I am aware that I
shall be obliged to draw more largely on the
reader's attention, than so immethodical a
miscellany as this can authorize; when in such
a work (the *Ecclesiastical Polity*) of such a
mind as Hooker's, the judicious author, though
no less admirable for the perspicuity than for
the port and dignity of his language,—and
though he wrote for men of learning in a
learned age,—saw nevertheless occasion to anticipate and guard against "complaints of obscurity," as often as he was to trace his subject "to the highest well-spring and fountain."
Which, (continues he) "because men are not
accustomed to, the pains we take are more needful a great deal, than acceptable; and the matters we handle, seem by reason of newness (till
the mind grow better acquainted with them)
dark and intricate." I would gladly therefore
spare both myself and others this labour, if I
knew how without it to present an intelligible
statement of my poetic creed,—not as my
opinions, which weigh for nothing, but as deductions from established premises conveyed
in such a form, as is calculated either to effect
a fundamental conviction, or to receive a
fundamental confutation. If I may dare once
more adopt the words of Hooker, "they, unto
whom we shall seem tedious, are in no wise
injured by us, because it is in their own hands
to spare that labour, which they are not willing
to endure." Those at least, let me be permitted
to add, who have taken so much pains to render
me ridiculous for a perversion of taste, and
have supported the charge by attributing
strange notions to me on no other authority
than their own conjectures, owe it to themselves as well as to me not to refuse their
attention to my own statement of the theory
which I do acknowledge; or shrink from the
trouble of examining the grounds on which I
rest it, or the arguments which I offer in its
justification.

CHAPTER XII

A chapter of requests and premonitions concerning the perusal or omission of the chapter that follows.

. . . I shall now proceed to the nature and *genesis* of the Imagination; but I must first take leave to notice, that after a more accurate perusal of Mr. Wordsworth's remarks on the Imagination, in his preface to the new edition of his poems, I find that my conclusions are not so consentient with his as, I confess, I had taken for granted. In an article contributed by me to Mr. Southey's *Omniana, On the soul and its organs of sense,* are the following sentences. "These (the human faculties) I would arrange under the different senses and powers: as the eye, the ear, the touch, &c.; the imitative power, voluntary and automatic; the imagination, or shaping and modifying power; the fancy, or the aggregative and associative power; the understanding, or the regulative, substantiating and realizing power; the speculative reason, *vis theoretica et scientifica,* or the power by which we produce or aim to produce unity, necessity, and universality in all our knowledge by means of principles *a priori;* the will, or practical reason; the faculty of choice (*Germanice,* Willkühr) and (distinct both from the moral will and the choice,) the *sensation* of volition, which I have found reason to include under the head of single and double touch." To this, as far as it relates to the subject in question, namely the words (*the aggregative and associative power*) Mr. Wordsworth's "objection is only that the definition is too general. To aggregate and to associate, to evoke and to combine, belong as well to the Imagination as to the Fancy." I reply, that if, by the power of evoking and combining, Mr. Wordsworth means the same as, and no more than, I meant by the aggregative and associative, I continue to deny, that it belongs at all to the Imagination; and I am disposed to conjecture, that he has mistaken the co-presence of Fancy with Imagination for the operation of the latter singly. A man may work with two very different tools at the same moment; each has its share in the work, but the work effected by each is distinct and different. But it will probably appear in the next chapter, that deeming it necessary to go back much further than Mr. Wordsworth's subject required or permitted, I have attached a meaning to both Fancy and Imagination, which he had not in view, at least while he was writing that preface. He will judge. Would to Heaven, I might meet with many such readers! I will conclude with the words of Bishop Jeremy Taylor: "He to whom all things are one, who draweth all things to one, and seeth all things in one, may enjoy true peace and rest of spirit."

CHAPTER XIII

On the imagination, or esemplastic power

Des Cartes, speaking as a naturalist, and in imitation of Archimedes, said, give me matter and motion and I will construct you the universe. We must of course understand him to have meant; I will render the construction of the universe intelligible. In the same sense the transcendental philosopher says; grant me a nature having two contrary forces, the one of which tends to expand infinitely, while the other strives to apprehend or *find* itself in this infinity, and I will cause the world of intelligences with the whole system of their representations to rise up before you. Every other science presupposes intelligence as already existing and complete: the philosopher contemplates it in its growth, and as it were represents its history to the mind from its birth to its maturity.

The venerable sage of Koenigsberg has preceded the march of this master-thought as an effective pioneer in his essay on the introduction of negative quantities into philosophy, published 1763. In this he has shown, that instead of assailing the science of mathematics by metaphysics, as Berkeley did in his *Analyst,* or of sophisticating it, as Wolf did, by the vain attempt of deducing the first principles of geometry from supposed deeper grounds of ontology, it behoved the metaphysician rather to examine whether the only province of knowledge, which man has succeeded in erecting into a pure science, might not furnish materials, or at least hints, for establishing and pacifying the unsettled, warring, and embroiled domain of philosophy. An imitation of the mathematical *method* had indeed been attempted with no better success than attended the essay of David to wear the armour of Saul. Another use however is possible and of far greater promise, namely, the actual application of the positions which had so wonderfully enlarged the discoveries of geometry, *mutatis mutandis,* to philosophical subjects. Kant having briefly illustrated the utility of such an attempt in the questions of space, motion, and infinitely small quantities, as employed by the mathematician, proceeds to the idea of negative quantities and the transfer of them to metaphysical investigation. Opposites, he well observes, are of two kinds, either logical, that is, such as are absolutely incompatible; or real, without being contradictory. The former he denominates *Nihil negativum irrepræsentabile,* the connection of which produces nonsense. A body in motion is something—*Aliquid cogitabile;* but a body, at one and the same time in motion and not in motion, is nothing, or, at most, air articulated into nonsense. But a motory force of a body in one direction, and an equal force of the same body in an opposite direction is not incompatible, and the result, namely, rest, is real and representable. For the purposes of mathematical *calculus* it is indifferent which force we term negative, and which positive, and consequently we appropriate the latter to that, which happens to be the principal object in our thoughts. Thus if a man's capital be ten and his debts eight, the subtraction will be the same, whether we call the capital negative debt, or the debt negative capital. But in as much as the latter stands practically in reference to the former, we of course represent the sum as 10–8. It is equally clear that two equal forces acting in opposite directions, both being finite and each distinguished from the other by its direction only, must neutralize or reduce each other to inaction. Now the transcendental philosophy demands; first, that two forces should be conceived which counteract each other by their essential nature; not only not in consequence of the accidental direction of each, but as prior to all direction, nay, as the primary forces from which the conditions of all possible directions are derivative and deducible: secondly, that these forces should be assumed to be both alike infinite, both alike indestructible. The problem will then be to discover the result or product of two such forces, as distinguished from the result of those forces which are finite, and derive their difference solely from the circumstance of their direction. When we have formed a scheme or outline of these two different kinds of force, and of their different results, by the process of discursive reasoning, it will then remain for us to elevate the *thesis* from notional to actual, by contemplating intuitively this one power with its two inherent indestructible yet counteracting forces, and the results or generations to which their interpenetration gives existence, in the living principle and in the process of our own self-consciousness. By what instrument this is possible the solution itself will discover, at the same time that it will reveal to and for whom it is possible. *Non omnia possumus omnes.* There is a philosophic no less than a poetic genius, which is differenced from the highest perfection of talent, not by degree but by kind.

The counteraction then of the two assumed forces does not depend on their meeting from opposite directions; the power which acts in them is indestructible; it is therefore inexhaustibly re-ebullient; and as something must be the result of these two forces, both alike infinite, and both alike indestructible; and as rest or neutralization cannot be this result; no other conception is possible, but that the product must be a *tertium aliquid,* or finite generation. Consequently this conception is necessary. Now this *tertium aliquid* can be no other than an inter-penetration of the counteracting powers, partaking of both.

* * * * * *

Thus far had the work been transcribed for the press, when I received the following letter from a friend, whose practical judgment I have had ample reason to estimate and revere, and whose taste and sensibility preclude all the excuses which my self-love might possibly have prompted me to set up in plea against the decision of advisers of equal good sense, but with less tact and feeling.

"Dear C.

"You ask my opinion concerning your Chapter on the Imagination, both as to the impressions it made on myself, and as to those which I think it will make on the Public, *i.e. that part of the public, who, from the title of the work and from its forming a sort of introduction to a volume of poems, are likely to constitute the great majority of your readers.*

"As to myself, and stating in the first place the effect on my understanding, *your opinions and method of argument were not only so new to me, but so directly the reverse of all*

I had ever been accustomed to consider as truth, that even if I had comprehended your premises sufficiently to have admitted them, and had seen the necessity of your conclusions, I should still have been in that state of mind, which in your note in Chap. IV. you have so ingeniously evolved, as the antithesis to that in which a man is, when he makes a bull. In your own words, I should have felt as if I had been standing on my head.

"The effect on my feelings, on the other hand, I cannot better represent, than by supposing myself to have known only our light airy modern chapels of ease, and then for the first time to have been placed, and left alone, in one of our largest Gothic cathedrals in a gusty moonlight night of autumn. 'Now in glimmer, and now in gloom;' often in palpable darkness not without a chilly sensation of terror; then suddenly emerging into broad yet visionary lights with coloured shadows of fantastic shapes, yet all decked with holy insignia and mystic symbols; and ever and anon coming out full upon pictures and stone-work images of great men, with whose names I was familiar, but which looked upon me with countenances and an expression, the most dissimilar to all I had been in the habit of connecting with those names. Those whom I had been taught to venerate as almost superhuman in magnitude of intellect, I found perched in little fret-work niches, as grotesque dwarfs; while the grotesques, in my hitherto belief, stood guarding the high altar with all the characters of apotheosis. In short, what I had supposed substances were thinned away into shadows, while everywhere shadows were deepened into substances:

If substance might be call'd that shadow seem'd,
For each seem'd either!

"Yet after all, I could not but repeat the lines which you had quoted from a MS. poem of your own in the FRIEND, and applied to a work of Mr. Wordsworth's though with a few of the words altered:

————An Orphic tale indeed,
A tale obscure of high and passionate thoughts
To a strange music chanted!

"Be assured, however, that I look forward anxiously to your great book on the Constructive Philosophy, which you have promised and announced: and that I will do my best to understand it. Only I will not promise to descend into the dark cave of Trophonius with you, there to rub my own eyes, in order to make the sparks and figured flashes, which I am required to see.

"So much for myself. But as for the Public I do not hesitate a moment in advising and urging you to withdraw the Chapter from the present work, and to reserve it for your announced treatises on the Logos or communicative intellect in Man and Deity. First, because imperfectly as I understand the present Chapter, I see clearly that you have done too much, and yet not enough. You have been obliged to omit so many links, from the necessity of compression, that what remains, looks (if I may recur to my former illustration) like the fragments of the winding steps of an old ruined tower. Secondly, a still stronger argument (at least one that I am sure will be more forcible with you) is, that your readers will have both right and reason to complain of you. This Chapter, which cannot, when it is printed, amount to so little as an hundred pages, will of necessity greatly increase the expense of the work; and every reader who, like myself, is neither prepared nor perhaps calculated for the study of so abstruse a subject so abstrusely treated, will, as I have before hinted, be almost entitled to accuse you of a sort of imposition on him. For who, he might truly observe, could from your title-page, to wit, "My Literary Life and Opinions," published too as introductory to a volume of miscellaneous poems, have anticipated, or even conjectured, a long treatise on Ideal Realism which holds the same relation in abstruseness to Plotinus, as Plotinus does to Plato. It will be well, if already you have not too much of metaphysical disquisition in your work, though as the larger part of the disquisition is historical, it will doubtless be both interesting and instructive to many to whose unprepared minds your speculations on the esemplastic power would be utterly unintelligible. Be assured, if you do publish this Chapter in the present work, you will be reminded of Bishop Berkeley's Siris, announced as an Essay on Tar-water, which beginning with Tar ends with the Trinity, the omne scibile forming the interspace. I say in the present work. In that greater work to which you have devoted so many years, and study so intense and various, it will be in its proper place. Your prospectus will have described and announced both *its contents and their nature; and if any persons purchase it, who feel no interest in the subjects of which it treats, they will have themselves only to blame.*

"I could add to these arguments one derived from pecuniary motives, and particularly from the probable effects on the sale of your present publication; but they would weigh little with you compared with the preceding. Besides, I have long observed, that arguments drawn from your own personal interests more often act on you as narcotics than as stimulants, and that in money concerns you have some small portion of pig-nature in your moral idiosyncrasy, and, like these amiable creatures, must occasionally be pulled backward from the boat in order to make you enter it. All success attend you, for if hard thinking and hard reading are merits, you have deserved it.

Your affectionate, &c."

In consequence of this very judicious letter, which produced complete conviction on my mind, I shall content myself for the present with stating the main result of the chapter, which I have reserved for that future publication, a detailed *prospectus* of which the reader will find at the close of the second volume.

The Imagination then I consider either as primary, or secondary. The primary Imagination I hold to be the living power and prime agent of all human perception, and as a repetition in the finite mind of the eternal act of creation in the infinite I AM. The secondary Imagination I consider as an echo of the former, co-existing with the conscious will, yet still as identical with the primary in the *kind* of its agency, and differing only in *degree*, and in the *mode* of its operation. It dissolves, diffuses, dissipates, in order to recreate: or where this process is rendered impossible, yet still at all events it struggles to idealize and to unify. It is essentially *vital*, even as all objects (*as* objects) are essentially fixed and dead.

FANCY, on the contrary, has no other counters to play with, but fixities and definites. The fancy is indeed no other than a mode of memory emancipated from the order of time and space; while it is blended with, and modified by that empirical phenomenon of the will, which we express by the word Choice. But equally with the ordinary memory the Fancy must receive all its materials ready made from the law of association.

CHAPTER XIV

Occasion of the Lyrical Ballads, and the objects originally proposed—Preface to the second edition—The ensuing controversy, its causes and acrimony—Philosophic definitions of a Poem and Poetry with scholia.

During the first year that Mr. Wordsworth and I were neighbours, our conversations turned frequently on the two cardinal points of poetry, the power of exciting the sympathy of the reader by a faithful adherence to the truth of nature, and the power of giving the interest of novelty by the modifying colours of imagination. The sudden charm, which accidents of light and shade, which moon-light or sunset diffused over a known and familiar landscape, appeared to represent the practicability of combining both. These are the poetry of nature. The thought suggested itself— (to which of us I do not recollect)—that a series of poems might be composed of two sorts. In the one, the incidents and agents were to be, in part at least, supernatural; and the excellence aimed at was to consist in the interesting of the affections by the dramatic truth of such emotions, as would naturally accompany such situations, supposing them real. And real in this sense they have been to every human being who, from whatever source of delusion, has at any time believed himself under supernatural agency. For the second class, subjects were to be chosen from ordinary life; the characters and incidents were to be such as will be found in every village and its vicinity, where there is a meditative and feeling mind to seek after them, or to notice them, when they present themselves.

In this idea originated the plan of the *Lyrical Ballads;* in which it was agreed, that my endeavours should be directed to persons and characters supernatural, or at least romantic; yet so as to transfer from our inward nature a human interest and a semblance of truth sufficient to procure for these shadows of imagination that willing suspension of disbelief for the moment, which constitutes poetic faith. Mr. Wordsworth, on the other hand, was to propose to himself as his object, to give the charm of novelty to things of every day, and to excite a feeling analogous to the supernatural, by awakening the mind's attention to the lethargy of custom, and directing it to the loveliness and the wonders of the world before us; an inexhaustible treasure, but for which, in consequence of the film of familiarity and selfish solicitude, we have eyes, yet see not, ears that hear not, and hearts that neither feel nor understand.

With this view I wrote *The Ancient Mariner,* and was preparing among other poems, *The Dark Ladie,* and the *Christabel,* in which I should have more nearly realized my ideal, than I had done in my first attempt. But Mr. Wordsworth's industry had proved so much more successful, and the number of his poems so much greater, that my compositions, instead of forming a balance, appeared rather an interpolation of heterogeneous matter. Mr. Wordsworth added two or three poems written in his own character, in the impassioned, lofty, and sustained diction, which is characteristic of his genius. In this form the *Lyrical Ballads* were published; and were presented by him, as an experiment, whether subjects, which from their nature rejected the usual ornaments and extra-colloquial style of poems in general, might not be so managed in the language of ordinary life as to produce the pleasurable interest, which it is the peculiar business of poetry to impart. To the second edition he added a preface of considerable length; in which, notwithstanding some passages of apparently a contrary import, he was understood to contend for the extension of this style to poetry of all kinds, and to reject as vicious and indefensible all phrases and forms of speech that were not included in what he (unfortunately, I think, adopting an equivocal expression) called the language of real life. From this preface, prefixed to poems in which it was impossible to deny the presence of original genius, however mistaken its direction might be deemed, arose the whole long-continued controversy. For from the conjunction of perceived power with supposed heresy I explain the inveteracy and in some instances, I grieve to say, the acrimonious passions, with which the controversy has been conducted by the assailants.

Had Mr. Wordsworth's poems been the silly, the childish things, which they were for a long time described as being: had they been really distinguished from the compositions of other poets merely by meanness of language and inanity of thought; had they indeed contained nothing more than what is found in the parodies and pretended imitations of them; they must have sunk at once, a dead weight, into the slough of oblivion, and have dragged the preface along with them. But year after year increased the number of Mr. Wordsworth's admirers. They were found too not in the lower classes of the reading public, but chiefly among young men of strong sensibility and meditative minds; and their admiration (inflamed perhaps in some degree by opposition) was distinguished by its intensity, I might almost say, by its religious fervour. These facts, and the intellectual energy of the author, which was more or less consciously felt, where it was outwardly and even boisterously denied, meeting with sentiments of aversion to his opinions, and of alarm at their consequences, produced an eddy of criticism, which would of itself have borne up the poems by the violence with which it whirled them round and round. With many parts of this preface in the sense attributed to them and which the words undoubtedly seem to authorize, I never concurred; but on the contrary objected to them as erroneous in principle, and as contradictory (in appearance at least) both to other parts of the same preface, and to the author's own practice in the greater part of the poems themselves. Mr. Wordsworth in his recent collection has, I find, degraded this prefatory disquisition to the end of his second volume, to be read or not at the reader's choice. But he has not, as far as I can discover, announced any change in his poetic creed. At all events, considering it as the source of a controversy, in which I have been honoured more than I deserve by the frequent conjunction of my name with his, I think it expedient to declare once for all, in what points I coincide with the opinions supported in that preface, and in what points I altogether differ. But in order to render myself intelligible I must previously, in as few words as possible, explain my views, first, of a Poem; and secondly, of Poetry itself, in kind, and in essence.

The office of philosophical disquisition consists in just distinction; while it is the privilege of the philosopher to preserve himself constantly aware, that distinction is not division. In order to obtain adequate notions of any truth, we must intellectually separate its distinguishable parts; and this is the technical process of philosophy. But having so done, we must then restore them in our conceptions to the unity, in which they actually co-exist; and this is the result of philosophy. A poem contains the same elements as a prose composition; the difference therefore must consist in a different combination of them, in consequence of a different object being proposed. According to the difference of the object will be the difference of the combination. It is possible, that the object may be merely to facilitate the recollection of any given facts or observations by artificial arrangement; and the composition will be a poem, merely because it is distinguished from prose by metre, or by rhyme, or by both conjointly. In this, the lowest sense, a man might attribute the name of a poem to the well-known enumeration of the days in the several months;

> Thirty days hath September,
> April, June, and November, &c.

and others of the same class and purpose. And as a particular pleasure is found in anticipating the recurrence of sounds and quantities, all compositions that have this charm super-added, whatever be their contents, *may* be entitled poems.

So much for the superficial form. A difference of object and contents supplies an additional ground of distinction. The immediate purpose may be the communication of truths; either of truth absolute and demonstrable, as in works of science; or of facts experienced and recorded, as in history. Pleasure, and that of the highest and most permanent kind, may result from the attainment of the end; but it is not itself the immediate end. In other works the communication of pleasure may be the immediate purpose; and though truth, either moral or intellectual, ought to be the ultimate end, yet this will distinguish the character of the author, not the class to which the work belongs. Blest indeed is that state of society, in which the immediate purpose would be baffled by the perversion of the proper ultimate end; in which no charm of diction or imagery could exempt the *Bathyllus* even of an Anacreon, or the *Alexis* of Virgil, from disgust and aversion!

But the communication of pleasure may be the immediate object of a work not metrically composed; and that object may have been in a high degree attained, as in novels and romances. Would then the mere superaddition of metre, with or without rhyme, entitle these to the name of poems? The answer is, that nothing can permanently please, which does not contain in itself the reason why it is so, and not otherwise. If metre be superadded, all other parts must be made consonant with it. They must be such, as to justify the perpetual and distinct attention to each part, which an exact correspondent recurrence of accent and sound are calculated to excite. The final definition then, so deduced, may be thus worded. A poem is that species of composition, which is opposed to works of science, by proposing for its *immediate* object pleasure, not truth; and from all other species—(having *this* object in common with it)—it is discriminated by proposing to itself such delight from the *whole,* as is compatible with a distinct gratification from each component *part.*

Controversy is not seldom excited in consequence of the disputants attaching each a different meaning to the same word; and in few instances has this been more striking, than in disputes concerning the present subject. If a man chooses to call every composition a poem, which is rhyme, or measure, or both, I must leave his opinion uncontroverted. The distinction is at least competent to characterize the writer's intention. If it were subjoined, that the whole is likewise entertaining or affecting, as a tale, or as a series of interesting reflections, I of course admit this as another fit ingredient of a poem, and an additional merit. But if the definition sought for be that of a *legitimate* poem, I answer, it must be one, the parts of which mutually support and explain each other; all in their proportion harmonizing with, and supporting the purpose and known influences of metrical arrangement. The philosophic critics of all ages coincide with the ultimate judgment of all countries, in equally denying the praises of a just poem, on the one hand, to a series of striking lines or distiches, each of which, absorbing the whole attention of the reader to itself, becomes disjoined from its context, and forms a separate whole, instead of a harmonizing part; and on the other hand, to an unsustained composition, from which the reader collects rapidly the general result unattracted by the component parts. The reader should be carried forward, not merely or chiefly by the mechanical impulse of curiosity, or by a restless desire to arrive at the final solution; but by the pleasureable activity of mind excited by the attractions of the journey itself. Like the motion of a serpent, which the Egyptians made the emblem of intellectual power; or like the path of sound through the air;—at every step he pauses and half recedes, and from the retrogressive movement collects the force which again carries him onward. *Præcipitandus est liber spiritus,* says Petronius most happily. The epithet, *liber,* here balances the preceding verb; and it is not easy to conceive more meaning condensed in fewer words.

But if this should be admitted as a satisfactory character of a poem, we have still to seek for a definition of poetry. The writings of Plato, and Jeremy Taylor, and Burnet's Theory of the Earth, furnish undeniable proofs that poetry of the highest kind may exist without metre, and even without the contradistinguishing objects of a poem. The first chapter of Isaiah—(indeed a very large portion of the whole book)—is poetry in the most emphatic sense; yet it would be not less irrational than strange to assert, that pleasure, and not truth was the immediate object of the prophet. In short, whatever specific import we attach to the word, Poetry, there will be found involved in it, as a necessary consequence, that a poem of any length neither can be, nor ought to be, all poetry. Yet if an harmonious whole is to be produced, the remaining parts must be preserved in keeping with the poetry; and this can be no otherwise effected than by such a studied selection and artificial arrangement, as will partake of one, though not a peculiar property of poetry. And this again can be no other than the property of exciting a more continuous and equal attention than the language of prose aims at, whether colloquial or written.

My own conclusions on the nature of poetry, in the strictest use of the word, have been in part anticipated in some of the remarks on the Fancy and Imagination in the early part of this work. What is poetry?—is so nearly the same question with, what is a poet?—that the answer to the one is involved in the solution of the other. For it is a distinction resulting from the poetic genius itself, which sustains and modifies the images, thoughts, and emotions of the poet's own mind.

The poet, described in ideal perfection, brings the whole soul of man into activity, with the subordination of its faculties to each other according to their relative worth and dignity. He diffuses a tone and spirit of unity, that blends, and (as it were) *fuses,* each into each, by that synthetic and magical power, to

which I would exclusively appropriate the name of Imagination. This power, first put in action by the will and understanding, and retained under their irremissive, though gentle and unnoticed, control, *laxis effertur habenis,* reveals itself in the balance or reconcilement of opposite or discordant qualities: of sameness, with difference; of the general with the concrete; the idea with the image; the individual with the representative; the sense of novelty and freshness with old and familiar objects; a more than usual state of emotion with more than usual order; judgment ever awake and steady self-possession with enthusiasm and feeling profound or vehement; and while it blends and harmonizes the natural and the artificial, still subordinates art to nature; the manner to the matter; and our admiration of the poet to our sympathy with the poetry. Doubtless, as Sir John Davies observes of the soul—(and his words may with slight alteration be applied, and even more appropriately, to the poetic Imagination)—

Doubtless this could not be, but that she turns
  Bodies to *spirit* by sublimation strange,
As fire converts to fire the things it burns,
  As we our food into our nature change.

From their gross matter she abstracts *their* forms,
  And draws a kind of quintessence from things;
Which to her proper nature she transforms
  To bear them light on her celestial wings.

Thus does she, when from *individual states*
  She doth abstract the universal kinds;
Which then re-clothed in divers names and fates
  Steal access through the senses to our minds.

Finally, Good Sense is the Body of poetic genius, Fancy its Drapery, Motion its Life, and Imagination the Soul that is everywhere, and in each; and forms all into one graceful and intelligent whole.

CHAPTER XVII

Examination of the tenets peculiar to Mr. Wordsworth—Rustic life (above all, low and rustic life) especially unfavourable to the formation of a human diction—The best parts of language the product of philosophers, not of clowns or shepherds—Poetry essentially ideal and generic —The language of Milton as much the language of real life, yea, incomparably more so than that of the cottager.

As far then as Mr. Wordsworth in his preface contended, and most ably contended, for a reformation in our poetic diction, as far as he has evinced the truth of passion, and the dramatic propriety of those figures and metaphors in the original poets, which, stripped of their justifying reasons, and converted into mere artifices of connection or ornament, constitute the characteristic falsity in the poetic style of the moderns; and as far as he has, with equal acuteness and clearness, pointed out the process by which this change was effected, and the resemblances between that state into which the reader's mind is thrown by the pleasurable confusion of thought from an unaccustomed train of words and images; and that state which is induced by the natural language of impassioned feeling; he undertook a useful task, and deserves all praise, both for the attempt and for the execution. The provocations to this remonstrance in behalf of truth and nature were still of perpetual recurrence before and after the publication of this preface. I cannot likewise but add, that the comparison of such poems of merit, as have been given to the public within the last ten or twelve years, with the majority of those produced previously to the appearance of that preface, leave no doubt on my mind, that Mr. Wordsworth is fully justified in believing his efforts to have been by no means ineffectual. Not only in the verses of those who have professed their admiration of his genius, but even of those who have distinguished themselves by hostility to his theory, and depreciation of his writings, are the impressions of his principles plainly visible. It is possible, that with these principles others may have been blended, which are not equally evident; and some which are unsteady and subvertible from the narrowness or imperfection of their basis. But it is more than possible, that these errors of defect or exaggeration, by kindling and feeding the controversy, may have conduced not only to the wider propagation of the accompanying truths, but that, by their frequent presentation to the mind in an excited state, they may have won for them a more permanent and practical result. A man will borrow a part from his opponent the more easily, if he feels himself justified in continuing to reject a part. While there remain important points in which he can still feel himself in the right, in which he still finds firm footing for continued resistance, he will gradually adopt those opinions, which were the least remote from his own convictions, as not less congruous with his own theory than with that which he reprobates. In like manner with a kind of instinctive prudence, he will abandon by little and little his weakest posts, till at length he seems to forget that they had ever belonged to him, or affects to consider them at most as accidental and "petty annexments," the removal of which leaves the citadel unhurt and unendangered.

My own differences from certain supposed parts of Mr. Wordsworth's theory ground themselves on the assumption, that his words had been rightly interpreted, as purporting that the proper diction for poetry in general consists altogether in a language taken, with due exceptions, from the mouths of men in real life, a language which actually constitutes the natural conversation of men under the influence of natural feelings. My objection is, first, that in any sense this rule is applicable only to certain classes of poetry; secondly, that even to these classes it is not applicable, except in such a sense, as hath never by any one (as far as I know or have read,) been denied or doubted; and lastly, that as far as, and in that degree in which it is practicable, it is yet as a rule useless, if not injurious, and therefore either need not, or ought not to be practised. The poet informs his reader, that he had generally chosen low and rustic life; but not as low and rustic, or in order to repeat that pleasure of doubtful moral effect, which persons of elevated rank and of superior refinement oftentimes derive from a happy imitation of the rude unpolished manners and discourse of their inferiors. For the pleasure so derived may be traced to three exciting causes. The first is the naturalness, in fact, of the things represented. The second is the apparent naturalness of the representation, as raised and qualified by an imperceptible infusion of the author's own knowledge and talent, which infusion does, indeed, constitute it an imitation as distinguished from a mere copy. The third cause may be found in the reader's conscious feeling of his superiority awakened by the contrast presented to him; even as for the same purpose the kings and great barons of yore retained, sometimes actual clowns and fools, but more frequently shrewd and witty fellows in that character. These, however, were not Mr. Wordsworth's objects. *He* chose low and rustic life, "because in that condition the essential passions of the heart find a better soil, in which they can attain their maturity, are less under restraint, and speak a plainer and more emphatic language; because in that condition of life our elementary feelings coexist in a state of greater simplicity, and consequently may be more accurately contemplated, and more forcibly communicated; because the manners of rural life germinate from those elementary feelings; and from the necessary character of rural occupations are more easily comprehended, and are more durable; and lastly, because in that condition the passions of men are incorporated with the beautiful and permanent forms of nature."

Now it is clear to me, that in the most interesting of the poems, in which the author is more or less dramatic, as "The Brothers," "Michael," "Ruth," "The Mad Mother," and others, the persons introduced are by no means taken from low or rustic life in the common acceptation of those words! and it is not less clear, that the sentiments and language, as far as they can be conceived to have been really transferred from the minds and conversation of such persons, are attributable to causes and circumstances not necessarily connected with "their occupations and abode." The thoughts, feelings, language, and manners of the shepherd-farmers in the vales of Cumberland and Westmoreland, as far as they are actually adopted in those poems, may be accounted for from causes, which will and do produce the same results in every state of life, whether in town or country. As the two principal I rank that independence, which raises a man above servitude, or daily toil for the profit of others, yet not above the necessity of industry and a frugal simplicity of domestic life; and the accompanying unambitious, but solid and religious, education, which has rendered few books familiar, but the Bible, and the Liturgy or Hymn book. To this latter cause, indeed, which is so far accidental, that it is the blessing of particular countries and a particular age, not the product of particular places or employments, the poet owes the show of probability, that his personages might really feel, think, and talk with any tolerable resemblance to his representation. It is an excellent remark of Dr. Henry More's, that "a man of confined education, but of good parts, by constant reading of the Bible will naturally form a

more winning and commanding rhetoric than those that are learned: the intermixture of tongues and of artificial phrases debasing *their* style."

It is, moreover, to be considered that to the formation of healthy feelings, and a reflecting mind, negations involve impediments not less formidable than sophistication and vicious intermixture. I am convinced, that for the human soul to prosper in rustic life a certain vantage-ground is prerequisite. It is not every man that is likely to be improved by a country life or by country labours. Education, or original sensibility, or both, must pre-exist, if the changes, forms, and incidents of nature are to prove a sufficient stimulant. And where these are not sufficient, the mind contracts and hardens by want of stimulants: and the man becomes selfish, sensual, gross, and hard-hearted. Let the management of the Poor Laws in Liverpool, Manchester, or Bristol be compared with the ordinary dispensation of the poor rates in agricultural villages, where the farmers are the overseers and guardians of the poor. If my own experience have not been particularly unfortunate, as well as that of the many respectable country clergymen with whom I have conversed on the subject, the result would engender more than scepticism concerning the desirable influences of low and rustic life in and for itself. Whatever may be concluded on the other side, from the stronger local attachments and enterprising spirit of the Swiss, and other mountaineers, applies to a particular mode of pastoral life, under forms of property that permit and beget manners truly republican, not to rustic life in general, or to the absence of artificial cultivation. On the contrary the mountaineers, whose manners have been so often eulogized, are in general better educated and greater readers than men of equal rank elsewhere. But where this is not the case, as among the peasantry of North Wales, the ancient mountains, with all their terrors and all their glories, are pictures to the blind, and music to the deaf.

I should not have entered so much into detail upon this passage, but here seems to be the point, to which all the lines of difference converge as to their source and centre;—I mean, as far as, and in whatever respect, my poetic creed *does* differ from the doctrines promulgated in this preface. I adopt with full faith, the principle of Aristotle, that poetry, as poetry, is essentially ideal, that it avoids and excludes all accident; that its apparent individualities of rank, character, or occupation must be representative of a class; and that the persons of poetry must be clothed with generic attributes, with the common attributes of the class: not with such as one gifted individual might possibly possess, but such as from his situation it is most probable before-hand that he would possess. If my premises are right and my deductions legitimate, it follows that there can be no poetic medium between the swains of Theocritus and those of an imaginary golden age.

The characters of the vicar and the shepherd-mariner in the poem of "The Brothers," and that of the shepherd of Green-head Ghyll in the "Michael," have all the verisimilitude and representative quality, that the purposes of poetry can require. They are persons of a known and abiding class, and their manners and sentiments the natural product of circumstances common to the class. Take Michael for instance:

An old man stout of heart, and strong of limb.
His bodily frame had been from youth to age
Of an unusual strength: his mind was keen,
Intense, and frugal, apt for all affairs,
And in his shepherd's calling he was prompt
And watchful more than ordinary men.
Hence he had learned the meaning of all winds,
Of blasts of every tone; and oftentimes
When others heeded not, He heard the South
Make subterraneous music, like the noise
Of bagpipers on distant Highland hills.
The Shepherd, at such warning, of his flock
Bethought him, and he to himself would say,
'The winds are now devising work for me!'
And truly, at all times, the storm, that drives
The traveller to a shelter, summoned him
Up to the mountains: he had been alone
Amid the heart of many thousand mists,
That came to him and left him on the heights.
So lived he, until his eightieth year was past.
And grossly that man errs, who should suppose
That the green valleys, and the streams and rocks,
Were things indifferent to the Shepherd's thoughts.
Fields, where with cheerful spirits he had breathed
The common air; the hills, which he so oft
Had climbed with vigorous steps; which had impressed
So many incidents upon his mind
Of hardship, skill or courage, joy or fear;
Which, like a book, preserved the memory
Of the dumb animals, whom he had saved,
Had fed or sheltered, linking to such acts,
So grateful in themselves, the certainty
Of honourable gain; these fields, these hills
Which were his living Being, even more
Than his own blood—what could they less? had laid

Strong hold on his affections, were to him
A pleasurable feeling of blind love,
The pleasure which there is in life itself.

On the other hand, in the poems which are pitched in a lower key, as the "Harry Gill," and "The Idiot Boy," the feelings are those of human nature in general; though the poet has judiciously laid the scene in the country, in order to place himself in the vicinity of interesting images, without the necessity of ascribing a sentimental perception of their beauty to the persons of his drama. In "The Idiot Boy," indeed, the mother's character is not so much the real and native product of a "situation where the essential passions of the heart find a better soil, in which they can attain their maturity and speak a plainer and more emphatic language," as it is an impersonation of an instinct abandoned by judgment. Hence the two following charges seem to me not wholly groundless: at least, they are the only plausible objections, which I have heard to that fine poem. The one is, that the author has not, in the poem itself, taken sufficient care to preclude from the reader's fancy the disgusting images of ordinary morbid idiocy, which yet it was by no means his intention to represent. He was even by the "burr, burr, burr," uncounteracted by any preceding description of the boy's beauty, assisted in recalling them. The other is, that the idiocy of the boy is so evenly balanced by the folly of the mother, as to present to the general reader rather a laughable burlesque on the blindness of anile dotage, than an analytic display of maternal affection in its ordinary workings.

In "The Thorn," the poet himself acknowledges in a note the necessity of an introductory poem, in which he should have portrayed the character of the person from whom the words of the poem are supposed to proceed: a superstitious man moderately imaginative, of slow faculties and deep feelings, "a captain of a small trading vessel, for example, who, being past the middle age of life, had retired upon an annuity, or small independent income, to some village or country town of which he was not a native, or in which he had not been accustomed to live. Such men having nothing to do become credulous and talkative from indolence." But in a poem, still more in a lyric poem—and the Nurse in *Romeo and Juliet* alone prevents me from extending the remark even to dramatic poetry, if indeed even the Nurse can be deemed altogether a case in point—it is not possible to imitate truly a dull and garrulous discourser, without repeating the effects of dullness and garrulity. However this may be, I dare assert, that the parts—(and these form the far larger portion of the whole)—which might as well or still better have proceeded from the poet's own imagination, and have been spoken in his own character, are those which have given, and which will continue to give, universal delight; and that the passages exclusively appropriate to the supposed narrator, such as the last couplet of the third stanza; the seven last lines of the tenth; and the five following stanzas, with the exception of the four admirable lines at the commencement of the fourteenth, are felt by many unprejudiced and unsophisticated hearts, as sudden and unpleasant sinkings from the height to which the poet had previously lifted them, and to which he again re-elevates both himself and his reader.

If then I am compelled to doubt the theory, by which the choice of characters was to be directed, not only *a priori*, from grounds of reason, but both from the few instances in which the poet himself need be supposed to have been governed by it, and from the comparative inferiority of those instances; still more must I hesitate in my assent to the sentence which immediately follows the former citation; and which I can neither admit as particular fact, nor as general rule. "The language, too, of these men has been adopted (purified indeed from what appear to be its real defects, from all lasting and rational causes of dislike or disgust) because such men hourly communicate with the best objects from which the best part of language is originally derived; and because, from their rank in society and the sameness and narrow circle of their intercourse, being less under the action of social vanity, they convey their feelings and notions in simple and unelaborated expressions." To this I reply; that a rustic's language, purified from all provincialism and grossness, and so far reconstructed as to be made consistent with the rules of grammar —(which are in essence no other than the laws of universal logic, applied to psychological materials)—will not differ from the language of any other man of common sense, however learned or refined he may be, except as far as the notions, which the rustic has to convey, are fewer and more indiscriminate. This will become still clearer, if we add the consideration—(equally important though less obvious)—that the rustic, from the more imperfect development of his faculties, and from the lower state of their cultivation, aims almost solely to convey insulated facts, either those of his scanty experience or his tradinal belief; while the educated man chiefly seeks to discover and express those connections of things, or those relative bearings of fact to fact, from which some more or less general law is deducible. For facts are valuable to a wise man, chiefly as they lead to the discovery of the indwelling law, which is the true being of things, the sole solution of their modes of existence, and in the knowledge of which consists our dignity and our power.

As little can I agree with the assertion, that from the objects with which the rustic hourly communicates the best part of language is formed. For first, if to communicate with an object implies such an acquaintance with it, as renders it capable of being discriminately reflected on, the distinct knowledge of an uneducated rustic would furnish a very scanty vocabulary. The few things and modes of action requisite for his bodily conveniences would alone be individualized; while all the rest of nature would be expressed by a small number of confused general terms. Secondly, I deny that the words and combinations of words derived from the objects, with which the rustic is familiar, whether with distinct or confused knowledge, can be justly said to form the best part of language. It is more than probable, that many classes of the brute creation possess discriminating sounds, by which they can convey to each other notices of such objects as concern their food, shelter, or safety. Yet we hesitate to call the aggregate of such sounds a language, otherwise than metaphorically. The best part of human language, properly so called, is derived from reflection on the acts of the mind itself. It is formed by a voluntary appropriation of fixed symbols to internal acts, to processes and results of imagination, the greater part of which have no place in the consciousness of uneducated man; though in civilized society, by imitation and passive remembrance of what they hear from their religious instructors and other superiors, the most uneducated share in the harvest which they neither sowed, nor reaped. If the history of the phrases in hourly currency among our peasants were traced, a person not previously aware of the fact would be surprised at finding so large a number, which three or four centuries ago were the exclusive property of the universities and the schools; and, at the commencement of the Reformation, had been transferred from the school to the pulpit, and thus gradually passed into common life. The extreme difficulty, and often the impossibility, of finding words for the simplest moral and intellectual processes of the languages of uncivilized tribes has proved perhaps the weightiest obstacle to the progress of our most zealous and adroit missionaries. Yet these tribes are surrounded by the same nature as our peasants are; but in still more impressive forms; and they are, moreover, obliged to particularize many more of them. When, therefore, Mr. Wordsworth adds, "accordingly, such a language"—(meaning, as before, the language of rustic life purified from provincialism)—"arising out of repeated experience and regular feelings, is a more permanent, and a far more philosophical language, than that which is frequently substituted for it by Poets, who think that they are conferring honour upon themselves and their art in proportion as they indulge in arbitrary and capricious habits of expression;" it may be answered, that the language, which he has in view, can be attributed to rustics with no greater right, than the style of Hooker or Bacon to Tom Brown or Sir Roger L'Estrange. Doubtless, if what is peculiar to each were omitted in each, the result must needs be the same. Further, that the poet, who uses an illogical diction, or a style fitted to excite only the low and changeable pleasure of wonder by means of groundless novelty, substitutes a language of folly and vanity, not for that of the rustic, but for that of good sense and natural feeling.

Here let me be permitted to remind the reader, that the positions, which I controvert, are contained in the sentences—"a selection of the real language of men;"—"the language of these men" (that is, men in low and rustic life) "has been adopted; I have proposed to myself to imitate, and, as far as is possible, to adopt the very language of men."

"Between the language of prose and that of metrical composition, there neither is, nor can be, any *essential difference:*" it is against these exclusively that my opposition is directed.

I object, in the very first instance, to an equivocation in the use of the word "real." Every man's language varies, according to the extent of his knowledge, the activity of his faculties, and the depth or quickness of his feelings. Every man's language has, first, its individualities; secondly, the common properties of the class to which he belongs; and thirdly, words and phrases of universal use. The language of Hooker, Bacon, Bishop Taylor, and Burke differs from the common language of the learned class only by the superior number and novelty of the thoughts and relations which they had to convey. The language of Algernon Sidney differs not at all from that, which every well-educated gentleman would wish to write, and (with due allowances for the undeliberateness, and less connected train, of thinking natural and proper to conversation) such as he would wish to talk. Neither one nor the other differ half as much from the general language of cultivated society, as the language of Mr. Wordsworth's homeliest composition differs from that of a common peasant. For "real" therefore, we must substitute ordinary, or *lingua communis.* And this, we have proved, is no more to be found in the phraseology of low and rustic life than in that of any other class. Omit the peculiarities of each and the result of course must be common to all. And assuredly the omissions and changes to be made in the language of rustics, before it could be transferred to any species of poem, except the drama or other professed imitation, are at least as numerous and weighty, as would be required in adapting to the same purpose the ordinary language of tradesmen and manufacturers. Not to mention, that the language so highly extolled by Mr. Wordsworth varies in every county, nay in every village, according to the accidental character of the clergyman, the existence or non-existence of schools; or even, perhaps, as the exciseman, publican, and barber happen to be, or not to be, zealous politicians, and readers of the weekly newspaper *pro bono publico.* Anterior to cultivation the *lingua communis* of every country, as Dante has well observed, exists every where in parts, and no where as a whole.

Neither is the case rendered at all more tenable by the addition of the words, "in a state of excitement." For the nature of a man's words, where he is strongly affected by joy, grief, or anger, must necessarily depend on the number and quality of the general truths, conceptions and images, and of the words expressing them, with which his mind had been previously stored. For the property of passion is not to create; but to set in increased activity. At least, whatever new connections of thoughts or images, or—(which is equally, if not more than equally, the appropriate effect of strong excitement)—whatever generalizations of truth or experience the heat of passion may produce; yet the terms of their conveyance must have pre-existed in his former conversations, and are only collected and crowded together by the unusual stimulation. It is indeed very possible to adopt in a poem the unmeaning repetitions, habitual phrases, and other blank counters, which an unfurnished or confused understanding interposes at short intervals, in order to keep hold of his subject, which is still slipping from him, and to give him time for recollection; or, in mere aid of vacancy, as in the scanty companies of a country stage the same player pops backwards and forwards, in order to prevent the appearance of empty spaces, in the procession of *Macbeth*, or *Henry VIII.* But what assistance to the poet, or ornament to the poem, these can supply, I am at a loss to conjecture. Nothing assuredly can differ either in origin or in mode more widely from the apparent tautologies of intense and turbulent feeling, in which the passion is greater and of longer endurance than to be exhausted or satisfied by a single representation of the image or incident exciting it. Such repetitions I admit to be a beauty of the highest kind; as illustrated by Mr. Wordsworth himself from the song of Deborah. *At her feet he bowed, he fell, he lay down: at her feet he bowed, he fell: where he bowed, there he fell down dead.* Judges v. 27.

CHAPTER XVIII

Language of metrical composition, why and wherein essentially different from that of prose—Origin and elements of metre—Its necessary consequences, and the conditions thereby imposed on the metrical writer in the choice of his diction.

I conclude, therefore, that the attempt is impracticable; and that, were it not imprac-

ticable, it would still be useless. For the very power of making the selection implies the previous possession of the language selected. Or where can the poet have lived? And by what rules could he direct his choice, which would not have enabled him to select and arrange his words by the light of his own judgment? We do not adopt the language of a class by the mere adoption of such words exclusively, as that class would use, or at least understand; but likewise by following the order, in which the words of such men are wont to succeed each other. Now this order, in the intercourse of uneducated men, is distinguished from the diction of their superiors in knowledge and power, by the greater disjunction and separation in the component parts of that, whatever it be, which they wish to communicate. There is a want of that prospectiveness of mind, that surview, which enables a man to foresee the whole of what he is to convey, appertaining to any one point; and by this means so to subordinate and arrange the different parts according to their relative importance, as to convey it at once, and as an organized whole.

Now I will take the first stanza, on which I have chanced to open, in the *Lyrical Ballads.* It is one the most simple and the least peculiar in its language.

> In distant countries have I been,
> And yet I have not often seen
> A healthy man, a man full grown,
> Weep in the public roads, alone.
> But such a one, on English ground,
> And in the broad highway, I met;
> Along the broad highway he came,
> His cheeks with tears were wet:
> Sturdy he seemed, though he was sad;
> And in his arms a lamb he had.

The words here are doubtless such as are current in all ranks of life; and of course not less so in the hamlet and cottage than in the shop, manufactory, college, or palace. But is this the *order*, in which the rustic would have placed the words? I am grievously deceived, if the following less compact mode of commencing the same tale be not a far more faithful copy. "I have been in a many parts, far and near, and I don't know that I ever saw before a man crying by himself in the public road; a grown man I mean, that was neither sick nor hurt," etc., etc. But when I turn to the following stanza in "The Thorn":

> At all times of the day and night
> This wretched woman thither goes;
> And she is known to every star,
> And every wind that blows:
> And there, beside the Thorn, she sits,
> When the blue day-light's in the skies,
> And when the whirlwind's on the hill,
> Or frosty air is keen and still,
> And to herself she cries,
> Oh misery! Oh misery!
> Oh woe is me! Oh misery!

and compare this with the language of ordinary men; or with that which I can conceive at all likely to proceed, in real life, from such a narrator, as is supposed in the note to the poem; compare it either in the succession of the images or of the sentences; I am reminded of the sublime prayer and hymn of praise, which Milton, in opposition to an established liturgy, presents as a fair specimen of common extemporary devotion, and such as we might expect to hear from every self-inspired minister of a conventicle! And I reflect with delight, how little a mere theory, though of his own workmanship, interferes with the processes of genuine imagination in a man of true poetic genius, who possesses, as Mr. Wordsworth, if ever man did, most assuredly does possess,

The Vision and the Faculty divine.

One point then alone remains, but that the most important; its examination having been, indeed, my chief inducement for the preceding inquisition. "There neither is nor can be any essential difference between the language of prose and metrical composition." Such is Mr. Wordsworth's assertion. Now prose itself, at least in all argumentative and consecutive works, differs, and ought to differ, from the language of conversation; even as reading ought to differ from talking. Unless therefore the difference denied be that of the mere words, as materials common to all styles of writing, and not of the style itself in the universally admitted sense of the term, it might be naturally presumed that there must exist a still greater between the ordonnance of poetic composition and that of prose, than is expected to distinguish prose from ordinary conversation.

There are not, indeed, examples wanting in the history of literature, of apparent paradoxes that have summoned the public wonder as new and startling truths, but which, on examination, have shrunk into tame and harmless truisms; as the eyes of a cat, seen in the dark, have been mistaken for flames of fire. But Mr. Wordsworth is among the last men, to whom a delusion of this kind would be attributed by anyone, who had enjoyed the slightest opportunity of understanding his mind and character. Where an objection has been anticipated by such an author as natural, his answer to it must needs be interpreted in some sense which either is, or has been, or is capable of being controverted. My object then must be to discover some other meaning for the term "essential difference" in this place, exclusive of the indistinction and community of the words themselves. For whether there ought to exist a class of words in the English, in any degree resembling the poetic dialect of the Greek and Italian, is a question of very subordinate importance. The number of such words would be small indeed, in our language; and even in the Italian and Greek, they consist not so much of different words, as of slight differences in the forms of declining and conjugating the same words; forms, doubtless, which having been, at some period more or less remote, the common grammatic flexions of some tribe or province, had been accidentally appropriated to poetry by the general admiration of certain master intellects, the first established lights of inspiration, to whom that dialect happened to be native.

Essence, in its primary signification, means the principle of individuation, the inmost principle of the possibility of any thing, as that particular thing. It is equivalent to the idea of a thing, whenever we use the word, idea, with philosophic precision. Existence, on the other hand, is distinguished from essence, by the superinduction of reality. Thus we speak of the essence, and essential properties of a circle; but we do not therefore assert, that any thing, which really exists, is mathematically circular. Thus too, without any tautology we contend for the existence of the Supreme Being; that is, for a reality correspondent to the idea. There is, next, a secondary use of the word essence, in which it signifies the point or ground of contra-distinction between two modifications of the same substance or subject. Thus we should be allowed to say, that the style of architecture of Westminster Abbey is essentially different from that of St. Paul, even though both had been built with blocks cut into the same form, and from the same quarry. Only in this latter sense of the term must it have been denied by Mr. Wordsworth (for in this sense alone is it affirmed by the general opinion) that the language of poetry (that is the formal construction, or architecture, of the words and phrases) is essentially different from that of prose. Now the burden of the proof lies with the oppugner, not with the supporters of the common belief. Mr. Wordsworth, in consequence, assigns as the proof of his position, "that not only the language of a large portion of every good poem, even of the most elevated character, must necessarily, except with reference to the metre, in no respect differ from that of good prose, but likewise that some of the most interesting parts of the best poems will be found to be strictly the language of prose, when prose is well written. The truth of this assertion might be demonstrated by innumerable passages from almost all the poetical writings, even of Milton himself." He then quotes Gray's sonnet—

In vain to me the smiling mornings shine,
And reddening Phœbus lifts his golden fire;
The birds in vain their amorous descant join,
Or cheerful fields resume their green attire.
These ears, alas! for other notes repine;
A different object do these eyes require;
My lonely anguish melts no heart but mine;
And in my breast the imperfect joys expire.
Yet morning smiles the busy race to cheer,
And new-born pleasure brings to happier men;
The fields to all their wonted tribute bear;
To warm their little loves the birds complain:
I fruitless mourn to him that cannot hear,
And weep the more, because I weep in vain.

and adds the following remark:—"It will easily be perceived, that the only part of this Sonnet which is of any value, is the lines printed in italics; it is equally obvious, that, except in the rhyme, and in the use of the single word 'fruitless' for fruitlessly, which is so far a defect, the language of these lines does in no respect differ from that of prose."

An idealist defending his system by the fact, that when asleep we often believe ourselves awake, was well answered by his plain neighbour, "Ah, but when awake do we ever believe ourselves asleep?" Things identical must be convertible. The preceding passage seems to rest on a similar sophism. For the question is not, whether there may not occur in prose an order of words, which would be equally proper

in a poem; nor whether there are not beautiful lines and sentences of frequent occurrence in good poems, which would be equally becoming as well as beautiful in good prose; for neither the one nor the other has ever been either denied or doubted by any one. The true question must be, whether there are not modes of expression, a construction, and an order of sentences, which are in their fit and natural place in a serious prose composition, but would be disproportionate and heterogeneous in metrical poetry; and, *vice versa*, whether in the language of a serious poem there may not be an arrangement both of words and sentences, and a use and selection of (what are called) figures of speech, both as to their kind, their frequency, and their occasions, which on a subject of equal weight would be vicious and alien in correct and manly prose. I contend, that in both cases this unfitness of each for the place of the other frequently will and ought to exist.

And first from the origin of metre. This I would trace to the balance in the mind effected by that spontaneous effort which strives to hold in check the workings of passion. It might be easily explained likewise in what manner this salutary antagonism is assisted by the very state, which it counteracts; and how this balance of antagonists became organized into metre (in the usual acceptation of that term), by a supervening act of the will and judgment, consciously and for the foreseen purpose of pleasure. Assuming these principles, as the *data* of our argument, we deduce from them two legitimate conditions, which the critic is entitled to expect in every metrical work. First, that, as the elements of metre owe their existence to a state of increased excitement, so the metre itself should be accompanied by the natural language of excitement. Secondly, that as these elements are formed into metre artificially, by a voluntary act, with the design and for the purpose of blending delight with emotion, so the traces of present volition should throughout the metrical language be proportionately discernible. Now these two conditions must be reconciled and co-present. There must be not only a partnership, but a union; an interpenetration of passion and of will, of spontaneous impulse and of voluntary purpose. Again, this union can be manifested only in a frequency of forms and figures of speech, (originally the offspring of passion, but now the adopted children of power).

greater than would be desired or endured, where the emotion is not voluntarily encouraged and kept up for the sake of that pleasure, which such emotion, so tempered and mastered by the will, is found capable of communicating. It not only dictates, but of itself tends to produce a more frequent employment of picturesque and vivifying language, than would be natural in any other case, in which there did not exist, as there does in the present, a previous and well understood, though tacit, compact between the poet and his reader, that the latter is entitled to expect, and the former bound to supply this species and degree of pleasurable excitement. We may in some measure apply to this union the answer of Polixenes, in the *Winter's Tale,* to Perdita's neglect of the streaked gilliflowers, because she had heard it said,

There is an art, which, in their piedness, shares
With great creating nature.
  Pol.   Say there be:
Yet nature is made better by no mean,
But nature makes that mean; so, o'er that art,
Which, you say, adds to nature, is an art,
That nature makes. You see, sweet maid, we marry
A gentler scion to the wildest stock;
And make conceive a bark of baser kind
By bud of nobler race. This is an art,
Which does mend nature,—change it rather; but
The art itself is nature.

Secondly, I argue from the effects of metre. As far as metre acts in and for itself, it tends to increase the vivacity and susceptibility both of the general feelings and of the attention. This effect it produces by the continued excitement of surprise, and by the quick reciprocations of curiosity still gratified and still re-excited, which are too slight indeed to be at any one moment objects of distinct consciousness, yet become considerable in their aggregate influence. As a medicated atmosphere, or as wine during animated conversation, they act powerfully, though themselves unnoticed. Where, therefore, correspondent food and appropriate matter are not provided for the attention and feelings thus roused there must needs be a disappointment felt; like that of leaping in the dark from the last step of a stair-case, when we had prepared our muscles for a leap of three or four.

The discussion on the powers of metre in the preface is highly ingenious and touches at all points on truth. But I cannot find any statement of its powers considered abstractly and separately. On the contrary Mr. Wordsworth seems always to estimate metre by the powers, which it exerts during, (and, as I think, in consequence of), its combination with other elements of poetry. Thus the previous difficulty is left unanswered, what the elements are, with which it must be combined, in order to produce its own effects to any pleasurable purpose. Double and tri-syllable rhymes, indeed, form a lower species of wit, and, attended to exclusively for their own sake, may become a source of momentary amusement; as in poor Smart's distich to the Welsh Squire who had promised him a hare:

Tell me, thou son of great Cadwallader!
Hast sent the hare? or hast thou swallow'd her?

But for any poetic purposes, metre resembles, (if the aptness of the simile may excuse its meanness), yeast, worthless or disagreeable by itself, but giving vivacity and spirit to the liquor with which it is proportionally combined.

The reference to "The Children in the Wood" by no means satisfies my judgment. We all willingly throw ourselves back for awhile into the feelings of our childhood. This ballad, therefore, we read under such recollections of our own childish feelings, as would equally endear to us poems, which Mr. Wordsworth himself would regard as faulty in the opposite extreme of gaudy and technical ornament. Before the invention of printing, and in a still greater degree, before the introduction of writing, metre, especially alliterative metre, (whether alliterative at the beginning of the words, as in *Pierce Plouman,* or at the end, as in rhymes,) possessed an independent value as assisting the recollection, and consequently the preservation, of any series of truths or incidents. But I am not convinced by the collation of facts, that "The Children in the Wood" owes either its preservation, or its popularity, to its metrical form. Mr. Marshal's repository affords a number of tales in prose inferior in pathos and general merit, some of as old a date, and many as widely popular. "Tom Hickathrift," "Jack the Giant-killer," "Goody Two-shoes," and "Little Red Riding-hood" are formidable rivals. And that they have continued in prose, cannot be fairly explained by the assumption, that the comparative meanness of their thoughts and images precluded even the humblest forms of metre. The scene of "Goody Two-shoes" in the church is perfectly susceptible of metrical narration; and, among the Θαυματα θαυμαστότατα even of the present age, I do not recollect a more astonishing image than that of the "whole rookery, that flew out of the giant's beard," scared by the tremendous voice, with which this monster answered the challenge of the heroic "Tom Hickathrift"!

If from these we turn to compositions universally, and independently of all early associations, beloved and admired; would the *Maria, The Monk,* or *The Poor Man's Ass* of Sterne, be read with more delight, or have a better chance of immortality, had they without any change in the diction been composed in rhyme, than in their present state? If I am not grossly mistaken, the general reply would be in the negative. Nay, I will confess, that, in Mr. Wordsworth's own volumes, the "Anecdote for Fathers," "Simon Lee," "Alice Fell," "Beggars," and "The Sailor's Mother," notwithstanding the beauties which are to be found in each of them where the poet interposes the music of his own thoughts, would have been more delightful to me in prose, told and managed, as by Mr. Wordsworth they would have been, in a moral essay or pedestrian tour.

Metre in itself is simply a stimulant of the attention, and therefore excites the question: Why is the attention to be thus stimulated? Now the question cannot be answered by the pleasure of the metre itself: for this we have shown to be conditional, and dependent on the appropriateness of the thoughts and expressions, to which the metrical form is superadded. Neither can I conceive any other answer that can be rationally given, short of this: I write in metre, because I am about to use a language different from that of prose. Besides, where the language is not such, how interesting soever the reflections are, that are capable of being drawn by a philosophic mind from the thoughts or incidents of the poem, the metre itself must often become feeble. Take the last three stanzas of "The Sailor's Mother," for instance. If I could for a moment abstract from the effect produced on the author's feelings, as a man, by the incident at the time of its real occurrence, I would dare appeal to his own judgment, whether in the

metre itself he found a sufficient reason for *their* being written *metrically?*

And, thus continuing, she said,
"I had a Son, who many a day
Sailed on the seas; but he is dead;
In Denmark he was cast away;
And I have travelled far as Hull to see
What clothes he might have left, or other property.

The Bird and Cage they both were his:
'Twas my Son's Bird; and neat and trim
He kept it: many voyages
This Singing-bird hath gone with him;
When last he sailed he left the Bird behind;
As it might be, perhaps, from bodings of his mind.

He to a Fellow-lodger's care
Had left it, to be watched and fed,
Till he came back again; and there
I found it when my Son was dead;
And now, God help me for my little wit!
I trail it with me, Sir! he took so much delight in it."

If disproportioning the emphasis we read these stanzas so as to make the rhymes perceptible, even tri-syllable rhymes could scarcely produce an equal sense of oddity and strangeness, as we feel here in finding *rhymes at all* in sentences so exclusively colloquial. I would further ask whether, but for that visionary state, into which the figure of the woman and the susceptibility of his own genius had placed the poet's imagination,—(a state, which spreads its influence and colouring over all, that co-exists with the exciting cause, and in which

The simplest, and the most familiar things
Gain a strange power of spreading awe around them,)

I would ask the poet whether he would not have felt an abrupt downfall in these verses from the preceding stanza?

The ancient spirit is not dead;
Old times, thought I, are breathing there;
Proud was I that my country bred
Such strength, a dignity so fair:
She begged an alms, like one in poor estate;
I looked at her again, nor did my pride abate.

It must not be omitted, and is besides worthy of notice, that those stanzas furnish the only fair instance that I have been able to discover in all Mr. Wordsworth's writings, of an actual adoption, or true imitation, of *the real and very language of low and rustic life,* freed from provincialisms.

Thirdly, I deduce the position from all the causes elsewhere assigned, which render metre the proper form of poetry, and poetry imperfect and defective without metre. Metre, therefore, having been connected with poetry most often and by a peculiar fitness, whatever else is combined with metre must, though it be not itself essentially poetic, have nevertheless some property in common with poetry, as an *intermedium* of affinity, a sort, (if I may dare borrow a well-known phrase from technical chemistry), of *mordaunt* between it and the super-added metre. Now poetry, Mr. Wordsworth truly affirms, does always imply passion: which word must be here understood in its most general sense, as an excited state of the feelings and faculties. And as every passion has its proper pulse, so will it likewise have its characteristic modes of expression. But where there exists that degree of genius and talent which entitles a writer to aim at the honours of a poet, the very act of poetic composition itself is, and is allowed to imply and to produce, an unusual state of excitement, which of course justifies and demands a correspondent difference of language, as truly, though not perhaps in as marked a degree, as the excitement of love, fear, rage, or jealousy. The vividness of the descriptions or declamations in Donne or Dryden, is as much and as often derived from the force and fervour of the describer, as from the reflections, forms or incidents, which constitute their subject and materials. The wheels take fire from the mere rapidity of their motion. To what extent, and under what modifications, this may be admitted to act, I shall attempt to define in an after remark on Mr. Wordsworth's reply to this objection, or rather on his objection to this reply, as already anticipated in his preface.

Fourthly, and as intimately connected with this, if not the same argument in a more general form, I adduce the high spiritual instinct of the human being impelling us to seek unity by harmonious adjustment, and thus establishing the principle that *all* the parts of an organized whole must be assimilated to the more *important* and *essential* parts. This and the preceding arguments may be strengthened by the reflection, that the composition of a poem is among the imitative arts; and that imitation, as opposed to copying, consists either in the interfusion of the same throughout the radically different, or of the different throughout a base radically the same.

Lastly, I appeal to the practice of the best poets, of all countries and in all ages, as authorizing the opinion, (deduced from all the foregoing,) that in every import of the word essential, which would not here involve a mere truism, there may be, is, and ought to be an *essential* difference between the language of prose and of metrical composition.

In Mr. Wordsworth's criticism of Gray's Sonnet, the reader's sympathy with his praise or blame of the different parts is taken for granted rather perhaps too easily. He has not, at least, attempted to win or compel it by argumentative analysis. In my conception at least, the lines rejected as of no value do, with the exception of the two first, differ as much and as little from the language of common life, as those which he has printed in italics as possessing genuine excellence. Of the five lines thus honourably distinguished, two of them differ from prose even more widely, than the lines which either precede or follow, in the position of the words.

A different object do these eyes require;
My lonely anguish melts no heart but mine;
And in my breast the imperfect joys expire.

But were it otherwise, what would this prove, but a truth, of which no man ever doubted?—*videlicet,* that there are sentences, which would be equally in their place both in verse and prose. Assuredly it does not prove the point, which alone requires proof; namely, that there are not passages, which would suit the one and not suit the other. The first line of this sonnet is distinguished from the ordinary language of men by the epithet to morning. For we will set aside, at present, the consideration, that the particular word "smiling" is hackneyed, and, as it involves a sort of personification, not quite congruous with the common and material attribute of *"shining."* And, doubtless, this adjunction of epithets for the purpose of additional description, where no particular attention is demanded for the quality of the thing, would be noticed as giving a poetic cast to a man's conversation. Should the sportsman exclaim, "Come boys! the rosy morning calls you up:"—he will be supposed to have some song in his head. But no one suspects this, when he says, "A wet morning shall not confine us to our beds." This then is either a defect in poetry, or it is not. Whoever should decide in the affirmative, I would request him to re-peruse any one poem, of any confessedly great poet from Homer to Milton, or from Æschylus to Shakespeare; and to strike out, (in thought I mean), every instance of this kind. If the number of these fancied erasures did not startle him; or if he continued to deem the work improved by their total omission; he must advance reasons of no ordinary strength and evidence, reasons grounded in the essence of human nature. Otherwise, I should not hesitate to consider him as a man not so much proof against all authority, as dead to it.

The second line,

And reddening Phœbus lifts his golden fire;—

has indeed almost as many faults as words. But then it is a bad line, not because the language is distinct from that of prose; but because it conveys incongruous images; because it confounds the cause and the effect, the real thing with the personified representative of the thing; in short, because it differs from the language of good sense! That the "Phœbus" is hackneyed, and a school-boy image, is an accidental fault, dependent on the age in which the author wrote, and not deduced from the nature of the thing. That it is part of an exploded mythology, is an objection more deeply grounded. Yet when the torch of ancient learning was re-kindled, so cheering were its beams, that our eldest poets, cut off by Christianity from all accredited machinery, and deprived of all acknowledged guardians and symbols of the great objects of nature, were naturally induced to adopt, as a poetic language, those fabulous personages, those forms of the supernatural in nature, which had given them such dear delight in the poems of their great masters. Nay, even at this day what scholar of genial taste will not so far sympathize with them, as to read with pleasure in Petrarch, Chaucer, or Spenser, what he would perhaps condemn as puerile in a modern poet?

I remember no poet, whose writings would safelier stand the test of Mr. Wordsworth's theory, than Spenser. Yet will Mr. Wordsworth say, that the style of the following stanza is either undistinguished from prose, and the language of ordinary life? Or that it is vicious, and that the stanzas are *blots* in *The Faery Queen?*

By this the northern wagoner had set
His sevenfold teme behind the stedfast starre,
That was in ocean waves yet never wet,
But firme is fixt and sendeth light from farre
To all that in the wild deep wandering arre:
And chearfull chaunticlere with his note shrill
Had warned once that Phœbus' fiery carre
In hast was climbing up the easterne hill,
Full envious that night so long his roome did fill.

At last the golden orientall gate
Of greatest heaven gan to open fayre,
And Phœbus fresh, as brydegrome to his mate,
Came dauncing forth, shaking his deawie hayre,
And hurl'd his glist'ring beams through gloomy ayre:
Which when the wakeful elfe perceived, streight way
He started up, and did him selfe prepayre
In sun-bright armes and battailous array;
For with that pagan proud he combat will that day.

On the contrary to how many passages, both in hymn books and in blank verse poems, could I, (were it not invidious), direct the reader's attention, the style of which is most unpoetic, because, and only because, it is the style of prose? He will not suppose me capable of having in my mind such verses, as

I put my hat upon my head
And walk'd into the Strand;
And there I met another man,
Whose hat was in his hand.

To such specimens it would indeed be a fair and full reply, that these lines are not bad, because they are unpoetic; but because they are empty of all sense and feeling; and that it were an idle attempt to prove that "an ape is not a Newton, when it is self-evident that he is not a man." But the sense shall be good and weighty, the language correct and dignified, the subject interesting and treated with feeling; and yet the style shall, notwithstanding all these merits, be justly blamable as prosaic, and solely because the words and the order of the words would find their appropriate place in prose, but are not suitable to metrical composition. The *Civil Wars* of Daniel is an instructive, and even interesting work; but take the following stanzas, (and from the hundred instances which abound I might probably have selected others far more striking):

And to the end we may with better ease
Discern the true discourse, vouchsafe to shew
What were the times foregoing near to these,
That these we may with better profit know.
Tell how the world fell into this disease;
And how so great distemperature did grow;
So shall we see with what degrees it came;
How things at full do soon wax out of frame.

Ten kings had from the Norman Conqu'ror reign'd
With intermix'd and variable fate,
When England to her greatest height attain'd
Of power, dominion, glory, wealth, and state;
After it had with much ado sustain'd
The violence of princes, with debate
For titles and the often mutinies
Of nobles for their ancient liberties.

For first, the Norman, conqu'ring all by might,
By might was forc'd to keep what he had got;
Mixing our customs and the form of right
With foreign constitutions, he had brought;
Mast'ring the mighty, humbling the poorer wight,
By all severest means that could be wrought;
And, making the succession doubtful, rent
His new-got state, and left it turbulent.

Will it be contended on the one side, that
these lines are mean and senseless? Or on
the other, that they are not prosaic, and for
that reason unpoetic? This poet's well-merited
epithet is that of the "well-languaged Daniel;"
but likewise, and by the consent of his contemporaries no less than of all succeeding
critics, "the prosaic Daniel." Yet those, who
thus designate this wise and amiable writer
from the frequent incorrespondency of his
diction to his metre in the majority of his
compositions, not only deem them valuable
and interesting on other accounts; but willingly admit, that there are to be found
throughout his poems, and especially in his
Epistles and in his *Hymen's Triumph,* many
and exquisite specimens of that style which,
as the *neutral ground* of prose and verse, is
common to both. A fine and almost faultless
extract, eminent as for other beauties, so for
its perfection in this species of diction, may
be seen in Lamb's *Dramatic Specimens,* a
work of various interest from the nature of
the selections themselves,—(all from the plays
of Shakespeare's contemporaries),—and deriving a high additional value from the notes,
which are full of just and original criticism,
expressed with all the freshness of originality.

Among the possible effects of practical adherence to a theory, that aims to identify the
style of prose and verse,—(if it does not
indeed claim for the latter a yet nearer resemblance to the average style of men in the
vivâ voce intercourse of real life)—we might
anticipate the following as not the least likely
to occur. It will happen, as I have indeed before observed, that the metre itself, the sole
acknowledged difference, will occasionally become metre to the eye only. The existence of

prosaisms, and that they detract from the
merit of a poem, *must* at length be conceded,
when a number of successive lines can be
rendered, even to the most delicate ear, un-
recognizable as verse, or as having even been
intended for verse, by simply transcribing
them as prose; when if the poem be in blank
verse, this can be effected without any alteration, or at most by merely restoring one or
two words to their proper places, from which
they have been transplanted [1] for no assigna-
ble cause or reason but that of the author's
convenience; but if it be in rhyme, by the
mere exchange of the final word of each line
for some other of the same meaning, equally
appropriate, dignified and euphonic.

The answer or objection in the preface to
the anticipated remark "that metre paves the

---

[1] As the ingenious gentleman under the influence of the Tragic Muse contrived to dislocate, "I
wish you a good morning, Sir! Thank you, Sir,
and I wish you the same," into two blank-verse
heroics:—

To you a morning good, good Sir! I wish.
You, Sir! I thank: to you the same wish I.

In those parts of Mr. Wordsworth's works
which I have thoroughly studied, I find fewer
instances in which this would be practicable than
I have met in many poems; where an approximation of prose has been sedulously and on system
guarded against. Indeed excepting the stanzas already quoted from *The Sailor's Mother,* I can
recollect but one instance: that is to say, a short
passage of four or five lines in *The Brothers,*
that model of English pastoral, which I never but
read with unclouded eye.—"James, pointing to its
summit, over which they had all purposed to return together, informed them that he would wait
for them there. They parted, and his comrades
passed that way some two hours after, but they
did not find him at the appointed place, *a circumstance of which they took no heed:* but one of
them, going by chance into the house, which at
this time was James's house, learnt *there,* that
nobody had seen him all that day." The only
change which has been made is in the position of
the little word *there* in two instances, the position
in the original being clearly such as is not adopted
in ordinary conversation. The other words printed
in italics were so marked because, though good
and genuine English, they are not the phraseology
of common conversation either in the word put
in apposition, or in the connection by the genitive
pronoun. Men in general would have said, "but
that was a circumstance they paid no attention to,
or took no notice of;" and the language is, on
the theory of the preface, justified only by the
narrator's being the Vicar. Yet if any ear *could*
suspect, that these sentences were ever printed as
metre, on those very words alone could the suspicion have been grounded.

way to other distinctions," is contained in the following words. "The distinction of rhyme and metre is regular and uniform, and not, like that produced by (what is usually called) poetic diction, arbitrary, and subject to infinite caprices, upon which no calculation whatever can be made. In the one case the reader is utterly at the mercy of the poet respecting what imagery or diction he may choose to connect with the passion." But is this a *poet*, of whom a poet is speaking? No surely! rather of a fool or madman: or at best of a vain or ignorant phantast! And might not brains so wild and so deficient make just the same havoc with rhymes and metres, as they are supposed to effect with modes and figures of speech? How is the reader at the mercy of such men? If he continue to read their nonsense, is it not his own fault? The ultimate end of criticism is much more to establish the principles of writing, than to furnish rules how to pass judgment on what has been written by others; if indeed it were possible that the two could be separated. But if it be asked, by what principles the poet is to regulate his own style, if he do not adhere closely to the sort and order of words which he hears in the market, wake, high-road, or plough-field? I reply; by principles, the ignorance or neglect of which would convict him of being no poet, but a silly or presumptuous usurper of the name. By the principles of grammar, logic, psychology. In one word by such a knowledge of the facts, material and spiritual, that most appertain to his art, as, if it have been governed and applied by good sense, and rendered instinctive by habit, becomes the representative and reward of our past conscious reasonings, insights, and conclusions, and acquires the name of Taste. By what *rule* that does not leave the reader at the poet's mercy, and the poet at his own, is the latter to distinguish between the language suitable to suppressed, and the language, which is characteristic of indulged, anger? Or between that of rage and that of jealousy? Is it obtained by wandering about in search of angry or jealous people in uncultivated society, in order to copy their words? Or not far rather by the power of imagination proceeding upon the *all in each* of human nature? By meditation, rather than by observation? And by the latter in consequence only of the former? As eyes, for which the former has pre-determined their field of vision, and to which, as to *its* organ, it communicates a microscopic power? There is not, I firmly believe, a man now living, who has, from his own inward experience, a clearer intuition, than Mr. Wordsworth himself, that the last mentioned are the true sources of *genial* discrimination. Through the same process and by the same creative agency will the poet distinguish the degree and kind of the excitement produced by the very act of poetic composition. As intuitively will he know, what differences of style it at once inspires and justifies, what intermixture of conscious volition is natural to that state; and in what instances such figures and colours of speech degenerate into mere creatures of an arbitrary purpose, cold technical artifices of ornament or connection. For, even as truth is its own light and evidence, discovering at once itself and falsehood, so is it the prerogative of poetic genius to distinguish by parental instinct its proper offspring from the changelings, which the gnomes of vanity or the fairies of fashion may have laid in its cradle or called by its names. Could a rule be given from without, poetry would cease to be poetry, and sink into a mechanical art. It would be μόρφωσις, not ποίησις. The rules of the Imagination are themselves the very powers of growth and production. The words to which they are reducible, present only the outlines and external appearance of the fruit. A deceptive counterfeit of the superficial form and colours may be elaborated; but the marble peach feels cold and heavy, and children only put it to their mouths. We find no difficulty in admitting as excellent, and the legitimate language of poetic fervour selfimpassioned, Donne's apostrophe to the Sun in the second stanza of his *Progress of the Soul*.

Thee, eye of heaven! this great Soul envies not;
By thy male force is all, we have, begot.
In the first East thou now beginn'st to shine,
Suck'st early balm and island spices there,
And wilt anon in thy loose-rein'd career
At Tagus, Po, Seine, Thames, and Danow dine,
And see at night this western world of mine:
Yet hast thou not more nations seen than she,
Who before thee one day began to be,
And, thy frail light being quench'd, shall long,
    long outlive thee.

Or the next stanza but one;

Great Destiny, the commissary of God,
That hast mark'd out a path and period
For every thing! Who, where we offspring took,
Our ways and ends see'st at one instant: thou
Knot of all causes! Thou, whose changeless brow
Ne'er smiles nor frowns! O! vouchsafe thou to
    look, 5
And shew my story in thy eternal book, etc.

As little difficulty do we find in excluding
from the honours of unaffected warmth and
elevation the madness prepense of pseudo- 10
poesy, or the startling hysteric of weakness
over-exerting itself, which bursts on the unprepared reader in sundry odes and apostro-
phes to abstract terms. Such are the Odes to
Jealousy, to Hope, to Oblivion, and the like, 15
in Dodsley's collection and the magazines of
that day, which seldom fail to remind me of
an Oxford copy of verses on the two "Sut-
tons," commencing with

    Inoculation, heavenly maid! descend! 20

It is not to be denied that men of undoubted talents, and even poets of true,
though not of first-rate, genius, have from a 25
mistaken theory deluded both themselves and
others in the opposite extreme. I once read
to a company of sensible and well-educated
women the introductory period of Cowley's
preface to his "Pindaric Odes," written in 30
imitation of the style and manner of the odes
of Pindar. "If," (says Cowley), "a man should
undertake to translate Pindar, word for word,
it would be thought that one madman had
translated another: as may appear, when he, 35
that understands not the original, reads the
verbal traduction of him into Latin prose,
than which nothing seems more raving." I
then proceeded with his own free version of
the second Olympic, composed for the chari- 40
table purpose of *rationalizing* the Theban
Eagle.

Queen of all harmonious things,
Dancing words and speaking strings,
What god, what hero, wilt thou sing?
What happy man to equal glories bring?
Begin, begin thy noble choice,
And let the hills around reflect the image of thy
    voice.
Pisa does to Jove belong,
Jove and Pisa claim thy song.
The fair first-fruits of war, th' Olympic games,
Alcides, offer'd up to Jove;
Alcides, too, thy strings may move,
But, oh! what man to join with these can worthy
    prove?

Join Theron boldly to their sacred names;
Theron the next honour claims;
Theron to no man gives place,
Is first in Pisa's and in Virtue's race;
Theron there, and he alone,
Ev'n his own swift forefathers has outgone.

One of the company exclaimed, with the
full assent of the rest, that if the original
were madder than this, it must be incurably
mad. I then translated the ode from the
Greek, and as nearly as possible, word for
word; and the impression was, that in the
general movement of the periods, in the form
of the connections and transitions, and in the
sober majesty of lofty sense, it appeared to
them to approach more nearly, than any
other poetry they had heard, to the style of
our Bible, in the prophetic books. The first
strophe will suffice as a specimen:

Ye harp-controlling hymns! (or) ye hymns
    the sovereigns of harps!
What God? what Hero?
What Man shall we celebrate?
Truly Pisa indeed is of Jove,
But the Olympiad (or the Olympic games)
    did Hercules establish,
The first-fruits of the spoils of war.
But Theron for the four-horsed car,
That bore victory to him,
It behoves us now to voice aloud:
The Just, the Hospitable,
The Bulwark of Agrigentum,
Of renowned fathers
The Flower, even him
Who preserves his native city erect and safe.

But are such rhetorical caprices condemna-
ble only for their deviation from the language
of real life? and are they by no other means
to be precluded, but by the rejection of all
distinctions between prose and verse, save
that of meter? Surely good sense, and a
moderate insight into the constitution of the
human mind, would be amply sufficient to
prove, that such language and such combinations are the native product neither of the
fancy nor of the imagination; that their
operation consists in the excitement of surprise by the juxta-position and *apparent* reconciliation of widely different or incompatible things. As when, for instance, the hills
are made to reflect the image of a *voice*.
Surely, no unusual taste is requisite to see
clearly, that this compulsory juxta-position is
not produced by the presentation of impressive or delightful forms to the inward vision,
nor by any sympathy with the modifying
powers with which the genius of the poet had

united and inspirited all the objects of his thought; that it is therefore a species of *wit,* a pure work of the *will,* and implies a leisure and self-possession both of thought and of feeling, incompatible with the steady fervour of a mind possessed and filled with the grandeur of its subject. To sum up the whole in one sentence. When a poem, or a part of a poem, shall be adduced, which is evidently vicious in the figures and contexture of its style, yet for the condemnation of which no reason can be assigned, except that it differs from the style in which men actually converse, then, and not till then, can I hold this theory to be either plausible, or practicable, or capable of furnishing either rule, guidance, or precaution, that might not, more easily and more safely, as well as more naturally, have been deduced in the author's own mind from considerations of grammar, logic, and the truth and nature of things, confirmed by the authority of works, whose fame is not of one country nor of one age.

Chapter XIX

Continuation—Concerning the real object which, it is probable, Mr. Wordsworth had before him in his critical preface—Elucidation and application of this.

It might appear from some passages in the former part of Mr. Wordsworth's preface, that he meant to confine his theory of style, and the necessity of a close accordance with the actual language of men, to those particular subjects from low and rustic life, which by way of experiment he had purposed to naturalize as a new species in our English poetry. But from the train of argument that follows; from the reference to Milton; and from the spirit of his critique on Gray's sonnet; those sentences appear to have been rather courtesies of modesty, than actual limitations of his system. Yet so groundless does this system appear on a close examination; and so strange and overwhelming [1] in its con-

sequences, that I cannot, and I do not, believe that the poet did ever himself adopt it in the unqualified sense, in which his expressions have been understood by others, and which, indeed, according to all the common laws of interpretation they seem to bear. What then did he mean? I apprehend, that in the clear perception, not unaccompanied with disgust or contempt, of the gaudy affectations of a style which passed current with too many for poetic diction, (though in truth it had as little pretensions to poetry, as to logic or common sense,) he narrowed his view for the time; and feeling a justifiable preference for the language of nature and of good sense, even in its humblest and least ornamented forms, he suffered himself to express, in terms at once too large and too exclusive, his predilection for a style the most remote possible from the false and showy splendour which he wished to explode. It is possible, that this predilection, at first merely comparative, deviated for a time into direct partiality. But the real object which he had in view, was, I doubt not, a species of excellence which had been long before most happily characterized by the judicious and amiable Garve, whose works are so justly beloved and esteemed by the Germans, in his remarks on Gellert, from which the following is literally translated. "The talent, that is required in order to make excellent verses, is perhaps greater than the philosopher is ready to admit, or would find it in his power to acquire: the talent to seek only the apt expression of the thought, and yet to find at the same time with it the rhyme and the metre. Gellert possessed this happy gift, if ever any one of our poets possessed it; and nothing perhaps contributed more to the great and universal impression which his fables made on their first publication, or conduces more to their continued popularity. It was a strange and curious phænomenon, and such as in Germany had been previously unheard of, to read verses in which everything was expressed just as one would wish to talk, and yet all dignified, attractive, and interesting; and all at the same time perfectly cor-

---

[1] I had in my mind the striking but untranslatable epithet, which the celebrated Mendelssohn applied to the great founder of the Critical Philosophy *"Der alleszermalmende* KANT," that is, the all-becrushing, or rather the *all-to-nothing-crushing* Kant. In the facility and force of compound epithets, the German from the number of its cases and inflections approaches to the Greek, that language so

"Bless'd in the happy marriage of sweet words."

It is in the woful harshness of its sounds alone that the German need shrink from the comparison.

rect as to the measure of the syllables and the rhyme. It is certain, that poetry when it has attained this excellence makes a far greater impression than prose. So much so indeed, that even the gratification which the very rhymes afford, becomes then no longer a contemptible or trifling gratification."

However novel this phænomenon may have been in Germany at the time of Gellert, it is by no means new, nor yet of recent existence in our language. Spite of the licentiousness with which Spenser occasionally compels the orthography of his words into a subservience to his rhymes, the whole *Fairy Queen* is an almost continued instance of this beauty. Waller's song "Go, lovely Rose," is doubtless familiar to most of my readers; but if I had happened to have had by me the Poems of Cotton, more but far less deservedly celebrated as the author of the *Virgil Travestied*, I should have indulged myself, and I think have gratified many, who are not acquainted with his serious works, by selecting some admirable specimens of this style. There are not a few poems in that volume, replete with every excellence of thought, image, and passion, which we expect or desire in the poetry of the milder muse; and yet so worded, that the reader sees no one reason either in the selection or the order of the words, why he might not have said the very same in an appropriate conversation, and cannot conceive how indeed he could have expressed such thoughts otherwise without loss or injury to his meaning.

But in truth our language is, and from the first dawn of poetry ever has been, particularly rich in compositions distinguished by this excellence. The final *e*, which is now mute, in Chaucer's age was either sounded or dropt indifferently. We ourselves still use either "beloved" or "belov'd" according as the rhyme, or measure, or the purpose of more or less solemnity may require. Let the reader then only adopt the pronunciation of the poet and of the court, at which he lived, both with respect to the final *e* and to the accentuation of the last syllable. . . .

In *The Excursion* the poet has introduced an old man, born in humble but not abject circumstances, who had enjoyed more than usual advantages of education, both from books and from the more awful discipline of nature. This person he represents, as having been driven by the restlessness of fervid feelings, and from a craving intellect to an itinerant life; and as having in consequence passed the larger portion of his time, from earliest manhood, in villages and hamlets from door to door,

A vagrant Merchant bent beneath his load.

Now whether this be a character appropriate to a lofty didactick poem, is perhaps questionable. It presents a fair subject for controversy; and the question is to be determined by the congruity or incongruity of such a character with what shall be proved to be the essential constituents of poetry. But surely the critic who, passing by all the opportunities which such a mode of life would present to such a man; all the advantages of the liberty of nature, of solitude, and of solitary thought; all the varieties of places and seasons, through which his track had lain, with all the varying imagery they bring with them; and lastly, all the observations of men,

Their manners, their enjoyments, and pursuits,
Their passions and their feelings——

which the memory of these yearly journeys must have given and recalled to such a mind —the critic, I say, who from the multitude of possible associations should pass by all these in order to fix his attention exclusively on the *pin-papers,* and *stay-tapes,* which *might* have been among the wares of his pack; this critic, in my opinion, cannot be thought to possess a much higher or much healthier state of moral feeling, than the Frenchmen above recorded.

CHAPTER XXII

The characteristic defects of Wordsworth's poetry, with the principles from which the judgment, that they are defects, is deduced—Their proportion to the beauties—For the greatest part characteristic of his theory only.

If Mr. Wordsworth have set forth principles of poetry which his arguments are insufficient to support, let him and those who have adopted his sentiments be set right by the confutation of those arguments, and by the substitution of more philosophical principles. And still let the due credit be given to the portion and importance of the truths, which are blended with his theory; truths, the too exclusive attention to which had occasioned its errors, by tempting him to carry those truths beyond their proper limits. If his mistaken theory have at all influenced his poetic compositions, let the effects be pointed out, and the instances given. But let it likewise be shown, how far the influence has acted; whether diffusively, or only by starts; whether the number and importance of the poems and passages thus infected be great or trifling compared with the sound portion; and lastly, whether they are inwoven into the texture of his works, or are loose and separable. The result of such a trial would evince beyond a doubt, what it is high time to announce decisively and aloud, that the supposed characteristics of Mr. Wordsworth's poetry, whether admired or reprobated; whether they are simplicity or simpleness; faithful adherence to essential nature, or wilful selections from human nature of its meanest forms and under the least attractive associations; are as little the real characteristics of his poetry at large, as of his genius and the constitution of his mind.

In a comparatively small number of poems he chose to try an experiment; and this experiment we will suppose to have failed. Yet even in these poems it is impossible not to perceive that the natural tendency of the poet's mind is to great objects and elevated conceptions. The poem entitled "Fidelity" is for the greater part written in language, as unraised and naked as any perhaps in the two volumes. Yet take the following stanza and compare it with the preceding stanzas of the same poem.

> There sometimes doth a leaping fish
> Send through the tarn a lonely cheer;
> The crags repeat the raven's croak,
> In symphony austere;
> Thither the rainbow comes—the cloud—
> And mists that spread the flying shroud;
> And sun-beams; and the sounding blast,
> That, if it could, would hurry past;
> But that enormous barrier holds it fast.

Or compare the four last lines of the concluding stanza with the former half.

> Yes, proof was plain that, since the day
> On which the Traveller thus had died,
> The Dog had watched about the spot,
> Or by his Master's side:
> *How nourish'd here through such long time*
> *He knows, who gave that love sublime,—*
> *And gave that strength of feeling, great*
> *Above all human estimate!*

Can any candid and intelligent mind hesitate in determining, which of these best represents the tendency and native character of the poet's genius? Will he not decide that the one was written because the poet *would* so write, and the other because he could not so entirely repress the force and grandeur of his mind, but that he must in some part or other of every composition write otherwise? In short, that his only disease is the being out of his element; like the swan, that, having amused himself, for a while, with crushing the weeds on the river's bank, soon returns to his own majestic movements on its reflecting and sustaining surface. Let it be observed that I am here supposing the imagined judge, to whom I appeal, to have already decided against the poet's theory, as far as it is different from the principles of the art, generally acknowledged.

I cannot here enter into a detailed examination of Mr. Wordsworth's works; but I will attempt to give the main results of my own judgment, after an acquaintance of many years, and repeated perusals. And though, to appreciate the defects of a great mind it is necessary to understand previously its characteristic excellences, yet I have already expressed myself with sufficient fulness, to preclude most of the ill effects that might arise from my pursuing a contrary arrangement. I will therefore commence with what I deem the prominent *defects* of his poems hitherto published.

The first characteristic, though only occasional defect, which I appear to myself to find in these poems is the *inconstancy* of the style. Under this name I refer to the sudden and unprepared transitions from lines or sentences of peculiar felicity—(at all events striking and original)—to a style, not only unimpassioned but undistinguished. He sinks too often and too abruptly to that style, which I should place in the second division of language, dividing it into the three species; first, that which is peculiar to poetry; second, that which is only proper in prose; and third, the neutral or common to both. There have been works, such as Cowley's "Essay on Cromwell," in which prose and verse are intermixed (not as in the "Consolation" of Boetius, or the *Argenis* of Barclay, by the insertion of poems supposed to have been spoken or composed on occasions previously related in prose, but) the poet passing from one to the other, as the nature of the thoughts or his own feelings dictated. Yet this mode of composition does not satisfy a cultivated taste. There is something unpleasant in the being thus obliged to alternate states of feeling so dissimilar, and this too in a species of writing, the pleasure from which is in part derived from the preparation and previous expectation of the reader. A portion of that awkwardness is felt which hangs upon the introduction of songs in our modern comic operas; and to prevent which the judicious Metastasio (as to whose exquisite taste there can be no hesitation, whatever doubts may be entertained as to his poetic genius) uniformly placed the *aria* at the end of the scene, at the same time that he almost always raises and impassions the style of the recitative immediately preceding. Even in real life, the difference is great and evident between words used as the arbitrary marks of thought, our smooth market-coin of intercourse, with the image and superscription worn out by currency; and those which convey pictures either borrowed from one outward object to enliven and particularize some other; or used allegorically to body forth the inward state of the person speaking; or such as are at least the exponents of his peculiar turn and unusual extent of faculty. So much so indeed, that in the social circles of private life we often find a striking use of the latter put a stop to the general flow of conversation, and by the excitement arising from concentred attention produce a sort of damp and interruption for some minutes after. But in the perusal of works of literary art, we prepare ourselves for such language; and the business of the writer, like that of a painter whose subject requires unusual splendour and prominence, is so to raise the lower and neutral tints, that what in a different style would be the commanding colours, are here used as the means of that gentle *degradation* requisite in order to produce the effect of a whole. Where this is not achieved in a poem, the metre merely reminds the reader of his claims in order to disappoint them; and where this defect occurs frequently, his feelings are alternately startled by anticlimax and hyperclimax.

I refer the reader to the exquisite stanzas cited for another purpose from "The blind Highland Boy"; and then annex, as being in my opinion instances of this *disharmony* in style, the two following:

And one, the rarest, was a shell,
Which he, poor child, had studied well:
The shell of a green turtle, thin
And hollow;—you might sit therein,
    It was so wide, and deep.

Our Highland Boy oft visited
The house which held this prize; and, led
By choice or chance, did thither come
One day, when no one was at home,
    And found the door unbarred.

Or page 172, vol. I.

'Tis gone forgotten, *let me do*
My best. There was a smile or two—
I can remember them, I see
The smiles worth all the world to me.
Dear Baby! I must lay thee down:
Thou troublest me with strange alarms;
Smiles hast thou, sweet ones of thine own:
I cannot keep thee in my arms;
For they confound me: *as it is,*
I have forgot those smiles of his!

Or page 269, vol. I.

Thou hast a nest, for thy love and thy rest
And though little troubled with sloth
Drunken lark! thou would'st be loth
To be such a traveller as I.
    Happy, happy liver!
With a soul as strong as a mountain river
Pouring out praise to th' Almighty giver,
Joy and jollity be with us both!
Hearing thee or else some other,
    As merry a brother
I on the earth will go plodding on
By myself cheerfully till the day is done.

The incongruity, which I appear to find in this passage, is that of the two noble lines in italics with the preceding and following. So vol. II. page 30.

Close by a Pond, upon the further side,
He stood alone; a minute's space I guess,
I watch'd him, he continuing motionless:
To the Pool's further margin then I drew;
He being all the while before me full in view.

Compare this with the repetition of the same image, in the next stanza but two.

And, still as I drew near with gentle pace,
Beside the little pond or moorish flood
Motionless as a Cloud the Old Man stood,
That heareth not the loud winds when they call;
And moveth altogether, if it move at all.

Or lastly, the second of the three following
stanzas, compared both with the first and the
third.

My former thoughts returned; the fear that kills;
And hope that is unwilling to be fed;
Cold, pain, and labour, and all fleshly ills;
And mighty Poets in their misery dead.
But now, perplex'd by what the Old Man had
   said,
My question eagerly did I renew,
"How is it that you live, and what is it you do?"

He with a smile did then his words repeat;
And said, that gathering Leeches far and wide
He travell'd; stirring thus about his feet
The waters of the Ponds where they abide.
"Once I could meet with them on every side;
"But they have dwindled long by slow decay;
"Yet still I persevere, and find them where I may."

While he was talking thus, the lonely place,
The Old Man's shape, and speech, all troubled me
In my mind's eye I seemed to see him pace
About the weary moors continually,
Wandering about alone and silently.

Indeed this fine poem is especially characteristic of the author. There is scarce a defect
or excellence in his writings of which it would
not present a specimen. But it would be unjust not to repeat that this defect is only occasional. From a careful reperusal of the two
volumes of poems, I doubt whether the ob-
jectionable passages would amount in the
whole to one hundred lines; not the eighth
part of the number of pages. In *The Excursion* the feeling of incongruity is seldom excited by the diction of any passage considered
in itself, but by the sudden superiority of
some other passage forming the context.

The second defect I can generalize with
tolerable accuracy, if the reader will pardon
an uncouth and new-coined word. There is,
I should say, not seldom a *matter-of-factness*
in certain poems. This may be divided into,
first, a laborious minuteness and fidelity in
the representation of objects, and their positions, as they appeared to the poet himself;
secondly, the insertion of accidental circumstances, in order to the full explanation of
his living characters, their dispositions and actions; which circumstances might be necessary to establish the probability of a statement in real life, where nothing is taken for
granted by the hearer; but appear superfluous in poetry, where the reader is willing
to believe for his own sake. To this *acci-
dentality* I object, as contravening the es-

sence of poetry, which Aristotle pronounces
to be σπουδαιότατον καὶ φιλοσοφώτατον γένος,
the most intense, weighty and philosophical
product of human art; adding, as the reason,
that it is the most catholic and abstract. The
following passage from Davenant's prefatory
letter to Hobbes well expresses this truth.
"When I considered the actions which I
meant to describe, (those inferring the persons), I was again persuaded rather to choose
those of a former age, than the present; and
in a century so far removed, as might preserve me from their improper examinations,
who know not the requisites of a poem, nor
how much pleasure they lose, (and even the
pleasures of heroic poesy are not unprofitable), who take away the liberty of a poet,
and fetter his feet in the shackles of an
historian. For why should a poet doubt in
story to mend the intrigues of fortune by
more delightful conveyances of probable fictions, because austere historians have entered into bond to truth? An obligation,
which were in poets as foolish and unnecessary, as is the bondage of false martyrs, who
lie in chains for a mistaken opinion. *But by
this I would imply, that truth, narrative and
past, is the idol of historians, (who worship
a dead thing), and truth operative, and by
effects continually alive, is the mistress of
poets, who hath not her existence in matter,
but in reason.*"

For this minute accuracy in the painting of
local imagery, the lines in *The Excursion,* pp.
96, 97, and 98, may be taken, if not as a
striking instance, yet as an illustration of my
meaning. It must be some strong motive—
(as, for instance, that the description was
necessary to the intelligibility of the tale)—
which could induce me to describe in a
number of verses what a draughtsman could
present to the eye with incomparably greater
satisfaction by half a dozen strokes of his
pencil, or the painter with as many touches of
his brush. Such descriptions too often occasion in the mind of a reader, who is determined to understand his author, a feeling
of labour, not very dissimilar to that, with
which he would construct a diagram, line by
line, for a long geometrical proposition. It
seems to be like taking the pieces of a dis-
sected map out of its box. We first look at
one part, and then at another, then join and
dove-tail them; and when the successive acts

of attention have been completed, there is a retrogressive effort of mind to behold it as a whole. The poet should paint to the imagination, not to the fancy; and I know no happier case to exemplify the distinction between these two faculties. Master-pieces of the former mode of poetic painting abound in the writings of Milton, for example:

The fig-tree; not that kind for fruit renown'd,
But such as at this day, to Indians known,
In Malabar or Decan spreads her arms
Branching so broad and long, that in the ground
The bended twigs take root, *and daughters grow
About the mother tree, a pillar'd shade
High over-arch'd and* ECHOING WALKS BETWEEN:
*There oft the Indian herdsman, shunning heat,
Shelters in cool, and tends his pasturing herds
At hoop-holes cut through thickest shade:*

This is creation rather than painting, or if painting, yet such, and with such co-presence of the whole picture flashed at once upon the eye, as the sun paints in a camera obscura. But the poet must likewise understand and command what Bacon calls the *vestigia communia* of the senses, the latency of all in each, and more especially as by a magical *penna duplex*, the excitement of vision by sound and the exponents of sound. Thus, "The echoing walks between," may be almost said to reverse the fable in tradition of the head of Memnon, in the Egyptian statue. Such may be deservedly entitled the *creative words* in the world of imagination.

The second division respects an apparent minute adherence to *matter-of-fact* in character and incidents; *a biographical* attention to probability, and an *anxiety* of explanation and retrospect. Under this head I shall deliver, with no feigned diffidence, the results of my best reflection on the great point of controversy between Mr. Wordsworth and his objectors; namely, on *the choice of his characters*. I have already declared, and, I trust justified, my utter dissent from the mode of argument which his critics have hitherto employed. To *their* question,—"Why did you choose such a character, or a character from such a rank of life?"—the poet might in my opinion fairly retort: why with the conception of my character did you make wilful choice of mean or ludicrous associations not furnished by me, but supplied from your own sickly and fastidious feelings? How was it, indeed, probable, that such arguments could

have any weight with an author, whose plan, whose guiding principle, and main object it was to attack and subdue that state of association, which leads us to place the chief value on those things on which man differs from man, and to forget or disregard the high dignities, which belong to Human Nature, the sense and the feeling, which may be, and ought to be, found in all ranks? The feelings with which, as Christians, we contemplate a mixed congregation rising or kneeling before their common Maker, Mr. Wordsworth would have us entertain at all times, as men, and as readers; and by the excitement of his lofty, yet prideless impartiality in poetry, he might hope to have encouraged its continuance in real life. The praise of good men be his! In real life, and, I trust, even in my imagination, I honour a virtuous and wise man, without reference to the presence or absence of artificial advantages. Whether in the person of an armed baron, a laurelled bard, or of an old Pedlar, or still older Leech-gatherer, the same qualities of head and heart must claim the same reverence. And even in poetry I am not conscious, that I have ever suffered my feelings to be disturbed or offended by any thoughts or images, which the poet himself has not presented.

But yet I object, nevertheless, and for the following reasons. First, because the object in view, as an *immediate* object, belongs to the moral philosopher, and would be pursued, not only more appropriately, but in my opinion with far greater probability of success, in sermons or moral essays, than in an elevated poem. It seems, indeed, to destroy the main fundamental distinction, not only between a poem and prose, but even between philosophy and works of fiction, inasmuch as it proposes *truth* for its immediate object, instead of *pleasure*. Now till the blessed time shall come, when truth itself shall be pleasure, and both shall be so united, as to be distinguishable in words only, not in feeling, it will remain the poet's office to proceed upon that state of association, which actually exists as general; instead of attempting first to make it what it ought to be, and then to let the pleasure follow. But here is unfortunately a small *hysteron-proteron*. For the communication of pleasure is the introductory means by which alone the poet must expect to moralize his readers. Secondly: though I were to admit, for a moment, *this* argument to be groundless: yet how is the moral effect to be produced, by merely attaching the name of some low profession to powers which are *least* likely, and to qualities which are assuredly not *more* likely, to be found in it? The Poet, speaking in his own person, may at once delight and improve us by sentiments, which teach us the independence of goodness, of wisdom, and even of genius, on the favours of fortune. And having made a due reverence before the throne of Antonine, he may bow with equal awe before Epictetus among his fellow-slaves—

—————————————and rejoice
In the plain presence of his dignity.

Who is not at once delighted and improved, when the Poet Wordsworth himself exclaims,

Oh! many are the Poets that are sown
By Nature; men endowed with highest gifts
The vision and the faculty divine,
Yet wanting the accomplishment of verse,
Nor having e'er, as life advanced, been led
By circumstance to take unto the height
The measure of themselves, these favoured
    Beings,
All but a scattered few, live out their time,
Husbanding that which they possess within,
And go to the grave, unthought of. Strongest
    minds
Are often those of whom the noisy world
Hears least.

To use a colloquial phrase, such sentiments, in such language, do one's heart good; though I for my part, have not the fullest faith in the truth of the observation. On the contrary I believe the instances to be exceedingly rare; and should feel almost as strong an objection to introduce such a character in a poetic fiction, as a pair of black swans on a lake, in a fancy landscape. When I think how many, and how much better books than Homer, or even than Herodotus, Pindar or Æschylus, could have read, are in the power of almost every man, in a country where almost every man is instructed to read and write; and how restless, how difficultly hidden, the powers of genius are; and yet find even in situations the most favourable, according to Mr. Wordsworth, for the formation of a pure and poetic language; in situations which ensure familiarity with the grandest objects of the imagination; but one Burns, among the

shepherds of Scotland, and not a single poet of humble life among those of English lakes and mountains; I conclude, that Poetic Genius is not only a very delicate but a very rare plant.

But be this as it may, the feelings with which,

I think of Chatterton, the marvellous Boy,
The sleepless Soul, that perished in his pride;
Of Burns, who walk'd in glory and in joy
Behind his plough, upon the mountain-side—

are widely different from those with which I should read a *poem,* where the author, having occasion for the character of a poet and a philosopher in the fable of his narration, had chosen to make him a chimney-sweeper; and then, in order to remove all doubts on the subject, had *invented* an account of his birth, parentage and education, with all the strange and fortunate accidents which had concurred in making him at once poet, philosopher, and sweep! Nothing, but biography, can justify this. If it be admissible even in a novel, it must be one in the manner of De Foe's, that were meant to pass for histories, not in the manner of Fielding's: in *The Life of Moll Flanders,* or *Colonel Jack,* not in a *Tom Jones,* or even a *Joseph Andrews.* Much less then can it be legitimately introduced in a poem, the characters of which, amid the strongest individualization, must still remain representative. The precepts of Horace, on this point, are grounded on the nature both of poetry and of the human mind. They are not more peremptory, than wise and prudent. For in the first place a deviation from them perplexes the reader's feelings, and all the circumstances which are feigned in order to make such accidents less improbable, divide and disquiet his faith, rather than aid and support it. Spite of all attempts, the fiction will appear, and unfortunately not as fictitious but as false. The reader not only knows, that the sentiments and language are the poet's own, and his own too in his artificial character, as poet; but by the fruitless endeavours to make him think the contrary, he is not even suffered to forget it. The effect is similar to that produced by an Epic Poet, when the fable and the characters are *derived* from Scripture history, as in *The Messiah of Klopstock,* or in *Cumberland's Calvary;* and not merely *suggested* by it as in the *Paradise Lost* of Milton. That illusion, contra-distinguished from delusion, that negative faith, which simply permits the images presented to work by their own force, without either denial or affirmation of their real existence by the judgment, is rendered impossible by their immediate neighbourhood to words and facts of known and absolute truth. A faith, which transcends even historic belief, must absolutely *put out* this mere poetic *analogon* of faith, as the summer sun is said to extinguish our household fires, when it shines full upon them. What would otherwise have been yielded to as pleasing fiction, is repelled as revolting falsehood. The effect produced in this latter case by the solemn belief of the reader, is in a less degree brought about in the instances, to which I have been objecting, by the baffled attempts of the author to *make* him believe.

Add to all the foregoing the seeming uselessness both of the project and of the anecdotes from which it is to derive support. Is there one word, for instance, attributed to the pedlar in *The Excursion,* characteristic of a *Pedlar?* One sentiment, that might not more plausibly, even without the aid of any previous explanation, have proceeded from any wise and beneficent old man, of a rank or profession in which the language of learning and refinement are natural and to be expected? Need the rank have been at all particularized, where nothing follows which the knowledge of that rank is to explain or illustrate? When on the contrary this information renders the man's language, feelings, sentiments, and information a riddle, which must itself be solved by episodes of anecdote? Finally when this, and this alone, could have induced a genuine Poet to inweave in a poem of the loftiest style, and on subjects the loftiest and of most universal interest, such minute matters of fact, (not unlike those furnished for the obituary of a magazine by the friends of some obscure "ornament of society lately deceased" in some obscure town,) as

Among the hills of Athol he was born:
There, on a small hereditary Farm,
An unproductive slip of rugged ground,
His Father dwelt; and died in poverty;
While He, whose lowly fortune I retrace,
The youngest of three sons, was yet a babe,
A little One—unconscious of their loss.
But ere he had outgrown his infant days
His widowed Mother, for a second Mate,

Espoused the teacher of the Village School;
Who on her offspring zealously bestowed
Needful instruction.

From his sixth year, the Boy of whom I
speak,
In summer tended cattle on the Hills;
But, through the inclement and the perilous
days
Of long-continuing winter, he repaired
To his Step-father's School,—&c.

For all the admirable passages interposed in this narration, might, with trifling alterations, have been far more appropriately, and with far greater verisimilitude, told of a poet in the character of a poet; and without incurring another defect which I shall now mention, and a sufficient illustration of which will have been here anticipated.

Third; an undue predilection for the *dramatic* form in certain poems, from which one or other of two evils result. Either the thoughts and diction are different from that of the poet, and then there arises an incongruity of style; or they are the same and indistinguishable, and then it presents a species of ventriloquism, where two are represented as talking, while in truth one man only speaks.

The fourth class of defects is closely connected with the former; but yet are such as arise likewise from an intensity of feeling disproportionate to such knowledge and value of the objects described, as can be fairly anticipated of men in general, even of the most cultivated classes; and with which therefore few only, and those few particularly circumstanced, can be supposed to sympathize: In this class, I comprise occasional prolixity, repetition, and an eddying, instead of progression, of thought. As instances, see pages 27, 28, and 62 of the Poems, Vol. I. and the first eighty lines of the VIth Book of *The Excursion.*

Fifth and last; thoughts and images too great for the subject. This is an approximation to what might be called mental bombast, as distinguished from verbal: for, as in the latter there is a disproportion of the expressions to the thoughts so in this there is a disproportion of thought to the circumstance and occasion. This, by the bye, is a fault of which none but a man of genius is capable. It is the awkwardness and strength of Hercules with the distaff of Omphale.

It is a well-known fact, that bright colours in motion both make and leave the strongest impressions on the eye. Nothing is more likely too, than that a vivid image or visual *spectrum,* thus originated, may become the link of association in recalling the feelings and images that had accompanied the original impression. But if we describe this in such lines, as

> They flash upon that inward eye,
> Which is the bliss of solitude!

in what words shall we describe the joy of retrospection, when the images and virtuous actions of a whole well-spent life, pass before that conscience which is indeed the *inward* eye: which is indeed *"the bliss of solitude?"* Assuredly we seem to sink most abruptly, not to say burlesquely, and almost as in a medley, from this couplet to—

> And then my heart with pleasure fills,
> And dances with the *daffodils.* Vol. I. p. 328.

The second instance is from Vol. II. page 12, where the poet having gone out for a day's tour of pleasure, meets early in the morning with a knot of Gipsies, who had pitched their blanket-tents and straw-beds, together with their children and asses, in some field by the road-side. At the close of the day on his return our tourist found them in the same place. "Twelve hours," says he,

> Twelve hours, twelve bounteous hours are
> 　　gone, while I
> Have been a traveller under open sky,
> Much witnessing of change and cheer,
> Yet as I left I find them here!

Whereat the poet, without seeming to reflect that the poor tawny wanderers might probably have been tramping for weeks together through road and lane, over moor and mountain, and consequently must have been right glad to rest themselves, their children and cattle, for one whole day; and overlooking the obvious truth, that such repose might be quite as necessary for them, as a walk of the same continuance was pleasing or healthful for the more fortunate poet; expresses his indignation in a series of lines, the diction and imagery of which would have been rather above, than below the mark, had they been applied to the immense empire of China improgressive for thirty centuries:

> The weary Sun betook himself to rest:—
> —Then issued Vesper from the fulgent west,
> Outshining, like a visible God,
> The glorious path in which he trod.
> And now, ascending, after one dark hour,
> And one night's diminution of her power,
> Behold the mighty Moon! this way
> She looks, as if at them—but they
> Regard not her:—oh, better wrong and strife,
> Better vain deeds or evil than such life!
> The silent Heavens have goings on:
> The stars have tasks!—but *these* have none!

The last instance of this defect, (for I know no other than these already cited) is from the Ode, page 351, Vol. II., where, speaking of a child, "a six years' Darling of a pigmy size," he thus addresses him:

> Thou best Philosopher, who yet dost keep
> Thy heritage, thou Eye among the blind,
> That, deaf and silent, read'st the eternal deep,
> Haunted for ever by the Eternal Mind,—
> Mighty Prophet! Seer blest!
> On whom those truths do rest,
> Which we are toiling all our lives to find!
> Thou, over whom thy Immortality
> Broods like the Day, a Master o'er a Slave,
> A Present which is not to be put by!

Now here, not to stop at the daring spirit of metaphor which connects the epithets "deaf and silent," with the apostrophized *eye:* or (if we are to refer it to the preceding word, "Philosopher"), the faulty and equivocal syntax of the passage; and without examining the propriety of making a "Master *brood* o'er a Slave," or "the *Day*" brood *at all;* we will merely ask, what does all this mean? In what sense is a child of that age a *Philosopher?* In what sense does he *read* "the eternal deep?" In what sense is he declared to be *"for ever haunted"* by the Supreme Being? or so inspired as to deserve the splendid titles of a *Mighty Prophet, a blessed Seer?* By reflection? by knowledge? by conscious intuition? or by *any* form or modification of consciousness? These would be tidings indeed; but such as would pre-suppose an immediate revelation to the inspired communicator, and require miracles to authenticate his inspiration. Children at this age give us no such information of themselves; and at what time were we dipped in the Lethe, which has produced such utter oblivion of a state so godlike? There are many of us that still possess some remembrances, more or less distinct, respecting themselves at six years old; pity that the worthless straws only should float, while treasures, compared with which all the mines of Golconda and Mexico were but straws, should be absorbed by some unknown gulf into some unknown abyss.

But if this be too wild and exorbitant to be suspected as having been the poet's meaning; if these mysterious gifts, faculties, and operations, are not accompanied with consciousness; who else is conscious of them? or how can it be called the child, if it be no part of the child's conscious being? For aught I know, the thinking Spirit within me may be *substantially* one with the principle of life, and of vital operation. For aught I know, it might be employed as a secondary agent in the marvellous organization and organic movements of my body. But, surely, it would be strange language to say, that *I* construct my *heart!* or that *I* propel the finer influences through my *nerves!* or that *I* compress my brain, and draw the curtains of sleep round my own eyes! Spinoza and Behmen were, on different systems, both Pantheists; and among the ancients there were philosophers, teachers of the ΕΝ ΚΑΙ ΠΑΝ, who not only taught that God was All, but that this All constituted God. Yet not even these would confound the *part, as* a part, with the whole, *as* the whole. Nay, in no system is the distinction between the individual and God, between the Modification, and the one only Substance, more sharply drawn, than in that of Spinoza. Jacobi indeed relates of Lessing, that, after a conversation with him at the house of the Poet, Gleim, (the Tyrtæus and Anacreon of the German Parnassus,) in which conversation Lessing had avowed privately to Jacobi his reluctance to admit any *personal* existence of the Supreme Being, or the *possibility* of personality except in a finite Intellect, and while they were sitting at table, a shower of rain came on unexpectedly. Gleim expressed his regret at the circumstance, because they had meant to drink their wine in the garden: upon which Lessing in one of his half-earnest, half-joking moods, nodded to Jacobi, and said, "It is *I*, perhaps, that am doing *that*," i.e. *raining!*—and Jacobi answered, "or perhaps I;" Gleim contented himself with staring at them both, without asking for any explanation.

So with regard to this passage. In what sense can the magnificent attributes, above quoted, be appropriated to a *child*, which would not make them equally suitable to a bee, or a *dog*, or a *field of corn:* or even to a ship, or to the wind and waves that propel it? The omnipresent Spirit works equally in them, as in the child; and the child is equally unconscious of it as they. It cannot surely be, that the four lines, immediately following, are to contain the explanation?

> To whom the grave
> Is but a lonely bed without the sense or sight
>   Of day or the warm light,
> A place of thought where we in waiting lie;—

Surely, it cannot be that this wonder-rousing apostrophe is but a comment on the little poem, "We are Seven?"—that the whole meaning of the passage is reducible to the assertion, that a child, who by the bye at six years old would have been better instructed in most Christian families, has no other notion of death than that of lying in a dark, cold place? And still, I hope, not as in a *place of thought!* not the frightful notion of lying *awake* in his grave! The analogy between death and sleep is too simple, too natural, to render so horrid a belief possible for children; even had they not been in the habit, as all Christian children are, of hearing the latter term used to express the former. But if the child's belief be only, that "he is not dead, but sleepeth:" wherein does it differ from that of his father and mother, or any other adult and instructed person? To form an idea of a thing's becoming nothing; or of nothing becoming a thing; is impossible to all finite beings alike, of whatever age, and however educated or uneducated. Thus it is with splendid paradoxes in general. If the words are taken in the common sense, they convey an absurdity; and if, in contempt of dictionaries and custom, they are so interpreted as to avoid the absurdity, the meaning dwindles into some bald truism. Thus you must at once understand the words *contrary* to their common import, in order to arrive at any *sense;* and *according* to their common import, if you are to receive from them any feeling of *sublimity* or *admiration.*

Though the instances of this defect in Mr. Wordsworth's poems are so few, that for themselves it would have been scarcely just to attract the reader's attention toward them; yet I have dwelt on it, and perhaps the more for this very reason. For being so very few, they cannot sensibly detract from the reputation of an author, who is even characterized by the number of profound truths in his writings, which will stand the severest analysis; and yet few as they are, they are exactly those passages which his *blind* admirers would be most likely, and best able, to imitate. But Wordsworth, where he is indeed Wordsworth, may be mimicked by copyists, he may be plundered by plagiarists; but he cannot be imitated, except by those who are not born to be imitators. For without his depth of feeling and his imaginative power his *sense* would want its vital warmth and peculiarity; and without his strong sense, his *mysticism* would become *sickly*—mere fog, and dimness!

To these defects which, as appears by the extracts, are only occasional, I may oppose, with far less fear of encountering the dissent of any candid and intelligent reader, the following (for the most part correspondent) excellencies. First, an austere purity of language both grammatically and logically; in short a perfect appropriateness of the words to the meaning. Of how high value I deem this, and how particularly estimable I hold the example at the present day, has been already stated: and in part too the reasons on which I ground both the moral and intellectual importance of habituating ourselves to a strict accuracy of expression. It is noticeable, how limited an acquaintance with the master-pieces of art will suffice to form a correct and even a sensitive taste, where none but master-pieces have been seen and admired: while on the other hand, the most correct notions, and the widest acquaintance with the works of excellence of all ages and countries, will not perfectly secure us against the contagious familiarity with the far more numerous offspring of tastelessness or of a perverted taste. If this be the case, as it notoriously is, with the arts of music and painting, much more difficult will it be, to avoid the infection of multiplied and daily examples in the practice of an art, which uses words, and words only, as its instruments. In poetry, in which every line, every phrase, may pass the ordeal of deliberation and deliberate choice, it is possible, and barely possible, to attain that *ultimatum* which I have ventured to propose as the infallible test of a blameless style; namely: its *untranslatableness* in words of the same language without injury to the meaning. Be it observed, however, that I include in the *meaning* of a word not only its correspondent object, but likewise all the

associations which it recalls. For language is framed to convey not the object alone, but likewise the character, mood and intentions of the person who is representing it. In poetry it *is* practicable to preserve the diction uncorrupted by the affectations and misappropriations, which promiscuous authorship, and reading not promiscuous only because it is disproportionally most conversant with the compositions of the day, have rendered general. Yet even to the poet, composing in his own province, it is an arduous work: and as the result and pledge of a watchful good sense of fine and luminous distinction, and of complete self-possession, may justly claim all the honour which belongs to an attainment equally difficult and valuable, and the more valuable for being rare. It is at *all* times the proper food of the understanding; but in an age of corrupt eloquence it is both food and antidote.

In prose I doubt whether it be even possible to preserve our style wholly unalloyed by the vicious phraseology which meets us everywhere, from the sermon to the newspaper, from the harangue of the legislator to the speech from the convivial chair, announcing a *toast* or sentiment. Our chains rattle, even while we are complaining of them. The poems of Boetius rise high in our estimation when we compare them with those of his contemporaries, as Sidonius Apollinaris, and others. They might even be referred to a purer age, but that the prose, in which they are set, as jewels in a crown of lead or iron, betrays the true age of the writer. Much however may be effected by education. I believe not only from grounds of reason, but from having in great measure assured myself of the fact by actual though limited experience, that, to a youth led from his first boyhood to investigate the meaning of every word and the reason of its choice and position, logic presents itself as an old acquaintance under new names.

On some future occasion, more especially demanding such disquisition, I shall attempt to prove the close connection between veracity and habits of mental accuracy; the beneficial after-effects of verbal precision in the preclusion of fanaticism, which masters the feelings more especially by indistinct watch-words; and to display the advantages which language alone, at least which language with incomparably greater ease and certainty than any other means, presents to the instructor of impressing modes of intellectual energy so constantly, so imperceptibly, and as it were by such elements and atoms, as to secure in due time the formation of a second nature. When we reflect, that the cultivation of the judgment is a positive command of the moral law, since the reason can give the *principle* alone, and the conscience bears witness only to the *motive*, while the application and effects must depend on the judgment: when we consider, that the greater part of our success and comfort in life depends on distinguishing the similar from the same, that which is peculiar in each thing from that which it has in common with others, so as still to select the most probable, instead of the merely possible or positively unfit, we shall learn to value earnestly and with a practical seriousness a mean, already prepared for us by nature and society, of teaching the young mind to think well and wisely by the same unremembered process and with the same never forgotten results, as those by which it is taught to speak and converse. Now how much warmer the interest is, how much more genial the feelings of reality and practicability, and thence how much stronger the impulses to imitation are, which a *contemporary* writer, and especially a contemporary *poet*, excites in youth and commencing manhood, has been treated of in the earlier pages of these sketches. I have only to add, that all the praise which is due to the exertion of such influence for a purpose so important, joined with that which must be claimed for the infrequency of the same excellence in the same perfection, belongs in full right to Mr. Wordsworth. I am far however from denying that we have poets whose *general* style possesses the same excellence, as Mr. Moore, Lord Byron, Mr. Bowles, and, in all his later and more important works, our laurel-honouring Laureate. But there are none, in whose works I do not appear to myself to find *more* exceptions, than in those of Wordsworth. Quotations or specimens would here be wholly out of place, and must be left for the critic who doubts and would invalidate the justice of this eulogy so applied.

The second characteristic excellence of Mr. Wordsworth's work is: a correspondent weight and sanity of the Thoughts and Sentiments,—won, not from books; but—from the poet's own meditative observation. They are *fresh* and have the dew upon them. His muse, at least when in her strength of wing, and

when she hovers aloft in her proper element,

> Makes audible a linked lay of truth,
> Of truth profound a sweet continuous lay,
> Not learnt, but native, her own natural notes!

Even throughout his smaller poems there is scarcely one, which is not rendered valuable by some just and original reflection.

See page 25, vol. II.: or the two following passages in one of his humblest compositions.

> O Reader! had you in your mind
> Such stores as silent thought can bring,
> O gentle Reader! you would find
> A tale in every thing;

and

> I've heard of hearts unkind, kind deeds
> With coldness still returning;
> Alas! the gratitude of men
> Has oftener left *me* mourning;

or in a still higher strain the six beautiful quatrains, page 134.

> Thus fares it still in our decay:
> And yet the wiser mind
> Mourns less for what age takes away
> Than what it leaves behind.

> The Blackbird in the summer trees,
> The Lark upon the hill,
> Let loose their carols when they please,
> Are quiet when they will.

> With Nature never do *they* wage
> A foolish strife; they see
> A happy youth, and their old age
> Is beautiful and free!

> But we are pressed by heavy laws;
> And often glad no more,
> We wear a face of joy, because
> We have been glad of yore.

> If there is one, who need bemoan
> His kindred laid in earth,
> The household hearts that were his own,
> It is the man of mirth.

> My days, my Friend, are almost gone,
> My life has been approved,
> And many love me; but by none
> Am I enough beloved;

or the sonnet on Buonaparte, page 202, vol. II. or finally (for a volume would scarce suffice to exhaust the instances,) the last stanza of the poem on the withered Celandine, vol. II. p. 312.

To be a Prodigal's Favorite—then, worse truth,
A Miser's Pensioner—behold our lot!
O Man! that from thy fair and shining youth
Age might but take the things Youth needed not.

Both in respect of this and of the former excellence, Mr. Wordsworth strikingly resembles Samuel Daniel, one of the golden writers of our golden Elizabethan age, now most causelessly neglected: Samuel Daniel, whose diction bears no mark of time, no distinction of age which has been, and as long as our language shall last, will be so far the language of the to-day and for ever, as that it is more intelligible to us, than the transitory fashions of our own particular age. A similar praise is due to his sentiments. No frequency of perusal can deprive them of their freshness. For though they are brought into the full daylight of every reader's comprehension; yet are they drawn up from depths which few in any age are privileged to visit, into which few in any age have courage or inclination to descend. If Mr. Wordsworth is not equally with Daniel alike intelligible to all readers of average understanding in all passages of his works, the comparative difficulty does not arise from the greater impurity of the ore, but from the nature and uses of the metal. A poem is not necessarily obscure, because it does not aim to be popular. It is enough, if a work be perspicuous to those for whom it is written, and

Fit audience find, though few.

To the "Ode on the Intimations of Immortality from Recollections of early Childhood" the poet might have prefixed the lines which Dante addresses to one of his own Canzoni—

Canzone, i' credo, che saranno radi
Color, che tua ragione intendan bene,
Tanto lor sei faticoso ed alto.

O lyric song, there will be few, I think,
Who may thy import understand aright:
Thou art for *them* so arduous and so high!

But the ode was intended for such readers only as had been accustomed to watch the flux and reflux of their inmost nature, to venture at times into the twilight realms of consciousness, and to feel a deep interest in modes of inmost being, to which they know that the attributes of time and space are inapplicable and alien, but which yet can not be conveyed, save in symbols of time and space. For such

readers the sense is sufficiently plain, and they will be as little disposed to charge Mr. Wordsworth with believing the Platonic pre-existence in the ordinary interpretation of the words, as I am to believe, that Plato himself ever meant or taught it.

> Πολλά δι ὑπ' ἀγκῶ-
> νος ὠκέα βέλη
> ἔνδον ἐντὶ φαρέτρας
> φωνᾶντα συνετοῖσιν· ἐς
> δὲ τὸ πὰν ἑρμηνέων
> χατίζει. σοφὸς ὁ πολ-
> λα εἰδὼς φυᾷ.
> μαθόντες δὲ λάβροι
> παγγλωσσια, κόρακες ὥς,
> ἄκραντα γαρύετον
> Διὸς πρὸς ὄρνιχα θεῖον.

Third (and wherein he soars far above Daniel) the sinewy strength and originality of single lines and paragraphs: the frequent *curiosa felicitas* of his diction, of which I need not here give specimens, having anticipated them in a preceding page. This beauty, and as eminently characteristic of Wordsworth's poetry, his rudest assailants have felt themselves compelled to acknowledge and admire.

Fourth; the perfect truth of nature in his images and descriptions as taken immediately from nature, and proving a long and genial intimacy with the very spirit which gives the physiognomic expression to all the works of nature. Like a green field reflected in a calm and perfectly transparent lake, the image is distinguished from the reality only by its greater softness and lustre. Like the moisture or the polish on a pebble, genius neither distorts nor false-colours its objects; but on the contrary brings out many a vein and many a tint, which escape the eye of common observation, thus raising to the rank of gems what had been often kicked away by the hurrying foot of the traveller on the dusty high road of custom.

Let me refer to the whole description of skating, vol. I. page 42 to 47, especially to the lines

So through the darkness and the cold we flew,
And not a voice was idle: with the din
Meanwhile the precipices rang aloud;
The leafless trees and every icy crag
Tinkled like iron; while the distant hills
Into the tumult sent an alien sound
Of melancholy, not unnoticed, while the stars,
Eastward, were sparkling clear, and in the west
The orange sky of evening died away.

Or to the poem on "The Green Linnet," vol. I. page 244. What can be more accurate yet more lovely than the two concluding stanzas?

Upon yon tuft of hazel trees,
That twinkle to the gusty breeze,
Behold him perched in ecstasies,
    Yet seeming still to hover;
There! where the flutter of his wings
Upon his back and body flings
Shadows and sunny glimmerings,
    That cover him all over.

While thus before my eyes he gleams,
A Brother of the Leaves he seems;
When in a moment forth he teems
    His little song in gushes:
As if it pleased him to disdain
And mock the Form which he did feign
While he was dancing with the train
    Of Leaves among the bushes.

Or the description of the blue-cap, and of the noontide silence, page 284; or the poem to the cuckoo, page 299; or, lastly, though I might multiply the references to ten times the number, to the poem, so completely Wordsworth's, commencing

Three years she grew in sun and shower—

Fifth: a meditative pathos, a union of deep and subtle thought with sensibility; a sympathy with man as man; the sympathy indeed of a contemplator, rather than a fellow-sufferer or co-mate, (*spectator, haud particeps*) but of a contemplator, from whose view no difference of rank conceals the sameness of the nature; no injuries of wind or weather, or toil, or even of ignorance, wholly disguise the human face divine. The superscription and the image of the Creator still remain legible to *him* under the dark lines, with which guilt or calamity had cancelled or cross-barred it. Here the Man and the Poet lose and find themselves in each other, the one as glorified, the latter as substantiated. In this mild and philosophic pathos, Wordsworth appears to me without a compeer. Such as he *is:* so he *writes.* See vol. I. page 134 to 136, or that most affecting composition, "The Affliction of Margaret —— of ——," page 165 to 168, which no mother, and, if I may judge by my own experience, no parent can read without a tear. Or turn to that genuine lyric, in the former edition, entitled, "The Mad Mother," page

174 to 178, of which I cannot refrain from quoting two of the stanzas, both of them for their pathos, and the former for the fine transition in the two concluding lines of the stanza, so expressive of that deranged state, in which, from the increased sensibility, the sufferer's attention is abruptly drawn off by every trifle, and in the same instant plucked back again by the one despotic thought, bringing home with it, by the blending, *fusing* power of Imagination and Passion, the alien object to which it had been so abruptly diverted, no longer an alien but an ally and an inmate.

Suck, little babe, oh suck again!
It cools my blood; it cools my brain;
Thy lips, I feel them, baby! they
Draw from my heart the pain away.
Oh! press me with thy little hand;
It loosens something at my chest:
About that tight and deadly band
I feel thy little fingers prest.
The breeze I see is in the tree!
It comes to cool my babe and me.

Thy father cares not for my breast,
'Tis thine, sweet baby, there to rest;
'Tis all thine own!—and if its hue
Be changed, that was so fair to view,
'Tis fair enough for thee, my dove!
My beauty, little child, is flown,
But thou wilt live with me in love;
And what if my poor cheek be brown?
'Tis well for me, thou canst not see
How pale and wan it else would be.

Last, and pre-eminently, I challenge for this poet the gift of Imagination in the highest and strictest sense of the word. In the play of *fancy*, Wordsworth, to my feelings, is not always graceful, and sometimes recondite. The *likeness* is occasionally too strange, or demands too peculiar a point of view, or is such as appears the creature of pre-determined research, rather than spontaneous presentation. Indeed his fancy seldom displays itself, as mere and unmodified fancy. But in imaginative power, he stands nearest of all modern writers to Shakespeare and Milton; and yet in a kind perfectly unborrowed and his own. To employ his own words, which are at once an instance and an illustration, he does indeed to all thoughts and to all objects—

——————————add the gleam,
The light that never was, on sea or land,
The consecration, and the Poet's dream.
. . . .

WILLIAM WORDSWORTH

COLERIDGE AND WORDSWORTH

Coleridge and Wordsworth were not only contemporaries but they were also intimate friends during the most productive years of both of their lives. Though the work of both was in a general way the product of the same intellectual and social movements, yet the character of the mind and of the art of each was utterly different from that of the other. Coleridge's mind was volatile, expansive, and soaring. It delighted in the remote and the eerie. It discovered meaning in fantasy and in conceptions accessible only to an imagination habitually roving on strange seas of thought and feeling. Wordsworth's mind was frugal, tenacious, and intense. It was firmly anchored in the actual and the familiar. It created beauty from facts essentially simple and in themselves common-place.

Real collaboration between two such persons was impossible. Their one attempt in *The Ancient Mariner* convinced both of its futility. Moreover, when each attempted to imitate the other, the results were not happy. Wordsworth's equivalent of *The Ancient Mariner* was *Goody Blake and Harry Gill* and Coleridge's effort to write a simple ballad in his friend's manner resulted in *The Three Graves,* the exaggerated simplicity of which is frequently silly.

Their collaboration was of a less literal and conscious sort. Ideas generated and impulses released in their endless hours of talk became in the mind of each an impulse toward artistic expression in his own peculiar fashion. Coleridge's spacious intelligence brought to their colloquies ideas and philosophic conceptions gleaned from wide reading in the literature of travel, science, and philosophy. These ideas were usually surrounded by a fog of abstruseness which Wordsworth's acute sense of reality did much to dispel. But they were also illuminated by brilliant gleams of insight which became in his friend's mind germinating truth. Wordsworth's moral stability, on the other hand, fortified Coleridge's will and tamed his mind to poetic accomplishment. He invariably awakened Coleridge's ambition and gave his vagrant fantasy an object and a goal.

The two poets, each thus inspired and controlled by the other, enormously enlarged the scope of English poetry and determined its direction for almost a hundred years. The simple dramas of homely men and women became one of the main subjects of English poetry. Different as their tone may be, such characteristic modern poems as Masefield's *The Everlasting Mercy* and Edgar Lee Masters' *The Spoon-River Anthology* are both written in the mode established by *The Lyrical Ballads.* Moreover, the exalted position which was given throughout the nineteenth century to Nature in poetry and to the emotional and moral value of her various sights and sounds, was due largely to the position which Nature assumed in the psychological system and the transcendental conceptions of these two men. Only very recently have these values ceased to be a source of inspiration for English and American poets. Wordsworth and Coleridge, therefore, can be said to have introduced into English poetry one of its rare, genuinely formative impulses.

WILLIAM WORDSWORTH

1770–1850

Almost all of Wordsworth's life and work is associated with the so-called Lake District of England. This is a descriptive term for a part of the hilly country of the Counties of Westmoreland and Cumberland. Grasmere, near which the poet lived for almost fifty years, is approximately the geographical center of the district. The region contains a number of mountain peaks from two thousand to three thousand feet in height, about which lie many lovely tarns and mountain lakes. In the village of Cockermouth in Cumberland County William Wordsworth was born on April 7, 1770.

He was the second child of a family of three brothers and one sister, Dorothy, who was to be his best-beloved companion during most of his life. His mother died when he was eight years old, and William and his elder brother Richard were sent to a simple but excellent classical school at Hawkshead on Esthwaite Water. This remained William's virtual home until his eighteenth year. The boys lived in the cottages of the dalesmen of the town and, except during the actual sessions of the school, they were left free to roam the countryside. In the wide rambles and solitary adventures thus wisely permitted the boys, Wordsworth established that affectionate intimacy with nature from which was to come both for him and for the world "rememberable things."

In 1783 the poet's father died. His principal legacy to his children was a sum of money owed him by Sir James Lowther, afterward Lord Lonsdale, who refused to pay it. This unjust refusal left the Wordsworth children almost without funds. The poet's maternal uncles, however, agreed to finance his course at St. John's College, Cambridge, and he entered the University in 1787. At that time the two principal disciplines of the place were mathematics and theology. It is small wonder, then, that his intellectual enthusiasm was aroused only by his reading in English, Latin, and Italian poets. His imagination, he tells us, slept. In January, 1791, he took his degree and left the University.

His artistic faculties were quickened during his long vacations. The summer of 1788 he spent at Hawkshead and in its immediate neighborhood. On one definite moment of this summer he decided to devote his life to Poetry. God spoke to him through Nature. As he trudged home from a merry rustic dance early in the morning, a glorious sunrise captured his soul for Beauty and in sacramental awe he there dedicated his life to her service.

The summer which was to prove most important for his career was that of 1790, when he took a long walking-trip on the Continent with a college friend named Robert Jones. They traversed France, the Valley of the Rhine, Switzerland, and visited the Italian Lakes. They observed life as tourists merely. The great political events shaking France at the time, Wordsworth, at least, beheld as from a remote distance. Only the scenes of their tour caught the poet's imagination. Three years later he dedicated to Jones a poetical account of this expedition called *Descriptive Sketches*.

After leaving college he idled for half a year in London, undecided about his career. In November, 1791, he sailed for France, ostensibly to learn French in order to fit himself for the office of a travelling tutor. He went first to Paris, where he observed various manifestations of the Revolution with only cursory interest. He soon set out for Orleans, a city on the Loire in the very heart of France. There and in the neighboring city of Blois he stayed until October, 1792. While there he fell in love with a young French woman of good family, named Annette Vallon. Although she later bore him a daughter, the two were never married. The intense emotional significance of this experience to Wordsworth is reflected in many of his poems, but particularly in *Vaudracour and Julia*.

On the Loire Wordsworth also was taught to sympathize with the Revolution. One of the army officers who formed his chief circle of friends at Blois, Michel Beaupuy, had espoused the popular cause. He instructed the poet in the political philosophy of which it was the expression. But he converted him only by showing him a hunger-bitten little girl and exclaiming, "It is against that we are fighting." After this instruction Wordsworth returned to Paris eager to play a part in the great events then unrolling. He hints that he was about to associate himself with the moderate Girondists when his uncle cut off his allowance and he reluctantly returned to England.

Information about Wordsworth during the critical years from 1793 to 1797 is very meagre. His position must have been precarious; he had neither home nor money. His uncles, shocked at the license of his conduct in France, forbade his sister Dorothy to associate with him. His mind and spirit were equally disturbed. He continued to espouse the cause of the Revolution and of France, even through the outrages of the Terror. When England, in 1793, declared war against France, he took sides with the enemy of his country. He professed revolutionary principles and associated with radicals in London. He turned his back on Christianity and traditional morality by adopting the rigorously logical, mechanistic philosophy of William Godwin. His mind was inordinately restless. The poems written during these years, or slightly later, *Guilt and Sorrow* (1793–4) and *The Borderers* (1796) reflect the state of turmoil through which he was passing.

In January, 1795, a friend left him a legacy of nine hundred pounds. Small though the sum was, it enfranchised Wordsworth. It put an end to his aimlessness; he determined to devote his life to poetry. Another friend offered him, rent-free, a house at Racedown, in Dorsetshire, about seven miles from the Channel. There Wordsworth moved with his sister Dorothy and began that intimate fellowship with her which lasted until his death. She gradually dispelled his pessimism by reawakening his interest in Nature, which she realized was the true source of his poetic inspiration.

Early during this residence at Racedown Wordsworth made the acquaintance of Coleridge. The latter was at once filled with enthusiasm for his new friend and soon persuaded him that they must live near each other. The Wordsworths accordingly took a house at Alfoxden, about four miles from Coleridge at Nether Stowey. Then the two poets saw each other every day and their powers were mutually stimulated through this association. They soon decided to write a poem together to be called *The Ancient Mariner*. Their powers, however, proved too much unlike to admit of successful collaboration. They substituted for this project, therefore, a joint volume in which each was given his appointed task. Wordsworth was to transform homely reality into art through the simple intensity of his imagination. Coleridge was to give verisimilitude to the wildest flights of his fancy. The volume was printed in September, 1798, as *Lyrical Ballads* and a second expanded edition was published in 1800, to which Wordsworth contributed a Preface in which he expressed the theories of poetry illustrated in the volume. Both the poems and the Preface are landmarks in the history of English poetry.

In September, 1798, Coleridge and the Wordsworths sailed for Germany. Once there, they separated. The Wordsworths went to Goslar where they suffered with the cold and longed for home. The poet's nostalgia expressed itself in a number of exquisite lyrics about England, among which were the Lucy Poems.

After returning to England, the Wordsworths rented a cottage on the shore of Grasmere Lake. It was an abandoned Inn, named *The Dove and Olive Branche.* They took possession of this Dove Cottage, as they called it, on December 21, 1799; and practically within sight of this house Wordsworth spent the remaining fifty years of his long career. From this moment his life can almost be said to be devoid of external incident. The joy of renewed association with Coleridge, who lived only thirteen miles away, constantly associated with his delight in the familiar beauty of the region, released in Wordsworth a flood of creative energy and made the years from 1800 to 1807 the most productive of his entire life.

Wordsworth's first great poems were written on two principal subjects—Nature and typical, intense psychological experiences of simple folk. He wrote of Nature in these early years first because he wished to describe, with sympathetic accuracy, flowers, birds and hills; but, most of all, because he worshipped her with actual religious fervor. His God was the Spirit of Nature and was invoked in many poems with the deep solemnity and exaltation associated with worship of the Deity. His second theme was the mind of man. He accepted the associationistic psychology of Locke and David Hartley. According to these philosophers the mind possesses no innate ideas. All knowledge, therefore, comes from experience and is all built upon sensations. By automatic and increasingly complex processes of association, the mind builds up all of its higher complexes, including even moral impulses. Many of his poems were written to reveal the mind of some utterly natural person at moments when its laws operated most clearly. The unsuccessful of these poems are over-simple, the best are filled with Wordsworth's characteristic emotions of reverence and enthusiasm.

In 1802, the Lord Lowther then holding the title paid with interest the debt which his father had long owed to the Wordsworth estate. The greater financial security which a larger income gave the poet enabled him to marry, on October 4, 1802, Mary Hutchinson, whom he had known since childhood. On his wedding journey he wrote two sonnets, one on a sunset and one on the imprisonment of Mary Queen of Scots in Bolton Chapel. Coleridge's wedding gift was *Dejection, an Ode.*

During the years immediately following his marriage, Wordsworth's principal poetic interest was the poem later called *The Prelude.* This was planned to serve as an introduction to a projected great poem in three parts, which was to be a systematic expression of his philosophy. *The Prelude* was devoted to a description of the origin and progress of the poet's powers up to the time when he felt himself qualified for the priest-like task of composing his *magnum opus.* The poem, constant'y revised throughout his life, was not published until after his death in

1850. Of the philosophical poem itself only a fragment of the first part was written, now published as *The Recluse.* The complete second part called *The Excursion* was published in 1814; the third part seems never to have been begun.

On the night of February 6, 1805, the ship of which his brother John was captain was wrecked and 270 persons were drowned. John Wordsworth stuck heroically to his post and, true to the best traditions of the sea, went down with his ship. Wordsworth's youthful buoyancy was thereafter always weighted with the grief of this death and his joy sobered. The deep distress not only humanized his soul but also made him lose confidence in the divinity of Nature. In *An Ode to Duty* and other poems written shortly after this loss he confesses that the guidance of Nature is not enough. From this time forward he mentions the names and the attributes of the Christian God more and more frequently and reveals his belief in Him.

In 1808 the Wordsworth family, having outgrown Dove Cottage, moved to a larger place not far away called Allan Bank. The house was spacious enough to accommodate the Wordsworths and also their constant guests. It was expected that Coleridge, who seldom now "domesticated" with his wife and his two boys, would form a permanent part of the household. In this place were written most of *The Excursion* and his patriotic sonnets. The family changed its residence twice more in the next few years. First in 1817 it moved to the Rectory at Grasmere and finally in 1819 to Rydal Mount, a spot which commanded a wide view of wood, lake and mountain. In this lovely spot Wordsworth lived until his death in 1850. Some of his leisure time during his first years in this place was spent in preparing his eldest son for college. He read Virgil with him and was greatly impressed with the poet's majesty and tenderness. Filled with the Roman's spirit of restrained passion, he wrote *Laodamia* and *Dion.*

Wordsworth's income was always small. The severity with which the influential reviews had criticized his poems had kept them from having a large audience and a profitable sale. He had long urged Lord Lonsdale to secure a government sinecure for him. Finally, in 1813, he was appointed Distributor of Stamps in Westmoreland County. The post was worth nearly five hundred pounds a year and the duties could be performed almost entirely by deputy.

During the later years of his life, Wordsworth exercised his poetical powers but fitfully. Politics became his main interest. From 1820 until the end of his life, conservatism grew upon him until any suggested political change filled him with panic and fear. He was opposed to Parliamentary Reform, because he believed that any enlargement of the franchise would lead inevitably to the national calamity of universal suffrage. He opposed Catholic Emancipation and the freedom of the press. He had a corresponding intolerance for the younger poets and their work. Not only Leigh Hunt and Moore, but also Byron,

Shelley, and Keats he regarded almost contemptuously. These views show how completely the ardent radical had been transformed into a timid conservative.

Fortunately his poetical ability did not suffer a corresponding decline. His technique and his powers of self-criticism grew with the years. Occasionally his deeper passion reawakened and enabled him to produce work of noble and exalted character. He continues in these later poems his perennial quest for spiritual tranquillity and peace. During these years he finds centers of quiet, as in the Ecclesiastical Sonnets, in the old, the settled and the traditional. Sonnets like *Mutability* and *Inside of King's College Chapel, Cambridge,* best express his later spirit of serenity. Wordsworth's work was very slowly recognized by the general public. But in 1839 Oxford paid a tribute to his reputation by conferring upon him the honorary degree of D.C.L. The audience on the occasion gave him an ovation said to have been exceeded at Oxford only by that extended to the Duke of Wellington a few years before. In 1843, upon the death of Southey, Wordsworth was appointed Poet Laureate with the understanding that official verse-making would not be expected of him. He lived two weeks beyond his eightieth birthday, dying on April 23, 1850. Although a monument to his memory was erected in Westminster Abbey, his body lies buried in Grasmere Churchyard.

SELECTED BIBLIOGRAPHY

TEXTS

Poetical Works, 5 Vols., ed. by Thomas Hutchinson, 1895.
The standard complete edition of his works.
Poetical Works, 1 Vol., ed. by Thomas Hutchinson, 1906.
The best one-volume edition.
Letters of the Wordsworth Family, 1787–1855, ed. by William Knight, 3 Vols., 1907.
Wordsworth, Dorothy, *Journals,* 2 Vols., 1897.
Detailed accounts of the life of Wordsworth and his sister during certain crucial years.

CRITICAL WORKS

Wordsworth, Christopher, *Memoir of William Wordsworth,* 2 Vols., 1851. The first biography, over-decorous and partial, but still indispensable.
Harper, G. M. C., *William Wordsworth,* 1916. The most recent authoritative life.
Legouis, Emile, *The Early Life of William Wordsworth,* translated by J. W. Matthews, 1921. A brilliant illuminative study of Wordsworth's formative years.
Garrod, H. W., *Wordsworth, Lectures and Essays,* 1923.

LINES

Left upon a Seat in a Yew-tree, which stands near the lake of Esthwaite, on a desolate part of the shore, commanding a beautiful prospect.

NAY, Traveller! rest. This lonely Yew-tree stands
Far from all human dwelling: what if here
No sparkling rivulet spread the verdant herb?
What if the bee love not these barren boughs?
Yet, if the wind breathe soft, the curling waves,
That break against the shore, shall lull thy mind
By one soft impulse saved from vacancy.
————————Who he was
That piled these stones and with the mossy sod
First covered, and here taught this aged Tree 10
With its dark arms to form a circling bower,
I well remember.—He was one who owned
No common soul. In youth by science nursed,
And led by nature into a wild scene
Of lofty hopes, he to the world went forth

A favoured Being, knowing no desire
Which genius did not hallow; 'gainst the taint
Of dissolute tongues, and jealousy, and hate,
And scorn,—against all enemies prepared,
All but neglect. The world, for so it thought, 20
Owed him no service; wherefore he at once
With indignation turned himself away,
And with the food of pride sustained his soul
In solitude.—Stranger! these gloomy boughs
Had charms for him; and here he loved to sit,
His only visitants a straggling sheep,
The stone-chat, or the glancing sand-piper:
And on these barren rocks, with fern and heath,
And juniper and thistle, sprinkled o'er,
Fixing his downcast eye, he many an hour 30
A morbid pleasure nourished, tracing here
An emblem of his own unfruitful life:
And, lifting up his head, he then would gaze
On the more distant scene,—how lovely 'tis
Thou seest,—and he would gaze till it became
Far lovelier, and his heart could not sustain
The beauty, still more beauteous! Nor, that time,

When nature had subdued him to herself,
Would he forget those Beings to whose minds
Warm from the labours of benevolence　　40
The world, and human life, appeared a scene
Of kindred loveliness: then he would sigh,
Inly disturbed, to think that others felt
What he must never feel: and so, lost Man!
On visionary views would fancy feed,
Till his eye streamed with tears. In this deep
　　vale
He died,—this seat his only monument.

If Thou be one whose heart the holy forms
Of young imagination have kept pure,
Stranger! henceforth be warned; and know
　　　that pride,　　　50
Howe'er disguised in its own majesty,
Is littleness; that he who feels contempt
For any living thing, hath faculties
Which he has never used; that thought with
　　him
Is in its infancy. The man whose eye
Is ever on himself doth look on one,
The least of Nature's works, one who might
　　move
The wise man to that scorn which wisdom
　　holds
Unlawful, ever. O be wiser, Thou!
Instructed that true knowledge leads to
　　love;　　　60
True dignity abides with him alone
Who, in the silent hour of inward thought,
Can still suspect, and still revere himself,
In lowliness of heart.

THE REVERIE OF POOR SUSAN

At the corner of Wood Street, when daylight
　　appears,
Hangs a Thrush that sings loud, it has sung
　　for three years:
Poor Susan has passed by the spot, and has
　　heard
In the silence of morning the song of the
　　Bird.

'Tis a note of enchantment; what ails her?
　　She sees
A mountain ascending, a vision of trees;
Bright volumes of vapour through Lothbury
　　glide,

And a river flows on through the vale of
　　Cheapside.

Green pastures she views in the midst of the
　　dale,
Down which she so often has tripped with
　　her pail;　　　10
And a single small cottage, a nest like a
　　dove's,
The one only dwelling on earth that she loves.

She looks, and her heart is in heaven: but they
　　fade,
The mist and the river, the hill and the shade:
The stream will not flow, and the hill will not
　　rise,
And the colours have all passed away from
　　her eyes!

A NIGHT PIECE

　　　　　——The sky is overcast
With a continuous cloud of texture close,
Heavy and wan, all whitened by the Moon,
Which through that veil is indistinctly seen,
A dull, contracted circle, yielding light
So feebly spread that not a shadow falls,
Chequering the ground—from rock, plant,
　　tree, or tower.
At length a pleasant instantaneous gleam
Startles the pensive traveller while he treads
His lonesome path, with unobserving eye　　10
Bent earthwards; he looks up—the clouds are
　　split
Asunder,—and above his head he sees
The clear Moon, and the glory of the heavens.
There in a black-blue vault she sails along,
Followed by multitudes of stars, that, small
And sharp, and bright, along the dark abyss
Drive as she drives: how fast they wheel
　　away,
Yet vanish not!—the wind is in the tree,
But they are silent;—still they roll along
Immeasurably distant; and the vault,　　20
Built round by those white clouds, enormous
　　clouds,
Still deepens its unfathomable depth.
At length the Vision closes; and the mind,
Not undisturbed by the delight it feels,
Which slowly settles into peaceful calm,
Is left to muse upon the solemn scene.

WE ARE SEVEN

——A SIMPLE Child,
That lightly draws its breath,
And feels its life in every limb,
What should it know of death?

I met a little cottage Girl:
She was eight years old, she said;
Her hair was thick with many a curl
That clustered round her head.

She had a rustic, woodland air,
And she was wildly clad: 10
Her eyes were fair, and very fair;
——Her beauty made me glad.

"Sisters and brothers, little maid,
How many may you be?"
"How many? Seven in all," she said,
And wondering looked at me.

"And where are they? I pray you tell."
She answered, "Seven are we;
And two of us at Conway dwell,
And two are gone to sea.   20

"Two of us in the church-yard lie,
My sister and my brother;
And, in the church-yard cottage, I
Dwell near them with my mother."

"You say that two at Conway dwell,
And two are gone to sea,
Yet ye are seven! I pray you tell,
Sweet Maid, how this may be."

Then did the little Maid reply,
"Seven boys and girls are we;   30
Two of us in the church-yard lie,
Beneath the church-yard tree."

"You run about, my little Maid,
Your limbs they are alive;
If two are in the church-yard laid,
Then ye are only five."

"Their graves are green, they may be seen,"
The little Maid replied,
"Twelve steps or more from my mother's
                                      door,
And they are side by side.   40

"My stockings there I often knit,
My kerchief there I hem;
And there upon the ground I sit,
And sing a song to them.

"And often after sun-set, Sir,
When it is light and fair,
I take my little porringer,
And eat my supper there.

"The first that died was sister Jane;
In bed she moaning lay,   50
Till God released her of her pain;
And then she went away.

"So in the church-yard she was laid;
And, when the grass was dry,
Together round her grave we played,
My brother John and I.

"And when the ground was white with snow,
And I could run and slide,
My brother John was forced to go,
And he lies by her side."   60

"How many are you, then," said I,
If they two are in heaven?"
Quick was the little Maid's reply,
"O Master! we are seven."

"But they are dead; those two are dead!
Their spirits are in heaven!"
'Twas throwing words away; for still
The little Maid would have her will,
And said, "Nay, we are seven!"

SIMON LEE

THE OLD HUNTSMAN;

With an incident in which he was concerned.

IN the sweet shire of Cardigan,
Not far from pleasant Ivor-hall,
An old Man dwells, a little man,——
'Tis said he once was tall.
Full five-and-thirty years he lived
A running huntsman merry;
And still the centre of his cheek
Is red as a ripe cherry.

No man like him the horn could sound,
And hill and valley rang with glee,   10
When Echo bandied, round and round,

The halloo of Simon Lee.
In those proud days, he little cared
For husbandry or tillage;
To blither tasks did Simon rouse
The sleepers of the village.

He all the country could outrun,
Could leave both man and horse behind;
And often, ere the chase was done,
He reeled, and was stone-blind.   20
And still there's something in the world
At which his heart rejoices;
For when the chiming hounds are out,
He dearly loves their voices!

But, oh the heavy change!—bereft
Of health, strength, friends, and kindred, see!
Old Simon to the world is left
In liveried poverty.
His Master's dead,—and no one now
Dwells in the Hall of Ivor;   30
Men, dogs, and horses, all are dead;
He is the sole survivor.

And he is lean and he is sick;
His body, dwindled and awry,
Rests upon ankles swoln and thick;
His legs are thin and dry.
One prop he has, and only one,
His wife, an aged woman,
Lives with him, near the waterfall,
Upon the village Common.   40

Beside their moss-grown hut of clay,
Not twenty paces from the door,
A scrap of land they have, but they
Are poorest of the poor.
This scrap of land he from the heath
Enclosed when he was stronger;
But what to them avails the land
Which he can till no longer?

Oft, working by her Husband's side,
Ruth does what Simon cannot do;   50
For she, with scanty cause for pride,
Is stouter of the two.
And, though you with your utmost skill
From labour could not wean them,
'Tis very, very little—all
That they can do between them.

Few months of life has he in store
As he to you will tell,
For still, the more he works, the more

Do his weak ankles swell.   60
My gentle Reader, I perceive
How patiently you've waited,
And now I fear that you expect
Some tale will be related.

O Reader, had you in your mind
Such stores as silent thought can bring,
O gentle Reader! you would find
A tale in every thing.
What more I have to say is short,
And you must kindly take it: 70
It is no tale; but, should you think,
Perhaps a tale you'll make it.

One summer-day I chanced to see
This old Man doing all he could
To unearth the root of an old tree,
A stump of rotten wood.
The mattock tottered in his hand;
So vain was his endeavour,
That at the root of the old tree
He might have worked for ever.   80

"You're overtasked, good Simon Lee,
Give me your tool," to him I said;
And at the word right gladly he
Received my proffered aid.
I struck, and with a single blow
The tangled root I severed,
At which the poor old Man so long
And vainly had endeavoured.

The tears into his eyes were brought.
And thanks and praises seemed to run   90
So fast out of his heart, I thought
They never would have done.
—I've heard of hearts unkind, kind deeds
With coldness still returning;
Alas! the gratitude of men
Hath oftener left me mourning.

GOODY BLAKE AND HARRY GILL

A TRUE STORY

OH! what's the matter? what's the matter?
What is't that ails young Harry Gill?
That evermore his teeth they chatter,
Chatter, chatter, chatter still!
Of waistcoats Harry has no lack,
Good duffle grey, and flannel fine;

He has a blanket on his back,
And coats enough to smother nine.

In March, December, and in July,
'Tis all the same with Harry Gill;   10
The neighbours tell, and tell you truly,
His teeth they chatter, chatter still.
At night, at morning, and at noon,
'Tis all the same with Harry Gill;
Beneath the sun, beneath the moon,
His teeth they chatter, chatter still!

Young Harry was a lusty drover,
And who so stout of limb as he?
His cheeks were red as ruddy clover;
His voice was like the voice of three.   20
Old Goody Blake was old and poor;
Ill fed she was, and thinly clad;
And any man who passed her door
Might see how poor a hut she had.

All day she spun in her poor dwelling:
And then her three hours' work at night,
Alas! 'twas hardly worth the telling,
It would not pay for candle-light.
Remote from sheltered village-green,
On a hill's northern side she dwelt,   30
Where from sea-blasts the hawthorns lean,
And hoary dews are slow to melt.

By the same fire to boil their pottage.
Two poor old Dames, as I have known,
Will often live in one small cottage;
But she, poor Woman, housed alone.
'Twas well enough, when summer came,
The long, warm, lightsome summer-day,
Then at her door the *canty* Dame
Would sit, as any linnet, gay.   40

But when the ice our streams did fetter,
Oh then how her old bones would shake!
You would have said, if you had met her,
'Twas a hard time for Goody Blake.
Her evenings then were dull and dead:
Sad case it was, as you may think,
For very cold to go to bed;
And then for cold not sleep a wink.

O joy for her! whene'er in winter
The winds at night had made a rout;   50
And scattered many a lusty splinter
And many a rotten bough about.
Yet never had she, well or sick,
As every man who knew her says,

A pile beforehand, turf or stick,
Enough to warm her for three days.

Now, when the frost was past enduring,
And made her poor old bones to ache,
Could any thing be more alluring
Than an old hedge to Goody Blake?   60
And, now and then, it must be said,
When her old bones were cold and chill,
She left her fire, or left her bed,
To seek the hedge of Harry Gill.

Now Harry he had long suspected
This trespass of old Goody Blake;
And vowed that she should be detected—
That he on her would vengeance take.
And oft from his warm fire he'd go,
And to the fields his road would take;   70
And there, at night, in frost and snow,
He watched to seize old Goody Blake.

And once, behind a rick of barley,
Thus looking out did Harry stand:
The moon was full and shining clearly,
And crisp with frost the stubble land.
—He hears a noise—he's all awake—
Again?—on tip-toe down the hill
He softly creeps—'tis Goody Blake;
She's at the hedge of Harry Gill!   80

Right glad was he when he beheld her:
Stick after stick did Goody pull:
He stood behind a bush of elder,
Till she had filled her apron full.
When with her load she turned about,
The by-way back again to take;
He started forward, with a shout,
And sprang upon poor Goody Blake.

And fiercely by the arm he took her,
And by the arm he held her fast,   90
And fiercely by the arm he shook her,
And cried, "I've caught you then at last!"
Then Goody, who had nothing said,
Her bundle from her lap let fall;
And, kneeling on the sticks, she prayed
To God that is the judge of all.

She prayed, her withered hand uprearing,
While Harry held her by the arm—
"God! who art never out of hearing,
O may he never more be warm!"   100
The cold, cold moon above her head,
Thus on her knees did Goody pray;

Young Harry heard what she had said:
And icy cold he turned away.

He went complaining all the morrow
That he was cold and very chill:
His face was gloom, his heart was sorrow,
Alas! that day for Harry Gill!
That day he wore a riding-coat,
But not a whit the warmer he: 110
Another was on Thursday brought,
And ere the Sabbath he had three.

'Twas all in vain, a useless matter,
And blankets were about him pinned;
Yet still his jaws and teeth they clatter,
Like a loose casement in the wind.
And Harry's flesh it fell away;
And all who see him say, 'tis plain,
That, live as long as live he may,
He never will be warm again.   120

No word to any man he utters,
A-bed or up, to young or old;
But ever to himself he mutters,
"Poor Harry Gill is very cold."
A-bed or up, by night or day;
His teeth they chatter, chatter still.
Now think, ye farmers all, I pray,
Of Goody Blake and Harry Gill!

THE OLD CUMBERLAND BEGGAR

The class of Beggars, to which the Old Man here
described belongs, will probably soon be extinct. It
consisted of poor, and, mostly, old and infirm persons,
who confined themselves to a stated round in their
neighbourhood, and had certain and fixed days, on
which, at different houses, they regularly received
alms, sometimes in money, but mostly in provisions.

I SAW an aged Beggar in my walk;
And he was seated, by the highway side,
On a low structure of rude masonry
Built at the foot of a huge hill, that they
Who lead their horses down the steep rough
    road
May thence remount at ease. The aged Man
Had placed his staff across the broad smooth
    stone
That overlays the pile; and, from a bag
All white with flour, the dole of village dames,
He drew his scraps and fragments, one by
    one;   10
And scanned them with a fixed and serious
    look

Of idle computation. In the sun,
Upon the second step of that small pile,
Surrounded by those wild unpeopled hills,
He sat, and ate his food in solitude:
And ever, scattered from his palsied hand,
That, still attempting to prevent the waste,
Was baffled still, the crumbs in little showers
Fell on the ground; and the small mountain
    birds,
Not venturing yet to peck their destined
    meal,   20
Approached within the length of half his
    staff.

Him from my childhood have I known;
    and then
He was so old, he seems not older now;
He travels on, a solitary Man,
So helpless in appearance, that for him
The sauntering Horseman throws not with a
    slack
And careless hand his alms upon the ground,
But stops,—that he may safely lodge the coin
Within the old Man's hat; nor quits him so,
But still, when he has given his horse the
    rein,   30
Watches the aged Beggar with a look
Sidelong, and half-reverted. She who tends
The toll-gate, when in summer at her door
She turns her wheel, if on the road she sees
The aged Beggar coming, quits her work,
And lifts the latch for him that he may pass.
The post-boy, when his rattling wheels o'er-
    take
The aged Beggar in the woody lane,
Shouts to him from behind; and, if thus
    warned
The old man does not change his course, the
    boy   40
Turns with less noisy wheels to the roadside,
And passes gently by, without a curse
Upon his lips or anger at his heart.

He travels on, a solitary Man;
His age has no companion. On the ground
His eyes are turned, and, as he moves along,
They move along the ground; and, evermore,
Instead of common and habitual sight
Of fields with rural works, of hill and dale,
And the blue sky, one little span of earth   50
Is all his prospect. Thus, from day to day,
Bow-bent, his eyes for ever on the ground,
He plies his weary journey; seeing still,
And seldom knowing that he sees, some straw,

Some scattered leaf, or marks which, in one
    track,
The nails of cart or chariot-wheel have left
Impressed on the white road,—in the same
    line,
At distance, still the same. Poor Traveller!
His staff trails with him; scarcely do his feet
Disturb the summer dust; he is so still   60
In look and motion, that the cottage curs,
Ere he has passed the door, will turn away,
Weary of barking at him. Boys and girls,
The vacant and the busy, maids and youths,
And urchins newly breeched—all pass him by:
Him even the slow-paced waggon leaves be-
    hind.

But deem not this Man useless.—States-
    men! ye
Who are so restless in your wisdom, ye
Who have a broom still ready in your hands
To rid the world of nuisances; ye proud,   70
Heart-swoln, while in your pride ye con-
    template
Your talents, power, or wisdom, deem him
    not
A burthen of the earth! 'Tis Nature's law
That none, the meanest of created things,
Of forms created the most vile and brute,
The dullest or most noxious, should exist
Divorced from good—a spirit and pulse of
    good,
A life and soul, to every mode of being
Inseparably linked. Then be assured
That least of all can aught—that ever
    owned   80
The heaven-regarding eye and front sublime
Which man is born to—sink, howe'er de-
    pressed,
So low as to be scorned without a sin;
Without offence to God cast out of view;
Like the dry remnant of a garden-flower
Whose seeds are shed, or as an implement
Worn out and worthless. While from door
    to door,
This old Man creeps, the villagers in him
Behold a record which together binds
Past deeds and offices of charity,   90
Else unremembered, and so keeps alive
The kindly mood in hearts which lapse of
    years,
And that half-wisdom half-experience gives,
Make slow to feel, and by sure steps resign
To selfishness and cold oblivious cares.
Among the farms and solitary huts,

Hamlets and thinly-scattered villages,
Where'er the aged Beggar takes his rounds,
The mild necessity of use compels
To acts of love; and habit does the work   100
Of reason; yet prepares that after-joy
Which reason cherishes. And thus the soul,
By that sweet taste of pleasure unpursued,
Doth find herself insensibly disposed
To virtue and true goodness.
                  Some there are,
By their good works exalted, lofty minds,
And meditative, authors of delight
And happiness, which to the end of time
Will live, and spread, and kindle: even such
    minds
In childhood, from this solitary Being,   110
Or from like wanderer, haply have received
(A thing more precious far than all that books
Or the solicitudes of love can do!)
That first mild touch of sympathy and
    thought,
In which they found their kindred with a
    world
Where want and sorrow were. The easy man
Who sits at his own door,—and, like the pear
That overhangs his head from the green wall,
Feeds in the sunshine; the robust and young,
The prosperous and unthinking, they who
    live   120
Sheltered, and flourish in a little grove
Of their own kindred;—all behold in him
A silent monitor, which on their minds
Must needs impress a transitory thought
Of self-congratulation, to the heart
Of each recalling his peculiar boons,
His charters and exemptions; and, perchance,
Though he to no one give the fortitude
And circumspection needful to preserve
His present blessings, and to husband up   130
The respite of the season, he, at least,
And 'tis no vulgar service, makes them felt.

Yet further.——Many, I believe, there are
Who live a life of virtuous decency,
Men who can hear the Decalogue and feel
No self-reproach; who of the moral law
Established in the land where they abide
Are strict observers; and not negligent
In acts of love to those with whom they
    dwell,
Their kindred, and the children of their
    blood.   140
Praise be to such, and to their slumbers peace!
—But of the poor man ask, the abject poor;

Go, and demand of him, if there be here
In this cold abstinence from evil deeds,
And these inevitable charities,
Wherewith to satisfy the human soul?
No—man is dear to man; the poorest poor
Long for some moments in a weary life
When they can know and feel that they have
        been,
Themselves, the fathers and the dealers-
        out   150
Of some small blessings; have been kind to
        such
As needed kindness, for this single cause,
That we have all of us one human heart.
—Such pleasure is to one kind Being known,
My neighbour, when with punctual care, each
        week,
Duly as Friday comes, though pressed herself
By her own wants, she from her store of meal
Takes one unsparing handful for the scrip
Of this old Mendicant, and, from her door
Returning with exhilarated heart,   160
Sits by her fire, and builds her hope in heaven.

   Then let him pass, a blessing on his head!
And while in that vast solitude to which
The tide of things has borne him, he appears
To breathe and live but for himself alone,
Unblamed, uninjured, let him bear about
The good which the benignant law of Heaven
Has hung around him: and, while life is his,
Still let him prompt the unlettered villagers
To tender offices and pensive thoughts.   170
—Then let him pass, a blessing on his head!
And, long as he can wander, let him breathe
The freshness of the valleys; let his blood
Struggle with frosty air and winter snows;
And let the chartered wind that sweeps the
        heath
Beat his grey locks against his withered face.
Reverence the hope whose vital anxiousness
Gives the last human interest to his heart.
May never HOUSE, misnamed of INDUSTRY,
Make him a captive!—for that pent-up din, 180
Those life-consuming sounds that clog the air,
Be his the natural silence of old age!
Let him be free of mountain solitudes;
And have around him, whether heard or not,
The pleasant melody of woodland birds.
Few are his pleasures: if his eyes have now
Been doomed so long to settle upon earth
That not without some effort they behold
The countenance of the horizontal sun,
Rising or setting, let the light at least   190

Find a free entrance to their languid orbs,
And let him, *where* and *when* he will, sit down
Beneath the trees, or on a grassy bank
Of highway side, and with the little birds
Share his chance-gathered meal; and, finally,
As in the eye of Nature he has lived,
So in the eye of Nature let him die!

LUCY GRAY;

OR, SOLITUDE

OFT I had heard of Lucy Gray:
And, when I crossed the wild,
I chanced to see at break of day
The solitary child.

No mate, no comrade Lucy knew;
She dwelt on a wide moor,
—The sweetest thing that ever grew
Beside a human door!

You yet may spy the fawn at play,
The hare upon the green;   10
But the sweet face of Lucy Gray
Will never more be seen.

"To-night will be a stormy night—
You to the town must go;
And take a lantern, Child, to light
Your mother through the snow."

"That, Father! will I gladly do:
'Tis scarcely afternoon—
The minster-clock has just struck two,
And yonder is the moon!"   20

At this the Father raised his hook,
And snapped a faggot-band;
He plied his work;—and Lucy took
The lantern in her hand.

Not blither is the mountain roe:
With many a wanton stroke
Her feet disperse the powdery snow,
That rises up like smoke.

The storm came on before its time:
She wandered up and down;   30
And many a hill did Lucy climb:
But never reached the town.

The wretched parents all that night
Went shouting far and wide;
But there was neither sound nor sight
To serve them for a guide.

At day-break on a hill they stood
That overlooked the moor;
And thence they saw the bridge of wood,
A furlong from their door.   40

They wept—and, turning homeward, cried,
"In heaven we all shall meet;"
—When in the snow the mother spied
The print of Lucy's feet.

Then downwards from the steep hill's edge
They tracked the footmarks small;
And through the broken hawthorn hedge,
And by the long stone-wall;

And then an open field they crossed:
The marks were still the same;   50
They tracked them on, nor ever lost;
And to the bridge they came.

They followed from the snowy bank
Those footmarks, one by one,
Into the middle of the plank;
And further there were none!

—Yet some maintain that to this day
She is a living child;
That you may see sweet Lucy Gray
Upon the lonesome wild.   60

O'er rough and smooth she trips along,
And never looks behind;
And sings a solitary song
That whistles in the wind.

MICHAEL

A PASTORAL POEM

IF from the public way you turn your steps
Up the tumultuous brook of Green-head
    Ghyll,
You will suppose that with an upright path
Your feet must struggle; in such bold ascent
The pastoral mountains front you, face to
    face.
But, courage! for around that boisterous
    brook

The mountains have all opened out them-
    selves,
And made a hidden valley of their own.
No habitation can be seen; but they
Who journey thither find themselves alone 10
With a few sheep, with rocks and stones, and
    kites
That overhead are sailing in the sky.
It is in truth an utter solitude;
Nor should I have made mention of this Dell
But for one object which you might pass by,
Might see and notice not. Beside the brook
Appears a straggling heap of unhewn stones!
And to that simple object appertains
A story—unenriched with strange events,
Yet not unfit, I deem, for the fireside,   20
Or for the summer shade. It was the first
Of those domestic tales that spake to me
Of Shepherds, dwellers in the valleys, men
Whom I already loved;—not verily
For their own sakes, but for the fields and
    hills
Where was their occupation and abode.
And hence this Tale, while I was yet a Boy
Careless of books, yet having felt the power
Of Nature, by the gentle agency
Of natural objects, led me on to feel   30
For passions that were not my own, and think
(At random and imperfectly indeed)
On man, the heart of man, and human life.
Therefore, although it be a history
Homely and rude, I will relate the same
For the delight of a few natural hearts;
And, with yet fonder feeling, for the sake
Of youthful Poets, who among these hills
Will be my second self when I am gone.

Upon the forest-side in Grasmere Vale   40
There dwelt a Shepherd, Michael was his
    name;
An old man, stout of heart, and strong of
    limb.
His bodily frame had been from youth to age
Of an unusual strength: his mind was keen,
Intense, and frugal, apt for all affairs,
And in his shepherd's calling he was prompt
And watchful more than ordinary men.
Hence had he learned the meaning of all
    winds,
Of blasts of every tone; and oftentimes,
When others heeded not, He heard the
    South   50
Make subterraneous music, like the noise
Of bagpipers on distant Highland hills.

The Shepherd, at such warning, of his flock
Bethought him, and he to himself would say,
"The winds are now devising work for me!"
And, truly, at all times, the storm, that drives
The traveller to a shelter, summoned him
Up to the mountains: he had been alone
Amid the heart of many thousand mists,
That came to him, and left him, on the
    heights.   60
So lived he till his eightieth year was past.
And grossly that man errs, who should sup-
    pose
That the green valleys, and the streams and
    rocks,
Were things indifferent to the Shepherd's
    thoughts.
Fields, where with cheerful spirits he had
    breathed
The common air; hills, which with vigorous
    step
He had so often climbed; which had im-
    pressed
So many incidents upon his mind
Of hardship, skill or courage, joy or fear;
Which, like a book, preserved the memory   70
Of the dumb animals, whom he had saved,
Had fed or sheltered, linking to such acts
The certainty of honourable gain;
Those fields, those hills—what could they
    less? had laid
Strong hold on his affections, were to him
A pleasurable feeling of blind love,
The pleasure which there is in life itself.

His days had not been passed in single-
    ness.
His Helpmate was a comely matron, old—
Though younger than himself full twenty
    years.   80
She was a woman of a stirring life,
Whose heart was in her house: two wheels she
    had
Of antique form; this large, for spinning wool;
That small, for flax; and, if one wheel had
    rest,
It was because the other was at work.
The Pair had but one inmate in their house,
An only Child, who had been born to them
When Michael, telling o'er his years, began
To deem that he was old,—in shepherd's
    phrase,
With one foot in the grave. This only Son,   90
With two brave sheep-dogs tried in many a
    storm,

The one of an inestimable worth,
Made all their household. I may truly say,
That they were as a proverb in the vale
For endless industry. When day was gone,
And from their occupations out of doors
The Son and Father were come home, even
    then,
Their labour did not cease; unless when all
Turned to the cleanly supper-board, and there,
Each with a mess of pottage and skimmed
    milk,   100
Sat round the basket piled with oaten cakes,
And their plain home-made cheese. Yet when
    the meal
Was ended, Luke (for so the Son was named)
And his old Father both betook themselves
To such convenient work as might employ
Their hands by the fire-side; perhaps to card
Wool for the Housewife's spindle, or repair
Some injury done to sickle, flail, or scythe,
Or other implement of house or field.
    Down from the ceiling, by the chimney's
    edge,   110
That in our ancient uncouth country style
With huge and black projection overbrowed
Large space beneath, as duly as the light
Of day grew dim the Housewife hung a lamp;
An aged utensil, which had performed
Service beyond all others of its kind.
Early at evening did it burn—and late,
Surviving comrade of uncounted hours,
Which, going by from year to year, had
    found,
And left, the couple neither gay perhaps   120
Nor cheerful, yet with objects and with
    hopes,
Living a life of eager industry.
And now, when Luke had reached his eight-
    eenth year,
There by the light of this old lamp they sate,
Father and Son, while far into the night
The Housewife plied her own peculiar work,
Making the cottage through the silent hours
Murmur as with the sound of summer flies.
This light was famous in its neighbourhood,
And was a public symbol of the life   130
That thrifty Pair had lived. For, as it chanced,
Their cottage on a plot of rising ground
Stood single, with large prospect, north and
    south,
High into Easedale, up to Dunmail-Raise,
And westward to the village near the lake;
And from this constant light, so regular,
And so far seen, the House itself, by all

Who dwelt within the limits of the vale,
Both old and young, was named THE EVE-
    NING STAR.

    Thus living on through such a length of
        years,   140
The Shepherd, if he loved himself, must needs
Have loved his Helpmate; but to Michael's
        heart
This son of his old age was yet more dear—
Less from instinctive tenderness, the same
Fond spirit that blindly works in the blood
        of all—
Than that a child, more than all other gifts
That earth can offer to declining man,
Brings hope with it, and forward-looking
        thoughts,
And stirrings of inquietude, when they
By tendency of nature needs must fail.   150
Exceeding was the love he bare to him,
His heart and his heart's joy! For often-
        times
Old Michael, while he was a babe in arms,
Had done him female service, not alone
For pastime and delight, as is the use
Of fathers, but with patient mind enforced
To acts of tenderness; and he had rocked
His cradle, as with a woman's gentle hand.

    And in a later time, ere yet the Boy
Had put on boy's attire, did Michael love, 160
Albeit of a stern unbending mind,
To have the Young-one in his sight, when he
Wrought in the field, or on his shepherd's stool
Sate with a fettered sheep before him
        stretched
Under the large old oak, that near his door
Stood single, and, from matchless depth of
        shade,
Chosen for the Shearer's covert from the sun,
Thence in our rustic dialect was called
The CLIPPING TREE, a name which yet it
        bears.
There, while they two were sitting in the
        shade,   170
With others round them, earnest all and
        blithe,
Would Michael exercise his heart with looks
Of fond correction and reproof bestowed
Upon the Child, if he disturbed the sheep
By catching at their legs, or with his shouts
Scared them, while they lay still beneath the
        shears.

And when by Heaven's good grace the boy
        grew up
A healthy Lad, and carried in his cheek
Two steady roses that were five years old;
Then Michael from a winter coppice cut   180
With his own hand a sapling, which he hooped
With iron, making it throughout in all
Due requisites a perfect shepherd's staff,
And gave it to the Boy; wherewith equipt
He as a watchman oftentimes was placed
At gate or gap, to stem or turn the flock;
And, to his office prematurely called,
There stood the urchin, as you will divine,
Something between a hindrance and a help;
And for this cause not always, I believe,   190
Receiving from his Father hire of praise;
Though nought was left undone which staff, or
        voice,
Or looks, or threatening gestures, could per-
        form.

    But soon as Luke, full ten years old, could
        stand
Against the mountain blasts; and to the
        heights,
Not fearing toil, or length of weary ways,
He with his Father daily went, and they
Were as companions, why should I relate
That objects which the Shepherd loved before
Were dearer now? that from the Boy there
        came   200
Feelings and emanations—things which were
Light to the sun and music to the wind;
And that the old Man's heart seemed born
        again?
    Thus in his Father's sight the Boy grew
        up:
And now, when he had reached his eighteenth
        year,
He was his comfort and his daily hope.

    While in this sort the simple household lived
From day to day, to Michael's ear there came
Distressful tidings. Long before the time
Of which I speak, the Shepherd had been
        bound   210
In surety for his brother's son, a man
Of an industrious life, and ample means;
But unforeseen misfortunes suddenly
Had prest upon him; and old Michael now
Was summoned to discharge the forfeiture,
A grievous penalty, but little less

Than half his substance. This unlooked-for
    claim,
At the first hearing for a moment took
More hope out of his life than he supposed
That any old man ever could have lost.   220
As soon as he had armed himself with
    strength
To look his trouble in the face, it seemed
The Shepherd's sole resource to sell at once
A portion of his patrimonial fields.
Such was his first resolve; he thought again,
And his heart failed him. "Isabel," said he,
Two evenings after he had heard the news,
"I have been toiling more than seventy years,
And in the open sunshine of God's love
Have we all lived; yet, if these fields of
    ours   230
Should pass into a stranger's hand, I think
That I could not lie quiet in my grave.
Our lot is a hard lot; the sun himself
Has scarcely been more diligent than I;
And I have lived to be a fool at last
To my own family. An evil man
That was, and made an evil choice, if he
Were false to us; and, if he were not false,
There are ten thousand to whom loss like this
Had been no sorrow. I forgive him;—but   240
'Twere better to be dumb than to talk thus.

"When I began, my purpose was to speak
Of remedies and of a cheerful hope.
Our Luke shall leave us, Isabel; the land
Shall not go from us, and it shall be free;
He shall possess it, free as is the wind
That passes over it. We have, thou know'st,
Another kinsman—he will be our friend
In this distress. He is a prosperous man,
Thriving in trade—and Luke to him shall
    go,   250
And with his kinsman's help and his own
    thrift
He quickly will repair this loss, and then
He may return to us. If here he stay,
What can be done? Where every one is poor,
What can be gained?"
               At this the old Man paused,
And Isabel sat silent, for her mind
Was busy, thinking back into past times.
There's Richard Bateman, thought she to her-
    self,
He was a parish-boy—at the church-door
They made a gathering for him, shillings,
    pence,   260
And halfpennies, wherewith the neighbours
    bought

A basket, which they filled with pedlar's
    wares;
And, with this basket on his arm, the lad
Went up to London, found a master there,
Who, out of many, chose the trusty boy
To go and overlook his merchandise
Beyond the seas; where he grew wondrous
    rich,
And left estates and monies to the poor,
And, at his birth-place, built a chapel floored
With marble, which he sent from foreign
    lands.   270
These thoughts, and many others of like sort,
Passed quickly through the mind of Isabel,
And her face brightened. The old Man was
    glad,
And thus resumed:—"Well, Isabel! this
    scheme
These two days has been meat and drink to
    me.
For more than we have lost is left us yet.
"We have enough—I wish indeed that I
Were younger;—but this hope is a good hope.
Make ready Luke's best garments, of the best
Buy for him more, and let us send him
    forth   280
To-morrow, or the next day, or to-night;
If he *could* go, the Boy should go to-night."

Here Michael ceased, and to the fields went
    forth
With a light heart. The Housewife for five
    days
Was restless morn and night, and all day long
Wrought on with her best fingers to prepare
Things needful for the journey of her son.
But Isabel was glad when Sunday came
To stop her in her work: for, when she lay
By Michael's side, she through the last two
    nights   290
Heard him, how he was troubled in his sleep:
And when they rose at morning she could
    see
That all his hopes were gone. That day at
    noon
She said to Luke, while they two by them-
    selves
Were sitting at the door, "Thou must not
    go:
We have no other Child but thee to lose,
None to remember—do not go away,
For if thou leave thy Father he will die."
The Youth made answer in a jocund voice;
And Isabel, when she had told her fears,   300

Recovered heart. That evening her best fare
Did she bring forth, and all together sat
Like happy people round a Christmas fire.

With daylight Isabel resumed her work;
And all the ensuing week the house appeared
As cheerful as a grove in Spring: at length
The expected letter from their kinsman came,
With kind assurances that he would do
His utmost for the welfare of the Boy;
To which, requests were added, that forth-
with   310
He might be sent to him. Ten times or more
The letter was read over; Isabel
Went forth to show it to the neighbours
round;
Nor was there at that time on English land
A prouder heart than Luke's. When Isabel
Had to her house returned, the old Man said,
"He shall depart to-morrow." To this word
The Housewife answered, talking much of
things
Which, if at such short notice he should go,
Would surely be forgotten. But at length   320
She gave consent, and Michael was at ease.

Near the tumultuous brook of Greenhead
Ghyll,
In that deep valley, Michael had designed
To build a Sheep-fold; and, before he heard
The tidings of his melancholy loss,
For this same purpose he had gathered up
A heap of stones, which by the streamlet's
edge
Lay thrown together, ready for the work.
With Luke that evening thitherward he
walked:
And soon as they had reached the place he
stopped,   330
And thus the old Man spake to him:—"My
son,
To-morrow thou wilt leave me: with full heart
I look upon thee, for thou art the same
That wert a promise to me ere thy birth,
And all thy life hast been my daily joy.
I will relate to thee some little part
Of our two histories; 'twill do thee good
When thou art from me, even if I should
touch
On things thou canst not know of.—After
thou
First cam'st into the world—as oft befalls   340
To new-born infants—thou didst sleep away

Two days, and blessings from thy Father's
tongue
Then fell upon thee. Day by day passed on,
And still I loved thee with increasing love.
Never to living ear came sweeter sounds
Than when I heard thee by our own fireside
First uttering, without words, a natural tune;
While thou, a feeding babe, didst in thy joy
Sing at thy Mother's breast. Month followed
month,
And in the open fields my life was passed   350
And on the mountains; else I think that thou
Hadst been brought up upon thy Father's
knees.
But we were playmates, Luke: among these
hills,
As well thou knowest, in us the old and young
Have played together, nor with me didst thou
Lack any pleasure which a boy can know."
Luke had a manly heart; but at these words
He sobbed aloud. The old Man grasped his
hand,
And said, "Nay, do not take it so—I see
That these are things of which I need not
speak.   360
—Even to the utmost I have been to thee
A kind and a good Father: and herein
I but repay a gift which I myself
Received at others' hands; for, though now
old
Beyond the common life of man, I still
Remember them who loved me in my youth.
Both of them sleep together: here they lived,
As all their Forefathers had done; and, when
At length their time was come, they were not
loth
To give their bodies to the family mould.   370
I wished that thou shouldst live the life they
lived,
But 'tis a long time to look back, my Son,
And see so little gain from threescore years.
These fields were burthened when they came
to me;
Till I was forty years of age, not more
Than half of my inheritance was mine.
I toiled and toiled; God blessed me in my
work,
And till these three weeks past the land was
free.
—It looks as if it never could endure
Another Master. Heaven forgive me, Luke,   380
If I judge ill for thee, but it seems good
That thou shouldst go."
                    At this the old Man paused;

Then, pointing to the stones near which they
    stood,
Thus, after a short silence, he resumed:
"This was a work for us; and now, my Son,
It is a work for me. But, lay one stone—
Here, lay it for me, Luke, with thine own
    hands.
Nay, Boy, be of good hope;—we both may
    live
To see a better day. At eighty-four
I still am strong and hale;—do thou thy
    part;   390
I will do mine.—I will begin again
With many tasks that were resigned to thee:
Up to the heights, and in among the storms,
Will I without thee go again, and do
All works that I was wont to do alone,
Before I knew thy face.—Heaven bless thee,
    Boy!
Thy heart these two weeks has been beating
    fast
With many hopes; it should be so—yes—
    yes—
I knew that thou couldst never have a wish
To leave me, Luke: thou hast been bound to
    me   400
Only by links of love: when thou art gone,
What will be left to us!—But I forget
My purposes. Lay now the corner-stone,
As I requested; and hereafter, Luke,
When thou art gone away, should evil men
Be thy companions, think of me, my Son,
And of this moment; hither turn thy thoughts,
And God will strengthen thee: amid all fear
And all temptation, Luke, I pray that thou
May'st bear in mind the life thy Fathers
    lived,   410
Who, being innocent, did for that cause
Bestir them in good deeds. Now, fare thee
    well—
When thou return'st, thou in this place wilt
    see
A work which is not here: a covenant
'Twill be between us; but, whatever fate
Befall thee, I shall love thee to the last,
And bear thy memory with me to the grave."

    The Shepherd ended here; and Luke
        stooped down,
And, as his Father had requested, laid
The first stone of the Sheep-fold. At the
    sight   420
The old Man's grief broke from him; to his
    heart

He pressed his Son, he kissed him and wept;
And to the house together they returned.
—Hushed was that House in peace, or seem-
    ing peace,
Ere the night fell:—with morrow's dawn the
    Boy
Began his journey, and, when he had reached
The public way, he put on a bold face;
And all the neighbours, as he passed their
    doors,
Came forth with wishes and with farewell
    prayers,
That followed him till he was out of sight. 430

    A good report did from their Kinsman
        come,
Of Luke and his well-doing: and the Boy
Wrote loving letters, full of wondrous news,
Which, as the Housewife phrased it, were
    throughout
"The prettiest letters that were ever seen."
Both parents read them with rejoicing hearts.
So, many months passed on: and once again
The Shepherd went about his daily work
With confident and cheerful thoughts; and
    now
Sometimes when he could find a leisure
    hour   440
He to that valley took his way, and there
Wrought at the Sheep-fold. Meantime Luke
    began
To slacken in his duty; and, at length,
He in the dissolute city gave himself
To evil courses: ignominy and shame
Fell on him, so that he was driven at last
To seek a hiding-place beyond the seas.

    There is a comfort in the strength of love;
'Twill make a thing endurable, which else
Would overset the brain, or break the
    heart: 450
I have conversed with more than one who well
Remember the old Man, and what he was
Years after he had heard this heavy news.
His bodily frame had been from youth to age
Of an unusual strength. Among the rocks
He went, and still looked up to sun and cloud,
And listened to the wind; and, as before,
Performed all kinds of labour for his sheep,
And for the land, his small inheritance.
And to that hollow dell from time to time 460
Did he repair, to build the Fold of which
His flock had need. 'Tis not forgotten yet
The pity which was then in every heart

For the old Man—and 'tis believed by all
That many and many a day he thither went,
And never lifted up a single stone.

There, by the Sheep-fold, sometimes was
    he seen
Sitting alone, or with his faithful Dog,
Then old, beside him, lying at his feet.
The length of full seven years, from time to
    time,   470
He at the building of this Sheep-fold wrought,
And left the work unfinished when he died.
Three years, or little more, did Isabel
Survive her Husband: at her death the estate
Was sold, and went into a stranger's hand.
The Cottage which was named the EVENING
    STAR
Is gone—the ploughshare has been through
    the ground
On which it stood; great changes have been
    wrought
In all the neighbourhood:—yet the oak is left
That grew beside their door; and the re-
    mains   480
Of the unfinished Sheep-fold may be seen
Beside the boisterous brook of Greenhead
    Ghyll.

RUTH

WHEN Ruth was left half desolate,
Her Father took another Mate;
And Ruth, not seven years old,
A slighted child, at her own will
Went wandering over dale and hill,
In thoughtless freedom, bold.

And she had made a pipe of straw,
And music from that pipe could draw
Like sounds of winds and floods;
Had built a bower upon the green,   10
As if she from her birth had been
An infant of the woods.

Beneath her father's roof, alone
She seemed to live; her thoughts her own;
Herself her own delight;
Pleased with herself, nor sad, nor gay;
And, passing thus the live-long day,
She grew to woman's height.

There came a Youth from Georgia's shore—
A military casque he wore,   20

With splendid feathers drest;
He brought them from the Cherokees;
The feathers nodded in the breeze,
And made a gallant crest.

From Indian blood you deem him sprung:
But no! he spake the English tongue,
And bore a soldier's name;
And, when America was free
From battle and from jeopardy,
He 'cross the ocean came.   30

With hues of genius on his cheek
In finest tones the Youth could speak:
—While he was yet a boy,
The moon, the glory of the sun,
The streams that murmur as they run,
Had been his dearest joy.

He was a lovely Youth! I guess
The panther in the wilderness
Was not so fair as he;
And, when he chose to sport and play,   40
No dolphin ever was so gay
Upon the tropic sea.

Among the Indians he had fought,
And with him many tales he brought
Of pleasure and of fear;
Such tales as told to any maid
By such a Youth, in the green shade,
Were perilous to hear.

He told of girls—a happy rout!
Who quit their fold with dance and shout,   50
Their pleasant Indian town,
To gather strawberries all day long;
Returning with a choral song
When daylight is gone down.

He spake of plants that hourly change
Their blossoms, through a boundless range
Of intermingling hues;
With budding, fading, faded flowers
They stand the wonder of the bowers
From morn to evening dews.   60

He told of the magnolia, spread
High as a cloud, high over head!
The cypress and her spire;
—Of flowers that with one scarlet gleam
Cover a hundred leagues, and seem
To set the hills on fire.

The Youth of green savannahs spake,
And many an endless, endless lake,
With all its fairy crowds
Of islands, that together lie   70
As quietly as spots of sky
Among the evening clouds.

"How pleasant," then he said, "it were
A fisher or a hunter there,
In sunshine or in shade
To wander with an easy mind;
And build a household fire, and find
A home in every glade!

"What days and what bright years! Ah me!
Our life were life indeed, with thee   80
So passed in quiet bliss,
And all the while," said he, "to know
That we were in a world of woe,
On such an earth as this!"

And then he sometimes interwove
Fond thoughts about a father's love:
"For there," said he, "are spun
Around the heart such tender ties,
That our own children to our eyes
Are dearer than the sun.   90

"Sweet Ruth! and could you go with me
My helpmate in the woods to be,
Our shed at night to rear;
Or run, my own adopted bride,
A sylvan huntress at my side,
And drive the flying deer!

"Beloved Ruth!"—No more he said.
The wakeful Ruth at midnight shed
A solitary tear:
She thought again—and did agree   100
With him to sail across the sea,
And drive the flying deer.

"And now, as fitting is and right,
We in the church our faith will plight,
A husband and a wife."
Even so they did; and I may say
That to sweet Ruth that happy day
Was more than human life.

Through dream and vision did she sink,
Delighted all the while to think   110
That on those lonesome floods,
And green savannahs, she should share
His board with lawful joy, and bear
His name in the wild woods.

But, as you have before been told,
This Stripling, sportive, gay, and bold,
And, with his dancing crest,
So beautiful, through savage lands
Had roamed about, with vagrant bands
Of Indians in the West.   120

The wind, the tempest roaring high,
The tumult of a tropic sky,
Might well be dangerous food
For him, a Youth to whom was given
So much of earth—so much of heaven,
And such impetuous blood.

Whatever in those climes he found
Irregular in sight or sound
Did to his mind impart
A kindred impulse, seemed allied   130
To his own powers, and justified
The workings of his heart.

Nor less, to feed voluptuous thought,
The beauteous forms of nature wrought,
Fair trees and gorgeous flowers;
The breezes their own languor lent;
The stars had feelings, which they sent
Into those favoured bowers.

Yet, in his worst pursuits I ween
That sometimes there did intervene   140
Pure hopes of high intent:
For passions linked to forms so fair
And stately needs must have their share
Of noble sentiment.

But ill he lived, much evil saw,
With men to whom no better law
Nor better life was known;
Deliberately, and undeceived,
Those wild men's vices he received,
And gave them back his own.   150

His genius and his moral frame
Were thus impaired, and he became
The slave of low desires:
A Man who without self-control
Would seek what the degraded soul
Unworthily admires.

And yet he with no feigned delight
Had wooed the Maiden, day and night
Had loved her, night and morn:
What could he less than love a Maid   160
Whose heart with so much nature played?
So kind and so forlorn!

Sometimes, most earnestly, he said,
"O Ruth! I have been worse than dead;
False thoughts, thoughts bold and vain,
Encompassed me on every side
When I, in confidence and pride,
Had crossed the Atlantic main.

"Before me shone a glorious world—
Fresh as a banner bright, unfurled   170
To music suddenly:
I looked upon those hills and plains,
And seemed as if let loose from chains,
To live at liberty.

"No more of this; for now, by thee,
Dear Ruth! more happily set free
With nobler zeal I burn;
My soul from darkness is released,
Like the whole sky when to the east
The morning doth return."   180

Full soon that better mind was gone:
No hope, no wish remained, not one,—
They stirred him now no more;
New objects did new pleasure give,
And once again he wished to live
As lawless as before.

Meanwhile, as thus with him it fared,
They for the voyage were prepared,
And went to the sea-shore,
But, when they thither came, the Youth
Deserted his poor Bride, and Ruth   191
Could never find him more.

God help thee, Ruth!—Such pains she had,
That she in half a year was mad,
And in a prison housed;
And there, with many a doleful song
Made of wild words, her cup of wrong
She fearfully caroused.

Yet sometimes milder hours she knew,
Nor wanted sun, nor rain, nor dew,   200
Nor pastimes of the May;
—They all were with her in her cell;
And a clear brook with cheerful knell
Did o'er the pebbles play.

When Ruth three seasons thus had lain,
There came a respite to her pain;
She from her prison fled;
But of the Vagrant none took thought;

And where it liked her best she sought
Her shelter and her bread.   210

Among the fields she breathed again:
The master-current of her brain
Ran permanent and free;
And, coming to the Bank of Tone,
There did she rest; and dwell alone
Under the greenwood tree.

The engines of her pain, the tools
That shaped her sorrows, rocks and pools,
And airs that gently stir
The vernal leaves—she loved them still;
Nor ever taxed them with the ill   221
Which had been done to her.

A Barn her *winter* bed supplies;
But, till the warmth of summer skies
And summer days is gone,
(And all do in this tale agree)
She sleeps beneath the greenwood tree,
And other home hath none.

An innocent life, yet far astray!
And Ruth will, long before her day,   230
Be broken down and old:
Sore aches she needs must have! but less
Of mind than body's wretchedness,
From damp, and rain, and cold.

If she is prest by want of food,
She from her dwelling in the wood
Repairs to a road-side;
And there she begs at one steep place
Where up and down with easy pace
The horsemen-travellers ride.   240

That oaten pipe of hers is mute,
Or thrown away; but with a flute
Her loneliness she cheers:
This flute, made of a hemlock stalk,
At evening in his homeward walk
The Quantock woodman hears.

I, too, have passed her on the hills
Setting her little water-mills
By spouts and fountains wild—
Such small machinery as she turned   250
Ere she had wept, ere she had mourned,
A young and happy Child!

Farewell! and when thy days are told,
Ill-fated Ruth, in hallowed mould

Thy corpse shall buried be,
For thee a funeral bell shall ring,
And all the congregation sing
A Christian psalm for thee.

LINES WRITTEN IN EARLY SPRING

I HEARD a thousand blended notes,
While in a grove I sate reclined,
In that sweet mood when pleasant thoughts
Bring sad thoughts to the mind.

To her fair works did Nature link
The human soul that through me ran;
And much it grieved my heart to think
What man has made of man.

Through primrose tufts, in that green bower,
The periwinkle trailed its wreaths;　　10
And 'tis my faith that every flower
Enjoys the air it breathes.

The birds around me hopped and played,
Their thoughts I cannot measure:—
But the least motion which they made,
It seemed a thrill of pleasure.

The budding twigs spread out their fan,
To catch the breezy air;
And I must think, do all I can,
That there was pleasure there.　　20

If this belief from heaven be sent,
If such be Nature's holy plan,
Have I not reason to lament
What man has made of man?

TO MY SISTER

IT is the first mild day of March:
Each minute sweeter than before,
The redbreast sings from the tall larch
That stands beside our door.

There is a blessing in the air,
Which seems a sense of joy to yield
To the bare trees, and mountains bare,
And grass in the green field.

My sister! ('tis a wish of mine)
Now that our morning meal is done,　　10

Make haste, your morning task resign;
Come forth and feel the sun.

Edward will come with you;—and, pray,
Put on with speed your woodland dress;
And bring no book: for this one day
We'll give to idleness.

No joyless forms shall regulate
Our living calendar:
We from to-day, my Friend, will date
The opening of the year.　　20

Love, now a universal birth,
From heart to heart is stealing,
From earth to man, from man to earth:
—It is the hour of feeling.

One moment now may give us more
Than years of toiling reason:
Our minds shall drink at every pore
The spirit of the season.

Some silent laws our hearts will make,
Which they shall long obey:　　30
We for the year to come may take
Our temper from to-day.

And from the blessed power that rolls
About, below, above,
We'll frame the measure of our souls:
They shall be tuned to love.

Then come, my Sister! come, I pray,
With speed put on your woodland dress;
And bring no book: for this one day
We'll give to idleness.　　40

EXPOSTULATION AND REPLY

"WHY, William, on that old grey stone,
Thus for the length of half a day,
Why, William, sit you thus alone,
And dream your time away?

"Where are your books?—that light bequeathed
To Beings else forlorn and blind!
Up! up! and drink the spirit breathed
From dead men to their kind.

"You look round on your Mother Earth,
As if she for no purpose bore you;　　10

As if you were her first-born birth,
And none had lived before you!"

One morning thus, by Esthwaite lake,
When life was sweet, I knew not why,
To me my good friend Matthew spake,
And thus I made reply:

"The eye—it cannot choose but see;
We cannot bid the ear be still;
Our bodies feel, where'er they be,
Against or with our will.   20

"Nor less I deem that there are Powers
Which of themselves our minds impress;
That we can feed this mind of ours
In a wise passiveness.

"Think you, 'mid all this mighty sum
Of things for ever speaking,
That nothing of itself will come,
But we must still be seeking?

"—Then ask not wherefore, here, alone,
Conversing as I may,   30
I sit upon this old grey stone,
And dream my time away."

THE TABLES TURNED

AN EVENING SCENE ON THE SAME SUBJECT

UP! up! my Friend, and quit your books;
Or surely you'll grow double:
Up! up! my Friend, and clear your looks;
Why all this toil and trouble?

The sun, above the mountain's head,
A freshening lustre mellow
Through all the long green fields has spread,
His first sweet evening yellow.

Books! 'tis a dull and endless strife:
Come, hear the woodland linnet,   10
How sweet his music! on my life,
There's more of wisdom in it.

And hark! how blithe the throstle sings!
He, too, is no mean preacher:
Come forth into the light of things,
Let Nature be your Teacher.

She has a world of ready wealth,
Our minds and hearts to bless—
Spontaneous wisdom breathed by health,
Truth breathed by cheerfulness.   20

One impulse from a vernal wood
May teach you more of man,
Of moral evil and of good,
Than all the sages can.

Sweet is the lore which Nature brings;
Our meddling intellect
Mis-shapes the beauteous forms of things:—
We murder to dissect.

Enough of Science and of Art;
Close up those barren leaves;   30
Come forth, and bring with you a heart
That watches and receives.

RESOLUTION AND INDEPENDENCE

I

THERE was a roaring in the wind all night;
The rain came heavily and fell in floods;
But now the sun is rising calm and bright;
The birds are singing in the distant woods;
Over his own sweet voice the Stock-dove
          broods;
The Jay makes answer as the Magpie chatters;
And all the air is filled with pleasant noise
          of waters.

II

All things that love the sun are out of doors;
The sky rejoices in the morning's birth;
The grass is bright with rain-drops;—on the
          moors
The hare is running races in her mirth;   11
And with her feet she from the plashy earth
Raises a mist; that, glittering in the sun,
Runs with her all the way, wherever she
          doth run.

III

I was a Traveller then upon the moor;
I saw the hare that raced about with joy;
I heard the woods and distant waters roar;
Or heard them not, as happy as a boy:
The pleasant season did my heart employ: 19

My old remembrances went from me wholly;
And all the ways of men, so vain and melan-
    choly.

IV

But, as it sometimes chanceth, from the
    might
Of joy in minds that can no further go,
As high as we have mounted in delight
In our dejection do we sink as low;
To me that morning did it happen so;
And fears and fancies thick upon me came;
Dim sadness—and blind thoughts, I knew
    not, nor could name.

V

I heard the sky-lark warbling in the sky;
And I bethought me of the playful hare: 30
Even such a happy Child of earth am I;
Even as these blissful creatures do I fare;
Far from the world I walk, and from all
    care;
But there may come another day to me—
Solitude, pain of heart, distress, and poverty.

VI

My whole life I have lived in pleasant thought,
As if life's business were a summer mood;
As if all needful things would come unsought
To genial faith, still rich in genial good;
But how can He expect that others should
Build for him, sow for him, and at his call 41
Love him, who for himself will take no heed
    at all?

VII

I thought of Chatterton, the marvellous Boy,
The sleepless Soul that perished in his pride;
Of Him who walked in glory and in joy
Following his plough, along the mountain-
    side:
By our own spirits are we deified:
We Poets in our youth begin in gladness;
But thereof come in the end despondency
    and madness.

VIII

Now, whether it were by peculiar grace, 50
A leading from above, a something given,

Yet it befell that, in this lonely place,
When I with these untoward thoughts had
    striven,
Beside a pool bare to the eye of heaven
I saw a Man before me unawares:
The oldest man he seemed that ever wore
    grey hairs.

IX

As a huge stone is sometimes seen to lie
Couched on the bald top of an eminence;
Wonder to all who do the same espy,
By what means it could thither come, and
    whence; 60
So that it seems a thing endued with sense:
Like a sea-beast crawled forth, that on a
    shelf
Of rock or sand reposeth, there to sun itself;

X

Such seemed this Man, not all alive nor
    dead,
Nor all asleep—in his extreme old age:
His body was bent double, feet and head
Coming together in life's pilgrimage;
As if some dire constraint of pain, or rage
Of sickness felt by him in times long past,
A more than human weight upon his frame
    had cast. 70

XI

Himself he propped, limbs, body, and pale
    face,
Upon a long grey staff of shaven wood:
And, still as I drew near with gentle pace,
Upon the margin of that moorish flood
Motionless as a cloud the old Man stood,
That heareth not the loud winds when they
    call;
And moveth all together, if it move at all.

XII

At length, himself unsettling, he the pond
Stirred with his staff, and fixedly did look
Upon the muddy water, which he conned,
As if he had been reading in a book: 81
And now a stranger's privilege I took;
And, drawing to his side, to him did say,
"This morning gives us promise of a glorious
    day."

XIII

A gentle answer did the old Man make,
In courteous speech which forth he slowly
    drew:
And him with further words I thus bespake,
"What occupation do you there pursue?
This is a lonesome place for one like you."
Ere he replied, a flash of mild surprise 90
Broke from the sable orbs of his yet-vivid
    eyes.

XIV

His words came feebly, from a feeble chest,
But each in solemn order followed each,
With something of a lofty utterance drest—
Choice word and measured phrase, above the
    reach
Of ordinary men; a stately speech;
Such as grave Livers do in Scotland use,
Religious men, who give to God and man
    their dues.

XV

He told, that to these waters he had come
To gather leeches, being old and poor: 100
Employment hazardous and wearisome!
And he had many hardships to endure:
From pond to pond he roamed, from moor to
    moor;
Housing, with God's good help, by choice or
    chance;
And in this way he gained an honest main-
    tenance.

XVI

The old Man still stood talking by my side;
But now his voice to me was like a stream
Scarce heard; nor word from word could I
    divide;
And the whole body of the Man did seem
Like one whom I had met with in a dream; 110
Or like a man from some far region sent,
To give me human strength, by apt admonish-
    ment.

XVII

My former thoughts returned: the fear that
    kills;
And hope that is unwilling to be fed;

Cold, pain, and labour, and all fleshly ills;
And mighty Poets in their misery dead.
—Perplexed, and longing to be comforted,
My question eagerly did I renew,
"How is it that you live, and what is it you
    do?"

XVIII

He with a smile did then his words repeat;
And said that, gathering leeches, far and
    wide 121
He travelled; stirring thus about his feet
The waters of the pools where they abide.
"Once I could meet with them on every
    side;
But they have dwindled long by slow decay;
Yet still I persevere, and find them where I
    may."

XIX

While he was talking thus, the lonely place,
The old Man's shape, and speech—all troubled
    me:
In my mind's eye I seemed to see him pace
About the weary moors continually, 130
Wandering about alone and silently.
While I these thoughts within myself pur-
    sued,
He, having made a pause, the same discourse
    renewed.

XX

And soon with this he other matter blended,
Cheerfully uttered, with demeanour kind,
But stately in the main; and, when he ended,
I could have laughed myself to scorn to find
In that decrepit Man so firm a mind.
"God," said I, "be my help and stay secure;
I'll think of the Leech-gatherer on the lonely
    moor!" 140

LINES

COMPOSED A FEW MILES ABOVE TINTERN ABBEY
ON REVISITING THE BANKS OF THE WYE
DURING A TOUR. JULY 13, 1798.

FIVE years have past; five summers, with the
    length
Of five long winters! and again I hear

These waters, rolling from their mountain-
    springs
With a soft inland murmur.—Once again
Do I behold these steep and lofty cliffs,
That on a wild secluded scene impress
Thoughts of more deep seclusion; and con-
    nect
The landscape with the quiet of the sky.
The day is come when I again repose
Here, under this dark sycamore, and view
These plots of cottage-ground, these orchard-
    tufts,   11
Which at this season, with their unripe fruits,
Are clad in one green hue, and lose them-
    selves
'Mid groves and copses. Once again I see
These hedge-rows, hardly hedge-rows, little
    lines
Of sportive wood run wild: these pastoral
    farms,
Green to the very door; and wreaths of
    smoke
Sent up, in silence, from among the trees!
With some uncertain notice, as might seem
Of vagrant dwellers in the houseless woods, 20
Or of some Hermit's cave, where by his fire
The Hermit sits alone.

                These beauteous forms,
Through a long absence, have not been to me
As is a landscape to a blind man's eye:
But oft, in lonely rooms, and 'mid the din
Of towns and cities, I have owed to them,
In hours of weariness, sensations sweet,
Felt in the blood, and felt along the heart;
And passing even into my purer mind,
With tranquil restoration:—feelings too   30
Of unremembered pleasure: such, perhaps,
As have no slight or trivial influence
On that best portion of a good man's life,
His little, nameless, unremembered, acts
Of kindness and of love. Nor less, I trust,
To them I may have owed another gift,
Of aspect more sublime; that blessed mood,
In which the burthen of the mystery,
In which the heavy and the weary weight
Of all this unintelligible world,   40
Is lightened:—that serene and blessed mood,
In which the affections gently lead us on,—
Until, the breath of this corporeal frame
And even the motion of our human blood
Almost suspended, we are laid asleep
In body, and become a living soul:
While with an eye made quiet by the power

Of harmony, and the deep power of joy,
We see into the life of things.

                             If this
Be but a vain belief, yet, oh! how oft— 50
In darkness and amid the many shapes
Of joyless daylight; when the fretful stir
Unprofitable, and the fever of the world,
Have hung upon the beatings of my heart—
How oft, in spirit, have I turned to thee,
O sylvan Wye! thou wanderer thro' the
    woods,
How often has my spirit turned to thee!

   And now, with gleams of half-extinguished
    thought,
With many recognitions dim and faint,
And somewhat of a sad perplexity,   60
The picture of the mind revives again:
While here I stand, not only with the sense
Of present pleasure, but with pleasing
    thoughts
That in this moment there is life and food
For future years. And so I dare to hope,
Though changed, no doubt, from what I was
    when first
I came among these hills; when like a roe
I bounded o'er the mountains, by the sides
Of the deep rivers, and the lonely streams,
Wherever nature led: more like a man   70
Flying from something that he dreads than
    one
Who sought the thing he loved. For nature
    then
(The coarser pleasures of my boyish days,
And their glad animal movements all gone
    by)
To me was all in all.—I cannot paint
What then I was. The sounding cataract
Haunted me like a passion: the tall rock,
The mountain, and the deep and gloomy
    wood,
Their colours and their forms, were then to
    me
An appetite; a feeling and a love,   80
That had no need of a remoter charm,
By thought supplied, nor any interest
Unborrowed from the eye.—That time is past,
And all its aching joys are now no more,
And all its dizzy raptures. Not for this
Faint I, nor mourn nor murmur; other gifts
Have followed; for such loss, I would believe,
Abundant recompense. For I have learned
To look on nature, not as in the hour

Of thoughtless youth; but hearing oftentimes
The still, sad music of humanity,   91
Nor harsh nor grating, though of ample
    power
To chasten and subdue. And I have felt
A presence that disturbs me with the joy
Of elevated thoughts; a sense sublime
Of something far more deeply interfused,
Whose dwelling is the light of setting suns,
And the round ocean and the living air,
And the blue sky, and in the mind of man:
A motion and a spirit, that impels   100
All thinking things, all objects of all thought,
And rolls through all things. Therefore am
    I still
A lover of the meadows and the woods,
And mountains; and of all that we behold
From this green earth; of all the mighty world
Of eye, and ear,—both what they half create,
And what perceive; well pleased to recog-
    nise
In nature and the language of the sense
The anchor of my purest thoughts, the nurse,
The guide, the guardian of my heart, and
    soul
Of all my moral being.   111

                          Nor perchance,
If I were not thus taught, should I the more
Suffer my genial spirits to decay:
For thou art with me here upon the banks
Of this fair river; thou my dearest Friend,
My dear, dear Friend; and in thy voice I
    catch
The language of my former heart, and read
My former pleasures in the shooting lights
Of thy wild eyes. Oh! yet a little while
May I behold in thee what I was once,
My dear, dear Sister! and this prayer I make,
Knowing that Nature never did betray   122
The heart that loved her; 'tis her privilege,
Through all the years of this our life, to lead
From joy to joy: for she can so inform
The mind that is within us, so impress
With quietness and beauty, and so feed
With lofty thoughts, that neither evil tongues,
Rash judgments, nor the sneers of selfish
    men,
Nor greetings where no kindness is, nor all
The dreary intercourse of daily life,   131
Shall e'er prevail against us, or disturb
Our cheerful faith, that all which we behold
Is full of blessings. Therefore let the moon
Shine on thee in thy solitary walk;

And let the misty mountain-winds be free
To blow against thee: and, in after years,
When these wild esctasies shall be matured
Into a sober pleasure; when thy mind
Shall be a mansion for all lovely forms,   140
Thy memory be as a dwelling-place
For all sweet sounds and harmonies; oh! then,
If solitude, or fear, or pain, or grief,
Should be thy portion, with what healing
    thoughts
Of tender joy wilt thou remember me,
And these my exhortations! Nor, perchance—
If I should be where I no more can hear
Thy voice, nor catch from thy wild eyes
    these gleams
Of past existence—wilt thou then forget
That on the banks of this delightful stream
We stood together; and that I, so long   151
A worshipper of Nature, hither came
Unwearied in that service: rather say
With warmer love—oh! with far deeper zeal
Of holier love. Nor wilt thou then forget
That after many wanderings, many years
Of absence, these steep woods and lofty cliffs,
And this green pastoral landscape, were to
    me
More dear, both for themselves and for thy
    sake!

NUTTING

——————————————————It seems a day
(I speak of one from many singled out)
One of those heavenly days that cannot die;
When, in the eagerness of boyish hope,
I left our cottage-threshold, sallying forth
With a huge wallet o'er my shoulders slung,
A nutting-crook in hand; and turned my
    steps
Tow'rd some far-distant wood, a Figure quaint,
Tricked out in proud disguise of cast-off
    weeds
Which for that service had been husbanded, 10
By exhortation of my frugal Dame—
Motley accoutrement, of power to smile
At thorns, and brakes, and brambles,—and
    in truth
More ragged than need was! O'er pathless
    rocks,
Through beds of matted fern, and tangled
    thickets,
Forcing my way, I came to one dear nook
Unvisited, where not a broken bough

Drooped with its withered leaves, ungracious
        sign
Of devastation; but the hazels rose
Tall and erect, with tempting clusters hung,
A virgin scene!—A little while I stood,   21
Breathing with such suppression of the heart
As joy delights in; and with wise restraint
Voluptuous, fearless of a rival, eyed
The banquet;—or beneath the trees I sate
Among the flowers, and with the flowers I
        played;
A tempter known to those who, after long
And weary expectation, have been blest
With sudden happiness beyond all hope.
Perhaps it was a bower beneath whose leaves
The violets of five seasons re-appear   31
And fade, unseen by any human eye;
Where fairy water-breaks do murmur on
For ever; and I saw the sparkling foam,
And—with my cheek on one of those green
        stones
That, fleeced with moss, under the shady
        trees,
Lay round me, scattered like a flock of sheep—
I heard the murmur and the murmuring
        sound,
In that sweet mood when pleasure loves to
        pay
Tribute to ease; and, of its joy secure,   40
The heart luxuriates with indifferent things,
Wasting its kindliness on stocks and stones,
And on the vacant air. Then up I rose,
And dragged to earth both branch and bough,
        with crash
And merciless ravage: and the shady nook
Of hazels, and the green and mossy bower,
Deformed and sullied, patiently gave up
Their quiet being: and unless I now
Confound my present feelings with the past,
Ere from the mutilated bower I turned   50
Exulting, rich beyond the wealth of kings,
I felt a sense of pain when I beheld
The silent trees, and saw the intruding sky.—
Then, dearest Maiden, move along these
        shades
In gentleness of heart; with gentle hand
Touch—for there is a spirit in the woods.

STRANGE FITS OF PASSION HAVE
I KNOWN

STRANGE fits of passion have I known:
And I will dare to tell,

But in the Lover's ear alone,
What once to me befell.

When she I loved looked every day
Fresh as a rose in June,
I to her cottage bent my way,
Beneath an evening-moon.

Upon the moon I fixed my eye,
All over the wide lea;   10
With quickening pace my horse drew nigh
Those paths so dear to me.

And now we reached the orchard-plot;
And, as we climbed the hill,
The sinking moon to Lucy's cot
Came near, and nearer still.

In one of those sweet dreams I slept,
Kind Nature's gentlest boon!
And all the while my eyes I kept
On the descending moon.   20

My horse moved on; hoof after hoof
He raised, and never stopped:
When down behind the cottage roof,
At once, the bright moon dropped.

What fond and wayward thoughts will slide
Into a Lover's head!
"O mercy!" to myself I cried,
"If Lucy should be dead!"

SHE DWELT AMONG THE UNTRODDEN
WAYS

SHE dwelt among the untrodden ways
    Beside the springs of Dove,
A Maid whom there were none to praise
    And very few to love:

A violet by a mossy stone
    Half hidden from the eye!
—Fair as a star, when only one
    Is shining in the sky.

She lived unknown, and few could know
    When Lucy ceased to be;   10
But she is in her grave, and, oh,
    The difference to me!

I TRAVELLED AMONG UNKNOWN
MEN

I TRAVELLED among unknown men,
    In lands beyond the sea;

Nor, England! did I know till then
What love I bore to thee.

'Tis past, that melancholy dream!
Nor will I quit thy shore
A second time; for still I seem
To love thee more and more.

Among thy mountains did I feel
The joy of my desire;　10
And she I cherished turned her wheel
Beside an English fire.

Thy mornings showed, thy nights concealed,
The bowers where Lucy played;
And thine too is the last green field
That Lucy's eyes surveyed.

THREE YEARS SHE GREW

Three years she grew in sun and shower,
Then Nature said, "A lovelier flower
On earth was never sown;
This Child I to myself will take;
She shall be mine, and I will make
A Lady of my own.

"Myself will to my darling be
Both law and impulse: and with me
The Girl, in rock and plain,
In earth and heaven, in glade and bower,
Shall feel an overseeing power　11
To kindle or restrain.

"She shall be sportive as the fawn
That wild with glee across the lawn
Or up the mountain springs;
And hers shall be the breathing balm,
And hers the silence and the calm
Of mute insensate things.

"The floating clouds their state shall lend
To her; for her the willow bend;　20
Nor shall she fail to see
Even in the motions of the Storm
Grace that shall mould the Maiden's form
By silent sympathy.

"The stars of midnight shall be dear
To her; and she shall lean her ear
In many a secret place
Where rivulets dance their wayward round,
And beauty born of murmuring sound
Shall pass into her face.　30

"And vital feelings of delight
Shall rear her form to stately height,
Her virgin bosom swell;
Such thoughts to Lucy I will give
While she and I together live
Here in this happy dell."

Thus Nature spake—The work was done—
How soon my Lucy's race was run!
She died, and left to me
This heath, this calm, and quiet scene;　40
The memory of what has been,
And never more will be.

A SLUMBER DID MY SPIRIT SEAL

A slumber did my spirit seal;
I had no human fears:
She seemed a thing that could not feel
The touch of earthly years.

No motion has she now, no force;
She neither hears nor sees;
Rolled round in earth's diurnal course,
With rocks, and stones, and trees.

THE TWO APRIL MORNINGS

We walked along, while bright and red
Uprose the morning sun;
And Matthew stopped, he looked, and said,
"The will of God be done!"

A village schoolmaster was he,
With hair of glittering grey;
As blithe a man as you could see
On a spring holiday.

And on that morning, through the grass,
And by the steaming rills,
We travelled merrily, to pass　10
A day among the hills.

"Our work," said I, "was well begun,
Then from thy breast what thought,
Beneath so beautiful a sun,
So sad a sigh has brought?"

A second time did Matthew stop;
And fixing still his eye
Upon the eastern mountain-top,
To me he made reply:　20

"Yon cloud with that long purple cleft
Brings fresh into my mind

A day like this which I have left
Full thirty years behind.

"And just above yon slope of corn
Such colours, and no other,
Were in the sky, that April morn,
Of this the very brother.

"With rod and line I sued the sport
Which that sweet season gave,   30
And, to the churchyard come, stopped short
Beside my daughter's grave.

"Nine summers had she scarcely seen,
The pride of all the vale;
And then she sang;—she would have been
A very nightingale.

"Six feet in earth my Emma lay;
And yet I loved her more,
For so it seemed, than till that day
I e'er had loved before.   40

"And, turning from her grave, I met,
Beside the churchyard yew,
A blooming Girl, whose hair was wet
With points of morning dew.

"A basket on her head she bare;
Her brow was smooth and white:
To see a child so very fair,
It was a pure delight!

"No fountain from its rocky cave
E'er tripped with foot so free;   50
She seemed as happy as a wave
That dances on the sea.

"There came from me a sigh of pain
Which I could ill confine;
I looked at her, and looked again:
And did not wish her mine!"

Matthew is in his grave, yet now,
Methinks, I see him stand,
As at that moment, with a bough
Of wilding in his hand.   60

THE FOUNTAIN

A CONVERSATION

WE talked with open heart, and tongue
Affectionate and true,
A pair of friends, though I was young,
And Matthew seventy-two.

We lay beneath a spreading oak,
Beside a mossy seat;
And from the turf a fountain broke,
And gurgled at our feet.

"Now, Matthew!" said I, "let us match
This water's pleasant tune   10
With some old border-song, or catch
That suits a summer's noon;

"Or of the church-clock and the chimes
Sing here beneath the shade,
That half-mad thing of witty rhymes
Which you last April made!"

In silence Matthew lay, and eyed
The spring beneath the tree;
And thus the dear old Man replied,
The grey-haired man of glee: 20

"No check, no stay, this Streamlet fears;
How merrily it goes!
'Twill murmur on a thousand years,
And flow as now it flows.

"And here, on this delightful day,
I cannot choose but think
How oft, a vigorous man, I lay
Beside this fountain's brink.

"My eyes are dim with childish tears,
My heart is idly stirred,   30
For the same sound is in my ears
Which in those days I heard.

"Thus fares it still in our decay:
And yet the wiser mind
Mourns less for what age takes away
Than what it leaves behind.

"The blackbird amid leafy trees,
The lark above the hill,
Let loose their carols when they please,
Are quiet when they will.   40

"With Nature never do *they* wage
A foolish strife; they see
A happy youth, and their old age
Is beautiful and free:

"But we are pressed by heavy laws;
And often, glad no more,
We wear a face of joy, because
We have been glad of yore.

"If there be one who need bemoan
His kindred laid in earth,   50
The household hearts that were his own;
It is the man of mirth.

"My days, my Friend, are almost gone,
My life has been approved,
And many love me! but by none
Am I enough beloved."

"Now both himself and me he wrongs,
The man who thus complains!
I live and sing my idle songs
Upon these happy plains;   60

"And, Matthew, for thy children dead
I'll be a son to thee!"
At this he grasped my hand, and said,
"Alas! that cannot be."

We rose up from the fountain-side;
And down the smooth descent
Of the green sheep-track did we glide;
And through the wood we went;

And, ere we came to Leonard's rock,
He sang those witty rhymes   70
About the crazy old church-clock,
And the bewildered chimes.

A POET'S EPITAPH

ART thou a Statist in the van
Of public conflicts trained and bred?
—First learn to love one living man;
Then may'st thou think upon the dead.

A Lawyer art thou?—draw not nigh!
Go, carry to some fitter place
The keenness of that practised eye,
The hardness of that sallow face.

Art thou a Man of purple cheer?
A rosy Man, right plump to see?   10
Approach; yet, Doctor, not too near,
This grave no cushion is for thee.

Or art thou one of gallant pride,
A Soldier and no man of chaff?
Welcome!—but lay thy sword aside,
And lean upon a peasant's staff.

Physician art thou?—one, all eyes,
Philosopher!—a fingering slave,
One that would peep and botanize
Upon his mother's grave?   20

Wrapt closely in thy sensual fleece,
O turn aside,—and take, I pray,
That he below may rest in peace,
Thy ever-dwindling soul, away!

A Moralist perchance appears;
Led, Heaven knows how! to this poor sod:
And he has neither eyes nor ears;
Himself his world, and his own God;

One to whose smooth-rubbed soul can cling
Nor form, nor feeling, great or small;   30
A reasoning, self-sufficing thing,
An intellectual All-in-all!

Shut close the door; press down the latch;
Sleep in thy intellectual crust;
Nor lose ten tickings of thy watch
Near this unprofitable dust.

But who is He, with modest looks,
And clad in homely russet brown?
He murmurs near the running brooks
A music sweeter than their own.   40

He is retired as noontide dew,
Or fountain in a noon-day grove;
And you must love him, ere to you
He will seem worthy of your love.

The outward shows of sky and earth,
Of hill and valley, he has viewed;
And impulses of deeper birth
Have come to him in solitude.

In common things that round us lie
Some random truths he can impart,—   50
The harvest of a quiet eye
That broods and sleeps on his own heart.

But he is weak; both Man and Boy,
Hath been an idler in the land;
Contented if he might enjoy
The things which others understand.

—Come hither in thy hour of strength;
Come, weak as is a breaking wave!
Here stretch thy body at full length;
Or build thy house upon this grave.   60

MATTHEW

In the School of —— is a tablet, on which are inscribed, in gilt letters, the Names of the several persons who have been Schoolmasters there since the foundation of the School, with the time at which they entered upon and quitted their office. Opposite to one of those Names the Author wrote the following lines.

IF Nature, for a favourite child,
In thee hath tempered so her clay,
That every hour thy heart runs wild,
Yet never once doth go astray,

Read o'er these lines; and then review
This tablet, that thus humbly rears
In such diversity of hue
Its history of two hundred years.

—When through this little wreck of fame,
Cipher and syllable! thine eye   10
Has travelled down to Matthew's name,
Pause with no common sympathy.

And if a sleeping tear should wake,
Then be it neither checked or stayed:
For Matthew a request I make
Which for himself he had not made.

Poor Matthew, all his frolics o'er,
Is silent as a standing pool;
Far from the chimney's merry roar,
And murmur of the village school.   20

The sighs which Matthew heaved were sighs
Of one tired out with fun and madness;
The tears which came to Matthew's eyes
Were tears of light, the dew of gladness.

Yet sometimes, when the secret cup
Of still and serious thought went round,
It seemed as if he drank it up—
He felt with spirit so profound.

—Thou soul of God's best earthly mould!
Thou happy Soul! and can it be   30
That these two words of glittering gold
Are all that must remain of thee?

TO THE DAISY

"Her divine skill taught me this,
That from every thing I saw
I could some instruction draw,
And raise pleasure to the height
Through the meanest object's sight.

By the murmur of a spring,
Or the least bough's rustelling;
By a Daisy whose leaves spread
Shut when Titan goes to bed;
Or a shady bush or tree;
She could more infuse in me
Than all Nature's beauties can
In some other wiser man."

G. WITHER.

IN youth from rock to rock I went,
From hill to hill in discontent
Of pleasure high and turbulent,
    Most pleased when most uneasy;
But now my own delights I make,—
My thirst at every rill can slake,
And gladly Nature's love partake
    Of Thee, sweet Daisy!

Thee Winter in the garland wears
That thinly decks his few grey hairs;   10
Spring parts the clouds with softest airs,
    That she may sun thee;
Whole Summer-fields are thine by right;
And Autumn, melancholy Wight!
Doth in thy crimson head delight
    When rains are on thee.

In shoals and bands, a morrice train,
Thou greet'st the traveller in the lane;
Pleased at his greeting thee again;
    Yet nothing daunted,   20
Nor grieved if thou be set at nought:
And oft alone in nooks remote
We meet thee, like a pleasant thought,
    When such are wanted.

Be violets in their secret mews
The flowers the wanton Zephyrs choose;
Proud be the rose, with rains and dews
    Her head impearling,
Thou liv'st with less ambitious aim,
Yet hast not gone without thy fame;   30
Thou art indeed by many a claim
    The Poet's darling.

If to a rock from rains he fly,
Or, some bright day of April sky,
Imprisoned by hot sunshine lie
    Near the green holly,
And wearily at length should fare;
He needs but look about, and there
Thou art!—a friend at hand, to scare
    His melancholy.   40

A hundred times, by rock or bower,
Ere thus I have lain couched an hour,

Have I derived from thy sweet power
  Some apprehension;
Some steady love; some brief delight;
Some memory that had taken flight;
Some chime of fancy wrong or right;
  Or stray invention.

If stately passions in me burn,
And one chance look to Thee should turn, 50
I drink out of an humbler urn
  A lowlier pleasure;
The homely sympathy that heeds
The common life our nature breeds;
A wisdom fitted to the needs
  Of hearts at leisure.

Fresh-smitten by the morning ray,
When thou art up, alert and gay,
Then, cheerful Flower! my spirts play
  With kindred gladness: 60
And when, at dusk, by dews opprest
Thou sink'st, the image of thy rest
Hath often eased my pensive breast
  Of careful sadness.

And all day long I number yet,
All seasons through, another debt,
Which I, wherever thou art met,
  To thee am owing;
An instinct call it, a blind sense;
A happy, genial influence,   70
Coming one knows not how, nor whence,
  Nor whither going.

Child of the Year! that round dost run
Thy pleasant course,—when day's begun
As ready to salute the sun
  As lark or leveret,
Thy long-lost praise thou shalt regain;
Nor be less dear to future men
Than in old time;—thou not in vain
  Art Nature's favourite.   80

TO THE SAME FLOWER

WITH little here to do or see
Of things that in the great world be,
Daisy! again I talk to thee,
  For thou art worthy,
Thou unassuming Common-place
Of Nature, with that homely face,
And yet with something of a grace
  Which love makes for thee!

Oft on the dappled turf at ease
I sit, and play with similes,   10
Loose types of things through all degrees,
  Thoughts of thy raising:
And many a fond and idle name
I give to thee, for praise or blame,
As is the humour of the game,
  While I am gazing.

A nun demure of lowly port;
Or sprightly maiden, of Love's court,
In thy simplicity the sport
  Of all temptations;   20
A queen in crown of rubies drest;
A starveling in a scanty vest;
Are all, as seems to suit thee best,
  Thy appellations.

A little Cyclops with one eye
Staring to threaten and defy,
That thought comes next—and instantly
  The freak is over,
The shape will vanish—and behold
A silver shield with boss of gold,   30
That spreads itself, some faery bold
  In fight to cover!

I see thee glittering from afar—
And then thou art a pretty star;
Not quite so fair as many are
  In heaven above thee!
Yet like a star, with glittering crest,
Self-poised in air thou seem'st to rest;—
May peace come never to his nest,
  Who shall reprove thee!   40

Bright *Flower!* for by that name at last,
When all my reveries are past,
I call thee, and to that cleave fast,
  Sweet silent creature!
That breath'st with me in sun and air,
Do thou, as thou art wont, repair
My heart with gladness, and a share
  Of thy meek nature!

THE GREEN LINNET

BENEATH these fruit-tree boughs that shed
Their snow-white blossoms on my head,
With brightest sunshine round me spread
  Of spring's unclouded weather,
In this sequestered nook how sweet
To sit upon my orchard-seat!

And birds and flowers once more to greet,
  My last year's friends together.

One have I marked, the happiest guest
In all this covert of the blest: 10
Hail to Thee, far above the rest
  In joy of voice and pinion!
Thou, Linnet! in thy green array,
Presiding Spirit here to-day,
Dost lead the revels of the May;
  And this is thy dominion.

While birds, and butterflies, and flowers,
Make all one band of paramours,
Thou, ranging up and down the bowers,
  Art sole in thy employment: 20
A Life, a Presence like the Air,
Scattering thy gladness without care,
Too blest with any one to pair;
  Thyself thy own enjoyment.

Amid yon tuft of hazel trees,
That twinkle to the gusty breeze,
Behold him perched in ecstasies,
  Yet seeming still to hover;
There! where the flutter of his wings
Upon his back and body flings   30
Shadows and sunny glimmerings,
  That cover him all over.

My dazzled sight he oft deceives,
A Brother of the dancing leaves;
Then flits, and from the cottage eaves
  Pours forth his song in gushes;
As if by that exulting strain
He mocked and treated with disdain
The voiceless Form he chose to feign,
  While fluttering in the bushes.   40

TO THE CUCKOO

O BLITHE New-comer! I have heard,
I hear thee and rejoice.
O Cuckoo! shall I call thee Bird,
Or but a wandering Voice?

While I am lying on the grass
Thy twofold shout I hear;
From hill to hill it seems to pass
At once far off, and near.

Though babbling only to the Vale,
Of sunshine and of flowers,   10

Thou bringest unto me a tale
Of visionary hours.

Thrice welcome, darling of the Spring!
Even yet thou art to me
No bird, but an invisible thing,
A voice, a mystery;

The same whom in my school-boy days
I listened to; that Cry
Which made me look a thousand ways
In bush, and tree, and sky.   20

To seek thee did I often rove
Through woods and on the green;
And thou wert still a hope, a love;
Still longed for, never seen.

And I can listen to thee yet;
Can lie upon the plain
And listen, till I do beget
That golden time again.

O blessèd Bird! the earth we pace
Again appears to be   30
An unsubstantial, faery place;
That is fit home for Thee!

TO A BUTTERFLY

STAY near me—do not take thy flight!
A little longer stay in sight!
Much converse do I find in thee,
Historian of my infancy!
Float near me; do not yet depart!
Dead times revive in thee:
Thou bring'st, gay creature as thou art!
A solemn image to my heart,
My father's family!

Oh! pleasant, pleasant were the days,   10
The time, when in our childish plays,
My sister Emmeline and I
Together chased the butterfly!
A very hunter did I rush
Upon the prey;—with leaps and springs
I followed on from brake to bush;
But she, God love her! feared to brush
The dust from off its wings.

I WANDERED LONELY

I WANDERED lonely as a cloud
That floats on high o'er vales and hills,

When all at once I saw a crowd,
A host, of golden daffodils;
Beside the lake, beneath the trees,
Fluttering and dancing in the breeze.

Continuous as the stars that shine
And twinkle on the milky way,
They stretched in never-ending line
Along the margin of a bay: 10
Ten thousand saw I at a glance,
Tossing their heads in sprightly dance.

The waves beside them danced; but they
Out-did the sparkling waves in glee:
A poet could not but be gay,
In such a jocund company.
I gazed—and gazed—but little thought
What wealth the show to me had brought:

For oft, when on my couch I lie
In vacant or in pensive mood,   20
They flash upon that inward eye
Which is the bliss of solitude;
And then my heart with pleasure fills,
And dances with the daffodils.

MY HEART LEAPS UP

My heart leaps up when I behold
    A rainbow in the sky:
So was it when my life began;
So is it now I am a man;
So be it when I shall grow old,
    Or let me die!
The Child is father of the Man;
And I could wish my days to be
Bound each to each by natural piety.

TO THE SMALL CELANDINE

Pansies, lilies, kingcups, daisies,
Let them live upon their praises;
Long as there's a sun that sets,
Primroses will have their glory;
Long as there are violets,
They will have a place in story:
There's a flower that shall be mine,
'Tis the little Celandine.

Eyes of some men travel far
For the finding of a star;   10
Up and down the heavens they go,
Men that keep a mighty rout!
I'm as great as they, I trow,

Since the day I found thee out,
Little Flower—I'll make a stir,
Like a sage astronomer.

Modest, yet withal an Elf
Bold, and lavish of thyself;
Since we needs must first have met
I have seen thee, high and low,   20
Thirty years or more, and yet
'Twas a face I did not know;
Thou hast now, go where I may,
Fifty greetings in a day.

Ere a leaf is on a bush,
In the time before the thrush
Has a thought about her nest,
Thou wilt come with half a call,
Spreading out thy glossy breast
Like a careless Prodigal;   30
Telling tales about the sun,
When we've little warmth, or none.

Poets, vain men in their mood!
Travel with the multitude:
Never heed them; I aver
That they all are wanton wooers;
But the thrifty cottager,
Who stirs little out of doors,
Joys to spy thee near her home:
Spring is coming, Thou art come!   40

Comfort have thou of thy merit,
Kindly, unassuming Spirit!
Careless of thy neighbourhood,
Thou dost show thy pleasant face
On the moor, and in the wood,
In the lane;—there's not a place,
Howsoever mean it be,
But 'tis good enough for thee.

Ill befall the yellow flowers,
Children of the flaring hours!   50
Buttercups, that will be seen,
Whether we will see or no;
Others, too, of lofty mien;
They have done as worldlings do,
Taken praise that should be thine,
Little, humble Celandine.

Prophet of delight and mirth,
Ill-requited upon earth;
Herald of a mighty band,
Of a joyous train ensuing,   60
Serving at my heart's command,

Tasks that are no tasks renewing,
I will sing, as doth behove,
Hymns in praise of what I love!

TO THE SAME FLOWER

PLEASURES newly found are sweet
When they lie about our feet:
February last, my heart
First at sight of thee was glad;
All unheard of as thou art,
Thou must needs, I think, have had,
Celandine! and long ago,
Praise of which I nothing know.

I have not a doubt but he,
Whosoe'er the man might be,   10
Who the first with pointed rays
(Workman worthy to be sainted)
Set the sign-board in a blaze,
When the rising sun he painted,
Took the fancy from a glance
At thy glittering countenance.

Soon as gentle breezes bring
News of winter's vanishing,
And the children build their bowers,
Sticking 'kerchief-plots of mould   20
All about with full-blown flowers,
Thick as sheep in shepherd's fold!
With the proudest thou art there,
Mantling in the tiny square.

Often have I sighed to measure
By myself a lonely pleasure,
Sighed to think I read a book
Only read, perhaps, by me;
Yet I long could overlook
Thy bright coronet and Thee,   30
And thy arch and wily ways,
And thy store of other praise.

Blithe of heart, from week to week
Thou dost play at hide-and-seek;
While the patient primrose sits
Like a beggar in the cold,
Thou, a flower of wiser wits,
Slip'st into thy sheltering hold;
Liveliest of the vernal train
When ye all are out again.   40

Drawn by what peculiar spell,
By what charm of sight or smell,

Does the dim-eyed curious Bee,
Labouring for her waxen cells,
Fondly settle upon Thee
Prized above all buds and bells
Opening daily at thy side,
By the season multiplied?

Thou art not beyond the moon,
But a thing "beneath our shoon:"   50
Let the bold Discoverer thrid
In his bark the polar sea;
Rear who will a pyramid;
Praise it is enough for me,
If there be but three or four
Who will love my little Flower.

AT THE GRAVE OF BURNS

1803

SEVEN YEARS AFTER HIS DEATH

I SHIVER, Spirit fierce and bold,
At thought of what I now behold:
As vapours breathed from dungeons cold
    Strike pleasure dead,
So sadness comes from out the mould
    Where Burns is laid.

And have I then thy bones so near,
And thou forbidden to appear?
As if it were thyself that's here
    I shrink with pain;   10
And both my wishes and my fear
    Alike are vain.

Off weight—nor press on weight!—away
Dark thoughts!—they came, but not to stay;
With chastened feelings would I pay
    The tribute due
To him, and aught that hides his clay
    From mortal view.

Fresh as the flower, whose modest worth
He sang, his genius "glinted" forth,   20
Rose like a star that touching earth,
    For so it seems,
Doth glorify its humble birth
    With matchless beams.

The piercing eye, the thoughtful brow,
The struggling heart, where be they now?—
Full soon the Aspirant of the plough,

The prompt, the brave,
Slept, with the obscurest, in the low
And silent grave.   30

I mourned with thousands, but as one
More deeply grieved, for He was gone
Whose light I hailed when first it shone,
And showed my youth
How Verse may build a princely throne
On humble truth.

Alas! where'er the current tends,
Regret pursues and with it blends,—
Huge Criffel's hoary top ascends
By Skiddaw seen,—   40
Neighbours we were, and loving friends
We might have been;

True friends though diversely inclined;
But heart with heart and mind with mind,
Where the main fibres are entwined,
Through Nature's skill,
May even by contraries be joined
More closely still.

The tear will start, and let it flow;
Thou "poor Inhabitant below,"   50
At this dread moment—even so—
Might we together
Have sate and talked where gowans blow,
Or on wild heather.

What treasures would have then been placed
Within my reach; of knowledge graced
By fancy what a rich repast!
But why go on?—
Oh! spare to sweep, thou mournful blast,
His grave grass-grown.   60

There, too, a Son, his joy and pride,
(Not three weeks past the Stripling died,)
Lies gathered to his Father's side,
Soul-moving sight!
Yet one to whom is not denied
Some sad delight.

For *he* is safe, a quiet bed
Hath early found among the dead,
Harboured where none can be misled,
Wronged, or distrest;   70
And surely here it may be said
That such are blest.

And oh for Thee, by pitying grace
Checked oft-times in a devious race,
May He, who halloweth the place
Where Man is laid,
Receive thy Spirit in the embrace
For which it prayed!

Sighing I turned away; but ere
Night fell I heard, or seemed to hear,   80
Music that sorrow comes not near,
A ritual hymn,
Chanted in love that casts out fear
By Seraphim.

STEPPING WESTWARD

While my Fellow-traveller and I were walking by the
side of Loch Ketterine, one fine evening after sunset, in our road to a Hut where, in the course of
our Tour, we had been hospitably entertained some
weeks before, we met, in one of the loneliest parts
of that solitary region, two well-dressed Women,
one of whom said to us, by way of greeting,
"What, you are stepping westward?"

"What, you are stepping westward?"—"Yea."
—T'would be a *wildish* destiny,
If we, who thus together roam
In a strange Land, and far from home,
Were in this place the guests of Chance:
Yet who would stop, or fear to advance,
Though home or shelter he had none,
With such a sky to lead him on?

The dewy ground was dark and cold;
Behind, all gloomy to behold;
And stepping westward seemed to be   10
A kind of *heavenly* destiny:
I liked the greeting; 'twas a sound
Of something without place or bound;
And seemed to give me spiritual right
To travel through that region bright.

The voice was soft, and she who spake
Was walking by her native lake:
The salutation had to me
The very sound of courtesy: 20
Its power was felt; and while my eye
Was fixed upon the glowing Sky,
The echo of the voice enwrought
A human sweetness with the thought
Of travelling through the world that lay
Before me in my endless way.

TO A HIGHLAND GIRL,

AT INVERSNEYDE, UPON LOCH LOMOND

SWEET Highland Girl, a very shower
Of beauty is thy earthly dower!
Twice seven consenting years have shed
Their utmost bounty on thy head:
And these grey rocks; that household lawn;
Those trees, a veil just half withdrawn;
This fall of water that doth make
A murmur near the silent lake;
This little bay; a quiet road
That holds in shelter thy Abode—   10
In truth together do ye seem
Like something fashioned in a dream;
Such Forms as from their covert peep
When earthly cares are laid asleep!
But, O fair Creature! in the light
Of common day, so heavenly bright,
I bless Thee, Vision as thou art,
I bless thee with a human heart;
God shield thee to thy latest years!
Thee, neither know I, nor thy peers;   20
And yet my eyes are filled with tears.

With earnest feeling I shall pray
For thee when I am far away:
For never saw I mien, or face,
In which more plainly I could trace
Benignity and home-bred sense
Ripening in perfect innocence.
Here scattered, like a random seed,
Remote from men, Thou dost not need
The embarrassed look of shy distress,   30
And maidenly shamefacedness:
Thou wear'st upon thy forehead clear
The freedom of a Mountaineer:
A face with gladness overspread!
Soft smiles, by human kindness bred!
And seemliness complete, that sways
Thy courtesies, about thee plays;
With no restraint, but such as springs
From quick and eager visitings
And thoughts that lie beyond the reach   40
Of thy few words of English speech:
A bondage sweetly brooked, a strife
That gives thy gestures grace and life!
So have I, not unmoved in mind,
Seen birds of tempest-loving kind—
Thus beating up against the wind.

What hand but would a garland cull
For thee who art so beautiful?

O happy pleasure! here to dwell
Beside thee in some heathy dell;   50
Adopt your homely ways, and dress,
A Shepherd, thou a Shepherdess!
But I could frame a wish for thee
More like a grave reality:
Thou art to me but as a wave
Of the wild sea; and I would have
Some claim upon thee, if I could,
Though but of common neighbourhood.
What joy to hear thee, and to see!
Thy elder Brother I would be,   60
Thy Father—anything to thee!

Now thanks to Heaven! that of its grace
Hath led me to this lonely place.
Joy have I had; and going hence
I bear away my recompense.
In spots like these it is we prize
Our Memory, feel that she hath eyes:
Then, why should I be loth to stir?
I feel this place was made for her;
To give new pleasure like the past,   70
Continued long as life shall last,
Nor am I loth, though pleased at heart,
Sweet Highland Girl! from thee to part;
For I, methinks, till I grow old,
As fair before me shall behold,
As I do now, the cabin small,
The lake, the bay, the waterfall;
And Thee, the Spirit of them all!

SHE WAS A PHANTOM OF DELIGHT

SHE was a Phantom of delight
When first she gleamed upon my sight;
A lovely Apparition, sent
To be a moment's ornament;
Her eyes as stars of Twilight fair;
Like Twilight's, too, her dusky hair;
But all things else about her drawn
From May-time and the cheerful Dawn;
A dancing Shape, an Image gay,
To haunt, to startle, and way-lay.   10

I saw her upon nearer view,
A Spirit, yet a Woman too!
Her household motions light and free,
And steps of virgin-liberty;
A countenance in which did meet
Sweet records, promises as sweet;
A Creature not too bright or good
For human nature's daily food;
For transient sorrows, simple wiles,
Praise, blame, love, kisses, tears, and smiles.   20

And now I see with eye serene
The very pulse of the machine;
A Being breathing thoughtful breath,
A Traveller between life and death;
The reason firm, the temperate will,
Endurance, foresight, strength, and skill;
A perfect Woman, nobly planned,
To warn, to comfort, and command;
And yet a Spirit still, and bright
With something of angelic light.   30

THE SOLITARY REAPER

BEHOLD her, single in the field,
Yon solitary Highland Lass!
Reaping and singing by herself;
Stop here, or gently pass!
Alone she cuts and binds the grain,
And sings a melancholy strain;
O listen! for the Vale profound
Is overflowing with the sound.

No Nightingale did ever chaunt
More welcome notes to weary bands   10
Of travellers in some shady haunt,
Among Arabian sands:
A voice so thrilling ne'er was heard
In spring-time from the Cuckoo-bird,
Breaking the silence of the seas
Among the farthest Hebrides.

Will no one tell me what she sings?—
Perhaps the plaintive numbers flow
For old, unhappy, far-off things,
And battles long ago: 20
Or is it some more humble lay,
Familiar matter of to-day?
Some natural sorrow, loss, or pain,
That has been, and may be again?

Whate'er the theme, the Maiden sang
As if her song could have no ending;
I saw her singing at her work,
And o'er the sickle bending;—
I listened, motionless and still;
And, as I mounted up the hill,   30
The music in my heart I bore,
Long after it was heard no more.

THE AFFLICTION OF MARGARET ——

I

WHERE art thou, my beloved Son,
Where art thou, worse to me than dead?
Oh find me, prosperous or undone!
Or, if the grave be now thy bed,
Why am I ignorant of the same,
That I may rest; and neither blame
Nor sorrow may attend thy name?

II

Seven years, alas! to have received
No tidings of an only child;
To have despaired, have hoped, believed,   10
And been for evermore beguiled;
Sometimes with thoughts of very bliss!
I catch at them, and then I miss;
Was ever darkness like to this?

III

He was among the prime in worth,
An object beauteous to behold;
Well born, well bred; I sent him forth
Ingenuous, innocent, and bold:
If things ensued that wanted grace,
As hath been said, they were not base;   20
And never blush was on my face.

IV

Ah! little doth the young-one dream,
When full of play and childish cares,
What power is in his wildest scream,
Heard by his mother unawares!
He knows it not, he cannot guess:
Years to a mother bring distress;
But do not make her love the less.

V

Neglect me! no, I suffered long   29
From that ill thought; and, being blind,
Said, "Pride shall help me in my wrong:
Kind mother have I been, as kind
As ever breathed:" and that is true;
I've wet my path with tears like dew,
Weeping for him when no one knew.

VI

My Son, if thou be humbled, poor,
Hopeless of honour and of gain,

Oh! do not dread thy mother's door;
Think not of me with grief and pain:
I now can see with better eyes; 40
And worldly grandeur I despise,
And fortune with her gifts and lies.

VII

Alas! the fowls of heaven have wings,
And blasts of heaven will aid their flight;
They mount—how short a voyage brings
The wanderers back to their delight!
Chains tie us down by land and sea;
And wishes, vain as mine, may be
All that is left to comfort thee.

VIII

Perhaps some dungeon hears thee groan, 50
Maimed, mangled by inhuman men;
Or thou upon a desert thrown
Inheritest the lion's den;
Or hast been summoned to the deep,
Thou, thou and all thy mates, to keep
An incommunicable sleep.

IX

I look for ghosts; but none will force
Their way to me; 'tis falsely said
That there was ever intercourse
Between the living and the dead; 60
For, surely, then I should have sight
Of him I wait for day and night,
With love and longings infinite.

X

My apprehensions come in crowds;
I dread the rustling of the grass;
The very shadows of the clouds
Have power to shake me as they pass:
I question things and do not find
One that will answer to my mind;
And all the world appears unkind. 70

XI

Beyond participation lie
My troubles, and beyond relief:
If any chance to heave a sigh,
They pity me, and not my grief.
Then come to me, my Son, or send
Some tidings that my woes may end;
I have no other earthly friend!

TO H. C.

SIX YEARS OLD

O THOU! whose fancies from afar are
 brought;
Who of thy words dost make a mock apparel,
And fittest to unutterable thought
The breeze-like motion and the self-born
 carol;
Thou faery voyager! that dost float
In such clear water, that thy boat
May rather seem
To brood on air than on an earthly stream;
Suspended in a stream as clear as sky,
Where earth and heaven do make one
 imagery; 10
O blessèd vision! happy child!
Thou art so exquisitely wild,
I think of thee with many fears
For what may be thy lot in future years.

I thought of times when Pain might be thy
 guest,
Lord of thy house and hospitality;
And Grief, uneasy lover! never rest
But when she sate within the touch of thee.
O too industrious folly!
O vain and causeless melancholy! 20
Nature will either end thee quite;
Or, lengthening out thy season of delight,
Preserve for thee, by individual right,
A young lamb's heart among the full-grown
 flocks.
What hast thou to do with sorrow,
Or the injuries of to-morrow?
Thou art a dew-drop, which the morn brings
 forth,
Ill fitted to sustain unkindly shocks,
Or to be trailed along the soiling earth;
A gem that glitters while it lives, 30
And no forewarning gives;
But, at the touch of wrong, without a strife
Slips in a moment out of life.

TO A SKY-LARK

Up with me! up with me into the clouds!
 For thy song, Lark, is strong;
Up with me, up with me into the clouds!
 Singing, singing,

With clouds and sky about thee ringing,
    Lift me, guide me, till I find
That spot which seems so to thy mind!

I have walked through wildernesses dreary,
And to-day my heart is weary;
Had I now the wings of a Faery,   10
Up to thee would I fly.
There is madness about thee, and joy divine
In that song of thine;
Lift me, guide me, high and high
To thy banqueting place in the sky.

        Joyous as morning,
Thou art laughing and scorning;
Thou hast a nest for thy love and thy rest,
And, though little troubled with sloth,
Drunken Lark! thou wouldst be loth   20
To be such a traveller as I.
Happy, happy Liver,
With a soul as strong as a mountain river
Pouring out praise to the almighty Giver,
Joy and jollity be with us both!

Alas! my journey, rugged and uneven,
Through prickly moors or dusty ways must
        wind;
But hearing thee, or others of thy kind,
As full of gladness and as free of heaven,
I, with my fate contented, will plod on,   30
And hope for higher raptures, when life's day
        is done.

TO A SKY-LARK

Ethereal minstrel! pilgrim of the sky!
Dost thou despise the earth where cares
        abound?
Or, while the wings aspire, are heart and eye
Both with thy nest upon the dewy ground?
Thy nest which thou canst drop into at will,
Those quivering wings composed, that music
        still!

Leave to the nightingale her shady wood;
A privacy of glorious light is thine;
Whence thou dost pour upon the world a
        flood
Of harmony, with instinct more divine;   10
Type of the wise who soar, but never roam;
True to the kindred points of Heaven and
        Home!

I GRIEVED FOR BUONAPARTÉ

I grieved for Buonaparté, with a vain
And an unthinking grief! The tenderest mood
Of that Man's mind—what can it be? what
        food
Fed his first hopes? what knowledge could he
        gain?
'Tis not in battles that from youth we train
The Governor who must be wise and good,
And temper with the sternness of the brain
Thoughts motherly, and meek as womanhood.
Wisdom doth live with children round her
        knees:
Books, leisure, perfect freedom, and the
        talk   10
Man holds with week-day man in the hourly
        walk
Of the mind's business: these are the degrees
By which true Sway doth mount; this is the
        stalk
True Power doth grow on; and her rights are
        these.

COMPOSED UPON WESTMINSTER BRIDGE, SEPTEMBER 3, 1802

Earth has not anything to show more fair:
Dull would he be of soul who could pass by
A sight so touching in its majesty:
This City now doth, like a garment, wear
The beauty of the morning; silent, bare,
Ships, towers, domes, theatres, and temples
        lie
Open unto the fields, and to the sky;
All bright and glittering in the smokeless air.
Never did sun more beautifully steep
In his first splendour, valley, rock, or hill;   10
Ne'er saw I, never felt, a calm so deep!
The river glideth at his own sweet will;
Dear God! the very houses seem asleep;
And all that mighty heart is lying still!

IT IS A BEAUTEOUS EVENING

It is a beauteous evening, calm and free,
The holy time is quiet as a Nun
Breathless with adoration; the broad sun
Is sinking down in its tranquillity;
The gentleness of heaven broods o'er the
        Sea:
Listen! the mighty Being is awake,
And doth with his eternal motion make
A sound like thunder—everlastingly.

Dear Child! dear Girl! that walkest with me
    here,
If thou appear untouched by solemn thought,
Thy nature is not therefore less divine: 11
Thou liest in Abraham's bosom all the year;
And worshipp'st at the Temple's inner shrine,
God being with thee when we know it not.

COMPOSED BY THE SEA-SIDE, NEAR CALAIS, AUGUST, 1802

FAIR Star of evening, Splendour of the west,
Star of my Country!—on the horizon's brink
Thou hangest, stooping, as might seem, to
    sink
On England's bosom; yet well pleased to rest,
Meanwhile, and be to her a glorious crest
Conspicuous to the Nations. Thou, I think,
Shouldst be my Country's emblem; and
    shouldst wink,
Bright Star! with laughter on her banners,
    drest
In thy fresh beauty. There! that dusky spot
Beneath thee, that is England; there she
    lies.   10
Blessings be on you both! one hope, one lot,
One life, one glory!—I, with many a fear
For my dear Country, many heartfelt sighs,
Among men who do not love her, linger here.

ON THE EXTINCTION OF THE VENETIAN REPUBLIC

ONCE did She hold the gorgeous east in fee;
And was the safeguard of the west: the worth
Of Venice did not fall below her birth,
Venice, the eldest Child of Liberty.
She was a maiden City, bright and free;
No guile seduced, no force could violate;
And, when she took unto herself a Mate,
She must espouse the everlasting Sea.
And what if she had seen those glories fade,
Those titles vanish, and that strength de-
    cay;   10
Yet shall some tribute of regret be paid
When her long life hath reached its final day:
Men are we, and must grieve when even the
    Shade
Of that which once was great is passed away.

TO TOUSSAINT L'OUVERTURE

TOUSSAINT, the most unhappy man of men!
Whether the whistling Rustic tend his plough
Within thy hearing, or thy head be now
Pillowed in some deep dungeon's earless
    den;—
O miserable Chieftain! where and when
Wilt thou find patience! Yet die not; do
    thou
Wear rather in thy bonds a cheerful brow:
Though fallen thyself, never to rise again,
Live, and take comfort. Thou hast left be-
    hind
Powers that will work for thee; air, earth,
    and skies;   10
There's not a breathing of the common wind
That will forget thee; thou hast great allies;
Thy friends are exultations, agonies,
And love, and man's unconquerable mind.

SEPTEMBER, 1802. NEAR DOVER

INLAND, within a hollow vale, I stood;
And saw, while sea was calm and air was
    clear,
The coast of France—the coast of France how
    near!
Drawn almost into frightful neighbourhood.
I shrunk; for verily the barrier flood
Was like a lake, or river bright and fair,
A span of waters; yet what power is there!
What mightiness for evil and for good!
Even so doth God protect us if we be
Virtuous and wise. Winds blow, and waters
    roll,   10
Strength to the brave, and Power, and Deity;
Yet in themselves are nothing! One decree
Spake laws to *them,* and said that by the soul
Only, the Nations shall be great and free.

LONDON, 1802

MILTON! thou shouldst be living at this hour:
England hath need of thee: she is a fen
Of stagnant waters: altar, sword, and pen,
Fireside, the heroic wealth of hall and bower,
Have forfeited their ancient English dower
Of inward happiness. We are selfish men;
Oh! raise us up, return to us again;
And give us manners, virtue, freedom, power.
Thy soul was like a Star, and dwelt apart;

Thou hadst a voice whose sound was like the
    sea: 10
Pure as the naked heavens, majestic, free,
So didst thou travel on life's common way,
In cheerful godliness; and yet thy heart
The lowliest duties on herself did lay.

WRITTEN IN LONDON, SEPTEMBER, 1802

O FRIEND! I know not which way I must look
For comfort, being, as I am, opprest,
To think that now our life is only drest
For show; mean handy-work of craftsman,
    cook,
Or groom!—We must run glittering like a
    brook
In the open sunshine, or we are unblest:
The wealthiest man among us is the best:
No grandeur now in nature or in book
Delights us. Rapine, avarice, expense,
This is idolatry; and these we adore: 10
Plain living and high thinking are no more:
The homely beauty of the good old cause
Is gone; our peace, our fearful innocence,
And pure religion breathing household laws.

GREAT MEN HAVE BEEN AMONG US

GREAT men have been among us; hands that
    penned
And tongues that uttered wisdom—better
    none:
The later Sidney, Marvel, Harrington,
Young Vane, and others who called Milton
    friend.
These moralists could act and comprehend:
They knew how genuine glory was put on;
Taught us how rightfully a nation shone
In splendour: what strength was, that would
    not bend
But in magnanimous meekness. France, 'tis
    strange,
Hath brought forth no such souls as we had
    then. 10
Perpetual emptiness! unceasing change!
No single volume paramount, no code,
No master spirit, no determined road;
But equally a want of books and men!

THE PRELUDE

BOOK FIRST

FAR better never to have heard the name
Of zeal and just ambition, than to live

Baffled and plagued by a mind that every
    hour
Turns recreant to her task; takes heart again,
Then feels immediately some hollow thought
Hang like an interdict upon her hopes.
This is my lot; for either still I find
Some imperfection in the chosen theme,
Or see of absolute accomplishment
Much wanting, so much wanting, in myself, 10
That I recoil and droop, and seek repose
In listlessness from vain perplexity,
Unprofitably travelling toward the grave,
Like a false steward who hath much received
And renders nothing back.

                      Was it for this
That one, the fairest of all rivers, loved
To blend his murmurs with my nurse's song,
And, from his alder shades and rocky falls,
And from his fords and shallows, sent a voice
That flowed along my dreams? For this,
    didst thou, 20
O Derwent! winding among grassy holms
Where I was looking on, a babe in arms,
Make ceaseless music that composed my
    thoughts
To more than infant softness, giving me
Amid the fretful dwellings of mankind
A foretaste, a dim earnest, of the calm
That Nature breathes among the hills and
    groves.

When he had left the mountains and re-
    ceived
On his smooth breast the shadow of those
    towers
That yet survive, a shattered monument 30
Of feudal sway, the bright blue river passed
Along the margin of our terrace walk;
A tempting playmate whom we dearly loved.
Oh, many a time have I, a five years' child,
In a small mill-race severed from his stream,
Made one long bathing of a summer's day;
Basked in the sun, and plunged and basked
    again
Alternate, all a summer's day, or scoured
The sandy fields, leaping through flowery
    groves
Of yellow ragwort; or when rock and hill, 40
The woods, and distant Skiddaw's lofty
    height,
Were bronzed with deepest radiance, stood
    alone
Beneath the sky, as if I had been born
On Indian plains, and from my mother's hut

Had run abroad in wantonness, to sport,
A naked savage, in the thunder shower.

    Fair seed-time had my soul, and I grew up
Fostered alike by beauty and by fear:
Much favoured in my birthplace, and no less
In that belovèd Vale to which erelong   50
We were transplanted—there were we let
    loose
For sports of wider range. Ere I had told
Ten birth-days, when among the mountain-
    slopes
Frost, and the breath of frosty wind, had
    snapped
The last autumnal crocus, 'twas my joy
With store of springes o'er my shoulder hung
To range the open heights where wood-cocks
    run
Among the smooth green turf. Through half
    the night,
Scudding away from snare to snare, I plied
That anxious visitation;—moon and stars 60
Were shining o'er my head. I was alone,
And seemed to be a trouble to the peace
That dwelt among them. Sometimes it be-
    fell
In these night wanderings, that a strong de-
    sire
O'erpowered my better reason, and the bird
Which was the captive of another's toil
Became my prey; and when the deed was
    done
I heard among the solitary hills
Low breathings coming after me, and sounds
Of undistinguishable motion, steps   70
Almost as silent as the turf they trod.

    Nor less when spring had warmed the cul-
    tured Vale,
Moved we as plunderers where the mother-
    bird
Had in high places built her lodge; though
    mean
Our object and inglorious, yet the end
Was not ignoble. Oh! when I have hung
Above the raven's nest, by knots of grass
And half-inch fissures in the slippery rock
But ill sustained, and almost (so it seemed)
Suspended by the blast that blew amain, 80
Shouldering the naked crag, oh, at that time
While on the perilous ridge I hung alone,
With what strange utterance did the loud dry
    wind

Blow through my ear! the sky seemed not a
    sky
Of earth—and with what motion moved the
    clouds!

    Dust as we are, the immortal spirit grows
Like harmony in music; there is a dark
Inscrutable workmanship that reconciles
Discordant elements, makes them cling to-
    gether
In one society. How strange that all   90
The terrors, pains, and early miseries,
Regrets, vexations, lassitudes interfused
Within my mind, should e'er have borne a
    part,
And that a needful part, in making up
The calm existence that is mine when I
Am worthy of myself! Praise to the end!
Thanks to the means which Nature deigned
    to employ;
Whether her fearless visitings, or those
That came with soft alarm, like hurtless light
Opening the peaceful clouds; or she would
    use   100
Severer interventions, ministry
More palpable, as best might suit her aim.

    One summer evening (led by her) I found
A little boat tied to a willow tree
Within a rocky cave, its usual home.
Straight I unloosed her chain, and stepping in
Pushed from the shore. It was an act of
    stealth
And troubled pleasure, nor without the voice
Of mountain-echoes did my boat move on;
Leaving behind her still, on either side, 110
Small circles glittering idly in the moon,
Until they melted all into one track
Of sparkling light. But now, like one who
    rows,
Proud of his skill, to reach a chosen point
With an unswerving line, I fixed my view
Upon the summit of a craggy ridge,
The horizon's utmost boundary; far above
Was nothing but the stars and the grey sky.
She was an elfin pinnace; lustily
I dipped my oars into the silent lake,   120
And, as I rose upon the stroke, my boat
Went heaving through the water like a swan;
When, from behind that craggy steep till
    then
The horizon's bound, a huge peak, black and
    huge,
As if with voluntary power instinct

Upreared its head. I struck and struck again,
And growing still in stature the grim shape
Towered up between me and the stars, and
    still,
For so it seemed, with purpose of its own
And measured motion like a living thing, 130
Strode after me. With trembling oars I
    turned,
And through the silent water stole my way
Back to the covert of the willow tree;
There in her mooring-place I left my bark,—
And through the meadows homeward went, in
    grave
And serious mood; but after I had seen
That spectacle, for many days, my brain
Worked with a dim and undetermined sense
Of unknown modes of being; o'er my thoughts
There hung a darkness, call it solitude   140
Or blank desertion. No familiar shapes
Remained, no pleasant images of trees,
Of sea or sky, no colours of green fields;
But huge and mighty forms, that do not live
Like living men, moved slowly through the
    mind
By day, and were a trouble to my dreams.

Wisdom and Spirit of the universe!
Thou Soul that art the eternity of thought,
That givest to forms and images a breath
And everlasting motion, not in vain   150
By day or star-light thus from my first dawn
Of childhood didst thou intertwine for me
The passions that build up our human soul;
Not with the mean and vulgar works of man,
But with high objects, with enduring things—
With life and nature—purifying thus
The elements of feeling and of thought,
And sanctifying, by such discipline,
Both pain and fear, until we recognise
A grandeur in the beatings of the heart.   160
Nor was this fellowship vouchsafed for me
With stinted kindness. In November days,
When vapours rolling down the valley made
A lonely scene more lonesome, among woods,
At noon and 'mid the calm of summer nights,
When, by the margin of the trembling lake,
Beneath the gloomy hills homeward I went
In solitude, such intercourse was mine;
Mine was it in the fields both day and night,
And by the waters, all the summer long.   170

And in the frosty season, when the sun
Was set, and visible for many a mile

The cottage windows blazed through twilight
    gloom,
I heeded not their summons: happy time
It was indeed for all of us—for me
It was a time of rapture! Clear and loud
The village clock tolled six,—I wheeled about,
Proud and exulting like an untired horse
That cares not for his home. All shod with
    steel,
We hissed along the polished ice in games   180
Confederate, imitative of the chase
And woodland pleasures,—the resounding
    horn,
The pack loud chiming, and the hunted hare.
So through the darkness and the cold we flew,
And not a voice was idle; with the din
Smitten, the precipices rang aloud;
The leafless trees and every icy crag
Tinkled like iron; while far distant hills
Into the tumult sent an alien sound
Of melancholy not unnoticed, while the
    stars   190
Eastward were sparkling clear, and in the
    west
The orange sky of evening died away.
Not seldom from the uproar I retired
Into a silent bay, or sportively
Glanced sideway, leaving the tumultuous
    throng,
To cut across the reflex of a star
That fled, and, flying still before me, gleamed
Upon the glassy plain; and oftentimes,
When we had given our bodies to the wind,
And all the shadowy banks on either side   200
Came sweeping through the darkness, spinning
    still
The rapid line of motion, then at once
Have I, reclining back upon my heels,
Stopped short; yet still the solitary cliffs
Wheeled by me—even as if the earth had
    rolled
With visible motion her diurnal round!
Behind me did they stretch in solemn train,
Feebler and feebler, and I stood and watched
Till all was tranquil as a dreamless sleep.

Ye Presences of Nature in the sky   210
And on the earth! Ye Visions of the hills!
And Souls of lonely places! can I think
A vulgar hope was yours when ye employed
Such ministry, when ye through many a year
Haunting me thus among my boyish sports,
On caves and trees, upon the woods and hills,
Impressed upon all forms the characters

Of danger or desire; and thus did make
The surface of the universal earth
With triumph and delight, with hope and
    fear,   220
Work like a sea?
            Not uselessly employed,
Might I pursue this theme through every
    change
Of exercise and play, to which the year
Did summon us in his delightful round.

We were a noisy crew; the sun in heaven
Beheld not vales more beautiful than ours;
Nor saw a band in happiness and joy
Richer, or worthier of the ground they trod.
I could record with no reluctant voice
The woods of autumn, and their hazel bow-
    ers   230
With milk-white clusters hung; the rod and
    line,
True symbol of hope's foolishness, whose
    strong
And unreproved enchantment led us on
By rocks and pools shut out from every star,
All the green summer, to forlorn cascades
Among the windings hid of mountain brooks.
—Unfading recollections! at this hour
The heart is almost mine with which I felt,
From some hill-top on sunny afternoons,
The paper kite high among fleecy clouds 240
Pull at her rein like an impetuous courser;
Or, from the meadows sent on gusty days,
Beheld her breast the wind, then suddenly
Dashed headlong, and rejected by the storm.

Ye lowly cottages wherein we dwelt,
A ministration of your own was yours;
Can I forget you, being as you were
So beautiful among the pleasant fields
In which ye stood? or can I here forget
The plain and seemly countenance with
    which   250
Ye dealt out your plain comforts? Yet had ye
Delights and exultations of your own.
Eager and never weary we pursued
Our home-amusements by the warm peat-fire
At evening, when with pencil, and smooth
    slate
In square divisions parcelled out and all
With crosses and with cyphers scribbled o'er,
We schemed and puzzled, head opposed to
    head
In strife too humble to be named in verse:
Or round the naked table, snow-white deal, 260
Cherry or maple, sate in close array,

And to the combat, Loo or Whist, led on
A thick-ribbed army; not, as in the world,
Neglected and ungratefully thrown by
Even for the very service they had wrought,
But husbanded through many a long campaign.
Uncouth assemblage was it, where no few
Had changed their functions; some, plebeian
    cards
Which Fate, beyond the promise of their
    birth,
Had dignified, and called to represent   270
The persons of departed potentates.
Oh, with what echoes on the board they fell!
Ironic diamonds,—clubs, hearts, diamonds,
    spades,
A congregation piteously akin!
Cheap matter offered they to boyish wit,
Those sooty knaves, precipitated down
With scoffs and taunts, like Vulcan out of
    heaven:
The paramount ace, a moon in her eclipse,
Queens gleaming through their splendour's last
    decay,
And monarchs surly at the wrongs sus-
    tained   280
By royal visages. Meanwhile abroad
Incessant rain was falling, or the frost
Raged bitterly, with keen and silent tooth;
And, interrupting oft that eager game,
From under Esthwaite's splitting fields of ice
The pent-up air, struggling to free itself,
Gave out to meadow-grounds and hills a loud
Protracted yelling, like the noise of wolves
Howling in troops along the Bothnic Main.

Nor, sedulous as I have been to trace 290
How Nature by extrinsic passion first
Peopled the mind with forms sublime or fair,
And made me love them, may I here omit
How other pleasures have been mine, and joys
Of subtler origin; how I have felt,
Not seldom even in that tempestuous time,
Those hallowed and pure motions of the sense
Which seem, in their simplicity, to own
An intellectual charm; that calm delight
Which, if I err not, surely must belong   300
To those first-born affinities that fit
Our new existence to existing things,
And, in our dawn of being, constitute
The bond of union between life and joy.

Yes, I remember when the changeful earth,
And twice five summers on my mind had
    stamped

The faces of the moving year, even then
I held unconscious intercourse with beauty
Old as creation, drinking in a pure
Organic pleasure from the silver wreaths   310
Of curling mist, or from the level plain
Of waters coloured by impending clouds.

The sands of Westmoreland, the creeks and
   bays
Of Cumbria's rocky limits, they can tell
How, when the Sea threw off his evening
   shade
And to the shepherd's hut on distant hills
Sent welcome notice of the rising moon,
How I have stood, to fancies such as these
A stranger, linking with the spectacle
No conscious memory of a kindred sight,   320
And bringing with me no peculiar sense
Of quietness or peace; yet have I stood,
Even while mine eye hath moved o'er many
   a league
Of shining water, gathering as it seemed,
Through every hair-breadth in that field of
   light,
New pleasure like a bee among the flowers.

Thus oft amid those fits of vulgar joy
Which, through all seasons, on a child's pur-
   suits
Are prompt attendants, 'mid that giddy bliss
Which, like a tempest, works along the
   blood   330
And is forgotten; even then I felt
Gleams like the flashing of a shield;—the
  · earth
And common face of Nature spake to me
Rememberable things; sometimes, 'tis true,
By chance collisions and quaint accidents
(Like those ill-sorted unions, work supposed
Of evil-minded fairies), yet not vain
Nor profitless, if haply they impressed
Collateral objects and appearances,
Albeit lifeless then, and doomed to sleep   340
Until maturer seasons called them forth
To impregnate and to elevate the mind.
—And if the vulgar joy by its own weight
Wearied itself out of the memory,
The scenes which were a witness of that joy
Remained in their substantial lineaments
Depicted on the brain, and to the eye
Were visible, a daily sight; and thus
By the impressive discipline of fear,
By pleasure and repeated happiness,   350
So frequently repeated, and by force

Of obscure feelings representative
Of things forgotten, these same scenes so
   bright,
So beautiful, so majestic in themselves,
Though yet the day was distant, did become
Habitually dear, and all their forms
And changeful colours by invisible links
Were fastened to the affections.
                        I began
My story early—not misled, I trust,
By an infirmity of love for days   360
Disowned by memory—ere the breath of
   spring
Planting my snowdrops among winter snows:
Nor will it seem to thee, O Friend! so prompt
In sympathy, that I have lengthened out
With fond and feeble tongue a tedious tale.
Meanwhile, my hope has been, that I might
   fetch
Invigorating thoughts from former years;
Might fix the wavering balance of my mind,
And haply meet reproaches too, whose power
May spur me on, in manhood now mature,   370
To honourable toil. Yet should these hopes
Prove vain, and thus should neither I be
   taught
To understand myself, nor thou to know
With better knowledge how the heart was
   framed
Of him thou lovest; need I dread from thee
Harsh judgments, if the song be loth to
   quit
Those recollected hours that have the charm
Of visionary things, those lovely forms
And sweet sensations that throw back our
   life,
And almost make remotest infancy   380
A visible scene, on which the sun is shining?

One end at least hath been attained; my
   mind
Hath been revived, and if this genial mood
Desert me not, forthwith shall be brought
   down
Through later years the story of my life.
The road lies plain before me;—'tis a theme
Single and of determined bounds; and hence
I choose it rather at this time, than work
Of ampler or more varied argument,
Where I might be discomfited and lost: 390
And certain hopes are with me, that to thee
This labour will be welcome, honoured
   Friend!

SCHOOL-TIME

BOOK SECOND

THUS far, O Friend! have we, though leaving
    much
Unvisited, endeavoured to retrace
The simple ways in which my childhood
    walked;
Those chiefly that first led me to the love
Of rivers, woods, and fields. The passion yet
Was in its birth, sustained as might befall
By nourishment that came unsought; for still
From week to week, from month to month,
    we lived
A round of tumult. Duly were our games   9
Prolonged in summer till the day-light failed:
No chair remained before the doors; the
    bench
And threshold steps were empty; fast asleep
The labourer, and the old man who had
    sate
A later lingerer; yet the revelry
Continued and the loud uproar: at last,
When all the ground was dark, and twinkling
    stars
Edged the black clouds, home and to bed we
    went,
Feverish with weary joints and beating
    minds.
Ah! is there one who ever has been young,
Nor needs a warning voice to tame the pride
Of intellect and virtue's self-esteem?   21
One is there, though the wisest and the best
Of all mankind, who covets not at times
Union that cannot be;—who would not give,
If so he might, to duty and to truth
The eagerness of infantine desire?
A tranquillising spirit presses now
On my corporeal frame, so wide appears
The vacancy between me and those days
Which yet have such self-presence in my
    mind,   30
That, musing on them, often do I seem
Two consciousnesses, conscious of myself
And of some other Being. A rude mass
Of native rock, left midway in the square
Of our small market village, was the goal
Or centre of these sports; and when, re-
    turned
After long absence, thither I repaired,
Gone was the old grey stone, and in its
    place
A smart Assembly-room usurped the ground

That had been ours. There let the fiddle
    scream,   40
And be ye happy! Yet, my Friends! I know
That more than one of you will think with
    me
Of those soft starry nights, and that old
    Dame
From whom the stone was named, who there
    had sate,
And watched her table with its huckster's
    wares
Assiduous, through the length of sixty years.

We ran a boisterous course; the year
    span round
With giddy motion. But the time approached
That brought with it a regular desire
For calmer pleasures, when the winning forms
Of Nature were collaterally attached   51
To every boyish sport, less grateful else
And languidly pursued.
                        When summer came,
Our pastime was, on bright half-holidays,
To sweep along the plain of Windermere
With rival oars; and the selected bourne
Was now an Island musical with birds
That sang and ceased not; now a Sister
    Isle
Beneath the oak's umbrageous covert, sown
With lilies of the valley like a field;   61
And now a third small Island, where sur-
    vived
In solitude the ruins of a shrine
Once to Our Lady dedicate, and served
Daily with chaunted rites. In such a race
So ended, disappointment could be none,
Uneasiness, or pain, or jealousy:
We rested in the shade, all pleased alike,
Conquered and conqueror. Thus the pride
    of strength,
And the vain-glory of superior skill,   70
Were tempered; thus was gradually pro-
    duced
A quiet independence of the heart;
And to my Friend who knows me I may
    add,
Fearless of blame, that hence for future days
Ensued a diffidence and modesty,
And I was taught to feel, perhaps too much,
The self-sufficing power of Solitude.

Our daily meals were frugal, Sabine fare!
More than we wished we knew the blessing
    then

Of vigorous hunger—hence corporeal strength
Unsapped by delicate viands; for, exclude 81
A little weekly stipend, and we lived
Through three divisions of the quartered year
In penniless poverty. But now to school
From the half-yearly holidays returned,
We came with weightier purses, that sufficed
To furnish treats more costly than the Dame
Of the old grey stone, from her scant board,
    supplied.
Hence rustic dinners on the cool green ground,
Or in the woods, or by a river's side   90
Or shady fountain's, while among the leaves
Soft airs were stirring, and the mid-day sun
Unfelt shone brightly round us in our joy.
Nor is my aim neglected if I tell
How sometimes, in the length of those half-
    years,
We from our funds drew largely;—proud to
    curb,
And eager to spur on, the galloping steed;
And with the courteous inn-keeper, whose
    stud
Supplied our want, we haply might employ
Sly subterfuge, if the adventure's bound
Were distant: some famed temple where of
    yore   101
The Druids worshipped, or the antique walls
Of that large abbey, where within the Vale
Of Nightshade, to St. Mary's honour built,
Stands yet a mouldering pile with fractured
    arch,
Belfry, and images, and living trees;
A holy scene!—Along the smooth green turf
Our horses grazed. To more than inland peace,
Left by the west wind sweeping overhead   109
From a tumultuous ocean, trees and towers
In that sequestered valley may be seen,
Both silent and both motionless alike;
Such the deep shelter that is there, and such
The safeguard for repose and quietness.

Our steeds remounted and the summons
    given,
With whip and spur we through the chauntry
    flew
In uncouth race, and left the cross-legged
    knight,
And the stone-abbot, and that single wren
Which one day sang so sweetly in the nave
Of the old church, that—though from recent
    showers   120
The earth was comfortless, and, touched by
    faint

Internal breezes, sobbings of the place
And respirations, from the roofless walls
The shuddering ivy dripped large drops—yet
    still
So sweetly 'mid the gloom the invisible bird
Sang to herself, that there I could have made
My dwelling-place, and lived for ever there
To hear such music. Through the walls we
    flew
And down the valley, and, a circuit made
In wantonness of heart, through rough and
    smooth   130
We scampered homewards. Oh, ye rocks and
    streams,
And that still spirit shed from evening air!
Even in this joyous time I sometimes felt
Your presence, when with slackened step we
    breathed
Along the sides of the steep hills, or when
Lighted by gleams of moonlight from the sea
We beat with thundering hoofs the level
    sand.

Midway on long Winander's eastern shore,
Within the crescent of a pleasant bay,
A tavern stood; no homely-featured house, 140
Primeval like its neighbouring cottages,
But 'twas a splendid place, the door beset
With chaises, grooms, and liveries, and within
Decanters, glasses, and the blood-red wine.
In ancient times, and ere the Hall was built
On the large island, had this dwelling been
More worthy of a poet's love, a hut,
Proud of its own bright fire and sycamore
    shade.
But—though the rhymes were gone that once
    inscribed
The threshold, and large golden characters, 150
Spread o'er the spangled sign-board, had dis-
    lodged
The old Lion and usurped his place, in slight
And mockery of the rustic painter's hand—
Yet, to this hour, the spot to me is dear
With all its foolish pomp. The garden lay
Upon a slope surmounted by a plain
Of a small bowling-green; beneath us stood
A grove, with gleams of water through the
    trees
And over the tree-tops; nor did we want   159
Refreshment, strawberries and mellow cream.
There, while through half an afternoon we
    played
On the smooth platform, whether skill pre-
    vailed

Or happy blunder triumphed, bursts of glee
Made all the mountains ring. But, ere night-
    fall,
When in our pinnace we returned at leisure
Over the shadowy lake, and to the beach
Of some small island steered our course with
    one,
The Minstrel of the Troop, and left him
    there,
And rowed off gently, while he blew his flute
Alone upon the rock—oh, then, the calm   170
And dead still water lay upon my mind
Even with a weight of pleasure, and the
    sky,
Never before so beautiful, sank down
Into my heart, and held me like a dream!
Thus were my sympathies enlarged, and thus
Daily the common range of visible things
Grew dear to me: already I began
To love the sun; a boy I loved the sun,
Not as I since have loved him, as a pledge
And surety of our earthly life, a light   180
Which we behold and feel we are alive;
Nor for his bounty to so many worlds—
But for this cause, that I had seen him lay
His beauty on the morning hills, had seen
The western mountain touch his setting orb,
In many a thoughtless hour, when, from excess
Of happiness, my blood appeared to flow
For its own pleasure, and I breathed with
    joy.
And, from like feelings, humble though
    intense,
To patriotic and domestic love   190
Analogous, the moon to me was dear;
For I could dream away my purposes,
Standing to gaze upon her while she hung
Midway between the hills, as if she knew
No other region, but belonged to thee,
Yea, appertained by a peculiar right
To thee and thy grey huts, thou one dear
    Vale!

    Those incidental charms which first at-
        tached
My heart to rural objects, day by day
Grew weaker, and I hasten on to tell   200
How Nature, intervenient till this time
And secondary, now at length was sought
For her own sake. But who shall parcel out
His intellect by geometric rules,
Split like a province into round and square?
Who knows the individual hour in which
His habits were first sown, even as a seed?

Who that shall point as with a wand and say
"This portion of the river of my mind   209
Came from yon fountain?" Thou, my Friend!
    art one
More deeply read in thy own thoughts; to
    thee
Science appears but what in truth she is,
Not as our glory and our absolute boast,
But as a succedaneum, and a prop
To our infirmity. No officious slave
Art thou of that false secondary power
By which we multiply distinctions, then
Deem that our puny boundaries are things
That we perceive, and not that we have made.
To thee, unblinded by these formal arts,
The unity of all hath been revealed,   221
And thou wilt doubt, with me less aptly
    skilled
Than many are to range the faculties
In scale and order, class the cabinet
Of their sensations, and in voluble phrase
Run through the history and birth of each
As a single independent thing.
Hard task, vain hope, to analyse the mind,
If each most obvious and particular thought,
Not in a mystical and idle sense,   230
But in the words of Reason deeply weighed,
Hath no beginning.
                    Blest the infant Babe,
(For with my best conjecture I would trace
Our Being's earthly progress,) blest the Babe,
Nursed in his Mother's arms, who sinks to
    sleep,
Rocked on his Mother's breast; who with his
    soul
Drinks in the feelings of his Mother's eye!
For him, in one dear Presence, there exists
A virtue which irradiates and exalts
Objects through widest intercourse of sense.
No outcast he, bewildered and depressed: 241
Along his infant veins are interfused
The gravitation and the filial bond
Of nature that connect him with the world.
Is there a flower, to which he points with
    hand
Too weak to gather it, already love
Drawn from love's purest earthly fount for
    him
Hath beautified that flower; already shades
Of pity cast from inward tenderness
Do fall around him upon aught that bears
Unsightly marks of violence or harm.   251
Emphatically such a Being lives,
Frail creature as he is, helpless as frail,

An inmate of this active universe:
For feeling has to him imparted power
That through the growing faculties of sense
Doth like an agent of the one great Mind
Create, creator and receiver both,
Working but in alliance with the works
Which it beholds.—Such, verily, is the first 260
Poetic spirit of our human life,
By uniform control of after years,
In most, abated or suppressed; in some,
Through every change of growth and of
     decay,
Pre-eminent till death.
                              From early days,
Beginning not long after that first time
In which, a Babe, by intercourse of touch
I held mute dialogues with my Mother's heart,
I have endeavoured to display the means
Whereby this infant sensibility,   270
Great birthright of our being, was in me
Augmented and sustained. Yet is a path
More difficult before me; and I fear
That in its broken windings we shall need
The chamois' sinews, and the eagle's wing:
For now a trouble came into my mind
From unknown causes. I was left alone
Seeking the visible world, nor knowing why.
The props of my affections were removed,
And yet the building stood, as if sustained 280
By its own spirit! All that I beheld
Was dear, and hence to finer influxes
The mind lay open, to a more exact
And close communion. Many are our joys
In youth, but oh! what happiness to live
When every hour brings palpable access
Of knowledge, when all knowledge is delight,
And sorrow is not there! The seasons came,
And every season wheresoe'er I moved
Unfolded transitory qualities,   290
Which, but for this most watchful power of
     love,
Had been neglected; left a register
Of permanent relations, else unknown.
Hence life, and change, and beauty, solitude
More active even than "best society"—
Society made sweet as solitude
By silent inobtrusive sympathies,
And gentle agitations of the mind
From manifold distinctions, difference
Perceived in things, where, to the unwatch-
     ful eye,   300
No difference is, and hence, from the same
     source,
Sublimer joy; for I would walk alone,

Under the quiet stars, and at that time,
Have felt whate'er there is of power in sound
To breathe an elevated mood, by form
Or image unprofaned; and I would stand,
In the night blackened with a coming storm,
Beneath some rock, listening to notes that
     are
The ghostly language of the ancient earth,
Or make their dim abode in distant winds. 310
Thence did I drink the visionary power;
And deem not profitless those fleeting moods
Of shadowy exultation: not for this,
That they are kindred to our purer mind
And intellectual life; but that the soul,
Remembering how she felt, but what she felt
Remembering not, retains an obscure sense
Of possible sublimity, whereto
With growing faculties she doth aspire,
With faculties still growing, feeling still   320
That whatsoever point they gain, they yet
Have something to pursue.
                              And not alone,
'Mid gloom and tumult, but no less 'mid
     fair
And tranquil scenes, that universal power
And fitness in the latent qualities
And essences of things, by which the mind
Is moved with feelings of delight, to me
Came strengthened with a superadded soul,
A virtue not its own. My morning walks
Were early;—oft before the hours of school
I travelled round our little lake, five miles 331
Of pleasant wandering. Happy time! more
     dear
For this, that one was by my side, a Friend,
Then passionately loved; with heart how full
Would he peruse these lines! For many years
Have since flowed in between us, and, our
     minds
Both silent to each other, at this time
We live as if those hours had never been.
Nor seldom did I lift our cottage latch
Far earlier, ere one smoke-wreath had risen 340
From human dwelling, or the vernal thrush
Was audible; and sate among the woods
Alone upon some jutting eminence,
At the first gleam of dawn-light, when the
     Vale,
Yet slumbering, lay in utter solitude.
How shall I seek the origin? where find
Faith in the marvellous things which then
     I felt?
Oft in these moments such a holy calm
Would overspread my soul, that bodily eyes

Were utterly forgotten, and what I saw   350
Appeared like something in myself, a dream,
A prospect in the mind.
                    'Twere long to tell
What spring and autumn, what the winter
        snows,
And what the summer shade, what day and
        night,
Evening and morning, sleep and waking,
        thought
From sources inexhaustible, poured forth
To feed the spirit of religious love
In which I walked with Nature. But let this
Be not forgotten, that I still retained
My first creative sensibility;   360
That by the regular action of the world
My soul was unsubdued. A plastic power
Abode with me; a forming hand, at times
Rebellious, acting in a devious mood;
A local spirit of his own, at war
With general tendency, but, for the most,
Subservient strictly to external things
With which it communed. An auxiliar light
Came from my mind, which on the setting sun
Bestowed new splendour; the melodious birds,
The fluttering breezes, fountains that run on   371
Murmuring so sweetly in themselves, obeyed
A like dominion, and the midnight storm
Grew darker in the presence of my eye:
Hence my obeisance, my devotion hence,
And hence my transport.
                    Nor should this, perchance,
Pass unrecorded, that I still had loved
The exercise and produce of a toil,
Than analytic industry to me
More pleasing, and whose character I deem
Is more poetic as resembling more   381
Creative agency. The song would speak
Of that interminable building reared
By observation of affinities
In objects where no brotherhood exists
To passive minds. My seventeenth year was
        come;
And, whether from this habit rooted now
So deeply in my mind, or from excess
In the great social principle of life
Coercing all things into sympathy,   390
To unorganic natures were transferred
My own enjoyments; or the power of truth
Coming in revelation, did converse
With things that really are; I, at this time,
Saw blessings spread around me like a sea.
Thus while the days flew by, and years passed
        on,

From Nature and her overflowing soul
I had received so much, that all my thoughts
Were steeped in feeling; I was only then
Contented, when with bliss ineffable   400
I felt the sentiment of Being spread
O'er all that moves and all that seemeth
        still;
O'er all that, lost beyond the reach of thought
And human knowledge, to the human eye
Invisible, yet liveth to the heart;
O'er all that leaps and runs, and shouts and
        sings,
Or beats the gladsome air; o'er all that glides
Beneath the wave, yea, in the wave itself,
And mighty depth of waters. Wonder not
If high the transport, great the joy I felt   410
Communing in this sort through earth and
        heaven
With every form of creature, as it looked
Towards the Uncreated with a countenance
Of adoration, with an eye of love.
One song they sang, and it was audible,
Most audible, then, when the fleshly ear,
O'ercome by humblest prelude of that strain,
Forgot her functions, and slept undisturbed.

If this be error, and another faith
Find easier access to the pious mind,   420
Yet were I grossly destitute of all
Those human sentiments that make this earth
So dear, if I should fail with grateful voice
To speak of you, ye mountains, and ye lakes
And sounding cataracts, ye mists and winds
That dwell among the hills where I was born.
If in my youth I have been pure in heart,
If, mingling with the world, I am content
With my own modest pleasures, and have lived
With God and Nature communing, removed
From little enmities and low desires,   431
The gift is yours; if in these times of fear
This melancholy waste of hopes o'erthrown,
If, 'mid indifference and apathy,
And wicked exultation when good men
On every side fall off, we know not how,
To selfishness, disguised in gentle names
Of peace and quiet and domestic love,
Yet mingled not unwillingly with sneers
On visionary minds; if, in this time   440
Of dereliction and dismay, I yet
Despair not of our nature, but retain
A more than Roman confidence, a faith
That fails not, in all sorrow my support,
The blessing of my life; the gift is yours,
Ye winds and sounding cataracts! 'tis yours,

Ye mountains! thine, O Nature! Thou hast
    fed
My lofty speculations; and in thee,
For this uneasy heart of ours, I find
A never-failing principle of joy   450
And purest passion.
                Thou, my Friend! wert reared
In the great city, 'mid far other scenes;
But we, by different roads, at length have
    gained
The self-same bourne. And for this cause to
    thee
I speak, unapprehensive of contempt,
The insinuated scoff of coward tongues,
And all that silent language which so oft
In conversation between man and man
Blots from the human countenance all trace
Of beauty and of love. For thou hast sought
The truth in solitude, and, since the days 461
That gave thee liberty, full long desired,
To serve in Nature's temple, thou hast been
The most assiduous of her ministers;
In many things my brother, chiefly here
In this our deep devotion.
                Fare thee well!
Health and the quiet of a healthful mind
Attend thee! seeking oft the haunts of men,
And yet more often living with thyself,
And for thyself, so haply shall thy days   470
Be many, and a blessing to mankind.

RESIDENCE AT CAMBRIDGE

BOOK THIRD

.   .   .   .

The Evangelist St. John my patron was:
Three Gothic courts are his, and in the first
Was my abiding-place, a nook obscure;
Right underneath, the College kitchens made
A humming sound, less tuneable than bees,
But hardly less industrious; with shrill notes
Of sharp command and scolding intermixed.
Near me hung Trinity's loquacious clock,
Who never let the quarters, night or day,
Slip by him unproclaimed, and told the
    hours   10
Twice over with a male and female voice.
Her pealing organ was my neighbour too;
And from my pillow, looking forth by light
Of moon or favouring stars, I could behold
The antechapel where the statue stood

Of Newton with his prism and silent face,
The marble index of a mind for ever
Voyaging through strange seas of Thought,
    alone.

    Of College labours, of the Lecturer's room
All studded round, as thick as chairs could
    stand,   20
With loyal students, faithful to their books,
Half-and-half idlers, hardy recusants,
And honest dunces—of important days,
Examinations, when the man was weighed
As in a balance! of excessive hopes,
Tremblings withal and commendable fears,
Small jealousies, and triumphs good or bad—
Let others that know more speak as they
    know.
Such glory was but little sought by me,
And little won. Yet from the first crude days 30
Of settling time in this untried abode,
I was disturbed at times by prudent thoughts,
Wishing to hope without a hope, some fears
About my future worldly maintenance,
And, more than all, a strangeness in the mind,
A feeling that I was not for that hour,
Nor for that place. But wherefore be cast
    down?
For (not to speak of Reason and her pure
Reflective acts to fix the moral law
Deep in the conscience, nor of Christian
    Hope,   40
Bowing her head before her sister Faith
As one far mightier), hither I had come,
Bear witness Truth, endowed with holy pow-
    ers
And faculties, whether to work or feel.
Oft when the dazzling show no longer new
Had ceased to dazzle, ofttimes did I quit
My comrades, leave the crowd, buildings and
    groves,
And as I paced alone the level fields
Far from those lovely sights and sounds sub-
    lime
With which I had been conversant, the mind 50
Drooped not; but there into herself returning,
With prompt rebound seemed fresh as hereto-
    fore.
At least I more distinctly recognised
Her native instincts: let me dare to speak
A higher language, say that now I felt
What independent solaces were mine,
To mitigate the injurious sway of place
Or circumstance, how far soever changed
In youth, or *to* be changed in after years.

As if awakened, summoned, roused, con-
        strained,   60
I looked for universal things; perused
The common countenance of earth and sky:
Earth, nowhere unembellished by some trace
Of that first Paradise whence man was driven;
And sky, whose beauty and bounty are ex-
        pressed
By the proud name she bears—the name of
        Heaven.
I called on both to teach me what they might;
Or, turning the mind in upon herself,
Pored, watched, expected, listened, spread my
        thoughts
And spread them with a wider creeping; felt 70
Incumbencies more awful, visitings
Of the Upholder of the tranquil soul,
That tolerates the indignities of Time,
And, from the centre of Eternity
All finite motions overruling, lives
In glory immutable. But peace! enough
Here to record that I was mounting now
To such community with highest truth—
A track pursuing, not untrod before,
From strict analogies by thought supplied 80
Or consciousnesses not to be subdued.
To every natural form, rock, fruits, or flower,
Even the loose stones that cover the highway,
I gave a moral life: I saw them feel,
Or linked them to some feeling: the great
        · mass
Lay bedded in a quickening soul, and all
That I beheld respired with inward meaning.
Add that whate'er of Terror or of Love
Or Beauty, Nature's daily face put on
From transitory passion, unto this   90
I was as sensitive as waters are
To the sky's influence in a kindred mood
Of passion; was obedient as a lute
That waits upon the touches of the wind.
Unknown, unthought of, yet I was most rich—
I had a world about me—'twas my own;
I made it, for it only lived to me,
And to the God who sees into the heart.
Such sympathies, though rarely, were betrayed
By outward gestures and by visible looks: 100
Some called it madness—so indeed it was,
If child-like fruitfulness in passing joy,
If steady moods of thoughtfulness matured
To inspiration, sort with such a name;
If prophecy be madness; if things viewed
By poets in old time, and higher up
By the first men, earth's first inhabitants,
May in these tutored days no more be seen

With undisordered sight. But leaving this,
It was no madness, for the bodily eye   110
Amid my strongest workings evermore
Was searching out the lines of difference
As they lie hid in all external forms,
Near or remote, minute or vast; an eye
Which, from a tree, a stone, a withered leaf,
To the broad ocean and the azure heavens
Spangled with kindred multitudes of stars,
Could find no surface where its power might
        sleep;
Which spake perpetual logic to my soul,
And by an unrelenting agency   120
Did bind my feelings even as in a chain.

    And here, O Friend! have I retraced my life
Up to an eminence, and told a tale
Of matters which not falsely may be called
The glory of my youth. Of genius, power,
Creation and divinity itself
I have been speaking, for my theme has been
What passed within me. Not of outward things
Done visibly for other minds, words, signs,
Symbols or actions, but of my own heart 130
Have I been speaking, and my youthful mind.
O Heavens! how awful is the might of souls,
And what they do within themselves while yet
The yoke of earth is new to them, the world
Nothing but a wild field where they were sown.
This is, in truth, heroic argument,
This genuine prowess, which I wished to touch
With hand however weak, but in the main
It lies far hidden from the reach of words.
Points have we all of us within our souls 140
Where all stand single; this I feel, and make
Breathings for incommunicable powers;
But is not each a memory to himself,
And, therefore, now that we must quit this
        theme,
I am not heartless, for there's not a man
That lives who hath not known his god-like
        hours,
And feels not what an empire we inherit
As natural beings in the strength of Nature.

.   .   .   .

SUMMER VACATION

Book Fourth

.   .   .   .

Among the favourites whom it pleased me
        well
To see again, was one by ancient right

Our inmate, a rough terrier of the hills;
By birth and call of nature pre-ordained
To hunt the badger and unearth the fox
Among the impervious crags, but having been
From youth our own adopted, he had passed
Into a gentler service. And when first
The boyish spirit flagged, and day by day
Along my veins I kindled with the stir,   10
The fermentation, and the vernal heat
Of poesy, affecting private shades
Like a sick Lover, then this dog was used
To watch me, an attendant and a friend,
Obsequious to my steps early and late,
Though often of such dilatory walk
Tired, and uneasy at the halts I made.
A hundred times when, roving high and low,
I have been harassed with the toil of verse,
Much pains and little progress, and at once 20
Some lovely Image in the song rose up
Full-formed, like Venus rising from the sea;
Then have I darted forwards to let loose
My hand upon his back with stormy joy,
Caressing him again and yet again.
And when at evening on the public way
I sauntered, like a river murmuring
And talking to itself when all things else
Are still, the creature trotted on before;
Such was his custom; but whene'er he met   30
A passenger approaching, he would turn
To give me timely notice, and straightway,
Grateful for that admonishment, I hushed
My voice, composed my gait, and, with the air
And mien of one whose thoughts are free, advanced
To give and take a greeting that might save
My name from piteous rumours, such as wait
On men suspected to be crazed in brain.

Those walks well worthy to be prized and
    loved—
Regretted!—that word, too, was on my
    tongue,
                                           40
But they were richly laden with all good,
And cannot be remembered but with thanks
And gratitude, and perfect joy of heart—
Those walks in all their freshness now came
    back
Like a returning Spring. When first I made
Once more the circuit of our little lake,
If ever happiness hath lodged with man,
That day consummate happiness was mine,
Wide-spreading, steady, calm, contemplative.
The sun was set, or setting, when I left   50

Our cottage door, and evening soon brought on
A sober hour, not winning or serene,
For cold and raw the air was, and untuned:
But as a face we love is sweetest then
When sorrow damps it, or, whatever look
It chance to wear, is sweetest if the heart
Have fulness in herself; even so with me
It fared that evening. Gently did my soul
Put off her veil, and, self-transmuted, stood
Naked, as in the presence of her God.   60
While on I walked, a comfort seemed to touch
A heart that had not been disconsolate:
Strength came where weakness was not known
    to be,
At least not felt; and restoration came
Like an intruder knocking at the door
Of unacknowledged weariness. I took
The balance, and with firm hand weighed myself.
—Of that external scene which round me lay,
Little, in this abstraction, did I see;
Remembered less; but I had inward hopes   70
And swellings of the spirit, was rapt and
    soothed,
Conversed with promises, had glimmering
    views
How life pervades the undecaying mind;
How the immortal soul with God-like power
Informs, creates, and thaws the deepest sleep
That time can lay upon her; how on earth,
Man, if he do but live within the light
Of high endeavours, daily spreads abroad
His being armed with strength that cannot fail.
Nor was there want of milder thoughts, of
    love,   80
Of innocence, and holiday repose;
And more than pastoral quiet, 'mid the stir
Of boldest projects, and a peaceful end
At last, or glorious, by endurance won.
Thus musing, in a wood I sate me down
Alone, continuing there to muse: the slopes
And heights meanwhile were slowly overspread
With darkness, and before a rippling breeze
The long lake lengthened out its hoary line,
And in the sheltered coppice where I sate,   90
Around me from among the hazel leaves,
Now here, now there, moved by the straggling
    wind,
Came ever and anon a breath-like sound,
Quick as the pantings of the faithful dog,
The off and on companion of my walk;
And such, at times, believing them to be,
I turned my head to look if he were there;

Then into solemn thought I passed once
    more.
 .   .   .   .
                         Yet in spite
Of pleasure won, and knowledge not with-
    held,   100
There was an inner falling off—I loved,
Loved deeply all that had been loved before,
More deeply even than ever: but a swarm
Of heady schemes jostling each other, gawds,
And feast and dance, and public revelry,
And sports and games (too grateful in them-
    selves,
Yet in themselves less grateful, I believe,
Than as they were a badge glossy and fresh
Of manliness and freedom) all conspired
To lure my mind from firm habitual quest 110
Of feeding pleasures, to depress the zeal
And damp those yearnings which had once
    been mine—
A wild, unworldly-minded youth, given up
To his own eager thoughts. It would demand
Some skill, and longer time than may be spared
To paint these vanities, and how they wrought
In haunts where they, till now, had been un-
    known.
It seemed the very garments that I wore
Preyed on my strength, and stopped the quiet
    stream
Of self-forgetfulness.
                Yes, that heartless chase 120
Of trivial pleasures was a poor exchange
For books and nature at that early age.
'Tis true, some casual knowledge might be
    gained
Of character or life; but at that time,
Of manners put to school I took small note,
And all my deeper passions lay elsewhere.
Far better had it been to exalt the mind
By solitary study, to uphold
Intense desire through meditative peace;
And yet, for chastisement of these regrets, 130
The memory of one particular hour
Doth here rise up against me. 'Mid a throng
Of maids and youths, old men, and matrons
    staid,
A medley of all tempers, I had passed
The night in dancing, gaiety, and mirth,
With din of instruments and shuffling feet,
And glancing forms, and tapers glittering,
And unaimed prattle flying up and down;
Spirits upon the stretch, and here and there
Slight shocks of young love-liking inter-
    spersed.   140

Whose transient pleasure mounted to the head,
And tingled through the veins. Ere we retired,
The cock had crowed, and now the eastern sky
Was kindling, not unseen, from humble copse
And open field, through which the pathway
    wound,
And homeward led my steps. Magnificent
The morning rose, in memorable pomp,
Glorious as e'er I had beheld—in front,
The sea lay laughing at a distance; near,
The solid mountains shone, bright as the
    clouds,   150
Grain-tinctured, drenched in empyrean light;
And in the meadows and the lower grounds
Was all the sweetness of a common dawn—
Dews, vapours, and the melody of birds,
And labourers going forth to till the fields,
Ah! need I say, dear Friend! that to the brim
My heart was full; I made no vows, but vows
Were then made for me; bond unknown to me
Was given, that I should be, else sinning
    greatly,
A dedicated Spirit. On I walked   160
In thankful blessedness, which yet survives.
 .   .   .   .

BOOKS

BOOK FIFTH

WHEN Contemplation, like the night-calm felt
Through earth and sky, spreads widely, and
    sends deep
Into the soul its tranquillising power,
Even then I sometimes grieve for thee, O
    Man,
Earth's paramount Creature! not so much for
    woes
That thou endurest; heavy though that weight
    be,
Cloud-like it mounts, or touched with light
    divine
Doth melt away; but for those palms achieved
Through length of time, by patient exercise
Of study and hard thought; there, there, it
    is   10
That sadness finds its fuel. Hitherto,
In progress through this Verse, my mind hath
    looked
Upon the speaking face of earth and heaven
As her prime teacher, intercourse with man
Established by the sovereign Intellect,
Who through that bodily image hath diffused,
As might appear to the eye of fleeting time,

A deathless spirit. Thou also, man! hast
    wrought,
For commerce of thy nature with herself,
Things that aspire to unconquerable life; 20
And yet we feel—we cannot choose but feel—
That they must perish. Tremblings of the
    heart
It gives, to think that our immortal being
No more shall need such garments; and yet
    man,
As long as he shall be the child of earth,
Might almost "weep to have" what he may
    lose,
Nor be himself extinguished, but survive,
Abject, depressed, forlorn, disconsolate.
A thought is with me sometimes, and I say,—
Should the whole frame of earth by inward
    throes 30
Be wrenched, or fire come down from far to
    scorch
Her pleasant habitations, and dry up
Old Ocean, in his bed left singed and bare,
Yet would the living Presence still subsist
Victorious, and composure would ensue,
And kindlings like the morning—presage sure
Of day returning and of life revived.
But all the meditations of mankind,
Yea, all the adamantine holds of truth
By reason built, or passion, which itself 40
Is highest reason in a soul sublime;
The consecrated works of Bard and Sage,
Sensuous or intellectual, wrought by men,
Twin labourers and heirs of the same hopes;
Where would they be? Oh! why hath not the
    Mind
Some element to stamp her image on
In nature somewhat nearer to her own?
Why, gifted with such powers to send abroad
Her spirit, must it lodge in shrines so frail?

    .   .   .   .   .   .

    Great and benign, indeed, must be the
    power 50
Of living nature, which could thus so long
Detain me from the best of other guides
And dearest helpers, left unthanked, unpraised,
Even in the time of lisping infancy;
And later down, in prattling childhood even,
While I was travelling back among those days,
How could I ever play an ingrate's part?
Once more should I have made those bowers
    resound,
By intermingling strains of thankfulness
With their own thoughtless melodies; at
    least 60

It might have well beseemed me to repeat
Some simply fashioned tale, to tell again,
In slender accents of sweet verse, some tale
That did bewitch me then, and soothes me
    now.
O Friend! O Poet! brother of my soul,
Think not that I could pass along untouched
By these remembrances. Yet wherefore speak?
Why call upon a few weak words to say
What is already written in the hearts
Of all that breathe?—what in the path of all 70
Drops daily from the tongue of every child,
Wherever man is found? The trickling tear
Upon the cheek of listening Infancy
Proclaims it, and the insuperable look
That drinks as if it never could be full.

    That portion of my story I shall leave
There registered: whatever else of power
Or pleasure sown, or fostered thus, may be
Peculiar to myself, let that remain
Where still it works, though hidden from all
    search 80
Among the depths of time. Yet is it just
That here, in memory of all books which lay
Their sure foundations in the heart of man,
Whether by native prose, or numerous verse,
That in the name of all inspirèd souls—
From Homer the great Thunderer, from the
    voice
That roars along the bed of Jewish song,
And that more varied and elaborate,
Those trumpet-tones of harmony that shake
Our shores in England,—from those loftiest
    notes 90
Down to the low and wren-like warblings,
    made
For cottagers and spinners at the wheel,
And sun-burnt travellers resting their tired
    limbs,
Stretched under wayside hedge-rows, ballad
    tunes,
Food for the hungry ears of little ones,
And of old men who have survived their
    joys—
'Tis just that in behalf of these, the works,
And of the men that framed them, whether
    known
Or sleeping nameless in their scattered graves,
That I should here assert their rights, attest 100
Their honours, and should, once for all, pro-
    nounce
Their benediction; speak of them as Powers
For ever to be hallowed; only less,

For what we are and what we may become,
Than Nature's self, which is the breath of
    God,
Or His pure Word by miracle revealed.

  .   .   .   .   .   .

    And when thereafter to my father's house
The holidays returned me, there to find
That golden store of books which I had left,
What joy was mine! How often in the
    course   110
Of those glad respites, though a soft west
    wind
Ruffled the waters to the angler's wish,
For a whole day together, have I lain
Down by thy side, O Derwent! murmuring
    stream,
On the hot stones, and in the glaring sun,
And there have read, devouring as I read,
Defrauding the day's glory, desperate!
Till with a sudden bound of smart reproach,
Such as an idler deals with in his shame,
I to the sport betook myself again.   120

    A gracious spirit o'er this earth presides,
And o'er the heart of man; invisibly
It comes, to works of unreproved delight,
And tendency benign, directing those
Who care not, know not, think not, what they
    do.
The tales that charm away the wakeful night
In Araby, romances; legends penned
For solace by dim light of monkish lamps;
Fictions, for ladies of their love, devised
By youthful squires; adventures endless,
    spun   130
By the dismantled warrior in old age,
Out of the bowels of those very schemes
In which his youth did first extravagate;
These spread like day, and something in the
    shape
Of these will live till man shall be no more.
Dumb yearnings, hidden appetites, are ours,
And *they must* have their food. Our childhood
    sits,
Our simple childhood, sits upon a throne
That hath more power than all the elements.
I guess not what this tells of Being past,   140
Nor what it augurs of the life to come;
But so it is; and, in that dubious hour—
That twilight—when we first begin to see
This dawning earth, to recognise, expect,
And, in the long probation that ensues,
The time of trial, ere we learn to live
In reconcilement with our stinted powers;

To endure this state of meagre vassalage,
Unwilling to forego, confess, submit,
Uneasy and unsettled, yoke-fellows   150
To custom, mettlesome, and not yet tamed
And humbled down—oh! then we feel, we
    feel,
We know where we have friends. Ye dream-
    ers, then,
Forgers of daring tales! we bless you then,
Impostors, drivellers, dotards, as the ape
Philosophy will call you: *then* we feel
With what, and how great might ye are in
    league,
Who make our wish, our power, our thought
    a deed,
An empire, a possession. .   .   .

    Here must we pause: this only let me
    add,   160
From heart-experience, and in humblest sense
Of modesty, that he, who in his youth
A daily wanderer among woods and fields
With living Nature hath been intimate,
Not only in that raw unpractised time
Is stirred to ecstasy, as others are,
By glittering verse; but further, doth receive,
In measure only dealt out to himself,
Knowledge and increase of enduring joy
From the great Nature that exists in works   170
Of mighty Poets. Visionary power
Attends the motions of the viewless winds,
Embodied in the mystery of words:
There, darkness makes abode, and all the host
Of shadowy things work endless changes,—
    there,
As in a mansion like their proper home,
Even forms and substances are circumfused
By that transparent veil with light divine,
And, through the turnings intricate of verse,
Present themselves as objects recognised,   180
In flashes, and with glory not their own.

CAMBRIDGE AND THE ALPS

BOOK SIXTH

  .   .   .   .   .   .

We questioned him again, and yet again;
But every word that from the peasant's lips
Came in reply, translated by our feelings,
Ended in this, *that we had crossed the Alps.*

    Imagination—here the Power so called
Through sad incompetence of human speech,

That awful Power rose from the mind's abyss
Like an unfathered vapour that enwraps,
At once, some lonely traveller. I was lost;
Halted without an effort to break through; 10
But to my conscious soul I now can say—
"I recognise thy glory:" in such strength
Of usurpation, when the light of sense
Goes out, but with a flash that has revealed
The invisible world, doth greatness make
    abode,
There harbours; whether we be young or old,
Our destiny, our being's heart and home,
Is with infinitude, and only there;
With hope it is, hope that can never die,
Effort, and expectation, and desire, 20
And something evermore about to be.
Under such banners militant, the soul
Seeks for no trophies, struggles for no spoils
That may attest her prowess, blest in thoughts
That are their own perfection and reward,
Strong in herself and in beatitude
That hides her, like the mighty flood of Nile
Poured from his fount of Abyssinian clouds
To fertilise the whole Egyptian plain.

The melancholy slackening that ensued 30
Upon those tidings by the peasant given
Was soon dislodged. Downwards we hurried
    fast,
And, with the half-shaped road which we had
    missed,
Entered a narrow chasm. The brook and
    road
Were fellow-travellers in this gloomy strait,
And with them did we journey several hours
At a slow pace. The immeasurable height
Of woods decaying, never to be decayed,
The stationary blasts of waterfalls,
And in the narrow rent at every turn 40
Winds thwarting winds, bewildered and for-
    lorn,
The torrents shooting from the clear blue sky,
The rocks that muttered close upon our ears,
Black drizzling crags that spake by the way-
    side
As if a voice were in them, the sick sight
And giddy prospect of the raving stream,
The unfettered clouds and region of the
    Heavens,
Tumult and peace, the darkness and the
    light—
Were all like workings of one mind, the
    features
Of the same face, blossoms upon one tree; 50

Characters of the great Apocalypse,
The types and symbols of Eternity,
Of first, and last, and midst, and without end.

.   .   .   .

RESIDENCE IN LONDON

BOOK SEVENTH

.   .   .   .

                            . . . From these sights
Take one,—that ancient festival, the Fair,
Holden where martyrs suffered in past time,
And named of St. Bartholomew; there, see
A work completed to our hands, that lays,
If any spectacle on earth can do,
The whole creative powers of man asleep!—
For once, the Muse's help will we implore,
And she shall lodge us, wafted on her wings,
Above the press and danger of the crowd,
Upon some showman's platform. What a
    shock 10
For eyes and ears! what anarchy and din,
Barbarian and infernal,—a phantasma,
Monstrous in colour, motion, shape, sight,
    sound!
Below, the open space, through every nook
Of the wide area, twinkles, is alive
With heads; the midway region, and above,
Is thronged with staring pictures and huge
    scrolls,
Dumb proclamations of the Prodigies;
With chattering monkeys dangling from their
    poles,
And children whirling in their roundabouts; 20
With those that stretch the neck and strain
    the eyes,
And crack the voice in rivalship, the crowd
Inviting; with buffoons against buffoons
Grimacing, writhing, screaming,—him who
    grinds
The hurdy-gurdy, at the fiddle weaves,
Rattles the salt-box, thumps the kettle-drum,
And him who at the trumpet puffs his cheeks,
The silver-collared Negro with his timbrel,
Equestrians, tumblers, women, girls, and boys,
Blue-breeched, pink-vested, with high-towering
    plumes.— 30
All moveables of wonder, from all parts,
Are here—Albinos, painted Indians, Dwarfs,
The Horse of knowledge, and the learned Pig,
The Stone-eater, the man that swallows fire,
Giants, Ventriloquists, the Invisible Girl,
The Bust that speaks and moves its goggling
    eyes,

The Wax-work, Clock-work, all the marvellous
      craft
Of modern Merlins, Wild Beasts, Puppet-
      shows,
All out-o'-the-way, far-fetched, perverted
      things,
All freaks of nature, all Promethean
      thoughts   40
Of man, his dulness, madness, and their feats
All jumbled up together, to compose
A Parliament of Monsters. Tents and Booths
Meanwhile, as if the whole were one vast mill,
Are vomiting, receiving on all sides,
Men, Women, three-years' Children, Babes
      in arms.

      Oh, blank confusion! true epitome
Of what the mighty City is herself,
To thousands upon thousands of her sons,
Living amid the same perpetual whirl   50
Of trivial objects, melted and reduced
To one identity, by differences
That have no law, no meaning, and no end—
Oppression, under which even highest minds
Must labour, whence the strongest are not
      free.
But though the picture weary out the eye,
By nature an unmanageable sight,
It is not wholly so to him who looks
In steadiness, who hath among least things
An under-sense of greatest; sees the parts   60
As parts, but with a feeling of the whole.
This, of all acquisitions, first awaits
On sundry and most widely different modes
Of education, nor with least delight
On that through which I passed. Attention
      springs,
And comprehensiveness and memory flow,
From early converse with the works of God
Among all regions; chiefly where appear
Most obviously simplicity and power.
Think, how the everlasting streams and
      woods,   70
Stretched and still stretching far and wide,
      exalt
The roving Indian, on his desert sands:
What grandeur not unfelt, what pregnant
      show
Of beauty, meets the sun-burnt Arab's eye:
And, as the sea propels, from zone to zone,
Its currents; magnifies its shoals of life
Beyond all compass; spreads, and sends aloft
Armies of clouds,—even so, its powers and
      aspects

Shape for mankind, by principles as fixed,
The views and aspirations of the soul   80
To majesty. Like virtue have the forms
Perennial of the ancient hills; nor less
The changeful language of their countenances
Quickens the slumbering mind, and aids the
      thoughts,
However multitudinous, to move
With order and relation. This, if still,
As hitherto, in freedom I may speak,
Not violating any just restraint,
As may be hoped, of real modesty,—
This did I feel, in London's vast domain.   90
The Spirit of Nature was upon me there;
The soul of Beauty and enduring Life
Vouchsafed her inspiration, and diffused,
Through meagre lines and colours, and the
      press
Of self-destroying, transitory things,
Composure, and ennobling Harmony.

RETROSPECT—LOVE OF NATURE
LEADING TO LOVE OF MAN

BOOK EIGHTH

.   .   .   .   .   .

      Yet deem not, Friend! that human kind
      with me
Thus early took a place pre-eminent;
Nature herself was, at this unripe time,
But secondary to my own pursuits
And animal activities, and all
Their trivial pleasures; and when these had
      drooped
And gradually expired, and Nature, prized
For her own sake, became my joy, even
      then—
And upwards through late youth, until not less
Than two-and-twenty summers had been
      told—   10
Was Man in my affections and regards
Subordinate to her, her visible forms
And viewless agencies: a passion, she,
A rapture often, and immediate love
Ever at hand; he, only a delight
Occasional, an accidental grace,
His hour being not yet come. Far less had
      then
The inferior creatures, beast or bird, attuned
My spirit to that gentleness of love,
(Though they had long been carefully ob-
      served),   20
Won from me those minute obeisances
Of tenderness, which I may number now

With my first blessings. Nevertheless, on these
The light of beauty did not fall in vain,
Or grandeur circumfuse them to no end.

But when that first poetic faculty
Of plain Imagination and severe,
No longer a mute influence of the soul,
Ventured, at some rash Muse's earnest call,
To try her strength among harmonious
    words;   30
And to book-notions and the rules of art
Did knowingly conform itself; there came
Among the simple shapes of human life
A wilfulness of fancy and conceit;
And Nature and her objects beautified
These fictions, as in some sort, in their turn,
They burnished her. From touch of this new
    power
Nothing was safe: the elder-tree that grew
Beside the well-known charnel-house had then
A dismal look: the yew-tree had its ghost,   40
That took his station there for ornament:
The dignities of plain occurrence then
Were tasteless, and truth's golden mean, a
    point
Where no sufficient pleasure could be found.
Then, if a widow, staggering with the blow
Of her distress, was known to have turned her
    steps
To the cold grave in which her husband slept,
One night, or haply more than one, through
    pain
Or half-insensate impotence of mind,
The fact was caught at greedily, and there   50
She must be visitant the whole year through,
Wetting the turf with never-ending tears.

Through quaint obliquities I might pursue
These cravings; when the foxglove, one by
    one,
Upwards through every stage of the tall stem,
Had shed beside the public way its bells,
And stood of all dismantled, save the last
Left at the tapering ladder's top, that seemed
To bend as doth a slender blade of grass
Tipped with a rain-drop, Fancy loved to
    seat,   60
Beneath the plant despoiled, but crested still
With this last relic, soon itself to fall,
Some vagrant mother, whose arch little ones,
All unconcerned by her dejected plight,
Laughed as with rival eagerness their hands
Gathered the purple cups that round them lay,
Strewing the turf's green slope.

Enough of humble arguments; recall,
My Song! those high emotions which thy
    voice
Has heretofore made known; that bursting
    forth   70
Of sympathy, inspiring and inspired,
When everywhere a vital pulse was felt,
And all the several frames of things, like
    stars,
Through every magnitude distinguishable,
Shone mutually indebted, or half lost
Each in the other's blaze, a galaxy
Of life and glory. In the midst stood Man,
Outwardly, inwardly contemplated,
As, of all visible natures, crown, though born
Of dust, and kindred to the worm; a Being, 80
Both in perception and discernment, first
In every capability of rapture,
Through the divine effect of power and love;
As, more than anything we know, instinct
With godhead, and, by reason and by will,
Acknowledging dependency sublime.

RESIDENCE IN FRANCE

Book Ninth

          . . . Yet not the less,
Hatred of absolute rule, where will of one
Is law for all, and of that barren pride
In them who, by immunities unjust,
Between the sovereign and the people stand,
His helper and not theirs, laid stronger hold
Daily upon me, mixed with pity too
And love; for where hope is, there love will be
For the abject multitude. And when we chanced
One day to meet a hunger-bitten girl,   10
Who crept along fitting her languid gait,
Unto a heifer's motion, by a cord
Tied to her arm, and picking thus from the
    lane
Its sustenance, while the girl with pallid hands
Was busy knitting in a heartless mood
Of solitude, and at the sight my friend
In agitation said, " 'Tis against *that*
That we are fighting," I with him believed
That a benignant spirit was abroad
Which might not be withstood, that poverty 20
Abject as this would in a little time
Be found no more, that we should see the
    earth
Unthwarted in her wish to recompense
The meek, the lowly, patient child of toil,

All institutes for ever blotted out
That legalised exclusion, empty pomp
Abolished, sensual state and cruel power
Whether by edict of the one or few;
And finally, as sum and crown of all,
Should see the people having a strong hand 30
In framing their own laws; whence better days
To all mankind.

    .   .   .   .   .

Oh, happy time of youthful lovers, (thus
The story might begin,) oh, balmy time,
In which a love-knot, on a lady's brow,
Is fairer than the fairest star in Heaven!
So might—and with that prelude *did* begin
The record; and, in faithful verse, was given
The doleful sequel.

    .   .   .   .   .

RESIDENCE IN FRANCE (*continued*)

BOOK TENTH

  .   .   .   .   .   .

    . . . In this frame of mind,
Dragged by a chain of harsh necessity,
So seemed it,—now I thankfully acknowledge,
Forced by the gracious providence of Heaven,—
To England I returned, else (though assured
That I both was and must be of small weight,
No better than a landsman on the deck
Of a ship struggling with a hideous storm)
Doubtless, I should have then made common cause
With some who perished; haply perished too, 10
A poor mistaken and bewildered offering,—
Should to the breast of Nature have gone back,
With all my resolutions, all my hopes,
A Poet only to myself, to men
Useless.

    .   .   .   .   .

What, then, were my emotions, when in arms
Britain put forth her free-born strength in league,
Oh, pity and shame! with those confederate Powers!
Not in my single self alone I found,
But in the minds of all ingenuous youth, 20
Change and subversion from that hour. No shock
Given to my moral nature had I known
Down to that very moment; neither lapse
Nor turn of sentiment that might be named

A revolution, save at this one time;
All else was progress on the self-same path
On which, with a diversity of pace,
I had been travelling: this a stride at once
Into another region.

    .   .   .   .   .   .

    When the proud fleet that bears the red-cross flag 30
In that unworthy service was prepared
To mingle, I beheld the vessels lie,
A brood of gallant creatures, on the deep;
I saw them in their rest, a sojourner
Through a whole month of calm and glassy days
In that delightful island which protects
Their place of convocation—there I heard,
Each evening, pacing by the still sea-shore,
A monitory sound that never failed,—
The sunset cannon. While the orb went down 40
In the tranquillity of nature, came
That voice, ill requiem! seldom heard by me
Without a spirit overcast by dark
Imaginations, sense of woes to come,
Sorrow for human kind, and pain of heart.

    .   .   .   .   .

Most melancholy at that time, O Friend!
Were my day-thoughts,—my nights were miserable;
Through months, through years, long after the last beat
Of those atrocities, the hour of sleep
To me came rarely charged with natural gifts, 50
Such ghastly visions had I of despair
And tyranny, and implements of death;
And innocent victims sinking under fear,
And momentary hope, and worn-out prayer,
Each in his separate cell, or penned in crowds
For sacrifice, and struggling with fond mirth
And levity in dungeons, where the dust
Was laid with tears. Then suddenly the scene
Changed, and the unbroken dream entangled me
In long orations, which I strove to plead 60
Before unjust tribunals,—with a voice
Labouring, a brain confounded, and a sense,
Death-like, of treacherous desertion, felt
In the last place of refuge—my own soul.

    .   .   .   .   .

    But as the ancient Prophets, borne aloft
In vision, yet constrained by natural laws
With them to take a troubled human heart,
Wanted not consolations, nor a creed

Of reconcilement, then when they denounced,
On towns and cities, wallowing in the abyss   70
Of their offences, punishment to come;
Or saw, like other men, with bodily eyes,
Before them, in some desolated place,
The wrath consummate and the threat ful-
    filled;
So, with devout humility be it said,
So, did a portion of that spirit fall
On me uplifted from the vantage-ground
Of pity and sorrow to a state of being
That through the time's exceeding fierceness
    saw
Glimpses of retribution, terrible,   80
And in the order of sublime behests:
But, even if that were not, amid the awe
Of unintelligible chastisement,
Not only acquiescences of faith
Survived, but daring sympathies with power,
Motions not treacherous or profane, else why
Within the folds of no ungentle breast
Their dread vibration to this hour prolonged?
Wild blasts of music thus could find their way
Into the midst of turbulent events;   90
So that worst tempests might be listened to.
Then was the truth received into my heart,
That, under heaviest sorrow earth can bring,
If from the affliction somewhere do not grow
Honour which could not else have been, a
    faith,
An elevation, and a sanctity,
If new strength be not given nor old restored,
The blame is ours, not Nature's. When a taunt
Was taken up by scoffers in their pride,
Saying, "Behold the harvest that we reap   100
From popular government and equality,"
I clearly saw that neither these nor aught
Of wild belief engrafted on their names
By false philosophy had caused the woe,
But a terrific reservoir of guilt
And ignorance filled up from age to age,
That could no longer hold its loathsome
    charge,
But burst and spread in deluge through the
    land.

·   ·   ·   ·   ·   ·

FRANCE (concluded)

BOOK ELEVENTH

·   ·   ·   ·   ·   ·

Depressed, bewildered thus, I did not walk
With scoffers, seeking light and gay revenge

From indiscriminate laughter, nor sate down
In reconcilement with an utter waste
Of intellect; such sloth I could not brook,
(Too well I loved, in that my spring of life,
Pains-taking thoughts, and truth, their dear
    reward)
But turned to abstract science, and there sought
Work for the reasoning faculty enthroned
Where the disturbances of space and time—   10
Whether in matters various, properties
Inherent, or from human will and power
Derived—find no admission. Then it was—
Thanks to the bounteous Giver of all good!—
That the belovèd Sister in whose sight
Those days were passed, now speaking in a
    voice
Of sudden admonition—like a brook
That did but *cross* a lonely road, and now
Is seen, heard, felt, and caught at every turn,
Companion never lost through many a
    league—   20
Maintained for me a saving intercourse
With my true self; for, though bedimmed
    and changed
Much, as it seemed, I was no further changed
Than as a clouded and a waning moon:
She whispered still that brightness would re-
    turn;
She, in the midst of all, preserved me still
A Poet, made me seek beneath that name,
And that alone, my office upon earth.

·   ·   ·   ·   ·   ·

                  Thus, O Friend!
Through times of honour and through times
    of shame
Descending, have I faithfully retraced   30
The perturbations of a youthful mind
Under a long-lived storm of great events—
A story destined for thy ear, who now,
Among the fallen of nations, dost abide
Where Etna, over hill and valley, casts
His shadow stretching towards Syracuse,
The city of Timoleon! Righteous Heaven!
How are the mighty prostrated! They first,
They first of all that breathe should have
    awaked
When the great voice was heard from out the
    tombs   40
Of ancient heroes. If I suffered grief
For ill-requited France, by many deemed
A trifler only in her proudest day;
Have been distressed to think of what she
    once
Promised, now is; a far more sober cause

Thine eyes must see of sorrow in a land,
To the reanimating influence lost
Of memory, to virtue lost and hope,
Though with the wreck of loftier years be-
        strewn.

But indignation works where hope is not, 50
And thou, O Friend! wilt be refreshed. There
        is
One great society alone on earth:
The noble Living and the noble Dead.

·   ·   ·   ·   ·   ·   ·

IMAGINATION AND TASTE, HOW
IMPAIRED AND RESTORED

BOOK TWELFTH

·   ·   ·   ·   ·   ·

There are in our existence spots of time,
That with distinct pre-eminence retain
A renovating virtue, whence—depressed
By false opinion and contentious thought,
Or aught of heavier or more deadly weight,
In trivial occupations, and the round
Of ordinary intercourse—our minds
Are nourished and invisibly repaired;
A virtue, by which pleasure is enhanced,
That penetrates, enables us to mount,   10
When high, more high, and lifts us up when
        fallen.
This efficacious spirit chiefly lurks
Among those passages of life that give
Profoundest knowledge to what point, and
        how,
The mind is lord and master—outward sense
The obedient servant of her will. Such mo-
        ments
Are scattered everywhere, taking their date
From our first childhood. I remember well,
That once, while yet my inexperienced hand
Could scarcely hold a bridle, with proud
        hopes   20
I mounted, and we journeyed towards the
        hills:
An ancient servant of my father's house
Was with me, my encourager and guide:
We had not travelled long, ere some mis-
        chance
Disjoined me from my comrade; and, through
        fear
Dismounting, down the rough and stony moor
I led my horse, and, stumbling on, at length
Came to a bottom, where in former times
A murderer had been hung in iron chains.

The gibbet-mast had mouldered down, the
        bones   30
And iron case were gone; but on the turf,
Hard by, soon after that fell deed was
        wrought,
Some unknown hand had carved the mur-
        derer's name.
The monumental letters were inscribed
In times long past; but still, from year to
        year
By superstition of the neighbourhood,
The grass is cleared away, and to this hour
The characters are fresh and visible:
A casual glance had shown them, and I fled,
Faltering and faint, and ignorant of the
        road: 40
Then, reascending the bare common, saw
A naked pool that lay beneath the hills,
The beacon on the summit, and, more near,
A girl, who bore a pitcher on her head,
And seemed with difficult steps to force her
        way
Against the blowing wind. It was, in truth,
An ordinary sight; but I should need
Colours and words that are unknown to man,
To paint the visionary dreariness
Which, while I looked all round for my lost
        guide,   50
Invested moorland waste and naked pool,
The beacon crowning the lone eminence,
The female and her garments vexed and
        tossed
By the strong wind. When, in the blessèd
        hours
Of early love, the loved one at my side,
I roamed, in daily presence of this scene,
Upon the naked pool and dreary crags,
And on the melancholy beacon, fell
A spirit of pleasure and youth's golden gleam;
And think ye not with radiance more sub-
        lime   60
For these remembrances, and for the power
They had left behind? So feeling comes in
        aid
Of feeling, and diversity of strength
Attends us, if but once we have been strong.
Oh! mystery of man, from what a depth
Proceed thy honours. I am lost, but see
In simple childhood something of the base
On which thy greatness stands; but this I
        feel,
That from thyself it comes, that thou must
        give,
Else never canst receive. The days gone by 70

Return upon me almost from the dawn
Of life: the hiding-places of man's power
Open; I would approach them, but they close.
I see by glimpses now; when age comes on,
May scarcely see at all; and I would give,
While yet we may, as far as words can give,
Substance and life to what I feel, enshrining,
Such is my hope, the spirit of the Past
For future restoration.

.   .   .   .   .   .

IMAGINATION AND TASTE, HOW IM-PAIRED AND RESTORED (*concluded*)

BOOK THIRTEENTH

.   .   .   .   .   .

. . . Above all
Were re-established now those watchful
    thoughts
Which, seeing little worthy or sublime
In what the Historian's pen so much delights
To blazon—power and energy detached
From moral purpose—early tutored me
To look with feelings of fraternal love
Upon the unassuming things that hold
A silent station in this beauteous world.

Thus moderated, thus composed, I found
Once more in Man an object of delight,
Of pure imagination, and of love;   10
And, as the horizon of my mind enlarged,
Again I took the intellectual eye
For my instructor, studious more to see
Great truths, than touch and handle little ones.
Knowledge was given accordingly; my trust
Became more firm in feelings that had stood
The test of such a trial; clearer far
My sense of excellence—of right and wrong:
The promise of the present time retired
Into its true proportion; sanguine schemes,   20
Ambitious projects, pleased me less; I sought
For present good in life's familiar face,
And built thereon my hopes of good to come.

.   .   .   .   .   .

Here, calling up to mind what then I saw,
A youthful traveller, and see daily now
In the familiar circuit of my home,
Here might I pause, and bend in reverence
To Nature, and the power of human minds,
To men as they are men within themselves.
How oft high service is performed within,   30
When all the external man is rude in show,—
Not like a temple rich with pomp and gold,
But a mere mountain chapel, that protects
Its simple worshippers from sun and shower.
Of these, said I, shall be my song; of these,
If future years mature me for the task,
Will I record the praises, making verse
Deal boldly with substantial things; in truth
And sanctity of passion, speak of these,
That justice may be done, obeisance paid   40
Where it is due: thus haply shall I teach,
Inspire; through unadulterated ears
Pour rapture, tenderness, and hope,—my
    theme
No other than the very heart of man,
As found among the best of those who live—
Not unexalted by religious faith,
Nor uninformed by books, good books, though
    few—
In Nature's presence: thence may I select
Sorrow, that is not sorrow, but delight;
And miserable love, that is not pain   50
To hear of, for the glory that redounds
Therefrom to human kind, and what we are.
Be mine to follow with no timid step
Where knowledge leads me: it shall be my
    pride
That I have dared to tread this holy ground,
Speaking no dream, but things oracular;
Matter not lightly to be heard by those
Who to the letter of the outward promise
Do read the invisible soul; by men adroit
In speech, and for communion with the
    world   60
Accomplished; minds whose faculties are then
Most active when they are most eloquent,
And elevated most when most admired.
Men may be found of other mould than these,
Who are their own upholders, to themselves
Encouragement, and energy, and will,
Expressing liveliest thoughts in lively words
As native passion dictates. Others, too,
There are among the walks of homely life
Still higher, men for contemplation framed,   70
Shy, and unpractised in the strife of phrase;
Meek men, whose very souls perhaps would
    sink
Beneath them, summoned to such intercourse:
Theirs is the language of the heavens, the
    power,
The thought, the image, and the silent joy:
Words are but under-agents in their souls;
When they are grasping with their greatest
    strength,
They do not breathe among them: this I speak
In gratitude to God, Who feeds our hearts

For His own service; knoweth, loveth us, 80
When we are unregarded by the world.

.   .   .   .

CONCLUSION

BOOK FOURTEENTH

IN one of those excursions (may they ne'er
Fade from remembrance!) through the North-
    ern tracts
Of Cambria ranging with a youthful friend,
I left Bethgelert's huts at couching-time,
And westward took my way, to see the sun
Rise, from the top of Snowdon. To the door
Of a rude cottage at the mountain's base
We came, and roused the shepherd who at-
    tends
The adventurous stranger's steps, a trusty
    guide;
Then, cheered by short refreshment, sallied
    forth.   10

It was a close, warm, breezeless summer
    night,
Wan, dull, and glaring, with a dripping fog
Low-hung and thick that covered all the sky;
But, undiscouraged, we began to climb
The mountain-side. The mist soon girt us
    round,
And, after ordinary travellers' talk
With our conductor, pensively we sank
Each into commerce with his private thoughts:
Thus did we breast the ascent, and by myself
Was nothing either seen or heard that
    checked   20
Those musings or diverted, save that once
The shepherd's lurcher, who, among the crags,
Had to his joy unearthed a hedgehog, teased
His coiled-up prey with barkings turbulent.
This small adventure, for even such it seemed
In that wild place and at the dead of night,
Being over and forgotten, on we wound
In silence as before. With forehead bent
Earthward, as if in opposition set
Against an enemy, I panted up   30
With eager pace, and no less eager thoughts.
Thus might we wear a midnight hour away,
Ascending at loose distance each from each,
And I, as chanced, the foremost of the band;
When at my feet the ground appeared to
    brighten,
And with a step or two seemed brighter still;
Nor was time given to ask or learn the cause,
For instantly a light upon the turf

Fell like a flash, and lo! as I looked up,
The Moon hung naked in a firmament   40
Of azure without cloud, and at my feet
Rested a silent sea of hoary mist.
A hundred hills their dusky backs upheaved
All over this still ocean; and beyond,
Far, far beyond, the solid vapours stretched,
In headlands, tongues, and promontory shapes,
Into the main Atlantic, that appeared
To dwindle, and give up his majesty,
Usurped upon far as the sight could reach.
Not so the ethereal vault; encroachment
    none   50
Was there, nor less; only the inferior stars
Had disappeared, or shed a fainter light
In the clear presence of the full-orbed Moon,
Who, from her sovereign elevation, gazed
Upon the billowy ocean, as it lay
All meek and silent, save that through a rift—
Not distant from the shore whereon we stood,
A fixed, abysmal, gloomy, breathing-place—
Mounted the roar of waters, torrents, streams
Innumerable, roaring with one voice!   60
Heard over earth and sea, and, in that hour,
For so it seemed, felt by the starry heavens.

When into air had partially dissolved
That vision, given to spirits of the night
And three chance human wanderers, in calm
    thought
Reflected, it appeared to me the type
Of a majestic intellect, its acts
And its possessions, what it has and craves,
What in itself it is, and would become.
There I beheld the emblem of a mind   70
That feeds upon infinity, that broods
Over the dark abyss, intent to hear
Its voices issuing forth to silent light
In one continuous stream; a mind sustained
By recognitions of transcendent power,
In sense conducting to ideal form,
In soul of more than mortal privilege.
One function, above all, of such a mind
Had Nature shadowed there, by putting forth,
'Mid circumstances awful and sublime,   80
That mutual domination which she loves
To exert upon the face of outward things,
So moulded, joined, abstracted, so endowed
With interchangeable supremacy,
That men, least sensitive, see, hear, perceive,
And cannot choose but feel. The power, which
    all
Acknowledge when thus moved, which Nature
    thus

To bodily sense exhibits, is the express
Resemblance of that glorious faculty
That higher minds bear with them as their
    own.   90
This is the very spirit in which they deal
With the whole compass of the universe:
They from their native selves can send abroad
Kindred mutations; for themselves create
A like existence; and, whene'er it dawns
Created for them, catch it, or are caught
By its inevitable mastery,
Like angels stopped upon the wing by sound
Of harmony from Heaven's remotest spheres.
Them the enduring and the transient both 100
Serve to exalt; they build up greatest things
From least suggestions; ever on the watch,
Willing to work and to be wrought upon,
They need not extraordinary calls
To rouse them; in a world of life they live,
By sensible impressions not enthralled,
But by their quickening impulse made more
    prompt
To hold fit converse with the spiritual world,
And with the generations of mankind
Spread over time, past, present, and to
    come,   110
Age after age, till Time shall be no more.
Such minds are truly from the Deity,
For they are Powers; and hence the highest
    bliss
That flesh can know is theirs—the conscious-
    ness
Of Whom they are, habitually infused
Through every image and through every
    thought,
And all affections by communion raised
From earth to heaven, from human to di-
    vine;
Hence endless occupation for the Soul,
Whether discursive or intuitive;   120
Hence cheerfulness for acts of daily life,
Emotions which best foresight need not fear,
Most worthy then of trust when most intense.
Hence, amid ills that vex and wrongs that
    crush
Our hearts—if here the words of Holy Writ
May with fit reverence be applied—that peace
Which passeth understanding, that repose
In moral judgments which from this pure
    source
Must come, or will by man be sought in vain.

  ·   ·   ·   ·   ·   ·   ·

  This spiritual Love acts not nor can exist 130
Without Imagination, which, in truth,

Is but another name for absolute power
And clearest insight, amplitude of mind,
And Reason in her most exalted mood.
This faculty hath been the feeding source
Of our long labour: we have traced the stream
From the blind cavern whence is faintly heard
Its natal murmur; followed it to light
And open day; accompanied its course
Among the ways of Nature, for a time   140
Lost sight of it bewildered and engulphed;
Then given it greeting as it rose once more
In strength, reflecting from its placid breast
The works of man and face of human life;
And lastly, from its progress have we drawn
Faith in life endless, the sustaining thought
Of human Being, Eternity, and God.

  Imagination having been our theme,
So also hath that intellectual Love,
For they are each in each, and cannot stand 150
Dividually.—Here must thou be, O Man!
Power to thyself; no Helper hast thou here;
Here keepest thou in singleness thy state:
No other can divide with thee this work:
No secondary hand can intervene
To fashion this ability; 'tis thine,
The prime and vital principle is thine
In the recesses of thy nature, far
From any reach of outward fellowship,
Else is not thine at all. But joy to him,   160
Oh, joy to him who here hath sown, hath laid
Here, the foundation of his future years!
For all that friendship, all that love can do,
All that a darling countenance can look
Or dear voice utter, to complete the man,
Perfect him, made imperfect in himself,
All shall be his: and he whose soul hath risen
Up to the height of feeling intellect
Shall want no humbler tenderness; his heart
Be tender as a nursing mother's heart;   170
Of female softness shall his life be full,
Of humble cares and delicate desires,
Mild interests and gentlest sympathies.

  Child of my parents! Sister of my soul!
Thanks in sincerest verse have been elsewhere
Poured out for all the early tenderness
Which I from thee imbibed: and 'tis most true
That later seasons owed to thee no less;
For, spite of thy sweet influence and the touch
Of kindred hands that opened out the
    springs   180
Of genial thought in childhood, and in spite
Of all that unassisted I had marked
In life or nature of those charms minute

That win their way into the heart by stealth
(Still to the very going-out of youth)
I too exclusively esteemed *that* love,
And sought *that* beauty, which, as Milton
    sings,
Hath terror in it. Thou didst soften down
This over-sternness; but for thee, dear Friend!
My soul, too reckless of mild grace, had
    stood   190
In her original self too confident,
Retained too long a countenance severe;
A rock with torrents roaring, with the clouds
Familiar, and a favourite of the stars:
But thou didst plant its crevices with flowers,
Hang it with shrubs that twinkle in the breeze,
And teach the little birds to build their nests
And warble in its chambers. At a time
When Nature, destined to remain so long
Foremost in my affections, had fallen back 200
Into a second place, pleased to become
A handmaid to a nobler than herself,
When every day brought with it some new
    sense
Of exquisite regard for common things,
And all the earth was budding with these gifts
Of more refined humanity, thy breath,
Dear Sister! was a kind of gentler spring
That went before my steps. Thereafter came
One whom with thee friendship had early
    paired;
She came, no more a phantom to adorn   210
A moment, but an inmate of the heart,
And yet a spirit, there for me enshrined
To penetrate the lofty and the low;
Even as one essence of pervading light
Shines, in the brightest of ten thousand stars
And the meek worm that feeds her lonely
    lamp
Couched in the dewy grass.
                      With such a theme,
Coleridge! with this my argument, of thee
Shall I be silent? O capacious Soul!
Placed on this earth to love and understand, 220
And from thy presence shed the light of love,
Shall I be mute, ere thou be spoken of?
Thy kindred influence to my heart of hearts
Did also find its way. Thus fear relaxed
Her overweening grasp; thus thoughts and
    things
In the self-haunting spirit learned to take
More rational proportions; mystery,
The incumbent mystery of sense and soul,
Of life and death, time and eternity,
Admitted more habitually a mild   230

Interposition—a serene delight
In closelier gathering cares, such as become
A human creature, howsoe'er endowed,
Poet, or destined for a humbler name.

Whether to me shall be allotted life,
And, with life, power to accomplish aught of
    worth,
That will be deemed no insufficient plea
For having given the story of myself,
Is all uncertain: but, beloved Friend!
When, looking back, thou seest, in clearer view
Than any liveliest sight of yesterday,   240
That summer, under whose indulgent skies,
Upon smooth Quantock's airy ridge we roved
Unchecked, or loitered 'mid her sylvan combs,
Thou in bewitching words, with happy heart,
Didst chaunt the vision of that Ancient Man,
The bright-eyed Mariner, and rueful woes
Didst utter of the Lady Christabel;
And I, associate with such labour, steeped
In soft forgetfulness the livelong hours,
Murmuring of him who, joyous hap, was
    found,   250
After the perils of his moonlight ride,
Near the loud waterfall; or her who sate
In misery near the miserable Thorn—
When thou dost to that summer turn thy
    thoughts,
And hast before thee all which then we were,
To thee, in memory of that happiness,
It will be known, by thee at least, my Friend!
Felt, that the history of a Poet's mind
Is labour not unworthy of regard;
To thee the work shall justify itself.   260

Oh! yet a few short years of useful life,
And all will be complete, thy race be run,
Thy monument of glory will be raised;
Then, though (too weak to tread the ways of
    truth)
This age fall back to old idolatry,
Though men return to servitude as fast
As the tide ebbs, to ignominy and shame,
By nations, sink together, we shall still
Find solace—knowing what we have learnt to
    know,
Rich in true happiness if allowed to be   270
Faithful alike in forwarding a day
Of firmer trust, joint labourers in the work
(Should Providence such grace to us vouch-
    safe)
Of their deliverance, surely yet to come.
Prophets of Nature, we to them will speak

A lasting inspiration, sanctified
By reason, blest by faith: what we have loved,
Others will love, and we will teach them how;
Instruct them how the mind of man becomes
A thousand times more beautiful than the
    earth   280
On which he dwells, above this frame of things
(Which, 'mid all revolution in the hopes
And fears of men, doth still remain un-
    changed)
In beauty exalted, as it is itself
Of quality and fabric more divine.

THE RECLUSE

PART FIRST

. . . .

While yet an innocent little one, with a heart
That doubtless wanted not its tender moods,
I breathed (for this I better recollect)
Among wild appetites and blind desires,
Motions of savage instinct my delight
And exaltation. Nothing at that time
So welcome, no temptation half so dear
As that which urged me to a daring feat,
Deep pools, tall trees, black chasms, and dizzy
    crags,
And tottering towers: I loved to stand and
    read   10
Their looks forbidding, read and disobey,
Sometimes in act and evermore in thought.
With impulses, that scarcely were by these
Surpassed in strength, I heard of danger met
Or sought with courage; enterprise forlorn
By one, sole keeper of his own intent,
Or by a resolute few, who for the sake
Of glory fronted multitudes in arms.
Yea, to this hour I cannot read a Tale
Of two brave vessels matched in deadly fight, 20
And fighting to the death, but I am pleased
More than a wise man ought to be; I wish,
Fret, burn, and struggle, and in soul am there.
But me hath Nature tamed, and bade to seek
For other agitations, or be calm;
Hath dealt with me as with a turbulent stream,
Some nursling of the mountains which she
    leads
Through quiet meadows, after he has learnt
His strength, and had his triumph and his joy,
His desperate course of tumult and of glee. 30
That which in stealth by Nature was per-
    formed
Hath Reason sanctioned: her deliberate Voice

Hath said; be mild, and cleave to gentle things,
Thy glory and thy happiness be there.
Nor fear, though thou confide in me, a want
Of aspirations that have been—of foes
To wrestle with, and victory to complete,
Bounds to be leapt, darkness to be explored;
All that inflamed thy infant heart, the love,
The longing, the contempt, the undaunted
    quest,   40
All shall survive, though changed their office,
    all
Shall live, it is not in their power to die.
    Then farewell to the Warrior's Schemes,
    farewell
The forwardness of soul which looks that way
Upon a less incitement than the Cause
Of Liberty endangered, and farewell
That other hope, long mine, the hope to fill
The heroic trumpet with the Muse's breath!
Yet in this peaceful Vale we will not spend
Unheard-of days, though loving peaceful
    thought,   50
A voice shall speak, and what will be the
    theme?
    On Man, on Nature, and on Human Life,
Musing in solitude, I oft perceive
Fair trains of imagery before me rise,
Accompanied by feelings of delight
Pure, or with no unpleasing sadness mixed;
And I am conscious of affecting thoughts
And dear remembrances, whose presence
    soothes
Or elevates the Mind, intent to weigh
The good and evil of our mortal state.   60
—To these emotions, whencesoe'er they come,
Whether from breath of outward circumstance,
Or from the Soul—an impulse to herself—
I would give utterance in numerous verse.
Of Truth, of Grandeur, Beauty, Love, and
    Hope,
And melancholy Fear subdued by Faith;
Of blessèd consolations in distress;
Of moral strength, and intellectual Power;
Of joy in widest commonalty spread;
Of the individual Mind that keeps her own 70
Inviolate retirement, subject there
To Conscience only, and the law supreme
Of that Intelligence which governs all—
I sing:—"fit audience let me find though few!"
    So prayed, more gaining than he asked, the
    Bard—
In holiest mood. Urania, I shall need
Thy guidance, or a greater Muse, if such
Descend to earth or dwell in highest heaven!

For I must tread on shadowy ground, must
    sink
Deep—and, aloft ascending, breathe in
    worlds   80
To which the heaven of heavens is but a veil.
All strength—all terror, single or in bands,
That ever was put forth in personal form—
Jehovah—with his thunder, and the choir
Of shouting Angels, and the empyreal
    thrones—
I pass them unalarmed. Not Chaos, not
The darkest pit of lowest Erebus,
Nor aught of blinder vacancy, scooped out
By help of dreams—can breed such fear and
    awe
As fall upon us often when we look   90
Into our Minds, into the Mind of Man—
My haunt, and the main region of my song
—Beauty—a living Presence of the earth,
Surpassing the most fair ideal Forms
Which craft of delicate Spirits hath composed
From earth's materials—waits upon my steps;
Pitches her tents before me as I move,
An hourly neighbour. Paradise, and groves
Elysian, Fortunate Fields—like those of old
Sought in the Atlantic Main—why should they
    be   100
A history only of departed things,
Or a mere fiction of what never was?
For the discerning intellect of Man,
When wedded to this goodly universe
In love and holy passion, shall find these
A simple produce of the common day.
—I, long before the blissful hour arrives,
Would chant, in lonely peace, the spousal
    verse
Of this great consummation:—and, by words
Which speak of nothing more than what we
    are,   110
Would I arouse the sensual from their sleep
Of Death, and win the vacant and the vain
To noble raptures; while my voice proclaims
How exquisitely the individual Mind
(And the progressive powers perhaps no less
Of the whole species) to the external World
Is fitted:—and how exquisitely, too—
Theme this but little heard of among men—
The external World is fitted to the Mind;
And the creation (by no lower name   120
Can it be called) which they with blended
    might
Accomplish:—this is our high argument.
—Such grateful haunts foregoing, if I oft
Must turn elsewhere—to travel near the tribes

And fellowships of men, and see ill sights
Of madding passions mutually inflamed;
Must hear Humanity in fields and groves
Pipe solitary anguish; or must hang
Brooding above the fierce confederate storm
Of sorrow, barricadoed evermore   130
Within the walls of cities—may these sounds
Have their authentic comment; that even
    these
Hearing, I be not downcast or forlorn!—
Descend, prophetic Spirit! that inspir'st
The human Soul of universal earth,
Dreaming on things to come; and dost possess
A metropolitan temple in the hearts
Of mighty Poets; upon me bestow
A gift of genuine insight; that my Song
With star-like virtue in its place may shine, 140
Shedding benignant influence, and secure
Itself from all malevolent effect
Of those mutations that extend their sway
Throughout the nether sphere!—

    •   •   •   •   •   •

ODE TO DUTY

"Jam non consilio bonus, sed more eò perductus, ut
non tantum rectè facere possim, sed nisi rectè facere
non possim."

STERN Daughter of the Voice of God!
O Duty! if that name thou love
Who art a light to guide, a rod
To check the erring, and reprove;
Thou, who art victory and law
When empty terrors overawe;
From vain temptations dost set free;
And calm'st the weary strife of frail human-
    ity!

There are who ask not if thine eye
Be on them; who, in love and truth,   10
Where no misgiving is, rely
Upon the genial sense of youth:
Glad Hearts! without reproach or blot;
Who do thy work, and know it not:
Oh! if through confidence misplaced
They fail, thy saving arms, dread Power!
    around them cast.

Serene will be our days and bright,
And happy will our nature be,
When love is an unerring light,
And joy its own security.   20

And they a blissful course may hold
Even now, who, not unwisely bold,
Live in the spirit of this creed;
Yet seek thy firm support, according to their
    need.

I, loving freedom, and untried;
No sport of every random gust,
Yet being to myself a guide,
Too blindly have reposed my trust:
And oft, when in my heart was heard
Thy timely mandate, I deferred   30
The task, in smoother walks to stray;
But thee I now would serve more strictly,
    if I may.

Through no disturbance of my soul,
Or strong compunction in me wrought,
I supplicate for thy control;
But in the quietness of thought:
Me this unchartered freedom tires;
I feel the weight of chance-desires:
My hopes no more must change their name,
I long for a repose that ever is the same. 40

[Yet not the less would I throughout
Still act according to the voice
Of my own wish; and feel past doubt
That my submissiveness was choice:
Not seeking in the school of pride
For "precepts over dignified,"
Denial and restraint I prize
No farther than they breed a second Will
    more wise.]

Stern Lawgiver! yet thou dost wear   50
The Godhead's most benignant grace;
Nor know we anything so fair
As is the smile upon thy face:
Flowers laugh before thee on their beds
And fragrance in thy footing treads;
Thou dost preserve the stars from wrong;
And the most ancient heavens, through thee,
    are fresh and strong.

To humbler functions, awful Power!
I call thee: I myself commend   60
Unto thy guidance from this hour;
Oh, let my weakness have an end!
Give unto me, made lowly wise,
The spirit of self-sacrifice;
The confidence of reason give;

And in the light of truth thy Bondman let
  me live!

ELEGIAC STANZAS

SUGGESTED BY A PICTURE OF PEELE CASTLE,
IN A STORM, PAINTED BY SIR GEORGE BEAU-
MONT.

I WAS thy neighbour once, thou rugged Pile!
Four summer weeks I dwelt in sight of thee:
I saw thee every day; and all the while
Thy Form was sleeping on a glassy sea.

So pure the sky, so quiet was the air!
So like, so very like, was day to day!
Whene'er I looked, thy Image still was there;
It trembled, but it never passed away.

How perfect was the calm! it seemed no
  sleep;   9
No mood, which season takes away, or brings:
I could have fancied that the mighty Deep
Was even the gentlest of all gentle Things.

Ah! THEN, if mine had been the Painter's
  hand,
To express what then I saw; and add the
  gleam,
The light that never was, on sea or land,
The consecration, and the Poet's dream;

I would have planted thee, thou hoary Pile
Amid a world how different from this!
Beside a sea that could not cease to smile;
On tranquil land, beneath a sky of bliss.   20

Thou shouldst have seemed a treasure-house
  divine
Of peaceful years; a chronicle of heaven;—
Of all the sunbeams that did ever shine
The very sweetest had to thee been given.

A Picture had it been of lasting ease,
Elysian quiet, without toil or strife;
No motion but the moving tide, a breeze,
Or merely silent Nature's breathing life.

Such, in the fond illusion of my heart,
Such Picture would I at that time have made:
And seen the soul of truth in every part, 31
A steadfast peace that might not be betrayed.

So once it would have been,—'tis so no more;
I have submitted to a new control:
A power is gone, which nothing can restore;
A deep distress hath humanised my Soul.

Not for a moment could I now behold
A smiling sea, and be what I have been:
The feeling of my loss will ne'er be old;
This, which I know, I speak with mind
      serene.   40

Then, Beaumont, Friend! who would have
      been the Friend,
If he had lived, of Him whom I deplore,
This work of thine I blame not, but com-
      mend;
This sea in anger, and that dismal shore.

O 'tis a passionate Work!—yet wise and well,
Well chosen is the spirit that is here;
That Hulk which labours in the deadly swell,
This rueful sky, this pageantry of fear!

And this huge Castle, standing here sublime,
I love to see the look with which it braves, 50
Cased in the unfeeling armour of old time,
The lightning, the fierce wind, and tram-
      pling waves.

Farewell, farewell the heart that lives alone,
Housed in a dream, at distance from the
      Kind!
Such happiness, wherever it be known,
Is to be pitied; for 'tis surely blind.

But welcome fortitude, and patient cheer,
And frequent sights of what is to be borne!
Such sights, or worse, as are before me here.—
Not without hope we suffer and we mourn. 60

CHARACTER OF THE HAPPY
WARRIOR

WHO is the happy Warrior? Who is he
That every man in arms should wish to be?
—It is the generous Spirit, who, when brought
Among the tasks of real life, hath wrought
Upon the plan that pleased his boyish thought:
Whose high endeavours are an inward light
That makes the path before him always bright:
Who, with a natural instinct to discern
What knowledge can perform, is diligent to
      learn;

Abides by this resolve, and stops not there, 10
But makes his moral being his prime care;
Who, doomed to go in company with Pain,
And Fear, and Bloodshed, miserable train!
Turns his necessity to glorious gain;
In face of these doth exercise a power
Which is our human nature's highest dower;
Controls them and subdues, transmutes, be-
      reaves
Of their bad influence, and their good re-
      ceives;
By objects, which might force the soul to
      abate
Her feeling, rendered more compassionate; 20
Is placable—because occasions rise
So often that demand such sacrifice;
More skilful in self-knowledge, even more
      pure,
As tempted more; more able to endure,
As more exposed to suffering and distress;
Thence, also, more alive to tenderness.
—'Tis he whose law is reason; who depends
Upon that law as on the best of friends;
Whence, in a state where men are tempted
      still
To evil for a guard against worse ill,   30
And what in quality or act is best
Doth seldom on a right foundation rest,
He labours good on good to fix, and owes
To virtue every triumph that he knows:
—Who, if he rise to station of command,
Rises by open means; and there will stand
On honourable terms, or else retire,
And in himself possesses his own desire;
Who comprehends his trust, and to the same
Keeps faithful with a singleness of aim;
And therefore does not stoop, nor lie in
      wait   41
For wealth, or honours, or for worldly state;
Whom they must follow; on whose head must
      fall,
Like showers of manna, if they come at all;
Whose powers shed round him in the common
      strife,
Or mild concerns of ordinary life,
A constant influence, a peculiar grace;
But who, if he be called upon to face
Some awful moment to which Heaven has
      joined
Great issues, good or bad for human kind, 50
Is happy as a Lover; and attired
With sudden brightness, like a Man inspired;
And, through the heat of conflict, keeps the
      law

In calmness made, and sees what he fore-
     saw;
Or if an unexpected call succeed,
Come when it will, is equal to the need:
—He who, though thus endued as with a sense
And faculty for storm and turbulence,
Is yet a Soul whose master-bias leans
To homefelt pleasures and to gentle scenes; 60
Sweet images! which, wheresoe'er he be,
Are at his heart; and such fidelity
It is his darling passion to approve;
More brave for this, that he hath much to
     love:—
'Tis, finally, the Man, who, lifted high,
Conspicuous object in a Nation's eye,
Or left unthought-of in obscurity,—
Who, with a toward or untoward lot,
Prosperous or adverse, to his wish or not—
Plays, in the many games of life, that one
Where what he most doth value must be
     won: 71
Whom neither shape of danger can dismay,
Nor thought of tender happiness betray;
Who, not content that former worth stand
     fast,
Looks forward, persevering to the last,
From well to better, daily self-surpast:
Who, whether praise of him must walk the
     earth
For ever, and to noble deeds give birth,
Or he must fall, to sleep without his fame,
And leave a dead unprofitable name— 80
Finds comfort in himself and in his cause;
And, while the mortal mist is gathering,
     draws
His breath in confidence of Heaven's ap-
     plause:
This is the happy Warrior; this is He
That every Man in arms should wish to be.

PERSONAL TALK

I

I AM not One who much or oft delight
To season my fireside with personal talk,—
Of friends, who live within an easy walk,
Or neighbours, daily, weekly, in my sight:
And, for my chance-acquaintance, ladies
     bright,
Sons, mothers, maidens withering on the
     stalk,
These all wear out of me, like Forms with
     chalk
Painted on rich men's floors, for one feast-
     night.
Better than such discourse doth silence long,
Long, barren silence, square with my desire; 10
To sit without emotion, hope, or aim,
In the loved presence of my cottage-fire,
And listen to the flapping of the flame,
Or kettle whispering its faint undersong.

II

"Yet life," you say, "is life; we have seen
     and see,
And with a living pleasure we describe;
And fits of sprightly malice do but bribe
The languid mind into activity.
Sound sense, and love itself, and mirth and
     glee
Are fostered by the comment and the gibe." 20
Even be it so: yet still among your tribe,
Our daily world's true Worldlings, rank not
     me!
Children are blest, and powerful; their world
     lies
More justly balanced; partly at their feet,
And part far from them:—sweetest melodies
Are those that are by distance made more
     sweet;
Whose mind is but the mind of his own
     eyes,
He is a Slave; the meanest we can meet!

III

Wings have we,—and as far as we can go
We may find pleasure: wilderness and wood, 30
Blank ocean and mere sky, support that mood
Which with the lofty sanctifies the low.
Dreams, books, are each a world; and books,
     we know,
Are a substantial world, both pure and good:
Round these, with tendrils strong as flesh and
     blood,
Our pastime and our happiness will grow.
There find I personal themes, a plenteous
     store,
Matter wherein right voluble I am,
To which I listen with a ready ear;
Two shall be named, pre-eminently dear,— 40
The gentle Lady married to the Moor;
And heavenly Una with her milk-white Lamb.

IV

Nor can I not believe but that hereby
Great gains are mine; for thus I live remote
From evil-speaking; rancour, never sought,
Comes to me not; malignant truth, or lie.
Hence have I genial seasons, hence have I
Smooth passions, smooth discourse, and joy-
ous thought:
And thus from day to day my little boat
Rocks in its harbour, lodging peaceably.   50
Blessings be with them—and eternal praise,
Who gave us nobler loves, and nobler cares—
The Poets, who on earth have made us heirs
Of truth and pure delight by heavenly lays!
Oh! might my name be numbered among
theirs,
Then gladly would I end my mortal days.

ODE

INTIMATIONS OF IMMORTALITY FROM RECOL-
LECTIONS OF EARLY CHILDHOOD

The Child is father of the Man;
And I could wish my days to be
Bound each to each by natural piety.

I

THERE was a time when meadow, grove, and
stream,
The earth, and every common sight,
To me did seem
Apparelled in celestial light,
The glory and the freshness of a dream.
It is not now as it hath been of yore;—
Turn wheresoe'er I may,
By night or day,
The things which I have seen I now can see
no more.

II

The Rainbow comes and goes,   10
And lovely is the Rose,
The Moon doth with delight
Look round her when the heavens are bare,
Waters on a starry night
Are beautiful and fair;
The sunshine is a glorious birth;
But yet I know, where'er I go,
That there hath past away a glory from the
earth.

III

Now, while the birds thus sing a joyous song,
And while the young lambs bound   20
As to the tabor's sound,
To me alone there came a thought of grief:
A timely utterance gave that thought relief,
And I again am strong:
The cataracts blow their trumpets from the
steep;
No more shall grief of mine the season wrong;
I hear the Echoes through the mountains
throng,
The Winds come to me from the fields of
sleep,
And all the earth is gay;
Land and sea   30
Give themselves up to jollity,
And with the heart of May
Doth every Beast keep holiday;—
Thou Child of Joy,
Shout round me, let me hear thy shouts, thou
happy Shepherd-boy!

IV

Ye blessèd Creatures, I have heard the call
Ye to each other make; I see
The heavens laugh with you in your jubilee;
My heart is at your festival,
My head hath its coronal,   40
The fulness of your bliss, I feel—I feel it all.
Oh evil day! if I were sullen
While Earth herself is adorning,
This sweet May-morning,
And the Children are culling
On every side,
In a thousand valleys far and wide,
Fresh flowers; while the sun shines
warm,
And the Babe leaps up on his Mother's arm:—
I hear, I hear, with joy I hear!   50
—But there's a Tree, of many, one,
A single Field which I have looked upon,
Both of them speak of something that is gone;
The Pansy at my feet
Doth the same tale repeat:
Whither is fled, the visionary gleam?
Where is it now, the glory and the dream?

V

Our birth is but a sleep and a forgetting:
The Soul that rises with us, our life's Star,

Hath had elsewhere its setting,   60
And cometh from afar:
Not in entire forgetfulness,
And not in utter nakedness,
But trailing clouds of glory do we come
From God, who is our home:
Heaven lies about us in our infancy!
Shades of the prison-house begin to close
    Upon the growing Boy,
But He beholds the light, and whence it flows,
    He sees it in his joy;   70
The Youth, who daily farther from the east
    Must travel, still is Nature's Priest,
    And by the vision splendid
    Is on his way attended;
At length the Man perceives it die away,
And fade into the light of common day.

VI

Earth fills her lap with pleasures of her own;
Yearnings she hath in her own natural kind,
And, even with something of a Mother's mind,
    And no unworthy aim,   80
    The homely Nurse doth all she can
To make her Foster-child, her Inmate Man,
    Forget the glories he hath known,
And that imperial palace whence he came.

VII

Behold the Child among his new-born blisses,
A six years' Darling of a pigmy size!
See, where 'mid work of his own hand he lies,
Fretted by sallies of his mother's kisses,
With light upon him from his father's eyes!
See, at his feet, some little plan or chart,   90
Some fragment from his dream of human
        life,
Shaped by himself with newly-learned art;
    A wedding or a festival,
    A mourning or a funeral;
    And this hath now his heart,
    And unto this he frames his song:
    Then will he fit his tongue
To dialogues of business, love, or strife;
    But it will not be long
    Ere this be thrown aside,   100
    And with new joy and pride
The little Actor cons another part;
Filling from time to time his "humorous
        stage"
With all the Persons, down to palsied Age,
That Life brings with her in her equipage;

As if his whole vocation
Were endless imitation.

VIII

Thou, whose exterior semblance doth belie
    Thy Soul's immensity;
Thou best Philosopher, who yet dost keep   110
Thy heritage, thou Eye among the blind,
That, deaf and silent, read'st the eternal deep,
Haunted for ever by the eternal mind,—
    Mighty Prophet! Seer blest!
    On whom those truths do rest,
Which we are toiling all our lives to find,
In darkness lost, the darkness of the grave;
Thou, over whom thy Immortality
Broods like the Day, a Master o'er a Slave,
A Presence which is not to be put by;   120
    [To whom the grave
Is but a lonely bed without the sense or sight
    Of day or the warm light,
A place of thought where we in waiting
        lie;]
Thou little Child, yet glorious in the might
Of heaven-born freedom on thy being's height,
Why with such earnest pains dost thou pro-
        voke
The years to bring the inevitable yoke,
Thus blindly with thy blessedness at strife?
Full soon thy Soul shall have her earthly
        freight,   130
And custom lie upon thee with a weight,
Heavy as frost, and deep almost as life!

IX

O joy! that in our embers
Is something that doth live,
That nature yet remembers
What was so fugitive!
The thought of our past years in me doth
        breed
Perpetual benediction: not indeed
For that which is most worthy to be blest;
Delight and liberty, the simple creed   140
Of Childhood, whether busy or at rest,
With new-fledged hope still fluttering in his
        breast:—
    Not for these I raise
    The song of thanks and praise;
But for those obstinate questionings
Of sense and outward things,
Fallings from us, vanishings;
Blank misgivings of a Creature

Moving about in worlds not realised,
High instincts before which our mortal Na-
    ture   150
Did tremble like a guilty Thing surprised:
    But for those first affections,
    Those shadowy recollections,
  Which, be they what they may,
Are yet the fountain-light of all our day,
Are yet a master-light of all our seeing;
    Uphold us, cherish, and have power to
    make
Our noisy years seem moments in the being
Of the eternal Silence: truths that wake,
    To perish never: 160
Which neither listlessness, nor mad endeavour,
    Nor Man nor Boy,
Nor all that is at enmity with joy,
Can utterly abolish or destroy!
    Hence in a season of calm weather
      Though inland far we be,
Our Souls have sight of that immortal sea
    Which brought us hither,
    Can in a moment travel thither,
And see the Children sport upon the shore, 170
And hear the mighty waters rolling evermore.

X

Then sing, ye Birds, sing, sing a joyous song!
    And let the young Lambs bound
    As to the tabor's sound!
We in thought will join your throng,
  Ye that pipe and ye that play,
  Ye that through your hearts to-day
  Feel the gladness of the May!
What though the radiance which was once so
    bright
Be now for ever taken from my sight,   180
    Though nothing can bring back the hour
Of splendour in the grass, of glory in the
    flower;
    We will grieve not, rather find
    Strength in what remains behind;
    In the primal sympathy
    Which having been must ever be;
    In the soothing thoughts that spring
    Out of human suffering;
    In the faith that looks through death,
In years that bring the philosophic mind. 190

XI

And O, ye Fountains, Meadows, Hills, and
    Groves,
Forebode not any severing of our loves!

Yet in my heart of hearts I feel your might;
I only have relinquished one delight
To live beneath your more habitual sway.
I love the Brooks which down their channels
    fret,
Even more than when I tripped lightly as
    they;
The innocent brightness of a new-born Day
    Is lovely yet;
The Clouds that gather round the setting
    sun   200
Do take a sober colouring from an eye
That hath kept watch o'er man's mortality;
Another race hath been, and other palms are
    won.
Thanks to the human heart by which we live,
Thanks to its tenderness, its joys, and fears,
To me the meanest flower that blows can
    give
Thoughts that do often lie too deep for tears.

THOUGHT OF A BRITON ON THE SUBJUGATION OF SWITZERLAND

Two Voices are there; one is of the sea,
One of the mountains; each a mighty Voice:
In both from age to age thou didst rejoice,
They were thy chosen music, Liberty!
There came a Tyrant, and with holy glee
Thou fought'st against him; but hast vainly
    striven:
Thou from thy Alpine holds at length art
    driven,
Where not a torrent murmurs heard by thee.
Of one deep bliss thine ear hath been bereft:
Then cleave, O cleave to that which still is
    left;   10
For, high-souled Maid, what sorrow would
    it be
That Mountain floods should thunder as be-
    fore,
And Ocean bellow from his rocky shore,
And neither awful Voice be heard by thee!

SONG AT THE FEAST OF BROUGHAM CASTLE,

UPON THE RESTORATION OF LORD CLIFFORD,
    THE SHEPHERD, TO THE ESTATES AND
    HONOURS OF HIS ANCESTORS.

HIGH in the breathless Hall the Minstrel sate,

And Emont's murmur mingled with the
    Song.—
The words of ancient time I thus translate,
A festal strain that hath been silent long:—

"From town to town, from tower to tower,
  The red rose is a gladsome flower.
Her thirty years of winter past,
The red rose is revived at last;
She lifts her head for endless spring,
For everlasting blossoming: 10
Both roses flourish, red and white:
In love and sisterly delight
The two that were at strife are blended,
And all old troubles now are ended.—
Joy! joy to both! but most to her
Who is the flower of Lancaster!
Behold her how She smiles to-day
On this great throng, this bright array!
Fair greeting doth she send to all
From every corner of the hall;   20
But chiefly from above the board
Where sits in state our rightful Lord,
A Clifford to his own restored!

"They came with banner, spear, and shield;
And it was proved in Bosworth-field.
Not long the Avenger was withstood—
Earth helped him with the cry of blood:
St. George was for us, and the might
Of blessed Angels crowned the right.
Loud voice the Land has uttered forth, 30
We loudest in the faithful north:
Our fields rejoice, our mountains ring,
Our streams proclaim a welcoming;
Our strong abodes and castles see
The glory of their loyalty.

"How glad is Skipton at this hour—
Though lonely, a deserted Tower;
Knight, squire, and yeoman, page and groom:
We have them at the feast of Brough'm.
How glad Pendragon—though the sleep 40
Of years be on her!—She shall reap
A taste of this great pleasure, viewing
As in a dream her own renewing.
Rejoiced is Brough, right glad, I deem,
Beside her little humble stream;
And she that keepeth watch and ward
Her statelier Eden's course to guard;
They both are happy at this hour,
Though each is but a lonely Tower:—
But here is perfect joy and pride   50
For one fair House by Emont's side,

This day, distinguished without peer,
To see her Master and to cheer—
Him, and his Lady-mother dear!

"Oh! it was a time forlorn
When the fatherless was born—
Give her wings that she may fly,
Or she sees her infant die!
Swords that are with slaughter wild
Hunt the Mother and the Child.   60
Who will take them from the light?
—Yonder is a man in sight—
Yonder is a house—but where?
No, they must not enter there.
To the caves, and to the brooks,
To the clouds of heaven she looks;
She is speechless, but her eyes
Pray in ghostly agonies.
Blissful Mary, Mother mild,
Maid and Mother undefiled,   70
Save a Mother and her Child!

"Now Who is he that bounds with joy
On Carrock's side, a Shepherd-boy?
No thoughts hath he but thoughts that pass
Light as the wind along the grass.
Can this be He who hither came
In secret, like a smothered flame?
O'er whom such thankful tears were shed
For shelter, and a poor man's bread!
God loves the Child; and God hath willed 80
That those dear words should be fulfilled,
The Lady's words, when forced away
The last she to her Babe did say:
'My own, my own, thy Fellow-guest
I may not be; but rest thee, rest,
For lowly shepherd's life is best!'

"Alas! when evil men are strong
No life is good, no pleasure long.
The Boy must part from Mosedale's groves,
And leave the Blencathara's rugged coves, 90
And quit the flowers that summer brings
To Glenderamakin's lofty springs;
Must vanish, and his careless cheer
Be turned to heaviness and fear.
—Give Sir Lancelot Threlkeld praise!
Hear it, good man, old in days!
Thou tree of covert and of rest
For this young Bird that is distrest;
Among thy branches safe he lay,
And he was free to sport and play,   100
When falcons were abroad for prey.

"A recreant harp, that sings of fear
And heaviness in Clifford's ear!
I said, when evil men are strong,
No life is good, no pleasure long,
A weak and cowardly untruth!
Our Clifford was a happy Youth,
And thankful through a weary time,
That brought him up to manhood's prime.
—Again he wanders forth at will,   110
And tends a flock from hill to hill:
His garb is humble; ne'er was seen
Such garb with such a noble mien;
Among the shepherd-grooms no mate
Hath he, a Child of strength and state!
Yet lacks not friends for simple glee,
Nor yet for higher sympathy.
To his side the fallow-deer
Came, and rested without fear;
The eagle, lord of land and sea,   120
Stooped down to pay him fealty;
And both the undying fish that swim
Through Bowscale-tarn did wait on him;
The pair were servants of his eye
In their immortality;
And glancing, gleaming, dark or bright,
Moved to and fro, for his delight.
He knew the rocks which Angels haunt
Upon the mountains visitant;
He hath kenned them taking wing: 130
And into caves where Faeries sing
He hath entered; and been told
By Voices how men lived of old.
Among the heavens his eye can see
The face of thing that is to be;
And, if that men report him right,
His tongue could whisper words of might.
—Now another day is come,
Fitter hope, and nobler doom;
He hath thrown aside his crook,   140
And hath buried deep his book;
Armour rusting in his halls
On the blood of Clifford calls;—
'Quell the Scot,' exclaims the Lance—
Bear me to the heart of France,
Is the longing of the Shield—
Tell thy name, thou trembling Field;
Field of death, where'er thou be,
Groan thou with our victory!
Happy day, and mighty hour,   150
When our Shepherd in his power,
Mailed and horsed, with lance and sword,
To his ancestors restored
Like a re-appearing Star,
Like a glory from afar,

First shall head the flock of war!"

Alas! the impassioned minstrel did not know
How, by Heaven's grace, this Clifford's heart
    was framed:
How he, long forced in humble walks to go,
Was softened into feeling, soothed, and
    tamed.   160

Love had he found in huts where poor men
    lie;
His daily teachers had been woods and rills,
The silence that is in the starry sky,
The sleep that is among the lonely hills.

In him the savage virtue of the Race,
Revenge, and all ferocious thoughts were
    dead:
Nor did he change; but kept in lofty place
The wisdom which adversity had bred.

Glad were the vales, and every cottage-hearth;
The Shepherd-lord was honoured more and
    more;   170
And, ages after he was laid in earth,
"The good Lord Clifford" was the name he
    bore.

LAODAMIA

"WITH sacrifice before the rising morn
Vows have I made by fruitless hope inspired;
And from the infernal Gods, 'mid shades for-
    lorn
Of night, my slaughtered Lord have I re-
    quired:
Celestial pity I again implore;—
Restore him to my sight—great Jove, re-
    store!"

So speaking, and by fervent love endowed
With faith, the Suppliant heavenward lifts
    her hands;
While, like the sun emerging from a cloud,
Her countenance brightens—and her eye ex-
    pands;   10
Her bosom heaves and spreads, her stature
    grows;
And she expects the issue in repose.

O terror! what hath she perceived?—O joy!
What doth she look on?—whom doth she be-
    hold?
Her Hero slain upon the beach of Troy?

His vital presence? his corporeal mould?
It is—if sense deceive her not—'tis He!
And a God leads him, wingèd Mercury!

Mild Hermes spake—and touched her with
    his wand
That calms all fear: "Such grace hath crowned
    thy prayer,   20
Laodamía! that at Jove's command
Thy Husband walks the paths of upper air:
He comes to tarry with thee three hours'
    space;
Accept the gift, behold him face to face!"

Forth sprang the impassioned Queen her Lord
    to clasp;
Again that consummation she essayed;
But unsubstantial Form eludes her grasp
As often as that eager grasp was made.
The Phantom parts—but parts to re-unite,
And re-assume his place before her sight.   30

"Protesiláus, lo! thy guide is gone!
Confirm, I pray, the vision with thy voice:
This is our palace,—yonder is thy throne;
Speak, and the floor thou tread'st on will re-
    joice.
Not to appal me have the gods bestowed
This precious boon; and blest a sad abode."

"Great Jove, Laodamía! doth not leave
His gifts imperfect:—Spectre though I be,
I am not sent to scare thee or deceive;
But in reward of thy fidelity.   40
And something also did my worth obtain;
For fearless virtue bringeth boundless gain.

"Thou knowest, the Delphic oracle foretold
That the first Greek who touched the Trojan
    strand
Should die; but me the threat could not with-
    hold:
A generous cause a victim did demand;
And forth I leapt upon the sandy plain;
A self-devoted chief—by Hector slain."

"Supreme of Heroes—bravest, noblest, best!
Thy matchless courage I bewail no more,   50
Which then, when tens of thousands were de-
    prest
By doubt, propelled thee to the fatal shore;
Thou found'st—and I forgive thee—here thou
    art—
A nobler counsellor than my poor heart.

"But thou, though capable of sternest deed,
Wert kind as resolute, and good as brave;
And he, whose power restores thee, hath de-
    creed
Thou shouldst elude the malice of the grave:
Redundant are thy locks, thy lips as fair
As when their breath enriched Thessalian
    air.   60

"No Spectre greets me,—no vain Shadow this;
Come, blooming Hero, place thee by my side!
Give, on this well-known couch, one nuptial
    kiss
To me, this day, a second time thy bride!"
Jove frowned in heaven: the conscious Parcæ
    threw
Upon those roseate lips a Stygian hue.

"This visage tells thee that my doom is past:
Nor should the change be mourned, even if
    the joys
Of sense were able to return as fast
And surely as they vanish. Earth destroys   70
Those raptures duly—Erebus disdains:
Calm pleasures there abide—majestic pains.

"Be taught, O faithful Consort, to control
Rebellious passion: for the Gods approve
The depth, and not the tumult, of the soul;
A fervent, not ungovernable, love.
Thy transports moderate; and meekly mourn
When I depart, for brief is my sojourn—"

"Ah wherefore?—Did not Hercules by force
Wrest from the guardian Monster of the
    tomb   80
Alcestis, a reanimated corse,
Given back to dwell on earth in vernal bloom?
Medea's spells dispersed the weight of years,
And Æson stood a youth 'mid youthful peers.

"The Gods to us are merciful—and they
Yet further may relent: for mightier far
Than strength of nerve and sinew, or the sway
Of magic potent over sun and star,
Is love, though oft to agony distrest,
And though his favourite seat be feeble
    woman's breast.   90

"But if thou goest, I follow—" "Peace!" he
    said,—
She looked upon him and was calmed and
    cheered;
The ghastly colour from his lips had fled;

In his deportment, shape, and mien, appeared
Elysian beauty, melancholy grace,
Brought from a pensive though a happy place.

He spake of love, such love as Spirits feel
In worlds whose course is equable and pure;
No fears to beat away—no strife to heal—
The past unsighed for, and the future sure; 100
Spake of heroic arts in graver mood
Revived, with finer harmony pursued;

Of all that is most beauteous—imaged there
In happier beauty; more pellucid streams,
An ampler ether, a diviner air,
And fields invested with purpureal gleams;
Climes which the sun, who shed the brightest
        day
Earth knows, is all unworthy to survey.

Yet there the Soul shall enter which hath
        earned   109
That privilege by virtue.—"Ill," said he,
"The end of man's existence I discerned,
Who from ignoble games and revelry
Could draw, when we had parted, vain de-
        light,
While tears were thy best pastime, day and
        night;

"And while my youthful peers before my eyes
(Each hero following his peculiar bent)
Prepared themselves for glorious enterprise
By martial sports,—or, seated in the tent,
Chieftains and kings in council were detained;
What time the fleet at Aulis lay enchained. 120

"The wished-for wind was given:—I then re-
        volved
The oracle, upon the silent sea;
And, if no worthier led the way, resolved
That, of a thousand vessels, mine should be
The foremost prow in pressing to the strand,—
Mine the first blood that tinged the Trojan
        sand.

"Yet bitter, oft-times bitter, was the pang
When of thy loss I thought, belovèd Wife!
On thee too fondly did my memory hang,
And on the joys we shared in mortal life,— 130
The paths which we had trod—these foun-
        tains, flowers;
My new-planned cities, and unfinished towers.

"But should suspense permit the Foe to cry,

'Behold they tremble!—haughty their array,
Yet of their number no one dares to die?'
In soul I swept the indignity away:
Old frailties then recurred:—but lofty
        thought,
In act embodied, my deliverance wrought.

"And Thou, though strong in love, art all too
        weak
In reason, in self-government too slow;   140
I counsel thee by fortitude to seek
Our blest re-union in the shades below.
The invisible world with thee hath sympa-
        thised;
Be thy affections raised and solemnised.

"Learn, by a mortal yearning, to ascend—
Seeking a higher object. Love was given,
Encouraged, sanctioned, chiefly for that end;
For this the passion to excess was driven—
That self might be annulled: her bondage
        prove
The fetters of a dream opposed to love."—

Aloud she shrieked! for Hermes reap-
        pears!   151
Round the dear Shade she would have clung
        —'tis vain:
The hours are past—too brief had they been
        years;
And him no mortal effort can detain:
Swift, toward the realms that know not
        earthly day,
He through the portal takes his silent way,
And on the palace-floor a lifeless corse She
        lay.

Thus, all in vain exhorted and reproved,
She perished; and, as for a wilful crime,
By the just Gods whom no weak pity
        moved,   160
Was doomed to wear out her appointed time,
Apart from happy Ghosts, that gather flowers
Of blissful quiet 'mid unfading bowers.

—Yet tears to human suffering are due;
And mortal hopes defeated and o'erthrown
Are mourned by man, and not by man alone,
As fondly he believes.—Upon the side
Of Hellespont (such faith was entertained)
A knot of spiry trees for ages grew
From out the tomb of him for whom she
        died;   170
And ever, when such stature they had gained

That Ilium's walls were subject to their view,
The trees' tall summits withered at the sight;
A constant interchange of growth and blight!

YARROW UNVISITED

See the various Poems the scene of which is laid
  upon the banks of the Yarrow; in particular, the
  exquisite Ballad of Hamilton beginning—
  "Busk ye, busk ye, my bonny, bonny Bride,
  Busk ye, busk ye, my winsome Marrow!"

FROM Stirling castle we had seen
The mazy Forth unravelled;
Had trod the banks of Clyde, and Tay,
And with the Tweed had travelled;
And when we came to Clovenford,
Then said my *"winsome Marrow,"*
"Whate'er betide, we'll turn aside,
And see the Braes of Yarrow."

"Let Yarrow folk, *frae* Selkirk town,
Who have been buying, selling,   10
Go back to Yarrow, 'tis their own;
Each maiden to her dwelling!
On Yarrow's banks let herons feed,
Hares couch, and rabbits burrow!
But we will downward with the Tweed,
Nor turn aside to Yarrow.

"There's Galla Water, Leader Haughs,
Both lying right before us;
And Dryborough, where with chiming Tweed
The lintwhites sing in chorus;   20
There's pleasant Tiviot-dale, a land
Made blithe with plough and harrow:
Why throw away a needful day
To go in search of Yarrow?

"What's Yarrow but a river bare,
That glides the dark hills under?
There are a thousand such elsewhere
As worthy of your wonder."
—Strange words they seemed of slight and
    scorn;
My True-love sighed for sorrow;   30
And looked me in the face, to think
I thus could speak of Yarrow!

"Oh! green," said I, "are Yarrow's holms,
And sweet is Yarrow flowing!
Fair hangs the apple frae the rock,
But we will leave it growing.
O'er hilly path, and open Strath,

We'll wander Scotland thorough;
But, though so near, we will not turn
Into the dale of Yarrow.   40

"Let beeves and home-bred kine partake
The sweets of Burn-mill meadow;
The swan on still St. Mary's Lake
Float double, swan and shadow!
We will not see them; will not go,
To-day, nor yet to-morrow;
Enough if in our hearts we know
There's such a place as Yarrow.

"Be Yarrow stream unseen, unknown!
It must, or we shall rue it: 50
We have a vision of our own:
Ah! why should we undo it?
The treasured dreams of times long past,
We'll keep them, winsome Marrow!
For when we're there, although 'tis fair,
'Twill be another Yarrow!

"If Care with freezing years should come,
And wandering seem but folly,—
Should we be loth to stir from home,
And yet be melancholy;   60
Should life be dull, and spirits low,
'Twill soothe us in our sorrow,
That earth hath something yet to show,
The bonny holms of Yarrow!"

YARROW VISITED

SEPTEMBER, 1814

AND is this—Yarrow?—*This* the Stream
Of which my fancy cherished,
So faithfully, a waking dream?
An image that hath perished!
O that some Minstrel's harp were near,
To utter notes of gladness,
And chase this silence from the air,
That fills my heart with sadness!

Yet why?—a silvery current flows
With uncontrolled meanderings;   10
Nor have these eyes by greener hills
Been soothed, in all my wanderings.
And, through her depths, Saint Mary's Lake
Is visibly delighted;
For not a feature of those hills
Is in the mirror slighted.

A blue sky bends o'er Yarrow vale,
Save where that pearly whiteness
Is round the rising sun diffused,
A tender hazy brightness;　　　　20
Mild dawn of promise! that excludes
All profitless dejection;
Though not unwilling here to admit
A pensive recollection.

Where was it that the famous Flower
Of Yarrow Vale lay bleeding?
His bed perchance was yon smooth mound
On which the herd is feeding:
And haply from this crystal pool,
Now peaceful as the morning,　　　　30
The Water-wraith ascended thrice—
And gave his doleful warning.

Delicious is the Lay that sings
The haunts of happy Lovers,
The path that leads them to the grove,
The leafy grove that covers:
And Pity sanctifies the Verse
That paints, by strength of sorrow,
The unconquerable strength of love;
Bear witness, rueful Yarrow!　　　　40

But thou, that didst appear so fair
To fond imagination,
Dost rival in the light of day
Her delicate creation:
Meek loveliness is round thee spread,
A softness still and holy;
The grace of forest charms decayed,
And pastoral melancholy.

That region left, the vale unfolds
Rich groves of lofty stature,　　　　50
With Yarrow winding through the pomp
Of cultivated nature;
And, rising from those lofty groves,
Behold a Ruin hoary!
The shattered front of Newark's Towers,
Renowned in Border story.

Fair scenes for childhood's opening bloom,
For sportive youth to stray in;
For manhood to enjoy his strength;
And age to wear away in!　　　　60
Yon cottage seems a bower of bliss,
A covert for protection
Of tender thoughts, that nestle there—
The brood of chaste affection.

How sweet, on this autumnal day,
The wild-wood fruits to gather,
And on my True-love's forehead plant
A crest of blooming heather!
And what if I enwreathed my own!
'Twere no offence to reason;　　　　70
The sober Hills thus deck their brows
To meet the wintry season.

I see—but not by sight alone,
Loved Yarrow, have I won thee;
A ray of fancy still survives—
Her sunshine plays upon thee!
Thy ever-youthful waters keep
A course of lively pleasure;
And gladsome notes my lips can breathe,
Accordant to the measure.　　　　80

The vapours linger round the Heights,
They melt, and soon must vanish;
One hour is theirs, no more is mine—
Sad thought, which I would banish,
But that I know, where'er I go,
Thy genuine image, Yarrow!
Will dwell with me—to heighten joy,
And cheer my mind in sorrow.

SURPRISED BY JOY

SURPRISED by joy—impatient as the Wind
I turned to share the transport— Oh! with
　　whom
But Thee, deep buried in the silent tomb,
That spot which no vicissitude can find?
Love, faithful love, recalled thee to my
　　mind—
But how could I forget thee? Through what
　　power,
Even for the least division of an hour,
Have I been so beguiled as to be blind
To my most grievous loss!—That thought's
　　return
Was the worst pang that sorrow ever bore, 10
Save one, one only, when I stood forlorn,
Knowing my heart's best treasure was no
　　more;
That neither present time, nor years unborn
Could to my sight that heavenly face restore.

DION

(SEE PLUTARCH)

[I]

[FAIR is the Swan, whose majesty, prevailing

O'er breezeless water, on Locarno's lake,
Bears him on while proudly sailing
He leaves behind a moon-illumined wake:
Behold! the mantling spirit of reserve
Fashions his neck into a goodly curve;
An arch thrown back between luxuriant wings
Of whitest garniture, like fir-tree boughs
To which, on some unruffled morning, clings
A flaky weight of winter's purest snows! 10
—Behold!—as with a gushing impulse heaves
That downy prow, and softly cleaves
The mirror of the crystal flood,
Vanish inverted hill, and shadowy wood,
And pendent rocks, where'er, in gliding state,
Winds the mute Creature without visible Mate
Or Rival, save the Queen of night
Showering down a silver light,
From heaven, upon her chosen Favourite!]

[II]

[So pure, so bright, so fitted to embrace
Where'er he turned, a natural grace 20
Of haughtiness without pretence,
     &c. &c. &c. (Ed. 1820, 1827, 1832).]

I

SERENE, and fitted to embrace,
Where'er he turned, a swan-like grace
Of haughtiness without pretence,
And to unfold a still magnificence,
Was princely Dion, in the power
And beauty of his happier hour.
And what pure homage *then* did wait
On Dion's virtues, while the lunar beam
Of Plato's genius, from its lofty sphere,
Fell round him in the grove of Academe, 10
Softening their inbred dignity austere—
  That he, not too elate
  With self-sufficing solitude,
But with majestic lowliness endued,
Might in the universal bosom reign,
And from affectionate observation gain
Help, under every change of adverse fate.

II

Five thousand warriors—O the rapturous day!
Each crowned with flowers, and armed with
    spear and shield,
Or ruder weapon which their course might
    yield, 20
To Syracuse advance in bright array.

Who leads them on?—The anxious people see
Long-exiled Dion marching at their head,
He also crowned with flowers of Sicily,
And in a white, far-beaming, corselet clad!
Pure transport undisturbed by doubt or fear
The gazers feel; and, rushing to the plain,
Salute those strangers as a holy train
Or blest procession (to the Immortals dear)
That brought their precious liberty again. 30
Lo! when the gates are entered, on each hand,
Down the long street, rich goblets filled with
    wine
    In seemly order stand,
On tables set, as if for rites divine;—
And, as the great Deliverer marches by,
He looks on festal ground with fruits be-
    strown;
And flowers are on his person thrown
  In boundless prodigality;
Nor doth the general voice abstain from
    prayer,
Invoking Dion's tutelary care, 40
As if a very Deity he were!

III

Mourn, hills and groves of Attica! and mourn
Ilissus, bending o'er thy classic urn!
Mourn, and lament for him whose spirit
    dreads
Your once sweet memory, studious walks and
    shades!
For him who to divinity aspired,
Not on the breath of popular applause,
But through dependence on the sacred laws
Framed in the schools where Wisdom dwelt
    retired,
Intent to trace the ideal path of right 50
(More fair than heaven's broad causeway
    paved with stars)
Which Dion learned to measure with sub-
    lime delight;—
But He hath overleaped the eternal bars;
And, following guides whose craft holds no
    consent
With aught that breathes the ethereal ele-
    ment,
Hath stained the robes of civil power with
    blood,
Unjustly shed, though for the public good.
Whence doubts that came too late, and wishes
    vain,
Hollow excuses, and triumphant pain;
And oft his cogitations sink as low 60

As, through the abysses of a joyless heart,
The heaviest plummet of despair can go—
But whence that sudden check? that fearful
    start!
        He hears an uncouth sound—
        Anon his lifted eyes
Saw, at a long-drawn gallery's dusky bound,
A Shape of more than mortal size
And hideous aspect, stalking round and round!
    A woman's garb, the Phantom wore,
    And fiercely swept the marble floor,— 70
    Like Auster whirling to and fro,
    His force on Caspian foam to try;
Or Boreas when he scours the snow
That skims the plains of Thessaly,
Or when aloft on Mænalus he stops
His flight, 'mid eddying pine-tree tops!

                    IV

So, but from toil less sign of profit reaping,
The sullen Spectre to her purpose bowed,
    Sweeping—vehemently sweeping—
No pause admitted, no design avowed!   80
"Avaunt, inexplicable Guest!—avaunt,"
Exclaimed the Chieftain—"let me rather see
The coronal that coiling vipers make;
The torch that flames with many a lurid flake,
And the long train of doleful pageantry
Which they behold, whom vengeful Furies
    haunt;
Who, while they struggle from the scourge to
    flee,
Move where the blasted soil is not unworn,
And, in their anguish, bear what other minds
    have borne!"

                    V

But Shapes, that come not at an earthly call, 90
Will not depart when mortal voices bid;
Lords of the visionary eye whose lid,
Once raised, remains aghast, and will not fall!
Ye Gods, thought He, that servile Implement
    Obeys a mystical intent!
Your Minister would brush away
The spots that to my soul adhere;
But should she labour night and day,
They will not, cannot disappear;
Whence angry perturbation,—and that look 100
Which no philosophy can brook!

                    VI

Ill-fated Chief! there are whose hopes are
    built

Upon the ruins of thy glorious name;
Who, through the portal of one moment's
    guilt,
Pursue thee with their deadly aim!
O matchless perfidy! portentous lust
Of monstrous crime!—that horror-striking
    blade,
Drawn in defiance of the Gods, hath laid
The noble Syracusan low in dust!
Shuddered the walls—the marble city wept—
And sylvan places heaved a pensive sigh; 111
But in calm peace the appointed Victim slept,
As he had fallen in magnanimity;
Of spirit too capacious to require
That Destiny her course should change; too
    just
To his own native greatness to desire
That wretched boon, days lengthened by mis-
    trust.
So were the hopeless troubles, that involved
The soul of Dion, instantly dissolved.
Released from life and cares of princely
    state,   120
He left this moral grafted on his Fate;
"Him only pleasure leads, and peace attends,
Him, only him, the shield of Jove defends,
Whose means are fair and spotless as his
    ends."

COMPOSED UPON AN EVENING OF
EXTRAORDINARY SPLENDOUR AND
BEAUTY

                    I

HAD this effulgence disappeared
With flying haste, I might have sent,
Among the speechless clouds, a look
Of blank astonishment;
But 'tis endued with power to stay,
And sanctify one closing day,
That frail Mortality may see—
What is?—ah no, but what can be!
Time was when fields and watery cove
With modulated echoes rang,   10
While choirs of fervent Angels sang
Their vespers in the grove;
Or, crowning, star-like, each some sovereign
    height,
Warbled, for heaven above and earth below,
Strains suitable to both.—Such holy rite,
Methinks, if audibly repeated now
From hill or valley, could not move

Sublimer transport, purer love,
Than doth this silent spectacle—the gleam—
The shadow—and the peace supreme!   20

II

No sound is uttered,—but a deep
And solemn harmony pervades
The hollow vale from steep to steep,
And penetrates the glades.
Far-distant images draw nigh,
Called forth by wondrous potency
Of beamy radiance, that imbues
Whate'er it strikes with gem-like hues!
In vision exquisitely clear,
Herds range along the mountain side;   30
And glistening antlers are descried;
And gilded flocks appear.
Thine is the tranquil hour, purpureal Eve!
But long as god-like wish, or hope divine,
Informs my spirit, ne'er can I believe
That this magnificence is wholly thine!
—From worlds not quickened by the sun
A portion of the gift is won;
An intermingling of Heaven's pomp is spread
On ground which British shepherds tread!   40

III

And if there be whom broken ties
Afflict, or injuries assail,
Yon hazy ridges to their eyes
Present a glorious scale,
Climbing suffused with sunny air,
To stop—no record hath told where!
And tempting Fancy to ascend,
And with immortal Spirits blend!
—Wings at my shoulders seem to play;
But, rooted here, I stand and gaze   50
On those bright steps that heavenward raise
Their practicable way.
Come forth, ye drooping old men, look abroad,
And see to what fair countries ye are bound!
And if some traveller, weary of his road,
Hath slept since noon-tide on the grassy
    ground,
Ye Genii! to his covert speed;
And wake him with such gentle heed
As may attune his soul to meet the dower
Bestowed on this transcendent hour!   60

IV

Such hues from their celestial Urn

Were wont to stream before mine eye,
Where'er it wandered in the morn
Of blissful infancy.
This glimpse of glory, why renewed?
Nay, rather speak with gratitude;
For, if a vestige of those gleams
Survived, 'twas only in my dreams.
Dread Power! whom peace and calmness serve
No less than Nature's threatening voice,   70
If aught unworthy be my choice,
From THEE if I would swerve;
Oh, let Thy grace remind me of the light
Full early lost, and fruitlessly deplored;
Which, at this moment, on my waking sight
Appears to shine, by miracle restored;
My soul, though yet confined to earth,
Rejoices in a second birth!
—'Tis past, the visionary splendour fades;
And night approaches with her shades.   80

YARROW REVISITED

The following Stanzas are a memorial of a day passed
with Sir Walter Scott and other Friends visiting
the Banks of the Yarrow under his guidance, immediately before his departure from Abbotsford,
for Naples.
The title "Yarrow Revisited" will stand in no need
of explanation for Readers acquainted with the
Author's previous poems suggested by that celebrated Stream.

I

THE gallant Youth, who may have gained,
    Or seeks, a "winsome Marrow,"
Was but an Infant in the lap
    When first I looked on Yarrow;
Once more, by Newark's Castle-gate
    Long left without a warder,
I stood, looked, listened, and with Thee,
    Great Minstrel of the Border!

Grave thoughts ruled wide on that sweet day,
    Their dignity installing   10
In gentle bosoms, while sere leaves
    Were on the bough, or falling;
But breezes played, and sunshine gleamed—
    The forest to embolden;
Reddened the fiery hues, and shot
    Transparence through the golden.

For busy thoughts the Stream flowed on
    In foamy agitation;
And slept in many a crystal pool

For quiet contemplation: 20
No public and no private care
  The freeborn mind enthralling,
We made a day of happy hours,
  Our happy days recalling.

Brisk Youth appeared, the Morn of Youth,
  With freaks of graceful folly,—
Life's temperate Noon, her sober Eve,
  Her Night not melancholy;
Past, present, future, all appeared
  In harmony united,   30
Like guests that meet, and some from far,
  By cordial love invited.

And if, as Yarrow, through the woods
  And down the meadow ranging,
Did meet us with unaltered face,
  Though we were changed and changing;
If, *then*, some natural shadows spread
  Our inward prospect over,
The soul's deep valley was not slow
  Its brightness to recover.   40

Eternal blessings on the Muse,
  And her divine employment!
The blameless Muse, who trains her Sons
  For hope and calm enjoyment;
Albeit sickness, lingering yet,
  Has o'er their pillow brooded;
And Care waylays their steps—a Sprite
  Not easily eluded.

For thee, O SCOTT! compelled to change
  Green Eildon-hill and Cheviot   50
For warm Vesuvio's vine-clad slopes;
  And leave thy Tweed and Tiviot
For mild Sorrento's breezy waves;
  May classic Fancy, linking
With native Fancy her fresh aid,
  Preserve thy heart from sinking!

Oh! while they minister to thee,
  Each vying with the other,
May Health return to mellow Age,
  With Strength, her venturous brother;   60
And Tiber, and each brook and rill
  Renowned in song and story,
With unimagined beauty shine,
  Nor lose one ray of glory!

For Thou, upon a hundred streams,
  By tales of love and sorrow,
Of faithful love, undaunted truth,

Hast shed the power of Yarrow;
And streams unknown, hills yet unseen,
  Wherever they invite Thee,   70
At parent Nature's grateful call,
  With gladness must requite Thee.

A gracious welcome shall be thine,
  Such looks of love and honour
As thy own Yarrow gave to me
  When first I gazed upon her;
Beheld what I had feared to see,
  Unwilling to surrender
Dreams treasured up from early days,
  The holy and the tender.   80

And what, for this frail world, were all
  That mortals do or suffer,
Did no responsive harp, no pen,
  Memorial tribute offer?
Yea, what were mighty Nature's self?
  Her features, could they win us,
Unhelped by the poetic voice
  That hourly speaks within us?

Nor deem that localised Romance
  Plays false with our affections;   90
Unsanctifies our tears—made sport
  For fanciful dejections:
Ah, no! the visions of the past
  Sustain the heart in feeling
Life as she is—our changeful Life,
  With friends and kindred dealing.

Bear witness, Ye, whose thoughts that day
  In Yarrow's groves were centred;
Who through the silent portal arch
  Of mouldering Newark entered;   100
And climb the winding stair that once
  Too timidly was mounted
By the "last Minstrel," (not the last!)
  Ere he his Tale recounted.

Flow on for ever, Yarrow Stream!
  Fulfil thy pensive duty,
Well pleased that future Bards should chant
  For simple hearts thy beauty;
To dream-light dear while yet unseen,
  Dear to the common sunshine,   110
And dearer still, as now I feel,
  To memory's shadowy moonshine!

THE WORLD IS TOO MUCH WITH US

THE world is too much with us; late and
    soon,

Getting and spending, we lay waste our pow-
ers:
Little we see in Nature that is ours;
We have given our hearts away, a sordid
boon!
This Sea that bares her bosom to the moon;
The winds that will be howling at all hours,
And are up-gathered now like sleeping flowers;
For this, for everything, we are out of tune;
It moves us not.—Great God! I'd rather be
A Pagan suckled in a creed outworn;   10
So might I, standing on this pleasant lea,
Have glimpses that would make me less for-
lorn;
Have sight of Proteus rising from the sea;
Or hear old Triton blow his wreathèd horn.

WHERE LIES THE LAND

WHERE lies the Land to which yon Ship must
go?
Fresh as a lark mounting at break of day,
Festively she puts forth in trim array;
Is she for tropic suns, or polar snow?
What boots the enquiry?—Neither friend nor
foe
She cares for; let her travel where she may,
She finds familiar names, a beaten way
Ever before her, and a wind to blow.
Yet still I ask, what haven is her mark?
And, almost as it was when the ships were
rare,   10
(From time to time, like Pilgrims, here and
there
Crossing the waters) doubt, and something
dark,
Of the old Sea some reverential fear,
Is with me at thy farewell, joyous Bark!

TO SLEEP

A FLOCK of sheep that leisurely pass by,
One after one; the sound of rain, and bees
Murmuring; the fall of rivers, winds and seas,
Smooth fields, white sheets of water, and pure
sky;
I have thought of all by turns, and yet do
lie
Sleepless! and soon the small birds' melodies
Must hear, first uttered from my orchard
trees;
And the first cuckoo's melancholy cry.

Even thus last night, and two nights more, I
lay
And could not win thee, Sleep! by any
stealth: 10
So do not let me wear to-night away:
Without Thee what is all the morning's
wealth?
Come, blessed barrier between day and day,
Dear mother of fresh thoughts and joyous
health!

EXCURSION

BOOK FIRST

THE WANDERER

Supine the wanderer lay,
His eyes as if in drowsiness half shut,
The shadows of the breezy elms above
Dappling his face. He had not heard the sound
Of my approaching steps, and in the shade
Unnoticed did I stand some minutes' space.
At length I hailed him, seeing that his hat
Was moist with water-drops, as if the brim
Had newly scooped a running stream. He rose,
And ere our lively greeting into peace   10
Had settled, " 'Tis," said I, "a burning day:
My lips are parched with thirst, but you, it
seems,
Have somewhere found relief." He, at the
word,
Pointing towards a sweet-briar, bade me climb
The fence where that aspiring shrub looked
out
Upon the public way. It was a plot
Of garden ground run wild, its matted weeds
Marked with the steps of those, whom, as they
passed,
The gooseberry trees that shot in long lank
slips,
Or currants, hanging from their leafless
stems,   20
In scanty strings, had tempted to o'erleap
The broken wall. I looked around, and there,
Where two tall hedge-rows of thick alder
boughs
Joined in a cold damp nook, espied a well
Shrouded with willow-flowers and plumy fern.
My thirst I slaked, and, from the cheerless
spot
Withdrawing, straightway to the shade re-
turned

Where sate the old Man on the cottage-
    bench;
And, while, beside him, with uncovered head,
I yet was standing, freely to respire,   30
And cool my temples in the fanning air,
Thus did he speak. "I see around me here
Things which you cannot see: we die, my
    Friend,
Nor we alone, but that which each man loved
And prized in his peculiar nook of earth
Dies with him, or is changed; and very soon
Even of the good is no memorial left.
—The Poets, in their elegies and songs
Lamenting the departed, call the groves,
They call upon the hills and streams to
    mourn,   40
And senseless rocks; nor idly; for they speak,
In these their invocations, with a voice
Obedient to the strong creative power
Of human passion. Sympathies there are
More tranquil, yet perhaps of kindred birth,
That steal upon the meditative mind,
And grow with thought. Beside yon spring I
    stood,
And eyed its waters till we seemed to feel
One sadness, they and I. For them a bond
Of brotherhood is broken: time has been   50
When, every day, the touch of human hand
Dislodged the natural sleep that binds them
    up
In mortal stillness; and they ministered
To human comfort. Stooping down to drink,
Upon the slimy foot-stone I espied
The useless fragment of a wooden bowl,
Green with the moss of years, and subject only
To the soft handling of the elements:
There let it lie—how foolish are such
    thoughts!
Forgive them;—never—never did my steps   60
Approach this door but she who dwelt within
A daughter's welcome gave me, and I loved
    her
As my own child. Oh, Sir! the good die first,
And they whose hearts are dry as summer
    dust
Burn to the socket. Many a passenger
Hath blessed poor Margaret for her gentle
    looks,
When she upheld the cool refreshment drawn
From that forsaken spring; and no one came
But he was welcome; no one went away
But that it seemed she loved him. She is
    dead,   70
The light extinguished of her lonely hut,

The hut itself abandoned to decay,
And she forgotten in the quiet grave.

"I speak," continued he, "of One whose
    stock
Of virtues bloomed beneath this lowly roof.
She was a Woman of a steady mind,
Tender and deep in her excess of love;
Not speaking much, pleased rather with the
    joy
Of her own thoughts: by some especial care
Her temper had been framed, as if to make   80
A Being, who by adding love to peace
Might live on earth a life of happiness.
Her wedded Partner lacked not on his side
The humble worth that satisfied her heart:
Frugal, affectionate, sober, and withal
Keenly industrious. She with pride would tell
That he was often seated at his loom,
In summer, ere the mower was abroad
Among the dewy grass,—in early spring,
Ere the last star had vanished.—They who
    passed   90
At evening, from behind the garden fence
Might hear his busy spade, which he would
    ply,
After his daily work, until the light
Had failed, and every leaf and flower were lost
In the dark hedges. So their days were spent
In peace and comfort; and a pretty boy
Was their best hope, next to the God in
    heaven.

"Not twenty years ago, but you I think
Can scarcely bear it now in mind, there came
Two blighting seasons, when the fields were
    left   100
With half a harvest. It pleased Heaven to add
A worse affliction in the plague of war;
This happy Land was stricken to the heart!
A Wanderer then among the cottages,
I, with my freight of winter raiment, saw
The hardships of the season: many rich
Sank down, as in a dream, among the poor;
And of the poor did many cease to be,
And their place knew them not. Meanwhile,
    abridged
Of daily comforts, gladly reconciled   110
To numerous self-denials, Margaret
Went struggling on through those calamitous
    years
With cheerful hope, until the second autumn,
When her life's Helpmate on a sick-bed lay,
Smitten with perilous fever. In disease

He lingered long; and, when his strength re-
turned,
He found the little he had stored, to meet
The hour of accident or crippling age,
Was all consumed. A second infant now
Was added to the troubles of a time 120
Laden, for them and all of their degree,
With care and sorrow: shoals of artisans
From ill-requited labour turned adrift
Sought daily bread from public charity,
They, and their wives and children—happier
far
Could they have lived as do the little birds
That peck along the hedge-rows, or the kite
That makes her dwelling on the mountain
rocks!

"A sad reverse it was for him who long
Had filled with plenty, and possessed in
peace, 130
This lonely Cottage. At the door he stood,
And whistled many a snatch of merry tunes
That had no mirth in them; or with his knife
Carved uncouth figures on the heads of
sticks—
Then, not less idly, sought, through every
nook
In house or gardens, any casual work
Of use or ornament; and with a strange,
Amusing, yet uneasy, novelty,
He mingled, where he might, the various tasks
Of summer, autumn, winter, and of spring. 140
But this endured not; his good humour soon
Became a weight in which no pleasure was:
And poverty brought on a petted mood
And a sore temper: day by day he drooped,
And he would leave his work—and to the
town
Would turn without an errand his slack steps;
Or wander here and there among the fields.
One while he would speak lightly of his babes,
And with a cruel tongue: at other times
He tossed them with a false unnatural joy: 150
And 'twas a rueful thing to see the looks
Of the poor innocent children. 'Every smile,'
Said Margaret to me, here beneath these trees,
'Made my heart bleed.' "
                    At this the Wanderer paused;
And, looking up to those enormous elms,
He said, " 'Tis now the hour of deepest noon,
At this still season of repose and peace,
This hour when all things which are not at
rest
Are cheerful; while this multitude of flies

With tuneful hum is filling all the air; 160
Why should a tear be on an old Man's cheek?
Why should we thus, with an untoward mind,
And in the weakness of humanity,
From natural wisdom turn our hearts away;
To natural comfort shut our eyes and ears;
And, feeding on disquiet, thus disturb
The calm of nature with our restless
thoughts?"

HE spake with somewhat of a solemn tone:
But, when he ended, there was in his face
Such easy cheerfulness, a look so mild 170
That for a little time it stole away
All recollection; and that simple tale
Passed from my mind like a forgotten sound.
A while on trivial things we held discourse,
To me soon tasteless. In my own despite,
I thought of that poor Woman as of one
Whom I had known and loved. He had re-
hearsed
Her homely tale with such familiar power,
With such an active countenance, an eye
So busy, that the things of which he spake 180
Seemed present; and, attention now relaxed,
A heart-felt chilliness crept along my veins.
I rose; and, having left the breezy shade,
Stood drinking comfort from the warmer
sun,
That had not cheered me long—ere, looking
round
Upon that tranquil Ruin, I returned,
And begged of the old Man that, for my
sake,
He would resume his story.

                                He replied,
"It were a wantonness, and would demand
Severe reproof, if we were men whose
hearts 190
Could hold vain dalliance with the misery
Even of the dead; contented thence to draw
A momentary pleasure, never marked
By reason, barren of all future good.
But we have known that there is often found
In mournful thoughts, and always might be
found
A power to virtue friendly; were't not so,
I am a dreamer among men, indeed
An idle dreamer! 'Tis a common tale,
An ordinary sorrow of man's life, 200
A tale of silent suffering, hardly clothed
In bodily form.—But without further bid-
ding

I will proceed.
                    While thus it fared with them,
To whom this cottage, till those hapless years,
Had been a blessèd home, it was my chance
To travel in a country far remote;
And when these lofty elms once more appeared
What pleasant expectations lured me on
O'er the flat Common!—With quick step I
    reached
The threshold, lifted with light hand the
    latch;   210
But, when I entered, Margaret looked at me
A little while; then turned her head away
Speechless,—and, sitting down upon a chair,
Wept bitterly. I wist not what to do,
Nor how to speak to her. Poor Wretch! at
    last
She rose from off her seat, and then,—O
    Sir!
I cannot *tell* how she pronounced my name:—
With fervent love, and with a face of grief
Unutterably helpless, and a look
That seemed to cling upon me, she enquired
If I had seen her husband. As she spake 221
A strange surprise and fear came to my
    heart,
Nor had I power to answer ere she told
That he had disappeared—not two months
    gone.
He left his house: two wretched days had
    past,
And on the third, as wistfully she raised
Her head from off her pillow, to look forth,
Like one in trouble, for returning light,
Within her chamber-casement she espied
A folded paper, lying as if placed   230
To meet her waking eyes. This tremblingly
She opened—found no writing, but beheld
Pieces of money carefully enclosed,
Silver and gold. 'I shuddered at the sight,'
Said Margaret, 'for I knew it was his hand
That must have placed it there; and ere
    that day
Was ended, that long anxious day, I learned,
From one who by my husband had been
    sent
With the sad news, that he had joined a
    troop
Of soldiers, going to a distant land.   240
—He left me thus—he could not gather heart
To take a farewell of me; for he feared
That I should follow with my babes, and
    sink
Beneath the misery of that wandering life.'

"This tale did Margaret tell with many
    tears:
And, when she ended, I had little power
To give her comfort, and was glad to take
Such words of hope from her own mouth as
    served
To cheer us both. But long we had not talked
Ere we built up a pile of better thoughts 250
And with a brighter eye she looked around
As if she had been shedding tears of joy.
We parted.—'Twas the time of early spring;
I left her busy with her garden tools;
And well remembered, o'er that fence she
    looked,
And, while I paced along the foot-way path,
Called out, and sent a blessing after me,
With tender cheerfulness, and with a voice
That seemed the very sound of happy
    thoughts.

"I roved o'er many a hill and many a
    dale,   260
With my accustomed load; in heat and cold,
Through many a wood and many an open
    ground,
In sunshine and in shade, in wet and fair,
Drooping or blithe of heart, as might befall;
My best companions now the driving winds,
And now the 'trotting brooks' and whispering
    trees,
And now the music of my own sad steps,
With many a short-lived thought that passed
    between,
And disappeared.
                    I journeyed back this way,
When, in the warmth of midsummer, the
    wheat   270
Was yellow; and the soft and bladed grass,
Springing afresh, had o'er the hay-field spread
Its tender verdure. At the door arrived,
I found that she was absent. In the shade,
Where now we sit, I waited her return.
Her cottage, then a cheerful object, wore
Its customary look,—only, it seemed,
The honeysuckle, crowding round the porch,
Hung down in heavier tufts; and that bright
    weed,
The yellow stone-crop, suffered to take root 280
Along the window's edge, profusely grew
Blinding the lower panes. I turned aside,
And strolled into her garden. It appeared
To lag behind the season, and had lost
Its pride of neatness. Daisy-flowers and thrift

Had broken their trim border-lines, and
   straggled
O'er paths they used to deck: carnations,
   once
Prized for surpassing beauty, and no less
For the peculiar pains they had required,
Declined their languid heads, wanting sup-
   port.   290
The cumbrous bind-weed, with its wreaths and
   bells,
Had twined about her two small rows of peas,
And dragged them to the earth.
                  Ere this an hour
Was wasted.—Back I turned my restless steps;
A stranger passed; and, guessing whom I
   sought,
He said that she was used to ramble far.—
The sun was sinking in the west; and now
I sate with sad impatience. From within
Her solitary infant cried aloud;
Then, like a blast that dies away self-
   stilled,   300
The voice was silent. From the bench I rose;
But neither could divert nor soothe my
   thoughts.
The spot, though fair, was very desolate—
The longer I remained, more desolate:
And, looking round me, now I first observed
The corner stones, on either side the porch,
With dull red stains discoloured, and stuck
   o'er
With tufts and hairs of wool, as if the sheep,
That fed upon the Common, thither came
Familiarly, and found a couching-place   310
Even at her threshold. Deeper shadows fell
From these tall elms; the cottage-clock struck
   eight;—
I turned, and saw her distant a few steps.
Her face was pale and thin—her figure, too,
Was changed. As she unlocked the door, she
   said,
'It grieves me you have waited here so long,
But, in good truth, I've wandered much of
   late;
And, sometimes—to my shame I speak—
   have need
Of my best prayers to bring me back again.'
While on the board she spread our evening
   meal,   320
She told me—interrupting not the work
Which gave employment to her listless
   hands—
That she had parted with her elder child;
To a kind master on a distant farm

Now happily apprenticed.—'I perceive
You look at me, and you have cause;
   to-day
I have been travelling far; and many days
About the fields I wander, knowing this
Only, that what I seek I cannot find;
And so I waste my time: for I am changed;   330
And to myself,' said she, 'have done much
   wrong
And to this helpless infant. I have slept
Weeping, and weeping have I waked; my
   tears
Have flowed as if my body were not such
As others are; and I could never die.
But I am now in mind and in my heart
More easy; and I hope,' said she, 'that God
Will give me patience to endure the things
Which I behold at home.'
               It would have grieved
Your very soul to see her. Sir, I feel   340
The story linger in my heart; I fear
'Tis long and tedious; but my spirit clings
To that poor Woman:—so familiarly
Do I perceive her manner, and her look,
And presence; and so deeply do I feel
Her goodness, that, not seldom, in my walks
A momentary trance comes over me;
And to myself I seem to muse on One
By sorrow laid asleep; or borne away,
A human being destined to awake   350
To human life, or something very near
To human life, when he shall come again
For whom she suffered. Yes, it would have
   grieved
Your very soul to see her: evermore
Her eyelids drooped, her eyes downward were
   cast;
And, when she at her table gave me food,
She did not look at me. Her voice was low,
Her body was subdued. In every act
Pertaining to her house-affairs, appeared
The careless stillness of a thinking mind   360
Self-occupied; to which all outward things
Are like an idle matter. Still she sighed,
But yet no motion of the breast was seen,
No heaving of the heart. While by the fire
We sate together, sighs came on my ear,
I knew not how, and hardly whence they came.

   "Ere my departure, to her care I gave,
For her son's use, some tokens of regard,
Which with a look of welcome she received;
And I exhorted her to place her trust   370

In God's good love, and seek his help by
     prayer.
I took my staff, and, when I kissed her babe,
The tears stood in her eyes. I left her then
With the best hope and comfort I could give:
She thanked me for my wish;—but for my
     hope
It seemed she did not thank me.
                                   I returned,
And took my rounds along this road again
When on its sunny bank the primrose flower
Peeped forth, to give an earnest of the Spring.
I found her sad and drooping: she had
     learned   380
No tidings of her husband; if he lived,
She knew not that he lived; if he were dead,
She knew not he was dead. She seemed the
     same
In person and appearance; but her house
Bespake a sleepy hand of negligence;
The floor was neither dry nor neat, the hearth
Was comfortless, and her small lot of books,
Which, in the cottage-window, heretofore
Had been piled up against the corner panes
In seemly order, now, with straggling leaves 390
Lay scattered here and there, open or shut,
As they had chanced to fall. Her infant Babe
Had from its mother caught the trick of
     grief,
And sighed among its playthings. I withdrew,
And once again entering the garden saw,
More plainly still, that poverty and grief
Were now come nearer to her: weeds defaced
The hardened soil, and knots of withered
     grass:
No ridges there appeared of clear black mould,
No winter greenness; of her herbs and
     flowers,   400
It seemed the better part were gnawed away
Or trampled into earth; a chain of straw,
Which had been twined about the slender
     stem
Of a young apple-tree, lay at its root;
The bark was nibbled round by truant sheep.
—Margaret stood near, her infant in her
     arms,
And, noting that my eye was on the tree,
She said, 'I fear it will be dead and gone
Ere Robert come again.' When to the House
We had returned together, she enquired   410
If I had any hope:—but for her babe
And for her little orphan boy, she said,
She had no wish to live, that she must die
Of sorrow. Yet I saw the idle loom

Still in its place; his Sunday garments hung
Upon the self-same nail; his very staff
Stood undisturbed behind the door.
                              And when,
In bleak December, I retraced this way,
She told me that her little babe was dead,
And she was left alone. She now, released 420
From her maternal cares, had taken up
The employment common through these wilds,
     and gained,
By spinning hemp, a pittance for herself;
And for this end had hired a neighbour's boy
To give her needful help. That very time
Most willingly she put her work aside,
And walked with me along the miry road,
Heedless how far; and, in such piteous sort
That any heart had ached to hear her, begged
That, wheresoe'er I went, I still would ask 430
For him whom she had lost. We parted then—
Our final parting; for from that time forth
Did many seasons pass ere I returned
Into this tract again.
                          Nine tedious years;
From their first separation, nine long years,
She lingered in unquiet widowhood;
A Wife and Widow. Needs must it have been
A sore heart-wasting! I have heard, my Friend,
That in yon arbour oftentimes she sate
Alone, through half the vacant sabbath day; 440
And, if a dog passed by, she still would quit
The shade, and look abroad. On this old
     bench
For hours she sate; and evermore her eye
Was busy in the distance, shaping things
That made her heart beat quick. You see
     that path,
Now faint,—the grass has crept o'er its grey
     line;
There, to and fro, she paced through many
     a day
Of the warm summer, from a belt of hemp
That girt her waist, spinning the long-drawn
     thread
With backward steps. Yet ever as there
     passed   450
A man whose garments showed the soldier's
     red,
Or crippled mendicant in soldier's garb,
The little child who sate to turn the wheel
Ceased from his task; and she with faltering
     voice
Made many a fond enquiry; and when they,
Whose presence gave no comfort, were gone
     by,

Her heart was still more sad. And by yon
    gate,
That bars the traveller's road, she often stood,
And when a stranger horseman came, the
    latch
Would lift, and in his face look wistfully: 460
Most happy, if, from aught discovered there
Of tender feeling, she might dare repeat
The same sad question. Meanwhile her poor
    Hut
Sank to decay; for he was gone, whose hand,
At the first nipping of October frost,
Closed up each chink, and with fresh bands
    of straw
Chequered the green-grown thatch. And so
    she lived
Through the long winter, reckless and alone;
Until her house by frost, and thaw, and rain,
Was sapped; and while she slept, the nightly
    damps 470
Did chill her breast; and in the stormy day
Her tattered clothes were ruffled by the wind,
Even at the side of her own fire. Yet still
She loved this wretched spot, nor would for
    worlds
Have parted hence; and still that length of
    road,
And this rude bench, one torturing hope en-
    deared,
Fast rooted at her heart: and here, my
    Friend,—
In sickness she remained; and here she died;
Last human tenant of these ruined walls!"

The old Man ceased: he saw that I was
    moved; 480
From that low bench, rising instinctively
I turned aside in weakness, nor had power
To thank him for the tale which he had told.
I stood, and leaning o'er the garden wall
Reviewed that Woman's sufferings; and it
    seemed
To comfort me while with a brother's love
I blessed her in the impotence of grief.
Then towards the cottage I returned; and
    traced
Fondly, though with an interest more mild,
That secret spirit of humanity 490
Which, 'mid the calm oblivious tendencies
Of nature, 'mid her plants, and weeds, and
    flowers,
And silent overgrowings, still survived.
The old Man, noting this, resumed, and said,
"My Friend! enough to sorrow you have given,

The purposes of wisdom ask no more:
Nor more would she have craved as due to
    One
Who, in her worst distress, had ofttimes felt
The unbounded might of prayer; and learned,
    with soul
Fixed on the Cross, that consolation springs,
From sources deeper far than deepest pain, 501
For the meek Sufferer. Why then should we
    read
The forms of things with an unworthy eye?
She sleeps in the calm earth, and peace is
    here.
I well remember that those very plumes,
Those weeds, and the high spear-grass on that
    wall,
By mist and silent rain-drops silvered o'er,
As once I passed, into my heart conveyed
So still an image of tranquillity,
So calm and still, and looked so beautiful 510
Amid the uneasy thoughts which filled my
    mind,
That what we feel of sorrow and despair
From ruin and from change, and all the grief
That passing shows of Being leave behind,
Appeared an idle dream, that could maintain,
Nowhere, dominion o'er the enlightened spirit
Whose meditative sympathies repose
Upon the breast of Faith. I turned away,
And walked along my road in happiness."

I SAW THE FIGURE OF A LOVELY MAID

I saw the figure of a lovely Maid
Seated alone beneath a darksome tree,
Whose fondly-overhanging canopy
Set off her brightness with a pleasing shade.
No Spirit was she; *that* my heart betrayed,
For she was one I loved exceedingly;
But while I gazed in tender reverie
(Or was it sleep that with my Fancy played?)
The bright corporeal presence—form and
    face—
Remaining still distinct grew thin and rare, 10
Like sunny mist;—at length the golden hair,
Shape, limbs, and heavenly features, keeping
    pace
Each with the other in a lingering race
Of dissolution, melted into air.

PLACES OF WORSHIP

As star that shines dependent upon star
Is to the sky while we look up in love;

As to the deep fair ships which though they
    move
Seem fixed, to eyes that watch them from
    afar;
As to the sandy desert fountains are,
With palm-groves shaded at wide intervals,
Whose fruit around the sun-burnt Native falls
Of roving tired or desultory war—
Such to this British Isle her christian Fanes,
Each linked to each for kindred services;
Her Spires, her Steeple-towers with glittering
    vanes   11
Far-kenned, her Chapels lurking among trees,
Where a few villagers on bended knees
Find solace which a busy world disdairs.

MUTABILITY

FROM low to high doth dissolution climb,
And sink from high to low, along a scale
Of awful notes, whose concord shall not
    fail;
A musical but melancholy chime,
Which they can hear who meddle not with
    crime,
Nor avarice, nor over-anxious care.
Truth fails not; but her outward forms that
    bear
The longest date do melt like frosty rime,
That in the morning whitened hill and plain
And is no more; drop like the tower sub-
    lime   10
Of yesterday, which royally did wear
His crown of weeds, but could not even sus-
    tain
Some casual shout that broke the silent air,
Or the unimaginable touch of Time.

INSIDE OF KING'S COLLEGE CHAPEL, CAMBRIDGE

TAX not the royal Saint with vain expense,
With ill-matched aims the Architect who
    planned—
Albeit labouring for a scanty band
Of white-robed Scholars only—this immense
And glorious Work of fine intelligence!
Give all thou canst; high Heaven rejects the
    lore
Of nicely-calculated less or more;

So deemed the man who fashioned for the
    sense
These lofty pillars, spread that branching roof
Self-poised, and scooped into ten thousand
    cells,   10
Where light and shade repose, where music
    dwells
Lingering—and wandering on as loth to die;
Like thoughts whose very sweetness yieldeth
    proof
That they were born for immortality.

THE SAME

WHAT awful pérspective! while from our
    sight
With gradual stealth the lateral windows hide
Their Portraitures, their stone-work glimmers,
    dyed
In the soft chequerings of a sleepy light.
Martyr, or King, or sainted Eremite,
Whoe'er ye be, that thus, yourselves unseen,
Imbue your prison-bars with solemn sheen,
Shine on, until ye fade with coming Night!—
But, from the arms of silence—list! O list!
The music bursteth into second life;   10
The notes luxuriate, every stone is kissed
By sound, or ghost of sound, in mazy strife;
Heart-thrilling strains, that cast, before the
    eye
Of the devout, a veil of ecstasy!

CONTINUED

THEY dreamt not of a perishable home
Who thus could build. Be mine, in hours of
    fear
Or grovelling thought, to seek a refuge here;
Or through the aisles of Westminster to roam;
Where bubbles burst, and folly's dancing foam
Melts, if it cross the threshold; where the
    wreath
Of awe-struck wisdom droops: or let my path
Lead to that younger Pile, whose sky-like dome
Hath typified by reach of daring art
Infinity's embrace; whose guardian crest,
The silent Cross, among the stars shall
    spread   11
As now, when She hath also seen her breast
Filled with mementos, satiate with its part
Of grateful England's overflowing Dead.

SELECTIONS FROM THE PROSE OF WORDSWORTH

A LETTER TO THE BISHOP OF LANDAFF
1793

MY LORD,

Reputation may not improperly be termed the moral life of man. Alluding to our natural existence, Addison, in a sublime allegory well known to your Lordship, has represented us as crossing an immense bridge, from whose surface from a variety of causes we disappear one after another, and are seen no more. Every one who enters upon public life has such a bridge to pass. Some slip through at the very commencement of their career from thoughtlessness, others pursue their course a little longer, till, misled by the phantoms of avarice and ambition, they fall victims to their delusion. Your Lordship was either seen, or supposed to be seen, continuing your way for a long time unseduced and undismayed; but those who now look for you will look in vain, and it is feared you have at last fallen, through one of the numerous trap-doors, into the tide of contempt, to be swept down to the ocean of oblivion.

It is not my intention to be illiberal; these latter expressions have been forced from me by indignation. Your Lordship has given a proof that even religious controversy may be conducted without asperity; I hope I shall profit by your example. At the same time, with a spirit which you may not approve—for it is a republican spirit—I shall not preclude myself from any truths, however severe, which I may think beneficial to the cause which I have undertaken to defend. You will not, then, be surprised when I inform you that it is only the name of its author which has induced me to notice an Appendix to a Sermon which you have lately given to the world, with a hope that it may have some effect in calming a perturbation which, you say, has been *excited* in the minds of the lower orders of the community. While, with a servility which has prejudiced many people against religion itself, the ministers of the Church of England have appeared as writers upon public measures only to be the advocates of slavery civil and religious, your Lordship stood almost alone as the defender of truth and political charity. The names of levelling prelate, bishop of the Dissenters, which were intended as a dishonour to your character, were looked upon by your friends—perhaps by yourself—as an acknowledgment of your possessing an enlarged and philosophical mind; and, like the generals in a neighbouring country, if it had been equally becoming your profession, you might have adopted, as an honourable title, a denomination intended as a stigma.

On opening your Appendix, your admirers will naturally expect to find an impartial statement of the grievances which harass this Nation, and a sagacious inquiry into the proper modes of redress. They will be disappointed. Sensible how large a portion of mankind receive opinions upon authority, I am apprehensive lest the doctrines which they will there find should derive a weight from your name to which they are by no means intrinsically entitled. I will therefore examine what you have advanced, from a hope of being able to do away any impression left on the minds of such as may be liable to confound with argument a strong prepossession for your Lordship's talents, experience, and virtues.

Before I take notice of what you appear to have laid down as principles, it may not be improper to advert to some incidental opinions found at the commencement of your political confession of faith.

At a period big with the fate of the human race I am sorry that you attach so much importance to the personal sufferings of the late royal martyr, and that an anxiety for the issue of the present convulsions should not have prevented you from joining in the idle cry of modish lamentation which has resounded from the Court to the cottage. You wish it to be supposed you are one of those who are unpersuaded of the guilt of Louis XVI. If you had attended to the history of the French Revolution as minutely as its importance demands, so far from stopping to bewail his death, you would rather have regretted that the blind fondness of his people had placed a human being in that monstrous situation which rendered him unaccountable before a human tribunal. A bishop, a man of philosophy and humanity as distinguished as your Lordship, declared at the opening of the National Convention—and twenty-five millions of men were convinced of the truth of the assertion—that there was not a citizen on the tenth of August who, if he could have dragged before the eyes of Louis the corse of one of his murdered brothers, might not have exclaimed to him: "Tyran, voilà ton ouvrage." Think of this, and you will not want consolation under any depression your spirits may feel at the contrast exhibited by Louis on the most splendid throne of the universe, and Louis alone in the tower of the Temple or on the scaffold. But there is a class of men who receive the news of the late execution with much more heartfelt sorrow than that which you, among such a multitude, so officiously express. The passion of pity is one of which, above all others, a Christian teacher should be cautious of cherishing the abuse when, under the influence of reason, it is regulated by the disproportion of the pain suffered to the guilt incurred. It is from the passon thus directed that the men of whom I have just spoken are afflicted by the catastrophe of the fallen monarch. They are sorry that the prejudice and weakness of mankind have made it necessary to force an individual into an unnatural situation, which requires more than human talents and human virtues, and at the same time precludes him from attaining even a moderate knowledge of common life, and from feeling a particular share in the interests of mankind. But, above all, these men lament that any combination of circumstances should have rendered it necessary or advisable to veil for a moment the statues of the laws, and that by such emergency the cause of twenty-five millions of people, I may say of the whole human race, should have been so materially injured. Any other sorrow for the death of Louis is irrational and weak.

In France royalty is no more. The person of the last anointed is no more also; and I flatter myself I am not alone, even in this *kingdom,* when I wish that it may please the Almighty neither by the hands of His priests nor His nobles (I allude to a striking passage of Racine) to raise his posterity to the rank of his ancestors, and reillume the torch of extinguished David.

You say: "I fly with terror and abhorrence even from the altar of Liberty, when I see it stained with the blood of the aged, of the innocent, of the defenceless sex, of the ministers of religion, and of the faithful adherents of a fallen monarch." What! have you so little knowledge of the nature of man as to be igno-

rant that a time of revolution is not the season of true Liberty? Alas, the obstinacy and perversion of man is such that she is too often obliged to borrow the very arms of Despotism to overthrow him, and, in order to reign in peace, must establish herself by violence. She deplores such stern necessity, but the safety of the people, her supreme law, is her consolation. This apparent contradiction between the principles of liberty and the march of revolutions; this spirit of jealousy, of severity, of disquietude, of vexation, indispensable from a state of war between the oppressors and oppressed, must of necessity confuse the ideas of morality, and contract the benign exertion of the best affections of the human heart. Political virtues are developed at the expense of moral ones; and the sweet emotions of compassion, evidently dangerous when traitors are to be punished, are too often altogether smothered. But is this a sufficient reason to reprobate a convulsion from which is to spring a fairer order of things? It is the province of education to rectify the erroneous notions which a habit of oppression, and even of resistance, may have created, and to soften this ferocity of character, proceeding from a necessary suspension of the mild and social virtues; it belongs to her to create a race of men who, truly free, will look upon their fathers as only enfranchised.

I proceed to the sorrow you express for the fate of the French priesthood. The measure by which that body was immediately stripped of part of its possessions, and a more equal distribution enjoined of the rest, does not meet with your Lordship's approbation. You do not question the right of the Nation over ecclesiastical wealth; you have voluntarily abandoned a ground which you were conscious was altogether untenable. Having allowed this right, can you question the propriety of exerting it at that particular period? The urgencies of the State were such as required the immediate application of a remedy. Even the clergy were conscious of such necessity; and aware, from the immunities they had long enjoyed, that the people would insist upon their bearing some share of the burden, offered of themselves a considerable portion of their superfluities. The Assembly was true to justice, and refused to compromise the interests of the Nation by accepting as a satisfaction the insidious offerings of compulsive charity. They enforced their right. They took from the clergy a large share of their wealth, and applied it to the alleviation of the national misery. Experience shows daily the wise employment of the ample provision which yet remains to them. While you reflect on the vast diminution which some men's fortunes must have undergone, your sorrow for these individuals will be diminished by recollecting the unworthy motives which induced the bulk of them to undertake the office, and the scandalous arts which enabled so many to attain the rank and enormous wealth which it has seemed necessary to annex to the charge of a Christian pastor. You will rather look upon it as a signal act of justice that they should thus unexpectedly be stripped of the rewards of their vices and their crimes. If you should lament the sad reverse by which the hero of the necklace has been divested of about 1,300,000 livres of annual revenue, you may find some consolation that a part of this prodigious mass of riches is gone to preserve from famine some thousands of curés, who were pining in villages unobserved by Courts.

I now proceed to principles. Your Lordship very properly asserts that "the liberty of man in a state of society consists in his being subject to no law but the law enacted by the general will of the society to which he belongs." You approved of the object which the French had in view when, in the infancy of the Revolution, they were attempting to destroy arbitrary power, and to erect a temple to Liberty on its remains. It is with surprise, then, that I find you afterwards presuming to dictate to the world a servile adoption of the British constitution. It is with indignation I perceive you "reprobate" a people for having imagined happiness and liberty more likely to flourish in the open field of a Republic than under the shade of Monarchy. You are therefore guilty of a most glaring contradiction. Twenty-five millions of Frenchmen have felt that they could have no security for their liberties under any modification of monarchical power. They have in consequence unanimously chosen a Republic. You cannot but observe that they have only exercised that right in which, by your own confession, liberty essentially resides.

As to your arguments, by which you pretend to justify your anathemas of a Republic—if arguments they may be called—they are so concise, that I cannot but transcribe them. "I dislike a Republic for this reason, because of all forms of government, scarcely excepting the most despotic, I think a Republic the most oppressive to the bulk of the people; they are deceived in it with a show of liberty, but they live in it under the most odious of all tyrannies—the tyranny of their equals."

This passage is a singular proof of that fatality by which the advocates of error furnish weapons for their own destruction: while it is merely *assertion* in respect to a justification of your aversion to Republicanism, a strong *argument* may be drawn from it in its favour. Mr. Burke, in a philosophic lamentation over the extinction of chivalry, told us that in those times vice lost half its evil by losing all its grossness. Infatuated moralist! Your Lordship excites compassion as labouring under the same delusion. Slavery is a bitter and a poisonous draught. We have but one consolation under it, that a Nation may dash the cup to the ground when she pleases. Do not imagine that by taking from its bitterness you weaken its deadly quality; no, by rendering it more palatable you contribute to its power of destruction. We submit without repining to the chastisements of Providence, aware that we are creatures, that opposition is vain and remonstrance impossible. But when redress is in our own power and resistance is rational, we suffer with the same humility from beings like ourselves, because we are taught from infancy that we were born in a state of inferiority to our oppressors, that they were sent into the world to scourge, and we to be scourged. Accordingly we see the bulk of mankind, actuated by these fatal prejudices, even more ready to lay themselves under the feet of *the great* than the great are to trample upon them. Now taking for granted, that in Republics men live under the tyranny of what you call their equals, the circumstance of this being the most odious of all tyrannies is what a Republican would boast of; as soon as tyranny becomes odious, the principal step is made towards its destruction. Reflecting on the degraded state of the mass of mankind, a philosopher will lament that oppression is not odious to them, that the iron, while it eats the soul, is not felt to enter into it. "Tout l'homme né dans l'esclavage naît pour l'esclavage, rien n'est plus certain; les esclaves perdent tout dans leurs fers, jusqu'au désir d'en sortir; ils aiment leur servitude, comme les compagnons d'Ulysse aimaient leur abrutissement."

I return to the quotation in which you reprobate Republicanism. Relying upon the temper of the times, you have surely thought little argument necessary to content what few will be hardy enough to support; the strongest of auxiliaries, imprisonment and the pillory, has left your arm little to perform. But the happiness of mankind is so closely connected with this subject, that I cannot suffer such considerations to deter me from throwing out a few hints, which may lead to a conclusion that a Republic legitimately constructed contains less of an oppressive principle than any other form of government.

Your Lordship will scarcely question that much of human misery, that the great evils which desolate States, proceed from the governors having an interest distinct from that of the governed. It should seem a natural deduction, that whatever has a tendency to identify the two must also in the same degree promote the general welfare. As the magnitude of almost all States prevents the possibility of their enjoying a pure democracy, philosophers—from a wish, as far as is in their power, to make the governors and the governed one—will turn their thoughts to the system of universal representation, and will annex an equal importance to the suffrage of every individual. Jealous of giving up no more of the authority of the people than is necessary, they will be solicitous of finding out some method by which the office of their delegates may be confined as much as is practicable to the proposing and deliberating upon laws rather than to enacting them; reserving to the people the power of finally inscribing them in the national code. Unless this is attended to, as soon as a people has chosen representatives it no longer has a political existence, except as it is understood to retain the privilege of annihilating the trust when it shall think proper, and of resuming its original power. Sensible that at the moment of election an interest distinct from that of the general body is created, an enlightened legislator will endeavour by every possible method to diminish the operation of such interest. The first and most natural mode that presents itself is that of shortening the regular duration of this trust, in order that the man who has betrayed it may soon be superseded by a more worthy successor. But this is not enough; aware of the possibility of imposition, and of the natural tendency of power to corrupt the heart of man, a sensible Republican will think it essential that the office of legislator be not intrusted to the same man for a succession of years. He will also be induced to this wise restraint by the grand principle of identification; he will be more sure of the virtue of the legislator by knowing that, in the capacity of private citizen, to-morrow he must either smart under the oppression or bless the justice of the law which he has enacted to-day.

Perhaps in the very outset of this inquiry the principle on which I proceed will be questioned, and I shall be told that the people are not the proper judges of their own welfare. But because under every government of modern times, till the foundation of the American Republic, the bulk of mankind have appeared incapable of discerning their true interests, no conclusion can be drawn against my principle. At this moment have we not daily the strongest proofs of the success with which, in what you call the best of all monarchical governments, the popular mind may be debauched? Left to the quiet exercise of their own judgment, do you think that the people would have thought it necessary to set fire to the house of the philosophic Priestley, and to hunt down his life like that of a traitor or a parricide? that, deprived almost of the necessaries of existence by the burden of their taxes, they would cry out, as with one voice, for a war from which not a single ray of consolation can visit them to compensate for the additional keenness with which they are about to smart under the scourge of labour, of cold, and of hunger?

Appearing, as I do, the advocate of Republicanism, let me not be misunderstood. I am well aware, from the abuse of the executive power in States, that there is not a single European nation but what affords a melancholy proof that if, at this moment, the original authority of the people should be restored, all that could be expected from such restoration would in the beginning be but a change of tyranny. Considering the nature of a Republic in reference to the present condition of Europe, your Lordship stops here; but a philosopher will extend his views much farther: having dried up the source from which flows the corruption of the public opinion, he will be sensible that the stream will go on gradually refining itself. I must add also, that the coercive power is of necessity so strong in all the old governments, that a people could not at first make an abuse of that liberty which a legitimate Republic supposes. The animal just released from its stall will exhaust the overflow of its spirits in a round of wanton vagaries; but it will soon return to itself, and enjoy its freedom in moderate and regular delight.

But, to resume the subject of universal representation, I ought to have mentioned before, that in the choice of its representatives a people will not immorally hold out wealth as a criterion of integrity, nor lay down as a fundamental rule, that to be qualified for the trying duties of legislation a citizen should be possessed of a certain fixed property. Virtues, talents, and acquirements are all that it will look for.

Having destroyed every external object of delusion, let us now see what makes the supposition necessary that the people will mislead themselves. Your Lordship respects "peasants and mechanics when they intrude not themselves into concerns for which their education has not fitted them."

Setting aside the idea of a peasant or mechanic being a legislator, what vast education is requisite to enable him to judge amongst his neighbours which is most qualified by his industry and integrity to be intrusted with the care of the interests of himself and of his fellow-citizens? But leaving this ground, as governments formed on such a plan proceed in a plain and open manner, their administration would require much less of what is usually called talents and experience, that is, of disciplined treachery and hoary Machiavelism; and at the same time, as it would no longer be their interest to keep the mass of the nation in ignorance, a moderate portion of useful knowledge would be universally disseminated. If your Lordship has travelled in the democratic cantons of Switzerland, you must have seen the herdsman with the staff in one hand and the book in the other. In the constituent Assembly of France was found a peasant whose sagacity was as distinguished as his integrity, whose blunt honesty overawed and baffled the refinements of hypocritical patriots. The people of Paris followed him with acclamations, and the name of Père Gerard will long be mentioned with admiration and respect through the eighty-three departments.

From these hints, if pursued further, might be demonstrated the expediency of the whole people "intruding themselves" on the office of legislation, and the wisdom of putting into force what they may claim as a right. But government is divided into two parts—the legislative and executive. The executive power you would lodge in the hands of an individual. Before we inquire into the propriety of this measure, it will be necessary to state the proper objects of the executive power in governments where the principle of universal representation is admitted. With regard to that portion of this power which is exerted in the application of the laws, it may be observed that much of it would be superseded. As laws, being but the expression of the general will, would be enacted only from an almost universal conviction of their utility, any resistance to such laws, any desire of eluding them, must proceed from a few refractory individuals. As far, then, as relates to the internal administration of the country, a Republic has a manifest advantage over a Monarchy, inasmuch as less force is requisite to compel obedience to its laws.

From the judicial tribunals of our own country, though we labour under a variety of partial and oppressive laws, we have an evident proof of the nullity of regal interference, as the king's name is confessedly a mere fiction, and justice is known to be most equitably administered when the judges are least dependent on the crown.

I have spoken of laws partial and oppressive; our penal code is so crowded with disproportioned penalties and indiscriminate severity that a conscientious man would sacrifice, in many instances, his respect for the laws to the common feelings of humanity; and there must be a strange vice in that legislation from which can proceed laws in whose execution a man cannot be instrumental without forfeiting his self-esteem and incurring the contempt of his fellow-citizens.

But to return from this digression: with regard to the other branches of the executive government, which relate rather to original measures than to administering the law, it may be observed that the power exercised in conducting them is distinguished by almost imperceptible shades from the legislative, and that all such as admit of open discussion and of the delay attendant on public deliberations are properly the province of the representative assembly. If this observation be duly attended to, it will appear that this part of the executive power will be extremely circumscribed, will be stripped almost entirely of a deliberative capacity, and will be reduced to a mere hand or instrument. As a Republican government would leave this power to a select body destitute of the means of corruption, and whom the people, continually contributing, could at all times bring to account or dismiss, will it not necessarily ensue that a body so selected and supported would perform their simple functions with greater efficacy and fidelity than the complicated concerns of royalty can be expected to meet with in the councils of princes; of men who from their wealth and interest have forced themselves into trust; and of statesmen, whose constant object is to exalt themselves by laying pitfalls for their colleagues and for their country.

I shall pursue this subject no further; but adopting your Lordship's method of argument, instead of continuing to demonstrate the superiority of a Republican executive government, I will repeat some of the objections which have been often made to monarchy, and have not been answered.

My first objection to regal government is its instability, proceeding from a variety of causes. Where monarchy is found in its greatest intensity, as in Morocco and Turkey, this observation is illustrated in a very pointed manner, and indeed is more or less striking as governments are more or less despotic. The reason is obvious: as the monarch is the chooser of his ministers, and as his own passions and caprice are in general the sole guides of his conduct, these ministers, instead of pursuing directly the one grand object of national welfare, will make it their chief study to vary their measures according to his humours. But a minister *may* be refractory: his successor will naturally run headlong into plans totally the reverse of the former system; for if he treads in the same path, he is well aware that a similar fate will attend him. This observation will apply to each succession of kings, who, from vanity and a desire of distinction, will in general studiously avoid any step which may lead to a suspicion that they are so spiritless as to imitate their predecessor. That a similar

instability is not incident to Republics is evident from their very constitution.

As from the nature of monarchy, particularly of hereditary monarchy, there must always be a vast disproportion between the duties to be performed and the powers that are to perform them; and as the measures of government, far from gaining additional vigour, are, on the contrary, enfeebled by being intrusted to one hand, what arguments can be used for allowing to the will of a single being a weight which, as history shows, will subvert that of the whole body politic? And this brings me to my grand objection to monarchy, which is drawn from THE ETERNAL NATURE OF MAN. The office of king is a trial to which human virtue is not equal. Pure and universal representation, by which alone liberty can be secured, cannot, I think, exist together with monarchy. It seems madness to expect a manifestation of the *general* will, at the same time that we allow to a *particular* will that weight which it must obtain in all governments that can with any propriety be called monarchical. They must war with each other till one of them is extinguished. It was so in France and . . .

I shall not pursue this topic further, but, as you are a teacher of purity of morals, I cannot but remind you of that atmosphere of corruption without which it should seem that courts cannot exist.

You seem anxious to explain what ought to be understood by the equality of men in a state of civil society; but your Lordship's success has not answered your trouble. If you had looked in the articles of the Rights of Man, you would have found your efforts superseded: "Equality, without which liberty cannot exist, is to be met with in perfection in that State in which no distinctions are admitted but such as have evidently for their object the general good;" "The end of government cannot be attained without authorising some members of the society to command, and of course without imposing on the rest the necessity of obedience."

Here, then, is an inevitable inequality, which may be denominated that of power. In order to render this as small as possible, a legislator will be careful not to give greater force to such authority than is essential to its due execution. Government is at best but a necessary evil. Compelled to place themselves in a state of subordination, men will obviously endeavour to prevent the abuse of that superiority to which they submit; accordingly they will cautiously avoid whatever may lead those in whom it is acknowledged to suppose they hold it as a right. Nothing will more effectually contribute to this than that the person in whom authority has been lodged should occasionally descend to the level of private citizen; he will learn from it a wholesome lesson, and the people will be less liable to confound the person with the power. On this principle hereditary authority will be proscribed; and on another also—that in such a system as that of hereditary authority, no security can be had for talents adequate to the discharge of the office, and consequently the people can only feel the mortification of being humbled without having protected themselves.

Another distinction will arise amongst mankind, which, though it may be easily modified by government, exists independent of it; I mean the distinction of wealth, which always will attend superior talents and industry. It cannot be denied that the security of individual property is one of the strongest and most natural motives to induce men to bow their necks to the yoke of civil government. In order to attain this end of security to property, a legislator will proceed with impartiality. He should not suppose that, when he has insured to their proprietors the possession of lands and movables against the depredation of the necessitous, nothing remains to be done. The history of all ages has demonstrated that wealth not only can secure itself, but includes even an oppressive principle. Aware of this, and that the extremes of poverty and riches have a necessary tendency to corrupt the human heart, he will banish from his code all laws such as the unnatural monster of primogeniture, such as encourage associations against labour in the form of corporate bodies, and indeed all that monopolising system of legislation, whose baleful influence is shown in the depopulation of the country and in the necessity which reduces the sad relicks to owe their very existence to the ostentatious bounty of their oppressors. If it is true in common life, it is still more true in governments, that we should be just before we are generous; but our legislators seem to have forgotten or despised this homely maxim. They have unjustly left unprotected that most important part of property, not less real because it has no material existence, that which ought to enable the labourer to provide food for himself and his family. I appeal to innumerable statutes, whose constant and professed object it is to lower the price of labour, to compel the workman to be *content* with arbitrary wages, evidently too small from the necessity of legal enforcement of the acceptance of them. Even from the astonishing amount of the sums raised for the support of one description of the poor may be concluded the extent and greatness of that oppression, whose effects have rendered it possible for the few to afford so much, and have shown us that such a multitude of our brothers exist in even helpless indigence. Your Lordship tells us that the science of civil government has received all the perfection of which it is capable. For my part, I am more enthusiastic. The sorrow I feel from the contemplation of this melancholy picture is not unconsoled by a comfortable hope that the class of wretches called mendicants will not much longer shock the feelings of humanity; that the miseries entailed upon the marriage of those who are not rich will no longer tempt the bulk of mankind to fly to that promiscuous intercourse to which they are impelled by the instincts of nature, and the dreadful satisfaction of escaping the prospect of infants, sad fruit of such intercourse, whom they are unable to support. If these flattering prospects be ever realised, it must be owing to some wise and salutary regulations counteracting that inequality among mankind which proceeds from the present *fixed* disproportion of their possessions.

I am not an advocate for the agrarian law nor for sumptuary regulations, but I contend that the people amongst whom the law of primogeniture exists, and among whom corporate bodies are encouraged, and immense salaries annexed to useless and indeed hereditary offices, is oppressed by an inequality in the distribution of wealth which does not necessarily attend men in a state of civil society.

Thus far we have considered inequalities inseparable from civil society. But other arbitrary distinctions exist among mankind, either from choice or usurpation. I allude to titles, to stars, ribbons, and garters, and other badges of fictitious superiority. Your Lordship will not question the grand principle on which this inquiry set out; I look upon it, then, as my duty to try the propriety of these distinctions by that criterion, and think it will be no difficult task to prove that these separations among mankind are absurd, impolitic, and immoral. Considering hereditary nobility as a reward for services rendered to the State—and it is to my charity that you owe the permission of taking up the question on this ground—what services can a man render to the State adequate to such a compensation that the making of laws, upon which the happiness of millions is to depend, shall be lodged in him and his posterity, however depraved may be their principles, however contemptible their understandings?

But here I may be accused of sophistry; I ought to subtract every idea of power from such distinction, though from the weakness of mankind it is impossible to disconnect them. What services, then, can a man render to society to compensate for the outrage done to the dignity of our nature when we bind ourselves to address him and his posterity with humiliating circumlocutions, calling him most noble, most honourable, most high, most august, serene, excellent, eminent, and so forth; when it is more than probable that such unnatural flattery will but generate vices which ought to consign him to neglect and solitude, or make him the perpetual object of the finger of scorn? And does not experience justify the observation, that where titles—a thing very rare—have been conferred as the rewards of merit, those to whom they have descended, far from being thereby animated to imitate their ancestor, have presumed upon that lustre which they supposed thrown round them, and, prodigally relying on such resources, lavished what alone was their own, their personal reputation?

It would be happy if this delusion were confined to themselves; but, alas, the world is weak enough to grant the indulgence which they assume. Vice, which is forgiven in one character, will soon cease to meet with sternness of rebuke when found in others. Even at first she will entreat pardon with confidence, assured that ere long she will be charitably supposed to stand in no need of it.

But let me ask you seriously, from the mode in which these distinctions are originally conferred, is it not almost necessary that, far from being the rewards of services rendered to the State, they should usually be the recompense of an industrious sacrifice of the general welfare to the particular aggrandisement of that power by which they are bestowed? Let us even alter their source, and consider them as proceeding from the Nation itself, and deprived of that hereditary quality; even here I should proscribe them, and for the most evident reason—that a man's past services are no sufficient security for his future character; he who to-day merits the civic wreath may to-morrow deserve the Tarpeian rock. Besides, where respect is not perverted, where the world is not taught to reverence men without regarding their conduct, the esteem of mankind will have a very different value, and, when a proper independence is secured, will be regarded as a sufficient recompense for services however important, and will be a much surer guarantee of the continuance of such virtues as may deserve it.

I have another strong objection to nobility, which is that it has a necessary tendency to dishonour labour, a prejudice which extends far beyond its own circle; that it binds down whole ranks of men to idleness, while it gives the enjoyment of a reward which exceeds the hopes of the most active exertions of human industry. The languid tedium of this noble repose must be dissipated, and gaming, with the tricking manoeuvres of the horse-race, afford occupation to hours which it would be happy for mankind had they been totally unemployed.

Reflecting on the corruption of the public manners, does your Lordship shudder at the prostitution which miserably deluges our streets? You may find the cause in our aristocratical prejudices. Are you disgusted with the hypocrisy and sycophancy of our intercourse in private life? You may find the cause in the necessity of dissimulation which we have established by regulations which oblige us to address as our superiors, indeed as our masters, men whom we cannot but internally despise. Do you lament that such large portions of mankind should stoop to occupations unworthy the dignity of their nature? You may find in the pride and luxury thought necessary to nobility how such servile arts are encouraged. Besides, where the most honourable of the Land do not blush to accept such offices as groom of the bedchamber, master of the hounds, lords in waiting, captain of the honourable band of gentlemen-pensioners is it astonishing that the bulk of the people should not ask of an occupation, what is it? but what may be gained by it?

If the long equestrian train of equipage should make your Lordship sigh for the poor who are pining in hunger, you will find that little is thought of snatching the bread from their mouths to eke out the *"necessary* splendour" of nobility.

I have not time to pursue this subject further, but am so strongly impressed with the baleful influence of aristocracy and nobility upon human happiness and virtue, that if, as I am persuaded, monarchy cannot exist without such supporters, I think that reason sufficient for the preference I have given to the Republican system.

It is with reluctance that I quit the subjects I have just touched upon; but the nature of this Address does not permit me to continue the discussion. I proceed to what more immediately relates to this Kingdom at the present crisis.

You ask with triumphant confidence, to what other law are the people of England subject than the general will of the society to which they belong? Is your Lordship to be told that acquiescence is not choice, and that obedience is not freedom? If there is a single man in Great Britain who has no suffrage in the election of a representative, the will of the society of which he is a member is not generally expressed; he is a Helot in that society. You answer the question, so confidently put, in this singular manner: "The King, we are all justly persuaded, has not the inclination—and we all know that, if he had the inclination, he has not the power—to substitute his will in the place of law. The House of Lords has no such power. The House of Commons has no such power." This passage, so artfully and unconstitutionally framed to agree with the delusions of the moment, cannot deceive a thinking reader. The expression of your full persuasion of the upright intentions of the King can only be the language of flattery. You are not to be told that it is constitutionally a maxim not to attribute to the person of the King the measures and misconduct of government. Had you chosen to speak, as you ought to have done, openly and explicitly, you must have expressed your just persuasion and implicit confidence in the integrity, moderation, and wisdom of his Majesty's ministers. Have you forgot the avowed ministerial maxim of Sir Robert Walpole? Are you ignorant of the overwhelming corruption of the present day?

You seem unconscious of the absurdity of separating what is inseparable even in imagination. Would it have been any consolation to the miserable Romans under the second triumvirate to have been asked insultingly, Is it Octavius, is it Anthony, or is it Lepidus that has caused this bitterness of affliction? and when the answer could not be returned with certainty, to have been reproached that their sufferings were imaginary? The fact is that the King *and* Lords *and* Commons, by what is termed the omnipotence of Parliament, have constitutionally the right of enacting whatever laws they please, in defiance of the petitions or remonstrances of the nation. They have the power of doubling our enormous debt of 240 millions, and *may* pursue measures which could never be supposed the emanation of the general will without concluding the people stripped of reason, of sentiment, and even of that first instinct which prompts them to preserve their own existence.

I congratulate your Lordship upon your enthusiastic fondness for the judicial proceedings of this country. I am happy to find you have passed through life without having your fleece torn from your back in the thorny labyrinth of litigation. But you have not lived always in colleges, and must have passed by some victims, whom it cannot be supposed, without a reflection on your heart, that you have forgotten. Here I am reminded of what I have said on the subject of representation—to be qualified for the office of legislation you should have felt like the bulk of mankind; their sorrows should be familiar to you, of which, if you are ignorant, how can you redress them? As a member of the assembly which, from a confidence in its experience, sagacity, and wisdom, the constitution has invested with the supreme appellant jurisdiction to determine the most doubtful points of an intricate jurisprudence, your Lordship cannot, I presume, be ignorant of the consuming expense of our never-ending process, the verbosity of unintelligible statutes, and the perpetual contrariety in our judicial decisions.

"The greatest freedom that can be enjoyed by man in a state of civil society, the greatest security that can be given with respect to the protection of his character, property, personal liberty, limb, and life, is afforded to every individual by our present constitution."

"Let it never be forgotten by ourselves, and let us impress the observation upon the hearts of our children, that we are in possession of both (liberty and equality), of as much of both as can be consistent with the end for which civil society was introduced among mankind."

Many of my readers will hardly believe me when I inform them that these passages are copied verbatim from your Appendix. Mr. Burke roused the indignation of all ranks of men when, by a refinement in cruelty superior to that which in the East yokes the living to the dead, he strove to persuade us that we and our posterity to the end of time were riveted to a constitution by the indissoluble compact of—a dead parchment, and were bound to cherish a corse at the bosom when reason might call aloud that it should be entombed. Your Lordship aims at the same detestable object by means more criminal, because more dangerous and insidious. Attempting to lull the people of England into a belief that any inquiries directed towards the nature of liberty and equality can in no other way lead to their happiness than by convincing them that they have already arrived at perfection in the science of government, what is your object but to exclude them for ever from the most fruitful field of human knowledge? Besides, it is another cause to execrate this doctrine that the consequence of such fatal delusion would be that they must entirely draw off their attention, not only from the government, but from their governors; that the stream of public vigilance, far from clearing and enriching the prospect of society, would by its stagnation consign it to barrenness, and by its putrefaction infect it with death. You have aimed an arrow at liberty and philosophy, the eyes of the human race; why, like the inveterate enemy of Philip, in putting your name to the shaft, did you not declare openly its destination?

As a teacher of religion, your Lordship cannot be ignorant of a class of breaches of duty · which may be denominated faults of omission. You profess to give your opinions upon the present turbulent crisis, expressing a wish that they may have some effect in tranquillising the minds of the people. Whence comes it, then, that the two grand causes of this working of the popular mind are passed over in silence? Your Lordship's conduct may bring to mind the story of a company of strolling comedians, who gave out the play of *Hamlet* as the performance of the evening. The audience were not a little surprised to be told, on the drawing up of the curtain, that from circumstances of particular convenience it was hoped they would dispense with the omission of the character of—Hamlet! But to be serious—for the subject is serious in the extreme—from your silence respecting the general call for a PARLIAMENTARY REFORM, supported by your assertion that we at present enjoy as great a portion of liberty and equality as is consistent with civil society, what can be supposed but that you are a determined enemy to the redress of what the people of England call and feel to be grievances?

From your omitting to speak upon the war, and your general disapprobation of French measures and French principles, expressed particularly at this moment, we are necessarily led also to conclude that you have no wish to dispel an infatuation which is now giving up to the sword so large a portion of the poor, and consigning the rest to the more slow and more painful consumption of want. I could excuse your silence on this point, as it would ill become an English bishop at the close of the eighteenth century to make the pulpit the vehicle of exhortations which would have disgraced the incendiary of the Crusades, the hermit Peter. But you have deprived yourself of the plea of decorum by giving no opinion on the REFORM OF THE LEGISLATURE. As undoubtedly you have some secret reason for the reservation of your sentiments on this latter head, I cannot but apply the same reason to the former. Upon what principle is your conduct to be explained? In some parts of England it is quaintly said, when a drunken man is seen reeling towards his home, that he has business on both sides of the road. Observing your Lordship's tortuous path, the spectators will be far from insinuating that you have partaken of Mr. Burke's intoxicating bowl; they will content themselves, shaking their heads as you stagger along, with remarking that you have business on both sides of the road.

The friends of Liberty congratulate themselves upon the odium under which they are at present labouring, as the causes which have produced it have obliged so many of her false adherents to disclaim with officious earnestness any desire to promote her interests; nor are they disheartened by the diminution which their body is supposed already to have sustained. Conscious that an enemy lurking in our ranks is ten times more formidable than when drawn out against us, that the unblushing aristocracy of a Maury or a Cazalès is far less dangerous than the insidious mask of patriotism assumed by a La Fayette or a Mirabeau, we thank you for your desertion. Political convulsions have been said particularly to call forth concealed abilities, but it has been seldom observed how vast is their consumption of them. Reflecting upon the fate of the greatest portion of the members of the constituent and legislative assemblies, we must necessarily be struck with a prodigious annihilation of human talents. Aware that this necessity is attached to a struggle for Liberty, we are the less sorry that we can expect no advantage from the mental endowments of your Lordship.

A LETTER TO JOHN WILSON
(CHRISTOPHER NORTH)

MY DEAR SIR,

Had it not been for a very amiable modesty you could not have imagined that your letter could give me any offence. It was on many accounts highly grateful to me. I was pleased to find that I had given so much pleasure to an ingenious and able mind, and I further considered the enjoyment which you had had from my Poems as an earnest that others might be delighted with them in the same, or a like manner. It is plain from your letter that the pleasure which I have given you has not been blind or unthinking; you have studied the poems, and prove that you have entered into the spirit of them. They have not given you a cheap or vulgar pleasure; therefore I feel that you are entitled to my kindest thanks for having done some violence to your natural diffidence in the communication which you have made to me.

There is scarcely any part of your letter that does not deserve particular notice; but partly from some constitutional infirmities, and partly from certain habits of mind, I do not write any letters unless upon business, not even to my dearest friends. Except during absence from my own family I have not written five letters of friendship during the last five years. I have mentioned this in order that I may retain your good opinion, should my letter be less minute than you are entitled to expect. You seem to be desirous of my opinion on the influence of natural objects in forming the character of Nations. This cannot be understood without first considering their influence upon men in general, first, with reference to such objects as are common to all countries; and, next, such as belong exclusively to any particular country, or in a greater degree to it than to another. Now it is manifest that no human being can be so besotted and debased by oppression, penury, or any other evil which unhumanizes man, as to be utterly insensible to the colours, forms, or smell of flowers, the [voices] and motions of birds and beasts, the appearances of the sky and heavenly bodies, the general warmth of a fine day, the terror and uncomfortableness of a storm, &c. &c. How dead soever many full-grown men may outwardly seem to these things, all are more or less affected by them; and in childhood, in the first practice and exercise of their senses, they must have been not the nourishers merely, but often the fathers of their passions. There cannot be a doubt that in tracts of country where images of danger, melancholy, grandeur, or loveliness, softness, and ease prevail, that they will make themselves felt powerfully in forming the characters of the people, so as to produce an uniformity or national character, where the nation is small and is not made up of men who, inhabiting different soils, climates, &c., by their civil usages and relations materially interfere with each other. It was so formerly, no doubt, in the Highlands of Scotland; but we cannot perhaps observe much of it in our own island at the present day, because, even in the most sequestered places, by manufactures, traffic, religion, law, interchange of inhabitants, &c., distinctions are done away, which would otherwise have been strong and obvious. This complex state of society does not, however, prevent the characters of individuals from frequently receiving a strong bias, not merely from the impressions of general nature, but also from local objects and images. But it seems that to produce these effects, in the degree in which we frequently find them to be produced, there must be a peculiar sensibility of original organization combining with moral accidents, as is exhibited in "The Brothers" and in "Ruth"; I mean, to produce this in a marked degree; not that I believe that any man was ever brought up in the country without loving it, especially in his better moments, or in a district of particular grandeur or beauty without feeling some stronger attachment to it on that account than he would otherwise have felt. I include, you will observe, in these considerations, the influence of climate, changes in the atmosphere and elements, and the labours and occupations which particular districts require.

You begin what you say upon "The Idiot Boy," with this observation, that nothing is a fit subject for poetry which does not please. But here follows a question, Does not please whom? Some have little knowledge of natural imagery of any kind, and, of course, little relish for it; some are disgusted with the very mention of the words pastoral poetry, sheep or shepherds; some cannot tolerate a poem with a ghost or any supernatural agency in it; others would shrink from an animated description of the pleasures of love, as from a thing carnal and libidinous; some cannot bear to see delicate and refined feelings ascribed to men in low conditions in society, because their vanity and self-love tell them that these belong only to themselves, and men like themselves in dress, station, and way of life; others are disgusted with the naked language of some of the most interesting passions of men, because either it is indelicate, or gross, or vulgar; as many fine ladies could not bear certain expressions in "The Mother" and "The Thorn" and, as in the instance of Adam Smith, who, we are told, could not endure the ballad of "Clym of the Clough," because the author had not written like a gentleman. Then there are professional and national prejudices for evermore. Some take no interest in the description of a particular passion or quality, as love of solitariness, we will say, genial activity of fancy, love of nature, religion, and so forth, because they have [little or] nothing of it in themselves; and so on without end. I return then to [the] question, please whom? or what? I answer, human nature as it has been [and ever] will be. But, where are we to find the best measure of this? I answer, [from with]in; by stripping our own hearts naked, and by looking out of ourselves to[wards men] who lead the simplest lives, and most according to nature; men who have never known false refinements, wayward and artificial desires, false criticisms, effeminate habits of thinking and feeling, or who having known these things have outgrown them. This latter class is the most to be depended upon, but it is very small in number. People in our rank in life are perpetually falling into one sad mistake, namely, that of supposing that human nature and the persons they associate with are one and the same thing. Whom do we generally associate with? Gentlemen, persons of fortune, professional men, ladies, persons who can afford to buy, or can easily procure books of half-a-guinea price, hot-pressed, and printed upon superfine paper. These persons are, it is true, a part of human nature, but we err lamentably if we suppose them to be fair representatives of the vast mass of human existence. And yet few ever consider books but with reference to their power of pleasing these persons and men of a higher rank; few descend lower, among cottages and fields, and among children. A man must have done this habitually before his judgment upon "The Idiot Boy" would be in any way decisive with me. I *know* I have done this myself habitually; I wrote the poem with exceeding delight and pleasure, and whenever I read it I read it with pleasure. You have given me praise for having reflected faithfully in my Poems the feelings of human nature. I would fain hope that I have done so. But a great Poet ought to do more than this; he ought, to a certain degree, to rectify men's feelings, to give them new compositions of feeling, to render their feelings more sane, pure, and permanent, in short, more consonant to nature, that is, to eternal nature, and the great moving spirit of things. He ought to travel before men occasionally as well as at their sides. I may illustrate this by a reference to natural objects. What false notions have prevailed from generation to generation of the true character of the Nightingale. As far as my Friend's Poem, in the *Lyrical Ballads*, is read, it will contribute greatly to rectify these. You will recollect a passage in Cowper, where, speaking of rural sounds, he says,

And *even* the boding Owl
That hails the rising moon has charms for me.

Cowper was passionately fond of natural objects, yet you see he mentions it as a marvellous thing that he could connect pleasure with the cry of the owl. In the same poem he speaks in the same manner of that beautiful plant, the gorse; making in some degree an amiable boast of his loving it *unsightly* and unsmooth as it is. There are many aversions of this kind, which, though they have some foundation in nature, have yet so slight a one, that, though they may have prevailed hundreds of years, a philosopher will look upon them as accidents. So with respect to many moral feelings, either of love or dislike. What excessive admiration was paid in former times to personal prowess and military success; it is so with the latter even at the present day, but surely not nearly so much as heretofore. So with regard to birth, and innumerable other modes of sentiment, civil and religious. But you will be inclined to ask by this time how all this applies to "The Idiot Boy." To this I can only say that the loathing and disgust which many people have at the sight of an idiot, is a feeling which, though having some foundation in human nature, is not necessarily attached to it in any virtuous degree, but is owing in a great measure to a false delicacy, and, if I may say it without rudeness, a certain want of comprehensiveness of thinking and feeling. Persons in the lower classes of society have little or nothing of this: if an idiot is born in a poor man's house, it must be taken care of, and cannot be boarded out, as it would be by gentlefolks, or sent to a public or private receptacle for such unfortunate beings. [Poor people] seeing frequently among their neighbours such objects, easily [forget] whatever there is of natural disgust about them, and have [therefore] a sane state, so that without pain or suffering they [perform] their duties towards them. I could with pleasure pursue this subject, but I must now strictly adopt the plan which I proposed to myself when I began to write this letter, namely, that of setting down a few hints or memorandums, which you will think of for my sake.

I have often applied to idiots, in my own mind, that sublime expression of scripture that *their life is hidden with God.* They are worshipped, probably from a feeling of this sort, in several parts of the East. Among the Alps, where they are numerous, they are considered, I believe, as a blessing to the family to which they belong. I have, indeed, often looked upon the conduct of fathers and mothers of the lower classes of society towards idiots as the great triumph of the human heart. It is there that we see the strength, disinterestedness, and grandeur of love; nor have I ever been able to contemplate an object that calls out so many excellent and virtuous sentiments without finding it hallowed thereby, and having something in me which bears down before it, like a deluge, every feeble sensation of disgust and aversion.

There are, in my opinion, several important mistakes in the latter part of your letter which I could have wished to notice; but I find myself much fatigued. These refer both to the Boy and the Mother. I must content myself simply with observing that it is probable that the principal cause of your dislike to this particular poem lies in the *word* Idiot. If there had been any such word in our language, *to which we had attached passion,* as lack-wit, half-wit, witless, &c., I should have certainly employed it in preference; but there is no such word. Observe (this is entirely in reference to this particular poem), my *Idiot* is not one of those who cannot articulate, and such as are usually disgusting in their persons:

Whether in cunning or in joy,
And then his words were not a few, &c.

and the last speech at the end of the poem. The *Boy* whom I had in my mind was by no means disgusting in his appearance, quite the contrary; and I have known several with imperfect faculties, who are handsome in their persons and features. There is one, at present, within a mile of my own house, remarkably so, though [he has something] of a stare and vacancy in his countenance. A friend of mine, knowing that some persons had a dislike to the poem, such as you have expressed, advised me to add a stanza, describing the person of the Boy [so as] entirely to separate him in the imaginations of my readers from that class of idiots who are disgusting in their persons; but the narration in the poem is so rapid and impassioned, that I could not find a place in which to insert the stanza without checking the progress of it, and [so leaving] a deadness upon the feeling. This poem has, I know, frequently produced the same effect as it did upon you and your friends; but there are many also to whom it affords exquisite delight, and who, indeed, prefer it to any other of my poems. This proves that the feelings there delineated are such as men *may* sympathize with. This is enough for my purpose. It is not enough for me as a Poet, to delineate merely such feelings as all men *do* sympathize with; but it is also highly desirable to add to these others, such as all men *may* sympathize with, and such as there is reason to believe they would be better and more moral beings if they did sympathize with.

I conclude with regret, because I have not said one half of [what I intended] to say; but I am sure you will deem my excuse sufficient, [when I] inform you that my head aches violently, and I am in other respects unwell. I must, however, again give you my warmest thanks for your kind letter. I shall be happy to hear from you again: and do not think it unreasonable that I should request a letter from you, when I feel that the answer which I may make to it will not perhaps be above three or four lines. This I mention to you with frankness, and you will not take it ill after what I have before said of my remissness in writing letters.

I am, dear Sir, with great respect, yours sincerely,

W. WORDSWORTH.
1800

PREFACE

TO THE SECOND EDITION OF SEVERAL OF THE FORE-
GOING POEMS, PUBLISHED, WITH AN ADDITIONAL
VOLUME, UNDER THE TITLE OF "LYRICAL BAL-
LADS"

Note.—In succeeding Editions, when the Collection was much enlarged and diversified, this Preface was transferred to the end of the Volumes as having little of a special application to their contents.

The first Volume of these Poems has already been submitted to general perusal. It was published as an experiment, which, I hoped, might be of some use to ascertain how far, by fitting to metrical arrangement a selection of the real language of men in a state of vivid sensation, that sort of pleasure and that quantity of pleasure may be imparted, which a Poet may rationally endeavour to impart.

I had formed no very inaccurate estimate of the probable effect of those Poems: I flattered myself that they who should be pleased with them would read them with more than common pleasure: and, on the other hand, I was well aware, that by those who should dislike them they would be read with more than common dislike. The result has differed from my expectation in this only, that a greater number have been pleased than I ventured to hope I should please.

.   .   .   .   .   .

Several of my Friends are anxious for the success of these Poems, from the belief that, if the views with which they were composed were indeed realised, a class of Poetry would be produced, well adapted to interest mankind permanently, and not unimportant in the quality and in the multiplicity of its moral relations: and on this account they have advised me to prefix a systematic defence of the theory upon which the Poems were written. But I was unwilling to undertake the task, knowing that on this occasion the Reader would look coldly upon my arguments, since I might be suspected of having been principally influenced by the selfish and foolish hope of *reasoning* him into an approbation of these particular Poems: and I was still more unwilling to undertake the task, because adequately to display the opinions, and fully to enforce the arguments, would require a space wholly disproportionate to a preface. For, to treat the subject with the clearness and coherence of which it is susceptible, it would be necessary to give a full account of the present state of the public taste in this country, and to determine how far this taste is healthy or depraved; which, again, could not be determined without pointing out in what manner language and the human mind act and re-act on each other, and without retracing the revolutions, not of literature alone, but likewise of society itself. I have therefore altogether declined to enter regularly upon this defence; yet I am sensible that there would be something like impropriety in abruptly obtruding upon the Public, without a few words of introduction, Poems so materially different from those upon which general approbation is at present bestowed.

It is supposed that by the act of writing in verse an Author makes a formal engagement that he will gratify certain known habits of association; that he not only thus apprises the Reader that certain classes of ideas and expressions will be found in his book, but that others will be carefully excluded. This exponent or symbol held forth by metrical language must in different eras of literature have excited very different expectations: for example, in the age of Catullus, Terence, and Lucretius, and that of Statius or Claudian; and in our own country, in the age of Shakspeare and Beaumont and Fletcher, and that of Donne and Cowley, or Dryden, or Pope. I will not take upon me to determine the exact import of the promise which, by the act of writing in verse, an Author in the present day makes to his reader; but it will undoubtedly appear to many persons that I have not fulfilled the terms of an engagement thus voluntarily contracted. They who have been accustomed to the gaudiness and inane phraseology of many modern writers, if they persist in reading this book to its conclusion, will, no doubt, frequently have to struggle with feelings of strangeness and awkwardness: they will look round for poetry, and will be induced to inquire by what species of courtesy these attempts can be permitted to assume that title. I hope, therefore, the reader will not censure me for attempting to state what I have proposed to myself to perform; and also (as far as the limits of a preface will permit) to explain some of the chief reasons which have determined me in the choice of my purpose: that at least he may be spared any unpleasant feeling of disappointment, and that I myself may be protected from one of the most dishonourable accusations which can be brought against an Author; namely, that of an indolence which prevents him from endeavouring to ascertain what is his duty, or, when his duty is ascertained, prevents him from performing it.

The principal object, then, proposed in these Poems, was to choose incidents and situations from common life, and to relate or describe them throughout, as far as was possible, in a selection of language really used by men, and, at the same time, to throw over them a certain colouring of imagination, whereby ordinary things should be presented to the mind in an unusual aspect; and further, and above all, to make these incidents and situations interesting by tracing in them, truly though not ostentatiously, the primary laws of our nature: chiefly, as far as regards the manner in which we associate ideas in a state of excitement. Humble and rustic life was generally chosen, because in that condition the essential passions of the heart find a better soil in which they can attain their maturity, are less under restraint, and speak a plainer and more emphatic language; because in that condition of life our elementary feelings co-exist in a state of greater simplicity, and, consequently, may be more accurately contemplated, and more forcibly communicated; because the manners of rural life germinate from those elementary feelings, and, from the necessary character of rural occupations, are more easily comprehended, and are more durable; and, lastly, because in that condition the passions of men are incorporated with the beautiful and permanent forms of nature. The language, too, of these men has been adopted (purified indeed from what appear to be its real defects, from all lasting and rational causes of dislike or disgust), because such men hourly communicate with the best objects from which the best part of language is originally derived; and because, from their rank in society and the sameness and narrow circle of their intercourse, being less under the influence of social vanity, they convey their feelings and notions in simple and unelaborated expressions. Accordingly, such a language, arising out of repeated experience and regular feelings, is a more permanent, and a far more philosophical language, than that which is frequently substituted for it by Poets, who think that they are conferring honour upon themselves and their art in proportion as they separate themselves from the sympathies of men, and indulge in arbitrary and capricious habits of expression, in order to furnish food for fickle tastes and fickle appetites of their own creation.[1]

I cannot, however, be insensible to the present outcry against the triviality and meanness, both of thought and language, which some of my contemporaries have occasionally introduced into their metrical compositions; and I acknowledge that this defect, where it exists, is more dishonourable to the Writer's own character than false refinement or arbitrary innovation, though I should contend at the same time that it is far less pernicious in the sum of its consequences. From such verses

[1] It is worth while here to observe that the affecting parts of Chaucer are almost always expressed in language pure and universally intelligible even to this day.

the Poems in these volumes will be found distinguished at least by one mark of difference, that each of them has a worthy *purpose*. Not that I always began to write with a distinct purpose formally conceived, but habits of meditation have, I trust, so prompted and regulated my feelings, that my descriptions of such objects as strongly excite those feelings will be found to carry along with them a *purpose*. If this opinion be erroneous, I can have little right to the name of a Poet. For all good poetry is the spontaneous overflow of powerful feelings: and though this be true, Poems to which any value can be attached were never produced on any variety of subjects but by a man who, being possessed of more than usual organic sensibility, had also thought long and deeply. For our continued influxes of feeling are modified and directed by our thoughts, which are indeed the representatives of all our past feelings; and as, by contemplating the relation of these general representatives to each other, we discover what is really important to men, so, by the repetition and continuance of this act, our feelings will be connected with important subjects, till at length, if we be originally possessed of much sensibility, such habits of mind will be produced that, by obeying blindly and mechanically the impulses of those habits, we shall describe objects, and utter sentiments, of such a nature, and in such connection with each other, that the understanding of the Reader must necessarily be in some degree enlightened, and his affections strengthened and purified.

It has been said that each of these Poems has a purpose. Another circumstance must be mentioned which distinguishes these Poems from the popular Poetry of the day; it is this, that the feeling therein developed gives importance to the action and situation, and not the action and situation to the feeling.

A sense of false modesty shall not prevent me from asserting that the Reader's attention is pointed to this mark of distinction, far less for the sake of these particular Poems than from the general importance of the subject. The subject is indeed important! For the human mind is capable of being excited without the application of gross and violent stimulants; and he must have a very faint perception of its beauty and dignity who does not know this, and who does not further know, that one being is elevated above another in proportion as

he possesses this capability. It has therefore appeared to me, that to endeavour to produce or enlarge this capability is one of the best services in which, at any period, a Writer can be engaged; but this service, excellent at all times, is especially so at the present day. For a multitude of causes, unknown to former times, are now acting with a combined force to blunt the discriminating powers of the mind, and, unfitting it for all voluntary exertion, to reduce it to a state of almost savage torpor. The most effective of these causes are the great national events which are daily taking place, and the increasing accumulation of men in cities, where the uniformity of their occupations produces a craving for extraordinary incident which the rapid communication of intelligence hourly gratifies. To this tendency of life and manners the literature and theatrical exhibitions of the country have conformed themselves. The invaluable works of our elder writers, I had almost said the works of Shakspeare and Milton, are driven into neglect by frantic novels, sickly and stupid German Tragedies, and deluges of idle and extravagant stories in verse.—When I think upon this degrading thirst after outrageous stimulation, I am almost ashamed to have spoken of the feeble endeavour made in these volumes to counteract it; and, reflecting upon the magnitude of the general evil, I should be oppressed with no dishonourable melancholy, had I not a deep impression of certain inherent and indestructible qualities of the human mind, and likewise of certain powers in the great and permanent objects that act upon it, which are equally inherent and indestructible; and were there not added to this impression a belief that the time is approaching when the evil will be systematically opposed by men of greater powers, and with far more distinguished success.

Having dwelt thus long on the subjects and aim of these Poems, I shall request the Reader's permission to apprise him of a few circumstances relating to their *style*, in order, among other reasons, that he may not censure me for not having performed what I never attempted. The Reader will find that personifications of abstract ideas rarely occur in these volumes, and are utterly rejected as an ordinary device to elevate the style and raise it above prose. My purpose was to imitate, and, as far as is possible, to adopt the very lan-

guage of men; and assuredly such personfica-
tions do not make any natural or regular part
of that language. They are, indeed, a figure of
speech occasionally prompted by passion, and
I have made use of them as such; but have
endeavoured utterly to reject them as a mechanical device of style, or as a family language which Writers in metre seem to lay
claim to by prescription. I have wished to
keep the Reader in the company of flesh and
blood, persuaded that by so doing I shall interest him. Others who pursue a different track
will interest him likewise; I do not interfere
with their claim, but wish to prefer a claim
of my own. There will also be found in these
volumes little of what is usually called poetic
diction; as much pains has been taken to avoid
it as is ordinarily taken to produce it; this has
been done for the reason already alleged, to
bring my language near to the language of men;
and further, because the pleasure which I have
proposed to myself to impart is of a kind very
different from that which is supposed by many
persons to be the proper object of poetry. Without being culpably particular, I do not know
how to give my Reader a more exact notion of
the style in which it was my wish and intention to write, than by informing him that I
have at all times endeavoured to look steadily at my subject; consequently there is, I
hope, in these Poems little falsehood of description, and my ideas are expressed in language fitted to their respective importance.
Something must have been gained by this practice, as it is friendly to one property of all
good poetry, namely, good sense: but it has
necessarily cut me off from a large portion
of phrases and figures of speech which from
father to son have long been regarded as the
common inheritance of Poets. I have also
thought it expedient to restrict myself still
further, having abstained from the use of
many expressions, in themselves proper and
beautiful, but which have been foolishly repeated by bad Poets, till such feelings of disgust are connected with them as it is scarcely
possible by any art of association to over-
power.

If in a poem there should be found a series
of lines, or even a single line, in which the
language, though naturally arranged, and according to the strict laws of metre, does not
differ from that of prose, there is a numerous
class of critics, who, when they stumble upon

these prosaisms, as they call them, imagine
that they have made a notable discovery, and
exult over the Poet as over a man ignorant of
his own profession. Now these men would
establish a canon of criticism which the Reader
will conclude he must utterly reject, if he
wishes to be pleased with these volumes. And
it would be a most easy task to prove to him
that not only the language of a large portion
of every good poem, even of the most elevated character, must necessarily, except with
reference to the metre, in no respect differ from
that of good prose, but likewise that some of
the most interesting parts of the best poems
will be found to be strictly the language of
prose when prose is well written. The truth of
this assertion might be demonstrated by innumerable passages from almost all the poetical
writings, even of Milton himself. To illustrate
the subject in a general manner, I will here
adduce a short composition of Gray, who was
at the head of those who, by their reasonings,
have attempted to widen the space of separation betwixt Prose and Metrical composition,
and was more than any other man curiously
elaborate in the structure of his own poetic
diction.

> In vain to me the smiling mornings shine,
> And reddening Phœbus lifts his golden fire;
> The birds in vain their amorous descant join,
> Or cheerful fields resume their green attire.
> These ears, alas! for other notes repine;
> *A different object do these eyes require;*
> *My lonely anguish melts no heart but mine;*
> *And in my breast the imperfect joys expire;*
> Yet morning smiles the busy race to cheer,
> And new-born pleasure brings to happier men;
> The fields to all their wonted tribute bear;
> To warm their little loves the birds complain.
> *I fruitless mourn to him that cannot hear,*
> *And weep the more because I weep in vain.*

It will easily be perceived, that the only part
of this Sonnet which is of any value is the
lines printed in Italics; it is equally obvious
that, except in the rhyme and in the use of the
single word "fruitless" for fruitlessly, which is
so far a defect, the language of these lines does
in no respect differ from that of prose.

By the foregoing quotation it has been shown
that the language of Prose may yet be well
adapted to Poetry; and it was previously asserted that a large portion of the language of
every good poem can in no respect differ from
that of good Prose. We will go further. It may
be safely affirmed that there neither is, nor can

be, any *essential* difference between the language of prose and metrical composition. We are fond of tracing the resemblance between Poetry and Painting, and, accordingly, we call them Sisters: but where shall we find bonds of connection sufficiently strict to typify the affinity betwixt metrical and prose composition? They both speak by and to the same organs; the bodies in which both of them are clothed may be said to be of the same substance, their affections are kindred, and almost identical, not necessarily differing even in degree; Poetry [1] sheds no tears "such as Angels weep," but natural and human tears; she can boast of no celestial ichor that distinguishes her vital juices from those of Prose; the same human blood circulates through the veins of them both.

If it be affirmed that rhyme and metrical arrangement of themselves constitute a distinction which overturns what has just been said on the strict affinity of metrical language with that of Prose, and paves the way for other artificial distinctions which the mind voluntarily admits, I answer that the language of such Poetry as is here recommended is, as far as is possible, a selection of the language really spoken by men; that this selection, wherever it is made with true taste and feeling, will of itself form a distinction far greater than would at first be imagined, and will entirely separate the composition from the vulgarity and meanness of ordinary life; and, if metre be superadded thereto, I believe that a dissimilitude will be produced altogether sufficient for the gratification of a rational mind. What other distinction would we have? Whence is it to come? And where is it to exist? Not, surely, where the Poet speaks through the mouths of his characters: it cannot be necessary here, either for elevation of style, or any of its supposed ornaments; for, if the Poet's subject be judiciously chosen, it will naturally, and upon fit occasion, lead him to passions, the language of which, if selected truly and judiciously, must

[1] I here use the word "Poetry" (though against my own judgment) as opposed to the word Prose, and synonymous with metrical composition. But much confusion has been introduced into criticism by this contradistinction of Poetry and Prose, instead of the more philosophical one of Poetry and Matter of Fact, or Science. The only strict antithesis to Prose is Metre; nor is this, in truth, a *strict* antithesis, because lines and passages of metre so naturally occur in writing prose, that it would be scarcely possible to avoid them, even were it desirable.

necessarily be dignified and variegated, and alive with metaphors and figures. I forbear to speak of an incongruity which would shock the intelligent Reader, should the Poet interweave any foreign splendour of his own with that which the passion naturally suggests: it is sufficient to say that such addition is unnecessary. And, surely, it is more probable that those passages, which with propriety abound with metaphors and figures, will have their due effect if, upon other occasions where the passions are of a milder character, the style also be subdued and temperate.

But, as the pleasure which I hope to give by the Poems now presented to the Reader must depend entirely on just notions upon this subject, and as it is in itself of high importance to our taste and moral feelings, I cannot content myself with these detached remarks. And if, in what I am about to say, it shall appear to some that my labour is unnecessary, and that I am like a man fighting a battle without enemies, such persons may be reminded that, whatever be the language outwardly holden by men, a practical faith in the opinions which I am wishing to establish is almost unknown. If my conclusions are admitted, and carried as far as they must be carried if admitted at all, our judgments concerning the works of the greatest Poets, both ancient and modern, will be far different from what they are at present, both when we praise and when we censure: and our moral feelings influencing and influenced by these judgments will, I believe, be corrected and purified.

Taking up the subject, then, upon general grounds, let me ask, what is meant by the word Poet? What is a Poet? To whom does he address himself? And what language is to be expected from him?—He is a man speaking to men: a man, it is true, endowed with more lively sensibility, more enthusiasm and tenderness, who has a greater knowledge of human nature, and a more comprehensive soul, than are supposed to be common among mankind; a man pleased with his own passions and volitions, and who rejoices more than other men in the spirit of life that is in him; delighting to contemplate similar volitions and passions as manifested in the goings-on of the Universe, and habitually impelled to create them where he does not find them. To these qualities he has added a disposition to be affected more than other men by absent things as if they were present; an ability of conjuring up in himself passions, which are indeed far from being the same as those produced by real events, yet (especially in those parts of the general sympathy which are pleasing and delightful) do more nearly resemble the passions produced by real events than anything which, from the motions of their own minds merely, other men are accustomed to feel in themselves:—whence, and from practice, he has acquired a greater readiness and power in expressing what he thinks and feels, and especially those thoughts and feelings which, by his own choice, or from the structure of his own mind, arise in him without immediate external excitement.

But whatever portion of this faculty we may suppose even the greatest Poet to possess, there cannot be a doubt that the language which it will suggest to him must often, in liveliness and truth, fall short of that which is uttered by men in real life under the actual pressure of those passions, certain shadows of which the Poet thus produces, or feels to be produced, in himself.

However exalted a notion we would wish to cherish of the character of a Poet, it is obvious that, while he describes and imitates passions, his employment is in some degree mechanical compared with the freedom and power of real and substantial action and suffering. So that it will be the wish of the Poet to bring his feelings near to those of the persons whose feelings he describes, nay, for short spaces of time, perhaps, to let himself slip into an entire delusion, and even confound and identify his own feelings with theirs; modifying only the language which is thus suggested to him by a consideration that he describes for a particular purpose, that of giving pleasure. Here, then, he will apply the principle of selection which has been already insisted upon. He will depend upon this for removing what would otherwise be painful or disgusting in the passion; he will feel that there is no necessity to trick out or to elevate nature: and the more industriously he applies this principle the deeper will be his faith that no words, which *his* fancy or imagination can suggest, will be to be compared with those which are the emanations of reality and truth.

But it may be said by those who do not object to the general spirit of these remarks, that, as it is impossible for the Poet to produce upon all occasions language as exquisitely fitted for the passion as that which the real passion itself suggests, it is proper that he should consider himself as in the situation of a translator, who does not scruple to substitute excellences of another kind for those which are unattainable by him; and endeavours occasionally to surpass his original, in order to make some amends for the general inferiority to which he feels that he must submit. But this would be to encourage idleness and unmanly despair. Further, it is the language of men who speak of what they do not understand; who talk of Poetry, as of a matter of amusement and idle pleasure; who will converse with us as gravely about a *taste* for Poetry, as they express it, as if it were a thing as indifferent as a taste for rope-dancing, or Frontiniac or Sherry. Aristotle, I have been told, has said, that Poetry is the most philosophic of all writing: it is so: its object is truth, not individual and local, but general and operative; not standing upon external testimony, but carried alive into the heart by passion; truth which is its own testimony, which gives competence and confidence to the tribunal to which it appeals, and receives them from the same tribunal. Poetry is the image of man and nature. The obstacles which stand in the way of the fidelity of the Biographer and Historian, and of their consequent utility, are incalculably greater than those which are to be encountered by the Poet who comprehends the dignity of his art. The Poet writes under one restriction only, namely, the necessity of giving immediate pleasure to a human Being possessed of that information which may be expected from him, not as a lawyer, a physician, a mariner, an astronomer, or a natural philosopher, but as a Man. Except this one restriction, there is no object standing between the Poet and the image of things; between this, and the Biographer and Historian, there are a thousand.

Nor let this necessity of producing immediate pleasure be considered as a degradation of the Poet's art. It is far otherwise. It is an acknowledgment of the beauty of the universe, an acknowledgment the more sincere because not formal, but indirect; it is a task light and easy to him who looks at the world in the spirit of love: further, it is a homage paid to the native and naked dignity of man, to the grand elementary principle of pleasure, by which he knows, and feels, and lives, and moves. We have no sympathy but what is propagated by pleasure: I would not be misunderstood; but wherever we sympathise with pain, it will be found that the sympathy is produced and carried on by subtle combinations with pleasure. We have no knowledge, that is, no general principles drawn from the contemplation of particular facts, but what has been built up by pleasure, and exists in us by pleasure alone. The Man of science, the Chemist and Mathematician, whatever difficulties and disgusts they may have had to struggle with, know and feel this. However painful may be the objects with which the Anatomist's knowledge is connected, he feels that his knowledge is pleasure; and where he has no pleasure he has no knowledge. What then does the Poet? He considers man and the objects that surround him as acting and re-acting upon each other, so as to produce an infinite complexity of pain and pleasure; he considers man in his own nature and in his ordinary life as contemplating this with a certain quantity of immediate knowledge, with certain convictions, intuitions, and deductions, which from habit acquire the quality of intuitions; he considers him as looking upon this complex scene of ideas and sensations, and finding everywhere objects that immediately excite in him sympathies which, from the necessities of his nature, are accompanied by an overbalance of enjoyment.

To this knowledge which all men carry about with them, and to these sympathies in which, without any other discipline than that of our daily life, we are fitted to take delight, the Poet principally directs his attention. He considers man and nature as essentially adapted to each other, and the mind of man as naturally the mirror of the fairest and most interesting properties of nature. And thus the Poet, prompted by this feeling of pleasure, which accompanies him through the whole course of his studies, converses with general nature, with affections akin to those which, through labour and length of time, the Man of science has raised up in himself, by conversing with those particular parts of nature which are the objects of his studies. The knowledge both of the Poet and the Man of science is pleasure; but the knowledge of the one cleaves to us as a necessary part of our existence, our natural and unalienable inheritance; the other is a personal and individual acquisition, slow to come to us, and by no habitual and direct sympathy connecting us with our fellow-beings. The Man of science seeks truth as a remote and unknown benefactor; he cherishes and loves it in his solitude: the Poet, singing a song in which all human beings join with him, rejoices in the presence of truth as our visible friend and hourly companion. Poetry is the breath and finer spirit of all knowledge; it is the impassioned expression which is in the countenance of all Science. Emphatically may it be said of the Poet, as Shakspeare hath said of man, "that he looks before and after." He is the rock of defence for human nature; an upholder and preserver, carrying everywhere with him relationship and love. In spite of difference of soil and climate, of language and manners, of laws and customs: in spite of things silently gone out of mind, and things violently destroyed; the Poet binds together by passion and knowledge the vast empire of human society, as it is spread over the whole earth and over all time. The objects of the Poet's thoughts are everywhere; though the eyes and senses of man are, it is true, his favourite guides, yet he will follow wheresoever he can find an atmosphere of sensation in which to move his wings. Poetry is the first and last of all knowledge—it is as immortal as the heart of man. If the labours of Men of science should ever create any material revolution, direct or indirect, in our condition, and in the impressions which we habitually receive, the Poet will sleep then no more than at present; he will be ready to follow the steps of the Man of science, not only in those general indirect effects, but he will be at his side, carrying sensation into the midst of the objects of the science itself. The remotest discoveries of the Chemist, the Botanist, or Mineralogist, will be as proper objects of the Poet's art as any upon which it can be employed, if the time should ever come when these things shall be familiar to us, and the relations under which they are contemplated by the followers of these respective sciences shall be manifestly and palpably material to us as enjoying and suffering beings. If the time should ever come when what is now called science, thus familiarised to men, shall be ready to put on, as it were, a form of flesh and blood, the Poet will lend his divine spirit to aid the transfiguration, and will welcome the Being thus produced as a dear and genuine inmate of the household of man.—It is not, then, to be supposed that any one, who holds that sublime notion of Poetry which I have attempted to convey, will break in upon the sanctity and truth of his pictures by transitory and accidental ornaments, and endeavour to excite admiration of himself by arts, the necessity of which must manifestly depend upon the assumed meanness of his subject.

What has been thus far said applies to Poetry in general, but especially to those parts of compositions where the Poet speaks through the mouths of his characters; and upon this point it appears to authorise the conclusion that there are few persons of good sense who would not allow that the dramatic parts of composition are defective in proportion as they deviate from the real language of nature, and are coloured by a diction of the Poet's own, either peculiar to him as an individual Poet or belonging simply to Poets in general; to a body of men who, from the circumstance of their compositions being in metre, it is expected will employ a particular language.

It is not, then, in the dramatic parts of composition that we look for this distinction of language; but still it may be proper and necessary where the Poet speaks to us in his own person and character. To this I answer by referring the Reader to the description before given of a Poet. Among the qualities there enumerated as principally conducing to form a Poet, is implied nothing differing in kind from other men, but only in degree. The sum of what was said is, that the Poet is chiefly distinguished from other men by a greater promptness to think and feel without immediate external excitement, and a greater power in expressing such thoughts and feelings as are produced in him in that manner. But these passions and thoughts and feelings are the general passions and thoughts and feelings of men. And with what are they connected? Undoubtedly with our moral sentiments and animal sensations, and with the causes which excite these; with the operations of the elements, and the appearances of the visible universe; with storm and sunshine, with the revolutions of the seasons, with cold and heat, with loss of friends and kindred, with injuries and resentments, gratitude and hope, with fear and sorrow. These, and the like, are the sensations and objects which the Poet describes, as they are the sensations of other men and the objects which interest them. The Poet thinks and feels in the spirit of human passions. How, then, can his language differ in any material degree from that of all other men who feel vividly and see clearly? It might be *proved* that it is impossible. But supposing that this were not the case, the Poet might then be allowed to use a peculiar language when expressing his feelings for his own gratification, or that of men like himself. But Poets do not write for Poets alone, but for men. Unless, therefore, we are advocates for that admiration which subsists upon ignorance, and that pleasure which arises from hearing what we do not understand, the Poet must descend from this supposed height; and, in order to excite rational sympathy, he must express himself as other men express themselves. To this it may be added, that while he is only selecting from the real language of men, or, which amounts to the same thing, composing accurately in the spirit of such selection, he is treading upon safe ground, and we know what we are to expect from him. Our feelings are the same with respect to metre; for, as it may be proper to remind the Reader, the distinction of metre is regular and uniform, and not, like that which is produced by what is usually called POETIC DICTION, arbitrary, and subject to infinite caprices, upon which no calculation whatever can be made. In the one case, the Reader is utterly at the mercy of the Poet, respecting what imagery or diction he may choose to connect with the passion; whereas, in the other, the metre obeys certain laws, to which the Poet and Reader both willingly submit because they are certain, and because no interference is made by them with the passion but such as the concurring testimony of ages has shown to heighten and improve the pleasure which co-exists with it.

It will now be proper to answer an obvious question, namely, Why, professing these opinions, have I written in verse? To this, in addition to such answer as is included in what has been already said, I reply, in the first place, Because, however I may have restricted myself, there is still left open to me what confessedly constitutes the most valuable object of all writing, whether in prose or verse; the great and universal passions of men, the most general and interesting of their occupations, and the entire world of nature before me—

to supply endless combinations of forms and imagery. Now, supposing for a moment that whatever is interesting in these objects may be as vividly described in prose, why should I be condemned for attempting to superadd to such description the charm which, by the consent of all nations, is acknowledged to exist in metrical language? To this, by such as are yet unconvinced, it may be answered that a very small part of the pleasure given by Poetry depends upon the metre, and that it is injudicious to write in metre, unless it be accompanied with the other artificial distinctions of style with which metre is usually accompanied, and that, by such deviation, more will be lost from the shock which will thereby be given to the Reader's associations than will be counterbalanced by any pleasure which he can derive from the general power of numbers. In answer to those who still contend for the necessity of accompanying metre with certain appropriate colours of style in order to the accomplishment of its appropriate end, and who also, in my opinion, greatly under-rate the power of metre in itself, it might, perhaps, as far as relates to these Volumes, have been almost sufficient to observe, that poems are extant, written upon more humble subjects, and in a still more naked and simple style, which have continued to give pleasure from generation to generation. Now, if nakedness and simplicity be a defect, the fact here mentioned affords a strong presumption that poems somewhat less naked and simple are capable of affording pleasure at the present day; and, what I wished chiefly to attempt, at present, was to justify myself for having written under the impression of this belief.

But various causes might be pointed out why, when the style is manly, and the subject of some importance, words metrically arranged will long continue to impart such a pleasure to mankind as he who proves the extent of that pleasure will be desirous to impart. The end of poetry is to produce excitement in coexistence with an overbalance of pleasure; but, by the supposition, excitement is an unusual and irregular state of the mind; ideas and feelings do not, in that state, succeed each other in accustomed order. If the words, however, by which this excitement is produced be in themselves powerful, or the images and feelings have an undue proportion of pain connected with them, there is some danger that the excitement may be carried beyond its proper bounds. Now the co-presence of something regular, something to which the mind has been accustomed in various moods and in a less excited state, cannot but have great efficacy in tempering and restraining the passion by an intertexture of ordinary feeling, and of feeling not strictly and necessarily connected with the passion. This is unquestionably true; and hence, though the opinion will at first appear paradoxical, from the tendency of metre to divest language, in a certain degree, of its reality, and thus to throw a sort of half-consciousness of unsubstantial existence over the whole composition, there can be little doubt but that more pathetic situations and sentiments, that is, those which have a greater proportion of pain connected with them, may be endured in metrical composition, especially in rhyme, than in prose. The metre of the old ballads is very artless, yet they contain many passages which would illustrate this opinion; and, I hope, if the following poems be attentively perused, similar instances will be found in them. This opinion may be further illustrated by appealing to the Reader's own experience of the reluctance with which he comes to the reperusal of the distressful parts of *Clarissa Harlowe*, or the *Gamester;* while Shakspeare's writings, in the most pathetic scenes, never act upon us, as pathetic, beyond the bounds of pleasure—an effect which, in a much greater degree than might at first be imagined, is to be ascribed to small, but continual and regular impulses of pleasurable surprise from the metrical arrangement.—On the other hand (what it must be allowed will much more frequently happen), if the Poet's words should be incommensurate with the passion, and inadequate to raise the Reader to a height of desirable excitement, then (unless the Poet's choice of his metre has been grossly injudicious), in the feelings of pleasure which the Reader has been accustomed to connect with metre in general, and in the feeling, whether cheerful or melancholy, which he has been accustomed to connect with that particular movement of metre, there will be found something which will greatly contribute to impart passion to the words, and to effect the complex end which the Poet proposes to himself.

If I had undertaken a SYSTEMATIC defence of the theory here maintained, it would have been my duty to develop the various causes upon which the pleasure received from metrical language depends. Among the chief of these causes is to be reckoned a principle which must be well known to those who have made any of the Arts the object of accurate reflection; namely, the pleasure which the mind derives from the perception of similitude in dissimilitude. This principle is the great spring of the activity of our minds, and their chief feeder. From this principle the direction of the sexual appetite, and all the passions connected with it, take their origin: it is the life of our ordinary conversation; and upon the accuracy with which similitude in dissimilitude, and dissimilitude in similitude, are perceived, depend our taste and our moral feelings. It would not be a useless employment to apply this principle to the consideration of metre, and to show that metre is hence enabled to afford much pleasure, and to point out in what manner that pleasure is produced. But my limits will not permit me to enter upon this subject, and I must content myself with a general summary.

I have said that poetry is the spontaneous overflow of powerful feelings: it takes its origin from emotion recollected in tranquillity; the emotion is contemplated till, by a species of re-action, the tranquillity gradually disappears, and an emotion, kindered to that which was before the subject of contemplation, is gradually produced, and does itself actually exist in the mind. In this mood successful composition generally begins, and in a mood similar to this it is carried on; but the emotion, of whatever kind, and in whatever degree, from various causes, is qualified by various pleasures, so that in describing any passions whatsoever, which are voluntarily described, the mind will, upon the whole, be in a state of enjoyment. If Nature be thus cautious to preserve in a state of enjoyment a being so employed, the Poet ought to profit by the lesson held forth to him, and ought especially to take care that, whatever passions he communicates to his Reader, those passions, if his Reader's mind be sound and vigorous, should always be accompanied with an over-balance of pleasure. Now the music of harmonious metrical language, the sense of difficulty overcome, and the blind association of pleasure which has been previously received from works of rhyme or metre of the same or similar construction, an indistinct perception perpetually renewed of language closely resembling that of real life, and yet, in the circumstance of metre, differing from it so widely—all these imperceptibly make up a complex feeling of delight, which is of the most important use in tempering the painful feeling always found intermingled with powerful descriptions of the deeper passions. This effect is always produced in pathetic and impassioned poetry; while, in lighter compositions, the ease and gracefulness with which the Poet manages his numbers are themselves confessedly a principal source of the gratification of the Reader. All that it is *necessary* to say, however, upon this subject, may be effected by affirming, what few persons will deny, that of two descriptions, either of passions, manners, or characters, each of them equally well executed, the one in prose and the other in verse, the verse will be read a hundred times where the prose is read once.

Having thus explained a few of my reasons for writing in verse, and why I have chosen subjects from common life, and endeavoured to bring my language near to the real language of men, if I have been too minute in pleading my own cause, I have at the same time been treating a subject of general interest; and for this reason a few words shall be added with reference solely to these particular poems, and to some defects which will probably be found in them. I am sensible that my associations must have sometimes been particular instead of general, and that, consequently, giving to things a false importance, I may have sometimes written upon unworthy subjects; but I am less apprehensive on this account, than that my language may frequently have suffered from those arbitrary connections of feelings and ideas with particular words and phrases from which no man can altogether protect himself. Hence I have no doubt that, in some instances, feelings, even of the ludicrous, may be given to my Readers by expressions which appeared to me tender and pathetic. Such faulty expressions, were I convinced they were faulty at present, and that they must necessarily continue to be so, I would willingly take all reasonable pains to correct. But it is dangerous to make these alterations on the simple authority of a few individuals, or even of certain classes of men; for where the understanding of an author is not convinced, or his feelings altered, this cannot be done without great injury to himself: for his own feelings are his stay and support; and, if he set them aside in one instance, he may be induced to repeat this act till his mind shall lose all confidence in itself, and become utterly debilitated. To this it may be added, that the critic ought never to forget that he is himself exposed to the same errors as the Poet, and, perhaps, in a much greater degree: for there can be no presumption in saying of most readers, that it is not probable they will be so well acquainted with the various stages of meaning through which words have passed, or with the fickleness or stability of the relations of particular ideas to each other; and, above all, since they are so much less interested in the subject, they may decide lightly and carelessly.

Long as the reader has been detained, I hope he will permit me to caution him against a mode of false criticism which has been applied to poetry, in which the language closely resembles that of life and nature. Such verses have been triumphed over in parodies, of which Dr. Johnson's stanza is a fair specimen:—

> I put my hat upon my head
> And walked into the Strand,
> And there I met another man
> Whose hat was in his hand.

Immediately under these lines let us place one of the most justly-admired stanzas of the "Babes in the Wood."

> These pretty Babes with hand in hand
> Went wandering up and down;
> But never more they saw the Man
> Approaching from the Town.

In both these stanzas the words, and the order of the words, in no respect differ from the most unimpassioned conversation. There are words in both, for example, "the Strand," and "the Town," connected with none but the most familiar ideas; yet the one stanza we admit as admirable, and the other as a fair example of the superlatively contemptible. Whence arises this difference? Not from the metre, not from the language, not from the order of the words; but the *matter* expressed in Dr. Johnson's stanza is contemptible. The proper method of treating trivial and simple verses, to which Dr. Johnson's stanza would be a fair parallelism, is not to say, this is a bad kind of poetry, or, this is not poetry; but, this wants sense; it is neither interesting in itself,

nor can *lead* to anything interesting; the images neither originate in that sane state of feeling which arises out of thought, nor can excite thought or feeling in the Reader. This is the only sensible manner of dealing with such verses. Why trouble yourself about the species till you have previously decided upon the genus? Why take pains to prove that an ape is not a Newton, when it is self-evident that he is not a man?

One request I must make of my Reader, which is, that in judging these Poems he would decide by his own feelings genuinely, and not by reflection upon what will probably be the judgment of others. How common is it to hear a person say, I myself do not object to this style of composition, or this or that expression, but, to such and such classes of people it will appear mean or ludicrous! This mode of criticism, so destructive of all sound unadulterated judgment, is almost universal: let the Reader then abide, independently, by his own feelings, and, if he finds himself affected, let him not suffer such conjectures to interfere with his pleasure.

If an Author, by any single composition, has impressed us with respect for his talents, it is useful to consider this as affording a presumption that on other occasions where we have been displeased he, nevertheless, may not have written ill or absurdly; and further, to give him so much credit for this one composition as may induce us to review what has displeased us with more care than we should otherwise have bestowed upon it. This is not only an act of justice, but, in our decisions upon poetry especially, may conduce, in a high degree, to the improvement of our own taste: for an *accurate* taste in poetry, and in all the other arts, as Sir Joshua Reynolds has observed, is an *acquired* talent, which can only be produced by thought and a long-continued intercourse with the best models of composition. This is mentioned, not with so ridiculous a purpose as to prevent the most inexperienced Reader from judging for himself (I have already said that I wish him to judge for himself), but merely to temper the rashness of decision, and to suggest that, if Poetry be a subject on which much time has not been bestowed, the judgment may be erroneous; and that, in many cases, it necessarily will be so.

Nothing would, I know, have so effectually contributed to further the end which I have in view, as to have shown of what kind the pleasure is, and how that pleasure is produced, which is confessedly produced by metrical composition essentially different from that which I have here endeavoured to recommend: for the Reader will say that he has been pleased by such composition; and what more can be done for him? The power of any art is limited; and he will suspect that, if it be proposed to furnish him with new friends, that can be only upon condition of his abandoning his old friends. Besides, as I have said, the Reader is himself conscious of the pleasure which he has received from such composition, composition to which he has peculiarly attached the endearing name of Poetry; and all men feel an habitual gratitude, and something of an honourable bigotry, for the objects which have long continued to please them: we not only wish to be pleased, but to be pleased in that particular way in which we have been accustomed to be pleased. There is in these feelings enough to resist a host of arguments; and I should be the less able to combat them successfully, as I am willing to allow that, in order entirely to enjoy the Poetry which I am recommending, it would be necessary to give up much of what is ordinarily enjoyed. But would my limits have permitted me to point out how this pleasure is produced, many obstacles might have been removed, and the Reader assisted in perceiving that the powers of language are not so limited as he may suppose; and that it is possible for poetry to give other enjoyments, of a purer, more lasting, and more exquisite nature. This part of the subject has not been altogether neglected, but it has not been so much my present aim to prove, that the interest excited by some other kinds of poetry is less vivid, and less worthy of the nobler powers of the mind, as to offer reasons for presuming that if my purpose were fulfilled, a species of poetry would be produced which is genuine poetry; in its nature well adapted to interest mankind permanently, and likewise important in the multiplicity and quality of its moral relations.

From what has been said, and from a perusal of the Poems, the Reader will be able clearly to perceive the object which I had in view: he will determine how far it has been attained, and, what is a much more important question, whether it be worth attaining: and upon the decision of these two ques-

tions will rest my claim to the approbation of the Public.

1802

APPENDIX

1802

Perhaps, as I have no right to expect that attentive perusal, without which, confined, as I have been, to the narrow limits of a preface, my meaning cannot be thoroughly understood, I am anxious to give an exact notion of the sense in which the phrase poetic diction has been used; and for this purpose, a few words shall here be added, concerning the origin and characteristics of the phraseology which I have condemned under that name.

The earliest poets of all nations generally wrote from passion excited by real events; they wrote naturally, and as men: feeling powerfully as they did, their language was daring, and figurative. In succeeding times, Poets, and Men ambitious of the fame of Poets, perceiving the influence of such language, and desirous of producing the same effect without being animated by the same passion, set themselves to a mechanical adoption of these figures of speech, and made use of them, sometimes with propriety, but much more frequently applied them to feelings and thoughts with which they had no natural connection whatsoever. A language was thus insensibly produced, differing materially from the real language of men in *any situation*. The Reader or Hearer of this distorted language found himself in a perturbed and unusual state of mind: when affected by the genuine language of passion he had been in a perturbed and unusual state of mind also: in both cases he was willing that his common judgment and understanding should be laid asleep, and he had no instinctive and infallible perception of the true to make him reject the false; the one served as a passport for the other. The emotion was in both cases delightful, and no wonder if he confounded the one with the other, and believed them both to be produced by the same or similiar causes. Besides, the Poet spake to him in the character of a man to be looked up to, a man of genius and authority. Thus, and from a variety of other causes, this distorted language was received with admiration; and Poets, it is probable, who had before contented themselves for the most part with misapplying only expressions which at first had been dictated by real passion, carried the abuse still further, and introduced phrases composed apparently in the spirit of the original figurative language of passion, yet altogether of their own invention, and characterised by various degrees of wanton deviation from good sense and nature.

It is indeed true that the language of the earliest Poets was felt to differ materially from ordinary language, because it was the language of extraordinary occasions; but it was really spoken by men, language which the Poet himself had uttered when he had been affected by the events which he described, or which he had heard uttered by those around him. To this language it is probable that metre of some sort or other was early superadded. This separated the genuine language of Poetry still further from common life, so that whoever read or heard the poems of these earliest Poets felt himself moved in a way in which he had not been accustomed to be moved in real life, and by causes manifestly different from those which acted upon him in real life. This was the great temptation to all the corruptions which have followed: under the protection of this feeling succeeding Poets constructed a phraseology which had one thing, it is true, in common with the genuine language of poetry, namely, that it was not heard in ordinary conversation; that it was unusual. But the first Poets, as I have said, spake a language which, though unusual, was still the language of men. This circumstance, however, was disregarded by their successors; they found that they could please by easier means: they became proud of modes of expression which they themselves had invented, and which were uttered only by themselves. In process of time metre became a symbol or promise of this unusual language, and whoever took upon him to write in metre, according as he possessed more or less of true poetic genius, introduced less or more of this adulterated phraseology into his compositions, and the true and the false were inseparably interwoven until, the taste of men becoming gradually perverted, this language was received as a natural language, and at length, by the influence of books upon men, did to a certain degree really become so. Abuses of this kind were imported from one nation to another, and with the progress of refinement this diction became daily more and more corrupt, thrusting out of sight the plain humanities of nature by a motley masquerade of tricks, quaintnesses, hieroglyphics, and enigmas.

It would not be uninteresting to point out the causes of the pleasure given by this extravagant and absurd diction. It depends upon a great variety of causes, but upon none, perhaps, more than its influence in impressing a notion of the peculiarity and exaltation of the Poet's character, and in flattering the Reader's self-love by bringing him nearer to a sympathy with that character; an effect which is accomplished by unsettling ordinary habits of thinking, and thus assisting the Reader to approach to that perturbed and dizzy state of mind in which if he does not find himself, he imagines that he is *balked* of a peculiar enjoyment which poetry can and ought to bestow.

The sonnet quoted from Gray in the Preface, except the lines printed in Italics, consists of little else but this diction, though not of the worst kind; and indeed, if one may be permitted to say so, it is far too common in the best writers, both ancient and modern. Perhaps in no way, by positive example, could more easily be given a notion of what I mean by the phrase *poetic diction* than by referring to a comparison between the metrical paraphrase which we have of passages in the Old and New Testament, and those passages as they exist in our common Translation. See Pope's "Messiah" throughout; Prior's "Did sweeter sounds adorn my flowing tongue," etc. "Though I speak with the tongues of men and of angels," etc. 1st Corinthians, chap. xiii. By way of immediate example, take the following of Dr. Johnson:—

Turn on the prudent Ant thy heedless eyes,
Observe her labours, Sluggard, and be wise;
No stern command, no monitory voice,
Prescribes her duties, or directs her choice;
Yet, timely provident, she hastes away
To snatch the blessings of a plenteous day;
When fruitful Summer loads the teeming plain,
She crops the harvest, and she stores the grain.
How long shall sloth usurp thy useless hours,
Unnerve thy vigour, and enchain thy powers?
While artful shades thy downy couch enclose,
And soft solicitation courts repose,
Amidst the drowsy charms of dull delight,
Year chases year with unremitted flight,
Till Want now following, fraudulent and slow,
Shall spring to seize thee, like an ambush'd foe.

From this hubbub of words pass to the original. "Go to the ant, thou sluggard; consider her ways, and be wise: which having no guide, overseer, or ruler, provideth her meat in the summer, and gathereth her food in the harvest. How long wilt thou sleep, O sluggard? when wilt thou arise out of thy sleep? Yet a little sleep, a little slumber, a little folding of the hands to sleep: so shall thy poverty come as one that travelleth, and thy want as an armed man." Proverbs, chap. vi.

One more quotation, and I have done. It is from Cowper's Verses supposed to be written by Alexander Selkirk:—

> Religion! what treasure untold
> Resides in that heavenly word!
> More precious than silver and gold,
> Or all that this earth can afford.
> But the sound of the church-going bell
> These valleys and rocks never heard,
> Ne'er sighed at the sound of a knell,
> Or smiled when a sabbath appeared.
>
> Ye winds, that have made me your sport,
> Convey to this desolate shore
> Some cordial endearing report
> Of a land I must visit no more.
> My Friends, do they now and then send
> A wish or a thought after me?
> O tell me I yet have a friend,
> Though a friend I am never to see.

This passage is quoted as an instance of three different styles of composition. The first four lines are poorly expressed; some Critics would call the language prosaic; the fact is, it would be bad prose, so bad, that it is scarcely worse in metre. The epithet "church-going" applied to a bell, and that by so chaste a writer as Cowper, is an instance of the strange abuses which Poets have introduced into their language, till they and their Readers take them as matters of course, if they do not single them out expressly as objects of admiration. The two lines "Ne'er sighed at the sound," etc., are, in my opinion, an instance of the language of passion wrested from its proper use, and, from the mere circumstance of the composition being in metre, applied upon an occasion that does not justify such violent expressions; and I should condemn the passage, though perhaps few Readers will agree with me, as vicious poetic diction. The last stanza is throughout admirably expressed: it would be equally good whether in prose or verse, except that the Reader has an exquisite pleasure in seeing such natural language so naturally connected with metre. The beauty of this stanza tempts me to conclude with a principle which ought never to be lost

sight of, and which has been my chief guide in all I have said,—namely, that in works of *imagination and sentiment,* for of these only have I been treating, in proportion as ideas and feelings are valuable, whether the composition be in prose or in verse, they require and exact one and the same language. Metre is but adventitious to composition, and the phraseology for which that passport is necessary, even where it may be graceful at all, will be little valued by the judicious.

LETTER TO LADY BEAUMONT

Coleorton, May 21, 1807.

My Dear Lady Beaumont,

Though I am to see you so soon, I cannot but write a word or two, to thank you for the interest you take in my poems, as evinced by your solicitude about their immediate reception. I write partly to thank you for this, and to express the pleasure it has given me, and partly to remove any uneasiness from your mind which the disappointments you sometimes meet with, in this labour of love, may occasion. I see that you have many battles to fight for me,—more than, in the ardour and confidence of your pure and elevated mind, you had ever thought of being summoned to; but be assured that this opposition is nothing more than what I distinctly foresaw that you and my other friends would have to encounter. I say this, not to give myself credit for an eye of prophecy, but to allay any vexatious thoughts on my account which this opposition may have produced in you.

It is impossible that any expectations can be lower than mine concerning the immediate effect of this little work upon what is called the public. I do not here take into consideration the envy and malevolence, and all the bad passions which always stand in the way of a work of any merit from a living poet; but merely think of the pure, absolute, honest ignorance in which all worldlings of every rank and situation must be enveloped, with respect to the thoughts, feelings, and images, on which the life of my poems depends. The things which I have taken, whether from within or without, what have they to do with routs, dinners, morning calls, hurry from door to door, from street to street, on foot or in carriage; with Mr. Pitt or Mr. Fox, Mr. Paul or Sir Francis Burdett, the Westminster election or the borough of Honiton? In a word—for I cannot stop to make my way through the hurry of images that present themselves to me—what have they to do with endless talking about things nobody cares anything for except as far as their own vanity is concerned, and this with persons they care nothing for but as their vanity or *selfishness* is concerned?—what have they to do (to say all at once) with a life without love? In such a life there can be no thought; for we have no thought (save thoughts of pain) but as far as we have love and admiration.

It is an awful truth, that there neither is, nor can be, any genuine enjoyment of poetry among nineteen out of twenty of those persons who live, or wish to live, in the broad light of the world—among those who either are, or are striving to make themselves, people of consideration in society. This is a truth, and an awful one, because to be incapable of a feeling of poetry, in my sense of the word, is to be without love of human nature and reverence for God.

Upon this I shall insist elsewhere; at present let me confine myself to my object, which is to make you, my dear friend, as easy-hearted as myself with respect to these poems. Trouble not yourself upon their present reception; of what moment is that compared with what I trust is their destiny?—to console the afflicted; to add sunshine to daylight, by making the happy happier; to teach the young and the gracious of every age to see, to think, and feel, and, therefore, to become more actively and securely virtuous; this is their office, which I trust they will faithfully perform, long after we (that is, all that is mortal of us) are mouldered in our graves. I am well aware how far it would seem to many I overrate my own exertions, when I speak in this way, in direct connexion with the volume I have just made public.

I am not, however, afraid of such censure, insignificant as probably the majority of those poems would appear to very respectable persons. I do not mean London wits and witlings, for these have too many foul passions about them to be respectable, even if they had more intellect than the benign laws of Providence will allow to such a heartless existence as theirs is; but grave, kindly-natured, worthy persons, who would be pleased if they could. I hope that these volumes are not without

some recommendations, even for readers of this class: but their imagination has slept; and the voice which is the voice of my poetry, without imagination, cannot be heard. Leaving these, I was going to say a word to such readers as Mr. ——. Such!—how would he be offended if he knew I considered him only as a representative of a class, and not an unique! "Pity," says Mr. —— "that so many trifling things should be admitted to obstruct the view of those that have merit." Now, let this candid judge take, by way of example, the sonnets, which, probably, with the exception of two or three other poems, for which I will not contend, appear to him the most trifling, as they are the shortest. I would say to him, omitting things of higher consideration, there is one thing which must strike you at once, if you will only read these poems,—that those "to Liberty," at least, have a connexion with, or a bearing upon, each other; and, therefore, if individually they want weight, perhaps, as a body, they may not be so deficient. At least, this ought to induce you to suspend your judgment, and qualify it so far as to allow that the writer aims at least at comprehensiveness.

But, dropping this, I would boldly say at once, that these sonnets, while they each fix the attention upon some important sentiment, separately considered, do, at the same time, collectively make a poem on the subject of civil liberty and national independence, which, either for simplicity of style or grandeur of moral sentiment, is, alas! likely to have few parallels in the poetry of the present day. Again, turn to the "Moods of my own Mind." There is scarcely a poem here of above thirty lines, and very trifling these poems will appear to many; but, omitting to speak of them individually, do they not, taken collectively, fix the attention upon a subject eminently poetical, viz., the interest which objects in nature derive from the predominance of certain affections, more or less permanent, more or less capable of salutary renewal in the mind of the being contemplating these objects? This is poetic, and essentially poetic. And why? Because it is creative.

But I am wasting words, for it is nothing more than you know; and if said to those for whom it is intended, it would not be understood.

I see by your last letter, that Mrs. Fermor has entered into the spirit of these "Moods of my own Mind." Your transcript from her letter gave me the greatest pleasure; but I must say that even she has something yet to receive from me. I say this with confidence, from her thinking that I have fallen below myself in the sonnet, beginning,

With ships the sea was sprinkled far and nigh.

As to the other which she objects to, I will only observe, that there is a misprint in the last line but two,

And *though* this wilderness

for

And *through* this wilderness,

that makes it unintelligible. This latter sonnet, for many reasons (though I do not abandon it), I will not now speak of; but upon the other, I could say something important in conversation, and will attempt now to illustrate it by a comment, which, I feel, will be inadequate to convey my meaning. There is scarcely one of my poems which does not aim to direct the attention to some moral sentiment, or to some general principle, or law of thought, or of our intellectual constitution. For instance, in the present case, who is there that has not felt that the mind can have no rest among a multitude of objects, of which it either cannot make one whole, or from which it cannot single out one individual whereupon may be concentrated the attention, divided among or distracted by a multitude? After a certain time, we must either select one image or object, which must put out of view the rest wholly, or must subordinate them to itself while it stands forth as a head:

How glowed the firmament
With living sapphires! Hesperus, that *led*
The starry host, rode brightest; till the moon,
Rising in clouded majesty, at length,
Apparent *Queen,* unveiled *her peerless* light,
And o'er the dark her silver mantle threw.

Having laid this down as a general principle, take the case before us. I am represented in the sonnet as casting my eyes over the sea, sprinkled with a multitude of ships, like the heavens with stars. My mind may be supposed to float up and down among them, in a kind of dreamy indifference with respect either to this or that one, only in a pleasurable state of feeling with respect to the whole prospect.

"Joyously it showed." This continued till that feeling may be supposed to have passed away, and a kind of comparative listlessness or apathy to have succeeded, as at this line,

Some veering up and down, one knew not why.

All at once, while I am in this state, comes forth an object, an individual; and my mind, sleepy and unfixed, is awakened and fastened in a moment.

Hesperus, that *led*
The starry host

is a poetical object, because the glory of his own nature gives him the pre-eminence the moment he appears. He calls forth the poetic faculty, receiving its exertions as a tribute. But this ship in the sonnet may, in a manner still more appropriate, be said to come upon a mission of the poetic spirit, because, in its own appearance and attributes, it is barely sufficiently distinguished to rouse the creative faculty of the human mind, to exertions at all times welcome, but doubly so when they come upon us when in a state of remissness. The mind being once fixed and roused, all the rest comes from itself; it is merely a lordly ship, nothing more:

This ship was nought to me, nor I to her,
Yet I pursued her with a lover's look.

My mind wantons with grateful joy in the exercise of its own powers, and, loving its own creation,

This ship to all the rest I did prefer,

making her a sovereign or a regent, and thus giving body and life to all the rest; mingling up this idea with fondness and praise—

where she comes the winds must stir;

and concluding the whole with,

On went she, and due north her journey took;

thus taking up again the reader with whom I began, letting him know how long I must have watched this favourite vessel, and inviting him to rest his mind as mine is resting.

Having said so much upon mere fourteen lines, which Mrs. Fermor did not approve, I cannot but add a word or two upon my satisfaction in finding that my mind has so much in common with hers, and that we participate so many of each other's pleasures. I collect this from her having singled out the two little poems, "The Daffodils," and "The Rock crowned with Snowdrops." I am sure that whoever is much pleased with either of these quiet and tender delineations must be fitted to walk through the recesses of my poetry with delight, and will there recognize, at every turn, something or other in which, and over which, it has that property and right which knowledge and love confer. The line,

Come, blessed barrier, &c.,

in the "Sonnet upon Sleep," which Mrs. F. points out, had before been mentioned to me by Coleridge, and, indeed, by almost everybody who had heard it, as eminently beautiful. My letter (as this second sheet, which I am obliged to take, admonishes me) is growing to an enormous length; and yet, saving that I have expressed my calm confidence that these poems will live, I have said nothing which has a particular application to the object of it, which was to remove all disquiet from your mind on account of the condemnation they may at present incur from that portion of my contemporaries who are called the public. I am sure, my dear Lady Beaumont, if you attach any importance to it, it can only be from an apprehension that it may affect me, upon which I have already set you at ease; or from a fear that this present blame is ominous of their future or final destiny. If this be the case, your tenderness for me betrays you. Be assured that the decision of these persons has nothing to do with the question; they are altogether incompetent judges. These people, in the senseless hurry of their idle lives, do not *read* books, they merely snatch a glance at them, that they may talk about them. And even if this were not so, never forget what, I believe, was observed to you by Coleridge, that every great and original writer, in proportion as he is great or original, must himself create the taste by which he is to be relished; he must teach the art by which he is to be seen; this, in a certain degree, even to all persons, however wise and pure may be their lives, and however unvitiated their taste. But for those who dip into books in order to give an opinion of them, or talk about them to take up an opinion—for this multitude of unhappy, and misguided, and misguiding beings, an entire regeneration must be produced; and if this be possible, it must be a work *of time*. To conclude, my ears are stone-dead to this idle buzz, and my flesh as insensible as iron to these petty stings; and, after what I have said, I am sure yours will be the same. I doubt not that you will share with me an invincible confidence that my writings (and among them these little poems) will co-operate with the benign tendencies in human nature and society, wherever found; and that they will, in their degree, be efficacious in making men wiser, better, and happier. Farewell! I will not apologize for this letter, though its length demands an apology. Believe me, eagerly wishing for the happy day when I shall see you and Sir George here,

Most affectionately yours,
W. WORDSWORTH.

ESSAY, SUPPLEMENTARY TO THE PREFACE

With the young of both sexes, Poetry is, like love, a passion; but, for much the greater part of those who have been proud of its power over their minds, a necessity soon arises of breaking the pleasing bondage; or it relaxes of itself;—the thoughts being occupied in domestic cares, or the time engrossed by business. Poetry then becomes only an occasional recreation, while to those whose existence passes away in a course of fashionable pleasure, it is a species of luxurious amusement. In middle and declining age, a scattered number of serious persons resort to poetry, as to religion, for a protection against the pressure of trivial employments, and as a consolation for the afflictions of life. And, lastly, there are many who, having been enamoured of this art in their youth, have found leisure, after youth was spent, to cultivate general literature; in which poetry has continued to be comprehended *as a study*.

Into the above classes the Readers of poetry may be divided; Critics abound in them all; but from the last only can opinions be collected of absolute value, and worthy to be depended upon, as prophetic of the destiny of a new work. The young, who in nothing can escape delusion, are especially subject to it in their intercourse with Poetry. The cause, not so obvious as the fact is unquestionable, is the same as that from which erroneous judgments in this art, in the minds of men of all ages, chiefly proceed; but upon Youth it operates with peculiar force. The appropriate business of poetry (which, nevertheless, if genuine, is as permanent as pure science), her appropriate employment, her privilege and her *duty,* is to treat of things not as they *are,* but as they appear; not as they exist in themselves, but as they *seem* to exist to the *senses,* and to the *passions.* What a world of delusion does this acknowledged obligation prepare for the inexperienced! what temptations to go astray are here held forth for them whose thoughts have been little disciplined by the understanding, and whose feelings revolt from the sway of reason!—When a juvenile Reader is in the height of his rapture with some vicious passage, should experience throw in doubts, or common sense suggest suspicions, a lurking consciousness that the realities of the Muse are but shows, and that her liveliest excitements are raised by transient shocks of conflicting feeling and successive assemblages of contradictory thoughts—is ever at hand to justify extravagance, and to sanction absurdity. But, it may be asked, as these illusions are unavoidable, and, no doubt, eminently useful to the mind as a process, what good can be gained by making observations, the tendency of which is to diminish the confidence of youth in its feelings, and thus to abridge its innocent and even profitable pleasures? The reproach implied in the question could not be warded off, if Youth were incapable of being delighted with what is truly excellent; or if these errors always terminated of themselves in due season. But, with the majority, though their force be abated, they continue through life. Moreover, the fire of youth is too vivacious an element to be extinguished or damped by a philosophical remark; and, while there is no danger that what has been said will be injurious or painful to the ardent and the confident, it may prove beneficial to those who, being enthusiastic, are, at the same time, modest and ingenuous. The intimation may unite with their own misgivings to regulate their sensibility, and to bring in, sooner than it would otherwise have arrived, a more discreet and sound judgment.

If it should excite wonder that men of ability, in later life, whose understandings have been rendered acute by practice in affairs, should be so easily and so far imposed upon when they happen to take up a new work in verse, this appears to be the cause;—that, having discontinued their attention to poetry, whatever progress may have been made in other departments of knowledge, they have not, as to this art, advanced in true discernment beyond the age of youth. If, then, a new poem fall in their way, whose attractions are of that kind which would have enraptured them during the heat of youth, the judgment not being improved to a degree that they shall be disgusted, they are dazzled; and prize and cherish the faults for having had power to make the present time vanish before them, and to throw the mind back, as by enchantment, into the happiest season of life. As they read, powers seem to be revived, passions are regenerated, and pleasures restored. The Book was probably taken up after an escape from the burden of business, and with a wish to forget the world, and all its vexations and anxieties. Having obtained this wish, and so much more, it is natural that they should make report as they have felt.

If Men of mature age, through want of practice, be thus easily beguiled into admiration of absurdities, extravagances, and misplaced ornaments, thinking it proper that their understandings should enjoy a holiday, while they are unbending their minds with verse, it may be expected that such Readers will resemble their former selves also in strength of prejudice, and an inaptitude to be moved by the unostentatious beauties of a pure style. In the higher poetry, an enlightened Critic chiefly looks for a reflection of the wisdom of the heart and the grandeur of the imagination. Wherever these appear, simplicity accompanies them; Magnificence herself, when legitimate, depending upon a simplicity of her own, to regulate her ornaments. But it is a well-known property of human nature, that our estimates are ever governed by comparisons, of which we are conscious with various degrees of distinctness. Is it not, then, inevitable (confining these observations to the effects of style merely) that an eye, accustomed to the glaring hues of diction by which such Readers are caught and excited, will for the most part be rather repelled than attracted by an original Work, the colouring of which is disposed according to a pure and refined scheme of harmony? It is in the fine arts as in the affairs of life, no man can *serve* (*i.e.* obey with zeal and fidelity) two Masters.

As Poetry is most just to its own divine origin when it administers the comforts and breathes the spirit of religion, they who have learned to perceive this truth, and who betake themselves to reading verse for sacred purposes, must be preserved from numerous illusions to which the two Classes of Readers, whom we have been considering, are liable. But as the mind grows serious from the weight of life, the range of its passions is contracted accordingly; and its sympathies become so exclusive that many species of high excellence wholly escape, or but languidly excite, its notice. Besides, men who read from religious or moral inclinations, even when the subject is of that kind which they approve, are beset with misconceptions and mistakes peculiar to themselves. Attaching so much importance to the truths which interest them, they are prone to over-rate the Authors by whom those truths are expressed and enforced. They come prepared to impart so much passion to the Poet's language, that they remain unconscious how little, in fact, they received from it. And, on the other hand, religious faith is to him who holds it so momentous a thing, and error appears to be attended with such tremendous consequences, that, if opinions touching upon religion occur which the Reader condemns, he not only cannot sympathise with them, however animated the expression, but there is, for the most part, an end put to all satisfaction and enjoyment. Love, if it before existed, is converted into dislike; and the heart of the Reader is set against the Author and his book. —To these excesses they, who from their professions ought to be the most guarded against them, are perhaps the most liable; I mean those sects whose religion, being from the calculating understanding, is cold and formal. For when Christianity, the religion of humility, is founded upon the proudest faculty of our nature, what can be expected but contradictions? Accordingly, believers of this cast are at one time contemptuous; at another, being troubled, as they are and must be, with inward misgivings, they are jealous and suspicious;—and at all seasons they are under temptations to supply, by the heat with which they defend their tenets, the animation which is wanting to the constitution of the religion itself.

Faith was given to man that his affections, detached from the treasures of time, might be inclined to settle upon those of eternity:— the elevation of his nature, which this habit produces on earth, being to him a presumptive evidence of a future state of existence, and giving him a title to partake of its holiness. The religious man values what he sees chiefly as an "imperfect shadowing forth" of what he is incapable of seeing. The concerns of religion refer to indefinite objects, and are too weighty for the mind to support them without relieving itself by resting a great part of the burthen upon words and symbols. The commerce between Man and his Maker cannot be carried on but by a process where much is represented in little, and the Infinite Being accommodates himself to a finite capacity. In all this may be perceived the affinity between religion and poetry; between religion—making up the deficiencies of reason by faith; and poetry— passionate for the instruction of reason; between religion—whose element is infinitude, and whose ultimate trust is the supreme of things, submitting herself to circumscription, and reconciled to substitutions; and poetry— ethereal and transcendent, yet incapable to sustain her existence without sensuous incarnation. In this community of nature may be perceived also the lurking incitements of kindred error;—so that we shall find that no poetry has been more subject to distortion than that species, the argument and scope of which is religious; and no lovers of the art have gone farther astray than the pious and the devout.

Whither then shall we turn for that union of qualifications which must necessarily exist before the decisions of a critic can be of absolute value? For a mind at once poetical and philosophical; for a critic whose affections are as free and kindly as the spirit of society, and whose understanding is severe as that of dispassionate government? Where are we to look for that initiatory composure of mind which no selfishness can disturb? For a natural sensibility that has been tutored into correctness without losing anything of its quickness; and for active faculties, capable of answering the demands which an Author of original imagination shall make upon them, associated with a judgment that cannot be duped into admiration by aught that is unworthy of it?—among those and those only, who, never having suffered their youthful love of poetry to remit much of its force, have applied to the consideration of the laws of this art the best power of their understandings. At the same time it must be observed that, as this Class comprehends the only judgments which are trustworthy, so does it include the most erroneous and perverse. For to be mistaught is worse than to be untaught; and no perverseness equals that which is supported by system, no errors are so difficult to root out as those which the understanding has pledged its credit to uphold. In this Class are contained censors, who, if they be pleased with what is good, are pleased with it only by imperfect glimpses, and upon false principles; who, should they generalise rightly to a certain point, are sure to suffer for it in the end; who, if they stumble upon a sound rule, are fettered by misapplying it, or by straining it too far; being incapable of perceiving when it ought to yield to one of higher order. In it are found critics too petulant to be passive to a genuine poet, and too feeble to grapple with him; men, who take upon them to report of the course which *he* holds when they are utterly unable to accompany,—confounded if he turn quick upon the wing, dismayed if he soar steadily "into the region;" —men of palsied imaginations and indurated hearts; in whose minds all healthy action is languid, who therefore feed as the many direct them, or, with the many, are greedy after vicious provocatives;—judges, whose censure is auspicious, and whose praise ominous! In this class meet together the two extremes of best and worst.

The observations presented in the foregoing series are of too ungracious a nature to have been made without reluctance; and, were it only on this account, I would invite the reader to try them by the test of comprehensive experience. If the number of judges who can be confidently relied upon be in reality so small, it ought to follow that partial notice only, or neglect, perhaps long continued, or attention wholly inadequate to their merits, must have been the fate of most works in the higher departments of poetry; and that, on the other hand, numerous productions have blazed into popularity, and have passed away, leaving scarcely a trace behind them: it will be further found, that when Authors shall have at length raised themselves into general admiration and maintained their ground, errors and prejudices have prevailed concerning their genius and their works, which the few who are conscious of those errors and prejudices would deplore; if they were not recompensed by perceiving that there are select Spirits for whom it is ordained that their fame shall be in the world

an existence like that of Virtue, which owes its being to the struggles it makes, and its vigour to the enemies whom it provokes;—a vivacious quality, ever doomed to meet with opposition, and still triumphing over it; and, from the nature of its dominion, incapable of being brought to the sad conclusion of Alexander, when he wept that there were no more worlds for him to conquer.

Let us take a hasty retrospect of the poetical literature of this Country for the greater part of the last two centuries, and see if the facts support these inferences.

Who is there that now reads the "Creation" of Dubartas? Yet all Europe once resounded with his praise; he was caressed by kings; and, when his Poem was translated into our language, the Faery Queen faded before it. The name of Spenser, whose genius is of a higher order than even that of Ariosto, is at this day scarcely known beyond the limits of the British Isles. And if the value of his works is to be estimated from the attention now paid to them by his countrymen, compared with that which they bestow on those of some other writers, it must be pronounced small indeed.

The laurel, meed of mighty conquerors
And poets *sage*—

are his own words; but his wisdom has, in this particular, been his worst enemy: while its opposite, whether in the shape of folly or madness, has been *their* best friend. But he was a great power, and bears a high name: the laurel has been awarded to him.

A dramatic Author, if he write for the stage, must adapt himself to the taste of the audience, or they will not endure him; accordingly the mighty genius of Shakspeare was listened to. The people were delighted; but I am not sufficiently versed in stage antiquities to determine whether they did not flock as eagerly to the representation of many pieces of contemporary Authors, wholly undeserving to appear upon the same boards. Had there been a formal contest for superiority among dramatic writers, that Shakspeare, like his predecessors Sophocles and Euripides, would have often been subject to the mortification of seeing the prize adjudged to sorry competitors, becomes too probable, when we reflect that the admirers of Settle and Shadwell were, in a later age, as numerous, and reckoned as respectable in point of talent, as those of Dryden. At all events, that Shakspeare stooped to accommodate himself to the People, is sufficiently apparent; and one of the most striking proofs of his almost omnipotent genius is, that he could turn to such glorious purpose those materials which the prepossessions of the age compelled him to make use of. Yet even this marvellous skill appears not to have been enough to prevent his rivals from having some advantage over him in public estimation; else how can we account for passages and scenes that exist in his works, unless upon a supposition that some of the grossest of them, a fact which in my own mind I have no doubt of, were foisted in by the Players, for the gratification of the many?

But that his Works, whatever might be their reception upon the stage, made but little impression upon the ruling Intellects of the time, may be inferred from the fact that Lord Bacon, in his multifarious writings, nowhere either quotes or alludes to him.[1]—His dramatic excellence enabled him to resume possession of the stage after the Restoration; but Dryden tells us that in his time two of the plays of Beaumont and Fletcher were acted for one of Shakspeare's. And so faint and limited was the perception of the poetic beauties of his dramas in the time of Pope, that, in his Edition of the Plays, with a view of rendering to the general reader a necessary service, he printed between inverted commas those passages which he thought most worthy of notice.

At this day, the French Critics have abated nothing of their aversion to this darling of our Nation: "the English, with their bouffon de Shakspeare," is as familiar an expression among them as in the time of Voltaire. Baron Grimm is the only French writer who seems to have perceived his infinite superiority to the first names of the French Theatre; an advantage which the Parisian critic owed to his German blood and German education. The most enlightened Italians, though well acquainted with our language, are wholly incompetent to measure the proportions of Shakspeare. The Germans only, of foreign nations, are approaching towards a knowledge and feeling of what he

is. In some respects they have acquired a superiority over the fellow-countrymen of the Poet: for among us it is a current, I might say an established opinion, that Shakspeare is justly praised when he is pronounced to be "a wild irregular genius, in whom great faults are compensated by great beauties." How long may it be before this misconception passes away, and it becomes universally acknowledged that the judgment of Shakspeare in the selection of his materials, and in the manner in which he has made them, heterogeneous as they often are, constitute a unity of their own, and contribute all to one great end, is not less admirable than his imagination, his invention, and his intuitive knowledge of human Nature!

There is extant a small Volume of miscellaneous poems, in which Shakspeare expresses his own feelings in his own person. It is not difficult to conceive that the Editor, George Steevens, should have been insensible to the beauties of one portion of that Volume, the Sonnets; though in no part of the writings of this Poet is found, in an equal compass, a greater number of exquisite feelings felicitously expressed. But, from regard to the Critic's own credit, he would not have ventured to talk of an [2] act of parliament not being strong enough to compel the perusal of those little pieces, if he had not known that the people of England were ignorant of the treasures contained in them: and if he had not, moreover, shared the too common propensity of human nature to exult over a supposed fall into the mire of a genius whom he had been compelled to regard with admiration, as an inmate of the celestial regions—"there sitting where he durst not soar."

Nine years before the death of Shakspeare, Milton was born; and early in life he published several small poems, which, though on their first appearance they were praised by a few of the judicious, were afterwards neglected to that degree, that Pope in his youth could borrow from them without risk of its being known. Whether these poems are at this day justly appreciated, I will not undertake to de-

[1] The learned Hakewill (a third edition of whose book bears date 1635), writing to refute the error "touching Nature's perpetual and universal decay," cites triumphantly the names of Ariosto, Tasso, Bartas, and Spenser, as instances that poetic genius had not degenerated; but he makes no mention of Shakspeare.

[2] This flippant insensibility was publicly reprehended by Mr. Coleridge in a course of Lectures upon Poetry given by him at the Royal Institution. For the various merits of thought and language in Shakspeare's Sonnets see Numbers 27, 29, 30, 32, 33, 54, 64, 66, 68, 73, 76, 86, 91, 92, 93, 97, 98, 105, 107, 108, 109, 111, 113, 114, 116, 117, 129, and many others.

cide: nor would it imply a severe reflection upon the mass of readers to suppose the contrary; seeing that a man of the acknowledged genius of Voss, the German poet, could suffer their spirit to evaporate; and could change their character, as is done in the translation made by him of the most popular of those pieces. At all events, it is certain that these Poems of Milton are now much read, and loudly praised; yet were they little heard of till more than 150 years after their publication; and of the Sonnets, Dr. Johnson, as appears from Boswell's Life of him, was in the habit of thinking and speaking as contemptuously as Steevens wrote upon those of Shakspeare.

About the time when the Pindaric odes of Cowley and his imitators, and the productions of that class of curious thinkers whom Dr. Johnson has strangely styled metaphysical Poets, were beginning to lose something of that extravagant admiration which they had excited, the Paradise Lost made its appearance. "Fit audience find though few," was the petition addressed by the Poet to his inspiring Muse. I have said elsewhere that he gained more than he asked; this I believe to be true; but Dr. Johnson has fallen into a gross mistake when he attempts to prove, by the sale of the work, that Milton's Countrymen were *"just to it"* upon its first appearance. Thirteen hundred Copies were sold in two years; an uncommon example, he asserts, of the prevalence of genius in opposition to so much recent enmity as Milton's public conduct had excited. But, be it remembered that, if Milton's political and religious opinions, and the manner in which he announced them, had raised him many enemies, they had procured him numerous friends; who, as all personal danger was passed away at the time of publication, would be eager to procure the master-work of a man whom they revered, and whom they would be proud of praising. Take, from the number of purchasers, persons of this class, and also those who wished to possess the Poem as a religious work, and but few, I fear, would be left who sought for it on account of its poetical merits. The demand did not immediately increase; "for," says Dr. Johnson, "many more readers" (he means persons in the habit of reading poetry) "than were supplied at first the Nation did not afford." How careless must a writer be who can make this assertion in the face of so many existing title-pages to belie it! Turning to my own shelves,

I find the folio of Cowley, seventh edition, 1681. A book near it is Flatman's Poems, fourth edition, 1686; Waller, fifth edition, same date. The Poems of Norris of Bemerton not long after went, I believe, through nine editions. What further demand there might be for these works I do not know; but I well remember that, twenty-five years ago, the booksellers' stalls in London swarmed with the folios of Cowley. This is not mentioned in disparagement of that able writer and amiable man; but merely to show that, if Milton's work were not more read, it was not because readers did not exist at the time. The early editions of the Paradise Lost were printed in a shape which allowed them to be sold at a low price, yet only three thousand copies of the Work were sold in eleven years; and the Nation, says Dr. Johnson, had been satisfied from 1623 to 1664, that is, forty-one years, with only two editions of the Works of Shakspeare, which probably did not together make one thousand Copies; facts adduced by the critic to prove the "paucity of Readers."—There were readers in multitudes; but their money went for other purposes, as their admiration was fixed elsewhere. We are authorized, then, to affirm that the reception of the Paradise Lost, and the slow progress of its fame, are proofs as striking as can be desired that the positions which I am attempting to establish are not erroneous.[1]—How amusing to shape to one's self such a critique as a Wit of Charles's days, or a Lord of the Miscellanies or trading Journalist of King William's time, would have brought forth, if he had set his faculties industriously to work upon this Poem, everywhere impregnated with *original* excellence.

So strange indeed are the obliquities of admiration, that they whose opinions are much influenced by authority will often be tempted to think that there are no fixed principles [2] in human nature for this art to rest upon. I have been honoured by being permitted to peruse

[1] Hughes is express upon this subject: in his dedication of Spenser's Works to Lord Somers, he writes thus: "It was your Lordship's encouraging a beautiful Edition of Paradise Lost that first brought that incomparable Poem to be generally known and esteemed."

[2] This opinion seems actually to have been entertained by Adam Smith, the worst critic, David Hume not excepted, that Scotland, a soil to which this sort of weed seems natural, has produced.

in MS. a tract composed between the period of the Revolution and the close of that century. It is the Work of an English Peer of high accomplishments, its object to form the character and direct the studies of his son. Perhaps nowhere does a more beautiful treatise of the kind exist. The good sense and wisdom of the thoughts, the delicacy of the feelings, and the charm of the style, are throughout equally conspicuous. Yet the Author, selecting among the Poets of his own country those whom he deems most worthy of his son's perusal, particularises only Lord Rochester, Sir John Denham, and Cowley. Writing about the same time, Shaftesbury, an author at present unjustly depreciated, describes the English Muses as only yet lisping in their cradles.

The arts by which Pope, soon afterwards, contrived to procure to himself a more general and a higher reputation than perhaps any English Poet ever attained during his life-time, are known to the judicious. And as well known is it to them, that the undue exertion of those arts is the cause why Pope has for some time held a rank in literature, to which, if he had not been seduced by an over-love of immediate popularity, and had confided more in his native genius, he never could have descended. He bewitched the nation by his melody, and dazzled it by his polished style, and was himself blinded by his own success. Having wandered from humanity in his Eclogues with boyish inexperience, the praise which these compositions obtained tempted him into a belief that Nature was not to be trusted, at least in pastoral Poetry. To prove this by example, he put his friend Gay upon writing those Eclogues, which their author intended to be burlesque. The instigator of the work, and his admirers, could perceive in them nothing but what was ridiculous. Nevertheless, though these Poems contain some detestable passages, the effect, as Dr. Johnson well observes, "of reality and truth became conspicuous even when the intention was to show them grovelling and degraded." The Pastorals, ludicrous to such as prided themselves upon their refinement, in spite of those disgusting passages, "became popular, and were read with delight, as just representations of rural manners and occupations."

Something less than sixty years after the publication of the Paradise Lost appeared Thomson's Winter; which was speedily followed by his other Seasons. It is a work of inspiration; much of it is written from himself, and nobly from himself. How was it received? "It was no sooner read," says one of his contemporary biographers, "than universally admired: those only excepted who had not been used to feel, or to look for anything in poetry, beyond a *point* of satirical or epigrammatic wit, a smart *antithesis* richly trimmed with rhyme, or the softness of an *elegiac* complaint. To such his manly classical spirit could not readily commend itself; till, after a more attentive perusal, they had got the better of their prejudices, and either acquired or affected a truer taste. A few others stood aloof, merely because they had long before fixed the articles of their poetical creed, and resigned themselves to an absolute despair of ever seeing anything new and original. These were somewhat mortified to find their notions disturbed by the appearance of a poet, who seemed to owe nothing but to nature and his own genius. But, in a short time, the applause became unanimous; every one wondering how so many pictures, and pictures so familiar, should have moved them but faintly to what they felt in his descriptions. His digressions too, the overflowings of a tender benevolent heart, charmed the reader no less; leaving him in doubt, whether he should more admire the Poet or love the Man."

This case appears to bear strongly against us:—but we must distinguish between wonder and legitimate admiration. The subject of the work is the changes produced in the appearances of nature by the revolution of the year: and, by undertaking to write in verse, Thomson pledged himself to treat his subject as became a Poet. Now it is remarkable that, excepting the nocturnal Reverie of Lady Winchilsea, and a passage or two in the Windsor Forest of Pope, the poetry of the period intervening between the publication of the Paradise Lost and the Seasons does not contain a single new image of external nature, and scarcely presents a familiar one from which it can be inferred that the eye of the Poet had been steadily fixed upon his object, much less that his feelings had urged him to work upon it in the spirit of genuine imagination. To what a low state knowledge of the most obvious and important phenomena had sunk, is evident from the style in which Dryden has executed a description of Night in one of his Tragedies, and Pope his translation of the celebrated moonlight scene in the Iliad. A blind man, in the habit of attending accurately to descriptions casually dropped from the lips of those around him, might easily depict these appearances with more truth. Dryden's lines are vague, bombastic, and senseless; [1] those of Pope, though he had Homer to guide him, are throughout false and contradictory. The verses of Dryden, once highly celebrated, are forgotten; those of Pope still retain their hold upon public estimation,—nay, there is not a passage of descriptive poetry, which at this day finds so many and such ardent admirers. Strange to think of an enthusiast, as may have been the case with thousands, reciting those verses under the cope of a moonlight sky, without having his raptures in the least disturbed by a suspicion of their absurdity!—If these two distinguished writers could habitually think that the visible universe was of so little consequence to a poet, that it was scarcely necessary for him to cast his eyes upon it, we may be assured that those passages of the elder poets which faithfully and poetically describe the phenomena of nature, were not at that time holden in much estimation, and that there was little accurate attention paid to those appearances.

Wonder is the natural product of Ignorance; and as the soil was *in such good condition* at the time of the publication of the Seasons, the crop was doubtless abundant. Neither individuals nor nations become corrupt all at once, nor are they enlightened in a moment. Thomson was an inspired poet, but he could not work miracles; in cases where the art of seeing had in some degree been learned, the teacher would further the proficiency of his pupils, but he could do little *more;* though so far does vanity assist men in acts of self-deception, that many would often fancy they recognised a likeness when they knew nothing of the original. Having shown that much of what his biographer deemed genuine admiration must in fact have been blind wonderment—how is the rest to be accounted for?—Thomson was fortunate in the very title of his poem, which seemed to bring

[1] CORTES *alone in a night-gown.*

All things are hush'd as Nature's self lay dead;
The mountains seem to nod their drowsy head.
The little Birds in dreams their songs repeat,
And sleeping Flowers beneath the Night-dew
  sweat:
Even Lust and Envy sleep; yet Love denies
Rest to my soul, and slumber to my eyes.
      DRYDEN'S *Indian Emperor.*

it home to the prepared sympathies of every one: in the next place, notwithstanding his high powers, he writes a vicious style; and his false ornaments are exactly of that kind which would be most likely to strike the undiscerning. He likewise abounds with sentimental commonplaces that, from the manner in which they were brought forward, bore an imposing air of novelty. In any well-used copy of the Seasons the book generally opens of itself with the rhapsody on love, or with one of the stories (perhaps Damon and Musidora); these also are prominent in our collections of Extracts, and are the parts of his Work which, after all, were probably most efficient in first recommending the author to general notice. Pope, repaying praises which he had received, and wishing to extol him to the highest, only styles him "an elegant and philosophical Poet;" nor are we able to collect any unquestionable proofs that the true characteristics of Thomson's genius as an imaginative poet [2] were perceived, till the elder Warton, almost forty years after the publication of the Seasons, pointed them out by a note in his Essay on the Life and Writings of Pope. In the Castle of Indolence (of which Gray speaks so coldly) these characteristics were almost as conspicuously displayed, and in verse more harmonious and diction more pure. Yet that fine poem was neglected on its appearance, and is at this day the delight only of a few!

When Thomson died, Collins breathed forth his regrets in an Elegiac Poem, in which he pronounces a poetical curse upon *him* who should regard with insensibility the place where the Poet's remains were deposited. The Poems of the mourner himself have now passed through innumerable editions, and are universally known; but if, when Collins died, the same kind of imprecation had been pronounced by a surviving admirer, small is the number whom it would not have comprehended. The notice which his poems attained during his lifetime was so small, and of course the sale so insignificant, that not long before his death he deemed it right to repay to the bookseller the

[2] Since these observations upon Thomson were written, I have perused the second edition of his Seasons, and find that even *that* does not contain the most striking passages which Warton points out for admiration; these, with other improvements, throughout the whole work, must have been added at a later period.

sum which he had advanced for them, and threw the edition into the fire.

Next in importance to the Seasons of Thomson, though at considerable distance from that work in order of time, come the Reliques of Ancient English Poetry, collected, new-modelled, and in many instances (if such a contradiction in terms may be used) composed by the Editor, Dr. Percy. This work did not steal silently into the world, as is evident from the number of legendary tales that appeared not long after its publication; and had been modelled, as the authors persuaded themselves, after the old Ballad. The Compilation was however ill suited to the then existing taste of city society; and Dr. Johnson, 'mid the little senate to which he gave laws, was not sparing in his exertions to make it an object of contempt. The critic triumphed, the legendary imitators were deservedly disregarded, and, as undeservedly, their ill-imitated models sank, in this country, into temporary neglect; while Bürger, and other able writers of Germany, were translating or imitating these Reliques, and composing, with the aid of inspiration thence derived, poems which are the delight of the German nation. Dr. Percy was so abashed by the ridicule flung upon his labours from the ignorance and insensibility of the persons with whom he lived, that, though while he was writing under a mask he had not wanted resolution to follow his genius into the regions of true simplicity and genuine pathos (as is evinced by the exquisite ballad of Sir Cauline and by many other pieces), yet when he appeared in his own person and character as a poetical writer, he adopted, as in the tale of the Hermit of Warkworth, a diction scarcely in any one of its features distinguishable from the vague, the glossy, and unfeeling language of his day. I mention this remarkable fact [1] with regret, esteeming the genius of Dr. Percy in this kind of writing superior to that of any other man by whom in modern times it has

[1] Shenstone, in his Schoolmistress, gives a still more remarkable instance of this timidity. On its first appearance, (see D'Israeli's 2d Series of the Curiosities of Literature) the Poem was accompanied with an absurd prose commentary, showing, as indeed some incongruous expressions in the text imply, that the whole was intended for burlesque. In subsequent editions the commentary was dropped, and the People have since continued to read in seriousness, doing for the Author what he had not courage openly to venture upon for himself.

been cultivated. That even Bürger (to whom Klopstock gave in my hearing a commendation which he denied to Goethe and Schiller, pronouncing him to be a genuine poet, and one of the few among the Germans whose works would last) had not the fine sensibility of Percy, might be shown from many passages, in which he has deserted his original only to go astray. For example,

> Now daye was gone, and night was come,
> And all were fast asleepe,
> All save the Lady Emeline,
> Who sate in her bowre to weepe:
> And soone she heard her true Love's voice
> Low whispering at the walle,
> Awake, awake, my dear Ladye,
> 'Tis I thy true-love call.

Which is thus tricked out and dilated:

> Als nun die Nacht Gebirg' und Thal
> Vermummt in Rabenschatten,
> Und Hochburgs Lampen überall
> Schon ausgeflimmert hatten,
> Und alles tief entschlafen war;
> Doch nur das Fräulein immerdar,
> Voll Fieberängst, noch wachte,
> Und seinen Ritter dachte:
> Da horch! Ein süsser Liebeston
> Kam leis' empor geflogen.
> "Ho, Trudchen, ho! Da bin ich schon!
> Frisch auf! Dich angezogen!"

But from humble ballads we must ascend to heroics.

All hail, Macpherson! hail to thee, Sire of Ossian! The Phantom was begotten by the snug embrace of an impudent Highlander upon a cloud of tradition—it travelled southward, where it was greeted with acclamation, and the thin Consistence took its course through Europe, upon the breath of popular applause. The Editor of the Reliques had indirectly preferred a claim to the praise of invention, by not concealing that his supplementary labours were considerable! how selfish his conduct, contrasted with that of the disinterested Gael, who, like Lear, gives his kingdom away, and is content to become a pensioner upon his own issue for a beggarly pittance!—Open this far-famed Book!—I have done so at random, and the beginning of the "Epic Poem Temora," in eight Books, presents itself. "The blue waves of Ullin roll in light. The green hills are covered with day. Trees shake their dusky heads in the breeze. Grey torrents pour their noisy streams. Two green hills with aged oaks surround a narrow plain. The blue course of a stream is there. On its banks stood Cairbar of Atha. His spear supports the king; the red eyes of his fear are sad. Cormac rises on his soul with all his ghastly wounds." Precious memorandums from the pocketbook of the blind Ossian!

If it be unbecoming, as I acknowledge that for the most part it is, to speak disrespectfully of Works that have enjoyed for a length of time a widely-spread reputation, without at the same time producing irrefragable proofs of their unworthiness, let me be forgiven upon this occasion.—Having had the good fortune to be born and reared in a mountainous country, from my very childhood I have felt the falsehood that pervades the volumes imposed upon the world under the name of Ossian. From what I saw with my own eyes, I knew that the imagery was spurious. In nature everything is distinct, yet nothing defined into absolute independent singleness. In Macpherson's work, it is exactly the reverse; everything (that is not stolen) is in this manner defined, insulated, dislocated, deadened,—yet nothing distinct. It will always be so when words are substituted for things. To say that the characters never could exist, that the manners are impossible, and that a dream has more substance than the whole state of society, as there depicted, is doing nothing more than pronouncing a censure which Macpherson defied; when, with the steeps of Morven before his eyes, he could talk so familiarly of his Car-borne heroes;— of Morven, which, if one may judge from its appearance at the distance of a few miles, contains scarcely an acre of ground sufficiently accommodating for a sledge to be trailed along its surface.—Mr. Malcolm Laing has ably shown that the diction of this pretended translation is a motley assemblage from all quarters; but he is so fond of making out parallel passages as to call poor Macpherson to account for his *"ands"* and his *"buts!"* and he has weakened his argument by conducting it as if he thought that every striking resemblance was a *conscious* plagiarism. It is enough that the coincidences are too remarkable for its being probable or possible that they could arise in different minds without communication between them. Now as the Translators of the Bible, and Shakspeare, Milton, and Pope, could not be indebted to Macpherson, it follows that he must have owed his fine feathers to them; unless we are prepared gravely to assert, with Madame de Staël, that many of the character-

istic beauties of our most celebrated English Poets are derived from the ancient Fingallian; in which case the modern translator would have been but giving back to Ossian his own. —It is consistent that Lucien Buonaparte, who could censure Milton for having surrounded Satan in the infernal regions with courtly and regal splendour, should pronounce the modern Ossian to be the glory of Scotland; —a country that has produced a Dunbar, a Buchanan, a Thomson, and a Burns! These opinions are of ill omen for the Epic ambition of him who has given them to the world.

Yet, much as those pretended treasures of antiquity have been admired, they have been wholly uninfluential upon the literature of the Country. No succeeding writer appears to have caught from them a ray of inspiration; no author, in the least distinguished, has ventured formally to imitate them—except the boy, Chatterton, on their first appearance. He had perceived, from the successful trials which he himself had made in literary forgery, how few critics were able to distinguish between a real ancient medal and a counterfeit of modern manufacture; and he set himself to the work of filling a magazine with *Saxon Poems,*— counterparts of those of Ossian, as like his as one of his misty stars is to another. This incapability to amalgamate with the literature of the Island is, in my estimation, a decisive proof that the book is essentially unnatural; nor should I require any other to demonstrate it to be a forgery, audacious as worthless.— Contrast, in this respect, the effect of Macpherson's publication with the Reliques of Percy, so unassuming, so modest in their pretensions!—I have already stated how much Germany is indebted to this latter work; and for our own country, its poetry has been absolutely redeemed by it. I do not think that there is an able writer in verse of the present day who would not be proud to acknowledge his obligations to the Reliques; I know that it is so with my friends; and, for myself, I am happy in this occasion to make a public avowal of my own.

Dr. Johnson, more fortunate in his contempt of the labours of Macpherson than those of his modest friend, was solicited not long after to furnish Prefaces, biographical and critical, for the works of some of the most eminent English Poets. The booksellers took upon themselves to make the collection; they referred probably to the most popular miscellanies, and, unquestionably, to their books of accounts; and decided upon the claim of authors to be admitted into a body of the most eminent from the familiarity of their names with the readers of that day, and by the profits which, from the sale of his works, each had brought and was bringing to the Trade. The Editor was allowed a limited exercise of discretion, and the Authors whom he recommended are scarcely to be mentioned without a smile. We open the volume of Prefatory Lives, and to our astonishment the *first* name we find is that of Cowley!—What is become of the morning-star of English Poetry? Where is the bright Elizabethan constellation? Or, if names be more acceptable than images, where is the ever-to-be-honoured Chaucer? where is Spenser? where Sidney? and, lastly, where he, whose rights as a poet, contradistinguished from those which he is universally allowed to possess as a dramatist, we have vindicated,—where Shakspeare?— These, and a multitude of others not unworthy to be placed near them, their contemporaries and successors, we have *not*. But in their stead, we have (could better be expected when precedence was to be settled by an abstract of reputation at any given period made, as in this case before us?) Roscommon, and Stepney, and Phillips, and Walsh, and Smith, and Duke, and King, and Spratt—Halifax, Granville, Sheffield, Congreve, Broome, and other reputed Magnates—metrical writers utterly worthless and useless, except for occasions like the present, when their productions are referred to as evidence what a small quantity of brain is necessary to procure a considerable stock of admiration, provided the aspirant will accommodate himself to the likings and fashions of his day.

As I do not mean to bring down this retrospect to our own times, it may with propriety be closed at the era of this distinguished event. From the literature of other ages and countries, proofs equally cogent might have been adduced, that the opinions announced in the former part of this Essay are founded upon truth. It was not an agreeable office, nor a prudent undertaking, to declare them; but their importance seemed to render it a duty. It may still be asked, where lies the particular relation of what has been said to these Volumes?—The question will be easily answered by the discerning Reader who is old enough to remember the taste that prevailed when some of these poems were first published, seventeen years ago; who has also observed to what degree the poetry of this Island has since that period been coloured by them; and who is further aware of the unremitting hostility with which, upon some principle or other, they have each and all been opposed. A sketch of my own notion of the constitution of Fame has been given; and, as far as concerns myself, I have cause to be satisfied. The love, the admiration, the indifference, the slight, the aversion, and even the contempt, with which these Poems have been received, knowing, as I do, the source within my own mind from which they have proceeded, and the labour and pains which, when labour and pains appeared needful, have been bestowed upon them, must all, if I think consistently, be received as pledges and tokens, bearing the same general impression, though widely different in value;—they are all proofs that for the present time I have not laboured in vain; and afford assurances, more or less authentic, that the products of my industry will endure.

If there be one conclusion more forcibly pressed upon us than another by the review which has been given of the fortunes and fate of poetical Works, it is this,—that every author, as far as he is great and at the same time *original*, has had the task of *creating* the taste by which he is to be enjoyed: so has it been, so will it continue to be. This remark was long since made to me by the philosophical Friend for the separation of whose poems from my own I have previously expressed my regret. The predecessors of an original Genius of a high order will have smoothed the way for all that he has in common with them;—and much he will have in common; but, for what is peculiarly his own, he will be called upon to clear and often to shape his own road:—he will be in the condition of Hannibal among the Alps.

And where lies the real difficulty of creating that taste by which a truly original poet is to be relished? Is it in breaking the bonds of custom, in overcoming the prejudices of false refinement, and displacing the aversions of inexperience? Or, if he labour for an object which here and elsewhere I have proposed to myself, does it consist in divesting the reader of the pride that induces him to dwell upon those points wherein men differ from each other, to the exclusion of those in which all men are alike, or the same; and in making him ashamed of the vanity that renders him insensible of the appropriate excellence which civil arrangements, less unjust than might appear, and Nature illimitable in her bounty, have conferred on men who may stand below him in the scale of society? Finally, does it lie in establishing that dominion over the spirits of readers by which they are to be humbled and humanised, in order that they may be purified and exalted?

If these ends are to be attained by the mere communication of *knowledge*, it does *not* lie here.—Taste, I would remind the reader, like Imagination, is a word which has been forced to extend its services far beyond the point to which philosophy would have confined them. It is a metaphor, taken from a *passive* sense of the human body, and transferred to things which are in their essence *not* passive,—to intellectual *acts* and *operations*. The word Imagination has been overstrained, from impulses honourable to mankind, to meet the demands of the faculty which is perhaps the noblest of our nature. In the instance of Taste, the process has been reversed; and from the prevalence of dispositions at once injurious and discreditable, being no other than that selfishness which is the child of apathy,—which, as Nations decline in productive and creative power, makes them value themselves upon a presumed refinement of judging. Poverty of language is the primary cause of the use which we make of the word Imagination; but the word Taste has been stretched to the sense which it bears in modern Europe by habits of self-conceit, inducing that inversion in the order of things whereby a passive faculty is made paramount among the faculties conversant with the fine arts. Proportion and congruity, the requisite knowledge being supposed, are subjects upon which taste may be trusted; it is competent to this office;—for in its intercourse with these the mind is *passive*, and is affected painfully or pleasurably as by an instinct. But the profound and the exquisite in feeling, the lofty and universal in thought and imagination; or, in ordinary language, the pathetic and the sublime;—are neither of them, accurately speaking, objects of a faculty which could ever without a sinking in the spirit of Nations have been designated by the metaphor—*Taste*. And why? Because without the exertion of a co-operating *power* in the mind of the Reader, there can be no

adequate sympathy with either of these emotions: without this auxiliary impulse, elevated or profound passion cannot exist.

Passion, it must be observed, is derived from a word which signifies *suffering;* but the connection which suffering has with effort, with exertion, and *action*, is immediate and inseparable. How strikingly is this property of human nature exhibited by the fact that, in popular language, to be in a passion is to be angry!— But,

Anger in hasty *words* or *blows*
Itself discharges on its foes.

To be moved, then, by a passion, is to be excited, often to external, and always to internal effort; whether for the continuance and strengthening of the passion, or for its suppression, accordingly as the course which it takes may be painful or pleasurable. If the latter, the soul must contribute to its support, or it never becomes vivid,—and soon languishes, and dies. And this brings us to the point. If every great poet with whose writings men are familiar, in the highest exercise of his genius, before he can be thoroughly enjoyed, has to call forth and to communicate *power*, this service, in a still greater degree, falls upon an original writer at his first appearance in the world.—Of genius the only proof is the act of doing well what is worthy to be done, and what was never done before: Of genius, in the fine arts, the only infallible sign is the widening the sphere of human sensibility for the delight, honour, and benefit of human nature. Genius is the introduction of a new element into the intellectual universe: or, if that be not allowed, it is the application of powers to objects on which they had not before been exercised, or the employment of them in such a manner as to produce effects hitherto unknown. What is all this but an advance, or a conquest, made by the soul of the poet? Is it to be supposed that the reader can make progress of this kind, like an Indian prince or general—stretched on his palanquin, and borne by slaves? No; he is invigorated and inspirited by his leader, in order that he may exert himself; for he cannot proceed in quiescence, he cannot be carried like a dead weight. Therefore to create taste is to call forth and bestow power, of which knowledge is the effect; and *there* lies the true difficulty.

As the pathetic participates of an *animal*

sensation, it might seem that, if the springs of this emotion were genuine, all men, possessed of competent knowledge of the facts and circumstances, would be instantaneously affected. And, doubtless, in the works of every true poet will be found passages of that species of excellence which is proved by effects immediate and universal. But there are emotions of the pathetic that are simple and direct, and others that are complex and revolutionary; some to which the heart yields with gentleness; others against which it struggles with pride; these varieties are infinite as the combinations of circumstance and the constitutions of character. Remember, also, that the medium through which, in poetry, the heart is to be affected is language; a thing subject to endless fluctuations and arbitrary associations. The genius of the poet melts these down for his purpose; but they retain their shape and quality to him who is not capable of exerting, within his own mind, a corresponding energy. There is also a meditative, as well as a human, pathos; an enthusiastic as well as an ordinary sorrow; a sadness that has its seat in the depths of reason, to which the mind cannot sink gently of itself—but to which it must descend by treading the steps of thought. And for the sublime,—if we consider what are the cares that occupy the passing day, and how remote is the practice and the course of life from the sources of sublimity in the soul of Man, can it be wondered that there is little existing preparation for a poet charged with a new mission to extend its kingdom, and to augment and spread its enjoyments?

Away, then, with the senseless iteration of the world *popular* applied to new works in poetry, as if there were no test of excellence in this first of the fine arts but that all men should run after its productions, as if urged by an appetite, or constrained by a spell!—The qualities of writing best fitted for eager reception are either such as startle the world into attention by their audacity and extravagance; or they are chiefly of a superficial kind, lying upon the surfaces of manners; or arising out of a selection and arrangement of incidents, by which the mind is kept upon the stretch of curiosity, and the fancy amused without the trouble of thought. But in everything which is to send the soul into herself, to be admonished of her weakness, or to be made conscious of her power; wherever life and nature are described as operated upon by the creative or abstracting virtue of the imagination; wherever the instinctive wisdom of antiquity and her heroic passions uniting, in the heart of the poet, with the meditative wisdom of later ages, have produced that accord of sublimated humanity, which is at once a history of the remote past and a prophetic enunciation of the remotest future; *there,* the poet must reconcile himself for a season to few and scattered hearers.—Grand thoughts (and Shakspeare must often have sighed over this truth), as they are most naturally and most fitly conceived in solitude, so can they not be brought forth in the midst of plaudits without some violation of their sanctity. Go to a silent exhibition of the productions of the sister Art, and be convinced that the qualities which dazzle at first sight, and kindle the admiration of the multitude, are essentially different from those by which permanent influence is secured. Let us not shrink from following up these principles as far as they will carry us, and conclude with observing that there never has been a period, and perhaps never will be, in which vicious poetry, of some kind or other, has not excited more zealous admiration, and been far more generally read, than good; but this advantage attends the good, that the *individual,* as well as the species, survives from age to age; whereas, of the depraved, though the species be immortal, the individual quickly *perishes;* the object of present admiration vanishes, being supplanted by some other as easily produced; which, though no better, brings with it at least the irritation of novelty,—with adaptation, more or less skilful, to the changing humours of the majority of those who are most at leisure to regard poetical works when they first solicit their attention.

Is it the result of the whole that, in the opinion of the Writer, the judgment of the People is not to be respected? The thought is most injurious; and, could the charge be brought against him, he would repel it with indignation. The People have already been justified, and their eulogium pronounced by implication, when it was said above that, of *good* poetry, the *individual,* as well as the species, *survives.* And how does it survive but through the People? What preserves it but their intellect and their wisdom?

—Past and future, are the wings
On whose support, harmoniously conjoined,

Moves the great Spirit of human knowledge—
MS.

The voice that issues from this Spirit, is that Vox Populi which the Deity inspires. Foolish must he be who can mistake for this a local acclamation, or a transitory outcry—transitory though it be for years, local though from a Nation. Still more lamentable is his error who can believe that there is anything of divine infallibility in the clamour of that small though loud portion of the community, ever governed by factitious influence, which, under the name of the Public, passes itself, upon the unthinking, for the People. Towards the Public, the Writer hopes that he feels as much deference as it is entitled to: but to the People, philosophically characterised, and to the embodied spirit of their knowledge, so far as it exists and moves, at the present, faithfully supported by its two wings, the past and the future, his devout respect, his reverence, is due. He offers it willingly and readily; and, this done, takes leave of his Readers, by assuring them that, if he were not persuaded that the contents of these Volumes, and the Work to which they are subsidiary, evince something of the "Vision and the Faculty divine"; and that, both in words and things, they will operate in their degree to extend the domain of sensibility for the delight, the honour, and the benefit of human nature, notwithstanding the many happy hours which he has employed in their composition, and the manifold comforts and enjoyments they have procured to him, he would not, if a wish could do it, save them from immediate destruction—from becoming at this moment, to the world, as a thing that had never been.
1815.

PREFACE TO THE EDITION OF 1815

The powers requisite for the production of poetry are: first, those of Observation and Description,—*i.e.*, the ability to observe with accuracy things as they are in themselves, and with fidelity to describe them, unmodified by any passion or feeling existing in the mind of the describer: whether the things depicted be actually present to the senses, or have a place only in the memory. This power, though indispensable to a Poet, is one which he employs only in submission to necessity, and never for a continuance of time: as its exercise supposes all the higher qualities of the mind to be passive, and in a state of subjection to external objects, much in the same way as a translator or engraver ought to be to his original. 2dly, Sensibility,—which, the more exquisite it is, the wider will be the range of a poet's perceptions; and the more will he be incited to observe objects, both as they exist in themselves and as re-acted upon by his own mind. (The distinction between poetic and human sensibility has been marked in the character of the Poet delineated in the original preface.) 3dly, Reflection,—which makes the Poet acquainted with the value of actions, images, thoughts, and feelings; and assists the sensibility in perceiving their connection with each other. 4thly, Imagination and Fancy,—to modify, to create, and to associate. 5thly, Invention,—by which characters are composed out of materials supplied by observation; whether of the Poet's own heart and mind, or of external life and nature; and such incidents and situations produced as are most impressive to the imagination, and most fitted to do justice to the characters, sentiments, and passions, which the Poet undertakes to illustrate. And, lastly, Judgment,—to decide how and where, and in what degree, each of these faculties ought to be exerted; so that the less shall not be sacrificed to the greater; nor the greater, slighting the less, arrogate, to its own injury, more than its due. By judgment, also, is determined what are the laws and appropriate graces of every species of composition.[1]

The materials of Poetry, by these powers collected and produced, are cast, by means of various moulds, into divers forms. The moulds may be enumerated, and the forms specified, in the following order. 1st, The Narrative,—including the Epopœia, the Historic Poem, the Tale, the Romance, the Mock-heroic, and, if the spirit of Homer will tolerate such neighbourhood, that dear production of our days, the metrical Novel. Of this Class, the distinguishing mark is, that the Narrator, however liberally his speaking agents be introduced, is himself the source from which everything primarily flows. Epic Poets, in order that their mode of composition may accord with the elevation of their subject, represent themselves

[1] As sensibility to harmony of numbers, and the power of producing it, are invariably attendants upon the faculties above specified, nothing has been said upon those requisites.

as *singing* from the inspiration of the Muse, "Arma virumque *cano;*" but this is a fiction, in modern times, of slight value: the Iliad or the Paradise Lost would gain little in our estimation by being chanted. The other poets who belong to this class are commonly content to *tell* their tale;—so that of the whole it may be affirmed that they neither require nor reject the accompaniment of music.

2dly, The Dramatic,—consisting of Tragedy, Historic Drama, Comedy, and Masque, in which the poet does not appear at all in his own person, and where the whole action is carried on by speech and dialogue of the agents; music being admitted only incidentally and rarely. The Opera may be placed here, inasmuch as it proceeds by dialogue; though depending, to the degree that it does, upon music, it has a strong claim to be ranked with the lyrical. The characteristic and impassioned Epistle, of which Ovid and Pope have given examples, considered as a species of monodrama, may, without impropriety, be placed in this class.

3dly, The Lyrical—containing the Hymn, the Ode, the Elegy, the Song, and the Ballad; in all which, for the production of their *full* effect, an accompaniment of music is indispensable.

4thly, The Idyllium,—descriptive chiefly either of the processes and appearances of external nature, as the Seasons of Thomson; or of characters, manners, and sentiments, as are Shenstone's Schoolmistress, The Cotter's Saturday Night of Burns, the Twa Dogs of the same Author; or of these in conjunction with the appearances of Nature, as most of the pieces of Theocritus, the Allegro and Penseroso of Milton, Beattie's Minstrel, Goldsmith's Deserted Village. The Epitaph, the Inscription, the Sonnet, most of the epistles of poets writing in their own persons, and all locodescriptive poetry, belong to this class.

5thly, Didactic,—the principal object of which is direct instruction; as the Poem of Lucretius, the Georgics of Virgil, The Fleece of Dyer, Mason's English Garden, etc.

And, lastly, philosophical Satire, like that of Horace and Juvenal; personal and occasional Satire rarely comprehending sufficient of the general in the individual to be dignified with the name of poetry.

Out of the three last has been constructed a composite order, of which Young's Night Thoughts, and Cowper's Task, are excellent examples.

It is deducible from the above, that poems, apparently miscellaneous, may with propriety be arranged either with reference to the powers of mind *predominant* in the production of them; or to the mould in which they are cast; or, lastly, to the subjects to which they relate. From each of these considerations, the following Poems have been divided into classes; which, that the work may more obviously correspond with the course of human life, and for the sake of exhibiting in it the three requisites of a legitimate whole, a beginning, a middle, and an end, have been also arranged, as far as it was possible, according to an order of time, commencing with Childhood, and terminating with Old Age, Death, and Immortality. My guiding wish was that the small pieces of which these volumes consist, thus discriminated, might be regarded under a two-fold view; as composing an entire work within themselves, and as adjuncts to the philosophical Poem, "The Recluse." This arrangement has long presented itself habitually to my own mind. Nevertheless, I should have preferred to scatter the contents of these volumes at random, if I had been persuaded that, by the plan adopted, anything material would be taken from the natural effect of the pieces, individually, on the mind of the unreflecting Reader. I trust there is a sufficient variety in each class to prevent this; while, for him who reads with reflection, the arrangement will serve as a commentary unostentatiously directing his attention to my purposes, both particular and general. But as I wish to guard against the possibility of misleading by this classification, it is proper first to remind the Reader that certain poems are placed according to the powers of mind, in the Author's conception, predominant in the production of them; *predominant,* which implies the exertion of other faculties in less degree. Where there is more imagination than fancy in a poem, it is placed under the head of imagination, and *vice versa.* Both the above classes might without impropriety have been enlarged from that consisting of "Poems founded on the Affections;" as might this latter from those, and from the class "proceeding from Sentiment and Reflection." The most striking characteristics of each piece, mutual illustration, variety, and proportion, have governed me throughout.

None of the other Classes, except those of Fancy and Imagination, require any particular notice. But a remark of general application may be made. All Poets, except the dramatic, have been in the practice of feigning that their works were composed to the music of the harp or lyre: with what degree of affectation this has been done in modern times, I leave to the judicious to determine. For my own part, I have not been disposed to violate probability so far, or to make such a large demand upon the Reader's charity. Some of these pieces are essentially lyrical; and, therefore, cannot have their due force without a supposed musical accompaniment; but, in much the greatest part, as a substitute for the classic lyre or romantic harp, I require nothing more than an animated or impassioned recitation, adapted to the subject. Poems, however humble in their kind, if they be good in that kind, cannot read themselves; the law of long syllable and short must not be so inflexible,—the letter of metre must not be so impassive to the spirit of versification,—as to deprive the Reader of all voluntary power to modulate, in subordination to the sense, the music of the poem;—in the same manner as his mind is left at liberty, and even summoned, to act upon its thoughts and images. But, though the accompaniment of a musical instrument be frequently dispensed with, the true Poet does not therefore abandon his privilege distinct from that of the mere Proseman;

> He murmurs near the running brooks
> A music sweeter than their own.

Let us come now to the consideration of the words Fancy and Imagination, as employed in the classification of the following Poems. "A man," says an intelligent author, "has imagination in proportion as he can distinctly copy in idea the impressions of sense: it is the faculty which *images* within the mind the phenomena of sensation. A man has fancy in proportion as he can call up, connect, or associate, at pleasure, those internal images (φαντάζειν is to cause to appear), so as to complete ideal representations of absent objects. Imagination is the power of depicting, and fancy of evoking and combining. The imagination is formed by patient observation; the fancy by a voluntary activity in shifting the scenery of the mind. The more accurate the imagination, the more safely may a painter, or a poet, undertake a delineation, or a description, without the presence of the objects to be characterised. The more versatile the fancy, the more original and striking will be the decorations produced."—*British Synonyms discriminated, by W. Taylor.*

Is not this as if a man should undertake to supply an account of a building, and be so intent upon what he had discovered of the foundation, as to conclude his task without once looking up at the superstructure? Here, as in other instances throughout the volume, the judicious Author's mind is enthralled by Etymology; he takes up the original word as his guide and escort, and too often does not perceive how soon he becomes its prisoner, without liberty to tread in any path but that to which it confines him. It is not easy to find out how imagination, thus explained, differs from distinct remembrance of images; or fancy from quick and vivid recollection of them: each is nothing more than a mode of memory. If the two words bear the above meaning, and no other, what term is left to designate that faculty of which the Poet is "all compact;" he whose eye glances from earth to heaven, whose spiritual attributes body forth what his pen is prompt in turning to shape; or what is left to characterise Fancy, as insinuating herself into the heart of objects with creative activity?— Imagination, in the sense of the word as giving title to a class of the following Poems, has no reference to images that are merely a faithful copy, existing in the mind, of absent external objects; but is a word of higher import, denoting operations of the mind upon those objects, and processes of creation or of composition, governed by certain fixed laws. I proceed to illustrate my meaning by instances. A parrot *hangs* from the wires of his cage by his beak or by his claws; or a monkey from the bough of a tree by his paws or his tail. Each creature does so literally and actually. In the first Eclogue of Virgil, the shepherd, thinking of the time when he is to take leave of his farm, thus addresses his goats:—

> Non ego vos posthac viridi projectus in antro
> Dumosa *pendere* procul de rupe videbo.

> ————half way down
> *Hangs* one who gathers samphire,

is the well-known expression of Shakspeare, delineating an ordinary image upon the cliffs of Dover. In these two instances is a slight exertion of the faculty which I denominate imagination, in the use of one word: neither the goats nor the samphire-gatherer do literally hang, as does the parrot or the monkey; but, presenting to the senses something of such an appearance, the mind in its activity, for its own gratification, contemplates them as hanging.

As when far off at sea a fleet descried
Hangs in the clouds, by equinoctial winds
Close sailing from Bengala, or the isles
Of Ternate or Tidore, whence merchants
    bring
Their spicy drugs; they on the trading flood
Through the wide Ethiopian to the Cape
Ply, stemming nightly toward the Pole:
    so seemed
Far off the flying Fiend.

Here is the full strength of the imagination involved in the word *hangs,* and exerted upon the whole image: First, the fleet, an aggregate of many ships, is represented as one mighty person, whose track, we know and feel, is upon the waters; but, taking advantage of its appearance to the senses, the Poet dares to represent it as *hanging in the clouds,* both for the gratification of the mind in contemplating the image itself, and in reference to the motion and appearance of the sublime objects to which it is compared.

From impressions of sight we will pass to those of sound; which, as they must necessarily be of a less definite character, shall be selected from these volumes:

Over his own sweet voice the Stock-dove *broods,*

of the same bird,

His voice was *buried* among trees,
Yet to be come at by the breeze;
O, Cuckoo! shall I call thee *Bird,*
Or but a wandering *Voice?*

The stock-dove is said to *coo,* a sound well imitating the note of the bird; but, by the intervention of the metaphor *broods,* the affections are called in by the imagination to assist in marking the manner in which the bird reiterates and prolongs her soft note, as if herself delighting to listen to it, and participating of a still and quiet satisfaction, like that which may be supposed inseparable from the continuous process of incubation. "His voice was buried among trees," a metaphor expressing the love of *seclusion* by which this Bird is marked; and characterising its note as not partaking of the shrill and the piercing, and therefore more easily deadened by the intervening shade; yet a note so peculiar and withal so pleasing, that the breeze, gifted with that love of the sound which the Poet feels, penetrates the shades in which it is entombed, and conveys it to the ear of the listener.

Shall I call thee Bird,
Or but a wandering Voice?

This concise interrogation characterises the seeming ubiquity of the voice of the cuckoo, and dispossesses the creature almost of a corporeal existence; the Imagination being tempted to this exertion of her power by a consciousness in the memory that the cuckoo is almost perpetually heard throughout the season of spring, but seldom becomes an object of sight.

Thus far of images independent of each other, and immediately endowed by the mind with properties that do not inhere in them, upon an incitement from properties and qualities the existence of which is inherent and obvious. These processes of imagination are carried on either by conferring additional properties upon an object, or abstracting from it some of those which it actually possesses, and thus enabling it to re-act upon the mind which hath performed the process like a new existence.

I pass from the Imagination acting upon an individual image to a consideration of the same faculty employed upon images in a conjunction by which they modify each other. The Reader has already had a fine instance before him in the passage quoted from Virgil, where the apparently perilous situation of the goat, hanging upon the shaggy precipice, is contrasted with that of the shepherd contemplating it from the seclusion of the cavern in which he lies stretched at ease and in security. Take these images separately, and how unaffecting the picture compared with that produced by their being thus connected with, and opposed to, each other!

As a huge stone is sometimes seen to lie
Couched on the bald top of an eminence,
Wonder to all who do the same espy
By what means it could thither come,
    and whence,
So that it seems a thing endued with sense,
Like a sea-beast crawled forth, which on a
    shelf
Of rock or sand reposeth, there to sun himself.

Such seemed this Man; not all alive or dead,
Nor all asleep, in his extreme old age.

*   *   *   *   *   *

Motionless as a cloud the old Man stood,
That heareth not the loud winds when they call,
And moveth altogether if it move at all.

In these images, the conferring, the abstracting, and the modifying powers of the Imagination, immediately and mediately acting, are all brought into conjunction. The stone is endowed with something of the power of life to approximate it to the sea-beast; and the sea-beast stripped of some of its vital qualities to assimilate it to the stone; which intermediate image is thus treated for the purpose of bringing the original image, that of the stone, to a nearer resemblance to the figure and condition of the aged Man; who is divested of so much of the indications of life and motion as to bring him to the point where the two objects unite and coalesce in just comparison. After what has been said, the image of the cloud need not be commented upon.

Thus far of an endowing or modifying power; but the Imagination also shapes and *creates;* and how? By innumerable processes; and in none does it more delight than in that of consolidating numbers into unity, and dissolving and separating unity into number,— alternations proceeding from, and governed by, a sublime consciousness of the soul in her own mighty and almost divine powers. Recur to the passage already cited from Milton. When the compact Fleet, as one Person, has been introduced "Sailing from Bengala," "They," *i.e.* the "merchants," representing the fleet resolved into a multitude of ships, "ply" their voyage towards the extremities of the earth: "So" (referring to the word "As" in the commencement) "seemed the flying Fiend;" the image of his Person acting to recombine the multitude of ships into one body,—the point from which the comparison set out. "So seemed," and to whom seemed? To the heavenly Muse who dictates the poem, to the eye of the Poet's mind, and to that of the Reader, present at one moment in the wide Ethiopian, and the next in the solitudes, then first broken in upon, of the infernal regions!

Modo me Thebis, modo ponit Athenis.

Hear again this mighty Poet,—speaking of the Messiah going forth to expel from heaven the rebellious angels,

Attended by ten thousand thousand Saints
He onward came: far off his coming shone,—

the retinue of Saints, and the Person of the Messiah himself, lost almost and merged in the splendour of that indefinite abstraction "His coming"!

As I do not mean here to treat this subject further than to throw some light upon the present Volumes, and especially upon one division of them, I shall spare myself and the Reader the trouble of considering the Imagination as it deals with thoughts and sentiments, as it regulates the composition of characters, and determines the course of actions: I will not consider it (more than I have already done by implication) as that power which, in the language of one of my most esteemed Friends, "draws all things to one; which makes things animate or inanimate, beings with their attributes, subjects with their accessories, take one colour and serve to one effect." [1] The grand storehouses of enthusiastic and meditative Imagination, of poetical, as contradistinguished from human and dramatic Imagination, are the prophetic and lyrical parts of the Holy Scriptures, and the works of Milton; to which I cannot forbear to add those of Spenser. I select these writers in preference to those of ancient Greece and Rome, because the anthropomorphism of the Pagan religion subjected the minds of the greatest poets in those countries too much to the bondage of definite form; from which the Hebrews were preserved by their abhorrence of idolatry. This abhorrence was almost as strong in our great epic Poet, both from circumstances of his life, and from the constitution of his mind. However imbued the surface might be with classical literature, he was a Hebrew in soul; and all things tended in him towards the sublime. Spenser, of a gentler nature, maintained his freedom by aid of his allegorical spirit, at one time inciting him to create persons out of abstractions; and, at another, by a superior effort of genius, to give the universality and permanence of abstractions to his human beings, by means of attributes and emblems that belong to the highest moral truths and the purest sensations,—of which his character of Una is a glorious example. Of the human and dramatic Imagination the works of Shakspeare are an inexhaustible source.

[1] Charles Lamb upon the genius of Hogarth.

I tax not you, ye Elements, with unkindness,
I never gave you kingdoms, call'd you Daughters!

And if, bearing in mind the many Poets distinguished by this prime quality, whose names I omit to mention, yet justified by recollection of the insults which the ignorant, the incapable, and the presumptuous, have heaped upon these and my other writings, I may be permitted to anticipate the judgment of posterity upon myself, I shall declare (censurable, I grant, if the notoriety of the fact above stated does not justify me) that I have given in these unfavourable times evidence of exertions of this faculty upon its worthiest objects, the external universe, the moral and religious sentiments of Man, his natural affections, and his acquired passions; which have the same ennobling tendency as the productions of men, in this kind, worthy to be holden in undying remembrance.

To the mode in which Fancy has already been characterised as the power of evoking and combining, or, as my friend Mr. Coleridge has styled it, "the aggregative and associative power," my objection is only that the definition is too general. To aggregate and to associate, to evoke and to combine, belong as well to the Imagination as to the Fancy; but either the materials evoked and combined are different, or they are brought together under a different law, and for a different purpose. Fancy does not require that the materials which she makes use of should be susceptible of change in their constitution from her touch; and, where they admit of modification, it is enough for her purpose if it be slight, limited, and evanescent. Directly the reverse of these are the desires and demands of the Imagination. She recoils from everything but the plastic, the pliant, and the indefinite. She leaves it to Fancy to describe Queen Mab as coming,

In shape no bigger than an agate-stone
On the fore-finger of an alderman.

Having to speak of stature, she does not tell you that her gigantic Angel was as tall as Pompey's Pillar; much less that he was twelve cubits or twelve hundred cubits high; or that his dimensions equalled those of Teneriffe or Atlas;—because these, and if they were a million times as high it would be the same, are bounded: The expression is, "His stature reached the sky!" the illimitable firmament! —When the Imagination frames a comparison, if it does not strike on the first presentation, a sense of the truth of the likeness, from the moment that it is perceived, grows—and continues to grow—upon the mind; the resemblance depending less upon outline of form and feature than upon expression and effect; less upon casual and outstanding than upon inherent and internal properties: moreover, the images invariably modify each other.— The law under which the processes of Fancy are carried on is as capricious as the accidents of things, and the effects are surprising, playful, ludicrous, amusing, tender, or pathetic, as the objects happen to be appositely produced or fortunately combined. Fancy depends upon the rapidity and profusion with which she scatters her thoughts and images; trusting that their number, and the felicity with which they are linked together, will make amends for the want of individual value: or she prides herself upon the curious subtilty and the successful elaboration with which she can detect their lurking affinities. If she can win you over to her purpose, and impart to you her feelings, she cares not how unstable or transitory may be her influence, knowing that it will not be out of her power to resume it upon an apt occasion. But the Imagination is conscious of an indestructible dominion;—the Soul may fall away from it, not being able to sustain its grandeur; but, if once felt and acknowledged, by no act of any other faculty of the mind can it be relaxed, impaired, or diminished.—Fancy is given to quicken and to beguile the temporal part of our nature, Imagination to incite and to support the eternal.—Yet is it not the less true that Fancy, as she is an active, is also, under her own laws and in her own spirit, a creative faculty. In what manner Fancy ambitiously aims at a rivalship with Imagination, and Imagination stoops to work with the materials of Fancy, might be illustrated from the compositions of all eloquent writers, whether in prose or verse; and chiefly from those of our own Country. Scarcely a page of the impassioned parts of Bishop Taylor's Works can be opened that shall not afford examples.—Referring the Reader to those inestimable volumes, I will content myself with placing a conceit (ascribed to Lord Chesterfield) in contrast with a passage from the Paradise Lost:—

The dews of the evening most carefully shun,
They are the tears of the sky for the loss of
   the sun.

After the transgression of Adam, Milton, with
other appearances of sympathising Nature, thus 5
marks the immediate consequence,

Sky lowered, and, muttering thunder, some
   sad drops
Wept at completing of the mortal sin.   10

The associating link is the same in each instance: Dew and rain, not distinguishable from
the liquid substance of tears, are employed as
indications of sorrow. A flash of surprise is 15
the effect in the former case; a flash of surprise, and nothing more; for the nature of
things does not sustain the combination. In
the latter, the effects from the act, of which
there is this immediate consequence and vis- 20
ible sign, are so momentous that the mind
acknowledges the justice and reasonableness
of the sympathy in nature so manifested; and
the sky weeps drops of water as if with
human eyes, as "Earth had before trembled 25
from her entrails, and Nature given a second
groan."

   Finally, I will refer to Cotton's "Ode upon
Winter," an admirable composition, though
stained with some peculiarities of the age in 30
which he lived, for a general illustration of
the characteristics of Fancy. The middle part
of this ode contains a most lively description
of the entrance of Winter, with his retinue, as
"A palsied king," and yet a military monarch, 35
—advancing for conquest with his army; the
several bodies of which, and their arms and
equipments, are described with a rapidity of
detail, and a profusion of *fanciful* comparisons, which indicate on the part of the poet 40
extreme activity of intellect, and a correspondent hurry of delightful feeling. Winter retires
from the foe into his fortress, where

    ——a magazine
Of sovereign juice is cellared in;   45
Liquor that will the siege maintain
Should Phœbus ne'er return again.

Though myself a water-drinker, I cannot resist the pleasure of transcribing what follows, 50
as an instance still more happy of Fancy employed in the treatment of feeling than, in its
preceding passages, the Poem supplies of her
management of forms.

'Tis that, that gives the poet rage,
And thaws the gelly'd blood of age;
Matures the young, restores the old,
And makes the fainting coward bold.

It lays the careful head to rest,
Calms palpitations in the breast,
Renders our lives' misfortune sweet;

  *   *   *   *   *

Then let the chill Sirocco blow,
And gird us round with hills of snow,
Or else go whistle to the shore,
And make the hollow mountains roar,

Whilst we together jovial sit
Careless, and crowned with mirth and wit,
Where, though bleak winds confine us home
Our fancies round the world shall roam.

We'll think of all the Friends we know,
And drink to all worth drinking to;
When having drunk all thine and mine,
We rather shall want healths than wine.

But where Friends fail us, we'll supply
Our friendships with our charity;
Men that remote in sorrows live,
Shall by our lusty brimmers thrive.

We'll drink the wanting into wealth,
And those that languish into health,
The afflicted into joy; th' opprest
Into security and rest.

The worthy in disgrace shall find
Favour return again more kind,
And in restraint who stifled lie,
Shall taste the air of liberty.

The brave shall triumph in success,
The lovers shall have mistresses,
Poor unregarded Virtue, praise,
And the neglected Poet, bays.

Thus shall our healths do others good,
Whilst we ourselves do all we would;
For, freed from envy and from care,
What would we be but what we are?

   When I sate down to write this Preface,
it was my intention to have made it more comprehensive; but, thinking that I ought rather
to apologise for detaining the reader so long,
I will here conclude.

POSTSCRIPT

1835

   In the present Volume, as in those that have
preceded it, the reader will have found occasionally opinions expressed upon the course
of public affairs, and feelings given vent to as

national interests excited them. Since nothing, I trust, has been uttered but in the spirit of reflective patriotism, those notices are left to produce their own effect; but, among the many objects of general concern, and the changes going forward, which I have glanced at in verse, are some especially affecting the lower orders of society: in reference to these, I wish here to add a few words in plain prose.

Were I conscious of being able to do justice to those important topics, I might avail myself of the periodical press for offering anonymously my thoughts, such as they are, to the world; but I feel that in procuring attention, they may derive some advantage, however small, from my name, in addition to that of being presented in a less fugitive shape. It is also not impossible that the state of mind which some of the foregoing poems may have produced in the reader, will dispose him to receive more readily the impression which I desire to make, and to admit the conclusions I would establish.

I. The first thing that presses upon my attention is the Poor-Law Amendment Act. I am aware of the magnitude and complexity of the subject, and the unwearied attention which it has received from men of far wider experience than my own; yet I cannot forbear touching upon one point of it, and to this I will confine myself, though not insensible to the objection which may reasonably be brought against treating a portion of this, or any other, great scheme of civil polity separately from the whole. The point to which I wish to draw the reader's attention is, that *all* persons who cannot find employment, or procure wages sufficient to support the body in health and strength, are entitled to a maintenance by law.

This dictate of humanity is acknowledged in the Report of the Commissioners: but is there not room for apprehension that some of the regulations of the new act have a tendency to render the principle nugatory by difficulties thrown in the way of applying it? If this be so, persons will not be wanting to show it, by examining the provisions of the act in detail,—an attempt which would be quite out of place here; but it will not, therefore, be deemed unbecoming in one who fears that the prudence of the head may, in framing some of those provisions, have supplanted the wis-

dom of the heart, to enforce a principle which cannot be violated without infringing upon one of the most precious rights of the English people, and opposing one of the most sacred claims of civilised humanity.

There can be no greater error, in this department of legislation, than the belief that this principle does by necessity operate for the degradation of those who claim, or are so circumstanced as to make it likely they may claim, through laws founded upon it, relief or assistance. The direct contrary is the truth: it may be unanswerably maintained that its tendency is to raise, not to depress; by stamping a value upon life, which can belong to it only where the laws have placed men who are willing to work, and yet cannot find employment, above the necessity of looking for protection against hunger and other natural evils, either to individual and casual charity, to despair and death, or to the breach of law by theft or violence.

And here, as, in the Report of the Commissioners, the fundamental principle has been recognised, I am not at issue with them any farther than I am compelled to believe that their "remedial measures" obstruct the application of it more than the interests of society require.

And, calling to mind the doctrines of political economy which are now prevalent, I cannot forbear to enforce the justice of the principle, and to insist upon its salutary operation.

And first for its justice: If self-preservation be the first law of our nature, would not every one in a state of nature be morally justified in taking to himself that which is indispensable to such preservation, where, by so doing, he would not rob another of that which might be equally indispensable to *his* preservation? And if the value of life be regarded in a right point of view, may it not be questioned whether this right of preserving life, at any expense short of endangering the life of another, does not survive man's entering into the social state; whether this right can be surrendered or forfeited, except when it opposes the divine law, upon any supposition of a social compact, or of any convention for the protection of mere rights of property?

But if it be not safe to touch the abstract question of man's right in a social state to help himself even in the last extremity, may we not still contend for the duty of a christian government, standing *in loco parentis* towards all its subjects, to make such effectual provisions, that no one shall be in danger of perishing either through the neglect or harshness of its legislation? Or, waiving this, is it not indisputable that the claim of the state to the allegiance involves the protection of the subject? And, as all rights in one party impose a correlative duty upon another, it follows that the right of the state to require the services of its members, even to the jeoparding of their lives in the common defence, establishes a right in the people (not to be gainsaid by utilitarians and economists) to public support when from any cause they may be unable to support themselves.

Let us now consider the salutary and benign operation of this principle. Here we must have recourse to elementary feelings of human nature, and to truths which from their very obviousness are apt to be slighted, till they are forced upon our notice by our own sufferings or those of others. In the Paradise Lost, Milton represents Adam, after the Fall, as exclaiming, in the anguish of his soul—

> Did I request Thee, Maker, from my clay
> To mould me man; did I solicit Thee
> From darkness to promote me?
> .   .   .   .   .   . My will
> Concurred not to my being.

Under how many various pressures of misery have men been driven thus, in a strain touching upon impiety, to expostulate with the Creator! and under few so afflictive as when the source and origin of earthly existence have been brought back to the mind by its impending close in the pangs of destitution. But as long as, in our legislation, due weight shall be given to this principle, no man will be forced to bewail the gift of life in hopeless want of the necessaries of life.

Englishmen have, therefore, by the progress of civilisation among them, been placed in circumstances more favourable to piety and resignation to the divine will than the inhabitants of other countries, where a like provision has not been established. And as Providence, in this care of our countrymen, acts through a human medium, the objects of that care must, in like manner, be more inclined towards a grateful love of their fellow-men. Thus, also, do stronger ties attach the people to their country, whether while they tread its soil, or, at a distance, think of their native land as an indulgent parent, to whose arms even they who have been imprudent and undeserving may, like the prodigal son, betake themselves, without fear of being rejected.

Such is the view of the case that would first present itself to a reflective mind; and it is in vain to show, by appeals to experience, in contrast with this view, that provisions founded upon the principle have promoted profaneness of life and dispositions the reverse of philanthropic, by spreading idleness, selfishness, and rapacity: for these evils have arisen, not as an inevitable consequence of the principle, but for want of judgment in framing laws based upon it; and, above all, from faults in the mode of administering the law. The mischief that has grown to such a height from granting relief in cases where proper vigilance would have shown that it was not required, or in bestowing it in undue measure, will be urged by no truly enlightened statesman as a sufficient reason for banishing the principle itself from legislation.

Let us recur to the miserable states of consciousness that it precludes.

There is a story told, by a traveller in Spain, of a female who, by a sudden shock of domestic calamity, was driven out of her senses, and ever after looked up incessantly to the sky, feeling that her fellow-creatures could do nothing for her relief. Can there be Englishmen who, with a good end in view, would, upon system, expose their brother Englishmen to a like necessity of looking upwards only; or downwards to the earth, after it shall contain no spot where the destitute can demand, by civil right, what by right of nature they are entitled to?

Suppose the objects of our sympathy not sunk into this blank despair, but wandering about as strangers in streets and ways, with the hope of succour from casual charity; what have we gained by such a change of scene? Woful is the condition of the famished Northern Indian, dependent, among winter snows, upon the chance-passage of a herd of deer, from which one, if brought down by his rifle-gun, may be made the means of keeping him and his companions alive. As miserable is that of some savage Islander, who, when the land has ceased to afford him sustenance, watches for food which the waves may cast up, or in vain endeavours to extract it from the inexplorable deep. But neither of these is in a state of wretchedness comparable to that which is so often endured in civilised society: multitudes, in all ages, have known it, of whom may be said:—

Homeless, near a thousand homes they stood,
And near a thousand tables pined, and wanted food.

Justly might I be accused of wasting time in an uncalled-for attempt to excite the feelings of the reader, if systems of political economy, widely spread, did not impugn the principle, and if the safeguards against such extremities were left unimpaired. It is broadly asserted by many, that every man who endeavours to find work *may* find it: were this assertion capable of being verified, there still would remain a question, what kind of work, and how far may the labourer be fit for it? For if sedentary work is to be exchanged for standing, and some light and nice exercise of the fingers, to which an artisan has been accustomed all his life, for severe labour of the arms, the best efforts would turn to little account, and occasion would be given for the unthinking and the unfeeling unwarrantably to reproach those who are put upon such employment as idle, froward, and unworthy of relief, either by law or in any other way! Were this statement correct, there would indeed be an end of the argument, the principle here maintained would be superseded. But, alas! it is far otherwise. That principle, applicable to the benefit of all countries, is indispensable for England, upon whose coast families are perpetually deprived of their support by shipwreck, and where large masses of men are so liable to be thrown out of their ordinary means of gaining bread, by changes in commercial intercourse, subject mainly or solely to the will of foreign powers; by new discoveries in arts and manufactures; and by reckless laws, in conformity with theories of political economy, which, whether right or wrong in the abstract, have proved a scourge to tens of thousands by the abruptness with which they have been carried into practice.

But it is urged,—refuse altogether compulsory relief to the able-bodied, and the number of those who stand in need of relief will steadily diminish through a conviction of an absolute necessity for greater forethought and more prudent care of a man's earnings. Undoubtedly it would, but so also would it, and in a much greater degree, if the legislative provisions were retained, and parochial relief administered under the care of the upper classes, as it ought to be. For it has been invariably found, that wherever the funds have been raised and applied under the superintendence of gentlemen and substantial proprietors, acting in vestries and as overseers, pauperism has diminished accordingly. Proper care in that quarter would effectually check what is felt in some districts to be one of the worst evils in the poor law system, viz. the readiness of small and needy proprietors to join in imposing rates that seemingly subject them to great hardships, while, in fact, this is done with a mutual understanding that the relief each is ready to bestow upon his still poorer neighbours will be granted to himself, or his relatives, should it hereafter be applied for.

But let us look to inner sentiments of a nobler quality, in order to know what we have to build upon. Affecting proofs occur in every one's experience, who is acquainted with the unfortunate and the indigent, of their unwillingness to derive their subsistence from aught but their own funds or labour, or to be indebted to parochial assistance for the attainment of any object, however dear to them. A case was reported, the other day, from a coroner's inquest, of a pair who, through the space of four years, had carried about their dead infant from house to house, and from lodging to lodging, as their necessities drove them, rather than ask the parish to bear the expense of its interment:—the poor creatures lived in the hope of one day being able to bury their child at their own cost. It must have been heart-rendering to see and hear the mother, who had been called upon to account for the state in which the body was found, make this deposition. By some, judging coldly, if not harshly, this conduct might be imputed to an unwarrantable pride, as she and her husband had, it is true, been once in prosperity. But examples, where the spirit of independence works with equal strength, though not with like miserable accompaniments, are frequently to be found even yet among the humblest peasantry and mechanics. There is not, then, sufficient cause for doubting that a like sense of honour may be revived among the people, and their ancient habits of independence restored, without resorting to those severities which the new Poor Law Act has introduced.

But even if the surfaces of things only are to be examined, we have a right to expect that lawgivers should take into account the various tempers and dispositions of mankind: while some are led, by the existence of a legislative provision, into idleness and extravagance, the economical virtues might be cherished in others by the knowledge that, if all their efforts fail, they have in the Poor Laws a "refuge from the storm and a shadow from the heat." Despondency and distraction are no friends to prudence: the springs of industry will relax, if cheerfulness be destroyed by anxiety; without hope men become reckless, and have a sullen pride in adding to the heap of their own wretchedness. He who feels that he is abandoned by his fellow-men will be almost irresistibly driven to care little for himself; will lose his self-respect accordingly, and with that loss what remains to him of virtue?

With all due deference to the particular experience and general intelligence of the individuals who framed the Act, and of those who in and out of parliament have approved of and supported it, it may be said that it proceeds too much upon the presumption that it is a labouring man's own fault if he be not, as the phrase is, beforehand with the world. But the most prudent are liable to be thrown back by sickness, cutting them off from labour, and causing to them expense: and who but has observed how distress creeps upon multitudes without misconduct of their own; and merely from a gradual fall in the price of labour, without a correspondent one in the price of provisions; so that men who may have ventured upon the marriage state with a fair prospect of maintaining their families in comfort and happiness, see them reduced to a pittance which no effort of theirs can increase? Let it be remembered, also, that there are thousands with whom vicious habits of expense are not the cause why they do not store up their gains; but they are generous and kindhearted, and ready to help their kindred and friends; moreover, they have a faith in Providence that those who have been prompt to assist others, will not be left destitute, should they themselves come to need. By acting from these blended feelings, numbers have rendered themselves incapable of standing up against a sudden reverse. Nevertheless, these men, in common with all who have the misfortune to be in want, if many theorists had their wish, would be thrown upon one or other of those three sharp points of condition before adverted to, from which the intervention of law has hitherto saved them.

All that has been said tends to show how the principle contended for makes the gift of life more valuable, and has, it may be hoped, led to the conclusion that its legitimate operation is to make men worthier of that gift: in other words, not to degrade but to exalt human nature. But the subject must not be dismissed without adverting to the indirect influence of the same principle upon the moral sentiments of a people among whom it is embodied in law. In our criminal jurisprudence there is a maxim, deservedly eulogised, that it is better that ten guilty persons should escape, than that one innocent man should suffer; so, also, might it be maintained, with regard to the Poor Laws, that it is better for the interests of humanity among the people at large, that ten undeserving should partake of the funds provided, than that one morally good man, through want of relief, should either have his principles corrupted or his energies destroyed; than that such a one should either be driven to do wrong or be cast to the earth in utter hopelessness. In France the English maxim of criminal jurisprudence is reversed; there, it is deemed better that ten innocent men should suffer than one guilty escape: in France there is no universal provision for the poor; and we may judge of the small value set upon human life in the metropolis of that country, by merely noticing the disrespect with which, after death, the body is treated, not by the thoughtless vulgar, but in schools of anatomy, presided over by men allowed to be, in their own art and in physical science, among the most enlightened in the world. In the East, where countries are overrun with population as with a weed, infinitely more respect is shown to the remains of the deceased; and what a bitter mockery is it, that this insensibility should be found where civil polity is so busy in minor regulations, and ostentatiously careful to gratify the luxurious propensities, whether social of intellectual, of the multitude! Irreligion is, no doubt, much concerned with this offensive disrespect shown to the bodies of the dead in France; but it is mainly attributable to the state in which so many of the living are left by the absence of compulsory provision for the indigent so humanely established by the law of England.

Sights of abject misery, perpetually recurring, harden the heart of the community. In the perusal of history and of works of fiction we are not, indeed, unwilling to have our commiseration excited by such objects of distress as they present to us; but, in the concerns of real life, men know that such emotions are not given to be indulged for their own sakes: there, the conscience declares to them that sympathy must be followed by action; and if there exist a previous conviction that the power to relieve is utterly inadequate to the demand, the eye shrinks from communication with wretchedness, and pity and compassion languish, like any other qualities that are deprived of their natural aliment. Let these considerations be duly weighed by those who trust to the hope that an increase of private charity, with all its advantages of superior discrimination, would more than compensate for the abandonment of those principles, the wisdom of which has been here insisted upon. How discouraging, also, would be the sense of injustice, which could not fail to arise in the minds of the well-disposed, if the burden of supporting the poor, a burden of which the selfish have hitherto by compulsion borne a share, should now, or hereafter, be thrown exclusively upon the benevolent.

By having put an end to the Slave Trade and Slavery, the British people are exalted in the scale of humanity; and they cannot but feel so, if they look into themselves, and duly consider their relation to God and their fellow-creatures. That was a noble advance; but a retrograde movement will assuredly be made, if ever the principle which has been here defended should be either avowedly abandoned or but ostensibly retained.

But, after all, there may be a little reason to apprehend permanent injury from any experiment that may be tried. On the one side will be human nature rising up in her own defence, and on the other prudential selfishness acting to the same purpose, from a conviction that, without a compulsory provision for the exigencies of the labouring multitude, that degree of ability to regulate the price of labour, which is indispensable for the reasonable interest of arts and manufactures, cannot, in Great Britain, be upheld.

II. In a poem of the foregoing collection allusion is made to the state of the workmen congregated in manufactories. In order to relieve many of the evils to which that class of society are subject, and to establish a better harmony between them and their employers, it would be well to repeal such laws as prevent the formation of joint-stock companies. There are, no doubt, many and great obstacles to the formation and salutary working of these societies, inherent in the mind of those whom they would obviously benefit. But the combinations of masters to keep down, unjustly, the price of labour would be fairly checked by them, as far as they were practicable; they would encourage economy, inasmuch as they would enable a man to draw profit from his savings, by investing them in buildings or machinery for processes of manufacture with which he was habitually connected. His little capital would then be working for him while he was at rest or asleep; he would more clearly perceive the necessity of capital for carrying on great works; he would better learn to respect the larger portions of it in the hands of others; he would be less tempted to join in unjust combinations; and, for the sake of his own property, if not for higher reasons, he would be slow to promote local disturbance or endanger public tranquillity; he would, at least, be loth to act in that way *knowingly:* for it is not to be denied that such societies might be nurseries of opinions unfavourable to a mixed constitution of government, like that of Great Britain. The democratic and republican spirit which they might be apt to foster would not, however, be dangerous in itself, but only as it might act without being sufficiently counterbalanced, either by landed proprietorship, or by a Church extending itself so as to embrace an ever-growing and ever-shifting population of mechanics and artisans. But if the tendencies of such societies would be to make the men prosper who might belong to them, rulers and legislators should rejoice in the result, and do their duty to the state by upholding and extending the influence of that Church to which it owes, in so great a measure, its safety, its prosperity, and its glory.

This, in the temper of the present times, may be difficult, but it is become indispensable, since large towns in great numbers have sprung up, and others have increased tenfold, with little or no dependence upon the gentry and the landed proprietors; and apart from those mitigated feudal institutions, which, till of late, have acted so powerfully upon the composition of the House of Commons. Now it may be affirmed that, in quarters where there is not an attachment to the Church, or the landed aristocracy, and a pride in supporting them, *there* the people will dislike both, and be ready, upon such incitements as are perpetually recurring, to join in attempts to overthrow them. There is no neutral ground here: from want of due attention to the state of society in large towns and manufacturing districts, and ignorance or disregard of these obvious truths, innumerable well-meaning persons became zealous supporters of a Reform Bill, the qualities and powers of which, whether destructive or constructive, they would otherwise have been afraid of; and even the framers of that bill, swayed as they might be by party resentments and personal ambition, could not have gone so far, had not they too been lamentably ignorant or neglectful of the same truths both of fact and philosophy.

But let that pass; and let no opponent of the bill be tempted to compliment his own foresight, by exaggerating the mischiefs and dangers that have sprung from it: let not time be wasted in profitless regrets; and let those party distinctions vanish to their very names that have separated men who, whatever course they may have pursued, have ever had a bond of union in the wish to save the limited monarchy and those other institutions that have, under Providence, rendered for so long a period of time this country the happiest and worthiest of which there is any record since the foundation of civil society.

III. A philosophic mind is best pleased when looking at religion in its spiritual bearing; as a guide of conduct, a solace under affliction, and a support amid the instabilities of mortal life: but the Church having been forcibly brought by political considerations to my notice, while treating of the labouring classes, I cannot forbear saying a few words upon that momentous topic.

There is a loud clamour for extensive change in that department. The clamour would be entitled to more respect if they who are the most eager to swell it with their voices were not generally the most ignorant of the real state of the Church and the service it renders to the community. *Reform* is the word employed.

Let us pause and consider what sense it is apt to carry, and how things are confounded by a lax use of it. The great religious Reformation, in the sixteenth century, did not profess to be a new construction, but a restoration of something fallen into decay, or put out of sight. That familiar and justifiable use of the word seems to have paved the way for fallacies with respect to the term reform, which it is difficult to escape from. Were we to speak of improvement and the correction of abuses, we should run less risk of being deceived ourselves or of misleading others. We should be less likely to fall blindly into the belief that the change demanded is a renewal of something that has existed before, and that, therefore, we have experience on our side; nor should we be equally tempted to beg the question that the change for which we are eager must be advantageous. From generation to generation, men are the dupes of words; and it is painful to observe that so many of our species are most tenacious of those opinions which they have formed with the least consideration. They who are the readiest to meddle with public affairs, whether in church or state, fly to generalities, that they may be eased from the trouble of thinking about particulars; and thus is deputed to mechanical instrumentality the work which vital knowledge only can do well.

"Abolish pluralities, have a resident incumbent in every parish," is a favourite cry; but, without adverting to other obstacles in the way of this specious scheme, it may be asked what benefit would accrue from its *indiscriminate* adoption to counterbalance the harm it would introduce, by nearly extinguishing the order of curates, unless the revenues of the church should grow with the population, and be greatly increased in many thinly-peopled districts, especially among the parishes of the North.

The order of curates is so beneficial, that some particular notice of it seems to be required in this place. For a church poor as, relatively to the numbers of people, that of England is, and probably will continue to be, it is no small advantage to have youthful servants, who will work upon the wages of hope and expectation. Still more advantageous is it to have, by means of this order, young men scattered over the country, who being more detached from the temporal concerns of the benefice, have more leisure for improvement and study, and are less subject to be brought into secular collision with those who are under their spiritual guardianship. The curate, if he reside at a distance from the incumbent, undertakes the requisite responsibilities of a temporal kind, in that modified way which prevents him, as a new-comer, from being charged with selfishness: while it prepares him for entering upon a benefice of his own with something of a suitable experience. If he should act under and in co-operation with a resident incumbent, the gain is mutual. His studies will probably be assisted; and his training, managed by a superior, will not be liable to relapse in matters of prudence, seemliness, or in any of the highest cares of his functions; and by way of return for these benefits to the pupil, it will often happen that the zeal of a middle-aged or declining incumbent will be revived, by being in near communion with the ardour of youth, when his own efforts may have languished through a melancholy consciousness that they have not produced as much good among his flock as, when he first entered upon the charge, he fondly hoped.

Let one remark, and that not the least important, be added. A curate, entering for the first time upon his office, comes from college after a course of expense, and with such inexperience in the use of money that in his new situation he is apt to fall unawares into pecuniary difficulties. If this happens to him, much more likely is it to happen to the youthful incumbent, whose relations, to his parishioners and to society, are more complicated; and, his income being larger and independent of another, a costlier style of living is required of him by public opinion. If embarrassment should ensue, and with that unavoidably some loss of respectability, his future usefulness will be proportionally impaired: not so with the curate, for he can easily remove and start afresh with a stock of experience and an unblemished reputation; whereas the early indiscretions of an incumbent being rarely forgotten, may be impediments to the efficacy of his ministry for the remainder of his life. The same observations would apply with equal force to doctrine. A young minister is liable to errors, from his notions being either too lax or overstrained. In both cases it would prove injurious that the error should be remembered, after study and reflection, with advancing years, shall have brought him to a clearer discernment of the truth, and better judgment in the application of it.

It must be acknowledged that, among the regulations of ecclesiastical polity, none at first view are more attractive than that which prescribes for every parish a resident incumbent. How agreeable to picture to one's self, as has been done by poets and romance-writers, from Chaucer down to Goldsmith, a man devoted to his ministerial office, with not a wish or a thought ranging beyond the circuit of its cares! Nor is it in poetry and fiction only that such characters are found; they are scattered, it is hoped not sparingly, over real life, especially in sequestered and rural districts, where there is but small influx of new inhabitants, and little change of occupation. The spirit of the Gospel, unaided by acquisitions of profane learning and experience in the world,—that spirit and the obligations of the sacred office may, in such situations, suffice to effect most of what is needful. But for the complex state of society that prevails in England much more is required, both in large towns and in many extensive districts of the country. A minister there should not only be irreproachable in manners and morals, but accomplished in learning, as far as is possible without sacrifice of the least of his pastoral duties. As necessary, perhaps more so, is it that he should be a citizen as well as a scholar; thoroughly acquainted with the structure of society and the constitution of civil government, and able to reason upon both with the most expert; all ultimately in order to support the truths of Christianity and to diffuse its blessings.

A young man coming fresh from the place of his education cannot have brought with him these accomplishments; and if the scheme of equalising church incomes, which many advisers are much bent upon, be realised, so that there should be little or no secular inducement for a clergyman to desire a removal from the spot where he may chance to have been first set down; surely not only opportunities for obtaining the requisite qualifications would be diminished, but the motives for desiring to obtain them would be proportionably weakened. And yet these qualifications are indispensable for the diffusion of that knowledge by which alone the political philosophy of the New Testament can be rightly expounded, and its precepts adequately enforced. In these times, when the press is daily exercising so great a power over the minds of the people, for wrong or for right as may happen, *that* preacher ranks among the first of benefactors who, without stooping to the direct treatment of current politics and passing events, can furnish infallible guidance through the delusions that surround them; and who, appealing to the sanctions of Scripture, may place the grounds of its injunctions in so clear a light that disaffection shall cease to be cultivated as a laudable propensity, and loyalty cleansed from the dishonour of a blind and prostrate obedience.

It is not, however, in regard to civic duties alone, that this knowledge in a minister of the Gospel is important; it is still more so for softening and subduing private and personal discontents. In all places, and at all times, men have gratuitously troubled themselves, because their survey of the dispensations of Providence has been partial and narrow; but now that readers are so greatly multiplied, men judge as they are *taught,* and repinings are engendered everywhere, by imputations being cast upon the government; and are prolonged or aggravated by being ascribed to misconduct or injustice in rulers, when the individual himself only is in fault. If a Christian pastor be competent to deal with these humours, as they may be dealt with, and by no members of society so successfully, both from more frequent and more favourable opportunities of intercourse, and by aid of the authority with which he speaks; he will be a teacher of moderation, a dispenser of the wisdom that blunts approaching distress by submission to God's will, and lightens, by patience, grievances which cannot be removed.

We live in times when nothing, of public good at least, is generally acceptable, but what we believe can be traced to preconceived intention and specific acts and formal contrivances of human understanding. A Christian instructor thoroughly accomplished would be a standing restraint upon such presumptuousness of judgment, by impressing the truth that

In the unreasoning progress of the world
A wiser spirit is at work for us,
A better eye than ours.   *MS.*

Revelation points to the purity and peace of a future world; but our sphere of duty is upon earth; and the relations of impure and conflicting things to each other must be understood, or we shall be perpetually going wrong, in all but goodness of intention; and goodness of intention will itself relax through frequent disappointment. How desirable, then, is it, that a minister of the Gospel should be versed in the knowledge of existing facts, and be accustomed to a wide range of social experience! Nor is it less desirable for the purpose of counterbalancing and tempering in his own mind that ambition with which spiritual power is as apt to be tainted as any other species of power which men covet or possess.

It must be obvious that the scope of the argument is to discourage an attempt which would introduce into the Church of England an equality of income and station, upon the model of that of Scotland. The sounder part of the Scottish nation know what good their ancestors derived from their church, and feel how deeply the living generation is indebted to it. They respect and love it, as accommodated in so great a measure to a comparatively poor country, through the far greater portion of which prevails a uniformity of employment; but the acknowledged deficiency of theological learning among the clergy of that church is easily accounted for by this very equality. What else may be wanting there it would be unpleasant to inquire, and might prove invidious to determine: one thing, however, is clear; that in all countries the temporalities of the Church Establishment should bear an analogy to the state of society, otherwise it cannot diffuse its influence through the whole community. In a country so rich and luxurious as England, the character of its clergy must unavoidably sink, and their influence be everywhere impaired, if individuals from the upper ranks, and men of leading talents, are to have no inducements to enter into that body but such as are purely spiritual. And this "tinge of secularity" is no reproach to the clergy, nor does it imply a deficiency of spiritual endowments. Parents and guardians, looking forward to sources of honourable maintenance for their children and wards, often direct their thoughts early towards the church, being determined partly by outward circumstances, and partly by indications of seriousness or intellectual fitness. It is natural that a boy or youth, with such a prospect before him, should turn his attention to those studies, and be led into those habits of reflection, which will in some degree tend to prepare him for the duties he is hereafter to undertake. As he draws nearer to the time when he will be called to these duties, he is both led and compelled to examine the Scriptures. He becomes more and more sensible of their truth. Devotion grows in him; and what might begin in temporal considerations, will end (as in a majority of instances we trust it does) in a spiritual-mindedness not unworthy of that Gospel, the lessons of which he is to teach, and the faith of which he is to inculcate. Not inappositely may be here repeated an observation which, from its obviousness and importance, must have been frequently made, viz. that the impoverishing of the clergy, and bringing their incomes much nearer to a level, would not cause them to become less worldly-minded: the emoluments, howsoever reduced, would be as eagerly sought for, but by men from lower classes in society; men who, by their manners, habits, abilities, and the scanty measure of their attainments, would unavoidably be less fitted for their station, and less competent to discharge its duties.

Visionary notions have in all ages been afloat upon the subject of best providing for the clergy; notions which have been sincerely entertained by good men, with a view to the improvement of that order, and eagerly caught at and dwelt upon by the designing, for its degradation and disparagement. Some are beguiled by what they call the *voluntary system,* not seeing (what stares one in the face at the very threshold) that they who stand in most need of religious instruction are unconscious of the want, and therefore cannot reasonably be expected to make any sacrifices in order to supply it. Will the licentious, the sensual, and the depraved, take from the means of their gratifications and pursuits, to support a discipline that cannot advance without uprooting the trees that bear the fruit which they devour so greedily? Will *they* pay the price of that seed whose harvest is to be reaped in an invisible world? A voluntary system for the religious exigencies of a people numerous and circumstanced as we are! Not more absurd would it be to expect that a knot of boys should draw upon the pittance of their pocket-money to build schools, or out of the abundance of their discretion be able to select fit masters to teach and keep them in order! Some, who clearly perceive the incompetence and folly of such a scheme for the agricultural part of the people, nevertheless think it fea-

sible in large towns, where the rich might subscribe for the religious instruction of the poor. Alas! they know little of the thick darkness that spreads over the streets and alleys of our large towns. The parish of Lambeth, a few years since, contained not more than one church and three or four small proprietary chapels, while dissenting chapels of every denomination were still more scantily found there; yet the inhabitants of the parish amounted at that time to upwards of 50,000. Were the parish church and the chapels of the Establishment existing there an *impediment* to the spread of the Gospel among that mass of people? Who shall dare to say so? But if any one, in the face of the fact which has just been stated, and in opposition to authentic reports to the same effect from various other quarters, should still contend that a voluntary system is sufficient for the spread and maintenance of religion, we would ask, what kind of religion? wherein would it differ, among the many, from deplorable fanaticism?

For the preservation of the Church Establishment, all men, whether they belong to it or not, could they perceive their true interest, would be strenuous; but how inadequate are its provisions for the needs of the country! and how much is it to be regretted that, while its zealous friends yield to alarms on account of the hostility of dissent, they should so much overrate the danger to be apprehended from that quarter, and almost overlook the fact that hundreds of thousands of our fellow-countrymen, though formally and nominally of the Church of England, never enter her places of worship, neither have they communication with her ministers! This deplorable state of things was partly produced by a decay of zeal among the rich and influential, and partly by a want of due expansive power in the constitution of the Establishment as regulated by law. Private benefactors, in their efforts to build and endow churches, have been frustrated or too much impeded by legal obstacles; these, where they are unreasonable or unfitted for the times, ought to be removed; and, keeping clear of intolerance and injustice, means should be used to render the presence and powers of the church commensurate with the wants of a shifting and still-increasing population.

This cannot be effected, unless the English Government vindicate the truth that, as her church exists for the benefit of all (though not in equal degree), whether of her communion or not, all should be made to contribute to its support. If this ground be abandoned, cause will be given to fear that a moral wound may be inflicted upon the heart of the English people, for which a remedy cannot be speedily provided by the utmost efforts which the members of the Church will themselves be able to make.

But let the friends of the church be of good courage. Powers are at work, by which, under Divine Providence, she may be strengthened and the sphere of her usefulness extended; not by alterations in her Liturgy, accommodated to this or that demand of finical taste, nor by cutting off this or that from her articles or Canons, to which the scrupulous or the overweening may object. Covert schism, and open nonconformity, would survive after alterations, however promising in the eyes of those whose subtilty had been exercised in making them. Latitudinarianism is the parhelion of liberty of conscience, and will ever successfully lay claim to a divided worship. Among Presbyterians, Socinians, Baptists, and Independents, there will always be found numbers who will tire of their several creeds, and some will come over to the Church. Conventicles may disappear, congregations in each denomination may fall into decay or be broken up, but the conquests which the National Church ought chiefly to aim at, lie among the thousands and tens of thousands of the unhappy outcasts who grow up with no religion at all. The wants of these cannot but be feelingly remembered. Whatever may be the disposition of the new constituencies under the reformed parliament, and the course which the men of their choice may be inclined or compelled to follow, it may be confidently hoped that individuals, acting in their private capacities, will endeavour to make up for the deficiencies of the legislature. Is it too much to expect that proprietors of large estates, where the inhabitants are without religious instruction, or where it is sparingly supplied, will deem it their duty to take part in this good work; and that thriving manufacturers and merchants will, in their several neighbourhoods, be sensible of the like obligation, and act upon it with generous rivalry?

Moreover, the force of public opinion is rapidly increasing, and some may bend to it, who are not so happy as to be swayed by a higher motive; especially they who derive large incomes from lay-impropriations in tracts of country where ministers are few and meagrely provided for. A claim still stronger may be acknowledged by those who, round their superb habitations, or elsewhere, walk over vast estates which were lavished upon their ancestors by royal favouritism or purchased at insignificant prices after church-spoliation; such proprietors, though not conscience-stricken (there is no call for that), may be prompted to make a return for which their tenantry and dependents will learn to bless their names. An impulse has been given; an accession of means from these several sources, co-operating with a *well*-considered change in the distribution of some parts of the property at present possessed by the church, a change scrupulously founded upon due respect to law and justice, will, we trust, bring about so much of what her friends desire, that the rest may be calmly waited for, with thankfulness for what shall have been obtained.

Let it not be thought unbecoming in a layman to have treated at length a subject with which the clergy are more intimately conversant. All may, without impropriety, speak of what deeply concerns all; nor need an apology be offered for going over ground which has been trod before so ably and so often: without pretending, however, to anything of novelty, either in matter or manner, something may have been offered to view which will save the writer from the imputation of having little to recommend his labour but goodness of intention.

It was with reference to thoughts and feelings expressed in verse, that I entered upon the above notices, and with verse I will conclude. The passage is extracted from my MSS. written above thirty years ago: it turns upon the individual dignity which humbleness of social condition does not preclude, but frequently promotes. It has no direct bearing upon clubs for the discussion of public affairs, nor upon political or trade-unions; but if a single workman—who, being a member of one of those clubs, runs the risk of becoming an agitator, or who, being enrolled in a union, must be left without a will of his own, and therefore a slave —should read these lines, and be touched by them, I should indeed rejoice, and little would I care for losing credit as a poet with intemperate critics, who think differently from me upon political philosophy or public measures,

if the sober-minded admit that, in general
views, my affections have been moved, and my
imagination exercised, under and *for* the guidance of reason.

Here might I pause, and bend in reverence
To Nature, and the power of human minds;
To men as they are men within themselves.
How oft high service is performed within,
When all the external man is rude in show;
Not like a temple rich with pomp and gold,
But a mere mountain chapel that protects
Its simple worshippers from sun and shower!
Of these, said I, shall be my song; of these,
If future years mature me for the task,
Will I record the praises, making verse
Deal boldly with substantial things—in truth
And sanctity of passion, speak of these,
That justice may be done, obeisance paid
Where it is due. Thus haply shall I teach,
Inspire, through unadulterated ears
Pour rapture, tenderness, and hope; my theme
No other than the very heart of man,
As found among the best of those who live,
Not unexalted by religious faith,
Nor uninformed by books, good books, though
    few,
In Nature's presence: thence may I select
Sorrow that is not sorrow, but delight,
And miserable love that is not pain
To hear of, for the glory that redounds

Therefrom to human kind, and what we are.
Be mine to follow with no timid step
Where knowledge leads me; it shall be my pride
That I have dared to tread this holy ground,
Speaking no dream, but things oracular,
Matter not lightly to be heard by those
Who to the letter of the outward promise
Do read the invisible soul; by men adroit
In speech, and for communion with the world
Accomplished, minds whose faculties are then
Most active when they are most eloquent,
And elevated most when most admired.
Men may be found of other mould than these;
Who are their own upholders, to themselves
Encouragement and energy, and will;
Expressing liveliest thoughts in lively words
As native passion dictates. Others, too,
There are, among the walks of homely life,
Still higher, men for contemplation framed;
Shy, and unpractised in the strife of phrase;
Meek men, whose very souls perhaps would sink
Beneath them, summoned to such intercourse.
Theirs is the language of the heavens, the power,
The thought, the image, and the silent joy:
Words are but under-agents in their souls;
When they are grasping with their greatest
    strength
They do not breathe among them; this I speak
In gratitude to God, who feeds our hearts
For his own service, knoweth, loveth us,
When we are unregarded by the world.

SIR WALTER SCOTT

WORDSWORTH AND SCOTT

Students of the great poets of the early nineteenth century should be as aware of the dissimilarity between authors as of the similarity. The practice of using the word *romantic* to describe all of the writers of the time has led us to assume among them a kinship which may in reality not exist. We must remember that *romantic* connotes individualism and difference as much as anything else. It is, in fact, a tricky term. If it is used as an expression which is supposed accurately to gather into a class certain writers who because of likeness give uniform distinction to a period, it is a very bad word indeed. If it is thought of as something less than a term which nevertheless suggests similarity in dissimilarity, then we may the more safely use it.

As Wordsworth said of Burns,

Neighbors we were, and loving friends
   We might have been;

so he might have said of Scott. They were within a year of the same age. One lived in the north of England, the other in the south of Scotland. The father of each was a lawyer; and there was about each a legal sanity concerning the universe. Both men were profoundly wholesome and strong in righteous purpose. And where one sought to employ the very language of men in transforming homely reality into lyrical ballads, the other transcribed ballads sung from the very tongues of men. But not for a moment could we think of Sir Walter rapt in prophetic trance under the light of a strange morning, hearing a voice which called him to song, a voice which he must obey or else sin greatly. And not for a moment can we think of William Wordsworth beginning the *Prelude* at the request of a young lady.

Between these two Romantics we find, then, certain similarities; but we find dissimilarities far greater. The work of the two men has in it all the difference which can exist between intense individuality profoundly dedicated and a most generous unconsciousness of self. Within the bones of one there burns a fire, and there are coals on his lips: he is a prophet. Within the bones of the other there is only healthy marrow, and he suffers from none of the afflicting exhalations of mighty poetic purpose. He is no idle singer of an empty day; but the day of Scott is a past day, glamorous and full of sound. The day of Wordsworth is unclocked eternity.

Wordsworth, then, was more keenly original than Scott. He was the kind of man to start a new movement in poetry and in thought, not to accept an old measure and with it sing the past. Wordsworth built within solitude and among mountains a place on which to stand, and standing there he turned the course of English poetry. He held communion with invisible forms, and straightened his passions sharply, and disciplined his emotions with severe thought. His was the hard power of vehemence controlled. His were the paradoxes of truth. He had no ear for the sound of the clarion, hearing rather "the still sad music of humanity." Where Scott was roused by a fife screaming war among rocky glens, Wordsworth was chastened and subdued and humanized by more ample music. Where Scott was objective and epic, Wordsworth was subjective, although above his subjectivism reigned a strong intelligence.

It is not that Wordsworth does not deal with the actual, but that he deals with it after his own nature. Scott depicts the actual in motion, Wordsworth stills it and passes it through his own mind. He re-creates the actual after the needs of his own fancy and imagination. With him the daisy becomes a nun demure, and the leech gatherer like to a stone that is like to a sea beast. In a sense, all of Wordsworth's children and men and women have in them the mind of the poet, and all the world of external nature into which he peers is invested with his own mind. He looks on mountains the better to contemplate himself. But Scott watches the act and does not care so much as to invade the mind of the actor. He rolls the deed soundingly before himself, but he does not concern himself intimately with the impulses from which the deed arose. The external event he gives us, but he does not stand brooding within the event, inviting attention to the feelings that steal along his blood. Scott is not the poet of his own mind, but the singer of the deeds of his race. The last entry which he made in the book of a little inn in Tyrol points this distinction shrewdly and finally: "Sir Walter Scott, for Scotland."

Had Wordsworth signed this book he might as justly have written, "William Wordsworth, for the Mind of Man." It is wrong to suggest that however intensely occupied he was with the imperial business of his own mind, he had no interest outside that mind. It was in reality the mind of man which he claimed as the main haunt and region of his song. And he was creatively concerned with the intimate affinity existing between that mind and nature. He was not, as has been said too often, merely a nature poet; he sang the high hymeneal chaunt of the wedding of nature to the mind of man. As he contemplated this mystic union his hours grew visionary and he became England's greatest philosophical poet. It was his poetic destiny to "tread on shadowy ground," to sink

Deep—and, aloft ascending, breathe in worlds
To which the heaven of heavens is but a veil.

Here Sir Walter cannot follow him. Wordsworth in respect of sublimity stands immeasurably above and beyond the man who chants the lays of chivalry with clarion couplets, who tells the heroic tale, who watches with bright-eyed, boyish wonder the panoplied processions of history. The reality of Wordsworth is in the truth wrought out of imagination; the reality of Scott is in the deed of the past delightedly and sympathetically spied upon by a bright intelligence.

It is rather from Coleridge, whose task was to give verisimilitude to fancy, that Sir Walter learned. In his 1830 introduction to *The Lay of the Last Minstrel*, referring to the similarity of his poem to *Christabel*, he says, "I am bound to make the acknowledgment due from the pupil to his master." What he meant becomes plain upon the briefest reading.

Christabel

Hush, beating heart of Christabel!
Jesu, Maria, shield her well.—11. 53, 4.

The Lay

Her bower that was guarded by word and by spell,
Deadly to hear, and deadly to tell—
Jesu Maria, shield us well!—C. I. 11. 3–5.

There are in *The Lay* few of the original subtleties spun of the internal lightning of Coleridge's mind, few of the miraculous cadences of wavering genius; but in a broad way the music of the one is the music of the other. Beyond this debt, however, Scott owed little to the eerie man who was amazed by the brightness of his own eyes.

Scott is, then, among the Romanticists, another individual. It is because of his individuality that he is important, that individuality being vital and sound. The business of the student is to seek his delightful peculiarities, being assured that he may treasure them once he finds them.

SIR WALTER SCOTT

1771–1832

On August 15, 1771, Walter Scott was born in Edinburgh. He was descended, as he tells us in his *Autobiography*, from Auld Wat of Harden, "whose name I have made to ring in many a Border ditty, and from his fair dame, the Flower of Yarrow; no bad genealogy for a Border Minstrel." His father was a steady and purposeful man, an attorney with what his son called, "a zeal for his clients which was almost ludicrous." His mother, a person of more lively temperament and imagination, was Anne Rutherford, daughter of Dr. John Rutherford, professor of medicine at the University of Edinburgh. The characteristics of both of the parents were united in their son.

Adorning the main street of Edinburgh today, its grey tracery of stone rising above Princess Park, stands a great monument to Walter Scott. Across the Park, immediately opposite, is the house of Allan Ramsay, the father of Scotch song; and beyond this, the stupendous Castle. Away to the left is Holyrood, where Mary Queen of Scots argued with John Knox and dined fatally with Riccio and stole down her secret stairway into the chapel, to pray. Here in this great hall Bonnie Prince Charlie danced; and here into this chapel Cromwell came marching, tumbling out and together half a dozen kings and queens. Still further beyond is Arthur's Seat, the eminence from which the great king is supposed to have viewed the city. In Edinburgh history turns back into lore, and lore and history mingle to form romance. Beyond the city lie the mountains, the lochs, and the glens of Scotland—a land of tales and ballads and songs. To these things Sir Walter was heir. He voiced the romance of his people, and so he is remembered—

The last of all the bards was he
Who sung of Border chivalry.

When Sir Walter was an infant of eighteen months he suffered from a fever which left him permanently lame in his right leg. As he continued to be a sickly child, his wise grandfather Rutherford sent him away from the city, beyond the Lammermuir Hills, to Sandy-Knowe, a farm in the valley of the Tweed. Here he lived an outdoor life from his third to his fifth year. His grandfather Scott, a hardy cattle-dealer owning the farm, determined to make a healthy boy out of him. "Among the odd remedies recurred to to aid my lameness," writes Sir Walter, "some one had recommended that so often as a sheep was killed for the use of the family, I should be stripped, and swathed up in the skin, warm as it was flayed from the carcase of the animal. In this Tartar-like habiliment I well remember lying upon the floor of the little parlor in the farmhouse, while my grandfather, a venerable old man with white hair, used every excitement to make me try to crawl." He continues: "My health was by this time a good deal confirmed by the country air, and the influence of that imperceptible and unfatiguing exercise to which the good sense of my grandfather had subjected me; for when the day was fine, I was usually carried out and laid down beside the old shepherd, among the crags or rocks round which he fed his sheep." Here, being impatient with his infirmity, he began to struggle and "to roll about in the grass all day long in the midst of the flock." Nature responded to his efforts, and began to return his strength.

But yet another boon was granted

By the green hill and clear blue heaven,

and that was the "poetic impulse." Before the opening eyes of the child lay the naked cliff and the shattered tower, the fair river winding "round holy Melrose," which were to be treasured by him always and recalled in the scenes of his romances. To his awakening consciousness were brought the partly-understood tales and ballads of the actual Border. He heard them first from the tongues of the people who lived in the land where the celebrated deeds were done. The scene, the story, and the song blended into something haunting and unforgettable, something which by the chances of blood and genius were to become a new force in our Romantic literature. All this, while Sir Walter is writing *Marmion,* he pauses to say to his friend William Erskine.

Thus while I ape the measure wild
Of tales that charm'd me yet a child,
Rude though they be, still with the chime
Return the thoughts of early time;
And feelings roused in life's first day,
Glow in the line, and prompt the lay.

No child was ever more father of the man than was this lame boy at Sandy-Knowe. He had scarcely grown to understand the tales of Border raids which were glorified in the memory of his grandmother Scott, or the legends of old Alison Wilson, or the marvelous lore of his vivacious mother, before, like all Scottish boys, he was sent to school. Of his indifferent scholarship it is unnecessary to speak. If he had no brains for Greek and few for Latin, he was all mind for the beautiful adventures of the *Faerie Queen,* for the fresh boldness of *As You Like It,* and the entrancing matter of Percy's *Reliques.* So important was the effect of the *Reliques* upon him that we should keep in mind what he wrote. "I remember well the spot where I read these volumes for the first time.—The summer-day sped onward so fast, that notwithstanding the sharp appetite of thirteen, I forgot the hour of dinner, was sought for with anxiety, and was found still entranced in my intellectual banquet. To read and to remember was in this instance the same thing." So literally was this true that when later the young romancer came to the more responsible affairs of life he was inclined to lament that "there was a period in his life, when a memory that ought to have been charged with more valuable matter, enabled him to recollect as many of these old songs as would have occupied several days in the recitation." And it was not long before he was confounding his boyhood friends with lengthy tales of knight-errants, no less marvelous than those which he had read.

At the age of fifteen the romancer fell ill. But it was a fortunate illness; for, said Scott, "There was at this time a circulating library in Edinburgh, founded, I believe, by the celebrated Allan Ramsay, which, besides containing a most respectable collection of books, of every description, was, as might have been expected, peculiarly rich in works of fiction." Sir Walter became "a glutton of books." Like his own Waverley "He . . . read, and stored in a memory of uncommon tenacity, much curious, though ill-arranged and miscellaneous information." Together with "the specious miracles of fiction" which brought satiety, he mingled "histories, memoirs, voyages, and travels." He did not know then, but later, after he had com-

pleted his many novels, he realized that he had been laying up a rich store for future use.

Already Sir Walter had begun to collect ballads, eagerly fixing them in his memory as he listened to their recitation by some acquaintance or friend. This was a practice very important in his case, not only because it confirmed in him his tendencies and schooled him in accuracy and in truth, but also because it projected him into his literary career. Having entered the law he had, in fact, given little promise of any literary ability until he was over thirty years of age. Then in 1832 he published the *Minstrelsy of the Scottish Border,* a compendious collection of ballads edited with an intelligence and sympathy which rivalled that of the great Bishop Percy. The *Minstrelsy* crowned worthily the work of many years and gave consummate expression to interests which through it were now made ready to come into new flower. The collecting done, Sir Walter turned to his first creative work of importance, *The Lay of the Last Minstrel.*

A student of the mind of Scott can do no better thing than read carefully the *Minstrelsy* with its memorable introduction. He will probably find that no man has yet lived who has had so inquiring and so illumined an eye when it comes to the affairs of Border history, no man with a heart so quick to the romance of the heroic past. These citizens of Jedburgh, these Mortons and Johnstons, these Buccleuchs and Lennoxes, these Armstrongs and Douglasses, these marchmen all, he knew them. He knew each long spear, each double-handed sword, each battle axe they carried. He knew the lone keeps which they called home, and the wild hills which they loved more than life. He could follow them on their dangerous midnight trails, their booty driven before them; and he could ride with them in their savage feuds when the blood lust was upon them. Behind them, far behind them, he could see the ancient British bring war against the Border—"and where they made solitude they called it peace." He could see the Saxon families fleeing northward before the Normans. He could see the armies of Bruce and Baliol and the guilty men of Turnbull with naked swords in their hands and with halters round their necks —all men of the Border, men, as Surrey wrote, "the boldest and the hottest, that I ever saw in any nation." Once the student brings up into his imagination the materials of the *Minstrelsy* he is ready to meet Walter Scott.

Before the mature poet wrote *The Lay of the Last Minstel,* however, he had limbered his hand with the writing of lesser poems. In 1795 he translated two ballads from the German of Gottfried Augustus Bürger, *William and Helen* and *The Wild Huntsman.* In 1797 he wrote *The Violet* and *To a Lady,* slight lyrics indeed, the first commemorating his rejection by Williamina Stuart. Then there came the more substantial and authentic ballads, such as *The Eve of Saint John* and *Cadyow Castle.* But all of the original work completed before 1805 gave the world little assurance of the man.

Nor is it at all probable that the man himself sensed the significance of the work he had done.

Sir Walter never valued his own poetry highly, or cared to have his own children read it. Surely he did not anticipate the fact that in five years nearly thirty thousand copies of the *Lay* would be sold in Scotland alone and that within eight years he would be offered the Laureateship of Great Britain. The critics of the day, not yet having the permission of his fame, were perplexed, and could see little of value in his work. Among them Francis Jeffrey gave the *Lay* twenty pages of space in the April number of the *Edinburgh Review*, but not twenty pages of commendation. Indeed, wrote Sir Walter to his friend Miss Seward, "the herd of critics . . . do not understand what I call poetry. Many of these gentlemen appear to me to be a sort of tinkers, who, unable to *make* pots and pans, set up for *menders* of them, and, God knows, often make two holes in patching one." But the new note had been sounded; and the student may measure the effect by reading [*infra*] the *Edinburgh Review* for August, 1810, and *Blackwood's* for July, 1818.

Sir Walter "the Scotchman" had blown his bugle. In 1808, when *Marmion* was published,

> He blew again so loud and clear

that all England listened. And two years later, when *The Lady of the Lake* left the press,

> the third blast rang with such a din
> That the echoes answer'd from Pentoun-linn,
> And all his riders came lightly in.

One can speak of his amazing success only in this poetical manner. Never had so many books of one man been bought by the English people. Scott had become the "Bard of the North," the "Great Minstrel."

Those longer poems written between 1813 and 1817—*Rokeby, The Bridal of Triermain, The Lord of the Isles,* and *Harold the Dauntless*—lack the spirit and the vividness of the earlier works. Andrew Lang gives an excellent critical summary: "The *Lay* is as much the best of all these as it is the freshest, the least premeditated, the most spontaneous, the most *disinterested*. More and more the latter poems become articles of manufacture—not, indeed, *Marmion,* composed during gallops on the hills, nor *The Lady of the Lake,* with all its enchanted memories of his romantic native land. But *Rokeby,* despite its lovely lyrics, is not spontaneous, and *The Lord of the Isles,* with all the vigor of its Bannockburn, is as much an article of commerce as *Anne of Geierstein.* So the world, seeking some new thing, turned to Byron, and Scott to Waverley." In this connection we should remember that the first two cantos of *Childe Harold,* the publication of which made Byron instantly famous, came out in 1812. We have elsewhere made reference to the characteristically generous attitude of Sir Walter, turning to praise the work of the man who had called him execrable, the very work which eclipsed his own.

However, had Byron never written, it is probable that Scott in those longer verse romances written after 1810 would have given evidences of an ebbing impetuosity. If "the sword outwears its sheath," surely it would be but natural for the genius of Sir Walter to outwear those octosyllabics in which it had for so long appeared. The new interests which came to be his, and the wider, more varied observations which he had to make on life would have required inevitably a medium of expression other than clarion couplets sounding on and on. At any rate, the genius of the author turned from verse to prose. It changed not itself, but its medium. The need now was no longer to paint a foray of clansmen, but on a ten league canvas to splash the march of crusaders. The need was no longer to sing of the Ladye of Branksome, for now there was to be ushered in a queen to a high festival played out above death. Armies and courts and nations in action, the heroic doings of six hundred years, these became the business of Sir Walter. Across the English world he released a flood of fiction rolling high, crested with fresh beauty. When in 1831 he paused, he had written, in addition to many volumes of miscellaneous work, over thirty stories and novels.

It is not within our purview to venture here an appraisal of the prose of this fecund and copious genius. Merely to recall the names of the novels written before *Waverley* is enough to make us aware that in the work of Sir Walter a new power has come into fiction, an essential force which can give even to history a living authenticity. His men and women have real hearts in them and if you prick them they bleed. The society which he portrays has organic life, the events have meaning. We do not for a moment suggest that the romancer became a realist and the passionate antiquarian a realistic historian. We are pointing merely to the truth that there is somewhat deeper in life than facts. There are meanings which draw facts together into patterns of significance; and it is with these meanings that Sir Walter deals. Under his touch the singular becomes universal, the past becomes permanent.

Since throughout his prose works the Minstrel scattered ballads and songs, never really bidding farewell to the harp of the north or failing to stroke its strings, we should perhaps point to certain general characteristics of his verse. Among them we shall not find the sublime and the mystical, the profound and the introspective, the ornate and the subtle. Nothing here is in itself speculative or in its expression polished. But if there is little reflection here, there is much action; if there is no brooding, there are deeds charged with hot, impetuous forces of life. It has been noticed, and rightly, that between the author of *Marmion* and the author of the *Iliad* there is a spiritual kinship. As for the songs which the minstrel wrote, Andrew Lang has made the final comment: "Scott, as a lyrist, is limited by his unconsciousness."

Great as is Sir Walter the epic poet and the novelist, it would be to exalt literature above life were we not to notice Sir Walter the man. Among all the literary figures of his age he alone stands clean of scars. It is true that he has been charged with pride in title and in possession. Yet no one has thought him vain and none found him ungenerous. When the test came by way of his financial involvement in the failure of Constable and Company, and his friend James Ballantyne the publisher, Scott met the test. The liability involved was £117,000. As a lawyer Scott knew that he could be held legally for only a fraction of this total; as a man of honor he undertook to make good to the creditors the entire sum. He was in his fifty-fifth year, and his health was breaking. To his diary on December 18, 1825, he confided this statement: "My extremity is come." But he met his extremity with work. In two years he had earned £40,000; and in the five years left, though the task killed him, he met the entire obligation. During these heroic years his concern was not for himself but for those dependent upon him—his family and those who lived "in the cottages at Abbotsford." Perhaps the most heroic story that Scott ever wrote, he wrote with his life.

In the autumn of 1832 he died. When on a morning in September his son-in-law was called into his room, "His eye was clear and calm. 'Lockhart,' he said, 'I have but a minute to speak to you. My dear, be a good man—be virtuous—be religious. Nothing else will give you any comfort when you come to lie here.'" Then he closed his eyes, requesting that other members of the family should not be disturbed, since they were weary with watching. He was buried in the Abbey of Dryburgh, among the scenes which he had loved.

Far may we search before we find
A heart so manly and so kind.

SELECTED BIBLIOGRAPHY

TEXTS

Complete Poetical Works, ed. by Horace E. Scudder, 1900.
Miscellaneous Prose Works, 30 Vols., 1834 ff.
Minstrelsy of the Scottish Border, ed. by T. F. Henderson, 4 Vols., 1902.
Journal: 1825–32, ed. by David Douglas, 2 Vols., 1893.

Familiar Letters, ed. by David Douglas, 2 Vols., 1893.

CRITICAL WORKS

Carlyle, Thomas, *Critical and Miscellaneous Essays,* 1838.
Lang, Andrew, *Sir Walter Scott,* 1906.
Lockhart, J. G., *Memoirs of the Life of Sir Walter Scott,* 1837–39.
Stephen, Leslie, *Hours in a Library,* I, 137, 1874.
Stevenson, R. L., *Memoirs and Portraits,* 1887.

THE VIOLET

THE violet in her green-wood bower,
　Where birchen boughs with hazels mingle,
May boast itself the fairest flower
　In glen, or copse, or forest dingle.

Though fair her gems of azure hue,
　Beneath the dew-drop's weight reclining;
I've seen an eye of lovelier blue,
　More sweet through wat'ry lustre shining.

The summer sun that dew shall dry,
　Ere yet the day be past its morrow;　10
Nor longer in my false love's eye
　Remain'd the tear of parting sorrow.

TO A LADY WITH FLOWERS FROM A ROMAN WALL

TAKE these flowers which, purple waving,
　On the ruin'd rampart grew,
Where, the sons of freedom braving,
　Rome's imperial standards flew.

Warriors from the breach of danger
　Pluck no longer laurels there;
They but yield the passing stranger
　Wild-flower wreaths for Beauty's hair.

THE MAID OF TORO

O, LOW shone the sun on the fair lake of Toro,
　And weak were the whispers that waved the dark wood,
All as a fair maiden, bewilder'd in sorrow,
　Sorely sigh'd to the breezes, and wept to the flood.
"O saints! from the mansions of bliss lowly bending;
　Sweet Virgin! who hearest the suppliant's cry,
Now grant my petition, in· anguish ascending,
　My Henry restore, or let Eleanor die!"

All distant and faint were the sounds of the battle,
　With the breezes they rise, with the breezes they fail,　10

Till the shout, and the groan, and the conflict's
    dread rattle,
And the chase's wild clamour, came loading
    the gale.
Breathless she gazed on the woodlands so
    dreary;
    Slowly approaching a warrior was seen;
Life's ebbing tide mark'd his footsteps so
    weary,
    Cleft was his helmet, and woe was his mien.

"O save thee, fair maid, for our armies are
    flying!
    O save thee, fair maid, for thy guardian is
    low!
Deadly cold on yon heath thy brave Henry is
    lying,
And fast through the woodland approaches
    the foe." 20
Scarce could he falter the tidings of sorrow,
    And scarce could she hear them, benumb'd
    with despair:
And when the sun sank on the sweet lake of
    Toro,
    For ever he set to the Brave and the Fair.

JOCK OF HAZELDEAN

I

"WHY weep ye by the tide, ladie?
    Why weep ye by the tide?
I'll wed ye to my youngest son,
    And ye sall be his bride:
And ye sall be his bride, ladie,
    Sae comely to be seen"—
But aye she loot the tears down fa'
    For Jock of Hazeldean.

II

"Now let this wilfu' grief be done,
    And dry that cheek so pale; 10
Young Frank is chief of Errington,
    And lord of Langley-dale;
His step is first in peaceful ha',
    His sword in battle keen"—
But aye she loot the tears down fa'
    For Jock of Hazeldean.

III

"A chain of gold ye sall not lack,
    Nor braid to bind your hair;
Nor mettled hound, nor managed hawk,

Nor palfrey fresh and fair; 20
And you, the foremost o' them a',
    Shall ride our forest queen"—
But aye she loot the tears down fa'
    For Jock of Hazeldean.

IV

The kirk was deck'd at morning-tide,
    The tapers glimmer'd fair;
The priest and bridegroom wait the bride,
    And dame and knight are there.
They sought her baith by bower and ha';
    The ladie was not seen! 30
She's o'er the Border, and awa'
    Wi' Jock of Hazeldean.

NORA'S VOW

I

HEAR what Highland Nora said,—
"The Earlie's son I will not wed,
Should all the race of nature die,
And none be left but he and I.
For all the gold, for all the gear,
And all the lands both far and near,
That ever valour lost or won,
I would not wed the Earlie's son."—

II

"A maiden's vows," old Callum spoke,
"Are lightly made and lightly broke; 10
The heather on the mountain's height
Begins to bloom in purple light;
The frost-wind soon shall sweep away
That lustre deep from glen and brae;
Yet Nora, ere its bloom be gone,
May blithely wed the Earlie's son."—

III

"The swan," she said, "the lake's clear breast
May barter for the eagle's nest;
The Awe's fierce stream may backward turn,
Ben-Cruaichan fall, and crush Kilchurn; 20
Our kilted clans, when blood is high,
Before their foes may turn and fly;
But I, were all these marvels done,
Would never wed the Earlie's son."

IV

Still in the water-lily's shade
Her wonted nest the wild-swan made;
Ben-Cruaichan stands as fast as ever,
Still downward foams the Awe's fierce river;
To shun the clash of foeman's steel,
No Highland brogue has turn'd the heel;   30
But Nora's heart is lost and won,
—She's wedded to the Earlie's son!

THE SUN UPON THE WEIRDLAW HILL

THE sun upon the Weirdlaw Hill,
    In Ettrick's vale, is sinking sweet;
The westland wind is hush and still,
    The lake lies sleeping at my feet.
Yet not the landscape to mine eye
Bears those bright hues that once it bore;
Though evening, with her richest dye,
    Flames o'er the hills of Ettrick's shore.

With listless look along the plain,
    I see Tweed's silver current glide,   10
And coldly mark the holy fane
    Of Melrose rise in ruin'd pride.
The quiet lake, the balmy air,
    The hill, the stream, the tower, the tree,—
Are they still such as once they were?
    Or is the dreary change in me?

Alas, the warp'd and broken board,
    How can it bear the painter's dye!
The harp of strain'd and tuneless chord,
    How to the minstrel's skill reply!   20
To aching eyes each landscape lowers,
    To feverish pulse each gale blows chill;
And Araby's or Eden's bowers
    Were barren as this moorland hill.

PROUD MAISIE

PROUD Maisie is in the wood,
    Walking so early;
Sweet Robin sits on the bush,
    Singing so rarely.

"Tell me, thou bonny bird,
    When shall I marry me?"—
"When six braw gentlemen
    Kirkward shall carry ye."

"Who makes the bridal bed,
    Birdie, say truly?"—   10
"The grey-headed sexton
    That delves the grave duly.

"The glow-worm o'er grave and stone
    Shall light thee steady.
The owl from the steeple sing,
    'Welcome, proud lady.' "

BORDER BALLAD

I

MARCH, march, Ettrick and Teviotdale,
    Why the deil dinna ye march forward in
        order?
March, march, Eskdale and Liddesdale,
    All the Blue Bonnets are bound for the
        Border.
        Many a banner spread,
        Flutters above your head,
    Many a crest that is famous in story.
        Mount and make ready then,
        Sons of the mountain glen,
    Fight for the Queen and our old Scottish
        glory.   10

II

Come from the hills where your hirsels are
        grazing,
    Come from the glen of the buck and the roe;
Come to the crag where the beacon is blazing,
    Come with the buckler, the lance, and the
        bow.
        Trumpets are sounding,
        War-steeds are bounding,
    Stand to your arms, and march in good
        order,
        England shall many a day
        Tell of the bloody fray,
    When the Blue Bonnets came over the
        Border.   20

THE TRUTH OF WOMAN

I

WOMAN'S faith, and woman's trust—
Write the characters in dust;

Stamp them on the running stream,
Print them on the moon's pale beam,
And each evanescent letter
Shall be clearer, firmer, better,
And more permanent, I ween,
Than the thing those letters mean.

II

I have strain'd the spider's thread
'Gainst the promise of a maid;   10
I have weigh'd a grain of sand
'Gainst her plight of heart and hand;
I told my true love of the token,
How her faith proved light, and her word was
    broken:
Again her word and truth she plight,
And I believed them again ere night.

THE EVE OF ST. JOHN

THE Baron of Smaylho'me rose with day,
  He spurr'd his courser on,
Without stop or stay, down the rocky way,
  That leads to Brotherstone.

He went not with the bold Buccleuch,
  His banner broad to rear;
He went not 'gainst the English yew,
  To lift the Scottish spear.

Yet his plate-jack was braced, and his helmet
    was laced,
  And his vaunt-brace of proof he wore; 10
At his saddle-gerthe was a good steel sperthe,
  Full ten pound weight and more.

The Baron return'd in three days' space,
  And his looks were sad and sour;
And weary was his courser's pace,
  As he reach'd his rocky tower.

He came not from where Ancram Moor
  Ran red with English blood;
Where the Douglas true, and the bold
    Buccleuch,
  'Gainst keen Lord Evers stood.   20

Yet was his helmet hack'd and hew'd,
  His action pierced and tore,
His axe and his dagger with blood imbrued,—
  But it was not English gore.

He lighted at the Chapellage,
  He held him close and still;
And he whistled thrice for his little foot-page,
  His name was English Will.

"Come thou hither, my little foot-page,
  Come hither to my knee;   30
Though thou art young, and tender of age,
  I think thou art true to me.

"Come, tell me all that thou hast seen,
  And look thou tell me true!
Since I from Smaylho'me tower have been,
  What did thy lady do?"—

"My lady, each night, sought the lonely light,
  That burns on the wild Watchfold;
For, from height to height, the beacons bright
  Of the English foemen told.   40

"The bittern clamour'd from the moss,
  The wind blew loud and shrill;
Yet the craggy pathway she did cross
  To the eiry Beacon Hill.

"I watch'd her steps, and silent came
  Where she sat her on a stone;—
No watchman stood by the dreary flame,
  It burnèd all alone.

"The second night I kept her in sight,
  Till to the fire she came,   50
And, by Mary's might! an Armed Knight
  Stood by the lonely flame.

"And many a word that warlike lord
  Did speak to my lady there;
But the rain fell fast, and loud blew the blast,
  And I heard not what they were.

"The third night there the sky was fair,
  And the mountain-blast was still,
As again I watch'd the secret pair,
  On the lonesome Beacon Hill.   60

"And I heard her name the midnight hour,
  And name this holy eve;
And say, 'Come this night to thy lady's bower;
  Ask no bold Baron's leave.

" 'He lifts his spear with the bold Buccleuch;
  His lady is all alone;
The door she'll undo, to her knight so true,
  On the eve of good St. John.'—

" 'I cannot come; I must not come;
   I dare not come to thee;   70
On the eve of St. John I must wander alone:
   In thy bower I may not be.'—

" 'Now, out on thee, fainthearted knight!
   Thou shouldst not say me nay;
For the eve is sweet, and when lovers meet,
   Is worth the whole summer's day.

" 'And I'll chain the blood-hound, and the
     warder shall not sound,
   And rushes shall be strewed on the stair;
So, by the black rood-stone, and by holy St.
     John,
   I conjure thee, my love, to be there!'—   80

" 'Though the blood-hound be mute, and the
     rush beneath my foot,
   And the warder his bugle should not blow,
Yet there sleepeth a priest in the chamber to
     the east,
   And my footstep he would know.'—

" 'O fear not the priest, who sleepeth to the
     east!
   For to Dryburgh the way he has ta'en;
And there to say mass, till three days do pass,
   For the soul of a knight that is slayne.'—

"He turn'd him around, and grimly he frown'd;
   Then he laughed right scornfully—   90
'He who says the mass-rite for the soul of that
     knight,
   May as well say mass for me:

" 'At the lone midnight hour, when bad spirits
     have power,
   In thy chamber will I be.'—
With that he was gone, and my lady left alone,
   And no more did I see."

Then changed, I trow, was that bold Baron's
     brow,
   From the dark to the blood-red high
"Now, tell me the mien of the knight thou hast
     seen,
   For, by Mary, he shall die!"—   100

"His arms shone full bright, in the beacon's
     red light:
   His plume it was scarlet and blue;
On his shield was a hound, in a silver leash
     bound,
   And his crest was a branch of the yew."—

"Thou liest, thou liest, thou little foot-page,
   Loud dost thou lie to me!
For that knight is cold, and now laid in the
     mould,
   All under the Eildon-tree."—

"Yet hear but my word, my noble lord!
   For I heard her name his name;   110
And that lady bright, she called the knight
   Sir Richard of Coldinghame."—

The bold Baron's brow then changed, I trow,
   From high blood-red to pale—
"The grave is deep and dark—and the corpse
     is stiff and stark—
   So I may not trust thy tale.

"Where fair Tweed flows round holy Melrose,
   And Eildon slopes to the plain,
Full three nights ago, by some secret foe,
   That gay gallant was slain.   120

"The varying light deceived thy sight,
   And the wild winds drown'd the name;
For the Dryburgh bells ring, and the white
     monks do sing,
   For Sir Richard of Coldinghame!"

He pass'd the court-gate, and he oped the
     tower-gate,
   And he mounted the narrow stair,
To the bartizan-seat, where, with maids that on
     her wait,
   He found his lady fair.

That lady sat in mournful mood;
   Look'd over hill and vale;   130
Over Tweed's fair flood, and Mertoun's wood,
   And all down Teviotdale.

"Now hail, now hail, thou lady bright!"—
   "Now hail, thou Baron true!
What news, what news, from Ancram fight?
   What news from the bold Buccleuch?"—

"The Ancram Moor is red with gore,
   For many a southron fell;
And Buccleuch has charged us, evermore,
   To watch our beacons well."—   140

The lady blush'd red, but nothing she said:
   Nor added the Baron a word:
Then she stepp'd down the stair to her chamber
     fair,
   And so did her moody lord.

In sleep the lady mourn'd, and the Baron toss'd
    and turn'd,
  And oft to himself he said,—
"The worms around him creep, and his bloody
    grave is deep . . .
  It cannot give up the dead!"—

It was near the ringing of matin-bell,
  The night was wellnigh done,   150
When a heavy sleep on that Baron fell,
  On the eve of good St. John.

The lady look'd through the chamber fair,
  By the light of a dying flame;
And she was aware of a knight stood there—
  Sir Richard of Coldinghame!

"Alas! away, away!" she cried,
  "For the holy Virgin's sake!"—
"Lady, I know who sleeps by thy side;
  But, lady, he will not awake.   160

"By Eildon-tree, for long nights three,
  In bloody grave have I lain;
The mass and the death-prayer are said for
    me,
  But, lady, they are said in vain.

"By the Baron's brand, near Tweed's fair
    strand,
  Most foully slain, I fell;
And my restless sprite on the beacon's height,
  For a space is doom'd to dwell.

"At our trysting-place, for a certain space,
  I must wander to and fro;   170
But I had not had power to come to thy bower
  Had'st thou not conjured me so."—

Love master'd fear—her brow she cross'd;
  "How, Richard, hast thou sped?
And art thou saved, or art thou lost?"—
  The vision shook his head!

"Who spilleth life, shall forfeit life;
  So bid thy lord believe:
That lawless love is guilt above,
  This awful sign receive."   180

He laid his left palm on an oaken beam;
  His right upon her hand;
The lady shrunk, and fainting sunk,
  For it scorch'd like a fiery brand.

The sable score, of fingers four,
  Remains on that board impress'd;
And for evermore that lady wore
  A covering on her wrist.

There is a nun in Dryburgh bower,
  Ne'er looks upon the sun;   190
There is a monk in Melrose tower,
  He speaketh word to none.

That nun, who ne'er beholds the day,
  That monk, who speaks to none—
That nun was Smaylho'me's Lady gay,
  That monk the bold Baron.

CADYOW CASTLE

WHEN princely Hamilton's abode
  Ennobled Cadyow's Gothic towers,
The song went round, the goblet flow'd,
  And revel sped the laughing hours.

Then, thrilling to the harp's gay sound,
  So sweetly rung each vaulted wall,
And echoed light the dancer's bound,
  As mirth and music cheer'd the hall.

But Cadyow's towers, in ruins laid,
  And vaults, by ivy mantled o'er,   10
Thrill to the music of the shade,
  Or echo Evan's hoarser roar.

Yet still, of Cadyow's faded fame,
  You bid me tell a minstrel tale,
And tune my harp, of Border frame,
  On the wild banks of Evandale.

For thou, from scenes of courtly pride,
  From pleasure's lighter scenes, canst turn,
To draw oblivion's pall aside,
  And mark the long-forgotten urn.   20

Then, noble maid! at thy command,
  Again the crumbled halls shall rise;
Lo! as on Evan's banks we stand,
  The past returns—the present flies.

Where, with the rock's wood cover'd side,
  Were blended late the ruins green,
Rise turrets in fantastic pride,
  And feudal banners flaunt between:

Where the rude torrent's brawling course
  Was shagg'd with thorn and tangling sloe,   30

The ashler buttress braves its force,
   And ramparts frown in battled row.

'Tis night—the shade of keep and spire
   Obscurely dance on Evan's stream;
And on the wave the warder's fire
   Is chequering the moonlight beam.

Fades slow their light; the east is grey;
   The weary warder leaves his tower;
Steeds snort; uncoupled stag-hounds bay,
   And merry hunters quit the bower.   40

The drawbridge falls—they hurry out—
   Clatters each plank and swinging chain,
As, dashing o'er, the jovial rout
   Urge the shy steed, and slack the rein.

First of his troop, the Chief rode on;
   His shouting merry-men throng behind;
The steed of princely Hamilton
   Was fleeter than the mountain wind.

From the thick copse the roebucks bound,
   The startled red-deer scuds the plain,   50
For the hoarse bugle's warrior-sound
   Has roused their mountain haunts again.

Through the huge oaks of Evandale,
   Whose limbs a thousand years have worn,
What sullen roar comes down the gale,
   And drowns the hunter's pealing horn?

Mightiest of all the beasts of chase,
   That roam in woody Caledon,
Crashing the forest in his race,
   The Mountain Bull comes thundering on. 60

Fierce, on the hunter's quiver'd band,
   He rolls his eyes of swarthy glow,
Spurns, with black hoof and horn, the sand,
   And tosses high his mane of snow.

Aim'd well, the Chieftain's lance has flown;
   Struggling in blood the savage lies;
His roar is sunk in hollow groan—
   Sound, merry huntsmen! sound the *pryse!*

'Tis noon—against the knotted oak
   The hunters rest the idle spear;   70
Curls through the trees the slender smoke,
   Where yeomen dight the woodland cheer.

Proudly the Chieftain mark'd his clan,
   On greenwood lap all careless thrown,

Yet miss'd his eye the boldest man
   That bore the name of Hamilton.

"Why fills not Bothwellhaugh his place,
   Still wont our weal and woe to share?
Why comes he not our sport to grace?
   Why shares he not our hunter's fare?"— 80

Stern Claud replied, with darkening face,
   (Grey Paisley's haughty lord was he,)
"At merry feast, or buxom chase,
   No more the warrior wilt thou see.

"Few suns have set since Woodhouselee
   Saw Bothwellhaugh's bright goblets foam,
When to his hearths, in social glee,
   The war-worn soldier turn'd him home.

"There, wan from her maternal throes,
   His Margaret, beautiful and mild,   90
Sate in her bower, a pallid rose,
   And peaceful nursed her new-born child.

"O change accursed! past are those days;
   False Murray's ruthless spoilers came,
And, for the hearth's domestic blaze,
   Ascends destruction's volumed flame.

"What sheeted phantom wanders wild,
   Where mountain Eske through woodland
     flows,
Her arms enfold a shadowy child—
   Oh! is it she, the pallid rose?   100

"The wilder'd traveller sees her glide,
   And hears her feeble voice with awe—
'Revenge,' she cries, 'on Murray's pride!
   And woe for injured Bothwellhaugh!' "

He ceased—and cries of rage and grief
   Burst mingling from the kindred band,
And half arose the kindling Chief,
   And half unsheathed his Arran brand.

But who, o'er bush, o'er stream and rock,
   Rides headlong, with resistless speed,   110
Whose bloody poniard's frantic stroke
   Drives to the leap his jaded steed;

Whose cheek is pale, whose eyeballs glare,
   As one some vision'd sight that saw,
Whose hands are bloody, loose his hair?—
   'Tis he! 'tis he! 'tis Bothwellhaugh.

From gory selle, and reeling steed,
   Sprung the fierce horseman with a bound,

And, reeking from the recent deed,
  He dash'd his carbine on the ground.   120

Sternly he spoke—" 'Tis sweet to hear
  In good greenwood the bugle blown,
But sweeter to Revenge's ear,
  To drink a tyrant's dying groan.

"Your slaughter'd quarry proudly trode,
  At dawning morn, o'er dale and down,
But prouder base-born Murray rode
  Through old Linlithgow's crowded town.

"From the wild Border's humbled side,
  In haughty triumph marched he,   130
While Knox relax'd his bigot pride,
  And smiled, the traitorous pomp to see.

"But can stern Power, with all his vaunt,
  Or Pomp, with all her courtly glare,
The settled heart of Vengeance daunt,
  Or change the purpose of Despair?

"With hackbut bent, my secret stand,
  Dark as the purposed deed, I chose,
And mark'd, where, mingling in his band,
  Troop'd Scottish pikes and English bows.   140

"Dark Morton, girt with many a spear,
  Murder's foul minion, led the van;
And clash'd their broadswords in the rear
  The wild Macfarlanes' plaided clan.

"Glencairn and stout Parkhead were nigh,
  Obsequious at their Regent's rein,
And haggard Lindesay's iron eye,
  That saw fair Mary weep in vain.

" 'Mid pennon'd spears, a steely grove,
  Proud Murray's plumage floated high;   150
Scarce could his trampling charger move,
  So close the minions crowded nigh.

"From the raised vizor's shade, his eye,
  Dark-rolling, glanced the ranks along,
And his steel truncheon, waved on high,
  Seem'd marshalling the iron throng.

"But yet his sadden'd brow confess'd
  A passing shade of doubt and awe;
Some fiend was whispering in his breast;
  'Beware of injured Bothwellhaugh!'   160

"The death-shot parts—the charger springs—
  Wild rises tumult's startling roar!
And Murray's plumy helmet rings—
  —Rings on the ground, to rise no more.

"What joy the raptured youth can feel,
  To hear her love the loved one tell—
Or he, who broaches on his steel
  The wolf, by whom his infant fell!

"But dearer to my injured eye
  To see in dust proud Murray roll;   170
And mine was ten times trebled joy,
  To hear him groan his felon soul.

"My Margaret's spectre glided near;
  With pride her bleeding victim saw;
And shriek'd in his death-deafen'd ear,
  'Remember injured Bothwellhaugh!'

"Then speed thee, noble Chatlerault!
  Spread to the wind thy banner'd tree!
Each warrior bend his Clydesdale bow!—
  Murray is fall'n, and Scotland free!"   180

Vaults every warrior to his steed;
  Loud bugles join their wild acclaim—
"Murray is fall'n, and Scotland freed!
  Couch, Arran! couch thy spear of flame!"

But, see! the minstrel vision fails—
  The glimmering spears are seen no more;
The shouts of war die on the gales,
  Or sink in Evan's lonely roar.

For the loud bugle, pealing high,
  The blackbird whistles down the vale,   190
And sunk in ivied ruins lie
  The banner'd towers of Evandale.

For Chiefs, intent on bloody deed,
  And Vengeance shouting o'er the slain,
Lo! high-born Beauty rules the steed,
  Or graceful guides the silken rein.

And long may Peace and Pleasure own
  The maids who list the minstrel's tale;
Nor e'er a ruder guest be known
  On the fair banks of Evandale!   200

ELSPETH'S BALLAD

THE herring loves the merry moon-light,
  The mackerel loves the wind,
But the oyster loves the dredging sang,
  For they come of a gentle kind.

Now haud your tongue, baith wife and carle,
  And listen great and sma',
And I will sing of Glenallan's Earl
  That fought on the red Harlaw.

The cronach's cried on Bennachie,
  And doun the Don and a',   10
And hieland and lawland may mournfu' be
  For the sair field of Harlaw.——

They saddled a hundred milk-white steeds,
  They hae bridled a hundred black,
With a chafron of steel on each horse's head,
  And a good knight upon his back.

They hadna ridden a mile, a mile,
  A mile, but barely ten,
When Donald came branking down the brae
  Wi' twenty thousand men.   20

Their tartans they were waving wide,
  Their glaives were glancing clear,
The pibrochs rung frae side to side,
  Would deafen ye to hear.

The great Earl in his stirrups stood,
  That Highland host to see:
"Now here a knight that's stout and good
  May prove a jeopardie:

"What would'st thou do, my squire so gay,
  That rides beside my reyne,—   30
Were ye Glenallan's Earl the day,
  And I were Roland Cheyne?

"To turn the rein were sin and shame,
  To fight were wond'rous peril,—
What would ye do now, Roland Cheyne,
  Were ye Glenallan's Earl?"——

"Were I Glenallan's Earl this tide,
  And ye were Roland Cheyne,
The spear should be in my horse's side,
  And the bridle upon his mane.   40

"If they hae twenty thousand blades,
  And we twice ten times ten,
Yet they hae but their tartan plaids,
  And we are mail-clad men.

"My horse shall ride through ranks sae rude,
  As through the moorland fern,—
Then ne'er let the gentle Norman blude
  Grow cauld for Highland kerne."

        .   .   .   .
      .   .   .   .

He turn'd him right and round again,
  Said, Scorn na at my mither;   50
Light loves I may get mony a ane,
  But minnie ne'er anither.

THE LAY OF THE LAST MINSTREL

INTRODUCTION

THE way was long, the wind was cold,
The Minstrel was infirm and old;
His wither'd cheek, and tresses gray,
Seem'd to have known a better day;
The harp, his sole remaining joy,
Was carried by an orphan boy.
The last of all the Bards was he,
Who sung of Border chivalry;
For, welladay! their date was fled,
His tuneful brethren all were dead;   10
And he, neglected and oppress'd,
Wish'd to be with them, and at rest.
No more on prancing palfrey borne,
He caroll'd, light as lark at morn;
No longer courted and caress'd,
High placed in hall, a welcome guest,
He pour'd, to lord and lady gay,
The unpremeditated lay:
Old times were changed, old manners gone;
A stranger fill'd the Stuarts' throne;   20
The bigots of the iron time
Had call'd his harmless art a crime.
A wandering Harper, scorn'd and poor,
He begg'd his bread from door to door.
And tuned, to please a peasant's ear,
The harp, a king had loved to hear.

  He pass'd where Newark's stately tower
Looks out from Yarrow's birchen bower;
The Minstrel gazed with wistful eye—
No humbler resting-place was nigh,   30
With hesitating step at last,
The embattled portal arch he pass'd,
Whose ponderous grate and massy bar
Had oft roll'd back the tide of war,
But never closed the iron door
Against the desolate and poor.
The Duchess marked his weary pace,
His timid mien, and reverend face,
And bade her page the menials tell,
That they should tend the old man well: 40
For she had known adversity,
Though born in such a high degree;
In pride of power, in beauty's bloom,
Had wept o'er Monmouth's bloody tomb!

When kindness had his wants supplied,
And the old man was gratified,
Began to rise his minstrel pride:
And he began to talk anon,
Of good Earl Francis, dead and gone,
And of Earl Walter, rest him, God! 50
A braver ne'er to battle rode;
And how full many a tale he knew,
Of the old warriors of Buccleuch:
And, would the noble Duchess deign
To listen to an old man's strain,
Though stiff his hand, his voice though weak,
He thought even yet, the sooth to speak,
That, if she loved the harp to hear,
He could make music to her ear.

The humble boon was soon obtain'd; 60
The Aged Minstrel audience gain'd.
But, when he reach'd the room of state,
Where she, with all her ladies, sate,
Perchance he wish'd his boon denied:
For, when to tune his harp he tried,
His trembling hand had lost the ease,
Which marks security to please;
And scenes, long past, of joy and pain,
Came wildering o'er his aged brain—
He tried to tune his harp in vain! 70
The pitying Duchess praised its chime,
And gave him heart, and gave him time,
Till every string's according glee
Was blended into harmony.
And then, he said, he would full fain
He could recall an ancient strain,
He never thought to sing again.
It was not framed for village churls,
But for high dames and mighty earls;
He had play'd it to King Charles the Good, 80
When he kept court in Holyrood;
And much he wish'd, yet fear'd, to try
The long-forgotten melody.
Amid the strings his fingers stray'd,
And an uncertain warbling made,
And oft he shook his hoary head.
But when he caught the measure wild,
The old man raised his face, and smiled;
And lighten'd up his faded eye,
With all a poet's ecstasy! 90
In varying cadence, soft or strong,
He swept the sounding chords along:
The present scene, the future lot,
His toils, his wants, were all forgot:
Cold diffidence, and age's frost,
In the full tide of song were lost;
Each blank, in faithless memory void,

The poet's glowing thought supplied;
And, while his harp responsive rung,
'Twas thus the LATEST MINSTREL sung. 100

CANTO FIRST

I

THE feast was over in Branksome tower,
And the Ladye had gone to her secret bower;
Her bower that was guarded by word and by
    spell,
Deadly to hear, and deadly to tell—
Jesu Maria, shield us well!
No living wight, save the Ladye alone,
Had dared to cross the threshold stone.

II

The tables were drawn, it was idlesse all;
    Knight, and page, and household squire,
Loiter'd through the lofty hall,
    Or crowded round the ample fire: 10
The stag-hounds, weary with the chase,
    Lay stretch'd upon the rushy floor,
And urged, in dreams, the forest race,
    From Teviot-stone to Eskdale-moor.

III

Nine-and-twenty knights of fame
    Hung their shields in Branksome-Hall;
Nine-and-twenty squires of name
    Brought them their steeds to bower from
        stall;
    Nine-and-twenty yeomen tall 20
    Waited, duteous, on them all:
    They were all knights of mettle true,
    Kinsmen to the bold Buccleuch.

IV

Ten of them were sheathed in steel,
With belted sword, and spur on heel:
They quitted not their harness bright,
Neither by day, nor yet by night:
        They lay down to rest,
        With corslet laced,
Pillow'd on buckler cold and hard; 30
        They carved at the meal
        With gloves of steel,
And they drank the red wine through the
        helmet barr'd.

V

Ten squires, ten yeomen, mail-clad men,
Waited the beck of the warder's ten;
Thirty steeds, both fleet and wight,
Stood saddled in stable day and night,
Barbed with frontlet of steel, I trow,
And with Jedwood-axe at saddlebow;
A hundred more fed free in stall:—   40
Such was the custom of Branksome-Hall.

VI

Why do these steeds stand ready dight?
Why watch these warriors, arm'd, by night?—
They watch, to hear the blood-hound baying:
They watch to hear the war-horn braying;
To see St. George's red cross streaming,
To see the midnight beacon gleaming:
They watch, against Southern force and guile,
   Lest Scroop, or Howard, or Percy's powers,
   Threaten Branksome's lordly towers,   50
From Warkworth, or Naworth, or merry
      Carlisle.

VII

Such is the custom of Branksome-Hall.—
   Many a valiant knight is here;
But he, the chieftain of them all,
His sword hangs rusting on the wall,
   Beside his broken spear.
   Bards long shall tell
   How Lord Walter fell!
When startled burghers fled, afar,
The furies of the Border war;   60
When the streets of high Dunedin
Saw lances gleam, and falchions redden,
And heard the slogan's deadly yell—
Then the Chief of Branksome fell.

VIII

Can piety the discord heal,
   Or stanch the death-feud's enmity?
Can Christian lore, can patriot zeal,
   Can love of blessed charity?
No! vainly to each holy shrine,
   In mutual pilgrimage, they drew;   70
Implored, in vain, the grace divine
   For chiefs, their own red falchions slew:
While Cessford owns the rule of Carr,
   While Ettrick boasts the line of Scott.

The slaughter'd chiefs, the mortal jar,
The havoc of the feudal war,
   Shall never, never be forgot!

IX

In sorrow o'er Lord Walter's bier
   The warlike foresters had bent;
And many a flower, and many a tear,   80
   Old Teviot's maids and matrons lent:
But o'er her warrior's bloody bier
The Ladye dropp'd nor flower nor tear!
Vengeance, deep-brooding o'er the slain,
   Had lock'd the source of softer woe;
And burning pride, and high disdain,
   Forbade the rising tear to flow;
Until, amid his sorrowing clan,
   Her son lisp'd from the nurse's knee—
"And if I live to be a man,   90
   My father's death revenged shall be!"
Then fast the mother's tears did seek
To dew the infant's kindling cheek.

X

All loose her negligent attire,
   All loose her golden hair,
Hung Margaret o'er her slaughter'd sire,
   And wept in wild despair,
But not alone the bitter tear
   Had filial grief supplied;
For hopeless love, and anxious fear,   100
   Had lent their mingled tide:
Nor in her mother's alter'd eye
Dared she to look for sympathy.
Her lover, 'gainst her father's clan,
   With Carr in arms had stood,
When Mathouse-burn to Melrose ran,
   All purple with their blood;
And well she knew, her mother dread,
Before Lord Cranstoun she should wed,
Would see her on her dying bed.   110

XI

Of noble race the Ladye came,
Her father was a clerk of fame,
   Of Bethune's line of Picardie:
He learn'd the art that none may name,
   In Padua, far beyond the sea.
Men said, he changed his mortal frame
   By feat of magic mystery;
For when, in studious mood, he paced

St. Andrew's cloister'd hall,
His form no darkening shadow traced   120
  Upon the sunny wall!

XII

And of his skill, as bards avow,
  He taught that Ladye fair,
Till to her bidding she could bow
  The viewless forms of air.
And now she sits in secret bower,
In old Lord David's western tower,
And listens to a heavy sound,
That moans the mossy turrets round.
Is it the roar of Teviot's tide,   130
That chafes against the scaur's red side?
Is it the wind that swings the oaks?
Is it the echo from the rocks?
What may it be, the heavy sound,
That moans old Branksome's turrets round?

XIII

At the sullen, moaning sound,
  The ban-dogs bay and howl;
And, from the turrets round,
  Loud whoops the startled owl.
In the hall, both squire and knight   140
  Swore that a storm was near,
And looked forth to view the night,
  But the night was still and clear!

XIV

From the sound of Teviot's tide,
Chafing with the mountain's side,
From the groan of the wind-swung oak,
From the sullen echo of the rock,
From the voice of the coming storm,
  The Ladye knew it well!
It was the Spirit of the Flood that spoke,   150
  And he called on the Spirit of the Fell.

XV

RIVER SPIRIT

"Sleep'st thou, brother?"—

MOUNTAIN SPIRIT

      —"Brother, nay—
On my hills the moon-beams play.
From Craik-cross to Skelfhill-pen,
By every rill, in every glen,
  Merry elves their morris pacing,

To aërial minstrelsy,
Emerald rings on brown heath tracing,
  Trip it deft and merrily.   160
Up, and mark their nimble feet!
Up, and list their music sweet!"—

XVI

RIVER SPIRIT

"Tears of an imprison'd maiden
  Mix with my polluted stream;
Margaret of Branksome, sorrow-laden,
  Mourns beneath the moon's pale beam.
Tell me, thou, who view'st the stars,
When shall cease these feudal jars?
What shall be the maiden's fate?
Who shall be the maiden's mate?"—   170

XVII

MOUNTAIN SPIRIT

"Arthur's slow wain his course doth roll,
In utter darkness round the pole;
The Northern Bear lowers black and grim;
Orion's studded belt is dim;
Twinkling faint, and distant far,
Shimmers through mist each planet star;
  Ill may I read their high decree!
But no kind influence deign they shower
On Teviot's tide, and Branksome's tower,
  Till pride be quell'd, and love be free."   180

XVIII

The unearthly voices ceast,
  And the heavy sound was still;
It died on the river's breast,
  It died on the side of the hill.
But round Lord David's tower
  The sound still floated near;
For it rung in the Ladye's bower,
  And it rung in the Ladye's ear.
She raised her stately head,
  And her heart throbb'd high with pride:—190
"Your mountains shall bend,
And your streams ascend,
  Ere Margaret be our foeman's bride!"

XIX

The Ladye sought the lofty hall,
  Where many a bold retainer lay,
And, with jocund din, among them all,
  Her son pursued his infant play.

A fancied moss-trooper, the boy
　The truncheon of a spear bestrode,
And round the hall, right merrily,　200
　In mimic foray rode.
Even bearded knights, in arms grown old,
　Share in his frolic gambols bore,
Albeit their hearts of rugged mould,
　Were stubborn as the steel they wore.
For the gray warriors prophesied,
　How the brave boy, in future war,
Should tame the Unicorn's pride,
　Exalt the Crescent and the Star.

XX

The Ladye forgot her purpose high,　210
　One moment, and no more;
One moment gazed with a mother's eye,
　As she paused at the arched door:
Then from amid the armed train,
She call'd to her William of Deloraine.

XXI

A stark moss-trooping Scott was he,
As e'er couch'd Border lance by knee;
Through Solway sands, through Tarras moss,
Blindfold, he knew the paths to cross;
By wily turns, by desperate bounds,　220
Had baffled Percy's best blood-hounds;
In Eske or Liddel, fords were none,
But he would ride them, one by one;
Alike to him was time or tide,
December's snow, or July's pride;
Alike to him was tide or time,
Moonless midnight, or matin prime:
Steady of heart, and stout of hand,
As ever drove prey from Cumberland;
Five times outlawed had he been,　230
By England's King, and Scotland's Queen.

XXII

"Sir William of Deloraine, good at need,
Mount thee on the wightest steed;
Spare not to spur, not stint to ride,
Until thou come to fair Tweedside;
And in Melrose's holy pile
Seek thou the Monk of St. Mary's aisle.
　Greet the Father well from me;
　　Say that the fated hour is come,
And to-night he shall watch with thee,　240
　　To win the treasure of the tomb:
For this will be St. Michael's night,

And, though stars be dim, the moon is bright;
And the Cross, of bloody red,
Will point to the grave of the mighty dead.

XXIII

"What he gives thee, see thou keep;
Stay not thou for food or sleep:
Be it scroll, or be it book,
Into it, Knight, thou must not look;
If thou readest, thou art lorn!　250
Better had'st thou ne'er been born."—

XXIV

"O swiftly can speed my dapple-gray steed,
　Which drinks of the Teviot clear;
Ere break of day," the Warrior 'gan say,
　"Again will I be here:
And safer by none may thy errand be done,
　Than, noble dame, by me;
Letter nor line know I never a one,
　Wer't my neck-verse at Hairibee."

XXV

Soon in his saddle sate he fast,　260
And soon the steep descent he past,
Soon cross'd the sounding barbican,
And soon the Teviot side he won.
Eastward the wooded path he rode,
Green hazels o'er his basnet nod;
He passed the Peel of Goldiland,
And cross'd old Borthwick's roaring strand;
Dimly he view'd the Moat-hill's mound,
Where Druid shades still flitted round;
In Hawick twinkled many a light;　270
Behind him soon they set in night;
And soon he spurr'd his courser keen
Beneath the tower of Hazeldean.

XXVI

The clattering hoofs the watchmen mark;—
"Stand, ho! thou courier of the dark."—
"For Branksome, ho!" the knight rejoin'd,
And left the friendly tower behind.
　He turn'd him now from Teviotside,
　　And, guided by the tinkling rill,
　Northward the dark ascent did ride,　280
　　And gained the moor at Horsliehill;
Broad on the left before him lay,
For many a mile, the Roman way.

XXVII

A moment now he slack'd his speed,
A moment breathed his panting steed;
Drew saddle-girth and corslet-band,
And loosen'd in the sheath his brand.
On Minto-crags the moonbeams glint,
Where Barnhill hew'd his bed of flint;
Who flung his outlaw'd limbs to rest,   290
Where falcons hang their giddy nest,
Mid cliffs, from whence his eagle eye
For many a league his prey could spy;
Cliffs, doubling, on their echoes borne,
The terrors of the robber's horn;
Cliffs, which, for many a later year,
The warbling Doric reed shall hear,
When some sad swain shall teach the grove,
Ambition is no cure for love!

XXVIII

Unchalleng'd, thence pass'd Deloraine,   300
To ancient Riddel's fair domain,
   Where Aill, from mountains freed,
Down from the lakes did raving come;
Each wave was crested with tawny foam,
   Like the mane of a chestnut steed.
In vain! no torrent, deep or broad,
Might bar the bold moss-trooper's road.

XXIX

At the first plunge the horse sunk low,
And the water broke o'er the saddlebow;
Above the foaming tide, I ween,   310
Scarce half the charger's neck was seen;
For he was barded from counter to tail,
And the rider was armed complete in mail;
Never heavier man and horse
Stemm'd a midnight torrent's force.
The warrior's very plume, I say,
Was daggled by the dashing spray;
Yet, through good heart, and Our Ladye's
      grace,
At length he gain'd the landing-place.

XXX

Now Bowden Moor the march-man won,   320
   And sternly shook his plumed head,
As glanced his eye o'er Halidon;
   For, on his soul the slaughter red
Of that unhallow'd morn arose,
When first the Scott and Carr were foes;

When royal James beheld the fray,
Prize to the victor of the day;
When Home and Douglas, in the van,
Bore down Buccleuch's retiring clan,
Till gallant Cessford's heart-blood dear   330
Reek'd on dark Elliot's Border spear.

XXXI

In bitter mood he spurred fast,
And soon the hated heath was past;
And far beneath, in lustre wan,
Old Melros' rose and fair Tweed ran:
Like some tall rock with lichens gray,
Seem'd dimly huge, the dark Abbaye.
When Hawick he pass'd, had curfew rung,
Now midnight lauds were in Melrose sung.
The sound, upon the fitful gale,   340
In solemn wise did rise and fail,
Like that wild harp, whose magic tone
Is waken'd by the winds alone.
But when Melrose he reach'd 'twas silence
      all;
He meetly stabled his steed in stall,
And sought the convent's lonely wall.

Here paused the harp; and with its swell
The Master's fire and courage fell;
Dejectedly, and low, he bow'd,
And, gazing timid on the crowd,   350
He seem'd to seek, in every eye,
If they approved his minstrelsy;
And, diffident of present praise,
Somewhat he spoke of former days,
And how old age, and wand'ring long,
Had done his hand and harp some wrong.
The Duchess, and her daughters fair,
And every gentle lady there,
Each after each, in due degree,
Gave praises to his melody;   360
His hand was true, his voice was clear,
And much they long'd the rest to hear.
Encouraged thus, the Aged Man,
After meet rest, again began.

CANTO SECOND

I

IF thou would'st view fair Melrose aright,
Go visit it by the pale moonlight;
For the gay beams of lightsome day

Gild, but to flout, the ruins gray.
When the broken arches are black in night,
And each shafted oriel glimmers white;
When the cold light's uncertain shower
Streams on the ruin'd central tower;
When buttress and buttress, alternately,
Seem framed of ebon and ivory;   10
When silver edges the imagery,
And the scrolls that teach thee to live and die;
When distant Tweed is heard to rave,
And the owlet to hoot o'er the dead man's
    grave,
Then go—but go alone the while—
Then view St. David's ruin'd pile;
And, home returning, soothly swear,
Was never scene so sad and fair!

II

Short halt did Deloraine make there;
Little reck'd he of the scene so fair: 20
With dagger's hilt, on the wicket strong,
He struck full loud, and struck full long.
The porter hurried to the gate—
"Who knocks so loud, and knocks so late?"
"From Branksome I," the warrior cried;
And straight the wicket open'd wide:
For Branksome's Chiefs had in battle stood,
    To fence the rights of fair Melrose;
And lands and livings, many a rood,
    Had gifted the shrine for their souls'
    repose.   30

III

Bold Deloraine his errand said;
The porter bent his humble head;
With torch in hand, and feet unshod,
And noiseless step, the path he trod;
The arched cloister, far and wide,
Rang to the warrior's clanking stride,
Till, stooping low his lofty crest,
He enter'd the cell of the ancient priest,
And lifted his barred aventayle,[1]
To hail the Monk of St. Mary's aisle.   40

IV

"The Ladye of Branksome greets thee by me;
    Says, that the fated hour is come,
And that to-night I shall watch with thee,

[1] *Aventayle*, visor of the helmet.

To win the treasure of the tomb."
From sackcloth couch the Monk arose,
    With toil his stiffen'd limbs he rear'd;
A hundred years had flung their snows
    On his thin locks and floating beard.

V

And strangely on the Knight look'd he,
    And his blue eyes gleam'd wild and wide;   50
"And, darest thou, Warrior! seek to see
    What heaven and hell alike would hide?
My breast, in belt of iron pent,
    With shirt of hair and scourge of thorn;
For threescore years, in penance spent,
    My knees those flinty stones have worn:
Yet all too little to atone
For knowing what should ne'er be known.
    Would'st thou thy every future year
        In ceaseless prayer and penance drie,   60
    Yet wait thy latter end with fear—
        Then, daring Warrior, follow me!"—

VI

"Penance, father, will I none;
Prayer know I hardly one;
For mass or prayer can I rarely tarry,
Save to patter an Ave Mary,
When I ride on a Border foray.
Other prayer can I none;
So speed me my errand, and let me be gone."—

VII

Again on the Knight look'd the Churchman
    old,   70
    And again he sighed heavily;
For he had himself been a warrior bold,
    And fought in Spain and Italy.
And he thought on the days that were long
    since by
When his limbs were strong, and his courage
    was high:—
Now, slow and faint, he led the way,
Where, cloister'd round, the garden lay;
The pillar'd arches were over their head,
And beneath their feet were the bones of the
    dead.

VIII

Spreading herbs, and flowerets bright,   80
Glisten'd with the dew of night;

Nor herb, nor floweret, glisten'd there,
But was carved in the cloister-arches as fair.
　The Monk gazed long on the lovely moon,
　　Then into the night he looked forth;
　And red and bright the streamers light
　　Were dancing in the glowing north.
So had he seen, in fair Castile,
　The youth in glittering squadrons start;
Sudden the flying jennet wheel,　　　90
　And hurl the unexpected dart.
He knew, by the streamers that shot so bright,
That spirits were riding the northern light.

IX

By a steel-clenched postern door,
　They enter'd now the chancel tall;
The darken'd roof rose high aloof
　On pillars lofty and light and small:
The key-stone, that lock'd each ribbed aisle,
Was a fleur-de-lys, or a quatre-feuille;
The corbells were carved grotesque and
　　grim;　　　　　　　　　　　100
And the pillars, with cluster'd shafts so trim,
With base and with capital flourish'd around,
Seem'd bundles of lances which garlands had
　　bound.

X

Full many a scutcheon and banner riven,
Shook to the cold night-wind of heaven,
　Around the screened altar's pale;
And there the dying lamps did burn,
Before thy low and lonely urn,
O gallant Chief of Otterburne!
　And thine, dark Knight of Liddesdale!　110
O fading honours of the dead!
O high ambition, lowly laid!

XI

The moon on the east oriel shone
Through slender shafts of shapely stone,
　By foliaged tracery combined;
Thou would'st have thought some fairy's hand
'Twixt poplars straight the ozier wand,
　In many a freakish knot, had twined;
Then framed a spell, when the work was done,
And changed the willow-wreaths to stone.　120
The silver light, so pale and faint,
Show'd many a prophet, and many a saint,
　Whose image on the glass was dyed;

Full in the midst, his Cross of Red
Triumphant Michael brandished,
　And trampled the Apostate's pride.
The moon-beam kiss'd the holy pane,
And threw on the pavement a bloody stain.

XII

They sate them down on a marble stone,—
　(A Scottish monarch slept below;)　　130
Thus spoke the Monk, in solemn tone:—
　"I was not always a man of woe;
For Paynim countries I have trod,
And fought beneath the Cross of God:
Now, strange to my eyes thine arms appear,
And their iron clang sounds strange to my ear.

XIII

"In these far climes it was my lot
To meet the wondrous Michael Scott:
　A wizard, of such dreaded fame,
That when, in Salamanca's cave,　　　140
Him listed his magic wand to wave,
　The bells would ring in Notre Dame!
Some of his skill he taught to me;
And, Warrior, I could say to thee
The words that cleft Eildon hills in three,
　And bridled the Tweed with a curb of stone:
But to speak them were a deadly sin;
And for having but thought them my heart
　　within,
A treble penance must be done.

XIV

"When Michael lay on his dying bed,　150
His conscience was awakened:
He bethought him of his sinful deed,
And he gave me a sign to come with speed:
I was in Spain when the morning rose,
But I stood by his bed ere evening close.
The words may not again be said,
That he spoke to me, on death-bed laid;
They would rend this Abbaye's massy nave,
And pile it in heaps above his grave.

XV

"I swore to bury his Mighty Book,　　160
That never mortal might therein look;
And never to tell where it was hid,
Save at his Chief of Branksome's need:
And when that need was past and o'er,

Again the volume to restore.
I buried him on St. Michael's night,
When the bell toll'd one, and the moon was
    bright,
And I dug his chamber among the dead,
When the floor of the chancel was stained red,
That his patron's cross might over him
    wave, 170
And scare the fiends from the Wizard's grave.

XVI

"It was a night of woe and dread,
When Michael in the tomb I laid!
Strange sounds along the chancel pass'd,
The banners waved without a blast"—
—Still spoke the Monk, when the bell toll'd
    one!—
I tell you, that a braver man
Than William of Deloraine, good at need,
Against a foe ne'er spurr'd a steed;
Yet somewhat was he chill'd with dread, 180
And his hair did bristle upon his head.

XVII

"Lo, Warrior! now, the Cross of Red
Points to the grave of the mighty dead;
Within it burns a wondrous light,
To chase the spirits that love the night:
That lamp shall burn unquenchably,
Until the eternal doom shall be."—
Slow moved the Monk to the broad flag-stone,
Which the bloody Cross was traced upon:
He pointed to a secret nook; 190
An iron bar the Warrior took;
And the Monk made a sign with his wither'd
    hand,
The grave's huge portal to expand.

XVIII

With beating heart to the task he went;
His sinewy frame o'er the grave-stone bent;
With bar of iron heaved amain,
Till the toil-drops fell from his brows, like
    rain.
It was by dint of passing strength,
That he moved the massy stone at length.
I would you had been there, to see 200
How the light broke forth so gloriously,
Stream'd upward to the chancel roof,
And through the galleries far aloof!
No earthly flame blazed e'er so bright:

It shone like heaven's own blessed light,
    And, issuing from the tomb,
Show'd the Monk's cowl, and visage pale,
Danced on the dark-brow'd Warrior's mail,
    And kiss'd his waving plume.

XIX

Before their eyes the Wizard lay, 210
As if he had not been dead a day.
His hoary beard in silver roll'd,
He seem'd some seventy winters old;
    A palmer's amice wrapp'd him round,
    With a wrought Spanish baldric bound,
      Like a pilgrim from beyond the sea:
His left hand held his Book of Might;
A silver cross was in his right;
    The lamp was placed beside his knee:
High and majestic was his look, 220
At which the fellest fiends had shook,
And all unruffled was his face:
They trusted his soul had gotten grace.

XX

Often had William of Deloraine
Rode through the battle's bloody plain,
And trampled down the warriors slain,
    And neither known remorse nor awe;
Yet now remorse and awe he own'd;
His breath came thick, his head swam round,
    When this strange scene of death he saw. 230
Bewilder'd and unnerved he stood,
And the priest pray'd fervently and loud:
With eyes averted prayed he;
He might not endure the sight to see,
Of the man he had loved so brotherly.

XXI

And when the priest his death-prayer had
    pray'd,
Thus unto Deloraine he said:—
"Now, speed thee what thou hast to do,
Or, Warrior, we may dearly rue;
For those, thou may'st not look upon, 240
Are gathering fast round the yawning
    stone!"—
Then Deloraine, in terror, took
From the cold hand the Mighty Book,
With iron clasp'd, and with iron bound:
He thought, as he took it, the dead man
    frown'd;

But the glare of the sepulchral light,
Perchance, had dazzled the warrior's sight.

XXII

When the huge stone sunk o'er the tomb,
The night return'd in double gloom;
For the moon had gone down, and the stars
    were few;   250
And, as the Knight and Priest withdrew,
With wavering steps and dizzy brain,
They hardly might the postern gain.
'Tis said, as through the aisles they pass'd,
They heard strange noises on the blast;
And through the cloister-galleries small,
Which at mid-height thread the chancel wall,
Loud sobs, and laughter louder, ran,
And voices unlike the voice of man;
As if the fiends kept holiday,   260
Because these spells were brought to day.
I cannot tell how the truth may be;
I say the tale as 'twas said to me.

XXIII

"Now, hie thee hence," the Father said,
"And when we are on death-bed laid,
O may our dear Ladye, and sweet St. John,
Forgive our souls for the deed we have
    done!"—
  The Monk return'd him to his cell,
    And many a prayer and penance sped;
  When the convent met at the noontide
    bell—   270
    The Monk of St. Mary's aisle was dead!
Before the cross was the body laid,
With hands clasp'd fast, as if still he pray'd.

XXIV

The Knight breathed free in the morning wind,
And strove his hardihood to find:
He was glad when he pass'd the tombstones
    gray,
Which girdle round the fair Abbaye;
For the mystic Book, to his bosom prest,
Felt like a load upon his breast;
And his joints, with nerves of iron twined, 280
Shook, like the aspen leaves in wind.
Full fain was he when the dawn of day
Began to brighten Cheviot grey;
He joy'd to see the cheerful light,
And he said Ave Mary, as well as he might.

XXV

The sun had brighten'd Cheviot gray,
  The sun had brighten'd the Carter's side;
And soon beneath the rising day
  Smiled Branksome Towers and Teviot's
    tide.
The wild birds told their warbling tale,   290
  And waken'd every flower that blows;
And peeped forth the violet pale,
  And spread her breast the mountain rose.
And lovelier than the rose so red,
  Yet paler than the violet pale,
She early left her sleepless bed,
  The fairest maid of Teviotdale.

XXVI

Why does fair Margaret so early awake,
  And don her kirtle so hastilie;
And the silken knots, which in hurry she would
    make,   300
  Why tremble her slender fingers to tie;
Why does she stop, and look often around,
  As she glides down the secret stair;
And why does she pat the shaggy blood-hound,
  As he rouses him up from his lair;
And, though she passes the postern alone,
  Why is not the watchman's bugle blown?

XXVII

The ladye steps in doubt and dread,
Lest her watchful mother hear her tread;
The lady caresses the rough blood-hound, 310
Lest his voice should waken the castle round;
The watchman's bugle is not blown,
For he was her foster-father's son;
And she glides through the greenwood at
    dawn of light
To meet Baron Henry, her own true knight.

XXVIII

The Knight and ladye fair are met,
And under the hawthorn's boughs are set.
A fairer pair were never seen
To meet beneath the hawthorn green.
He was stately, and young, and tall;   320
Dreaded in battle, and loved in hall:
And she, when love, scarce told, scarce hid,
Lent to her cheek a livelier red;
When the half sigh her swelling breast
Against the silken ribbon prest;

When her blue eyes their secret told,
Though shaded by her locks of gold—
Where would you find the peerless fair,
With Margaret of Branksome might compare!

XXIX

And now, fair dames, methinks I see   330
You listen to my minstrelsy;
Your waving locks ye backward throw,
And sidelong bend your necks of snow;
Ye ween to hear a melting tale,
Of two true lovers in a dale;
  And how the Knight, with tender fire,
    To paint his faithful passion strove;
  Swore he might at her feet expire,
    But never, never cease to love;
And how she blush'd, and how she sigh'd, 340
And, half consenting, half denied,
And said that she would die a maid;—
Yet, might the bloody feud be stay'd,
Henry of Cranstoun, and only he,
Margaret of Branksome's choice should be.

XXX

Alas! fair dames, your hopes are vain!
My harp has lost the enchanting strain;
Its lightness would my age reprove:
My hairs are grey, my limbs are old,
My heart is dead, my veins are cold: 350
I may not, must not, sing of love.

XXXI

Beneath an oak, moss'd o'er by eld,
The Baron's Dwarf his courser held,
  And held his crested helm and spear:
That Dwarf was scarce an earthly man,
If the tales were true that of him ran
  Through all the Border, far and near.
'Twas said, when the Baron a-hunting rode
Through Reedsdale's glens, but rarely trod,
  He heard a voice cry, "Lost! lost! lost!" 360
And, like tennis-ball by racket toss'd,
  A leap, of thirty feet and three,
Made from the gorse this elfin shape,
Distorted like some dwarfish ape,
  And lighted at Lord Cranstoun's knee.
Lord Cranstoun was some whit dismay'd;
'Tis said that five good miles he rade,
  To rid him of his company;
But where he rode one mile, the Dwarf ran
    four,
And the Dwarf was first at the castle door. 370

XXXII

Use lessens marvel, it is said:
This elvish Dwarf with the Baron staid;
Little he ate, and less he spoke,
Nor mingled with the menial flock:
And oft apart his arms he toss'd,
And often mutter'd "Lost! lost! lost!"
  He was waspish, arch, and litherlie,
    But well Lord Cranstoun served he:
And he of his service was full fain;
For once he had been ta'en or slain,   380
  An it had not been for his ministry.
All between Home and Hermitage,
Talk'd of Lord Cranstoun's Goblin-Page.

XXXIII

For the Baron went on pilgrimage,
And took with him this elvish Page,
  To Mary's Chapel of the Lowes:
For there, beside our Ladye's lake,
An offering he had sworn to make,
  And he would pay his vows.
But the Ladye of Branksome gather'd a
    band   390
Of the best that would ride at her command:
  The trysting place was Newark Lee.
Wat of Harden came thither amain,
And thither came John of Thirlestane,
And thither came William of Deloraine;
  They were three hundred spears and three.
Through Douglas-burn, up Yarrow stream,
Their horses prance, their lances gleam.
They came to St. Mary's lake ere day;
But the chapel was void, and the Baron
    away.   400
They burn'd the chapel for very rage,
And cursed Lord Cranstoun's Goblin-Page.

XXXIV

And now, in Branksome's good green wood,
As under the aged oak he stood,
The Baron's courser pricks his ears,
As if a distant noise he hears.
The Dwarf waves his long lean arm on high,
And signs to the lovers to part and fly;
No time was then to vow or sigh.
Fair Margaret through the hazel grove, 410
Flew like the startled cushat-dove:
The Dwarf the stirrup held and rein;
Vaulted the Knight on his steed amain,

And, pondering deep that morning's scene,
Rode eastward through the hawthorns green.

While thus he pour'd the lengthen'd tale
The Minstrel's voice began to fail:
Full slyly smiled the observant page,
And gave the wither'd hand of age
A goblet, crown'd with mighty wine,   420
The blood of Velez' scorched vine.
He raised the silver cup on high,
And, while the big drop fill'd his eye,
Pray'd God to bless the Duchess long,
And all who cheer'd a son of song.
The attending maidens smiled to see
How long, how deep, how zealously,
The precious juice the Minstrel quaff'd;
And he, embolden'd by the draught,
Look'd gaily back to them, and laugh'd.   430
The cordial nectar of the bowl
Swell'd his old veins, and cheer'd his soul;
A lighter, livelier prelude ran,
Ere thus his tale again began.

CANTO THIRD

I

AND said I that my limbs were old,
And said that my blood was cold,
And that my kindly fire was fled,
And my poor wither'd heart was dead,
  And that I might not sing of love?—
How could I to the dearest theme,
That ever warm'd a minstrel's dream,
  So foul, so false a recreant prove!
How could I name love's very name,
Nor wake my heart to notes of flame!   10

II

In peace, Love tunes the shepherd's reed;
In war, he mounts the warrior's steed;
In halls, in gay attire is seen;
In hamlets, dances on the green.
Love rules the court, the camp, the grove,
And men below, and saints above;
For love is heaven, and heaven is love.

III

So thought Lord Cranstoun, as I ween,
While, pondering deep the tender scene,
He rode through Branksome's hawthorn
  green.
  But the page shouted wild and shrill,
    And scarce his helmet could he don,
  When downward from the shady hill
    A stately knight came pricking on.
That warrior's steed, so dapple-gray,
Was dark with sweat, and splashed with clay;
  His armour red with many a stain:
He seem'd in such a weary plight,
As if he had ridden the live-long night;
  For it was William of Deloraine.

IV

But no whit weary did he seem,
When, dancing in the sunny beam,
He mark'd the crane on the Baron's crest;
For his ready spear was in his rest.
  Few were the words, and stern and high,
    That mark'd the foemen's feudal hate;
  For question fierce, and proud reply,
    Gave signal soon of dire debate.
Their very coursers seem'd to know
That each was other's mortal foe,   4
And snorted fire, when wheel'd around,
To give each knight his vantage-ground.

V

In rapid round the Baron bent;
  He sigh'd a sigh, and pray'd a prayer;
The prayer was to his patron saint,
  The sigh was to his ladye fair.
Stout Deloraine nor sigh'd nor pray'd,
Nor saint, nor ladye, call'd to aid;
But he stoop'd his head, and couch'd his spear
And spurred his steed to full career.   5
The meeting of these champions proud
Seem'd like the bursting thunder-cloud.

VI

Stern was the dint the Borderer lent!
The stately Baron backwards bent;
Bent backwards to his horse's tail,
And his plumes went scattering on the gale;
The tough ash spear, so stout and true,
Into a thousand flinders flew.
But Cranstoun's lance, of more avail,
Pierced through, like silk, the Borderer's
  mail;   60
Through shield, and jack, and acton, past,
Deep in his bosom broke at last.—

till sate the warrior saddle-fast,
ill, stumbling in the mortal shock,
Down went the steed, the girthing broke,
Hurl'd on a heap lay man and horse.
The Baron onward pass'd his course;
Nor knew—so giddy roll'd his brain—
His foe lay stretch'd upon the plain.

VII

But when he rein'd his courser round,   70
And saw his foeman on the ground
  Lie senseless as the bloody clay,
He bade his page to stanch the wound,
  And there beside the warrior stay,
And tend him in his doubtful state,
And lead him to Branksome castle-gate:
His noble mind was inly moved
For the kinsman of the maid he loved.
This shalt thou do without delay:
No longer here myself may stay;   80
Unless the swifter I speed away,
Short shrift will be at my dying day."

VIII

Away in speed Lord Cranstoun rode;
The Goblin Page behind abode;
His lord's command he ne'er withstood,
Though small his pleasure to do good.
As the corslet off he took,
The dwarf espied the Mighty Book!
Much he marvell'd a knight of pride,
Like a book-bosom'd priest should ride: 90
He thought not to search or stanch the wound,
Until the secret he had found.

IX

The iron band, the iron clasp,
Resisted long the elfin grasp:
For when the first he had undone,
It closed as he the next begun.
Those iron clasps, that iron band,
Would not yield to unchristen'd hand,
Till he smear'd the cover o'er
With the Borderer's curdled gore;   100
A moment then the volume spread,
And one short spell therein he read,
It had much of glamour might,
Could make a ladye seem a knight;
The cobwebs on a dungeon wall
Seem tapestry in lordly hall;

A nut-shell seem a gilded barge,
A sheeling seem a palace large,
And youth seem age, and age seem youth—
All was delusion, nought was truth.   110

X

He had not read another spell,
When on his cheek a buffet fell,
So fierce, it stretch'd him on the plain,
Beside the wounded Deloraine.
From the ground he rose dismay'd,
And shook his huge and matted head;
One word he mutter'd, and no more,
"Man of age, thou smitest sore!"—
No more the Elfin Page durst try
Into the wondrous Book to pry;   120
The clasps, though smear'd with Christian
    gore,
Shut faster than they were before.
He hid it underneath his cloak.—
Now, if you ask who gave the stroke,
I cannot tell, so mot I thrive;
It was not given by man alive.

XI

Unwillingly himself he address'd,
To do his master's high behest:
He lifted up the living corse,
And laid it on the weary horse;   130
He led him into Branksome Hall,
Before the beards of the warders all;
And each did after swear and say,
There only pass'd a wain of hay.
He took him to Lord David's tower,
Even to the Ladye's secret bower;
And, but that stronger spells were spread,
And the door might not be opened,
He had laid him on her very bed.
Whate'er he did of gramarye,   140
Was always done maliciously;
He flung the warrior on the ground,
And the blood well'd freshly from the wound.

XII

As he repass'd the outer court,
He spied the fair young child at sport:
He thought to train him to the wood;
For, at a word, be it understood,
He was always for ill, and never for good.
Seem'd to the boy, some comrade gay
Led him forth to the woods to play;   150

On the drawbridge the warders stout
Saw a terrier and lurcher passing out.

XIII

He led the boy o'er bank and fell,
   Until they came to a woodland brook;
The running stream dissolved the spell,
   And his own elvish shape he took.
Could he have had his pleasure vilde,
He had crippled the joints of the noble child;
Or, with his fingers long and lean,
Had strangled him in fiendish spleen: 160
But his awful mother he had in dread,
And also his power was limited;
So he but scowl'd on the startled child,
And darted through the forest wild;
The woodland brook he bounding cross'd,
And laugh'd, and shouted, "Lost! lost! lost!"

XIV

Full sore amazed at the wondrous change,
   And frighten'd as a child might be,
At the wild yell and visage strange,
   And the dark words of gramarye,   170
The child, amidst the forest bower,
Stood rooted like a lily flower;
   And when at length, with trembling pace,
     He sought to find where Branksome lay,
He fear'd to see that grisly face
     Glare from some thicket on his way.
Thus, starting oft, he journey'd on,
And deeper in the wood is gone,—
For aye the more he sought his way,
The farther still he went astray,—   180
Until he heard the mountains round
Ring to the baying of a hound.

XV

And hark! and hark! the deep-mouth'd bark
   Comes nigher still, and nigher:
Bursts on the path a dark blood-hound,
His tawny muzzle track'd the ground,
   And his red eye shot fire.
Soon as the wilder'd child saw he,
He flew at him right furiouslie.
I ween you would have seen with joy   190
The bearing of the gallant boy,
When, worthy of his noble sire,
His wet cheek glow'd 'twixt fear and ire!
He faced the blood-hound manfully,
And held his little bat on high;

So fierce he struck, the dog, afraid,
At cautious distance hoarsely bay'd,
   But still in act to spring;
When dash'd an archer through the glade,
And when he saw the hound was stay'd,   20
   He drew his tough bow-string;
But a rough voice cried, "Shoot not, hoy!
Ho! shoot not, Edward—'Tis a boy!"

XVI

The speaker issued from the wood,
And check'd his fellow's surly mood,
   And quell'd the ban-dog's ire:
He was an English yeoman good,
   And born in Lancashire.
Well could he hit a fallow-deer
   Five hundred feet him fro;   210
With hand more true, and eye more clear,
   No archer bended bow.
His coal-black hair, shorn round and close,
   Set off his sun-burn'd face:
Old England's sign, St. George's cross,
   His barret-cap did grace;
His bugle-horn hung by his side,
   All in a wolf-skin baldric tied;
And his short falchion, sharp and clear,
Had pierced the throat of many a deer.   220

XVII

His kirtle, made of forest green,
   Reach'd scantly to his knee;
And, at his belt, of arrows keen
   A furbish'd sheaf bore he;
His buckler, scarce in breadth a span,
   No larger fence had he;
He never counted him a man,
   Would strike below the knee:
His slacken'd bow was in his hand,
And the leash, that was his blood-hound's
     band.   230

XVIII

He would not do the fair child harm,
But held him with his powerful arm,
That he might neither fight nor flee;
For when the Red-Cross spied he,
The boy strove long and violently.
"Now, by St. George," the archer cries,
"Edward, methinks we have a prize!
This boy's fair face, and courage free,
Show he is come of high degree."—

XIX

"Yes! I am come of high degree,   240
For I am the heir of bold Buccleuch;
And, if thou dost not set me free,
False Southron, thou shalt dearly rue!
For Walter of Harden shall come with speed,
And William of Deloraine, good at need,
And every Scott, from Esk to Tweed;
And, if thou dost not let me go,
Despite thy arrows, and thy bow,
I'll have thee hang'd to feed the crow!"—

XX

"Gramercy, for thy good-will, fair boy!   250
My mind was never set so high;
But if thou art chief of such a clan,
And art the son of such a man,
And ever comest to thy command,
    Our wardens had need to keep good order;
My bow of yew to a hazel wand,
    Thou'lt make them work upon the Border.
Meantime, be pleased to come with me,
For good Lord Dacre shalt thou see;
I think our work is well begun,   260
When we have taken thy father's son."

XXI

Although the child was led away,
In Branksome still he seem'd to stay,
For so the Dwarf his part did play;
And, in the shape of that young boy,
He wrought the castle much annoy.
The comrades of the young Buccleuch
He pinch'd, and beat, and overthrew;
Nay, some of them he wellnigh slew.
He tore Dame Maudlin's silken tire,   270
And, as Sym Hall stood by the fire,
He lighted the match of his bandelier,
And wofully scorch'd the hackbuteer.
It may be hardly thought or said,
The mischief that the urchin made,
Till many of the castle guess'd,
That the young Baron was possess'd!

XXII

Well I ween the charm he held
The noble Ladye had soon dispell'd;
But she was deeply busied then   280
To tend the wounded Deloraine.
    Much she wonder'd to find him lie,
On the stone threshold stretch'd along;
She thought some spirit of the sky
    Had done the bold moss-trooper wrong;
Because, despite her precept dread,
Perchance he in the Book had read;
But the broken lance in his bosom stood,
And it was earthly steel and wood.

XXIII

She drew the splinter from the wound,   290
    And with a charm she stanch'd the blood;
She bade the gash be cleansed and bound:
    No longer by his couch she stood;
But she has ta'en the broken lance,
    And wash'd it from the clotted gore,
    And salved the splinter o'er and o'er.
William of Deloraine, in trance,
    Whene'er she turn'd it round and round,
    Twisted as if she gall'd his wound.
    Then to her maidens she did say,   300
    That he should be whole man and sound,
    Within the course of a night and day.
Full long she toil'd; for she did rue
Mishap to friend so stout and true.

XXIV

So pass'd the day—the evening fell,
'Twas near the time of curfew bell;
The air was mild, the wind was calm,
The stream was smooth, the dew was balm;
E'en the rude watchman, on the tower,
Enjoy'd and bless'd the lovely hour.   310
Far more fair Margaret loved and bless'd
The hour of silence and of rest.
On the high turret sitting lone,
She waked at times the lute's soft tone;
Touch'd a wild note, and all between
Thought of the bower of hawthorns green.
Her golden hair stream'd free from band,
Her fair cheek rested on her hand,
Her blue eyes sought the west afar,
For lovers love the western star.   320

XXV

Is yon the star, o'er Penchryst Pen,
That rises slowly to her ken,
And, spreading broad its wavering light,
Shakes its loose tresses on the night?
Is yon red glare the western star?—
O, 'tis the beacon-blaze of war!
Scarce could she draw her tighten'd breath,
For well she knew the fire of death!

XXVI

The Warder view'd it blazing strong,
And blew his war-note loud and long,   330
Till, at the high and haughty sound,
Rock, wood, and river, rung around.
The blast alarm'd the festal hall,
And startled forth the warriors all;
Far downward, in the castle-yard,
Full many a torch and cresset glared;
And helms and plumes, confusedly toss'd,
Were in the blaze half-seen, half-lost;
And spears in wild disorder shook,
Like reeds beside a frozen brook.   340

XXVII

The Seneschal, whose silver hair
Was redden'd by the torches' glare,
Stood in the midst, with gesture proud,
And issued forth his mandates loud:—
"On Penchryst glows a bale of fire,
And three are kindling on Priesthaughswire;
      Ride out, ride out,
      The foe to scout!
Mount, mount for Branksome, every man!
Thou, Todrig, warn the Johnstone clan,   350
      That ever are true and stout—
Ye need not send to Liddesdale;
For when they see the blazing bale,
Elliots and Armstrongs never fail.—
Ride, Alton, ride, for death and life!
And warn the Warder of the strife.
Young Gilbert, let our beacon blaze,
Our kin, and clan, and friends, to raise."

XXVIII

Fair Margaret, from the turret head,
Heard, far below, the coursers' tread,   360
      While loud the harness rung,
As to their seats, with clamour dread,
      The ready horsemen sprung:
And trampling hoofs, and iron coats,
And leaders' voices, mingled notes,
      And out! and out!
      In hasty route,
      The horsemen gallop'd forth;
Dispersing to the south to scout,
      And east, and west, and north,   370
To view their coming enemies,
And warn their vassals and allies.

XXIX

The ready page, with hurried hand,
Awaked the need-fire's slumbering brand,
      And ruddy blush'd the heaven:
For a sheet of flame, from the turret high,
Waved like a blood-flag on the sky,
      All flaring and uneven;
And soon a score of fires, I ween,
From height, and hill, and cliff, were seen;   380
Each with warlike tidings fraught;
Each from each the signal caught;
Each after each they glanced to sight,
As stars arise upon the night.
They gleam'd on many a dusky tarn,
Haunted by the lonely earn;
On many a cairn's gray pyramid,
Where urns of mighty chiefs lie hid;
Till high Dunedin the blazes saw,
From Soltra and Dumpender Law;   390
And Lothian heard the Regent's order,
That all should bowne them for the Border.

XXX

The livelong night in Branksome rang
      The ceaseless sound of steel;
The castle-bell, with backward clang,
      Sent forth the larum peal;
Was frequent heard the heavy jar,
Where massy stone and iron bar
Were piled on echoing keep and tower,
To whelm the foe with deadly shower;   400
Was frequent heard the changing guard,
And watch-word from the sleepless ward;
While, wearied by the endless din,
Blood-hound and ban-dog yell'd within.

XXXI

The noble Dame, amid the broil,
Shared the gray Seneschal's high toil,
And spoke of danger with a smile;
Cheer'd the young knights, and council sage
Held with the chiefs of riper age.
No tidings of the foe were brought,   410
Nor of his numbers knew they aught,
Nor what in time of truce he sought.
      Some said, that there were thousands ten;
And others ween'd that it was nought
      But Leven Clans, or Tynedale men,
Who came to gather in black-mail;
And Liddesdale, with small avail,
      Might drive them lightly back agen.

o pass'd the anxious night away,
nd welcome was the peep of day.   420

---

eased the high sound—the listening throng
pplaud the Master of the Song;
nd marvel much, in helpless age,
o hard should be his pilgrimage.
lad he no friend—no daughter dear,
lis wandering toil to share and cheer;
lo son to be his father's stay,
nd guide him on the rugged way?
Ay, once he had—but he was dead!"—
pon the harp he stoop'd his head,   430
nd busied himself the strings withal,
o hide the tear that fain would fall.
n solemn measure, soft and slow,
rose a father's notes of woe.

CANTO FOURTH

I

WEET Teviot! on thy silver tide
  The glaring bale-fires blaze no more;
lo longer steel-clad warriors ride
  Along thy wild and willow'd shore;
Vhere'er thou wind'st, by dale or hill,
ll, all is peaceful, all is still,
  As if thy waves, since Time was born,
ince first they roll'd upon the Tweed,
lad only heard the shepherd's reed,
  Nor started at the bugle-horn.   10

II

nlike the tide of human time,
  Which, though it change in ceaseless flow,
etains each grief, retains each crime
  Its earliest course was doom'd to know;
nd, darker as it downward bears,
s stain'd with past and present tears.
  Low as that tide has ebb'd with me,
: still reflects to Memory's eye
he hour my brave, my only boy,
  Fell by the side of great Dundee.   20
Vhy, when the volleying musket play'd
gainst the bloody Highland blade,
Vhy was not I beside him laid!—
nough—he died the death of fame;
nough—he died with conquering Græme.

III

low over Border, dale and fell,
  Full wide and far was terror spread;

For pathless marsh, and mountain cell,
  The peasant left his lowly shed.
The frighten'd flocks and herds were pent   30
Beneath the peel's rude battlement;
And maids and matrons dropp'd the tear,
While ready warriors seized the spear.
From Branksome's towers, the watchman's eye
Dun wreaths of distant smoke can spy,
  Which, curling in the rising sun,
  Show'd southern ravage was begun.

IV

Now loud the heedful gate-ward cried—
  "Prepare ye all for blows and blood!
Watt Tinlinn, from the Liddel-side,   40
  Comes wading through the flood.
Full oft the Tynedale snatchers knock
  At his lone gate, and prove the lock;
It was but last St. Barnabright
They sieged him a whole summer night,
But fled at morning; well they knew,
In vain he never twang'd the yew.
Right sharp has been the evening shower,
That drove him from his Liddel tower;
And, by my faith," the gate-ward said,   50
"I think 'twill prove a Warden-Raid."

V

While thus he spoke, the bold yeoman
Enter'd the echoing barbican.
He led a small and shaggy nag,
That through a bog, from hag to hag,
Could bound like any Billhope stag.
It bore his wife and children twain;
A half-clothed serf was all their train;
His wife, stout, ruddy, and dark-brow'd,
Of silver brooch and bracelet proud,   60
Laugh'd to her friends among the crowd.
He was of stature passing tall,
But sparely form'd, and lean withal;
A batter'd morion on his brow;
A leather jack, as fence enow,
On his broad shoulders loosely hung;
A border axe behind was slung;
His spear, six Scottish ells in length,
  Seem'd newly dyed with gore;
His shafts and bow, of wondrous strength,   70
  His hardy partner bore.

VI

Thus to the Ladye did Tinlinn show
The tidings of the English foe:—

"Belted Will Howard is marching here,
And hot Lord Dacre, with many a spear,
And all the German hackbut-men,
Who have long lain at Askerten:
They cross'd the Liddel at curfew hour,
And burn'd my little lonely tower:
The fiend receive their souls therefor!   80
It had not been burnt this year and more.
Barn-yard and dwelling, blazing bright,
Served to guide me on my flight;
But I was chased the livelong night.
Black John of Akeshaw, and Fergus Græme,
Fast upon my traces came,
Until I turn'd at Priesthaugh Scrogg,
And shot their horses in the bog,
Slew Fergus with my lance outright—
I had him long at high despite: 90
He drove my cows last Fastern's night.

VII

Now weary scouts from Liddesdale,
Fast hurrying in, confirm'd the tale;
    As far as they could judge by ken,
        Three hours would bring to Teviot's strand
    Three thousand armed Englishmen—
        Meanwhile, full many a warlike band,
From Teviot, Aill, and Ettrick shade,
Came in, their Chief's defence to aid.
    There was saddling and mounting in haste,   100
        There was pricking o'er moor and lea;
    He that was last at the trysting-place
        Was but lightly held of his gaye ladye.

VIII

From fair St. Mary's silver wave,
    From dreary Gamescleugh's dusky height,
His ready lances Thirlestane brave
    Array'd beneath a banner bright.
The tressured fleur-de-luce he claims,
To wreathe his shield, since royal James,
Encamp'd by Fala's mossy wave,   110
The proud distinction grateful gave,
    For faith 'mid feudal jars;
What time, save Thirlestane alone,
Of Scotland's stubborn barons none
    Would march to southern wars;
And hence, in fair remembrance worn,
Yon sheaf of spears his crest has borne:
Hence his high motto shines reveal'd—
"Ready, aye ready," for the field.

IX

An aged Knight, to danger steel'd,   120
    With many a moss-trooper, came on;
And azure in a golden field,
The stars and cresent graced his shield,
    Without the bend of Murdieston.
Wide lay his lands round Oakwood tower,
And wide round haunted Castle-Ower;
High over Borthwick's mountain flood,
His wood-embosom'd mansion stood;
In the dark glen, so deep below,
The herds of plunder'd England low;   130
His bold retainers' daily food,
And bought with danger, blows, and blood.
Marauding chief! his sole delight
The moonlight raid, the morning fight;
Not even the Flower of Yarrow's charms,
In youth, might tame his rage for arms;
And still, in age, he spurn'd at rest,
And still his brows the helmet press'd,
Albeit the blanched locks below
Were white as Dinlay's spotless snow;   140
    Five stately warriors drew the sword
        Before their father's band;
    A braver knight than Harden's lord
        Ne'er belted on a brand.

X

Scotts of Eskdale, a stalwart band,
    Came trooping down the Todshawhill;
By the sword they won their land,
    And by the sword they hold it still.
Hearken, Ladye, to the tale,
How thy sires won fair Eskdale.—   150
Earl Morton was lord of that valley fair,
The Beattisons were his vassals there.
The Earl was gentle, and mild of mood,
The vassals were warlike, and fierce, and rude;
High of heart, and haughty of word,
Little they reck'd of a tame liege lord.
The Earl into fair Eskdale came,
Homage and seignory to claim:
Of Gilbert the Galliard a heriot he sought,
Saying, "Give thy best steed, as a vassal ought."   160
—"Dear to me is my bonny white steed,
Oft has he help'd me at pinch of need;
Lord and Earl though thou be, I trow,
I can rein Bucksfoot better than thou."—
Word on word gave fuel to fire,
Till so highly blazed the Beattison's ire,
But that the Earl the flight had ta'en,

The vassals there their lord had slain.
Sore he plied both whip and spur,
As he urged his steed through Eskdale
    muir;   170
And it fell down a weary weight,
Just on the threshold of Branksome gate.

XI

The Earl was a wrathful man to see,
Full fain avenged would he be.
In haste to Branksome's Lord he spoke,
Saying—"Take these traitors to thy yoke;
For a cast of hawks, and a purse of gold,
All Eskdale I'll sell thee, to have and hold:
Beshrew thy heart, of the Beattisons' clan
If thou leavest on Eske a landed man;   180
But spare Woodkerrick's lands alone,
For he lent me his horse to escape upon."
A glad man then was Branksome bold,
Down he flung him the purse of gold;
To Eskdale soon he spurr'd amain,
And with him five hundred riders has ta'en.
He left his merrymen in the mist of the hill,
And bade them hold them close and still;
And alone he wended to the plain,
To meet with the Galliard and all his train.190
To Gilbert the Galliard thus he said:—
"Know thou me for thy liege-lord and head,
Deal not with me as with Morton tame,
For Scotts play best at the roughest game.
Give me in peace my heriot due,
Thy bonny white steed, or thou shalt rue.
If my horn I three times wind,
Eskdale shall long have the sound in mind."—

XII

Loudly the Beattison laugh'd in scorn;
"Little care we for thy winded horn.   200
Ne'er shall it be the Galliard's lot,
To yield his steed to a haughty Scott.
Wend thou to Branksome back on foot,
With rusty spur and miry boot."—
He blew his bugle so loud and hoarse
That the dun deer started at fair Craikcross;
He blew again so loud and clear,
Through the gray mountain-mist there did
    lances appear;
And the third blast rang with such a din,
That the echoes answer'd from Pentoun-
    linn,   210
And all his riders came lightly in.
Then had you seen a gallant shock,

When saddles were emptied, and lances broke!
For each scornful word the Galliard had said,
A Beattison on the field was laid.
His own good sword the chieftain drew,
And he bore the Galliard through and through;
Where the Beattisons' blood mix'd with the
    rill,
The Galliard's-Haugh men call it still.
The Scotts have scatter'd the Beattison clan, 220
In Eskdale they left but one landed man.
The valley of Eske, from the mouth to the
    source,
Was lost and won for that bonny white horse.

XIII

Whitslade the Hawk, and Headshaw came,
And warriors more than I may name;
From Yarrow-cleugh to Hindhaugh-swair,
    From Woodhouselie to Chester-glen,
Troop'd man and horse, and bow and spear;
    Their gathering word was Bellenden.
And better hearts o'er Border sod
To siege or rescue never rode.   230
    The Ladye mark'd the aids come in,
        And high her heart of pride arose:
    She bade her youthful son attend,
    That he might know his father's friend,
        And learn to face his foes.
    "The boy is ripe to look on war;
        I saw him draw a cross-bow stiff,
    And his true arrow struck afar
        The raven's nest upon the cliff;   240
The red cross, on a southern breast,
Is broader than the raven's nest:
Thou, Whitslade, shalt teach him his weapon
    to wield,
And o'er him hold his father's shield."

XIV

Well may you think, the wily page
Cared not to face the Ladye sage.
He counterfeited childish fear,
And shriek'd, and shed full many a tear,
    And moan'd and plain'd in manner wild.
        The attendants to the Ladye told,   250
    Some fairy, sure, had changed the child,
        That wont to be so free and bold.
Then wrathful was the noble dame;
She blush'd blood-red for very shame:—
"Hence! ere the clan his faintness view;
Hence with the weakling to Buccleuch!—
Watt Tinlinn, thou shalt be his guide

To Rangleburn's lonely side.—
Sure some fell fiend has cursed our line,
That coward should e'er be son of mine!"— 260

XV

A heavy task Watt Tinlinn had,
To guide the counterfeited lad.
Soon as the palfrey felt the weight
Of that ill-omen'd elfish freight,
He bolted, sprung, and rear'd amain,
Nor heeded bit, nor curb, nor rein.
　　It cost Watt Tinlinn mickle toil
　　To drive him but a Scottish mile;
　　　But as a shallow brook they cross'd,
　　The elf, amid the running stream,　　270
　　　His figure changed, like form in dream,
　　　　And fled, and shouted, "Lost! lost! lost!"
Full fast the urchin ran and laugh'd,
But faster still a cloth-yard shaft
Whistled from startled Tinlinn's yew,
And pierced his shoulder through and through.
Although the imp might not be slain,
And though the wound soon heal'd again,
Yet, as he ran, he yell'd for pain;
And Watt of Tinlinn, much aghast,　　280
Rode back to Branksome fiery fast.

XVI

Soon on the hill's steep verge he stood,
That looks o'er Branksome's towers and wood;
And martial murmurs, from below,
Proclaim'd the approaching southern foe.
Through the dark wood, in mingled tone,
Were Border pipes and bugles blown;
The coursers' neighing he could ken,
A measured tread of marching men;
While broke at times the solemn hum,　　290
The Almayn's sullen kettle-drum;
　　And banners tall, of crimson sheen,
　　　Above the copse appear;
　　And, glistening through the hawthorns green,
　　　Shine helm, and shield, and spear.

XVII

Light forayers, first, to view the ground,
Spurr'd their fleet coursers loosely round;
　　Behind, in close array, and fast,
　　　The Kendal archers, all in green,
　　Obedient to the bugle blast,　　300
　　　Advancing from the wood were seen.

To back and guard the archer band,
Lord Dacre's bill-men were at hand:
A hardy race, on Irthing bred,
With kirtles white, and crosses red,
Array'd beneath the banner tall,
That stream'd o'er Acre's conquer'd wall;
And minstrels, as they march'd in order,
Play'd, "Noble Lord Dacre, he dwells on the
　　Border."

XVIII

Behind the English bill and bow,　　310
The mercenaries, firm and slow,
　　Moved on to fight, in dark array,
By Conrad led of Wolfenstein,
Who brought the band from distant Rhine,
　　And sold their blood for foreign pay.
The camp their home, their law the sword,
They knew no country, own'd no lord:
They were not arm'd like England's sons,
But bore the levin-darting guns;
Buff coats, all frounced and 'broider'd o'er,　　320
And morsing-horns and scarfs they wore;
Each better knee was bared, to aid
The warriors in the escalade;
All, as they march'd, in rugged tongue,
Songs of Teutonic feuds they sung.

XIX

But louder still the clamour grew,
And louder still the minstrels blew,
When, from beneath the greenwood tree,
Rode forth Lord Howard's chivalry;
His men-at-arms, with glaive and spear,　　330
Brought up the battle's glittering rear,
There many a youthful knight, full keen
To gain his spurs, in arms was seen;
With favour in his crest, or glove,
Memorial of his ladye-love.
So rode they forth in fair array,
Till full their lengthen'd lines display;
Then call'd a halt, and made a stand,
And cried, "St. George, for merry Eng-
　　land!"

XX

Now every English eye, intent　　340
On Branksome's armed towers was bent;
So near they were, that they might know
The straining harsh of each cross-bow;
On battlement and bartizan

Gleam'd axe, and spear, and partisan;
Falcon and culver, on each tower,
Stood prompt their deadly hail to shower;
And flashing armour frequent broke
From eddying whirls of sable smoke,
Where upon tower and turret head,   350
The seething pitch and molten lead
Reek'd, like a witch's caldron red.
While yet they gaze, the bridges fall,
The wicket opes, and from the wall
Rides forth the hoary Seneschal.

XXI

Armed he rode, all save the head,
His white beard o'er his breast-plate spread;
Unbroke by age, erect his seat,
He ruled his eager courser's gait;
Forced him, with chasten'd fire, to prance,   360
And, high curvetting, slow advance:
In sign of truce, his better hand
Display'd a peeled willow wand;
His squire, attending in the rear,
Bore high a gauntlet on a spear.
When they espied him riding out,
Lord Howard and Lord Dacre stout
Sped to the front of their array,
To hear what this old knight should say.

XXII

"Ye English warden lords, of you   370
Demands the Ladye of Buccleuch,
Why, 'gainst the truce of Border tide,
In hostile guise ye dare to ride,
With Kendal bow, and Gilsland brand,
And all yon mercenary band,
Upon the bounds of fair Scotland?
My Ladye reads you swith return;
And, if but one poor straw you burn,
Or do our towers so much molest,
As scare one swallow from her nest,   380
St. Mary! but we'll light a brand
Shall warm your hearths in Cumberland."—

XXIII

A wrathful man was Dacre's lord,
But calmer Howard took the word:
"May't please thy Dame, Sir Seneschal,
To seek the castle's outward wall,
Our pursuivant-at-arms shall show
Both why we came, and when we go."—
The message sped, the noble Dame
To the wall's outward circle came;   390
Each chief around lean'd on his spear,
To see the pursuivant appear.
All in Lord Howard's livery dress'd,
The lion argent deck'd his breast;
He led a boy of blooming hue—
O sight to meet a mother's view!
It was the heir of great Buccleuch.
Obeisance meet the herald made,
And thus his master's will he said:—

XXIV

"It irks, high Dame, my noble Lords,   400
'Gainst ladye fair to draw their swords;
But yet they may not tamely see,
All through the Western Wardenry,
Your law-contemning kinsmen ride,
And burn and spoil the Border-side;
And ill beseems your rank and birth
To make your towers a flemens-firth.
We claim from thee William of Deloraine,
That he may suffer march-treason pain.
It was but last St. Cuthbert's even   410
He prick'd to Stapleton on Leven,
Harried the lands of Richard Musgrave,
And slew his brother by dint of glaive.
Then, since a lone and widow'd Dame
These restless riders may not tame,
Either receive within thy towers
Two hundred of my master's powers,
Or straight they sound their warrison,
And storm and spoil thy garrison:
And this fair boy, to London led,   420
Shall good King Edward's page be bred."

XXV

He ceased—and loud the boy did cry,
And stretch'd his little arms on high;
Implored for aid each well-known face,
And strove to seek the Dame's embrace.
A moment changed that Ladye's cheer,
Gush'd to her eye the unbidden tear;
She gazed upon the leaders round,
And dark and sad each warrior frown'd;
Then, deep within her sobbing breast   430
She lock'd the struggling sigh to rest;
Unalter'd and collected stood,
And thus replied, in dauntless mood:—

XXVI

"Say to your Lords of high emprize,
Who war on women and on boys,

That either William of Deloraine
Will cleanse him, by oath, of march-treason
          stain,
Or else he will the combat take
'Gainst Musgrave, for his honour's sake.
No knight in Cumberland so good,   440
But William may count with him kin and blood.
Knighthood he took of Douglas' sword,
When English blood swell'd Ancram's ford;
And but Lord Dacre's steed was wight,
And bare him ably in the flight,
Himself had seen him dubb'd a knight.
For the young heir of Branksome's line,
God be his aid, and God be mine;
Through me no friend shall meet his doom;
Here, while I live, no foe finds room.   450
     Then, if thy Lords their purpose urge,
        Take our defiance loud and high;
     Our slogan is their lyke-wake dirge,
        Our moat, the grave where they shall lie."

XXVII

Proud she look'd round, applause to claim—
Then lighten'd Thirlestane's eye of flame;
     His bugle Wat of Harden blew;
Pensils and pennons wide were flung,
To heaven the Border slogan rung,
     "St. Mary for the young Buccleuch!"   460
The English war-cry answer'd wide,
     And forward bent each southern spear;
Each Kendal archer made a stride,
     And drew the bowstring to his ear;
Each minstrel's war-note loud was blown:—
But, ere a gray-goose shaft had flown,
     A horseman gallop'd from the rear.

XXVIII

"Ah! noble Lords!" he breathless said,
"What treason has your march betray'd?
What make you here, from aid so far,   470
Before you walls, around you war?
Your foemen triumph in the thought,
That in the toils the lion's caught.
Already on dark Ruberslaw
The Douglas holds his weapon-schaw;
The lances, waving in his train,
Clothe the dun heath like autumn grain;
And on the Liddel's northern strand,
To bar retreat to Cumberland,
Lord Maxwell ranks his merry-men good,   480
Beneath the eagle and the rood;
     And Jedwood, Eske, and Teviotdale,

Have to proud Angus come;
And all the Merse and Lauderdale
     Have risen with haughty Home.
An exile from Northumberland,
     In Liddesdale I've wander'd long;
But still my heart was with merry England,
     And cannot brook my country's wrong;
And hard I've spurr'd all night, to show   490
The mustering of the coming foe."

XXIX

"And let them come!" fierce Dacre cried;
"For soon yon crest, my father's pride,
That swept the shores of Judah's sea,
And waved in gales of Galilee,
From Branksome's highest towers display'd,
Shall mock the rescue's lingering aid!—
Level each harquebuss on row;
Draw, merry archers, draw the bow;
Up, bill-men, to the walls, and cry,   500
Dacre for England, win or die!"—

XXX

"Yet hear," quoth Howard, "calmly hear,
Nor deem my words the words of fear:
For who, in field or foray slack,
Saw the blanche lion e'er fall back?
But thus to risk our Border flower
In strife against a kingdom's power,
Ten thousand Scots 'gainst thousands three,
Certes, were desperate policy.
Nay, take the terms the Ladye made,   510
Ere conscious of the advancing aid:
Let Musgrave meet fierce Deloraine
In single fight, and, if he gain,
He gains for us; but if he's cross'd,
'Tis but a single warrior lost:
The rest, retreating as they came,
Avoid defeat, and death, and shame."

XXXI

Ill could the haughty Dacre brook
His brother Warden's sage rebuke;
And yet his forward step he staid,   520
And slow and sullenly obey'd.
But ne'er again the Border side
Did these two lords in friendship ride;
And this slight discontent, men say,
Cost blood upon another day.

XXXII

The pursuivant-at-arms again
　Before the castle took his stand;
His trumpet call'd, with parleying strain,
　The leaders of the Scottish band;
And he defied, in Musgrave's right,　　530
Stout Deloraine to single fight;
A gauntlet at their feet he laid,
And thus the terms of fight he said:—
"If in the lists good Musgrave's sword
Vanquish the Knight of Deloraine,
Your youthful chieftain, Branksome's Lord,
　Shall hostage for his clan remain:
If Deloraine foil good Musgrave,
The boy his liberty shall have.
　Howe'er it falls, the English band,　　540
Unharming Scots, by Scots unharm'd,
In peaceful march, like men unarm'd,
　Shall straight retreat to Cumberland."

XXXIII

Unconscious of the near relief,
The proffer pleased each Scottish chief,
　Though much the Ladye sage gainsay'd;
For though their hearts were brave and true,
From Jedwood's recent sack they knew,
　How tardy was the Regent's aid:
And you may guess the noble Dame　　550
　Durst not the secret prescience own,
Sprung from the art she might not name,
　By which the coming help was known.
Closed was the compact, and agreed
　That lists should be enclosed with speed,
Beneath the castle, on a lawn:
They fix'd the morrow for the strife,
On foot, with Scottish axe and knife,
　At the fourth hour from peep of dawn;
When Deloraine, from sickness freed,　　560
Or else a champion in his stead,
Should for himself and chieftain stand,
Against stout Musgrave, hand to hand.

XXXIV

I know right well, that, in their lay,
Full many minstrels sing and say,
　Such combat should be made on horse,
On foaming steed, in full career,
With brand to aid, when as the spear
　Should shiver in the course:
But he, the jovial Harper, taught　　570
Me, yet a youth, how it was fought,
　In guise which now I say;

He knew each ordinance and clause
Of Black Lord Archibald's battle-laws,
　In the old Douglas' day.
He brook'd not, he, that scoffing tongue
Should tax his minstrelsy with wrong,
　Or call his song untrue:
For this, when they the goblet plied,
And such rude taunt had chafed his pride,　　580
　The Bard of Ruell he slew.
On Teviot's side, in fight they stood,
And tuneful hands were stain'd with blood;
Where still the thorn's white branches wave,
Memorial o'er his rival's grave.

XXXV

Why should I tell the rigid doom,
That dragg'd my master to his tomb;
　How Ousenam's maidens tore their hair,
Wept till their eyes were dead and dim,
And wrung their hands for love of him,　　590
　Who died at Jedwood Air?
He died!—his scholars, one by one,
To the cold silent grave are gone;
And I, alas! survive alone,
To muse o'er rivalries of yore,
And grieve that I shall hear no more
The strains, with envy heard before;
For, with my minstrel brethren fled,
My jealousy of song is dead.

———

He paused: the listening dames again　　600
Applaud the hoary Minstrel's strain.
With many a word of kindly cheer,—
In pity half, and half sincere,—
Marvell'd the Duchess how so well
His legendary song could tell—
Of ancient deeds, so long forgot;
Of feuds, whose memory was not;
Of forests, now laid waste and bare;
Of towers, which harbour now the hare;
Of manners, long since changed and gone;　　610
Of chiefs, who under their gray stone
So long had slept, that fickle Fame
Had blotted from her rolls their name,
And twined round some new minion's head
The fading wreath for which they bled;
In sooth, 'twas strange, this old man's verse
Could call them from their marble hearse.

The Harper smiled, well-pleased; for ne'er
Was flattery lost on poet's ear:

A simple race! they waste their toil   620
For the vain tribute of a smile;
E'en when in age their flame expires,
Her dulcet breath can fan its fires:
Their drooping fancy wakes at praise,
And strives to trim the short-lived blaze.

Smiled then, well-pleased, the Aged Man,
And thus his tale continued ran.

Canto Fifth

I

CALL it not vain:—they do not err,
  Who say, that when the Poet dies,
Mute Nature mourns her worshipper,
  And celebrates his obsequies:
Who say, tall cliff, and cavern lone,
For the departed Bard make moan;
That mountains weep in crystal rill;
That flowers in tears of balm distil;
Through his loved groves that breezes sigh,
And oaks, in deeper groan, reply;   10
And rivers teach their rushing wave
To murmur dirges round his grave.

II

Not that, in sooth, o'er mortal urn
Those things inanimate can mourn;
But that the stream, the wood, the gale,
Is vocal with the plaintive wail
Of those, who, else forgotten long,
Lived in the poet's faithful song,
And, with the poet's parting breath,
Whose memory feels a second death.   20
The Maid's pale shade, who wails her lot,
That love, true love, should be forgot,
From rose and hawthorn shakes the tear
Upon the gentle Minstrel's bier:
The phantom Knight, his glory fled,
Mourns o'er the field he heap'd with dead:
Mounts the wild blast that sweeps amain,
And shrieks along the battle-plain.
The Chief, whose antique crownlet long
Still sparkled in the feudal song,   30
Now, from the mountain's misty throne,
Sees, in the thanedom once his own,
His ashes undistinguish'd lie,
His place, his power, his memory die:
His groans the lonely caverns fill,
His tears of rage impel the rill:

All mourn the Minstrel's harp unstrung,
Their name unknown, their praise unsung.

III

Scarcely the hot assault was staid,
The terms of truce were scarcely made,   40
When they could spy, from Branksome's tow-
    ers,
The advancing march of martial powers.
Thick clouds of dust afar appear'd,
And trampling steeds were faintly heard;
Bright spears, above the columns dun,
Glanced momentary to the sun;
And feudal banners fair display'd
The bands that moved to Branksome's aid.

IV

Vails not to tell each hardy clan,
  From the fair Middle Marches came;   50
The Bloody Heart blazed in the van,
  Announcing Douglas, dreaded name!
Vails not to tell what steeds did spurn,
Where the Seven Spears of Wedderburne
  Their men in battle-order set;
And Swinton laid the lance in rest,
That tamed of yore the sparkling crest
  Of Clarence's Plantagenet.
Nor list I say what hundreds more,
From the rich Merse and Lammermore,   60
And Tweed's fair borders, to the war,
Beneath the crest of Old Dunbar,
  And Hepburn's mingled banners come,
Down the steep mountain glittering far,
  And shouting still, "A Home! a Home!"

V

Now squire and knight, from Branksome sent,
On many a courteous message went;
To every chief and lord they paid
Meet thanks for prompt and powerful aid;
And told them,—how a truce was made,   70
  And how a day of fight was ta'en
'Twixt Musgrave and stout Deloraine;
    And how the Ladye pray'd them dear,
  That all would stay the fight to see,
  And deign, in love and courtesy,
    To taste of Branksome cheer.
Nor, while they bade to feast each Scot,
Were England's noble Lords forgot.
Himself, the hoary Seneschal
Rode forth, in seemly terms to call   80
Those gallant foes to Branksome Hall.

Accepted Howard, than whom knight
Was never dubb'd, more bold in fight;
Nor, when from war and armour free,
More famed for stately courtesy:
But angry Dacre rather chose
In his pavilion to repose.

VI

Now, noble Dame, perchance you ask,
  How these two hostile armies met?
Deeming it were no easy task   90
  To keep the truce which here was set;
Where martial spirits, all on fire,
Breathed only blood and mortal ire.—
By mutual inroads, mutual blows,
By habit, and by nation, foes,
  They met on Teviot's strand;
They met and sate them mingled down
Without a threat, without a frown,
  As brothers meet in foreign land:
The hands, the spear that lately grasp'd,   100
Still in the mailed gauntlet clasp'd,
  Were interchanged in greeting dear;
Visors were raised, and faces shown,
And many a friend, to friend made known,
  Partook of social cheer.
Some drove the jolly bowl about;
  With dice and draughts some chased the day;
And some, with many a merry shout,
In riot, revelry, and rout,
  Pursued the foot-ball play.   110

VII

Yet, be it known, had bugles blown,
  Or sign of war been seen,
Those bands, so fair together ranged,
Those hands, so frankly interchanged,
  Had dyed with gore the green:
The merry shout by Teviot-side
Had sunk in war-cries wild and wide,
  And in the groan of death;
And whingers, now in friendship bare,
The social meal to part and share,   120
  Had found a bloody sheath,
'Twixt truce and war, such sudden change
Was not infrequent, nor held strange,
  In the old Border-day:
But yet on Branksome's towers and town,
In peaceful merriment, sunk down
  The sun's declining ray.

VIII

The blithsome signs of wassel gay
Decay'd not with the dying day;
Soon through the latticed windows tall   130
Of lofty Branksome's lordly hall,
Divided square by shafts of stone,
Huge flakes of ruddy lustre shone;
Nor less the gilded rafters rang
With merry harp and beakers' clang:
  And frequent, on the darkening plain,
    Loud hollo, whoop, or whistle ran,
  As bands, their stragglers to regain,
    Give the shrill watchword of their clan;
And revellers, o'er their bowls, proclaim   140
Douglas or Dacre's conquering name.

IX

Less frequent heard, and fainter still,
  At length the various clamours died:
And you might hear, from Branksome hill,
  No sound but Teviot's rushing tide;
Save when the changing sentinel
The challenge of his watch could tell;
And save, where, through the dark profound,
The clanging axe and hammer's sound
  Rung from the nether lawn;   150
For many a busy hand toil'd there,
Strong pales to shape, and beams to square,
The lists' dread barriers to prepare
  Against the morrow's dawn.

X

Margaret from hall did soon retreat,
  Despite the Dame's reproving eye;
Nor mark'd she, as she left her seat,
  Full many a stifled sigh;
For many a noble warrior strove
To win the Flower of Teviot's love,   160
  And many a bold ally,—
With throbbing head and anxious heart,
All in her lonely bower apart,
  In broken sleep she lay:
By times, from silken couch she rose;
While yet the banner'd hosts repose,
  She view'd the dawning day:
Of all the hundreds sunk to rest,
First woke the loveliest and the best.

XI

She gazed upon the inner court,   170
  Which in the tower's tall shadow lay;

Where coursers' clang, and stamp, and snort,
  Had rung the livelong yesterday;
Now still as death; till stalking slow,—
  The jingling spurs announced his tread,—
A stately warrior pass'd below;
  But when he raised his plumed head—
    Blessed Mary! can it be?—
Secure, as if in Ousenam bowers,   179
He walks through Branksome's hostile towers,
  With fearless step and free.
She dared not sign, she dared not speak—
Oh! if one page's slumbers break,
  His blood the price must pay!
Not all the pearls Queen Mary wears,
Not Margaret's yet more precious tears,
  Shall buy his life a day.

XII

Yet was his hazard small; for well
You may bethink you of the spell
  Of that sly urchin page;   190
This to his lord he did impart,
And made him seem, by glamour art,
  A knight from Hermitage.
Unchallenged thus, the warder's post,
The court, unchallenged, thus he cross'd,
  For all the vassalage:
But O! what magic's quaint disguise
Could blind fair Margaret's azure eyes!
  She started from her seat;
While with surprise and fear she strove,   200
And both could scarcely master love—
  Lord Henry's at her feet.

XIII

Oft have I mused, what purpose bad
That foul malicious urchin had
  To bring this meeting round;
For happy love's a heavenly sight,
And by a vile malignant sprite
  In such no joy is found;
And oft I've deem'd, perchance he thought
Their erring passion might have wrought   210
  Sorrow, and sin, and shame;
And death to Cranstoun's gallant Knight,
And to the gentle ladye bright,
  Disgrace, and loss of fame.
But earthly spirit could not tell
The heart of them that loved so well.
True love's the gift which God has given
To man alone beneath the heaven:
  It is not fantasy's hot fire,

Whose wishes, soon as granted, fly;   220
It liveth not in fierce desire,
  With dead desire it doth not die;
It is the secret sympathy,
The silver link, the silken tie,
Which heart to heart, and mind to mind,
In body and in soul can bind.—
Now leave we Margaret and her Knight,
To tell you of the approaching fight.

XIV

Their warning blasts the bugles blew,
  The pipe's shrill port aroused each clan;   230
In haste, the deadly strife to view,
  The trooping warriors eager ran:
Thick round the lists their lances stood,
Like blasted pines in Ettrick wood;
To Branksome many a look they threw,
The combatants' approach to view,
And bandied many a word of boast,
About the knight each favour'd most.

XV

Meantime full anxious was the Dame;
For now arose disputed claim,   240
Of who should fight for Deloraine,
'Twixt Harden and 'twixt Thirlestane:
  They 'gan to reckon kin and rent,
And frowning brow on brow was bent;
  But yet not long the strife—for, lo!
Himself, the Knight of Deloraine,
Strong, as it seem'd, and free from pain,
  In armour sheath'd from top to toe,
Appear'd, and craved the combat due.
The Dame her charm successful knew,   250
And the fierce chiefs their claims withdrew.

XVI

When for the lists they sought the plain,
The stately Ladye's silken rein
  Did noble Howard hold;
Unarm'd by her side he walk'd,
And much, in courteous phrase, they talk'd
  Of feats of arms of old.
Costly his garb—his Flemish ruff
Fell o'er his doublet, shaped of buff,
  With satin slash'd and lined;   260
Tawny his boot, and gold his spur,
His cloak was all of Poland fur,
  His hose with silver twined;
His Bilboa blade, by Marchmen felt,

Hung in a broad and studded belt;
Hence, in rude phrase, the Borderers still
Call'd noble Howard, Belted Will.

XVII

Behind Lord Howard and the Dame,
Fair Margaret on her palfrey came,
    Whose foot-cloth swept the ground: 270
White was her wimple, and her veil,
And her loose locks a chaplet pale
    Of whitest roses bound;
The lordly Angus, by her side,
In courtesy to cheer her tried;
Without his aid, her hand in vain
Had strove to guide her broider'd rein.
He deem'd, she shudder'd at the sight
Of warriors met for mortal fight;
But cause of terror, all unguess'd,   280
Was fluttering in her gentle breast,
When, in their chairs of crimson placed,
The Dame and she the barriers graced.

XVIII

Prize of the field, the young Buccleuch,
An English knight led forth to view;
Scarce rued the boy his present plight,
So much he long'd to see the fight.
Within the lists, in knightly pride,
High Home and haughty Dacre ride;
Their leading staffs of steel they wield,   290
As marshals of the mortal field;
While to each knight their care assign'd
Like vantage of the sun and wind.
Then heralds hoarse did loud proclaim,
In King and Queen, and Warden's name,
    That none, while lasts the strife,
Should dare, by look, or sign, or word,
Aid to a champion to afford,
    On peril of his life;
And not a breath the silence broke,   300
Till thus the alternate Heralds spoke:—

XIX

ENGLISH HERALD

"Here standeth Richard of Musgrave,
    Good knight and true, and freely born,
Amends from Deloraine to crave,
    For foul despiteous scathe and scorn.
He sayeth, that William of Deloraine
    Is traitor false by Border laws;

This with his sword he will maintain,
    So help him God, and his good cause!"

XX

SCOTTISH HERALD

"Here standeth William of Deloraine,   310
Good knight and true, of noble strain,
Who sayeth, that foul treason's stain,
    Since he bore arms, ne'er soil'd his coat;
    And that, so help him God above!
    He will on Musgrave's body prove,
He lies most foully in his throat."

LORD DACRE

"Forward, brave champions, to the fight!
Sound trumpets!"——

LORD HOME

——"God defend the right!"—

Then, Teviot! how thine echoes rang,
When bugle-sound and trumpet-clang   320
    Let loose the martial foes,
And in mid list, with shield poised high,
And measured step and wary eye,
    The combatants did close.

XXI

Ill would it suit your gentle ear,
Ye lovely listeners, to hear
How to the axe the helms did sound,
And blood pour'd down from many a wound;
For desperate was the strife and long,
And either warrior fierce and strong.   330
But, were each dame a listening knight,
I well could tell how warriors fight!
For I have seen war's lightning flashing,
Seen the claymore with bayonet clashing,
Seen through red blood the war-horse dashing,
And scorn'd, amid the reeling strife,
To yield a step for death or life.—

XXII

'Tis done, 'tis done! that fatal blow
    Has stretch'd him on the bloody plain;
He strives to rise—Brave Musgrave, no!   340
    Thence never shalt thou rise again!
He chokes in blood—some friendly hand
Undo the visor's barred band,

Unfix the gorget's iron clasp,
And give him room for life to gasp!—
O, bootless aid!—haste, holy Friar,
Haste, ere the sinner shall expire!
Of all his guilt let him be shriven,
And smooth his path from earth to heaven!

XXIII

In haste the holy Friar sped;—   350
His naked foot was dyed with red,
As through the lists he ran;
Unmindful of the shouts on high,
That hail'd the conqueror's victory,
    He raised the dying man;
Loose waved his silver beard and hair,
As o'er him he kneel'd down in prayer;
And still the crucifix on high
He holds before his darkening eye;
And still he bends an anxious ear,   360
His faltering penitence to hear;
    Still props him from the bloody sod,
Still, even when soul and body part,
Pours ghostly comfort on his heart,
    And bids him trust in God!
Unheard he prays;—the death-pang's o'er!
Richard of Musgrave breathes no more.

XXIV

As if exhausted in the fight,
Or musing o'er the piteous sight,
    The silent victor stands;   370
His beaver did he not unclasp,
Mark'd not the shouts, felt not the grasp
    Of gratulating hands.
When lo! strange cries of wild surprise,
Mingled with seeming terror, rise
    Among the Scottish bands;
And all, amid the throng'd array,
In panic haste gave open way
To a half-naked ghastly man,
Who downward from the castle ran: 380
He cross'd the barriers at a bound,
And wild and haggard look'd around,
    As dizzy, and in pain;
And all, upon the armed ground,
    Knew William of Deloraine!
Each ladye sprung from seat with speed;
Vaulted each marshal from his steed;
    "And who art thou," they cried,
"Who hast this battle fought and won?"—
His plumed helm was soon undone—   390
    "Cranstoun of Teviot-side!

For this fair prize I've fought and won,"—
And to the Ladye led her son.

XXV

Full oft the rescued boy she kiss'd,
And often press'd him to her breast;
For, under all her dauntless show,
Her heart had throbb'd at every blow;
Yet not Lord Cranstoun deign'd she greet,
Though low he kneeled at her feet.
Me lists not tell what words were made,   400
What Douglas, Home, and Howard said—
    —For Howard was a generous foe—
And how the clan united pray'd
    The Ladye would the feud forego,
And deign to bless the nuptial hour
Of Cranstoun's Lord and Teviot's Flower.

XXVI

She look'd to river, look'd to hill,
    Thought on the Spirit's prophecy,
Then broke her silence stern and still,—
    "Not you, but Fate, has vanquish'd me.   410
Their influence kindly stars may shower
On Teviot's tide and Branksome's tower,
    For pride is quell'd, and love is free."—
She took fair Margaret by the hand,
Who, breathless, trembling, scarce might stand,
    That hand to Cranstoun's lord gave she:—
"As I am true to thee and thine,
Do thou be true to me and mine!
    This clasp of love our bond shall be;
For this is your betrothing day,   420
And all these noble lords shall stay,
    To grace it with their company."—

XXVII

All as they left the listed plain,
Much of the story she did gain;
How Cranstoun fought with Deloraine,
And of his page, and of the Book
Which from the wounded knight he took;
And how he sought her castle high,
That morn, by help of gramarye;
How, in Sir William's armour dight,   430
Stolen by his page, while slept the knight,
He took on him the single fight.
But half his tale he left unsaid,
And linger'd till he join'd the maid.—
Cared not the Ladye to betray
Her mystic arts in view of day;

But well she thought, ere midnight came,
Of that strange page the pride to tame,
From his foul hands the Book to save,
And send it back to Michael's grave.—   440
Needs not to tell each tender word
'Twixt Margaret and 'twixt Cranstoun's lord;
Nor how she told of former woes,
And how her bosom fell and rose,
While he and Musgrave bandied blows.—
Needs not these lovers' joys to tell:
One day, fair maids, you'll know them well.

XXVIII

William of Deloraine, some chance
Had waken'd from his death-like trance;
  And taught that, in the listed plain,   450
Another, in his arms and shield,
Against fierce Musgrave axe did wield,
  Under the name of Deloraine.
Hence, to the field, unarm'd, he ran,
And hence his presence scared the clan,
Who held him for some fleeting wraith,
And not a man of blood and breath.
  Not much this new ally he loved,
  Yet, when he saw what hap had proved,
    He greeted him right heartilie: 460
He would not waken old debate,
For he was void of rancorous hate,
    Though rude, and scant of courtesy;
In raids he spilt but seldom blood,
Unless when men-at-arms withstood,
Or, as was meet, for deadly feud.
He ne'er bore grudge for stalwart blow,
Ta'en in fair fight from gallant foe:
  And so 'twas seen of him, e'en now,   469
    When on dead Musgrave he look'd down;
  Grief darken'd on his rugged brow,
    Though half disguised with a frown;
And thus, while sorrow bent his head,
His foeman's epitaph he made.

XXIX

"Now, Richard Musgrave, liest thou here!
  I ween, my deadly enemy;
For, if I slew thy brother dear,
  Thou slew'st a sister's son to me;
And when I lay in dungeon dark,
  Of Naworth Castle, long months three,   480
Till ransom'd for a thousand mark,
  Dark Musgrave, it was long of thee.
And, Musgrave, could our fight be tried,
  And thou wert now alive, as I,

Nor mortal man should us divide,
  Till one, or both of us, did die:
Yet rest thee God! for well I know
I ne'er shall find a nobler foe.
In all the northern counties here,
Whose word is Snaffle, spur, and spear,   490
Thou wert the best to follow gear!
'Twas pleasure, as we look'd behind,
To see how thou the chase could'st wind,
Cheer the dark blood-hound on his way,
And with the bugle rouse the fray!
I'd give the lands of Deloraine,
Dark Musgrave were alive again."—

XXX

So mourn'd he, till Lord Dacre's band
Were bowning back to Cumberland.   499
They raised brave Musgrave from the field,
And laid him on his bloody shield;
On levell'd lances, four and four,
By turns, the noble burden bore.
Before, at times, upon the gale,
Was heard the Minstrel's plaintive wail;
Behind, four priests, in sable stole,
Sung requiem for the warrior's soul:
Around, the horsemen slowly rode;
With trailing pikes the spearmen trode;
And thus the gallant knight they bore,   510
Through Liddesdale to Leven's shore;
Thence to Holme Coltrame's lofty nave,
And laid him in his father's grave.

————

The harp's wild notes, though hush'd the song,
The mimic march of death prolong;
Now seems it far, and now a-near,
Now meets, and now eludes the ear;
Now seems some mountain side to sweep,
Now faintly dies in valley deep;
Seems now as if the Minstrel's wail,   520
Now the sad requiem, loads the gale;
Last, o'er the warrior's closing grave,
Rung the full choir in choral stave.

After due pause, they bade him tell,
Why he, who touch'd the harp so well,
Should thus, with ill-rewarded toil,
Wander a poor and thankless soil,
When the more generous Southern Land
Would well requite his skilful hand.

  The Aged Harper, howsoe'er   530
His only friend, his harp, was dear,

Liked not to hear it rank'd so high
Above his flowing poesy:
Less liked he still, that scornful jeer
Misprised the land he loved so dear;
High was the sound, as thus again
The Bard resumed his minstrel strain.

CANTO SIXTH

I

BREATHES there the man, with soul so dead,
Who never to himself hath said,
   This is my own, my native land!
Whose heart hath ne'er within him burn'd,
As home his footsteps he hath turn'd,
   From wandering on a foreign strand!
If such there breathe, go, mark him well;
For him no Minstrel raptures swell;
High though his titles, proud his name,
Boundless his wealth as wish can claim;   10
Despite those titles, power, and pelf,
The wretch, concentred all in self,
Living, shall forfeit fair renown,
And, doubly dying, shall go down
To the vile dust, from whence he sprung,
Unwept, unhonour'd, and unsung.

II

O Caledonia! stern and wild,
Meet nurse for a poetic child!
Land of brown heath and shaggy wood,
Land of the mountain and the flood,   20
Land of my sires! what mortal hand
Can e'er untie the filial band,
That knits me to thy rugged strand!
Still, as I view each well-known scene,
Think what is now, and what hath been,
Seems as, to me, of all bereft,
Sole friends thy woods and streams were left;
And thus I love them better still,
Even in extremity of ill.
By Yarrow's streams still let me stray,   30
Though none should guide my feeble way;
Still feel the breeze down Ettrick break,
Although it chill my wither'd cheek;
Still lay my head by Teviot Stone,
Though there, forgotten and alone,
The Bard may draw his parting groan.

III

Not scorn'd like me! to Branksome Hall
The Minstrels came, at festive call;
Trooping they came, from near and far,
The jovial priests of mirth and war;   40
Alike for feast and fight prepared,
Battle and banquet both they shared.
Of late, before each martial clan,
They blew their death-note in the van,
But now, for every merry mate,
Rose the portcullis' iron grate;
They sound the pipe, they strike the string,
They dance, they revel, and they sing,
Till the rude turrets shake and ring.

IV

Me lists not at this tide declare   50
   The splendour of the spousal rite,
How muster'd in the chapel fair
   Both maid and matron, squire and knight;
Me lists not tell of owches rare,
Of mantles green, and braided hair,
And kirtles furr'd with miniver;
What plumage waved the altar round,
How spurs and ringing chainlets sound;
And hard it were for bard to speak
The changeful hue of Margaret's cheek;   60
That lovely hue which comes and flies,
As awe and shame alternate rise!

V

Some bards have sung, the Ladye high
Chapel or altar came not nigh;
Nor durst the rites of spousal grace,
So much she fear'd each holy place.
False slanders these:—I trust right well
She wrought not by forbidden spell;
For mighty words and signs have power
O'er sprites in planetary hour: 70
Yet scarce I praise their venturous part,
Who tamper with such dangerous art.
   But this for faithful truth I say,
     The Ladye by the altar stood.
   Of sable velvet her array,
     And on her head a crimson hood,
With pearls embroider'd and entwined,
Guarded with gold, with ermine lined;
A merlin sat upon her wrist
Held by a leash of silken twist.   80

VI

The spousal rites were ended soon:
'Twas now the merry hour of noon,
And in the lofty arched hall
Was spread the gorgeous festival.
Steward and squire, with heedful haste,
Marshall'd the rank of every guest;
Pages, with ready blade, were there,
The mighty meal to carve and share:
O'er capon, heron-shew, and crane,
And princely peacock's gilded train,   90
And o'er the boar-head, garnish'd brave,
And cygnet from St. Mary's wave;
O'er ptarmigan and venison,
The priest had spoke his benison.
Then rose the riot and the din,
Above, beneath, without, within!
For, from the lofty balcony,
Rung trumpet, shalm, and psaltery:
Their clanging bowls old warriors quaff'd,
Loudly they spoke, and loudly laugh'd;   100
Whisper'd young knights, in tone more mild,
To ladies fair, and ladies smiled.
The hooded hawks, high perch'd on beam,
The clamour join'd with whistling scream,
And flapp'd their wings, and shook their bells,
In concert with the stag-hounds' yells.
Round go the flasks of ruddy wine,
From Bourdeaux, Orleans, or the Rhine;
Their tasks the busy sewers ply,
And all is mirth and revelry.   110

VII

The Goblin Page, omitting still
No opportunity of ill,
Strove now, while blood ran hot and high,
To rouse debate and jealousy;
Till Conrad, Lord of Wolfenstein,
By nature fierce, and warm with wine,
And now in humour highly cross'd,
About some steeds his band had lost,
High words to words succeeding still,
Smote, with his gauntlet, stout Hunthill;   120
A hot and hardy Rutherford,
Whom men called Dickon Draw-the-sword.
He took it on the page's saye,
Hunthill had driven these steeds away.
Then Howard, Home, and Douglas rose,
The kindling discord to compose:
Stern Rutherford right little said,
But bit his glove, and shook his head.—
A fortnight thence, in Inglewood,

Stout Conrad, cold, and drench'd in blood,   130
His bosom gored with many a wound,
Was by a woodman's lyme-dog found;
Unknown the manner of his death,
Gone was his brand, both sword and sheath;
But ever from that time, 'twas said,
That Dickon wore a Cologne blade.

VIII

The dwarf, who fear'd his master's eye
Might his foul treachery espie,
Now sought the castle buttery,
Where many a yeoman, bold and free,   140
Revell'd as merrily and well
As those that sat in lordly selle.
Watt Tinlinn, there, did frankly raise
The pledge to Arthur Fire-the-Braes;
And he, as by his breeding bound,
To Howard's merry-men sent it round.
To quit them, on the English side,
Red Roland Forster loudly cried,
"A deep carouse to yon fair bride!"—
At every pledge, from vat and pail,   150
Foam'd forth in floods the nut-brown ale;
While shout the riders every one;
Such day of mirth ne'er cheer'd their clan,
Since old Buccleuch the name did gain,
When in the cleuch the buck was ta'en.

IX

The wily page, with vengeful thought,
  Remember'd him of Tinlinn's yew,
And swore, it should be dearly bought
  That ever he the arrow drew.
First, he the yeoman did molest,   160
With bitter gibe and taunting jest;
Told, how he fled at Solway strife,
And how Hob Armstrong cheer'd his wife;
Then, shunning still his powerful arm,
At unawares he wrought him harm;
From trencher stole his choicest cheer,
Dash'd from his lips his can of beer;
Then, to his knee sly creeping on,
With bodkin pierced him to the bone:
The venom'd wound, and festering joint,   170
Long after rued that bodkin's point.
The startled yeoman swore and spurn'd,
And board and flagons overturn'd.
Riot and clamour wild began;
Back to the hall the Urchin ran;
Took in a darkling nook his post,
And grinn'd, and mutter'd, "Lost! lost! lost!"

X

By this, the Dame, lest farther fray
Should mar the concord of the day,
Had bid the Minstrels tune their lay. 180
And first stept forth old Albert Græme,
The Minstrel of that ancient name:
Was none who struck the harp so well,
Within the Land Debateable;
Well friended, too, his hardy kin,
Whoever lost, were sure to win;
They sought the beeves that made their broth,
In Scotland and in England both.
In homely guise, as nature bade,
His simple song the Borderer said. 190

XI

ALBERT GRÆME

It was an English ladye bright,
  (The sun shines fair on Carlisle wall,)
And she would marry a Scottish knight,
  For Love will still be lord of all.

Blithely they saw the rising sun,
  When he shone fair on Carlisle wall;
But they were sad ere day was done,
  Though Love was still the lord of all.

Her sire gave brooch and jewel fine,
  Where the sun shines fair on Carlisle wall; 200
Her brother gave but a flask of wine,
  For ire that Love was lord of all.

For she had lands, both meadow and lea,
  Where the sun shines fair on Carlisle wall,
And he swore her death, ere he would see
  A Scottish knight the lord of all!

XII

That wine she had not tasted well,
  (The sun shines fair on Carlisle wall,)
When dead, in her true love's arms, she fell,
  For Love was still the lord of all! 210

He pierced her brother to the heart,
  Where the sun shines fair on Carlisle wall:—
So perish all would true love part,
  That Love may still be lord of all!

And then he took the cross divine,
  (Where the sun shines fair on Carlisle wall,)
And died for her sake in Palestine,
  So Love was still the lord of all.

Now all ye lovers, that faithful prove,
  (The sun shines fair on Carlisle wall,) 220
Pray for their souls who died for love,
  For Love shall still be lord of all!

XIII

As ended Albert's simple lay,
  Arose a bard of loftier port;
For sonnet, rhyme, and roundelay,
  Renown'd in haughty Henry's court:
There rung thy harp, unrivall'd long,
Fitztraver of the silver song!
  The gentle Surrey loved his lyre—
    Who has not heard of Surrey's fame? 230
  His was the hero's soul of fire,
    And his the bard's immortal name,
And his was love, exalted high
By all the glow of chivalry.

XIV

They sought, together, climes afar,
  And oft, within some olive grove,
When even came with twinkling star,
  They sung of Surrey's absent love.
His step the Italian peasant stay'd,
  And deem'd, that spirits from on high, 240
Round where some hermit saint was laid,
  Were breathing heavenly melody;
So sweet did harp and voice combine,
To praise the name of Geraldine.

XV

Fitztraver! O what tongue may say
  The pangs thy faithful bosom knew,
When Surrey, of the deathless lay,
  Ungrateful Tudor's sentence slew?
Regardless of the tryant's frown,
His harp call'd wrath and vengeance down. 250
He left, for Naworth's iron towers,
Windsor's green glades, and courtly bowers,
And faithful to his patron's name,
  With Howard still Fitztraver came;
Lord William's foremost favourite he,
And chief of all his minstrelsy.

XVI

FITZTRAVER

'Twas All-soul's eve, and Surrey's heart beat
  high;
  He heard the midnight bell with anxious
    start,
Which told the mystic hour, approaching nigh,
  When wise Cornelius promised, by his art, 260
To show to him the ladye of his heart,
  Albeit betwixt them roar'd the ocean grim;
Yet so the sage had hight to play his part,
  That he should see her form in life and limb,
And mark, if still she loved, and still she
    thought of him.

XVII

Dark was the vaulted room of gramarye,
  To which the wizard led the gallant Knight,
Save that before a mirror, huge and high,
  A hallow'd taper shed a glimmering light
On mystic implements of magic might;   270
  On cross, and character, and talisman,
And almagest, and altar, nothing bright:
  For fitful was the lustre, pale and wan,
As watchlight by the bed of some departing
    man.

XVIII

But soon, within that mirror huge and high,
  Was seen a self-emitted light to gleam;
And forms upon its breast the Earl 'gan spy,
  Cloudy and indistinct, as feverish dream;
Till, slow arranging, and defined, they seem
  To form a lordly and a lofty room,   280
Part lighted by a lamp with silver beam,
  Placed by a couch of Agra's silken loom,
And part by moonshine pale, and part was hid
    in gloom.

XIX

Fair all the pageant—but how passing fair
  The slender form, which lay on couch of
    Ind!
O'er her white bosom stray'd her hazel hair,
  Pale her dear cheek, as if for love she pined;
All in her night-robe loose she lay reclined,
  And, pensive, read from tablet eburnine,
Some strain that seem'd her inmost soul to
    find:—   290

That favour'd strain was Surrey's raptured
    line,
That fair and lovely form, the Lady Geraldine.

XX

Slow roll'd the clouds upon the lovely form,
  And swept the goodly vision all away—
So royal envy roll'd the murky storm
  O'er my beloved Master's glorious day.
Thou jealous, ruthless tyrant! Heaven repay
  On thee, and on thy children's latest line,
The wild caprice of thy despotic sway,
  The gory bridal bed, the plunder'd shrine, 300
The murder'd Surrey's blood, the tears of
    Geraldine!

XXI

Both Scots, and Southern chiefs, prolong
Applauses of Fitztraver's song;
These hated Henry's name as death,
And those still held the ancient faith.—
Then, from his seat, with lofty air,
Rose Harold, bard of brave St. Clair;
St. Clair, who, feasting high at Home,
Had with that lord to battle come.
Harold was born where restless seas   310
Howl round the storm-swept Orcades;
Where erst St. Clairs held princely sway
O'er isle and islet, strait and bay;—
Still nods their palace to its fall,
Thy pride and sorrow, fair Kirkwall!—
Thence oft he mark'd fierce Pentland rave,
As if grim Odin rode her wave;
And watch'd, the whilst, with visage pale,
And throbbing heart, the struggling sail;
For all of wonderful and wild   320
Had rapture for the lonely child.

XXII

And much of wild and wonderful
In these rude isles might fancy cull;
For thither came, in times afar,
Stern Lochlin's sons of roving war,
The Norsemen, train'd to spoil and blood,
Skill'd to prepare the raven's food;
Kings of the main their leaders brave,
Their barks the dragons of the wave.
And there, in many a stormy vale,   330
The Scald had told his wondrous tale;
And many a Runic column high
Had witness'd grim idolatry.

And thus had Harold, in his youth,
Learn'd many a Saga's rhyme uncouth,—
Of that Sea-Snake, tremendous curl'd,
Whose monstrous circle girds the world;
Of those dread Maids, whose hideous yell
Maddens the battle's bloody swell;
Of Chiefs, who, guided through the gloom 340
By the pale death-lights of the tomb,
Ransack'd the graves of warriors old,
Their falchions wrench'd from corpses' hold,
Waked the deaf tomb with war's alarms,
And bade the dead arise to arms!
With war and wonder all on flame,
To Roslin's bowers young Harold came,
Where, by sweet glen and greenwood tree,
He learn'd a milder minstrelsy;
Yet something of the Northern spell 350
Mix'd with the softer numbers well.

XXIII

HAROLD

O listen, listen, ladies gay!
  No haughty feat of arms I tell;
Soft is the note, and sad the lay,
  That mourns the lovely Rosabelle.

—"Moor, moor the barge, ye gallant crew!
  And, gentle ladye, deign to stay!
Rest thee in Castle Ravensheuch,
  Nor tempt the stormy firth to-day.

"The blackening wave is edged with white: 360
  To inch and rock the sea-mews fly;
The fishers have heard the Water-Sprite,
  Whose screams forbode that wreck is nigh.

"Last night the gifted Seer did view
  A wet shroud swathed round ladye gay;
Then stay thee, Fair, in Ravensheuch:
  Why cross the gloomy firth to-day?"—

" 'Tis not because Lord Lindesay's heir
  To-night at Roslin leads the ball,
But that my ladye-mother there 370
  Sits lonely in her castle-hall.

" 'Tis not because the ring they ride,
  And Lindesay at the ring rides well,
But that my sire the wine will chide,
  If 'tis not fill'd by Rosabelle."—

O'er Roslin all that dreary night,
  A wondrous blaze was seen to gleam;

'Twas broader than the watch-fire's light,
  And redder than the bright moon-beam.

It glared on Roslin's castled rock, 380
  It ruddied all the copse-wood glen;
'Twas seen from Dryden's groves of oak,
  And seen from cavern'd Hawthornden.

Seem'd all on fire that chapel proud,
  Where Roslin's chiefs uncoffin'd lie,
Each Baron, for a sable shroud,
  Sheathed in his iron panoply.

Seem'd all on fire within, around,
  Deep sacristy and altar's pale;
Shone every pillar foliage-bound, 390
  And glimmer'd all the dead men's mail.

Blazed battlement and pinnet high,
  Blazed every rose-carved buttress fair—
So still they blaze, when fate is nigh
  The lordly line of high St. Clair.

There are twenty of Roslin's barons bold
  Lie buried within that proud chapelle;
Each one the holy vault doth hold—
  But the sea holds lovely Rosabelle!

And each St. Clair was buried there, 400
  With candle, with book, and with knell;
But the sea-caves rung, and the wild winds
    sung,
  The dirge of lovely Rosabelle.

XXIV

So sweet was Harold's piteous lay,
  Scarce mark'd the guests the darken'd hall,
Though, long before the sinking day,
  A wondrous shade involved them all:
It was not eddying mist or fog,
Drain'd by the sun from fen or bog;
  Of no eclipse had sages told; 410
And yet, as it came on apace,
Each one could scarce his neighbour's face,
  Could scarce his own stretch'd hand behold,
A secret horror check'd the feast,
And chill'd the soul of every guest;
Even the high Dame stood half aghast,
She knew some evil on the blast;
The elvish page fell to the ground,
And, shuddering, mutter'd, "Found! found!
    found!"

XXV

Then sudden, through the darken'd air 420
  A flash of lightning came;
So broad, so bright, so red the glare,
  The castle seem'd on flame.
Glanced every rafter of the hall,
Glanced every shield upon the wall;
Each trophied beam, each sculptured stone,
Were instant seen, and instant gone;
Full through the guests' bedazzled band
Resistless flash'd the levin-brand,
And fill'd the hall with smouldering smoke, 430
As on the elvish page it broke.
  It broke with thunder long and loud,
  Dismay'd the brave, appall'd the proud,—
    From sea to sea the larum rung;
  On Berwick wall, and at Carlisle withal,
    To arms the startled warders sprung.
When ended was the dreadful roar,
The elvish dwarf was seen no more!

XXVI

Some heard a voice in Branksome Hall,
Some saw a sight, not seen by all; 440
That dreadful voice was heard by some,
Cry, with loud summons, "GYLBIN, COME!"
  And on the spot where burst the brand,
    Just where the page had flung him down,
  Some saw an arm, and some a hand,
    And some the waving of a gown.
The guests in silence pray'd and shook,
And terror dimm'd each lofty look.
But none of all the astonish'd train
Was so dismay'd as Deloraine; 450
His blood did freeze, his brain did burn,
'Twas fear'd his mind would ne'er return;
  For he was speechless, ghastly, wan,
  Like him of whom the story ran,
  Who spoke the spectre-hound in Man.
At length, by fits, he darkly told,
With broken hint, and shuddering cold—
  That he had seen, right certainly,
A shape with amice wrapp'd around,
With a wrought Spanish baldric bound, 460
  Like pilgrim from beyond the sea;
And knew—but how it matter'd not—
It was the wizard, Michael Scott.

XXVII

The anxious crowd, with horror pale,
All trembling heard the wondrous tale;

No sound was made, no word was spoke,
Till noble Angus silence broke;
  And he a solemn sacred plight
Did to St. Bride of Douglas make,
That he a pilgrimage would take 470
To Melrose Abbey, for the sake
  Of Michael's restless sprite.
Then each, to ease his troubled breast,
To some bless'd saint his prayers address'd:
Some to St. Modan made their vows,
Some to St. Mary of the Lowes,
Some to the Holy Rood of Lisle,
Some to our Ladye of the Isle;
Each did his patron witness make,
That he such pilgrimage would take, 480
And monks should sing, and bells should toll,
All for the weal of Michael's soul.
While vows were ta'en, and prayers were
  pray'd,
'Tis said the noble dame, dismay'd,
Renounced, for aye, dark magic's aid.

XXVIII

Nought of the bridal will I tell,
Which after in short space befell;
Nor how brave sons and daughters fair
Bless'd Teviot's Flower, and Cranstoun's heir:
After such dreadful scene, 'twere vain 490
To wake the note of mirth again.
  More meet it were to mark the day
  Of penitence and prayer divine,
  When pilgrim-chiefs, in sad array,
  Sought Melrose' holy shrine.

XXIX

With naked foot, and sackcloth vest,
And arms enfolded on his breast,
  Did every pilgrim go;
The standers-by might hear uneath,
Footstep, or voice, or high-drawn breath, 500
  Through all the lengthen'd row:
No lordly look, nor martial stride,
Gone was their glory, sunk their pride,
  Forgotten their renown;
Silent and slow, like ghosts they glide
To the high altar's hallow'd side,
  And there they knelt them down:
Above the suppliant chieftains wave
The banners of departed brave;
Beneath the letter'd stones were laid 510
The ashes of their fathers dead;

From many a garnish'd niche around,
Stern saints and tortured martyrs frown'd.

XXX

And slow up the dim aisle afar,
With sable cowl and scapular,
And snow-white stoles, in order due,
The holy Fathers, two and two,
   In long procession came;
Taper and host, and book they bare,
And holy banner, flourish'd fair   520
   With the Redeemer's name.
Above the prostrate pilgrim band
The mitred Abbot stretch'd his hand,
   And bless'd them as they kneel'd;
With holy cross he sign'd them all,
And pray'd they might be sage in hall,
   And fortunate in field.
Then mass was sung, and prayers were said,
And solemn requiem for the dead;
And bells toll'd out their mighty peal,   530
For the departed spirit's weal;
And ever in the office close
The hymn of intercession rose;
And far the echoing aisles prolong
The awful burthen of the song,—
   DIES IRÆ, DIES ILLA,
   SOLVET SÆCLUM IN FAVILLA;
While the pealing organ rung;
   Were it meet with sacred strain
   To close my lay, so light and vain,   540
Thus the holy Fathers sung.

XXXI

HYMN FOR THE DEAD

That day of wrath, that dreadful day,
When heaven and earth shall pass away,
What power shall be the sinner's stay?
How shall he meet that dreadful day?

When, shrivelling like a parched scroll,
The flaming heavens together roll;
When louder yet, and yet more dread,
Swells the high trump that wakes the dead!

Oh! on that day, that wrathful day,   550
When man to judgment wakes from clay,
Be THOU the trembling sinner's stay,
Though heaven and earth shall pass away!

Hush'd is the harp—the Minstrel gone.
And did he wander forth alone?
Alone, in indigence and age,
To linger out his pilgrimage?
No; close beneath proud Newark's tower,
Arose the Minstrel's lowly bower;
A simple hut; but there was seen   560
The little garden hedged with green,
The cheerful hearth, and lattice clean.
There shelter'd wanderers, by the blaze,
Oft heard the tale of other days;
For much he loved to ope his door,
And give the aid he begg'd before.
So pass'd the winter's day; but still,
When summer smiled on sweet Bowhill,
And July's eve, with balmy breath,
Waved the blue-bells on Newark heath;   570
When throstles sung in Harehead-shaw,
And corn was green on Carterhaugh,
And flourish'd, broad, Blackandro's oak,
The aged Harper's soul awoke!
Then would he sing achievements high,
And circumstance of chivalry,
Till the rapt traveller would stay,
Forgetful of the closing day;
And noble youths, the strain to hear,
Forsook the hunting of the deer;   580
And Yarrow, as he roll'd along,
Bore burden to the Minstrel's song.

SONGS FROM "THE LADY OF THE LAKE"

1. SOLDIER, REST!

Soldier, rest! thy warfare o'er
   Sleep the sleep that knows not breaking;
Dream of battled fields no more,
   Days of danger, nights of waking.
In our isle's enchanted hall,
   Hands unseen thy couch are strewing,
Fairy strains of music fall,
   Every sense in slumber dewing.
Soldier, rest! thy warfare o'er,
Dream of fighting fields no more;   10
Sleep the sleep that knows not breaking,
Morn of toil, nor night of waking.

No rude sound shall reach thine ear,
   Armor's clang of war-steed champing,
Trump nor pibroch summon here
   Mustering clan or squadron tramping.

Yet the lark's shrill fife may come
  At the daybreak from the fallow,
And the bittern sound his drum,
  Booming from the sedgy shallow.   20
Ruder sounds shall none be near,
Guards nor warders challenge here,
Here's no war-steed's neigh and champing,
Shouting clans or squadrons stamping.

Huntsman, rest! thy chase is done;
  While our slumbrous spells assail ye,
Dream not, with the rising sun,
  Bugles here shall sound reveillé.
Sleep! the deer is in his den;
  Sleep! thy hounds are by thee lying: 30
Sleep! nor dream in yonder glen
  How thy gallant steed lay dying.
Huntsman, rest! thy chase is done;
Think not of the rising sun,
For at dawning to assail ye
Here no bugles sound reveillé.

2. BOAT SONG

Hail to the Chief who in triumph advances!
  Honored and blessed be the ever-green Pine!
Long may the tree, in his banner that glances,
  Flourish, the shelter and grace of our line!
    Heaven send it happy dew,
    Earth lend it sap anew,
Gayly to bourgeon, and broadly to grow,
    While every Highland glen
    Sends back our shout again,
Roderigh Vich Alpine dhu, ho! ieroe!   10

Ours is no sapling, chance-sown by the fountain,
  Blooming at Beltane, in winter to fade;
When the whirlwind has stripped every leaf on the mountain,
  The more shall Clan-Alpine exult in her shade.
    Moored in the rifted rock,
    Proof to the tempest's shock,
Firmer he roots him the ruder it blows;
    Menteith and Breadalbane, then,
    Echo his praise again,
Roderigh Vich Alpine dhu, ho! ieroe!   20

Proudly our pibroch has thrilled in Glen Fruin,
  And Bannochar's groans to our slogan replied;
Glen Luss and Ross-dhu, they are smoking in ruin,

And the best of Loch Lomond lie dead on her side.
    Widow and Saxon maid
    Long shall lament our raid,
Think of Clan-Alpine with fear and with woe;
    Lennox and Leven-glen
    Shake when they hear again,
Roderigh Vich Alpine dhu, ho! ieroe!   30

Row, vassals, row, for the pride of the Highlands!
  Stretch to your oars for the ever-green Pine!
O! that the rosebud that graces yon islands
  Were wreathed in a garland around him to twine!
    O that some seedling gem,
    Worthy such noble stem,
Honored and blessed in their shadow might grow!
    Loud should Clan-Alpine then
    Ring from her deepmost glen,
Roderigh Vich Alpine dhu, ho! ieroe!   40

3. CORONACH

He is gone on the mountain,
  He is lost to the forest,
Like a summer-dried fountain,
  When our need was the sorest.
The font, reappearing,
  From the rain-drops shall borrow,
But to us comes no cheering,
  To Duncan no morrow!

The hand of the reaper
  Takes ears that are hoary,   10
But the voice of the weeper
  Wails manhood in glory.
The autumn winds rushing
  Waft the leaves that are searest,
But our flower was in flushing,
  When blighting was nearest.

Fleet foot on the correi,
  Sage counsel in cumber,
Red hand in the foray,
  How sound is thy slumber!   20
Like the dew on the mountain,
  Like the foam on the river,
Like the bubble on the fountain,
  Thou art gone, and forever!

4. Harp of the North

Harp of the North, farewell! The hills grow
    dark,
  On purple peaks a deeper shade descending;
In twilight copse the glow-worm lights her
    spark,
  The deer, half-seen, are to the covert wend-
    ing.
Resume thy wizard elm! the fountain lending,
  And the wild breeze, thy wilder minstrelsy;
Thy numbers sweet with nature's vespers
    blending,
  With distant echo from the fold and lea,
And herd-boy's evening pipe, and hum of
    housing bee.

Yet, once again, farewell, thou Minstrel
    Harp!   10
  Yet, once again, forgive my feeble sway,
And little reck I of the censure sharp

May idly cavil at an idle lay.
Much have I owed thy strains on life's long
    way,
  Through secret woes the world has never
    known,
When on the weary night dawned wearier day,
  And bitterer was the grief devoured alone.
That I o'erlive such woes, Enchantress! is
    thine own.

Hark! as my lingering footsteps slow retire,
  Some Spirit of the Air has waked thy
    string!   20
'Tis now a seraph bold, with touch of fire,
  'Tis now the brush of Fairy's frolic wing.
Receding now, the dying numbers ring
  Fainter and fainter down the rugged dell,
And now the mountain breezes scarcely bring
  A wandering witch-note of the distant spell—
And now, 'tis silent all!—Enchantress, fare
    thee well!

LORD BYRON

SCOTT AND BYRON

When Byron wrote of Scott, "This person is at present the most profound explorer of bathos —the most impudent and execrable of literary poachers—silly—venal—grovelling," he was himself both impudent and silly. He had taken offense at Henry Brougham's criticism of his *Hours of Idleness* [*infra*] and, mistakenly thinking that Scott had written it, he struck his friend. For Sir Walter was his friend, as Byron later came to know; and the younger poet learned from the older something of how a tale might be told. But it would have been strangely humiliating to the dangerous boy who wrote the *English Bards and Scotch Reviewers* had he realized that the man whom he had proclaimed "the most profound explorer of bathos" were to explore his own poetry and write of it the most understanding review of the early century [*infra*].

We have said that the young Byron in attacking Scott was both impudent and silly, and we might make no more of the matter were there not something revealing in his attitude. His impudence was the impudence of pride that had been wounded; his silliness was the savage silliness of a nature exposed to pain by its own sensitiveness, and of one which being cut attempts the desperate cure of satire. We may mark these characteristics in Byron well, for they will explain much of him. There never seems to be a solid, unshifting center in the man; but there seem to be in him wild and changing energies which are released alike by pride and by pain.

Where Scott to us seems wholesome and consistent with himself, Byron seems somewhat fevered and afflicted with deep contradictions. He glories in being "a good hater;" but he struggles to dramatize his loneliness as he passes from his wife's love, from the adoration of his people, from the adulation of his race into darkness. His progress is always away from his own need. Boasting that there is that within him which would tire Torture and Time, he cries out when he is amerced. With head cocked stiff he stands staring at God, a Cain or a Satan; yet to have his Bible near him when he sleeps is a comfort to him. Because he needs the brightness and beauty of women, he touches them only to dim and to spoil them. He is an aristocrat of the aristocrats, and yet he goes up to a dirty field and gives away his breath for an uncertain republicanism. Being of a warrior race, he keeps his pistols near at hand; but he confesses ruefully that it is because he is afraid of pain. His nature is tortured by the incompleteness of its paradoxes.

Both Scott and Byron were lame before they could attempt walking. Whether the lameness led to a compensatory delight in strong action—a vicarious satisfaction—we need not decide. Still there is something almost preternaturally alive in each of them, something that thrills at a glorious deed. Each of these men could write a song which would stir like a trumpet, although the work of each might have in it little more than machine magic. At their best, in the rush and tumult of their passions, neither is a thinker. It is not the argument that makes the meter, but an over-flood of poetic passion. Consequently each gives us a pleasure which we should not analyze and cannot question. But Byron, introspective and self-occupied even to misanthropy, is greater in this than Scott the master of unconsciousness. When the balancing is finished, we must see that the one was a poet out of the necessity of his own nature, while the other could bid farewell to his harp and turn naturally to prose.

These considerations lead to two others more important; namely, that it was largely out of the torture imposed by the incomplete paradoxes in his nature and out of the sympathetic energies of his egotism that Byron wrote. Had his mind been one of perfect poise and perfect power, balanced therefore and at ease, he never would have written the thing that most distinguishes him, great satire. In Byron, as in Swift, there was a Setebosian power seeking ease in satire. It was not by chance that Byron thought it "Better to err with Pope, than shine with Pye;" it was because a pre-determining condition of nature discovered to him a satisfying similarity in Pope. Like likes like, congratulating itself by approving itself in others.

Between the satiric mood which arises out of a sense of imperfect power, and egotism which springs from a desire for complete power there is a close relationship. It is, however, with egotism that one finds a necessitous energy. And it is energy, astonishing, attractive, overmastering, which more than all else characterizes Byron's poetry. Among Romanticists he is the poet of the magnificent self.

GEORGE NOEL GORDON,

LORD BYRON

1788–1824

The birth of Lord Byron was to have taken place among his mother's relatives in Scotland and she was on her way from France when, after nearly precipitating the event at sea, he was born in a temporary London lodging, January 22, 1788. The incalculable being thus bustled into the world was descended from a race of rovers and fighters; or as he characteristically put it, "a line of cut-throat ancestors." Seven Byrons fought for King Charles at Edgehill, and the walls of Newstead Abbey, the family seat in Nottinghamshire, still show the effects of Cromwell's cannon. Admiral John Byron, grandfather of the poet, was a famous seaman and a picturesque character, known to all the navy as "Foul-weather Jack." Byron's father was a captain in the guards; a cousin of his father died of wounds received in Spain, leaving Byron, at the age of six, heir presumptive to his grand-uncle, the "wicked Lord Byron" of Newstead, renowned for acts of violence; and the cousin who succeeded Byron in the title, became an admiral in the navy. Byron's mother, Catharine Gordon, boasted descent from Scottish kings, but more immediately belonged to a branch of "the mad Gordons of Gight." She had married, three years before Byron's birth, "mad Jack Byron," a handsome, careless scamp for whom England was usually out of bounds because of his debts. He had made away with the bulk of his wife's property before the birth of their child, and died when Byron was three years old. Byron's half-sister Augusta was Jack Byron's daughter by a previous marriage with a marchioness whom he had induced to elope from her husband and had served much as he did Byron's mother.

With this background of wildness and irregularity, Byron was subjected to an impoverished and badly managed childhood. His mother, though in some ways an estimable woman, was an ill-disciplined person who early lost his respect by extravagances of temper and alternate tyranny and indulgence. When enraged she was capable of hurling objects at him, apparently with very bad aim, rolling after him in hopeless pursuit, reviling the entire Byron family in shocking language, and twitting him with his lameness—a point on which Byron was so sensitive that, after he became a person to be reckoned with, it was never noticed in his presence. Byron, for his part, retaliated with impish defiance, mocking and mimicking her absurdities of speech and gait and laughing fiendishly at her impotence. In times of peace, Mrs. Byron was foolishly indulgent and effusive and Byron as he grew up found these moods even harder to bear than the fits of violence. By the time he was fourteen he had become entirely callous to his mother's reproaches and indifferent to her commands, and saw her only

on the shortest possible visits. Doubtless Byron would have been a handful for any mother; but he was an impressionable child and a sensible woman might have molded him differently and perhaps modified his conception of the entire sex.

There was nothing in Byron's childhood, and there was little in his later surroundings to inculcate an ideal of self-control. This humble virtue was not highly regarded by his generation or by his class. The words of Byron's tutor at Cambridge which so delighted his friend Matthews, "Lord Byron, Sir, is a young gentleman of *tumultuous passions*," were very likely pronounced with an accent of awed admiration. Here was a lord that *was* a lord! And so it was with much of the wildness and irregularity of Byron's early life. From the time he inherited his title, at the age of ten, he was intensely conscious of its implications, and the freedom of behavior which he allowed himself did not exceed the license that was taken for granted and considered a sign of spirit in a young man of rank. On the other hand, he was equally responsive to the ideals of honorable, manly, and intrepid behavior which he conceived to be incumbent upon one who had been born to his station in life. Thus, at school, though he was often indolent and mischievous, he could always be successfully managed if courteously treated and appealed to on grounds of manliness and honor. Irritated by his relative poverty, he was sometimes too vigilant against affronts to his rank and personal dignity; but his fiercest resentments were reserved for the least suspicion of tyranny, whether toward himself or others. Byron's record at school, and particularly at Harrow where he spent what he called "the most romantic period" of his life—from his fourteenth to his eighteenth year—was a rather gallant one. He joined heartily in all manly sports for which he was not hopelessly incapacitated, "made" the school cricket team, was a good horseman, fond of dogs and pets, and was a crack swimmer. He was direct and open, if sometimes too defiant, toward the masters, chivalrous, if a bit lordly, toward younger boys, and had generous friendships among his equals. An indifferent scholar, he was brilliant in declamation and was picked by the masters to enter public life and make his mark as a speaker.

In 1805, Byron left Harrow—perhaps the only place he ever parted from with deep sorrow—and entered Trinity College, Cambridge. His residence at Cambridge was very irregular. He was lonely during the first year and "miserable over leaving Harrow." He was then absent for nearly a year, then present and absent by fits, finally, surprisingly enough, taking his M.A. degree, in July, 1808. During his second period of residence, he made one of a small inner circle of brilliant, gay, but—as things went then—entirely decent men, of whom Hobhouse, afterward Lord Broughton, remained through life his most confidential friend and took charge of the strange funeral when Byron's body was brought back from Greece in 1824. At Harrow Byron had begun, in a small way, the dangerous practice of borrowing money on his expectations, and though his annual allowance had been increased to five hundred pounds when he entered Trinity, he went recklessly in debt while there. Long before he finished at Cambridge he had considered leaving England as a means of escaping these embarrassments until his affairs could be set in order. Much of the melancholy and excessive irritability of his next few years was caused by the fact that, with considerable ultimate resources, he was constantly haunted by the dread of financial disaster.

Meanwhile he had made his bow as an author. During his long absence from Cambridge, while apparently knocking about England in an idle and expensive fashion, he had been straightening out old verses and writing new ones for four different arrangements of his Juvenilia that were printed between the end of 1806 and the middle of 1808, the collection best known as *Hours of Idleness* (1807). The lackadaisical attitude suggested in the title, the feebleness of some of the poems, together with the allusion to his rank and the apology, thinly veiling a claim to precocity, of Byron's preface, made the book an easy target for any reviewer who chose to be cheaply funny at the expense of an ambitious boy. The *Edinburgh Review* could not resist the opportunity to polish off a lord under the pretense of chastising a presumptuous poetaster. Byron was, as he said, "cut to atoms." But he was ready for them. Within a year he replied with *English Bards and Scotch Reviewers*. They had drawn the fire of a born fighter. He adopted the tactics recommended by his boxing master for informal occasions: "Mill away right and left; don't stop to pick out your friends." That is, he vigorously pitched into everybody, poets and critics, big and little, landing with damaging accuracy on their vulnerable spots. That Byron's first satire was an astonishing performance for a young man who had just celebrated his twenty-first birthday is evident from the fact that it at least challenges comparison with the similar works of Dryden and Pope. The dullest reviewer now apprehended that there was a new literary force to be reckoned with. Having taken his seat in the House of Lords, and attaching his name and a preface to a second edition, Byron let it be known that any who claimed the privilege of resorting to other than literary weapons would find him at their disposal on his return and departed on his travels.

Byron's tour was not the conventional round of the baths and show places of the continent. After a few weeks in Portugal and Spain, he proceeded up the Mediterranean, to Constantinople, visiting Albania, Asia Minor and the Troad, and much of Greece, and spending many months at Athens. During his travels in the interior and especially in Albania, he went among wild and lawless peoples, taking all risks with coolness, facing hardships with a composure that bordered on delight, and putting to shame the whinings of his English servants. It was always so with Byron; action and danger brought out his best qualities. After two of the most cheerful years of his life, he returned to England, thinned by a fever, but hard and handsome as a pirate of fiction, his mind freshened with a new enthusiasm for classical antiquity and stocked with exotic pictures of Eastern scenery and manners. Yet, once in England again, his deep-seated melancholy returned; the ineradicable discontent and sense of futility were always there, beneath "the light war of mocking words," ready to prompt him at any moment "to deeds eternity cannot annul."

Byron had kept a new kind of log-book of his travels, consisting of a series of sketches and reflections in Spenserian verse, suggested by the scenes through which he had passed, all strung on a slender thread of narrative and characterization, the hero a modified projection of his own submerged and darker self. He avowed that it had not been intended for publication; but friends insisted, and in the spring of 1812, almost simultaneously with his first address in the House of Lords, he published the first two cantos of *Childe Harold's Pilgrimage*. The sensation which followed was the most extraordinary in literary history, taking into account its suddenness, its intensity, and its significance. Byron's vivid words, "I awoke one morning and found myself famous," graphic as they are, express only one aspect of the matter. The effect was out of all proportion to the final literary value of this particular poem; yet the public were not wrong in feeling the authentic presence of a new man of genius. It was not a case of mere literary acclaim. It might have been a matter of small moment that Byron was admitted instantaneously to equality with the best writers of the age or that he became for a season or two the latest thrill of the fashionable fast set that immediately took him up. The important thing was that Byron became almost over night a national figure. What Lord Byron thought, what Lord Byron did and said, became matters of serious concern,—not merely to romantic ladies who found "that pale face their fate" or to social dandies who aped his picturesque negligences of costume and his distracted faraway air; they became of concern to serious or ambitious men who made it their affair to watch over the policies and morals of the nation. Men of conservative principles are quick to detect what they call "a dangerous man," an enemy of the existing order of things. Byron was such a force, or at least a portent, a social and political symbol. He was, indeed, though they knew it not, nor he, the potential author of *Don Juan* and *The Vision of Judgment*.

Byron, it must be remembered, was only twenty-four, a mere schoolboy and a provincial as to social experience, with his full share of superficial vanity mixed with more solid pride. He loved gay and beautiful women and loved the company of able and witty men, and he had been, considering his rank, in social obscuration all his life. To dine with Rogers, Campbell, and Moore, visit Leigh Hunt in prison, exchange tokens with Walter Scott, and sit over the cups till morning with the renowned, old, but still bibulous and brilliant author of *The School for Scandal* and call him "Sherry" might have gone to the head of even a prudent young man, and no one could accuse Byron of being that. For some three seasons he drifted. He was never quite content to be, but he allowed himself to be, the idol of fashionable society, "a lion" as he afterward contemptuously called himself, "a ball-room bard, a foolscap, hot-press darling." He spun his oriental experiences and observations into dark-eyed romantic tales of love and lawlessness, through which he wove the fascination of a more or less real melancholy and a mysterious reputation for wickedness. *The Giaour, The Bride of Abydos, The Corsair, Lara,* are all for the most part mere philanderings with the muse, and bear about the same relation to Byron's real poetry that the flirtations and amours with which the same period was crowded have to a real passion.

Yet through all the triumphs and indiscretions of this period, Byron seems to have scented danger from afar. He felt the hollowness of his pleasures and the insecurity of his popularity. He thought that marriage would stabilize him and chose and won Miss Millbanke, one of the most correct ladies in the kingdom, too correct for Byron, as was soon proved. There is no doubt that Byron at this stage really wished to be a regular citizen, to regulate his affairs, perpetuate his line, and be a sound British subject. It was not to be. After a year came the mysterious separation. It became known that his wife had left him and refused to return. Then the storm broke. The lurking envy, the hidden malice, and all the suspended detestation of what Byron stood for, both good and evil, were let loose upon him. From being the most flattered, he became the most execrated person alive in England. Almost he might have said, that he "awoke one morning" and found himself infamous. A little less than five years had elapsed since he returned from his first pilgrimage, when he left England again, this time never to return alive.

Byron's life was in ruins, so far as he identified his life with a career at home, the headship of a great family, and an honorable place in the continuous history of his country. It is from this point of view that the separation is the grand turning point in Byron's career, not as he supposed, or pretended, because of violence to his personal affections. The shock called out all the real lion in his nature and stirred his genius to its depths. He knew that he had sinned; but he felt that his punishment, though not more than he could bear, was more than he deserved. His society had cast him out; he knew that society, now, to the core, and he felt that he had been the victim of its seductions first of all, and then of its insincerity, its bigotry, its hypocrisy, and its injustice. He paraded himself in earnest as the devil's disciple and at the same time he put forth, with all the abandonment of a glorious despair, the incomparable energy and the cunning fascination of his genius to bring it again to his feet, only to unmask its viciousness and to "spurn it lying low." Such a purpose was not explicit in Byron's consciousness, but it gradually revealed itself in the direction that he took. And all the time, this conflict was accompanied by an ever burning warfare within his own nature which is not always distinctly legible on the surface, but which glows behind the bars of his most passionate and most mocking poetry.

It is hard to realize that when Byron left England he had but eight more years to live, and that practically all which is deeply significant in his voluminous production, was the product of those years. That he ever, at any time, abandoned himself to the complete degradation that his enemies pretended is refuted by a list of his works, with dates. He went first, by way of Belgium and the Rhine, to Switzerland. There he met Shelley, who had also been exiled by public opinion, and formed an intimacy which was continued, with interruptions, until Shelley's death only two years before his own. From Switzerland he sent back almost immediately *The Prisoner of Chillon* and toward the end of the year the third canto of *Childe Harold,* which is really a poem by itself combining impressions of Waterloo, the Rhine, and the Alps, with passionate reflections upon recent events and his own recent misfortunes. But there were too many English in Switzerland and Byron crossed over into Italy, arriving in November at Venice, where he "sought him out a home by a remoter sea" for the following three years. In 1819, he removed to Ravenna to be near the Countess Guiccioli, with whom he had formed a permanent *liaison.* At Venice, Byron had completed *Manfred,* which again reflects his impressions of the Alps, and had written the fourth canto of *Childe Harold* which records his Italian impressions, particularly of Venice and of Rome; both poems, again, are filled with echoes of his own passionate grief and defiance. More important still he had discovered his richest power in the familiar, realistic, and comic vein of *Beppo* and of *Don Juan,* of which last, two cantos had been completed by July, 1819.

At Ravenna, he wrote three more cantos of *Don Juan, The Prophecy of Dante* which he once called "the best thing he ever wrote," *The Vision of Judgment,* and half a dozen "Mysteries" and plays, of which the most notable was *Cain,* which Shelley pronounced "apocalyptic," probably because he liked the bold scepticism (then, but no longer, intensely blasphemous) of its theological speculations. In 1821, for political reasons Byron and the Guiccioli removed to Pisa, where Byron and Shelley were neighbors for nine months, continuing their intimacy until Shelley was drowned, July, 1822. Later Byron removed to Genoa, and remained there until his departure for Greece. He had laid aside *Don Juan* for nearly a year at the request of the Guiccioli but resumed it at Pisa with a promise "to be good" and his last literary energies were devoted to the closing cantos of his unfinished masterpiece. The statement of Taine that Byron was played out at the time he ceased writing and that his genius was on the decline has been often repeated. There never was a greater error. Some of Byron's most sincere, most powerful, and most engaging verse is to be found in the later cantos of *Don Juan* and some of his swiftest prose belongs to the last months of his life, busy as he was with his preparations for Greece.

On July 14, 1823, with all his available resources, some ten thousand pounds, converted into currency and packed in a trunk, Byron embarked for Greece. Byron sincerely hated oppression and he sincerely hated the established dynasties of Europe. He did not join in the rejoicing over Waterloo, but was furious at the fall of Napoleon, not only because he recognized in him a kindred spirit, notwithstanding his "hero had sunk into a king," but because he hated to see him beaten by "three stupid, legitimate old dynastic boobies of regular sovereigns." And the movement for Greek freedom enlisted his enthusiasm, not because he had great faith in the patriots, but because it was a war with tyranny and because it gave a practical outlet for his energies such as he had dreamed of but never yet found; and not less than either, because (and it is one of the charming things about Byron that has made many men love him) he never ceased to be in some measure the lively schoolboy for whom, among other things, there would always be an immortal glamour about "the glory that was Greece and the grandeur that was Rome." Yet, as his conduct proved, Byron did not go to Greece to play, nor yet, as some have thought, to die; he went expecting to work and, if possible, to fight. It was fated otherwise. Taken with fever among the malarial swamps and amid the inconceivable rains of Missolonghi, he yet stuck to his post and gave his life in the service of liberty as directly as if he had fallen in a cavalry charge.

The end came April 19, 1824. Byron had always loved a storm. As the last breath left his body the most terrific thunder-storm that had been known for years broke over the camp and wrapped its blinding curtain about the final scene. As Byron had foreseen, his "name" and also his body were barred "from out the temple where the dead are honored by the Nations." He was buried with his ancestors in a little church at Hucknall Torkard, near Newstead Abbey.

SELECTED BIBLIOGRAPHY

TEXTS

The Works of Lord Byron, 1898–1904.
 Poetry, 7 Vols., ed. by E. H. Coleridge.
 Letters and Journals, 6 Vols., ed. by R. E. Prothero.
  The standard edition, fully and ably annotated.
The Poetical Works, ed. by E. H. Coleridge, 1905.
  The best one-volume edition.
Cambridge edition, ed. by P. E. More.
  An excellent text, with noteworthy introduction.

CRITICAL WORKS

Arnold, M., "Byron," *Essays in Criticism,* Second Series, 1888.
  A brilliant appreciation.
Drinkwater, John, *The Pilgrim of Eternity,* 1925.
  Best of the recent lives of Byron.
Elton, O., *Survey of English Literature, 1780–1830,* 1912. Comprehensive and sound.
Mayne, E. C., *Byron,* 2 Vols., 1912.
  Excellent.

SONNET ON CHILLON

ETERNAL Spirit of the chainless Mind!
 Brightest in dungeons, Liberty! thou art,
 For there thy habitation is the heart—
The heart which love of thee alone can bind;
And when thy sons to fetters are consign'd—
 To fetters, and the damp vault's dayless gloom,
 Their country conquers with their martyrdom,
And Freedom's fame finds wings on every wind.
Chillon! thy prison is a holy place,
 And thy sad floor an altar—for 't was trod,
Until his very steps have left a trace   11
 Worn, as if thy cold pavement were a sod,
By Bonnivard! May none those marks efface!
 For they appeal from tyranny to God.

THE PRISONER OF CHILLON

I

My hair is grey, but not with years,
 Nor grew it white
 In a single night,
As men's have grown from sudden fears:
My limbs are bow'd, though not with toil,
 But rusted with a vile repose,
For they have been a dungeon's spoil,
 And mine has been the fate of those

To whom the goodly earth and air 9
Are bann'd, and barr'd—forbidden fare:
But this was for my father's faith
I suffer'd chains and courted death;
That father perish'd at the stake
For tenets he would not forsake;
And for the same his lineal race
In darkness found a dwelling-place;
We were seven—who now are one,
 Six in youth, and one in age,
Finish'd as they had begun,
 Proud of Persecution's rage; 20
One in fire, and two in field,
Their belief with blood have seal'd,
Dying as their father died,
For the God their foes denied;
Three were in a dungeon cast,
Of whom this wreck is left the last.

II

There are seven pillars of Gothic mould,
In Chillon's dungeons deep and old,
There are seven columns, massy and grey,
Dim with a dull imprison'd ray, 30
A sunbeam which hath lost its way,
And through the crevice and the cleft
Of the thick wall is fallen and left;
Creeping o'er the floor so damp,
Like a marsh's meteor lamp:
And in each pillar there is a ring,
 And in each ring there is a chain;
That iron is a cankering thing,
 For in these limbs its teeth remain,
With marks that will not wear away, 40
Till I have done with this new day,
Which now is painful to these eyes,
Which have not seen the sun so rise
For years—I cannot count them o'er,
I lost their song and heavy score,
When my last brother droop'd and died,
And I lay living by his side.

III

They chain'd us each to a column stone,
And we were three—yet, each alone;
We could not move a single pace, 50
We could not see each other's face,
But with that pale and livid light
That made us strangers in our sight:
And thus together—yet apart,
Fetter'd in hand, but join'd in heart,
'T was still some solace, in the dearth

Of the pure elements of earth,
To hearken to each other's speech,
And each turn comforter to each
With some new hope, or legend old, 60
Or song heroically bold;
But even these at length grew cold.
Our voices took a dreary tone,
An echo of the dungeon stone,
 A grating sound, not full and free,
 As they of yore were wont to be:
 It might be fancy, but to me
They never sounded like our own.

IV

I was the eldest of the three,
 And to uphold and cheer the rest 70
 I ought to do—and did my best—
And each did well in his degree.
 The youngest, whom my father loved,
Because our mother's brow was given
To him, with eyes as blue as heaven—
 For him my soul was sorely moved;
And truly might it be distress'd
To see such bird in such a nest;
For he was beautiful as day—
 (When day was beautiful to me 80
 As to young eagles, being free)—
 A polar day, which will not see
A sunset till its summer's gone,
 Its sleepless summer of long light,
The snow-clad offspring of the sun:
 And thus he was as pure and bright,
And in his natural spirit gay,
With tears for nought but others' ills,
And then they flow'd like mountain rills,
Unless he could assuage the woe 90
Which he abhorr'd to view below.

V

The other was as pure of mind,
But form'd to combat with his kind;
Strong in his frame, and of a mood
Which 'gainst the world in war had stood,
And perish'd in the foremost rank
 With joy:—but not in chains to pine:
His spirit wither'd with their clank,
 I saw it silently decline—
 And so perchance in sooth did mine: 100
But yet I forced it on to cheer
Those relics of a home so dear.
He was a hunter of the hills,
 Had follow'd there the deer and wolf;

To him his dungeon was a gulf,
And fetter'd feet the worst of ills.

VI

Lake Leman lies by Chillon's walls:
A thousand feet in depth below
Its massy waters meet and flow;
Thus much the fathom-line was sent   110
From Chillon's snow-white battlement,
   Which round about the wave inthrals:
A double dungeon wall and wave
Have made—and like a living grave
Below the surface of the lake
The dark vault lies wherein we lay,
We heard it ripple night and day;
   Sounding o'er our heads it knock'd;
And I have felt the winter's spray
Wash through the bars when winds were
      high   120
And wanton in the happy sky;
   And then the very rock hath rock'd,
   And I have felt it shake, unshock'd,
Because I could have smiled to see
The death that would have set me free.

VII

I said my nearer brother pined,
I said his mighty heart declined,
He loathed and put away his food;
It was not that 't was coarse and rude,
For we were used to hunter's fare,   130
And for the like had little care:
The milk drawn from the mountain goat
Was changed for water from the moat,
Our bread was such as captives' tears
Have moisten'd many a thousand years,
Since man first pent his fellow men
Like brutes within an iron den;
But what were these to us or him?
These wasted not his heart or limb;
My brother's soul was of that mould   140
Which in a palace had grown cold,
Had his free breathing been denied
The range of the steep mountain's side;
But why delay the truth?—he died.
I saw, and could not hold his head,
Nor reach his dying hand—nor dead,—
Though hard I strove, but strove in vain,
To rend and gnash my bonds in twain.
He died, and they unlock'd his chain,
And scoop'd for him a shallow grave   150
Even from the cold earth of our cave,

I begg'd them as a boon to lay
His corse in dust whereon the day
Might shine—it was a foolish thought,
But then within my brain it wrought,
That even in death his freeborn breast
In such a dungeon could not rest.
I might have spared my idle prayer—
They coldly laugh'd, and laid him there:
The flat and turfless earth above   160
The being we so much did love;
His empty chain above it leant,
Such murder's fitting monument!

VIII

But he, the favourite and the flower,
Most cherish'd since his natal hour,
His mother's image in fair face,
The infant love of all his race,
His martyr'd father's dearest thought,
My latest care, for whom I sought
To hoard my life, that his might be   170
Less wretched now, and one day free;
He, too, who yet had held untired
A spirit natural or inspired—
He, too, was struck, and day by day
Was wither'd on the stalk away.
Oh, God! it is a fearful thing
To see the human soul take wing
In any shape, in any mood:
I've seen it rushing forth in blood,
I've seen it in the breaking ocean   180
Strive with a swoln convulsive motion,
I've seen the sick and ghastly bed
Of Sin delirious with its dread;
But these were horrors—this was woe
Unmix'd with such—but sure and slow:
He faded, and so calm and meek,
So softly worn, so sweetly weak,
So tearless, yet so tender, kind,
And grieved for those he left behind;
With all the while a cheek whose bloom   190
Was as a mockery of the tomb,
Whose tints as gently sunk away
As a departing rainbow's ray;
An eye of most transparent light,
That almost made the dungeon bright,
And not a word of murmur, not
A groan o'er his untimely lot,—
A little talk of better days,
A little hope my own to raise,
For I was sunk in silence—lost   200
In this last loss, of all the most;
And then the sighs he would suppress

Of fainting nature's feebleness,
More slowly drawn, grew less and less:
I listen'd, but I could not hear;
I call'd, for I was wild with fear;
I knew 't was hopeless, but my dread
Would not be thus admonished;
I call'd, and thought I heard a sound—
I burst my chain with one strong bound,   210
And rush'd to him:—I found him not,
I only stirr'd in this black spot,
I only lived, *I* only drew
The accursed breath of dungeon-dew;
The last, the sole, the dearest link
Between me and the eternal brink,
Which bound me to my failing race,
Was broken in this fatal place.
One on the earth, and one beneath—
My brothers—both had ceased to breathe: 220
I took that hand which lay so still,
Alas! my own was full as chill;
I had not strength to stir, or strive,
But felt that I was still alive—
A frantic feeling, when we know
That what we love shall ne'er be so.
     I know not why
     I could not die,
I had no earthly hope but faith,
And that forbade a selfish death.   230

IX

What next befell me then and there
   I know not well—I never knew—
First came the loss of light, and air,
   And then of darkness too:
I had no thought, no feeling—none—
Among the stones I stood a stone,
And was, scarce conscious what I wist,
As shrubless crags within the mist;
For all was blank, and bleak, and grey;
It was not night, it was not day;   240
It was not even the dungeon-light,
So hateful to my heavy sight,
But vacancy absorbing space,
And fixedness without a place;
There were no stars, no earth, no time,
No check, no change, no good, no crime,
But silence, and a stirless breath
Which neither was of life nor death;
A sea of stagnant idleness,
Blind, boundless, mute, and motionless!   250

X

A light broke in upon my brain,—
   It was the carol of a bird;
It ceased, and then it came again,
   The sweetest song ear ever heard,
And mine was thankful till my eyes
Ran over with the glad surprise,
And they that moment could not see
I was the mate of misery;
But then by dull degrees came back
My senses to their wonted track;   260
I saw the dungeon walls and floor
Close slowly round me as before,
I saw the glimmer of the sun
Creeping as it before had done,
But through the crevice where it came
That bird was perch'd, as fond and tame,
   And tamer than upon the tree;
A lovely bird, with azure wings,
And song that said a thousand things,
   And seem'd to say them all for me!   270
I never saw its like before,
I ne'er shall see its likeness more:
It seem'd like me to want a mate,
But was not half so desolate,
And it was come to love me when
None lived to love me so again,
And cheering from my dungeon's brink,
Had brought me back to feel and think.
I know not if it late were free,
   Or broke its cage to perch on mine,   280
But knowing well captivity,
   Sweet bird! I could not wish for thine!
Or if it were, in winged guise,
   A visitant from Paradise;
For—Heaven forgive that thought! the while
Which made me both to weep and smile—
I sometimes deem'd that it might be
My brother's soul come down to me;
But then at last away it flew,
And then 't was mortal well I knew,   290
For he would never thus have flown,
And left me twice so doubly lone,
Lone as the corse within its shroud,
Lone as a solitary cloud,—
   A single cloud on a sunny day,
While all the rest of heaven is clear,
A frown upon the atmosphere,
That hath no business to appear
   When skies are blue, and earth is gay.

XI

A kind of change came in my fate,   300

My keepers grew compassionate;
I know not what had made them so,
They were inured to sights of woe,
But so it was:—my broken chain
With links unfasten'd did remain,
And it was liberty to stride
Along my cell from side to side,
And up and down, and then athwart,
And tread it over every part;
And round the pillars one by one,   310
Returning where my walk begun,
Avoiding only, as I trod,
My brothers' graves without a sod;
For if I thought with heedless tread
My step profaned their lowly bed,
My breath came gaspingly and thick,
And my crush'd heart fell blind and sick.

XII

I made a footing in the wall,
  It was not therefrom to escape,
For I had buried one and all   320
  Who loved me in a human shape;
And the whole earth would henceforth be
A wider prison unto me:
No child, no sire, no kin had I,
No partner in my misery;
I thought of this, and I was glad,
For thought of them had made me mad;
But I was curious to ascend
To my barr'd windows, and to bend
Once more, upon the mountains high,   330
The quiet of a loving eye.

XIII

I saw them, and they were the same,
They were not changed like me in frame;
I saw their thousand years of snow
On high—their wide long lake below,
And the blue Rhone in fullest flow;
I heard the torrents leap and gush
O'er channell'd rock and broken bush;
I saw the white-wall'd distant town,
And whiter sails go skimming down;   340
And then there was a little isle,
Which in my very face did smile,
  The only one in view;
A small green isle, it seem'd no more,
Scarce broader than my dungeon floor,
But in it there were three tall trees,
And o'er it blew the mountain breeze,
And by it there were waters flowing,

And on it there were young flowers growing,
  Of gentle breath and hue.   350
The fish swam by the castle wall,
And they seem'd joyous each and all;
The eagle rode the rising blast,
Methought he never flew so fast
As then to me he seem'd to fly;
And then new tears came in my eye,
And I felt troubled—and would fain
I had not left my recent chain;
And when I did descend again,
The darkness of my dim abode   360
Fell on me as a heavy load;
It was as is a new-dug grave,
Closing o'er one we sought to save,—
And yet my glance, too much opprest,
Had almost need of such a rest.

XIV

It might be months, or years, or days,
  I kept no count, I took no note,
I had no hope my eyes to raise,
  And clear them of their dreary mote;
At last men came to set me free;   370
  I ask'd not why, and reck'd not where;
It was at length the same to me,
Fetter'd or fetterless to be,
  I learn'd to love despair.
And thus when they appear'd at last,
And all my bonds aside were cast,
These heavy walls to me had grown
A hermitage—and all my own!
And half I felt as they were come
To tear me from a second home: 380
With spiders I had friendship made,
And watch'd them in their sullen trade,
Had seen the mice by moonlight play,
And why should I feel less than they?
We were all inmates of one place,
And I, the monarch of each race,
Had power to kill—yet, strange to tell!
In quiet we had learn'd to dwell;
My very chains and I grew friends.
So much a long communion tends   390
To make us what we are:—even I
Regain'd my freedom with a sigh.

EPISTLE TO AUGUSTA

I

My sister! my sweet sister! if a name
Dearer and purer were, it should be thine;

Mountains and seas divide us, but I claim
No tears, but tenderness to answer mine:
Go where I will, to me thou art the same—
A loved regret which I would not resign.
There yet are two things in my destiny,—
A world to roam through, and a home with
thee.

II

The first were nothing—had I still the last,
It were the haven of my happiness;   10
But other claims and other ties thou hast,
And mine is not the wish to make them
less.
A strange doom is thy father's son's, and
past
Recalling, as it lies beyond redress;
Reversed for him our grandsire's fate of
yore,—
He had no rest at sea, nor I on shore.

III

If my inheritance of storms hath been
In other elements, and on the rocks
Of perils, overlook'd or unforeseen,   19
I have sustain'd my share of worldly shocks,
The fault was mine; nor do I seek to
screen
My errors with defensive paradox;
I have been cunning in mine overthrow,
The careful pilot of my proper woe.

IV

Mine were my faults, and mine be their
reward.
My whole life was a contest, since the day
That gave me being, gave me that which
marr'd
The gift,—a fate, or will, that walk'd
astray;
And I at times have found the struggle
hard,
And thought of shaking off my bonds of
clay: 30
But now I fain would for a time survive,
If but to see what next can well arrive.

V

Kingdoms and empires in my little day
I have outlived, and yet I am not old;

And when I look on this, the petty spray
Of my own years of trouble, which have
roll'd
Like a wild bay of breakers, melts away:
Something—I know not what—does still
uphold
A spirit of slight patience;—not in vain,
Even for its own sake, do we purchase pain. 40

VI

Perhaps the workings of defiance stir
Within me—or perhaps a cold despair,
Brought on when ills habitually recur,—
Perhaps a kinder clime, or purer air,
(For even to this may change of soul refer,
And with light armour we may learn to
bear,)
Have taught me a strange quiet, which was
not
The chief companion of a calmer lot.

VII

I feel almost at times as I have felt
In happy childhood; trees, and flowers, and
brooks,   50
Which do remember me of where I dwelt
Ere my young mind was sacrificed to books,
Come as of yore upon me, and can melt
My heart with recognition of their looks;
And even at moments I could think I see
Some living thing to love—but none like thee.

VIII

Here are the Alpine landscapes which create
A fund for contemplation;—to admire
Is a brief feeling of a trivial date;
But something worthier do such scenes in-
spire: 60
Here to be lonely is not desolate,
For much I view which I could most desire,
And, above all, a lake I can behold
Lovelier, not dearer, than our own of old.

IX

Oh that thou wert but with me!—but I
grow
The fool of my own wishes, and forget
The solitude which I have vaunted so
Has lost its praise in this but one regret;
There may be others which I less may
show;—

I am not of the plaintive mood, and yet 70
I feel an ebb in my philosophy,
And the tide rising in my alter'd eye.

X

I did remind thee of our own dear Lake,
By the old Hall which may be mine no
    more.
Leman's is fair; but think not I forsake
The sweet remembrance of a dearer shore:
Sad havoc Time must with my memory
    make,
Ere *that* or *thou* can fade these eyes before;
Though, like all things which I have loved,
    they are
Resign'd for ever, or divided far.   80

XI

The world is all before me; I but ask
Of Nature that with which she will com-
    ply—
It is but in her summer's sun to bask,
To mingle with the quiet of her sky,
To see her gentle face without a mask,
And never gaze on it with apathy.
She was my early friend, and now shall be
My sister—till I look again on thee.

XII

I can reduce all feelings but this one;
And that I would not;—for at length I
    see   90
Such scenes as those wherein my life be-
    gun.
The earliest—even the only paths for me—
Had I but sooner learnt the crowd to shun,
I had been better than I now can be;
The passions which have torn me would
    have slept;
I had not suffer'd, and *thou* hadst not wept.

XIII

With false Ambition what had I to do?
Little with Love, and least of all with Fame;
And yet they came unsought, and with me
    grew,
And made me all which they can make—a
    name.   100
Yet this was not the end I did pursue;
Surely I once beheld a nobler aim.

But all is over—I am one the more
To baffled millions which have gone before.

XIV

And for the future, this world's future may
From me demand but little of my care;
I have outlived myself by many a day;
Having survived so many things that were;
My years have been no slumber, but the
    prey
Of ceaseless vigils; for I had the share   110
Of life which might have fill'd a century,
Before its fourth in time had pass'd me by.

XV

And for the remnant which may be to come
I am content; and for the past I feel
Not thankless,—for within the crowded sum
Of struggles, happiness at times would
    steal,
And for the present, I would not benumb
My feelings further.—Nor shall I conceal
That with all this I still can look around,
And worship Nature with a thought pro-
    found.   '   120

XVI

For thee, my own sweet sister, in thy heart
I know myself secure, as thou in mine;
We were and are—I am, even as thou art—
Beings who ne'er each other can resign;
It is the same, together or apart,
From life's commencement to its slow de-
    cline
We are entwined—let death come slow or
    fast,
The tie which bound the first endures the last!

THE DREAM

I

Our life is two-fold: Sleep hath its own
    world,
A boundary between the things misnamed
Death and existence: Sleep hath its own
    world,
And a wide realm of wild reality.
And dreams in their developments have
    breath,

And tears, and tortures, and the touch of joy;
They leave a weight upon our waking
    thoughts,
They take a weight from off our waking toils,
They do divide our being; they become
A portion of ourselves as of our time,   10
And look like heralds of eternity;
They pass like spirits of the past,—they
    speak
Like Sibyls of the future: they have power—
The tyranny of pleasure and of pain;
They make us what we were not—what they
    will,
And shake us with the vision that's gone by,
The dread of vanish'd shadows— Are they so?
Is not the past all shadow?—What are they?
Creations of the mind?—The mind can make
Substance, and people planets of its own   20
With beings brighter than have been, and give
A breath to forms which can outlive all flesh.
I would recall a vision which I dream'd
Perchance in sleep—for in itself a thought,
A slumbering thought, is capable of years,
And curdles a long life into one hour.

II

I saw two beings in the hues of youth
Standing upon a hill, a gentle hill,
Green and of mild declivity, the last
As 't were the cape of a long ridge of such, 30
Save that there was no sea to lave its base,
But a most living landscape, and the wave
Of woods and corn-fields, and the abodes of
    men
Scatter'd at intervals, and wreathing smoke
Arising from such rustic roofs;—the hill
Was crown'd with a peculiar diadem
Of trees, in circular array, so fix'd,
Not by the sport of nature, but of man:
These two, a maiden and a youth, were there
Gazing—the one on all that was beneath   40
Fair as herself—but the boy gazed on her;
And both were young, and one was beautiful:
And both were young—yet not alike in youth.
As the sweet moon on the horizon's verge,
The maid was on the eve of womanhood;
The boy had fewer summers, but his heart
Had far outgrown his years, and to his eye
There was but one beloved face on earth,
And that was shining on him: he had look'd
Upon it till it could not pass away;   50
He had no breath, no being, but in hers;
She was his voice; he did not speak to her,
But trembled on her words; she was his sight,
For his eye follow'd hers, and saw with hers,
Which colour'd all his objects:—he had
    ceased
To live within himself; she was his life,
The ocean to the river of his thoughts,
Which terminated all: upon a tone,
A touch of hers, his blood would ebb and flow,
And his cheek change tempestuously—his
    heart   60
Unknowing of its cause of agony.
But she in these fond feelings had no share:
Her sighs were not for him; to her he was
Even as a brother—but no more; 't was much,
For brotherless she was, save in the name
Her infant friendship had bestow'd on him;
Herself the solitary scion left
Of a time-honour'd race.—It was a name
Which pleased him, and yet pleased him not
    —and why?
Time taught him a deep answer—when she
    loved   70
Another; even *now* she loved another,
And on the summit of that hill she stood
Looking afar if yet her lover's steed
Kept pace with her expectancy, and flew.

III

A change came o'er the spirit of my dream.
There was an ancient mansion, and before
Its walls there was a steed caparison'd:
Within an antique Oratory stood
The Boy of whom I spake;—he was alone,
And pale, and pacing to and fro: anon   80
He sate him down, and seized a pen, and
    traced
Words which I could not guess of; then he
    lean'd
His bow'd head on his hands, and shook as
    't were
With a convulsion—then arose again,
And with his teeth and quivering hands did
    tear
What he had written, but he shed no tears,
And he did calm himself, and fix his brow
Into a kind of quiet: as he paused,
The Lady of his love re-entered there;
She was serene and smiling then, and yet   90
She knew she was by him beloved,—she knew,
For quickly comes such knowledge, that his
    heart
Was darken'd with her shadow, and she saw
That he was wretched, but she saw not all.

He rose, and with a cold and gentle grasp
He took her hand; a moment o'er his face
A tablet of unutterable thoughts
Was traced, and then it faded, as it came;
He dropp'd the hand he held, and with slow
    steps
Retired, but not as bidding her adieu,   100
For they did part with mutual smiles; he
    pass'd
From out the massy gate of that old Hall,
And mounting on his steed he went his way;
And ne'er repass'd that hoary threshold more.

IV

A change came o'er the spirit of my dream.
The Boy was sprung to manhood: in the
    wilds
Of fiery climes he made himself a home,
And his soul drank their sunbeams: he was
    girt
With strange and dusky aspects; he was not
Himself like what he had been; on the sea 110
And on the shore he was a wanderer:
There was a mass of many images
Crowded like waves upon me, but he was
A part of all; and in the last he lay
Reposing from the noontide sultriness,
Couch'd among fallen columns, in the shade
Of ruin'd walls that had survived the names
Of those who rear'd them; by his sleeping side
Stood camels grazing, and some goodly steeds
Were fasten'd near a fountain; and a man 120
Clad in a flowing garb did watch the while,
While many of his tribe slumber'd around:
And they were canopied by the blue sky,
So cloudless, clear, and purely beautiful,
That God alone was to be seen in heaven.

V

A change came o'er the spirit of my dream.
The Lady of his love was wed with One
Who did not love her better:—in her home,
A thousand leagues from his,—her native
    home,
She dwelt, begirt with growing Infancy,   130
Daughters and sons of Beauty,—but behold!
Upon her face there was the tint of grief,
The settled shadow of an inward strife,
And an unquiet* drooping of the eye,
As if its lid were charged with unshed tears.
What could her grief be?—she had all she
    loved,
And he who had so loved her was not there
To trouble with bad hopes, or evil wish,

Or ill-repress'd affliction, her pure thoughts.
What could her grief be?—she had loved
    him not,   140
Nor given him cause to deem himself be-
    loved,
Nor could he be a part of that which prey'd
Upon her mind—a spectre of the past.

VI

A change came o'er the spirit of my dream.
The Wanderer was return'd.—I saw him
    stand
Before an Altar—with a gentle bride;
Her face was fair, but was not that which
    made
The Starlight of his Boyhood;—as he stood
Even at the altar, o'er his brow there came
The self-same aspect, and the quivering
    shock   150
That in the antique Oratory shook
His bosom in its solitude; and then—
As in that hour—a moment o'er his face
The tablet of unutterable thoughts
Was traced,—and then it faded as it came,
And he stood calm and quiet, and he spoke
The fitting vows, but heard not his own
    words,
And all things reel'd around him; he could see
Not that which was, nor that which should
    have been—   159
But the old mansion, and the accustom'd hall,
And the remember'd chambers, and the place,
The day, the hour, the sunshine, and the
    shade,
All things pertaining to that place and hour,
And her who was his destiny,—came back
And thrust themselves between him and the
    light:
What business had they there at such a time?

VII

A change came o'er the spirit of my dream.
The Lady of his love:—Oh! she was changed
As by the sickness of the soul; her mind 169
Had wander'd from its dwelling, and her eyes
They had not their own lustre, but the look
Which is not of the earth; she was become
The queen of a fantastic realm; her thoughts
Were combinations of disjointed things;
And forms impalpable and unperceived
Of others' sight familiar were to hers.
And this the world calls frenzy; but the wise

Have a far deeper madness, and the glance
Of melancholy is a fearful gift;
What is it but the telescope of truth?   180
Which strips the distance of its fantasies,
And brings life near in utter nakedness,
Making the cold reality too real!

VIII

A change came o'er the spirit of my dream.
The Wanderer was alone as heretofore,
The beings which surrounded him were gone,
Or were at war with him; he was a mark
For blight and desolation, compass'd round
With Hatred and Contention; Pain was mix'd
In all which was served up to him, until,   190
Like to the Pontic monarch of old days,
He fed on poisons, and they had no power,
But were a kind of nutriment; he lived
Through that which had been death to many
    men,
And made him friends of mountains: with
    the stars
And the quick Spirit of the Universe
He held his dialogues; and they did teach
To him the magic of their mysteries;
To him the book of Night was open'd wide,
And voices from the deep abyss reveal'd   200
A marvel and a secret— Be it so.

IX

My dream was past; it had no further change.
It was of a strange order, that the doom
Of these two creatures should be thus traced
    out
Almost like a reality—the one
To end in madness—both in misery.

CHILDE HAROLD'S PILGRIMAGE

CANTO THE THIRD

"Afin que cette application vous forçât de penser
à autre chose; il n'y a en vérité de remède que
celui-là et le temps."
Lettre du Roi de Prusse à D'Alembert, Sept. 7, 1776.

I

Is thy face like thy mother's, my fair
    child!
ADA! sole daughter of my house and heart?

When last I saw thy young blue eyes they
    smiled,
And then we parted,—not as now we part
But with a hope.—
            Awaking with a start,
The waters heave around me; and on
    high
The winds lift up their voices: I depart,
Whither I know not; but the hour's gone
    by,
When Albion's lessening shores could grieve
    or glad mine eye.

II

Once more upon the waters! yet once
    more!   10
And the waves bound beneath me as a
    steed
That knows his rider. Welcome to their
    roar!
Swift be their guidance, wheresoe'er it
    lead!
Though the strain'd mast should quiver as
    a reed,
And the rent canvas fluttering strew the
    gale,
Still must I on; for I am as a weed,
Flung from the rock, on Ocean's foam to
    sail
Where'er the surge may sweep, the tempest's
    breath prevail.

III

In my youth's summer I did sing of One,
The wandering outlaw of his own dark
    mind;   20
Again I seize the theme, then but begun,
And bear it with me, as the rushing wind
Bears the cloud onwards: in that Tale I
    find
The furrows of long thought, and dried-up
    tears,
Which, ebbing, leave a sterile track behind,
O'er which all heavily the journeying years
Plod the last sands of life,—where not a
    flower appears.

IV

Since my young days of passion—joy, or
    pain,

Perchance my heart and harp have lost a
    string,
And both may jar: it may be, that in vain
I would essay as I have sung to sing.   31
Yet, though a dreary strain, to this I
    cling;
So that it wean me from the weary dream
Of selfish grief or gladness—so it fling
Forgetfulness around me—it shall seem
To me, though to none else, a not ungrateful
    theme.

V

He, who grown aged in this world of woe,
In deeds, not years, piercing the depths
    of life,
So that no wonder waits him; nor below 39
Can love or sorrow, fame, ambition, strife,
Cut to his heart again with the keen knife
Of silent, sharp endurance: he can tell
Why thought seeks refuge in lone caves,
    yet rife
With airy images, and shapes which dwell
Still unimpair'd, though old, in the soul's
    haunted cell.

VI

'T is to create, and in creating live
A being more intense that we endow
With form our fancy, gaining as we give
The life we image, even as I do now.
What am I? Nothing: but not so art thou, 50
Soul of my thought! with whom I traverse
    earth,
Invisible but gazing, as I glow
Mix'd with thy spirit, blended with thy
    birth,
And feeling still with thee in my crush'd
    feelings' dearth.

VII

Yet must I think less wildly:—I *have*
    thought
Too long and darkly, till my brain became,
In its own eddy boiling and o'erwrought,
A whirling gulf of phantasy and flame:
And thus, untaught in youth my heart to
    tame,
My springs of life were poison'd. 'T is
    too late!   60

Yet am I changed; though still enough
    the same
In strength to bear what time cannot
    abate,
And feed on bitter fruits without accusing
    Fate.

VIII

Something too much of this:—but now
    't is past,
And the spell closes with its silent seal.
Long absent HAROLD re-appears at last;
He of the breast which fain no more would
    feel,
Wrung with the wounds which kill not,
    but ne'er heal;
Yet Time, who changes all, had alter'd
    him
In soul and aspect as in age: years steal 70
Fire from the mind as vigour from the
    limb;
And life's enchanted cup but sparkles near
    the brim.

IX

His had been quaff'd too quickly, and he
    found
The dregs were wormwood; but he fill'd
    again,
And from a purer fount, on holier ground,
And deem'd its spring perpetual; but in
    vain!
Still round him clung invisibly a chain
Which gall'd for ever, fettering though un-
    seen,
And heavy though it clank'd not; worn
    with pain,
Which pined although it spoke not, and
    grew keen,   80
Entering with every step he took through
    many a scene.

X

Secure in guarded coldness, he had mix'd
Again in fancied safety with his kind,
And deem'd his spirit now so firmly fix'd
And sheath'd with an invulnerable mind,
That, if no joy, no sorrow lurk'd behind;
And he, as one, might 'midst the many
    stand

Unheeded, searching through the crowd to
    find
Fit speculation; such as in strange land
He found in wonder-works of God and Na-
    ture's hand.   90

XI

But who can view the ripen'd rose, nor
    seek
To wear it? who can curiously behold
The smoothness and the sheen of beauty's
    cheek,
Nor feel the heart can never all grow old?
Who can contemplate Fame through clouds
    unfold
The star which rises o'er her steep, nor
    climb?
Harold, once more within the vortex, roll'd
On with the giddy circle, chasing Time,
Yet with a nobler aim than in his youth's
    fond prime.

XII

But soon he knew himself the most unfit 100
Of men to herd with Man; with whom he
    held
Little in common; untaught to submit
His thoughts to others, though his soul
    was quell'd
In youth by his own thoughts; still un-
    compell'd,
He would not yield dominion of his mind
To spirits against whom his own rebell'd;
Proud though in desolation; which could
    find
A life within itself, to breathe without man-
    kind.

XIII

Where rose the mountains, there to him
    were friends;
Where roll'd the ocean, thereon was his
    home;   110
Where a blue sky, and glowing clime, ex-
    tends,
He had the passion and the power to
    roam;
The desert, forest, cavern, breaker's foam,
Were unto him companionship; they spake
A mutual language, clearer than the tome

Of his land's tongue, which he would oft
    forsake
For Nature's pages glass'd by sunbeams on
    the lake.

XIV

Like the Chaldean, he could watch the
    stars,
Till he had peopled them with beings
    bright
As their own beams; and earth, and earth-
    born jars,   120
And human frailties, were forgotten quite:
Could he have kept his spirit to that flight
He had been happy; but this clay will
    sink
Its spark immortal, envying it the light
To which it mounts, as if to break the
    link
That keeps us from yon heaven which woos
    us to its brink.

XV

But in Man's dwellings he became a thing
Restless and worn, and stern and weari-
    some,
Droop'd as a wild-born falcon with clipt
    wing,
To whom the boundless air alone were
    home: 130
Then came his fit again, which to o'er-
    come,
As eagerly the barr'd-up bird will beat
His breast and beak against his wiry dome
Till the blood tinge his plumage, so the
    heat
Of his impeded soul would through his bosom
    eat.

XVI

Self-exiled Harold wanders forth again,
With nought of hope left, but with less
    of gloom;
The very knowledge that he lived in vain,
That all was over on this side the tomb,
Had made Despair a smilingness assume,
Which, though 't were wild,—as on the
    plunder'd wreck   141
When mariners would madly meet their
    doom

With draughts intemperate on the sinking
    deck,—
Did yet inspire a cheer, which he forbore to
    check.

XVII

Stop!—for thy tread is on an Empire's
    dust!
An Earthquake's spoil is sepulchred below!
Is the spot mark'd with no colossal bust?
Nor column trophied for triumphal show?
None; but the moral's truth tells simpler
    so,
As the ground was before, thus let it be;—
How that red rain hath made the harvest
    grow!   151
And is this all the world has gain'd by thee,
Thou first and last of fields! king-making
    Victory?

XVIII

And Harold stands upon this place of skulls,
The grave of France, the deadly Waterloo!
How in an hour the power which gave
    annuls
Its gifts, transferring fame as fleeting too!
In "pride of place" here last the eagle
    flew,
Then tore with bloody talon the rent plain,
Pierced by the shaft of banded nations
    through;   160
Ambition's life and labours all were vain;
He wears the shatter'd links of the world's
    broken chain.

XIX

Fit retribution! Gaul may champ the bit
And foam in fetters;—but is Earth more
    free?
Did nations combat to make *One* submit;
Or league to teach all kings true sover-
    eignty?
What! shall reviving Thraldom again be
The patch'd-up idol of enlighten'd days?
Shall we, who struck the Lion down, shall
    we
Pay the Wolf homage? proffering lowly
    gaze   170
And servile knees to thrones? No; *prove*
    before ye praise!

XX

If not, o'er one fallen despot boast no
    more!
In vain fair cheeks were furrow'd with hot
    tears
For Europe's flowers long rooted up before
The trampler of her vineyards; in vain
    years
Of death, depopulation, bondage, fears,
Have all been borne, and broken by the
    accord
Of roused-up millions; all that most en-
    dears
Glory, is when the myrtle wreathes a sword
Such as Harmodius drew on Athens' tyrant
    lord.   180

XXI

There was a sound of revelry by night,
And Belgium's capital had gather'd then
Her Beauty and her Chivalry, and bright
The lamps shone o'er fair women and
    brave men;
A thousand hearts beat happily; and when
Music arose with its voluptuous swell,
Soft eyes look'd love to eyes which spake
    again,
And all went merry as a marriage bell;
But hush! hark! a deep sound strikes like
    a rising knell!

XXII

Did ye not hear it?—No; 't was but the
    wind,   190
Or the car rattling o'er the stony street;
On with the dance! let joy be unconfined;
No sleep till morn, when Youth and Pleas-
    ure meet
To chase the glowing Hours with flying
    feet—
But hark!—that heavy sound breaks in
    once more,
As if the clouds its echo would repeat;
And nearer, clearer, deadlier than before!
Arm! Arm! it is—it is—the cannon's open-
    ing roar!

XXIII

Within a window'd niche of that high hall
Sate Brunswick's fated chieftain; he did
    hear   200

That sound the first amidst the festival,
And caught its tone with Death's prophetic
ear;
And when they smiled because he deem'd
it near,
His heart more truly knew that peal too
well
Which stretch'd his father on a bloody
bier,
And roused the vengeance blood alone could
quell;
He rush'd into the field, and, foremost fighting, fell.

XXIV

Ah! then and there was hurrying to and
fro,
And gathering tears, and tremblings of distress,
And cheeks all pale, which but an hour
ago   210
Blush'd at the praise of their own loveliness;
And there were sudden partings, such as
press
The life from out young hearts, and choking sighs
Which ne'er might be repeated; who could
guess
If ever more should meet those mutual
eyes,
Since upon night so sweet such awful morn
could rise!

XXV

And there was mounting in hot haste: the
steed,
The mustering squadron, and the clattering
car,
Went pouring forward with impetuous
speed,
And swiftly forming in the ranks of
war;   220
And the deep thunder peal on peal afar;
And near, the beat of the alarming drum
Roused up the soldier ere the morning
star;
While throng'd the citizens with terror
dumb,
Or whispering, with white lips—"The foe!
they come! they come!"

XXVI

And wild and high the "Cameron's gather-
ing" rose!
The war-note of Lochiel, which Albyn's
hills
Have heard, and heard, too, have her Saxon
foes:—
How in the noon of night that pibroch
thrills,
Savage and shrill! But with the breath
which fills   230
Their mountain-pipe, so fill the moun-
taineers
With the fierce native daring which instils
The stirring memory of a thousand years,
And Evan's, Donald's fame rings in each
clansman's ears!

XXVII

And Ardennes waves above them her green
leaves,
Dewy with nature's tear-drops as they
pass,
Grieving, if aught inanimate e'er grieves,
Over the unreturning brave,—alas!
Ere evening to be trodden like the grass
Which now beneath them, but above shall
grow   240
In its next verdure, when this fiery mass
Of living valour, rolling on the foe
And burning with high hope shall moulder
cold and low.

XXVIII

Last noon beheld them full of lusty life,
Last eve in Beauty's circle proudly gay,
The midnight brought the signal-sound of
strife,
The morn the marshalling in arms,—the
day
Battle's magnificently stern array!
The thunder-clouds close o'er it, which
when rent
The earth is cover'd thick with other
clay,   250
Which her own clay shall cover, heap'd
and pent,
Rider and horse,—friend, foe,—in one red
burial blent!

XXIX

Their praise is hymn'd by loftier harps
    than mine:
Yet one I would select from that proud
    throng,
Partly because they blend me with his line,
And partly that I did his sire some wrong,
And partly that bright names will hallow
    song;
And his was of the bravest, and when
    shower'd
The death-bolts deadliest the thinn'd files
    along,
Even where the thickest of war's tempest
    lower'd,   260
They reach'd no nobler breast than thine,
    young gallant Howard!

XXX

There have been tears and breaking hearts
    for thee,
And mine were nothing had I such to give;
But when I stood beneath the fresh green
    tree,
Which living waves where thou didst cease
    to live,
And saw around me the wide field revive
With fruits and fertile promise, and the
    Spring
Came forth her work of gladness to con-
    trive,
With all her reckless birds upon the wing,
I turn'd from all she brought to those she
    could not bring.   270

XXXI

I turn'd to thee, to thousands, of whom
    each
And one as all a ghastly gap did make
In his own kind and kindred, whom to
    teach
Forgetfulness were mercy for their sake;
The Archangel's trump, not Glory's, must
    awake
Those whom they thirst for; though the
    sound of Fame
May for a moment soothe, it cannot slake
The fever of vain longing, and the name
So honour'd but assumes a stronger, bitterer
    claim.

XXXII

They mourn, but smile at length; and,
    smiling, mourn,   280
The tree will wither long before it fall;
The hull drives on, though mast and sail
    be torn;
The roof-tree sinks, but moulders on the
    hall
In massy hoariness; the ruin'd wall
Stands when its wind-worn battlements are
    gone;
The bars survive the captive they enthral;
The day drags through, though storms
    keep out the sun;
And thus the heart will break, yet brokenly
    live on:

XXXIII

Even as a broken mirror, which the glass
In every fragment multiplies; and makes 290
A thousand images of one that was,
The same, and still the more, the more it
    breaks;
And thus the heart will do which not for-
    sakes,
Living in shatter'd guise; and still, and cold,
And bloodless, with its sleepless sorrow
    aches,
Yet withers on till all without is old,
Showing no visible sign, for such things are
    untold.

XXXIV

There is a very life in our despair,
Vitality of poison,—a quick root
Which feeds these deadly branches; for it
    were   300
As nothing did we die; but Life will suit
Itself to Sorrow's most detested fruit,
Like to the apples on the Dead Sea's shore,
All ashes to the taste: Did man compute
Existence by enjoyment, and count o'er
Such hours 'gainst years of life,—say, would
    he name threescore?

XXXV

The Psalmist number'd out the years of
    man:
They are enough; and if thy tale be *true*,
Thou, who didst grudge him even that
    fleeting span,

More than enough, thou fatal Waterloo! 310
Millions of tongues record thee, and anew
Their children's lips shall echo them, and
    say—
"Here, where the sword united nations
    drew,
Our countrymen were warring on that
    day!"
And this is much, and all which will not
    pass away.

XXXVI

There sunk the greatest, nor the worst of
    men,
Whose spirit, antithetically mixt,
One moment of the mightiest, and again
On little objects with like firmness fixt;
Extreme in all things! hadst thou been
    betwixt,   320
Thy throne had still been thine, or never
    been;
For daring made thy rise as fall: thou
    seek'st
Even now to re-assume the imperial mien,
And shake again the world, the Thunderer
    of the scene!

XXXVII

Conqueror and captive of the earth art
    thou!
She trembles at thee still, and thy wild
    name
Was ne'er more bruited in men's minds
    than now
That thou art nothing, save the jest of
    Fame,
Who woo'd thee once, thy vassal, and
    became
The flatterer of thy fierceness, till thou
    wert   330
A god unto thyself; nor less the same
To the astounded kingdoms all inert,
Who deem'd thee for a time whate'er thou
    didst assert.

XXXVIII

Oh, more or less than man—in high or
    low
Battling with nations, flying from the field;

Now making monarchs' necks thy foot-
    stool, now
More than thy meanest soldier taught to
    yield;
An empire thou couldst crush, command,
    rebuild,
But govern not thy pettiest passion, nor,
However deeply in men's spirits skill'd, 340
Look through thine own, nor curb the lust
    of war,
Nor learn that tempted Fate will leave the
    loftiest star.

XXXIX

Yet well thy soul hath brook'd the turning
    tide
With that untaught innate philosophy,
Which be it wisdom, coldness, or deep
    pride,
Is gall and wormwood to an enemy.
When the whole host of hatred stood hard
    by,
To watch and mock thee shrinking, thou
    hast smiled
With a sedate and all-enduring eye;—
When Fortune fled her spoil'd and favourite
    child,   350
He stood unbow'd beneath the ills upon him
    piled.

XL

Sager than in thy fortunes; for in them
Ambition steel'd thee on too far to show
That just habitual scorn, which could con-
    temn
Men and their thoughts; 't was wise to
    feel, not so
To wear it ever on thy lip and brow,
And spurn the instruments thou wert to
    use
Till they were turn'd unto thine overthrow:
'Tis but a worthless world to win or lose;
So hath it proved to thee, and all such lot
    who choose.   360

XLI

If, like a tower upon a headland rock,
Thou hadst been made to stand or fall
    alone,
Such scorn of man had help'd to brave the
    shock;

But men's thoughts were the steps which
    paved thy throne,
Their admiration thy best weapon shone;
The part of Philip's son was thine, not
    then
(Unless aside thy purple had been thrown)
Like stern Diogenes to mock at men;
For sceptred cynics earth were far too wide
    a den.

XLII

But quiet to quick bosoms is a hell,   370
And *there* hath been thy bane; there is a
    fire
And motion of the soul which will not
    dwell
In its own narrow being, but aspire
Beyond the fitting medium of desire;
And, but once kindled, quenchless ever-
    more,
Preys upon high adventure, nor can tire
Of aught but rest; a fever at the core,
Fatal to him who bears, to all who ever bore.

XLIII

This makes the madmen who have made
    men mad
By their contagion; Conquerors and
    Kings,   380
Founders of sects and systems, to whom
    add
Sophists, Bards, Statesmen, all unquiet
    things
Which stir too strongly the soul's secret
    springs,
And are themselves the fools to those they
    fool;
Envied, yet how unenviable! what stings
Are theirs! One breast laid open were a
    school
Which would unteach mankind the lust to
    shine or rule:

XLIV

Their breath is agitation, and their life
A storm whereon they ride, to sink at last,
And yet so nursed and bigoted to strife, 390
That should their days, surviving perils
    past,
Melt to calm twilight, they feel overcast
With sorrow and supineness, and so die;

Even as a flame unfed, which runs to waste
With its own flickering, or a sword laid by,
Which eats into itself, and rusts ingloriously.

XLV

He who ascends to mountain-tops, shall
    find
The loftiest peaks most wrapt in clouds
    and snow;
He who surpasses or subdues mankind,
Must look down on the hate of those
    below.   400
Though high *above* the sun of glory glow,
And far *beneath* the earth and ocean spread,
Round him are icy rocks, and loudly blow
Contending tempests on his naked head,
And thus reward the toils which to those
    summits led.

XLVI

Away with these! true Wisdom's world
    will be
Within its own creation, or in thine,
Maternal Nature! for who teems like thee,
Thus on the banks of thy majestic Rhine?
There Harold gazes on a work divine,   410
A blending of all beauties; streams and
    dells,
Fruit, foliage, crag, wood, cornfield, moun-
    tain, vine,
And chiefless castles breathing stern fare-
    wells
From gray but leafy walls, where Ruin greenly
    dwells.

XLVII

And there they stand, as stands a lofty
    mind,
Worn, but unstooping to the baser crowd,
All tenantless, save to the crannying wind,
Or holding dark communion with the crowd.
There was a day when they were young
    and proud;
Banners on high, and battles pass'd be-
    low;   420
But they who fought are in a bloody shroud,
And those which waved are shredless dust
    ere now,
And the bleak battlements shall bear no
    future blow.

XLVIII

Beneath those battlements, within those
    walls,
Power dwelt amidst her passions; in proud
    state
Each robber chief upheld his armèd halls,
Doing his evil will, nor less elate
Than mightier heroes of a longer date.
What want these outlaws conquerors should
    have
But history's purchased page to call them
    great?   430
A wider space, an ornamented grave?
Their hopes were not less warm, their souls
    were full as brave.

XLIX

In their baronial feuds and single fields,
What deeds of prowess unrecorded died!
And Love, which lent a blazon to their
    shields,
With emblems well devised by amorous
    pride,
Through all the mail of iron hearts would
    glide;
But still their flame was fierceness, and
    drew on
Keen contest and destruction near allied,
And many a tower for some fair mischief
    won,   440
Saw the discolour'd Rhine beneath its ruin
    run.

L

But Thou, exulting and abounding river!
Making thy waves a blessing as they flow
Through banks whose beauty would endure
    for ever
Could man but leave thy bright creation so,
Nor its fair promise from the surface mow
With the sharp scythe of conflict,—then
    to see
Thy valley of sweet waters, were to know
Earth paved like Heaven; and to seem
    such to me,
Even now what wants thy stream?—that it
    should Lethe be.   450

LI

A thousand battles have assail'd thy banks,

But these and half their fame have pass'd
    away,
And Slaughter heap'd on high his welter-
    ing ranks;
Their very graves are gone, and what are
    they?
Thy tide wash'd down the blood of yester-
    day,
And all was stainless, and on thy clear
    stream
Glass'd, with its dancing light, the sunny
    ray;
But o'er the blacken'd memory's blighting
    dream
Thy waves would vainly roll, all sweeping
    as they seem.

LII

Thus Harold inly said, and pass'd along,   460
Yet not insensible to all which here
Awoke the jocund birds to early song
In glens which might have made even exile
    dear:
Though on his brow were graven lines
    austere,
And tranquil sternness, which had ta'en the
    place
Of feelings fierier far but less severe,
Joy was not always absent from his face,
But o'er it in such scenes would steal with
    transient trace.

LIII

Nor was all love shut from him, though
    his days
Of passion had consumed themselves to
    dust.   470
It is in vain that we would coldly gaze
On such as smile upon us; the heart must
Leap kindly back to kindness, though dis-
    gust
Hath wean'd it from all wordlings: thus
    he felt,
For there was soft remembrance, and sweet
    trust
In one fond breast, to which his own would
    melt,
And in its tenderer hour on that his bosom
    dwelt.

LIV

And he had learn'd to love,—I know not
    why,

For this in such as him seems strange of
    mood,—
The helpless looks of blooming infancy, 480
Even in its earliest nurture; what subdued,
To change like this, a mind so far imbued
With scorn of man, it little boots to know;
But thus it was; and though in solitude
Small power the nipp'd affections have to
    grow,
In him this glow'd when all beside had ceased
    to glow.

LV

And there was one soft breast, as hath
    been said,
Which unto his was bound by stronger ties
Than the church links withal; and, though
    unwed,
That love was pure, and, far above dis-
    guise, 490
Had stood the test of mortal enmities
Still undivided, and cemented more
By peril, dreaded most in female eyes;
But this was firm, and from a foreign shore
Well to that heart might his these absent
    greetings pour!

1

The castled crag of Drachenfels
Frowns o'er the wide and winding Rhine,
Whose breast of waters broadly swells
Between the banks which bear the vine,
And hills all rich with blossom'd trees,
And fields which promise corn and wine,
And scatter'd cities crowning these, 502
Whose far white walls along them shine,
Have strew'd a scene, which I should see
With double joy wert *thou* with me.

2

And peasant girls, with deep blue eyes,
And hands which offer early flowers,
Walk smiling o'er this paradise;
Above, the frequent feudal towers
Through green leaves lift their walls of
    gray; 510
And many a rock which steeply lowers,
And noble arch in proud decay,
Look o'er this vale of vintage-bowers;
But one thing want these banks of
    Rhine,—
Thy gentle hand to clasp in mine!

3

I send the lilies given to me;
Though long before thy hand they touch,
I know that they must wither'd be,
But yet reject them not as such;
For I have cherish'd them as dear, 520
Because they yet may meet thine eye,
And guide thy soul to mine even here,
When thou behold'st them drooping nigh,
And know'st them gather'd by the Rhine,
And offer'd from my heart to thine!

4

The river nobly foams and flows,
The charm of this enchanted ground,
And all its thousand turns disclose
Some fresher beauty varying round:
The haughtiest breast its wish might
    bound 530
Through life to dwell delighted here;
Nor could on earth a spot be found
To nature and to me so dear,
Could thy dear eyes in following mine
Still sweeten more these banks of Rhine!

LVI

By Coblentz, on a rise of gentle ground,
There is a small and simple pyramid,
Crowning the summit of the verdant
    mound;
Beneath its base are heroes' ashes hid,
Our enemy's—but let not that forbid 540
Honour to Marceau! o'er whose early tomb
Tears, big tears, gush'd from the rough
    soldier's lid,
Lamenting and yet envying such a doom,
Falling for France, whose rights he battled
    to resume.

LVII

Brief, brave, and glorious was his young
    career,—
His mourners were two hosts, his friends
    and foes;
And fitly may the stranger lingering here
Pray for his gallant spirit's bright repose;
For he was Freedom's champion, one of
    those,
The few in number, who had not o'er-
    stept 550

The charter to chastise which she bestows
On such as wield her weapons; he had
  kept
The whiteness of his soul, and thus men o'er
  him wept.

LVIII

Here Ehrenbreitstein, with her shatter'd
  wall
Black with the miner's blast, upon her
  height
Yet shows of what she was, when shell
  and ball
Rebounding idly on her strength did light:
A tower of victory! from whence the flight
Of baffled foes was watch'd along the plain:
But Peace destroy'd what War could never
  blight,   560
And laid those proud roofs bare to Sum-
  mer's rain—
On which the iron shower for years had
  pour'd in vain.

LIX

Adieu to thee, fair Rhine! How long de-
  lighted
The stranger fain would linger on his way!
Thine is a scene alike where souls united
Or lonely Contemplation thus might stray;
And could the ceaseless vultures cease to
  prey
On self-condemning bosoms, it were here,
Where Nature, nor too sombre nor too
  gay,
Wild but not rude, awful yet not austere,
Is to the mellow Earth as Autumn to the
  year.   571

LX

Adieu to thee again! a vain adieu!
There can be no farewell to scene like
  thine;
The mind is colour'd by thy every hue;
And if reluctantly the eyes resign
Their cherish'd gaze upon thee, lovely
  Rhine!
'T is with the thankful heart of parting
  praise;
More mighty spots may rise, more glaring
  shine,
But none unite in one attaching maze

The brilliant, fair, and soft,—the glories of
  old days.   580

LXI

The negligently grand, the fruitful bloom
Of coming ripeness, the white city's sheen,
The rolling stream, the precipice's gloom,
The forest's growth, and Gothic walls be-
  tween,
The wild rocks shaped as they had turrets
  been,
In mockery of man's art; and these withal
A race of faces happy as the scene,
Whose fertile bounties here extend to all,
Still springing o'er thy banks, though Em-
  pires near them fall.   589

LXII

But these recede. Above me are the Alps,
The palaces of Nature, whose vast walls
Have pinnacled in clouds their snowy scalps,
And throned Eternity in icy halls
Of cold sublimity, where forms and falls
The avalanche—the thunderbolt of snow!
All that expands the spirit, yet appals,
Gather around these summits, as to show
How Earth may pierce to Heaven, yet leave
  vain man below.

LXIII

But ere these matchless heights I dare to
  scan,
There is a spot should not be pass'd in
  vain,—   600
Morat! the proud, the patriot field! where
  man
May gaze on ghastly trophies of the slain,
Nor blush for those who conquer'd on that
  plain;
Here Burgundy bequeath'd his tombless
  host,
A bony heap, through ages to remain,
Themselves their monument;—the Stygian
  coast
Unsepulchred they roam'd, and shriek'd each
  wandering ghost.

LXIV

While Waterloo with Cannæ's carnage vies,

Morat and Marathon twin names shall
   stand;   609
They were true Glory's stainless victories,
Won by the unambitious heart and hand
Of a proud, brotherly, and civic band,
All unbought champions in no princely
   cause
Of vice-entail'd Corruption; they no land
Doom'd to bewail the blasphemy of laws
Making kings' rights divine, by some Dra-
   conic clause.

LXV

By a lone wall a lonelier column rears
A gray and grief-worn aspect of old days;
'Tis the last remnant of the wreck of years,
And looks as with the wild-bewilder'd
   gaze   620
Of one to stone converted by amaze,
Yet still with consciousness; and there it
   stands
Making a marvel that it not decays,
When the coeval pride of human hands,
Levell'd Adventicum, hath strew'd her sub-
   ject lands.

LXVI

And there—oh! sweet and sacred be the
   name!—
Julia—the daughter, the devoted—gave
Her youth to Heaven; her heart, beneath
   a claim
Nearest to Heaven's, broke o'er a father's
   grave.
Justice is sworn 'gainst tears, and hers
   would crave   630
The life she lived in; but the judge was
   just,
And then she died on him she could not
   save.
Their tomb was simple, and without a bust,
And held within their urn one mind, one
   heart, one dust.

LXVII

But these are deeds which should not pass
   away,
And names that must not wither, though
   the earth
Forgets her empires with a just decay,

The enslavers and the enslaved, their death
   and birth;
This high, the mountain-majesty of worth
Should be, and shall, survivor of its woe 640
And from its immortality look forth
In the sun's face, like yonder Alpine snow,
Imperishably pure beyond all things below.

LXVIII

Lake Leman woos me with its crystal face,
The mirror where the stars and mountains
   view
The stillness of their aspect in each trace
Its clear depth yields of their far height and
   hue:
There is too much of man here, to look
   through
With a fit mind the might which I behold;
But soon in me shall Loneliness renew 650
Thoughts hid, but not less cherish'd than
   of old,
Ere mingling with the herd had penn'd me in
   their fold.

LXIX

To fly from, need not be to hate, man-
   kind:
All are not fit with them to stir and toil,
Nor is it discontent to keep the mind
Deep in its fountain, lest it overboil
In the hot throng, where we become the
   spoil
Of our infection, till too late and long
We may deplore and struggle with the coil,
In wretched interchange of wrong for
   wrong   660
Midst a contentious world, striving where
   none are strong.

LXX

There, in a moment we may plunge our
   years
In fatal penitence, and in the blight
Of our own soul turn all our blood to tears,
And colour things to come with hues of
   Night;
The race of life becomes a hopeless flight
To those that walk in darkness: on the
   sea
The boldest steer but where their ports
   invite;

But there are wanderers o'er Eternity
Whose bark drives on and on, and anchor'd
    ne'er shall be.   670

LXXI

Is it not better, then, to be alone,
And love Earth only for its earthly sake?
By the blue rushing of the arrowy Rhone,
Or the pure bosom of its nursing lake,
Which feeds it as a mother who doth make
A fair but froward infant her own care,
Kissing its cries away as these awake;—
Is it not better thus our lives to wear,
Than join the crushing crowd, doom'd to in-
    flict or bear?

LXXII

I live not in myself, but I become   680
Portion of that around me; and to me
High mountains are a feeling, but the hum
Of human cities torture: I can see
Nothing to loathe in nature, save to be
A link reluctant in a fleshly chain,
Class'd among creatures, when the soul can
    flee,
And with the sky, the peak, the heaving
    plain
Of ocean, or the stars, mingle, and not in
    vain.

LXXIII

And thus I am absorb'd, and this is life:
I look upon the peopled desert past,   690
As on a place of agony and strife,
Where, for some sin, to sorrow I was cast,
To act and suffer, but remount at last
With a fresh pinion; which I feel to spring,
Though young, yet waxing vigorous as the
    blast
Which it would cope with, on delighted
    wing,
Spurning the clay-cold bonds which round
    our being cling.

LXXIV

And when, at length, the mind shall be all
    free
From what it hates in this degraded form,
Reft of its carnal life, save what shall be   700
Existent happier in the fly and worm,—

When elements to elements conform,
And dust is as it should be, shall I not
Feel all I see, less dazzling, but more
    warm?
The bodiless thought? the Spirit of each
    spot?
Of which, even now, I share at times the
    immortal lot?

LXXV

Are not the mountains, waves, and skies,
    a part
Of me and of my soul, as I of them?
Is not the love of these deep in my heart
With a pure passion? should I not con-
    temn   710
All objects, if compared with these? and
    stem
A tide of suffering, rather than forego
Such feelings for the hard and worldly
    phlegm
Of those whose eyes are only turn'd below,
Gazing upon the ground, with thoughts which
    dare not glow?

LXXVI

But this is not my theme; and I return
To that which is immediate, and require
Those who find contemplation in the urn,
To look on One, whose dust was once all
    fire,
A native of the land where I respire   720
The clear air for a while—a passing guest,
Where he became a being,—whose desire
Was to be glorious; 't was a foolish quest,
The which to gain and keep, he sacrificed all
    rest.

LXXVII

Here the self-torturing sophist, wild Rous-
    seau,
The apostle of affliction, he who threw
Enchantment over passion, and from woe
Wrung overwhelming eloquence, first drew
The breath which made him wretched; yet
    he knew   729
How to make madness beautiful, and cast
O'er erring deeds and thoughts a heavenly
    hue
Of words, like sunbeams, dazzling as they
    past

The eyes, which o'er them shed tears feelingly and fast.

LXXVIII

His love was passion's essence:—as a tree
On fire by lightning, with ethereal flame
Kindled he was, and blasted; for to be
Thus, and enamour'd, were in him the same.
But his was not the love of living dame,
Nor of the dead who rise upon our dreams,
But of ideal beauty, which became   740
In him existence, and o'erflowing teems
Along his burning page, distemper'd though
it seems.

LXXIX

This breathed itself to life in Julie, *this*
Invested her with all that's wild and sweet;
This hallow'd, too, the memorable kiss
Which every morn his fever'd lip would
greet,
From hers, who but with friendship his
would meet;
But to that gentle touch through brain and
breast
Flash'd the thrill'd spirit's love-devouring
heat;
In that absorbing sigh perchance more
blest   750
Than vulgar minds may be with all they seek
possest.

LXXX

His life was one long war with self-sought
foes,
Or friends by him self-banish'd; for his
mind
Had grown Suspicion's sanctuary, and
chose,
For its own cruel sacrifice, the kind,
'Gainst whom he raged with fury strange
and blind.
But he was phrensied,—wherefore, who
may know?
Since cause might be which skill could
never find;
But he was phrensied by disease or woe,
To that worst pitch of all, which wears a
reasoning show.   760

LXXXI

For then he was inspired, and from him
came,
As from the Pythian's mystic cave of yore,
Those oracles which set the world in flame,
Nor ceased to burn till kingdoms were no
more:
Did he not this for France? which lay be-
fore
Bow'd to the inborn tyranny of years?
Broken, and trembling to the yoke she
bore,
Till by the voice of him and his compeers
Roused up to too much wrath, which follows
o'ergrown fears?

LXXXII

They made themselves a fearful monu-
ment!   770
The wreck of old opinions—things which
grew,
Breathed from the birth of time: the veil
they rent,
And what behind it lay, all earth shall
view.
But good with ill they also overthrew,
Leaving but ruins, wherewith to rebuild
Upon the same foundation, and renew
Dungeons and thrones, which the same hour
refill'd,
As heretofore, because ambition was self-
will'd.

LXXXIII

But this will not endure, nor be endured!
Mankind have felt their strength, and made
it felt.   780
They might have used it better, but, allured
By their new vigour, sternly have they
dealt
On one another; pity ceased to melt
With her once natural charities. But they,
Who in oppression's darkness caved had
dwelt,
They were not eagles, nourish'd with the
day;
What marvel then, at times, if they mistook
their prey?

LXXXIV

What deep wounds ever closed without a
scar?

The heart's bleed longest, and but heal to
    wear
That which disfigures it; and they who
    war   790
With their own hopes, and have been van-
    quish'd, bear
Silence, but not submission: in his lair
Fix'd Passion holds his breath, until the
    hour
Which shall atone for years; none need
    despair:
It came, it cometh, and will come,—the
    power
To punish or forgive—in *one* we shall be
    slower.

LXXXV

Clear, placid Leman! thy contrasted lake,
With the wild world I dwelt in, is a thing
Which warns me, with its stillness, to for-
    sake   799
Earth's troubled waters for a purer spring.
This quiet sail is as a noiseless wing
To waft me from distraction; once I loved
Torn ocean's roar, but thy soft murmuring
Sounds sweet as if a Sister's voice reproved,
That I with stern delights should e'er have
    been so moved.

LXXXVI

It is the hush of night, and all between
Thy margin and the mountains, dusk, yet
    clear,
Mellow'd and mingling, yet distinctly seen,
Save darken'd Jura, whose capt heights
    appear
Precipitously steep; and drawing near, 810
There breathes a living fragrance from the
    shore,
Of flowers yet fresh with childhood; on
    the ear
Drops the light drip of the suspended oar,
Or chirps the grasshopper one good-night
    carol more;

LXXXVII

He is an evening reveller, who makes
His life an infancy, and sings his fill;
At intervals, some bird from out the brakes
Starts into voice a moment, then is still.
There seems a floating whisper on the hill,

But that is fancy, for the starlight dews 820
All silently their tears of love instil,
Weeping themselves away, till they infuse
Deep into nature's breast the spirit of her
    hues.

LXXXVIII

Ye stars! which are the poetry of heaven!
If in your bright leaves we would read the
    fate
Of men and empires,—'t is to be forgiven,
That in our aspirations to be great,
Our destinies o'erleap their mortal state,
And claim a kindred with you; for ye are
A beauty and a mystery, and create   830
In us such love and reverence from afar,
That fortune, fame, power, life, have named
    themselves a star.

LXXXIX

All heaven and earth are still—though not
    in sleep,
But breathless, as we grow when feeling
    most;
And silent, as we stand in thoughts too
    deep:—
All heaven and earth are still: From the
    high host
Of stars, to the lull'd lake and mountain-
    coast,
All is concenter'd in a life intense,
Where not a beam, nor air, nor leaf is lost,
But hath a part of being, and a sense, 840
Of that which is of all Creator and defence.

XC

Then stirs the feeling infinite, so felt
In solitude, where we are *least* alone;
A truth, which through our being then doth
    melt,
And purifies from self: it is a tone,
The soul and source of music, which makes
    known
Eternal harmony, and sheds a charm
Like to the fabled Cytherea's zone,
Binding all things with beauty;—'t would
    disarm
The spectre Death, had he substantial power
    to harm.   850

XCI

Not vainly did the early Persian make
His altar the high places, and the peak
Of earth-o'ergazing mountains, and thus
   take
A fit and unwall'd temple, there to seek
The Spirit, in whose honour shrines are
   weak,
Uprear'd by human hands. Come and com-
   pare
Columns and idol-dwellings, Goth or Greek,
With Nature's realms of worship, earth and
   air,
Nor fix on fond abodes to circumscribe thy
   pray'r!

XCII

The sky is changed!—and such a change!
   Oh night,   860
And storm, and darkness, ye are wondrous
   strong,
Yet lovely in your strength, as is the light
Of a dark eye in woman! Far along,
From peak to peak, the rattling crags
   among
Leaps the live thunder! Not from one lone
   cloud,
But every mountain now hath found a
   tongue,
And Jura answers, through her misty
   shroud,
Back to the joyous Alps, who call to her
   aloud!

XCIII

And this is in the night:—Most glorious
   night!   869
Thou wert not sent for slumber! let me be
A sharer in thy fierce and far delight,—
A portion of the tempest and of thee!
How the lit lake shines, a phosphoric sea,
And the big rain comes dancing to the
   earth!
And now again 't is black,—and now, the
   glee
Of the loud hills shakes with its mountain-
   mirth,
As if they did rejoice o'er a young earth-
   quake's birth.

XCIV

Now, where the swift Rhone cleaves his
   way between
Heights which appear as lovers who have
   parted   879
In hate, whose mining depths so intervene,
That they can meet no more, though
   broken-hearted;
Though in their souls, which thus each other
   thwarted,
Love was the very root of the fond rage
Which blighted their life's bloom, and then
   departed:
Itself expired, but leaving them an age
Of years all winters,—war within themselves
   to wage.

XCV

Now, where the quick Rhone thus hath
   cleft his way,
The mightiest of the storms hath taken his
   stand:
For here, not one, but many, make their
   play,
And fling their thunder-bolts from hand to
   hand,   890
Flashing and cast around; of all the band,
The brightest through these parted hills
   hath fork'd
His lightnings,—as if he did understand,
That in such gaps as desolation work'd,
There the hot shaft should blast whatever
   therein lurk'd.

XCVI

Sky, mountains, river, winds, lake, light-
   nings! ye!
With night, and clouds, and thunder, and
   a soul
To make these felt and feeling, well may be
Things that have made me watchful; the
   far roll
Of your departing voices, is the knoll   900
Of what in me is sleepless,—if I rest.
But where of ye, O tempests! is the goal?
Are ye like those within the human breast?
Or do ye find, at length, like eagles, some
   high nest?

XCVII

Could I embody and unbosom now

That which is most within me,—could I
    wreak
My thoughts upon expression, and thus
    throw
Soul, heart, mind, passions, feelings, strong
    or weak,
All that I would have sought, and all I
    seek,
Bear, know, feel, and yet breathe—into *one*
    word,   910
And that one word were Lightning, I would
    speak;
But as it is, I live and die unheard,
With a most voiceless thought, sheathing it
    as a sword.

XCVIII

The morn is up again, the dewy morn,
With breath all incense, and with cheek all
    bloom,
Laughing the clouds away with playful
    scorn,
And living as if earth contain'd no tomb,—
And glowing into day: we may resume
The march of our existence: and thus I,
Still on thy shores, fair Leman! may find
    room   920
And food for meditation, nor pass by
Much, that may give us pause, if ponder'd
    fittingly.

XCIX

Clarens! sweet Clarens, birthplace of deep
    Love!
Thine air is the young breath of passionate
    thought;
Thy trees take root in Love; the snows
    above
The very Glaciers have his colours caught,
And sun-set into rose-hues sees them
    wrought
By rays which sleep there lovingly: the
    rocks,
The permanent crags, tell here of Love,
    who sought   929
In them a refuge from the worldly shocks,
Which stir and sting the soul with hope that
    woos, then mocks.

C

Clarens! by heavenly feet thy paths are
    trod,—

Undying Love's, who here ascends a throne
To which the steps are mountains; where
    the god
Is a pervading life and light,—so shown
Not on those summits solely, nor alone
In the still cave and forest; o'er the flower
His eye is sparkling, and his breath hath
    blown,
His soft and summer breath, whose tender
    power
Passes the strength of storms in their most
    desolate hour.   940

CI

All things are here of *him;* from the black
    pines,
Which are his shade on high, and the loud
    roar
Of torrents, where he listeneth, to the vines
Which slope his green path downward to
    the shore,
Where the bow'd waters meet him, and
    adore,
Kissing his feet with murmurs; and the
    wood,
The covert of old trees, with trunks all
    hoar,
But light leaves, young as joy, stands where
    it stood,
Offering to him, and his, a populous solitude.

CII

A populous solitude of bees and birds, 950
And fairy-form'd and many-colour'd things,
Who worship him with notes more sweet
    than words,
And innocently open their glad wings,
Fearless and full of life: the gush of
    springs,
And fall of lofty fountains, and the bend
Of stirring branches, and the bud which
    brings
The swiftest thought of beauty, here extend,
Mingling, and made by Love, unto one mighty
    end.

CIII

He who hath loved not, here would learn
    that lore,   959
And make his heart a spirit; he who knows
That tender mystery, will love the more;

For this is Love's recess, where vain men's
    woes,
And the world's waste, have driven him far
    from those,
For 't is his nature to advance or die;
He stands not still, but or decays, or grows
Into a boundless blessing, which may vie
With the immortal lights, in its eternity!

CIV

'T was not for fiction chose Rousseau this
    spot,
Peopling it with affections; but he found
It was the scene which Passion must allot
To the mind's purified beings; 't was the
    ground   971
Where early Love his Psyche's zone un-
    bound,
And hallow'd it with loveliness: 't is lone,
And wonderful, and deep, and hath a sound,
And sense, and sight of sweetness; here
    the Rhone
Hath spread himself a couch, the Alps have
    rear'd a throne.

CV

Lausanne! and Ferney! ye have been the
    abodes
Of names which unto you bequeath'd a
    name;
Mortals, who sought and found, by danger-
    ous roads,
A path to perpetuity of fame: 980
They were gigantic minds, and their steep
    aim
Was, Titan-like, on daring doubts to pile
Thoughts which should call down thunder,
    and the flame
Of Heaven again assail'd, if Heaven the
    while
On man and man's research could deign do
    more than smile.

CVI

The one was fire and fickleness, a child
Most mutable in wishes, but in mind
A wit as various,—gay, grave, sage, or
    wild,—
Historian, bard, philosopher, combined;
He multiplied himself among mankind, 990
The Proteus of their talents: But his own

Breathed most in ridicule,—which, as the
    wind,
Blew where it listed, laying all things
    prone,—
Now to o'erthrow a fool, and now to shake
    a throne.

CVII

The other, deep and slow, exhausting
    thought,
And hiving wisdom with each studious year,
In meditation dwelt, with learning wrought,
And shaped his weapon with an edge severe,
Sapping a solemn creed with solemn sneer;
The lord of irony,—that master-spell, 1000
Which stung his foes to wrath, which grew
    from fear,
And doom'd him to the zealot's ready Hell,
Which answers to all doubts so eloquently
    well.

CVIII

Yet, peace be with their ashes,—for by
    them,
If merited, the penalty is paid;
It is not ours to judge,—far less condemn;
The hour must come when such things
    shall be made
Known unto all, or hope and dread allay'd
By slumber, on one pillow, in the dust,
Which, thus much we are sure, must lie
    decay'd;   1010
And when it shall revive, as is our trust,
'T will be to be forgiven, or suffer what is
    just.

CIX

But let me quit man's works, again to read
His Maker's, spread around me, and sus-
    pend
This page, which from my reveries I feed,
Until it seems prolonging without end.
The clouds above me to the white Alps
    tend,
And I must pierce them, and survey what-
    e'er
May be permitted, as my steps I bend
To their most great and growing region,
    where   1020
The earth to her embrace compels the powers
    of air.

CX

Italia! too, Italia! looking on thee,
Full flashes on the soul the light of ages,
Since the fierce Carthaginian almost won
  thee,
To the last halo of the chiefs and sages
Who glorify thy consecrated pages;
Thou wert the throne and grave of empires;
  still,
The fount at which the panting mind as-
  suages
Her thirst of knowledge, quaffing there her
  fill,
Flows from the eternal source of Rome's im-
  perial hill.   1030

CXI

Thus far have I proceeded in a theme
Renew'd with no kind auspices:—to feel
We are not what we have been, and to
  deem
We are not what we should be, and to steel
The heart against itself; and to conceal,
With a proud caution, love, or hate, or
  aught,—
Passion or feeling, purpose, grief or zeal,—
Which is the tyrant spirit of our thought,
Is a stern task of soul:—No matter,—it is
  taught.

CXII

And for these words, thus woven into
  song,   1040
It may be that they are a harmless wile,—
The colouring of the scenes which fleet
  along,
Which I would seize, in passing, to beguile
My breast, or that of others, for a while.
Fame is the thirst of youth, but I am not
So young as to regard men's frown or smile,
As loss or guerdon of a glorious lot;
I stood and stand alone,—remember'd or for-
  got.

CXIII

I have not loved the world, nor the world
  me;
I have not flatter'd its rank breath, nor
  bow'd   1050
To its idolatries a patient knee,
Nor coin'd my cheek to smiles, nor cried
  aloud
In worship of an echo; in the crowd
They could not deem me one of such; I
  stood
Among them, but not of them; in a shroud
Of thoughts which were not their thoughts,
  and still could,
Had I not filed my mind, which thus itself
  subdued.

CXIV

I have not loved the world, nor the world
  me,—
But let us part fair foes; I do believe,
Though I have found them not, that there
  may be   1060
Words which are things, hopes which will
  not deceive,
And virtues which are merciful, nor weave
Snares for the failing; I would also deem
O'er others' griefs that some sincerely
  grieve;
That two, or one, are almost what they
  seem,
That goodness is no name, and happiness no
  dream.

CXV

My daughter! with thy name this song be-
  gun;
My daughter! with thy name thus much
  shall end;
I see thee not, I hear thee not, but none
Can be so wrapt in thee; thou art the
  friend   1070
To whom the shadows of far years extend:
Albeit my brow thou never shouldst behold,
My voice shall with thy future visions blend,
And reach into thy heart, when mine is
  cold,
A token and a tone, even from thy father's
  mould.

CXVI

To aid thy mind's development, to watch
Thy dawn of little joys, to sit and see
Almost thy very growth, to view thee catch
Knowledge of objects,—wonders yet to
  thee!
To hold thee lightly on a gentle knee,   1080

And print on thy soft cheek a parent's
kiss,—
This, it should seem, was not reserved for
me;
Yet this was in my nature: as it is,
I know not what is there, yet something like
to this.

CXVII

Yet, though dull Hate as duty should be
taught,
I know that thou wilt love me; though my
name
Should be shut from thee, as a spell still
fraught
With desolation, and a broken claim:
Though the grave closed between us,—
't were the same,
I know that thou wilt love me; though to
drain   1090
My blood from out thy being were an aim,
And an attainment,—all would be in vain,—
Still thou wouldst love me, still that more
than life retain.

CXVIII

The child of love, though born in bitterness,
And nurtured in convulsion. Of thy sire
These were the elements, and thine no less.
As yet such are around thee, but thy fire
Shall be more temper'd, and thy hope far
higher.
Sweet be thy cradled slumbers! O'er the
sea
And from the mountains where I now
respire,   1100
Fain would I waft such blessing upon thee,
As, with a sigh, I deem thou might'st have
been to me.

MANFRED:

A DRAMATIC POEM

"There are more things in heaven and earth,
Horatio,
Than are dreamt of in your philosophy."

MANFRED.   WITCH OF THE ALPS.
CHAMOIS HUNTER.   ARIMANES.
ABBOT OF ST. MAURICE.   NEMESIS.
MANUEL.   THE DESTINIES.
HERMAN.   SPIRITS, &c.

*The Scene of the Drama is amongst the Higher Alps
—partly in the Castle of Manfred, and partly in the
Mountains.*

ACT I

SCENE I.—MANFRED *alone.—Scene, a Gothic
Gallery.—Time, Midnight.*

Man. The lamp must be replenish'd, but
even then
It will not burn so long as I must watch:
My slumbers—if I slumber—are not sleep,
But a continuance of enduring thought,
Which then I can resist not: in my heart
There is a vigil, and these eyes but close
To look within; and yet I live, and bear
The aspect and the form of breathing men.
But grief should be the instructor of the
wise;
Sorrow is knowledge: they who know the
most   10
Must mourn the deepest o'er the fatal truth,
The Tree of Knowledge is not that of Life.
Philosophy and science, and the springs
Of wonder, and the wisdom of the world,
I have essay'd, and in my mind there is
A power to make these subject to itself—
But they avail not: I have done men good,
And I have met with good even among men—
But this avail'd not: I have had my foes,
And none have baffled, many fallen before
me—   20
But this avail'd not:—Good, or evil, life,
Powers, passions, all I see in other beings,
Have been to me as rain unto the sands,
Since that all-nameless hour. I have no
dread,
And feel the curse to have no natural fear,
Nor fluttering throb, that beats with hopes or
wishes,
Or lurking love of something on the earth.
Now to my task.—
          Mysterious agency!
Ye spirits of the unbounded Universe!
Whom I have sought in darkness and in
light—   30
Ye, who do compass earth about, and dwell
In subtler essence—ye, to whom the tops
Of mountains inaccessible are haunts,
And earth's and ocean's caves familiar
things—
I call upon ye by the written charm
Which gives me power upon you— Rise!
Appear!
          [*A pause.*
They come not yet.—Now by the voice of
him
Who is the first among you—by this sign,

Which makes you tremble—by the claims of
    him
Who is undying,—Rise! Appear!—Appear! 40
                [*A pause.*
If it be so—Spirits of earth and air,
Ye shall not thus elude me: by a power,
Deeper than all yet urged, a tyrant-spell,
Which had its birthplace in a star condemn'd,
The burning wreck of a demolish'd world,
A wandering hell in the eternal space;
By the strong curse which is upon my soul,
The thought which is within me and around
    me,
I do compel ye to my will— Appear!
    [*A star is seen at the darker end of the
    gallery: it is stationary; and a voice
    is heard singing.*

FIRST SPIRIT

Mortal! to thy bidding bow'd,   50
From my mansion in the cloud,
Which the breath of twilight builds,
And the summer's sunset gilds
With the azure and vermilion,
Which is mix'd for my pavilion;
Though thy quest may be forbidden,
On a star-beam I have ridden:
To thine adjuration bow'd,
Mortal—be thy wish avow'd!

Voice of the SECOND SPIRIT

Mont Blanc is the monarch of mountains; 60
    They crown'd him long ago
On a throne of rocks, in a robe of clouds,
    With a diadem of snow.
Around his waist are forests braced,
    The Avalanche in his hand;
But ere it fall, that thundering ball
    Must pause for my command.
The Glacier's cold and restless mass
    Moves onward day by day;
But I am he who bids it pass,   70
    Or with its ice delay.
I am the spirit of the place,
    Could make the mountain bow
And quiver to his cavern'd base—
    And what with me wouldst *Thou?*

Voice of the THIRD SPIRIT

In the blue depth of the waters,
    Where the wave hath no strife,

Where the wind is a stranger,
    And the sea-snake hath life,
Where the Mermaid is decking   80
    Her green hair with shells,
Like the storm on the surface
    Came the sound of thy spells;
O'er my calm Hall of Coral
    The deep echo roll'd—
To the Spirit of Ocean
    Thy wishes unfold!

FOURTH SPIRIT

Where the slumbering earthquake
    Lies pillow'd on fire,
And the lakes of bitumen   90
    Rise boilingly higher;
Where the roots of the Andes
    Strike deep in the earth,
As their summits to heaven
    Shoot soaringly forth;
I have quitted my birthplace,
    Thy bidding to bide—
Thy spell hath subdued me,
    Thy will be my guide!

FIFTH SPIRIT

I am the Rider of the wind,   100
    The Stirrer of the storm;
The hurricane I left behind
    Is yet with lightning warm;
To speed to thee, o'er shore and sea
    I swept upon the blast:
The fleet I met sail'd well, and yet
    'T will sink ere night be past.

SIXTH SPIRIT

My dwelling is the shadow of the night,
Why doth thy magic torture me with light?

SEVENTH SPIRIT

The star which rules thy destiny   110
Was ruled, ere earth began, by me:
It was a world as fresh and fair
As e'er revolved round sun in air;
Its course was free and regular,
Space bosom'd not a lovelier star.
The hour arrived—and it became
A wandering mass of shapeless flame,
A pathless comet, and a curse,
The menace of the universe;

Still rolling on with innate force,   120
Without a sphere, without a course,
A bright deformity on high,
The monster of the upper sky!
And thou! beneath its influence born—
Thou worm! whom I obey and scorn—
Forced by a power (which is not thine,
And lent thee but to make thee mine)
For this brief moment to descend,
Where these weak spirits round thee bend,
And parley with a thing like thee—   130
What wouldst thou, Child of Clay! with me?

The Seven Spirits

Earth, ocean, air, night, mountains, winds, thy star,
  Are at thy beck and bidding, Child of Clay!
Before thee at thy quest their spirits are—
  What wouldst thou with us, son of mortals—say?

Man. Forgetfulness——
First Spirit. Of what—of whom—and why?
Man. Of that which is within me; read it there—
Ye know it, and I cannot utter it.
  Spirit. We can but give thee that which we possess: 139
Ask of us subjects, sovereignty, the power
O'er earth—the whole, or portion—or a sign
Which shall control the elements, whereof
We are the dominators,—each and all,
These shall be thine.
  Man.   Oblivion, self-oblivion!
Can ye not wring from out the hidden realms
Ye offer so profusely what I ask?
  Spirit. It is not in our essence, in our skill;
But—thou may'st die.
  Man.   Will death bestow it on me?
  Spirit. We are immortal, and do not forget;
We are eternal; and to us the past   150
Is, as the future, present. Art thou answer'd?
  Man. Ye mock me—but the power which brought ye here
Hath made you mine. Slaves, scoff not at my will!
The mind, the spirit, the Promethean spark,
The lightning of my being, is as bright,
Pervading, and far darting as your own,
And shall not yield to yours, though coop'd in clay!
Answer, or I will teach you what I am.
  Spirit. We answer as we answer'd; our reply
Is even in thine own words.
  Man.   Why say ye so?
  Spirit. If as thou say'st, thine essence be as ours,   161
We have replied in telling thee, the thing
Mortals call death hath nought to do with us.
  Man. I then have call'd ye from your realms in vain!
Ye cannot, or ye will not, aid me.
  Spirit.   Say,
What we possess we offer; it is thine;
Bethink ere thou dismiss us; ask again;
Kingdom, and sway, and strength, and length of days——
  Man. Accursed! what have I to do with days?
They are too long already.—Hence—begone!
  Spirit. Yet pause: being here, our will would do thee service;   171
Bethink thee, is there then no other gift
Which we can make not worthless in thine eyes?
  Man. No, none: yet stay—one moment, ere we part,
I would behold ye face to face. I hear
Your voices, sweet and melancholy sounds,
As music on the waters; and I see
The steady aspect of a clear large star;
But nothing more. Approach me as ye are,
Or one, or all, in your accustom'd forms.   180
  Spirit. We have no forms, beyond the elements
Of which we are the mind and principle:
But choose a form—in that we will appear.
  Man. I have no choice; there is no form on earth
Hideous or beautiful to me. Let him,
Who is most powerful of ye, take such aspect
As unto him may seem most fitting—Come!
  Seventh Spirit (appearing in the shape of a beautiful female figure). Behold!
  Man. Oh God! if it be thus, and *thou*
Art not a madness and a mockery,
I yet might be most happy. I will clasp thee,   190
And we again will be——
                    [*The figure vanishes.*
                    My heart is crush'd!
                    [Manfred *falls senseless.*

(A voice is heard in the Incantation which follows.)

When the moon is on the wave,
　And the glow-worm in the grass,
And the meteor on the grave,
　And the wisp on the morass;
When the falling stars are shooting,
And the answer'd owls are hooting,
And the silent leaves are still
In the shadow of the hill,
Shall my soul be upon thine, 200
With a power and with a sign.

Though thy slumber may be deep,
Yet thy spirit shall not sleep;
There are shades which will not vanish,
There are thoughts thou canst not banish;
By a power to thee unknown,
Thou canst never be alone;
Thou art wrapt as with a shroud,
Thou art gather'd in a cloud;
And for ever shalt thou dwell 210
In the spirit of this spell.

Though thou seest me not pass by,
Thou shalt feel me with thine eye
As a thing that, though unseen,
Must be near thee, and hath been;
And when in that secret dread
Thou hast turn'd around thy head,
Thou shalt marvel I am not
As thy shadow on the spot,
And the power which thou dost feel 220
Shall be what thou must conceal.

And a magic voice and verse
Hath baptized thee with a curse;
And a spirit of the air
Hath begirt thee with a snare;
In the wind there is a voice
Shall forbid thee to rejoice;
And to thee shall night deny
All the quiet of her sky;
And the day shall have a sun, 230
Which shall make thee wish it done.

From thy false tears I did distil
An essence which hath strength to kill;
From thy own heart I then did wring
The black blood in its blackest spring;
From thy own smile I snatch'd the snake,
For there it coil'd as in a brake;
From thy own lip I drew the charm
Which gave all these their chiefest harm;

In proving every poison known, 240
I found the strongest was thine own.

By thy cold breast and serpent smile,
By thy unfathom'd gulfs of guile,
By that most seeming virtuous eye,
By thy shut soul's hypocrisy;
By the perfection of thine art
Which pass'd for human thine own heart;
By thy delight in others' pain,
And by thy brotherhood of Cain,
I call upon thee! and compel 250
Thyself to be thy proper Hell!

And on thy head I pour the vial
Which doth devote thee to this trial;
Nor to slumber, nor to die,
Shall be in thy destiny;
Though thy death shall still seem near
To thy wish, but as a fear;
Lo! the spell now works around thee
And the clankless chain hath bound thee;
O'er thy heart and brain together 260
Hath the word been pass'd—now wither!

SCENE II

*The Mountain of the Jungfrau.—Time, Morning.—*MANFRED *alone upon the Cliffs.*

Man. The spirits I have raised abandon me,
The spells which I have studied baffle me,
The remedy I reck'd of tortured me;
I lean no more on superhuman aid;
It hath no power upon the past, and for
The future, till the past be gulf'd in darkness,
It is not of my search.—My mother Earth!
And thou fresh breaking Day, and you, ye Mountains.
Why are ye beautiful? I cannot love ye.
And thou, the bright eye of the universe, 10
That openest over all, and unto all
Art a delight—thou shin'st not on my heart.
And you, ye crags, upon whose extreme edge
I stand, and on the torrent's brink beneath
Behold the tall pines dwindled as to shrubs
In dizziness of distance; when a leap,
A stir, a motion, even a breath, would bring
My breast upon its rocky bosom's bed
To rest for ever—wherefore do I pause?
I feel the impulse—yet I do not plunge; 20
I see the peril—yet do not recede;
And my brain reels—and yet my foot is firm:

There is a power upon me which withholds,
And makes it my fatality to live,—
If it be life to wear within myself
This barrenness of spirit, and to be
My own soul's sepulchre, for I have ceased
To justify my deeds unto myself—
The last infirmity of evil. Ay,
Thou winged and cloud-cleaving minister, 30
               [*An eagle passes.*
Whose happy flight is highest into heaven,
Well may'st thou swoop so near me—I should be
Thy prey, and gorge thine eaglets; thou art gone
Where the eye cannot follow thee; but thine
Yet pierces downward, onward, or above,
With a pervading vision.—Beautiful!
How beautiful is all this visible world!
How glorious in its action and itself!
But we, who name ourselves its sovereigns, we,
Half dust, half deity, alike unfit 40
To sink or soar, with our mix'd essence make
A conflict of its elements, and breathe
The breath of degradation and of pride,
Contending with low wants and lofty will,
Till our mortality predominates,
And men are—what they name not to themselves,
And trust not to each other. Hark! the note,
     [*The Shepherd's pipe in the distance
     is heard.*
The natural music of the mountain reed——
For here the patriarchal days are not
A pastoral fable—pipes in the liberal air, 50
Mix'd with the sweet bells of the sauntering herd;
My soul would drink those echoes. Oh, that I were
The viewless spirit of a lovely sound,
A living voice, a breathing harmony,
A bodiless enjoyment—born and dying,
With the blest tone which made me!

Enter from below a CHAMOIS HUNTER.

Chamois Hunter.   Even so
This way the chamois leapt: her nimble feet
Have baffled me; my gains to-day will scarce
Repay my break-neck travail.—What is here?
Who seems not of my trade, and yet hath reach'd 60

A height which none even of our mountaineers,
Save our best hunters, may attain: his garb
Is goodly, his mien manly, and his air
Proud as a free-born peasant's, at this distance:
I will approach him nearer.
    Man. (not perceiving the other). To be thus—
Grey-hair'd with anguish, like these blasted pines,
Wrecks of a single winter, barkless, branchless,
A blighted trunk upon a cursed root,
Which but supplies a feeling to decay—
And to be thus, eternally but thus,   70
Having been otherwise! Now furrow'd o'er
With wrinkles, plough'd by moments,—not by years,—
And hours, all tortured into ages—hours
Which I outlive!—Ye toppling crags of ice!
Ye avalanches, whom a breath draws down
In mountainous o'erwhelming, come and crush me!
I hear ye momently above, beneath,
Crash with a frequent conflict; but ye pass,
And only fall on things that still would live;
On the young flourishing forest, or the hut
And hamlet of the harmless villager.   81
    C. Hun. The mists begin to rise from up the valley;
I'll warn him to descend, or he may chance
To lose at once his way and life together.
    Man. The mists boil up around the glaciers; clouds
Rise curling fast beneath me, white and sulphury,
Like foam from the roused ocean of deep Hell,
Whose every wave breaks on a living shore,
Heap'd with the damn'd like pebbles.—I am giddy.
    C. Hun. I must approach him cautiously; if near,   90
A sudden step will startle him, and he
Seems tottering already.
    Man.   Mountains have fallen,
Leaving a gap in the clouds, and with the shock
Rocking their Alpine brethren; filling up
The ripe green valleys with destruction's splinters;
Damming the rivers with a sudden dash,

Which crush'd the waters into mist and made
Their fountains find another channel—thus,
Thus, in its old age, did Mount Rosenberg—
Why stood I not beneath it?   100
    C. Hun.   Friend! have a care,
Your next step may be fatal!—for the love
Of him who made you, stand not on that brink!
    Man. (*not hearing him*)   Such would have
       been for me a fitting tomb;
My bones had then been quiet in their depth;
They had not then been strewn upon the rocks
For the wind's pastime—as thus—thus they shall be—
In this one plunge.—Farewell, ye opening heavens!
Look not upon me thus reproachfully—
You were not meant for me—Earth! take these atoms!
    [*As* MANFRED *is in act to spring from*
    the cliff, the CHAMOIS HUNTER *seizes*
    and retains him with a sudden grasp.
    C. Hun. Hold, madman!—though aweary
      of thy life,   110
Stain not our pure vales with thy guilty blood:
Away with me———I will not quit my hold.
    Man. I am most sick at heart—nay, grasp
      me not—
I am all feebleness—the mountains whirl
Spinning around me———I grow blind———
      What art thou?
    C. Hun. I'll answer that anon. Away with
      me—
The clouds grow thicker—there—now lean on me—
Place your foot here—here, take this staff, and cling
A moment to that shrub—now give me your
      hand,   119
And hold fast by my girdle—softly—well—
The Chalet will be gain'd within an hour:
Come on, we'll quickly find a surer footing,
And something like a pathway, which the torrent
Hath wash'd since winter.—Come, 't is bravely done—
You should have been a hunter.—Follow me.
    [*As they descend the rocks with*
    difficulty, the scene closes.

ACT II

SCENE I.—*A Cottage amongst the Bernese*
Alps.

MANFRED *and the* CHAMOIS HUNTER.

    C. Hun. No, no—yet pause—thou must
      not yet go forth:
Thy mind and body are alike unfit
To trust each other, for some hours, at least;
When thou art better, I will be thy guide—
But whither?
    Man.   It imports not: I do know
My route full well, and need no further guidance.
    C. Hun. Thy garb and gait bespeak thee
      of high lineage—
One of the many chiefs, whose castled crag
Look o'er the lower valleys—which of these
May call thee lord? I only know their portals;
My way of life leads me but rarely down
To bask by the huge hearths of those old halls,
Carousing with the vassals; but the paths,
Which step from out our mountains to their doors,
I know from childhood—which of these is thine?
    Man. No matter.
    C. Hun. Well, sir, pardon me the question,
And be of better cheer. Come, taste my wine;
'T is of an ancient vintage; many a day
'T has thaw'd my veins among our glaciers, now
Let it do thus for thine— Come, pledge me fairly.   20
    Man. Away, away! there's blood upon the brim!
Will it then never—never sink in the earth?
    C. Hun. What dost thou mean? thy senses
      wander from thee.
    Man. I say 't is blood—my blood! the pure
      warm stream
Which ran in the veins of my fathers, and in ours
When we were in our youth, and had one heart,
And loved each other as we should not love,
And this was shed: but still it rises up,

Colouring the clouds, that shut me out from
    heaven,
Where thou art not—and I shall never be.   30
  C. Hun. Man of strange words, and some
    half-maddening sin,
Which makes thee people vacancy, whate'er
Thy dread and sufferance be, there's comfort
    yet—
The aid of holy men, and heavenly pa-
    tience—
  Man. Patience and patience! Hence—that
    word was made
For brutes of burthen, not for birds of prey;
Preach it to mortals of a dust like thine,—
I am not of thine order.
  C. Hun.   Thanks to Heaven!
I would not be of thine for the free fame
Of William Tell; but whatsoe'er thine ill,   40
It must be borne, and these wild starts are
    useless.
  Man. Do I not bear it?—Look on me—I
    live.
  C. Hun. This is convulsion, and no health-
    ful life.
  Man. I tell thee, man! I have lived many
    years,
Many long years, but they are nothing now
To those which I must number: ages—ages—
Space and eternity—and consciousness,
With the fierce thirst of death—and still
    unslaked!
  C. Hun. Why, on thy brow the seal of
    middle age
Hath scarce been set; I am thine elder far.   50
  Man. Think'st thou existence doth depend
    on time?
It doth; but actions are our epochs: mine
Have made my days and nights imperishable,
Endless, and all alike, as sands on the shore,
Innumerable atoms; and one desert,
Barren and cold, on which the wild waves
    break,
But nothing rests, save carcasses and wrecks,
Rocks, and the salt-surf weeds of bitterness.
  C. Hun. Alas! he's mad—but yet I must
    not leave him.
  Man. I would I were—for then the things
    I see   60
Would be but a distemper'd dread.
  C. Hun.   What is it
That thou dost see, or think thou look'st
    upon?
  Man. Myself, and thee—a peasant of the
    Alps—

Thy humble virtues, hospitable home,
And spirit patient, pious, proud, and free;
Thy self-respect, grafted on innocent thoughts;
Thy days of health, and nights of sleep; thy
    toils,
By danger dignified, yet guiltless; hopes
Of cheerful old age and a quiet grave,
With cross and garland over its green turf,   70
And thy grandchildren's love for epitaph;
This do I see—and then I look within—
It matters not—my soul was scorch'd already!
  C. Hun. And wouldst thou then exchange
    thy lot for mine?
  Man. No, friend! I would not wrong thee,
    nor exchange
My lot with living being: I can bear—
However wretchedly, 't is still to bear—
In life what others could not brook to dream,
But perish in their slumber.
  C. Hun.   And with this—
This cautious feeling for another's pain,   80
Canst thou be black with evil?—say not so.
Can one of gentle thoughts have wreak'd re-
    venge
Upon his enemies?
  Man.   Oh! no, no, no!
My injuries came down on those who loved
    me—
On those whom I best loved: I never quell'd
An enemy, save in my just defence—
But my embrace was fatal.
  C. Hun.   Heaven give thee rest!
And penitence restore thee to thyself;
My prayers shall be for thee.
  Man.   I need them not—
But can endure thy pity. I depart—   90
'T is time—farewell!—Here's gold, and thanks
    for thee—
No words—it is thy due.—Follow me not—
I know my path—the mountain peril's past:
And once again I charge thee, follow not!
                 [*Exit* MANFRED.

SCENE II

A lower Valley in the Alps.—A Cataract.

Enter MANFRED.

It is not noon—the sunbow's rays still arch
The torrent with the many hues of heaven,
And roll the sheeted silver's waving column
O'er the crag's headlong perpendicular,
And fling its lines of foaming light along,

And to and fro, like the pale courser's tail,
The Giant steed, to be bestrode by Death,
As told in the Apocalypse. No eyes
But mine now drink this sight of loveliness;
I should be sole in this sweet solitude,   10
And with the Spirit of the place divide
The homage of these waters.—I will call her.

> [MANFRED *takes some of the water into
> the palm of his hand, and flings it
> into the air, muttering the adjuration.
> After a pause, the Witch of the Alps
> rises beneath the arch of the sunbow
> of the torrent.*

Beautiful Spirit! with thy hair of light,
And dazzling eyes of glory, in whose form
The charms of earth's least mortal daughters
    grow
To an unearthly stature, in an essence
Of purer elements; while the hues of youth,—
Carnation'd like a sleeping infant's cheek,
Rock'd by the beating of her mother's heart,
Or the rose tints, which summer's twilight
    leaves   20
Upon the lofty glacier's virgin snow,
The blush of earth embracing with her
    heaven,—
Tinge thy celestial aspect, and make tame
The beauties of the sunbow which bends o'er
    thee.
Beautiful Spirit! in thy calm clear brow,
Wherein is glass'd serenity of soul,
Which of itself shows immortality,
I read that thou wilt pardon to a Son
Of Earth, whom the abstruser powers permit
At times to commune with them—if that he 30
Avail him of his spells—to call thee thus,
And gaze on thee a moment.
   Witch,   Son of Earth!
I know thee, and the powers which give thee
    power;
I know thee for a man of many thoughts,
And deeds of good and ill, extreme in both,
Fatal and fated in thy sufferings.
I have expected this—what wouldst thou
    with me?
   Man. To look upon thy beauty—nothing
    further.
The face of the earth hath madden'd me,
    and I
Take refuge in her mysteries, and pierce   40
To the abodes of those who govern her—
But they can nothing aid me. I have sought
From them what they could not bestow, and
    now

I search no further.
   Witch.   What could be the quest
Which is not in the power of the most power-
    ful,
The rulers of the invisible?
   Man.   A boon;
But why should I repeat it? 't were in vain.
   Witch. I know not that; let thy lips utter
    it.
   Man. Well, though it torture me, 't is but
    the same;
My pang shall find a voice. From my youth
    upwards   50
My spirit walk'd not with the souls of men,
Nor look'd upon the earth with human eyes;
The thirst of their ambition was not mine,
The aim of their existence was not mine;
My joys, my griefs, my passions, and my
    powers,
Made me a stranger; though I wore the form,
I had no sympathy with breathing flesh,
Nor midst the creatures of clay that girded
    me
Was there but one who—but of her anon.
I said with men, and with the thoughts of
    men,   60
I held but slight communion; but instead,
My joy was in the wilderness,—to breathe
The difficult air of the iced mountain's top,
Where the birds dare not build, nor insect's
    wing
Flit o'er the herbless granite; or to plunge
Into the torrent, and to roll along
On the swift whirl of the new breaking
    wave
Of river-stream, or ocean, in their flow.
In these my early strength exulted; or
To follow through the night the moving
    moon,   70
The stars and their development; or catch
The dazzling lightnings till my eyes grew
    dim;
Or to look, list'ning, on the scatter'd leaves,
While Autumn winds were at their evening
    song.
These were my pastimes, and to be alone;
For if the beings, of whom I was one,—
Hating to be so,—cross'd me in my path,
I felt myself degraded back to them,
And was all clay again. And then I dived,   79
In my lone wanderings, to the caves of death,
Searching its cause in its effect; and drew
From wither'd bones, and skulls, and heap'd
    up dust,

Conclusions most forbidden. Then I pass'd
The nights of years in sciences untaught,
Save in the old time; and with time and toil,
And terrible ordeal, and such penance
As in itself hath power upon the air,
And spirits that do compass air and earth,
Space, and the peopled infinite, I made
Mine eyes familiar with Eternity, 90
Such as, before me, did the Magi, and
He who from out their fountain dwellings
    raised
Eros and Anteros, at Gadara,
As I do thee;—and with my knowledge grew
The thirst of knowledge, and the power and
    joy
Of this most bright intelligence, until—
  Witch. Proceed.
  Man.   Oh! I but
Thus prolong'd my words,
Boasting these idle attributes, because
As I approach the core of my heart's grief—
But to my task. I have not named to thee 100
Father or mother, mistress, friend, or being,
With whom I wore the chain of human ties;
If I had such, they seem'd not such to me;
Yet there was one—
  Witch.   Spare not thyself—proceed.
  Man. She was like me in lineaments; her
    eyes,
Her hair, her features, all, to the very tone
Even of her voice, they said were like to
    mine;
But soften'd all, and temper'd into beauty;
She had the same lone thoughts and wander-
    ings, 109
The quest of hidden knowledge, and a mind
To comprehend the universe: nor these
Alone, but with them gentler powers than
    mine,
Pity, and smiles, and tears—which I had not;
And tenderness—but that I had for her;
Humility—and that I never had.
Her faults were mine—her virtues were her
    own—
I loved her, and destroy'd her!
  Witch.   With thy hand?
  Man. Not with my hand, but heart, which
    broke her heart;
It gazed on mine, and wither'd. I have shed
Blood, but not hers—and yet her blood was
    shed; 120
I saw—and could not stanch it.
  Witch.   And for this—
A being of the race thou dost despise,

The order, which thine own would rise
    above,
Mingling with us and ours,—thou dost forego
The gifts of our great knowledge, and shrink'st
    back
To recreant mortality—— Away!
  Man. Daughter of Air! I tell thee, since
    that hour—
But words are breath—look on me in my
    sleep,
Or watch my watchings— Come and sit by
    me!
My solitude is solitude no more, 130
But peopled with the Furies;—I have gnash'd
My teeth in darkness till returning morn,
Then cursed myself till sunset;—I have
    pray'd
For madness as a blessing—'tis denied me.
I have affronted death—but in the war
Of elements the waters shrunk from me,
And fatal things pass'd harmless; the cold
    hand
Of an all-pitiless demon held me back,
Back by a single hair, which would not break.
In fantasy, imagination, all 140
The affluence of my soul—which one day
    was
A Crœsus in creation—I plunged deep,
But, like an ebbing wave, it dash'd me back
Into the gulf of my unfathom'd thought.
I plunged amidst mankind— Forgetfulness
I sought in all, save where 't is to be found,
And that I have to learn; my sciences,
My long-pursued and superhuman art,
Is mortal here: I dwell in my despair—
And live—and live for ever.
  Witch.   It may be
That I can aid thee.
  Man.   To do this thy power 151
Must wake the dead, or lay me low with
    them.
Do so—in any shape—in any hour—
With any torture—so it be the last.
  Witch. That is not in my province; but if
    thou
Wilt swear obedience to my will, and do
My bidding, it may help thee to thy wishes.
  Man. I will not swear— Obey! and whom?
    the spirits
Whose presence I command, and be the slave
Of those who served me— Never! 160
  Witch.   Is this all?
Hast thou no gentler answer?—Yet bethink
    thee,

And pause ere thou rejectest.

Man.   I have said it.

Witch. Enough! I may retire then—say!

Man.   Retire!

[*The* WITCH *disappears.*

Man. (alone). We are the fools of time
    and terror: Days
Steal on us, and steal from us; yet we live,
Loathing our life, and dreading still to die.
In all the days of this detested yoke—
This vital weight upon the struggling heart,
Which sinks with sorrow, or beats quick with
    pain,   169
Or joy that ends in agony or faintness—
In all the days of past and future, for
In life there is no present, we can number
How few—how less than few—wherein the
    soul
Forbears to pant for death, and yet draws
    back
As from a stream in winter, though the chill
Be but a moment's. I have one resource
Still in my science—I can call the dead,
And ask them what it is we dread to be:
The sternest answer can but be the Grave, 179
And that is nothing. If they answer not——
The buried Prophet answered to the Hag
Of Endor; and the Spartan Monarch drew
From the Byzantine maid's unsleeping spirit
An answer and his destiny—he slew
That which he loved, unknowing what he slew,
And died unpardon'd—though he call'd in
    aid
The Phyxian Jove, and in Phigalia roused
The Arcadian Evocators to compel
The indignant shadow to depose her wrath,
Or fix her term of vengeance—she replied 190
In words of dubious import, but fulfill'd.
If I had never lived, that which I love
Had still been living; had I never loved,
That which I love would still be beautiful,
Happy and giving happiness. What is she?
What is she now?—a sufferer for my sins—
A thing I dare not think upon—or nothing.
Within few hours I shall not call in vain—
Yet in this hour I dread the thing I dare:
Until this hour I never shrunk to gaze   200
On spirit, good or evil—now I tremble,
And feel a strange cold thaw upon my heart.
But I can act even what I most abhor,
And champion human fears.—The night ap-
    proaches.   [*Exit.*

SCENE III

The Summit of the Jungfrau Mountain.

Enter FIRST DESTINY.

The moon is rising broad, and round, and
    bright;
And here on snows, where never human foot
Of common mortal trod, we nightly tread
And leave no traces: o'er the savage sea,
The glassy ocean of the mountain ice,
We skim its rugged breakers, which put on
The aspect of a tumbling tempest's foam,
Frozen in a moment—a dead whirlpool's
    image:
And this most steep fantastic pinnacle,
The fretwork of some earthquake—where the
    clouds   10
Pause to repose themselves in passing by—
Is sacred to our revels, or our vigils;
Here do I wait my sisters, on our way
To the Hall of Arimanes, for to-night
Is our great festival—'t is strange they come
    not.

A Voice without, singing.

The Captive Usurper,
    Hurl'd down from the throne,
Lay buried in torpor,
    Forgotten and lone;
I broke through his slumbers,   20
    I shiver'd his chain,
I leagued him with numbers—
    He's Tyrant again!
With the blood of a million he'll answer my
    care,
With a nation's destruction—his flight and
    despair.

Second Voice, without.

The ship sail'd on, the ship sail'd fast,
But I left not a sail, and I left not a mast;
There is not a plank of the hull or the deck,
And there is not a wretch to lament o'er his
    wreck;
Save one, whom I held, as he swam, by the
    hair,   30
And he was a subject well worthy my care;
A traitor on land, and a pirate at sea—
But I saved him to wreak further havoc for
    me!

FIRST DESTINY, *answering.*

The city lies sleeping;
  The morn, to deplore it,
May dawn on it weeping:
  Sullenly, slowly,
The black plague flew o'er it—
  Thousands lie lowly;
Tens of thousands shall perish;   40
  The living shall fly from
The sick they should cherish;
  But nothing can vanquish
The touch that they die from.
  Sorrow and anguish,
And evil and dread,
  Envelop a nation;
The blest are the dead,
  Who see not the sight
Of their own desolation;   50
This work of a night—
This wreck of a realm—this deed of my doing—
For ages I've done, and shall still be renewing!

Enter the SECOND *and* THIRD DESTINIES.

The Three

Our hands contain the hearts of men,
  Our footsteps are their graves;
We only give to take again
  The spirits of our slaves!

First Des. Welcome!—Where's Nemesis?
Second Des.   At some great work;
But what I know not, for my hands were full.
Third Des. Behold she cometh.

Enter NEMESIS.

First Des.   Say, where hast thou been? 60
My sisters and thyself are slow to-night.
Nem. I was detain'd repairing shatter'd thrones,
Marrying fools, restoring dynasties,
Avenging men upon their enemies,
And making them repent their own revenge;
Goading the wise to madness; from the dull
Shaping out oracles to rule the world
Afresh, for they were waxing out of date,
And mortals dared to ponder for themselves,
To weigh kings in the balance, and to speak

Of freedom, the forbidden fruit.—Away! 71
We have outstay'd the hour—mount we our clouds!

    [Exeunt.

SCENE IV

The Hall of Arimanes—Arimanes on his Throne, a Globe of Fire, surrounded by the Spirits.

Hymn of the SPIRITS.

Hail to our Master!—Prince of Earth and Air!
  Who walks the clouds and waters—in his hand
The sceptre of the elements, which tear
  Themselves to chaos at his high command!
He breatheth—and a tempest shakes the sea;
  He speaketh—and the clouds reply in thunder;
He gazeth—from his glance the sunbeams flee;
  He moveth—earthquakes rend the world asunder.
Beneath his footsteps the volcanoes rise;
  His shadow is the Pestilence; his path   10
The comets herald through the crackling skies;
  And planets turn to ashes at his wrath.
To him War offers daily sacrifice;
  To him Death pays his tribute; Life is his,
With all its infinite of agonies—
  And his the spirit of whatever is!

Enter the DESTINIES *and* NEMESIS.

First Des. Glory to Arimanes! on the earth
His power increaseth—both my sisters did
His bidding, nor did I neglect my duty!
  Second Des. Glory to Arimanes! we who bow   20
The necks of men, bow down before his throne!
  Third Des. Glory to Arimanes! we await
His nod!
  Nem. Sovereign of Sovereigns! we are thine,
And all that liveth, more or less, is ours,
And most things wholly so; still to increase
Our power, increasing thine, demands our care,
And we are vigilant. Thy late commands
Have been fulfill'd to the utmost.

Enter MANFRED.

A Spirit.   What is here?
A mortal!—Thou most rash and fatal wretch,
Bow down and worship!
    Second Spirit.   I do know the man—
A Magician of great power, and fearful skill! 31
     Third Spirit. Bow down and worship,
       slave!—What, know'st thou not
Thine and our Sovereign?—Tremble, and
       obey!
    All the Spirits. Prostrate thyself, and thy
       condemned clay,
Child of the Earth! or dread the worst.
    Man.   I know it;
And yet ye see I kneel not.
     Fourth Spirit.   'T will be taught thee.
    Man. 'T is taught already;—many a night
       on the earth,
On the bare ground, have I bow'd down my
       face,
And strew'd my head with ashes; I have
       known   40
The fulness of humiliation, for
I sunk before my vain despair, and knelt
To my own desolation.
     Fifth Spirit.   Dost thou dare
Refuse to Arimanes on his throne
What the whole earth accords, beholding not
The terror of his glory?—Crouch, I say.
    Man. Bid *him* bow down to that which is
       above him,
The overruling Infinite—the Maker
Who made him not for worship—let him
       kneel,
And we will kneel together.
    The Spirits.   Crush the worm!
Tear him in pieces!—
    First Des. Hence! Avaunt!—he's mine. 50
Prince of the Powers invisible! This man
Is of no common order, as his port
And presence here denote; his sufferings
Have been of an immortal nature, like
Our own; his knowledge, and his powers and
       will,
As far as is compatible with clay,
Which clogs the ethereal essence, have been
       such
As clay hath seldom borne; his aspirations
Have been beyond the dwellers of the earth,
And they have only taught him what we
       know—   60
That knowledge is not happiness, and science
But an exchange of ignorance for that

Which is another kind of ignorance.
This is not all—the passions, attributes
Of earth and heaven, from which no power
       nor being,
Nor breath from the worm upwards is exempt
Have pierced his heart, and in their conse-
       quence
Made him a thing which I, who pity not,
Yet pardon those who pity. He is mine,
And thine, it may be; be it so, or not,   70
No other Spirit in this region hath
A soul like his—or power upon his soul.
    Nem. What doth he here then?
    First Des.   Let him answer that
    Man. Ye know what I have known; and
       without power
I could not be amongst ye: but there are
Powers deeper still beyond—I come in quest
Of such, to answer unto what I seek.
    Nem. What wouldst thou?
    Man.   Thou canst not reply to me
Call up the dead—my question is for them. 7
    Nem. Great Arimanes, doth thy will avouch
The wishes of this mortal?
    Ari.   Yea.
    Nem.   Whom wouldst thou
Uncharnel?
    Man.   One without a tomb—call up
Astarte.

NEMESIS.

Shadow! or Spirit!
    Whatever thou art,
Which still doth inherit
    The whole or a part
Of the form of thy birth,
    Of the mould of thy clay,
Which return'd to the earth,   90
    Re-appear to the day!
Bear what thou borest,
    The heart and the form,
And the aspect thou worest
    Redeem from the worm.
Appear!—Appear!—Appear!
Who sent thee there requires thee here!
    [*The Phantom of* ASTARTE *rises*
            and stands in the midst
    Man. Can this be death? there's bloom
       upon her cheek;
But now I see it is no living hue,   99
But a strange hectic—like the unnatural red
Which Autumn plants upon the perish'd leaf.
It is the same! Oh, God! that I should dread

To look upon the same—Astarte!—No,
I cannot speak to her—but bid her speak—
Forgive me or condemn me.

NEMESIS.

By the power which hath broken
   The grave which enthrall'd thee,
Speak to him who hath spoken,
   Or those who have call'd thee!
Man.   She is silent, 110
And in that silence I am more than answer'd.
Nem. My power extends no further. Prince
   of Air!
It rests with thee alone—command her voice.
Ari. Spirit—obey this sceptre!
Nem.   Silent still!
She is not of our order, but belongs
To the other powers. Mortal! thy quest is
   vain,
And we are baffled also.
Man.   Hear me, hear me—
Astarte! my beloved! speak to me:
I have so much endured—so much endure—
Look on me! the grave hath not changed thee
   more
Than I am changed for thee. Thou lovedst
   me   120
Too much, as I loved thee: we were not made
To torture thus each other, though it were
The deadliest sin to love as we have loved.
Say that thou loath'st me not—that I do
   bear
This punishment for both—that thou wilt be
One of the blessed—and that I shall die;
For hitherto all hateful things conspire
To bind me in existence—in a life
Which makes me shrink from immortality—
A future like the past. I cannot rest.   130
I know not what I ask, nor what I seek:
I feel but what thou art, and what I am;
And I would hear yet once before I perish
The voice which was my music—Speak to me!
For I have call'd on thee in the still night,
Startled the slumbering birds from the hush'd
   boughs,
And woke the mountain wolves, and made the
   caves
Acquainted with thy vainly echoed name,
Which answer'd me—many things answer'd
   me—
Spirits and men—but thou wert silent all. 140
Yet speak to me! I have outwatch'd the stars,
And gazed o'er heaven in vain in search of
   thee.

Speak to me! I have wander'd o'er the earth,
And never found thy likeness—Speak to me!
Look on the fiends around—they feel for me:
I fear them not, and feel for thee alone—
Speak to me! though it be in wrath;—but
   say—
I reck not what—but let me hear thee once—
This once—once more!
   Phantom of Astarte. Manfred!
   Man.   Say on, say on—
I live but in the sound—it is thy voice!   150
   Phan. Manfred! To-morrow ends thine
   earthly ills.
Farewell!
   Man. Yet one word more—am I forgiven?
   Phan. Farewell!
   Man.   Say, shall we meet again?
   Phan.   Farewell!
   Man. One word for mercy! Say, thou
   lovest me.
   Phan. Manfred!
             [*The Spirit of* ASTARTE *disappears.*
   Nem. She's gone, and will not be recall'd;
Her words will be fulfill'd. Return to the
   earth.
   A Spirit. He is convulsed.—This is to be a
   mortal
And seek the things beyond mortality.
   Another Spirit. Yet, see, he mastereth him-
   self, and makes
His torture tributary to his will.   160
Had he been one of us, he would have made
An awful spirit.
   Nem.   Hast thou further question
Of our great sovereign, or his worshippers?
   Man. None.
   Nem.   Then for a time farewell.
   Man. We meet then! Where? On the
   earth?—
Even as thou wilt: and for the grace ac-
   corded
I now depart a debtor. Fare ye well!
                 [*Exit* MANFRED.
   (*Scene closes.*)

ACT III

SCENE I.—*A Hall in the Castle of Manfred.*

MANFRED *and* HERMAN.

Man. What is the hour?
Her.   It wants but one till sunset

And promises a lovely twilight.
Man.   Say,
Are all things so disposed of in the tower
As I directed?
Her.   All, my lord, are ready:
Here is the key and casket.
Man.   It is well:
Thou may'st retire.

[*Exit* HERMAN.

Man. (*alone*). There is a calm upon me—
Inexplicable stillness! which till now
Did not belong to what I knew of life.
If that I did not know philosophy
To be of all our vanities the motliest,   10
The merest word that ever fool'd the ear
From out the schoolman's jargon, I should
     deem
The golden secret, the sought "Kalon," found,
And seated in my soul. It will not last,
But it is well to have known it, though but
     once;
It hath enlarged my thoughts with a new
     sense,
And I within my tablets would note down
That there is such a feeling. Who is there?

Re-enter HERMAN.

Her. My lord, the abbot of St. Maurice
     craves
To greet your presence.

Enter the ABBOT OF ST. MAURICE.

Abbot.   Peace be with Count Manfred!
Man. Thanks, holy father! welcome to
     these walls;   21
Thy presence honours them, and blesseth
     those
Who dwell within them.
Abbot.   Would it were so, Count!—
But I would fain confer with thee alone.
Man. Herman, retire.—What would my
     reverend guest?
Abbot. Thus, without prelude:—Age and
     zeal, my office,
And good intent, must plead my privilege;
Our near, though not acquainted neighbour-
     hood,
May also be my herald. Rumours strange,
And of unholy nature, are abroad,   30
And busy with thy name; a noble name
For centuries: may he who bears it now
Transmit it unimpair'd!

Man.   Proceed,—I listen.
Abbot. 'T is said thou holdest converse with
     the things
Which are forbidden to the search of man;
That with the dwellers of the dark abodes,
The many evil and unheavenly spirits
Which walk the valley of the shade of death,
Thou communest. I know that with mankind,
Thy fellows in creation, thou dost rarely   40
Exchange thy thoughts, and that thy solitude
Is as an anchorite's, were it but holy.
Man. And what are they who do avouch
     these things?
Abbot. My pious brethren—the scared
     peasantry—
Even thy own vassals—who do look on thee
With most unquiet eyes. Thy life's in peril.
Man. Take it.
Abbot.   I come to save, and not destroy:
I would not pry into thy secret soul;
But if these things be sooth, there still is
     time
For penitence and pity: reconcile thee   50
With the true church, and through the church
     to heaven.
Man. I hear thee. This is my reply: what-
     e'er
I may have been, or am, doth rest between
Heaven and myself. I shall not choose a
     mortal
To be my mediator. Have I sinn'd
Against your ordinances? prove and pun-
     ish!
Abbot. My son! I did not speak of punish-
     ment,
But penitence and pardon;—with thyself
The choice of such remains—and for the last,
Our institutions and our strong belief   60
Have given me power to smooth the path
     from sin
To higher hope and better thoughts; the first
I leave to heaven,—"Vengeance is mine
     alone!"
So saith the Lord, and with all humbleness
His servant echoes back the awful word.
Man. Old man! there is no power in holy
     men,
Nor charm in prayer, nor purifying form
Of penitence, nor outward look, nor fast,
Nor agony—nor, greater than all these,
The innate tortures of that deep despair,   70
Which is remorse without the fear of hell,
But all in all sufficient to itself
Would make a hell of heaven—can exorcise

From out the unbounded spirit the quick
sense
Of its own sins, wrongs, sufferance, and re-
venge
Upon itself; there is no future pang
Can deal that justice on the self-condemn'd
He deals on his own soul.

Abbot. All this is well;
For this will pass away, and be succeeded
By an auspicious hope, which shall look up 80
With calm assurance to that blessed place,
Which all who seek may win, whatever be
Their earthly errors, so they be atoned:
And the commencement of atonement is
The sense of its necessity. Say on—
And all our church can teach thee shall be
taught;
And all we can absolve thee shall be pardon'd.

Man. When Rome's sixth emperor was near
his last,
The victim of a self-inflicted wound,
To shun the torments of a public death 90
From senates once his slaves, a certain soldier,
With show of loyal pity, would have stanch'd
The gushing throat with his officious robe;
The dying Roman thrust him back, and said—
Some empire still in his expiring glance—
"It is too late—is this fidelity?"

Abbot. And what of this?

Man. I answer with the Roman—
"It is too late!"

Abbot. It never can be so,
To reconcile thyself with thy own soul,
And thy own soul with heaven. Hast thou
no hope? 100

'T is strange—even those who do despair
above,
Yet shape themselves some fantasy on earth,
To which frail twig they cling, like drowning
men.

Man. Ay—father! I have had those earthly
visions,
And noble aspirations in my youth,
To make my own the mind of other men,
The enlightener of nations; and to rise
I knew not whither—it might be to fall;
But fall, even as the mountain-cataract,
Which having leapt from its more dazzling
height, 110
Even in the foaming strength of its abyss,
(Which casts up misty columns that become
Clouds raining from the re-ascended skies,)
Lies low but mighty still.—But this is past,
My thoughts mistook themselves.

Abbot. And wherefore so?

Man. I could not tame my nature down;
for he
Must serve who fain would sway; and soothe,
and sue,
And watch all time, and pry into all place,
And be a living lie, who would become
A mighty thing amongst the mean, and such 120
The mass are; I disdain'd to mingle with
A herd, though to be leader—and of wolves.
The lion is alone, and so am I.

Abbot. And why not live and act with other
men?

Man. Because my nature was averse from
life;
And yet not cruel; for I would not make,
But find a desolation. Like the wind,
The red-hot breath of the most lone simoom,
Which dwells but in the desert, and sweeps
o'er
The barren sands which bear no shrubs to
blast, 130
And revels o'er their wild and arid waves,
And seeketh not, so that it is not sought,
But being met is deadly,—such hath been
The course of my existence; but there came
Things in my path which are no more.

Abbot. Alas!
I 'gin to fear that thou art past all aid
From me and from my calling; yet so young,
I still would——

Man. Look on me! there is an order
Of mortals on the earth, who do become
Old in their youth, and die ere middle age,
Without the violence of warlike death; 141
Some perishing of pleasure, some of study,
Some worn with toil, some of mere weariness,
Some of disease, and some insanity,
And some of wither'd or of broken hearts;
For this last is a malady which slays
More than are number'd in the lists of Fate,
Taking all shapes, and bearing many names.
Look upon me! for even of all these things
Have I partaken; and of all these things, 150
One were enough; then wonder not that I
Am what I am, but that I ever was,
Or having been, that I am still on earth.

Abbot. Yet, hear me still——

Man. Old man! I do respect
Thine order, and revere thine years; I deem
Thy purpose pious, but it is in vain:
Think me not churlish; I would spare thy-
self,
Far more than me, in shunning at this time

All further colloquy—and so—farewell.

[*Exit* MANFRED.

Abbot. This should have been a noble crea-
     ture: he   160
Hath all the energy which would have made
A goodly frame of glorious elements,
Had they been wisely mingled; as it is,
It is an awful chaos—light and darkness,
And mind and dust, and passions and pure
     thoughts
Mix'd, and contending without end or order,—
All dormant or destructive: he will perish,
And yet he must not; I will try once more.
For such are worth redemption; and my duty
Is to dare all things for a righteous end.   170
I 'll follow him—but cautiously, though surely.

SCENE II

Another Chamber.

MANFRED *and* HERMAN.

Her. My lord, you bade me wait on you at
     sunset:
He sinks behind the mountain.
Man.   Doth he so?
I will look on him. [MANFRED *advances to the*
                    Window of the Hall.
                       Glorious Orb! the idol
Of early nature, and the vigorous race
Of undiseased mankind, the giant sons
Of the embrace of angels, with a sex
More beautiful than they, which did draw
     down
The erring spirits who can ne'er return.—
Most glorious orb! that wert a worship, ere
The mystery of thy making was reveal'd!   10
Thou earliest minister of the Almighty,
Which gladden'd, on their mountain tops, the
     hearts
Of the Chaldean shepherds, till they pour'd
Themselves in orisons! Thou material God!
And representative of the Unknown—
Who chose thee for his shadow! Thou chief
     star!
Centre of many stars! which mak'st our earth
Endurable, and temperest the hues
And hearts of all who walk within thy rays!
Sire of the seasons! Monarch of the climes, 20
And those who dwell in them! for near or
     far,
Our inborn spirits have a tint of thee
Even as our outward aspects;—thou dost rise,

And shine, and set in glory. Fare thee well!
I ne'er shall see thee more. As my first
     glance
Of love and wonder was for thee, then take
My latest look; thou wilt not beam on one
To whom the gifts of life and warmth have
     been
Of a more fatal nature. He is gone:
I follow.   30

[*Exit* MANFRED.

SCENE III

*The Mountains—The Castle of Manfred at
some distance—A Terrace before a Tower—
Time, Twilight.*

HERMAN, MANUEL, *and other Dependants of*
MANFRED.

Her. 'T is strange enough; night after
     night, for years,
He hath pursued long vigils in this tower,
Without a witness. I have been within it,—
So have we all been oft-times; but from it,
Or its contents, it were impossible
To draw conclusions absolute, of aught
His studies tend to. To be sure, there is
One chamber where none enter: I would give
The fee of what I have to come these three
     years,
To pore upon its mysteries.   10
Manuel.   'T were dangerous;
Content thyself with what thou know'st al-
     ready.
Her. Ah. Manuel! thou art elderly and
     wise,
And couldst say much; thou hast dwelt within
     the castle—
How many years is 't?
Manuel.   Ere Count Manfred's birth,
I served his father, whom he nought re-
     sembles.
Her. There be more sons in like predica-
     ment.
But wherein do they differ?
Manuel.   I speak not
Of features or of form, but mind and habits;
Count Sigismund was proud, but gay and
     free,—
A warrior and a reveller; he dwelt not   20
With books and solitude, nor made the night
A gloomy vigil, but a festal time,
Merrier than day; he did not walk the rocks

And forests like a wolf, nor turn aside
From men and their delights.

Her.   Beshrew the hour,
But those were jocund times! I would that
     such
Would visit the old walls again; they look
As if they had forgotten them.

Manuel.   These walls
Must change their chieftain first. Oh! I have
     seen
Some strange things in them, Herman.   30

Her.   Come, be friendly;
Relate me some to while away our watch:
I've heard thee darkly speak of an event
Which happen'd hereabouts, by this same
     tower.

Manuel. That was a night indeed! I do
     remember
'T was twilight, as it may be now, and such
Another evening;—yon red cloud, which rests
On Eigher's pinnacle, so rested then,—
So like that it might be the same; the wind
Was faint and gusty, and the mountain snows
Began to glitter with the climbing moon;   40
Count Manfred was, as now, within his
     tower,—
How occupied, we knew not, but with him
The sole companion of his wanderings
And watchings—her, whom of all earthly
     things
That lived, the only thing he seem'd to
     love,—
As he, indeed, by blood was bound to do,
The lady Astarte, his—
                    Hush! who comes here?

Enter the ABBOT.

Abbot. Where is your master?

Her.   Yonder in the tower.

Abbot. I must speak with him.

Manuel.   'T is impossible;
He is most private, and must not be thus   50
Intruded on.

Abbot.   Upon myself I take
The forfeit of my fault, if fault there be—
But I must see him.

Her.   Thou hast seen him once
This eve already.

Abbot.   Herman! I command thee,
Knock, and apprize the Count of my ap-
     proach.

Her. We dare not.

Abbot.   Then it seems I must be herald
Of my own purpose.

Manuel.   Reverend father, stop—
I pray you pause.

Abbot.   Why so?

Manuel.   But step this way,
And I will tell you further.

                    [*Exeunt.*

SCENE IV

Interior of the Tower.

MANFRED *alone.*

The stars are forth, the moon above the tops
Of the snow-shining mountains.—Beautiful!
I linger yet with Nature, for the Night
Hath been to me a more familiar face
Than that of man; and in her starry shade
Of dim and solitary loveliness,
I learn'd the language of another world.
I do remember me, that in my youth,
When I was wandering,—upon such a night
I stood within the Coliseum's wall,   10
'Midst the chief relics of almighty Rome;
The trees which grew along the broken
     arches
Waved dark in the blue midnight, and the
     stars
Shone through the rents of ruin; from afar
The watch-dog bay'd beyond the Tiber; and
More near from out the Cæsars' palace came
The owl's long cry, and, interruptedly,
Of distant sentinels the fitful song
Begun and died upon the gentle wind.   19
Some cypresses beyond the time-worn breach
Appear'd to skirt the horizon, yet they stood
Within a bowshot. Where the Cæsars dwelt,
And dwell the tuneless birds of night, amidst
A grove which springs through levell'd battle-
     ments,
And twines its roots with the imperial hearths,
Ivy usurps the laurel's place of growth;
But the gladiators' bloody Circus stands,
A noble wreck in ruinous perfection,
While Cæsar's chambers, and the Augustan
     halls,
Grovel on earth in indistinct decay.   30
And thou didst shine, thou rolling moon, upon
All this, and cast a wide and tender light,
Which soften'd down the hoar austerity
Of rugged desolation, and fill'd up,
As 't were anew, the gaps of centuries;

Leaving that beautiful which still was so,
And making that which was not, till the place
Became religion, and the heart ran o'er
With silent worship of the great of old,—
The dead but sceptred sovereigns, who still
    rule   40
Our spirits from their urns.
                        'T was such a night!
'T is strange that I recall it at this time;
But I have found our thoughts take wildest
    flight
Even at the moment when they should array
Themselves in pensive order.

Enter the ABBOT.

    Abbot.   My good lord!
I crave a second grace for this approach:
But yet let not my humble zeal offend
By its abruptness—all it hath of ill
Recoils on me; its good in the effect
May light upon your head—could I say
    heart—   50
Could I touch *that,* with words or prayers, I
    should
Recall a noble spirit which hath wander'd;
But is not yet all lost.
    Man.   Thou know'st me not;
My days are number'd, and my deeds re-
    corded:
Retire, or 't will be dangerous—Away!
    Abbot. Thou dost not mean to menace me?
    Man.   Not I;
I simply tell thee peril is at hand,
And would preserve thee.
    Abbot.   What dost thou mean?
    Man.   Look there!
What dost thou see?
    Abbot.   Nothing.
    Man.   Look there I say,
And steadfastly;—now tell me what thou
    seest?   60
    Abbot. That which should shake me, but
        I fear it not:
I see a dusk and awful figure rise,
Like an infernal god, from out the earth;
His face wrapt in a mantle, and his form
Robed as with angry clouds: he stands be-
    tween
Thyself and me—but I do fear him not.
    Man. Thou hast no cause—he shall not
        harm thee—but
His sight may shock thine old limbs into
    palsy.

I say to thee— Retire!
    Abbot.   And I reply—   6
Never—till I have battled with this fiend:—
What doth he here?
    Man.   Why—ay—what doth he here?
I did not send for him,—he is unbidden.
    Abbot. Alas! lost mortal! what with guests
        like these
Hast thou to do? I tremble for thy sake:
Why doth he gaze on thee, and thou on him?
Ah! he unveils his aspect: on his brow
The thunder-scars are graven: from his eye
Glares forth the immortality of hell—
Avaunt!—
    Man.   Pronounce—what is thy mission?
    Spirit.   Come!
    Abbot. What art thou, unknown being?
        answer!—speak!   80
    Spirit. The genius of this mortal.—Come!
't is time.
    Man. I am prepared for all things, but deny
The power which summons me. Who sent thee
    here?
    Spirit. Thou'lt know anon— Come! come!
    Man.   I have commanded
Things of an essence greater far than thine,
And striven with thy masters. Get thee hence!
    Spirit. Mortal! thine hour is come— Away!
    I say.
    Man. I knew, and know my hour is come,
        but not
To render up my soul to such as thee:
Away! I'll die as I have lived—alone.   90
    Spirit. Then I must summon up my breth-
        ren.—Rise!
                [Other Spirits rise up.
    Abbot. Avaunt! ye evil ones!—Avaunt! I
        say;
Ye have no power where piety hath power,
And I do charge ye in the name——
    Spirit.   Old man!
We know ourselves, our mission, and thine
    order;
Waste not thy holy words on idle uses,
It were in vain: this man is forfeited.
Once more I summon him—Away, Away!
    Man. I do defy ye,—though I feel my soul
Is ebbing from me, yet I do defy ye;   100
Nor will I hence, while I have earthly breath
To breathe my scorn upon ye—earthly
    strength
To wrestle, though with spirits; what ye take
Shall be ta'en limb by limb.
    Spirit.   Reluctant mortal!

Is this the Magian who would so pervade
The world invisible, and make himself
Almost our equal? Can it be that thou
Art thus in love with life? the very life
Which made thee wretched!

   Man.   Thou false fiend, thou liest!
My life is in its last hour,—*that* I know,   110
Nor would redeem a moment of that hour;
I do not combat against death, but thee
And thy surrounding angels; my past power,
Was purchased by no compact with thy crew,
But by superior science—penance, daring,
And length of watching, strength of mind,
    and skill
In knowledge of our fathers—when the earth
Saw men and spirits walking side by side,
And gave ye no supremacy: I stand
Upon my strength—I do defy—deny—   120
Spurn back, and scorn ye!—

   Spirit.   But thy many crimes
Have made thee——

   Man.   What are they to such as thee?
Must crimes be punish'd but by other crimes,
And greater criminals?—Back to thy hell!
Thou hast no power upon me, *that* I feel;
Thou never shalt possess me, *that* I know:
What I have done is done; I bear within
A torture which could nothing gain from
    thine:
The mind which is immortal makes itself
Requital for its good or evil thoughts,— 130
Is its own origin of ill and end
And its own place and time: its innate sense,
When stripp'd of this mortality, derives
No colour from the fleeting things without,
But is absorb'd in sufferance or in joy,
Born from the knowledge of its own desert.
Thou didst not tempt me, and thou couldst
    not tempt me;
I have not been thy dupe, nor am thy prey—
But was my own destroyer, and will be   139
My own hereafter.—Back, ye baffled fiends!—
The hand of death is on me—but not yours!
          [*The Demons disappear.*

   Abbot. Alas! how pale thou art—thy lips
    are white—
And thy breast heaves—and in thy gasping
    throat
The accents rattle: Give thy prayers to
    heaven—
Pray—albeit but in thought,—but die not
    thus.

   Man. 'T is over—my dull eyes can fix thee
    not;

But all things swim around me, and the earth
Heaves as it were beneath me. Fare thee
    well!
Give me thy hand.

   Abbot.   Cold—cold—even to the heart—
But yet one prayer— Alas! how fares it with
    thee?   150

   Man. Old man! 't is not so difficult to die.
               [MANFRED *expires.*

   Abbot. He's gone—his soul hath ta'en its
    earthless flight;
Whither? I dread to think—but he is gone.

DON JUAN

Canto the Second

I

Oh ye! who teach the ingenuous youth of
    nations,
   Holland, France, England, Germany, or
    Spain,
I pray ye flog them upon all occasions,
   It mends their morals, never mind the pain:
The best of mothers and of educations
   In Juan's case were but employ'd in vain,
Since, in a way that's rather of the oddest, he
Became divested of his native modesty.

II

Had he but been placed in a public school,
   In the third form, or even in the fourth, 10
His daily task had kept his fancy cool,
   At least, had he been nurtured in the
    north;
Spain may prove an exception to the rule,
   But then exceptions always prove its
    worth—
A lad of sixteen causing a divorce
Puzzled his tutors very much, of course.

III

I can't say that it puzzles me at all,
   If all things be consider'd; first, there was
His lady-mother, mathematical,
   A——never mind;—his tutor, an old ass; 20
A pretty woman—(that's quite natural,
   Or else the thing had hardly come to pass)
A husband rather old, not much in unity

With his young wife—a time, and opportunity.

IV

Well—well; the world must turn upon its
  axis,
  And all mankind turn with it, heads or
  tails,
And live and die, make love and pay our
  taxes,
  And as the veering wind shifts, shift our
  sails;
The king commands us, and the doctor
  quacks us,
  The priest instructs, and so our life ex-
  hales,   30
A little breath, love, wine, ambition, fame,
Fighting, devotion, dust,—perhaps a name.

V

I said, that Juan had been sent to Cadiz—
  A pretty town, I recollect it well—
'T is there the mart of the colonial trade is,
  (Or was, before Peru learn'd to rebel,)
And such sweet girls—I mean, such graceful
  ladies,
  Their very walk would make your bosom
  swell;
I can't describe it, though so much it strike,
Nor liken it—I never saw the like: 40

VI

An Arab horse, a stately stag, a barb
  New broke, a cameleopard, a gazelle,
No—none of these will do;—and then their
  garb,
  Their veil and petticoat— Alas! to dwell
Upon such things would very near absorb
  A canto—then their feet and ankles,—well
Thank Heaven I've got no metaphor quite
  ready,
(And so, my sober Muse—come, let's be
  steady—

VII

Chaste Muse!—well, if you must, you must)
  —the veil
  Thrown back a moment with the glancing
  hand,   50

While the o'erpowering eye, that turns you
  pale,
  Flashes into the heart:—Ah sunny land
Of love! when I forget you, may I fail
  To——say my prayers—but never was
  there plann'd
A dress through which the eyes give such a
  volley,
Excepting the Venetian Fazzioli.

VIII

But to our tale: the Donna Inez sent
  Her son to Cadiz only to embark;
To stay there had not answer'd her intent,
  But why?—we leave the reader in the
  dark—   60
'T was for a voyage the young man was
  meant,
  As if a Spanish ship were Noah's ark,
To wean him from the wickedness of earth,
And send him like a dove of promise forth.

IX

Don Juan bade his valet pack his things
  According to direction, then received
A lecture and some money: for four springs
  He was to travel; and though Inez grieved
(As every kind of parting has its stings),
  She hoped he would improve—perhaps be-
  lieved: 70
A letter, too, she gave (he never read it)
Of good advice—and two or three of credit.

X

In the mean time, to pass her hours away,
  Brave Inez now set up a Sunday school
For naughty children, who would rather play
  (Like truant rogues) the devil, or the fool;
Infants of three years old were taught that
  day,
  Dunces were whipt, or set upon a stool:
The great success of Juan's education
Spurr'd her to teach another generation.   80

XI

Juan embark'd—the ship got under way,
  The wind was fair, the water passing
  rough;
A devil of a sea rolls in that bay,

As I who've cross'd it oft, know well
    enough;
And, standing upon deck, the dashing spray
    Flies in one's face, and makes it weather-
        tough:
And there he stood to take, and take again,
His first—perhaps his last—farewell of Spain.

XII

I can't but say it is an awkward sight
    To see one's native land receding through
The growing waters; it unmans one quite, 91
    Especially when life is rather new:
I recollect Great Britain's coast looks white,
    But almost every other country's blue,
When gazing on them, mystified by distance,
We enter on our nautical existence.

XIII

So Juan stood, bewilder'd on the deck:
    The wind sung, cordage strain'd, and sail-
        ors swore,
And the ship creak'd, the town became a
        speck,
    From which away so fair and fast they
        bore. 100
The best of remedies is a beef-steak
    Against sea-sickness: try it, sir, before
You sneer, and I assure you this is true,
For I have found it answer—so may you.

XIV

Don Juan stood, and, gazing from the stern,
    Beheld his native Spain receding far:
First partings form a lesson hard to learn,
    Even nations feel this when they go to
        war;
There is a sort of unexprest concern, 109
    A kind of shock that sets one's heart ajar;
At leaving even the most unpleasant people
And places, one keeps looking at the steeple.

XV

But Juan had got many things to leave,
    His mother, and a mistress, and no wife,
So that he had much better cause to grieve
    Than many persons more advanced in life;
And if we now and then a sigh must heave
    At quitting even those we quit in strife,

No doubt we weep for those the heart en-
    dears— 119
That is, till deeper griefs congeal our tears.

XVI

So Juan wept, as wept the captive Jews
    By Babel's waters, still remembering Sion:
I'd weep,—but mine is not a weeping Muse,
    And such light griefs are not a thing to
        die on;
Young men should travel, if but to amuse
    Themselves; and the next time their serv-
        ants tie on
Behind their carriages their new portmanteau,
Perhaps it may be lined with this my canto.

XVII

And Juan wept, and much he sigh'd and
        thought,
    While his salt tears dropp'd into the salt
        sea, 130
"Sweets to the sweet"; (I like so much to
        quote;
    You must excuse this extract,—'t is where
        she,
The Queen of Denmark, for Ophelia brought
    Flowers to the grave;) and, sobbing often,
        he
Reflected on his present situation,
And seriously resolved on reformation.

XVIII

"Farewell, my Spain! a long farewell!" he
        cried,
    "Perhaps I may revisit thee no more,
But die, as many an exiled heart hath died,
    Of its own thirst to see again thy shore: 140
Farewell, where Guadalquivir's waters glide!
    Farewell, my mother! and, since all is o'er,
Farewell, too, dearest Julia!—(here he drew
Her letter out again, and read it through.)

XIX

"And oh! if e'er I should forget, I swear—
    But that's impossible, and cannot be—
Sooner shall this blue ocean melt to air,
    Sooner shall earth resolve itself to sea,
Than I resign thine image, oh, my fair!
    Or think of anything, excepting thee; 150
A mind diseased no remedy can physic—

(Here the ship gave a lurch, and he grew
    sea-sick.)

XX

"Sooner shall heaven kiss earth—(here he fell
    sicker)
  Oh, Julia! what is every other woe?—
(For God's sake let me have a glass of liquor;
  Pedro, Battista, help me down below.)
Julia, my love—(you rascal, Pedro, quicker)—
  Oh, Julia!—(this curst vessel pitches so)—
Beloved Julia, hear me still beseeching!"
(Here he grew inarticulate with retching.) 160

XXI

He felt that chilling heaviness of heart,
  Or rather stomach, which, alas! attends,
Beyond the best apothecary's art,
  The loss of love, the treachery of friends,
Or death of those we dote on, when a part
  Of us dies with them as each fond hope
    ends:
No doubt he would have been much more
    pathetic,
But the sea acted as a strong emetic.

XXII

Love's a capricious power: I've known it
  hold
  Out through a fever caused by its own
    heat, 170
But be much puzzled by a cough and cold,
  And find a quinsy very hard to treat;
Against all noble maladies he's bold,
  But vulgar illnesses don't like to meet,
Nor that a sneeze should interrupt his sigh,
Nor inflammations redden his blind eye.

XXIII

But worst of all is nausea, or a pain
  About the lower region of the bowels;
Love, who heroically breathes a vein,
  Shrinks from the application of hot towels,
And purgatives are dangerous to his reign, 181
  Sea-sickness death: his love was perfect,
    how else
Could Juan's passion, while the billows roar,
Resist his stomach, ne'er at sea before?

XXIV

The ship, call'd the most holy "Trinidada,"
  Was steering duly for the port Leghorn;
For there the Spanish family Moncada
  Were settled long ere Juan's sire was born:
They were relations, and for them he had a
  Letter of introduction, which the morn 190
Of his departure had been sent him by
His Spanish friends for those in Italy.

XXV

His suite consisted of three servants and
  A tutor, the licentiate Pedrillo,
Who several languages did understand,
  But now lay sick and speechless on his
    pillow,
And, rocking in his hammock, long'd for land,
  His headache béing increased by every bil-
    low;
And the waves oozing through the port-hole
  made
His berth a little damp, and him afraid. 200

XXVI

'T was not without some reason, for the wind
  Increased at night, until it blew a gale;
And though 't was not much to a naval mind,
  Some landsmen would have look'd a little
    pale,
For sailors are, in fact, a different kind:
  At sunset they began to take in sail,
For the sky show'd it would come on to blow,
And carry away, perhaps, a mast or so.

XXVII

At one o'clock the wind with sudden shift
  Threw the ship right into the trough of
    the sea, 210
Which struck her aft, and made an awkward
  rift,
  Started the stern-post, also shatter'd the
Whole of her stern-frame, and, ere she could
  lift
  Herself from out her present jeopardy,
The rudder tore away: 't was time to sound
The pumps, and there were four feet water
    found.

XXVIII

One gang of people instantly was put
    Upon the pumps, and the remainder set
To get up part of the cargo, and what not;
    But they could not come at the leak as
        yet;   220
At last they did get at it really, but
    Still their salvation was an even bet:
The water rush'd through in a way quite
        puzzling,
While they thrust sheets, shirts, jackets, bales
        of muslin,

XXIX

Into the opening; but all such ingredients
    Would have been vain, and they must have
        gone down,
Despite of all their efforts and expedients.
    But for the pumps: I'm glad to make them
        known
To all the brother tars who may have need
        hence,
    For fifty tons of water were upthrown   230
By them per hour, and they all had been un-
        done,
But for the maker, Mr. Mann, of London.

XXX

As day advanced the weather seem'd to abate,
    And then the leak they reckon'd to reduce,
And keep the ship afloat, though three feet
        yet
    Kept two hand and one chain-pump still
        in use.
The wind blew fresh again: as it grew late
    A squall came on, and while some guns
        broke loose,
A gust—which all descriptive power tran-
        scends—
Laid with one blast the ship on her beam
    ends.   240

XXXI

There she lay, motionless, and seem'd upset;
    The water left the hold, and wash'd the
        decks,
And made a scene men do not soon forget;
    For they remember battles, fires, and
        wrecks,
Or any other thing that brings regret,

Or breaks their hopes, or hearts, or heads,
        or necks;
Thus drownings are much talk'd of by the
        divers,
And swimmers, who may chance to be sur-
        vivors.

XXXII

Immediately the masts were cut away,
    Both main and mizen: first the mizen
        went,   250
The main-mast follow'd; but the ship still
        lay
    Like a mere log, and baffled our intent.
Foremast and bowsprit were cut down, and
        they
    Eased her at last (although we never meant
To part with all till every hope was blighted),
And then with violence the old ship righted.

XXXIII

It may be easily supposed, while this
    Was going on, some people were unquiet,
That passengers would find it much amiss
    To lose their lives, as well as spoil their
        diet;   260
That even the able seaman, deeming his
    Days nearly o'er, might be disposed to riot,
As upon such occasions tars will ask
For grog, and sometimes drink rum from the
        cask.

XXXIV

There's nought, no doubt, so much the spirit
        calms
    As rum and true religion: thus it was,
Some plunder'd, some drank spirits, some
        sung psalms,
    The high wind made the treble, and as bass
The hoarse harsh waves kept time; fright
        cured the qualms
    Of all the luckless landsmen's sea-sick
        maws: 270
Strange sounds of wailing, blasphemy, devo-
        tion,
Clamour'd in chorus to the roaring ocean.

XXXV

Perhaps more mischief had been done, but for
    Our Juan, who, with sense beyond his
        years,

Got to the spirit-room, and stood before
　It with a pair of pistols; and their fears,
As if Death were more dreadful by his door
　Of fire than water, spite of oaths and tears,
Kept still aloof the crew, who, ere they sunk,
Thought it would be becoming to die
　　drunk.   280

XXXVI

"Give us more grog," they cried, "for it will
　　be
　All one an hour hence." Juan answer'd,
　　"No!
'T is true that death awaits both you and me,
　But let us die like men, not sink below
Like brutes:"—and thus his dangerous post
　　kept he,
　And none liked to anticipate the blow;
And even Pedrillo, his most reverend tutor,
Was for some rum a disappointed suitor.

XXXVII

The good old gentleman was quite aghast,
　And made a loud and pious lamentation; 290
Repented all his sins, and made a last
　Irrevocable vow of reformation;
Nothing should tempt him more (this peril
　　past)
　To quit his academic occupation,
In cloisters of the classic Salamanca,
To follow Juan's wake, like Sancho Panca.

XXXVIII

But now there came a flash of hope once
　　more;
　Day broke, and the wind lull'd: the masts
　　were gone;
The leak increased; shoals round her, but no
　　shore,
　The vessel swam, yet still she held her
　　own.   300
They tried the pumps again, and though be-
　　fore
　Their desperate efforts seem'd all useless
　　grown,
A glimpse of sunshine set some hands to
　　bale—
The stronger pump'd, the weaker thrumm'd
　a sail.

XXXIX

Under the vessel's keel the sail was pass'd,
　And for the moment it had some effect;
But with a leak, and not a stick of mast,
　Nor rag of canvas, what could they expect?
But still 't is best to struggle to the last,
　'T is never too late to be wholly wreck'd: 310
And though 't is true that man can only die
　　once,
'T is not so pleasant in the Gulf of Lyons.

XL

There winds and waves had hurl'd them, and
　　from thence,
　Without their will, they carried them away;
For they were forced with steering to dis-
　　pense,
　And never had as yet a quiet day
On which they might repose, or even com-
　　mence
　A jurymast or rudder, or could say
The ship would swim an hour, which, by good
　　luck,
Still swam—though not exactly like a duck. 320

XLI

The wind, in fact, perhaps, was rather less,
　But the ship labour'd so, they scarce could
　　hope
To weather out much longer; the distress
　Was also great with which they had to
　　cope
For want of water, and their solid mess
　Was scant enough: in vain the telescope
Was used—nor sail nor shore appear'd in
　　sight,
Nought but the heavy sea, and coming night.

XLII

Again the weather threaten'd,—again blew
　A gale, and in the fore and after hold   330
Water appear'd; yet, though the people knew
　All this, the most were patient, and some
　　bold,
Until the chains and leathers were worn
　　through
　Of all our pumps:—a wreck complete she
　　roll'd,
At mercy of the waves, whose mercies are
Like human beings during civil war.

XLIII

Then came the carpenter, at last, with tears
  In his rough eyes, and told the captain, he
Could do no more: he was a man in years,
  And long had voyaged through many a
      stormy sea,   340
And if he wept at length, they were not fears
  That made his eyelids as a woman's be,
But he, poor fellow, had a wife and children,
Two things for dying people quite bewildering.

XLIV

The ship was evidently settling now
  Fast by the head; and, all distinction gone,
Some went to prayers again, and made a vow
  Of candles to their saints—but there were
    none
To pay them with; and some look'd o'er the
    bow;
  Some hoisted out the boats; and there was
    one   350
That begged Pedrillo for an absolution,
Who told him to be damn'd—in his con-
    fusion.

XLV

Some lash'd them in their hammocks; some
    put on
  Their best clothes, as if going to a fair;
Some cursed the day on which they saw the
    sun,
  And gnash'd their teeth, and howling, tore
    their hair;
And others went on as they had begun,
  Getting the boats out, being well aware
That a tight boat will live in a rough sea,
Unless with breakers close beneath her lee. 360

XLVI

The worst of all was, that in their condition,
  Having been several days in great distress,
'T was difficult to get out such provision
  As now might render their long suffering
    less:
Men, even when dying, dislike inanition;
  Their stock was damaged by the weather's
    stress:
Two casks of biscuit, and a keg of butter,
Were all that could be thrown into the cutter.

XLVII

But in the long-boat they contrived to stow
  Some pounds of bread, though injured by
    the wet;   370
Water, a twenty-gallon cask or so;
  Six flasks of wine: and they contrived to
    get
A portion of their beef up from below,
  And with a piece of pork, moreover, met,
But scarce enough to serve them for a
    luncheon—
Then there was rum, eight gallons in a
    puncheon.

XLVIII

The other boats, the yawl and pinnace, had
  Been stove in the beginning of the gale;
And the long-boat's condition was but bad,
  As there were but two blankets for a sail,
And one oar for a mast, which a young lad 381
  Threw in by good luck over the ship's rail;
And two boats could not hold, far less be
    stored,
To save one half the people then on board.

XLIX

'T was twilight, and the sunless day went
    down
  Over the waste of waters; like a veil,
Which, if withdrawn, would but disclose the
    frown
  Of one whose hate is mask'd but to assail.
Thus to their hopeless eyes the night was
    shown,
  And grimly darkled o'er the faces pale, 390
And the dim desolate deep: twelve days had
    Fear
Been their familiar, and now Death was here.

L

Some trial had been making at a raft,
  With little hope in such a rolling sea,
A sort of thing at which one would have
    laugh'd,
  If any laughter at such times could be,
Unless with people who too much have
    quaff'd,
  And have a kind of wild and horrid glee,
Half epileptical, and half hysterical:—

Their preservation would have been a miracle.   400

LI

At half-past eight o'clock, booms, hencoops,
    spars,
    And all things, for a chance, had been cast
      loose
That still could keep afloat the struggling
    tars,
    For yet they strove, although of no great
      use:
There was no light in heaven but a few stars,
    The boats put off o'ercrowded with their
      crews;
She gave a heel, and then a lurch to port,
And, going down head foremost—sunk, in
    short.

LII

Then rose from sea to sky the wild farewell—
    Then shriek'd the timid, and stood still the
      brave—   410
Then some leap'd overboard with dreadful
    yell,
    As eager to anticipate their grave;
And the sea yawn'd around her like a hell,
    And down she suck'd with her the whirling
      wave,
Like one who grapples with his enemy,
And strives to strangle him before he die.

LIII

And first one universal shriek there rush'd.
    Louder than the loud ocean, like a crash
Of echoing thunder; and then all was hush'd,
    Save the wild wind and the remorseless
      dash   420
Of billows; but at intervals there gush'd,
    Accompanied with a convulsive splash,
A solitary shriek, the bubbling cry
Of some strong swimmer in his agony.

LIV

The boats, as stated, had got off before,
    And in them crowded several of the crew;
And yet their present hope was hardly more
    Than what it had been, for so strong it
      blew
There was slight chance of reaching any
    shore;

And then they were too many, though so
    few—   430
Nine in the cutter, thirty in the boat,
Were counted in them when they got afloat.

LV

All the rest perish'd; near two hundred souls
    Had left their bodies; and what's worse,
      alas!
When over Catholics the ocean rolls,
    They must wait several weeks before a
      mass
Takes off one peck of purgatorial coals,
    Because, till people know what's come to
      pass,
They won't lay out their money on the
    dead—
It costs three francs for every mass that's
    said.   440

LVI

Juan got into the long-boat, and there
    Contrived to help Pedrillo to a place;
It seem'd as if they had exchanged their
    care,
    For Juan wore the magisterial face
Which courage gives, while poor Pedrillo's
    pair
    Of eyes were crying for their owner's case:
Battista, though (a name called shortly Tita),
Was lost by getting at some aqua-vita.

LVII

Pedro, his valet, too, he tried to save,
    But the same cause, conducive to his loss, 450
Left him so drunk, he jump'd into the wave,
    As o'er the cutter's edge he tried to cross,
And so he found a wine-and-watery grave;
    They could not rescue him although so
      close,
Because the sea ran higher every minute,
And for the boat—the crew kept crowding
    in it.

LVIII

A small old spaniel—which had been Don
    Jóse's,
    His father's, whom he loved, as ye may
      think,
For on such things the memory reposes

With tenderness—stood howling on the
  brink, 460
Knowing, (dogs have such intellectual noses!)
  No doubt the vessel was about to sink;
And Juan caught him up, and ere he stepp'd
Off threw him in, then after him he leap'd.

LIX

He also stuff'd his money where he could
  About his person, and Pedrillo's too,
Who let him do, in fact, whate'er he would,
  Not knowing what himself to say, or do,
As every rising wave his dread renew'd;
  But Juan trusting they might still get
    through, 470
And deeming there were remedies for any ill,
Thus re-embark'd his tutor and his spaniel.

LX

'T was a rough night, and blew so stiffly yet,
  That the sail was becalm'd between the
    seas,
Though on the wave's high top too much to
    set,
  They dared not take it in for all the breeze:
Each sea curl'd o'er the stern, and kept
    them wet,
  And made them bale without a moment's
    ease,
So that themselves as well as hopes were
    damp'd,
And the poor little cutter quickly swamp'd. 480

LXI

Nine souls more went in her: the long-boat
  still
  Kept above water, with an oar for mast,
Two blankets stitch'd together, answering ill
  Instead of sail, were to the oar made fast:
Though every wave roll'd menacing to fill,
  And present peril all before surpass'd,
They grieved for those who perish'd with the
    cutter,
And also for the biscuit-casks and butter.

LXII

The sun rose red and fiery, a sure sign
  Of the continuance of the gale: to run 490
Before the sea until it should grow fine,
  Was all that for the present could be done:
A few tea-spoonfuls of their rum and wine

Were served out to the people, who begun
  To faint, and damaged bread wet through the
    bags,
And most of them had little clothes but rags.

LXIII

They counted thirty, crowded in a space
  Which left scarce room for motion or ex-
    ertion;
They did their best to modify their case,
  One-half sat up, though numb'd with the
    immersion, 500
While t 'other half were laid down in their
    place,
  At watch and watch; thus, shivering like
    the tertian
Ague in its cold fit, they fill'd their boat,
With nothing but the sky for a great coat.

LXIV

'T is very certain the desire of life
  Prolongs it: this is obvious to physicians,
When patients, neither plagued with friends
    nor wife,
  Survive through very desperate conditions,
Because they still can hope, nor shines the
    knife
  Nor shears of Atropos before their vi-
    sions: 510
Despair of all recovery spoils longevity,
And makes men's miseries of alarming brevity.

LXV

'T is said that persons living on annuities
  Are longer lived than others,—God knows
    why,
Unless to plague the grantors,—yet so true
    it is,
  That some, I really think, *do* never die;
Of any creditors the worst a Jew it is,
  And *that's* their mode of furnishing supply:
In my young days they lent me cash that
    way,
Which I found very troublesome to pay. 520

LXVI

'T is thus with people in an open boat,
  They live upon the love of life, and bear
More than can be believed, or even thought,

And stand like rocks the tempest's wear
    and tear;
And hardship still has been the sailor's lot,
    Since Noah's ark went cruising here and
        there;
She had a curious crew as well as cargo,
Like the first old Greek privateer, the Argo.

LXVII

But man is a carnivorous production,
    And must have meals, at least one meal a
        day;   530
He cannot live, like woodcocks, upon suction,
    But, like the shark and tiger, must have
        prey;
Although his anatomical construction
    Bears vegetables, in a grumbling way,
Your labouring people think beyond all ques-
    tion
Beef, veal, and mutton, better for digestion.

LXVIII

And thus it was with this our hapless crew;
    For on the third day there came on a
        calm,
And though at first their strength it might
    renew,
    And lying on their weariness like balm, 540
Lull'd them like turtles sleeping on the blue
    Of ocean, when they woke they felt a
        qualm,
And fell all ravenously on their provision,
Instead of hoarding it with due precision.

LXIX

The consequence was easily foreseen—
    They ate up all they had, and drank their
        wine,
In spite of all remonstrances, and then
    On what, in fact, next day were they to
        dine?
They hoped the wind would rise, these foolish
    men!
    And carry them to shore; these hopes
        were fine,   550
But as they had but one oar, and that brittle,
It would have been more wise to save their
    victual.

LXX

The fourth day came, but not a breath of
    air,

And Ocean slumber'd like an unwean'd
    child:
The fifth day, and their boat lay floating
    there,
    The sea and sky were blue, and clear, and
        mild—
With their one oar (I wish they had had a
    pair)
    What could they do? and hunger's rage
        grew wild:
So Juan's spaniel, spite of his entreating,
Was kill'd, and portion'd out for present eat-
    ing.   560

LXXI

On the sixth day they fed upon his hide,
    And Juan, who had still refused, because
The creature was his father's dog that died,
    Now feeling all the vulture in his jaws,
With some remorse received (though first
    denied)
    As a great favour one of the fore-paws,
Which he divided with Pedrillo, who
Devour'd it, longing for the other too.

LXXII

The seventh day, and no wind—the burning
    sun
    Blister'd and scorch'd, and, stagnant on
        the sea,   570
They lay like carcasses; and hope was none,
    Save in the breeze that came not: savagely
They glared upon each other—all was done,
    Water, and wine, and food,—and you might
        see
The longings of the cannibal arise
(Although they spoke not) in their wolfish
    eyes.

LXXIII

At length one whisper'd his companion, who
    Whisper'd another, and thus it went round,
And then into a hoarser murmur grew,
    An ominous, and wild, and desperate
        sound;   580
And when his comrade's thought each suf-
    ferer knew,
    'T was but his own, suppress'd till now, he
        found:
And out they spoke of lots for flesh and blood,
And who should die to be his fellow's food.

LXXIV

But ere they came to this, they that day
    shared
    Some leathern caps, and what remain'd of
      shoes;
And then they look'd around them, and de-
    spair'd,
    And none to be the sacrifice would choose;
At length the lots were torn up, and prepared.
    But of materials that must shock the
    Muse—   590
Having no paper, for the want of better,
They took by force from Juan Julia's letter.

LXXV

Then lots were made, and mark'd, and mix'd,
    and handed
    In silent horror, and their distribution
Lull'd even the savage hunger which de-
    manded,
    Like the Promethean vulture, this pollu-
      tion;
None in particular had sought or plann'd it,
    'T was nature gnaw'd them to this reso-
      lution,
By which none were permitted to be neuter—
And the lot fell on Juan's luckless tutor. 600

LXXVI

He but requested to be bled to death:
    The surgeon had his instruments, and bled
Pedrillo, and so gently ebb'd his breath,
    You hardly could perceive when he was
    dead.
He died as born, a Catholic in faith,
    Like most in the belief in which they're
    bred,
And first a little crucifix he kiss'd,
And then held out his jugular and wrist.

LXXVII

The surgeon, as there was no other fee,
    Had his first choice of morsels for his
    pains;   610
But being thirstiest at the moment, he
    Preferr'd a draught from the fast-flowing
    veins:
Part was divided, part thrown in the sea,
    And such things as the entrails and the
    brains

Regaled two sharks, who follow'd o'er the
    billow—
The sailors ate the rest of poor Pedrillo.

LXXVIII

The sailors ate him, all save three or four,
    Who were not quite so fond of animal
    food;
To these was added Juan, who, before
    Refusing his own spaniel, hardly could 620
Feel now his appetite increased much more;
    'T was not to be expected that he should,
Even in extremity of their disaster,
Dine with them on his pastor and his master.

LXXIX

'Twas better that he did not; for in fact,
    The consequence was awful in the extreme;
For they, who were most ravenous in the act,
    Went raging mad— Lord! how they did
    blaspheme!
And foam, and roll, with strange convulsions
    rack'd,
    Drinking salt-water like a mountain-
    stream;   630
Tearing, and grinning, howling, screeching,
    swearing,
And, with hyæna-laughter, died despairing.

LXXX

Their numbers were much thinn'd by this
    infliction,
    And all the rest were thin enough, Heaven
    knows;
And some of them had lost their recollection,
    Happier than they who still perceived their
    woes;
But others ponder'd on a new dissection,
    As if not warn'd sufficiently by those
Who had already perish'd, suffering madly,
For having used their appetites so sadly. 640

LXXXI

And next they thought upon the master's
    mate,
    As fattest; but he saved himself, because,
Besides being much averse from such a fate,
    There were some other reasons: the first
    was,
He had been rather indisposed of late;

And that which chiefly proved his saving
  clause,
Was a small present made to him at Cadiz,
By general subscription of the ladies.

LXXXII

Of Poor Pedrillo something still remain'd,
  But was used sparingly,—some were
    afraid,   650
And others still their appetites constrain'd,
  Or but at times a little supper made;
All except Juan, who throughout abstain'd,
  Chewing a piece of bamboo, and some lead:
At length they caught two boobies, and a
    noddy,
And then they left off eating the dead body.

LXXXIII

And if Pedrillo's fate should shocking be,
  Remember Ugolino condescends
To eat the head of his arch-enemy
  The moment after he politely ends   660
His tale: if foes be food in hell, at sea
  'T is surely fair to dine upon our friends,
When shipwreck's short allowance grows too
    scanty,
Without being much more horrible than
    Dante.

LXXXIV

And the same night there fell a shower of
    rain,
  For which their mouths gaped, like the
    cracks of earth
When dried to summer dust; till taught by
    pain,
  Men really know not what good water's
    worth;
If you had been in Turkey or in Spain,
  Or with a famish'd boat's-crew had your
    berth,   670
Or in the desert heard the camel's bell,
You'd wish yourself where Truth is—in a
    well.

LXXXV

It pour'd down torrents, but they were no
    richer,
  Until they found a ragged piece of sheet,

Which served them as a sort of spongy
    pitcher,
  And when they deem'd its moisture was
    complete,
They wrung it out, and though a thirsty
    ditcher
  Might not have thought the scanty draught
    so sweet
As a full pot of porter, to their thinking
They ne'er till now had known the joys of
    drinking.   680

LXXXVI

And their baked lips, with many a bloody
    crack,
  Suck'd in the moisture, which like nectar
    stream'd;
Their throats were ovens, their swoln tongues
    were black
  As the rich man's in hell, who vainly
    scream'd
To beg the beggar, who could not rain back
  A drop of dew, when every drop had seem'd
To taste of heaven— If this be true, indeed,
Some Christians have a comfortable creed.

LXXXVII

There were two fathers in this ghastly crew,
  And with them their two sons, of whom
    the one   690
Was more robust and hardy to the view,
  But he died early; and when he was gone,
His nearest messmate told his sire, who threw
  One glance at him, and said, "Heaven's
    will be done!"
I can do nothing," and he saw him thrown
Into the deep without a tear or groan.

LXXXVIII

The other father had a weaklier child,
  Of a soft cheek, and aspect delicate;
But the boy bore up long, and with a mild
  And patient spirit held aloof his fate; 700
Little he said, and now and then he smiled,
  As if to win a part from off the weight
He saw increasing on his father's heart,
With the deep deadly thought, that they
    must part.

LXXXIX

And o'er him bent his sire, and never raised
  His eyes from off his face, but wiped the
    foam
From his pale lips, and ever on him gazed,
  And when the wish'd-for shower at length
    was come,
And the boy's eyes, which the dull film half
    glazed,
  Brighten'd, and for a moment seem'd to
    roam,   710
He squeezed from out a rag some drops of
    rain
Into his dying child's mouth—but in vain.

XC

The boy expired—the father held the clay,
  And look'd upon it long, and when at last
Death left no doubt, and the dead burthen lay
  Stiff on his heart, and pulse and hope were
    past,
He watch'd it wistfully, until away
  'T was borne by the rude wave wherein
    't was cast;
Then he himself sunk down all dumb and
    shivering,
And gave no sign of life, save his limbs'
    quivering.   720

XCI

Now overhead a rainbow, bursting through
  The scattering clouds, shone, spanning the
    dark sea,
Resting its bright base on the quivering
    blue;
  And all within its arch appear'd to be
Clearer than that without, and its wide hue
  Wax'd broad and waving, like a banner
    free,
Then changed like to a bow that's bent, and
    then
Forsook the dim eyes of these shipwreck'd
    men.

XCII

It changed, of course; a heavenly chameleon,
  The airy child of vapour and the sun, 730
Brought forth in purple, cradled in vermilion,
  Baptized in molten gold, and swathed in
    dun,
Glittering like crescents o'er a Turk's pavilion,
  And blending every colour into one,
Just like a black eye in a recent scuffle
(For sometimes we must box without the
    muffle).

XCIII

Our shipwreck'd seamen thought it a good
    omen—
  It is as well to think so, now and then;
'T was an old custom of the Greek and Ro-
    man,   739
  And may become of great advantage when
Folks are discouraged; and most surely no
    men
  Had greater need to nerve themselves again
Than these, and so this rainbow look'd like
    hope—
Quite a celestial kaleidoscope.

XCIV

About this time a beautiful white bird,
  Web-footed, not unlike a dove in size
And plumage (probably it might have err'd
  Upon its course), pass'd oft before their
    eyes,
And tried to perch, although it saw and
    heard
  The men within the boat, and in this
    guise   750
It came and went, and flutter'd round them
    till
Night fell:—this seem'd a better omen still.

XCV

But in this case I also must remark,
  'T was well this bird of promise did not
    perch,
Because the tackle of our shatter'd bark
  Was not so safe for roosting as a church;
And had it been the dove from Noah's ark,
  Returning there from her successful search,
Which in their way that moment chanced to
    fall,
They would have eat her, olive-branch and
    all.   760

XCVI

With twilight it again came on to blow,
  But not with violence; the stars shone out,

The boat made way; yet now they were so
 low,
 They knew not where nor what they were
  about;
Some fancied they saw land, and some said
 "No!"
 The frequent fog-banks gave them cause to
  doubt—
Some swore that they heard breakers, others
 guns,
And all mistook about the latter once.

XCVII

As morning broke, the light wind died away,
 When he who had the watch sung out and
  swore,   770
If 't was not land that rose with the sun's ray,
 He wished that land he never might see
  more:
And the rest rubb'd their eyes, and saw a
 bay,
 Or thought they saw, and shaped their
  course for shore;
For shore it was, and gradually grew
Distinct, and high, and palpable to view.

XCVIII

And then of these some part burst into tears,
 And others, looking with a stupid stare,
Could not yet separate their hopes from fears,
 And seem'd as if they had not further
  care;   780
While a few pray'd—(the first time for some
 years)—
 And at the bottom of the boat three were
Asleep: they shook them by the hand and
 head,
And tried to awaken them, but found them
 dead.

XCIX

The day before, fast sleeping on the water,
 They found a turtle of the hawk's-bill kind,
And by good fortune, gliding softly, caught
 her,
 Which yielded a day's life, and to their
  mind
Proved even still a more nutritious matter,
 Because it left encouragement behind: 790
They thought that in such perils, more than
 chance
Had sent them this for their deliverance.

C

The land appear'd a high and rocky coast,
 And higher grew the mountains as they
  drew,
Set by a current, toward it: they were lost
 In various conjectures, for none knew
To what part of the earth they had been tost,
 So changeable had been the winds that
  blew;
Some thought it was Mount Ætna, some the
 highlands
Of Candia, Cyprus, Rhodes, or other
 islands.   800

CI

Meantime the current, with a rising gale,
 Still set them onwards to the welcome
  shore,
Like Charon's bark of spectres, dull and pale:
 Their living freight was now reduced to
  four,
And three dead, whom their strength could
 not avail
 To heave into the deep with those before,
Though the two sharks still follow'd them,
 and dash'd
The spray into their faces as they splash'd.

CII

Famine, despair, cold, thirst, and heat, had
 done
 Their work on them by turns, and thinn'd
  them to   810
Such things a mother had not known her son
 Amidst the skeletons of that gaunt crew;
By night chill'd, by day scorch'd, thus one
 by one
 They perish'd, until wither'd to these few,
But chiefly by a species of self-slaughter,
In washing down Pedrillo with salt water.

CIII

As they drew nigh the land, which now was
 seen
 Unequal in its aspect here and there,
They felt the freshness of its growing green,
 That waved in forest-tops, and smooth'd
  the air,   820
And fell upon their glazed eyes like a screen

From glistening waves, and skies so hot
    and bare—
Lovely seem'd any object that should sweep
Away the vast, salt, dread, eternal deep.

CIV

The shore look'd wild, without a trace of
    man,
  And girt by formidable waves; but they
Were mad for land, and thus their course
    they ran,
  Though right ahead the roaring breakers
    lay:
A reef between them also now began
  To show its boiling surf and bounding
    spray,   830
But finding no place for their landing better,
They ran the boat for shore,—and overset
  her.

CV

But in his native stream, the Guadalquivir,
  Juan to lave his youthful limbs was wont;
And having learnt to swim in that sweet river,
  Had often turn'd the art to some account:
A better swimmer you could scarce see ever,
  He could, perhaps, have pass'd the Helles-
    pont,
As once (a feat on which ourselves we prided)
Leander, Mr. Ekenhead, and I did.   840

CVI

So here, though faint, emaciated, and stark,
  He buoy'd his boyish limbs, and strove to
    ply
With the quick wave, and gain, ere it was
    dark,
  The beach which lay before him, high and
    dry:
The greatest danger here was from a shark,
  That carried off his neighbour by the thigh;
As for the other two, they could not swim,
So nobody arrived on shore but him.

CVII

Nor yet had he arrived but for the oar, 849
  Which, providentially for him, was wash'd
Just as his feeble arms could strike no more,
  And the hard wave o'erwhelm'd him as
    't was dash'd

Within his grasp; he clung to it, and sore
  The waters beat while he thereto was lash'd;
At last, with swimming, wading, scrambling,
    he
Roll'd on the beach, half senseless, from the
    sea:

CVIII

There, breathless, with his digging nails he
    clung
  Fast to the sand, lest the returning wave,
From whose reluctant roar his life he wrung,
  Should suck him back to her insatiate
    grave: 860
And there he lay, full length, where he was
    flung,
  Before the entrance of a cliff-worn cave,
With just enough of life to feel its pain,
And deem that it was saved, perhaps in vain.

CIX

With slow and staggering effort he arose,
  But sunk again upon his bleeding knee
And quivering hand; and then he look'd for
    those
  Who long had been his mates upon the
    sea;
But none of them appear'd to share his woes,
  Save one, a corpse, from out the famish'd
    three,   870
Who died two days before, and now had
    found
An unknown barren beach for burial-ground.

CX

And as he gazed, his dizzy brain spun
    fast,
  And down he sunk; and as he sunk, the
    sand
Swam round and round, and all his senses
    pass'd:
  He fell upon his side, and his stretch'd
    hand
Droop'd dripping on the oar (their jury-
    mast),
  And, like a wither'd lily, on the land
His slender frame and pallid aspect lay,
As fair a thing as e'er was form'd of clay. 880

CXI

How long in his damp trance young Juan lay
  He knew not, for the earth was gone for
    him,
And time had nothing more of night nor
    day
  For his congealing blood, and senses dim;
And how this heavy faintness pass'd away
  He knew not, till each painful pulse and
    limb,
And tingling vein, seem'd throbbing back to
    life,
For Death, though vanquish'd, still retired
    with strife.

CXII

His eyes he open'd, shut, again unclosed,
  For all was doubt and dizziness; he
    thought   890
He still was in the boat, and had but dozed,
  And felt again with his despair o'erwrought,
And wish'd it death in which he had reposed,
  And then once more his feelings back were
    brought,
And slowly by his swimming eyes was seen
A lovely female face of seventeen.

CXIII

'T was bending close o'er his, and the small
    mouth
  Seem'd almost prying into his for breath;
And chafing him, the soft warm hand of youth
  Recall'd his answering spirits back from
    death;   900
And, bathing his chill temples, tried to soothe
  Each pulse to animation, till beneath
Its gentle touch and trembling care, a sigh
To these kind efforts made a low reply.

CXIV

Then was the cordial pour'd, and mantle flung
  Around his scarce-clad limbs; and the fair
    arm
Raised higher the faint head which o'er it
    hung;
  And her transparent cheek, all pure and
    warm,
Pillow'd his death-like forehead; then she
    wrung

His dewy curls, long drench'd by every
    storm;   910
And watch'd with eagerness each throb that
    drew
A sigh from his heaved bosom—and hers, too.

CXV

And lifting him with care into the cave,
  The gentle girl, and her attendant,—one
Young, yet her elder, and of brow less grave,
  And more robust of figure—then begun
To kindle fire, and as the new flames gave
  Light to the rocks that roof'd them, which
    the sun
Had never seen, the maid, or whatsoe'er
She was, appear'd distinct, and tall, and
    fair.   920

CXVI

Her brow was overhung with coins of gold,
  That sparkled o'er the auburn of her hair,
Her clustering hair, whose longer locks were
    roll'd
  In braids behind; and though her stature
    were
Even of the highest for a female mould,
  They nearly reach'd her heel; and in her
    air
There was a something which bespoke com-
    mand,
As one who was a lady in the land.

CXVII

Her hair, I said, was auburn; but her eyes
  Were black as death, their lashes the same
    hue,   930
Of downcast length, in whose silk shadow
    lies
  Deepest attraction; for when to the view
Forth from its raven fringe the full glance
    flies,
  Ne'er with such force the swiftest arrow
    flew;
'T is as the snake late coil'd, who pours his
    length,
And hurls at once his venom and his strength.

CXVIII

Her brow was white and low, her cheek's pure
    dye
  Like twilight rosy still with the set sun;

Short upper lip—sweet lips! that make us
    sigh
    Ever to have seen such; for she was one 940
Fit for the model of a statuary
    (A race of mere impostors, when all's
        done—
I've seen much finer women, ripe and real,
Than all the nonsense of their stone ideal).

CXIX

I'll tell you why I say so, for 't is just
    One should not rail without a decent cause:
There was an Irish lady, to whose bust
    I ne'er saw justice done, and yet she was
A frequent model; and if e'er she must
    Yield to stern Time and Nature's wrinkling
        laws,   950
They will destroy a face which mortal thought
Ne'er compass'd, nor less mortal chisel
    wrought.

CXX

And such was she, the lady of the cave:
    Her dress was very different from the
        Spanish,
Simpler, and yet of colours not so grave;
    For, as you know, the Spanish women banish
Bright hues when out of doors, and yet, while
    wave
    Around them (what I hope will never
        vanish)
The basquina and the mantilla, they
Seem at the same time mystical and gay. 960

CXXI

But with our damsel this was not the case:
    Her dress was many-colour'd, finely spun;
Her locks curl'd negligently round her face,
    But through them gold and gems profusely
        shone:
Her girdle sparkled, and the richest lace
    Flow'd in her veil, and many a precious
        stone
Flash'd on her little hand; but, what was
    shocking,
Her small snow feet had slippers, but no
    stocking.

CXXII

The other female's dress was not unlike,

But of inferior materials: she   970
Had not so many ornaments to strike,
    Her hair had silver only, bound to be
Her dowry; and her veil, in form alike,
    Was coarser; and her air, though firm less
        free;
Her hair was thicker, but less long; her eyes
As black, but quicker, and of smaller size.

CXXIII

And these two tended him, and cheer'd him
    both
    With food and raiment, and those soft at-
        tentions,
Which are—(as I must own)—of female
    growth,
    And have ten thousand delicate inven-
        tions: 980
They made a most superior mess of broth,
    A thing which poesy but seldom mentions,
But the best dish that e'er was cook'd since
    Homer's
Achilles order'd dinner for new comers.

CXXIV

I'll tell you who they were, this female pair,
    Lest they should seem princesses in dis-
        guise;
Besides, I hate all mystery, and that air
    Of clap-trap, which your recent poets prize;
And so, in short, the girls they really were
    They shall appear before your curious
        eyes,   990
Mistress and maid; the first was only daugh-
    ter
Of an old man, who lived upon the water.

CXXV

A fisherman he had been in his youth,
    And still a sort of fisherman was he;
But other speculations were, in sooth,
    Added to his connexion with the sea,
Perhaps not so respectable, in truth:
    A little smuggling, and some piracy,
Left him, at last, the sole of many masters
Of an ill-gotten million of piastres.   1000

CXXVI

A fisher, therefore, was he,—though of men,
    Like Peter the Apostle,—and he fish'd

For wandering merchant vessels, now and
then,
    And sometimes caught as many as he
    wish'd;
The cargoes he confiscated, and gain
    He sought in the slave-market too, and
    dish'd
Full many a morsel for that Turkish trade,
By which, no doubt, a good deal may be made.

CXXVII

He was a Greek, and on his isle had built
    (One of the wild and smaller Cyclades) 1010
A very handsome house from out his guilt,
    And there he lived exceedingly at ease;
Heaven knows what cash he got, or blood he
    spilt,
    A sad old fellow was he, if you please;
But this I know, it was a spacious building,
Full of barbaric carving, paint, and gilding.

CXXVIII

He had an only daughter, call'd Haidée,
    The greatest heiress of the Eastern Isles;
Besides, so very beautiful was she,
    Her dowry was as nothing to her smiles: 1020
Still in her teens, and like a lovely tree
    She grew to womanhood, and between
    whiles
Rejected several suitors, just to learn
How to accept a better in his turn.

CXXIX

And walking out upon the beach, below
    The cliff,—towards sunset, on that day she
    found,
Insensible,—not dead, but nearly so,—
    Don Juan, almost famish'd, and half
    drown'd;
But being naked, she was shock'd, you know,
    Yet deem'd herself in common pity
    bound, 1030
As far as in her lay, "to take him in,
A stranger" dying, with so white a skin.

CXXX

But taking him into her father's house
    Was not exactly the best way to save,
But like conveying to the cat the mouse,
    Or people in a trance into their grave;

Because the good old man had so much
    "vous,"
    Unlike the honest Arab thieves so brave,
He would have hospitably cured the stranger
And sold him instantly when out of dan-
    ger.   1040

CXXXI

And therefore, with her maid, she thought it
    best
    (A virgin always on her maid relies)
To place him in the cave for present rest:
    And when, at last, he open'd his black eyes,
Their charity increased about their guest;
    And their compassion grew to such a size,
It open'd half the turnpike gates to heaven—
(St. Paul says, 't is the toll which must be
    given).

CXXXII

They made a fire,—but such a fire as they
    Upon the moment could contrive with
    such   1050
Materials as were cast up round the bay,—
    Some broken planks, and oars, that to the
    touch
Were nearly tinder, since so long they lay
    A mast was almost crumbled to a crutch;
But, by God's grace, here wrecks were in
    such plenty,
That there was fuel to have furnish'd twenty.

CXXXIII

He had a bed of furs, and a pelisse,
    For Haidée stripp'd her sables off to make
His couch; and, that he might be more at
    ease,
    And warm, in case by chance he should
    awake,   1060
They also gave a petticoat apiece,
    She and her maid,—and promised by day-
    break
To pay him a fresh visit, with a dish
For breakfast, of eggs, coffee, bread, and
    fish.

CXXXIV

And thus they left him to his lone repose;
    Juan slept like a top, or like the dead,
Who sleep at last, perhaps (God only knows),

Just for the present; and in his lull'd head
Not even a vision of his former woes
    Throbb'd in accursed dreams, which some-
      times spread   1070
Unwelcome visions of our former years,
Till the eye, cheated, opens thick with tears.

CXXXV

Young Juan slept all dreamless:—but the
    maid,
    Who smooth'd his pillow, as she left the
      den
Look'd back upon him, and a moment staid,
    And turn'd, believing that he call'd again.
He slumber'd; yet she thought, at least she
    said
    (The heart will slip, even as the tongue
      and pen),
He had pronounced her name—but she forgot
That at this moment Juan knew it not. 1080

CXXXVI

And pensive to her father's house she went,
    Enjoining silence strict to Zoe, who
Better than her knew what, in fact, she meant,
    She being wiser by a year or two:
A year or two's an age when rightly spent,
    And Zoe spent hers, as most women do,
In gaining all that useful sort of knowledge
Which is acquired in Nature's good old college.

CXXXVII

The morn broke, and found Juan slumbering
    still
    Fast in his cave, and nothing clash'd
      upon   1090
His rest: the rushing of the neighbouring rill,
    And the young beams of the excluded sun,
Troubled him not, and he might sleep his
    fill;
    And need he had of slumber yet, for none
Had suffer'd more—his hardships were com-
    parative
To those related in my grand-dad's "Narra-
    tive."

CXXXVIII

Not so Haidée: she sadly toss'd and tumbled,
    And started from her sleep, and, turning
    o'er,
Dream'd of a thousand wrecks, o'er which she
    stumbled,
    And handsome corpses strew'd upon the
      shore;   1100
And woke her maid so early that she grumbled
    And call'd her father's old slaves up, who
    swore
In several oaths—Armenian, Turk, and
    Greek—
They knew not what to think of such a freak.

CXXXIX

But up she got, and up she made them get,
    With some pretence about the sun, that
    makes
Sweet skies just when he rises, or is set;
    And 't is, no doubt, a sight to see when
    breaks
Bright Phœbus, while the mountains still are
    wet
    With mist, and every bird with him
    awakes,   1110
And night is flung off like a mourning suit
Worn for a husband,—or some other brute.

CXL

I say, the sun is a most glorious sight:
    I've seen him rise full oft, indeed of late
I have sat up on purpose all the night,
    Which hastens, as physicians say, one's
    fate;
And so all ye, who would be in the right
    In health and purse, begin your day to
    date
From daybreak, and when coffin'd at four-
    score
Engrave upon the plate, you rose at four. 1120

CXLI

And Haidée met the morning face to face;
    Her own was freshest, though a feverish
    flush
Had dyed it with the headlong blood, whose
    race
    From heart to cheek is curb'd into a blush,
Like to a torrent which a mountain's base,
    That overpowers some Alpine river's rush,
Checks to a lake, whose waves in circles
    spread;
Or the Red Sea—but the sea is not red.

CXLII

And down the cliff the island virgin came,
  And near the cave her quick light footsteps
    drew,   1130
While the sun smiled on her with his first
    flame,
  And young Aurora kiss'd her lips with dew,
Taking her for a sister; just the same
  Mistake you would have made on seeing
    the two,
Although the mortal, quite as fresh and fair,
Had all the advantage, too, of not being air.

CXLIII

And when into the cavern Haidée stepp'd
  All timidly, yet rapidly, she saw
That like an infant Juan sweetly slept;
  And then she stopp'd, and stood as if in
    awe   1140
(For sleep is awful), and on tiptoe crept
  And wrapt him closer, lest the air, too raw,
Should reach his blood, then o'er him still as
    death
Bent, with hush'd lips, that drank his scarce-
    drawn breath.

CXLIV

And thus like to an angel o'er the dying
  Who die in righteousness, she lean'd; and
    there
All tranquilly the shipwreck'd boy was lying,
  As o'er him lay the calm and stirless air:
But Zoe the meantime some eggs was frying,
  Since, after all, no doubt the youthful
    pair   1150
Must breakfast, and betimes—lest they should
    ask it,
She drew out her provision from the basket.

CXLV

She knew that the best feelings must have
    victual,
  And that a shipwreck'd youth would hungry
    be;
Besides, being less in love, she yawn'd a little,
  And felt her veins chill'd by the neigh-
    bouring sea;
And so, she cook'd their breakfast to a tittle;
  I can't say that she gave them any tea,

But there were eggs, fruit, coffee, bread, fish,
    honey,
With Scio wine,—and all for love, not
    money.   1160

CXLVI

And Zoe, when the eggs were ready, and
  The coffee made, would fain have waken'd
    Juan;
But Haidée stopp'd her with her quick small
    hand,
  And without word, a sign her finger drew
    on
Her lip, which Zoe needs must understand;
  And, the first breakfast spoilt, prepared a
    new one,
Because her mistress would not let her break
That sleep which seem'd as it would ne'er
    awake.

CXLVII

For still he lay, and on his thin worn cheek
  A purple hectic play'd like dying day   1170
On the snow-tops of distant hills; the streak
  Of sufferance yet upon his forehead lay,
Where the blue veins look'd shadowy, shrunk,
    and weak;
  And his black curls were dewy with the
    spray,
Which weigh'd upon them yet, all damp and
    salt,
Mix'd with the stony vapours of the vault.

CXLVIII

And she bent o'er him, and he lay beneath,
  Hush'd as the babe upon its mother's breast,
Droop'd as the willow when no winds can
    breathe,   1179
  Lull'd like the depth of ocean when at rest,
Fair as the crowning rose of the whole wreath,
  Soft as the callow cygnet in its nest;
In short, he was a very pretty fellow,
Although his woes had turn'd him rather
    yellow.

CXLIX

He woke, and gazed, and would have slept
    again,
  But the fair face which met his eyes for-
    bade

Those eyes to close, though weariness and
    pain
  Had further sleep a further pleasure made;
For woman's face was never form'd in vain
  For Juan, so that even when he pray'd 1190
He turn'd from grisly saints, and martyrs
    hairy,
To the sweet portraits of the Virgin Mary.

CL

And thus upon his elbow he arose,
  And look'd upon the lady, in whose cheek
The pale contended with the purple rose,
  As with an effort she began to speak;
Her eyes were eloquent, her words would pose,
  Although she told him, in good modern
    Greek,
With an Ionian accent, low and sweet,   1199
That he was faint, and must not talk, but eat.

CLI

Now Juan could not understand a word,
  Being no Grecian; but he had an ear,
And her voice was the warble of a bird,
  So soft, so sweet, so delicately clear,
That finer, simpler music ne'er was heard;
  The sort of sound we echo with a tear,
Without knowing why—an overpowering tone,
Whence melody descends as from a throne.

CLII

And Juan gazed as one who is awoke
  By a distant organ, doubting if he be 1210
Not yet a dreamer, till the spell is broke
  By the watchman, or some such reality,
Or by one's early valet's cursed knock;
  At least it is a heavy sound to me,
Who like a morning slumber—for the night
Shows stars and women in a better light.

CLIII

And Juan, too, was help'd out from his dream,
  Or sleep, or whatsoe'er it was, by feeling
A most prodigious appetite; the steam
  Of Zoe's cookery no doubt was stealing 1220
Upon his senses, and the kindling beam
  Of the new fire, which Zoe kept up, kneel-
    ing,
To stir her viands, made him quite awake
And long for food, but chiefly a beef-steak.

CLIV

But beef is rare within these oxless isles;
  Goat's flesh there is, no doubt, and kid, and
    mutton,
And, when a holiday upon them smiles,
  A joint upon their barbarous spits they
    put on:
But this occurs but seldom, between whiles,
  For some of these are rocks with scarce a
    hut on;   1230
Others are fair and fertile, among which
This, though not large, was one of the most
    rich.

CLV

I say that beef is rare, and can't help thinking
  That the old fable of the Minotaur—
From which our modern morals, rightly
    shrinking,
  Condemn the royal lady's taste who wore
A cow's shape for a mask—was only (sinking
  The allegory) a mere type, no more,
That Pasiphae promoted breeding cattle,
To make the Cretans bloodier in battle.   1240

CLVI

For we all know that English people are
  Fed upon beef—I won't say much of beer,
Because 't is liquor only, and being far
  From this my subject, has no business here;
We know, too, they are very fond of war,
  A pleasure—like all pleasures—rather dear;
So were the Cretans—from which I infer
That beef and battles both were owing to her.

CLVII

But to resume. The languid Juan raised
  His head upon his elbow, and he saw   1250
A sight on which he had not lately gazed,
  As all his later meals had been quite raw,
Three or four things, for which the Lord he
    praised,
  And, feeling still the famish'd vulture gnaw,
He fell upon whate'er was offer'd, like
A priest, a shark, an alderman, or pike.

CLVIII

He ate, and he was well supplied; and she,

Who watch'd him like a mother, would have
fed
Him past all bounds, because she smiled to
see   1259
Such appetite in one she had deem'd dead:
But Zoe, being older than Haidée,
Knew (by tradition, for she ne'er had read)
That famish'd people must be slowly nurst,
And fed by spoonfuls, else they always burst.

CLIX

And so she took the liberty to state,
Rather by deeds than words, because the
case
Was urgent, that the gentleman, whose fate
Had made her mistress quit her bed to
trace
The sea-shore at this hour, must leave his
plate,
Unless he wish'd to die upon the place— 1270
She snatch'd it, and refused another morsel,
Saying, he had gorged enough to make a horse
ill.

CLX

Next they—he being naked, save a tatter'd
Pair of scarce decent trowsers—went to
work,
And in the fire his recent rags they scatter'd,
And dress'd him, for the present, like a
Turk,
Or Greek—that is, although it not much mat-
ter'd,
Omitting turban, slippers, pistols, dirk,—
They furnish'd him, entire, except some
stitches,   1279
With a clean shirt, and very spacious breeches.

CLXI

And then fair Haidée tried her tongue at
speaking,
But not a word could Juan comprehend,
Although he listen'd so that the young Greek
in
Her earnestness would ne'er have made an
end;
And, as he interrupted not, went eking
Her speech out to her protégé and friend,
Till pausing at the last her breath to take,
She saw he did not understand Romaic.

CLXII

And then she had recourse to nods, and signs,
And smiles, and sparkles of the speaking
eye,   1290
And read (the only book she could) the lines
Of his fair face, and found, by sympathy,
The answer eloquent, where the soul shines
And darts in one quick glance a long reply;
And thus in every look she saw exprest
A world of words, and things at which she
guess'd.

CLXIII

And now, by dint of fingers and of eyes,
And words repeated after her, he took
A lesson in her tongue; but by surmise,
No doubt, less of her language than her
look: 1300
As he who studies fervently the skies
Turns oftener to the stars than to his book,
Thus Juan learn'd his alpha beta better
From Haidée's glance than any graven letter.

CLXIV

'T is pleasing to be school'd in a strange
tongue
By female lips and eyes—that is, I mean,
When both the teacher and the taught are
young,
As was the case, at least, where I have
been;
They smile so when one's right, and when
one's wrong
They smile still more, and then there inter-
vene   1310
Pressure of hands, perhaps even a chaste
kiss;—
I learn'd the little that I know by this:

CLXV

That is, some words of Spanish, Turk, and
Greek,
Italian not at all, having no teachers;
Much English I cannot pretend to speak,
Learning that language chiefly from its
preachers,
Barrow, South, Tillotson, whom every week
I study, also Blair, the highest reachers
Of eloquence in piety and prose—
I hate your poets, so read none of those. 1320

CLXVI

As for the ladies, I have nought to say,
　A wanderer from the British world of
　　fashion,
Where I, like other "dogs, have had my day,"
　Like other men, too, may have had my
　　passion—
But that, like other things, has pass'd away,
　And all her fools whom I *could* lay the lash
　　on:
Foes, friends, men, women, now are nought
　　to me
But dreams of what has been, no more to be.

CLXVII

Return we to Don Juan. He begun
　To hear new words, and to repeat them;
　　but　　　　　　　　　　　　　　　1330
Some feelings, universal as the sun,
　Were such as could not in his breast be
　　shut
More than within the bosom of a nun:
　He was in love,—as you would be, no doubt,
With a young benefactress,—so was she,
Just in the way we very often see.

CLXVIII

And every day by daybreak—rather early
　For Juan, who was somewhat fond of rest—
She came into the cave, but it was merely
　To see her bird reposing in his nest;　　1340
And she would softly stir his locks so curly,
　Without disturbing her yet slumbering
　　guest,
Breathing all gently o'er his cheek and mouth,
As o'er a bed of roses the sweet south.

CLXIX

And every morn his colour freshlier came,
　And every day help'd on his convalescence;
'T was well, because health in the human
　　frame
　Is pleasant, besides being true love's es-
　　sence,
For health and idleness to passion's flame
　Are oil and gunpowder; and some good
　　lessons　　　　　　　　　　　　　　1350
Are also learnt from Ceres and from Bacchus,
Without whom Venus will not long attack us.

CLXX

While Venus fills the heart (without heart
　　really
　Love, though good always, is not quite so
　　good),
Ceres presents a plate of vermicelli,—
　For love must be sustain'd like flesh and
　　blood,
While Bacchus pours out wine, or hands a
　　jelly:
　Eggs, oysters, too, are amatory food;
But who is their purveyor from above
Heaven knows,—it may be Neptune, Pan, or
　Jove.　　　　　　　　　　　　　　1360

CLXXI

When Juan woke he found some good things
　　ready,
　A bath, a breakfast, and the finest eyes
That ever made a youthful heart less steady,
　Besides her maid's, as pretty for their size;
But I have spoken of all this already—
　And repetition's tiresome and unwise,—
Well—Juan, after bathing in the sea,
Came always back to coffee and Haidée.

CLXXII

Both were so young, and one so innocent,
　That bathing pass'd for nothing; Juan
　　seem'd　　　　　　　　　　　　　1370
To her, as 't were, the kind of being sent,
　Of whom these two years she had nightly
　　dream'd,
A something to be loved, a creature meant
　To be her happiness, and whom she
　　deem'd
To render happy: all who joy would win
Must share it,—Happiness was born a twin.

CLXXIII

It was such pleasure to behold him, such
　Enlargement of existence to partake
Nature with him, to thrill beneath his touch,
　To watch him slumbering, and to see him
　　wake;　　　　　　　　　　　　　1380
To live with him for ever were too much;
　But then the thought of parting made her
　　quake:
He was her own, her ocean-treasure, cast
Like a rich wreck—her first love, and her last.

CLXXIV

And thus a moon roll'd on, and fair Haidée
  Paid daily visits to her boy, and took
Such plentiful precautions, that still he
  Remain'd unknown within his craggy nook;
At last her father's prows put out to sea,
  For certain merchantmen upon the look, 1390
Not as of yore to carry off an Io,
But three Ragusan vessels bound for Scio.

CLXXV

Then came her freedom, for she had no
    mother,
  So that, her father being at sea, she was
Free as a married woman, or such other
  Female, as where she likes may freely pass,
Without even the encumbrance of a brother,
  The freest she that ever gazed on glass:
I speak of Christian lands in this comparison,
Where wives, at least, are seldom kept in gar-
    rison. 1400

CLXXVI

Now she prolong'd her visits and her talk
  (For they must talk), and he had learnt to
    say
So much as to propose to take a walk,—
  For little had he wander'd since the day
On which, like a young flower snapp'd from
    the stalk,
  Drooping and dewy on the beach he lay,—
And thus they walk'd out in the afternoon,
And saw the sun set opposite the moon.

CLXXVII

It was a wild and breaker-beaten coast,
  With cliffs above, and a broad sandy
    shore, 1410
Guarded by shoals and rocks as by an host,
  With here and there a creek, whose aspect
    wore
A better welcome to the tempest-tost;
  And rarely ceased the haughty billow's roar,
Save on the dead long summer days, which
    make
The outstretch'd ocean glitter like a lake.

CLXXVIII

And the small ripple spilt upon the beach
  Scarcely o'erpass'd the cream of your
    champagne,
When o'er the brim the sparkling bumpers
    reach,
  That spring-dew of the spirit! the heart's
    rain! 1420
Few things surpass old wine; and they may
    preach
  Who please,—the more because they preach
    in vain,—
Let us have wine and women, mirth and
    laughter,
Sermons and soda-water the day after.

CLXXIX

Man, being reasonable, must get drunk;
  The best of life is but intoxication:
Glory, the grape, love, gold, in these are
    sunk
  The hopes of all men, and of every nation;
Without their sap, how branchless were the
    trunk
  Of life's strange tree, so fruitful on occa-
    sion! 1430
But to return,—Get very drunk; and when
You wake with headache, you shall see what
    then.

CLXXX

Ring for your valet—bid him quickly bring
  Some hock and soda-water, then you'll
    know
A pleasure worthy Xerxes the great king;
  For not the blest sherbet, sublimed with
    snow,
Nor the first sparkle of the desert spring,
  Nor Burgundy in all its sunset glow,
After long travel, ennui, love, or slaughter,
Vie with that draught of hock and soda-
    water. 1440

CLXXXI

The coast—I think it was the coast that I
  Was just describing— Yes, it *was* the
    coast—
Lay at this period quiet as the sky,
  The sands untumbled, the blue waves un-
    tost,

And all was stillness, save the sea-bird's cry,
  And dolphin's leap, and little billow crost
By some low rock or shelve, that made it fret
Against the boundary it scarcely wet.

CLXXXII

And forth they wander'd, her sire being gone,
  As I have said, upon an expedition; 1450
And mother, brother, guardian, she had none,
  Save Zoe, who, although with due precision
She waited on her lady with the sun,
  Thought daily service was her only mission,
Bringing warm water, wreathing her long
    tresses,
And asking now and then for cast-off dresses.

CLXXXIII

It was the cooling hour, just when the rounded
  Red sun sinks down behind the azure hill,
Which then seems as if the whole earth it
    bounded,
  Circling all nature, hush'd, and dim, and
    still, 1460
With the far mountain-crescent half sur-
    rounded
  On one side, and the deep sea calm and
    chill,
Upon the other, and the rosy sky,
With one star sparkling through it like an eye.

CLXXXIV

And thus they wander'd forth, and hand in
    hand,
  Over the shining pebbles and the shells,
Glided along the smooth and harden'd sand,
  And in the worn and wild receptacles
Work'd by the storms, yet work'd as it were
    plann'd, 1469
  In hollow halls, with sparry roofs and cells,
They turn'd to rest; and, each clasp'd by an
    arm,
Yielded to the deep twilight's purple charm.

CLXXXV

They look'd up to the sky, whose floating glow
  Spread like a rosy ocean, vast and bright;
They gazed upon the glittering sea below,
  Whence the broad moon rose circling into
    sight;

They heard the waves splash, and the wind
    so low,
  And saw each other's dark eyes darting light
Into each other—and, beholding this, 1479
Their lips drew near, and clung into a kiss;

CLXXXVI

A long, long kiss, a kiss of youth, and love,
  And beauty, all concentrating like rays
Into one focus, kindled from above;
  Such kisses as belong to early days,
Where heart, and soul, and sense, in concert
    move,
  And the blood's lava, and the pulse a
    blaze,
Each kiss a heart-quake,—for a kiss's strength,
I think it must be reckon'd by its length.

CLXXXVII

By length I mean duration; theirs endured
  Heaven knows how long—no doubt they
    never reckon'd; 1490
And if they had, they could not have secured
  The sum of their sensations to a second:
They had not spoken; but they felt allured,
  As if their souls and lips each other beck-
    on'd,
Which, being join'd, like swarming bees they
    clung—
Their hearts the flowers from whence the
    honey sprung.

CLXXXVIII

They were alone, but not alone as they
  Who shut in chambers think it loneliness;
The silent ocean, and the starlight bay,
  The twilight glow, which momently grew
    less, 1500
The voiceless sands, and dropping caves, that
    lay
  Around them, made them to each other
    press,
As if there were no life beneath the sky
Save theirs, and that their life could never
    die.

CLXXXIX

They fear'd no eyes nor ears on that lone
    beach,

They felt no terrors from the night; they were
All in all to each other; though their speech
  Was broken words, they *thought* a language there,—
And all the burning tongues that passions teach
Found in one sigh the best interpreter 1510
Of nature's oracle—first love,—that all
Which Eve has left her daughters since her fall.

CXC

Haidée spoke not of scruples, ask'd no vows,
  Nor offer'd any; she had never heard
Of plight and promises to be a spouse,
  Or perils by a loving maid incurr'd;
She was all which pure ignorance allows,
  And flew to her young mate like a young bird,
And never having dreamt of falsehood, she
Had not one word to say of constancy. 1520

CXCI

She loved, and was beloved—she adored,
  And she was worshipp'd; after nature's fashion,
Their intense souls, into each other pour'd,
  If souls could die, had perish'd in that passion,—
But by degrees their senses were restored,
  Again to be o'ercome, again to dash on;
And, beating 'gainst *his* bosom, Haidée's heart
Felt as if never more to beat apart.

CXCII

Alas! they were so young, so beautiful,
  So lonely, loving, helpless, and the hour 1530
Was that in which the heart is always full,
  And, having o'er itself no further power,
Prompts deeds eternity cannot annul,
  But pays off moments in an endless shower
Of hell-fire—all prepared for people giving
Pleasure or pain to one another living.

CXCIII

Alas! for Juan and Haidée! they were
  So loving and so lovely—till then never,
Excepting our first parents, such a pair 1539
  Had run the risk of being damn'd for ever;

And Haidée, being devout as well as fair,
  Had, doubtless, heard about the Stygian river,
And hell and purgatory—but forgot
Just in the very crisis she should not.

CXCIV

They look upon each other, and their eyes
  Gleam in the moonlight; and her white arm clasps
Round Juan's head, and his around her lies
  Half buried in the tresses which it grasps;
She sits upon his knee, and drinks his sighs,
  He hers, until they end in broken gasps; 1550
And thus they form a group that's quite antique,
Half naked, loving, natural, and Greek.

CXCV

And when those deep and burning moments pass'd,
  And Juan sunk to sleep within her arms,
She slept not, but all tenderly, though fast,
  Sustain'd his head upon her bosom's charms;
And now and then her eye to heaven is cast
  And then on the pale cheek her breast now warms,
Pillow'd on her o'erflowing heart, which pants
With all it granted, and with all it grants. 1560

CXCVI

An infant when it gazes on a light,
  A child the moment when it drains the breast,
A devotee when soars the Host in sight,
  An Arab with a stranger for a guest,
A sailor when the prize has struck in fight,
  A miser filling his most hoarded chest,
Feel rapture; but not such true joy are reaping
As they who watch o'er what they love while sleeping.

CXCVII

For there it lies so tranquil, so beloved,
  All that it hath of life with us is living; 1570
So gentle, stirless, helpless, and unmoved,
  And all unconscious of the joy 't is giving;
All it hath felt, inflicted, pass'd, and proved,

Hush'd into depths beyond the watcher's
  diving;
There lies the thing we love with all its
  errors
And all its charms, like death without its
  terrors.

CXCVIII

The lady watch'd her lover—and that hour
  Of Love's, and Night's, and Ocean's soli-
  tude,
O'erflow'd her soul with their united power;
  Amidst the barren sand and rocks so rude
She and her wave-worn love had made their
  bower,   1581
  Where nought upon their passion could in-
  trude,
And all the stars that crowded the blue space
Saw nothing happier than her glowing face.

CXCIX

Alas! the love of women! it is known
  To be a lovely and a fearful thing;
For all of theirs upon that die is thrown,
  And if 't is lost, life hath no more to bring
To them but mockeries of the past alone,   1589
  And their revenge is as the tiger's spring,
Deadly, and quick, and crushing; yet, as
  real
Torture is theirs, what they inflict they feel.

CC

They are right; for man, to man so oft
  unjust,
  Is always so to women; one sole bond
Awaits them, treachery is all their trust;
  Taught to conceal, their bursting hearts
  despond
Over their idol, till some wealthier lust
  Buys them in marriage—and what rests
  beyond?
A thankless husband, next a faithless lover,
Then dressing, nursing, praying, and all's over.

CCI

Some take a lover, some take drams or
  prayers,   1601
  Some mind their household, others dissipation,
Some run away, and but exchange their cares,

Losing the advantage of a virtuous station;
  Few changes e'er can better their affairs,
  Theirs being an unnatural situation,
From the dull palace to the dirty hovel:
Some play the devil, and then write a novel.

CCII

Haidée was Nature's bride, and knew not
  this:
  Haidée was Passion's child, born where the
  sun   1610
Showers triple light, and scorches even the
  kiss
  Of his gazelle-eyed daughters; she was one
Made but to love, to feel that she was his
  Who was her chosen: what was said or
  done
Elsewhere was nothing. She had nought to
  fear,
Hope, care, nor love beyond,—her heart beat
  here.

CCIII

And oh! that quickening of the heart, that
  beat!
  How much it costs us! yet each rising throb
Is in its cause as its effect so sweet,
  That Wisdom, ever on the watch to rob   1620
Joy of its alchemy, and to repeat
  Fine truths; even Conscience, too, has a
  tough job
To make us understand each good old maxim,
So good—I wonder Castlereagh don't tax 'em.

CCIV

And now 't was done—on the lone shore were
  plighted
  Their hearts; the stars, their nuptial
  torches, shed
Beauty upon the beautiful they lighted:
  Ocean their witness, and the cave their bed,
By their own feelings hallow'd and united,
  Their priest was Solitude, and they were
  wed: 1630
And they were happy, for to their young eyes
Each was an angel, and earth paradise.

CCV

Oh, Love! of whom great Cæsar was the
  suitor,

Titus the master, Antony the slave,
Horace, Catullus, scholars, Ovid tutor,
   Sappho the sage blue-stocking, in whose
      grave
All those may leap who rather would be
      neuter—
   (Leucadia's rock still overlooks the wave)—
Oh, Love! thou art the very god of evil,
For, after all, we cannot call thee devil. 1640

CCVI

Thou mak'st the chaste connubial state pre-
      carious,
   And jestest with the brows of mightiest
      men:
Cæsar and Pompey, Mahomet, Belisarius,
   Have much employ'd the muse of history's
      pen:
Their lives and fortunes were extremely va-
      rious,
   Such worthies Time will never see again;
Yet to these four in three things the same
      luck holds,
They all were heroes, conquerors, and
      cuckolds.

CCVII

Thou mak'st philosophers; there's Epicurus
   And Aristippus, a material crew!   1650
Who to immoral courses would allure us
   By theories quite practicable too;
If only from the devil they would insure us,
   How pleasant were the maxim (not quite
      new),
"Eat, drink, and love; what can the rest avail
      us?"
So said the royal sage Sardanapalus.

CCVIII

But Juan! had he quite forgotten Julia?
   And should he have forgotten her so soon?
I can't but say it seems to me most truly a
   Perplexing question; but, no doubt, the
      moon   1660
Does these things for us, and whenever newly a
   Strong palpitation rises, 't is her boon,
Else how the devil is it that fresh features
Have such a charm for us poor human crea-
      tures?

CCIX

I hate inconstancy—I loathe, detest,
   Abhor, condemn, abjure the mortal made
Of such quicksilver clay that in his breast
   No permanent foundation can be laid;
Love, constant love, has been my constant
      guest,   1669
   And yet last night, being at a masquerade,
I saw the prettiest creature, fresh from Milan,
Which gave me some sensations like a villain.

CCX

But soon Philosophy came to my aid,
   And whisper'd, "Think of every sacred tie!"
"I will, my dear Philosophy!" I said,
   "But then her teeth, and then, oh, Heaven!
      her eye!
I'll just inquire if she be wife or maid,
   Or neither—out of curiosity."
"Stop!" cried Philosophy, with air so Grecian
(Though she was masqued then as a fair
      Venetian);   1680

CCXI

"Stop!" so I stopp'd.—But to return: that
      which
   Men call inconstancy is nothing more
Than admiration due where nature's rich
   Profusion with young beauty covers o'er
Some favour'd object; and as in the niche
   A lovely statue we almost adore,
This sort of adoration of the real
Is but a heightening of the "beau ideal."

CCXII

'T is the perception of the beautiful,
   A fine extension of the faculties,   1690
Platonic, universal, wonderful,
   Drawn from the stars, and filter'd through
      the skies,
Without which life would be extremely dull;
   In short, it is the use of our own eyes,
With one or two small senses added, just
To hint that flesh is form'd of fiery dust.

CCXIII

Yet 't is a painful feeling, and unwilling,
   For surely if we always could perceive
In the same object graces quite as killing

As when she rose upon us like an Eve, 1700
'T would save us many a heart-ache, many
    a shilling
(For we must get them any how, or grieve),
Whereas, if one sole lady pleased for ever,
How pleasant for the heart, as well as liver!

CCXIV

The heart is like the sky, a part of heaven,
    But changes night and day, too, like the
    sky;
Now o'er it clouds and thunder must be driven,
    And darkness and destruction as on high:
But when it hath been scorch'd and pierced,
    and riven,
    Its storms expire in water-drops; the eye
Pours forth at last the heart's blood turn'd to
    tears, 1711
Which make the English climate of our years.

CCXV

The liver is the lazaret of bile,
    But very rarely executes its function,
For the first passion stays there such a while,
    That all the rest creep in and form a junc-
    tion,
Like knots of vipers on a dunghill's soil,
    Rage, fear, hate, jealousy, revenge, com-
    punction,
So that all mischiefs spring up from this
    entrail,
Like earthquakes from the hidden fire call'd
    "central." 1720

CCXVI

In the mean time, without proceeding more
    In this anatomy, I've finish'd now
Two hundred and odd stanzas as before,
    That being about the number I'll allow
Each canto of the twelve, or twenty-four;
    And, laying down my pen, I make my bow,
Leaving Don Juan and Haidée to plead
For them and theirs with all who deign to
    read.

EXTRACTS FROM DON JUAN
DISILLUSION
(*Canto I, ccxiv–ccxvii*)

No more—no more— Oh! never more on me
    The freshness of the heart can fall like dew,

Which out of all the lovely things we see
    Extracts emotions beautiful and new;
Hived in our bosoms like the bag o' the bee.
    Think'st thou the honey with those objects
    grew?
Alas! 'twas not in them, but in thy power
To double even the sweetness of a flower.

No more—no more— Oh! never more, my
    heart,
    Canst thou be my sole world, my universe!
Once all in all, but now a thing apart, 11
    Thou canst not be my blessing or my curse:
The illusion's gone for ever, and thou art
Insensible, I trust, but none the worse,
And in thy stead I've got a deal of judgment,
Though heaven knows how it ever found a
    lodgment.

My days of love are over; me no more
    The charms of maid, wife, and still less of
    widow,
Can make the fool of which they made be-
    fore,— 19
    In short, I must not lead the life I did do;
The credulous hope of mutual minds is o'er,
    The copious use of claret is forbid too,
So for a good old-gentlemanly vice,
I think I must take up with avarice.

Ambition was my idol, which was broken
    Before the shrines of Sorrow, and of Pleas-
    ure;
And the two last have left me many a token
    O'er which reflection may be made at lei-
    sure;
Now, like Friar Bacon's brazen head, I've
    spoken,
    "Time is, Time was, Time's past":—a
    chymic treasure 30
Is glittering youth, which I have spent be-
    times—
My heart in passion, and my head on rhymes.

(*Canto IV, iii–iv*)

As boy, I thought myself a clever fellow,
    And wish'd that others held the same
    opinion;
They took it up when my days grew more
    mellow,
    And other minds acknowledged my domin-
    ion:
Now my sere fancy "falls into the yellow
    Leaf," and Imagination droops her pinion,

And the sad truth which hovers o'er my desk
Turns what was once romantic to burlesque. 40

And if I laugh at any mortal thing,
'Tis that I may not weep; and if I weep,
'Tis that our nature cannot always bring
Itself to apathy, for we must steep
Our hearts first in the depths of Lethe's
spring,
Ere what we least wish to behold will sleep:
Thetis baptized her mortal son in Styx;
A mortal mother would on Lethe fix.

FAME

(Canto I, ccxviii–ccxviii)

WHAT is the end of fame? 't is but to fill
A certain portion of uncertain paper:
Some liken it to climbing up a hill,
Whose summit, like all hills, is lost in
vapour;
For this men write, speak, preach, and heroes
kill,
And bards burn what they call their "mid-
night taper,"
To have, when the original is dust,
A name, a wretched picture, and worse bust.

What are the hopes of man? Old Egypt's King
Cheops erected the first pyramid, 10
And largest, thinking it was just the thing
To keep his memory whole, and mummy
hid;
But somebody or other, rummaging,
Burglariously broke his coffin's lid:
Let not a monument give you or me hopes,
Since not a pinch of dust remains of Cheops.

(Canto III, lxxxviii–lxxxix)

BUT words are things, and a small drop of ink,
Falling like dew, upon a thought, produces
That which makes thousands, perhaps millions
think; [uses
'Tis strange, the shortest letter which man
Instead of speech, may form a lasting link
Of ages; to what straits old Time reduces
Frail man, when paper—even a rag like this,
Survives himself, his tomb, and all that's his!

And when his bones are dust, his grave a
blank, 10
His station, generation, even his nation,
Become a thing, or nothing, save to rank

In chronological commemoration,
Some dull MS. oblivion long has sank,
Or graven stone found in a barrack's station
In digging the foundation of a closet,
May turn his name up, as a rare deposit.

POETICAL COMMANDMENTS

(Canto I, cciv–ccvi)

IF ever I should condescend to prose,
I'll write poetical commandments, which
Shall supersede beyond all doubt all those
That went before; in these I shall enrich
My text with many things that no one knows,
And carry precept to the highest pitch:
I'll call the work "Longinus o'er a Bottle,
Or, Every Poet his own Aristotle."

Thou shalt believe in Milton, Dryden, Pope;
Thou shalt not set up Wordsworth, Coleridge,
Southey; 10
Because the first is crazed beyond all hope,
The second drunk, the third so quaint and
mouthy:
With Crabbe it may be difficult to cope,
And Campbell's Hippocrene is somewhat
drouthy:
Thou shalt not steal from Samuel Rogers, nor
Commit—flirtation with the muse of Moore.

Thou shalt not covet Mr. Sotheby's Muse,
His Pegasus, nor anything that's his;
Thou shalt not bear false witness like "the
Blues"— 19
(There's one, at least, is very fond of this);
Thou shalt not write, in short, but what I
choose;
This is true criticism, and you may kiss—
Exactly as you please, or not,—the rod;
But if you don't, I'll lay it on, by G—d!

LOVE AND THE POETS

(Canto III, viii–xi)

THERE'S doubtless something in domestic
doings,
Which forms, in fact, true love's antithesis;
Romances paint at full length people's woo-
ings,
But only give a bust of marriages;
For no one cares for matrimonial cooings,
There's nothing wrong in a connubial kiss:
Think you, if Laura had been Petrarch's wife,
He would have written sonnets all his life?

All tragedies are finish'd by a death,
   All comedies are ended by a marriage;   10
The future states of both are left to faith,
   For authors fear description might disparage
The worlds to come of both, or fall beneath,
   And then both worlds would punish their
      miscarriage;
So leaving each their priest and prayer-book
     ready,
They say no more of Death or of the Lady.

The only two that in my recollection
   Have sung of heaven and hell, or marriage,
    are
Dante and Milton, and of both the affection 19
   Was hapless in their nuptials, for some bar
Of fault or temper ruin'd the connection
   (Such things, in fact, it don't ask much to
    mar);
But Dante's Beatrice and Milton's Eve
   Were not drawn from their spouses, you con-
    ceive.

Some persons say that Dante meant theology
   By Beatrice, and not a mistress—I,
Although my opinion may require apology,
   Deem this a commentator's phantasy;
Unless, indeed, it was from his own knowledge
   he   29
   Decided thus, and show'd good reason why;
I think that Dante's more abstruse ecstatics
Meant to personify the mathematics.

DEVOTION

(*Canto III, cii–cviii*)

AVE MARIA! blessed be the hour!
   The time, the clime, the spot, where I so
    oft
Have felt that moment in its fullest power
   Sink o'er the earth so beautiful and soft,
While swung the deep bell in the distant
    tower,
   Or the faint dying day-hymn stole aloft,
And not a breath crept through the rosy air,
And yet the forest leaves seem'd stirr'd with
    prayer.

Ave Maria! 'tis the hour of prayer!
   Ave Maria! 'tis the hour of love!   10
Ave Maria! may our spirits dare
   Look up to thine and to thy Son's above!
Ave Maria! oh that face so fair!

Those downcast eyes beneath the Almighty
    dove—
What though 'tis but a pictured image strike,
That painting is no idol,—'tis too like.

Some kinder casuists are pleased to say,
   In nameless print—that I have no devo-
    tion;
But set those persons down with me to pray,
   And you shall see who has the properest
    notion   20
Of getting into heaven the shortest way;
   My altars are the mountains and the ocean,
Earth, air, stars,—all that springs from the
    great Whole,
Who hath produced, and will receive the soul.

Sweet hour of twilight!—in the solitude
   Of the pine forest, and the silent shore
Which bounds Ravenna's immemorial wood,
   Rooted where once the Adrian wave flow'd
    o'er,
To where the last Cæsarean fortress stood,
   Evergreen forest! which Boccaccio's lore 30
And Dryden's lay made haunted ground to me,
How have I loved the twilight hour and thee!

The shrill cicadas, people of the pine,
   Making their summer lives one ceaseless
    song,
Were the sole echoes, save my steed's and
    mine,
   And vesper bell's that rose the boughs
    along;
The spectre huntsman of Onesti's line,
   His hell-dogs, and their chase, and the fair
    throng
Which learn'd from this example not to fly
From a true lover,—shadow'd my mind's
    eye.   40

Oh, Hesperus! thou bringest all good things—
   Home to the weary, to the hungry cheer,
To the young bird the parent's brooding wings,
   The welcome stall to the o'erlabour'd steer;
Whate'er of peace about our hearthstone
    clings,
   Whate'er our household gods protect of
    dear,
Are gather'd round us by thy look of rest;
Thou bring'st the child, too, to the mother's
    breast.

Soft hour! which wakes the wish and melts
    the heart

Of those who sail the seas, on the first
    day   50
When they from their sweet friends are torn
    apart;
Or fills with love the pilgrim on his way
As the far bell of vespers makes him start,
    Seeming to weep the dying day's decay;
Is this a fancy which our reason scorns?
Ah! surely nothing dies but something mourns!

LEARNED LADIES

(Canto IV, cx–cxi)

OH! "darkly, deeply, beautifully blue,"
    As some one somewhere sings about the
        sky,
And I, ye learned ladies, say of you;
    They say your stockings are so—(Heaven
        knows why,
I have examined few pairs of that hue);
    Blue as the garters which serenely lie
Round the patrician left-legs, which adorn
The festal midnight, and the levée morn.

Yet some of you are most seraphic creatures—
    But times are alter'd since, a rhyming
        lover,   10
You read my stanzas, and I read your fea-
    tures:
And—but no matter, all those things are
    over;
Still I have no dislike to learned natures,
    For sometimes such a world of virtues
        cover;
I knew one woman of that purple school,
The loveliest, chastest, best, but—quite a fool.

VANITAS VANITATUM

(Canto VII, i–vi)

O LOVE! O Glory! what are you who fly
    Around us ever, rarely to alight?
There's not a meteor in the Polar sky
    Of such transcendent and more fleeting
        flight.
Chill, and chain'd to cold earth, we lift on
    high
    Our eyes in search of either lovely light;
A thousand and a thousand colours they
Assume, then leave us on our freezing way.

And such as they are, such my present tale is,
    A nondescript and ever-varying rhyme,   10

A versified Aurora Borealis,
    Which flashes o'er a waste and icy clime.
When we know what all are, we must bewail
    us,
    But ne'ertheless I hope it is no crime
To laugh at *all* things—for I wish to know
What, after *all*, are *all* things—but a *show?*

They accuse me—*Me*—the present writer of
    The present poem—of—I know not what—
A tendency to under-rate and scoff
    At human power and virtue, and all that; 20
And this they say in language rather rough.
    Good God! I wonder what they would be
        at!
I say no more than hath been said in Dante's
    Verse, and by Solomon and by Cervantes;

By Swift, by Machiavel, by Rochefoucault,
    By Fénélon, by Luther, and by Plato;
By Tillotson, and Wesley, and Rousseau,
    Who knew this life was not worth a potato.
'T is not their fault, nor mine, if this be so,—
    For my part, I pretend not to be Cato, 30
Nor even Diogenes.—We live and die,
But which is best, you know no more than I.

Socrates said, our only knowledge was
    "To know that nothing could be known";
        a pleasant
Science enough, which levels to an ass
    Each man of wisdom, future, past, or
        present.
Newton (that proverb of the mind), alas!
    Declared, with all his grand discoveries
        recent,
That he himself felt only "like a youth   39
Picking up shells by the great ocean—Truth."

Ecclesiastes said, "that all is vanity"—
    Most modern preachers say the same, or
        show it
By their examples of true Christianity:
    In short, all know, or very soon may know
        it;
And in this scene of all-confess'd inanity,
    By saint, by sage, by preacher, and by poet,
Must I restrain me, through the fear of
    strife,
From holding up the nothingness of life?

HIS POLITICS

(Canto IX, xxiv–xxv)

AND I will war, at least in words (and—
    should

My chance so happen—deeds), with all who
  war
With Thought;—and of Thought's foes by
  far most rude,
Tyrants and sycophants have been and are.
I know not who may conquer: if I could
  Have such a prescience, it should be no bar
To this my plain, sworn, downright detesta-
  tion
Of every despotism in every nation.

It is not that I adulate the people:
  Without *me*, there are demagogues enough,
And infidels, to pull down every steeple,   10
  And set up in their stead some proper
  stuff.
Whether they may sow scepticism to reap
  hell,
  As is the Christian dogma rather rough,
I do not know;—I wish men to be free
As much from mobs as kings—from you as
  me.

WELLINGTON

(*Canto IX, i–iv*)

OH, Wellington! (or "Villainton"—for Fame
  Sounds the heroic syllables both ways;
France could not even conquer your great
  name,
  But punn'd it down to this facetious
  phrase—
Beating or beaten she will laugh the same,)
  You have obtain'd great pensions and much
  praise:
Glory like yours should any dare gainsay,
Humanity would rise, and thunder "Nay!"

I don't think that you used Kinnaird quite
  well
  In Marinèt's affair—in fact 't was shabby,   10
And like some other things won't do to tell
  Upon your tomb in Westminster's old abbey.
Upon the rest 't is not worth while to dwell,
  Such tales being for the tea-hours of some
  tabby;
But though your years as *man* tend fast to
  zero,
In fact your grace is still but a *young hero*.

Though Britain owes (and pays you too) so
  much,

Yet Europe doubtless owes you greatly
  more:
You have repair'd Legitimacy's crutch,
  A prop not quite so certain as before: 20
The Spanish, and the French, as well as
  Dutch,
  Have seen, and felt, how strongly you
  restore;
And Waterloo has made the world your
  debtor
(I wish your bards would sing it rather bet-
  ter).

You are "the best of cut-throats":—do not
  start;
  The phrase is Shakespeare's, and not mis-
  applied: —
War's a brain-spattering, windpipe-slitting art,
  Unless her cause by right be sanctified.
If you have acted *once* a generous part,
  The world, not the world's masters, will
  decide,   30
And I shall be delighted to learn who,
Save you and yours, have gain'd by Waterloo?

LONDON TOWN

(*Canto X, lxxxii*)

A MIGHTY mass of brick, and smoke, and
  shipping,
  Dirty and dusky, but as wide as eye
Could reach, with here and there a sail just
  skipping
  In sight, then lost amidst the forestry
Of masts; a wilderness of steeples peeping
  On tiptoe through their sea-coal canopy;
A huge, dun cupola, like a foolscap crown
On a fool's head—and there is London Town!

MONEY

(*Canto XII, xii–xiv*)

How beauteous are rouleaus! how charming
  chests
  Containing ingots, bags of dollars, coins
(Not of old victors, all whose heads and crests
  Weigh not the thin ore where their visage
  shines,
But) of fine unclipt gold, where dully rests
  Some likeness, which the glittering cirque
  confines,
Of modern, reigning, sterling, stupid stamp:
Yes! ready money *is* Aladdin's lamp.

"Love rules the camp, the court, the grove,—for love
    Is heaven, and heaven is love":—so sings the bard;   10
Which it were rather difficult to prove
(A thing with poetry in general hard).
Perhaps there may be something in "the grove,"
    At least it rhymes to "love": but I'm prepared
To doubt (no less than landlords of their rental)
If "courts" and "camps" be quite so sentimental.

But if Love don't, *Cash* does, and Cash alone:
    Cash rules the grove, and fells it too besides;
Without cash, camps were thin, and courts were none;
    Without cash, Malthus tells you—"take no brides."   20
So Cash rules Love the ruler, on his own
    High ground, as virgin Cynthia sways the tides:
And as for "Heaven being Love," why not say honey
Is wax? Heaven is not Love, 'tis Matrimony.

THE LAKE AT NEWSTEAD

(*Canto XIII, lvii–lviii*)

BEFORE the mansion lay a lucid lake,
    Broad as transparent, deep, and freshly fed
By a river, which its soften'd way did take
    In currents through the calmer water spread
Around: the wildfowl nestled in the brake
    And sedges, brooding in their liquid bed:
The woods sloped downwards to its brink, and stood
With their green faces fix'd upon the flood.

Its outlet dash'd into a deep cascade,
    Sparkling with foam, until again subsiding,
Its shriller echoes—like an infant made   10
    Quiet—sank into softer ripples, gliding
Into a rivulet: and thus allay'd,
    Pursued its course, now gleaming, and now hiding
Its windings through the woods; now clear, now blue,
According as the skies their shadows threw.

"MARY"

(*Canto V, iv*)

I HAVE a passion for the name of "Mary,"
    For once it was a magic sound to me;
And still it half calls up the realms of fairy,
    Where I beheld what never was to be;
All feelings changed, but this was last to vary,
    A spell from which even yet I am not quite free:
But I grow sad—and let a tale grow cold,
Which must not be pathetically told.

LIFE

(*Canto XV, xcix*)

BETWEEN two worlds life hovers like a star,
    'Twixt night and morn, upon the horizon's verge.
How little do we know that which we are!
    How less what we may be! The eternal surge
Of time and tide rolls on, and bears afar
    Our bubbles; as the old burst, new emerge,
Lash'd from the foam of ages; while the graves
Of empires heave but like some passing waves.

THE VISION OF JUDGMENT

I

SAINT PETER sat by the celestial gate:
    His keys were rusty, and the lock was dull,
So little trouble had been given of late;
    Not that the place by any means was full,
But since the Gallic era "eighty-eight"
    The devils had ta'en a longer, stronger pull,
And "a pull together," as they say
At sea—which drew most souls another way.

II

The angels all were singing out of tune,
    And hoarse with having little else to do,   10
Excepting to wind up the sun and moon,
    Or curb a runaway young star or two,
Or wild colt of a comet, which too soon
    Broke out of bounds o'er th' ethereal blue,
Splitting some planet with its playful tail,
As boats are sometimes by a wanton whale.

III

The guardian seraphs had retired on high,
  Finding their charges past all care below;
Terrestrial business fill'd nought in the sky
  Save the recording angel's black bureau; 20
Who found, indeed, the facts to multiply
  With such rapidity of vice and woe,
That he had stripp'd off both his wings in
    quills,
And yet was in arrear of human ills.

IV

His business so augmented of late years,
  That he was forced, against his will no
    doubt,
(Just like those cherubs, earthly ministers,)
  For some resource to turn himself about,
And claim the help of his celestial peers,
  To aid him ere he should be quite worn
    out   30
By the increased demand for his remarks:
Six angels and twelve saints were named his
    clerks.

V

This was a handsome board—at least for
    heaven;
  And yet they had even then enough to do,
So many conquerors' cars were daily driven,
  So many kingdoms fitted up anew;
Each day too slew its thousands six or seven,
  Till at the crowning carnage, Waterloo,
They threw their pens down in divine dis-
    gust—
The page was so besmear'd with blood and
    dust.   40

VI

This by the way; 't is not mine to record
  What angels shrink from: even the very
    devil
On this occasion his own work abhorr'd,
  So surfeited with the infernal revel:
Though he himself had sharpen'd every sword,
  It almost quench'd his innate thirst of evil.
(Here Satan's sole good work deserves in-
    sertion—
'Tis, that he has both generals in reversion.)

VII

Let's skip a few short years of hollow peace,
  Which peopled earth no better, hell as
    wont,   50
And heaven none—they form the tyrant's
    lease,
  With nothing but new names subscribed
    upon 't;
'T will one day finish: meantime they in-
    crease,
  "With seven heads and ten horns," and all
    in front,
Like Saint John's foretold beast; but ours
    are born
Less formidable in the head than horn.

VIII

In the first year of freedom's second dawn
  Died George the Third; although no tyrant,
    one
Who shielded tyrants, till each sense with-
    drawn
  Left him nor mental nor external sun: 60
A better farmer ne'er brush'd dew from
    lawn,
  A worse king never left a realm undone!
He died—but left his subjects still behind,
One half as mad—an t'other no less blind.

IX

He died! his death made no great stir on
    earth:
  His burial made some pomp; there was
    profusion
Of velvet, gilding, brass, and no great dearth
  Of aught but tears—save those shed by
    collusion.
For these things may be bought at their true
    worth;
  Of elegy there was the due infusion—   70
Bought also; and the torches, cloaks, and
    banners,
Heralds, and relics of old Gothic manners,

X

Form'd a sepulchral melodrame. Of all
  The fools who flock'd to swell or see the
    show,
Who cared about the corpse? The funeral
  Made the attraction, and the black the woe.

There throbb'd not there a thought which
　　pierced the pall;
And when the gorgeous coffin was laid low,
It seem'd the mockery of hell to fold
The rottenness of eighty years in gold.　　80

XI

So mix his body with the dust! It might
　　Return to what it *must* far sooner, were
The natural compound left alone to fight
　　Its way back into earth, and fire, and air;
But the unnatural balsams merely blight
　　What nature made him at his birth, as bare
As the mere million's base unmummied clay—
Yet all his spices but prolong decay.

XII

He's dead—and upper earth with him has
　　done;
　　He's buried; save the undertaker's bill, 90
Or lapidary scrawl, the world is gone
　　For him, unless he left a German will:
But where's the proctor who will ask his son?
　　In whom his qualities are reigning still,
Except that household virtue, most uncommon,
Of constancy to a bad, ugly woman.

XIII

"God save the king!" It is a large economy
　　In God to save the like; but if he will
Be saving, all the better; for not one am I
　　Of those who think damnation better still:
I hardly know too if not quite alone am I　101
　　In this small hope of bettering future ill
By circumscribing, with some slight restric-
　　tion,
The eternity of hell's hot jurisdiction.

XIV

I know this is unpopular; I know
　　'T is blasphemous; I know one may be
　　damn'd
For hoping no one else may e'er be so;
　　I know my catechism; I know we're
　　cramm'd
With the best doctrines till we quite o'erflow;
　　I know that all save England's church have
　　shamm'd,　　　　　　　　　　　　　110
And that the other twice two hundred churches

And synagogues have made a *damn'd* bad
　　purchase.

XV

God help us all! God help me too! I am,
　　God knows, as helpless as the devil can
　　wish,
And not a whit more difficult to damn,
　　Than is to bring to land a late-hook'd fish,
Or to the butcher to purvey the lamb;
　　Not that I'm fit for such a noble dish,
As one day will be that immortal fry
Of almost everybody born to die.　　120

XVI

Saint Peter sat by the celestial gate,
　　And nodded o'er his keys; when, lo! there
　　came
A wondrous noise he had not heard of late—
　　A rushing sound of wind, and stream, and
　　flame;
In short, a roar of things extremely great,
　　Which would have made aught save a saint
　　exclaim;
But he, with first a start and then a wink,
Said, "There's another star gone out, I
　　think!"

XVII

But ere he could return to his repose,
　　A cherub flapp'd his right wing o'er his
　　eyes —　　　　　　　　　　　　　　130
At which St. Peter yawn'd, and rubb'd his
　　nose:
　　"Saint porter," said the angel, "prithee
　　rise!"
Waving a goodly wing, which glow'd, as glows
　　An earthly peacock's tail, with heavenly
　　dyes:
To which the saint replied, "Well, what's the
　　matter?
Is Lucifer come back with all this clatter?"

XVIII

"No," quoth the cherub; "George the Third
　　is dead."
　　"And who *is* George the Third?" replied
　　the apostle:
"What George? what Third?" "The king of
　　England," said

The angel. "Well! he won't find kings to
    jostle   140
Him on his way; but does he wear his head?
    Because the last we saw here had a tustle,
And ne'er would have got into heaven's good
    graces,
Had he not flung his head in all our faces.

XIX

"He was, if I remember, king of France;
    That head of his, which could not keep a
        crown
On earth, yet ventured in my face to advance
    A claim to those of martyrs—like my own:
If I had had my sword, as I had once   149
    When I cut ears off, I had cut him down;
But having but my *keys,* and not my brand,
I only knock'd his head from out his hand.

XX

"And then he set up such a headless howl,
    That all the saints came out and took him
        in;
And there he sits by St. Paul, cheek by jowl;
    That fellow Paul—the parvenù! The skin
Of St. Bartholomew, which makes his cowl
    In heaven, and upon earth redeem'd his sin,
So as to make a martyr, never sped
Better than did this weak and wooden head. 160

XXI

"But had it come up here upon its shoulders,
    There would have been a different tale to
        tell:
The fellow-feeling in the saints beholders
    Seems to have acted on them like a spell,
And so this very foolish head heaven solders
    Back on its trunk: it may be very well,
And seems the custom here to overthrow
Whatever has been wisely done below."

XXII

The angel answer'd, "Peter! do not pout:
    The king who comes has head and all en-
        tire,   170
And never knew much what it was about—
    He did as doth the puppet—by its wire,
And will be judged like all the rest, no doubt:
    My business and your own is not to inquire

Into such matters, but to mind our cue—
Which is to act as we are bid to do."

XXIII

While thus they spake, the angelic caravan,
    Arriving like a rush of mighty wind,
Cleaving the fields of space, as doth the swan
    Some silver stream (say Ganges, Nile, or
        Inde,   180
Or Thames, or Tweed), and 'midst them an
    old man
With an old soul, and both extremely blind,
Halted before the gate, and in his shroud
Seated their fellow-traveller on a cloud.

XXIV

But bringing up the rear of this bright host
    A Spirit of a different aspect waved
His wings, like thunder-clouds above some
        coast
    Whose barren beach with frequent wrecks
        is paved;
His brow was like the deep when tempest-
        toss'd;
    Fierce and unfathomable thoughts engraved
Eternal wrath on his immortal face,   191
And *where* he gazed a gloom pervaded space.

XXV

As he drew near, he gazed upon the gate
    Ne'er to be enter'd more by him or Sin,
With such a glance of supernatural hate,
    As made Saint Peter wish himself within;
He patter'd with his keys at a great rate,
    And sweated through his apostolic skin:
Of course his perspiration was but ichor,
Or some such other spiritual liquor.   200

XXVI

The very cherubs huddled all together,
    Like birds when soars the falcon; and they
        felt
A tingling to the tip of every feather,
    And form'd a circle like Orion's belt
Around their poor old charge; who scarce
        knew whither
    His guards had led him, though they gently
        dealt
With royal manes (for by many stories,
And true, we learn the angels all are **Tories**).

XXVII

As things were in this posture, the gate flew
    Asunder, and the flashing of its hinges   210
Flung over space an universal hue
    Of many-colour'd flame, until its tinges
Reach'd even our speck of earth, and made a new
    Aurora borealis spread its fringes
O'er the North Pole; the same seen, when ice-bound,
    By Captain Parry's crew, in "Melville's Sound."

XXVIII

And from the gate thrown open issued beaming
    A beautiful and mighty Thing of Light,
Radiant with glory, like a banner streaming
    Victorious from some world-o'erthrowing fight: 220
My poor comparisons must needs be teeming
    With earthly likenesses, for here the night
Of clay obscures our best conceptions, saving
Johanna Southcote, or Bob Southey raving.

XXIX

'T was the archangel Michael; all men know
    The make of angels and archangels, since
There's scarce a scribbler has not one to show,
    From the fiends' leader to the angels' prince;
There also are some altar-pieces, though
    I really can't say that they much evince   230
One's inner notions of immortal spirits;
But let the connoisseurs explain *their* merits.

XXX

Michael flew forth in glory and in good;
    A goodly work of him from whom all glory
And good arise; the portal past—he stood;
    Before him the young cherubs and saints hoary—
(I say *young*, begging to be understood
    By looks, not years; and should be very sorry   238
To state, they were not older than St. Peter,
But merely that they seem'd a little sweeter).

XXXI

The cherubs and the saints bow'd down before

That arch-angelic hierarch, the first
    Of essences angelical, who wore
The aspect of a god; but this ne'er nursed
    Pride in his heavenly bosom, in whose core
No thought, save for his Master's service, durst
    Intrude, however glorified and high;
He knew him but the viceroy of the sky.

XXXII

He and the sombre, silent Spirit met—
    They knew each other both for good and ill;   250
Such was their power, that neither could forget
    His former friend and future foe; but still
There was a high, immortal, proud regret
    In either's eye, as if 't were less their will
Than destiny to make the eternal years
Their date of war, and their "champ clos" the spheres.

XXXIII

But here they were in neutral space: we know
    From Job, that Satan hath the power to pay
A heavenly visit thrice a year or so;
    And that the "sons of God," like those of clay,   260
Must keep him company; and we might show
    From the same book, in how polite a way
The dialogue is held between the Powers
Of Good and Evil—but 't would take up hours.

XXXIV

And this is not a theologic tract,
    To prove with Hebrew and with Arabic,
If Job be allegory or a fact,
    But a true narrative; and thus I pick
From out the whole but such and such an act
    As sets aside the slightest thought of trick.
'T is every tittle true, beyond suspicion,   271
And accurate as any other vision.

XXXV

The spirits were in neutral space, before
    The gate of heaven; like eastern thresholds is

The place where Death's grand cause is argued
o'er,
  And souls despatch'd to that world or to
this;
And therefore Michael and the other wore
  A civil aspect: though they did not kiss,
Yet still between his Darkness and his Bright-
ness
There pass'd a mutual glance of great polite-
ness.   280

XXXVI

The Archangel bow'd, not like a modern beau,
  But with a graceful Oriental bend,
Pressing one radiant arm just where below
  The heart in good men is supposed to tend;
He turn'd as to an equal, not too low,
  But kindly; Satan met his ancient friend
With more hauteur, as might an old Castilian
Poor noble meet a mushroom rich civilian.

XXXVII

He merely bent his diabolic brow
  An instant; and then raising it, he stood 290
In act to assert his right or wrong, and show
  Cause why King George by no means could
or should
Make out a case to be exempt from woe
  Eternal, more than other kings, endued
With better sense and hearts, whom history
mentions,
Who long have "paved hell with their good
intentions."

XXXVIII

Michael began: "What wouldst thou with
this man,
  Now dead, and brought before the Lord?
What ill
Hath he wrought since his mortal race began,
  That thou canst claim him? Speak! and
do thy will,   300
If it be just: if in this earthly span
  He hath been greatly failing to fufiil
His duties as a king and mortal, say,
And he is thine; if not, let him have way."

XXXIX

"Michael!" replied the Prince of Air, "even
here,

Before the Gate of him thou servest, must
  I claim my subject: and will make appear
That as he was my worshipper in dust,
  So shall he be in spirit, although dear
To thee and thine, because nor wine nor lust
  Were of his weaknesses; yet on the throne 311
He reign'd o'er millions to serve me alone.

XL

"Look to our earth, or rather mine; it was,
  Once, more thy master's: but I triumph not
In this poor planet's conquest; nor, alas!
  Need he thou servest envy me my lot:
With all the myriads of bright worlds which
pass
  In worship round him, he may have forgot
Yon weak creation of such paltry things:
I think few worth damnation save their
kings,—   320

XLI

"And these but as a kind of quit-rent, to
  Assert my right as lord: and even had
I such an inclination, 't were (as you
  Well know) superfluous; they are grown
so bad,
That hell has nothing better left to do
  Than leave them to themselves: so much
more mad
And evil by their own internal curse,
Heaven cannot make them better, nor I
worse.

XLII

"Look to the earth, I said, and say again:
  When this old, blind, mad, helpless, weak,
poor worm   330
Began in youth's first bloom and flush to
reign,
  The world and he both wore a different
form,
And much of earth and all the watery plain
  Of ocean call'd him king: through many a
storm
His isles had floated on the abyss of time;
For the rough virtues chose them for their
clime.

XLIII

"He came to his sceptre young; he leaves it
old:

Look to the state in which he found his
    realm,
And left it; and his annals too behold,
    How to a minion first he gave the helm; 340
How grew upon his heart a thirst for gold,
    The beggar's vice, which can but over-
        whelm
The meanest hearts; and for the rest, but
    glance
Thine eye along America and France.

XLIV

" 'T is true, he was a tool from first to last
    (I have the workmen safe); but as a tool
So let him be consumed. From out the past
    Of ages, since mankind have known the
        rule
Of monarchs—from the bloody rolls amass'd
    Of sin and slaughter—from the Cæsar's
        school,   350
Take the worst pupil; and produce a reign
More drench'd with gore, more cumber'd with
    the slain.

XLV

"He ever warr'd with freedom and the free:
    Nations as men, home subjects, foreign
        foes,
So that they utter'd the word 'Liberty!'
    Found George the Third their first oppon-
        ent. Whose
History was ever stain'd as his will be
    With national and individual woes?
I grant his household abstinence; I grant
His neutral virtues, which most monarchs
    want;   360

XLVI

"I know he was a constant consort; own
    He was a decent sire, and middling lord.
All this is much, and most upon a throne;
    As temperance, if at Apicius' board,
Is more than at an anchorite's supper shown.
    I grant him all the kindest can accord;
And this was well for him, but not for those
Millions who found him what oppression
    chose.

XLVII

"The New World shook him off; the Old yet
    groans   369

Beneath what he and his prepared, if not
Completed: he leaves heirs on many thrones
To all his vices, without what begot
Compassion for him—his tame virtues;
    drones
Who sleep, or despots who have now forgot
A lesson which shall be re-taught them, wake
Upon the thrones of earth; but let them
    quake!

XLVIII

"Five millions of the primitive, who hold
    The faith which makes ye great on earth,
        implored
A *part* of that vast *all* they held of old,— 379
    Freedom to worship—not alone your Lord,
Michael, but you, and you, Saint Peter! Cold
    Must be your souls, if you have not ab-
        horr'd
The foe to Catholic participation
In all the license of a Christian nation.

XLIX

"True! he allow'd them to pray God; but as
    A consequence of prayer, refused the law
Which would have placed them upon the same
    base
    With those who did not hold the saints in
        awe."
But here Saint Peter started from his place,
    And cried, "You may the prisoner with-
        draw: 390
Ere heaven shall ope her portals to this
    Guelph,
While I am guard, may I be damn'd myself!

L

"Sooner will I with Cerberus exchange
    My office (and *his* is no sinecure)
Than see this royal Bedlam bigot range
    The azure fields of heaven, of that be sure!"
"Saint!" replied Satan, "you do well to
    avenge
    The wrongs he made your satellites en-
        dure;
And if to this exchange you should be given,
I'll try to coax *our* Cerberus up to heaven!"

LI

Here Michael interposed: "Good saint! and
    devil!   401

Pray, not so fast; you both outrun dis-
    cretion.
Saint Peter! you were wont to be more civil!
    Satan! excuse this warmth of his expres-
    sion,
And condescension to the vulgar's level:
    Even saints sometimes forget themselves in
    session.
Have you got more to say?"—"No."—"If you
    please,
I'll trouble you to call your witnesses."

LII

Then Satan turn'd and waved his swarthy
    hand,
    Which stirr'd with its electric qualities 410
Clouds farther off than we can understand,
    Although we find him sometimes in our
    skies;
Infernal thunder shook both sea and land
    In all the planets, and hell's batteries
Let off the artillery, which Milton mentions
As one of Satan's most sublime inventions.

LIII

This was a signal unto such damn'd souls
    As have the privilege of their damnation
Extended far beyond the mere controls
    Of worlds past, present, or to come; no
    station   420
Is theirs particularly in the rolls
    Of hell assign'd; but where their inclina-
    tion
Or business carries them in search of game,
    They may range freely—being damn'd the
    same.

LIV

They're proud of this—as very well they
    may,
    It being a sort of knighthood, or gilt key
Stuck in their loins; or like to an "entrée"
    Up the back stairs, or such free-masonry.
I borrow my comparisons from clay,
    Being clay myself. Let not those spirits be
Offended with such base low likenesses;   431
We know their posts are nobler far than these.

LV

When the great signal ran from heaven to
    hell—

About ten million times the distance reck-
    on'd
From our sun to its earth, as we can tell
    How much time it takes up, even to a
    second,
For every ray that travels to dispel
    The fogs of London, through which, dimly
    beacon'd,
The weathercocks are gilt some thrice a year,
If that the *summer* is not too severe: 440

LVI

I say that I can tell—'t was half a minute;
    I know the solar beams take up more time
Ere, pack'd up for their journey, they begin
    it;
    But then their telegraph is less sublime,
And if they ran a race, they would not win it
    'Gainst Satan's couriers bound for their
    own clime.
The sun takes up some years for every ray
To reach its goal—the devil not half a day.

LVII

Upon the verge of space, about the size
    Of half-a-crown, a little speck appear'd   450
(I've seen a something like it in the skies
    In the Ægean, ere a squall); it near'd,
And, growing bigger, took another guise;
    Like an aërial ship it tack'd, and steer'd,
Or *was* steer'd (I am doubtful of the gram-
    mar
Of the last phrase, which makes the stanza
    stammer;—

LVIII

But take your choice): and then it grew a
    cloud;
    And so it was—a cloud of witnesses,
But such a cloud! No land e'er saw a crowd
    Of locusts numerous as the heavens saw
    these;   460
They shadow'd with their myriads space;
    their loud
    And varied cries were like those of wild
    geese
(If nations may be liken'd to a goose),
And realised the phrase of "hell broke loose."

LIX

Here crash'd a sturdy oath of stout John Bull,

Who damn'd away his eyes as heretofore:
There Paddy brogued "By Jasus!"—"What's
    your wull?"
The temperate Scot exclaim'd: the French
    ghost swore
In certain terms I shan't translate in full,
    As the first coachman will; and 'midst the
    war,   470
The voice of Jonathan was heard to express,
"Our President is going to war, I guess."

LX

Besides there were the Spaniard, Dutch, and
    Dane;
    In short, an universal shoal of shades,
From Otaheite's isle to Salisbury Plain,
    Of all climes and professions, years and
    trades,
Ready to swear against the good king's reign,
    Bitter as clubs in cards are against spades:
All summon'd by this grand "subpœna," to
Try if kings mayn't be damn'd like me or
    you.   480

LXI

When Michael saw this host, he first grew
    pale,
    As angels can; next, like Italian twilight,
He turn'd all colours—as a peacock's tail,
    Or sunset streaming through a Gothic sky-
    light
In some old abbey, or a trout not stale,
    Or distant lightning on the horizon *by* night,
Or a fresh rainbow, or a grand review
Of thirty regiments in red, green, and blue.

LXII

Then he address'd himself to Satan: "Why—
    My good old friend, for such I deem you,
    though   490
Our different parties make us fight so shy,
    I ne'er mistake you for a *personal* foe;
Our difference is *political,* and I
    Trust that, whatever may occur below,
You know my great respect for you: and this
Makes me regret whate'er you do amiss—

LXIII

"Why, my dear Lucifer, would you abuse
    My call for witnesses? I did not mean

That you should half of earth and hell pro-
    duce;
    'Tis even superfluous, since two honest,
    clean,   500
True testimonies are enough: we lose
    Our time, nay, our eternity, between
The accusation and defence: if we
Hear both, 't will stretch our immortality."

LXIV

Satan replied, "To me the matter is
    Indifferent, in a personal point of view:
I can have fifty better souls than this
    With far less trouble than we have gone
    through
Already; and I merely argued his
    Late majesty of Britain's case with you 510
Upon a point of form: you may dispose
Of him: I've kings enough below, God
    knows!"

LXV

Thus spoke the Demon (late call'd "multi-
    faced"
    By multo-scribbling Southey). "Then we'll
    call
One or two persons of the myriads placed
    Around our congress, and dispense with all
The rest," quoth Michael: "Who may be so
    graced
    As to speak first? there's choice enough—
    who shall
It be?" Then Satan answer'd, "There are
    many;
But you may choose Jack Wilkes as well as
    any."   520

LXVI

A merry, cock-eyed, curious-looking sprite
    Upon the instant started from the throng,
Dress'd in a fashion now forgotten quite;
    For all the fashions of the flesh stick long
By people in the next world; where unite
    All the costumes since Adam's, right or
    wrong,
From Eve's fig-leaf down to the petticoat,
Almost as scanty, of days less remote.

LXVII

The spirit look'd around upon the crowds

Assembled, and exclaim'd, "My friends of
    all   530
The spheres, we shall catch cold amongst
    these clouds;
So let's to business: why this general call?
If those are freeholders I see in shrouds,
And 't is for an election that they bawl,
Behold a candidate with unturn'd coat!
Saint Peter, may I count upon your vote?"

LXVIII

"Sir," replied Michael, "you mistake; these
    things
Are of a former life, and what we do
Above is more august; to judge of kings
    Is the tribunal met: so now you know." 540
"Then I presume those gentlemen with
    wings,"
    Said Wilkes, "are cherubs; and that soul
    below
Looks much like George the Third, but to my
    mind
A good deal older— Bless me! is he blind?"

LXIX

"He is what you behold him, and his doom
    Depends upon his deeds," the Angel said;
"If you have aught to arraign in him, the
    tomb
Gives license to the humblest beggar's
    head
To lift itself against the loftiest."—"Some,"
    Said Wilkes, "don't wait to see them laid
    in lead,   550
For such a liberty—and I, for one,
Have told them what I thought beneath the
    sun."

LXX

"*Above* the sun repeat, then, what thou hast
    To urge against him," said the Archangel.
        "Why,"
Replied the spirit, "since old scores are past,
    Must I turn evidence? In faith, not I.
Besides, I beat him hollow at the last,
    With all his Lords and Commons: in the
    sky
I don't like ripping up old stories, since
His conduct was but natural in a prince. 560

LXXI

"Foolish, no doubt, and wicked, to oppress
    A poor unlucky devil without a shilling;
But then I blame the man himself much less
    Than Bute and Grafton, and shall be un-
    willing
To see him punish'd here for their excess,
    Since they were both damn'd long ago, and
    still in
Their place below: for me, I have forgiven,
And vote his 'habeas corpus' into heaven."

LXXII

"Wilkes," said the Devil, "I understand all
    this;
    You turn'd to half a courtier ere you died,
And seem to think it would not be amiss 571
    To grow a whole one on the other side
Of Charon's ferry; you forget that *his*
    Reign is concluded; whatsoe'er betide,
He won't be sovereign more: you've lost your
    labour,
For at the best he will but be your neighbour.

LXXIII

"However, I knew what to think of it,
    When I beheld you in your jesting way,
Flitting and whispering round about the spit
    Where Belial, upon duty for the day, 580
With Fox's lard was basting William Pitt,
    His pupil; I knew what to think, I say:
That fellow even in hell breeds farther ills;
I'll have him *gagg'd*—'t was one of his own
    bills.

LXXIV

"Call Junius!" From the crowd a shadow
    stalk'd,
    And at the name there was a general
    squeeze,
So that the very ghosts no longer walk'd
    In comfort, at their own aërial ease,
But were all ramm'd, and jamm'd (but to be
    balk'd,
    As we shall see), and jostled hands and
    knees,   590
Like wind compress'd and pent within a
    bladder,
Or like a human colic, which is sadder.

LXXV

The shadow came—a tall, thin, grey-hair'd
    figure,
  That look'd as it had been a shade on
    earth;
Quick in its motions, with an air of vigour,
  But nought to mark its breeding or its
    birth;
Now it wax'd little, then again grew bigger,
  With now an air of gloom, or savage mirth;
But as you gazed upon its features, they
Changed every instant—to *what*, none could
    say.   600

LXXVI

The more intently the ghosts gazed, the less
  Could they distinguish whose the features
    were;
The Devil himself seem'd puzzled even to
    guess;
  They varied like a dream—now here, now
    there;
And several people swore from out the press,
  They knew him perfectly; and one could
    swear
He was his father: upon which another
Was sure he was his mother's cousin's
    brother:

LXXVII

Another, that he was a duke, or knight,
  An orator, a lawyer, or a priest,   610
A nabob, a man-midwife; but the wight
  Mysterious changed his countenance at
    least
As oft as they their minds; though in full
    sight
  He stood, the puzzle only was increased;
The man was a phantasmagoria in
Himself—he was so volatile and thin.

LXXVIII

The moment that you had pronounced him
    one,
  Presto! his face changed, and he was
    another;
And when that change was hardly well put on,
  It varied, till I don't think his own mother
(If that he had a mother) would her son 621

Have known, he shifted so from one to
    t' other;
Till guessing from a pleasure grew a task,
At this epistolary "Iron Mask."

LXXIX

For sometimes he like Cerberus would seem—
  "Three gentlemen at once" (as sagely says
Good Mrs. Malaprop); then you might deem
  That he was not even *one;* now many rays
Were flashing round him; and now a thick
    steam
  Hid him from sight—like fogs on London
    days: 630
Now Burke, now Tooke, he grew to people's
    fancies,
And certes often like Sir Philip Francis.

LXXX

I've an hypothesis—'t is quite my own;
  I never let it out till now, for fear
Of doing people harm about the throne,
  And injuring some minister or peer,
On whom the stigma might perhaps be blown;
  It is—my gentle public, lend thine ear!
'T is, that what Junius we are wont to call
Was *really, truly,* nobody at all.   640

LXXXI

I don't see wherefore letters should not be
  Written without hands, since we daily view
Them written without heads; and books, we
    see,
  Are fill'd as well without the latter too:
And really till we fix on somebody
  For certain sure to claim them as his due,
Their author, like the Niger's mouth, will
    bother
The world to say if *there* be mouth or author.

LXXXII

"And who and what art thou?" the Arch-
    angel said.
  "For *that* you may consult my title-page,"
Replied this mighty shadow of a shade: 651
  "If I have kept my secret half an age,
I scarce shall tell it now."—"Canst thou up-
    braid,"
  Continued Michael, "George Rex, or allege

Aught further?" Junius answer'd, "You had
better
First ask him for *his* answer to my letter:

LXXXIII

"My charges upon record will outlast
  The brass of both his epitaph and tomb."
"Repent'st thou not," said Michael, "of some
    past   659
  Exaggeration? something which may doom
Thyself if false, as him if true? Thou wast
  Too bitter—is it not so?—in thy gloom
Of passion?"—"Passion!" cried the phantom
    dim,
  "I loved my country, and I hated him.

LXXXIV

"What I have written, I have written: let
  The rest be on his head or mine!" So
    spoke
Old "Nominis Umbra"; and while speaking
    yet,
  Away he melted in celestial smoke.
Then Satan said to Michael, "Don't forget
  To call George Washington, and John
    Horne Tooke,   670
And Franklin";—but at this time there was
    heard
  A cry for room, though not a phantom stirr'd.

LXXXV

At length with jostling, elbowing, and the aid
  Of cherubim appointed to that post,
The devil Asmodeus to the circle made
  His way, and look'd as if his journey cost
Some trouble. When his burden down he laid,
  "What's this?" cried Michael; "why, 'tis
    not a ghost?"
"I know it," quoth the incubus; "but he
Shall be one, if you leave the affair to me. 680

LXXXVI

"Confound the renegado! I have sprain'd
  My left wing, he's so heavy; one would
    think
Some of his works about his neck were
    chain'd.
  But to the point; while hovering o'er the
    brink
Of Skiddaw (where as usual it still rain'd),

I saw a taper, far below me, wink,
And stooping, caught this fellow at a libel—
No less on history than the Holy Bible.

LXXXVII

"The former is the devil's scripture, and
  The latter yours, good Michael: so the
    affair   690
Belongs to all of us, you understand.
  I snatch'd him up just as you see him there,
And brought him off for sentence out of
    hand:
  I've scarcely been ten minutes in the air—
At least a quarter it can hardly be:
I dare say that his wife is still at tea."

LXXXVIII

Here Satan said, "I know this man of old,
  And have expected him for some time here;
A sillier fellow you will scarce behold,
  Or more conceited in his petty sphere: 700
But surely it was not worth while to fold
  Such trash below your wing, Asmodeus
    dear:
We had the poor wretch safe (without being
    bored
With carriage) coming of his own accord.

LXXXIX

"But since he 's here, let's see what he has
    done."
  "Done!" cried Asmodeus, "he anticipates
The very business you are now upon,
  And scribbles as if head clerk to the Fates.
Who knows to what his ribaldry may run,
  When such an ass as this, like Balaam's,
    prates?"   710
"Let's hear," quoth Michael, "what he has
    to say:
You know we 're bound to that in every way."

XC

Now the bard, glad to get an audience, which
  By no means often was his case below,
Began to cough, and hawk, and hem, and
    pitch
  His voice into that awful note of woe
To all unhappy hearers within reach
  Of poets when the tide of rhyme's in flow;
But stuck fast with his first hexameter.
Not one of all whose gouty feet would stir. 720

XCI

But ere the spavin'd dactyls could be spurr'd
  Into recitative, in great dismay
Both cherubim and seraphim were heard
  To murmur loudly through their long array;
And Michael rose ere he could get a word
  Of all his founder'd verses under way,
And cried, "For God's sake stop, my friend! 't were best—
Non Di, non homines—you know the rest."

XCII

A general bustle spread throughout the throng,
  Which seem'd to hold all verse in detestation;   730
The angels had of course enough of song
  When upon service; and the generation
Of ghosts had heard too much in life, not long
  Before, to profit by a new occasion:
The monarch, mute till then, exclaim'd, "What! what!
Pye come again? No more—no more of that!"

XCIII

The tumult grew; an universal cough
  Convulsed the skies, as during a debate,
When Castlereagh had been up long enough
  (Before he was first minister of state,   740
I mean—the *slaves hear now*); some cried
      "Off, off!"
  As at a farce; till, grown quite desperate,
The bard Saint Peter pray'd to interpose
(Himself an author) only for his prose.

XCIV

The varlet was not an ill-favour'd knave;
  A good deal like a vulture in the face,
With a hook nose and a hawk's eye, which gave
  A smart and sharper-looking sort of grace
To his whole aspect, which, though rather grave,
  Was by no means so ugly as his case;   750
But that, indeed, was hopeless as can be,
Quite a poetic felony *"de se."*

XCV

Then Michael blew his trump, and still'd the noise

XCVI

With one still greater, as is yet the mode
  On earth besides; except some grumbling voice,
    Which now and then will make a slight inroad
Upon decorous silence, few will twice
    Lift up their lungs when fairly overcrow'd;
And now the bard could plead his own bad cause,
With all the attitudes of self-applause.   760

XCVI

He said—(I only give the heads)—he said,
  He meant no harm in scribbling; 't was his way
Upon all topics; 't was, besides, his bread,
  Of which he butter'd both sides; 't would delay
Too long the assembly (he was pleased to dread),
  And take up rather more time than a day,
To name his works—he would but cite a few—
"Wat Tyler"—"Rhymes on Blenheim"—"Waterloo."

XCVII

He had written praises of a regicide;
  He had written praises of all kings whatever;   770
He had written for republics far and wide,
  And then against them bitterer than ever;
For pantisocracy he once had cried
  Aloud, a scheme less moral than 't was clever;
Then grew a hearty anti-jacobin—
Had turn'd his coat—and would have turn'd his skin.

XCVIII

He had sung against all battles, and again
  In their high praise and glory; he had call'd
Reviewing "the ungentle craft," and then
  Become as base a critic as e'er crawl'd—   780
Fed, paid, and pamper'd by the very men
  By whom his muse and morals had been maul'd:
He had written much blank verse, and blanker prose,
And more of both than anybody knows.

XCIX

He had written Wesley's life:—here turning
    round
  To Satan, "Sir, I'm ready to write yours,
In two octavo volumes, nicely bound,
  With notes and preface, all that most al-
    lures
The pious purchaser; and there's no ground
  For fear, for I can choose my own re-
    viewers: 790
So let me have the proper documents,
That I may add you to my other saints."

C

Satan bow'd, and was silent. "Well, if you,
  With amiable modesty, decline
My offer, what says Michael? There are few
  Whose memoirs could be render'd more
    divine.
Mine is a pen of all work; not so new
  As it was once, but I would make you
    shine
Like your own trumpet. By the way, my own
Has more of brass in it, and is as well
    blown.   800

CI

"But talking about trumpets, here's my
    Vision!
  Now you shall judge, all people; yes, you
    shall
Judge with my judgment, and by my decision
Be guided who shall enter heaven or fall.
I settle all these things by intuition,
  Times present, past, to come, heaven, hell,
    and all,
Like King Alfonso. When I thus see double,
I save the Deity some worlds of trouble."

CII

He ceased, and drew forth an MS.; and no
  Persuasion on the part of devils, saints, 810
Or angels, now could stop the torrent; so
  He read the first three lines of the con-
    tents;
But at the fourth, the whole spiritual show
  Had vanish'd, with variety of scents,
Ambrosial and sulphureous, as they sprang,
Like lightning, off from his "melodious
    twang."

CIII

Those grand heroics acted as a spell:
  The angels stopp'd their ears and plied their
    pinions;
The devils ran howling, deafen'd, down to
    hell;
  The ghosts fled, gibbering, for their own
    dominions—   820
(For 't is not yet decided where they dwell,
  And I leave every man to his opinions);
Michael took refuge in his trump—but, lo!
His teeth were set on edge, he could not
    blow!

CIV

Saint Peter, who has hitherto been known
  For an impetuous saint, upraised his keys,
And at the fifth line knock'd the poet down;
  Who fell like Phæton, but more at ease,
Into his lake, for there he did not drown;
  A different web being by the Destinies 830
Woven for the Laureate's final wreath, when-
    e'er
Reform shall happen either here or there.

CV

He first sank to the bottom—like his works,
  But soon rose to the surface—like himself;
For all corrupted things are buoy'd like corks,
  By their own rottenness, light as an elf,
Or wisp that flits o'er a morass: he lurks,
  It may be, still, like dull books on a shelf,
In his own den, to scrawl some "Life" or
    "Vision,"
As Welborn says—"the devil turn'd pre-
    cisian."   840

CVI

As for the rest, to come to the conclusion
  Of this true dream, the telescope is gone
Which kept my optics free from all delusion,
  And show'd me what I in my turn have
    shown;
All I saw farther, in the last confusion,
  Was, that King George slipp'd into heaven
    for one;
And when the tumult dwindled to a calm,
I left him practising the hundredth psalm.

THE ISLES OF GREECE

(*From Don Juan, Canto III*)

1

THE isles of Greece, the isles of Greece!
  Where burning Sappho loved and sung,
Where grew the arts of war and peace,
  Where Delos rose, and Phœbus sprung!
Eternal summer gilds them yet,
But all, except their sun, is set.

2

The Scian and the Teian muse,
  The hero's harp, the lover's lute,
Have found the fame your shores refuse:
  Their place of birth alone is mute   10
To sounds which echo further west
Than your sires' "Islands of the Blest."

3

The mountains look on Marathon—
  And Marathon looks on the sea;
And musing there an hour alone,
  I dream'd that Greece might still be free;
For standing on the Persians' grave,
I could not deem myself a slave.

4

A king sate on the rocky brow
  Which looks o'er sea-born Salamis;   20
And ships, by thousands, lay below,
  And men in nations;—all were his!
He counted them at break of day—
And when the sun set where were they?

5

And where are they? and where art thou,
  My country? On thy voiceless shore
The heroic lay is tuneless now—
  The heroic bosom beats no more!
And must thy lyre, so long divine,
Degenerate into hands like mine?   30

6

'T is something, in the dearth of fame,
  Though link'd among a fetter'd race,
To feel at least a patriot's shame,
  Even as I sing, suffuse my face;
For what is left the poet here?
For Greeks a blush—for Greece a tear.

7

Must *we* but weep o'er days more blest?
  Must *we* but blush?—Our fathers bled.
Earth! render back from out thy breast
  A remnant of our Spartan dead!   40
Of the three hundred grant but three,
To make a new Thermopylæ!

8

What, silent still? and silent all?
  Ah! no;—the voices of the dead
Sound like a distant torrent's fall,
  And answer, "Let one living head,
But one arise,—we come, we come!"
'T is but the living who are dumb.

9

In vain—in vain: strike other chords;
  Fill high the cup with Samian wine!   50
Leave battles to the Turkish hordes,
  And shed the blood of Scio's vine!
Hark! rising to the ignoble call—
How answers each bold Bacchanal!

10

You have the Pyrrhic dance as yet;
  Where is the Pyrrhic phalanx gone?
Of two such lessons, why forget
  The nobler and the manlier one?
You have the letters Cadmus gave—
Think ye he meant them for a slave?   60

11

Fill high the bowl with Samian wine!
  We will not think of themes like these!
It made Anacreon's song divine:
  He served—but served Polycrates—
A tyrant; but our masters then
Were still, at least, our countrymen.

12

The tyrant of the Chersonese
  Was freedom's best and bravest friend;
That tyrant was Miltiades!

Oh! that the present hour would lend   70
Another despot of the kind!
Such chains as his were sure to bind.

13

Fill high the bowl with Samian wine!
    On Suli's rock, and Parga's shore,
Exists the remnant of a line
    Such as the Doric mothers bore;
And there, perhaps, some seed is sown,
The Heracleidan blood might own.

14

Trust not for freedom to the Franks—
    They have a king who buys and sells;   80
In native swords, and native ranks,
    The only hope of courage dwells:
But Turkish force, and Latin fraud,
Would break your shield, however broad.

15

Fill high the bowl with Samian wine!
    Our virgins dance beneath the shade—
I see their glorious black eyes shine;
    But gazing on each glowing maid,
My own the burning tear-drop laves,
To think such breasts must suckle slaves.   90

16

Place me on Sunium's marbled steep,
    Where nothing, save the waves and I,
May hear our mutual murmurs sweep;
    There, swan-like, let me sing and die:
A land of slaves shall ne'er be mine—
Dash down yon cup of Samian wine!

SHE WALKS IN BEAUTY

I

SHE walks in beauty, like the night
    Of cloudless climes and starry skies;
And all that's best of dark and bright
    Meet in her aspect and her eyes:
Thus mellow'd to that tender light
    Which heaven to gaudy day denies.

II

One shade the more, one ray the less,
    Had half impair'd the nameless grace
Which waves in every raven tress,
    Or softly lightens o'er her face;   10
Where thoughts serenely sweet express
    How pure, how dear their dwelling-place.

III

And on that cheek, and o'er that brow,
    So soft, so calm, yet eloquent,
The smiles that win, the tints that glow,
    But tell of days in goodness spent,
A mind at peace with all below,
    A heart whose love is innocent!

THE DESTRUCTION OF SENNACHERIB

I

THE Assyrian came down like the wolf on
        the fold,
And his cohorts were gleaming in purple and
        gold;
And the sheen of their spears was like stars
        on the sea,
When the blue wave rolls nightly on deep
        Galilee.

II

Like the leaves of the forest when Summer is
        green,
That host with their banners at sunset were
        seen:
Like the leaves of the forest when Autumn
        hath blown,
That host on the morrow lay wither'd and
        strown.

III

For the Angel of Death spread his wings on
        the blast,
And breathed in the face of the foe as he
        pass'd;   10
And the eyes of the sleepers wax'd deadly and
        chill,
And their hearts but once heaved, and for
        ever grew still!

IV

And there lay the steed with his nostril all
    wide,
But through it there roll'd not the breath of
    his pride;
And the foam of his gasping lay white on
    the turf,
And cold as the spray of the rock-beating
    surf.

V

And there lay the rider distorted and pale,
With the dew on his brow, and the rust on
    his mail:
And the tents were all silent, the banners
    alone,
The lances unlifted, the trumpet unblown. ₂₀

VI

And the widows of Ashur are loud in their
    wail,
And the idols are broke in the temple of
    Baal;
And the might of the Gentile, unsmote by
    the sword,
Hath melted like snow in the glance of the
    Lord!

SO, WE'LL GO NO MORE A ROVING

I

So, we'll go no more a roving
    So late into the night,
Though the heart be still as loving,
    And the moon be still as bright.

II

For the sword outwears its sheath,
    And the soul wears out the breast,
And the heart must pause to breathe,
    And love itself have rest.

III

Though the night was made for loving,
    And the day return too soon, ₁₀
Yet we'll go no more a roving
    By the light of the moon.

ON THIS DAY I COMPLETE MY THIRTY-SIXTH YEAR

MISSOLONGHI, Jan. 22, 1824.

'TIS time this heart should be unmoved,
    Since others it hath ceased to move:
Yet, though I cannot be beloved,
    Still let me love!

My days are in the yellow leaf;
    The flowers and fruits of love are gone;
The worm, the canker, and the grief
    Are mine alone!

The fire that on my bosom preys
    Is lone as some volcanic isle; ₁₀
No torch is kindled at its blaze—
    A funeral pile.

The hope, the fear, the jealous care,
    The exalted portion of the pain
And power of love, I cannot share,
    But wear the chain.

But 'tis not *thus*—and 'tis not *here*—
    Such thoughts should shake my soul, nor
    now,
Where glory decks the hero's bier,
    Or binds his brow. ₂₀

The sword, the banner, and the field,
    Glory and Greece, around me see!
The Spartan, borne upon his shield,
    Was not more free.

Awake! (not Greece—she *is* awake!)
    Awake, my spirit! Think through *whom*
Thy life-blood tracks its parent lake,
    And then strike home!

Tread those reviving passions down,
    Unworthy manhood!—unto thee ₃₀
Indifferent should the smile or frown
    Of beauty be.

If thou regrett'st thy youth, *why live?*
    The land of honourable death
Is here:—up to the field, and give
    Away thy breath!

Seek out—less often sought than found—
    A soldier's grave, for thee the best;
Then look around, and choose thy ground,
    And take thy rest. ₄₀

PERCY BYSSHE SHELLEY

BYRON AND SHELLEY

About the middle of May, 1816, a memorable party of English travelers arrived at the Hotel d'Angleterre, in the outskirts of Geneva. It consisted of a man not quite twenty-four years of age, two girlish, but intellectual looking, young women, both under twenty, and a year-old child. The tall, slight figure of the young man had an habitual stoop, with head thrust forward, as if flying before the wind or pursuing some flying object, and when he moved, his irregular step and quick, erratic but often graceful gestures suggested the movements of a bird or other wild creature unaware of human observation. His head, though unusually small, seemed large because of a profusion of wavy brown hair, already a little streaked with gray, which he kept in a state of supreme disorder by running his fingers through it rapidly at every transition of thought. The face was fair and ruddy, irregular but with fine mouth and eyes, the lips delicately molded, the eyes deep blue, large, and changeable. His voice was high-pitched and tense, rising in animated conversation to something like a shriek, but in reading or when affected by beauty or pathos sinking to low, well-modulated tones. The entire individuality: posture, movement, face, eyes, and voice, seemed to denote a spirit singularly pure, natural, eager and intent. The two women, were in striking contrast to each other: the one golden-haired, wide-browed, with pale transparent face and spiritual features; the other dark, almost Latin in appearance, with prominent eyes, full, rounded features, petulant and passionate. The man, need it be said? was Shelley, and the fair-haired lady was Mary Godwin who had now been the companion of Shelley's flittings for some two years. The Italianate lady was Mary's step-sister, Jane, or as she preferred, Claire Clairmont. It was this last, in all probability, who had maneuvered the present stop, for she probably knew something of the itinerary of a second party.

Lord Byron had embarked for Ostend near the end of April, with four male companions of whom three were servants, taking with him a huge English coach, built in imitation of one captured from Napoleon. The bill for this affair, some two thousand pounds, had been one of the many horrors of his last weeks in England. He had, however, exchanged it for a lighter carriage at Brussels and proceeding by easy stages through Belgium and up the Rhine, arrived at the above-mentioned hotel on May 27. During Byron's last days in London, Claire Clairmont, having approached him by subterfuges in a long siege of letters, had finally attained her object of securing him as her lover. Thus, through the secret machinations of a mistress, Byron met Shelley, an event of far greater importance than his second *rencontre* with Claire; though the consequence of the intrigue in the shape of his natural daughter Allegra, was to be the occasion of much correspondence and numerous visits between the two poets. They invariably spent most of their time, however, upon other and less private topics.

For three months Byron and Shelley were daily companions among the Alps and on the waters of "clear placid Leman." Then Shelley returned to England, carrying with him the manuscript of the Third Canto of *Childe Harold*, which Byron entrusted to his care and editorship. Two years later, they met again in Venice, when Shelley and his household, at Byron's invitation, occupied for several weeks his picturesque villa among the Euganean Hills, a sojourn associated with some of Shelley's most beautiful creations. Another three years passed, years of surpassing interest in the literary activity of both, before Byron again induced Shelley to visit him, this time at the palace of the Guiccioli in Ravenna. Shelley arrived at ten in the evening and they sat up the rest of the night, discussing politics, personal affairs, and literature. Shelley stayed ten days, repeating this program every night. As a result of this visit, Byron—whose affiliation with the patriotic society of the Carbonari was beginning to make Ravenna too hot for him —chose Pisa, where the Shelleys were then living, as his next place of residence.

Accordingly, in the late autumn of 1821, Byron "with seven servants, five carriages, nine horses, a monkey, a bull-dog, a mastiff, two cats, three pet fowls, and some hens," crossed the mountains from Ravenna to Pisa and took possession of the Lanfranchi Palace. There for nine months Shelley was his neighbor and the frequent companion of his ridings, sailings, pistol-shootings, billiards, and other amusements. It was at this time that he declared Shelley "the most companionable man under thirty" that he had ever met. Shelley, on the other hand, wearied of the intimacy at times. His pure and delicate nature could not but be wounded by the grossness and levity that sometimes marred Byron's always witty conversation; and his deeply serious spirit was offended by the futility of some of Byron's amusements. The question of Allegra was always a source of contention between them. Byron accepted the care of the child; but he

389

relentlessly refused to see or to correspond with its mother,—for reasons not hard to guess. Shelley became the intermediary between the two parents. It was a trying responsibility, and the fact that the intimacy of the two poets survived this ordeal speaks volumes for the essential soundness of their fundamental respect for each other. Both were keen and unflinching critics and each knew the other thoroughly, so that their judgments of one another stand among the most valuable testimonials of each. Shelley never recanted his belief that Byron's was a mighty, if a darkened spirit and that he was, in his later writings, a supremely great poet. And Byron never ceased to reiterate that Shelley was "the *best* man" that he had ever known. After the weird scene on the wild sea-beach when Byron was of the small group that superintended the burning of Shelley's body, he wrote to Murray: "You were all brutally mistaken about Shelley who was without exception the *best* and least selfish man I ever knew." And to Moore, "There is another man gone about whom the world was ill-naturedly, and ignorantly, and brutally mistaken. It will perhaps do him justice *now* when he can be no better for it." If Byron did rather less than full justice to Shelley's poetical merit, he came far nearer than most of his generation; and so far as he erred, it was an error of judgment, and not a want of generosity. There was no mean literary jealousy on either side.

And wide as the poles asunder as Byron and Shelley were in many respects, they had certain very fundamental enthusiasms and detestations in common, always granting that Shelley had the greater abundance of admiration and Byron the more abounding hatred. If, in any of their all-night talks, they had compared notes on what each was doing in the spring of 1812, they would have found that while Shelley, aged nineteen, was saving Ireland with his *Address to the Irish People* and other tracts, Byron, aged twenty-four, was addressing the House of Lords, first, in vigorous defense of the wretched Frame-breakers of Nottingham, and second, in favor of Catholic emancipation and of political and economic justice to the Irish people. And they would have found that some of their sentiments and even their phrases were practically interchangeable. Both belonged to that younger generation of radicals who rebelled against the establishment of the same old dynastic tyrannies in Europe after the fall of Napoleon; both saw with dismay men like Wordsworth, Southey, and Coleridge, who had found it bliss to be alive and heaven to be young when the French Revolution began, slumping into stodgy reactionaries in their old age. Only, Byron saw it with furious anger and contempt, Shelley with more of sorrow and pity. Yet Shelley's basic code could not be more tersely phrased than in Byron's characteristic lines,

"I wish men to be *free*
As much from mobs as kings, from *you* as *me*."

Both suffered and were in some degree impractical in their "war with those who war with thought"; Byron because he could not, or would not control his own selfish passions and was too arrogant to conciliate mankind; Shelley because in his own abounding love and perfect purity of mind, he over-estimated the capacity of human nature to respond to absolute reason and dwell in his rarefied altitudes of ideal beauty and unselfish desire. The practical compromises by which the world is run, however, belong to its worldly men, not to its poets, and of this one Byron said "He was the *least* worldly-minded person I ever met."

PERCY BYSSHE SHELLEY

1792–1822

Of Shelley more than any other poet one feels that he should have been exhaled into the world at some indeterminate place and hour, instead of having been, as he was, substantially born August 4, 1792, at Field Place, in the county of Sussex. His family were landed gentry and his father Timothy Shelley had accumulated by his own diligence and capacity a large fortune, amounting at the time of his death to three hundred thousand pounds. It has been said of him that he was "in no sense a bad man, but he was everything which the poet's father ought not to have been." He was, in fact, a typical blindly conservative man of affairs and of property. His principles, religious, political, social, and moral, were simply the routine standards of the English squirearchy, which lived by tradition and not by thinking. And he had the misfortune of having to deal with a son and heir who attempted to live by pure reason, and for whom he became as the apotheosis of everything that had to be eradicated from the world. No more solid explanation has been discovered for the mysterious antipathy and religion of insubordination toward his father which seems to have possessed Shelley in his late boyhood and youth and, in fact, through life.

After a visionary childhood among his sisters, so composed of make-believe that it seems imaginary, Shelley began disgracing himself at Eton, where he was at odds with his masters about his duties and with the general run of his fellows about the traditions of the place and its sports for which he cared nothing, still preferring his childhood occupation of sailing paper boats upon any convenient stand of water. Yet he already had passionate friendships with idealized companions, he already "loved all waste and solitary places" of nature, and he became infatuated with the romantic and miraculous aspects of science, performing, privately, perilous and explosive experiments and declaring, with prophetic insight, that natural science was destined to revolutionize the life of mankind.

In the autumn of 1810, when he was just turned eighteen, Shelley entered University College, Oxford. Here again he "refused to keep the beaten track of prescribed studies" or to follow any ordinary routine of life. He paid little attention to his associates; but he attached to himself one of the most brilliant among them, Jefferson Hogg, whose able and circumstantial "Life" of Shelley contains a graphic account of that extraordinary being at this stage of his development. His striking personal beauty, his vehement but intermittent intellectual energy, his moral sanctity and all-embracing benevolence, and the spontaneous unconventionality combined with perfect "gentility" of his manners and habits are set vividly and convincingly before us. Hogg's description of Shelley's eccentric practice of sleeping in his clothes during the early evening may be taken as representative:

"He would sleep from two to four hours, often so soundly that his slumbers resembled a deep lethargy; he lay occasionally upon the sofa, but more commonly stretched upon the rug before a large fire, like a cat; and his little round head was exposed to such a fierce heat, that I used to wonder how he was able to bear it. Sometimes I have interposed some shelter, but rarely with any permanent effect; for the sleeper usually contrived to turn himself, and to roll again into the spot where the fire glowed the brightest. . . . At six he would suddenly compose himself, even in the midst of a most animated narrative, or of earnest discussion; and he would lie buried in entire forgetfulness, in a sweet and mighty oblivion, until ten, when he would suddenly start up, and, rubbing his eyes with great violence, and passing his fingers swiftly through his long hair, would enter at once into a vehement argument, or begin to recite verses, either of his own composition or from the works of others, with a rapidity and an energy that were often quite painful."

But Shelley's stay at Oxford was of short duration. To his interest in science he had added a passion for metaphysics. He devoured the writings of the French and English sceptics of the Eighteenth century and, with characteristic abandon, temporarily accepted their doctrine and discipline entire. To believe, with Shelley, was to act, and accordingly in the spring of 1811, he published and began circulating a tract entitled *The Necessity of Atheism.* He was expelled, not so much for his publication as for insubordination in refusing to declare whether he was or was not its author. Hogg voluntarily implicated himself and the two friends left Oxford together. This was the first of the series of short flights of which the remainder of Shelley's brief life was composed. His father refused to receive him at Field Place unless he would break off all association with Hogg, which Shelley, with unnecessary impertinence, refused to do. The rupture was never healed, and Shelley was henceforth a wanderer; though heir to a great estate of which his father could not legally deprive him, he was, so long as his father lived, without a home.

Within a few months and while negotiating with his father, Shelley followed his first imprudence with another which had even more serious consequences. In London he had become acquainted with Harriet Westbrook, a pleasant, good-looking school-girl, daughter of a coffee-house keeper. Shelley was certainly not deeply in love with her, for he thought himself still in love with a cousin; but Harriet was evidently smitten with him, and without perhaps consciously scheming to do so, she hurried matters by complaining to Shelley of the tyranny of her home and school and throwing herself upon his protection. With typical chivalry and resentment of tyranny, but with equal lack of good judgment, Shelley accepted the responsibility and the two children ran away to Edinburgh where Shelley compromised with his principles sufficiently to be legally married, under the Scotch law. After this escapade, Timothy Shelley gave up all hope of his son; ordinary immorality he could have condoned, and he said as much; but a misalliance shook the very foundations of his social system.

For a year or so Shelley, aside from money troubles, enjoyed his nomadic existence with Harriet. Within two years they were in all three kingdoms and twice in Ireland. As they moved from place to place Shelley bought books and continued his studies leaving the books behind when they moved on, so that Hogg declares that a considerable library could have been founded with the books that Shelley scattered about the British Isles. But his head was filled with schemes for the political rehabilitation of the world and he selected Ireland as his first field of practical endeavor. He wrote an *Address to the Irish People* which he had printed and carried to Dublin in person, distributing it on the streets and from the window of his hotel. Finding his efforts to reform the world less productive of immediate results than he had anticipated, he crossed to the coast of Wales where he continued his propaganda by occasionally setting afloat his documents in boxes and bottles,—a method of publication irresistibly suggestive of his earlier exploits with paper boats.

As Shelley and Harriet drew into the third year of married life the sympathy between them perceptibly cooled. Shelley had soon found the bottom of his girl wife's mind and heart. She ceased to simulate an interest in his intellectual pursuits and idealistic schemes; she had yearnings for a more settled and pretentious mode of living than they could afford; and she resented it when Shelley found sympathetic companionship with more intellectual women than herself. In the summer of 1814, Shelley, acting in accordance with his avowed principles, notified her that they no longer had enough in common to justify their living together and summarily left her. There is little doubt that his decision was influenced by the fact that he had already fallen in love with another woman. Less than two months after separating from Harriet, Shelley eloped to France with Mary Godwin, the fair-haired, *spirituelle* daughter of Mary Wollstonecraft, author of *The Rights of Women,* and William Godwin, author of Shelley's Bible, *Political Justice.* The behavior of Shelley and Mary can only be fairly judged in the light of the revolutionary doctrines which both accepted for gospel, and even so it raises grave questions. Shortly after Shelley left her, Harriet gave birth to his second child and two years later she drowned herself in the Serpentine river. The most charitable judgment that can be passed upon Shelley in this painful situation is that penned long after by Mary Shelley herself: "It will be sufficient to say that, in all he did, he at the time of doing it believed himself justified to his own conscience."

Shelley had always "scribbled," had in fact published two romances and a volume of verse in his Eton-Oxford period. But even when he published *Queen Mab,* in 1813, he had not yet turned his mind in earnest to the mastery of poetic form. Shelley is unlike most great poets, in that the ethic rather than the physique of art first carried him away. The poet in Shelley, strictly speaking, did not come to birth until after his union with Mary Godwin. Some of his characteristic diction and imagery are perceptible in *Queen Mab;* but its blank verse is dull and unmodulated. The genius for rhythm which is one of Shelley's peculiar attributes emerges in *Alastor; or the Spirit of Solitude* which he composed after an expedition on the Thames while he and Mary were summering near Windsor Forest in 1815, and when he believed himself under sentence of death from consumption. This, too, was the first of many fine poems in which Shelley gives ethereal body to that ideal beauty and perfect love, which in all human souls,

"Burns bright or dim, as each are mirrors of
The fire for which all thirst."

Only with Spenser—and then with the substitution of Spenser's large serenity for the swiftness and intensity of Shelley—has this Platonic concept found equally effective adaptation in English poetry.

Deep and bitter experience was teaching Shelley the wide gulf that exists between abstract speculation and the practical workings of the world; but simultaneously he was discovering the art and the joy of embodying his abstract conceptions in beautiful forms that might, as he hoped, serve as an intermediary between the two. The idea he was now forming of the nature and usefulness of poetry he embodied, some four years later, in his thoughtful and eloquent *Defence of Poetry,* and a knowledge of this essay is indispensable to an understanding of Shelley's intellectual character and of the spirit in which he accepted for himself this form of service to mankind. The following sentences, in which the teachings both of Wordsworth and of Plato seem discernible, epitomize Shelley's doctrine and also

illustrate his command of a rich and persuasive prose:

"The cultivation of poetry is never more to be desired than at periods when, from an excess of the selfish and calculating principle, the accumulation of the materials of external life exceeds the quantity of the power of assimilating them to the internal laws of human nature.

.   .   .   .   .

"Poetry is the record of the best and happiest moments of the happiest and best minds. We are aware of evanescent visitations of thought and feeling sometimes associated with place or person, sometimes regarding our own mind alone, and always arising unforeseen and departing unbidden, but elevating and delightful beyond all expression: so that even in the desire and the regret they leave, there cannot but be pleasure, participating as it does in the nature of its object. It is as it were the interpenetration of a diviner nature through our own; but its footsteps are like those of a wind over the sea, which the coming calm erases, and whose traces remain only, as on the wrinkled sand which paves it. These and corresponding conditions of being are experienced principally by those of the most delicate sensibility and the most enlarged imagination; and the state of mind produced by them is at war with every base desire. The enthusiasm of virtue, love, patriotism, and friendship, is essentially linked with such emotions; and whilst they last, self appears as what it is, an atom to a universe. Poets are not only subject to these experiences as spirits of the most refined organization, but they can colour all that they combine with the evanescent hues of this ethereal world; a word, a trait in the representation of a scene or a passion, will touch the enchanted chord, and reanimate, in those who have ever experienced these emotions, the sleeping, the cold, the buried image of the past. Poetry thus makes immortal all that is best and most beautiful in the world; it arrests the vanishing apparitions which haunt the interlunations of life, and veiling them, or in language or in form, sends them forth among mankind, bearing sweet news of kindred joy to those with whom their sisters abide—abide, because there is no portal of expression from the caverns of the spirit which they inhabit into the universe of things. Poetry redeems from decay the visitations of the divinity in man."

Although Shelley hardly relaxed his studies in political and metaphysical speculation, and never ceased to dally with thoughts of achievement in these fields, he had to all intents and purposes accepted his poetical vocation by the summer of 1816 when he was with Byron in the Alps of Switzerland. The year and a half following his return was agitated by a series of shocking and disturbing events. First came the suicide of Mary's half-sister, Fanny Imlay, then Harriet's disappearance, the finding of her body, the scandal of Allegra's birth, and then for months the suspense of his suit in Chancery for the possession of Harriet's children, then Lord Eldon's condemnation of Shelley's character and decision against him. Yet, though all these shocks and anxieties were shattering his health, Shelley continued to write, composing a large part of *Rosalind and Helen* and publishing his ambitious revolutionary epic, *The Revolt of Islam,* poems which show no abatement of his iconoclastic fervor. Surrounded by public detestation and assailed by superficial doubts though he was, nothing could shake Shelley's innermost belief in his own powers or his faith either in the purity of his own intentions or the soundness of his views. Nevertheless, he decided to seek a less hostile environment for his family and a more favorable climate not only for his peace of mind but his health of body. On March 12, 1818, he took his last look at the shores of England and with Mary, now legally his wife, Claire Clairmont and her child he crossed to the continent and went direct to Milan. The remaining four years of his life belong to Italy; but they belong, also, to the history of supreme achievements in English poetry.

Under Italian skies Shelley's health improved and his genius flowered. He went little into society, but he had friends. He was free to come and go, could concentrate on his studies in languages, literature, and philosophy and for his lighter hours had the companionship of a few free sympathetic spirits. He had domestic sorrows in the death of his two children and constant anxiety over Claire and her troubles; but the ghastly abominations of his earlier experiences were not repeated. His visit to Byron at Venice, in 1818, led to his interesting poem in the familiar *genre, Julian and Maddalo,* which contains a striking description of the child Allegra, and one of the most significant delineations of Byron's powerful but complex and baffling personality to be found in literature. While at Byron's villa in the Euganean Hills he wrote the sublime first act of *Prometheus Unbound,* which was continued at Rome the following spring and finished at Florence in the autumn of the same year, 1819. This poem combines Shelley's philosophical and ethical conceptions with his dramatic fire and his power of sustained lyric flight in a more comprehensive manner than any other of his poems. How clear he had now become as to the nature and purpose of his own poetry may be seen in the following extract from the preface to this poem:

"Didactic poetry is my abhorrence; nothing can be equally well expressed in prose that is not tedious and supererogatory in verse. My purpose has hitherto been simply to familiarise the highly refined imagination of the more select classes of poetical readers with beautiful idealisms of moral excellence; aware that until the mind can love, and admire, and trust, and hope, and endure, reasoned principles of moral conduct are seeds cast upon the highway of life which the unconscious passenger tramples into dust."

This year, 1819, has been called Shelley's *annus mirabilis,* for besides completing the *Prometheus,* he wrote in this year *The Masque of Anarchy, Peter Bell the Third,* the famous *Ode to the West Wind,* and *The Cenci,* the last rated by many good judges as the most competent poetic tragedy in English since the days of Shakespeare.

In the winter of 1819–20, the Shelleys moved, for the milder climate, to Pisa. Claire now being absent, they were shortly followed, as we have seen, by Byron and his astonishing household. Rather quickly there formed at Pisa a little world of liberal and cultivated Britons of which Shelley and Byron might be described as the magnetic poles. There was the brigandish Trelawney who, as a picturesque athlete and rover, rather out-Byroned the Byron of early days. There was the literary leech, Shelley's second cousin, Captain Medwin. There was the good Irish Count, Taafe, for whose Dante translation and commentary Byron interceded with mischievous good nature, writing to Murray: "He'll *die* if it isn't published, and he'll be *damned* if it is." There was the Greek patriot, Prince Mavrocordato, and so forth. Especially sympathetic to Shelley were the Gisbornes, not far away at Leghorn; and constantly at hand were his new friends, a young English officer Edward Williams and his exquisite wife Jane, with her guitar, celebrated in Shelley's lyrics. Toward the end, Leigh Hunt came over from England, with a wife and six children, at Byron's expense, to help Byron and Shelley launch a magazine, *The Liberal.* Within a few months after Hunt's arrival, Shelley and Williams were drowned, the circle was broken up, Byron was off for Greece, and Hunt was out of a job.

No long works comparable in sustained excellence with *Prometheus Unbound* and *The Cenci* were produced by Shelley during the last two and a half years of his life. Some of his finest lyrics, however, were the product of these years. Such are *To a Skylark, To Night,* and the concluding *Chorus* of his choric drama, *Hellas.* These are, indeed, very nearly perfect. *The Sensitive Plant, The Witch of Atlas,* and *Epipsychidion,* all pieces of considerable length, contain much fine poetry but contain also an esoteric element that is a bit baffling to mere mortals, though these poems are accepted as major pieces by thorough-going Shelleyans. *The Triumph of Life* upon which he was engaged at the time of his death is an impressive fragment; but it is impossible to guess exactly where the poet meant to leave us at the end, if indeed he knew himself, and it is doubtful if it could have been so developed as to rank among his masterpieces. It lacks the perfect clarity which Shelley's best things, however diffuse, always possess. Several larger projects, such as his historical drama *Charles the First,* were left unfinished partly because they hung heavily on his hands. The satires in which Shelley more or less challenged Byron on his own ground are confessed failures. It is the conventional view that, while contact with Shelley from the first stimulated Byron to take a higher range, Byron's influence upon Shelley's poetry was almost negligible. This can hardly be the case. Shelley recognized in *Don Juan* what he, as he said, had "long preached, something wholly new and relative to the age, and yet surpassingly beautiful." There are many evidences in his later poems, notably in *Julian and Maddalo* and the *Letter to Maria Gisborne,* that he was experimenting with the direct and colloquial style, the possibilities of which Byron had so conclusively demonstrated. The finer parts of *Don Juan* proved that poetry need not be either vague or metaphorical in order to be "surpassingly beautiful." At the same time, Shelley was earnestly re-examining the entire doctrine and discipline of his philosophy with a view to bringing it into a more vital relation with the realities of normal human experience. In this transitional state as to both the content and style of his poetry, his "best and happiest moments" were available only for relatively short flights.

Of these, the longest and most important is that which links his name inseparably with the name of Keats. In the death of Keats, so similar to that which he had anticipated for himself when he wrote his *Alastor,* and in the unjust treatment of Keats by the reviewers, so similar to that which he was at the moment suffering, Shelley was provided with a subject with which he could imaginatively identify himself and give a free rein to his own assured style. As a result, *Adonais* takes its place, if not as he thought, as his "most perfect," certainly as one of his most perfect poems. Shelley's poems are full of his premonitions of an early death; it is therefore a less surprising coincidence that the closing stanzas of *Adonais* are almost a prophetic description of his own end which came only a few months after the stanzas were written.

On July 8, 1822, Shelley and Williams sailed out of the harbor at Leghorn bound for Lerici in Shelley's sailboat the *Ariel.* About ten miles from the shore they were struck by a terrific squall and when the squall had passed watchers on the shore could no longer make them out. Ten days later their bodies were found half-buried in the sands of the shore. Trelawny, Hunt, and Byron superintended their cremation on the beach. Shelley's ashes and heart were placed in an urn and buried in the Protestant cemetery at Rome, which he had beautifully described in *Adonais.*

SELECTED BIBLIOGRAPHY

TEXTS

Works in Verse and Prose, ed. by H. B. Forman, 8 Vols., 1880.
　　The standard edition.
Poems, Cambridge edition, ed. by G. E. Woodberry, 1901.
　　Best one-volume edition of the poems.
Poems, ed. by C. D. Locock, 2 Vols., 1911.

CRITICAL WORKS

Bradley, A. C., *Shelley's View of Poetry,* Oxford Lectures on Poetry, 1909.
Clutton-Brock, A., *Shelley, the Man and the Poet,* 1910.
　　An interesting interpretation.
Dowden, E., *Life of Shelley,* 2 Vols., 1896.
　　The standard life.
Elton, O., *Survey of English Literature, 1780–1830,* 1912.
Symonds, J. A., *Shelley,* Men of Letters Series, 1887.
　　A good short biography.

QUEEN MAB

A PHILOSOPHICAL POEM, WITH NOTES

ECRASEZ L'INFAME!—*Correspondance de Voltaire.*

Avia Pieridum peragro loca, nullius ante
Trita solo; juvat integros accedere fonteis;
Atque haurire: juvatque novos decerpere flores.
. 　.　 .　 .　 .　 .　 .　 .
Unde prius nulli velarint tempora musae.
Primum quod magnis doceo de rebus; et arctis
Religionum animos nodis exsolvere pergo.—*Lucret.* lib. iv.

Δος που στω, και κοσμον κινησω.—*Archimedes.*

TO HARRIET

Whose is the love that gleaming through the
　　world,
Wards off the poisonous arrow of its scorn?
　　Whose is the warm and partial praise,
　　Virtue's most sweet reward?

Beneath whose looks did my reviving soul
Riper in truth and virtuous daring grow?

Whose eyes have I gazed fondly on,
And loved mankind the more?

HARRIET! on thine:—thou wert my purer
　　mind;
Thou wert the inspiration of my song;　　10
　　Thine are these early wilding flowers,
　　Though garlanded by me.

Then press into thy breast this pledge of love;
And know, though time may change and years
　　may roll,
　　Each floweret gathered in my heart
　　It consecrates to thine.

QUEEN MAB

I

How wonderful is Death,
　　Death and his brother Sleep!
One, pale as yonder waning moon
　　With lips of lurid blue;

The other, rosy as the morn
　When throned on ocean's wave
　It blushes o'er the world:
Yet both so passing wonderful!

Hath then the gloomy Power
Whose reign is in the tainted sepulchres   10
　Seized on her sinless soul?
　Must then that peerless form
Which love and admiration cannot view
Without a beating heart, those azure veins
Which steal like streams along a field of snow,
　That lovely outline, which is fair
　As breathing marble, perish?
　Must putrefaction's breath
Leave nothing of this heavenly sight
But loathsomeness and ruin?   20
Spare nothing but a gloomy theme,
On which the lightest heart might moralize?
　Or is it only a sweet slumber
　Stealing o'er sensation,
Which the breath of roseate morning
　Chaseth into darkness?
　Will Ianthe wake again,
And give that faithful bosom joy
Whose sleepless spirit waits to catch
Light, life and rapture from her smile?   30

　Yes! she will wake again,
Although her glowing limbs are motionless,
　And silent those sweet lips,
　Once breathing eloquence,
That might have soothed a tiger's rage,
Or thawed the cold heart of a conqueror.
　Her dewy eyes are closed,
And on their lids, whose texture fine
Scarce hides the dark blue orbs beneath,
　The baby Sleep is pillowed: 40
　Her golden tresses shade
　The bosom's stainless pride,
Curling like tendrils of the parasite
　Around a marble column.

　Hark! whence that rushing sound?
　'Tis like the wondrous strain
That round a lonely ruin swells,
Which, wandering on the echoing shore,
　The enthusiast hears at evening:
'Tis softer than the west wind's sigh;   50
'Tis wilder than the unmeasured notes
Of that strange lyre whose strings
The genii of the breezes sweep:
　Those lines of rainbow light
Are like the moonbeams when they fall
Through some cathedral window, but the tints

Are such as may not find
Comparison on earth.

Behold the chariot of the Fairy Queen!
Celestial coursers paw the unyielding air;   60
Their filmy pennons at her word they furl,
And stop obedient to the reins of light:
　These the Queen of Spells drew in,
　She spread a charm around the spot,
And leaning graceful from the aethereal car,
　Long did she gaze, and silently,
　Upon the slumbering maid.

Oh! not the visioned poet in his dreams,
When silvery clouds float through the 'wildered
　　brain,
When every sight of lovely, wild and grand   70
　Astonishes, enraptures, elevates,
　When fancy at a glance combines
　The wondrous and the beautiful,—
So bright, so fair, so wild a shape
　Hath ever yet beheld,
As that which reined the coursers of the air,
　And poured the magic of her gaze
　Upon the maiden's sleep.

　The broad and yellow moon
　Shone dimly through her form—   80
That form of faultless symmetry;
The pearly and pellucid car
　Moved not the moonlight's line:
　'Twas not an earthly pageant:
Those who had looked upon the sight,
　Passing all human glory,
　Saw not the yellow moon,
　Saw not the mortal scene,
　Heard not the night-wind's rush,
　Heard not an earthly sound,   90
　Saw but the fairy pageant,
　Heard but the heavenly strains
That filled the lonely dwelling.

The Fairy's frame was slight, yon fibrous
　　cloud,
That catches but the palest tinge of even,
And which the straining eye can hardly seize
When melting into eastern twilight's shadow,
Were scarce so thin, so slight; but the fair
　　star
That gems the glittering coronet of morn,
Sheds not a light so mild, so powerful,   100
As that which, bursting from the Fairy's
　　form,
Spread a purpureal halo round the scene,
　Yet with an undulating motion,
　Swayed to her outline gracefully.

From her celestial car
The Fairy Queen descended,
And thrice she waved her wand
Circled with wreaths of amaranth:
    Her thin and misty form
    Moved with the moving air,   110
    And the clear silver tones,
    As thus she spoke, were such
As are unheard by all but gifted ear.

Fairy

"Stars! your balmiest influence shed!
Elements! your wrath suspend!
Sleep, Ocean, in the rocky bounds
    That circle thy domain!
Let not a breath be seen to stir
Around yon grass-grown ruin's height,
    Let even the restless gossamer   120
    Sleep on the moveless air!
    Soul of Ianthe! thou,
Judged alone worthy of the envied boon,
That waits the good and the sincere; that waits
Those who have struggled, and with resolute
        will
Vanquished earth's pride and meanness, burst
        the chains,
The icy chains of custom, and have shone
The day-stars of their age;—Soul of Ianthe!
    Awake! arise!"

    Sudden arose   130
    Ianthe's Soul; it stood
All beautiful in naked purity,
The perfect semblance of its bodily frame.
Instinct with inexpressible beauty and grace,
    Each stain of earthliness
    Had passed away, it reassumed
    Its native dignity, and stood
    Immortal amid ruin.

    Upon the couch the body lay
    Wrapped in the depth of slumber: 140
Its features were fixed and meaningless,
    Yet animal life was there,
And every organ yet performed
Its natural functions: 'twas a sight
Of wonder to behold the body and soul.
    The self-same lineaments, the same
    Marks of identity were there:
Yet, oh, how different! One aspires to Heaven,
Pants for its sempiternal heritage,
And ever-changing, ever-rising still,   150
    Wantons in endless being.
The other, for a time the unwilling sport
Of circumstance and passion, struggles on;

Fleets through its sad duration rapidly:
Then, like an useless and worn-out machine,
    Rots, perishes, and passes.

Fairy

"Spirit! who hast dived so deep;
Spirit! who hast soared so high;
Thou the fearless, thou the mild,
Accept the boon thy worth hath earned,   160
    Ascend the car with me."

Spirit

"Do I dream? Is this new feeling
But a visioned ghost of slumber?
    If indeed I am a soul,
A free, a disembodied soul,
    Speak again to me."

Fairy

"I am the Fairy MAB: to me 'tis given
The wonders of the human world to keep:
The secrets of the immeasurable past,
In the unfailing consciences of men,   170
Those stern, unflattering chroniclers, I find:
The future, from the causes which arise
In each event, I gather: not the sting
Which retributive memory implants
In the hard bosom of the selfish man;
Nor that ecstatic and exulting throb
Which virtue's votary feels when he sums up
The thoughts and actions of a well-spent day,
Are unforeseen, unregistered by me:
And it is yet permitted me, to rend   180
The veil of mortal frailty, that the spirit,
Clothed in its changeless purity, may know
How soonest to accomplish the great end
For which it hath its being, and may taste
That peace, which in the end all life will share.
This is the meed of virtue; happy Soul,
    Ascend the car with me!"

    The chains of earth's immurement
        Fell from Ianthe's spirit;
They shrank and brake like bandages of
            straw   190
    Beneath a wakened giant's strength.
    She knew her glorious change,
And felt in apprehension uncontrolled
    New raptures opening round:
Each day-dream of her mortal life,
Each frenzied vision of the slumbers
    That closed each well-spent day,
    Seemed now to meet reality.

    The Fairy and the Soul proceeded;
    The silver clouds disparted;   200

And as the car of magic they ascended,
  Again the speechless music swelled,
  Again the coursers of the air
Unfurled their azure pennons, and the Queen
  Shaking the beamy reins
  Bade them pursue their way.

    The magic car moved on.
  The night was fair, and countless stars
  Studded Heaven's dark blue vault,—
    Just o'er the eastern wave   210
  Peeped the first faint smile of morn:—
    The magic car moved on—
    From the celestial hoofs
The atmosphere in flaming sparkles flew,
  And where the burning wheels
Eddied above the mountain's loftiest peak,
  Was traced a line of lightning.
  Now it flew far above a rock,
    The utmost verge of earth,
  The rival of the Andes, whose dark brow 220
  Lowered o'er the silver sea.

  Far, far below the chariot's path,
    Calm as a slumbering babe,
    Tremendous Ocean lay.
  The mirror of its stillness showed
    The pale and waning stars,
    The chariot's fiery track,
  And the gray light of morn
  Tinging those fleecy clouds
    That canopied the dawn.   230
Seemed it, that the chariot's way
Lay through the midst of an immense concave,
Radiant with million constellations, tinged
    With shades of infinite colour,
    And semicircled with a belt
  Flashing incessant meteors.

    The magic car moved on.
  As they approached their goal
  The coursers seemed to gather speed;
The sea no longer was distinguished; earth 240
  Appeared a vast and shadowy sphere;
    The sun's unclouded orb
    Rolled through the black concave;
    Its rays of rapid light
Parted around the chariot's swifter course,
  And fell, like ocean's feathery spray
    Dashed from the boiling surge
    Before a vessel's prow.

    The magic car moved on.
  Earth's distant orb appeared   250
The smallest light that twinkles in the heaven;

  Whilst round the chariot's way
    Innumerable systems rolled,
    And countless spheres diffused
    An ever-varying glory.
  It was a sight of wonder: some
  Were hornèd like the crescent moon;
  Some shed a mild and silver beam
  Like Hesperus o'er the western sea;
  Some dashed athwart with trains of flame, 260
  Like worlds to death and ruin driven;
Some shone like suns, and, as the chariot
    passed,
    Eclipsed all other light.

    Spirit of Nature! here!
In this interminable wilderness
Of worlds, at whose immensity
    Even soaring fancy staggers,
    Here is thy fitting temple.
    Yet not the lightest leaf
That quivers to the passing breeze   270
    Is less instinct with thee:
    Yet not the meanest worm
That lurks in graves and fattens on the dead
    Less shares thy eternal breath.
    Spirit of Nature! thou!
    Imperishable as this scene,
    Here is thy fitting temple.

      II

If solitude hath ever led thy steps
    To the wild Ocean's echoing shore,
    And thou hast lingered there,
    Until the sun's broad orb
  Seemed resting on the burnished wave,
    Thou must have marked the lines
    Of purple gold, that motionless
    Hung o'er the sinking sphere:
  Thou must have marked the billowy clouds
  Edged with intolerable radiancy   10
    Towering like rocks of jet
    Crowned with a diamond wreath.
    And yet there is a moment,
    When the sun's highest point
Peeps like a star o'er Ocean's western edge,
When those far clouds of feathery gold,
    Shaded with deepest purple, gleam
    Like islands on a dark blue sea;
Then has thy fancy soared above the earth,
    And furled its wearied wing   20
    Within the Fairy's fane.

    Yet not the golden islands
    Gleaming in yon flood of light,

Nor the feathery curtains
Stretching o'er the sun's bright couch,
Nor the burnished Ocean waves
Paving that gorgeous dome,
So fair, so wonderful a sight
As Mab's aethereal palace could afford.
Yet likest evening's vault, that faery Hall!   30
As Heaven, low resting on the wave, it spread
Its floors of flashing light,
Its vast and azure dome,
Its fertile golden islands
Floating on a silver sea;
Whilst suns their mingling beamings darted
Through clouds of circumambient darkness,
And pearly battlements around
Looked o'er the immense of Heaven.

The magic car no longer moved.   40
The Fairy and the Spirit
Entered the Hall of Spells:
Those golden clouds
That rolled in glittering billows
Beneath the azure canopy
With the aethereal footsteps trembled not:
The light and crimson mists,
Floating to strains of thrilling melody
Through that unearthly dwelling,
Yielded to every movement of the will.   50
Upon their passive swell the Spirit leaned,
And, for the varied bliss that pressed around,
Used not the glorious privilege
Of virtue and of wisdom.

"Spirit!" the Fairy said,
And pointed to the gorgeous dome,
"This is a wondrous sight
And mocks all human grandeur;
But, were it virtue's only meed, to dwell
In a celestial palace, all resigned   60
To pleasurable impulses, immured
Within the prison of itself, the will
Of changeless Nature would be unfulfilled.
Learn to make others happy. Spirit, come!
This is thine high reward:—the past shall rise;
Thou shalt behold the present; I will teach
The secrets of the future!"

The Fairy and the Spirit
Approached the overhanging battlement.—
Below lay stretched the universe!   70
There, far as the remotest line
That bounds imagination's flight,
Countless and unending orbs
In mazy motion intermingled,

Yet still fulfilled immutably
Eternal Nature's law.
Above, below, around,
The circling systems formed
A wilderness of harmony;
Each with undeviating aim,   80
In eloquent silence, through the depths of space
Pursued its wondrous way.

There was a little light
That twinkled in the misty distance:
None but a spirit's eye
Might ken that rolling orb;
None but a spirit's eye,
And in no other place
But that celestial dwelling, might behold
Each action of this earth's inhabitants.   90
But matter, space and time
In those aëreal mansions cease to act;
And all-prevailing wisdom, when it reaps
The harvest of its excellence, o'er-bounds
Those obstacles, of which an earthly soul
Fears to attempt the conquest.

The Fairy pointed to the earth.
The Spirit's intellectual eye
Its kindred beings recognized.
The thronging thousands, to a passing view,   100
Seemed like an ant-hill's citizens.
How wonderful! that even
The passions, prejudices, interests,
That sway the meanest being, the weak touch
That moves the finest nerve,
And in one human brain
Causes the faintest thought, becomes a link
In the great chain of Nature.

"Behold," the Fairy cried,
"Palmyra's ruined palaces!—   110
Behold! where grandeur frowned;
Behold! where pleasure smiled;
What now remains?—the memory
Of senselessness and shame—
What is immortal there?
Nothing—it stands to tell
A melancholy tale, to give
An awful warning: soon
Oblivion will steal silently
The remnant of its fame.   120
Monarchs and conquerors there
Proud o'er prostrate millions trod—
The earthquakes of the human race;
Like them, forgotten when the ruin
That marks their shock is past.

"Beside the eternal Nile,
The Pyramids have risen.
Nile shall pursue his changeless way:
Those Pyramids shall fall;
Yea! not a stone shall stand to tell   130
The spot whereon they stood!
Their very site shall be forgotten,
As is their builder's name!

"Behold yon sterile spot;
Where now the wandering Arab's tent
Flaps in the desert-blast.
There once old Salem's haughty fane
Reared high to Heaven its thousand golden
   domes,
And in the blushing face of day
Exposed its shameful glory.   140
Oh! many a widow, many an orphan cursed
The building of that fane; and many a father,
Worn out with toil and slavery, implored
The poor man's God to sweep it from the earth,
And spare his children the detested task
Of piling stone on stone, and poisoning
   The choicest days of life,
   To soothe a dotard's vanity.
There an inhuman and uncultured race
Howled hideous praises to their Demon-
   God;   150
They rushed to war, tore from the mother's
   womb
The unborn child,—old age and infancy
Promiscuous perished; their victorious arms
Left not a soul to breathe. Oh! they were
   fiends:
But what was he who taught them that the
   God
Of nature and benevolence hath given
A special sanction to the trade of blood?
His name and theirs are fading, and the tales
Of this barbarian nation, which imposture
Recites till terror credits, are pursuing   160
   Itself into forgetfulness.

"Where Athens, Rome, and Sparta stood,
There is a moral desert now:
The mean and miserable huts,
The yet more wretched palaces,
Contrasted with those ancient fanes,
Now crumbling to oblivion;
The long and lonely colonnades,
Through which the ghost of Freedom stalks,
   Seem like a well-known tune,   170
Which in some dear scene we have loved to
   hear,

Remembered now in sadness.
But, oh! how much more changed,
How gloomier is the contrast
Of human nature there!
Where Socrates expired, a tyrant's slave,
A coward and a fool, spreads death around—
   Then, shuddering, meets his own.
Where Cicero and Antoninus lived,
   A cowled and hypocritical monk   180
   Prays, curses and deceives.

"Spirit, ten thousand years
   Have scarcely passed away,
Since, in the waste where now the savage drinks
His enemy's blood, and aping Europe's sons,
   Wakes the unholy song of war,
   Arose a stately city,
Metropolis of the western continent:
   There, now, the mossy column-stone,
Indented by Time's unrelaxing grasp,   190
   Which once appeared to brave
   All, save its country's ruin;
   There the wide forest scene,
Rude in the uncultivated loveliness
   Of gardens long run wild,
Seems, to the unwilling sojourner, whose steps
   Chance in that desert has delayed,
Thus to have stood since earth was what it is.
   Yet once it was the busiest haunt,
Whither, as to a common centre, flocked   200
   Strangers, and ships, and merchandise:
   Once peace and freedom blessed
   The cultivated plain:
   But wealth, that curse of man,
Blighted the bud of its prosperity:
Virtue and wisdom, truth and liberty,
Fled, to return not, until man shall know
   That they alone can give the bliss
   Worthy a soul that claims
   Its kindred with eternity.   210

"There's not one atom of yon earth
   But once was living man;
Nor the minutest drop of rain,
That hangeth in its thinnest cloud,
   But flowed in human veins:
And from the burning plains
   Where Libyan monsters yell,
From the most gloomy glens
   Of Greenland's sunless clime,
To where the golden fields   220
   Of fertile England spread
   Their harvest to the day,
Thou canst not find one spot
Whereon no city stood.

"How strange is human pride!
I tell thee that those living things,
To whom the fragile blade of grass,
    That springeth in the morn
    And perisheth ere noon,
    Is an unbounded world;   230
I tell thee that those viewless beings,
Whose mansion is the smallest particle
    Of the impassive atmosphere,
    Think, feel and live like man;
That their affections and antipathies,
    Like his, produce the laws
    Ruling their moral state;
    And the minutest throb
That through their frame diffuses
    The slightest, faintest motion,   240
    Is fixed and indispensable
    As the majestic laws
    That rule yon rolling orbs."

The Fairy paused. The Spirit,
In ecstasy of admiration, felt
All knowledge of the past revived; the events
    Of old and wondrous times,
Which dim tradition interruptedly
Teaches the credulous vulgar, were unfolded
In just perspective to the view;   250
    Yet dim from their infinitude.
    The Spirit seemed to stand
High on an isolated pinnacle;
The flood of ages combating below,
The depth of the unbounded universe
    Above, and all around
    Nature's unchanging harmony.

                    III

"FAIRY!" the Spirit said,
    And on the Queen of Spells
    Fixed her aethereal eyes,
"I thank thee. Thou hast given
A boon which I will not resign, and taught
A lesson not to be unlearned. I know
The past, and thence I will essay to glean
A warning for the future, so that man
May profit by his errors, and derive
    Experience from his folly: 10
For, when the power of imparting joy
Is equal to the will, the human soul
    Requires no other Heaven."

                    Mab
"Turn thee, surpassing Spirit!
Much yet remains unscanned.

Thou knowest how great is man,
Thou knowest his imbecility:
Yet learn thou what he is:
Yet learn the lofty destiny
Which restless time prepares   20
    For every living soul.

"Behold a gorgeous palace, that, amid
Yon populous city rears its thousand towers
And seems itself a city. Gloomy troops
Of sentinels, in stern and silent ranks,
Encompass it around: the dweller there
Cannot be free and happy; hearest thou not
The curses of the fatherless, the groans
Of those who have no friend? He passes on:
The King, the wearer of a gilded chain   30
That binds his soul to abjectness, the fool
Whom courtiers nickname monarch, whilst a
        slave
Even to the basest appetites—that man
Heeds not the shriek of penury; he smiles
At the deep curses which the destitute
Mutter in secret, and a sullen joy
Pervades his bloodless heart when thousands
        groan
But for those morsels which his wantonness
Wastes in unjoyous revelry, to save
All that they love from famine: when he
        hears   40
The tale of horror, to some ready-made face
Of hypocritical assent he turns,
Smothering the glow of shame, that, spite of
        him,
Flushes his bloated cheek.
                        Now to the meal
Of silence, grandeur, and excess, he drags
His palled unwilling appetite. If gold,
Gleaming around, and numerous viands culled
From every clime, could force the loathing
        sense
To overcome satiety,—if wealth
The spring it draws from poisons not,—or
        vice,   50
Unfeeling, stubborn vice, converteth not
Its food to deadliest venom; then that king
Is happy; and the peasant who fulfils
His unforced task, when he returns at even,
And by the blazing faggot meets again
Her welcome for whom all his toil is sped,
Tastes not a sweeter meal.
                        Behold him now
Stretched on the gorgeous couch; his fevered
        brain
Reels dizzily awhile: but ah! too soon

The slumber of intemperance subsides,   60
And conscience, that undying serpent, calls
Her venomous brood to their nocturnal task.
Listen! he speaks! oh! mark that frenzied
        eye—
Oh! mark that deadly visage."

King
                                "No cessation!
Oh! must this last for ever? Awful Death,
I wish, yet fear to clasp thee!—Not one mo-
        ment
Of dreamless sleep! O dear and blessèd peace!
Why dost thou shroud thy vestal purity
In penury and dungeons? wherefore lurkest
With danger, death, and solitude; yet
        shunn'st   70
The palace I have built thee? Sacred peace!
Oh visit me but once, but pitying shed
One drop of balm upon my withered soul."

The Fairy
"Vain man! that palace is the virtuous heart,
And Peace defileth not her snowy robes
In such a shed as thine. Hark! yet he mutters;
His slumbers are but varied agonies,
They prey like scorpions on the springs of life.
There needeth not the hell that bigots frame
To punish those who err: earth in itself   80
Contains at once the evil and the cure;
And all-sufficing Nature can chastise
Those who transgress her law,—she only knows
How justly to proportion to the fault
The punishment it merits.
                                Is it strange
That this poor wretch should pride him in his
        woe?
Take pleasure in his abjectness, and hug
The scorpion that consumes him? Is it strange
That, placed on a conspicuous throne of thorns,
Grasping an iron sceptre, and immured   90
Within a splendid prison, whose stern bounds
Shut him from all that's good or dear on earth,
His soul asserts not its humanity?
That man's mild nature rises not in war
Against a king's employ? No—'tis not strange.
He, like the vulgar, thinks, feels, acts and lives
Just as his father did; the unconquered powers
Of precedent and custom interpose
Between a *king* and virtue. Stranger yet,
To those who know not Nature, nor deduce 100
The future from the present, it may seem,
That not one slave, who suffers from the crimes
Of this unnatural being; not one wretch,

Whose children famish, and whose nuptial bed
Is earth's unpitying bosom, rears an arm
To dash him from his throne!
                                Those gilded flies
That, basking in the sunshine of a court,
Fatten on its corruption!—what are they?
—The drones of the community; they feed
On the mechanic's labour: the starved hind 110
For them compels the stubborn glebe to yield
Its unshared harvests; and yon squalid form,
Leaner than fleshless misery, that wastes
A sunless life in the unwholesome mine,
Drags out in labour a protracted death,
To glut their grandeur; many faint with toil,
That few may know the cares and woe of sloth.

"Whence, think'st thou, kings and parasites
        arose?
Whence that unnatural line of drones, who heap
Toil and unvanquishable penury   120
On those who build their palaces, and bring
Their daily bread?—From vice, black loath-
        some vice;
From rapine, madness, treachery, and wrong;
From all that 'genders misery, and makes
Of earth this thorny wilderness; from lust,
Revenge, and murder. . . . And when Reason's
        voice,
Loud as the voice of Nature, shall have waked
The nations; and mankind perceive that vice
Is discord, war, and misery; that virtue
Is peace, and happiness and harmony;   130
When man's maturer nature shall disdain
The playthings of its childhood;—kingly glare
Will lose its power to dazzle; its authority
Will silently pass by; the gorgeous throne
Shall stand unnoticed in the regal hall,
Fast falling to decay; whilst falsehood's trade
Shall be as hateful and unprofitable
As that of truth is now.
                                Where is the fame
Which the vainglorious mighty of the earth
Seek to eternize? Oh! the faintest sound   140
From Time's light footfall, the minutest wave
That swells the flood of ages, whelms in
        nothing
The unsubstantial bubble. Ay! to-day
Stern is the tyrant's mandate, red the gaze
That flashes desolation, strong the arm
That scatters multitudes. To-morrow comes!
That mandate is a thunder-peal that died
In ages past; that gaze, a transient flash
On which the midnight closed, and on that
        arm

The worm has made his meal.
                    The virtuous man, 150
Who, great in his humility, as kings
Are little in their grandeur; he who leads
Invincibly a life of resolute good,
And stands amid the silent dungeon-depths
More free and fearless than the trembling
        judge,
Who, clothed in venal power, vainly strove
To bind the impassive spirit;—when he falls,
His mild eye beams benevolence no more:
Withered the hand outstretched but to relieve;
Sunk Reason's simple eloquence, that rolled 160
But to appal the guilty. Yes! the grave
Hath quenched that eye, and Death's relentless
        frost
Withered that arm: but the unfading fame
Which Virtue hangs upon its votary's tomb;
The deathless memory of that man, whom
        kings
Call to their mind and tremble; the remem-
        brance
With which the happy spirit contemplates
Its well-spent pilgrimage on earth,
Shall never pass away.

"Nature rejects the monarch, not the man; 170
The subject, not the citizen: for kings
And subjects, mutual foes, forever play
A losing game into each other's hands,
Whose stakes are vice and misery. The man
Of virtuous soul commands not, nor obeys.
Power, like a desolating pestilence,
Pollutes whate'er it touches; and obedience,
Bane of all genius, virtue, freedom, truth,
Makes slaves of men, and, of the human frame,
A mechanized automaton.
                    When Nero,   180
High over flaming Rome, with savage joy
Lowered like a fiend, drank with enraptured ear
The shrieks of agonizing death, beheld
The frightful desolation spread, and felt
A new-created sense within his soul
Thrill to the sight, and vibrate to the sound;
Think'st thou his grandeur had not overcome
The force of human kindness? and, when
        Rome,
With one stern blow, hurled not the tyrant
        down,
Crushed not the arm red with her dearest
        blood,   190
Had not submissive abjectness destroyed
Nature's suggestions?
                    Look on yonder earth:

The golden harvests spring; the unfailing sun
Sheds light and life; the fruits, the flowers, the
        trees,
Arise in due succession; all things speak
Peace, harmony, and love. The universe,
In Nature's silent eloquence, declares
That all fulfil the works of love and joy,—
All but the outcast, Man. He fabricates
The sword which stabs his peace; he cherish-
        eth   200
The snakes that gnaw his heart; he raiseth up
The tyrant, whose delight is in his woe,
Whose sport is in his agony. Yon sun,
Lights it the great alone? Yon silver beams,
Sleep they less sweetly on the cottage thatch
Than on the dome of kings? Is mother Earth
A step-dame to her numerous sons, who earn
Her unshared gifts with unremitting toil;
A mother only to those puling babes
Who, nursed in ease and luxury, make men 210
The playthings of their babyhood, and mar,
In self-important childishness, that peace
Which men alone appreciate?

        "Spirit of Nature! no.
The pure diffusion of thy essence throbs
    Alike in every human heart.
        Thou, aye, erectest there
    Thy throne of power unappealable:
    Thou art the judge beneath whose nod
Man's brief and frail authority   220
        Is powerless as the wind
        That passeth idly by.
    Thine the tribunal which surpasseth
        The show of human justice,
            As God surpasses man.

        "Spirit of Nature! thou
Life of interminable multitudes;
    Soul of those mighty spheres
Whose changeless paths through Heaven's deep
        silence lie;
        Soul of that smallest being,   230
        The dwelling of whose life
    Is one faint April sun-gleam;—
    Man, like these passive things,
Thy will unconsciously fulfilleth:
    Like theirs, his age of endless peace,
        Which time is fast maturing,
        Will swiftly, surely come;
And the unbounded frame, which thou per-
        vadest,
        Will be without a flaw
    Marring its perfect symmetry.   240

IV

"How beautiful this night! the balmiest sigh,
Which vernal zephyrs breathe in evening's ear,
Were discord to the speaking quietude
That wraps this moveless scene. Heaven's ebon
vault,
Studded with stars unutterably bright,
Through which the moon's unclouded grandeur
rolls,
Seems like a canopy which love had spread
To curtain her sleeping world. Yon gentle hills,
Robed in a garment of untrodden snow;
Yon darksome rocks, whence icicles depend, 10
So stainless, that their white and glittering
spires
Tinge not the moon's pure beam; yon castled
steep,
Whose banner hangeth o'er the time-worn
tower
So idly, that rapt fancy deemeth it
A metaphor of peace;—all form a scene
Where musing Solitude might love to lift
Her soul above this sphere of earthliness;
Where Silence undisturbed might watch alone,
So cold, so bright, so still.
The orb of day,
In southern climes, o'er ocean's waveless
field   20
Sinks sweetly smiling: not the faintest breath
Steals o'er the unruffled deep; the clouds of
eve
Reflect unmoved the lingering beam of day;
And vesper's image on the western main
Is beautifully still. To-morrow comes:
Cloud upon cloud, in dark and deepening
mass,
Roll o'er the blackened waters; the deep roar
Of distant thunder mutters awfully;
Tempest unfolds its pinion o'er the gloom
That shrouds the boiling surge; the pitiless
fiend,   30
With all his winds and lightnings, tracks his
prey;
The torn deep yawns,—the vessel finds a grave
Beneath its jaggèd gulf.
Ah! whence yon glare
That fires the arch of Heaven?—that dark red
smoke
Blotting the silver moon? The stars are
quenched
In darkness, and the pure and spangling snow
Gleams faintly through the gloom that gathers
round!

Hark to that roar, whose swift and deaf'ning
peals
In countless echoes through the mountains
ring,
Startling pale Midnight on her starry
throne!   40
Now swells the intermingling din; the jar
Frequent and frightful of the bursting bomb;
The falling beam, the shriek, the groan, the
shout,
The ceaseless clangour, and the rush of men
Inebriate with rage:—loud, and more loud
The discord grows; till pale Death shuts the
scene,
And o'er the conqueror and the conquered
draws
His cold and bloody shroud.—Of all the men
Whom day's departing beam saw blooming
there,
In proud and vigorous health; of all the
hearts   50
That beat with anxious life at sunset there;
How few survive, how few are beating now!
All is deep silence, like the fearful calm
That slumbers in the storm's portentous pause;
Save when the frantic wail of widowed love
Comes shuddering on the blast, or the faint
moan
With which some soul bursts from the frame
of clay
Wrapped round its struggling powers.
The gray morn
Dawns on the mournful scene; the sulphurous
smoke
Before the icy wind slow rolls away,   60
And the bright beams of frosty morning
dance
Along the spangling snow. There tracks of
blood
Even to the forest's depth, and scattered arms,
And lifeless warriors, whose hard lineaments
Death's self could change not, mark the dread-
ful path
Of the outsallying victors: far behind,
Black ashes note where their proud city stood.
Within yon forest is a gloomy glen—
Each tree which guards its darkness from the
day,
Waves o'er a warrior's tomb.
I see thee shrink, 70
Surpassing Spirit!—wert thou human else?
I see a shade of doubt and horror fleet
Across thy stainless features: yet fear not:
This is no unconnected misery,

Nor stands uncaused, and irretrievable.
Man's evil nature, that apology
Which kings who rule, and cowards who crouch,
　　set up
For their unnumbered crimes, sheds not the
　　blood
Which desolates the discord-wasted land.
From kings, and priests, and statesmen, war
　　arose,　　　　　　　　　　　　　80
Whose safety is man's deep unbettered woe,
Whose grandeur his debasement. Let the axe
Strike at the root, the poison-tree will fall;
And where its venomed exhalations spread
Ruin, and death, and woe, where millions lay
Quenching the serpent's famine, and their
　　bones
Bleaching unburied in the putrid blast,
A garden shall arise, in loveliness
Surpassing fabled Eden.
　　　　　　　　　　　　Hath Nature's soul,
That formed this world so beautiful, that
　　spread　　　　　　　　　　　　90
Earth's lap with plenty, and life's smallest
　　chord
Strung to unchanging unison, that gave
The happy birds their dwelling in the grove,
That yielded to the wanderers of the deep
The lovely silence of the unfathomed main,
And filled the meanest worm that crawls in
　　dust
With spirit, thought, and love; on Man alone,
Partial in causeless malice, wantonly
Heaped ruin, vice, and slavery; his soul
Blasted with withering curses; placed afar　100
The meteor-happiness, that shuns his grasp,
But serving on the frightful gulf to glare,
Rent wide beneath his footsteps?
　　　　　　　　　　　　　Nature!—no!
Kings, priests, and statesmen, blast the human
　　flower
Even in its tender bud; their influence darts
Like subtle poison through the bloodless veins
Of desolate society. The child,
Ere he can lisp his mother's sacred name,
Swells with the unnatural pride of crime, and
　　lifts
His baby-sword even in a hero's mood.　　110
This infant-arm becomes the bloodiest scourge
Of devastated earth; whilst specious names,
Learned in soft childhood's unsuspecting hour,
Serve as the sophisms with which manhood
　　dims
Bright Reason's ray, and sanctifies the sword
Upraised to shed a brother's innocent blood.

Let priest-led slaves cease to proclaim that
　　man
Inherits vice and misery, when Force
And Falsehood hang even o'er the cradled babe,
Stifling with rudest grasp all natural good.　120

"Ah! to the stranger-soul, when first it peeps
From its new tenement, and looks abroad
For happiness and sympathy, how stern
And desolate a tract is this wide world!
How withered all the buds of natural good!
No shade, no shelter from the sweeping storms
Of pitiless power! On its wretched frame,
Poisoned, perchance, by the disease and woe
Heaped on the wretched parent whence it
　　sprung
By morals, law, and custom, the pure winds　130
Of Heaven, that renovate the insect tribes,
May breathe not. The untainting light of day
May visit not its longings. It is bound
Ere it has life: yea, all the chains are forged
Long ere its being: all liberty and love
And peace is torn from its defencelessness;
Cursed from its birth, even from its cradle
　　doomed
To abjectness and bondage!

"Throughout this varied and eternal world
Soul is the only element: the block　　　140
That for uncounted ages has remained
The moveless pillar of a mountain's weight
Is active, living spirit. Every grain
Is sentient both in unity and part,
And the minutest atom comprehends
A world of loves and hatreds; these beget
Evil and good: hence truth and falsehood
　　spring;
Hence will and thought and action, all the
　　germs
Of pain or pleasure, sympathy or hate,
That variegate the eternal universe.　　150
Soul is not more polluted than the beams
Of Heaven's pure orb, ere round their rapid
　　lines
The taint of earth-born atmospheres arise.

"Man is of soul and body, formed for deeds
Of high resolve, on fancy's boldest wing
To soar unwearied, fearlessly to turn
The keenest pangs to peacefulness, and taste
The joys which mingled sense and spirit yield.
Or he is formed for abjectness and woe,
To grovel on the dunghill of his fears,　　160
To shrink at every sound, to quench the flame
Of natural love in sensualism, to know

That hour as blessed when on his worthless
    days
The frozen hand of Death shall set its seal,
Yet fear the cure, though hating the disease.
The one is man that shall hereafter be;
The other, man as vice has made him now.

"War is the statesman's game, the priest's de-
    light,
The lawyer's jest, the hired assassin's trade,
And, to those royal murderers, whose mean
    thrones   170
Are bought by crimes of treachery and gore,
The bread they eat, the staff on which they
    lean.
Guards, garbed in blood-red livery, surround
Their palaces, participate the crimes
That force defends, and from a nation's rage
Secure the crown, which all the curses reach
That famine, frenzy, woe and penury breathe.
These are the hired bravos who defend
The tyrant's throne—the bullies of his fear:
These are the sinks and channels of worst
    vice,   180
The refuse of society, the dregs
Of all that is most vile: their cold hearts blend
Deceit with sternness, ignorance with pride,
All that is mean and villanous, with rage
Which hopelessness of good, and self-contempt,
Alone might kindle; they are decked in wealth,
Honour and power, then are sent abroad
To do their work. The pestilence that stalks
In gloomy triumph through some eastern land
Is less destroying. They cajole with gold,   190
And promises of fame, the thoughtless youth
Already crushed with servitude: he knows
His wretchedness too late, and cherishes
Repentance for his ruin, when his doom
Is sealed in gold and blood!
Those too the tyrant serve, who, skilled to
    snare
The feet of Justice in the toils of law,
Stand, ready to oppress the weaker still;
And right or wrong will vindicate for gold,
Sneering at public virtue, which beneath   200
Their pitiless tread lies torn and trampled,
    where
Honour sits smiling at the sale of truth.

"Then grave and hoary-headed hypocrites,
Without a hope, a passion, or a love,
Who, through a life of luxury and lies,
Have crept by flattery to the seats of power,
Support the system whence their honours
    flow. . . .
They have three words:—well tyrants know
    their use,
Well pay them for the loan, with usury
Torn from a bleeding world!—God, Hell, and
    Heaven.   210
A vengeful, pitiless, and almighty fiend,
Whose mercy is a nickname for the rage
Of tameless tigers hungering for blood.
Hell, a red gulf of everlasting fire,
Where poisonous and undying worms prolong
Eternal misery to those hapless slaves
Whose life has been a penance for its crimes.
And Heaven, a meed for those who dare be-
    lie
Their human nature, quake, believe, and cringe
Before the mockeries of earthly power.   220

"These tools the tyrant tempers to his work,
Wields in his wrath, and as he wills destroys,
Omnipotent in wickedness: the while
Youth springs, age moulders, manhood tamely
    does
His bidding, bribed by short-lived joys to lend
Force to the weakness of his trembling arm.

"They rise, they fall; one generation comes
Yielding its harvest to destruction's scythe.
It fades, another blossoms: yet behold!
Red glows the tyrant's stamp-mark on its
    bloom,   230
Withering and cankering deep its passive prime.
He has invented lying words and modes,
Empty and vain as his own coreless heart;
Evasive meanings, nothings of much sound,
To lure the heedless victim to the toils
Spread round the valley of its paradise.

"Look to thyself, priest, conqueror, or prince!
Whether thy trade is falsehood, and thy lusts
Deep wallow in the earnings of the poor,
With whom thy Master was:—or thou de-
    light'st   240
In numbering o'er the myriads of thy slain,
All misery weighing nothing in the scale
Against thy short-lived fame: or thou dost
    load
With cowardice and crime the groaning land,
A pomp-fed king. Look to thy wretched self!
Ay, art thou not the veriest slave that e'er
Crawled on the loathing earth? Are not thy
    days
Days of unsatisfying listlessness?

Dost thou not cry, ere night's long rack is o'er,
'When will the morning come?' Is not thy
    youth   250
A vain and feverish dream of sensualism?
Thy manhood blighted with unripe disease?
Are not thy views of unregretted death
Drear, comfortless, and horrible? Thy mind,
Is it not morbid as thy nerveless frame,
Incapable of judgement, hope, or love?
And dost thou wish the errors to survive
That bar thee from all sympathies of good,
After the miserable interest
Thou hold'st in their protraction? When the
    grave   260
Has swallowed up thy memory and thyself,
Dost thou desire the bane that poisons earth
To twine its roots around thy coffined clay,
Spring from thy bones, and blossom on thy
    tomb,
That of its fruit thy babes may eat and die?

V

"THUS do the generations of the earth
Go to the grave, and issue from the womb,
Surviving still the imperishable change
That renovates the world; even as the leaves
Which the keen frost-wind of the waning year
Has scattered on the forest soil, and heaped
For many seasons there—though long they
    choke,
Loading with loathsome rottenness the land,
All germs of promise, yet when the tall trees
From which they fell, shorn of their lovely
    shapes,   10
Lie level with the earth to moulder there,
They fertilize the land they long deformed,
Till from the breathing lawn a forest springs
Of youth, integrity, and loveliness,
Like that which gave it life, to spring and die.
Thus suicidal selfishness, that blights
The fairest feelings of the opening heart,
Is destined to decay, whilst from the soil
Shall spring all virtue, all delight, all love,
And judgement cease to wage unnatural war 20
With passion's unsubduable array.
Twin-sister of religion, selfishness!
Rival in crime and falsehood, aping all
The wanton horrors of her bloody play;
Yet frozen, unimpassioned, spiritless,
Shunning the light, and owning not its name,
Compelled, by its deformity, to screen
With flimsy veil of justice and of right,
Its unattractive lineaments, that scare
All, save the brood of ignorance: at once 30

The cause and the effect of tyranny;
Unblushing, hardened, sensual, and vile;
Dead to all love but of its abjectness,
With heart impassive by more noble powers
Than unshared pleasure, sordid gain, or fame;
Despising its own miserable being,
Which still it longs, yet fears to disenthrall.

"Hence commerce springs, the venal inter-
    change
Of all that human art or nature yield;
Which wealth should purchase not, but want
    demand,   40
And natural kindness hasten to supply
From the full fountain of its boundless love,
For ever stifled, drained, and tainted now.
Commerce! beneath whose poison-breathing
    shade
No solitary virtue dares to spring,
But Poverty and Wealth with equal hand
Scatter their withering curses, and unfold
The doors of premature and violent death,
To pining famine and full-fed disease,
To all that shares the lot of human life, 50
Which poisoned, body and soul, scarce drags
    the chain,
That lengthens as it goes and clanks behind.

"Commerce has set the mark of selfishness,
The signet of its all-enslaving power
Upon a shining ore, and called it gold:
Before whose image bow the vulgar great,
The vainly rich, the miserable proud,
The mob of peasants, nobles, priests, and
    kings,
And with blind feelings reverence the power
That grinds them to the dust of misery. 60
But in the temple of their hireling hearts
Gold is a living god, and rules in scorn
All earthly things but virtue.

"Since tyrants, by the sale of human life,
Heap luxuries to their sensualism, and fame
To their wide-wasting and insatiate pride,
Success has sanctioned to a credulous world
The ruin, the disgrace, the woe of war.
His hosts of blind and unresisting dupes
The despot numbers; from his cabinet 70
These puppets of his schemes he moves at will,
Even as the slaves by force or famine driven,
Beneath a vulgar master, to perform
A task of cold and brutal drudgery;—
Hardened to hope, insensible to fear,
Scarce living pulleys of a dead machine,
Mere wheels of work and articles of trade,

That grace the proud and noisy pomp of
 wealth!

'The harmony and happiness of man
Yields to the wealth of nations; that which
 lifts   80
His nature to the heaven of its pride,
Is bartered for the poison of his soul;
The weight that drags to earth his towering
 hopes,
Blighting all prospect but of selfish gain,
Withering all passion but of slavish fear,
Extinguishing all free and generous love
Of enterprise and daring, even the pulse
That fancy kindles in the beating heart
To mingle with sensation, it destroys,—
Leaves nothing but the sordid lust of self, 90
The grovelling hope of interest and gold,
Unqualified, unmingled, unredeemed
Even by hypocrisy.
     And statesmen boast
Of wealth! The wordy eloquence, that lives
After the ruin of their hearts, can gild
The bitter poison of a nation's woe,
Can turn the worship of the servile mob
To their corrupt and glaring idol, Fame,
From Virtue, trampled by its iron tread,
Although its dazzling pedestal be raised 100
Amid the horrors of a limb-strewn field,
With desolated dwellings smoking round.
The man of ease, who, by his warm fireside,
To deeds of charitable intercourse,
And bare fulfilment of the common laws
Of decency and prejudice, confines
The struggling nature of his human heart,
Is duped by their cold sophistry; he sheds
A passing tear perchance upon the wreck
Of earthly peace, when near his dwelling's
 door   110
The frightful waves are driven,—when his son
Is murdered by the tyrant, or religion
Drives his wife raving mad. But the poor man,
Whose life is misery, and fear, and care;
Whom the morn wakens but to fruitless toil;
Who ever hears his famished offspring's scream,
Whom their pale mother's uncomplaining gaze
For ever meets, and the proud rich man's eye
Flashing command, and the heart-breaking
 scene
Of thousands like himself;—he little heeds 120
The rhetoric of tyranny; his hate
Is quenchless as his wrongs; he laughs to scorn
The vain and bitter mockery of words,
Feeling the horror of the tyrant's deeds,

And unrestrained but by the arm of power,
That knows and dreads his enmity.

"The iron rod of Penury still compels
Her wretched slave to bow the knee to wealth,
And poison, with unprofitable toil,
A life too void of solace to confirm 130
The very chains that bind him to his doom.
Nature, impartial in munificence,
Has gifted man with all-subduing will.
Matter, with all its transitory shapes,
Lies subjected and plastic at his feet,
That, weak from bondage, tremble as they
 tread.
How many a rustic Milton has passed by,
Stifling the speechless longings of his heart,
In unremitting drudgery and care!
How many a vulgar Cato has compelled 140
His energies, no longer tameless then,
To mould a pin, or fabricate a nail!
How many a Newton, to whose passive ken
Those mighty spheres that gem infinity
Were only specks of tinsel, fixed in Heaven
To light the midnights of his native town!

"Yet every heart contains perfection's germ:
The wisest of the sages of the earth,
That ever from the stores of reason drew
Science and truth, and virtue's dreadless
 tone,   150
Were but a weak and inexperienced boy,
Proud, sensual, unimpassioned, unimbued
With pure desire and universal love,
Compared to that high being, of cloudless
 brain,
Untainted passion, elevated will,
Which Death (who even would linger long in
 awe
Within his noble presence, and beneath
His changeless eyebeam) might alone subdue.
Him, every slave now dragging through the
 filth
Of some corrupted city his sad life, 160
Pining with famine, swoln with luxury,
Blunting the keenness of his spiritual sense
With narrow schemings and unworthy cares,
Or madly rushing through all violent crime,
To move the deep stagnation of his soul,—
Might imitate and equal.
     But mean lust
Has bound its chains so tight around the earth,
That all within it but the virtuous man
Is venal: gold or fame will surely reach
The price prefixed by selfishness, to all 170
But him of resolute and unchanging will;

Whom, nor the plaudits of a servile crowd,
Nor the vile joys of tainting luxury,
Can bribe to yield his elevated soul
To Tyranny or Falsehood, though they wield
With blood-red hand the sceptre of the world.

"All things are sold: the very light of Heaven
Is venal; earth's unsparing gifts of love,
The smallest and most despicable things
That lurk in the abysses of the deep,   180
All objects of our life, even life itself,
And the poor pittance which the laws allow
Of liberty, the fellowship of man,
Those duties which his heart of human love
Should urge him to perform instinctively,
Are bought and sold as in a public mart
Of undisguising sefishness, that sets
On each its price, the stamp-mark of her reign.
Even love is sold; the solace of all woe
Is turned to deadliest agony, old age   190
Shivers in selfish beauty's loathing arms,
And youth's corrupted impulses prepare
A life of horror from the blighting bane
Of commerce; whilst the pestilence that springs
From unenjoying sensualism, has filled
All human life with hydra-headed woes.

"Falsehood demands but gold to pay the pangs
Of outraged conscience; for the slavish priest
Sets no great value on his hireling faith:
A little passing pomp, some servile souls,   200
Whom cowardice itself might safely chain,
Or the spare mite of avarice could bribe
To deck the triumph of their languid zeal,
Can make him minister to tyranny.
More daring crime requires a loftier meed:
Without a shudder, the slave-soldier lends
His arm to murderous deeds, and steels his
               heart,
When the dread eloquence of dying men,
Low mingling on the lonely field of fame,
Assails that nature, whose applause he sells   210
For the gross blessings of a patriot mob,
For the vile gratitude of heartless kings,
And for a cold world's good word,—viler still!

"There is a nobler glory, which survives
Until our being fades, and, solacing
All human care, accompanies its change;
Deserts not virtue in the dungeon's gloom,
And, in the precincts of the palace, guides
Its footsteps through that labyrinth of crime;
Imbues his lineaments with dauntlessness,   220
Even when, from Power's avenging hand, he
               takes

Its sweetest, last and noblest title—death;
—The consciousness of good, which neither
               gold,
Nor sordid fame, nor hope of heavenly bliss
Can purchase; but a life of resolute good,
Unalterable will, quenchless desire
Of universal happiness, the heart
That beats with it in unison, the brain,
Whose ever wakeful wisdom toils to change
Reason's rich stores for its eternal weal.   230

"This commerce of sincerest virtue needs
No mediative signs of selfishness,
No jealous intercourse of wretched gain,
No balancings of prudence, cold and long;
In just and equal measure all is weighed,
One scale contains the sum of human weal,
And one, the good man's heart.
                                How vainly seek
The selfish for that happiness denied
To aught but virtue! Blind and hardened, they,
Who hope for peace amid the storms of
               care,   240
Who covet power they know not how to use,
And sigh for pleasure they refuse to give,—
Madly they frustrate still their own designs;
And, where they hope that quiet to enjoy
Which virtue pictures, bitterness of soul,
Pining regrets, and vain repentances,
Disease, disgust, and lassitude, pervade
Their valueless and miserable lives.

"But hoary-headed Selfishness has felt
Its death-blow, and is tottering to the grave: 250
A brighter morn awaits the human day,
When every transfer of earth's natural gifts
Shall be a commerce of good words and works;
When poverty and wealth, the thirst of fame,
The fear of infamy, disease and woe,
War with its million horrors, and fierce hell
Shall live but in the memory of Time,
Who, like a penitent libertine, shall start,
Look back, and shudder at his younger years."

VI

      ALL touch, all eye, all ear,
The Spirit felt the Fairy's burning speech.
     O'er the thin texture of its frame,
The varying periods painted changing glows,
         As on a summer even,
When soul-enfolding music floats around,
     The stainless mirror of the lake
     Re-images the eastern gloom,
Mingling convulsively its purple hues
         With sunset's burnished gold.   10

Then thus the Spirit spoke:
"It is a wild and miserable world!
  Thorny, and full of care,
Which every fiend can make his prey at will.
  O Fairy! in the lapse of years,
    Is there no hope in store?
    Will yon vast suns roll on
Interminably, still illuming
The night of so many wretched souls,
    And see no hope for them?   20
Will not the universal Spirit e'er
Revivify this withered limb of Heaven?"

    The Fairy calmly smiled
In comfort, and a kindling gleam of hope
  Suffused the Spirit's lineaments.
"Oh! rest thee tranquil; chase those fearful
      doubts,
Which ne'er could rack an everlasting soul,
That sees the chains which bind it to its doom.
Yes! crime and misery are in yonder earth,
    Falsehood, mistake, and lust;   30
    But the eternal world
Contains at once the evil and the cure.
Some eminent in virtue shall start up,
    Even in perversest time:
The truths of their pure lips, that never die,
Shall bind the scorpion falsehood with a wreath
    Of ever-living flame,
Until the monster sting itself to death.

    "How sweet a scene will earth become!
Of purest spirits a pure dwelling-place,   40
Symphonious with the planetary spheres;
When man, with changeless Nature coalescing,
Will undertake regeneration's work,
When its ungenial poles no longer point
    To the red and baleful sun
    That faintly twinkles there.

    "Spirit! on yonder earth,
  Falsehood now triumphs; deadly power
Has fixed its seal upon the lip of truth!
  Madness and misery are there!   50
The happiest is most wretched! Yet confide,
Until pure health-drops, from the cup of joy,
Fall like a dew of balm upon the world.
Now, to the scene I show, in silence turn,
And read the blood-stained charter of all woe,
Which Nature soon, with re-creating hand,
Will blot in mercy from the book of earth.
How bold the flight of Passion's wandering
      wing,
How swift the step of Reason's firmer tread,

How calm and sweet the victories of life,   60
How terrorless the triumph of the grave!
How powerless were the mightiest monarch's
      arm,
Vain his loud threat, and impotent his frown!
How ludicrous the priest's dogmatic roar!
The weight of his exterminating curse
How light! and his affected charity,
To suit the pressure of the changing times,
What palpable deceit!—but for thy aid,
Religion! but for thee, prolific fiend,
Who peoplest earth with demons, Hell with
      men,   70
And Heaven with slaves!

    "Thou taintest all thou look'st upon!—the
      stars,
Which on thy cradle beamed so brightly sweet,
Were gods to the distempered playfulness
Of thy untutored infancy: the trees,
The grass, the clouds, the mountains, and the
      sea,
All living things that walk, swim, creep, or fly,
Were gods: the sun had homage, and the moon
Her worshipper. Then thou becam'st, a boy,
More daring in thy frenzies: every shape,   80
Monstrous or vast, or beautifully wild,
Which, from sensation's relics, fancy culls;
The spirits of the air, the shuddering ghost,
The genii of the elements, the powers
That give a shape to Nature's varied works,
Had life and place in the corrupt belief
Of thy blind heart: yet still thy youthful hands
Were pure of human blood. Then manhood
      gave
Its strength and ardour to thy frenzied brain;
Thine eager gaze scanned the stupendous
      scene,   90
Whose wonders mocked the knowledge of thy
      pride:
Their everlasting and unchanging laws
Reproached thine ignorance. Awhile thou
      stoodst
Baffled and gloomy; then thou didst sum up
The elements of all that thou didst know;
The changing seasons, winter's leafless reign,
The budding of the Heaven-breathing trees,
The eternal orbs that beautify the night,
The sunrise, and the setting of the moon,
Earthquakes and wars, and poisons and dis-
      ease,   100
And all their causes, to an abstract point
Converging, thou didst bend and called it God!
The self-sufficing, the omnipotent,

The merciful, and the avenging God!
Who, prototype of human misrule, sits
High in Heaven's realm, upon a golden throne,
Even like an earthly king; and whose dread work,
Hell, gapes for ever for the unhappy slaves
Of fate, whom He created, in his sport,
To triumph in their torments when they fell!   110
Earth heard the name; Earth trembled, as the smoke
Of His revenge ascended up to Heaven,
Blotting the constellations; and the cries
Of millions, butchered in sweet confidence
And unsuspecting peace, even when the bonds
Of safety were confirmed by wordy oaths
Sworn in His dreadful name, rung through the land;
Whilst innocent babes writhed on thy stubborn spear,
And thou didst laugh to hear the mother's shriek
Of maniac gladness, as the sacred steel   120
Felt cold in her torn entrails!

"Religion! thou wert then in manhood's prime:
But age crept on: one God would not suffice
For senile puerility; thou framedst
A tale to suit thy dotage, and to glut
Thy misery-thirsting soul, that the mad fiend
Thy wickedness had pictured might afford
A plea for sating the unnatural thirst
For murder, rapine, violence, and crime,
That still consumed thy being, even when   130
Thou heardst the step of Fate;—that flames might light
Thy funeral scene, and the shrill horrent shrieks
Of parents dying on the pile that burned
To light their children to thy paths, the roar
Of the encircling flames, the exulting cries
Of thine apostles, loud commingling there,
     Might sate thine hungry ear
     Even on the bed of death!

"But now contempt is mocking thy gray hairs;
Thou art descending to the darksome grave,   140
Unhonoured and unpitied, but by those
Whose pride is passing by like thine, and sheds,
Like thine, a glare that fades before the sun
Of truth, and shines but in the dreadful night
That long has lowered above the ruined world.

"Throughout these infinite orbs of mingling light,

Of which yon earth is one, is wide diffused
A Spirit of activity and life,
That knows no term, cessation, or decay;
That fades not when the lamp of earthly life,   150
Extinguished in the dampness of the grave,
Awhile there slumbers, more than when the babe
In the dim newness of its being feels
The impulses of sublunary things,
And all is wonder to unpractised sense:
But, active, steadfast, and eternal, still
Guides the fierce whirlwind, in the tempest roars,
Cheers in the day, breathes in the balmy groves
Strengthens in health, and poisons in disease
And in the storm of change, that ceaselessly   160
Rolls round the eternal universe, and shakes
Its undecaying battlement, presides,
Apportioning with irresistible law
The place each spring of its machine shall fill;
So that when waves on waves tumultuous heap
Confusion to the clouds, and fiercely driven
Heaven's lightnings scorch the uprooted ocean-fords,
Whilst, to the eye of shipwrecked mariner,
Lone sitting on the bare and shuddering rock,
All seems unlinked contingency and chance: 170
No atom of this turbulence fulfils
A vague and unnecessitated task,
Or acts but as it must and ought to act.
Even the minutest molecule of light,
That in an April sunbeam's fleeting glow
Fulfils its destined, though invisible work,
The universal Spirit guides; nor less,
When merciless ambition, or mad zeal,
Has led two hosts of dupes to battlefield,
That, blind, they there may dig each other's graves,   180
And call the sad work glory, does it rule
All passions: not a thought, a will, an act,
No working of the tyrant's moody mind,
Nor one misgiving of the slaves who boast
Their servitude, to hide the shame they feel,
Nor the events enchaining every will,
That from the depths of unrecorded time
Have drawn all-influencing virtue, pass
Unrecognized, or unforeseen by thee,
Soul of the Universe! eternal spring   190
Of life and death, of happiness and woe,
Of all that chequers the phantasmal scene
That floats before our eyes in wavering light,
Which gleams but on the darkness of our prison,

Whose chains and massy walls
We feel, but cannot see.

"Spirit of Nature! all-sufficing Power,
Necessity! thou mother of the world!
Unlike the God of human error, thou
Requir'st no prayers or praises; the caprice 200
Of man's weak will belongs no more to thee
Than do the changeful passions of his breast
To thy unvarying harmony: the slave,
Whose horrible lusts spread misery o'er the
world,
And the good man, who lifts, with virtuous
pride,
His being, in the sight of happiness,
That springs from his own works; the poison-
tree,
Beneath whose shade all life is withered up,
And the fair oak, whose leafy dome affords
A temple where the vows of happy love 210
Are registered, are equal in thy sight:
No love, no hate thou cherishest; revenge
And favouritism, and worst desire of fame
Thou know'st not: all that the wide world con-
tains
Are but thy passive instruments, and thou
Regard'st them all with an impartial eye,
Whose joy or pain thy nature cannot feel,
Because thou hast not human sense,
Because thou art not human mind.

"Yes! when the sweeping storm of time 220
Has sung its death-dirge o'er the ruined fanes
And broken altars of the almighty Fiend
Whose name usurps thy honours, and the
blood
Through centuries clotted there, has floated
down
The tainted flood of ages, shalt thou live
Unchangeable! A shrine is raised to thee,
Which, nor the tempest-breath of time,
Nor the interminable flood,
Over earth's slight pageant rolling,
Availeth to destroy,— 230
The sensitive extension of the world.
That wondrous and eternal fane,
Where pain and pleasure, good and evil join,
To do the will of strong necessity,
And life, in multitudinous shapes,
Still pressing forward where no term can be,
Like hungry and unresting flame
Curls round the eternal columns of its
strength."

VII

Spirit

"I WAS an infant when my mother went
To see an atheist burned. She took me there:
The dark-robed priests were met around the
pile;
The multitude was gazing silently;
And as the culprit passed with dauntless mien,
Tempered disdain in his unaltering eye,
Mixed with a quiet smile, shone calmly forth:
The thirsty fire crept round his manly limbs;
His resolute eyes were scorched to blindness
soon;
His death-pang rent my heart! the insensate
mob 10
Uttered a cry of triumph, and I wept.
'Weep not, child!' cried my mother, 'for that
man
Has said, There is no God.'"

Fairy

"There is no God!
Nature confirms the faith his death-groan
sealed:
Let heaven and earth, let man's revolving race,
His ceaseless generations tell their tale;
Let every part depending on the chain
That links it to the whole, point to the hand
That grasps its term! let every seed that falls
In silent eloquence unfold its store 20
Of argument; infinity within,
Infinity without, belie creation;
The exterminable spirit it contains
Is nature's only God; but human pride
Is skilful to invent most serious names
To hide its ignorance. The name of God
Has fenced about all crime with holiness,
Himself the creature of His worshippers,
Whose names and attributes and passions
change,
Seeva, Buddh, Foh, Jehovah, God, or Lord, 30
Even with the human dupes who build His
shrines,
Still serving o'er the war-polluted world
For desolation's watchword; whether hosts
Stain His death-blushing chariot-wheels, as on
Triumphantly they roll, whilst Brahmins raise
A sacred hymn to mingle with the groans;
Or countless partners of His power divide
His tyranny to weakness; or the smoke
Of burning towns, the cries of female helpless-
ness,

Unarmed old age, and youth, and infancy,   40
Horribly massacred, ascend to Heaven
In honour of His name; or, last and worst,
Earth groans beneath religion's iron age,
And priests dare babble of a God of peace,
Even whilst their hands are red with guiltless
     blood,
Murdering the while, uprooting every germ
Of truth, exterminating, spoiling all,
Making the earth a slaughter-house!

     "O Spirit! through the sense
By which thy inner nature was apprised   50
  Of outward shows, vague dreams have rolled,
  And varied reminiscences have waked
     Tablets that never fade;
  All things have been imprinted there,
  The stars, the sea, the earth, the sky,
  Even the unshapeliest lineaments
     Of wild and fleeting visions
       Have left a record there
       To testify of earth.

"These are my empire, for to me is given   60
The wonders of the human world to keep,
And Fancy's thin creations to endow
With manner, being, and reality;
Therefore a wondrous phantom, from the
     dreams
Of human error's dense and purblind faith,
I will evoke, to meet thy questioning.
     Ahasuerus, rise!"

     A strange and woe-worn wight
     Arose beside the battlement,
       And stood unmoving there.   70
His inessential figure cast no shade
     Upon the golden floor;
His port and mien bore mark of many years,
And chronicles of untold ancientness
Were legible within his beamless eye:
  Yet his cheek bore the mark of youth;
Freshness and vigour knit his manly frame;
The wisdom of old age was mingled there
  With youth's primaeval dauntlessness;
     And inexpressible woe,   80
Chastened by fearless resignation, gave
An awful grace to his all-speaking brow.

Spirit
"Is there a God?"

Ahasuerus
"Is there a God!—ay, an almighty God,
And vengeful as almighty! Once His voice

Was heard on earth: earth shuddered at the
     sound;
The fiery-visaged firmament expressed
Abhorrence, and the grave of Nature yawned
To swallow all the dauntless and the good
That dared to hurl defiance at His throne,   90
Girt as it was with power. None but slaves
Survived,—cold-blooded slaves, who did the
     work
Of tyrannous omnipotence; whose souls
No honest indignation ever urged
To elevated daring, to one deed
Which gross and sensual self did not pollute.
These slaves built temples for the omnipotent
     Fiend,
Gorgeous and vast: the costly altars smoked
With human blood, and hideous paeans rung
Through all the long-drawn aisles. A murderer
     heard   100
His voice in Egypt, one whose gifts and arts
Had raised him to his eminence in power,
Accomplice of omnipotence in crime,
And confidant of the all-knowing one.
     These were Jehovah's words:—

"From an eternity of idleness
I, God, awoke; in seven days' toil made earth
From nothing; rested, and created man:
I placed him in a Paradise, and there
Planted the tree of evil, so that he   110
Might eat and perish, and My soul procure
Wherewith to sate its malice, and to turn,
Even like a heartless conqueror of the earth,
All misery to My fame. The race of men
Chosen to My honour, with impunity
May sate the lusts I planted in their heart.
Here I command thee hence to lead them on,
Until, with hardened feet, their conquering
     troops
Wade on the promised soil through woman's
     blood,
And make My name be dreaded through the
     land.   120
Yet ever-burning flame and ceaseless woe
Shall be the doom of their eternal souls,
With every soul on this ungrateful earth,
Virtuous or vicious, weak or strong,—even all
Shall perish, to fulfil the blind revenge
(Which you, to men, call justice) of their
     God."
               The murderer's brow
Quivered with horror.
               "God omnipotent,
Is there no mercy? must our punishment

Be endless? will long ages roll away,
And see no term? Oh! wherefore hast Thou
made   130
In mockery and wrath this evil earth?
Mercy becomes the powerful—be but just:
O God! repent and save."

    "One way remains:
I will beget a Son, and He shall bear
The sins of all the world; He shall arise
In an unnoticed corner of the earth,
And there shall die upon a cross, and purge
The universal crime; so that the few
On whom My grace descends, those who are
marked   140
As vessels to the honour of their God,
May credit this strange sacrifice, and save
Their souls alive: millions shall live and die,
Who ne'er shall call upon their Saviour's name,
But, unredeemed, go to the gaping grave.
Thousands shall deem it an old woman's tale,
Such as the nurses frighten babes withal:
These in a gulf of anguish and of flame
Shall curse their reprobation endlessly,
Yet tenfold pangs shall force them to avow, 150
Even on their beds of torment, where they
howl,
My honour, and the justice of their doom.
What then avail their virtuous deeds, their
thoughts
Of purity, with radiant genius bright,
Or lit with human reason's earthly ray?
Many are called, but few will I elect.
Do thou My bidding, Moses!"
    Even the murderer's cheek
Was blanched with horror, and his quivering
lips
Scarce faintly uttered—"O almighty One,
I tremble and obey!"   160

"O Spirit! centuries have set their seal
On this heart of many wounds, and loaded
brain,
Since the Incarnate came: humbly He came,
Veiling His horrible Godhead in the shape
Of man, scorned by the world, His name un-
heard,
Save by the rabble of His native town,
Even as a parish demagogue. He led
The crowd; He taught them justice, truth, and
peace,
In semblance; but He lit within their souls
The quenchless flames of zeal, and blessed the
sword   170

He brought on earth to satiate with the blood
Of truth and freedom His malignant soul.
At length His mortal frame was led to death.
I stood beside Him: on the torturing cross
No pain assailed His unterrestrial sense;
And yet He groaned. Indignantly I summed
The massacres and miseries which His name
Had sanctioned in my country, and I cried,
'Go! Go!' in mockery.
A smile of godlike malice reillumed   180
His fading lineaments.—'I go,' He cried,
'But thou shalt wander o'er the unquiet earth
Eternally.'——The dampness of the grave
Bathed my imperishable front. I fell,
And long lay tranced upon the charmèd soil.
When I awoke Hell burned within my brain,
Which staggered on its seat; for all around
The mouldering relics of my kindred lay,
Even as the Almighty's ire arrested them,
And in their various attitudes of death   190
My murdered children's mute and eyeless
skulls
Glared ghastily upon me.
    But my soul,
From sight and sense of the polluting woe
Of tyranny, had long learned to prefer
Hell's freedom to the servitude of Heaven.
Therefore I rose, and dauntlessly began
My lonely and unending pilgrimage,
Resolved to wage unweariable war
With my almighty Tyrant, and to hurl
Defiance at His impotence to harm   200
Beyond the curse I bore. The very hand
That barred my passage to the peaceful grave
Has crushed the earth to misery, and given
Its empire to the chosen of His slaves.
These have I seen, even from the earliest
dawn
Of weak, unstable and precarious power,
Then preaching peace, as now they practise
war;
So, when they turned but from the massacre
Of unoffending infidels, to quench
Their thirst for ruin in the very blood   210
That flowed in their own veins, and pitiless
zeal
Froze every human feeling, as the wife
Sheathed in her husband's heart the sacred
steel,
Even whilst its hopes were dreaming of her
love;
And friends to friends, brothers to brothers
stood
Opposed in bloodiest battle-field, and war,

Scarce satiable by fate's last death-draught,
    waged,
Drunk from the winepress of the Almighty's
    wrath;
Whilst the red cross, in mockery of peace,
Pointed to victory! When the fray was
    done,   220
No remnant of the exterminated faith
Survived to tell its ruin, but the flesh,
With putrid smoke poisoning the atmosphere,
That rotted on the half-extinguished pile.

"Yes! I have seen God's worshippers unsheathe
The sword of His revenge, when grace de-
    scended,
Confirming all unnatural impulses,
To sanctify their desolating deeds;
And frantic priests waved the ill-omened cross
O'er the unhappy earth: then shone the sun 230
On showers of gore from the upflashing steel
Of safe assassination, and all crime
Made stingless by the Spirits of the Lord,
And blood-red rainbows canopied the land.

"Spirit, no year of my eventful being
Has passed unstained by crime and misery,
Which flows from God's own faith. I've
    marked His slaves
With tongues whose lives are venomous, beguile
The insensate mob, and, whilst one hand was
    red
With murder, feign to stretch the other out 240
For brotherhood and peace; and that they now
Babble of love and mercy, whilst their deeds
Are marked with all the narrowness and crime
That Freedom's young arm dare not yet
    chastise,
Reason may claim our gratitude, who now
Establishing the imperishable throne
Of truth, and stubborn virtue, maketh vain
The unprevailing malice of my Foe,
Whose bootless rage heaps torments for the
    brave,
Adds impotent eternities to pain,   250
Whilst keenest disappointment racks His
    breast
To see the smiles of peace around them play,
To frustrate or to sanctify their doom.

"Thus have I stood,—through a wild waste of
    years
Struggling with whirlwinds of mad agony,
Yet peaceful, and serene, and self-enshrined,
Mocking my powerless Tyrant's horrible curse
With stubborn and unalterable will,

Even as a giant oak, which Heaven's fierce
    flame
Had scathèd in the wilderness, to stand   260
A monument of fadeless ruin there;
Yet peacefully and movelessly it braves
The midnight conflict of the wintry storm,
    As in the sunlight's calm its spreads
    Its worn and withered arms on high
To meet the quiet of a summer's noon."

    The Fairy waved her wand:
    Ahasuerus fled
Fast as the shapes of mingled shade and mist
That lurk in the glens of a twilight grove, 270
    Flee from the morning beam:
    The matter of which dreams are made
Not more endowed with actual life
Than this phantasmal portraiture
Of wandering human thought.

VIII

The Fairy

"THE Present and the Past thou hast beheld:
It was a desolate sight. Now, Spirit, learn
    The secrets of the Future.—Time!
Unfold the brooding pinion of thy gloom,
Render thou up thy half-devoured babes,
And from the cradles of eternity,
Where millions lie lulled to their portioned
    sleep
By the deep murmuring stream of passing
    things,
Tear thou that gloomy shroud.—Spirit, behold
    Thy glorious destiny!"   10

    Joy to the Spirit came.
Through the wide rent in Time's eternal veil,
Hope was seen beaming through the mists of
    fear:
    Earth was no longer Hell;
    Love, freedom, health, had given
Their ripeness to the manhood of its prime,
    And all its pulses beat
Symphonious to the planetary spheres:
    Then dulcet music swelled
Concordant with the life-strings of the soul; 20
It throbbed in sweet and languid beatings
    there,
Catching new life from transitory death,—
Like the vague sighings of a wind at even,
That wakes the wavelets of the slumbering sea
And dies on the creation of its breath,
And sinks and rises, fails and swells by fits:

Was the pure stream of feeling
  That sprung from these sweet notes,
And o'er the Spirit's human sympathies
With mild and gentle motion calmly flowed. 30

  Joy to the Spirit came,—
  Such joy as when a lover sees
The chosen of his soul in happiness,
  And witnesses her peace
Whose woe to him were bitterer than death,
  Sees her unfaded cheek
Glow mantling in first luxury of health,
  Thrills with her lovely eyes,
Which like two stars amid the heaving main
  Sparkle through liquid bliss.   40

Then in her triumph spoke the Fairy Queen:
"I will not call the ghost of ages gone
To unfold the frightful secrets of its lore;
  The present now is past,
And those events that desolate the earth
Have faded from the memory of Time,
Who dares not give reality to that
Whose being I annul. To me is given
The wonders of the human world to keep,
Space, matter, time, and mind. Futurity   50
Exposes now its treasure; let the sight
Renew and strengthen all thy failing hope.
O human Spirit! spur thee to the goal
Where virtue fixes universal peace,
And midst the ebb and flow of human things,
Show somewhat stable, somewhat certain still,
A lighthouse o'er the wild of dreary waves.

"The habitable earth is full of bliss;
Those wastes of frozen billows that were
    hurled
By everlasting snowstorms round the poles, 60
Where matter dared not vegetate or live,
But ceaseless frost round the vast solitude
Bound its broad zone of stillness, are unloosed;
And fragrant zephyrs there from spicy isles
Ruffle the placid ocean-deep, that rolls
Its broad, bright surges to the sloping sand,
Whose roar is wakened into echoings sweet
To murmur through the Heaven-breathing
    groves
And melodize with man's blest nature there.

"Those deserts of immeasurable sand,   70
Whose age-collected fervours scarce allowed
A bird to live, a blade of grass to spring,
Where the shrill chirp of the green lizard's love
Broke on the sultry silentness alone,
Now teem with countless rills and shady woods,

Cornfields and pastures and white cottages;
And where the startled wilderness beheld
A savage conquerer stained in kindred blood,
A tigress sating with the flesh of lambs
The unnatural famine of her toothless cubs, 80
Whilst shouts and howlings through the desert
    rang,
Sloping and smooth the daisy-spangled lawn,
Offering sweet incense to the sunrise, smiles
To see a babe before his mother's door,
  Sharing his morning's meal
  With the green and golden basilisk
    That comes to lick his feet.

"Those trackless deeps, where many a weary
    sail
Has seen above the illimitable plain,
Morning on night, and night on morning rise, 90
Whilst still no land to greet the wanderer
    spread
Its shadowy mountains on the sun-bright sea,
Where the loud roarings of the tempest-waves
So long have mingled with the gusty wind
In melancholy loneliness, and swept
The desert of those ocean solitudes,
But vocal to the sea-bird's harrowing shriek,
The bellowing monster, and the rushing storm,
Now to the sweet and many-mingling sounds
Of kindliest human impulses respond.   100
Those lonely realms bright garden-isles be-
    gem,
With lightsome clouds and shining seas be-
    tween,
And fertile valleys, resonant with bliss,
Whilst green woods overcanopy the wave,
Which like a toil-worn labourer leaps to shore,
To meet the kisses of the flow'rets there.

"All things are recreated, and the flame
Of consentaneous love inspires all life:
The fertile bosom of the earth gives suck
To myriads, who still grow beneath her care, 110
Rewarding her with their pure perfectness:
The balmy breathings of the wind inhale
Her virtues, and diffuse them all abroad:
Health floats amid the gentle atmosphere,
Glows in the fruits, and mantles on the stream:
No storms deform the beaming brow of
    Heaven,
Nor scatter in the freshness of its pride
The foliage of the ever-verdant trees;
But fruits are ever ripe, flowers ever fair,
And Autumn proudly bears her matron
    grace,   120
Kindling a flush on the fair cheek of Spring,

Whose virgin bloom beneath the ruddy fruit
Reflects its tint, and blushes into love.

"The lion now forgets to thirst for blood:
There might you see him sporting in the sun
Beside the dreadless kid; his claws are
        sheathed,
His teeth are harmless, custom's force has
        made
His nature as the nature of a lamb.
Like passion's fruit, the nightshade's tempting
        bane
Poisons no more the pleasure it bestows: 130
All bitterness is past; the cup of joy
Unmingled mantles to the goblet's brim,
And courts the thirsty lips it fled before.

"But chief, ambiguous Man, he that can know
More misery, and dream more joy than all;
Whose keen sensations thrill within his breast
To mingle with a loftier instinct there,
Lending their power to pleasure and to pain,
Yet raising, sharpening, and refining each;
Who stands amid the ever-varying world,   140
The burthen or the glory of the earth;
He chief perceives the change, his being notes
The gradual renovation, and defines
Each movement of its progress on his mind.

"Man, where the gloom of the long polar night
Lowers o'er the snow-clad rocks and frozen
        soil,
Where scarce the hardiest herb that braves the
        frost
Basks in the moonlight's ineffectual glow,
Shrank with the plants, and darkened with the
        night;
His chilled and narrow energies, his heart,   150
Insensible to courage, truth, or love,
His stunted stature and imbecile frame,
Marked him for some abortion of the earth,
Fit compeer of the bears that roamed around,
Whose habits and enjoyments were his own:
His life a feverish dream of stagnant woe,
Whose meagre wants, but scantily fulfilled,
Apprised him ever of the joyless length
Which his short being's wretchedness had
        reached;
His death a pang which famine, cold and toil   160
Long on the mind, whilst yet the vital spark
Clung to the body stubbornly, had brought:
All was inflicted here that Earth's revenge
Could wreak on the infringers of her law;
One curse alone was spared—the name of God.

"Nor where the tropics bound the realms of
        day
With a broad belt of mingling cloud and flame,
Where blue mists through the unmoving at-
        mosphere
Scattered the seeds of pestilence, and fed
Unnatural vegetation, where the land   170
Teemed with all earthquake, tempest and
        disease,
Was Man a nobler being; slavery
Had crushed him to his country's blood-stained
        dust;
Or he was bartered for the fame of power,
Which all internal impulses destroying,
Makes human will an article of trade;
Or he was changed with Christians for their
        gold,
And dragged to distant isles, where to the
        sound
Of the flesh-mangling scourge, he does the
        work
Of all polluting luxury and wealth,   180
Which doubly visits on the tyrants' heads
The long-protracted fulness of their woe;
Or he was led to legal butchery,
To turn to worms beneath that burning sun,
Where kings first leagued against the rights of
        men,
And priests first traded with the name of God.

"Even where the milder zone afforded Man
A seeming shelter, yet contagion there,
Blighting his being with unnumbered ills,
Spread like a quenchless fire; nor truth till
        late   190
Availed to arrest its progress, or create
That peace which first in bloodless victory
        waved
Her snowy standard o'er this favoured clime:
There man was long the train-bearer of slaves,
The mimic of surrounding misery,
The jackal of ambition's lion-rage,
The bloodhound of religion's hungry zeal.

"Here now the human being stands adorning
This loveliest earth with taintless body and
        mind;
Blessed from his birth with all bland im-
        pulses,   200
Which gently in his noble bosom wake
All kindly passions and all pure desires.
Him, still from hope to hope the bliss pursuing
Which from the exhaustless lore of human weal

Dawns on the virtuous mind, the thoughts that
  rise
In time-destroying infiniteness, gift
With self-enshrined eternity, that mocks
The unprevailing hoariness of age,
And man, once fleeting o'er the transient scene
Swift as an unremembered vision, stands 210
Immortal upon earth: no longer now
He slays the lamb that looks him in the face,
And horribly devours his mangled flesh,
Which, still avenging Nature's broken law,
Kindled all putrid humours in his frame,
All evil passions, and all vain belief,
Hatred, despair, and loathing in his mind,
The germs of misery, death, disease, and crime.
No longer now the wingèd habitants,
That in the woods their sweet lives sing
  away, 220
Flee from the form of man; but gather round,
And prune their sunny feathers on the hands
Which little children stretch in friendly sport
Towards these dreadless partners of their play.
All things are void of terror: Man has lost
His terrible prerogative, and stands
An equal amidst equals: happiness
And science dawn though late upon the earth;
Peace cheers the mind, health renovates the
  frame;
Disease and pleasure cease to mingle here, 230
Reason and passion cease to combat there;
Whilst each unfettered o'er the earth extend
Their all-subduing energies, and wield
The sceptre of a vast dominion there;
Whilst every shape and mode of matter lends
Its force to the omnipotence of mind,
Which from its dark mine drags the gem of
  truth
To decorate its Paradise of peace."

IX

"O HAPPY Earth! reality of Heaven!
To which those restless souls that ceaselessly
Throng through the human universe, aspire;
Thou consummation of all mortal hope!
Thou glorious prize of blindly-working will!
Whose rays, diffused throughout all space and
  time,
Verge to one point and blend for ever there:
Of purest spirits thou pure dwelling-place!
Where care and sorrow, impotence and crime,
Languor, disease, and ignorance dare not
  come: 10
O happy Earth, reality of Heaven!

"Genius has seen thee in her passionate dreams,
And dim forebodings of thy loveliness
Haunting the human heart, have there en-
  twined
Those rooted hopes of some sweet place of
  bliss
Where friends and lovers meet to part no
  more.
Thou art the end of all desire and will,
The product of all action; and the souls
That by the paths of an aspiring change
Have reached thy haven of perpetual peace, 20
There rest from the eternity of toil
That framed the fabric of thy perfectness.

"Even Time, the conqueror, fled thee in his
  fear;
That hoary giant, who, in lonely pride,
So long had ruled the world, that nations fell
Beneath his silent footstep. Pyramids,
That for millenniums had withstood the tide
Of human things, his storm-breath drove in
  sand
Across that desert where their stones survived
The name of him whose pride had heaped them
  there. 30
Yon monarch, in his solitary pomp,
Was but the mushroom of a summer day,
That his light-wingèd footstep pressed to dust:
Time was the king of earth: all things gave
  way
Before him, but the fixed and virtuous will,
The sacred sympathies of soul and sense,
That mocked his fury and prepared his fall.

"Yet slow and gradual dawned the morn of
  love;
Long lay the clouds of darkness o'er the scene,
Till from its native Heaven they rolled away: 40
First, Crime triumphant o'er all hope careered
Unblushing, undisguising, bold and strong;
Whilst Falsehood, tricked in Virtue's attributes,
Long sanctified all deeds of vice and woe,
Till done by her own venomous sting to death,
She left the moral world without a law,
No longer fettering Passion's fearless wing,
Nor searing Reason with the brand of God.
Then steadily the happy ferment worked;
Reason was free; and wild though Passion went
Through tangled glens and wood-embosomed
  meads, 51
Gathering a garland of the strangest flowers,
Yet like the bee returning to her queen,
She bound the sweetest on her sister's brow,

Who meek and sober kissed the sportive child,
No longer trembling at the broken rod.

"Mild was the slow necessity of death:
The tranquil spirit failed beneath its grasp,
Without a groan, almost without a fear,
Calm as a voyager to some distant land,   60
And full of wonder, full of hope as he.
The deadly germs of languor and disease
Died in the human frame, and Purity
Blessed with all gifts her earthly worshippers.
How vigorous then the athletic form of age!
How clear its open and unwrinkled brow!
Where neither avarice, cunning, pride, nor care,
Had stamped the seal of gray deformity
On all the mingling lineaments of time.
How lovely the intrepid front of youth!   70
Which meek-eyed courage decked with freshest
    grace;
Courage of soul, that dreaded not a name,
And elevated will, that journeyed on
Through life's phantasmal scene in fearlessness,
With virtue, love, and pleasure, hand in hand.

"Then, that sweet bondage which is Freedom's
    self,
And rivets with sensation's softest tie
The kindred sympathies of human souls,
Needed no fetters of tyrannic law:
Those delicate and timid impulses   80
In Nature's primal modesty arose,
And with undoubted confidence disclosed
The growing longings of its dawning love,
Unchecked by dull and selfish chastity,
That virtue of the cheaply virtuous,
Who pride themselves in senselessness and
    frost.
No longer prostitution's venomed bane
Poisoned the springs of happiness and life;
Woman and man, in confidence and love,
Equal and free and pure together trod   90
The mountain-paths of virtue, which no more
Were stained with blood from many a pilgrim's
    feet.

"Then, where, through distant ages, long in
    pride
The palace of the monarch-slave had mocked
Famine's faint groan, and Penury's silent tear,
A heap of crumbling ruins stood, and threw
Year after year their stones upon the field,
Wakening a lonely echo; and the leaves
Of the old thorn, that on the topmost tower
Usurped the royal ensign's grandeur, shook   100

In the stern storm that swayed the topmost
    tower
And whispered strange tales in the Whirl-
    wind's ear.

"Low through the lone cathedral's roofless
    aisles
The melancholy winds a death-dirge sung:
It were a sight of awfulness to see
The works of faith and slavery, so vast,
So sumptuous, yet so perishing withal!
Even as the corpse that rests beneath its wall.
A thousand mourners deck the pomp of death
To-day, the breathing marble glows above   110
To decorate its memory, and tongues
Are busy of its life: to-morrow, worms
In silence and in darkness seize their prey.

"Within the massy prison's mouldering courts,
Fearless and free the ruddy children played,
Weaving gay chaplets for their innocent brows
With the green ivy and the red wall-flower,
That mock the dungeon's unavailing gloom;
The ponderous chains, and gratings of strong
    iron,
There rusted amid heaps of broken stone   120
That mingled slowly with their native earth:
There the broad beam of day, which feebly
    once
Lighted the cheek of lean Captivity
With a pale and sickly glare, then freely shone
On the pure smiles of infant playfulness:
No more the shuddering voice of hoarse
    Despair
Pealed through the echoing vaults, but sooth-
    ing notes
Of ivy-fingered winds and gladsome birds
And merriment were resonant around.

"These ruins soon left not a wreck behind: 130
Their elements, wide scattered o'er the globe,
To happier shapes were moulded, and became
Ministrant to all blissful impulses:
Thus human things were perfected, and earth,
Even as a child beneath its mother's love,
Was strengthened in all excellence, and grew
Fairer and nobler with each passing year.

"Now Time his dusky pennons o'er the scene
Closes in steadfast darkness, and the past
Fades from our charmèd sight. My task is
    done: 140
Thy lore is learned. Earth's wonders are thine
    own,

With all the fear and all the hope they bring.
My spells are passed: the present now recurs.
Ah me! a pathless wilderness remains
Yet unsubdued by man's reclaiming hand.

.   .   .   .

"Fear not then, Spirit, Death's disrobing hand,
So welcome when the tyrant is awake,
So welcome when the bigot's hell-torch burns;
'Tis but the voyage of a darksome hour,
The transient gulf-dream of a startling sleep.
Death is no foe to Virtue: earth has seen
Love's brightest roses on the scaffold bloom,
Mingling with Freedom's fadeless laurels there,
And presaging the truth of visioned bliss.
Are there not hopes within thee, which this scene
Of linked and gradual being has confirmed?
Whose stingings bade thy heart look further still,
When, to the moonlight walk by Henry led,
Sweetly and sadly thou didst talk of death?
And will thou rudely tear them from thy breast,
Listening supinely to a bigot's creed,
Or tamely crouching to the tyrant's rod,
Whose iron thongs are red with human gore?
Never: but bravely bearing on, thy will
Is destined an eternal war to wage   190
With tyranny and falsehood, and uproot
The germs of misery from the human heart.
Thine is the hand whose piety would soothe
The thorny pillow of unhappy crime,
Whose impotence an easy pardon gains,
Watching its wanderings as a friend's disease:
Thine is the brow whose mildness would defy
Its fiercest rage, and brave its sternest will,
When fenced by power and master of the world.
Thou art sincere and good; of resolute mind, 200
Free from heart-withering custom's cold control,
Of passion lofty, pure and unsubdued.
Earth's pride and meanness could not vanquish thee,
And therefore art thou worthy of the boon
Which thou hast now received: Virtue shall keep
Thy footsteps in the path that thou hast trod,
And many days of beaming hope shall bless
Thy spotless life of sweet and sacred love.
Go, happy one, and give that bosom joy
Whose sleepless spirit waits to catch   210
Light, life and rapture from thy smile."

.   .   .   .

The Body and the Soul united then,
A gentle start convulsed Ianthe's frame:
Her veiny eyelids quietly unclosed;
Moveless awhile the dark blue orbs remained:
She looked around in wonder and beheld
Henry, who kneeled in silence by her couch,
Watching her sleep with looks of speechless love,
And the bright beaming stars
That through the casement shone.   240

ALASTOR

OR

THE SPIRIT OF SOLITUDE

Nondum amabam, et amare amabam, quaerebam quid amarem, amans amare.—Confess. St. August.

EARTH, ocean, air, belovèd brotherhood!
If our great Mother has imbued my soul
With aught of natural piety to feel
Your love, and recompense the boon with mine;
If dewy morn, and odorous noon, and even,
With sunset and its gorgeous ministers,
And solemn midnight's tingling silentness;
If autumn's hollow sighs in the sere wood,
And winter robing with pure snow and crowns
Of starry ice the grey grass and bare boughs;
If spring's voluptuous pantings when she breathes   11
Her first sweet kisses, have been dear to me;
If no bright bird, insect, or gentle beast
I consciously have injured, but still loved
And cherished these my kindred; then forgive
This boast, belovèd brethren, and withdraw
No portion of your wonted favour now!

Mother of this unfathomable world!
Favour my solemn song, for I have loved
Thee ever, and thee only; I have watched   20
Thy shadow, and the darkness of thy steps,
And my heart ever gazes on the depth
Of thy deep mysteries. I have made my bed
In charnels and on coffins, where black death
Keeps record of the trophies won from thee,
Hoping to still these obstinate questionings
Of thee and thine, by forcing some lone ghost
Thy messenger, to render up the tale
Of what we are. In lone and silent hours,

When night makes a weird sound of its own
    stillness,   30
Like an inspired and desperate alchymist
Staking his very life on some dark hope,
Have I mixed awful talk and asking looks
With my most innocent love, until strange
    tears
Uniting with those breathless kisses, made
Such magic as compels the charmèd night
To render up thy charge: . . . and, though
    ne'er yet
Thou hast unveiled thy inmost sanctuary,
Enough from incommunicable dream,
And twilight phantasms, and deep noon-day
    thought,   40
Has shone within me, that serenely now
And moveless, as a long-forgotten lyre
Suspended in the solitary dome
Of some mysterious and deserted fane,
I wait thy breath, Great Parent, that my
    strain
May modulate with murmurs of the air,
And motions of the forests and the sea,
And voice of living beings, and woven hymns
Of night and day, and the deep heart of man.

There was a Poet whose untimely tomb   50
No human hands with pious reverence reared,
But the charmed eddies of autumnal winds
Built o'er his mouldering bones a pyramid
Of mouldering leaves in the waste wilder-
    ness:—
A lovely youth,—no mourning maiden decked
With weeping flowers, or votive cypress
    wreath,
The lone couch of his everlasting sleep:—
Gentle, and brave, and generous,—no lorn
    bard
Breathed o'er his dark fate one melodious
    sigh:
He lived, he died, he sung, in solitude.   60
Strangers have wept to hear his passionate
    notes,
And virgins, as unknown he passed, have
    pined
And wasted for fond love of his wild eyes.
The fire of those soft orbs has ceased to burn,
And Silence, too enamoured of that voice,
Locks its mute music in her rugged cell.

By solemn vision, and bright silver dream,
His infancy was nurtured. Every sight
And sound from the vast earth and ambient
    air,

Sent to his heart its choicest impulses.   70
The fountains of divine philosophy
Fled not his thirsting lips, and all of great,
Or good, or lovely, which the sacred past
In truth or fable consecrates, he felt
And knew. When early youth had passed, he
    left
His cold fireside and alienated home
To seek strange truths in undiscovered lands.
Many a wide waste and tangled wilderness
Has lured his fearless steps; and he has bought
With his sweet voice and eyes, from savage
    men,   80
His rest and food. Nature's most secret steps
He like her shadow has pursued, where'er
The red volcano overcanopies
Its fields of snow and pinnacles of ice
With burning smoke, or where bitumen lakes
On black bare pointed islets ever beat
With sluggish surge, or where the secret
    caves
Rugged and dark, winding among the springs
Of fire and poison, inaccessible
To avarice or pride, their starry domes   90
Of diamond and of gold expand above
Numberless and immeasurable halls,
Frequent with crystal column, and clear
    shrines
Of pearl, and thrones radiant with chrysolite.
Nor had that scene of ampler majesty
Than gems or gold, the varying roof of
    heaven
And the green earth lost in his heart its claims
To love and wonder; he would linger long
In lonesome vales, making the wild his home,
Until the doves and squirrels would partake 100
From his innocuous hand his bloodless food,
Lured by the gentle meaning of his looks,
And the wild antelope, that starts whene'er
The dry leaf rustles in the brake, suspend
Her timid steps to gaze upon a form
More graceful than her own.
                 His wandering step
Obedient to high thoughts, has visited
The awful ruins of the days of old:
Athens, and Tyre, and Balbec, and the waste
Where stood Jerusalem, the fallen towers 110
Of Babylon, the eternal pyramids,
Memphis and Thebes, and whatsoe'er of
    strange
Sculptured on alabaster obelisk,
Or jasper tomb, or mutilated sphynx,
Dark Æthiopia in her desert hills
Conceals. Among the ruined temples there,

Stupendous columns, and wild images
Of more than man, where marble daemons watch
The Zodiac's brazen mystery, and dead men
Hang their mute thoughts on the mute walls around,   120
He lingered, poring on memorials
Of the world's youth, through the long burning day
Gazed on those speechless shapes, nor, when the moon
Filled the mysterious halls with floating shades
Suspended he that task, but ever gazed
And gazed, till meaning on his vacant mind
Flashed like strong inspiration, and he saw
The thrilling secrets of the birth of time.

Meanwhile an Arab maiden brought his food,
Her daily portion, from her father's tent,   130
And spread her matting for his couch, and stole
From duties and repose to tend his steps:—
Enamoured, yet not daring for deep awe
To speak her love:—and watched his nightly sleep,
Sleepless herself, to gaze upon his lips
Parted in slumber, whence the regular breath
Of innocent dreams arose: then, when red morn
Made paler the pale moon, to her cold home
Wildered, and wan, and panting, she returned.

The Poet wandering on, through Arabie   140
And Persia, and the wild Carmanian waste,
And o'er the aërial mountains which pour down
Indus and Oxus from their icy caves,
In joy and exultation held his way;
Till in the vale of Cashmire, far within
Its loneliest dell, where odorous plants entwine
Beneath the hollow rocks a natural bower,
Beside a sparkling rivulet he stretched
His languid limbs. A vision on his sleep   150
There came, a dream of hopes that never yet
Had flushed his cheek. He dreamed a veilèd maid
Sate near him, talking in low solemn tones.
Her voice was like the voice of his own soul
Heard in the calm of thought; its music long,
Like woven sounds of streams and breezes, held
His inmost sense suspended in its web
Of many-coloured woof and shifting hues.

Knowledge and truth and virtue were her theme,
And lofty hopes of divine liberty,
Thoughts the most dear to him, and poesy,   160
Herself a poet. Soon the solemn mood
Of her pure mind kindled through all her frame
A permeating fire: wild numbers then
She raised, with voice stifled in tremulous sobs
Subdued by its own pathos: her fair hands
Were bare alone, sweeping from some strange harp
Strange symphony, and in their branching veins
The eloquent blood told an ineffable tale.
The beating of her heart was heard to fill
The pauses of her music, and her breath,   170
Tumultuously accorded with those fits
Of intermitted song. Sudden she rose,
As if her heart impatiently endured
Its bursting burthen: at the sound he turned,
And saw by the warm light of their own life
Her glowing limbs beneath the sinuous veil
Of woven wind, her outspread arms now bare,
Her dark locks floating in the breath of night,
Her beamy bending eyes, her parted lips   179
Outstretched, and pale, and quivering eagerly.
His strong heart sunk and sickened with excess
Of love. He reared his shuddering limbs and quelled
His gasping breath, and spread his arms to meet
Her panting bosom: . . . she drew back a while,
Then, yielding to the irresistible joy,
With frantic gesture and short breathless cry
Folded his frame in her dissolving arms.
Now blackness veiled his dizzy eyes, and night
Involved and swallowed up the vision; sleep,
Like a dark flood suspended in its course,   190
Rolled back its impulse on his vacant brain.

Roused by the shock he started from his trance—
The cold white light of morning, the blue moon
Low in the west, the clear and garish hills,
The distinct valley and the vacant woods,
Spread round him where he stood. Whither have fled
The hues of heaven that canopied his bower,
Of yesternight? The sounds that soothed his sleep,

The mystery and the majesty of Earth,
The joy, the exultation? His wan eyes   200
Gaze on the empty scene as vacantly
As ocean's moon looks on the moon in heaven.
The spirit of sweet human love has sent
A vision to the sleep of him who spurned
Her choicest gifts. He eagerly pursues
Beyond the realms of dream that fleeting
      shade;
He overleaps the bounds. Alas! Alas!
Were limbs, and breath, and being interwined
Thus treacherously? Lost, lost, for ever lost,
In the wide pathless desert of dim sleep,   210
That beautiful shape! Does the dark gate of
      death
Conduct to thy mysterious paradise,
O Sleep? Does the bright arch of rainbow
      clouds,
And pendent mountains seen in the calm lake,
Lead only to a black and watery depth,
While death's blue vault, with loathliest va-
      pours hung,
Where every shade which the foul grave ex-
      hales
Hides its dead eye from the detested day,
Conduct, O Sleep, to thy delightful realms?
This doubt with sudden tide flowed on his
      heart,   220
The insatiate hope which it awakened, stung
His brain even like despair.

                              While daylight held
The sky, the Poet kept mute conference
With his still soul. At night the passion came,
Like the fierce fiend of a distempered dream,
And shook him from his rest, and led him
      forth
Into the darkness.—As an eagle grasped
In folds of the green serpent, feels her breast
Burn with the poison, and precipitates
Through night and day, tempest, and calm,
      and cloud,   230
Frantic with dizzying anguish, her blind flight
O'er the wild aëry wilderness: thus driven
By the bright shadow of that lovely dream,
Beneath the cold glare of the desolate night,
Through tangled swamps and deep precipitous
      dells,
Startling with careless step the moonlight
      snake,
He fled. Red morning dawned upon his flight,
Shedding the mockery of its vital hues
Upon his cheek of death. He wandered on
Till vast Aornos seen from Petra's steep   240
Hung o'er the low horizon like a cloud;

Through Balk, and where the desolated tombs
Of Parthian kings scatter to every wind
Their wasting dust, wildly he wandered on,
Day after day a weary waste of hours,
Bearing within his life the brooding care
That ever fed on its decaying flame.
And now his limbs were lean; his scattered
      hair
Sered by the autumn of strange suffering
Sung dirges in the wind; his listless hand   250
Hung like dead bone within its withered skin;
Life, and the lustre that consumed it, shone
As in a furnace burning secretly
From his dark eyes alone. The cottagers,
Who ministered with human charity
His human wants, beheld with wondering awe
Their fleeting visitant. The mountaineer,
Encountering on some dizzy precipice
That spectral form, deemed that the Spirit
      of wind
With lightning eyes, and eager breath, and
      feet   260
Disturbing not the drifted snow, had paused
In its career: the infant would conceal
His troubled visage in his mother's robe
In terror at the glare of those wild eyes,
To remember their strange light in many a
      dream
Of after-times; but youthful maidens, taught
By nature, would interpret half the woe
That wasted him, would call him with false
      names
Brother, and friend, would press his pallid
      hand
At parting, and watch, dim through tears, the
      path   270
Of his departure from their father's door.

   At length upon the lone Chorasmian shore
He paused, a wide and melancholy waste
Of putrid marshes. A strong impulse urged
His steps to the sea-shore. A swan was there,
Beside a sluggish stream among the reeds.
It rose as he approached, and with strong
      wings
Scaling the upward sky, bent its bright course
High over the immeasurable main.
His eyes pursued its flight.—'Thou hast a
      home,   280
Beautiful bird; thou voyagest to thine home,
Where thy sweet mate will twine her downy
      neck
With thine, and welcome thy return with eyes
Bright in the lustre of their own fond joy.

And what am I that I should linger here,
With voice far sweeter than thy dying notes,
Spirit more vast than thine, frame more
    attuned
To beauty, wasting these surpassing powers
In the deaf air, to the blind earth, and heaven
That echoes not my thoughts?' A gloomy
    smile   290
Of desperate hope wrinkled his quivering lips.
For sleep, he knew, kept most relentlessly
Its precious charge, and silent death exposed,
Faithless perhaps as sleep, a shadowy lure,
With doubtful smile mocking its own strange
    charms.

    Startled by his own thoughts he looked
    around.
There was no fair fiend near him, not a sight
Or sound of awe but in his own deep mind.
A little shallop floating near the shore   299
Caught the impatient wandering of his gaze.
It had been long abandoned, for its sides
Gaped wide with many a rift, and its frail
    joints
Swayed with the undulations of the tide.
A restless impulse urged him to embark
And meet lone Death on the drear ocean's
    waste;
For well he knew that mighty Shadow loves
The slimy caverns of the populous deep.

    The day was fair and sunny, sea and sky
Drank its inspiring radiance, and the wind
Swept strongly from the shore, blackening the
    waves.
Following his eager soul, the wanderer   311
Leaped in the boat, he spread his cloak aloft
On the bare mast, and took his lonely seat,
And felt the boat speed o'er the tranquil sea
Like a torn cloud before the hurricane.

    As one that in a silver vision floats
Obedient to the sweep of odorous winds
Upon resplendent clouds, so rapidly
Along the dark and ruffled waters fled
The straining boat.—A whirlwind swept it
    on,   320
With fierce gusts and precipitating force,
Through the white ridges of the chafèd sea.
The waves arose. Higher and higher still
Their fierce necks writhed beneath the tem-
    pest's scourge
Like serpents struggling in a vulture's grasp.
Calm and rejoicing in the fearful war

Of wave ruining on wave, and blast on blast
Descending, and black flood on whirlpool
    driven
With dark obliterating course, he sate:
As if their genii were the ministers   330
Appointed to conduct him to the light
Of those belovèd eyes, the Poet sate
Holding the steady helm. Evening came on,
The beams of sunset hung their rainbow hues
High 'mid the shifting domes of sheeted spray
That canopied his path o'er the waste deep;
Twilight, ascending slowly from the east,
Entwined in duskier wreaths her braided locks
O'er the fair front and radiant eyes of day;
Night followed, clad with stars. On every
    side   340
More horribly the multitudinous streams
Of ocean's mountainous waste to mutual war
Rushed in dark tumult thundering, as to mock
The calm and spangled sky. The little boat
Still fled before the storm; still fled, like foam
Down the steep cataract of a wintry river;
Now pausing on the edge of the riven wave;
Now leaving far behind the bursting mass
That fell, convulsing ocean: safely fled—
As if that frail and wasted human form,   350
Had been an elemental god.
                      At midnight
The moon arose: and lo! the ethereal cliffs
Of Caucasus, whose icy summits shone
Among the stars like sunlight, and around
Whose caverned base the whirlpools and the
    waves
Bursting and eddying irresistibly
Rage and resound for ever.—Who shall
    save?—
The boat fled on,—the boiling torrent drove,—
The crags closed round with black and jaggèd
    arms,
The shattered mountain overhung the sea,   360
And faster still, beyond all human speed,
Suspended on the sweep of the smooth wave,
The little boat was driven. A cavern there
Yawned, and amid its slant and winding
    depths
Ingulfed the rushing sea. The boat fled on
With unrelaxing speed.—'Vision and Love!'
The Poet cried aloud, 'I have beheld
The path of thy departure. Sleep and death
Shall not divide us long!'
                The boat pursued
The windings of the cavern. Daylight shone 370
At length upon that gloomy river's flow;
Now, where the fiercest war among the waves

Is calm, on the unfathomable stream
The boat moved slowly. Where the mountain,
   riven,
Exposed those black depths to the azure sky,
Ere yet the flood's enormous volume fell
Even to the base of Caucasus, with sound
That shook the everlasting rocks, the mass
Filled with one whirlpool all that ample chasm:
Stair above stair the eddying waters rose,   380
Circling immeasurably fast, and laved
With alternating dash the gnarlèd roots
Of mighty trees, that stretched their giant arms
In darkness over it. I' the midst was left,
Reflecting, yet distorting every cloud,
A pool of treacherous and tremendous calm.
Seized by the sway of the ascending stream,
With dizzy swiftness, round, and round, and
   round,
Ridge after ridge the straining boat arose,
Till on the verge of the extremest curve,   390
Where, through an opening of the rocky bank,
The waters overflow, and a smooth spot
Of glassy quiet mid those battling tides
Is left, the boat paused shuddering.—Shall it
   sink
Down the abyss? Shall the reverting stress
Of that resistless gulf embosom it?
Now shall it fall?—A wandering stream of
   wind,
Breathed from the west, has caught the ex-
   panded sail,
And, lo! with gentle motion, between banks
Of mossy slope, and on a placid stream,   400
Beneath a woven grove it sails, and, hark!
The ghastly torrent mingles its far roar,
With the breeze murmuring in the musical
   woods.
Where the embowering trees recede, and leave
A little space of green expanse, the cove
Is closed by meeting banks, whose yellow
   flowers
For ever gaze on their own drooping eyes,
Reflected in the crystal calm. The wave
Of the boat's motion marred their pensive
   task,
Which nought but vagrant bird, or wanton
   wind,   410
Or falling spear-grass, or their own decay
Had e'er disturbed before. The Poet longed
To deck with their bright hues his withered
   hair,
But on his heart its solitude returned,
And he forbore. Not the strong impulse hid

In those flushed cheeks, bent eyes, and shad-
   owy frame
Had yet performed its ministry: it hung
Upon his life, as lightning in a cloud
Gleams, hovering ere it vanish, ere the floods
Of night close over it.

                         The noonday sun   420
Now shone upon the forest, one vast mass
Of mingling shade, whose brown magnificence
A narrow vale embosoms. There, huge caves,
Scooped in the dark base of their aëry rocks
Mocking its moans, respond and roar for ever.
The meeting boughs and implicated leaves
Wove twilight o'er the Poet's path, as led
By love, or dream, or god, or mightier Death,
He sought in Nature's dearest haunt, some
   bank,
Her cradle, and his sepulchre. More dark   430
And dark the shades accumulate. The oak,
Expanding its immense and knotty arms,
Embraces the light beech. The pyramids
Of the tall cedar overarching, frame
Most solemn domes within, and far below,
Like clouds suspended in an emerald sky,
The ash and the acacia floating hang
Tremulous and pale. Like restless serpents,
   clothed
In rainbow and in fire, the parasites,
Starred with ten thousand blossoms, flow
   around   440
The grey trunks, and, as gamesome infants'
   eyes,
With gentle meanings, and most innocent
   wiles,
Fold their beams round the hearts of those
   that love,
These twine their tendrils with the wedded
   boughs
Uniting their close union; the woven leaves
Make net-work of the dark blue light of day,
And the night's noontide clearness, mutable
As shapes in the weird clouds. Soft mossy
   lawns
Beneath these canopies extend their swells,
Fragrant with perfumed herbs, and eyed with
   blooms
Minute yet beautiful. One darkest glen   450
Sends from its woods of musk-rose, twined
   with jasmine,
A soul-dissolving odour, to invite
To some more lovely mystery. Through the
   dell,
Silence and Twilight here, twin-sisters, keep

Their noonday watch, and sail among the
    shades,
Like vaporous shapes half seen; beyond, a
    well,
Dark, gleaming, and of most translucent wave,
Images all the woven boughs above,
And each depending leaf, and every speck   460
Of azure sky, darting between their chasms;
Nor aught else in the liquid mirror laves
Its portraiture, but some inconstant star
Between one foliaged lattice twinkling fair,
Or, painted bird, sleeping beneath the moon,
Or gorgeous insect floating motionless,
Unconscious of the day, ere yet his wings
Have spread their glories to the gaze of noon.

Hither the Poet came. His eyes beheld
Their own wan light through the reflected
    lines   470
Of his thin hair, distinct in the dark depth
Of that still fountain; as the human heart,
Gazing in dreams over the gloomy grave,
Sees its own treacherous likeness there. He
    heard
The motion of the leaves, the grass that
    sprung
Startled and glanced and trembled even to feel
An unaccustomed presence, and the sound
Of that sweet brook that from the secret
    springs
Of that dark fountain rose. A Spirit seemed
To stand beside him—clothed in no bright
    robes   480
Of shadowy silver or enshrining light,
Borrowed from aught the visible world affords
Of grace, or majesty, or mystery;—
But, undulating woods, and silent well,
And leaping rivulet, and evening gloom
Now deepening the dark shades, for speech
    assuming,
Held commune with him, as if he and it
Were all that was,—only . . . when his regard
Was raised by intense pensiveness, . . . two
    eyes,
Two starry eyes, hung in the gloom of
    thought,   490
And seemed with their serene and azure smiles
To beckon him.

Obedient to the light
That shone within his soul, he went, pursuing
The windings of the dell.—The rivulet

Wanton and wild, through many a green ravine
Beneath the forest flowed. Sometimes it fell
Among the moss with hollow harmony
Dark and profound. Now on the polished
    stones
It danced; like childhood laughing as it went:
Then, through the plain in tranquil wander-
    ings crept,   500
Reflecting every herb and drooping bud
That overhung its quietness.— 'O Stream!
Whose source is inaccessibly profound,
Whither do thy mysterious waters tend?
Thou imagest my life. Thy darksome stillness,
Thy dazzling waves, thy loud and hollow gulfs,
Thy searchless fountain, and invisible course
Have each their type in me: and the wide sky,
And measureless ocean may declare as soon
What oozy cavern or what wandering cloud 510
Contains thy waters, as the universe
Tell where these living thoughts reside, when
    stretched
Upon thy flowers my bloodless limbs shall
    waste
I' the passing wind!'

                    Beside the grassy shore
Of the small stream he went; he did impress
On the green moss his tremulous step, that
    caught
Strong shuddering from his burning limbs. As
    one
Roused by some joyous madness from the
    couch
Of fever, he did move; yet, not like him
Forgetful of the grave, where, when the flame
Of his frail exultation shall be spent,   520
He must descend. With rapid steps he went
Beneath the shade of trees, beside the flow
Of the wild babbling rivulet; and now
The forest's solemn canopies were changed
For the uniform and lightsome evening sky.
Grey rocks did peep from the spare moss, and
    stemmed
The struggling brook: tall spires of windle-
    strae
Threw their thin shadows down the rugged
    slope,
And nought but gnarled roots of ancient
    pines   530
Branchless and blasted, clenched with grasping
    roots
The unwilling soil. A gradual change was here,
Yet ghastly. For, as fast years flow away,

The smooth brow gathers, and the hair grows
    thin
And white, and where irradiate dewy eyes
Had shone, gleam stony orbs:—so from his
    steps
Bright flowers departed, and the beautiful
    shade
Of the green groves, with all their odorous
    winds
And musical motions. Calm, he still pursued
The stream, that with a larger volume now 540
Rolled through the labyrinthine dell; and
    there
Fretted a path through its descending curves
With its wintry speed. On every side now rose
Rocks, which, in unimaginable forms,
Lifted their black and barren pinnacles
In the light of evening, and, its precipice
Obscuring the ravine, disclosed above,
Mid toppling stones, black gulfs and yawning
    caves,
Whose windings gave ten thousand various
    tongues
To the loud stream. Lo! where the pass ex-
    pands   550
Its stony jaws, the abrupt mountain breaks,
And seems, with its accumulated crags,
To overhang the world: for wide expand
Beneath the wan stars and descending moon
Islanded seas, blue mountains, mighty streams,
Dim tracts and vast, robed in the lustrous
    gloom
Of leaden-coloured even, and fiery hills
Mingling their flames with twilight, on the
    verge
Of the remote horizon. The near scene,
In naked and severe simplicity,   560
Made contrast with the universe. A pine,
Rock-rooted, stretched athwart the vacancy
Its swinging boughs, to each inconstant blast
Yielding one only response, at each pause
In most familiar cadence, with the howl
The thunder and the hiss of homeless streams
Mingling its solemn song, whilst the broad
    river,
Foaming and hurrying o'er its rugged path,
Fell into that immeasurable void
Scattering its waters to the passing winds. 570

Yet the grey precipice and solemn pine
And torrent, were not all;—one silent nook
Was there. Even on the edge of that vast
    mountain,
Upheld by knotty roots and fallen rocks,

It overlooked in its serenity
The dark earth, and the bending vault of
    stars.
It was a tranquil spot, that seemed to smile
Even in the lap of horror. Ivy clasped
The fissured stones with its entwining arms,
And did embower with leaves for ever green,
And berries dark, the smooth and even space
Of its inviolated floor, and here   582
The children of the autumnal whirlwind bore,
In wanton sport, those bright leaves, whose
    decay,
Red, yellow, or ethereally pale,
Rivals the pride of summer. 'Tis the haunt
Of every gentle wind, whose breath can teach
The wilds to love tranquillity. One step,
One human step alone, has ever broken
The stillness of its solitude:—one voice 590
Alone inspired its echoes;—even that voice
Which hither came, floating among the winds,
And led the loveliest among human forms
To make their wild haunts the depository
Of all the grace and beauty that endued
Its motions, render up its majesty,
Scatter its music on the unfeeling storm,
And to the damp leaves and blue cavern
    mould,
Nurses of rainbow flowers and branching moss,
Commit the colours of that varying cheek, 600
That snowy breast, those dark and drooping
    eyes.

    The dim and hornèd moon hung low, and
        poured
A sea of lustre on the horizon's verge
That overflowed its mountains. Yellow mist
Filled the unbounded atmosphere, and drank
Wan moonlight even to fulness: not a star
Shone, not a sound was heard; the very winds,
Danger's grim playmates, on that precipice
Slept, clasped in his embrace.—O, storm of
    death!
Whose sightless speed divides this sullen
    night: 610
And thou, colossal Skeleton, that, still
Guiding its irresistible career
In thy devastating omnipotence,
Art king of this frail world, from the red
    field
Of slaughter, from the reeking hospital,
The patriot's sacred couch, the snowy bed
Of innocence, the scaffold and the throne,
A mighty voice invokes thee. Ruin calls
His brother Death. A rare and regal prey

He hath prepared, prowling around the world; 620
Glutted with which thou mayst repose, and men
Go to their graves like flowers or creeping worms
Nor ever more offer at thy dark shrine
The unheeded tribute of a broken heart.

When on the threshold of the green recess
The wanderer's footsteps fell, he knew that death
Was on him. Yet a little, ere it fled,
Did he resign his high and holy soul
To images of the majestic past,
That paused within his passive being now, 630
Like winds that bear sweet music, when they breathe
Through some dim latticed chamber. He did place
His pale lean hand upon the rugged trunk
Of the old pine. Upon an ivied stone
Reclined his languid head, his limbs did rest,
Diffused and motionless, on the smooth brink
Of that obscurest chasm;—and thus he lay,
Surrendering to their final impulses
The hovering powers of life. Hope and despair,
The torturers, slept; no mortal pain or fear 640
Marred his repose, the influxes of sense,
And his own being unalloyed by pain,
Yet feebler and more feeble, calmly fed
The stream of thought, till he lay breathing there
At peace, and faintly smiling:—his last sight
Was the great moon, which o'er the western line
Of the wide world her mighty horn suspended,
With whose dun beams inwoven darkness seemed
To mingle. Now upon the jaggèd hills
It rests, and still as the divided frame 650
Of the vast meteor sunk, the Poet's blood,
That ever beat in mystic sympathy
With nature's ebb and flow, grew feebler still:
And when two lessening points of light alone
Gleamed through the darkness, the alternate gasp
Of his faint respiration scarce did stir
The stagnate night:—till the minutest ray
Was quenched, the pulse yet lingered in his heart.
It paused—it fluttered. But when heaven remained
Utterly black, the murky shades involved 660

An image, silent, cold, and motionless,
As their own voiceless earth and vacant air.
Even as a vapour fed with golden beams
That ministered on sunlight, ere the west
Eclipses it, was now that wondrous frame—
No sense, no motion, no divinity—
A fragile lute, on whose harmonious strings
The breath of heaven did wander—a bright stream
Once fed with many-voicèd waves—a dream
Of youth, which night and time have quenched for ever, 670
Still, dark, and dry, and unremembered now.
O, for Medea's wondrous alchemy,
Which wheresoe'er it fell made the earth gleam
With bright flowers, and the wintry boughs exhale
From vernal blooms fresh fragrance! O, that God,
Profuse of poisons, would concede the chalice
Which but one living man has drained, who now,
Vessel of deathless wrath, a slave that feels
No proud exemption in the blighting curse
He bears, over the world wanders for ever, 680
Lone as incarnate death! O, that the dream
Of dark magician in his visioned cave,
Raking the cinders of a crucible
For life and power, even when his feeble hand
Shakes in its last decay, were the true law
Of this so lovely world! But thou art fled
Like some frail exhalation; which the dawn
Robes in its golden beams,—ah! thou hast fled!
The brave, the gentle, and the beautiful,
The child of grace and genius. Heartless things 690
Are done and said i' the world, and many worms
And beasts and men live on, and mighty Earth
From sea and mountain, city and wilderness,
In vesper low or joyous orison,
Lifts still its solemn voice:—but thou art fled—
Thou canst no longer know or love the shapes
Of this phantasmal scene, who have to thee
Been purest ministers, who are, alas!
Now thou art not. Upon those pallid lips
So sweet even in their silence, on those eyes
That image sleep in death, upon that form 701
Yet safe from the worm's outrage, let no tear
Be shed—not even in thought. Nor, when those hues

Are gone, and those divinest lineaments,
Worn by the senseless wind, shall live alone
In the frail pauses of this simple strain,
Let not high verse, mourning the memory
Of that which is no more, or painting's woe
Or sculpture, speak in feeble imagery
Their own cold powers. Art and eloquence, 710
And all the shows o' the world are frail and vain
To weep a loss that turns their lights to shade.
It is a woe too 'deep for tears,' when all
Is reft at once, when some surpassing Spirit,
Whose light adorned the world around it, leaves
Those who remain behind, not sobs or groans,
The passionate tumult of a clinging hope;
But pale despair and cold tranquillity,
Nature's vast frame, the web of human things,
Birth and the grave, that are not as they were. 720

PROMETHEUS UNBOUND

A LYRICAL DRAMA
IN FOUR ACTS

AUDISNE HAEC AMPHIARAE, SUB TERRAM
ABDITE?

DRAMATIS PERSONÆ

PROMETHEUS.
DEMOGORGON.
JUPITER.
THE EARTH.
OCEAN.
APOLLO.
MERCURY.
ASIA }
PANTHEA. } Ocean-
IONE } ides.
HERCULES.
THE PHANTASM OF JUPITER.
THE SPIRIT OF THE EARTH.
THE SPIRIT OF THE MOON.
SPIRITS OF THE HOURS.
FAUNS. FURIES. SPIRITS. ECHOES.

ACT I

SCENE.—*A Ravine of Icy Rocks in the Indian Caucasus.* PROMETHEUS *is discovered bound to the Precipice.* PANTHEA *and* IONE *are seated at his feet. Time, night. During the Scene, morning slowly breaks.*

Prometheus. Monarch of Gods and Dæmons, and all Spirits
But One, who throng those bright and rolling worlds
Which Thou and I alone of living things

Behold with sleepless eyes! regard this Earth
Made multitudinous with thy slaves, whom thou
Requitest for knee-worship, prayer, and praise,
And toil, and hecatombs of broken hearts,
With fear and self-contempt and barren hope.
Whilst me, who am thy foe, eyeless in hate,
Hast thou made reign and triumph, to thy scorn, 10
O'er mine own misery and thy vain revenge.
Three thousand years of sleep-unsheltered hours,
And moments aye divided by keen pangs
Till they seemed years, torture and solitude,
Scorn and despair,—these are mine empire:—
More glorious far than that which thou surveyest
From thine unenvied throne, O Mighty God!
Almighty, had I deigned to share the shame
Of thine ill tyranny, and hung not here 19
Nailed to this wall of eagle-baffling mountain,
Black, wintry, dead, unmeasured; without herb,
Insect, or beast, or shape or sound of life.
Ah me! alas, pain, pain ever, for ever!

No change, no pause, no hope! Yet I endure.
I ask the Earth, have not the mountains felt?
I ask yon Heaven, the all-beholding Sun,
Has it not seen? The Sea, in storm or calm,
Heaven's ever-changing Shadow, spread below,
Have its deaf waves not heard my agony?
Ah me! alas, pain, pain ever, for ever! 30

The crawling glaciers pierce me with the spears
Of their moon-freezing crystals, the bright chains
Eat with their burning cold into my bones.
Heaven's wingèd hound, polluting from thy lips
His beak in poison not his own, tears up
My heart; and shapeless sights come wandering by,
The ghastly people of the realm of dream,
Mocking me: and the Earthquake-fiends are charged
To wrench the rivets from my quivering wounds 39
When the rocks split and close again behind:
While from their loud abysses howling throng
The genii of the storm, urging the rage
Of whirlwind, and afflict me with keen hail.
And yet to me welcome is day and night,

Whether one breaks the hoar frost of the
    morn,
Or starry, dim, and slow, the other climbs
The leaden-coloured east; for then they lead
The wingless, crawling hours, one among whom
—As some dark Priest hales the reluctant vic-
    tim—   49
Shall drag thee, cruel King, to kiss the blood
From these pale feet, which then might
    trample thee
If they disdained not such a prostrate slave.
Disdain! Ah no! I pity thee. What ruin
Will hunt thee undefended through wide
    Heaven!
How will thy soul, cloven to its depth with
    terror,
Gape like a hell within! I speak in grief,
Not exultation, for I hate no more,
As then ere misery made me wise. The curse
Once breathed on thee I would recall. Ye
    Mountains,
Whose many-voicèd Echoes, through the mist
Of cataracts, flung the thunder of that spell! 61
Ye icy Springs, stagnant with wrinkling frost,
Which vibrated to hear me, and then crept
Shuddering through India! Thou serenest Air,
Through which the Sun walks burning without
    beams!
And ye swift Whirlwinds, who on poisèd
    wings
Hung mute and moveless o'er yon hushed
    abyss,
As thunder, louder than your own, made rock
The orbèd world! If then my words had
    power,
Though I am changed so that aught evil wish
Is dead within; although no memory be   71
Of what is hate, let them not lose it now!
What was that curse? for ye all heard me
    speak.

First Voice (from the Mountains)
Thrice three hundred thousand years
  O'er the Earthquake's couch we stood:
Oft, as men convulsed with fears,
  We trembled in our multitude.

Second Voice (from the Springs)
Thunderbolts had parched our water,
  We had been stained with bitter blood,
And had run mute, 'mid shrieks of slaughter,
  Thro' a city and a solitude.   81

Third Voice (from the Air)
I had clothed, since Earth uprose,
  Its wastes in colours not their own,
And oft had my serene repose
  Been cloven by many a rending groan.

Fourth Voice (from the Whirlwinds)
We had soared beneath these mountains
  Unresting ages; nor had thunder,
Nor yon volcano's flaming fountains,
  Nor any power above or under
Ever made us mute with wonder.   90

First Voice
But never bowed our snowy crest
As at the voice of thine unrest.

Second Voice
Never such a sound before
To the Indian waves we bore.
A pilot asleep on the howling sea
Leaped up from the deck in agony,
And heard, and cried, 'Ah, woe is me!'
And died as mad as the wild waves be.

Third Voice
By such dread words from Earth to Heaven
My still realm was never riven: 100
When its wound was closed, there stood
Darkness o'er the day like blood.

Fourth Voice
And we shrank back: for dreams of ruin
To frozen caves our flight pursuing
Made us keep silence—thus—and thus—
Though silence is as hell to us.

The Earth. The tongueless Caverns of the
    craggy hills
Cried, 'Misery!' then; the hollow Heaven re-
    plied,
'Misery!' And the Ocean's purple waves,
Climbing the land, howled to the lashing
    winds,   110
And the pale nations heard it, 'Misery!'
  Prometheus. I hear a sound of voices: not
    the voice
Which I gave forth. Mother, thy sons and
    thou
Scorn him, without whose all-enduring will
Beneath the fierce omnipotence of Jove,
Both they and thou had vanished, like thin
    mist

Unrolled on the morning wind. Know ye not
   me,
The Titan? He who made his agony
The barrier to your else all-conquering foe?
Oh, rock-embosomed lawns, and snow-fed
   streams,   120
Now seen athwart frore vapours, deep below,
Through whose o'ershadowing woods I wan-
   dered once
With Asia, drinking life from her loved eyes;
Why scorns the spirit which informs ye, now
To commune with me? me alone, who checked,
As one who checks a fiend-drawn charioteer,
The falsehood and the force of him who
   reigns
Supreme, and with the groans of pining slaves
Fills your dim glens and liquid wildernesses:
Why answer ye not, still? Brethren!
   The Earth.   They dare not
   Prometheus. Who dares? for I would hear
      that curse again.   131
Ha, what an awful whisper rises up!
'Tis scarce like sound: it tingles through the
   frame
As lightning tingles, hovering ere it strike.
Speak, Spirit! from thine inorganic voice
I only know that thou art moving near
And love. How cursed I him?
   The Earth.   How canst thou hear
Who knowest not the language of the dead?
   Prometheus. Thou art a living spirit; speak
      as they.
   The Earth. I dare not speak like life, lest
      Heaven's fell King   140
Should hear, and link me to some wheel of
   pain
More torturing than the one whereon I roll.
Subtle thou art and good, and though the
   Gods
Hear not this voice, yet thou art more than
   God,
Being wise and kind: earnestly hearken now.
   Prometheus. Obscurely through my brain,
      like shadows dim,
Sweep awful thoughts, rapid and thick. I feel
Faint, like one mingled in entwining love;
Yet 'tis not pleasure.
   The Earth.   No, thou canst not hear:
Thou art immortal, and this tongue is known
Only to those who die.   151
   Prometheus.   And what art thou,
O, melancholy Voice?
   The Earth.   I am the Earth,
Thy mother; she within whose stony veins,

To the last fibre of the loftiest tree
Whose thin leaves trembled in the frozen air,
Joy ran, as blood within a living frame,
When thou didst from her bosom, like a cloud
Of glory, arise, a spirit of keen joy!
And at thy voice her pining sons uplifted
Their prostrate brows from the polluting dust,
And our almighty Tyrant with fierce dread 161
Grew pale, until his thunder chained thee here.
Then, see those million worlds which burn and
   roll
Around us: their inhabitants beheld
My spherèd light wane in wide Heaven; the
   sea
Was lifted by strange tempest, and new fire
From earthquake-rifted mountains of bright
   snow
Shook its portentous hair beneath Heaven's
   frown;
Lightning and Inundation vexed the plains;
Blue thistles bloomed in cities; foodless toads
Within voluptuous chambers panting crawled:
When Plague had fallen on man, and beast,
   and worm,   172
And Famine; and black blight on herb and
   tree;
And in the corn, and vines, and meadow-
   grass,
Teemed ineradicable poisonous weeds
Draining their growth, for my wan breast
   was dry
With grief; and the thin air, my breath,
   was stained
With the contagion of a mother's hate
Breathed on her child's destroyer; ay, I heard
Thy curse, the which, if thou rememberest
   not,   180
Yet my innumerable seas and streams,
Mountains, and caves, and winds, and yon
   wide air,
And the inarticulate people of the dead,
Preserve, a treasured spell. We meditate
In secret joy and hope those dreadful words,
But dare not speak them.
   Prometheus.   Venerable mother!
All else who live and suffer take from thee
Some comfort; flowers, and fruits, and happy
   sounds,
And love, though fleeting; these may not be
   mine.
But mine own words, I pray, deny me not. 190
   The Earth. They shall be told. Ere Babylon
      was dust,
The Magus Zoroaster, my dead child,

Met his own image walking in the garden.
That apparition, sole of men, he saw.
For know there are two worlds of life and
  death:
One that which thou beholdest; but the other
Is underneath the grave, where do inhabit
The shadows of all forms that think and live
Till death unite them and they part no more;
Dreams and the light imaginings of men, 200
And all that faith creates or love desires,
Terrible, strange, sublime and beauteous
  shapes.
There thou art, and dost hang, a writhing
  shade,
'Mid whirlwind-peopled mountains; all the
  gods
Are there, and all the powers of nameless
  worlds,
Vast, sceptred phantoms; heroes, men, and
  beasts;
And Demogorgon, a tremendous gloom;
And he, the supreme Tyrant, on his throne
Of burning gold. Son, one of these shall utter
The curse which all remember. Call at will 210
Thine own ghost, or the ghost of Jupiter,
Hades or Typhon, or what mightier Gods
From all-prolific Evil, since thy ruin
Have sprung, and trampled on my prostrate
  sons.
Ask, and they must reply: so the revenge
Of the Supreme may sweep through vacant
  shades,
As rainy wind through the abandoned gate
Of a fallen palace.
Prometheus.   Mother, let not aught
Of that which may be evil, pass again
My lips, or those of aught resembling me. 220
Phantasm of Jupiter, arise, appear!

Ione

My wings are folded o'er mine ears:
  My wings are crossèd o'er mine eyes:
Yet through their silver shade appears,
  And through their lulling plumes arise,
A Shape, a throng of sounds;
  May it be no ill to thee
O thou of many wounds!
Near whom, for our sweet sister's sake,
Ever thus we watch and wake.   230

Panthea

The sound is of whirlwind underground,
  Earthquake, and fire, and mountains
  cloven;

The shape is awful like the sound,
  Clothed in dark purple, star-inwoven.
A sceptre of pale gold
  To stay steps proud, o'er the slow cloud
His veinèd hand doth hold.
Cruel he looks, but calm and strong,
Like one who does, not suffers wrong.

Phantasm of Jupiter. Why have the secret
  powers of this strange world   240
Driven me, a frail and empty phantom, hither
On direst storms? What unaccustomed sounds
Are hovering on my lips, unlike the voice
With which our pallid race hold ghastly talk
In darkness? And, proud sufferer, who art
  thou?
Prometheus. Tremendous Image, as thou art
  must be
He whom thou shadowest forth. I am his foe,
The Titan. Speak the words which I would
  hear,
Although no thought inform thine empty voice.
The Earth. Listen! And though your echoes
  must be mute,   250
Gray mountains, and old woods, and haunted
  springs,
Prophetic caves, and isle-surrounding streams,
Rejoice to hear what yet ye cannot speak.
Phantasm. A spirit seizes me and speaks
  within:
It tears me as fire tears a thunder-cloud.
Panthea. See, how he lifts his mighty looks,
  the Heaven
Darkens above.
Ione.   He speaks! O shelter me!
Prometheus. I see the curse on gestures
  proud and cold,
And looks of firm defiance, and calm hate, 259
And such despair as mocks itself with smiles,
Written as on a scroll: yet speak: Oh, speak!

Phantasm

Fiend, I defy thee! with a calm, fixed mind,
  All that thou canst inflict I bid thee do;
Foul Tyrant both of Gods and Human-kind,
  One only being shalt thou not subdue.
Rain then thy plagues upon me here,
  Ghastly disease, and frenzying fear;
And let alternate frost and fire
  Eat into me, and be thine ire
Lightning, and cutting hail, and legioned
  forms   270
Of furies, driving by upon the wounding
  storms.

Ay, do thy worst. Thou art omnipotent.
 O'er all things but thyself I gave thee
  power,
And my own will. Be thy swift mischiefs
  sent
 To blast mankind, from yon ethereal
  tower.
Let thy malignant spirit move
In darkness over those I love:
On me and mine I imprecate
The utmost torture of thy hate;
And thus devote to sleepless agony, 280
This undeclining head while thou must reign
 on high.

But thou, who art the God and Lord: O,
 thou,
 Who fillest with thy soul this world of
  woe,
To whom all things of Earth and Heaven do
 bow
 In fear and worship: all-prevailing foe!
I curse thee! let a sufferer's curse
Clasp thee, his torturer, like remorse;
Till thine Infinity shall be
A robe of envenomed agony;
And thine Omnipotence a crown of pain, 290
To cling like burning gold round thy dissolv-
 ing brain.

Heap on thy soul, by virtue of this Curse,
 Ill deeds, then be thou damned, beholding
  good;
Both infinite as is the universe,
 And thou, and thy self-torturing solitude.
An awful image of calm power
Though now thou sittest, let the hour
Come, when thou must appear to be
That which thou art internally;
And after many a false and fruitless crime
Scorn track thy lagging fall through bound-
 less space and time. 301

Prometheus. Were these my words, O Parent?
The Earth.   They were thine.
Prometheus. It doth repent me: words are
  quick and vain;
Grief for a while is blind, and so was mine.
I wish not living thing to suffer pain.

The Earth
Misery, Oh misery to me,
That Jove at length should vanquish thee.
Wail, howl aloud, Land and Sea,
The Earth's rent heart shall answer ye.

Howl, Spirits of the living and the dead, 310
Your refuge, your defence lies fallen and
vanquishèd.

First Echo
Lies fallen and vanquishèd!

Second Echo
Fallen and vanquishèd!

Ione
Fear not: 'tis but some passing spasm,
 The Titan is unvanquished still.
But see, where through the azure chasm
 Of yon forked and snowy hill
Trampling the slant winds on high
 With golden-sandalled feet, that glow
Under plumes of purple dye, 320
Like rose-ensanguined ivory,
 A Shape comes now,
Stretching on high from his right hand
 A serpent-cinctured wand.

Panthea. 'Tis Jove's world-wandering herald, Mercury.

Ione
And who are those with hydra tresses
 And iron wings that climb the wind,
Whom the frowning God represses
 Like vapours steaming up behind,
Clanging loud, an endless crowd— 330

Panthea
These are Jove's tempest-walking hounds,
 Whom he gluts with groans and blood,
When charioted on sulphurous cloud
 He bursts Heaven's bounds.

Ione
Are they now led, from the thin dead
On new pangs to be fed?

Panthea
The Titan looks as ever, firm, not
 proud.

First Fury. Ha! I scent life!
Second Fury. Let me but look into his eyes!
Third Fury. The hope of torturing him
  smells like a heap
Of corpses to a death-bird after battle. 340
First Fury. Darest thou delay, O Herald!
 take cheer, Hounds
Of Hell: what if the Son of Maia soon

Should make us food and sport—who can
please long
The Omnipotent?
   Mercury. Back to your towers of iron,
And gnash, beside the streams of fire and
wail,
Your foodless teeth. Geryon, arise! and
Gorgon,
Chimæra, and thou Sphinx, subtlest of fiends
Who ministered to Thebes Heaven's poisoned
wine,
Unnatural love, and more unnatural hate:
These shall perform your task.
   First Fury.   Oh, mercy! mercy! 350
We die with our desire: drive us not back!
   Mercury. Crouch then in silence.
                 Awful Sufferer!
To thee unwilling, most unwillingly
I come, by the great Father's will driven
down,
To execute a doom of new revenge.
Alas! I pity thee, and hate myself
That I can do no more: aye from thy sight
Returning, for a season, Heaven seems Hell,
So thy worn form pursues me night and
day,
Smiling reproach. Wise art thou, firm and
good,
                      360
But vainly wouldst stand forth alone in strife
Against the Omnipotent; as yon clear lamps
That measure and divide the weary years
From which there is no refuge, long have
taught
And long must teach. Even now thy Tor-
turer arms
With the strange might of unimagined pains
The powers who scheme slow agonies in Hell,
And my commission is to lead them here,
Or what more subtle, foul, or savage fiends
People the abyss, and leave them to their
task. 370
Be it not so! there is a secret known
To thee, and to none else of living things,
Which may transfer the sceptre of wide
Heaven,
The fear of which perplexes the Supreme:
Clothe it in words, and bid it clasp his throne
In intercession; bend thy soul in prayer,
And like a suppliant in some gorgeous fane,
Let the will kneel within thy haughty heart:
For benefits and meek submission tame
The fiercest and the mightiest.
   Prometheus.   Evil minds 380
Change good to their own nature. I gave all

He has; and in return he chains me here
Years, ages, night and day: whether the Sun
Split my parched skin, or in the moony night
The crystal-wingèd snow cling round my
hair:
Whilst my belovèd race is trampled down
By his thought-executing ministers.
Such is the tyrant's recompense: 'tis just:
He who is evil can receive no good;
And for a world bestowed, or a friend lost, 390
He can feel hate, fear, shame; not gratitude:
He but requites me for his own misdeed.
Kindness to such is keen reproach, which
breaks
With bitter stings the light sleep of Revenge.
Submission, thou dost know I cannot try:
For what submission but that fatal word,
The death-seal of mankind's captivity,
Like the Sicilian's hair-suspended sword,
Which trembles o'er his crown, would he
accept, 399
Or could I yield? Which yet I will not yield.
Let others flatter Crime, where it sits throned
In brief Omnipotence: secure are they:
For Justice, when triumphant, will weep down
Pity, not punishment, on her own wrongs,
Too much avenged by those who err. I wait,
Enduring thus, the retributive hour
Which since we spake is even nearer now.
But hark, the hell-hounds clamour: fear de-
lay:
Behold! Heaven lowers under thy Father's
frown.
   Mercury. Oh, that we might be spared: I
to inflict 410
And thou to suffer! Once more answer me:
Thou knowest not the period of Jove's power?
   Prometheus. I know but this, that it must
come.
   Mercury.   Alas!
Thou canst not count thy years to come of
pain?
   Prometheus. They last while Jove must
reign: nor more, nor less
Do I desire or fear.
   Mercury.   Yet pause, and plunge
Into Eternity, where recorded time,
Even all that we imagine, age on age,
Seems but a point, and the reluctant mind
Flags wearily in its unending flight, 420
Till it sink, dizzy, blind, lost, shelterless;
Perchance it has not numbered the slow years
Which thou must spend in torture, unre-
prieved?

Prometheus. Perchance no thought can
count them, yet they pass.
Mercury. If thou might'st dwell among the
Gods the while
Lapped in voluptuous joy?
Prometheus.　　　　　　I would not quit
This bleak ravine, these unrepentant pains.
Mercury. Alas! I wonder at, yet pity thee.
Prometheus. Pity the self-despising slaves
of Heaven,
Not me, within whose mind sits peace serene,
As light in the sun, throned: how vain is
talk!　　　　　　　　　　　431
Call up the fiends.
Ione.　　　　　O, sister, look! White fire
Has cloven to the roots yon huge snow-
loaded cedar;
How fearfully God's thunder howls behind!
Mercury. I must obey his words and thine:
alas!
Most heavily remorse hangs at my heart!
Panthea. See where the child of Heaven,
with wingèd feet,
Runs down the slanted sunlight of the dawn.
Ione. Dear sister, close thy plumes over
thine eyes
Lest thou behold and die: they come: they
come　　　　　　　　　　　440
Blackening the birth of day with countless
wings,
And hollow underneath, like death.
First Fury.　　　　　　　Prometheus!
Second Fury. ·Immortal Titan!
Third Fury. Champion of Heaven's slaves!
Prometheus. He whom some dreadful voice
invokes is here,
Prometheus, the chained Titan. Horrible
forms,
What and who are ye? Never yet there came
Phantasms so foul through monster-teeming
Hell
From the all-miscreative brain of Jove;
Whilst I behold such execrable shapes,
Methinks I grow like what I contemplate, 450
And laugh and stare in loathsome sym-
pathy.
First Fury. We are the ministers of pain,
and fear,
And disappointment, and mistrust, and hate,
And clinging crime; and as lean dogs pursue
Through wood and lake some struck and sob-
bing fawn,
We track all things that weep, and bleed, and
live,

When the great King betrays them to our
will.
Prometheus. Oh! many fearful natures in
one name,
I know ye; and these lakes and echoes know
The darkness and the clangour of your wings.
But why more hideous than your loathèd
selves　　　　　　　　　　　461
Gather ye up in legions from the deep?
Second Fury. We knew not that: Sisters,
rejoice, rejoice!
Prometheus. Can aught exult in its de-
formity?
Second Fury. The beauty of delight makes
lovers glad,
Gazing on one another: so are we.
As from the rose which the pale priestess
kneels
To gather for her festal crown of flowers
The aëreal crimson falls, flushing her cheek,
So from our victim's destined agony　　470
The shade which is our form invests us
round,
Else we are shapeless as our mother Night.
Prometheus. I laugh your power, and his
who sent you here,
To lowest scorn. Pour forth the cup of pain.
First Fury. Thou thinkest we will rend thee
bone from bone,
And nerve from nerve, working like fire
within?
Prometheus. Pain is my element, as hate is
thine;
Ye rend me now: I care not.
Second Fury.　　　　　　　Dost imagine
We will but laugh into thy lidless eyes?
Prometheus. I weigh not what ye do, but
what ye suffer,　　　　　　　480
Being evil. Cruel was the power which called
You, or aught else so wretched, into light.
Third Fury. Thou think'st we will live
through thee, one by one,
Like animal life, and though we can obscure
not
The soul which burns within, that we will
dwell
Beside it, like a vain loud multitude
Vexing the self-content of wisest men:
That we will be dread thought beneath thy
brain,
And foul desire round thine astonished heart,
And blood within thy labyrinthine veins　490
Crawling like agony?
Prometheus.　　　　　Why, ye are thus now;

Yet am I king over myself, and rule
The torturing and conflicting throngs within,
As Jove rules you when Hell grows mutinous.

Chorus of Furies

From the ends of the earth, from the ends of
 the earth,
Where the night has its grave and the morn-
 ing its birth,
   Come, come, come!
Oh, ye who shake hills with the scream of
 your mirth,
When cities sink howling in ruin; and ye
Who with wingless footsteps trample the
 sea,   500
And close upon Shipwreck and Famine's track,
Sit chattering with joy on the foodless wreck;
   Come, come, come!
 Leave the bed, low, cold, and red,
 Strewed beneath a nation dead;
 Leave the hatred, as in ashes
  Fire is left for future burning:
 It will burst in bloodier flashes
  When ye stir it, soon returning:
 Leave the self-contempt implanted 510
 In young spirits, sense-enchanted,
  Misery's yet unkindled fuel:
 Leave Hell's secrets half unchanted,
  To the maniac dreamer; cruel
 More than ye can be with hate
  Is he with fear.
   Come, come, come!
We are steaming up from Hell's wide gate
And we burthen the blast of the atmosphere,
But vainly we toil till ye come here. 520

Ione. Sister, I hear the thunder of new
 wings.
Panthea. These solid mountains quiver with
 the sound
Even as the tremulous air: their shadows
 make
The space within my plumes more black than
 night.

First Fury

Your call was as a wingèd car
Driven on whirlwinds fast and far;
It rapped us from red gulfs of war.

Second Fury

From wide cities, famine-wasted;

Third Fury

Groans half heard, and blood untasted;

Fourth Fury

Kingly conclaves stern and cold, 530
Where blood with gold is bought and sold;

Fifth Fury

From the furnace, white and hot,
In which—

A Fury

   Speak not: whisper not:
I know all that ye would tell,
But to speak might break the spell
Which must bend the Invincible,
 The stern of thought;
He yet defies the deepest power of Hell.

A Fury

Tear the veil!

Another Fury

  It is torn.

Chorus

   The pale stars of the morn
Shine on a misery, dire to be borne. 540
Dost thou faint, mighty Titan? We laugh thee
 to scorn.
Dost thou boast the clear knowledge thou
 waken'dst for man?
Then was kindled within him a thirst which
 outran
Those perishing waters; a thirst of fierce
 fever,
Hope, love, doubt, desire, which consume him
 for ever.
 One came forth of gentle worth
 Smiling on the sanguine earth;
 His words outlived him, like swift poison
  Withering up truth, peace, and pity.
 Look! where round the wide horizon 550
  Many a million-peopled city
 Vomits smoke in the bright air.
 Hark that outcry of despair!
 'Tis his mild and gentle ghost
  Wailing for the faith he kindled:
 Look again, the flames almost
  To a glow-worm's lamp have dwindled:
The survivors round the embers
 Gather in dread.
   Joy, joy, joy! 560

Past ages crowd on thee, but each one remembers,
And the future is dark, and the present is
spread
Like a pillow of thorns for thy slumberless
head.

Semichorus I

Drops of bloody agony flow
From his white and quivering brow.
Grant a little respite now:
See a disenchanted nation
Springs like day from desolation;
To Truth its state is dedicate,
And Freedom leads it forth, her mate;   570
A legioned band of linkèd brothers
Whom Love calls children—

Semichorus II

'Tis another's:
See how kindred murder kin:
'Tis the vintage-time for death and sin:
Blood, like new wine, bubbles within:
Till Despair smothers
The struggling world, which slaves and tyrants
win.
[All the FURIES *vanish, except one.*
Ione. Hark, sister! what a low yet dreadful
groan
Quite unsuppressed is tearing up the heart
Of the good Titan, as storms tear the deep, 580
And beasts hear the sea moan in inland caves.
Darest thou observe how the fiends torture
him?
Panthea. Alas! I looked forth twice, but will
no more.
Ione. What didst thou see?
Panthea.   A woful sight: a youth
With patient looks nailed to a crucifix.
Ione. What next?
Panthea. The heaven around, the earth be-
low
Was peopled with thick shapes of human
death,
All horrible, and wrought by human hands,
And some appeared the work of human hearts.
For men were slowly killed by frowns and
smiles: 590
And other sights too foul to speak and live
Were wandering by. Let us not tempt worse
fear
By looking forth: those groans are grief
enough

Fury. Behold an emblem: those who do
endure
Deep wrongs for man, and scorn, and chains,
but heap
Thousandfold torment on themselves and him.
Prometheus. Remit the anguish of that
lighted stare;
Close those wan lips; let that thorn-wounded
brow
Stream not with blood; it mingles with thy
tears!
Fix, fix those tortured orbs in peace and
death,   600
So thy sick throes shake not that crucifix,
So those pale fingers play not with thy gore.
O, horrible! Thy name I will not speak,
It hath become a curse. I see, I see
The wise, the mild, the lofty, and the just,
Whom thy slaves hate for being like to thee,
Some hunted by foul lies from their heart's
home,
An early-chosen, late-lamented home;
As hooded ounces cling to the driven hind;
Some linked to corpses in unwholesome cells:
Some—hear I not the multitude laugh
loud?—   611
Impaled in lingering fire: and mighty realms
Float by my feet, like sea-uprooted isles,
Whose sons are kneaded down in common
blood
By the red light of their own burning homes.
Fury. Blood thou canst see, and fire; and
canst hear groans;
Worse things, unheard, unseen, remain behind.
Prometheus. Worse?
Fury. In each human heart terror survives
The ravin it has gorged: the loftiest fear
All that they would disdain to think were
true: 620
Hypocrisy and custom make their minds
The fanes of many a worship, now outworn.
They dare not devise good for man's estate,
And yet they know not that they do not dare.
The good want power, but to weep barren
tears.
The powerful goodness want: worse need for
them.
The wise want love; and those who love want
wisdom;
And all best things are thus confused to ill.
Many are strong and rich, and would be just,
But live among their suffering fellow-men   630
As if none felt: they know not what they
do.

Prometheus. Thy words are like a cloud of
    wingèd snakes;
And yet I pity those they torture not.
Fury. Thou pitiest them? I speak no more!
                        [*Vanishes.*
Prometheus.   Ah woe!
Ah woe! Alas! pain, pain ever, for ever!
I close my tearless eyes, but see more clear
Thy works within my woe-illumèd mind,
Thou subtle tyrant! Peace is in the grave.
The grave hides all things beautiful and good:
I am a God and cannot find it there,   640
Nor would I seek it: for, though dread re-
    venge,
This is defeat, fierce king, not victory.
The sights with which thou torturest gird my
    soul
With new endurance, till the hour arrives
When they shall be no types of things which
    are.
Panthea. Alas! what sawest thou more?
Prometheus.   There are two woes:
To speak, and to behold; thou spare me one.
Names are there, Nature's sacred watchwords,
    they
Were borne aloft in bright emblazonry;
The nations thronged around, and cried aloud,
As with one voice, Truth, liberty, and love! 651
Suddenly fierce confusion fell from heaven
Among them: there was strife, deceit, and
    fear:
Tyrants rushed in, and did divide the spoil.
This was the shadow of the truth I saw.
   The Earth. I felt thy torture, son; with
    such mixed joy
As pain and virtue give. To cheer thy state
I bid ascend those subtle and fair spirits,
Whose homes are the dim caves of human
    thought,
And who inhabit, as birds wing the wind, 660
Its world-surrounding æther: they behold
Beyond that twilight realm, as in a glass,
The future: may they speak comfort to thee!
   Panthea. Look, sister, where a troop of
    spirits gather,
Like flocks of clouds in spring's delightful
    weather,
Thronging in the blue air!
   Ione.   And see! more come,
Like fountain-vapours when the winds are
    dumb,
That climb up the ravine in scattered lines.
And, hark! is it the music of the pines?
Is it the lake? Is it the waterfall?   670

Panthea. 'Tis something sadder, sweeter far
    than all.

Chorus of Spirits

From unremembered ages we
Gentle guides and guardians be
Of heaven-oppressed mortality;
And we breathe, and sicken not,
The atmosphere of human thought:
Be it dim, and dank, and gray,
Like a storm-extinguished day,
Travelled o'er by dying gleams;
  Be it bright as all between   680
Cloudless skies and windless streams,
  Silent, liquid, and serene;
As the birds within the wind,
  As the fish within the wave,
As the thoughts of man's own mind
  Float through all above the grave;
We make there our liquid lair,
Voyaging cloudlike and unpent
Through the boundless element:
Thence we bear the prophecy   690
Which begins and ends in thee!
Ione. More yet come, one by one: the air
    around them
Looks radiant as the air around a star.

First Spirit

On a battle-trumpet's blast
I fled hither, fast, fast, fast,
'Mid the darkness upward cast.
From the dust of creeds outworn,
From the tyrant's banner torn,
Gathering 'round me, onward borne,
There was mingled many a cry—   700
Freedom! Hope! Death! Victory!
Till they faded through the sky;
And one sound, above, around,
One sound beneath, around, above,
Was moving; 'twas the soul of Love;
'Twas the hope, the prophecy,
Which begins and ends in thee.

Second Spirit

A rainbow's arch stood on the sea,
Which rocked beneath, immovably;
And the triumphant storm did flee,   710
Like a conqueror, swift and proud,
Between, with many a captive cloud,
A shapeless, dark and rapid crowd,
Each by lightning riven in half:
I heard the thunder hoarsely laugh:
Mighty fleets were strewn like chaff

And spread beneath a hell of death
O'er the white waters. I alit
On a great ship lightning-split,
And speeded hither on the sigh   720
Of one who gave an enemy,
His plank, then plunged aside to die.

Third Spirit

I sate beside a sage's bed,
And the lamp was burning red
Near the book where he had fed,
When a Dream with plumes of flame,
To his pillow hovering came,
And I knew it was the same
Which had kindled long ago
Pity, eloquence, and woe;   730
And the world awhile below
Wore the shade, its lustre made.
It has borne me here as fleet
As Desire's lightning feet:
I must ride it back ere morrow,
Or the sage will wake in sorrow.

Fourth Spirit

On a poet's lips I slept
Dreaming like a love-adept
In the sound his breathing kept;
Nor seeks nor finds he mortal blisses,   740
But feeds on the aëreal kisses
Of shapes that haunt thought's wildernesses.
He will watch from dawn to gloom
The lake-reflected sun illume
The yellow bees in the ivy-bloom,
Nor heed nor see, what things they be;
But from these create he can
Forms more real than living man,
Nurslings of immortality!
One of these awakened me,   750
And I sped to succour thee.

Ione

Behold'st thou not two shapes from the east
      and west
Come, as two doves to one belovèd nest,
Twin nurslings of the all-sustaining air
On swift still wings glide down the atmos-
      phere?
And, hark! their sweet, sad voices! 'tis despair
Mingled with love and then dissolved in sound.
      Panthea. Canst thou speak, sister? all my
            words are drowned.
      Ione. Their beauty gives me voice. See how
            they float
On their sustaining wings of skiey grain,   760

Orange and azure deepening into gold:
Their soft smiles light the air like a star's fire.

Chorus of Spirits

Hast thou beheld the form of Love?

Fifth Spirit

                        As over wide dominions
I sped, like some swift cloud that wings the
      wide air's wildernesses,
That planet-crested shape swept by on
      lightning-braided pinions,
Scattering the liquid joy of life from his
      ambrosial tresses:
His footsteps paved the world with light; but
      as I passed 'twas fading,
And hollow Ruin yawned behind: great
      sages bound in madness,
And headless patriots, and pale youths who
      perished, unupbraiding,
Gleamed in the night. I wandered o'er, till
      thou, O King of sadness,   770
Turned by thy smile the worst I saw to
      recollected gladness.

Sixth Spirit

Ah, sister! Desolation is a delicate thing:
      It walks not on the earth, it floats not on
            the air,
But treads with lulling footstep, and fans with
      silent wing
      The tender hopes which in their hearts the
            best and gentlest bear;
Who, soothed to false repose by the fanning
      plumes above
      And the music-stirring motion of its soft
            and busy feet,
Dream visions of aëreal joy, and call the mon-
      ster, Love,
      And wake, and find the shadow Pain, as he
            whom now we greet.

Chorus

Though Ruin now Love's shadow be,   780
Following him, destroyingly,
      On Death's white and wingèd steed,
Which the fleetest cannot flee,
      Trampling down both flower and weed,
Man and beast, and foul and fair,
Like a tempest through the air;
Thou shalt quell this horseman grim,
Woundless though in heart or limb.

      Prometheus. Spirits! how know ye this
            shall be?

Chorus

In the atmosphere we breathe,   790
As buds grow red when the snow-storms flee,
   From Spring gathering up beneath,
Whose mild winds shake the elder brake,
And the wandering herdsmen know
That the white-thorn soon will blow:
   Wisdom, Justice, Love, and Peace,
   When they struggle to increase,
     Are to us as soft winds be
     To shepherd boys, the prophecy
     Which begins and ends in thee.   800

Ione. Where are the Spirits fled?
Panthea.   Only a sense
Remains of them, like the omnipotence
Of music, when the inspired voice and lute
Languish, ere yet the responses are mute,
Which through the deep and labyrinthine soul,
Like echoes through long caverns, wind and
   roll.
   Prometheus. How fair these airborn shapes!
   and yet I feel
Most vain all hope but love; and thou art far,
Asia! who, when my being overflowed,
Wert like a golden chalice to bright wine   810
Which else had sunk into the thirsty dust.
All things are still: alas! how heavily
This quiet morning weighs upon my heart;
Though I should dream I could even sleep
   with grief
If slumber were denied not. I would fain
Be what it is my destiny to be,
The saviour and the strength of suffering man,
Or sink into the original gulf of things:
There is no agony, and no solace left;
Earth can console, Heaven can torment no
   more.   820
   Panthea. Hast thou forgotten one who
   watches thee
The cold dark night, and never sleeps but
   when
The shadow of thy spirit falls on her?
   Prometheus. I said all hope was vain but
   love: thou lovest.
   Panthea. Deeply in truth; but the eastern
   star looks white,
And Asia waits in that far Indian vale,
The scene of her sad exile; rugged once
And desolate and frozen, like this ravine;
But now invested with fair flowers and herbs,
And haunted by sweet airs and sounds, which
   flow   830
Among the woods and waters, from the æther

Of her transforming presence, which would
   fade
If it were mingled not with thine. Farewell!
   END OF THE FIRST ACT.

ACT II

SCENE I.—*Morning. A lovely Vale in the Indian Caucasus.* ASIA *alone.*

   Asia. From all the blasts of heaven thou
   hast descended:
Yes, like a spirit, like a thought, which makes
Unwonted tears throng to the horny eyes,
And beatings haunt the desolated heart,
Which should have learnt repose: thou hast
   descended
Cradled in tempests; thou dost wake, O
   Spring!
O child of many winds! As suddenly
Thou comest as the memory of a dream,
Which now is sad because it hath been sweet;
Like genius, or like joy which riseth up   10
As from the earth, clothing with golden clouds
The desert of our life.
This is the season, this the day, the hour;
At sunrise thou shouldst come, sweet sister
   mine,
Too long desired, too long delaying, come!
How like death-worms the wingless moments
   crawl!
The point of one white star is quivering still
Deep in the orange light of widening morn
Beyond the purple mountains: through a
   chasm
Of wind-divided mist the darker lake   20
Reflects it: now it wanes: it gleams again
As the waves fade, and as the burning threads
Of woven cloud unravel in pale air:
'Tis lost! and through yon peaks of cloud-like
   snow
The roseate sunlight quivers: hear I not
The Æolian music of her sea-green plumes
Winnowing the crimson dawn?
              [PANTHEA *enters.*
              I feel, I see
Those eyes which burn through smiles that
   fade in tears,
Like stars half quenched in mists of silver
   dew.
Belovèd and most beautiful, who wearest   30
The shadow of that soul by which I live,
How late thou art! the spherèd sun had
   climbed

The sea; my heart was sick with hope, before
The printless air felt thy belated plumes.
  Panthea. Pardon, great Sister! but my wings
    were faint
With the delight of a remembered dream,
As are the noontide plumes of summer winds
Satiate with sweet flowers. I was wont to
    sleep
Peacefully, and awake refreshed and calm
Before the sacred Titan's fall, and thy   40
Unhappy love, had made, through use and
    pity,
Both love and woe familiar to my heart
As they had grown to thine: erewhile I slept
Under the glaucous caverns of old Ocean
Within dim bowers of green and purple moss,
Our young Ione's soft and milky arms
Locked then, as now, behind my dark, moist
    hair,
While my shut eyes and cheek were pressed
    within
The folded depth of her life-breathing bosom:
But not as now, since I am made the wind 50
Which fails beneath the music that I bear
Of thy most wordless converse; since dis-
    solved
Into the sense with which love talks, my rest
Was troubled and yet sweet; my waking hours
Too full of care and pain.
  Asia.   Lift up thine eyes,
And let me read thy dream.
  Panthea.   As I have said
With our sea-sister at his feet I slept.
The mountain mists, condensing at our voice
Under the moon, had spread their snowy
    flakes,   59
From the keen ice shielding our linkèd sleep.
Then two dreams came. One, I remember not.
But in the other his pale wound-worn limbs
Fell from Prometheus, and the azure night
Grew radiant with the glory of that form
Which lives unchanged within, and his voice
    fell
Like music which makes giddy the dim brain,
Faint with intoxication of keen joy:
'Sister of her whose footsteps pave the world
With loveliness—more fair than aught but
    her,
Whose shadow thou art—lift thine eyes on
    me.'   70
I lifted them: the overpowering light
Of that immortal shape was shadowed o'er
By love; which, from his soft and flowing
    limbs,

And passion-parted lips, and keen, faint eyes,
Steamed forth like vaporous fire; an atmos-
    phere
Which wrapped me in its all-dissolving power,
As the warm æther of the morning sun
Wraps ere it drinks some cloud of wandering
    dew.
I saw not, heard not, moved not, only felt
His presence flow and mingle through my
    blood   80
Till it became his life, and his grew mine,
And I was thus absorbed, until it passed,
And like the vapours when the sun sinks
    down,
Gathering again in drops upon the pines,
And tremulous as they, in the deep night
My being was condensed; and as the rays
Of thought were slowly gathered, I could hear
His voice, whose accents lingered ere they
    died
Like footsteps of weak melody: thy name
Among the many sounds alone I heard   90
Of what might be articulate; though still
I listened through the night when sound was
    none.
Ione wakened then, and said to me:
'Canst thou divine what troubles me to-night?
I always knew what I desired before,
Nor ever found delight to wish in vain.
But now I cannot tell thee what I seek;
I know not; something sweet, since it is
    sweet   98
Even to desire; it is thy sport, false sister;
Thou hast discovered some enchantment old,
Whose spells have stolen my spirit as I slept
And mingled it with thine: for when just now
We kissed, I felt within thy parted lips
The sweet air that sustained me, and the
    warmth
Of the life-blood, for loss of which I faint,
Quivered between our intertwining arms.'
I answered not, for the Eastern star grew
    pale,
But fled to thee.
  Asia.   Thou speakest, but thy words
Are as the air: I feel them not: Oh, lift
Thine eyes, that I may read his written soul!
  Panthea. I lift them though they droop be-
    neath the load   111
Of that they would express: what canst thou
    see
But thine own fairest shadow imaged there?
  Asia. Thine eyes are like the deep, blue,
    boundless heaven

Contracted to two circles underneath
Their long, fine lashes; dark, far, measureless,
Orb within orb, and line through line inwoven.
 Panthea. Why lookest thou as if a spirit
  passed?
 Asia. There is a change: beyond their in-
  most depth
I see a shade, a shape: 'tis He, arrayed 120
In the soft light of his own smiles, which
  spread
Like radiance from the cloud-surrounded
  moon.
Prometheus, it is thine! depart not yet!
Say not those smiles that we shall meet again
Within that bright pavilion which their beams
Shall build o'er the waste world? The dream is
  told.
What shape is that between us? Its rude hair
Roughens the wind that lifts it, its regard
Is wild and quick, yet 'tis a thing of air,
For through its gray robe gleams the golden
  dew 130
Whose stars the noon has quenched not.
 Dream.   Follow! Follow!
 Panthea. It is mine other dream.
 Asia.   It disappears.
 Panthea. It passes now into my mind. Me-
  thought
As we sate here, the flower-infolding buds
Burst on yon lightning-blasted almond-tree,
When swift from the white Scythian wilder-
  ness
A wind swept forth wrinkling the Earth with
  frost:
I looked, and all the blossoms were blown
  down;
But on each leaf was stamped, as the blue
  bells
Of Hyacinth tell Apollo's written grief, 140
O, FOLLOW, FOLLOW!
 Asia.   As you speak, your words
Fill, pause by pause, my own forgotten sleep
With shapes. Methought among these lawns
  together
We wandered, underneath the young gray
  dawn,
And multitudes of dense white fleecy clouds
Were wandering in thick flocks along the
  mountains
Shepherded by the slow, unwilling wind;
And the white dew on the new-bladed grass,
Just piercing the dark earth, hung silently;
And there was more which I remember not:
But on the shadows of the morning clouds, 151

Athwart the purple mountain slope, was writ-
  ten
FOLLOW, O, FOLLOW! as they vanished by;
And on each herb, from which Heaven's dew
  had fallen,
The like was stamped, as with a withering
  fire;
A wind arose among the pines; it shook
The clinging music from their boughs, and
  then
Low, sweet, faint sounds, like the farewell of
  ghosts,
Were heard: O, FOLLOW, FOLLOW, FOLLOW ME!
And then I said: 'Panthea, look on me.' 160
Still I saw, FOLLOW, FOLLOW!
 Echo.   Follow, follow!
 Panthea. The crags, this clear spring morn-
  ing, mock our voices
As they were spirit-tongued.
 Asia.   It is some being
Around the crags. What fine clear sounds! O,
  list!

   Echoes (unseen)
  Echoes we: listen!
   We cannot stay:
  As dew-stars glisten
   Then fade away—
    Child of Ocean! 170

 Asia. Hark! Spirits speak. The liquid re-
  sponses
Of their aërial tongues yet sound.
 Panthea.   I hear.

   Echoes
  O, follow, follow,
   As our voice recedeth
  Through the caverns hollow,
   Where the forest spreadeth;

   (*More distant.*)
  O, follow, follow!
  Through the caverns hollow,
  As the song floats thou pursue,
  Where the wild bee never flew, 180
  Through the noontide darkness deep,
  By the odour-breathing sleep
  Of faint night flowers, and the waves
  At the fountain-lighted caves
  While our music, wild and sweet,
  Mocks thy gently falling feet,
    Child of Ocean!

 Asia. Shall we pursue the sound? It grows
  more faint
And distant.

Panthea. List! the strain floats nearer now.

Echoes

In the world unknown   190
　Sleeps a voice unspoken;
By thy step alone
　Can its rest be broken;
　　Child of Ocean!

Asia. How the notes sink upon the ebbing
　wind!

Echoes

O, follow, follow!
　Through the caverns hollow,
As the song floats thou pursue,
By the woodland noontide dew;
By the forest, lakes, and fountains,   200
Through the many-folded mountains;
To the rents, and gulfs, and chasms,
Where the Earth resposed from spasms,
On the day when He and thou
Parted, to commingle now:
　　Child of Ocean!

Asia. Come, sweet Panthea, link thy hand
　in mine,
And follow, ere the voices fade away.

SCENE II.—*A Forest, intermingled with
Rocks and Caverns.* ASIA *and* PANTHEA
*pass into it. Two young Fauns are sitting
on a Rock listening.*

Semichorus I of Spirits

The path through which that lovely twain
　Have passed, by cedar, pine, and yew,
　And each dark tree that ever grew,
　Is curtained out from Heaven's wide blue;
Nor sun, nor moon, nor wind, nor rain,
　Can pierce its interwoven bowers,
　Nor aught, save where some cloud of dew,
Drifted along the earth-creeping breeze,
Between the trunks of the hoar trees,
　Hangs each a pearl in the pale flowers 10
　Of the green laurel, blown anew;
And bends, and then fades silently,
One frail and fair anemone:
Or when some star of many a one
That climbs and wanders through steep night,
Has found the cleft through which alone
Beams fall from high those depths upon
Ere it is borne away, away,
By the swift Heavens that cannot stay,
It scatters drops of golden light,   20
Like lines of rain that ne'er unite:

And the gloom divine is all around,
And underneath is the mossy ground.

Semichorus II

There the voluptuous nightingales,
　Are awake through all the broad noonday.
When one with bliss or sadness fails,
　And through the windless ivy-boughs,
Sick with sweet love, droops dying away
On its mate's music-panting bosom;
Another from the swinging blossom,   30
　Watching to catch the languid close
　Of the last strain, then lifts on high
　The wings of the weak melody,
'Till some new strain of feeling bear
　The song, and all the woods are mute;
When there is heard through the dim air
　The rush of wings, and rising there
Like many a lake-surrounded flute,
Sounds overflow the listener's brain
So sweet, that joy is almost pain.   40

Semichorus I

There those enchanted eddies play
　Of echoes, music-tongued, which draw,
　By Demogorgon's mighty law,
　With melting rapture, or sweet awe,
All spirits on that secret way;
　As inland boats are driven to Ocean
Down streams made strong with mountain-
　　thaw:
　And first there comes a gentle sound
　To those in talk or slumber bound,
And wakes the destined soft emotion,—   50
Attracts, impels them; those who saw
　Say from the breathing earth behind
　There steams a plume-uplifting wind
Which drives them on their path, while they
　Believe their own swift wings and feet
The sweet desires within obey:
And so they float upon their way,
Until, still sweet, but loud and strong,
The storm of sound is driven along,
　Sucked up and hurrying: as they fleet   60
　Behind, its gathering billows meet
And to the fatal mountain bear
Like clouds amid the yielding air.

First Faun. Canst thou imagine where those
　spirits live
Which make such delicate music in the woods?
We haunt within the least frequented caves
And closest coverts, and we know these wilds,
Yet never meet them, though we hear them
　oft:

Where may they hide themselves?
Second Faun.   'Tis hard to tell:
I have heard those more skilled in spirits
    say,   70
The bubbles, which the enchantment of the
    sun
Sucks from the pale faint water-flowers that
    pave
The oozy bottom of clear lakes and pools,
Are the pavilions where such dwell and float
Under the green and golden atmosphere
Which noontide kindles through the woven
    leaves;
And when these burst, and the thin fiery air,
The which they breathed within those lucent
    domes,
Ascends to flow like meteors through the
    night,
They ride on them, and rein their headlong
    speed,   80
And bow their burning crests, and glide in
    fire
Under the waters of the earth again.
    First Faun. If such live thus, have others
    other lives,
Under pink blossoms or within the bells
Of meadow flowers, or folded violets deep,
Or on their dying odours, when they die,
Or in the sunlight of the spherèd dew?
    Second Faun. Ay, many more which we
    may well divine.
But, should we stay to speak, noontide would
    come,
And thwart Silenus find his goats undrawn, 90
And grudge to sing those wise and lovely
    songs
Of Fate, and Chance, and God, and Chaos old,
And Love, and the chained Titan's woful
    doom,
And how he shall be loosed, and make the
    earth
One brotherhood: delightful strains which
    cheer
Our solitary twilights, and which charm
To silence the unenvying nightingales.

SCENE III.—A PINNACLE OF ROCK AMONG
    MOUNTAINS. ASIA *and* PANTHEA.

    Panthea. Hither the sound has borne us—
    to the realm
Of Demogorgon, and the mighty portal,
Like a volcano's meteor-breathing chasm,
Whence the oracular vapour is hurled up

Which lonely men drink wandering in their
    youth,
And call truth, virtue, love, genius, or joy,
That maddening wine of life, whose dregs
    they drain
To deep intoxication; and uplift,
Like Mænads who cry loud, Evoe! Evoe!
The voice which is contagion to the world. 10
    Asia. Fit throne for such a Power! Mag-
    nificent!
How glorious art thou, Earth! And if thou be
The shadow of some spirit lovelier still,
Though evil stain its work, and it should be
Like its creation, weak yet beautiful,
I could fall down and worship that and thee.
Even now my heart adoreth: Wonderful!
Look, sister, ere the vapour dim thy brain:
Beneath is a wide plain of billowy mist,
As a lake, paving in the morning sky,   20
With azure waves which burst in silver light,
Some Indian vale. Behold it, rolling on
Under the curdling winds, and islanding
The peak whereon we stand, midway, around,
Encinctured by the dark and blooming forests,
Dim twilight-lawns, and stream-illumèd caves,
And wind-enchanted shapes of wandering
    mist;
And far on high the keen sky-cleaving moun-
    tains
From icy spires of sun-like radiance fling
The dawn, as lifted Ocean's dazzling spray, 30
From some Atlantic islet scattered up,
Spangles the wind with lamp-like water-drops.
The vale is girdled with their walls, a howl
Of cataracts from their thaw-cloven ravines,
Satiates the listening wind, continuous, vast,
Awful as silence. Hark! the rushing snow!
The sun-awakened avalanche! whose mass,
Thrice sifted by the storm, had gathered there
Flake after flake, in heaven-defying minds
As thought by thought is piled, till some great
    truth   40
Is loosened, and the nations echo round,
Shaken to their roots, as do the mountains
    now.
    Panthea. Look how the gusty sea of mist is
    breaking
In crimson foam, even at our feet! it rises
As Ocean at the enchantment of the moon
Round foodless men wrecked on some oozy
    isle.
    Asia. The fragments of the cloud are scat-
    tered up;
The wind that lifts them disentwines my hair;

Its billows now sweep o'er mine eyes; my
    brain
Grows dizzy; see'st thou shapes within the
    mist? 50
Panthea. A countenance with beckoning
    smiles: there burns
An azure fire within its golden locks!
Another and another: hark! they speak!

Song of Spirits.

To the deep, to the deep,
    Down, down!
Through the shade of sleep,
Through the cloudy strife
Of Death and of Life;
Through the veil and the bar
Of things which seem and are 60
Even to the steps of the remotest throne,
    Down, down!

While the sound whirls around,
    Down, down!
As the fawn draws the hound,
As the lightning the vapour,
As a weak moth the taper;
Death, despair; love, sorrow;
Time both; to-day, to-morrow;
As steel obeys the spirit of the stone, 70
    Down, down!

Through the gray, void abysm,
    Down, down!
Where the air is no prism,
And the moon and stars are not,
And the cavern-crags wear not
The radiance of Heaven,
Nor the gloom to Earth given,
Where there is One pervading, One alone,
    Down, down! 80

In the depth of the deep,
    Down, down!
Like veiled lightning asleep,
Like the spark nursed in embers,
The last look Love remembers,
Like a diamond, which shines
On the dark wealth of mines,
A spell is treasured but for thee alone.
    Down, down!

We have bound thee, we guide thee; 90
    Down, down!
With the bright form beside thee;
Resist not the weakness,

Such strength is in meekness
That the Eternal, the Immortal,
Must unloose through life's portal
The snake-like Doom coiled underneath his
    throne
    By that alone.

SCENE IV.—THE CAVE OF DEMOGORGON.
ASIA *and* PANTHEA.

Panthea. What veilèd form sits on that
    ebon throne?
Asia. The veil has fallen.
Panthea.   I see a mighty darkness
Filling the seat of power, and rays of gloom
Dart round, as light from the meridian sun.
—Ungazed upon and shapeless; neither limb,
Nor form, nor outline; yet we feel it is
A living Spirit.
Demogorgon. Ask what thou wouldst know.
Asia. What canst thou tell?
Demogorgon. All things thou dar'st de-
    mand.
Asia. Who made the living world?
Demogorgon.   God.
Asia.   Who made all
That it contains? thought, passion, reason,
    will, 10
Imagination?
Demogorgon. God: Almighty God.
Asia. Who made that sense which, when the
    winds of Spring
In rarest visitation, or the voice
Of one belovèd heard in youth alone,
Fills the faint eyes with falling tears which
    dim
The radiant looks of unbewailing flowers,
And leaves this peopled earth a solitude
When it returns no more?
Demogorgon.   Merciful God.
Asia. And who made terror, madness, crime,
    remorse,
Which from the links of the great chain of
    things, 20
To every thought within the mind of man
Sway and drag heavily, and each one reels
Under the load towards the pit of death:
Abandoned hope, and love that turns to hate;
And self-contempt, bitterer to drink than
    blood;
Pain, whose unheeded and familiar speech
Is howling, and keen shrieks, day after day;
And Hell, or the sharp fear of Hell?
Demogorgon.   He reigns.

Asia. Utter his name: a world pining in
pain
Asks but his name: curses shall drag him
down.   30
Demogorgon. He reigns.
Asia.   I feel, I know it: who?
Demogorgon.   He reigns.
Asia. Who reigns? There was the Heaven
and Earth at first,
And Light and Love; then Saturn, from
whose throne
Time fell, an envious shadow: such the state
Of the earth's primal spirits beneath his sway,
As the calm joy of flowers and living leaves
Before the wind or sun has withered them
And semivital worms! but he refused
The birthright of their being, knowledge,
power,
The skill which wields the elements, the
thought   40
Which pierces this dim universe like light,
Self-empire, and the majesty of love;
For thirst of which they fainted. Then Prome-
theus
Gave wisdom, which is strength, to Jupiter,
And with this law alone, 'Let man be free,'
Clothed him with the dominion of wide
Heaven.
To know nor faith, nor love, nor law; to be
Omnipotent but friendless is to reign;
And Jove now reigned; for on the race of
man
First famine, and then toil, and then dis-
ease,   50
Strife, wounds, and ghastly death unseen be-
fore,
Fell; and the unseasonable seasons drove
With alternating shafts of frost and fire,
Their shelterless, pale tribes to mountain
caves:
And in their desert hearts fierce wants he
sent,
And mad disquietudes, and shadows idle
Of unreal good, which levied mutual war,
So ruining the lair wherein they raged.
Prometheus saw, and waked the legioned hopes
Which sleep within folded Elysian flowers, 60
Nepenthe, Moly, Amaranth, fadeless blooms,
That they might hide with thin and rainbow
wings
The shape of Death; and Love he sent to bind
The disunited tendrils of that vine
Which bears the wine of life, the human
heart;

And he tamed fire which, like some beast of
prey,
Most terrible, but lovely, played beneath
The frown of man; and tortured to his will
Iron and gold, the slaves and signs of power,
And gems and poisons, and all subtlest forms
Hidden beneath the mountains and the waves.
He gave man speech, and speech created
thought,   72
Which is the measure of the universe,
And Science struck the thrones of earth and
heaven,
Which shook, but fell not; and the harmonious
mind
Poured itself forth in all-prophetic song;
And music lifted up the listening spirit
Until it walked, exempt from mortal care,
Godlike, o'er the clear billows of sweet sound;
And human hands first mimicked and then
mocked,   80
With moulded limbs more lovely than its own,
The human form, till marble grew divine;
And mothers, gazing, drank the love men see
Reflected in their race, behold, and perish.
He told the hidden power of herbs and springs,
And Disease drank and slept. Death grew like
sleep.
He taught the implicated orbits woven
Of the wide-wandering stars; and how the sun
Changes his lair, and by what secret spell
The pale moon is transformed, when her
broad eye   90
Gazes not on the interlunar sea:
He taught to rule, as life directs the limbs,
The tempest-wingèd chariots of the Ocean,
And the Celt knew the Indian. Cities then
Were built, and through their snow-like
columns flowed
The warm winds, and the azure æther shone,
And the blue sea and shadowy hills were seen.
Such, the alleviations of his state,
Prometheus gave to man, for which he hangs
Withering in destined pain: but who rains
down   100
Evil, the immedicable plague, which, while
Man looks on his creation like a God
And sees that it is glorious, drives him on,
The wreck of his own will, the scorn of earth,
The outcast, the abandoned, the alone?
Not Jove: while yet his frown shook Heaven,
ay, when
His adversary from adamantine chains
Cursed him, he trembled like a slave. De-
clare

Who is his master? Is he too a slave?

Demogorgon. All spirits are enslaved which
     serve things evil: 110
Thou knowest if Jupiter be such or no.

Asia. Whom calledst thou God?

Demogorgon.   I spoke but as ye speak,
For Jove is the supreme of living things.

Asia. Who is the master of the slave?

Demogorgon.   If the abysm
Could vomit forth its secrets. . . . But a
     voice
Is wanting, the deep truth is imageless;
For what would it avail to bid thee gaze
On the revolving world? What to bid speak
Fate, Time, Occasion, Chance, and Change?
     To these
All things are subject but eternal Love.   120

Asia. So much I asked before, and my
     heart gave
The response thou hast given; and of such
     truths
Each to itself must be the oracle.
One more demand; and do thou answer me
As mine own soul would answer, did it know
That which I ask. Prometheus shall arise
Henceforth the sun of this rejoicing world:
When shall the destined hour arrive?

Demogorgon.   Behold!

Asia. The rocks are cloven, and through the
     purple night
I see cars drawn by rainbow-wingèd steeds 130
Which trample the dim winds: in each there
     stands
A wild-eyed charioteer urging their flight.
Some look behind, as fiends pursued them
     there,
And yet I see no shapes but the keen stars:
Others, with burning eyes, lean forth, and
     drink
With eager lips the wind of their own speed,
As if the thing they loved fled on before,
And now, even now, they clasped it. Their
     bright locks
Stream like a comet's flashing hair: they all 139
Sweep onward.

Demogorgon. These are the immortal Hours,
Of whom thou didst demand. One waits for
     thee.

Asia. A spirit with a dreadful countenance
Checks its dark chariot by the craggy gulf.
Unlike thy brethren, ghastly charioteer,
Who art thou? Whither wouldst thou bear
     me? Speak!

Spirit. I am the shadow of a destiny

More dread than is my aspect: ere yon planet
Has set, the darkness which ascends with me
Shall wrap in lasting night heaven's kingless
     throne.

Asia. What meanest thou?   150

Panthea.   That terrible shadow floats
Up from its throne, as may the lurid smoke
Of earthquake-ruined cities o'er the sea.
Lo! it ascends the car; the coursers fly
Terrified: watch its path among the stars
Blackening the night!

Asia.   Thus I am answered: strange!

Panthea. See, near the verge, another
     chariot stays;
An ivory shell inlaid with crimson fire,
Which comes and goes within its sculptured
     rim
Of delicate strange tracery; the young spirit
That guides it has the dove-like eyes of
     hope;   160
How its soft smiles attract the soul! as light
Lures wingèd insects through the lampless air.

Spirit

My coursers are fed with the lightning,
    They drink of the whirlwind's stream,
And when the red morning is bright'ning
    They bathe in the fresh sunbeam;
    They have strength for their swiftness I
     deem,
Then ascend with me, daughter of Ocean.

I desire: and their speed makes night kindle;
    I fear: they outstrip the Typhoon;   170
Ere the cloud piled on Atlas can dwindle
    We encircle the earth and the moon:
    We shall rest from long labours at noon:
Then ascend with me, daughter of Ocean.

SCENE V.—*The Car pauses within a Cloud on
the top of a snowy Mountain.* ASIA,
PANTHEA, *and the* SPIRIT OF THE HOUR.

Spirit

On the brink of the night and the morning
    My coursers are wont to respire;
But the Earth has just whispered a warning
    That their flight must be swifter than fire:
    They shall drink the hot speed of desire!

Asia. Thou breathest on their nostrils, but
     my breath
Would give them swifter speed.

Spirit.   Alas! it could not.

Panthea. Oh Spirit! pause, and tell whence
  is the light
Which fills this cloud? the sun is yet unrisen.
  Spirit. The sun will rise not until noon.
    Apollo   10
Is held in heaven by wonder; and the light
Which fills this vapour, as the aëreal hue
Of fountain-gazing roses fills the water,
Flows from thy mighty sister.
  Panthea.   Yes, I feel—
  Asia. What is it with thee, sister? Thou art
    pale.
  Panthea. How thou art changed! I dare not
    look on thee;
I feel but see thee not. I scarce endure
The radiance of thy beauty. Some good change
Is working in the elements, which suffer
Thy presence thus unveiled. The Nereids tell
That on the day when the clear hyaline   21
Was cloven at thine uprise, and thou didst
  stand
Within a veinèd shell, which floated on
Over the calm floor of the crystal sea,
Among the Ægean isles, and by the shores
Which bear thy name; love, like the atmos-
  phere
Of the sun's fire filling the living world,
Burst from thee, and illumined earth and
  heaven
And the deep ocean and the sunless caves
And all that dwells within them; till grief
  cast   30
Eclipse upon the soul from which it came:
Such art thou now; nor is it I alone,
Thy sister, thy companion, thine own chosen
  one,
But the whole world which seeks thy sym-
  pathy.
Hearest thou not sounds i' the air which speak
  the love
Of all articulate beings? Feelest thou not
The inanimate winds enamoured of thee?
  List!
                                    [*Music.*
  Asia. Thy words are sweeter than aught else
    but his
Whose echoes they are: yet all love is sweet,
Given or returned. Common as light is love,
And its familiar voice wearies not ever.   41
Like the wide heaven, the all-sustaining air,
It makes the reptile equal to the God:
They who inspire it most are fortunate,
As I am now; but those who feel it most
Are happier still, after long sufferings,

As I shall soon become.
  Panthea.   List! Spirits speak.

Voice in the Air, singing.
Life of Life! thy lips enkindle
  With their love the breath between them;
And thy smiles before they dwindle   50
  Make the cold air fire; then screen them
In those looks, where whoso gazes
Faints, entangled in their mazes.

Child of Light! thy limbs are burning
  Through the vest which seems to hide them;
As the radiant lines of morning
  Through the clouds ere they divide them;
And this atmosphere divinest
Shrouds thee wheresoe'er thou shinest.

Fair are others; none beholds thee,   60
  But thy voice sounds low and tender
Like the fairest, for it folds thee
  From the sight, that liquid splendour,
And all feel, yet see thee never,
As I feel now, lost for ever!

Lamp of Earth! where'er thou movest
  Its dim shapes are clad with brightness,
And the souls of whom thou lovest
  Walk upon the winds with lightness,
Till they fail, as I am failing,   70
Dizzy, lost, yet unbewailing!

Asia
My soul is an enchanted boat,
  Which, like a sleeping swan, doth float
Upon the silver waves of thy sweet singing;
  And thine doth like an angel sit
  Beside a helm conducting it,
Whilst all the winds with melody are ringing.
  It seems to float ever, for ever,
  Upon that many-winding river,
  Between mountains, woods, abysses,   80
  A paradise of wildernesses!
Till, like one in slumber bound,
Borne to the ocean, I float down, around,
Into a sea profound, of ever-spreading sound:

  Meanwhile thy spirit lifts its pinions
  In music's most serene dominions;
Catching the winds that fan that happy
  heaven.
  And we sail on, away, afar,
  Without a course, without a star,
But, by the instinct of sweet music driven; 90

Till through Elysian garden islets
By thee, most beautiful of pilots,
Where never mortal pinnace glided,
The boat of my desire is guided:
Realms where the air we breathe is love,
Which in the winds and on the waves doth
    move,
Harmonizing this earth with what we feel
    above.

We have passed Age's icy caves,
And Manhood's dark and tossing waves,
And Youth's smooth ocean, smiling to betray:
Beyond the glassy gulfs we flee   101
Of shadow-peopled Infancy,
Through Death and Birth, to a diviner day;
A paradise of vaulted bowers,
Lit by downward-gazing flowers,
And watery paths that wind between
Wildernesses calm and green,
Peopled by shapes too bright to see,
And rest, having beheld; somewhat like thee;
Which walk upon the sea, and chant melodi-
    ously!   110

END OF THE SECOND ACT

ACT III

SCENE I.—*Heaven.* JUPITER *on his Throne;*
THETIS *and the other Deities assembled.*

Jupiter. Ye congregated powers of heaven,
    who share
The glory and the strength of him ye serve,
Rejoice! henceforth I am omnipotent,
All else had been subdued to me; alone
The soul of man, like unextinguished fire,
Yet burns towards heaven with fierce re-
    proach, and doubt,
And lamentation, and reluctant prayer,
Hurling up insurrection, which might make
Our antique empire insecure, though built
On eldest faith, and hell's coeval, fear;   10
And though my curses through the pendulous
    air,
Like snow on herbless peaks, fall flake by
    flake,
And cling to it; though under my wrath's
    night
It climbs the crags of life, step after step,
Which wound it, as ice wounds unsandalled
    feet,
It yet remains supreme o'er misery,

Aspiring, unrepressed, yet soon to fall:
Even now have I begotten a strange wonder,
That fatal child, the terror of the earth,
Who waits but till the destined hour arrive, 20
Bearing from Demogorgon's vacant throne
The dreadful might of ever-living limbs
Which clothed that awful spirit unbeheld,
To redescend, and trample out the spark.
Pour forth heaven's wine, Idæan Ganymede,
And let it fill the Dædal cups like fire,
And from the flower-inwoven soil divine
Ye all-triumphant harmonies arise,
As dew from earth under the twilight stars:
Drink! be the nectar circling through your
    veins   30
The soul of joy, ye ever-living Gods,
Till exultation burst in one wide voice
Like music from Elysian winds.
                      And thou
Ascend beside me, veilèd in the light
Of the desire which makes thee one with me,
Thetis, bright image of eternity!
When thou didst cry, 'Insufferable might!
God! Spare me! I sustain not the quick
    flames,
The penetrating presence; all my being,
Like him whom the Numidian seps did thaw
Into a dew with poison, is dissolved,   41
Sinking through its foundations': even then
Two mighty spirits, mingling, made a third
Mightier than either, which, unbodied now,
Between us floats, felt, although unbeheld,
Waiting the incarnation, which ascends,
(Hear ye the thunder of the fiery wheels
Griding the winds?) from Demogorgon's
    throne.
Victory! victory! Feel'st thou not, O world,
The earthquake of his chariot thundering up 50
Olympus?
      [*The Car of the* HOUR *arrives.* DEMO-
      GORGON *descends, and moves towards*
      the Throne of JUPITER.
Awful shape, what art thou? Speak!
Demogorgon. Eternity. Demand no direr
    name.
Descend, and follow me down the abyss.
I am thy child, as thou wert Saturn's child;
Mightier than thee: and we must dwell to-
    gether
Henceforth in darkness. Lift thy lightnings
    not.
The tyranny of heaven none may retain,
Or reassume, or hold, succeeding thee:
Yet if thou wilt, as 'tis the destiny

Of trodden worms to writhe till they are dead,
Put forth thy might.   61
 Jupiter.   Detested prodigy!
Even thus beneath the deep Titanian prisons
I trample thee! thou lingerest?
                          Mercy! mercy!
No pity, no release, no respite! Oh,
That thou wouldst make mine enemy my
    judge,
Even where he hangs, seared by my long re-
    venge,
On Caucasus! he would not doom me thus.
Gentle, and just, and dreadless, is he not
The monarch of the world? What then art
    thou?
No refuge! no appeal!
                   Sink with me then, 70
We two will sink on the wide waves of ruin,
Even as a vulture and a snake outspent
Drop, twisted in inextricable fight,
Into a shoreless sea. Let hell unlock
Its mounded oceans of tempestuous fire,
And whelm on them into the bottomless void
This desolated world, and thee, and me,
The conqueror and the conquered, and the
    wreck
Of that for which they combated.
                              Ai! Ai!
The elements obey me not. I sink   80
Dizzily down, ever, for ever, down.
And, like a cloud, mine enemy above
Darkens my fall with victory! Ai, Ai!

SCENE II.—*The Mouth of a great River in
the Island Atlantis.* OCEAN *is discovered
reclining near the Shore;* APOLLO *stands
beside him.*

 Ocean. He fell, thou sayest, beneath his
    conqueror's frown?
 Apollo. Ay, when the strife was ended which
    made dim
The orb I rule, and shook the solid stars,
The terrors of his eye illumined heaven
With sanguine light, through the thick ragged
    skirts
Of the victorious darkness, as he fell:
Like the last glare of day's red agony,
Which, from a rent among the fiery clouds,
Burns far along the tempest-wrinkled deep.
 Ocean. He sunk to the abyss? To the dark
    void?   10
 Apollo. An eagle so caught in some bursting
    cloud

On Caucasus, his thunder-baffled wings
Entangled in the whirlwind, and his eyes
Which gazed on the undazzling sun, now
    blinded
By the white lightning, while the ponderous
    hail
Beats on his struggling form, which sinks at
    length
Prone, and the aëreal ice clings over it.
 Ocean. Henceforth the fields of heaven-
    reflecting sea
Which are my realm, will heave, unstained
    with blood,
Beneath the uplifting winds, like plains of
    corn   20
Swayed by the summer air; my streams will
    flow
Round many-peopled continents, and round
Fortunate isles; and from their glassy thrones
Blue Proteus and his humid nymphs shall
    mark
The shadow of fair ships, as mortals see
The floating bark of the light-laden moon
With that white star, its sightless pilot's crest,
Borne down the rapid sunset's ebbing sea;
Tracking their path no more by blood and
    groans,
And desolation, and the mingled voice   30
Of slavery and command; but by the light
Of wave-reflected flowers, and floating odours,
And music soft, and mild, free, gentle voices,
And sweetest music, such as spirits love.
 Apollo. And I shall gaze not on the deeds
    which make
My mind obscure with sorrow, as eclipse
Darkens the sphere I guide; but list, I hear
The small, clear, silver lute of the young Spirit
That sits i' the morning star.
 Ocean.   Thou must away;
Thy steeds will pause at even, till when fare-
    well: 40
The loud deep calls me home even now to
    feed it
With azure calm out of the emerald urns
Which stand for ever full beside my throne.
Behold the Nereids under the green sea,
Their wavering limbs borne on the wind-like
    stream,
Their white arms lifted o'er their streaming
    hair
With garlands pied and starry sea-flower
    crowns,
Hastening to grace their mighty sister's joy.
                   [*A sound of waves is heard.*

It is the unpastured sea hungering for calm.
Peace, monster; I come now. Farewell.
Apollo.   Farewell. 50

SCENE III.—*Caucasus.* PROMETHEUS HER-
    CULES, IONE, *the* EARTH, SPIRITS, ASIA,
    and PANTHEA, *borne in the Car with the*
    SPIRIT OF THE HOUR. HERCULES *unbinds*
    PROMETHEUS, *who descends.*

Hercules. Most glorious among Spirits, thus
    doth strength
To wisdom, courage, and long-suffering love,
And thee, who art the form they animate,
Minister like a slave.
    Prometheus.   Thy gentle words
Are sweeter even than freedom long desired
And long delayed.
                        Asia, thou light of life,
Shadow of beauty unbeheld: and ye,
Fair sister nymphs, who made long years of
    pain
Sweet to remember, through your love and
    care:
Henceforth we will not part. There is a cave,
All overgrown with trailing odorous plants, 11
Which curtain out the day with leaves and
    flowers,
And paved with veinèd emerald, and a foun-
    tain
Leaps in the midst with an awakening sound.
From its curved roof the mountain's frozen
    tears
Like snow, or silver, or long diamond spires,
Hang downward, raining forth a doubtful
    light:
And there is heard the ever-moving air,
Whispering without from tree to tree, and
    birds,
And bees; and all around are mossy seats, 20
And the rough walls are clothed with long soft
    grass;
A simple dwelling, which shall be our own;
Where we will sit and talk of time and
    change,
As the world ebbs and flows, ourselves un-
    changed.
What can hide man from mutability?
And if ye sigh, then I will smile; and thou,
Ione, shalt chant fragments of sea-music,
Until I weep, when ye shall smile away
The tears she brought, which yet were sweet
    to shed.   29

We will entangle buds and flowers and beams
Which twinkle on the fountain's brim, and
    make
Strange combinations out of common things,
Like human babes in their brief innocence;
And we will search, with looks and words
    of love,
For hidden thoughts, each lovelier than the
    last,
Our unexhausted spirits; and like lutes
Touched by the skill of the enamoured wind,
Weave harmonies divine, yet ever new,
From difference sweet where discord cannot
    be;
And hither come, sped on the charmèd winds,
Which meet from all the points of heaven, as
    bees   41
From every flower aëreal Enna feeds,
At their known island-homes in Himera,
The echoes of the human world, which tell
Of the low voice of love, almost unheard,
And dove-eyed pity's murmured pain, and
    music,
Itself the echo of the heart, and all
That tempers or improves man's life, now
    free;
And lovely apparitions,—dim at first,
Then radiant, as the mind, arising bright   50
From the embrace of beauty (whence the
    forms
Of which these are the phantoms) casts on
    them
The gathered rays which are reality—
Shall visit us, the progeny immortal
Of Painting, Sculpture, and rapt Poesy,
And arts, though unimagined, yet to be.
The wandering voices and the shadows these
Of all that man becomes, the mediators
Of that best worship, love, by him and us
Given and returned; swift shapes and sounds,
    which grow   60
More fair and soft as man grows wise and
    kind,
And, veil by veil, evil and error fall:
Such virtue has the cave and place around.
    [*Turning to the* SPIRIT OF THE HOUR.
For thee, fair Spirit, one toil remains. Ione,
Give her that curvèd shell, which Proteus
    old
Made Asia's nuptial boon, breathing within it
A voice to be accomplished, and which thou
Didst hide in grass under the hollow rock.
    Ione. Thou most desired Hour, more loved
    and lovely

Than all thy sisters, this is the mystic shell; 70
See the pale azure fading into silver
Lining it with a soft yet glowing light:
Looks it not like lulled music sleeping there?
　　Spirit. It seems in truth the fairest shell
　　　of Ocean:
Its sound must be at once both sweet and
　　strange.
　　Prometheus. Go, borne over the cities of
　　　mankind
On whirlwind-footed coursers: once again
Outspeed the sun around the orbèd world;
And as thy chariot cleaves the kindling air,
Thou breathe into the many-folded shell, 　80
Loosening its mighty music; it shall be
As thunder mingled with clear echoes: then
Return; and thou shalt dwell beside our cave.
And thou, O, Mother Earth!—
　　The Earth. 　　　　　　I hear, I feel;
Thy lips are on me, and their touch runs
　　down
Even to the adamantine central gloom
Along these marble nerves; 'tis life, 'tis joy,
And through my withered, old, and icy frame
The warmth of an immortal youth shoots
　　down
Circling. Henceforth the many children fair 90
Folded in my sustaining arms; all plants,
And creeping forms, and insects rainbow-
　　winged,
And birds, and beasts, and fish, and human
　　shapes,
Which drew disease and pain from my wan
　　bosom,
Draining the poison of despair, shall take
And interchange sweet nutriment; to me
Shall they become like sister-antelopes
By one fair dam, snow-white and swift as
　　wind,
Nursed among lilies near a brimming stream.
The dew-mists of my sunless sleep shall
　　float 　　　　　　　　　　　　　100
Under the stars like balm: night-folded flowers
Shall suck unwithering hues in their repose:
And men and beasts in happy dreams shall
　　gather
Strength for the coming day, and all its joy:
And death shall be the last embrace of her
Who takes the life she gave, even as a mother
Folding her child, says, 'Leave me not again.'
　　Asia. Oh, mother! wherefore speak the name
　　　of death?
Cease they to love, and move, and breathe,
　　and speak,

Who die?
　　The Earth. It would avail not to reply; 110
Thou art immortal, and this tongue is known
But to the uncommunicating dead.
Death is the veil which those who live call
　　life:
They sleep, and it is lifted: and meanwhile
In mild variety the seasons mild
With rainbow-skirted showers, and odorous
　　winds,
And long blue meteors cleansing the dull night,
And the life-kindling shafts of the keen sun's
All-piercing bow, and the dew-mingled rain 120
Of the calm moonbeams, a soft influence mild,
Shall clothe the forests and the fields, ay, even
The crag-built deserts of the barren deep,
With ever-living leaves, and fruits, and
　　flowers.
And thou! There is a cavern where my spirit
Was panted forth in anguish whilst thy pain
Made my heart mad, and those who did in-
　　hale it
Became mad too, and built a temple there,
And spoke, and were oracular, and lured
The erring nations round to mutual war.
And faithless faith, such as Jove kept with
　　thee; 　　　　　　　　　　　　130
Which breath now rises, as amongst tall weeds
A violet's exhalation, and it fills
With a serener light and crimson air
Intense, yet soft, the rocks and woods around;
It feeds the quick growth of the serpent vine,
And the dark linkèd ivy tangling wild,
And budding, blown, or odour-faded blooms
Which star the winds with points of coloured
　　light,
As they rain through them, and bright golden
　　globes
Of fruit, suspended in their own green heaven,
And through their veinèd leaves and amber
　　stems 　　　　　　　　　　　　140
The flowers whose purple and translucid bowls
Stand ever mantling with aëreal dew,
The drink of spirits: and it circles round,
Like the soft waving wings of noonday dreams,
Inspiring calm and happy thoughts, like
　　mine,
And thou art thus restored. This cave is thine.
Arise! Appear!
[A SPIRIT *rises in the likeness of a winged*
　　child.
　　　　　　　　This is my torch-bearer;
Who let his lamp out in old time gazing
On eyes from which he kindled it anew 　150

With love, which is as fire, sweet daughter
　　mine,
For such is that within thine own. Run, way-
　　ward,
And guide this company beyond the peak
Of Bacchic Nysia, Mænad-haunted mountain,
And beyond Indus and its tribute rivers,
Trampling the torrent streams and glassy lakes
With feet unwet, unwearied, undelaying,
And up the green ravine, across the vale,
Beside the windless and crystalline pool,
Where ever lies, on unerasing waves,　　　160
The image of a temple, built above,
Distinct with column, arch, and architrave,
And palm-like capital, and over-wrought,
And populous with most living imagery,
Praxitelean shapes, whose marble smiles
Fill the hushed air with everlasting love.
It is deserted now, but once it bore
Thy name, Prometheus; there the emulous
　　youths
Bore to thy honour through the divine gloom
The lamp which was thine emblem; even as
　　those　　　170
Who bear the untransmitted torch of hope
Into the grave, across the night of life,
As thou hast borne it most triumphantly
To this far goal of Time. Depart, farewell.
Beside that temple is the destined cave.

SCENE IV.—*A Forest. In the Background a
Cave.* PROMETHEUS, ASIA, PANTHEA,
IONE, *and the* SPIRIT OF THE EARTH.

Ione. Sister, it is not earthly: how it glides
Under the leaves! how on its head there burns
A light, like a green star, whose emerald
　　beams
Are twined with its fair hair! how, as it
　　moves,
The splendour drops in flakes upon the grass!
Knowest thou it?
　　Panthea.　　　It is the delicate spirit
That guides the earth through heaven. From
　　afar
The populous constellations call that light
The loveliest of the planets; and sometimes
It floats along the spray of the salt sea,　　10
Or makes its chariot of a foggy cloud,
Or walks through fields or cities while men
　　sleep,
Or o'er the mountain tops, or down the rivers,
Or through the green waste wilderness, as
　　now,

Wondering at all it sees. Before Jove reigned
It loved our sister Asia, and it came
Each leisure hour to drink the liquid light
Out of her eyes, for which it said it thirsted
As one bit by a dipsas, and with her
It made its childish confidence, and told her　20
All it had known or seen, for it saw much,
Yet idly reasoned what it saw; and called
　　her—
For whence it sprung it knew not, nor do I—
Mother, dear mother.
　　The Spirit of the Earth (running to Asia).
　　Mother, dearest mother;
May I then talk with thee as I was wont?
May I then hide my eyes in thy soft arms,
After thy looks have made them tired of
　　joy?
May I then play beside thee the long noons,
When work is none in the bright silent air?
　　Asia. I love thee, gentlest being, and hence-
　　forth　　　30
Can cherish thee unenvied: speak, I pray:
Thy simple talk once solaced, now delights.
　　Spirit of the Earth. Mother, I am grown
　　wiser, though a child
Cannot be wise like thee, within this day;
And happier too; happier and wiser both.
Thou knowest that toads, and snakes, and
　　loathly worms,
And venomous and malicious beasts, and
　　boughs
That bore ill berries in the woods, were ever
An hindrance to my walks o'er the green
　　world:
And that, among the haunts of humankind,　40
Hard-featured men, or with proud, angry looks,
Or cold, staid gait, or false and hollow smiles,
Or the dull sneer of self-loved ignorance,
Or other such foul masks, with which ill
　　thoughts
Hide that fair being whom we spirits call
　　man;
And women too, ugliest of all things evil,
(Though fair, even in a world where thou art
　　fair,
When good and kind, free and sincere like
　　thee),
When false or frowning made me sick at
　　heart
To pass them, though they slept, and I un-
　　seen.　　　50
Well, my path lately lay through a great city
Into the woody hills surrounding it:
A sentinel was sleeping at the gate:

When there was heard a sound, so loud, it
    shook
The towers amid the moonlight, yet more
    sweet
Than any voice but thine, sweetest of all;
A long, long sound, as it would never end:
And all the inhabitants leaped suddenly
Out of their rest, and gathered in the streets,
Looking in wonder up to Heaven, while yet 60
The music pealed along. I hid myself
Within a fountain in the public square,
Where I lay like the reflex of the moon
Seen in a wave under green leaves; and soon
Those ugly human shapes and visages
Of which I spoke as having wrought me pain,
Passed floating through the air, and fading still
Into the winds that scattered them; and those
From whom they passed seemed mild and
    lovely forms
After some foul disguise had fallen, and all 70
Were somewhat changed, and after brief sur-
    prise
And greetings of delighted wonder, all
Went to their sleep again: and when the dawn
Came, wouldst thou think that toads, and
    snakes, and efts,
Could e'er be beautiful? yet so they were,
And that with little change of shape or hue:
All things had put their evil nature off:
I cannot tell my joy, when o'er a lake
Upon a drooping bough with nightshade
    twined,
I saw two azure halcyons clinging downward
And thinning one bright bunch of amber ber-
    ries, 81
With quick long beaks, and in the deep there
    lay
Those lovely forms imaged as in a sky;
So, with my thoughts full of these happy
    changes,
We meet again, the happiest change of all.
    Asia. And never will we part, till thy chaste
    sister
Who guides the frozen and inconstant moon
Will look on thy more warm and equal light
Till her heart thaw like flakes of April snow
And love thee.
    Spirit of the Earth. What; as Asia loves
    Prometheus? 90
    Asia. Peace, wanton, thou art yet not old
    enough.
Think ye by gazing on each other's eyes
To multiply your lovely selves, and fill
With spherèd fires the interlunar air?

    Spirit of the Earth. Nay, mother, while my
    sister trims her lamp
'Tis hard I should go darkling.
    Asia.   Listen; look!
    [*The* SPIRIT OF THE HOUR *enters.*
    Prometheus. We feel what thou hast heard
    and seen: yet speak.
    Spirit of the Hour. Soon as the sound had
    ceased whose thunder filled
The abysses of the sky and the wide earth,
There was a change: the impalpable thin air
And the all-circling sunlight were trans-
    formed, 101
As if the sense of love dissolved in them
Had folded itself round the spherèd world.
My vision then grew clear, and I could see
Into the mysteries of the universe:
Dizzy as with delight I floated down,
Winnowing the lightsome air with languid
    plumes,
My coursers sought their birthplace in the
    sun,
Where they henceforth will live exempt from
    toil,
Pasturing flowers of vegetable fire; 110
And where my moonlike car will stand within
A temple, gazed upon by Phidian forms
Of thee, and Asia, and the Earth, and me,
And you fair nymphs looking the love we
    feel,—
In memory of the tidings it has borne,—
Beneath a dome fretted with graven flowers,
Poised on twelve columns of resplendent stone,
And open to the bright and liquid sky.
Yoked to it by an amphisbaenic snake 119
The likeness of those wingèd steeds will mock
The flight from which they find repose. Alas,
Whither has wandered now my partial tongue
When all remains untold which ye would hear?
As I have said, I floated to the earth:
It was, as it is still, the pain of bliss
To move, to breathe, to be; I wandering went
Among the haunts and dwellings of mankind,
And first was disappointed not to see
Such mighty change as I had felt within
Expressed in outward things; but soon I
    looked, 130
And behold, thrones were kingless, and men
    walked
One with the other even as spirits do,
None fawned, none trampled; hate, disdain, or
    fear,
Self-love or self-contempt, on human brows
No more inscribed, as o'er the gate of hell,

'All hope abandon ye who enter here';
None frowned, none trembled, none with eager
　　fear
Gazed on another's eye of cold command,
Until the subject of a tyrant's will
Became, worse fate, the abject of his own, 140
Which spurred him, like an outspent horse,
　　to death.
None wrought his lips in truth-entangling lines
Which smiled the lie his tongue disdained to
　　speak;
None, with firm sneer, trod out in his own
　　heart
The sparks of love and hope till there re-
　　mained
Those bitter ashes, a soul self-consumed,
And the wretch crept a vampire among men,
Infecting all with his own hideous ill;
None talked that common, false, cold, hollow
　　talk
Which makes the heart deny the *yes* it
　　breathes,   150
Yet question that unmeant hypocrisy
With such a self-mistrust as has no name.
And women, too, frank, beautiful, and kind
As the free heaven which rains fresh light
　　and dew
On the wide earth, past; gentle radiant forms,
From custom's evil taint exempt and pure;
Speaking the wisdom once they could not
　　think,
Looking emotions once they feared to feel,
And changed to all which once they dared
　　not be,
Yet being now, made earth like heaven; nor
　　pride,   160
Nor jealousy, nor envy, nor ill shame,
The bitterest of those drops of treasured gall,
Spoilt the sweet taste of the nepenthe, love.

Thrones, altars, judgment-seats, and prisons;
　　wherein,
And beside which, by wretched men were
　　borne
Sceptres, tiaras, swords, and chains, and tomes
Of reasoned wrong, glozed on by ignorance,
Were like those monstrous and barbaric
　　shapes,
The ghosts of a no-more-remembered fame,
Which, from their unworn obelisks, look forth
In triumph o'er the palaces and tombs   171
Of those who were their conquerors: moulder-
　　ing round,
These imaged to the pride of kings and priests

A dark yet mighty faith, a power as wide
As is the world it wasted, and are now
But an astonishment; even so the tools
And emblems of its last captivity,
Amid the dwellings of the peopled earth,
Stand, not o'erthrown, but unregarded now.
And those foul shapes, abhorred by god and
　　man,—   180
Which, under many a name and many a form
Strange, savage, ghastly, dark and execrable,
Were Jupiter, the tyrant of the world;
And which the nations, panic-stricken, served
With blood, and hearts broken by long hope,
　　and love
Dragged to his altars soiled and garlandless,
And slain amid men's unreclaiming tears,
Flattering the thing they feared, which fear
　　was hate,—
Frown, mouldering fast, o'er their abandoned
　　shrines:
The painted veil, by those who were, called
　　life,   190
Which mimicked, as with colours idly spread,
All men believed or hoped, is torn aside;
The loathsome mask has fallen, the man re-
　　mains
Sceptreless, free, uncircumscribed, but man
Equal, unclassed, tribeless, and nationless,
Exempt from awe, worship, degree, the king
Over himself; just, gentle, wise: but man
Passionless?——no, yet free from guilt or
　　pain,
Which were, for his will made or suffered
　　them,
Nor yet exempt, though ruling them like
　　slaves,   200
From chance, and death, and mutability,
The clogs of that which else might oversoar
The loftiest star of unascended heaven,
Pinnacled dim in the intense inane.

END OF THE THIRD ACT

ACT IV

SCENE.—*A Part of the Forest near the Cave
of* PROMETHEUS. PANTHEA *and* IONE *are
sleeping: they awaken gradually during
the first Song.*

Voice of unseen Spirits
The pale stars are gone!
For the sun, their swift shepherd,
To their folds them compelling,

In the depths of the dawn,
Hastes, in meteor-eclipsing array, and they flee
Beyond his blue dwelling,
As fawns flee the leopard.
But where are ye?

*A Train of dark Forms and Shadows passes
by confusedly, singing*
Here, oh, here:
We bear the bier   10
Of the Father of many a cancelled year!
Spectres we
Of the dead Hours be,
We bear Time to his tomb in eternity.

Strew, oh, strew
Hair, not yew!
Wet the dusty pall with tears, not dew!
Be the faded flowers
Of Death's bare bowers
Spread on the corpse of the King of Hours!   20

Haste, oh, haste!
As shades are chased,
Trembling, by day, from heaven's blue waste.
We melt away,
Like dissolving spray,
From the children of a diviner day,
With the lullaby
Of winds that die
On the bosom of their own harmony!

Ione
What dark forms were they?   30

Panthea
The past Hours weak and gray,
With the spoil which their toil
Raked together
From the conquest but One could foil.

Ione
Have they passed?

Panthea
They have passed;
They outspeeded the blast,
While 'tis said, they are fled:

Ione
Whither, oh, whither?

Panthea
To the dark, to the past, to the dead.

Voice of unseen Spirits
Bright clouds float in heaven,   40
Dew-stars gleam on earth,
Waves assemble on ocean,
They are gathered and driven
By the storm of delight, by the panic of glee!
They shake with emotion,
They dance in their mirth.
But where are ye?

The pine boughs are singing
Old songs with new gladness,
The billows and fountains   50
Fresh music are flinging,
Likes the notes of a spirit from land and from
sea;
The storms mock the mountains
With the thunder of gladness.
But where are ye?

Ione. What charioteers are these?
Panthea.   Where are their chariots?

Semichorus of Hours
The voice of the Spirits of Air and of Earth
Have drawn back the figured curtain of
sleep
Which covered our being and darkened our
birth
In the deep.

A Voice
In the deep?

Semichorus II
          Oh, below the deep.   60

Semichorus I
An hundred ages we had been kept
Cradled in visions of hate and care,
And each one who waked as his brother slept,
Found the truth—

Semichorus II
          Worse than his visions were!

Semichorus I
We have heard the lute of Hope in sleep;
We have known the voice of Love in
dreams;
We have felt the wand of Power, and leap—

Semichorus II
As the billows leap in the morning beams!

Chorus

Weave the dance on the floor of the breeze,
  Pierce with song heaven's silent light,   70
Enchant the day that too swiftly flees,
  To check its flight ere the cave of Night.

Once the hungry Hours were hounds
  Which chased the day like a bleeding deer,
And it limped and stumbled with many
    wounds
  Through the nightly dells of the desert year.

But now, oh weave the mystic measure
  Of music, and dance, and shapes of light,
Let the Hours, and the spirits of might and
    pleasure,
  Like the clouds and sunbeams, unite.

A Voice
              Unite!   80
Panthea. See, where the Spirits of the human mind
Wrapped in sweet sounds, as in bright veils,
approach.

Chorus of Spirits
  We join the throng
  Of the dance and the song,
By the whirlwind of gladness borne along,
  As the flying-fish leap
  From the Indian deep,
And mix with the sea-birds, half asleep.

Chorus of Hours
Whence come ye, so wild and so fleet,
For sandals of lightning are on your feet, 90
And your wings are soft and swift as thought,
And your eyes are as love which is veilèd not?

Chorus of Spirits
  We come from the mind
  Of human kind
Which was late so dusk, and obscene, and
    blind,
  Now 'tis an ocean
  Of clear emotion,
A heaven of serene and mighty motion.

  From that deep abyss   100
  Of wonder and bliss,
Whose caverns are crystal palaces;
  From those skiey towers
  Where Thought's crowned powers
Sit watching your dance, ye happy Hours!

  From the dim recesses
  Of woven caresses,
Where lovers catch ye by your loose tresses;
  From the azure isles,
  Where sweet Wisdom smiles,
Delaying your ships with her siren wiles. 110

  From the temples high
  Of Man's ear and eye,
Roofed over Sculpture and Poesy;
  From the murmurings
  Of the unsealed springs
Where Science bedews her Dædal wings.

  Years after years,
  Through blood, and tears,
And a thick hell of hatreds, and hopes, and
    fears;
  We waded and flew,   120
  And the islets were few
Where the bud-blighted flowers of happiness
    grew.

  Our feet now, every palm,
  Are sandalled with calm,
And the dew of our wings is a rain of balm;
  And, beyond our eyes,
  The human love lies
Which makes all it gazes on Paradise.

Chorus of Spirits and Hours
  Then weave the web of the mystic measure;
From the depths of the sky and the ends of
    the earth,
  Come, swift Spirits of might and of pleas-
    ure,   131
Fill the dance and the music of mirth,
  As the waves of a thousand streams rush by
  To an ocean of splendour and harmony!

Chorus of Spirits
  Our spoil is won,
  Our task is done,
We are free to dive, or soar, or run;
  Beyond and around,
  Or within the bound
Which clips the world with darkness round.

  We'll pass the eyes   141
  Of the starry skies
Into the hoar deep to colonize:
  Death, Chaos, and Night,
  From the sound of our flight,
Shall flee, like mist from a tempest's might.

And Earth, Air, and Light,
And the Spirit of Might,
Which drives round the stars in their fiery
　　flight;
And Love, Thought, and Breath,　150
The powers that quell Death,
Wherever we soar shall assemble beneath.

And our singing shall build
In the void's loose field
A world for the Spirit of Wisdom to wield;
We will take our plan
From the new world of man,
And our work shall be called the Promethean.

Chorus of Hours

Break the dance, and scatter the song;
Let some depart, and some remain.　160

Semichorus I

We, beyond heaven, are driven along:

Semichorus II

Us the enchantments of earth retain:

Semichorus I

Ceaseless, and rapid, and fierce, and free,
With the Spirits which build a new earth and
　　sea,
And a heaven where yet heaven could never
　　be;

Semichorus II

Solemn, and slow, and serene, and bright,
Leading the Day and outspeeding the Night,
With the powers of a world of perfect light;

Semichorus I

We whirl, singing loud, round the gathering
　　sphere,
Till the trees, and the beasts, and the clouds
　　appear　170
From its chaos made calm by love, not fear.

Semichorus II

We encircle the ocean and mountains of earth,
And the happy forms of its death and birth
Change to the music of our sweet mirth.

Chorus of Hours and Spirits

Break the dance, and scatter the song,
Let some depart, and some remain,
Wherever we fly we lead along
In leashes, like starbeams, soft yet strong,

The clouds that are heavy with love's sweet
　　rain.

Panthea. Ha! they are gone!
Ione.　　　　　Yet feel you no delight　180
From the past sweetness?
Panthea.　　　　As the bare green hill
When some soft cloud vanishes into rain,
Laughs with a thousand drops of sunny water
To the unpavilioned sky!
Ione.　　　　　Even whilst we speak
New notes arise. What is that awful sound?
Panthea. 'Tis the deep music of the rolling
　　world
Kindling within the strings of the waved air
Æolian modulations.
Ione.　　　　　Listen too,
How every pause is filled with under-notes,
Clear, silver, icy, keen, awakening tones,　190
Which pierce the sense, and live within the
　　soul,
As the sharp stars pierce winter's crystal air
And gaze upon themselves within the sea.
Panthea. But see where through two open-
　　ings in the forest
Which hanging branches overcanopy,
And where two runnels of a rivulet,
Between the close moss violet-inwoven,
Have made their path of melody, like sisters
Who part with sighs that they may meet in
　　smiles,
Turning their dear disunion to an isle　200
Of lovely grief, a wood of sweet sad thoughts;
Two visions of strange radiance float upon
The ocean-like enchantment of strong sound,
Which flows intenser, keener, deeper yet
Under the ground and through the windless
　　air.
Ione. I see a chariot like that thinnest boat,
In which the Mother of the Months is borne
By ebbing light into her western cave,
When she upsprings from interlunar dreams;
O'er which is curved an orblike canopy　210
Of gentle darkness, and the hills and woods,
Distinctly seen through that dusk aery veil,
Regard like shapes in an enchanter's glass;
Its wheels are solid clouds, azure and gold,
Such as the genii of the thunderstorm
Pile on the floor of the illumined sea
When the sun rushes under it; they roll
And move and grow as with an inward wind;
Within it sits a wingèd infant, white
Its countenance, like the whiteness of bright
　　snow,　220

Its plumes are as feathers of sunny frost,
Its limbs gleam white, through the wind-
   flowing folds
Of its white robe, woof of ethereal pearl.
Its hair is white, the brightness of white light
Scattered in strings; yet its two eyes are
   heavens
Of liquid darkness, which the Deity
Within seems pouring, as a storm is poured
From jaggèd clouds, out of their arrowy
   lashes,
Tempering the cold and radiant air around,
With fire that is not brightness; in its hand
It sways a quivering moonbeam, from whose
   point   231
A guiding power directs the chariot's prow
Over its wheelèd clouds, which as they roll
Over the grass, and flowers, and waves, wake
   sounds,
Sweet as a singing rain of silver dew.
   Panthea. And from the other opening in
   the wood
Rushes, with loud and whirlwind harmony,
A sphere, which is as many thousand spheres,
Solid as crystal, yet through all its mass
Flow, as through empty space, music and
   light: 240
Ten thousand orbs involving and involved,
Purple and azure, white, and green, and
   golden,
Sphere within sphere; and every space between
Peopled with unimaginable shapes,
Such as ghosts dream dwell in the lampless
   deep,
Yet each inter-transpicuous, and they whirl
Over each other with a thousand motions,
Upon a thousand sightless axles spinning,
And with the force of self-destroying swift-
   ness,
Intensely, slowly, solemnly roll on,   250
Kindling with mingled sounds, and many tones,
Intelligible words and music wild.
With mighty whirl the multitudinous orb
Grinds the bright brook into an azure mist
Of elemental subtlety, like light;
And the wild odour of the forest flowers,
The music of the living grass and air,
The emerald light of leaf-entangled beams
Round its intense yet self-conflicting speed,
Seem kneaded into one aëreal mass   260
Which drowns the sense. Within the orb itself,
Pillowed upon its alabaster arms,
Like to a child o'erwearied with sweet toil,
On its own folded wings, and wavy hair,

The Spirit of the Earth is laid asleep,
And you can see its little lips are moving,
Amid the changing light of their own smiles,
Like one who talks of what he loves in dream.
   Ione. 'Tis only mocking the orb's harmony.
   Panthea. And from a star upon its forehead,
   shoot,   270
Like swords of azure fire, or golden spears
With tyrant-quelling myrtle overtwined,
Embleming heaven and earth united now,
Vast beams like spokes of some invisible wheel
Which whirl as the orb whirls, swifter than
   thought,
Filling the abyss with sun-like lightenings,
And perpendicular now, and now transverse,
Pierce the dark soil, and as they pierce and
   pass,
Make bare the secrets of the earth's deep
   heart;
Infinite mines of adamant and gold,   280
Valueless stones, and unimagined gems,
And caverns on crystalline columns poised
With vegetable silver overspread;
Wells of unfathomed fire, and water springs
Whence the great sea, even as a child is fed,
Whose vapours clothe earth's monarch
   mountain-tops
With kingly, ermine snow. The beams flash on
And make appear the melancholy ruins
Of cancelled cycles; anchors, beaks of ships;
Planks turned to marble; quivers, helms, and
   spears,   290
And gorgon-headed targes, and the wheels
Of scythèd chariots, and the emblazonry
Of trophies, standards, and armorial beasts,
Round which death laughed, sepulchred em-
   blems
Of dead destruction, ruin within ruin!
The wrecks beside of many a city vast,
Whose population which the earth grew over
Was mortal, but not human; see, they lie,
Their monstrous works, and uncouth skeletons,
Their statues, homes and fanes; prodigious
   shapes   300
Huddled in gray annihilation, split,
Jammed in the hard, black deep; and over
   these,
The anatomies of unknown wingèd things,
And fishes which were isles of living scale,
And serpents, bony chains, twisted around
The iron crags, or within heaps of dust
To which the tortuous strength of their last
   pangs
Had crushed the iron crags: and over these

The jagged alligator, and the might
Of earth-convulsing behemoth, which once 310
Were monarch beasts, and on the slimy
     shores,
And weed-overgrown continents of earth,
Increased and multiplied like summer worms
On an abandoned corpse, till the blue globe
Wrapped deluge round it like a cloak, and
     they
Yelled, gasped, and were abolished; or some
     God
Whose throne was in a comet, passed, and
     cried,
'Be not!' And like my words they were no
     more.

The Earth

The joy, the triumph, the delight, the mad-
     ness!
The boundless, overflowing, bursting glad-
     ness, 320
The vaporous exultation not to be confined!
Ha! ha! the animation of delight
Which wraps me, like an atmosphere of
     light,
And bears me as a cloud is borne by its own
     wind.

The Moon

Brother mine, calm wanderer,
Happy globe of land and air,
Some Spirit is darted like a beam from thee,
Which penetrates my frozen frame,
And passes with the warmth of flame,
With love, and odour, and deep melody 330
     Through me, through me!

The Earth

Ha! ha! the caverns of my hollow moun-
     tains,
My cloven fire-crags, sound-exulting foun-
     tains
Laugh with a vast and inextinguishable
     laughter.
The oceans, and the deserts, and the
     abysses,
And the deep air's unmeasured wildernesses,
Answer from all their clouds and billows,
     echoing after.

They cry aloud as I do. Sceptred curse,
Who all our green and azure universe
Threatenedst to muffle round with black
     destruction, sending 340

A solid cloud to rain hot thunderstones,
And splinter and knead down my children's
     bones,
All I bring forth, to one void mass battering
     and blending,—

Until each crag-like tower, and storied
     column,
Palace, and obelisk, and temple solemn,
My imperial mountains crowned with cloud,
     and snow, and fire;
My sea-like forests, every blade and
     blossom
Which finds a grave or cradle in my bosom,
Were stamped by thy strong hate into a life-
     less mire:

How art thou sunk, withdrawn, covered,
     drunk up 350
By thirsty nothing, as the brackish cup
Drained by a desert-troop, a little drop for all;
And from beneath, around, within, above,
Filling thy void annihilation, love
Burst in like light on caves cloven by the
     thunder-ball.

The Moon

The snow upon my lifeless mountains
Is loosened into living fountains,
My solid oceans flow, and sing, and shine:
A spirit from my heart bursts forth,
It clothes with unexpected birth 360
My cold bare bosom: Oh! it must be thine
     On mine, on mine!

Gazing on thee I feel, I know
Green stalks burst forth, and bright flowers
     grow,
And living shapes upon my bosom move:
Music is in the sea and air,
Wingèd clouds soar here and there,
Dark with the rain new buds are dreaming of:
     'Tis love, all love!

The Earth

It interpenetrates my granite mass, 370
Through tangled roots and trodden clay
     doth pass
Into the utmost leaves and delicatest flowers;
Upon the winds, among the clouds 'tis
     spread,
It wakes a life in the forgotten dead,
They breathe a spirit up from their obscurest
     bowers.

And like a storm bursting its cloudy prison

With thunder, and with whirlwind, has arisen
Out of the lampless caves of unimagined being:
With earthquake shock and swiftness making shiver
Thought's stagnant chaos, unremoved for ever,   380
Till hate, and fear, and pain, light-vanquished shadows, fleeing,

Leave Man, who was a many-sided mirror,
Which could distort to many a shape of error,
This true fair world of things, a sea reflecting love;
Which over all his kind, as the sun's heaven
Gliding o'er ocean, smooth, serene, and even,
Darting from starry depths radiance and life, doth move:

Leave Man, even as a leprous child is left,
Who follows a sick beast to some warm cleft
Of rocks, through which the might of healing springs is poured;   390
Then when it wanders home with rosy smile,
Unconscious, and its mother fears awhile
It is a spirit, then, weeps on her child restored.

Man, oh, not men! a chain of linkèd thought,
Of love and might to be divided not,
Compelling the elements with adamantine stress;
As the sun rules, even with a tyrant's gaze,
The unquiet republic of the maze
Of planets, struggling fierce towards heaven's free wilderness.

Man, one harmonious soul of many a soul,
Whose nature is its own divine control,   401
Where all things flow to all, as rivers to the sea;
Familiar acts are beautiful through love;
Labour, and pain, and grief, in life's green grove
Sport like tame beasts, none knew how gentle they could be!

His will, with all mean passions, bad delights,
And selfish cares, its trembling satellites,
A spirit ill to guide, but mighty to obey,

Is as a tempest-wingèd ship, whose helm
Love rules, through waves which dare not overwhelm,   410
Forcing life's wildest shores to own its sovereign sway.

All things confess his strength. Through the cold mass
Of marble and of colour his dreams pass;
Bright threads whence mothers weave the robes their children wear;
Language is a perpetual Orphic song,
Which rules with Dædal harmony a throng
Of thoughts and forms, which else senseless and shapeless were.

The lightning is his slave; heaven's utmost deep
Gives up her stars, and like a flock of sheep
They pass before his eye, are numbered, and roll on!   420
The tempest is his steed, he strides the air;
And the abyss shouts from her depth laid bare,
Heaven, hast thou secrets? Man unveils me; I have none.

The Moon
The shadow of white death has passed
From my path in heaven at last,
A clinging shroud of solid frost and sleep;
And through my newly-woven bowers,
Wander happy paramours,
Less mighty, but as mild as those who keep
    Thy vales more deep.   430

The Earth
As the dissolving warmth of dawn may fold
A half unfrozen dew-globe, green, and gold,
And crystalline, till it becomes a wingèd mist,
And wanders up the vault of the blue day,
Outlives the moon, and on the sun's last ray
Hangs o'er the sea, a fleece of fire and amethyst.

The Moon
Thou art folded, thou art lying
In the light which is undying
Of thine own joy, and heaven's smile divine;
All suns and constellations shower   440
On thee a light, a life, a power
Which doth array thy sphere; thou pourest thine
    On mine, on mine!

The Earth

I spin beneath my pyramid of night,
Which points into the heavens dreaming de-
    light,
Murmuring victorious joy in my enchanted
    sleep;
As a youth lulled in love-dreams faintly
    sighing,
Under the shadow of his beauty lying,
Which round his rest a watch of light and
    warmth doth keep.

The Moon

As in the soft and sweet eclipse,   450
When soul meets soul on lovers' lips,
High hearts are calm, and brightest eyes are
    dull;
So when thy shadow falls on me,
Then am I mute and still, by thee
Covered; of thy love, Orb most beautiful,
      Full, oh, too full!

Thou art speeding round the sun
Brightest world of many a one;
Green and azure sphere which shinest
With a light which is divinest   460
Among all the lamps of Heaven
To whom life and light is given;
I, thy crystal paramour
Borne beside thee by a power
Like the polar Paradise,
Magnet-like of lovers' eyes;
I, a most enamoured maiden
Whose weak brain is overladen
With the pleasure of her love,
Maniac-like around thee move   470
Gazing, an insatiate bride,
On thy form from every side
Like a Mænad, round the cup
Which Agave lifted up
In the weird Cadmæan forest.
Brother, wheresoe'er thou soarest
I must hurry, whirl and follow,
Through the heavens wide and hollow,
Sheltered by the warm embrace
Of thy soul from hungry space,   480
Drinking from thy sense and sight
Beauty, majesty, and might,
As a lover or a chameleon
Grows like what it looks upon,
As a violet's gentle eye
Gazes on the azure sky
Until its hue grows like what it beholds,
As a gray and watery mist

Glows like solid amethyst
Athwart the western mountain it enfolds, 490
When the sunset sleeps
Upon its snow—

The Earth

And the weak day weeps
    That it should be so.
Oh, gentle Moon, the voice of thy delight
Falls on me like thy clear and tender light
Soothing the seaman, borne the summer night,
    Through isles for ever calm;
Oh, gentle Moon, thy crystal accents pierce
The caverns of my pride's deep universe, 500
Charming the tiger joy, whose tramplings
    fierce
Made wounds which need thy balm.
Panthea. I rise as from a bath of sparkling
    water,
A bath of azure light, among dark rocks,
Out of the stream of sound.
Ione.   Ah me! sweet sister,
The stream of sound has ebbed away from us,
And you pretend to rise out of its wave,
Because your words fall like the clear, soft
    dew
Shaken from a bathing wood-nymph's limbs
    and hair.
Panthea. Peace! peace! A mighty Power,
    which is as darkness,   510
Is rising out of Earth, and from the sky
Is showered like night, and from within the
    air
Bursts, like eclipse which had been gathered
    up
Into the pores of sunlight: the bright visions,
Wherein the singing spirits rode and shone,
Gleam like pale meteors through a watery
    night.
Ione. There is a sense of words upon mine
    ear.
Panthea. An universal sound like words:
    Oh, list!

Demogorgon

Thou, Earth, calm empire of a happy soul,
    Sphere of divinest shapes and harmonies, 520
Beautiful orb! gathering as thou dost roll
    The love which paves thy path along the
    skies:

The Earth

I hear: I am as a drop of dew that dies.

Demogorgon

Thou, Moon, which gazest on the nightly
    Earth
With wonder, as it gazes upon thee;
Whilst each to men, and beasts, and the swift
    birth
Of birds, is beauty, love, calm, harmony:

The Moon

I hear: I am a leaf shaken by thee!

Demogorgon

Ye Kings of suns and stars, Dæmons and
    Gods,
Æthereal Dominations, who possess   530
Elysian, windless, fortunate abodes
    Beyond Heaven's constellated wilderness:

A Voice from above

Our great Republic hears, we are blest, and
    bless.

Demogorgon

Ye happy Dead, whose beams of brightest
    verse
Are clouds to hide, not colours to portray,
Whether your nature is that universe
    Which once ye saw and suffered—

A Voice from beneath
                        Or as they
Whom we have left, we change and pass away.

Demogorgon

Ye elemental Genii, who have homes
    From man's high mind even to the central
        stone   540
Of sullen lead; from heaven's star-fretted
        domes
    To the dull weed some sea-worm battens
        on:

A confused Voice

We hear: thy words waken Oblivion.

Demogorgon

Spirits, whose homes are flesh: ye beasts and
    birds,
Ye worms, and fish; ye living leaves and
    buds;
Lightning and wind; and ye untameable herds,
    Meteors and mists, which throng air's soli-
        tudes:—

A Voice

Thy voice to us is wind among still woods.

Demogorgon

Man, who wert once a despot and a slave;
    A dupe and a deceiver; a decay;   550
A traveller from the cradle to the grave
    Through the dim night of this immortal
        day:

All

Speak: thy strong words may never pass
    away.

Demogorgon

This is the day, which down the void abysm
At the Earth-born's spell yawns for Heaven's
        despotism,
    And Conquest is dragged captive through
        the deep:
Love, from its awful throne of patient power
In the wise heart, from the last giddy hour
    Of dread endurance, from the slippery,
        steep,
And narrow verge of crag-like agony, springs
And folds over the world its healing wings. 561

Gentleness, Virtue, Wisdom, and Endurance,
These are the seals of that most firm as-
        surance
    Which bars the pit over Destruction's
        strength;
And if, with infirm hand, Eternity,
Mother of many acts and hours, should free
    The serpent that would clasp her with its
        length;
These are the spells by which to reassume
An empire o'er the disentangled doom.

To suffer woes which Hope thinks infinite; 570
To forgive wrongs darker than death or night;
    To defy Power, which seems omnipotent;
To love, and bear; to hope till Hope creates
From its own wreck the thing it contemplates;
Neither to change, nor falter, nor repent;
This, like thy glory, Titan, is to be
Good, great and joyous, beautiful and free;
This is alone Life, Joy, Empire, and Victory.

THE MASK OF ANARCHY

WRITTEN ON THE OCCASION OF THE MASSACRE AT MANCHESTER

I

As I lay asleep in Italy
There came a voice from over the Sea,
And with great power it forth led me
To walk in the visions of Poesy.

II

I met Murder on the way—
He had a mask like Castlereagh—
Very smooth he looked, yet grim;
Seven blood-hounds followed him:

III

All were fat; and well they might
Be in admirable plight,
For one by one, and two by two,
He tossed them human hearts to chew
Which from his wide cloak he drew.

IV

Next came Fraud, and he had on,
Like Eldon, an ermined gown;
His big tears, for he wept well,
Turned to mill-stones as they fell.

V

And the little children, who
Round his feet played to and fro,
Thinking every tear a gem,
Had their brains knocked out by them.

VI

Clothed with the Bible, as with light,
And the shadows of the night,
Like Sidmouth, next, Hypocrisy
On a crocodile rode by.

VII

And many more Destructions played
In this ghastly masquerade,
All disguised, even to the eyes,
Like Bishops, lawyers, peers, or spies.

VIII

Last came Anarchy: he rode
On a white horse, splashed with blood;
He was pale even to the lips,
Like Death in the Apocalypse.

IX

And he wore a kingly crown;
And in his grasp a sceptre shone;
On his brow this mark I saw—
"I AM GOD, AND KING, AND LAW!"

X

With a pace stately and fast,
Over English land he passed,
Trampling to a mire of blood
The adoring multitude.

. . . . . .

XXII

When one fled past, a maniac maid
And her name was Hope, she said:
But she looked more like Despair,
And she cried out in the air:

XXIII

"My father Time is weak and gray
With waiting for a better day;
See how idiot-like he stands,
Fumbling with his palsied hands!

XXIV

"He has had child after child,
And the dust of death is piled
Over every one but me—
Misery, oh, Misery!"

XXV

Then she lay down in the street,
Right before the horses' feet,
Expecting, with a patient eye,
Murder, Fraud, and Anarchy.

XXVI

When between her and her foes
A mist, a light, an image rose,
Small at first, and weak, and frail
Like the vapour of a vale:

XXVII

Till as clouds grow on the blast,
Like tower-crowned giants striding fast,
And glare with lightnings as they fly,
And speak in thunder to the sky,

XXVIII

It grew—a Shape arrayed in mail
Brighter than the viper's scale,
And upborne on wings whose grain
Was as the light of sunny rain.

XXIX

On its helm, seen far away,
A planet, like the Morning's, lay;
And those plumes its light rained through
Like a shower of crimson dew.

XXX

With step as soft as wind it passed
O'er the heads of men—so fast
That they knew the presence there,　120
And looked,—but all was empty air.

XXXI

As flowers beneath May's footstep waken,
As stars from Night's loose hair are shaken,
As waves arise when loud winds call,
Thoughts sprung where'er that step did fall.

XXXII

And the prostrate multitude
Looked—and ankle-deep in blood,
Hope, that maiden most serene,
Was walking with a quiet mien:

XXXIII

And Anarchy, the ghastly birth,　130
Lay dead earth upon the earth;
The Horse of Death tameless as wind
Fled, and with his hoofs did grind
To dust the murderers thronged behind.

XXXIV

A rushing light of clouds and splendour,
A sense awakening and yet tender
Was heard and felt—and at its close
These words of joy and fear arose:

．　．　．　．　．　．

XXXVII

"Men of England, heirs of Glory,
Heroes of unwritten story,
Nurslings of one mighty Mother,
Hopes of her, and one another;　150

XXXVIII

"Rise like Lions after slumber
In unvanquishable number,

Shake your chains to earth like dew
Which in sleep had fallen on you—
Ye are many—they are few.

XXXIX

"What is Freedom?—ye can tell
That which slavery is, too well—
For its very name has grown
To an echo of your own.

XL

" 'Tis to work and have such pay　160
As just keeps life from day to day
In your limbs, as in a cell
For the tyrants' use to dwell,

XLI

"So that ye for them are made
Loom, and plough, and sword, and spade,
With or without your own will bent
To their defence and nourishment.

XLII

" 'Tis to see your children weak
With their mothers pine and peak,
When the winter winds are bleak,—　170
They are dying whilst I speak.

XLIII

" 'Tis to hunger for such diet
As the rich man in his riot
Casts to the fat dogs that lie
Surfeiting beneath his eye;

XLIV

" 'Tis to let the Ghost of Gold
Take from Toil a thousandfold
More than e'er its substance could
In the tyrannies of old.

XLV

"Paper coin—that forgery　180
Of the title-deeds, which ye
Hold to something of the worth
Of the inheritance of Earth.

XLVI

" 'Tis to be a slave in soul
And to hold no strong control
Over your own wills, but be
All that others make of ye.

XLVII

"And at length when ye complain
With a murmur weak and vain
'Tis to see the Tyrant's crew   190
Ride over your wives and you—
Blood is on the grass like dew.

XLVIII

"Then it is to feel revenge
Fiercely thirsting to exchange
Blood for blood—and wrong for wrong—
Do not thus when ye are strong.

XLIX

"Birds find rest, in narrow nest
When weary of their wingèd quest;
Beasts find fare, in woody lair
When storm and snow are in the air.   200

L

"Asses, swine, have litter spread
And with fitting food are fed;
All things have a home but one—
Thou, Oh, Englishman, hast none!

LI

"This is Slavery—savage men,
Or wild beasts within a den
Would endure not as ye do—
But such ills they never knew.

LII

"What art thou Freedom? O! could slaves
Answer from their living graves   210
This demand—tyrants would flee
Like a dream's dim imagery:

LIII

"Thou art not, as impostors say,
A shadow soon to pass away,
A superstition, and a name
Echoing from the cave of Fame.

LIV

"For the labourer thou art bread,
And a comely table spread
From his daily labour come
In a neat and happy home.   220

LV

"Thou art clothes, and fire, and food
For the trampled multitude—
No—in countries that are free
Such starvation cannot be
As in England now we see.

LVI

"To the rich thou art a check,
When his foot is on the neck
Of his victim, thou dost make
That he treads upon a snake.

LVII

"Thou art Justice—ne'er for gold   230
May thy righteous laws be sold
As laws are in England—thou
Shield'st alike the high and low.

LVIII

"Thou art Wisdom—Freemen never
Dream that God will damn for ever
All who think those things untrue
Of which Priests make such ado.

LIX

"Thou art Peace—never by thee
Would blood and treasure wasted be
As tyrants wasted them, when all   240
Leagued to quench thy flame in Gaul.

LX

"What if English toil and blood
Was poured forth, even as a flood?
It availed, Oh, Liberty,
To dim, but not extinguish thee.

LXI

"Thou art Love—the rich have kissed
Thy feet, and like him following Christ,
Give their substance to the free
And through the rough world follow thee,

LXII

"Or turn their wealth to arms, and make   250
War for thy belovèd sake
On wealth, and war, and fraud—whence they
Drew the power which is their prey.

LXIII

"Science, Poetry, and Thought
Are thy lamps; they make the lot
Of the dwellers in a cot
So serene, they curse it not.

LXIV

"Spirit, Patience, Gentleness,
All that can adorn and bless
Art thou—let deeds, not words, express   260
Thine exceeding loveliness.

LXV

"Let a great Assembly be
Of the fearless and the free
On some spot of English ground
Where the plains stretch wide around.

LXVI

"Let the blue sky overhead,
The green earth on which ye tread,
All that must eternal be
Witness the solemnity.

LXVII

"From the corners uttermost   270
Of the bounds of English coast;
From every hut, village, and town
Where those who live and suffer moan
For others' misery or their own,

LXVIII

"From the workhouse and the prison
Where pale as corpses newly risen,
Women, children, young and old
Groan for pain, and weep for cold—

LXIX

"From the haunts of daily life
Where is waged the daily strife   280

With common wants and common cares
Which sows the human heart with tares—

LXX

"Lastly from the palaces
Where the murmur of distress
Echoes, like the distant sound
Of a wind alive around

LXXI

"Those prison halls of wealth and fashion,
Where some few feel such compassion
For those who groan, and toil, and wail
As must make their brethren pale—   290

LXXII

"Ye who suffer woes untold,
Or to feel, or to behold
Your lost country bought and sold
With a price of blood and gold—

LXXIII

"Let a vast assembly be,
And with great solemnity
Declare with measured words that ye
Are, as God has made ye, free—

LXXIV

"Be your strong and simple words
Keen to wound as sharpened swords,   300
And wide as targes let them be,
With their shade to cover ye.

LXXV

"Let the tyrants pour around
With a quick and startling sound,
Like the loosening of a sea,
Troops of armed emblazonry.

LXXVI

"Let the charged artillery drive
Till the dead air seems alive
With the clash of clanging wheels,
And the tramp of horses' heels.   310

LXXVII

"Let the fixèd bayonet
Gleam with sharp desire to wet

Its bright point in English blood
Looking keen as one for food.

. . . .

LXXXIV

"And if then the tyrants dare 340
Let them ride among you there,
Slash, and stab, and maim, and hew,—
What they like, that let them do.

LXXXV

"With folded arms and steady eyes,
And little fear, and less surprise,
Look upon them as they slay
Till their rage has died away.

LXXXVI

"Then they will return with shame
To the place from which they came,
And the blood thus shed will speak 350
In hot blushes on their cheek.

LXXXVII

"Every woman in the land
Will point at them as they stand—
They will hardly dare to greet
Their acquaintance in the street.

LXXXVIII

"And the bold, true warriors
Who have hugged Danger in wars
Will turn to those who would be free,
Ashamed of such base company.

LXXXIX

"And that slaughter to the Nation 360
Shall steam up like inspiration,
Eloquent, oracular;
A volcano heard afar.

XC

"And these words shall then become
Like Oppression's thundered doom
Ringing through each heart and brain,
Heard again—again—again—

XCI

"Rise like Lions after slumber
In unvanquishable number—
Shake your chains to earth like dew 370
Which in sleep had fallen on you—
Ye are many—they are few."

ADONAIS

I

I WEEP for Adonais—he is dead!
O, weep for Adonais! though our tears
Thaw not the frost which binds so dear a
head!
And thou, sad Hour, selected from all years
To mourn our loss, rouse thy obscure com-
peers,
And teach them thine own sorrow, say:
"With me
Died Adonais; till the Future dares
Forget the Past, his fate and fame shall be
An echo and a light unto eternity!"

II

Where wert thou, mighty Mother, when he
lay, 10
When thy Son lay, pierced by the shaft
which flies
In darkness? where was lorn Urania
When Adonais died? With veilèd eyes,
'Mid listening Echoes, in her Paradise
She sate, while one, with soft enamoured
breath
Rekindled all the fading melodies,
With which, like flowers that mock the corse
beneath,
He had adorned and hid the coming bulk of
Death.

III

Oh, weep for Adonais—he is dead!
Wake, melancholy Mother, wake and weep!
Yet wherefore? Quench within their burning
bed 21
Thy fiery tears, and let thy loud heart keep
Like his, a mute and uncomplaining sleep;
For he is gone, where all things wise and
fair

Descend;—oh, dream not that the amorous Deep
Will yet restore him to the vital air;
Death feeds on his mute voice, and laughs at our despair.

IV

Most musical of mourners, weep again!
Lament anew, Urania!—He died,
Who was the Sire of an immortal strain, 30
Blind, old, and lonely, when his country's pride,
The priest, the slave, and the liberticide,
Trampled and mocked with many a loathèd rite
Of lust and blood; he went, unterrified,
Into the gulf of death; but his clear Sprite
Yet reigns o'er earth; the third among the sons of light.

V

Most musical of mourners, weep anew!
Not all to that bright station dared to climb;
And happier they their happiness who knew,
Whose tapers yet burn through that night of time 40
In which suns perished; others more sublime,
Struck by the envious wrath of man or god,
Have sunk, extinct in their refulgent prime;
And some yet live, treading the thorny road,
Which leads, through toil and hate, to Fame's serene abode.

VI

But now, thy youngest, dearest one, has perished—
The nursling of thy widowhood, who grew,
Like a pale flower by some sad maiden cherished,
And fed with true-love tears, instead of dew;
Most musical of mourners, weep anew! 50
Thy extreme hope, the loveliest and the last,
The bloom, whose petals nipped before they blew
Died on the promise of the fruit, is waste;

The broken lily lies—the storm is overpast.

VII

To that high Capital, where kingly Death
Keeps his pale court in beauty and decay,
He came; and bought, with price of purest breath,
A grave among the eternal.—Come away!
Haste, while the vault of blue Italian day
Is yet his fitting charnel-roof! while still 60
He lies, as if in dewy sleep he lay;
Awake him not! surely he takes his fill
Of deep and liquid rest, forgetful of all ill.

VIII

He will awake no more, oh, never more!—
Within the twilight chamber spreads apace
The shadow of white Death, and at the door
Invisible Corruption waits to trace
His extreme way to her dim dwelling-place;
The eternal Hunger sits, but pity and awe
Soothe her pale rage, nor dares she to deface 70
So fair a prey, till darkness, and the law
Of change, shall o'er his sleep the mortal curtain draw.

IX

Oh, weep for Adonais!—The quick Dreams,
The passion-wingèd Ministers of thought,
Who were his flocks, whom near the living streams
Of his young spirit he fed, and whom he taught
The love which was its music, wander not,—
Wander no more, from kindling brain to brain,
But droop there, whence they sprung; and mourn their lot
Round the cold heart, where, after their sweet pain, 80
They ne'er will gather strength, or find a home again.

X

And one with trembling hands clasps his cold head,
And fans him with her moonlight wings, and cries;
'Our love, our hope, our sorrow, is not dead;

See, on the silken fringe of his faint eyes,
Like dew upon a sleeping flower, there lies
A tear some Dream has loosened from his
    brain.'
Lost Angel of a ruined Paradise!
She knew not 'twas her own; as with no
    stain
She faded, like a cloud which had outwept its
    rain.   90

XI

One from a lucid urn of starry dew
Washed his light limbs as if embalming
    them;
Another clipped her profuse locks, and
    threw
The wreath upon him, like an anadem,
Which frozen tears instead of pearls be-
    gem;
Another in her wilful grief would break
Her bow and wingèd reeds, as if to stem
A greater loss with one which was more
    weak;
And dull the barbèd fire against his frozen
    cheek.

XII

Another Splendour on his mouth alit,   100
That mouth, whence it was wont to draw
    the breath
Which gave it strength to pierce the guarded
    wit,
And pass into the panting heart beneath
With lightning and with music: the damp
    death
Quenched its caress upon his icy lips;
And, as a dying meteor stains a wreath
Of moonlight vapour, which the cold night
    clips,
It flushed through his pale limbs, and passed
    to its eclipse.

XIII

And others came . . . Desires and Adora-
    tions,
Wingèd Persuasions and veiled Destinies, 110
Splendours, and Glooms, and glimmering In-
    carnations
Of hopes and fears, and twilight Phantasies;
And Sorrow, with her family of Sighs,
And Pleasure, blind with tears, led by the
    gleam

Of her own dying smile instead of eyes,
Came in slow pomp;—the moving pomp
    might seem
Like pageantry of mist on an autumnal stream.

XIV

All he had loved, and moulded into thought,
From shape, and hue, and odour, and sweet
    sound,
Lamented Adonais. Morning sought   120
Her eastern watch-tower, and her hair un-
    bound,
Wet with the tears which should adorn the
    ground,
Dimmed the aëreal eyes that kindle day;
Afar the melancholy thunder moaned,
Pale Ocean in unquiet slumber lay,
And the wild Winds flew round, sobbing in
    their dismay.

XV

Lost Echo sits amid the voiceless moun-
    tains,
And feeds her grief with his remembered
    lay,
And will no more reply to winds or foun-
    tains,
Or amorous birds perched on the young
    green spray,   130
Or herdsman's horn, or bell at closing day;
Since she can mimic not his lips, more dear
Than those for whose disdain she pined
    away
Into a shadow of all sounds:—a drear
Murmur, between their songs, is all the wood-
    men hear.

XVI

Grief made the young Spring wild, and she
    threw down
Her kindling buds, as if she Autumn were,
Or they dead leaves; since her delight is
    flown,
For whom should she have waked the sullen
    year?
To Phœbus was not Hyacinth so dear   140
Nor to himself Narcissus, as to both
Thou, Adonais: wan they stand and sere,
Amid the faint companions of their youth,
With dew all turned to tears; odour, to sigh-
    ing ruth.

XVII

Thy spirit's sister, the lorn nightingale
Mourns not her mate with such melodious
    pain;
Not so the eagle, who like thee could scale
Heaven, and could nourish in the sun's do-
    main
Her mighty youth with morning, doth com-
    plain,
Soaring and screaming round her empty
    nest,   150
As Albion wails for thee: the curse of
    Cain
Light on his head who pierced thy innocent
    breast,
And scared the angel soul that was its earthly
    guest!

XVIII

Ah, woe is me! Winter is come and gone,
But grief returns with the revolving year;
The airs and streams renew their joyous
    tone;
The ants, the bees, the swallows reappear;
Fresh leaves and flowers deck the dead
    Season's bier;
The amorous birds now pair in every brake,
And build their mossy homes in field and
    brere;   160
And the green lizard, and the golden snake,
Like unimprisoned flames, out of their trance
    awake.

XIX

Through wood and stream and field and hill
    and Ocean
A quickening life from the Earth's heart has
    burst
As it has ever done, with change and mo-
    tion,
From the great morning of the world when
    first
God dawned on Chaos; in its stream im-
    mersed,
The lamps of Heaven flash with a softer
    light;
All baser things pant with life's sacred
    thirst;
Diffuse themselves; and spend in love's de-
    light,   170

The beauty and the joy of their renewèd
    might.

XX

The leprous corpse, touched by this spirit
    tender,
Exhales itself in flowers of gentle breath;
Like incarnations of the stars, when splen-
    dour
Is changed to fragrance, they illumine
    death
And mock the merry worm that wakes be-
    neath;
Nought we know, dies. Shall that alone
    which knows
Be as a sword consumed before the sheath
By sightless lightning?—the intense atom
    glows
A moment, then is quenched in a most cold
    repose.   180

XXI

Alas! that all we loved of him should be,
But for our grief, as if it had not been,
And grief itself be mortal! Woe is me!
Whence are we, and why are we? of what
    scene
The actors or spectators? Great and mean
Meet massed in death, who lends what life
    must borrow.
As long as skies are blue, and fields are
    green,
Evening must usher night, night urge the
    morrow,
Month follow month with woe, and year wake
    year to sorrow.

XXII

He will awake no more, oh, never more! 190
'Wake thou,' cried Misery, 'childless
    Mother, rise
Out of thy sleep, and slake, in thy heart's
    core,
A wound more fierce than his, with tears
    and sighs.'
And all the Dreams that watched Urania's
    eyes,
And all the Echoes whom their sister's song
Had held in holy silence, cried: 'Arise!'
Swift as a Thought by the snake Memory
    stung,

From her ambrosial rest the fading Splendour
   sprung.

XXIII

She rose like an autumnal Night, that
   springs
Out of the East, and follows wild and drear
The golden Day, which, on eternal wings, 201
Even as a ghost abandoning a bier,
Had left the Earth a corpse. Sorrow and
   fear
So struck, so roused, so rapped Urania;
So saddened round her like an atmosphere
Of stormy mist; so swept her on her way
Even to the mournful place where Adonais
   lay.

XXIV

Out of her secret Paradise she sped,
Through camps and cities rough with stone,
   and steel,
And human hearts, which to her aëry tread
Yielding not, wounded the invisible   211
Palms of her tender feet where'er they fell:
And barbèd tongues, and thoughts more
   sharp than they,
Rent the soft Form they never could repel,
Whose sacred blood, like the young tears of
   May,
Paved with eternal flowers that undeserving
   way.

XXV

In the death-chamber for a moment Death,
Shamed by the presence of that living
   Might,
Blushed to annihilation, and the breath
Revisited those lips, and Life's pale light 220
Flashed through those limbs, so late her
   dear delight.
'Leave me not wild and drear and comfort-
   less,
As silent lightning leaves the starless night!
Leave me not!' cried Urania: her distress
Roused Death: Death rose and smiled, and
   met her vain caress.

XXVI

'Stay yet awhile! speak to me once again;
Kiss me, so long but as a kiss may live;

And in my heartless breast and burning
   brain
That word, that kiss, shall all thoughts else
   survive,
With food of saddest memory kept alive,
Now thou art dead, as if it were a part   231
Of thee, my Adonais! I would give
All that I am to be as thou now art!
But I am chained to Time, and cannot thence
   depart!

XXVII

'O gentle child, beautiful as thou wert,
Why didst thou leave the trodden paths of
   men
Too soon, and with weak hands though
   mighty heart
Dare the unpastured dragon in his den?
Defenceless as thou wert, oh, where was
   then
Wisdom the mirrored shield, or scorn the
   spear?   240
Or hadst thou waited the full cycle, when
Thy spirit should have filled its crescent
   sphere,
The monsters of life's waste had fled from
   thee like deer.

XXVIII

'The herded wolves, bold only to pursue;
The obscene ravens, clamorous o'er the
   dead;
The vultures to the conqueror's banner true
Who feed where Desolation first has fed,
And whose wings rain contagion;—how they
   fled,
When, like Apollo, from his golden bow
The Pythian of the age one arrow sped 250
And smiled!—The spoilers tempt no sec-
   ond blow,
They fawn on the proud feet that spurn them
   lying low.

XXIX

'The sun comes forth, and many reptiles
   spawn;
He sets, and each ephemeral insect then
Is gathered into death without a dawn,
And the immortal stars awake again;
So is it in the world of living men:
A godlike mind soars forth, in its delight

Making earth bare and veiling heaven, and when
It sinks, the swarms that dimmed or shared its light   260
Leave to its kindred lamps the spirit's awful night.'

XXX

Thus ceased she: and the mountain shepherds came,
Their garlands sere, their magic mantles rent;
The Pilgrim of Eternity, whose fame
Over his living head like Heaven is bent,
An early but enduring monument,
Came, veiling all the lightnings of his song
In sorrow; from her wilds Ierne sent
The sweetest lyrist of her saddest wrong,
And Love taught Grief to fall like music from his tongue.   270

XXXI

Midst others of less note, came one frail Form,
A phantom among men; companionless
As the last cloud of an expiring storm
Whose thunder is its knell; he, as I guess,
Had gazed on Nature's naked loveliness,
Actæon-like, and now he fled astray
With feeble steps o'er the world's wilderness,
And his own thoughts, along that rugged way,
Pursued, like raging hounds, their father and their prey.

XXXII

A pardlike Spirit beautiful and swift—   280
A Love in desolation masked;—a Power
Girt round with weakness;—it can scarce uplift
The weight of the superincumbent hour;
It is a dying lamp, a falling shower,
A breaking billow;—even whilst we speak
Is it not broken? On the withering flower
The killing sun smiles brightly: on a cheek
The life can burn in blood, even while the heart may break.

XXXIII

His head was bound with pansies overblown,
And faded violets, white, and pied, and blue;   290
And a light spear topped with a cypress cone,
Round whose rude shaft dark ivy-tresses grew
Yet dripping with the forest's noonday dew,
Vibrated, as the ever-beating heart
Shook the weak hand that grasped it; of that crew
He came the last, neglected and apart;
A herd-abandoned deer struck by the hunter's dart.

XXXIV

All stood aloof, and at his partial moan
Smiled through their tears; well knew that gentle band
Who in another's fate now wept his own,   300
As in the accents of an unknown land
He sung new sorrow; sad Urania scanned
The Stranger's mien, and murmured: 'Who art thou?'
He answered not, but with a sudden hand
Made bare his branded and ensanguined brow,
Which was like Cain's or Christ's—oh! that it should be so!

XXXV

What softer voice is hushed over the dead?
Athwart what brow is that dark mantle thrown?
What form leans sadly o'er the white death-bed,
In mockery of monumental stone,   310
The heavy heart heaving without a moan?
If it be He, who, gentlest of the wise,
Taught, soothed, loved, honoured the departed one,
Let me not vex, with inharmonious sighs,
The silence of that heart's accepted sacrifice.

XXXVI

Our Adonais has drunk poison—oh!
What deaf and viperous murderer could crown

Life's early cup with such a draught of
woe?
The nameless worm would now itself dis-
own:
It felt, yet could escape, the magic tone 320
Whose prelude held all envy, hate, and
wrong,
But what was howling in one breast alone,
Silent with expectation of the song,
Whose master's hand is cold, whose silver
lyre unstrung.

XXXVII

Live thou, whose infamy is not thy fame!
Live! fear no heavier chastisement from me,
Thou noteless blot on a remembered name!
But be thyself, and know thyself to be!
And ever at thy season be thou free
To spill the venom when thy fangs o'er-
flow: 330
Remorse and Self-contempt shall cling to
thee;
Hot Shame shall burn upon thy secret brow,
And like a beaten hound tremble thou shalt—
as now.

XXXVIII

Nor let us weep that our delight is fled
Far from these carrion kites that scream
below;
He wakes or sleeps with the enduring dead;
Thou canst not soar where he is sitting
now—
Dust to the dust! but the pure spirit shall
flow
Back to the burning fountain whence it
came,
A portion of the Eternal, which must glow
Through time and change, unquenchably
the same, 341
Whilst thy cold embers choke the sordid
hearth of shame.

XXXIX

Peace, peace! he is not dead, he doth not
sleep—
He hath awakened from the dream of life—
'Tis we, who lost in stormy visions, keep
With phantoms an unprofitable strife,
And in mad trance, strike with our spirit's
knife

Invulnerable nothings.—*We* decay
Like corpses in a charnel; fear and grief
Convulse us and consume us day by day, 350
And cold hopes swarm like worms within our
living clay.

XL

He has outsoared the shadow of our night;
Envy and calumny and hate and pain,
And that unrest which men miscall delight,
Can touch him not and torture not again;
From the contagion of the world's slow
stain
He is secure, and now can never mourn
A heart grown cold, a head grown gray in
vain;
Nor, when the spirit's self has ceased to
burn,
With sparkless ashes load an unlamented urn.

XLI

He lives, he wakes—'tis Death is dead, not
he; 361
Mourn not for Adonais.—Thou young
Dawn,
Turn all thy dew to splendour, for from
thee
The spirit thou lamentest is not gone;
Ye caverns and ye forests, cease to moan!
Cease, ye faint flowers and fountains, and
thou Air,
Which like a mourning veil thy scarf hadst
thrown
O'er the abandoned Earth, now leave it
bare
Even to the joyous stars which smile on its
despair! 369

XLII

He is made one with Nature: there is heard
His voice in all her music, from the moan
Of thunder, to the song of night's sweet
bird;
He is a presence to be felt and known
In darkness and in light, from herb and
stone,
Spreading itself where'er that Power may
move
Which has withdrawn his being to its own;
Which wields the world with never-wearied
love,
Sustains it from beneath, and kindles it above.

XLIII

He is a portion of the loveliness
Which once he made more lovely: he doth
    bear   380
His part, while the one Spirit's plastic
    stress
Sweeps through the dull dense world, com-
    pelling there,
All new successions to the forms they wear;
Torturing th' unwilling dross that checks its
    flight
To its own likeness, as each mass may
    bear;
And bursting in its beauty and its might
From trees and beasts and men into the
    Heaven's light.

XLIV

The splendours of the firmament of time
May be eclipsed, but are extinguished not;
Like stars to their appointed height they
    climb,   390
And death is a low mist which cannot blot
The brightness it may veil. When lofty
    thought
Lifts a young heart above its mortal lair,
And love and life contend in it, for what
Shall be its earthly doom, the dead live
    there
And move like winds of light on dark and
    stormy air.

XLV

The inheritors of unfulfilled renown
Rose from their thrones, built beyond mor-
    tal thought,
Far in the Unapparent. Chatterton
Rose pale,—his solemn agony had not   400
Yet faded from him; Sidney, as he fought
And as he fell and as he lived and loved
Sublimely mild, a Spirit without spot,
Arose; and Lucan, by his death approved:
Oblivion as they rose shrank like a thing re-
    proved.

XLVI

And many more, whose names on Earth
    are dark,
But whose transmitted effluence cannot die
So long as fire outlives the parent spark,

Rose, robed in dazzling immortality.   409
'Thou art become as one of us,' they cry,
'It was for thee yon kingless sphere has long
Swung blind in unascended majesty,
Silent alone amid an Heaven of Song.
Assume thy wingèd throne, thou Vesper of
    our throng!'

XLVII

Who mourns for Adonais? Oh, come forth,
Fond wretch! and know thyself and him
    aright.
Clasp with thy panting soul the pendulous
    Earth;
As from a centre, dart thy spirit's light   418
Beyond all worlds, until its spacious might
Satiate the void circumference: then shrink
Even to a point within our day and night;
And keep thy heart light lest it make thee
    sink
When hope has kindled hope, and lured thee
    to the brink.

XLVIII

Or go to Rome, which is the sepulchre,
Oh, not of him, but of our joy: 'tis nought
That ages, empires, and religions there
Lie buried in the ravage they have wrought;
For such as he can lend,—they borrow not
Glory from those who made the world
    their prey;   429
And he is gathered to the kings of thought
Who waged contention with their time's de-
    cay,
And of the past are all that cannot pass away.

XLIX

Go thou to Rome,—at once the Paradise,
The grave, the city, and the wilderness;
And where its wrecks like shattered moun-
    tains rise,
And flowering weeds, and fragrant copses
    dress
The bones of Desolation's nakedness
Pass, till the spirit of the spot shall lead
Thy footsteps to a slope of green access
Where, like an infant's smile, over the
    dead   440
A light of laughing flowers along the grass is
    spread;

L

And gray walls moulder round, on which
    dull Time
Feeds, like slow fire upon a hoary brand;
And one keen pyramid with wedge sub-
    lime,
Pavilioning the dust of him who planned
This refuge for his memory, doth stand
Like flame transformed to marble; and be-
    neath,
A field is spread, on which a newer band
Have pitched in Heaven's smile their camp
    of death,
Welcoming him we lose with scarce extin-
    guished breath.   450

LI

Here pause: these graves are all too young
    as yet
To have outgrown the sorrow which con-
    signed
Its charge to each; and if the seal is set,
Here, on one fountain of a mourning mind,
Break it not thou! too surely shalt thou
    find
Thine own well full, if thou returnest home,
Of tears and gall. From the world's bitter
    wind
Seek shelter in the shadow of the tomb.
What Adonais is, why fear we to become?

LII

The One remains, the many change and
    pass;   460
Heaven's light forever shines, Earth's
    shadows fly;
Life, like a dome of many-coloured glass,
Stains the white radiance of Eternity,
Until Death tramples it to fragments.—
    Die,
If thou wouldst be with that which thou
    dost seek!
Follow where all is fled!—Rome's azure sky,
Flowers, ruins, statues, music, words, are
    weak
The glory they transfuse with fitting truth to
    speak.

LIII

Why linger, why turn back, why shrink, my
    Heart?

Thy hopes are gone before: from all things
    here   470
They have departed; thou shouldst now de-
    part!
A light is passed from the revolving year,
And man, and woman; and what still is
    dear
Attracts to crush, repels to make thee
    wither.
The soft sky smiles,—the low wind whispers
    near:
'Tis Adonais calls! oh, hasten thither,
No more let Life divide what Death can join
    together.

LIV

That Light whose smile kindles the Uni-
    verse,
That Beauty in which all things work and
    move,
That Benediction which the eclipsing Curse
Of birth can quench not, that sustaining
    Love   481
Which through the web of being blindly
    wove
By man and beast and earth and air and
    sea,
Burns bright or dim, as each are mirrors of
The fire for which all thirst; now beams on
    me,
Consuming the last clouds of cold mortality.

LV

The breath whose might I have invoked in
    song
Descends on me; my spirit's bark is driven,
Far from the shore, far from the trembling
    throng
Whose sails were never to the tempest
    given;   490
The massy earth and spherèd skies are
    riven!
I am borne darkly, fearfully, afar;
Whilst, burning through the inmost veil of
    Heaven,
The soul of Adonais, like a star,
Beacons from the abode where the Eternal
    are.

HYMN TO INTELLECTUAL BEAUTY

I

THE awful shadow of some unseen Power
  Floats though unseen among us,—visiting
  This various world with as inconstant wing
As summer winds that creep from flower to
    flower,—
Like moonbeams that behind some piny moun-
    tain shower,
    It visits with inconstant glance
    Each human heart and countenance;
Like hues and harmonies of evening,—
    Like clouds in starlight widely spread,—
    Like memory of music fled,— 10
    Like aught that for its grace may be
Dear, and yet dearer for its mystery.

II

Spirit of BEAUTY, that dost consecrate
  With thine own hues all thou dost shine
    upon
    Of human thought or form,—where art thou
    gone?
Why dost thou pass away and leave our state,
This dim vast vale of tears, vacant and deso-
    late?
    Ask why the sunlight not for ever
    Weaves rainbows o'er yon mountain-
    river,
Why aught should fail and fade that once is
    shown, 20
    Why fear and dream and death and birth
    Cast on the daylight of this earth
    Such gloom,—why man has such a scope
For love and hate, despondency and hope?

III

No voice from some sublimer world hath ever
  To sage or poet these responses given—
  Therefore the names of Demon, Ghost, and
    Heaven,
Remain the records of their vain endeavour,
Frail spells—whose uttered charm might not
    avail to sever,
    From all we hear and all we see, 30
    Doubt, chance, and mutability.
Thy light alone—like mist o'er mountains
    driven,
    Or music by the night-wind sent
    Through strings of some still instrument.

Or moonlight on a midnight stream,
Gives grace and truth to life's unquiet dream.

IV

Love, Hope, and Self-esteem, like clouds de-
    part
  And come, for some uncertain moments
    lent.
Man were immortal, and omnipotent,
Didst thou, unknown, and awful as thou art,
Keep with thy glorious train firm state within
    his heart. 41
    Thou messenger of sympathies,
    That wax and wane in lovers' eyes—
Thou—that to human thought art nourish-
    ment,
    Like darkness to a dying flame!
    Depart not as thy shadow came,
    Depart not—lest the grave should be,
Like life and fear, a dark reality.

V

While yet a boy I sought for ghosts, and sped
  Through many a listening chamber, cave
    and ruin, 50
  And starlight wood, with fearful steps pur-
    suing
Hopes of high talk with the departed dead.
I called on poisonous names with which our
    youth is fed;
    I was not heard—I saw them not—
    When musing deeply on the lot
Of life, at that sweet time when winds are
    wooing
    All vital things that wake to bring
    News of birds and blossoming,—
    Sudden, thy shadow fell on me;
I shrieked, and clasped my hands in ecstasy!

VI

I vowed that I would dedicate my powers 61
  To thee and thine—have I not kept the
    vow?
  With beating heart and streaming eyes, even
    now
I call the phantoms of a thousand hours
Each from his voiceless grave: they have in
    visioned bowers
    Of studious zeal or love's delight
    Outwatched with me the envious night—
They know that never joy illumed my brow

Unlinked with hope that thou wouldst
free
This world from its dark slavery,   70
That thou—O awful Loveliness,
Wouldst give whate'er these words cannot express.

VII

The day becomes more solemn and serene,
  When noon is past—there is a harmony
  In autumn, and a lustre in its sky,
Which through the summer is not heard or
    seen,
As if it could not be, as if it had not been!
  Thus let thy power, which like the truth
  Of nature on my passive youth
Descended, to my onward life supply   80
  Its calm—to one who worships thee,
  And every form containing thee,
Whom, Spirit fair, thy spells did bind
To fear himself, and love all human kind.

OZYMANDIAS

I met a traveller from an antique land
Who said: Two vast and trunkless legs of
    stone
Stand in the desert . . . Near them, on the
    sand,
Half sunk, a shattered visage lies, whose
    frown,
And wrinkled lip, and sneer of cold command,
Tell that its sculptor well those passions read
Which yet survive, stamped on these lifeless
    things,
The hand that mocked them, and the heart
    that fed:
And on the pedestal these words appear:
'My name is Ozymandias, king of kings: 10
Look on my works, ye Mighty, and despair!'
Nothing beside remains. Round the decay
Of that colossal wreck, boundless and bare
The lone and level sands stretch far away.

THE INDIAN SERENADE

I

I arise from dreams of thee
In the first sweet sleep of night,

When the winds are breathing low,
And the stars are shining bright:
I arise from dreams of thee,
And a spirit in my feet
Hath led me—who knows how?
To thy chamber window, Sweet!

II

The wandering airs they faint
On the dark, the silent stream—   10
The Champak odours fail
Like sweet thoughts in a dream;
The nightingale's complaint,
It dies upon her heart;—
As I must on thine,
Oh, belovèd as thou art!

III

Oh lift me from the grass!
I die! I faint! I fail!
Let thy love in kisses rain
On my lips and eyelids pale.   20
My cheek is cold and white, alas!
My heart beats loud and fast;—
Oh! press it to thine own again,
Where it will break at last.

LINES WRITTEN AMONG THE
EUGANEAN HILLS

Many a green isle needs must be
In the deep wide sea of Misery,
Or the mariner, worn and wan,
Never thus could voyage on—
Day and night, and night and day,
Drifting on his dreary way,
With the solid darkness black
Closing round his vessel's track;
Whilst above the sunless sky,
Big with clouds, hangs heavily,   10
And behind the tempest fleet
Hurries on with lightning feet,
Riving sail, and cord, and plank,
Till the ship has almost drank
Death from the o'er-brimming deep;
And sinks down, down, like that sleep
When the dreamer seems to be
Weltering through eternity;
And the dim low line before
Of a dark and distant shore   20
Still recedes, as ever still

Longing with divided will,
But no power to seek or shun,
He is ever drifted on
O'er the unreposing wave
To the haven of the grave.
What, if there no friends will greet;
What, if there no heart will meet
His with love's impatient beat;
Wander wheresoe'r he may,   30
Can he dream before that day
To find refuge from distress
In friendship's smile, in love's caress?
Then 'twill wreak him little woe
Whether such there be or no:
Senseless is the breast, and cold,
Which relenting love would fold;
Bloodless are the veins and chill
Which the pulse of pain did fill;
Every little living nerve   40
That from bitter words did swerve
Round the tortured lips and brow,
Are like sapless leaflets now
Frozen upon December's bough.

On the beach of a northern sea
Which tempests shake eternally,
As once the wretch there lay to sleep,
Lies a solitary heap,
One white skull and seven dry bones,
On the margin of the stones,   50
Where a few gray rushes stand,
Boundaries of the sea and land:
Nor is heard one voice of wail
But the sea-mews, as they sail
O'er the billows of the gale;
Or the whirlwind up and down
Howling, like a slaughtered town,
When a king in glory rides
Through the pomp of fratricides:
Those unburied bones around   60
There is many a mournful sound;
There is no lament for him,
Like a sunless vapour, dim,
Who once clothed with life and thought
What now moves nor murmurs not.

Ay, many flowering islands lie
In the waters of wide Agony:
To such a one this morn was led,
My bark by soft winds piloted:
'Mid the mountains Euganean   70
I stood listening to the paean
With which the legioned rooks did hail
The sun's uprise majestical;

Gathering round with wings all hoar,
Through the dewy mist they soar
Like gray shades, till the eastern heaven
Bursts, and then, as clouds of even,
Flecked with fire and azure, lie
In the unfathomable sky,
So their plumes of purple grain,   80
Starred with drops of golden rain,
Gleam above the sunlight woods,
As in silent multitudes
On the morning's fitful gale
Through the broken mist they sail,
And the vapours cloven and gleaming
Follow, down the dark steep streaming,
Till all is bright, and clear, and still,
Round the solitary hill.

Beneath is spread like a green sea   90
The waveless plain of Lombardy,
Bounded by the vaporous air,
Islanded by cities fair;
Underneath Day's azure eyes
Ocean's nursling, Venice lies,
A peopled labyrinth of walls,
Amphitrite's destined halls,
Which her hoary sire now paves
With his blue and beaming waves.
Lo! the sun upsprings behind,   100
Broad, red, radiant, half-reclined
On the level quivering line
Of the waters crystalline;
And before that chasm of light,
As within a furnace bright,
Column, tower, and dome, and spire,
Shine like obelisks of fire,
Pointing with inconstant motion
From the altar of dark ocean
To the sapphire-tinted skies;   110
As the flames of sacrifice
From the marble shrines did rise,
As to pierce the dome of gold
Where Apollo spoke of old.

Sun-girt City, thou hast been
Ocean's child, and then his queen;
Now is come a darker day,
And thou soon must be his prey,
If the power that raised thee here
Hallow so thy watery bier.   120
A less dread ruin then than now,
With thy conquest-branded brow
Stooping to the slave of slaves
From thy throne, among the waves
Wilt thou be, when the sea-mew

Flies, as once before it flew,
O'er thine isles depopulate,
And all is in its ancient state,
Save where many a palace gate
With green sea-flowers overgrown   130
Like a rock of Ocean's own,
Topples o'er the abandoned sea
As the tides change sullenly.
The fisher on his watery way,
Wandering at the close of day,
Will spread his sail and seize his oar
Till he pass the gloomy shore,
Lest thy dead should, from their sleep
Bursting o'er the starlight deep,
Lead a rapid masque of death   140
O'er the waters of his path.

Those who alone thy towers behold
Quivering through aëreal gold,
As I now behold them here,
Would imagine not they were
Sepulchres, where human forms,
Like pollution-nourished worms,
To the corpse of greatness cling,
Murdered, and now mouldering:
But if Freedom should awake   150
In her omnipotence, and shake
From the Celtic Anarch's hold
All the keys of dungeons cold,
Where a hundred cities lie
Chained like thee, ingloriously,
Thou and all thy sister band
Might adorn this sunny land,
Twining memories of old time
With new virtues more sublime;
If not, perish thou and they!—   160
Clouds which stain truth's rising day
By her sun consumed away—
Earth can spare ye: while like flowers,
In the waste of years and hours,
From your dust new nations spring
With more kindly blossoming.

Perish—let there only be
Floating o'er thy heartless sea
As the garment of thy sky
Clothes the world immortally,   170
One remembrance, more sublime
Than the tattered pall of time,
Which scarce hides thy visage wan;—
That a tempest-cleaving Swan
Of the songs of Albion,
Driven from his ancestral streams
By the might of evil dreams,

Found a nest in thee; and Ocean
Welcomed him with such emotion
That its joy grew his, and sprung   180
From his lips like music flung
O'er a mighty thunder-fit,
Chastening terror:—what though yet
Poesy's unfailing River,
Which through Albion winds forever
Lashing with melodious wave
Many a sacred Poet's grave,
Mourn its latest nursling fled?
What though thou with all thy dead
Scarce can for this fame repay   190
Aught thine own? oh, rather say
Though thy sins and slaveries foul
Overcloud a sunlike soul?
As the ghost of Homer clings
Round Scamander's wasting springs;
As divinest Shakespeare's might
Fills Avon and the world with light
Like omniscient power which he
Imaged 'mid mortality;
As the love from Petrarch's urn,   200
Yet amid yon hills doth burn,
A quenchless lamp by which the heart
Sees things unearthly;—so thou art,
Mighty spirit—so shall be
The City that did refuge thee.

Lo, the sun floats up the sky
Like thought-wingèd Liberty,
Till the universal light
Seems to level plain and height;
From the sea a mist has spread,   210
And the beams of morn lie dead
On the towers of Venice now,
Like its glory long ago.
By the skirts of that gray cloud
Many-domèd Padua proud
Stands, a peopled solitude,
'Mid the harvest-shining plain,
Where the peasant heaps his grain
In the garner of his foe,
And the milk-white oxen slow   220
With the purple vintage strain,
Heaped upon the creaking wain,
That the brutal Celt may swill
Drunken sleep with savage will;
And the sickle to the sword
Lies unchanged, though many a lord,
Like a weed whose shade is poison,
Overgrows this region's foison,
Sheaves of whom are ripe to come
To destruction's harvest-home: 230

Men must reap the things they sow,
Force from force must ever flow,
Or worse; but 'tis a bitter woe
That love or reason cannot change
The despot's rage, the slave's revenge.
Padua, thou within whose walls
Those mute guests at festivals,
Son and Mother, Death and Sin,
Played at dice for Ezzelin,
Till Death cried, "I win, I win!"   240
And Sin cursed to lose the wager,
But Death promised, to assuage her,
That he would petition for
Her to be made Vice-Emperor,
When the destined years were o'er,
Over all between the Po
And the eastern Alpine snow,
Under the mighty Austrian.
Sin smiled so as Sin only can,
And since that time, ay, long before,   250
Both have ruled from shore to shore,—
That incestuous pair, who follow
Tyrants as the sun the swallow,
As Repentance follows Crime,
And as changes follow Time.

In thine halls the lamp of learning,
Padua, now no more is burning;
Like a meteor, whose wild way
Is lost over the grave of day,
Its gleams betrayed and to betray: 260
Once remotest nations came
To adore that sacred flame,
When it lit not many a hearth
On this cold and gloomy earth:
Now new fires from antique light
Spring beneath the wide world's might;
But their spark lies dead in thee,
Trampled out by Tyranny.
As the Norway woodman quells,
In the depth of piny dells,   270
One light flame among the brakes,
While the boundless forest shakes,
And its mighty trunks are torn
By the fire thus lowly born:
The spark beneath his feet is dead,
He starts to see the flames it fed
Howling through the darkened sky
With a myriad tongues victoriously,
And sinks down in fear: so thou,
O Tyranny, beholdest now   280
Light around thee, and thou hearest
The loud flames ascend, and fearest:

Grovel on the earth; ay, hide
In the dust thy purple pride!

Noon descends around me now:
'Tis the noon of autumn's glow,
When a soft and purple mist
Like a vaporous amethyst,
Or an air-dissolvèd star
Mingling light and fragrance, far   290
From the curved horizon's bound
To the point of Heaven's profound,
Fills the overflowing sky;
And the plains that silent lie
Underneath, the leaves unsodden
Where the infant Frost has trodden
With his morning-wingèd feet,
Whose bright print is gleaming yet;
And the red and golden vines,
Piercing with their trellised lines   300
The rough, dark-skirted wilderness;
The dun and bladed grass no less,
Pointing from this hoary tower
In the windless air; the flower
Glimmering at my feet; the line
Of the olive-sandalled Apennine
In the south dimly islanded;
And the Alps, whose snows are spread
High between the clouds and sun;
And of living things each one;   310
And my spirit which so long
Darkened this swift stream of song,—
Interpenetrated lie
By the glory of the sky:
Be it love, light, harmony,
Odour, or the soul of all
Which from Heaven like dew doth fall,
Or the mind which feeds this verse
Peopling the lone universe.

Noon descends, and after noon   320
Autumn's evening meets me soon,
Leading the infantine moon,
And that one star, which to her
Almost seems to minister
Half the crimson light she brings
From the sunset's radiant springs:
And the soft dreams of the morn
(Which like wingèd winds had borne
To that silent isle, which lies
Mid remembered agonies,   330
The frail bark of this lone being)
Pass, to other sufferers fleeing,
And its ancient pilot, Pain,
Sits beside the helm again.

Other flowering isles must be
In the sea of Life and Agony:
Other spirits float and flee
O'er that gulf: even now, perhaps,
On some rock the wild wave wraps,
With folded wings they waiting sit   340
For my bark, to pilot it
To some calm and blooming cove,
Where for me, and those I love,
May a windless bower be built,
Far from passion, pain, and guilt,
In a dell mid lawny hills,
Which the wild sea-murmur fills,
And soft sunshine, and the sound
Of old forests echoing round,
And the light and the smell divine   350
Of all flowers that breathe and shine:
We may live so happy there,
That the Spirits of the Air,
Envying us, may even entice
To our healing Paradise
The polluting multitude;
But their rage would be subdued
By that clime divine and calm,
And the winds whose wings rain balm
On the uplifted soul, and leaves   360
Under which the bright sea heaves;
While each breathless interval
In their whisperings musical
The inspired soul supplies
With its own deep melodies;
And, the love which heals all strife
Circling, like the breath of life,
All things in that sweet abode
With its own mild brotherhood
They, not it, would change; and soon   370
Every sprite beneath the moon
Would repent its envy vain,
And the earth grow young again.

STANZAS

WRITTEN IN DEJECTION, NEAR NAPLES

I

THE sun is warm, the sky is clear,
  The waves are dancing fast and bright,
Blue isles and snowy mountains wear
  The purple noon's transparent might,
  The breath of the moist earth is light,
Around its unexpanded buds;
  Like many a voice of one delight,
The winds, the birds, the ocean floods,
The City's voice itself, is soft like Solitude's.

II

I see the Deep's untrampled floor   9
  With green and purple seaweeds strown;
I see the waves upon the shore,
  Like light dissolved in star-showers,
    thrown:
  I sit upon the sands alone,—
The lightning of the noontide ocean
  Is flashing round me, and a tone
Arises from its measured motion,
How sweet! did any heart now share in my
    emotion.

III

Alas! I have nor hope nor health,
  Nor peace within nor calm around,   20
Nor that content surpassing wealth
  The sage in meditation found,
  And walked with inward glory crowned—
Nor fame, nor power, nor love, nor leisure.
  Others I see whom these surround—
Smiling they live, and call life pleasure;—
To me that cup has been dealt in another
    measure.

IV

Yet now despair itself is mild,
  Even as the winds and waters are;
I could lie down like a tired child,   30
  And weep away the life of care
  Which I have borne and yet must bear,
Till death like sleep might steal on me,
  And I might feel in the warm air
My cheek grow cold, and hear the sea
Breathe o'er my dying brain its last monotony.

V

Some might lament that I were cold,
  As I, when this sweet day is gone,
Which, my lost heart, too soon grown old,
  Insults with this untimely moan;   40
  They might lament—for I am one
Whom men love not,—and yet regret,
  Unlike this day, which, when the sun
Shall on its stainless glory set,
Will linger, though enjoyed, like joy in mem-
    ory yet.

ODE TO THE WEST WIND

I

O WILD West Wind, thou breath of Autumn's
  being,
Thou, from whose unseen presence the leaves
  dead
Are driven, like ghosts from an enchanter
  fleeing,

Yellow, and black, and pale, and hectic red,
Pestilence-stricken multitudes: O thou,
Who chariotest to their dark wintry bed

The wingèd seeds, where they lie cold and
  low,
Each like a corpse within its grave, until
Thine azure sister of the Spring shall blow

Her clarion o'er the dreaming earth, and fill 10
(Driving sweet buds like flocks to feed in air)
With living hues and odours plain and hill:

Wild Spirit, which art moving everywhere;
Destroyer and preserver; hear, oh, hear!

II

Thou on whose stream, mid the steep sky's
  commotion,
Loose clouds like earth's decaying leaves are
  shed,
Shook from the tangled boughs of Heaven and
  Ocean,

Angels of rain and lightning: there are spread
On the blue surface of thine aëry surge,
Like the bright hair uplifted from the head 20

Of some fierce Mænad, even from the dim
  verge
Of the horizon to the zenith's height,
The locks of the approaching storm. Thou
  dirge

Of the dying year, to which this closing night
Will be the dome of a vast sepulchre,
Vaulted with all thy congregated might

Of vapours, from whose solid atmosphere
Black rain, and fire, and hail will burst: oh,
  hear!

III

Thou who didst waken from his summer
  dreams
The blue Mediterranean, where he lay,   30
Lulled by the coil of his crystàlline streams,

Beside a pumice isle in Baiae's bay,
And saw in sleep old palaces and towers
Quivering within the wave's intenser day,

All overgrown with azure moss and flowers
So sweet, the sense faints picturing them!
  Thou
For whose path the Atlantic's level powers

Cleave themselves into chasms, while far below
The sea-blooms and the oozy woods which
  wear
The sapless foliage of the ocean, know   40

Thy voice, and suddenly grow gray with fear,
And tremble and despoil themselves: oh, hear!

IV

If I were a dead leaf thou mightest bear;
If I were a swift cloud to fly with thee;
A wave to pant beneath thy power, and share

The impulse of thy strength, only less free
Than thou, O uncontrollable! If even
I were as in my boyhood, and could be

The comrade of thy wanderings over Heaven,
As then, when to outstrip thy skiey speed 50
Scarce seemed a vision; I would ne'er have
  striven

As thus with thee in prayer in my sore need.
Oh, lift me as a wave, a leaf, a cloud!
I fall upon the thorns of life! I bleed!

A heavy weight of hours has chained and
  bowed
One too like thee: tameless, and swift, and
  proud.

V

Make me thy lyre, even as the forest is:
What if my leaves are falling like its own!
The tumult of thy mighty harmonies

Will take from both a deep, autumnal tone, 60
Sweet though in sadness. Be thou, Spirit fierce,
My spirit! Be thou me, impetuous one!

Drive my dead thoughts over the universe
Like withered leaves to quicken a new birth!
And, by the incantation of this verse,

Scatter, as from an unextinguished hearth
Ashes and sparks, my words among mankind!
Be through my lips to unawakened earth

The trumpet of a prophecy! O, Wind,
If Winter comes, can Spring be far behind? 70

THE CLOUD

I BRING fresh showers for the thirsting flowers,
  From the seas and the streams;
I bear light shade for the leaves when laid
  In their noonday dreams.
From my wings are shaken the dews that waken
  The sweet buds every one,
When rocked to rest on their mother's breast,
  As she dances about the sun.
I wield the flail of the lashing hail,
  And whiten the green plains under, 10
And then again I dissolve it in rain,
  And laugh as I pass in thunder.

I sift the snow on the mountains below,
  And their great pines groan aghast;
And all the night 'tis my pillow white,
  While I sleep in the arms of the blast.
Sublime on the towers of my skiey bowers,
  Lightning my pilot sits;
In a cavern under is fettered the thunder,
  It struggles and howls at fits; 20
Over earth and ocean, with gentle motion,
  This pilot is guiding me,
Lured by the love of the genii that move
  In the depths of the purple sea;
Over the rills, and the crags, and the hills,
  Over the lakes and the plains,
Wherever he dream, under mountain or stream,
  The Spirit he loves remains;
And I all the while bask in Heaven's blue smile,
  Whilst he is dissolving in rains. 30

The sanguine Sunrise, with his meteor eyes,
  And his burning plumes outspread,
Leaps on the back of my sailing rack,
  When the morning star shines dead;
As on the jag of a mountain crag,
  Which an earthquake rocks and swings,
An eagle alit one moment may sit
  In the light of its golden wings.
And when Sunset may breathe, from the lit sea beneath,
  Its ardours of rest and of love, 40
And the crimson pall of eve may fall
  From the depth of Heaven above,
With wings folded I rest, on mine aëry nest,
  As still as a brooding dove.

That orbèd maiden with white fire laden,
  Whom mortals call the Moon,
Glides glimmering o'er my fleece-like floor,
  By the midnight breezes strewn;
And wherever the beat of her unseen feet,
  Which only the angels hear, 50
May have broken the woof of my tent's thin roof,
  The stars peep behind her and peer;
And I laugh to see them whirl and flee,
  Like a swarm of golden bees,
When I widen the rent in my wind-built tent,
  Till the calm rivers, lakes, and seas,
Like strips of the sky fallen through me on high,
  Are each paved with the moon and these.

I bind the Sun's throne with a burning zone,
  And the Moon's with a girdle of pearl; 60
The volcanoes are dim, and the stars reel and swim,
  When the whirlwinds my banner unfurl.
From cape to cape, with a bridge-like shape,
  Over a torrent sea,
Sunbeam-proof, I hang like a roof,—
  The mountains its columns be.
The triumphal arch through which I march
  With hurricane, fire, and snow,
When the Powers of the air are chained to my chair,
  Is the million-coloured bow; 70
The sphere-fire above its soft colours wove,
  While the moist Earth was laughing below.

I am the daughter of Earth and Water,
  And nursling of the Sky;

I pass through the pores of the ocean and
    shores;
    I change, but cannot die.
For after the rain when with never a stain
    The pavilion of Heaven is bare,
And the winds and sunbeams with their con-
    vex gleams
    Build up the blue dome of air,   80
I silently laugh at my own cenotaph,
    And out of the caverns of rain,
Like a child from the womb, like a ghost
    from the tomb,
    I arise and unbuild it again.

TO A SKYLARK

HAIL to thee, blithe Spirit!
    Bird thou never wert,
That from Heaven, or near it,
    Pourest thy full heart
In profuse strains of unpremeditated art.

Higher still and higher
    From the earth thou springest
Like a cloud of fire;
    The blue deep thou wingest,
And singing still dost soar, and soaring ever
    singest.   10

In the golden lightning
    Of the sunken sun,
O'er which clouds are bright'ning,
    Thou dost float and run;
Like an unbodied joy whose race is just be-
    gun.

The pale purple even
    Melts around thy flight;
Like a star of Heaven,
    In the broad daylight
Thou art unseen, but yet I hear thy shrill
    delight,   20

Keen as are the arrows
    Of that silver sphere,
Whose intense lamp narrows
    In the white dawn clear
Until we hardly see—we feel that it is there.

All the earth and air
    With thy voice is loud,
As, when night is bare,
    From one lonely cloud

The moon rains out her beams, and Heaven
    is overflowed.   30

What thou art we know not;
    What is most like thee?
From rainbow clouds there flow not
    Drops so bright to see
As from thy presence showers a rain of
    melody.

Like a Poet hidden
    In the light of thought,
Singing hymns unbidden,
    Till the world is wrought
To sympathy with hopes and fears it heeded
    not: 40

Like a high-born maiden
    In a palace-tower,
Soothing her love-laden
    Soul in secret hour
With music sweet as love, which overflows
    her bower:

Like a glow-worm golden
    In a dell of dew,
Scattering unbeholden
    Its aëreal hue
Among the flowers and grass, which screen
    it from the view!   50

Like a rose embowered
    In its own green leaves,
By warm winds deflowered,
    Till the scent it gives
Makes faint with too much sweet those heavy-
    wingèd thieves:

Sound of vernal showers
    On the twinkling grass,
Rain-awakened flowers,
    All that ever was
Joyous, and clear, and fresh, thy music doth
    surpass: 60

Teach us, Sprite or Bird,
    What sweet thoughts are thine:
I have never heard
    Praise of love or wine
That panted forth a flood of rapture so divine.

Chorus Hymeneal,
    Or triumphal chant,
Matched with thine would be all

But an empty vaunt,
A thing wherein we feel there is some hidden
    want. 70

What objects are the fountains
  Of thy happy strain?
What fields, or waves, or mountains?
  What shapes of sky or plain?
What love of thine own kind? what ignorance
    of pain?

With thy clear keen joyance
  Languor cannot be:
Shadow of annoyance
  Never came near thee:
Thou lovest—but ne'er knew love's sad
    satiety. 80

Waking or asleep,
  Thou of death must deem
Things more true and deep
  Than we mortals dream,
Or how could thy notes flow in such a crystal
    stream?

We look before and after,
  And pine for what is not:
Our sincerest laughter
  With some pain is fraught;
Our sweetest songs are those that tell of
    saddest thought. 90

Yet if we could scorn
  Hate, and pride, and fear;
If we were things born
  Not to shed a tear,
I know not how thy joy we ever should come
    near.

Better than all measures
  Of delightful sound,
Better than all treasures
  That in books are found,
Thy skill to poet were, thou scorner of the
    ground! 100

Teach me half the gladness
  That thy brain must know,
Such harmonious madness
  From my lips would flow
The world should listen then—as I am listen-
    ing now.

ODE TO LIBERTY

Yet, Freedom, yet, thy banner, torn but flying,
Streams like a thunder-storm against the
    wind.—BYRON.

I

A GLORIOUS people vibrated again
  The lightning of the nations: Liberty
From heart to heart, from tower to tower,
    o'er Spain,
  Scattering contagious fire into the sky,
Gleamed. My soul spurned the chains of its
    dismay,
    And in the rapid plumes of song
    Clothed itself, sublime and strong;
As a young eagle soars the morning clouds
    among,
    Hovering inverse o'er its accustomed prey;
      Till from its station in the Heaven of
      fame 10
The Spirit's whirlwind rapped it, and the ray
  Of the remotest sphere of living flame
Which paves the void was from behind it
    flung,
    As foam from a ship's swiftness, when there
    came
  A voice out of the deep: I will record the
    same.

II

The Sun and the serenest Moon sprang forth:
  The burning stars of the abyss were hurled
Into the depths of Heaven. The daedal earth,
  That island in the ocean of the world,
Hung in its cloud of all-sustaining air: 20
    But this divinest universe
    Was yet a chaos and a curse,
For thou wert not: but, power from worst
    producing worse,
    The spirit of the beasts was kindled there,
    And of the birds, and of the watery forms,
  And there was war among them, and de-
    spair,
    Within them, raging without truce or
    terms:
The bosom of their violated nurse
    Groaned, for beasts warred on beasts, and
    worms on worms,
    And men on men; each heart was as a hell
    of storms. 30

III

Man, the imperial shape, then multiplied
His generations under the pavilion
Of the Sun's throne: palace and pyramid,
Temple and prison, to many a swarming
million
Were, as to mountain-wolves their raggèd
caves.
This human living multitude
Was savage, cunning, blind, and rude,
For thou wert not; but o'er the populous
solitude,
Like one fierce cloud over a waste of waves,
Hung Tyranny; beneath, sate deified 40
The sister-pest, congregator of slaves;
Into the shadow of her pinions wide
Anarchs and priests, who feed on gold and
blood
Till with the stain their inmost souls are
dyed,
Drove the astonished herds of men from
every side.

IV

The nodding promotories, and blue isles,
And cloud-like mountains, and dividuous
waves
Of Greece, basked glorious in the open smiles
Of favouring Heaven: from their enchanted
caves
Prophetic echoes flung dim melody. 50
On the unapprehensive wild
The vine, the corn, the olive mild,
Grew savage yet, to human use unreconciled;
And, like unfolded flowers beneath the sea,
Like the man's thought dark in the in-
fant's brain,
Like aught that is which wraps what is to
be,
Art's deathless dreams lay veiled by
many a vein
Of Parian stone; and, yet a speechless child,
Verse murmured, and Philosophy did strain
Her lidless eyes for thee; when o'er the
Ægean main 60

V

Athens arose: a city such as vision
Builds from the purple crags and silver
towers
Of battlemented cloud, as in derision

Of kingliest masonry: the ocean-floors
Pave it; the evening sky pavilions it;
Its portals are inhabited
By thunder-zonèd winds, each head
Within its cloudy wings with sun-fire gar-
landed,—
A divine work! Athens, diviner yet,
Gleamed with its crest of columns, on
the will 70
Of man, as on a mount of diamond, set;
For thou wert, and thine all-creative skill
Peopled, with forms that mock the eternal
dead
In marble immortality, that hill
Which was thine earliest throne and latest
oracle.

VI

Within the surface of Time's fleeting river
Its wrinkled image lies, as then it lay
Immovably unquiet, and for ever
It trembles, but it cannot pass away!
The voices of thy bards and sages thunder 80
With an earth-awakening blast
Through the caverns of the past:
(Religion veils her eyes; Oppression shrinks
aghast:)
A wingèd sound of joy, and love, and won-
der,
Which soars where Expectation never flew,
Rending the veil of space and time asunder!
One ocean feeds the clouds, and streams,
and dew;
One Sun illumines Heaven; one Spirit vast
With life and love make chaos ever new,
As Athens doth the world with thy delight
renew. 90

VII

Then Rome was, and from thy deep bosom
fairest,
Like a wolf-cub from a Cadmæan Mænad,
She drew the milk of greatness, though thy
dearest
From that Elysian food was yet unweanèd;
And many a deed of terrible uprightness
By thy sweet love was sanctified;
And in thy smile, and by thy side,
Saintly Camillus lived, and firm Atilius died.
But when tears stained thy robe of vestal
whiteness, 99
And gold profaned thy Capitolian throne,

Thou didst desert, with spirit-wingèd light-
ness,
    The senate of the tyrants: they sunk
      prone
Slaves of one tyrant: Palatinus sighed
Faint echoes of Ionian song; that tone
Thou didst delay to hear, lamenting to dis-
own

VIII

From what Hyrcanian glen or frozen hill,
  Or piny promontory of the Arctic main,
Or utmost islet inaccessible,
  Didst thou lament the ruin of thy reign,
Teaching the woods and waves, and desert
    rocks,   110
    And every Naiad's ice-cold urn,
    To talk in echoes sad and stern
Of that sublimest lore which man had dared
    unlearn?
For neither didst thou watch the wizard
    flocks
    Of the Scald's dreams, nor haunt the
      Druid's sleep.
What if the tears rained through thy shat-
    tered locks
    Were quickly dried? for thou didst groan,
      not weep,
When from its sea of death, to kill and burn,
The Galilean serpent forth did creep,
And made thy world an undistinguishable
    heap.   120

IX

A thousand years the Earth cried, 'Where art
    thou?'
And then the shadow of thy coming fell
On Saxon Alfred's olive-cinctured brow:
  And many a warrior-peopled citadel,
Like rocks which fire lifts out of the flat deep,
    Arose in sacred Italy,
    Frowning o'er the tempestuous sea
Of kings, and priests, and slaves, in tower-
    crowned majesty;
    That multitudinous anarchy did sweep
    And burst around their walls, like idle
      foam,   130
    Whilst from the human spirit's deepest
    deep
    Strange melody with love and awe struck
      dumb
Dissonant arms; and Art, which cannot die,

With divine wand traced on our earthly
    home
Fit imagery to pave Heaven's everlasting
    dome.

X

Thou huntress swifter than the Moon! thou
    terror
    Of the world's wolves! thou bearer of the
      quiver,
Whose sunlike shafts pierce tempest-wingèd
    Error,
    As light may pierce the clouds when they
      dissever
In the calm regions of the orient day!   140
    Luther caught thy wakening glance;
    Like lightning, from his leaden lance
Reflected, it dissolved the visions of the trance
    In which, as in a tomb, the nations lay;
    And England's prophets hailed thee as
      their queen,
In songs whose music cannot pass away,
    Though it must flow forever: not unseen
Before the spirit-sighted countenance
    Of Milton didst thou pass, from the sad
      scene
    Beyond whose night he saw, with a dejected
      mien.   150

XI

The eager hours and unreluctant years
    As on a dawn-illumined mountain stood,
Trampling to silence their loud hopes and
      fears,
    Darkening each other with their multitude,
And cried aloud, 'Liberty!' Indignation
    Answered Pity from her cave;
    Death grew pale within the grave,
And Desolation howled to the destroyer, Save!
    When like Heaven's Sun girt by the exhala-
      tion   159
    Of its own glorious light, thou didst arise,
Chasing thy foes from nation unto nation
    Like shadows: as if day had cloven the
      skies
At dreaming midnight o'er the western wave,
    Men started, staggering with a glad surprise,
    Under the lightnings of thine unfamiliar
      eyes.

XII

Thou Heaven of earth! what spells could pall
    thee then

In ominous eclipse? a thousand years
Bred from the slime of deep Oppression's den,
   Dyed all thy liquid light with blood and
      tears,
Till thy sweet stars could weep the stain away;
     How like Bacchanals of blood   171
      Round France, the ghastly vintage,
      stood
Destruction's sceptred slaves, and Folly's
     mitred brood!
     When one, like them, but mightier far than
      they,
      The Anarch of thine own bewildered
       powers,
     Rose: armies mingled in obscure array,
      Like clouds with clouds, darkening the
       sacred bowers
Of serene Heaven. He, by the past pursued,
     Rests with those dead, but unforgotten
      hours,
     Whose ghosts scare victor kings in their
      ancestral towers.   180

XIII

England yet sleeps: was she not called of old?
Spain calls her now, as with its thrilling
     thunder
Vesuvius wakens Ætna, and the cold
   Snow-crags by its reply are cloven in sun-
     der:
O'er the lit waves every Æolian isle
     From Pithecusa to Pelorus
      Howls, and leaps, and glares in chorus:
They cry, 'Be dim; ye lamps of Heaven sus-
     pended o'er us!'
     Her chains are threads of gold, she need but
      smile
     And they dissolve; but Spain's were links
      of steel,   190
Till bit to dust by virtue's keenest file.
   Twins of a single destiny! appeal
To the eternal years enthroned before us
   In the dim West; impress us from a seal,
All ye have thought and done! Time cannot
     dare conceal.

XIV

Tomb of Arminius! render up thy dead
   Till, like a standard from a watch-tower's
     staff,
His soul may stream over the tyrant's head;
   Thy victory shall be his epitaph,

Wild Bacchanal of truth's mysterious wine, 200
     King-deluded Germany,
      His dead spirit lives in thee.
Why do we fear or hope? thou art already
     free!
And thou, lost Paradise of this divine
     And glorious world! thou flowery wil-
      derness!
Thou island of eternity! thou shrine
     Where Desolation, clothed with loveliness,
Worships the thing thou wert! O Italy,
     Gather thy blood into thy heart; repress
     The beasts who make their dens thy sacred
      palaces.   210

XV

Oh, that the free would stamp the impious
     name
Of KING into the dust! or write it there,
So that this blot upon the page of fame
   Were as a serpent's path, which the light air
Erases, and the flat sands close behind!
     Ye the oracle have heard:
      Lift the victory-flashing sword,
And cut the snaky knots of this foul gordian
     word,
     Which, weak itself as stubble, yet can bind
      Into a mass, irrefragably firm,   220
     The axes and the rods which awe mankind;
      The sound has poison in it, 'tis the sperm
Of what makes life foul, cankerous, and ab-
     horred;
     Disdain not thou, at thine appointed term,
     To set thine armèd heel on this reluctant
      worm.

XVI

Oh, that the wise from their bright minds
     would kindle
Such lamps within the dome of this dim
     world,
That the pale name of PRIEST might shrink
     and dwindle
   Into the hell from which it first was hurled,
A scoff of impious pride from fiends im-
     pure;   230
     Till human thoughts might kneel alone,
      Each before the judgment-throne
Of its own aweless soul, or of the Power un-
     known!
     Oh, that the words which make the thoughts
     obscure

From which they spring, as clouds of
glimmering dew
From a white lake blot Heaven's blue portraiture,
Were stripped of their thin masks and
various hue
And frowns and smiles and splendours not
their own,
Till in the nakedness of false and true
They stand before the Lord, each to receive
its due! 240

XVII

He who taught man to vanquish whatsoever
Can be between the cradle and the grave
Crowned him the King of Life. Oh, vain en-
deavour!
If on his own high will, a willing slave,
He has enthroned the oppression and the op-
pressor;
What if earth can clothe and feed
Amplest millions at their need,
And power in thought be as the tree within
the seed?
Or what if Art, an ardent intercessor,
Driving on fiery wings to Nature's throne,
Checks the great mother stooping to caress
her, 251
And cries: 'Give me, thy child, dominion
Over all height and depth'? if Life can breed
New wants, and wealth from those who toil
and groan,
Rend of thy gifts and hers a thousandfold
for one!

XVIII

Come thou, but lead out of the inmost cave
Of man's deep spirit, as the morning-star
Beckons the Sun from the Eoan wave,
Wisdom. I hear the pennons of her car
Self-moving, like cloud chariot by flame; 260
Comes she not, and come ye not,
Rulers of eternal thought,
To judge, with solemn truth, life's ill-
apportioned lot?
Blind Love, and equal Justice, and the Fame
Of what has been, the Hope of what
will be?
O Liberty! if such could be thy name
Wert thou disjoined from these, or they
from thee:
If thine or theirs were treasures to be bought

By blood or tears, have not the wise and
free
Wept tears, and blood like tears?—The
solemn harmony 270

XIX

Paused, and the Spirit of that mighty singing
To its abyss was suddenly withdrawn;
Then, as a wild swan, when sublimely winging
Its path athwart the thunder-smoke of dawn,
Sinks headlong through the aëreal golden light
On the heavy-sounding plain,
When the bolt has pierced its brain;
As summer clouds dissolve, unburthened of
their rain;
As a far taper fades with fading night, 279
As a brief insect dies with dying day,—
My song, its pinions disarrayed of might,
Drooped; o'er it closed the echoes far
away
Of the great voice which did its flight sustain,
As waves which lately paved his watery way
Hiss round a drowner's head in their tem-
pestuous play.

FROM HELLAS

Chorus

THE world's great age begins anew,
The golden years return,
The earth doth like a snake renew
Her winter weeds outworn:
Heaven smiles, and faiths and empires gleam,
Like wrecks of a dissolving dream.

A brighter Hellas rears its mountains
From waves serener far;
A new Peneus rolls his fountains
Against the morning star. 10
Where fairer Tempes bloom, there sleep
Young Cyclads on a sunnier deep.

A loftier Argo cleaves the main,
Fraught with a later prize;
Another Orpheus sings again,
And loves, and weeps, and dies.
A new Ulysses leaves once more
Calypso for his native shore.

Oh, write no more the tale of Troy,
If earth Death's scroll must be! 20

Nor mix with Laian rage the joy
  Which dawns upon the free:
Although a subtler Sphinx renew
Riddles of death Thebes never knew.

Another Athens shall arise,
  And to remoter time
Bequeath, like sunset to the skies,
  The splendour of its prime;
And leave, if nought so bright may live,
All earth can take or Heaven can give.   30

Saturn and Love their long repose
  Shall burst, more bright and good
Than all who fell, than One who rose,
  Than many unsubdued:
Not gold, not blood, their altar dowers,
But votive tears and symbol flowers.

Oh, cease! must hate and death return?
  Cease! must men kill and die?
Cease! drain not to its dregs the urn
  Of bitter prophecy.   40
The world is weary of the past,
Oh, might it die or rest at last!

TO NIGHT

I

Swiftly walk o'er the western wave,
  Spirit of Night!
Out of the misty eastern cave,
Where, all the long and lone daylight,
Thou wovest dreams of joy and fear,
Which make thee terrible and dear,—
  Swift be thy flight!

II

Wrap thy form in a mantle gray,
  Star-inwrought!
Blind with thine hair the eyes of Day;   10
Kiss her until she be wearied out,
Then wander o'er city, and sea, and land,
Touching all with thine opiate wand—
  Come, long-sought!

III

When I arose and saw the dawn,
  I sighed for thee;
When light rode high, and the dew was gone,

And noon lay heavy on flower and tree,
And the weary Day turned to his rest,
Lingering like an unloved guest,   20
  I sighed for thee.

IV

Thy brother Death came, and cried,
  Wouldst thou me?
Thy sweet child sleep, the filmy-eyed,
Murmured like a noontide bee,
Shall I nestle near thy side?
Wouldst thou me?—and I replied,
  No, not thee!

V

Death will come when thou art dead,
  Soon, too soon—   30
Sleep will come when thou art fled;
Of neither would I ask the boon
I ask of thee, belovèd Night—
Swift be thine approaching flight,
  Come soon, soon!

TO ———

Music, when soft voices die,
  Vibrates in the memory—
Odours, when sweet violets sicken,
  Live within the sense they quicken.

Rose leaves, when the rose is dead,
  Are heaped for the belovèd's bed;
And so thy thoughts, when thou art gone,
  Love itself shall slumber on.

A LAMENT

I

O world! O life! O time!
  On whose last steps I climb,
  Trembling at that where I had stood before;
When will return the glory of your prime?
  No more— Oh, never more!

II

Out of the day and night
  A joy has taken flight;
Fresh spring, and summer, and winter hoar,

Move my faint heart with grief, but with de-
    light
    No more— Oh, never more!   10

TO ———

I

ONE word is too often profaned
    For me to profane it,
One feeling too falsely disdained
    For thee to disdain it;
One hope is too like despair
    For prudence to smother,
And pity from thee more dear
    Than that from another.

II

I can give not what men call love,
    But wilt thou accept not   10
The worship the heart lifts above
    And the Heavens reject not,—
The desire of the moth for the star,
    Of the night for the morrow,
The devotion to something afar,
        From the sphere of our sorrow?

LINES: "WHEN THE LAMP IS SHATTERED"

I

WHEN the lamp is shattered
The light in the dust lies dead—
    When the cloud is scattered
The rainbow's glory is shed.
    When the lute is broken,
Sweet tones are remembered not;
    When the lips have spoken,
Loved accents are soon forgot.

II

    As music and splendour
Survive not the lamp and the lute,   10
    The heart's echoes render
No song when the spirit is mute:—
    No song but sad dirges,
Like the wind through a ruined cell,
    Or the mournful surges
That ring the dead seaman's knell.

III

    When hearts have once mingled
Love first leaves the well-built nest;
    The weak one is singled
To endure what it once possessed.   20
    O Love! who bewailest
The frailty of all things here,
    Why choose you the frailest
For your cradle, your home, and your bier?

IV

    Its passions will rock thee
As the storms rock the ravens on high;
    Bright reason will mock thee,
Like the sun from a wintry sky.
    From thy nest every rafter
Will rot, and thine eagle home   30
    Leave thee naked to laughter,
When leaves fall and cold winds come.

A DIRGE

    ROUGH wind, that moanest loud
        Grief too sad for song;
    Wild wind, when sullen cloud
        Knells all the night long;
    Sad storm, whose tears are vain,
    Bare woods, whose branches strain,
    Deep caves and dreary main, —
        Wail, for the world's wrong!

SELECTIONS FROM THE PROSE OF SHELLEY

ESSAY ON CHRISTIANITY
1815

The Being who has influenced in the most memorable manner the opinions and the fortunes of the human species, is Jesus Christ. At this day, his name is connected with the devotional feelings of two hundred millions of the race of man. The institutions of the most civilized portion of the globe derive their authority from the sanction of his doctrines; he is the hero, the God, of our popular religion. His extraordinary genius, the wide and rapid effect of his unexampled doctrines, his invincible gentleness and benignity, the devoted love borne to him by his adherents, suggested a persuasion to them that he was something divine. The supernatural events which the historians of this wonderful man subsequently asserted to have been connected with every gradation of his career, established the opinion.

His death is said to have been accompanied by an accumulation of tremendous prodigies. Utter darkness fell upon the earth, blotting the noonday sun; dead bodies, arising from their graves, walked through the public streets, and an earthquake shook the astonished city, rending the rocks of the surrounding mountains. The philosopher may attribute the application of these events to the death of a reformer, or the events themselves to a visitation of that universal Pan who——

. . . .

The thoughts which the word "God" suggests to the human mind are susceptible of as many variations as human minds themselves. The Stoic, the Platonist, and the Epicurean, the Polytheist, the Dualist, and the Trinitarian, differ infinitely in their conceptions of its meaning. They agree only in considering it the most awful and most venerable of names, as a common term devised to express all of mystery, or majesty, or power, which the invisible world contains. And not only has every sect distinct conceptions of the application of this name, but scarcely two individuals of the same sect, who exercise in any degree the freedom of their judgement, or yield themselves with any candour of feeling to the influences of the visible world, find perfect coincidence of opinion to exist between them. It is [interesting] to inquire in what acceptation Jesus Christ employed this term.

We may conceive his mind to have been predisposed on this subject to adopt the opinions of his countrymen. Every human being is indebted for a multitude of his sentiments to the religion of his early years. Jesus Christ probably [studied] the historians of his country with the ardour of a spirit seeking after truth. They were undoubtedly the companions of his childish years, the food and nutriment and materials of his youthful meditations. The sublime dramatic poem entitled *Job* had familiarized his imagination with the boldest imagery afforded by the human mind and the material world. *Ecclesiastes* had diffused a seriousness and solemnity over the frame of his spirit, glowing with youthful hope, and [had] made audible to his listening heart

The still, sad music of humanity,
Not harsh or grating, but of ample power
To chasten and subdue.

He had contemplated this name as having been profanely perverted to the sanctioning of the most enormous and abominable crimes. We can distinctly trace, in the tissue of his doctrines, the persuasion that God is some universal Being, differing from man and the mind of man. According to Jesus Christ, God is neither the Jupiter, who sends rain upon the earth; nor the Venus, through whom all living things are produced; nor the Vulcan, who presides over the terrestrial element of fire; nor the Vesta, that preserves the light which is enshrined in the sun and moon and stars. He is neither the Proteus nor the Pan of the material world. But the word God, according to the acceptation of Jesus Christ, unites all the attributes which these denominations contain, and is the [interpoint] and overruling Spirit of all the energy and wisdom included within the circle of existing things. It is important to observe that the author of the Christian system had a conception widely differing from the gross imaginations of the vulgar relatively to the ruling Power of the universe. He everywhere represents this Power as something mysteriously and illimitably prevading the frame of things. Nor do his doctrines practically assume any proposition which they theoretically deny. They do not represent God as a limitless and inconceivable mystery; affirming, at the same time, his existence as a Being subject to passion and capable——

. . . .

"Blessed are the pure in heart, for they shall see God." Blessed are those who have preserved internal sanctity of soul; who are conscious of no secret deceit; who are the same in act as they are in desire; who conceal no thought, no tendencies of thought, from their own conscience; who are faithful and sincere witnesses, before the tribunal of their own judgements, of all that passes within their mind. Such as these shall see God. What! after death, shall their awakened eyes behold the King of Heaven? Shall they stand in awe before the golden throne on which He sits, and gaze upon the venerable countenance of the paternal Monarch? Is this the reward of the virtuous and the pure? These are the idle dreams of the visionary, or the pernicious representations of impostors, who have fabricated from the very materials of wisdom a cloak for their own dwarfish or imbecile conceptions.

Jesus Christ has said no more than the most excellent philosophers have felt and expressed —that virtue is its own reward. It is true that such an expression as he has used was prompted by the energy of genius, and was the overflowing enthusiasm of a poet; but it is not the less literally true [because] clearly repugnant to the mistaken conceptions of the multitude. God, it has been asserted, was contemplated by Jesus Christ as every poet and every philosopher must have contemplated that mysterious principle. He considered that venerable word to express the overruling Spirit of the collective energy of the moral and material world. He affirms, therefore, no more than that a simple, sincere mind is the indispensable requisite of true science and true happiness. He affirms that a being of pure and gentle habits will not fail, in every thought, in every object of every thought, to be aware of benignant visitings from the invisible energies by which he is surrounded.

Whosoever is free from the contamination of luxury and licence, may go forth to the fields and to the woods, inhaling joyous renovation from the breath of Spring, or catching from the odours and sounds of Autumn some diviner mood of sweetest sadness, which improves the softened heart. Whosoever is no deceiver or destroyer of his fellow men—no liar, no flatterer, no murderer—may walk among his species, deriving, from the communion with all which they contain of beautiful or of majestic, some intercourse with the Universal God. Whosoever has maintained with his own heart the strictest correspondence of confidence, who dares to examine and to estimate every imagination which suggests itself to his mind—whosoever is that which he designs to become, and only aspires to that which the divinity of his own nature shall consider and approve—he has already seen God.

We live and move and think; but we are not the creators of our own origin and existence. We are not the arbiters of every motion of our own complicated nature; we are not the masters of our own imaginations and moods of mental being. There is a Power by which we are surrounded, like the atmosphere in which some motionless lyre is suspended, which visits with its breath our silent chords at will.

Our most imperial and stupendous qualities —those on which the majesty and the power of humanity is erected—are, relatively to the inferior portion of its mechanism, active and imperial; but they are the passive slaves of some higher and more omnipotent Power. This Power is God; and those who have seen God have, in the period of their purer and more perfect nature, been harmonized by their own will to so exquisite [a] consentaneity of power as to give forth divinest melody, when the breath of universal being sweeps over their frame. That those who are pure in heart shall see God, and that virtue is its own reward, may be considered as equivalent assertions. The former of these propositions is a metaphorical repetition of the latter. The advocates of literal interpretation have been the most efficacious enemies of those doctrines whose nature they profess to venerate. Thucydides, in particular, affords a number of instances calculated——

.   .   .   .

Tacitus says, that the Jews held God to be something eternal and supreme, neither subject to change nor to decay; therefore, they permit no statues in their cities or their temples. The universal Being can only be described or defined by negatives which deny his subjection to the laws of all inferior existences. Where indefiniteness ends, idolatry and anthropomorphism begin. God is, as Lucan has expressed,

> Quocunque vides, quodcunque moveris,
> Et caelum et virtus.

The doctrine of what some fanatics have termed "a peculiar Providence"—that is, of some power beyond and superior to that which ordinarily guides the operations of the Universe, interfering to punish the vicious and reward the virtuous—is explicitly denied by Jesus Christ. The absurd and execrable doctrine of vengeance, in *all its shapes,* seems to have been contemplated by this great moralist with the profoundest disapprobation; nor would he permit the most venerable of names to be perverted into a sanction for the meanest and most contemptible propensities incident to the nature of man. "Love your enemies, bless those who curse you, that ye may be the sons of your Heavenly Father, who makes the sun to shine on the good and on the evil, and the rain to fall on the just and unjust." How monstrous a calumny have not impostors dared to advance against the mild and gentle author of this just sentiment, and against the whole tenor of his doctrines and his life, overflowing with benevolence and forbearance and compassion! They have represented him asserting that the Omnipotent God —that merciful and benignant Power who scatters equally upon the beautiful earth all the elements of security and happiness—whose influences are distributed to all whose natures admit of a participation in them—who sends to the weak and vicious creatures of his will all the benefits which they are capable of sharing—that this God has devised a scheme whereby the body shall live after its apparent dissolution, and be rendered capable of indefinite torture. He is said to have compared the agonies which the vicious shall then endure to the excruciations of a living body bound among the flames, and being consumed sinew by sinew, and bone by bone.

And this is to be done, not because it is supposed (and the supposition would be sufficiently detestable) that the moral nature of the sufferer would be improved by his tortures —it is done because it *is just* to be done. My neighbour, or my servant, or my child, has done me an injury, and it is just that he should suffer an injury in return. Such is the doctrine which Jesus Christ summoned his whole resources of persuasion to oppose. "Love your enemy, bless those who curse you": such, he says, is the practice of God, and such must ye imitate if ye would be the children of God.

Jesus Christ would hardly have cited, as an example of all that is gentle and beneficent and compassionate, a Being who shall deliberately scheme to inflict on a large portion of the human race tortures indescribably intense and indefinitely protracted: who shall inflict them, too, without any mistake as to the true nature of pain—without any view to future good— merely because it is just.

This, and no other, is justice:—to consider, under all the circumstances and consequences of a particular case, how the greatest quantity and purest quality of happiness will ensue from any action; [this] is to be just, and there

is no other justice. The distinction between justice and mercy was first imagined in the courts of tyrants. Mankind receive every relaxation of their tyranny as a circumstance of grace or favour.

Such was the clemency of Julius Caesar, who, having achieved by a series of treachery and bloodshed the ruin of the liberties of his country, receives the fame of mercy because, possessing the power to slay the noblest men of Rome, he restrained his sanguinary soul, arrogating to himself as a merit an abstinence from actions which if he had committed, he would only have added one other atrocity to his deeds. His assassins understood justice better. They saw the most virtuous and civilized community of mankind under the insolent dominion of one wicked man; and they murdered him. They destroyed the usurper of the liberties of their countrymen, not because they hated him, not because they would revenge the wrongs which they had sustained (Brutus, it is said, was his most familiar friend; most of the conspirators were habituated to domestic intercourse with the man whom they destroyed): it was in affection, inextinguishable love for all that is venerable and dear to the human heart, in the names of Country, Liberty, and Virtue; it was in a serious and solemn and reluctant mood, that these holy patriots murdered their father and their friend. They would have spared his violent death, if he could have deposited the rights which he had assumed. His own selfish and narrow nature necessitated the sacrifices they made. They required that he should change all those habits which debauchery and bloodshed had twined around the fibres of his inmost frame of thought; that he should participate with them and with his country those privileges which, having corrupted by assuming to himself, he would no longer value. They would have sacrificed their lives if they could have made him worthy of the sacrifice. Such are the feelings which Jesus Christ asserts to belong to the ruling Power of the world. He desireth not the death of a sinner: he makes the sun to shine upon the just and unjust.

The nature of a narrow and malevolent spirit is so essentially incompatible with happiness as to render it inaccessible to the influences of the benignant God. All that his own perverse propensities will permit him to receive, that God abundantly pours forth upon him. If there is the slightest overbalance of happiness, which can be allotted to the most atrocious offender, consistently with the nature of things, that is rigidly made his portion by the ever-watchful Power of God. In every case, the human mind enjoys the utmost pleasure which it is capable of enjoying. God is represented by Jesus Christ as the Power from which, and through which, the streams of all that is excellent and delightful flow; the Power which models, as they pass, all the elements of this mixed universe to the purest and most perfect shape which it belongs to their nature to assume. Jesus Christ attributes to this Power the faculty of Will. How far such a doctrine, in its ordinary sense, may be philosophically true, or how far Jesus Christ intentionally availed himself of a metaphor easily understood, is foreign to the subject to consider. This much is certain, that Jesus Christ represents God as the fountain of all goodness, the eternal enemy of pain and evil, the uniform and unchanging motive of the salutary operations of the material world. The supposition that this cause is excited to action by some principle analogous to the human will, adds weight to the persuasion that it is foreign to its beneficent nature to inflict the slightest pain. According to Jesus Christ, and according to the indisputable facts of the case, some evil spirit has dominion in this imperfect world. But there will come a time when the human mind shall be visited exclusively by the influences of the benignant Power. Men shall die, and their bodies shall rot under the ground; all the organs through which their knowledge and their feelings have flowed, or in which they have originated, shall assume other forms, and become ministrant to purposes the most foreign from their former tendencies. There is a time when we shall neither be heard or be seen by the multitude of beings like ourselves by whom we have been so long surrounded. They shall go to graves; where then?

It appears that we moulder to a heap of senseless dust; to a few worms, that arise and perish, like ourselves. Jesus Christ asserts that these appearances are fallacious, and that a gloomy and cold imagination alone suggests the conception that thought can cease to be. Another and a more extensive state of being, rather than the complete extinction of being, will follow from that mysterious change which we call Death. There shall be no misery, no pain, no fear. The empire of evil spirits ex-

tends not beyond the boundaries of the grave. The unobscured irradiations from the fountain-fire of all goodness shall reveal all that is mysterious and unintelligible, until the mutual communications of knowledge and of happiness throughout all thinking natures constitute a harmony of good that ever varies and never ends.

This is Heaven, when pain and evil cease, and when the Benignant Principle, untrammelled and uncontrolled, visits in the fullness of its power the universal frame of things. Human life, with all its unreal ills and transitory hopes, is as a dream, which departs before the dawn, leaving no trace of its evanescent hues. All that it contains of pure or of divine visits the passive mind in some serenest mood. Most holy are the feelings through which our fellow beings are rendered dear and [venerable] to the heart. The remembrance of their sweetness, and the completion of the hopes which they [excite], constitute, when we awaken from the sleep of life, the fulfilment of the prophecies of its most majestic and beautiful visions.

We die, says Jesus Christ; and, when we awaken from the languor of disease, the glories and the happiness of Paradise are around us. All evil and pain have ceased for ever. Our happiness also corresponds with, and is adapted to, the nature of what is most excellent in our being. We see God, and we see that he is good. How delightful a picture, even if it be not true! How magnificent is the conception which this bold theory suggests to the contemplation, even if it be no more than the imagination of some sublimest and most holy poet, who, impressed with the loveliness and majesty of his own nature, is impatient and discontented with the narrow limits which this imperfect life and the dark grave have assigned for ever as his melancholy portion. It is not to be believed that Hell, or punishment, was the conception of this daring mind. It is not to be believed that the most prominent group of this picture, which is framed so heart-moving and lovely—the accomplishment of all human hope, the extinction of all morbid fear and anguish—would consist of millions of sensitive beings enduring, in every variety of torture which Omniscient vengeance could invent, immortal agony.

Jesus Christ opposed with earnest eloquence the panic fears and hateful superstitions which have enslaved mankind for ages. Nations had risen against nations, employing the subtlest devices of mechanism and mind to waste, and excruciate, and overthrow. The great community of mankind had been subdivided into ten thousand communities, each organized for the ruin of the other. Wheel within wheel, the vast machine was instinct with the restless spirit of desolation. Pain had been inflicted; therefore, pain should be inflicted in return. Retaliation of injuries is the only remedy which can be applied to violence, because it teaches the injurer the true nature of his own conduct, and operates as a warning against its repetition. Nor must the same measure of calamity be returned as was received. If a man borrows a certain sum from me, he is bound to repay that sum. Shall no more be required of the enemy who destroys my reputation, or ravages my fields? It is just that he should suffer ten times the loss which he has inflicted, that the legitimate consequences of his deed may never be obliterated from his remembrance, and that others may clearly discern and feel the danger of invading the peace of human society. Such reasonings, and the impetuous feelings arising from them, have armed nation against nation, family against family, man against man.

An Athenian soldier, in the Ionian army which had assembled for the purpose of vindicating the liberty of the Asiatic Greeks, accidentally set fire to Sardis. The city, being composed of combustible materials, was burned to the ground. The Persians believed that this circumstance of aggression made it their duty to retaliate on Athens. They assembled successive expeditions on the most extensive scale. Every nation of the East was united to ruin the Grecian States. Athens was burned to the ground, the whole territory laid waste, and every living thing which it contained [destroyed]. After suffering and inflicting incalculable mischiefs, they desisted from their purpose only when they became impotent to effect it. The desire of revenge for the aggression of Persia outlived, among the Greeks, that love of liberty which had been their most glorious distinction among the nations of mankind; and Alexander became the instrument of its completion. The mischiefs attendant on this consummation of fruitless ruin are too manifold and too tremendous to be related. If all the thought which had been expended on the construction of engines of agony and death

—the modes of aggression and defence, the raising of armies, and the acquirement of those arts of tyranny and falsehood without which mixed multitudes could neither be led nor governed—had been employed to promote the true welfare and extend the real empire of man, how different would have been the present situation of human society! how different the state of knowledge in physical and moral science, upon which the power and happiness of mankind essentially depend! What nation has the example of the desolation of Attica by Mardonius and Xerxes, or the extinction of the Persian empire by Alexander of Macedon, restrained from outrage? Was not the pretext of this latter system of spoliation derived immediately from the former? Had revenge in this instance any other effect than to increase, instead of diminishing, the mass of malice and evil already existing in the world?

The emptiness and folly of retaliation are apparent from every example which can be brought forward. Not only Jesus Christ, but the most eminent professors of every sect of philosophy, have reasoned against this futile superstition. Legislation is, in one point of view, to be considered as an attempt to provide against the excesses of this deplorable mistake. It professes to assign the penalty of all private injuries, and denies to individuals the right of vindicating their proper cause. This end is certainly not attained without some accommodation to the propensities which it desires to destroy. Still, it recognizes no principle but the production of the greatest eventual good with the least immediate injury; and regards the torture, or the death, of any human being as unjust, of whatever mischief he may have been the author, so that the result shall not more than compensate for the immediate pain.

Mankind, transmitting from generation to generation the legacy of accumulated vengeances, and pursuing with the feelings of duty the misery of their fellow beings, have not failed to attribute to the Universal Cause a character analogous with their own. The image of this invisible, mysterious Being is more or less excellent and perfect—resembles more or less its original—in proportion to the perfection of the mind on which it is impressed. Thus, that nation which has arrived at the highest step in the scale of moral progression will believe most purely in that God, the knowledge of whose real attributes is considered as the firmest basis of the true religion. The reason of the belief of each individual, also, will be so far regulated by his conceptions of what is good. Thus, the conceptions which any nation or individual entertains of the God of its popular worship may be inferred from their own actions and opinions, which are the subjects of their approbation among their fellow men. Jesus Christ instructed his disciples to be perfect, as their Father in Heaven is perfect, declaring at the same time his belief that human perfection requires the refraining from revenge and retribution in any of its various shapes.

The perfection of the human and the divine character is thus asserted to be the same. Man, by resembling God, fulfils most accurately the tendencies of his nature; and God comprehends within himself all that constitutes human perfection. Thus, God is a model through which the excellence of man is to be estimated, whilst the *abstract* perfection of the human character is the type of the *actual* perfection of the divine. It is not to be believed that a person of such comprehensive views as Jesus Christ could have fallen into so manifest a contradiction as to assert that men would be tortured after death by that Being whose character is held up as a model to human kind, because he is incapable of malevolence and revenge. All the arguments which have been brought forward to justify retribution fail, when retribution is destined neither to operate as an example to other agents, nor to the offender himself. How feeble such reasoning is to be considered, has been already shown; but it is the character of an evil Daemon to consign the beings whom he has endowed with sensation to unprofitable anguish. The peculiar circumstances attendant on the conception of God casting sinners to burn in Hell for ever, combine to render that conception the most perfect specimen of the greatest imaginable crime. Jesus Christ represented God as the principle of all good, the source of all happiness, the wise and benevolent Creator and Preserver of all living things. But the interpreters of his doctrines have confounded the good and the evil principle. They observed the emanations of their universal natures to be inextricably entangled in the world, and, trembling before the power of the cause of all things, addressed to it such flattery as is acceptable to the ministers of human tyranny, attributing love and wisdom to those energies which they felt to be exerted indifferently for the purposes of benefit and calamity.

Jesus Christ expressly asserts that distinction between the good and evil principle which it has been the practice of all theologians to confound. How far his doctrines, or their interpretation, may be true, it would scarcely have been worth while to inquire if the one did not afford an example and an incentive to the attainment of true virtue, whilst the other holds out a sanction and apology for every species of mean and cruel vice.

It cannot be precisely ascertained in what degree Jesus Christ accommodated his doctrines to the opinions of his auditors; or in what degree he really said all that he is related to have said. He has left no written record of himself, and we are compelled to judge from the imperfect and obscure information which his biographers (persons certainly of very undisciplined and undiscriminating minds) have transmitted to posterity. These writers (our only guides) impute sentiments to Jesus Christ which flatly contradict each other. They represent him as narrow, superstitious, and exquisitely vindictive and malicious. They insert, in the midst of a strain of impassioned eloquence or sagest exhortation, a sentiment only remarkable for its naked and drivelling folly. But it is not difficult to distinguish the inventions by which these historians have filled up the interstices of tradition, or corrupted the simplicity of truth, from the real character of their rude amazement. They have left sufficiently clear indications of the genuine character of Jesus Christ to rescue it for ever from the imputations cast upon it by their ignorance and fanaticism. We discover that he is the enemy of oppression and of falsehood; that he is the advocate of equal justice; that he is neither disposed to sanction bloodshed nor deceit, under whatsoever pretences their practice may be vindicated. We discover that he was a man of meek and majestic demeanour, calm in danger; of natural and simple thought and habits; beloved to adoration by his adherents; unmoved, solemn, and severe.

It is utterly incredible that this man said, that if you hate your enemy, you would find it to your account to return him good for evil, since, by such a temporary oblivion of vengeance, you would heap coals of fire on his head. Where such contradictions occur, a favourable construction is warranted by the general innocence of manners and comprehensiveness of views which he is represented to possess. The rule of criticism to be adopted in judging of the life, actions, and words of a man who has acted any conspicuous part in the revolutions of the world, should not be narrow. We ought to form a general image of his character and of his doctrines, and refer to this whole the distinct portions of actions and speech by which they are diversified. It is not here asserted that no contradictions are to be admitted to have taken place in the system of Jesus Christ, between doctrines promulgated in different states of feeling or information, or even such as are implied in the enunciation of a scheme of thought, various and obscure through its immensity and depth. It is not asserted that no degree of human indignation ever hurried him, beyond the limits which his calmer mood had placed, to disapprobation against vice and folly. Those deviations from the history of his life are alone to be vindicated, which represent his own essential character in contradiction with itself.

Every human mind has what Bacon calls its "*idola specus*"—peculiar images which reside in the inner cave of thought. These constitute the essential and distinctive character of every human being; to which every action and every word have intimate relation; and by which, in depicting a character, the genuineness and meaning of these words and actions are to be determined. Every fanatic or enemy of virtue is not at liberty to misrepresent the greatest geniuses and most heroic defenders of all that is valuable in this mortal world. History, to gain any credit, must contain some truth, and that truth shall thus be made a sufficient indication of prejudice and deceit.

With respect to the miracles which these biographers have related, I have already declined to enter into any discussion on their nature or their existence. The supposition of their falsehood or their truth would modify in no degree the hues of the picture which is attempted to be delineated. To judge truly of the moral and philosophical character of Socrates, it is not necessary to determine the question of the familiar Spirit which [it] is supposed that he believed to attend on him. The power of the human mind, relatively to intercourse with or dominion over the invisible

world, is doubtless an interesting theme of discussion; but the connexion of the instance of Jesus Christ with the established religion of the country in which I write, renders it dangerous to subject oneself to the imputation of introducing new Gods or abolishing old ones; nor is the duty of mutual forbearance sufficiently understood to render it certain that the metaphysician and the moralist, even though he carefully sacrifice a cock to Esculapius, may not receive something analogous to the bowl of hemlock for the reward of his labours. Much, however, of what his [Christ's] biographers have asserted is not to be rejected merely because inferences inconsistent with the general spirit of his system are to be adduced from its admission. Jesus Christ did what every other reformer who has produced any considerable effect upon the world has done. He accommodated his doctrines to the prepossessions of those whom he addressed. He used a language for this view sufficiently familiar to our comprehensions. He said,—However new or strange my doctrines may appear to you, they are in fact only the restoration and re-establishment of those original institutions and ancient customs of your own law and religion. The constitutions of your faith and policy, although perfect in their origin, have become corrupt and altered, and have fallen into decay. I profess to restore them to their pristine authority and splendour. "Think not that I am come to destroy the Law and the Prophets. I am come not to destroy, but to fulfil. Till heaven and earth pass away, one jot or one tittle shall in nowise pass away from the Law, till all be fulfilled." Thus, like a skilful orator (see Cicero, *De Oratore*), he secures the prejudices of his auditors, and induces them, by his professions of sympathy with their feelings, to enter with a willing mind into the exposition of his own. The art of persuasion differs from that of reasoning; and it is of no small moment, to the success even of a true cause, that the judges who are to determine on its merits should be free from those national and religious predilections which render the multitude both deaf and blind.

Let not this practice be considered as an unworthy artifice. It were best for the cause of reason that mankind should acknowledge no authority but its own; but it is useful, to a certain extent, that they should not consider those institutions which they have been habituated to reverence as opposing any obstacle to its admission. All reformers have been compelled to practise this misrepresentation of their own true feelings and opinions. It is deeply to be lamented that a word should ever issue from human lips which contains the minutest alloy of dissimulation, or simulation, or hypocrisy, or exaggeration, or anything but the precise and rigid image which is present to the mind, and which ought to dictate the expression. But the practice of utter sincerity towards other men would avail to no good end, if they were incapable of practising it towards their own minds. In fact, truth cannot be communicated until it is perceived. The interests, therefore, of truth require that an orator should, as far as possible, produce in his hearers that state of mind on which alone his exhortations could fairly be contemplated and examined.

Having produced this favourable disposition of mind, Jesus Christ proceeds to qualify, and finally to abrogate, the system of the Jewish law. He descants upon its insufficiency as a code of moral conduct, which it professed to be, and absolutely selects the law of retaliation as an instance of the absurdity and immorality of its institutions. The conclusion of the speech is in a strain of the most daring and most impassioned speculation. He seems emboldened by the success of his exculpation to the multitude, to declare in public the utmost singularity of his faith. He tramples upon all received opinions, on all the cherished luxuries and superstitions of mankind. He bids them cast aside the claims of custom and blind faith by which they have been encompassed from the very cradle of their being, and receive the imitator and minister of the Universal God.

EQUALITY OF MANKIND

"The spirit of the Lord is upon me, because he hath chosen me to preach the gospel to the poor: He hath sent me to heal the brokenhearted, to preach deliverance to the captives and recovery of sight to the blind, and to set at liberty them that are bruised" (Luke iv. 18). This is an enunciation of all that Plato and Diogenes have speculated upon the equality of mankind. They saw that the great majority of the human species were reduced to the situation of squalid ignorance and moral imbecility, for the purpose of purveying for the luxury of a few, and contributing to the satisfaction of their thirst for power. Too mean-spirited and too feeble in resolve to attempt the conquest of their own evil passions and of the difficulties of the material world, men sought dominion over their fellow men, as an easy method to gain that apparent majesty and power which the instinct of their nature requires. Plato wrote the scheme of a republic, in which law should watch over the equal distribution of the external instruments of unequal power—honours, property, &c. Diogenes devised a nobler and a more worthy system of opposition to the system of the slave and tyrant. He said: "It is in the power of each individual to level the inequality which is the topic of the complaint of mankind. Let him be aware of his own worth, and the station which he occupies in the scale of moral beings. Diamonds and gold, palaces and sceptres, derive their value from the opinion of mankind. The only sumptuary law which can be imposed on the use and fabrication of these instruments of mischief and deceit, these symbols of successful injustice, is the law of opinion. Every man possesses the power, in this respect, to legislate for himself. Let him be well aware of his own worth and moral dignity. Let him yield in meek reverence to any wiser or worthier than he, so long as he accords no veneration to the splendour of his apparel, the luxury of his food, the multitude of his flatterers and slaves. It is because, mankind, ye value and seek the empty pageantry of wealth and social power, that ye are enslaved to its possessions. Decrease your physical wants; learn to live, so far as nourishment and shelter are concerned, like the beasts of the forest and the birds of the air; ye will need not to complain, that other individuals of your species are surrounded by the diseases of luxury and the vices of subserviency and oppression." With all those who are truly wise, there will be an entire community, not only of thoughts and feelings, but also of external possessions. Insomuch, therefore, as ye live [wisely], ye may enjoy the community of whatsoever benefits arise from the inventions of civilized life. They are of value only for purposes of mental power; they are of value only as they are capable of being shared and applied to the common advantage of philosophy; and if there be no love among men, whatever institutions they may frame must be subservient to the same purpose—to the continuance of inequality. If there be no love among men, it is best that he who sees through the hollowness of their professions should fly from their society, and suffice to his own soul. In wisdom, he will thus lose nothing; in power, he will gain everything. In proportion to the love existing among men, so will be the community of property and power. Among true and real friends, all is common; and, were ignorance and envy and superstition banished from the world, all mankind would be friends. The only perfect and genuine republic is that which comprehends every living being. Those distinctions which have been artificially set up, of nations, societies, families, and religions, are only general names, expressing the abhorrence and contempt with which men blindly consider their fellow men. I love my country; I love the city in which I was born, my parents, my wife, and the children of my care; and to this city, this woman, and this nation, it is incumbent on me to do all the benefit in my power. To what do these distinctions point, but to an evident denial of the duty which humanity imposes on you, of doing every possible good to every individual, under whatever denomination he may be comprehended, to whom you have the power of doing it? You ought to love all mankind; nay, every individual of mankind. You ought not to love the individuals of your domestic circle less, but to love those who exist beyond it more. Once make the feelings of confidence and of affection universal, and the distinctions of property and power will vanish; nor are they to be abolished without substituting something equivalent in mischief to them, until all mankind shall acknowledge an entire community of rights.

But, as the shades of night are dispelled by the faintest glimmerings of dawn, so shall the minutest progress of the benevolent feelings disperse, in some degree, the gloom of tyranny, and [curb the] ministers of mutual suspicion and abhorrence. Your physical wants are few, whilst those of your mind and heart cannot be numbered or described, from their multitude and complication. To secure the gratification of the former, you have made yourselves the bond-slaves of each other.

They have cultivated these meaner wants to so great an excess as to judge nothing so valuable or desirable [as] what relates to their gratification. Hence has arisen a system of passions which loses sight of the end they were originally awakened to attain. Fame, power, and gold, are loved for their own sakes—are worshipped with a blind, habitual idolatry. The pageantry of empire, and the fame of irresistible might, are contemplated by the possessor with unmeaning complacency, without a retrospect to the properties which first made him consider them of value. It is from the cultivation of the most contemptible properties of human nature that discord and torpor and indifference, by which the moral universe is disordered, essentially depend. So long as these are the ties by which human society is connected, let it not be admitted that they are fragile.

Before man can be free, and equal, and truly wise, he must cast aside the chains of habit and superstition; he must strip sensuality of its pomp, and selfishness of its excuses, and contemplate actions and objects as they really are. He will discover the wisdom of universal love; he will feel the meanness and the injustice of sacrificing the reason and the liberty of his fellow men to the indulgence of his physical appetites, and becoming a party to their degradation by the consummation of his own.

Such, with those differences only incidental to the age and state of society in which they were promulgated, appear to have been the doctrines of Jesus Christ. It is not too much to assert that they have been the doctrines of every just and compassionate mind that ever speculated on the social nature of man. The dogma of the equality of mankind has been advocated, with various success, in different ages of the world. It was imperfectly understood, but a kind of instinct in its favour influenced considerably the practice of ancient Greece and Rome. Attempts to establish usages founded on this dogma have been made in modern Europe, in several instances, since the revival of literature and the arts. Rousseau has vindicated this opinion with all the eloquence of sincere and earnest faith; and is, perhaps, the philosopher among the moderns who, in the structure of his feelings and understanding, resembles most nearly the mysterious sage of Judea. It is impossible to read those passionate words in which Jesus Christ upbraids the pusillanimity and sensuality of mankind, without being strongly reminded of the more connected and systematic enthusiasm of Rousseau. "No man," says Jesus Christ, "can serve two masters. Take, therefore, no thought for to-morrow, for the morrow shall take thought for the things of itself. Sufficient unto the day is the evil thereof." If we would profit by the wisdom of a sublime and poetical mind, we must beware of the vulgar error of interpreting literally every expression it employs. Nothing can well be more remote from truth than the literal and strict construction of such expressions as Jesus Christ delivers, or than [to imagine that] it were best for man that he should abandon all his acquirements in physical and intellectual science, and depend on the spontaneous productions of nature for his subsistence. Nothing is more obviously false than that the remedy for the inequality among men consists in their return to the condition of savages and beasts. Philosophy will never be understood if we approach the study of its mysteries with so narrow and illiberal conceptions of its universality. Rousseau certainly did not mean to persuade the immense population of his country to abandon all the arts of life, destroy their habitations and their temples, and become the inhabitants of the woods. He addressed the most enlightened of his compatriots, and endeavoured to persuade them to set the example of a pure and simple life, by placing in the strongest point of view his conceptions of the calamitous and diseased aspect which, overgrown as it is with the vices of sensuality and selfishness, is exhibited by civilized society. Nor can it be believed that Jesus Christ endeavoured to prevail on the inhabitants of Jerusalem neither to till their fields, nor to frame a shelter against the sky, nor to provide food for the morrow. He simply exposes, with the passionate rhetoric of enthusiastic love towards all human beings, the miseries and mischiefs of that system which makes all things subservient to the subsistence of the material frame of man. He warns them that no man can serve two masters—God and Mammon; that it is impossible at once to be high-minded and just and wise, and to comply with the accustomed forms of human society, seek power, wealth, or empire, either from the idolatry of habit, or as the direct instruments of sensual gratification. He instructs them that clothing and food and shelter are not, as they suppose, the true end of human life, but only certain means, to be valued in proportion to their subserviency to that end. These means it is right of every human being to possess, and that in the same degree. In this respect, the fowls of the air and the lilies of the field are examples for the imitation of mankind. They are clothed and fed by the Universal God. Permit, therefore, the Spirit of this benignant Principle to visit your intellectual frame, or, in other words, become just and pure. When you understand the degree of attention which the requisitions of your physical nature demand, you will perceive how little labour suffices for their satisfaction. Your Heavenly Father knoweth you have need of these things. The universal Harmony, or Reason, which makes your passive frame of thought its dwelling, in proportion to the purity and majesty of its nature will instruct you, if ye are willing to attain that exalted condition, in what manner to possess all the objects necessary for your material subsistence. All men are [impelled] to become thus pure and happy. All men are called to participate in the community of Nature's gifts. The man who has fewest bodily wants approaches nearest to the Divine Nature. Satisfy these wants at the cheapest rate, and expend the remaining energies of your nature in the attainment of virtue and knowledge. The mighty frame of the wonderful and lovely world is the food of your contemplation, and living beings who resemble your own nature, and are bound to you by similarity of sensations, are destined to be the nutriment of your affection; united, they are the consummation of the widest hopes your mind can contain. Ye can expend thus no labour on mechanism consecrated to luxury and pride. How abundant will not be your progress in all that truly ennobles and extends human nature! By rendering yourselves thus worthy, ye will be as free in your imaginations as the swift and many-coloured fowls of the air, and as beautiful in pure simplicity as the lilies of the field. In proportion as mankind becomes wise—yes, in exact proportion to that wisdom—should be the extinction of the unequal system under which they now subsist. Government is, in fact, the mere badge of their depravity. They are so little aware of the inestimable benefits of mutual love as to indulge, without thought, and almost without motive, in the worst excesses of selfishness and malice. Hence, without graduating human society into a scale of empire and subjection, its very existence has become impossible. It is necessary that universal benevolence should supersede the regulations of precedent and prescription, before these regulations can safely be abolished. Meanwhile, their very subsistence depends on the system of injustice and violence which they have been devised to palliate. They suppose men endowed with the power of deliberating and determining for their equals; whilst these men, as frail and as ignorant as the multitude whom they rule, possess, as a practical consequence of this power, the right which they of necessity exercise to prevent (together with their own) the physical and moral and intellectual nature of all mankind.

It is the object of wisdom to equalize the distinctions on which this power depends, by exhibiting in their proper worthlessness the objects, a contention concerning which renders its existence a necessary evil. The evil, in fact, is virtually abolished wherever *justice* is practised; and it is abolished in precise proportion to the prevalence of true virtue.

The whole frame of human things is infected by an insidious poison. Hence it is that man is blind in his understanding, corrupt in his moral sense, and diseased in his physical functions. The wisest and most sublime of the ancient poets saw this truth, and embodied their conception of its value in retrospect to the earliest ages of mankind. They represented equality as the reign of Saturn, and taught that mankind had gradually degenerated from the virtue which enabled them to enjoy or maintain this happy state. Their doctrine was philosophically false. Later and more correct observations have instructed us that uncivilized man is the most pernicious and miserable of beings, and that the violence and injustice, which are the genuine indications of real inequality, obtain in the society of these beings without palliation. Their imaginations of a happier state of human society were referred, in truth, to the Saturnian period; they ministered, indeed, to thoughts of despondency and sorrow. But they were the children of airy hope—the prophets and parents of man's futurity. Man was once as a wild beast; he has become a moralist, a metaphysician, a poet, and an astronomer. Lucretius or Virgil might have referred the comparison to themselves; and, as a proof of the progress of the nature of man, challenged a comparison with

the cannibals of Scythia.[1] The experience of the ages which have intervened between the present period and that in which Jesus Christ taught, tends to prove his doctrine, and to illustrate theirs. There is more equality because there is more justice, and there is more justice because there is more universal knowledge.

To the accomplishment of such mighty hopes were the views of Jesus Christ extended; such did he believe to be the tendency of his doctrines—the abolition of artificial distinctions among mankind, so far as the love which it becomes all human beings to bear towards each other, and the knowledge of truth from which that love will never fail to be produced, avail to their destruction. A young man came to Jesus Christ, struck by the miraculous dignity and simplicity of his character, and attracted by the words of power which he uttered. He demanded to be considered as one of the followers of his creed. "Sell all that thou hast," replied the philosopher; "give it to the poor, and follow me." But the young man had large possessions, and he went away sorrowing.

The system of equality was attempted, after Jesus Christ's death, to be carried into effect by his followers. "They that believed had all things in common; they sold their possessions and goods, and parted them to all men, as every man had need; and they continued daily with one accord in the temple, and, breaking bread from house to house, did eat their meat with gladness and singleness of heart." (Acts ii.)

The practical application of the doctrines of strict justice to a state of society established in its contempt, was such as might have been expected. After the transitory glow of enthusiasm had faded from the minds of men, precedent and habit resumed their empire; they broke like a universal deluge on one shrinking and solitary island. Men to whom birth had allotted ample possession, looked with complacency on sumptuous apartments and luxurious food, and those ceremonials of delusive majesty which surround the throne of power and the court of wealth. Men from whom these things were withheld by their condition, began again to gaze with stupid envy on pernicious splendour; and, by desiring the false greatness of another's state, to sacrifice the intrinsic

[1] Jesus Christ foresaw what the poets retrospectively imagined.

dignity of their own. The demagogues of the infant republic of the Christian sect, attaining, through eloquence or artifice, to influence amongst its members, first violated (under the pretence of watching over their integrity) the institutions established for the common and equal benefit of all. These demagogues artfully silenced the voice of the moral sense among them by engaging them to attend, not so much to the cultivation of a virtuous and happy life in this mortal scene, as to the attainment of a fortunate condition after death; not so much to the consideration of those means by which the state of man is adorned and improved, as an inquiry into the secrets of the connexion between God and the world—things which, they well knew, were not to be explained, or even to be conceived. The system of equality which they established necessarily fell to the ground, because it is a system that must result from, rather than precede, the moral improvement of human kind. It was a circumstance of no moment that the first adherents of the system of Jesus Christ cast their property into a common stock. The same degree of real community of property could have subsisted without this formality, which served only to extend a temptation of dishonesty to the treasurers of so considerable a patrimony. Every man, in proportion to his virtue, considers himself, with respect to the great community of mankind, as the steward and guardian of their interests in the property which he chances to possess. Every man, in proportion to his wisdom, sees the manner in which it is his duty to employ the resources which the consent of mankind has entrusted to his discretion. Such is the [annihilation] of the unjust inequality of powers and conditions existing in the world; and so gradually and inevitably is the progress of equality accommodated to the progress of wisdom and of virtue among mankind.

Meanwhile, some benefit has not failed to flow from the imperfect attempts which have been made to erect a system of equal rights to property and power upon the basis of arbitrary institutions. They have undoubtedly, in every case, from the instability of their formation, failed. Still, they constitute a record of those epochs at which a true sense of justice suggested itself to the understandings of men, so that they consented to forgo all the cherished delights of luxury, all the habitual gratifications arising out of the possession or the expectation of power, all the superstitions with which the accumulated authority of ages had made them dear and venerable. They are so many trophies erected in the enemy's land, to mark the limits of the victorious progress of truth and justice.

Jesus Christ did not fail to advert to the——

END

A DEFENCE OF POETRY
1821

PART I

According to one mode of regarding those two classes of mental action, which are called reason and imagination, the former may be considered as mind contemplating the relations borne by one thought to another, however produced; and the latter, as mind acting upon those thoughts so as to colour them with its own light, and composing from them, as from elements, other thoughts, each containing within itself the principle of its own integrity. The one is the τὸ ποιεῖν, or the principle of synthesis, and has for its objects those forms which are common to universal nature and existence itself; the other is the τὸ λογίζειν, or principle of analysis, and its action regards the relations of things, simply as relations; considering thoughts, not in their integral unity, but as the algebraical representations which conduct to certain general results. Reason is the enumeration of quantities already known; imagination is the perception of the value of those quantities, both separately and as a whole. Reason respects the differences, and imagination the similitudes of things. Reason is to the imagination as the instrument to the agent, as the body to the spirit, as the shadow to the substance.

Poetry, in a general sense, may be defined to be "the expression of the imagination": and poetry is connate with the origin of man. Man is an instrument over which a series of external and internal impressions are driven, like the alternations of an ever-changing wind over an Aeolian lyre, which move it by their motion to ever-changing melody. But there is a principle within the human being, and perhaps within all sentient beings, which acts otherwise than in the lyre, and produces not melody alone, but harmony, by an internal adjustment of the sounds or motions thus excited to the impressions which excite them. It is as if the lyre could accommodate its chords to the motions of that which strikes them, in a determined proportion of sound; even as the musician can accommodate his voice to the sound of the lyre. A child at play by itself will express its delight by its voice and motions; and every inflexion of tone and every gesture will bear exact relation to a corresponding antitype in the pleasurable impressions which awakened it; it will be the reflected image of that impression; and as the lyre trembles and sounds after the wind has died away, so the child seeks, by prolonging in its voice and motions the duration of the effect, to prolong also a consciousness of the cause. In relation to the objects which delight a child, these expressions are what poetry is to higher objects. The savage (for the savage is to ages what the child is to years) expresses the emotions produced in him by surrounding objects in a similar manner; and language and gesture, together with plastic or pictorial imitation, become the image of the combined effect of those objects, and of his apprehension of them. Man in society, with all his passions and his pleasures, next becomes the object of the passions and pleasures of man; an additional class of emotions produces an augmented treasure of expressions; and language, gesture, and the imitative arts, become at once the representation and the medium, the pencil and the picture, the chisel and the statue, the chord and the harmony. The social sympathies, or those laws from which, as from its elements, society results, begin to develop themselves from the moment that two human beings coexist; the future is contained within the present, as the plant within the seed; and equality, diversity, unity, contrast, mutual dependence, become the principles alone capable of affording the motives according to which the will of a social being is determined to action, inasmuch as he is social; and constitute pleasure in sensation, virtue in sentiment, beauty in art, truth in reasoning, and love in the intercourse of kind. Hence men, even in the infancy of society, observe a certain order in their words and actions, distinct from that of the objects and the impressions represented by them, all expression being subject to the laws of that from which it proceeds. But let us dismiss those more general considerations which might involve an inquiry into the principles of society itself, and restrict our view to the manner in which the imagination is expressed upon its forms.

In the youth of the world, men dance and sing and imitate natural objects, observing in these actions, as in all others, a certain rhythm or order. And, although all men observe a similar, they observe not the same order, in the motions of the dance, in the melody of the song, in the combinations of language, in the series of their imitations of natural objects. For there is a certain order or rhythm belonging to each of these classes of mimetic representation, from which the hearer and the spectator receive an intenser and purer pleasure than from any other: the sense of an approximation to this order has been called taste by modern writers. Every man in the infancy of art observes an order which approximates more or less closely to that from which this highest delight results: but the diversity is not sufficiently marked, as that its gradations should be sensible, except in those instances where the predominance of this faculty of approximation to the beautiful (for so we may be permitted to name the relation between this highest pleasure and its cause) is very great. Those in whom it exists in excess are poets, in the most universal sense of the word; and the pleasure resulting from the manner in which they express the influence of society or nature upon their own minds, communicates itself to others, and gathers a sort of reduplication from that community. Their language is vitally metaphorical; that is, it marks the before unapprehended relations of things and perpetuates their apprehension, until the words which represent them become, through time, signs for portions or classes of thoughts instead of pictures of integral thoughts; and then if no new poets should arise to create afresh the associations which have been thus disorganized, language will be dead to all the nobler purposes of human intercourse. These similitudes or relations are finely said by Lord Bacon to be "the same footsteps of nature impressed upon the various subjects of the world"; and he considers the faculty which perceives them as the storehouse of axioms common to all knowledge. In the infancy of society every author is necessarily a poet, because language itself is poetry; and to be a poet is to apprehend the true and the beautiful, in a word, the good which exists in the relation, subsisting, first between existence and perception, and secondly between perception and expression. Every original language near to its source is in itself the chaos of a cyclic poem: the copiousness of lexicography and the distinctions of grammar are the works of a later age, and are merely the catalogue and the form of the creations of poetry.

But poets, or those who imagine and express this indestructible order, are not only the authors of language and of music, of the dance, and architecture, and statuary, and painting; they are the institutors of laws, and the founders of civil society, and the inventors of the arts of life, and the teachers, who draw into a certain propinquity with the beautiful and the true, that partial apprehension of the agencies of the invisible world which is called religion. Hence all original religions are allegorical, or susceptible of allegory, and, like Janus, have a double face of false and true. Poets, according to the circumstances of the age and nation in which they appeared, were called, in the earlier epochs of the world, legislators, or prophets: a poet essentially comprises and unites both these characters. For he not only beholds intensely the present as it is, and discovers those laws according to which present things ought to be ordered, but he beholds the future in the present, and his thoughts are the germs of the flower and the fruit of latest time. Not that I assert poets to be prophets in the gross sense of the word, or that they can foretell the form as surely as they foreknow the spirit of events: such is the pretence of superstition, which would make poetry an attribute of prophecy, rather than prophecy an attribute of poetry. A poet participates in the eternal, the infinite, and the one; as far as relates to his conceptions, time and place and number are not. The grammatical forms which express the moods of time, and the difference of persons, and the distinction of place, are convertible with respect to the highest poetry without injuring it as poetry; and the choruses of Aeschylus, and the book of *Job,* and Dante's *Paradise,* would afford more than any other writings, examples of this fact, if the limits of this essay did not forbid citation. The creations of sculpture, painting, and music, are illustrations still more decisive.

Language, colour, form, and religious and civil habits of action, are all the instruments and materials of poetry; they may be called poetry by that figure of speech which considers the effect as a synonym of the cause. But poetry in a more restricted sense expresses those arrangements of language, and especially metrical language, which are created by that imperial faculty, whose throne is curtained within the invisible nature of man. And this springs from the nature itself of language, which is a more direct representation of the actions and passions of our internal being, and is susceptible of more various and delicate combinations, than colour, form, or motion, and is more plastic and obedient to the control of that faculty of which it is the creation. For language is arbitrarily produced by the imagination, and has relation to thoughts alone; but all other materials, instruments, and conditions of art, have relations among each other, which limit and interpose between conception and expression. The former is as a mirror which reflects, the latter as a cloud which enfeebles, the light of which both are mediums of communication. Hence the fame of sculptors, painters, and musicians, although the intrinsic powers of the great masters of these arts may yield in no degree to that of those who have employed language as the hieroglyphic of their thoughts, has never equalled that of poets in the restricted sense of the term; as two performers of equal skill will produce unequal effects from a guitar and a harp. The fame of legislators and founders of religions, so long as their institutions last, alone seems to exceed that of poets in the restricted sense; but it can scarcely be a question, whether, if we deduct the celebrity which their flattery of the gross opinions of the vulgar usually conciliates, together with that which belonged to them in their higher character of poets, any excess will remain.

We have thus circumscribed the word poetry within the limits of that art which is the most familiar and the most perfect expression of the faculty itself. It is necessary, however, to make the circle still narrower, and to determine the distinction between measured and unmeasured language; for the popular division into prose and verse is inadmissible in accurate philosophy.

Sounds as well as thoughts have relation both between each other and towards that which they represent, and a perception of the order of those relations has always been found connected with a perception of the order of the relations of thoughts. Hence the language of poets has ever affected a certain uniform and harmonious recurrence of sound, without which it were not poetry, and which is scarcely less indispensable to the communication of its influence, than the words themselves, without reference to that peculiar order. Hence the vanity of translation; it were as wise to cast a violet into a crucible that you might discover the formal principle of its colour and odour, as seek to transfuse from one language into another the creations of a poet. The plant must spring again from its seed, or it will bear no flower—and this is the burthen of the curse of Babel.

An observation of the regular mode of the recurrence of harmony in the language of poetical minds, together with its relation to music, produced metre, or a certain system of traditional forms of harmony and language. Yet it is by no means essential that a poet should accommodate his language to this traditional form, so that the harmony, which is its spirit, be observed. The practice is indeed convenient and popular, and to be preferred, especially in such composition as includes much action: but every great poet must inevitably innovate upon the example of his predecessors in the exact structure of his peculiar versification. The distinction between poets and prose writers is a vulgar error. The distinction between philosophers and poets has been anticipated. Plato was essentially a poet —the truth and splendour of his imagery, and the melody of his language, are the most intense that it is possible to conceive. He rejected the measure of the epic, dramatic, and lyrical forms, because he sought to kindle a harmony in thoughts divested of shape and action, and he forbore to invent any regular plan of rhythm which would include, under determinate forms, the varied pauses of his style. Cicero sought to imitate the cadence of his periods, but with little success. Lord Bacon was a poet. His language has a sweet and majestic rhythm, which satisfies the sense, no less than the almost superhuman wisdom of his philosophy satisfies the intellect; it is a strain which distends, and then bursts the circumference of the reader's mind, and pours itself forth together with it into the universal element with which it has perpetual sympathy. All the authors of revolutions in opinion are not only necessarily poets as they are inventors, nor even as their words unveil the permanent analogy of things by images which participate in the life of truth; but as their periods are harmonious and rhythmical, and contain in themselves the elements of verse; being the echo of the eternal music. Nor are those supreme poets, who have employed traditional forms of rhythm on account of the form and action of their subjects, less capable of perceiving and teaching the truth of things, than those who have omitted that form. Shakespeare, Dante, and Milton (to confine ourselves to modern writers) are philosophers of the very loftiest power.

A poem is the very image of life expressed in its eternal truth. There is this difference between a story and a poem, that a story is a catalogue of detached facts, which have no other connexion than time, place, circumstance, cause and effect; the other is the creation of actions according to the unchangeable forms of human nature, as existing in the mind of the Creator, which is itself the image of all other minds. The one is partial, and applies only to a definite period of time, and a certain combination of events which can never again recur; the other is universal, and contains within itself the germ of a relation to whatever motives or actions have place in the possible varieties of human nature. Time, which destroys the beauty and the use of the story of particular facts, stripped of the poetry which should invest them, augments that of poetry, and for ever develops new and wonderful applications of the eternal truth which it contains. Hence epitomes have been called the moths of just history; they eat out the poetry of it. A story of particular facts is as a mirror which obscures and distorts that which should be beautiful: poetry is a mirror which makes beautiful that which is distorted.

The parts of a composition may be poetical, without the composition as a whole being a poem. A single sentence may be considered as a whole, though it may be found in the midst of a series of unassimilated portions: a single word even may be a spark of inextinguishable thought. And thus all the great historians, Herodotus, Plutarch, Livy, were poets; and although the plan of these writers, especially that of Livy, restrained them from developing this faculty in its highest degree, they made copious and ample amends for their subjection, by filling all the interstices of their subjects with living images.

Having determined what is poetry, and who are poets, let us proceed to estimate its effects upon society.

Poetry is ever accompanied with pleasure: all spirits on which it falls open themselves to receive the wisdom which is mingled with its delight. In the infancy of the world, neither poets themselves nor their auditors are fully aware of the excellence of poetry: for it acts in a divine and unapprehended manner, beyond and above consciousness; and it is reserved for future generations to contemplate and measure the mighty cause and effect in all the strength and splendour of their union. Even in modern times, no living poet ever arrived at the fullness of his fame; the jury which sits in judgement upon a poet, belonging as he does to all time, must be composed of his peers: it must be impanelled by Time from the selectest of the wise of many generations. A poet is a nightingale, who sits in darkness and sings to cheer its own solitude with sweet sounds; his auditors are as men entranced by the melody of an unseen musician, who feel that they are moved and softened, yet know not whence or why. The poems of Homer and his contemporaries were the delight of infant Greece; they were the elements of that social system which is the column upon which all succeeding civilization has reposed. Homer embodied the ideal perfection of his age in human character; nor can we doubt that those who read his verses were awakened to an ambition of becoming like to Achilles, Hector, and Ulysses: the truth and beauty of friendship, patriotism, and persevering devotion to an object, were unveiled to the depths in these immortal creations: the sentiments of the auditors must have been refined and enlarged by a sympathy with such great and lovely impersonations, until from admiring they imitated, and from imitation they identified themselves with the objects of their admiration. Nor let it be objected, that these characters are remote from moral perfection, and that they can by no means be considered as edifying patterns for general imitation. Every epoch, under names more or less specious, has deified its peculiar errors; Revenge is the naked idol of the worship of a semi-barbarous age; and Self-deceit is the veiled image of unknown evil, before which luxury and satiety lie prostrate. But a poet considers the vices of his contemporaries as a temporary dress in which his creations must be arrayed, and which cover without concealing the eternal proportions of their beauty. An epic or dramatic personage is understood to wear them around his soul, as he may the ancient armour or the modern uniform around his body; whilst it is easy to conceive a dress more graceful than either. The beauty of the internal nature cannot be so far concealed by its accidental vesture, but that the spirit of its form shall communicate itself to the very disguise, and indicate the shape it hides from the manner in which it is worn. A majestic form and graceful motions will express themselves through the most barbarous and tasteless costume. Few poets of the highest class have chosen to exhibit the beauty of their conceptions in its naked truth and splendour; and it is doubtful whether the alloy of costume, habit, &c., be not necessary to temper this planetary music for mortal ears.

The whole objection, however, of the immorality of poetry rests upon a misconception of the manner in which poetry acts to produce the moral improvement of man. Ethical science arranges the elements which poetry has created, and propounds schemes and proposes examples of civil and domestic life: nor is it for want of admirable doctrines that men hate, and despise, and censure, and deceive, and subjugate one another. But poetry acts in another and diviner manner. It awakens and enlarges the mind itself by rendering it the receptacle of a thousand unapprehended combinations of thought. Poetry lifts the veil from the hidden beauty of the world, and makes familiar objects be as if they were not familiar; it reproduces all that it represents, and the impersonations clothed in its Elysian light stand thenceforward in the minds of those who have once contemplated them, as memorials of that gentle and exalted content which extends itself over all thoughts and actions with which it coexists. The great secret of morals is love; or a going out of our own nature, and an identification of ourselves with the beautiful which exists in thought, action, or person, not our own. A man, to be greatly good, must imagine intensely and comprehensively; he must put himself in the place of another and of many others; the pains and pleasures of his species must become his own. The great instrument of moral good is the imagination; and poetry administers to the effect by acting upon the cause. Poetry enlarges the circumference of the imagination by replenishing it with thoughts of ever new delight, which have the power of attracting and assimilating to their own nature all other thoughts, and which form new intervals and interstices whose void for ever craves fresh food. Poetry strengthens the faculty which is the organ of the moral nature of man, in the same manner as exercise strengthens a limb. A poet therefore would do ill to embody his own conceptions of right and wrong, which are usually those of his place and time, in his poetical creations, which participate in neither. By this assumption of the inferior office of interpreting the effect, in which perhaps after all he might acquit himself but imperfectly, he would resign a glory in a participation in the cause. There was little danger that Homer, or any of the eternal poets, should have so far misunderstood themselves as to have abdicated this throne of their widest dominion. Those in whom the poetical faculty, though great, is less intense, as Euripides, Lucan, Tasso, Spenser, have frequently affected a moral aim, and the effect of their poetry is diminished in exact proportion to the degree in which they compel us to advert to this purpose.

Homer and the cyclic poets were followed at a certain interval by the dramatic and lyrical poets of Athens, who flourished contemporaneously with all that is most perfect in the kindred expressions of the poetical faculty; architecture, painting, music, the dance, sculpture, philosophy, and, we may add, the forms of civil life. For although the scheme of Athenian society was deformed by many imperfections which the poetry existing in chivalry and Christianity has erased from the habits and institutions of modern Europe; yet never at any other period has so much energy, beauty, and virtue, been developed; never was blind strength and stubborn form so disciplined and rendered subject to the will of man, or that will less repugnant to the dictates of the beautiful and the true, as during the century which preceded the death of Socrates. Of no other epoch in the history of our species have we records and fragments stamped so visibly with the image of the divinity in man. But

it is poetry alone, in form, in action, or in language, which has rendered this epoch memorable above all others, and the storehouse of examples to everlasting time. For written poetry existed at that epoch simultaneously with the other arts, and it is an idle inquiry to demand which gave and which received the light, which all, as from a common focus, have scattered over the darkest periods of succeeding time. We know no more of cause and effect than a constant conjunction of events: poetry is ever found to co-exist with whatever other arts contribute to the happiness and perfection of man. I appeal to what has already been established to distinguish between the cause and the effect.

It was at the period here adverted to, that the drama had its birth; and however a succeeding writer may have equalled or surpassed those few great specimens of the Athenian drama which have been preserved to us, it is indisputable that the art itself never was understood or practised according to the true philosophy of it, as at Athens. For the Athenians employed language, action, music, painting, the dance, and religious institutions, to produce a common effect in the representation of the highest idealisms of passion and of power; each division in the art was made perfect in its kind by artists of the most consummate skill, and was disciplined into a beautiful proportion and unity one towards the other. On the modern stage a few only of the elements capable of expressing the image of the poet's conception are employed at once. We have tragedy without music and dancing; and music and dancing without the highest impersonations of which they are the fit accompaniment, and both without religion and solemnity. Religious institution has indeed been usually banished from the stage. Our system of divesting the actor's face of a mask, on which the many expressions appropriated to his dramatic character might be moulded into one permanent and unchanging expression, is favourable only to a partial and inharmonious effect; it is fit for nothing but a monologue, where all the attention may be directed to some great master of ideal mimicry. The modern practice of blending comedy with tragedy, though liable to great abuse in point of practice, is undoubtedly an extension of the dramatic circle; but the comedy should be as in *King Lear,* universal, ideal, and sublime. It is perhaps the intervention of this principle which determines the balance in favour of *King Lear* against the *Oedipus Tyrannus* or the *Agamemnon,* or, if you will, the trilogies with which they are connected; unless the intense power of the choral poetry, especially that of the latter, should be considered as restoring the equilibrium. *King Lear,* if it can sustain this comparison, may be judged to be the most perfect specimen of the dramatic art existing in the world; in spite of the narrow conditions to which the poet was subjected by the ignorance of the philosophy of the drama which has prevailed in modern Europe. Calderon, in his religious *Autos,* has attempted to fulfil some of the high conditions of dramatic representation neglected by Shakespeare; such as the establishing a relation between the drama and religion, and the accommodating them to music and dancing; but he omits the observation of conditions still more important, and more is lost than gained by the substitution of the rigidly-defined and ever-repeated idealisms of a distorted superstition for the living impersonations of the truth of human passion.

But I digress.—The connexion of scenic exhibitions with the improvement or corruption of the manners of men, has been universally recognized: in other words, the presence or absence of poetry in its most perfect and universal form, has been found to be connected with good and evil in conduct or habit. The corruption which has been imputed to the drama as an effect, begins, when the poetry employed in its constitution ends: I appeal to the history of manners whether the periods of the growth of the one and the decline of the other have not corresponded with an exactness equal to any example of moral cause and effect.

The drama at Athens, or wheresoever else it may have approached to its perfection, ever co-existed with the moral and intellectual greatness of the age. The tragedies of the Athenian poets are as mirrors in which the spectator beholds himself, under a thin disguise of circumstance, stript of all but that ideal perfection and energy which every one feels to be the internal type of all that he loves, admires, and would become. The imagination is enlarged by a sympathy with pains and passions so mighty, that they distend in their conception the capacity of that by which they are conceived; the good affections are strengthened by pity, indignation, terror, and sorrow; and an exalted calm is prolonged from the satiety of this high exercise of them into the tumult of familiar life: even crime is disarmed of half its horror and all its contagion by being represented as the fatal consequence of the unfathomable agencies of nature; error is thus divested of its wilfulness; men can no longer cherish it as the creation of their choice. In a drama of the highest order there is little food for censure or hatred; it teaches rather self-knowledge and self-respect. Neither the eye nor the mind can see itself, unless reflected upon that which it resembles. The drama, so long as it continues to express poetry, is as a prismatic and many-sided mirror, which collects the brightest rays of human nature and divides and reproduces them from the simplicity of these elementary forms, and touches them with majesty and beauty, and multiplies all that it reflects, and endows it with the power of propagating its like wherever it may fall.

But in periods of the decay of social life, the drama sympathizes with that decay. Tragedy becomes a cold imitation of the form of the great masterpieces of antiquity, divested of all harmonious accompaniment of the kindred arts; and often the very form misunderstood, or a weak attempt to teach certain doctrines, which the writer considers as moral truths; and which are usually no more than specious flatteries of some gross vice or weakness, with which the author, in common with his auditors, are infected. Hence what has been called the classical and domestic drama. Addison's *Cato* is a specimen of the one; and would it were not superfluous to cite examples of the other! To such purposes poetry cannot be made subservient. Poetry is a sword of lightning, ever unsheathed, which consumes the scabbard that would contain it. And thus we observe that all dramatic writings of this nature are unimaginative in a singular degree; they affect sentiment and passion, which, divested of imagination, are other names for caprice and appetite. The period in our own history of the grossest degradation of the drama is the reign of Charles II, when all forms in which poetry had been accustomed to be expressed became hymns to the triumph of kingly power over liberty and virtue. Milton stood alone illuminating an age unworthy of him. At such periods the calculating principle pervades all the forms of dramatic exhibition, and poetry ceases to be expressed upon them. Comedy loses its ideal universality: wit succeeds to humour; we laugh from self-complacency and triumph, instead of pleasure; malignity, sarcasm, and contempt, succeed to sympathetic merriment; we hardly laugh, but we smile. Obscenity, which is ever blasphemy against the divine beauty in life, becomes, from the very veil which it assumes, more active if less disgusting: it is a monster for which the corruption of society for ever brings forth new food, which it devours in secret.

The drama being that form under which a greater number of modes of expression of poetry are susceptible of being combined than any other, the connexion of poetry and social good is more observable in the drama than in whatever other form. And it is indisputable that the highest perfection of human society has ever corresponded with the highest dramatic excellence; and that the corruption or the extinction of the drama in a nation where it has once flourished, is a mark of a corruption of manners, and an extinction of the energies which sustain the soul of social life. But, as Machiavelli says of political institutions, that life may be preserved and renewed, if men should arise capable of bringing back the drama to its principles. And this is true with respect to poetry in its most extended sense: all language, institution and form, require not only to be produced but to be sustained: the office and character of a poet participates in the divine nature as regards providence, no less than as regards creation.

Civil war, the spoils of Asia, and the fatal predominance first of the Macedonian, and then of the Roman arms, were so many symbols of the extinction or suspension of the creative faculty in Greece. The bucolic writers, who found patronage under the lettered tyrants of Sicily and Egypt, were the latest representatives of its most glorious reign. Their poetry is intensely melodious; like the odour of the tuberose, it overcomes and sickens the spirit with excess of sweetness; whilst the poetry of the preceding age was as a meadow-gale of June, which mingles the fragrance of all the flowers of the field, and adds a quickening and harmonizing spirit of its own, which endows the sense with a power of sustaining its extreme delight. The bucolic and erotic delicacy in written poetry is correlative with that softness in statuary, music, and the kindred arts, and even in manners and institutions, which distinguished the epoch to which I now refer. Nor is it the poetical faculty itself, or any misapplication of it, to which this want of harmony is to be imputed. An equal sensibility to the influence of the senses and the affections is to be found in the writings of Homer and Sophocles: the former, especially, has clothed sensual and pathetic images with irresistible attractions. Their superiority over these succeeding writers consists in the presence of those thoughts which belong to the inner faculties of our nature, not in the absence of those which are connected with the external: their incomparable perfection consists in a harmony of the union of all. It is not what the erotic poets have, but what they have not, in which their imperfection consists. It is not inasmuch as they were poets, but inasmuch as they were not poets, that they can be considered with any plausibility as connected with the corruption of their age. Had that corruption availed so as to extinguish in them the sensibility to pleasure, passion, and natural scenery, which is imputed to them as an imperfection, the last triumph of evil would have been achieved. For the end of social corruption is to destroy all sensibility to pleasure; and, therefore, it is corruption. It begins at the imagination and the intellect as at the core, and distributes itself thence as a paralysing venom, through the affections into the very appetites, until all become a torpid mass in which hardly sense survives. At the approach of such a period, poetry ever addresses itself to those faculties which are the last to be destroyed, and its voice is heard, like the footsteps of Astraea, departing from the world. Poetry ever communicates all the pleasure which men are capable of receiving: it is ever still the light of life; the source of whatever of beautiful or generous or true can have place in an evil time. It will readily be confessed that those among the luxurious citizens of Syracuse and Alexandria, who were delighted with the poems of Theocritus, were less cold, cruel, and sensual than the remnant of their tribe. But corruption must utterly have destroyed the fabric of human society before poetry can ever cease. The sacred links of that chain have never been entirely disjoined, which descending through the minds of many men is attached to those great minds, whence as from a magnet the invisible effluence is sent forth, which at once connects, animates, and sustains the life of all. It is the faculty which contains within itself the seeds at once of its own and of social renovation. And let us not circumscribe the effects of the bucolic and erotic poetry within the limits of the sensibility of those to whom it was addressed. They may have perceived the beauty of those immortal compositions, simply as fragments and isolated portions: those who are more finely organized, or born in a happier age, may recognize them as episodes to that great poem, which all poets, like the co-operating thoughts of one great mind, have built up since the beginning of the world.

The same revolutions within a narrower sphere had place in ancient Rome; but the actions and forms of its social life never seem to have been perfectly saturated with the poetical element. The Romans appear to have considered the Greeks as the selectest treasuries of the selectest forms of manners and of nature, and to have abstained from creating in measured language, sculpture, music, or architecture, anything which might bear a particular relation to their own condition, whilst it should bear a general one to the universal constitution of the world. But we judge from partial evidence, and we judge perhaps partially. Ennius, Varro, Pacuvius, and Accius, all great poets, have been lost. Lucretius is in the highest, and Virgil in a very high sense, a creator. The chosen delicacy of expressions of the latter, are as a mist of light which conceal from us the intense and exceeding truth of his conceptions of nature. Livy is instinct with poetry. Yet Horace, Catullus, Ovid, and generally the other great writers of the Virgilian age, saw man and nature in the mirror of Greece. The institutions also, and the religion of Rome were less poetical than those of Greece, as the shadow is less vivid than the substance. Hence poetry in Rome, seemed to follow, rather than accompany, the perfection of political and domestic society. The true poetry of Rome lived in its institutions; for whatever of beautiful, true, and majestic, they contained, could have sprung only from the faculty which creates the order in which they consist. The life of Camillus, the death of Regulus; the expectation of the senators, in their godlike state, of the victorious Gauls:

the refusal of the republic to make peace with Hannibal, after the battle of Cannae, were not the consequences of a refined calculation of the probable personal advantage to result from such a rhythm and order in the shows of life, to those who were at once the poets and the actors of these immortal dramas. The imagination beholding the beauty of this order, created it out of itself according to its own idea; the consequence was empire, and the reward everliving fame. These things are not the less poetry *quia carent vate sacro*. They are the episodes of that cyclic poem written by Time upon the memories of men. The Past, like an inspired rhapsodist, fills the theatre of everlasting generations with their harmony.

At length the ancient system of religion and manners had fulfilled the circle of its revolutions. And the world would have fallen into utter anarchy and darkness, but that there were found poets among the authors of the Christian and chivalric systems of manners and religion, who created forms of opinion and action never before conceived; which, copied into the imaginations of men, become as generals to the bewildered armies of their thoughts. It is foreign to the present purpose to touch upon the evil produced by these systems: except that we protest, on the ground of the principles already established, that no portion of it can be attributed to the poetry they contain.

It is probable that the poetry of Moses, Job, David, Solomon, and Isaiah, had produced a great effect upon the mind of Jesus and his disciples. The scattered fragments preserved to us by the biographers of this extraordinary person, are all instinct with the most vivid poetry. But his doctrines seem to have been quickly distorted. At a certain period after the prevalence of a system of opinions founded upon those promulgated by him, the three forms into which Plato had distributed the faculties of mind underwent a sort of apotheosis, and became the object of the worship of the civilized world. Here it is to be confessed that "Light seems to thicken", and

The crow makes wing to the rooky wood,
Good things of day begin to droop and drowse,
And night's black agents to their preys do rouze.

But mark how beautiful an order has sprung from the dust and blood of this fierce chaos! how the world, as from a resurrection, balancing itself on the golden wings of knowledge and of hope, has reassumed its yet unwearied flight into the heaven of time. Listen to the music, unheard by outward ears, which is as a ceaseless and invisible wind, nourishing its everlasting course with strength and swiftness.

The poetry in the doctrines of Jesus Christ, and the mythology and institutions of the Celtic conquerors of the Roman empire, outlived the darkness and the convulsions connected with their growth and victory, and blended themselves in a new fabric of manners and opinion. It is an error to impute the ignorance of the dark ages to the Christian doctrines or the predominance of the Celtic nations. Whatever of evil their agencies may have contained sprang from the extinction of the poetical principle, connected with the progress of despotism and superstition. Men, from causes too intricate to be here discussed, had become insensible and selfish: their own will had become feeble, and yet they were its slaves, and thence the slaves of the will of others: lust, fear, avarice, cruelty, and fraud, characterized a race amongst whom no one was to be found capable of *creating* in form, language, or institution. The moral anomalies of such a state of society are not justly to be charged upon any class of events immediately connected with them, and those events are most entitled to our approbation which could dissolve it most expeditiously. It is unfortunate for those who cannot distinguish words from thoughts, that many of these anomalies have been incorporated into our popular religion.

It was not until the eleventh century that the effects of the poetry of the Christian and chivalric systems began to manifest themselves. The principle of equality had been discovered and applied by Plato in his *Republic*, as the theoretical rule of the mode in which the materials of pleasure and of power, produced by the common skill and labour of human beings, ought to be distributed among them. The limitations of this rule were asserted by him to be determined only by the sensibility of each, or the utility to result to all. Plato, following the doctrines of Timaeus and Pythagoras, taught also a moral and intellectual system of doctrine, comprehending at once the past, present, and the future condition of man. Jesus Christ divulged the sacred and eternal truths contained in these views to mankind, and Christianity, in its abstract purity, became the exoteric expression of the esoteric doctrines of the poetry and wisdom of antiquity. The incorporation of the Celtic nations with the exhausted population of the south, impressed upon it the figure of the poetry existing in their mythology and institutions. The result was a sum of the action and reaction of all the causes included in it; for it may be assumed as a maxim that no nation or religion can supersede any other without incorporating into itself a portion of that which it supersedes. The abolition of personal and domestic slavery, and the emancipation of women from a great part of the degrading restraints of antiquity, were among the consequences of these events.

The abolition of personal slavery is the basis of the highest political hope that it can enter into the mind of man to conceive. The freedom of women produced the poetry of sexual love. Love became a religion, the idols of whose worship were ever present. It was as if the statues of Apollo and the Muses had been endowed with life and motion, and had walked forth among their worshippers; so that earth became peopled by the inhabitants of a diviner world. The familiar appearance and proceedings of life became wonderful and heavenly, and a paradise was created as out of the wrecks of Eden. And as this creation itself is poetry, so its creators were poets; and language was the instrument of their art: "Galeotto fù il libro, e chi lo scrisse." The Provençal Trouveurs, or inventors, preceded Petrarch, whose verses are as spells, which unseal the inmost enchanted fountains of the delight which is in the grief of love. It is impossible to feel them without becoming a portion of that beauty which we contemplate: it were superfluous to explain how the gentleness and the elevation of mind connected with these sacred emotions can render men more amiable, more generous and wise, and lift them out of the dull vapours of the little world of self. Dante understood the secret things of love even more than Petrarch. His *Vita Nuova* is an inexhaustible fountain of purity of sentiment and language: it is the idealized history of that period, and those intervals of his life which were dedicated to love. His apotheosis of Beatrice in Paradise, and the gradations of his own love and her loveliness, by which as by steps he feigns himself to have ascended to the throne of the Supreme Cause, is the most glorious imagination of modern poetry. The acutest critics have justly reversed the judgement of the vulgar, and the order of the great acts of the "Divine Drama", in the measure of the admiration which they accord to the Hell, Purgatory, and Paradise. The latter is a perpetual hymn of everlasting love. Love, which found a worthy poet in Plato alone of all the ancients, has been celebrated by a chorus of the greatest writers of the renovated world; and the music has penetrated the caverns of society, and its echoes still drown the dissonance of arms and superstition. At successive intervals, Ariosto, Tasso, Shakespeare, Spenser, Calderon, Rousseau, and the great writers of our own age, have celebrated the dominion of love, planting as it were trophies in the human mind of that sublimest victory over sensuality and force. The true relation borne to each other by the sexes into which human kind is distributed, has become less misunderstood; and if the error which confounded diversity with inequality of the powers of the two sexes has been partially recognized in the opinions and institutions of modern Europe, we owe this great benefit to the worship of which chivalry was the law, and poets the prophets.

The poetry of Dante may be considered as the bridge thrown over the stream of time, which unites the modern and ancient world. The distorted notions of invisible things which Dante and his rival Milton have idealized, are merely the mask and the mantle in which these great poets walk through eternity enveloped and disguised. It is a difficult question to determine how far they were conscious of the distinction which must have subsisted in their minds between their own creeds and that of the people. Dante at least appears to wish to mark the full extent of it by placing Riphaeus, whom Virgil calls *justissimus unus*, in Paradise, and observing a most heretical caprice in his distribution of rewards and punishments. And Milton's poem contains within itself a philosophical refutation of that system, of which, by a strange and natural antithesis, it has been a chief popular support. Nothing can exceed the energy and magnificence of the character of Satan as expressed in *Paradise Lost*. It is a mistake to suppose that he could ever have been intended for the popular personification of evil. Implacable hate, patient cunning, and a sleepless refine-

ment of device to inflict the extremest anguish on an enemy, these things are evil; and, although venial in a slave, are not to be forgiven in a tyrant; although redeemed by much that ennobles his defeat in one subdued, are marked by all that dishonours his conquest in the victor. Milton's Devil as a moral being is as far superior to his God, as one who perseveres in some purpose which he has conceived to be excellent in spite of adversity and torture, is to one who in the cold security of undoubted triumph inflicts the most horrible revenge upon his enemy, not from any mistaken notion of inducing him to repent of a perseverance in enmity, but with the alleged design of exasperating him to deserve new torments. Milton has so far violated the popular creed (if this shall be judged to be a violation) as to have alleged no superiority of moral virtue to his God over his Devil. And this bold neglect of a direct moral purpose is the most decisive proof of the supremacy of Milton's genius. He mingled as it were the elements of human nature as colours upon a single pallet, and arranged them in the composition of his great picture according to the laws of epic truth; that is, according to the laws of that principle by which a series of actions of the external universe and of intelligent and ethical beings is calculated to excite the sympathy of succeeding generations of mankind. The *Divina Commedia* and *Paradise Lost* have conferred upon modern mythology a systematic form; and when change and time shall have added one more superstition to the mass of those which have arisen and decayed upon the earth, commentators will be learnedly employed in elucidating the religion of ancestral Europe, only not utterly forgotten because it will have been stamped with the eternity of genius.

Homer was the first and Dante the second epic poet: that is, the second poet, the series of whose creations bore a defined and intelligible relation to the knowledge and sentiment and religion of the age in which he lived, and of the ages which followed it: developing itself in correspondence with their development. For Lucretius had limed the wings of his swift spirit in the dregs of the sensible world; and Virgil, with a modesty that ill became his genius, had affected the fame of an imitator, even whilst he created anew all that he copied; and none among the flock of mock-birds, though their notes were sweet, Apollonius Rhodius, Quintus Calaber, Nonnus, Lucan, Statius, or Claudian, have sought even to fulfil a single condition of epic truth. Milton was the third epic poet. For if the title of epic in its highest sense be refused to the *Aeneid*, still less can it be conceded to the *Orlando Furioso*, the *Gerusalemme Liberata*, the *Lusiad*, or the *Fairy Queen*.

Dante and Milton were both deeply penetrated with the ancient religion of the civilized world; and its spirit exists in their poetry probably in the same proportion as its forms survived in the unreformed worship of modern Europe. The one preceded and the other followed the Reformation at almost equal intervals. Dante was the first religious reformer, and Luther surpassed him rather in the rudeness and acrimony, than in the boldness of his censures of papal usurpation. Dante was the first awakener of entranced Europe; he created a language, in itself music and persuasion, out of a chaos of inharmonious barbarisms. He was the congregator of those great spirits who presided over the resurrection of learning; the Lucifer of that starry flock which in the thirteenth century shone forth from republican Italy, as from a heaven, into the darkness of the benighted world. His very words are instinct with spirit; each is as a spark, a burning atom of inextinguishable thought; and many yet lie covered in the ashes of their birth, and pregnant with a lightning which has yet found no conductor. All high poetry is infinite; it is as the first acorn, which contained all oaks potentially. Veil after veil may be undrawn, and the inmost naked beauty of the meaning never exposed. A great poem is a fountain for ever overflowing with the waters of wisdom and delight; and after one person and one age has exhausted all its divine effluence which their peculiar relations enable them to share, another and yet another succeeds, and new relations are ever developed, the source of an unforeseen and an unconceived delight.

The age immediately succeeding to that of Dante, Petrarch, and Boccaccio, was characterized by a revival of painting, sculpture, and architecture. Chaucer caught the sacred inspiration, and the superstructure of English literature is based upon the materials of Italian invention.

But let us not be betrayed from a defence into a critical history of poetry and its influence on society. Be it enough to have pointed out the effects of poets, in the large and true sense of the word, upon their own and all succeeding times.

But poets have been challenged to resign the civic crown to reasoners and mechanists, on another plea. It is admitted that the exercise of the imagination is most delightful, but it is alleged that that of reason is more useful. Let us examine as the grounds of this distinction, what is here meant by utility. Pleasure or good, in a general sense, is that which the consciousness of a sensitive and intelligent being seeks, and in which, when found, it acquiesces. There are two kinds of pleasure, one durable, universal and permanent; the other transitory and particular. Utility may either express the means of producing the former or the latter. In the former sense, whatever strengthens and purifies the affections, enlarges the imagination, and adds spirit to sense, is useful. But a narrower meaning may be assigned to the word utility, confining it to express that which banishes the importunity of the wants of our animal nature, the surrounding men with security of life, the dispersing the grosser delusions of superstition, and the conciliating such a degree of mutual forbearance among men as may consist with the motives of personal advantage.

Undoubtedly the promoters of utility, in this limited sense, have their appointed office in society. They follow the footsteps of poets, and copy the sketches of their creations into the book of common life. They make space, and give time. Their exertions are of the highest value, so long as they confine their administration of the concerns of the inferior powers of our nature within the limits due to the superior ones. But whilst the sceptic destroys gross superstitions, let him spare to deface, as some of the French writers have defaced, the eternal truths charactered upon the imaginations of men. Whilst the mechanist abridges, and the political economist combines labour, let them beware that their speculations, for want of correspondence with those first principles which belong to the imagination, do not tend, as they have in modern England, to exasperate at once the extremes of luxury and want. They have exemplified the saying, "To him that hath, more shall be given; and from him that hath not, the little that he hath shall be taken away." The rich have become richer, and the poor have become poorer; and the vessel of the state is driven between the Scylla and Charybdis of anarchy and despotism. Such are the effects which must ever flow from an unmitigated exercise of the calculating faculty.

It is difficult to define pleasure in its highest sense; the definition involving a number of apparent paradoxes. For, from an inexplicable defect of harmony in the constitution of human nature, the pain of the inferior is frequently connected with the pleasures of the superior portions of our being. Sorrow, terror, anguish, despair itself, are often the chosen expressions of an approximation to the highest good. Our sympathy in tragic fiction depends on this principle; tragedy delights by affording a shadow of the pleasure which exists in pain. This is the source also of the melancholy which is inseparable from the sweetest melody. The pleasure that is in sorrow is sweeter than the pleasure of pleasure itself. And hence the saying, "It is better to go to the house of mourning, than to the house of mirth." Not that this highest species of pleasure is necessarily linked with pain. The delight of love and friendship, the ecstasy of the admiration of nature, the joy of the perception and still more of the creation of poetry, is often wholly unalloyed.

The production and assurance of pleasure in this highest sense is true utility. Those who produce and preserve this pleasure are poets or poetical philosophers.

The exertions of Locke, Hume, Gibbon, Voltaire, Rousseau,[1] and their disciples, in favour of oppressed and deluded humanity, are entitled to the gratitude of mankind. Yet it is easy to calculate the degree of moral and intellectual improvement which the world would have exhibited, had they never lived. A little more nonsense would have been talked for a century or two; and perhaps a few more men, women, and children, burnt as heretics. We might not at this moment have been congratulating each other on the abolition of the Inquisition in Spain. But it exceeds all imagination to conceive what would have been the moral condition of the world if neither Dante, Petrarch, Boccaccio, Chaucer, Shakespeare,

[1] Although Rousseau has been thus classed, he was essentially a poet. The others, even Voltaire, were mere reasoners.

Calderon, Lord Bacon, nor Milton, had ever existed; if Raphael and Michael Angelo had never been born; if the Hebrew poetry had never been translated; if a revival of the study of Greek literature had never taken place; if no monuments of ancient sculpture had been handed down to us; and if the poetry of the religion of the ancient world had been extinguished together with its belief. The human mind could never, except by the intervention of these excitements, have been awakened to the invention of the grosser sciences, and that application of analytical reasoning to the aberrations of society, which it is now attempted to exalt over the direct expression of the inventive and creative faculty itself.

We have more moral, political and historical wisdom, than we know how to reduce into practice; we have more scientific and economical knowledge than can be accommodated to the just distribution of the produce which it multiplies. The poetry in these systems of thought, is concealed by the accumulation of facts and calculating processes. There is no want of knowledge respecting what is wisest and best in morals, government, and political economy, or at least, what is wiser and better than what men now practise and endure. But we let *I dare not* wait upon *I would,* like the poor cat in the adage." We want the creative faculty to imagine that which we know; we want the generous impulse to act that which we imagine; we want the poetry of life: our calculations have outrun conception; we have eaten more than we can digest. The cultivation of those sciences which have enlarged the limits of the empire of man over the external world, has, for want of the poetical faculty, proportionally circumscribed those of the internal world; and man, having enslaved the elements, remains himself a slave. To what but a cultivation of the mechanical arts in a degree disproportioned to the presence of the creative faculty, which is the basis of all knowledge, is to be attributed the abuse of all invention for abridging and combining labour, to the exasperation of the inequality of mankind? From what other cause has it arisen that the discoveries which should have lightened, have added a weight to the curse imposed on Adam? Poetry, and the principle of Self, of which money is the visible incarnation, are the God and Mammon of the world.

The functions of the poetical faculty are

two-fold; by one it creates new materials of knowledge and power and pleasure; by the other it engenders in the mind a desire to reproduce and arrange them according to a certain rhythm and order which may be called the beautiful and the good. The cultivation of poetry is never more to be desired than at periods when, from an excess of the selfish and calculating principle, the accumulation of the materials of external life exceed the quantity of the power of assimilating them to the internal laws of human nature. The body has then become too unwieldy for that which animates it.

Poetry is indeed something divine. It is at once the centre and circumference of knowledge; it is that which comprehends all science, and that to which all science must be referred. It is at the same time the root and blossom of all other systems of thought; it is that from which all spring, and that which adorns all; and that which, if blighted, denies the fruit and the seed, and withholds from the barren world the nourishment and the succession of the scions of the tree of life. It is the perfect and consummate surface and bloom of all things; it is as the odour and the colour of the rose to the texture of the elements which compose it, as the form and splendour of unfaded beauty to the secrets of anatomy and corruption. What were virtue, love, patriotism, friendship—what were the scenery of this beautiful universe which we inhabit; what were our consolations on this side of the grave— and what were our aspirations beyond it, if poetry did not ascend to bring light and fire from those eternal regions where the owl-winged faculty of calculation dare not ever soar? Poetry is not like reasoning, a power to be exerted according to the determination of the will. A man cannot say, "I will compose poetry." The greatest poet even cannot say it; for the mind in creation is as a fading coal, which some invisible influence, like an inconstant wind, awakens to transitory brightness; this power arises from within, like the colour of a flower which fades and changes as it is developed, and the conscious portions of our natures are unprophetic either of its approach or its departure. Could this influence be durable in its original purity and force, it is impossible to predict the greatness of the results; but when composition begins, inspiration is already on the decline, and the most

glorious poetry that has ever been communicated to the world is probably a feeble shadow of the original conceptions of the poet. I appeal to the greatest poets of the present day, whether it is not an error to assert that the finest passages of poetry are produced by labour and study. The toil and the delay recommended by critics, can be justly interpreted to mean no more than a careful observation of the inspired moments, and an artificial connexion of the spaces between their suggestions by the inter-texture of conventional expressions; a necessity only imposed by the limitedness of the poetical faculty itself; for Milton conceived the *Paradise Lost* as a whole before he executed it in portions. We have his own authority also for the muse having "dictated" to him the "unpremeditated song." And let this be an answer to those who would allege the fifty-six various readings of the first line of the *Orlando Furioso*. Compositions so produced are to poetry what mosaic is to painting. This instinct and intuition of the poetical faculty is still more observable in the plastic and pictorial arts; a great statue or picture grows under the power of the artist as a child in the mother's womb; and the very mind which directs the hands in formation is incapable of accounting to itself for the origin, the gradations, or the media of the process.

Poetry is the record of the best and happiest moments of the happiest and best minds. We are aware of evanescent visitations of thought and feeling sometimes associated with place or person, sometimes regarding our own mind alone, and always arising unforeseen and departing unbidden, but elevating and delightful beyond all expression: so that even in the desire and regret they leave, there cannot but be pleasure, participating as it does in the nature of its object. It is as it were the interpenetration of a diviner nature through our own; but its footsteps are like those of a wind over the sea, which the coming calm erases, and whose traces remain only, as on the wrinkled sand which paves it. These and corresponding conditions of being are experienced principally by those of the most delicate sensibility and the most enlarged imagination; and the state of mind produced by them is at war with every base desire. The enthusiasm of virtue, love, patriotism, and friendship, is essentially linked with such emotions; and whilst they last, self appears as what it is, an atom to a universe. Poets are not only subject to these experiences as spirits of the most refined organization, but they can colour all that they combine with the evanescent hues of this ethereal world; a word, a trait in the representation of a scene or a passion, will touch the enchanted chord, and reanimate, in those who have ever experienced these emotions, the sleeping, the cold, the buried image of the past. Poetry thus makes immortal all that is best and most beautiful in the world; it arrests the vanishing apparitions which haunt the interlunations of life, and veiling them, or in language or in form, sends them forth among mankind, bearing sweet news of kindred joy to those with whom their sisters abide—abide, because there is no portal of expression from the caverns of the spirit which they inhabit into the universe of things. Poetry redeems from decay the visitations of the divinity in man.

Poetry turns all things to loveliness; it exalts the beauty of that which is most beautiful, and it adds beauty to that which is most deformed; it marries exultation and horror, grief and pleasure, eternity and change; it subdues to union under its light yoke, all irreconcilable things. It transmutes all that it touches, and every form moving within the radiance of its presence is changed by wondrous sympathy to an incarnation of the spirit which it breathes: its secret alchemy turns to potable gold the poisonous waters which flow from death through life; it strips the veil of familiarity from the world, and lays bare the naked and sleeping beauty, which is the spirit of its forms.

All things exist as they are perceived; at least in relation to the percipient. "The mind is its own place, and of itself can make a heaven of hell, a hell of heaven." But poetry defeats the curse which binds us to be subjected to the accident of surrounding impressions. And whether it spreads its own figured curtain, or withdraws life's dark veil from before the scene of things, it equally creates for us a being within our being. It makes us the inhabitants of a world to which the familiar world is a chaos. It reproduces the common universe of which we are portions and percipients, and it purges from our inward sight the film of familiarity which obscures from us the wonder of our being. It compels us to feel that which we perceive, and to imagine that which we know. It creates anew the universe, after it has been annihilated in our minds by the recurrence of impressions blunted by reiteration. It justifies the bold and true words of Tasso: *Non merita nome di creatore, se non Iddio ed il Poeta.*

A poet, as he is the author to others of the highest wisdom, pleasure, virtue and glory, so he ought personally to be the happiest, the best, the wisest, and the most illustrious of men. As to his glory, let time be challenged to declare whether the fame of any other institutor of human life be comparable to that of a poet. That he is the wisest, the happiest, and the best, inasmuch as he is a poet, is equally incontrovertible: the greatest poets have been men of the most spotless virtue, of the most consummate prudence, and, if we would look into the interior of their lives, the most fortunate of men: and the exceptions, as they regard those who possessed the poetic faculty in a high yet inferior degree, will be found on consideration to confine rather than destroy the rule. Let us for a moment stoop to the arbitration of popular breath, and usurping and uniting in our own persons the incompatible characters of accuser, witness, judge, and executioner, let us decide without trial, testimony, or form, that certain motives of those who are "there sitting where we dare not soar," are reprehensible. Let us assume that Homer was a drunkard, that Virgil was a flatterer, that Horace was a coward, that Tasso was a madman, that Lord Bacon was a peculator, that Raphael was a libertine, that Spenser was a poet laureate. It is inconsistent with this division of our subject to cite living poets, but posterity has done ample justice to the great names now referred to. Their errors have been weighed and found to have been dust in the balance; if their sins "were as scarlet, they are now white as snow": they have been washed in the blood of the mediator and redeemer, Time. Observe in what a ludicrous chaos the imputations of real or fictitious crime have been confused in the contemporary calumnies against poetry and poets; consider how little is, as it appears—or appears, as it is; look to your own motives, and judge not, lest ye be judged.

Poetry, as has been said, differs in this respect from logic, that it is not subject to the control of the active powers of the mind, and that its birth and recurrence have no necessary connexion with the consciousness or will. It is presumptuous to determine that these are the necessary conditions of all mental causation, when mental effects are experienced unsusceptible of being referred to them. The frequent 5 recurrence of the poetical power, it is obvious to suppose, may produce in the mind a habit of order and harmony correlative with its own nature and with its effects upon other minds. But in the intervals of inspiration, and they 10 may be frequent without being durable, a poet becomes a man, and is abandoned to the sudden reflux of the influences under which others habitually live. But as he is more delicately organized than other men, and sensible to pain 15 and pleasure, both his own and that of others, in a degree unknown to them, he will avoid the one and pursue the other with an ardour proportioned to this difference. And he renders himself obnoxious to calumny, when he neg- 20 lects to observe the circumstances under which these objects of universal pursuit and flight have disguised themselves in one another's garments.

But there is nothing necessarily evil in this 25 error, and thus cruelty, envy, revenge, avarice, and the passions purely evil, have never formed any portion of the popular imputations on the lives of poets.

I have thought it most favourable to the 30 cause of truth to set down these remarks according to the order in which they were suggested to my mind, by a consideration of the subject itself, instead of observing the formality of a polemical reply; but if the view which 35 they contain be just, they will be found to involve a refutation of the arguers against poetry, so far at least as regards the first division of the subject. I can readily conjecture what should have moved the gall of some 40 learned and intelligent writers who quarrel with certain versifiers; I confess myself, like them, unwilling to be stunned by the Theseids of the hoarse Codri of the day. Bavius and Maevius undoubtedly are, as they ever were, 45 insufferable persons. But it belongs to a philosophical critic to distinguish rather than confound.

The first part of these remarks has related to poetry in its elements and principles; and it 50 has been shown, as well as the narrow limits assigned them would permit, that what is called poetry, in a restricted sense, has a common source with all other forms of order and of beauty, according to which the materials of human life are susceptible of being arranged, and which is poetry in a universal sense.

The second part will have for its object an application of these principles to the present state of the cultivation of poetry, and a defence of the attempt to idealize the modern forms of manners and opinions, and compel them into a subordination to the imaginative and creative faculty. For the literature of England, an energetic development of which has ever preceded or accompanied a great and free development of the national will, has arisen as it were from a new birth. In spite of the low-thoughted envy which would undervalue contemporary merit, our own will be a memorable age in intellectual achievements, and we live among such philosophers and poets as surpass beyond comparison any who have appeared since the last national struggle for civil and religious liberty. The most unfailing herald, companion, and follower of the awakening of a great people to work a beneficial change in opinion or institution, is poetry. At such periods there is an accumulation of the power of communicating and receiving intense and impassioned conceptions respecting man and nature. The persons in whom this power resides may often, as far as regards many portions of their nature, have little apparent correspondence with that spirit of good of which they are the ministers. But even whilst they deny and abjure, they are yet compelled to serve, the power which is seated on the throne of their own soul. It is impossible to read the compositions of the most celebrated writers of the present day without being startled with the electric life which burns within their words. They measure the circumference and sound the depths of human nature with a comprehensive and all-penetrating spirit, and they are themselves perhaps the most sincerely astonished at its manifestations; for it is less their spirit than the spirit of the age. Poets are the hierophants of an unapprehended inspiration; the mirrors of the gigantic shadows which futurity casts upon the present; the words which express what they understand not; the trumpets which sing to battle, and feel not what they inspire; the influence which is moved not, but moves. Poets are the unacknowledged legislators of the world.

A PHILOSOPHICAL VIEW OF REFORM
circ. 1820

CHAPTER I
INTRODUCTION

Those who imagine that their personal interest is directly or indirectly concerned in maintaining the power in which they are clothed by the existing institutions of English Government do not acknowledge the necessity of a material change in those institutions. With this exception, there is no inhabitant of the British Empire of mature age and perfect understanding not fully persuaded of the necessity of Reform.

From the dissolution of the Roman Empire, that vast and successful scheme for the enslaving *of* the most civilised portion of mankind, to the epoch of the French Revolution, have succeeded a series of schemes, on a smaller scale, operating to the same effect. Names borrowed from the life and opinions of Jesus Christ were employed as symbols of domination and imposture; and a system of liberty and equality—for such was the system planted by that great Reformer—was perverted to support oppression. Not his doctrines, for they are too simple and direct to be susceptible of such perversion, but the mere names. Such was the origin of the Catholic Church, which, together with the several dynasties then beginning to consolidate themselves in Europe, means, being interpreted, a plan according to which the cunning and selfish few have employed the fears and hopes of the ignorant many to the establishment of their own power and the destruction of the real interests of all.

The Republics and municipal Governments of Italy opposed for some time a systematic and effectual resistance to the all-surrounding tyranny. The Lombard League defeated the armies of the despot in open field, and until Florence was betrayed to those polished tyrants, the Medici, Freedom had one citadel wherein it could find refuge from a world which was its enemy. Florence, long balanced, divided and weakened the strength of the Empire and the Popedom. To this cause, if to anything, was due the undisputed superiority of Italy in literature and the arts over all its contemporary nations, that union of energy and of beauty which distinguishes from all other poets the writings of Dante, that restlessness of fervid power which expressed itself in painting and sculpture, and in daring architectural forms, and from which, and conjointly from the creations of Athens, its predecessor and its image, Raphael and Michael Angelo drew the inspiration which created those forms and colours now the astonishment of the world. The father of our own literature, Chaucer, wrought from the simple and powerful language of a nursling of this Republic the basis of our own literature. And thus we owe, among other causes, the exact condition belonging to intellectual existence to the generous disdain of submission which burned in the bosoms of men who filled a distant generation and inhabited other lands.

When this resistance was overpowered, as what resistance to fraud and tyranny has not been overpowered? another was even then maturing. The progress of philosophy and civilization which ended in that imperfect emancipation of mankind from the yoke of priests and kings called the Reformation, had already commenced. Exasperated by their long sufferings, inflamed by the sparks of that superstition from the flames of which they were emerging, the poor rose against their natural enemies, the rich, and repaid with bloody interest the tyranny of ages. One of the signs of the times was that the oppressed peasantry rose like the negro slaves of West Indian plantations, and murdered their tyrants when they were unaware. So dear is power that the tyrants themselves neither then, nor now, nor ever, left or leave a path to freedom but through their own blood. The contest then waged under the names of religion which have seldom been any more than popular and visible symbols which express power in some shape or other, asserted by one party and disclaimed by the other, ended; and the result, though partial and imperfect, is perhaps the most animating that the philanthropist can contemplate in the history of man. The Republic of Holland, which has been so long an armoury of the arrows of learning by which superstition has been wounded even to death, was established by this contest. What though the name of Republic—and by whom but by conscience-stricken tyrants would it be extinguished—is no more? The Republics of Switzerland derived from this event their consolidation and their union.

From England then first began to pass away

the stain of conquest. The exposure of a certain portion of religious imposture drew with it an enquiry into political imposture, and was attended with an extraordinary exertion of the energies of intellectual power. Shakespeare and Lord Bacon and the great writers of the age of Elizabeth and James I were at once the effects of the new spirit in men's minds, and the causes of its more complete development. By rapid gradations the nation was conducted to the temporary abolition of aristocracy and episcopacy, and *to* the mighty example which, "in teaching nations how to live", England afforded to the world—of bringing to public justice one of those chiefs of a conspiracy of privileged murderers and robbers whose impunity had been the consecration of crime. [The maxim that criminals should be pitied and reformed, not detested and punished, alone affords a source of. . . .]

After the selfish passions and temporizing interests of men had enlisted themselves to produce and establish the Restoration of Charles II the unequal combat was renewed under the reign of his successor, and that compromise between the unextinguishable spirit of Liberty, and the ever watchful spirit of fraud and tyranny, called the Revolution had place. On this occasion monarchy and aristocracy and episcopacy were at once established and limited by law. Unfortunately they lost no more in extent of power than they gained in security of possession. Meanwhile those by whom they were established acknowledged and declared that the Will of the People was the source from which those powers, in this instance, derived the right to subsist. A man has no right to be a King or a Lord or a Bishop but so long as it is for the benefit of the People and so long as the People judge that it is for their benefit that he should impersonate that character. The solemn establishment of this maxim as the basis of our constitutional law, more than any beneficial and energetic application of it to the circumstances of the era of its promulgation, was the fruit of that vaunted event. Correlative with this series of events in England was the commencement of a new epoch in the history of the progress of civilization and society.

That superstition which has disguised itself under the name of the system of Jesus subsisted under all its forms, even where it had been separated from those things especially considered as abuses by the multitude, in the shape of an intolerant and oppressive hierarchy. Catholics massacred Protestants and Protestants proscribed Catholics, and extermination was the sanction of each faith within the limits of the power of its professors. The New Testament is in everyone's hand, and the few who ever read it with the simple sincerity of an unbiassed judgement may perceive how distinct from the opinions of any of those professing themselves orthodox were the doctrines and the actions of Jesus Christ. At the period of the Reformation this test was applied, this judgement formed of the then existing hierarchy, and the same compromise was then made between the spirit of truth and the spirit of imposture after the struggle which ploughed up the area of the human mind, as was made in the particular instance of England between the spirit of freedom and the spirit of tyranny at that event called the Revolution. In both instances the maxims so solemnly recorded remain as trophies of our difficult and incomplete victory, planted on the enemies' soil. *The will of the People to change their government is an acknowledged right in the Constitution of England.* The protesting against religious dogmas which present themselves to his mind as false is the inalienable prerogative of every human being.

The new epoch was marked by the commencement of deeper enquiries into the point of human nature than are compatible with an unreserved belief in any of those popular mistakes upon which popular systems of faith with respect to the cause and agencies of the universe, with all their superstructure of political and religious tyranny, are built. Lord Bacon, Spinoza, Hobbes, Boyle, Montaigne, regulated the reasoning powers, criticized the history, exposed the past errors by illustrating their causes and their connexion, and anatomized the inmost nature of social man. Then, with a less interval of time than of genius, followed Locke and the philosophers of his exact and intelligible but superficial school. Their illustrations of some of the minor consequences of the doctrines established by the sublime genius of their predecessors were correct, popular, simple and energetic. Above all, they indicated inferences the most incompatible with the popular religions and the established governments of Europe. [Philosophy went now into the enchanted forest of the demons of worldly power, as the pioneer of the overgrowth of ages.] Berkeley and Hume, and Hartley at a later age, following the traces of these inductions, have clearly established the certainty of our ignorance with respect to those obscure questions which under the name of religious truths have been the watch-words of contention and symbols of unjust power ever since they were distorted by the narrow passions of the immediate followers of Jesus from that meaning to which philosophers are even now restoring them. A crowd of writers in France seized upon the most popular topics of these doctrines, and developing those particular portions of the new philosophy which conducted to inferences at war with the dreadful oppressions under which that country groaned, made familiar to mankind the falsehood of the mediaeval pretences of their religious and political oppressors. Considered as philosophers their error seems to have consisted chiefly in a limitation of view; they told the truth, but not the whole truth. This might have arisen from the terrible sufferings of their countrymen inviting them rather to apply a portion of what had already been discovered to their immediate relief, than to pursue one interest, the abstractions of thought, as the great philosophers who preceded them had done, for the sake of a future and more universal advantage. Whilst that philosophy which, burying itself in the obscure part of our nature, regards the truth and falsehood of dogmas relating to the cause of the universe, and the nature and manner of man's relation with it, was thus stripping Power of its darkest mask, Political Philosophy, or that which considers the relations of man as a social being, was assuming a precise form. That philosophy indeed sprang from and maintained a connexion with that other as its parent. What would Swift and Bolingbroke and Sidney and Locke and Montesquieu, or even Rousseau, not to speak of political philosophers of our own age, Godwin and Bentham, have been but for Lord Bacon, Montaigne and Spinoza, and the other great luminaries of the preceding epoch? Something excellent and eminent, no doubt, the least of these would have been, but something different from and inferior to what they are. A series

of these writers illustrated with more or less success the principles of human nature as applied to man in political society. A thirst for accommodating the existing forms according to which mankind are found divided to those rules of freedom and equality which have been discovered as being the elementary principles according to which the happiness resulting from the social union ought to be produced and distributed, was kindled by these enquiries. Contemporary with this condition of the intellect all the powers of mankind, though in most cases under forms highly inauspicious *began* to develop themselves with uncommon energy. The mechanical sciences attained to a degree of perfection which, though obscurely foreseen by Lord Bacon, it had been accounted madness to have prophesied in a preceding age. Commerce was pursued with a perpetually increasing vigour, and the same area of the Earth was perpetually compelled to furnish more and more subsistence. The means and sources of knowledge were thus increased together with knowledge itself, and the instruments of knowledge. The benefit of this increase of the powers of man became, in consequence of the inartificial forms into which mankind was distributed, an instrument of his additional evil. The capabilities of happiness were increased, and applied to the augmentation of misery. Modern society is thus an engine assumed to be for useful purposes, whose force is by a system of subtle mechanism augmented to the highest pitch, but which, instead of grinding corn or raising water acts against itself and is perpetually wearing away or breaking to pieces the wheels of which it is composed. The result of the labours of the political philosophers has been the establishment of the principle of Utility as the substance, and liberty and equality as the forms according to which the concerns of human life ought to be administered. By this test the various institutions regulating political society have been tried, and as the undigested growth of the private passions, errors, and interests of barbarians and oppressors have been condemned. And many new theories, more or less perfect, but all superior to the mass of evil which they would supplant, have been given to the world.

The system of government in the United States of America was the first practical illustration of the new philosophy. Sufficiently remote, it will be confessed, from the accuracy of ideal excellence is that representative system which will soon cover the extent of that vast Continent. But it is scarcely less remote from the insolent and contaminating tyrannies under which, with some limitation of the terms as regards England, Europe groaned at the period of the successful rebellion of America. America holds forth the victorious example of an immensely populous, and as far as the external arts of life are concerned, a highly civilized community administered according to republican forms. It has no king, that is it has no officer to whom wealth and from whom corruption flow. It has no hereditary oligarchy, that is it acknowledges no order of men privileged to cheat and insult the rest of the members of the State, and who inherit the right of legislating and judging which the principles of human nature compel them to exercise to their own profit and to the detriment of those not included within their peculiar class. It has no established Church, that is no system of opinions respecting the abstrusest questions which can be the topics of human thought, founded in an age of error and fanaticism, and opposed by law to all other opinions, defended by prosecutions, and sanctioned by enormous grants given to idle priests and forced from the unwilling hands of those who have an interest in the cultivation and improvement of the soil. It has no false representation, whose consequences are captivity, confiscation, infamy and ruin, but a true representation. The will of the many is represented in the assemblies and by the officers entrusted with the administration of the executive power almost as directly as the will of one person can be represented by the will of another. [This is not the place for dilating upon the inexpressible advantages (if such advantages require any manifestation) of a self-governing Society, or one which approaches it in the degree of the Republic of the United States.] Lastly, it has an institution by which it is honourably distinguished from all other governments which ever existed. It constitutionally acknowledges the progress of human improvement, and is framed under the limitation of the probability of more simple views of political science being rendered applicable to human life. There is a law by which the constitution is reserved for revision every ten years. Every other set of men who have assumed the office of legislation, and framing institutions for future ages, with far less right to such an assumption than the founders of the American Republic, *regarded* their work as the wisest and the best that could possibly have been produced: these illustrious men looked upon the past history of their species and saw that it was the history of his mistakes, and his sufferings arising from his mistakes; they observed the superiority of their own work to all the works which had preceded it, and they judged it possible that other political institutions would be discovered having the same relation to those which they had established which they bear to those which have preceded them. They provided therefore for the application of these contingent discoveries to the social state without the violence and misery attendant upon such change in less modest and more imperfect governments. The United States, as we would have expected from theoretical deduction, affords an example, compared with the old governments of Europe and Asia, of a free, happy and strong people.[1] Nor let it be said that they owe their superiority rather to the situation than to their government. Give them a king, and let that king waste in luxury, riot and bribery the same sum which now serves for the entire expenses of their government. Give them an aristocracy, and let that aristocracy legislate for the people. Give them a priesthood, and let them bribe with a tenth of the produce of the soil a certain set of men to say a certain set of words. Pledge the larger portion of them by financial subterfuges to pay the half of their property or earnings to another portion, and let the proportion of those who enjoy the fruits of the toil of others without toiling themselves be three instead of one. Give them a Court of Chancery and let

[1] Its error consists not in the not representing the will of the people as it is, but in not providing for the full development and the most salutary condition of that will. For two conditions are necessary to a theoretically perfect government, and one of them alone is adequately fulfilled by the most perfect of practical governments, the Republic of the United States: to represent the will of the people as it is. To provide that that will should be as wise and just as possible. In a certain extent the mere representation of public will produces in itself a wholesome condition of it, and in this extent America fulfils imperfectly and indirectly the last and most important condition of perfect government.

the property, the liberty and the interest in the dearest concerns, the exercise of the sacred rights of a social being depend upon the will of one of the most servile creations of that kingly and oligarchical and priestly power to which every man, in proportion as he is of an enquiring and philosophic mind and of a sincere and honourable disposition is a natural and necessary enemy. Give then, as you must if you give them these things, a great standing army to cut down the people if they murmur. If any American should see these words, his blood would run cold at the imagination of such a change. He well knows that the prosperity and happiness of the United States if subjected to such institutions *would* be no more.

The just and successful Revolt of America corresponded with a state of public opinion in Europe of which it was the first result. The French Revolution was the second. The oppressors of mankind had enjoyed (O that we could say suffered) a long and undisturbed reign in France, and to the pining famine, the shelterless destitution of the inhabitants of that country had been added and heaped up insult harder to bear than misery. For the feudal system (the immediate causes and conditions of its institution having become obliterated) had degenerated into an instrument not only of oppression but of contumely, and both were unsparingly inflicted. Blind in the possession of strength, drunken as with the intoxication of ancestral greatness, the rulers perceived not that increase of knowledge in the subject which made its exercise insecure. They called soldiers to hew down the people when their power was already past. The tyrants were, as usual, the aggressors. The oppressed, having been rendered brutal, ignorant, servile and bloody by slavery, having had the intellectual thirst, excited in them by the progress of civilization, satiated from fountains of literature poisoned by the spirit and the form of monarchy, arose to take a dreadful revenge on their oppressors. Their desire to wreak revenge, to this extent, in itself a mistake, a crime, a calamity, arose from the same source as their other miseries and errors, and affords an additional proof of the necessity of that long-delayed change which it accompanied and disgraced. If a just and necessary revolution could have been accomplished with as little expense of happiness and order in a country governed by despotic as *in* one governed by free laws, equal liberty and justice would lose their chief recommendations and tyranny be divested of its most revolting attributes. Tyranny entrenches itself within the existing interests of the best and most refined citizens of a nation and says "If you dare trample upon these, be free." Though these terrible conditions shall not be evaded, the world is no longer in a temper to decline the challenge.

The French were what their literature is (excepting Montaigne and Rousseau, and some few of the . . .) weak, superficial, vain, with little imagination, and with passions as well as judgements cleaving to the external forms of things. Not that *they* are organically different from the inhabitants of the nations who have become . . . or rather not that their organical differences, whatever they may amount to, incapacitate them from arriving at the exercise of the highest powers to be attained by man. Their institutions made them what they were. Slavery and superstition, contumely and the tame endurance of contumely, and the habits engendered from generation to generation out of this transmitted inheritance of wrong, created the thing which has extinguished what has been called the likeness of God in man. The Revolution in France overthrew the heirarchy, the aristocarcy and the monarchy, and the whole of that peculiarly insolent and oppressive system on which they were based. But as it only partially extinguished those passions which are the spirit of these forms a reaction took place which has restored in a certain limited degree the old system. In a degree, indeed, exceedingly limited, and stript of all its antient terrors, the hope of the Monarchy of France, with his teeth drawn and his claws pared, may *succeed in* maintaining the formal witness of most imperfect and insecure dominion. The usurpation of Bonaparte and then the Restoration of the Bourbons were the shapes in which this reaction clothed itself, and the heart of every lover of liberty was struck as with palsy on the succession of these events. But reversing the proverbial expression of Shakespeare, it may be the good which the Revolutionists did lives after them, their ills are interred with their bones. But the military project of government of the great tyrant having failed, and there being even no attempt—and, if there were any attempt, there being not the remotest possibility of re-establishing the enormous system of tyranny abolished by the Revolution, France is, as it were, regenerated. Its legislative assemblies are in a certain limited degree representations of the popular will, and the executive power is hemmed in by jealous laws. France occupies in this respect the same situation as was occupied by England at the restoration of Charles II. It has undergone a revolution (unlike in the violence and calamities which attended it, because unlike in the abuses which it was excited to put down) which may be paralleled with that in our own country which ended in the death of Charles I. The authors of both Revolutions proposed a greater and more glorious object than the degraded passions of their countrymen permitted them to attain. But in both cases abuses were abolished which never since have dared to show their face. There remains in the natural order of human things that the tyranny and perfidy of the reigns of Charles II and James II (for these were less the result of the disposition of particular men than the vices which would have been engendered in any but an extraordinary man by the natural necessities of their situation) perhaps under a milder form and within a shorter period should produce the institution of a Government in France which may bear the same relation to the state of political knowledge existing at the present day, as the Revolution under William III bore to the state of political knowledge existing at that period.

Germany, which is, among the great nations of Europe, one of the latest civilized, with the exception of Russia, is rising with the fervour of a vigorous youth to the assertion of those rights for which it has that desire arising from knowledge, the surest pledge of victory. The deep passion and the bold and Aeschylean vigour of the imagery of their poetry, the enthusiasm, however distorted, the purity, truth and comprehensiveness of their religious sentiments, their language which is the many-sided mirror of every changing thought, their sincere, bold and liberal spirit of criticism, their subtle and deep philosophy mingling fervid intuitions into truth with obscure error (for the period of just distinction is yet to come) and their taste and power in the plastic arts, prove that they are a great People. And every great nation either has *been* or is or will be free. The panic-stricken tyrants of that country promised to their subjects that their governments should be administered according to republican forms, they retaining merely the right of hereditary chief magistracy in their families. This promise, made in danger, the oppressors dream that they can break in security. And everything in consequence wears in Germany the aspect of rapidly maturing revolution.

In Spain and in the dependencies of Spain good and evil in the forms of Despair and Tyranny are struggling face to face. That great people have been delivered bound hand and foot to be trampled upon and insulted by a traitorous and sanguinary tyrant, a monster who makes credible all that might have been doubted in the history of Nero, Christiern, Muley Ismael or Ezzelin—the persons who have thus delivered them were that hypocritical knot of conspiring tyrants, who proceeded upon the credit they gained by putting down the only tyrant among them who was not a hypocrite, to undertake the administration of those *arrondissements* of consecrated injustice and violence which they deliver to those who the nearest resemble them under the name of the "kingdoms of the earth". This action signed a sentence of death, confiscation, exile or captivity against every philosopher and patriot in Spain. The tyrant Ferdinand, he whose name is held a proverb of execration, found natural allies in all the priests and military chiefs and a few of the most dishonourable of that devoted country. And the consequences of military despotism and the black, stagnant, venomous hatred which priests in common with eunuchs seek every opportunity to wreak upon the portion of mankind exempt from their own unmanly disqualifications is slavery. And what is slavery—in its mildest form hideous, and, so long as one amiable or great attribute survives in its victims, rankling and intolerable, but in its darkest shape as it now exhibits itself in Spain it is the essence of all and more than all the evil for the sake of an exemption from which mankind submit to the mighty calamity of government. It is a system of insecurity of property, and of person, of prostration of conscience and understanding, it is famine heaped upon the greater number and contumely heaped upon all, defended by unspeakable tortures employed not merely as punishments but as precautions, by want, death and captivity, and the application to political purposes of the execrated and enormous instruments of religious cruelty. Those men of understanding, integrity, and courage who rescued their country from one tyrant are exiled from it by his successor and his enemy and their legitimate king. Tyrants, however they may squabble among themselves, have common friends and foes. The taxes are levied at the point of the sword. Armed insurgents occupy all the defensible mountains of the country. The dungeons are peopled thickly, and persons of every sex and age have the fibres of their frame torn by subtle torments. Boiling water (such is an article in the last news from Spain) is poured upon the legs of a noble Spanish lady newly delivered, slowly and cautiously, that she may confess what she knows of a conspiracy against the tyrant, and she dies, as constant as the slave Epicharis, imprecating curses upon her torturers and passionately calling upon her children. These events, in the present condition of the understanding and sentiment of mankind, are the rapidly passing shadows, which forerun successful insurrection, the ominous comets of our republican poet perplexing great monarchs with fear of change.—Spain, having passed through an ordeal severe in proportion to the wrongs and errors which it is kindled to erase must of necessity be renovated. Spain produced Calderon and Cervantes, what else did it but breathe, thro the tumult of the despotism and superstition which invested them, the prophecy of a glorious consummation?

The independents of South America are as it were already free. Great Republics are about to consolidate themselves in a portion of the globe sufficiently vast and fertile to nourish more human beings than at present occupy, with the exception perhaps of China, the remainder of the inhabited earth. Some indefinite arrears of misery and blood remain to be paid to the Moloch of oppression. These, to the last drop and groan it will inflict by its *ministers*. But not the less are they inevitably enfranchised. The Great Monarchies of Asia cannot, let us confidently hope, remain unshaken by the earthquake which is shaking to dust the "mountainous strongholds" of the tyrants of the Western world.

Revolutions in the political and religious state of the Indian peninsula seem to be accomplishing, and it cannot be doubted but the zeal of the missionaries of what is called the Christian faith will produce beneficial innovation there, even by the application of dogmas and forms of what is here an outworn incumbrance. The Indians have been enslaved and cramped in the most severe and paralysing forms which were ever devised by man; some of this new enthusiasm ought to be kindled among them to consume it and leave them free, and even if the doctrines of Jesus do not penetrate through the darkness of that which those who profess to be his followers call Christianity, there will yet be a number of social forms modelled upon those European feelings from which it has taken its colour substituted to those according to which they are at present cramped, and from which, when the time for complete emancipation shall arrive, their disengagement may be less difficult, and under which their progress to it may be the less imperceptibly slow. Many native Indians have acquired, it is said, a competent knowledge in the arts and philosophy of Europe, and Locke and Hume and Rousseau are familiarly talked of in Brahminical society. But the thing to be sought is that they should, as they would if they were free, attain to a system of arts and literature of their own.— Of Persia we know little, but that it has been the theatre of sanguinary contests for power, and that it is now at peace. The Persians appear to be from organization a beautiful refined and impassioned people and would probably soon be infected by the contagion of good. The Turkish Empire is in its last stage of ruin, and it cannot be doubted but that the time is approaching when the deserts of Asia Minor and of Greece will be colonized by the overflowing population of countries less enslaved and debased, and that the climate and the scenery which was the birthplace of all that is wise and beautiful will not remain for ever the spoil of wild beasts and unlettered Tartars.—In Syria and Arabia the spirit of human intellect has roused a sect of people called Wahabees, who maintain the Unity of God, and the equality of man, and their enthusiasm must go on "conquering and to conquer" even if it must be repressed in its present shape.—Egypt having but a nominal dependence upon Constantinople is under the government of Ottoman Bey, a person of enlightened views who is introducing European literature and art, and is thus beginning that change which Time, the great innovator, will accomplish in that degraded country; and by the same means its sublime and enduring monuments may excite lofty emotions in the hearts of the posterity of those who now contemplate them without admiration.—The Jews, that wonderful people which has preserved so long the symbols of their union may reassume their ancestral seats and . . .

Lastly, in the West Indian islands, first from the disinterested yet necessarily cautious measures of the English Nation, and then from the infection of the spirit of Liberty in France, the deepest stain upon civilized man is fading away. Two nations of free negroes are already established; one, in pernicious mockery of the usurpation over France, an empire, the other a republic; both animating yet terrific spectacles to those who inherit around them the degradation of slavery and the spirit of dominion.

Such is a slight sketch of the general condition of the hopes and aspirations of the human race to which they have been conducted after the obliteration of the Greek republics by the successful tyranny of Rome,—its internal liberty having been first abolished,—and by those miseries and superstitions consequent upon them, which compelled the human race to begin anew its difficult and obscure career of producing, according to the forms of society, the greatest portion of good.

Meanwhile England, the particular object for the sake of which these general considerations have been stated on the present occasion, has arrived, like the nations which surround it, at a crisis in its destiny. The literature of England, an energetic development of which has ever followed or preceded a great and free development of the national will, has arisen, as it were, from a new birth. In spite of that low-thoughted envy which would underrate, thro a fear of comparison with its own insignificance, the eminence of contemporary merit, it is felt by the British that this is in intellectual achievements a memorable age, and we live among such philosophers and poets as surpass beyond comparison any who have appeared in our nation since its last struggle for liberty. For the most unfailing herald, or companion, or follower, of an universal employment of the sentiments of a nation to the production of a beneficial change is poetry, meaning by poetry an intense and impassioned power of communicating intense and impassioned impressions respecting man and nature. The persons in whom this power takes its abode may often, as far as regards many portions of their nature, have little correspondence with the spirit of good of which it is the minister. But although they may deny and abjure, they are yet compelled to serve that which is seated on the throne of their own soul. And whatever systems they may have professed by support, they actually advance the interests of Liberty. It is impossible to read the productions of our most celebrated writers, whatever may be their system relating to thought or expression, without being startled by the electric life which there is in their words. They measure the circumference or sound the depths of human nature with a comprehensive and all-penetrating spirit at which they are themselves perhaps most sincerely astonished, for it *is* less their own spirit than the spirit of their age. They are the priests of an unapprehended inspiration, the mirrors of gigantic shadows which futurity casts upon the present; the words which express what they conceive not; the trumpet which sings to battle and feels not what it inspires; the influence which is moved not but moves. Poets and philosophers are the unacknowledged legislators of the world.

But, omitting these more abstracted considerations, has there not been and is there not in England a desire of change arising from the profound sentiment of the exceeding inefficiency of the existing institutions to provide for the physical and intellectual happiness of the people? It is proposed in this work (1) to state and examine the present condition of this desire, (2) to elucidate its causes and its object, (3) to show the practicability and utility, nay the necessity of change, (4) to examine the state of parties as regards it, and (5) to state the probable, the possible, and the desirable mode in which it should be accomplished.

CHAPTER II

ON THE SENTIMENT OF THE NECESSITY OF CHANGE

Two circumstances arrest the attention of those who turn their regard to the present political condition of the English nation—first, that there is an almost universal sentiment of the approach of some change to be wrought in the institutions of the government, and secondly, the necessity and the desirableness of such a change. From the first of these propositions, it being matter of fact, no person addressing the public can dissent. The latter, from a general belief in which the former flows and on which it depends, is matter of opinion, but *one* which to the mind of all, excepting those interested in maintaining the contrary is a doctrine so clearly established that even they, admitting that great abuses exist, are compelled to impugn it by insisting upon the specious topic, that popular violence, by which they alone could be remedied, would be more injurious than the continuance of those abuses. But as those who argue thus derive for the most part great advantage and convenience from the continuance of these abuses, their estimation of the mischiefs of popular violence as compared with the mischiefs of tyrannical and fraudulent forms of government are likely, from the known principles of human nature, to be exaggerated. Such an estimate comes too with a worse grace from them, who if they would, in opposition to their own unjust advantage, take the lead in reform, might spare the nation from the inconveniences of the temporary dominion of the poor, who by means of that degraded condition which their insurrection would be designed to ameliorate, are sufficiently incapable of discerning their own glorious and permanent advantage, tho' surely less incapable than those whose interests consist in proposing to themselves an object perfectly opposite *to* and utterly incompatible with that advantage. These persons propose to us the dilemma of submitting to a despotism which is notoriously gathering like an avalanche year by year, or taking the risk of something which it must be confessed bears the aspect of revolution. To this alternative we are reduced by the selfishness of those who taunt us with it. And the history of the world teaches us not to hesitate an instant in the decision, if indeed the power of decision be not already past.

The establishment of King William III on the throne of England has already been referred to as a compromise between liberty and despotism. The Parliament of which that event was the act had ceased to be in an emphatic sense a representation of the people. The Long Parliament was the organ of the will of all classes of people in England since it effected the complete revolution in a tyranny consecrated by time. But since its meeting and since its dissolution a great change had taken place in England. Feudal manners and institutions having become obliterated, monopolies and patents having been abolished, property and personal liberty having been rendered secure, the nation advanced rapidly towards the acquirement of the elements of national prosperity. Population increased, a greater number of hands were employed in the labours of agriculture and commerce, towns arose where villages had been, and the proportion borne by those whose labour produced the materials of subsistence and enjoyment to those who claim for themselves a superfluity of these materials began to increase indefinitely. A fourth class therefore made its appearance in the nation, the unrepresented multitude. Nor was it so much that villages which sent no members to Parliament became great cities, and that towns which had been considerable enough to send members dwindled from local circumstances into villages. This cause no doubt contributed to the general effect of rendering the Commons' House a less complete representation of the people. Yet had this been all, though it had ceased to be a legal and actual it might still have been a virtual Representation of the People. But universally the nation became multiplied into a denomination *which* had no constitutional presence in the State. This denomination had not existed before, or had existed only to a degree in which its interests were sensibly interwoven with that of those who enjoyed a constitutional presence. Thus the proportion borne by the Englishmen who possessed the faculty of suffrage to those who were excluded from that faculty at the several periods of 1641 and 1688 had changed by the operation of these causes from 1 to 8 to 1 to 20. The rapid and effectual progress by which it changed from 1 to 20 to one to many hundreds in the interval between 1688 and 1819 is a process, to those familiar with the history of the political economy of that period, which is rendered by these principles sufficiently intelligible. The number therefore of those who have influence on the government, even if numerically the same as at the former period, was relatively different. And a sufficiently just measure is afforded of the degree in which a country is enslaved or free, by the consideration of the relative number of individuals who are admitted to the exercise of political rights. Meanwhile another cause was operating of a deeper and more extensive nature. The *class* who compose the Lords must, by the advantages of their situation as the great landed proprietors, possess a considerable influence over nomination to the Commons. This influence, from an original imperfection in the equal distribution of suffrage, was always enormous, but it is only since it has been combined with the cause before stated that it has appeared to be fraught with consequences incompatible with public liberty. In 1641 this influence was almost wholly inoperative to pervert the counsels of the nation from its own advantage. But at that epoch the enormous tyranny of the agents of the royal power weighed equally upon all denominations of men, and united all counsels to extinguish it; add to which, the nation, as stated before, was in a very considerable degree fairly represented in Parliament. The common danger which was the bond of union between the aristocracy and the people having been destroyed, the former systematized their influence through the permanence of hereditary right, whilst the latter were losing power by the inflexibility of the institutions which forbade a just accommodation to their numerical increase. After the operations of these causes had commenced, the accession of William III placed a seal upon forty years of Revolution.

The government of this country at the period of 1688 was regal, tempered by aristocracy, for what conditions of democracy attach to an assembly one portion of which was imperfectly nominated by less than a twentieth part of the people, and another perfectly nominated by the nobles? For the nobility, having by the assistance of the people imposed close limitations upon the royal power, finding that power to be its natural ally and the people (for the people from the increase of their numbers acquired greater and more important rights whilst the organ through which those rights might be asserted grew feebler in proportion to the increase of the cause of those rights and of their importance) its natural enemy, made the Crown the mask and pretence of their own authority. At this period began that despotism of the oligarchy of party, which under colour of administering the execu-

tive power lodged in the king, represented in truth the interest of the rich. When it is said by political reasoners, speaking of the interval between 1688 and the present time, that the royal power progressively increased, they use an expression which suggests a very imperfect and partial idea. The power which has increased is that entrusted with the administration of affairs, composed of men responsible to the aristocratical assemblies, or to the reigning party in those assemblies, which represents those orders of the nation which are privileged, and will retain power as long as it pleases them and must be divested of power as soon as it ceases to please them. The power which has increased therefore is the power of the rich. The name and office of king is merely the mask of this power, and is a kind of stalking-horse used to conceal these "catchers of men", whilst they lay their nets. Monarchy is only the string which ties the robber's bundle. Though less contumelious and abhorrent from the dignity of human nature than an absolute monarchy, an oligarchy of this nature exacts more of suffering from the people because it reigns both by the opinion generated by imposture, and the force which that opinion places within its grasp.

At the epoch adverted to, the device of public credit was first systematically applied as an instrument of government. It was employed at the accession of William III less as a resource for meeting the financial exigencies of the state than as a bond to connect those in the possession of property with those who had, by taking advantage of an accident of party, acceded to power. In the interval elapsed since that period it has accurately fulfilled the intention of its establishment, and has continued to add strength to the government even until the present crisis. Now this device is one of those execrable contrivances of misrule which overbalance the materials of common advantage produced by the progress of civilization and increase the number of those who are idle in proportion to those who work, whilst it increases, through the factitious wants of those indolent, privileged persons, the quantity of work to be done. The rich, no longer being able to rule by force, have invented this scheme that they may rule by fraud. The most despotic governments of antiquity were strangers to this invention, which is a compendious method of extorting from the people far more than praetorian guards, and arbitrary tribunals, and excise officers created judges in the last resort, would ever wring. Neither the Persian monarchy nor the Roman empire, where the will of one person was acknowledged as unappealable law, ever extorted a twentieth part the proportion now extorted from the property and labour of the inhabitants of Great Britain. The precious metals have been from the earliest records of civilization employed as the signs of labour and the titles to an unequal distribution of its produce. The *Government of* a country is necessarily entrusted with the affixing to certain portions of these metals a stamp, by which to mark their genuineness; no other is considered as current coin, nor can be a legal tender. The reason of this is that no alloyed coin should pass current, and thereby depreciate the genuine, and by augmenting the price of the articles which are the produce of labour defraud the holders of that which is genuine of the advantages legally belonging to them. If the Government itself abuses the trust reposed in it to debase the coin, in order that it may derive advantage from the unlimited multiplication of the mark entitling the holder to command the labour and property of others, the gradations by which it sinks, as labour rises, to the level of their comparative values, produces public confusion and misery. The foreign exchange meanwhile instructs the Government how temporary was its resource. This mode of making the distribution of the sign of labour a source of private aggrandisement at the expense of public confusion and loss was not wholly unknown to the nations of antiquity.

But the modern scheme of public credit is a far subtler and more complicated contrivance of misrule. All great transactions of personal property in England are managed by signs and that is by the authority of the possessor expressed upon paper, thus representing in a compendious form his right to so much gold, which represents his right to so much labour. A man may write on a piece of paper what he pleases; he may say he is worth a thousand when he is not worth a hundred pounds. If he can make others believe this, he has credit for the sum to which his name is attached. And so long as this credit lasts, he can enjoy all the advantages which would arise out of the actual possession of that sum he is believed to possess. He can lend two hundred to this man and three to that other, and his bills, among those who believe that he possesses this sum, pass like money. Of course in the same proportion as bills of this sort, beyond the actual goods or gold and silver possessed by the drawer, pass current, they defraud those who have gold and silver and goods of the advantages legally attached to the possession of them, and they defraud the labourer and artizan of the advantages attached to increasing the nominal price of labour, and such a participation in them as their industry *might* command, whilst they render wages fluctuating and add to the toil of the cultivator and manufacturer.

The existing government of England in substituting a currency of paper for one of gold has had no need to depreciate the currency by alloying the coin of the country; they have merely fabricated pieces of paper on which they promise to pay a certain sum. The holders of these papers came for payment in some representation of property universally exchangeable. They then declared that the persons who held the office for that payment could not be forced by law to pay. They declared subsequently that these pieces of paper were the current coin of the country. Of this nature are all such transactions of companies and banks as consist in the circulation of promissory notes to a greater amount than the actual property possessed by those whose names they bear. They have the effect of augmenting the prices of provision, and of benefiting at the expense of the community the speculators in this traffic. One of the vaunted effects of this system is to increase the national industry, that is, to increase the labours of the poor and those luxuries of the rich which they supply. To make a manufacturer work 16 hours when he only worked 8. To turn children into lifeless and bloodless machines at an age when otherwise they would be at play before the cottage doors of their parents. To augment indefinitely the proportion of those who enjoy the profit of the labour of others, as compared with those who exercise this labour. . . .

The consequences of this transaction have been the establishment of a new aristocracy, which has its basis in funds as the old one has its basis in force. The hereditary landowners in England derived their title from royal grants—they are fiefs bestowed by conquerors, or church-lands. Long usage has consecrated the abstraction of the word aristocracy from its primitive meaning to that ordinary sense which signifies that class of persons who possess a right to the produce of the labour of others, without dedicating to the common service any labour in return. This class of persons, whose existence is a prodigious anomaly in the social system, has ever constituted an inseparable portion of it, and there has never been an approach in practice towards any plan of political society modelled on equal justice, at least in the complicated mechanism of modern life. Mankind seem to acquiesce, as in a necessary condition of the imbecility of their own will and reason, in the existence of an aristocracy. With reference to this imbecility, it has doubtless been the instrument of great social advantage, although that advantage would have been greater which might have been produced according to the forms of a just distribution of the goods and evils of life. The object therefore of all enlightened legislation, and administration, is to enclose within the narrowest practicable limits this order of drones. The effect of the financial impostures of the modern rulers of England has been to increase the number of the drones. Instead of one aristocracy, the condition *to* which, in the present state of human affairs, the friends of virtue and liberty are willing to subscribe as to an inevitable evil, they have supplied us with two aristocracies. The one, consisting in great land proprietors, and wealthy merchants who receive and interchange the produce of this country with the produce of other countries: in this, because all other great communities have as yet acquiesced in it, we acquiesce. Connected with the members of it is a certain generosity and refinement of manners and opinion which, although neither philosophy nor virtue, has been that acknowledged substitute for them which at least is a religion which makes respected those venerable names. The other aristocracy is one of attornies and excisemen and directors and government pensioners, usurers, stockjobbers, country bankers, with their dependents and descendants. These are a set of pelting wretches in whose employment there is nothing to exercise even to their distortion the more majestic faculties of the soul. Though at the bottom it is all trick, there is something frank and magnificent in the chivalrous

disdain of infamy connected with a gentleman. There is something to which—until you see through the base falsehood upon which all inequality is founded—it is difficult for the imagination to refuse its respect, in the faithful and direct dealings of the substantial merchant. But in the habits and lives of this new aristocracy created out of an increase in public calamities, and whose existence must be determined by their termination, there is nothing to qualify our disapprobation. They eat and drink and sleep, and in the intervals of these things performed with most vexatious ceremony and accompaniments they cringe and lie. They poison the literature of the age in which they live by requiring either the antitype of their own mediocrity in books, or such stupid and distorted and inharmonious idealisms as alone have the power to stir their torpid imaginations. Their hopes and fears are of the narrowest description. Their domestic affections are feeble, and they have no others. They think of any commerce with their species but as a means, never as an end, and as a means to the basest forms of personal advantage.

If this aristocracy had arisen from a false and depreciated currency to the exclusion of the other, its existence would have been a moral calamity and disgrace, but it would not have constituted an oppression. But the hereditary aristocracy who had the political administration of affairs took the measures which created this other for purposes peculiarly its own. Those measures were so contrived as in no manner to diminish the wealth and power of the contrivers. The lord does not spare himself one luxury, but the peasant and artizan are assured of many *necessary* things. To support the system of social order according to its supposed unavoidable constitution, those from whose labour all those external accommodations which distinguish a civilized being from a savage arise, worked, before the institution of this double aristocracy, light hours. And of these only the healthy were compelled to labour, the efforts of the old, the sick and the immature being dispensed with, and they maintained by the labour of the sane, for such is the plain English of the poor-rates. That labour procured a competent share of the decencies of life, and society seemed to extend the benefits of its institution even to its most unvalued instrument. Although deprived of those resources of sentiment and knowledge which might have been their lot could the wisdom of the institutions of social forms have established a system of strict justice, yet they earned by their labour a competency in those external materials of life which, and not the loss of moral and intellectual excellence, is supposed to be the legitimate object of the desires and murmurs of the poor. Since the institution of this double aristocracy, how-ever, they have often worked not ten but twenty hours a day. Not that the poor have rigidly worked twenty hours, but that the worth of the labour of twenty hours now, in food and clothing, is equivalent to the worth of ten hours then. And because twenty hours cannot, from the nature of the human frame, be exacted from those who before performed ten, the aged and the sickly are compelled either to work or starve. Children who were exempted from labour are put in requisition, and the vigorous promise of the coming generation blighted by premature exertion. For fourteen hours' labour, which they do perforce, they receive—no matter in what nominal amount—the price of seven. They eat less bread, wear worse clothes, are more ignorant, immoral, miserable and desperate. This then is the condition of the lowest and largest class, from whose labour the whole materials of life are wrought, of which the others are only the receivers or the consumers. They are more superstitious, for misery on earth begets a diseased expectation and panic-stricken faith in miseries beyond the grave. "God", they argue, "rules this world as well as that; and assuredly since his nature is immutable, and his powerful will unchangeable, he rules them by the same laws." The gleams of hope which speak of Paradise seem like the flames of Milton's hell only to make darkness visible, and all things take their colour from what surrounds them. They become revengeful—

But the condition of all classes of society, excepting those within the privileged pale, is singularly unprosperous, and even they experience the reaction of their own short-sighted tyranny in all those sufferings and deprivations which are not of a distinctly physical nature, in the loss of dignity, simplicity and energy, and in the possession of all those qualities which distinguish a slave-driver from a proprietor. Right government being an institution for the purpose of securing such a moderate degree of happiness to men as has been experimentally practicable, the sure character of misgovernment is misery, and first discontent and, if that be despised, then insurrection, as the legitimate expression of that misery. The public right to demand happiness is a principle of nature; the labouring classes, when they cannot get food for their labour, are impelled to take it by force. Laws and assemblies and courts of justice and delegated powers placed in balance and in opposition are the means and the form, but public happiness is the substance and the end of political institutions. Whenever this is attained in a nation, not from external force, but from the internal arrangement and divisions of the common burthens of defence and maintenance, then there is oppression. And then arises an alternative between Reform, or the institution of a military Despotism, or a Revolution in which parties, one striving after ill-digested systems of democracy, and the other clinging to the outworn abuses of power, leave the few who aspire to more than the former and who would overthrow the latter at whatever expense, to wait *for* that modified advantage which, with the temperance and the toleration which both regard as a crime, might have resulted from the occasion which they let pass in a far more signal manner.

The propositions which are the consequences or the corollaries of the preceding reasoning, and to which it seems to have conducted us are:—

—That the majority of the people of England are destitute and miserable, ill-clothed, ill-fed, ill-educated.

—That they know this, and that they are impatient to procure a reform of the cause of this abject and wretched state.

—That the cause of this misery is the unequal distribution which, under the form of the national debt, has been surreptitiously made of the products of their labour and the products of the labour of their ancestors; for all property is the produce of labour.

—That the cause of that cause is a defect in the government.

—That if they knew nothing of their condition, but believed that all they endured and all they were deprived of arose from the unavoidable conditions of human life, this belief being an error, and *one* the endurance of which enforces an injustice, every enlightened and honourable person, whatever may be the imagined interest of his peculiar class, ought to excite them to the discovery of the true state of the case, and to the temperate but irresistible vindication of their rights.

A Reform in England is most just and necessary. What ought to be that reform?

A writer of the present day (a priest of course, for his doctrines are those of a eunuch and of a tyrant) has stated that the evils of the poor arise from an excess of population, and after they have been stript naked by the tax-gatherer and reduced to bread and tea and fourteen hours of hard labour by their masters, and after the frost has bitten their defenceless limbs, and the cramp has wrung like a disease within their bones, and hunger and the suppressed revenge of hunger has stamped the ferocity of want like the mark of Cain upon their countenance, that the last tie by which Nature holds them to the benignant earth whose plenty is garnered up in the strongholds of their tyrants, is to be divided; that the single alleviation of their sufferings and their scorns, the one thing which made it impossible to degrade them below the beasts, which amid all their crimes and miseries yet separated a cynical and unmanly contamination, an anti-social cruelty, from all the soothing, elevating and harmonious gentleness of the sexual intercourse and the humanizing charities of domestic life which are its appendages—that this is to be obliterated. They are required to abstain from marrying under penalty of starvation. And it is threatened to deprive them of that property which is as strictly their birthright as a gentleman's land is his birthright, without giving them any compensation but the insulting advice to conquer, with minds undisciplined in the habits of higher gratification, a propensity which persons of the most consummate wisdom have been unable to resist, and which it is difficult to admire a person for having resisted. The doctrine of this writer is that the principle of population, when under no dominion of moral restraint, *is* outstripping the sustenance produced by the labour of man, and that not in proportion to the number of inhabitants, but operating equally in a thinly peopled community as in one where the population is enormous, being not a prevention but a check. So far a man might have been conducted by a train of reasoning which, though it may be shown to be defective, would argue in the reasoner no selfish or slavish feelings. But he has the hardened insolence to propose as a remedy that the poor should be compelled (for what except compulsion is a threat of the confiscation of those funds which by the institutions of their country had been set apart for their sustenance in sickness or destitution?) to abstain from sexual intercourse, while the rich are to be permitted to add as many mouths to consume the products of the labours of the poor as they please. [The rights of all men are intrinsically and originally equal and they forgo the assertion of all of them only that they may the more securely enjoy a portion.] If any new disadvantages are found to attach to the condition of social existence, those disadvantages ought not to be borne exclusively by one class of men, nor especially by that class whose ignorance leads them to exaggerate the advantages of sensual enjoyment, whose callous habits render domestic endearments more important to dispose them to resist the suggestion to violence and cruelty by which their situation ever exposes them to be tempted, and all whose other enjoyments are limited and few, whilst their sufferings are various and many. In this sense I cannot imagine how the advocates of equality could so readily have conceded that the unlimited operation of the principle of population affects the truth of these theories. On the contrary, the more heavy and certain are the evils of life, the more injustice is there in casting the burden of them exclusively on one order in the community. They seem to have conceded it merely because their opponents have insolently assumed it. Surely it is enough that the rich should possess to the exclusion of the poor all other luxuries and comforts, and wisdom and refinement, the least envied but the most deserving of envy among all their privileges!

What is the Reform that we desire? Before we aspire after theoretical perfection in the amelioration of our political state, it is necessary that we possess those advantages which we have been cheated of, and *of* which the experience of modern times has proved that nations even under the present *conditions* are susceptible. We would regain these. We would establish some form of government which might secure us against such a series of events as have conducted us to a persuasion that the forms according to which it is now administered are inadequate to that purpose.

We would abolish the national debt.

We would disband the standing army.

We would, with every possible regard to the existing rights of the holders, abolish sinecures.

We would, with every possible regard to the existing interests of the holders, abolish tithes, and make all religions, all forms of opinion respecting the origin and government of the Universe, equal in the eye of the law.

We would make justice cheap, certain and speedy, and extend the institution of juries to every possible occasion of jurisprudence.

The national debt was contracted chiefly in two liberticide wars, undertaken by the privileged classes of the country—the first for the ineffectual purpose of tyrannizing over one portion of their subjects, the second, in order to extinguish the resolute spirit of obtaining their rights in another. The labour which this money represents, and that which is represented by the money wrung for purposes of the same detestable character out of the people since the commencement of the American war would, if properly employed, have covered our land with monuments of architecture exceeding the sumptuousness and the beauty of Egypt and Athens; it might have made every peasant's cottage, surrounded with its garden, a little paradise of comfort, with every convenience desirable in civilized life; neat tables and chairs, good beds, and a collection of useful books; and our ships manned by sailors well-paid and well-clothed, might have kept watch round this glorious island against the less enlightened nations which assuredly would have envied, until they could have imitated, its prosperity. But the labour which is expressed by these sums has been diverted from these purposes of human happiness to the promotion of slavery, and that attempt at dominion, and a great portion of the sum in question is debt and must be paid. Is it to remain unpaid for ever, an eternal rent-charge upon the land from which the inhabitants of these islands draw their subsistence? This were to pronounce the perpetual institution of two orders of aristocracy, and men are in a temper to endure one with some reluctance. Is it to be paid now? If so what are the funds, or when and how is it to be paid? The fact is that the national debt is a debt not contracted by the whole nation towards a portion of it, but a debt contracted by the whole mass of the privileged classes towards one particular portion of those classes. If the principal were paid, the whole property of those who possess property must be valued and the public creditor, whose property would have been included in this estimate, satisfied out of the proceeds. It has been said that all the land in the nation is mortgaged for the amount of the national debt. This is a partial statement. Not only all the land in the nation, but all the property of whatever denomination, all the houses and the furniture and the goods and every article of merchandise, and the property which is represented by the very money lent by the fundholder, who is bound to pay a certain portion as debtor whilst he is entitled to receive another certain portion as creditor. The property of the rich is mortgaged: to use the language of the law, let the mortgagee foreclose.

If the principal of this debt were paid, it would be the rich who alone could, and justly they ought to pay it. It would be a mere transfer among persons of property. Such a gentleman must lose a third of his estate, such a citizen a fourth of his money in the funds; the persons who borrowed would have paid, and the juggling and complicated system of paper finance be suddenly at an end. As it is, the interest is chiefly paid by those who had no hand in the borrowing, and who are sufferers in other respects from the consequences of those transactions in which the money was spent.

The payment of the principal of what is called the national debt, which it is pretended is so difficult a problem, is only difficult to those who do not see who is the debtor, and who the creditor, and who the wretched sufferers from whom they both wring the taxes which under the form of interest is given by the former and accepted by the latter. It is from the labour of those who have no property that all the persons who possess property think to extort the perpetual interest of a debt, the whole of which the latter know they could not persuade the former to pay, but by conspiring with them in an imposture which makes the third class pay what the first neither received by their sanction nor spent for their benefit and what the second never lent to them. They would both shift from themselves and their posterity to the labour of the present and of all succeeding generations the payment of the interest of their own debt, because the payment of the principal would be no more than a compromise and transfer of property between each other, by which the nation would be spared 44 millions a year, which now is paid to maintain in luxury and indolence the public debtors and to protect them from the demand of their creditors upon them, who, being part of the same body, and owing as debtors whilst they possess a claim as creditors, agree to abstain from demanding the principal which they must all unite to pay, for the sake of receiving an enormous interest which is principally wrung out of those who had no concern whatever in the transaction. One of the first acts of a reformed government would undoubtedly be an effectual scheme for compelling these to compromise their debt between themselves.

When I speak of persons of property I mean not every man who possesses any right of property; I mean the rich. Every man whose scope in society has a plebeian and intelligible utility, whose personal exertions are more valuable to him than his capital; every tradesman who is not a monopolist, all surgeons and physicians, and artists, and farmers, all those persons whose profits spring from honourably and honestly exerting their own skill and wisdom or strength in greater abundance than from the employment of money to take advantage of their fellow-citizens' starvation for their profit, are those who pay, as well as those more obviously understood by the labouring classes, the interest of the national debt. It is the interest of all these persons as well as that of the poor to insist upon the payment of the principal.

For this purpose the form ought to be as simple and succinct as possible. The operations deciding who was to pay, at what time, and how much, and to whom, divested of financial chicanery, are problems readily to be determined. The common tribunals may be invested with legal jurisdiction to award the proportion due upon the several claim of each.

Labour and skill and the immediate wages of labour and skill is a property of the most sacred and indisputable right, and the foundation of all other property. And the right *of a man* to property in the exertion of his own bodily and mental faculties, or on the produce and free reward from and for that exertion is the most *inalienable of rights*. If however he takes by violence and appropriates to himself through fraudulent cunning, or receives from another property so acquired, his claim to that property is of a far inferior force. We may acquiesce, if we evidently perceive an overbalance of public advantage in submission under this claim; but if any public emergency should arise, at which it might be necessary to satisfy, by a tax on capital, the claims of a part of the nation by a contribution from such national resources as may with the least injustice be appropriated to that purpose, assuredly it would not be on labour and skill, the foundation of all property, nor on the profits and savings of labour and skill, which are property itself, but on such possessions which can only be called property in a modified sense, as have from their magnitude and their nature an evident origin in violence or imposture.

Thus there are two descriptions of property which, without entering into the subtleties of a more refined moral theory as applicable to the existing forms of society, are entitled to two very different measures of forbearance and regard. And this forbearance and regard have by political institutions usually been accorded by an inverse reason from what is just and natural. Labour, industry, economy, skill, genius, or any similar powers honourably and innocently exerted are the foundations of one description of property, and all true political institutions ought to defend every man in the exercise of his discretion with respect to property so acquired. Of this kind is the principal part of the property enjoyed by those who are but one degree removed from the class which subsists by daily labour. [Yet there are instances of persons in this class who have produced their property by fraudulent and violent means, as there are instances in the other of persons who have acquired their property by innocent or honourable exertion. All political science abounds with limitations and exceptions.]—Property thus acquired men leave to their children. Absolute right becomes weakened by descent, just because it is only to avoid the greater evil of arbitrarily interfering with the discretion of every man in matters of property that the great evil of acknowledging any person to have an exclusive right to property who has not created it by his skill or labour is admitted, and secondly because the mode of its having been originally acquired is forgotten, and it is confounded with property acquired in a very different manner; and the principle upon which all property justly exists, after the great principle of the general advantage, becomes thus disregarded and misunderstood. Yet the privilege of disposing of property by will is one necessarily connected with the existing forms of domestic life; and exerted merely by those who having acquired property by industry or who preserve it by economy, would never produce any great and invidious inequality of fortune. A thousand accidents would perpetually tend to level the accidental elevation, and the signs of property would perpetually recur to those whose deserving skill might attract or whose labour might create it.

But there is another species of property which has its foundation in usurpation, or imposture, or violence, without which, by the nature of things, immense possessions of gold or land could never have been accumulated. Of this nature is the principal part of the property enjoyed by the aristocracy and by the great fundholders, the majority of whose ancestors never either deserved it by their skill and talents or acquired and created it by their personal labour. It could not be that they deserved it, for if the honourable exertion of the most glorious and imperial faculties of our nature had been the criterion of the possession of property the posterity of Shakespeare, of Milton, of Hampden, would be the wealthiest proprietors in England. It could not be that they acquired it by legitimate industry, for, besides that the real mode of acquisition is matter of history, no honourable profession or honest trade, nor the hereditary exercise of it, ever in such numerous instances accumulated so much as the masses of property enjoyed by the ruling orders in England. They were either grants from the feudal sovereigns whose right to what they granted was founded upon conquest or oppression, both a denial of all right; or they were lands of the antient Catholic clergy which according to the most acknowledged principles of public justice reverted to the nation at their suppression, or they were the products of patents and monopolies, an exercise of sovereignty which it is astonishing that political theorists have not branded as the most pernicious and odious to the interests of a commercial nation; or in later times such property has been accumulated by dishonourable cunning and the taking advantage of a fictitious paper currency to obtain an unfair power over labour and the fruits of labour.

Property thus accumulated, being transmitted from father to son, acquires, as property of the more legitimate kind loses, force and sanction, but in a very limited manner. For not only on an examination and recurrence to first principles is it seen to have been founded on a violation of all that to which the latter owes its sacredness, but it is felt in its existence and perpetuation as a public burthen, and known as a rallying point to the ministers of tyranny, having the property of a snowball, gathering as it rolls, and rolling until it bursts.

The national debt, as has been stated, is a debt contracted by a particular class in the nation towards a portion of that class. It is sufficiently clear that this debt was not contracted for the purpose of the public advantage. Besides there was no authority in the nation competent to a measure of this nature. The usual vindication of national debts is that they are in an overwhelming measure contracted for the purpose of defence against a common danger, for the vindication of the rights and liberties of posterity, *and that* it is just that posterity should bear the burthen of payment. This reasoning is most fallacious. The history of nations presents us with a succession of extraordinary emergencies, and thro their present imperfect organization their existence is perpetually threatened by new and unexpected combinations and developments of foreign or internal force. Imagine a situation of equal emergency to occur to England as that which the ruling party assume to have occurred as their excuse for burthening the nation with the perpetual payment of £45,000,000 annually. Suppose France, Russia, and Germany were to enter into a league against Britain, the one to avenge its injuries, the second to satisfy its ambition, the third to soothe its jealousy. Could the nation bear £90,000,000 of yearly interest? must there be twice as many luxurious and idle persons? must the labourer receive for 28 hours' work what he now receives for 14, what he once received for seven? . . .

What is meant by a Reform of Parliament? If England were a Republic governed by one assembly; if there were no chamber of hereditary aristocracy which is at once an actual and a virtual representation of all who attain through rank or wealth superiority over their countrymen; if there were no king who is as the rallying point of those whose tendency is at once to *gather* and to confer that power which is consolidated at the expense of the nation, then . . .

The advocates of universal suffrage have reasoned correctly that no individual who is governed can be denied a direct share in the government of his country without supreme injustice. If one pursues the train of reasonings which have conducted to this conclusion, we discover that systems of social order still more incompatible than universal suffrage with any reasonable hope of instant accomplishment appear to be that which should result from a just combination of the elements of social life. I do not understand why those reasoners who propose at any price an immediate appeal to universal suffrage, because it is that which it is injustice to withhold, do not insist, on the same ground, on the immediate abolition, for instance, of monarchy and aristocracy, and the levelling of inordinate wealth, and an agrarian distribution, including the parks and chases of the rich, of the uncultivated districts of the country. No doubt the institution of universal suffrage would by necessary consequence *immediately* tend to the *temporary* abolition of these forms; because it is impossible that the people, having attained the power, should fail to see, what the demagogues now conceal from them, the legitimate consequence of the doctrines through which they had attained it. A Republic, however just in its principle and glorious in its object, would through the violence and sudden change which must attend it, incur a great risk of being as rapid in its decline as in its growth. It is better that they should be instructed in the whole truth; that they should see the clear grounds of their rights, the objects to which they ought to tend; and be impressed with the just persuasion that patience and reason and endurance *are the means of* a calm yet irresistible progress. A civil war, which might be engendered by the passions attending on this mode of reform, would confirm in the mass of the nation those military habits which have been already introduced by our tyrants, and with which liberty is incompatible. From the moment that a man is a soldier, he becomes a slave. He is taught obedience; his will is no longer, which is the most sacred prerogative of men, guided by his own judgement. He is taught to despise human life and human suffering; this is the universal distinction of slaves. He is more degraded than a murderer; he is like the bloody knife which has stabbed and feels not: a murderer we may abhor and despise; a soldier, is by profession, beyond abhorrence and below contempt.

CHAPTER III

PROBABLE MEANS

That the House of Commons should reform itself, uninfluenced by any fear that the people would, on their refusal, assume to itself that office, seems a contradiction. What need of Reform if it expresses the will and watches over the interests of the public? And if, as is sufficiently evident, it despises that will and neglects that interest, what motives would incite it to institute a reform which the aspect of the times renders indeed sufficiently perilous, but without which there will speedily be no longer anything in England to distinguish it from the basest and most abject community of slaves that ever existed. . . .

The great principle of Reform consists in every individual giving his consent to the institution and the continuous existence of the social system which is instituted for his advantage and for the advantage of others in his situation. As in a great nation this is practically impossible, masses of individuals consent to qualify other individuals, whom they delegate to superintend their concerns. These delegates have constitutional authority to exercise the functions of sovereignty; they unite in the highest degree the legislative and executive functions. A government that is founded on any other basis is a government of fraud or force and ought on the first convenient occasion to be overthrown. The first principle of political reform is the natural equality of men, not with relation to their property but to their rights. That equality in possessions which Jesus Christ so passionately taught is a moral rather than a political truth and is such as social institutions cannot without mischief inflexibly secure. Morals and politics can only be considered as portions of the same science, with relation to a system of such absolute perfection as Plato and Rousseau and other reasoners have asserted, and as Godwin has with irresistible eloquence systematised and developed. Equality in possessions must be the last result of the utmost refinements of civilization; it is one of the conditions of that system of society towards which, with whatever hope of ultimate success, it is our duty to tend. We may and ought to advert to it as to the elementary principle, as to the goal, unattainable, perhaps, by us but which, as it were, we revive in our posterity to pursue. We derive tranquillity and courage and grandeur of soul from contemplating an object which is, because we will it, and may be, because we hope and desire it, and must be if succeeding generations of the enlightened sincerely and earnestly seek it.

But our present business is with the difficult and unbending realities of actual life, and when we have drawn inspiration from the great object of our hopes it becomes us with patience and resolution to apply ourselves to accommodating our theories to immediate practice.

That Representative Assembly called the House of Commons ought questionless to be immediately nominated by the great mass of the people. The aristocracy and those who unite in their own persons the vast privileges conferred by the possession of inordinate wealth are sufficiently represented by the House of Peers and by the King. Those theorists who admire and would put into action the mechanism of what is called the British Constitution would acquiesce in this view of the question. For if the House of Peers be a permanent representation of the privileged classes, if the regal power be no more than another form, and a form still more advisedly to be *so* regarded, of the same representation, whilst the House of Commons is not chosen by the mass of the population, what becomes of that democratic element upon the presence of which it has been supposed that the waning superiority of England over the surrounding nations has depended?

Any sudden attempt at universal suffrage would produce an immature attempt at a Republic. It is better that an object so inexpressibly great and sacred should never have been attempted than that it should be attempted and fail. It is no prejudice to the ultimate establishment of the boldest political innovations that we temporize so that when they shall be accomplished they may be rendered permanent.

Considering the population of Great Britain and Ireland as twenty millions and the representative assembly at five hundred, each member ought to be the expression of the will of 40,000 persons; of these two-thirds would consist of women and children and persons under age; the actual number of voters therefore for each member would be 13,333. The whole extent of the empire might be divided into five hundred electoral departments or parishes, and the inhabitants assemble on a certain day to exercise their rights of suffrage.

Mr. Bentham and other writers have urged the admission of females to the right of suffrage; this attempt seems somewhat immature. Should my opinion be the result of despondency, the writer of these pages would be the last to withhold his vote from any system which might tend to an equal and full development of the capacities of all living beings.

The system of voting by ballot which some reasoners have recommended is attended with obvious inconveniences. It withdraws the elector from the eye of his country, and his neighbours, and permits him to conceal the motives of his vote, which, if concealed, cannot but be dishonourable; when, if he had known that he had to render a public account of his conduct, he would never have permitted them to guide him. There is in this system of voting by ballot and of electing a member of the *Representative Assembly* as a churchwarden is elected something too mechanical. The elector and the elected ought to meet one another face to face, and interchange the meanings of actual presence and share some common impulses, and, in a degree, understand each other. There ought to be the common sympathy of the excitements of a popular assembly among the electors themselves. The imagination would thus be strongly excited and a mass of generous and enlarged and popular sentiments be awakened, which would give the vitality of . . .

That republican boldness of censuring and judging one another which has indeed existed in England under the title of "public opinion", though perverted from its true uses into an instrument of prejudice and calumny, would then be applied to its genuine purpose. Year by year the people would become more susceptible of assuming forms of government more simple and beneficial.

It is in this publicity of the exercise of

sovereignty that the difference between the republics of Greece and the monarchies of Asia
consisted.

If the existing government shall compel the
nation to take the task of reform into its own
hands, one of the most obvious consequences
of such a circumstance would be the abolition
of monarchy and aristocracy. Why, it will
then be argued, if the subsisting condition of
social forms is to be thrown into confusion,
should these things be endured? Is it because
we think that an hereditary king is cheaper
and wiser than an elected President, or a
House of Lords and a Bench of Bishops an institution modelled by the wisdom of the most
refined and civilized periods, beyond which
the wit of mortal man can furnish nothing
more perfect? In case the subsisting Government should compel the people to revolt to
establish a representative assembly in defiance
of them, and to assume in that assembly an
attitude of resistance and defence, this question would probably be answered in a very
summary manner. No friend of mankind and
of his country can desire that such a crisis
should suddenly arrive; but still less, once
having arrived, can he hesitate under what
banner to array his person and his power. At
the peace, Europe would have been contented
with strict economy and severe retrenchment,
and some direct and intelligible plan for producing that equilibrium between the capitalists
and the landholders which is derisively styled
the payment of the national debt: had this
system been adopted, they probably would
have refrained from exacting Parliamentary
Reform, the only secure guarantee that it would
have been pursued. Two years ago it might
still have been possible to have commenced a
system of gradual reform. The people were
then insulted, tempted and betrayed, and the
petitions of a million of men rejected with
disdain. Now they are more miserable, more
hopeless, more impatient of their misery. Above
all, they have become more universally aware
of the true sources of their misery. It is possible that the period of conciliation is past,
and that after having played with the confidence and cheated the expectations of the
people, their passions will be too little under
discipline to allow them to wait the slow,
gradual and certain operation of such a Reform as we can imagine the constituted authorities to concede.

Upon the issue of this question depends the
species of reform which a philosophical mind
should regard with approbation. If Reform
shall be begun by this existing government, let
us be contented with a limited *beginning,* with
any whatsoever opening; let the rotten
boroughs be disfranchised and their rights
transferred to the unenfranchised cities and
districts of the nation; it is no matter how
slow, gradual and cautious be the change; we
shall demand more and more with firmness and
moderation, never anticipating but never de-
ferring the moment of successful opposition,
so that the people may become habituated to
exercising the functions of sovereignty, in proportion as they acquire the possession of it. If
this reform could begin from within the Houses
of Parliament, as constituted at present, it
appears to me that what is called moderate
reform, that is a suffrage whose qualification
should be the possession of a certain small
property, and triennial parliaments, would be
a system in which for the sake of obtaining
without bloodshed or confusion ulterior improvements of a more important character, all
reformers ought to acquiesce. Not that such
are first principles, or that they would produce
a system of perfect social institutions or one
approaching to *such.* But nothing is more idle
than to reject a limited benefit because we
cannot without great sacrifices obtain an unlimited one. We might thus reject a Representative Republic, if it were obtainable, on
the plea that the imagination of man can conceive of something more absolutely perfect.
Towards whatever we regard as perfect, undoubtedly it is no less our duty than it is our
nature to press forward; this is the generous
enthusiasm which accomplishes not indeed the
consummation after which it aspires, but one
which approaches it in a degree far nearer than
if the whole powers had not been developed
by a delusion.—It is in politics rather than in
religion that faith is meritorious.

If the Houses of Parliament obstinately
and perpetually refuse to concede any reform
to the people, my vote is for universal suffrage
and equal representation. But, it is asked, how
shall this be accomplished in defiance of and in
opposition to the constituted authorities of
the nation, they who possess whether with or
without its consent the command of a standing
army and of a legion of spies and police officers, and hold the strings of that complicated

mechanism with which the hopes and fears of men are moved like puppets? They would disperse any assembly really chosen by the people, they would shoot and hew down any multitude, without regard to sex or age, as the Jews did the Canaanites, which might be collected in its defence, they would calumniate, imprison, starve, ruin and expatriate every person who wrote or acted or thought or might be suspected to think against them; misery and extermination would fill the country from one end to another.

This question I would answer by another. Will you endure to pay the half of your earnings to maintain in luxury and idleness the confederation of your tyrants as the reward of a successful conspiracy to defraud and oppress you? Will you make your tame cowardice and the branding record of it the everlasting inheritance of your posterity? Not only this, but will you render by your torpid endurance this condition of things as permanent as the system of caste in India, by which the same horrible injustice is perpetrated under another form?

Assuredly no Englishmen by whom these propositions are understood will answer in the affirmative; and the opposite side of the alternative remains.

When the majority in any nation arrive at a conviction that it is their duty and their interest to divest the minority of a power employed to their disadvantage, and the minority are sufficiently mistaken as to believe that their superiority is tenable, a struggle must ensue. If the majority are enlightened, united, impelled by a uniform enthusiasm and animated by a distinct and powerful appreciation of their object, and feel confidence in their undoubted power—the struggle is merely nominal. The minority perceive the approaches of the development of an irresistible force, by the influence of the public opinion of their weakness, on those political forms of which no government but an absolute despotism is devoid. They divest themselves of their usurped distinctions; the public tranquillity is not disturbed by the revolution.

But these conditions may only be imperfectly fulfilled by the state of a people grossly oppressed and impotent to cast off the load. Their enthusiasm may have been subdued by the killing weight of toil and suffering; they may be panic-stricken and disunited by their oppressors, and the demagogues, the influence of fraud may have been sufficient to weaken the union of classes which compose them by suggesting jealousies, and the position of the conspirators, although it is to be forced by repeated assaults, may be tenable until the siege can be vigorously urged. The true patriot will endeavour to enlighten and to unite the nation and animate it with enthusiasm and confidence. For this purpose he will be indefatigable in promulgating political truth. He will endeavour to rally round one standard the divided friends of liberty, and make them forget the subordinate objects with regard to which they differ by appealing to that respecting which they are all agreed. He will promote such open confederation among men of principle and spirit as may tend to make their intentions and their efforts converge to a common centre. He will discourage all secret associations, which have a tendency, by making the nation's will develop itself in a partial and premature manner, to cause tumult and confusion. He will urge the necessity of exciting the people frequently to exercise their right of assembling, in such limited numbers as that all present may be actual parties to the proceedings of the day. Lastly, if circumstances had collected a considerable number as at Manchester on the memorable 16th of August, if the tyrants command the troops to fire upon them or cut them down unless they disperse, he will exhort them peaceably to defy the danger, and to expect without resistance the onset of the cavalry, and wait with folded arms the event of the fire of the artillery and receive with unshrinking bosoms the bayonets of the charging battalions. Men are every day persuaded to incur greater perils for a less manifest advantage. And this, not because active resistance is not justifiable when all other means shall have failed, but because in this instance temperance and courage would produce greater advantages than the most decisive victory. In the first place, the soldiers are men and Englishmen, and it is not to be believed that they would massacre an unresisting multitude of their countrymen drawn up in unarmed array before them, and bearing in their looks the calm, deliberate resolution to perish rather than abandon the assertion of their rights. In the confusion of flight the ideas of the soldier become confused, and he massacres those who fly from him by the instinct of his trade. In the struggles of conflict and resistance he is irritated by a sense of his own danger, he is flattered by an apprehension of his own magnanimity in incurring it, he considers the blood of his countrymen at once the price of his valour, the pledge of his security. He applauds himself by reflecting that these base and dishonourable motives will gain him credit among his comrades and his officers who are animated by the same. But if he should observe neither resistance nor flight he would be reduced to confusion and indecision. Thus far, his ideas were governed by the same law as those of a dog who chases a flock of sheep to the corner of a field, and keeps aloof when they make a parade of resistance. But the soldier is a man and an Englishman. This unexpected reception would probably throw him back upon a recollection of the true nature of the measures of which he was made the instrument, and the enemy might be converted into the ally.

The patriot will be foremost to publish the boldest truths in the most fearless manner, yet without the slightest tincture of personal malignity. He would encourage all others to the same efforts and assist them to the utmost of his power with the resources both of his intellect and fortune. He would call upon them to despise imprisonment and persecution and lose no opportunity of bringing public opinion and the power of the tyrants into circumstances of perpetual contest and opposition.

All might however be ineffectual to produce so uniform an impulse of the national will as to preclude a further struggle. The strongest argument, perhaps, for the necessity of Reform, is the inoperative and unconscious abjectness to which the purposes of a considerable mass of the people are reduced. They neither know nor care—They are sinking into a resemblance with the Hindoos and the Chinese, who were once men as they are. Unless the cause which renders them passive subjects instead of active citizens be removed, they will sink with accelerated gradations into that barbaric and unnatural civilization which destroys all the differences among men. It is in vain to exhort us to wait until all men shall desire Freedom whose real interest will consist in its establishment. It is in vain to hope to enlighten them whilst their tyrants employ the utmost artifices of all their complicated engine to perpetuate the infection of every species of fanaticism and error from generation to generation.

The advocates of Reform ought indeed to leave no effort unexerted, and they ought to be indefatigable in exciting all men to examine.

But if they wait until those neutral politicians whose opinions represent the actions of this class are persuaded that some effectual reform is necessary, the occasion will have passed or will never arrive, and the people will have exhausted their strength in ineffectual expectation and will have sunk into incurable supineness. It was principally the *effect of* a similar quietism that the populous and extensive nations of Asia have fallen into their existing decrepitude; and that anarchy, insecurity, ignorance and barbarism, the symptoms of the confirmed disease of monarchy, have reduced nations of the most delicate physical and intellectual organization and under the most fortunate climates of the globe to a blank in the history of man.

The reasoners who *incline to* the opinion that it is not sufficient that the innovators should produce a majority in the nation, but that we ought to expect such an unanimity as would preclude anything amounting to a serious dispute, are prompted to this view of the question by the dread of anarchy and massacre. Infinite and inestimable calamities belong to oppression, but the most fatal of them all is that mine of unexploded mischief which it has practiced beneath the foundations of society, and with which, "pernicious to one touch" it threatens to involve the ruin of the entire building together with its own. But delay merely renders this mischief more tremendous, not the less inevitable. For the utmost may now be the crisis of the social disease *which* is rendered thus periodical, chronic and incurable.

The savage brutality of the populace is proportioned to the arbitrary character of their government, and tumults and insurrections soon, as in Constantinople, become consistent with the permanence of the causing evil, of which they might have been the critical determination.

The public opinion in England ought first to be excited to action, and the durability of those forms within which the oppressors entrench themselves brought perpetually to the test of its operation. No law or institution can last if this opinion be decisively pronounced against it. For this purpose government ought to be defied, in cases of questionable result, to prosecute for political libel. All questions relating to the jurisdiction of magistrates and courts of law respecting which any doubt could be raised ought to be agitated with indefatigable pertinacity. Some two or three of the popular leaders have shown the best spirit in this respect; they only want system and co-operation. The taxgatherer ought to be compelled in every practicable instance to distrain, whilst the right to impose taxes, as was the case in the beginning of the resistance to the tyranny of Charles I is formally contested by an overwhelming multitude of defendants before the courts of common law. Confound the subtlety of lawyers with the subtlety of the law. The nation would thus be excited to develop itself, and to declare whether it acquiesced in the existing forms of government. The manner in which all questions of this nature might be decided would develop the occasions, and afford a prognostic as to the success, of more decisive measures. Simultaneously with this active and vigilant system of opposition, means ought to be taken of solemnly conveying the sense of large bodies and various denominations of the people in a manner the most explicit to the existing depositaries of power. Petitions, couched in the actual language of the petitioners, and emanating from distinct assemblies, ought to load the tables of the House of Commons. The poets, philosophers and artists ought to remonstrate, and the memorials entitled their petitions might shew the universal conviction they entertain of the inevitable connection between national prosperity and freedom, and the cultivation of the imagination and the cultivation of scientific truth, and the profound development of moral and metaphysical enquiry. Suppose the memorials to be severally written by Godwin, Hazlitt and Bentham and Hunt, they would be worthy of the age and of the cause; radiant and irresistible like the meridian sun they would strike all but the eagles who dared to gaze upon its beams with blindness and confusion. These appeals of solemn and emphatic argument from those who have already a predestined existence among posterity, would appal the enemies of mankind by their echoes from every corner of the world in which the majestic literature of England is cultivated; it would be like a voice from beyond the dead of those who will live in the memories of men,

when they must be forgotten; it would be Eternity warning Time.

Let us hope that at this stage of the progress of Reform, the oppressors would feel their impotence and reluctantly and imperfectly concede some limited portion of the rights of the people, and disgorge some morsels of their undigested prey. In this case, the people ought to be exhorted by everything ultimately dear to them to pause until by the exercise of those rights which they have regained they become fitted to demand more. It is better that we gain what we demand by a process of negociation which should occupy twenty years than that by communicating a sudden shock to the interests of those who are the depositaries and dependents of power we should incur the calamity which their revenge might inflict upon us by giving the signal of civil war. If, after all, they consider the chance of personal ruin, and the infamy of figuring on the page of history as the promoters of civil war preferable to resigning any portion how small soever of their usurped authority, we are to recollect that we possess a right beyond remonstrance. It has been acknowledged by the most approved writers on the English constitution, which has in this instance *been* merely *a* declaration of the superior decisions of eternal justice, that we possess a right of resistance. The claim of the reigning family is founded upon a memorable exertion of this solemnly recorded right.

The last resort of resistance is undoubtedly insurrection. The right of insurrection is derived from the employment of armed force to counteract the will of the nation. Let the government disband the standing army, and the purpose of resistance would be sufficiently fulfilled by the incessant agitation of the points of dispute before the courts of common law, and by an unwarlike display of the irresistible number and union of the people.

Before we enter into a consideration of the measures which might terminate in civil war, let us for a moment consider the nature and the consequences of war. This is the alternative which the unprincipled cunning of the tyrants has presented to us, and which we must not shun. There is secret sympathy between Destruction and Power, between Monarchy and War; and the long experience of all the history of all recorded time teaches us with what success they have played into each other's hands. War is a kind of superstition; the pageantry of arms and badges corrupts the imagination of men. How far more appropriate would be the symbols of an inconsolable grief —muffled drums, and melancholy music, and arms reversed, and the livery of sorrow rather than of blood. When men mourn at funerals for what do they mourn in comparison with the calamities which they hasten with every circumstance of festivity to suffer and to inflict! Visit in imagination the scene of a field of battle or a city taken by assault, collect into one group the groans and the distortions of the innumerable dying, the inconsolable grief and horror of their surviving friends, the hellish exultation and unnatural drunkenness of destruction of the conquerors, the burning of the harvests and the obliteration of the traces of cultivation—to this, in a civil war, is to be added the sudden disruption of the bonds of social life, and "father against son".

If there had never been war, there could never have been tyranny in the world; tyrants take advantage of the mechanical organization of armies to establish and defend their encroachments. It is thus that the mighty advantages of the French Revolution have been almost compensated by a succession of tyrants (for demagogues, oligarchies, usurpers and legitimate kings are merely varieties of the same class) from Robespierre to Louis XVIII. War, waged from whatever motive, extinguishes the sentiment of reason and justice in the mind. The motive is forgotten, or only adverted to in a mechanical and habitual manner. A sentiment of confidence in brute force and in a contempt of death and danger is considered the highest virtue, when in truth, and however indispensable, they are merely the means and the instrument, highly capable of being perverted to destroy the cause they were assumed to promote. It is a foppery the most intolerable to an amiable and philosophical mind. It is like what some reasoners have observed of religious faith; no fallacious and indirect motive to action can subsist in the mind without weakening the effect of those which are genuine and true. The person who thinks it virtuous to believe, will think a less degree of virtue attaches to good actions than if he had considered it as indifferent. The person who has been accustomed to subdue men by force will be less inclined to the trouble of convincing or persuading them.

These brief considerations suffice to show that the true friend of mankind and of his country would hesitate before he recommended measures which tend to bring down so heavy a calamity as war.

I imagine however that before the English Nation shall arrive at that new point of moral and political degradation now occupied by the Chinese, it will be necessary to appeal to an exertion of physical strength. If the madness of parties admits no other mode of determining the question at issue, . . .

When the people shall have obtained, by whatever means, the victory over their oppressors and when persons appointed by them shall have taken their seats in the Representative Assembly of the nation, and assumed the control of public affairs according to constitutional rules, there will remain the great task of accommodating all that can be preserved of antient forms with the improvements of the knowledge of a more enlightened age, in legislation, jurisprudence, government and religious and academical institutions. The settlement of the national debt is on the principles before elucidated merely *an* arrangement of form, and however necessary and important is an affair of mere arithmetical proportions readily determined; nor can I see how those who, being deprived of their unjust advantages, will probably inwardly murmur, can oppose one word of open expostulation to a measure of such irrefragable justice.

There is one thing which certain vulgar agitators endeavour to flatter the most uneducated part of the people by assiduously proposing, which they ought not to do nor to require; and that is Retribution. Men having been injured, desire to injure in return. This is falsely called an universal law of human nature; it is a law from which many are exempt, and all in proportion to their virtue and cultivation. The savage is more revengeful than the civilized man, the ignorant and uneducated than the person of a refined and cultivated intellect; the generous and . . .

END OF MS.

JOHN KEATS

SHELLEY AND KEATS

Though Shelley and Keats were contemporaries, and were slightly acquainted, they were never friends. Keats's pride made him shrink from a relationship which the uninformed might interpret as social and financial dependence. Besides, he regarded Shelley as a careless artist, and Shelley considered his work to be deficient in intellectual content. The truth is that the enthusiasm for the French Revolution which had become a creative force in the minds of the other romanticists, did not touch the feelings of Keats. In that sense he seems to belong to a later time than that of Shelley.

Revolutionary social idealisms do not affect his work. He is insular, hardly aware of France and her age of boundless horizons. His effort is directed almost entirely toward the attainment of fullness of personal experience. At first he seeks and finds opulence of sensation in Nature and in Greek legend. Then he becomes more vividly aware than any of his contemporaries of the tragedy which mutability holds for the sensi-

tive individual. Shelley, the idealist, could believe "The one remains, the many change and pass." Keats, held by the very vividness of his senses in its world, feels that his life is built upon shifting sands. He therefore searches eagerly for centers of security and quietude outside the flux of nature. At times he seems to have discovered such havens in the perennial beauty of Nature or in the timeless glory of art. Yet at other times, at the very moment of apprehending beauty, he is most keenly aware of the fleeting insubstantial character of all things. Then melancholy descends upon him.

Keats's conception of beauty as largely gorgeous and decorative was to become an important article of later poetic creeds, and his sorrowful preoccupation with mutability was to haunt the emotional life of Tennyson and many another poet of the nineteenth century. In these respects Keats is not to be grouped with the bold romanticists. In important particulars, he cuts himself off sharply from them and starts poetry in the direction of the ardent melancholy poets of a later age.

JOHN KEATS

1795–1821

John Keats was born in London in October, 1795, over a livery stable of which his father was the manager. In this unpromising atmosphere appeared miraculously the English poet who possessed the keenest of artistic sensibilities and the surest of instincts for beauty. The father was ambitious for his children and sent John with his younger brother George to an excellent school at Enfield, ten miles from London. He was then a small, sturdy, but high-tempered boy, distinguished at first largely by his love of fighting. Suddenly at the age of fourteen he developed a passionate love of reading, which he indulged to the exclusion of all other interests. Charles Cowden Clarke, the son of the head-master and both then and later a guide to his reading, says that within a few months he completely exhausted the resources of the school-library. He also undertook for his own delight a prose translation of the Æneid and of various French classics.

Soon after Keats went to school, his father was killed in an accident and in 1810 his mother died of consumption. The poet thus clearly inherited a tendency to tuberculosis. The tie between the

boy and his mother had been very close and her death affected profoundly his ardent nature. When Keats was nearly sixteen years old, his guardian, a hard-headed, unsympathetic man, withdrew him from school and apprenticed him to a surgeon. Keats apparently made no protest. His duties were not exacting, so that he found ample time to gratify his passion for reading. Once a week he used to walk out to his old school and read with his friend Cowden Clarke. On one memorable day his literary mentor introduced him to Spenser and from *The Faerie Queene* came his first inspiration to write poetry.

In 1814 he went up to London to continue his medical training, in the approved fashion, in the hospitals. During the two years of his study there poetry gradually became his chief interest. He read Shakespeare, Milton, Chatterton, Burns, and Wordsworth, and began to write verses for himself and Cowden Clarke. Still he never became a lax student of medicine and gained competence, even skill, as a surgeon. In 1815 Cowden Clarke showed some of Keats's poetic efforts to Leigh Hunt. This man was a poet and a journalist. He was editor of a liberal paper called *The Examiner* and had just completed a two-years term in prison for calling the Prince Regent "a fat Adonis of forty." While there he continued to edit his paper and to write poetry full of color and languid sensuous charm, expressive of an exclamatory but infectious delight in all sorts of beauty. Hunt was much taken with Keats's poems and immediately published one of them, a sonnet *To Solitude,* in his journal. The appearance of this poem in print probably made Keats decide to give up surgery as a career. He passed his medical examinations, but never practised his profession. Indeed he felt a sort of exuberant joy in his release for the achievement in poetry which he confidently believed was now possible.

Hunt and Keats soon met and became enthusiastic friends. The young man found in Hunt's house an atmosphere of easy gaiety and much enthusiastic talk about poetry. The influence of the older man upon his new friend for a few months was strong and not always healthful. He gave Keats strong encouragement, but little criticism or discipline. He rather stimulated his native tendency to luxuriate in the purely sensuous aspects of Nature and of fable. He also communicated to his work a tone of vulgar fire-side familiarity, which led a hostile critic to brand the practice of the two as of the "Cockney School." In this atmosphere of gushing enthusiasm for his work Keats became, as he afterwards realized, "a pet lamb in a sentimental farce." Hunt's influence is to be discerned in "I stood tip-toe," in the sonnets "Keen fitful gusts" and *The Grasshopper and the Cricket,* and particularly in the free-form of the heroic couplet in which *Sleep and Poetry* and *Endymion* were written. Hunt's enthusiasm was also largely responsible for the publication of Keats's first volume in March, 1817.

At the time the public was absorbed in other poets, in Scott, Moore, and Byron. The book sold poorly; even the small first edition was not exhausted. Except for a brief notice in *The Monthly Review,* the press ignored it. The disappointment over this reception, however, merely drove Keats forward to greater artistic effort for the poem *Endymion* which occupied him most of the year 1817. This was a long flowery narrative in which is retold a Greek tale of the nightly descent of the Moon-Goddess to embrace her mortal lover *Endymion.* The poem is also an allegory, a kind of parable of the soul's tortuous pursuit of ideal beauty.

The poem was published in 1818 and the reviewers in both of the most influential magazines, Blackwoods and The Quarterly Review, attacked it savagely. These writers, in the approved manner of the age, indulged in vulgar and humiliating personalities. At first Keats was greatly discouraged by these criticisms and declared that he would write no more. But he soon realized that he must regard them as mere annoyances and that he must devote himself to his chosen career with unabated energy. The tradition that these hostile reviews utterly crushed Keats's spirit and were at least indirectly responsible for his death—his soul, as Byron put it, "snuffed out with an article"—is false and unfair to Keats as a man. During 1817 he was at

work on *Isabella; or, The Pot of Basil,* a narrative founded on one of the Tales of the Decameron and intended for a volume of poetic adaptations of Boccaccio. Though not free from his early discursive luxuriousness, in structure, the poem shows some of the firmness which characterizes his later work.

The year 1818 was a difficult one for Keats. He bade farewell to his brother George and his wife, who left England to live in Kentucky; and he nursed his brother Tom, who died of consumption, through his last illness. This brother's death was a severe blow to Keats. It left him singularly alone in the world and accentuated in him a native tendency to morbidity. Fortunately his friend Brown invited Keats to live with him. While there he met a young girl eighteen years old, named Fanny Brawne, and almost immediately fell in love with her. The feeling which she aroused in Keats was always a little feverish, so that some of the poems written under the influence of this passion are over-sensuous and unrestrained. Yet Keats's glorious outburst of poetry which began in January, 1819, was undoubtedly stimulated by his engagement to this Fanny Brawne. *The Eve of Saint Agnes, La Belle Dame Sans Merci,* and his five most beautiful Odes are all expressions of the brief ecstasy which came when he realized that his love was reciprocated. The first of these poems is usually regarded as the most complete expression of his genius. In it he follows most intelligently the advice which he once gave to Shelley to "load every rift with ore." The sensuous splendor with which love is here associated does not enervate the emotion. It rather endows it with the romance and idealism which comes to every sensitive youth whom love first awakens to beauty. The odes are all the voice, in different keys, of an identical melancholy. Keats, more than any of his contemporaries, was vividly conscious of the ceaseless change and decay in Nature and in the life of man. This sad fact of mortality weighed upon his spirit and found almost perfect expression in these flawless lyrics.

Hyperion, too, was probably completed in this year 1819. The poem was begun as an answer to the strictures made by the critics upon *Endymion.* For the flaccid sensuousness of that poem he sought to substitute simple grandeur of manner. He chose a story of the dethronement of the elder gods of Greece by a younger race of immortals, more strong in beauty and humanity. The mythological narrative was suggested by *Paradise Lost,* but in the vagueness of its outlines and of its allegorical implications it was written in the manner of no one but Keats. After composing only two books and a part of the third, he believed that he was only successfully imitating Milton's manner and immediately abandoned the work. These poems written during 1819 appeared in a volume published in June, 1820. The criticisms of this book were more generous; even the hostile Jeffrey of *The Edinburgh Review* finding much to praise in it.

By this time, however, poor Keats could take but little delight in this belated recognition. In

February, 1820, he suffered from a hemorrhage of the lungs, the first unmistakable manifestation of the disease that had been latently consuming him for almost two years. He was enough of a doctor to recognize the serious nature of his situation and to say to his friend Brown "That blood is my death warrant; I must die." From this moment he declined rapidly and pathetically into death. In August he accepted the verdict of the doctors that his sole chance for recovery lay in spending the winter in Italy. He made his plans accordingly, but "as a soldier marches up to a battery." He went with a young painter named Severn, who had won the Gold Medal of the Royal Academy the year before. While on board the boat waiting for favorable winds, he expressed the agony and passion of his spirit when he realized that he was leaving Fanny Brawne forever, in a sonnet, "Bright star, would I were steadfast as thou art."

When Shelley heard that Keats had landed at Naples, he sent him a cordial invitation to visit him at Pisa. Severn, however, was bound for Rome and Keats preferred to stay with him. At first the invalid seemed to improve and he began to plan for a projected poem on Sabrina. But on December 10th came a final relapse which left no doubt of the near approach of death. When Keats fully realized this fact, he at first was filled with despair. In this mood he begged Severn to allow him to end his life with laudanum. His friend's resolute refusal changed his feelings to pathetic acquiescence and a longing for the peace of death. "Doctor," he said, "when will this posthumous life of mine come

to an end?" Again he murmured to his friend Severn, "I feel the flowers growing over me." On February 23, 1821, he sank quietly into death, a mere youth, only twenty-five years old. Three days later he was buried in the Protestant Cemetery in Rome.

SELECTED BIBLIOGRAPHY

TEXTS

Complete Works, 4 Vols., ed. by G. H. Buxton Forman, 1883.
New Edition, 1889.
The standard complete edition.
Poetical Works, I Vol., ed. by E. de Selincourt, 1905.
The best one-volume edition.

CRITICAL WORKS

Colvin, Sidney, *John Keats*, 1917.
The standard biography.
Lowell, Amy, *John Keats*, 2 Vols., 1924.
A very full and sympathetic study of his life and work.
Fausset, H. I. A., *Keats, A Study in Development*, 1922.
A study of the growth of Keats's mind in its relation to his art.
de Selincourt, Ernest, *Keats*, 1922.
Arnold, Matthew, *Essays in Criticism, Second Series*, 1888.
A famous, but partly unsympathetic essay.

I STOOD TIP-TOE UPON A LITTLE HILL

"Places of nestling green for Poets made."
STORY OF RIMINI.

I STOOD tip-toe upon a little hill,
The air was cooling, and so very still,
That the sweet buds which with a modest pride
Pull droopingly, in slanting curve aside,
Their scantly leav'd, and finely tapering stems,
Had not yet lost those starry diadems
Caught from the early sobbing of the morn.
The clouds were pure and white as flocks new shorn,
And fresh from the clear brook; sweetly they slept
On the blue fields of heaven, and then there crept   10
A little noiseless noise among the leaves,
Born of the very sigh that silence heaves:
For not the faintest motion could be seen
Of all the shades that slanted o'er the green.
There was wide wand'ring for the greediest eye,

To peer about upon variety;
Far round the horizon's crystal air to skim,
And trace the dwindled edgings of its brim;
To picture out the quaint, and curious bending
Of a fresh woodland alley, never ending;   20
Or by the bowery clefts, and leafy shelves,
Guess where the jaunty streams refresh themselves.
I gazed awhile, and felt as light, and free
As though the fanning wings of Mercury
Had play'd upon my heels: I was light-hearted,
And many pleasures to my vision started;
So I straightway began to pluck a posey
Of luxuries bright, milky, soft and rosy.

A bush of May flowers with the bees about them;
Ah, sure no tasteful nook would be without them;   30
And let a lush laburnum oversweep them,
And let long grass grow round the roots to keep them

Moist, cool and green; and shade the violets,
That they may bind the moss in leafy nets.

A filbert hedge with wild briar overtwin'd,
And clumps of woodbine taking the soft wind
Upon their summer thrones; there too should
        be
The frequent chequer of a youngling tree,
That with a score of light green brethren
        shoots
From the quaint mossiness of aged roots: 40
Round which is heard a spring-head of clear
        waters
Babbling so wildly of its lovely daughters
The spreading blue bells; it may haply mourn
That such fair clusters should be rudely torn
From their fresh beds, and scatter'd thought-
        lessly
By infant hands, left on the path to die.

Open afresh your round of starry folds,
Ye ardent marigolds!
Dry up the moisture from your golden lids,
For great Apollo bids   50
That in these days your praises should be sung
On many harps, which he has lately strung;
And when again your dewiness he kisses,
Tell him, I have you in my world of blisses:
So haply when I rove in some far vale,
His mighty voice may come upon the gale.

Here are sweet peas, on tip-toe for a flight:
With wings of gentle flush o'er delicate white,
And taper fingers catching at all things,
To bind them all about with tiny rings.   60

Linger awhile upon some bending planks
That lean against a streamlet's rushy banks,
And watch intently Nature's gentle doings:
They will be found softer than ring-dove's
        cooings.
How silent comes the water round that bend;
Not the minutest whisper does it send
To the o'erhanging sallows: blades of grass
Slowly across the chequer'd shadows pass.
Why, you might read two sonnets, ere they
        reach
To where the hurrying freshnesses aye preach
A natural sermon o'er their pebbly beds;   71
Where swarms of minnows show their little
        heads,
Staying their wavy bodies 'gainst the streams,
To taste the luxury of sunny beams

Temper'd with coolness. How they ever
        wrestle
With their own sweet delight, and ever nestle
Their silver bellies on the pebbly sand.
If you but scantily hold out the hand,
That very instant not one will remain;   80
But turn your eye, and they are there again,
The ripples seem right glad to reach those
        cresses,
And cool themselves among the em'rald
        tresses;
The while they cool themselves, they freshness
        give,
And moisture, that the bowery green may live:
So keeping up an interchange of favors,
Like good men in the truth of their behaviors
Sometimes goldfinches one by one will drop
From low-hung branches; little space they
        stop;
But sip, and twitter, and their feathers sleek;
Then off at once, as in a wanton freak: 90
Or perhaps, to show their black, and golden
        wings,
Pausing upon their yellow flutterings.
Were I in such a place, I sure should pray
That nought less sweet, might call my
        thoughts away,
Than the soft rustle of a maiden's gown
Fanning away the dandelion's down;
Than the light music of her nimble toes
Patting against the sorrel as she goes.
How she would start, and blush, thus to be
        caught
Playing in all her innocence of thought.   100
O let me lead her gently o'er the brook,
Watch her half-smiling lips, and downward
        look;
O let me for one moment touch her wrist;
Let me one moment to her breathing list;
And as she leaves me may she often turn
Her fair eyes looking through her locks au-
        burne.
What next? A tuft of evening primroses,
O'er which the mind may hover till it dozes;
O'er which it well might take a pleasant sleep,
But that 'tis ever startled by the leap   110
Of buds into ripe flowers; or by the flitting
Of diverse moths, that aye their rest are quit-
        ting;
Or by the moon lifting her silver rim
Above a cloud, and with a gradual swim
Coming into the blue with all her light.
O Maker of sweet poets, dear delight
Of this fair world, and all its gentle livers;

Spangler of clouds, halo of crystal rivers,
Mingler with leaves, and dew and tumbling
    streams,
Closer of lovely eyes to lovely dreams, 120
Lover of loneliness, and wandering,
Of upcast eye, and tender pondering!
Thee must I praise above all other glories
That smile us on to tell delightful stories.
For what has made the sage or poet write
But the fair paradise of Nature's light?
In the calm grandeur of a sober line,
We see the waving of the mountain pine;
And when a tale is beautifully staid,
We feel the safety of a hawthorn glade: 130
When it is moving on luxurious wings,
The soul is lost in pleasant smotherings:
Fair dewy roses brush against our faces,
And flowering laurels spring from diamond
    vases;
O'er head we see the jasmine and sweet briar,
And bloomy grapes laughing from green at-
    tire;
While at our feet, the voice of crystal bubbles
Charms us at once away from all our troubles:
So that we feel uplifted from the world,
Walking upon the white clouds wreath'd and
    curl'd. 140
So felt he, who first told, how Psyche went
On the smooth wind to realms of wonder-
    ment;
What Psyche felt, and Love, when their full
    lips
First touch'd; what amorous, and fondling
    nips
They gave each other's cheeks; with all their
    sighs,
And how they kist each other's tremulous
    eyes:
The silver lamp,—the ravishment,—the won-
    der—
The darkness,—loneliness,—the fearful thun-
    der;
Their woes gone by, and both to heaven up-
    flown,
To bow for gratitude before Jove's throne. 150
So did he feel, who pull'd the boughs aside,
That we might look into a forest wide,
To catch a glimpse of Fauns, and Dryades
Coming with softest rustle through the trees;
And garlands woven of flowers wild, and
    sweet,
Upheld on ivory wrists, or sporting feet:
Telling us how fair, trembling Syrinx fled
Arcadian Pan, with such a fearful dread.

Poor nymph,—poor Pan,—how he did weep
    to find,
Naught but a lovely sighing of the wind 160
Along the reedy stream; a half heard strain,
Full of sweet desolation—balmy pain.

What first inspir'd a bard of old to sing
Narcissus pining o'er the untainted spring?
In some delicious ramble, he had found
A little space, with boughs all woven round;
And in the midst of all, a clearer pool
Than e'er reflected in its pleasant cool,
The blue sky here, and there, serenely peeping
Through tendril wreaths fantastically creep-
    ing. 170
And on the bank a lonely flower he spied,
A meek and forlorn flower, with naught of
    pride,
Drooping its beauty o'er the watery clearness,
To woo its own sad image into nearness:
Deaf to light Zephyrus it would not move;
But still would seem to droop, to pine, to
    love.
So while the poet stood in this sweet spot,
Some fainter gleaming o'er his fancy shot;
Nor was it long ere he had told the tale
Of young Narcissus, and sad Echo's bale. 180

Where had he been, from whose warm head
    out-flew
That sweetest of all songs, that ever new,
That aye refreshing, pure deliciousness,
Coming ever to bless
The wanderer by moonlight? to him bringing
Shapes from the invisible world, unearthly
    singing
From out the middle air, from flowery nests,
And from the pillowy silkiness that rests
Full in the speculation of the stars.
Ah! surely he had burst our mortal bars; 190
Into some wond'rous region he had gone,
To search for thee, divine Endymion!

He was a Poet, sure a lover too,
Who stood on Latmus' top, what time there
    blew
Soft breezes from the myrtle vale below;
And brought in faintness, solemn, sweet, and
    slow
A hymn from Dian's temple; while upswelling,
The incense went to her own starry dwelling.

But though her face was clear as infant's eyes,
Though she stood smiling o'er the sacrifice, 200
The Poet wept at her so piteous fate,
Wept that such beauty should be desolate:
So in fine wrath some golden sounds he won,
And gave meek Cynthia her Endymion.

Queen of the wide air; thou most lovely
        queen
Of all the brightness that mine eyes have
        seen!
As thou exceedest all things in thy shine,
So every tale, does this sweet tale of thine.
O for three words of honey, that I might
Tell but one wonder of thy bridal night! 210
Where distant ships do seem to show their
        keels
Phœbus awhile delay'd his mighty wheels,
And turn'd to smile upon thy bashful eyes,
Ere he his unseen pomp would solemnize.
The evening weather was so bright, and clear,
That men of health were of unusual cheer;
Stepping like Homer at the trumpet's call,
Or young Apollo on the pedestal:
And lovely women were as fair and warm,
As Venus looking sideways in alarm. 220
The breezes were ethereal, and pure,
And crept through half closed lattices to cure
The languid sick; it cool'd their fever'd sleep,
And sooth'd them into slumbers full and deep.
Soon they awoke clear ey'd: nor burnt with
        thirsting,
Nor with hot fingers, nor with temples burst-
        ing:
And springing up, they met the wond'ring
        sight
Of their dear friends, nigh foolish with de-
        light;
Who feel their arms, and breasts, and kiss and
        stare,
And on their placid foreheads part the hair. 230
Young men, and maidens at each other gaz'd
With hands held back, and motionless, amaz'd
To see the brightness in each other's eyes;
And so they stood, fill'd with a sweet surprise,
Until their tongues were loos'd in poesy.
Therefore no lover did of anguish die:
But the soft numbers, in that moment spoken,
Made silken ties, that never may be broken.
Cynthia! I cannot tell the greater blisses,
That follow'd thine, and thy dear shepherd's
        kisses: 240
Was there a poet born?—but now no more,
My wand'ring spirit must no farther soar.—

EPISTLES

"Among the rest a shepheard (though but young
Yet hartned to his pipe) with all the skill
His few yeeres could, began to fit his quill."
                        Britannia's Pastorals.—BROWNE.

TO GEORGE FELTON MATHEW

SWEET are the pleasures that to verse belong,
And doubly sweet a brotherhood in song;
Nor can remembrance, Mathew! bring to view
A fate more pleasing, a delight more true
Than that in which the brother Poets joy'd,
Who with combined powers, their wit employ'd
To raise a trophy to the drama's muses.
The thought of this great partnership diffuses
Over the genius loving heart, a feeling
Of all that's high, and great, and good, and
        healing.   10

Too partial friend! fain would I follow thee
Past each horizon of fine poesy;
Fain would I echo back each pleasant note
As o'er Sicilian seas, clear anthems float
'Mong the light skimming gondolas far parted,
Just when the sun his farewell beam has
        darted:
But 'tis impossible; far different cares
Beckon me sternly from soft "Lydian airs,"
And hold my faculties so long in thrall,
That I am oft in doubt whether at all   20
I shall see again Phœbus in the morning:
Or flush'd Aurora in the roseate dawning!
Or a white Naiad in a rippling stream;
Or a rapt seraph in a moonlight beam;
Or again witness what with thee I've seen,
The dew by fairy feet swept from the green,
After a night of some quaint jubilee
Which every elf and fay had come to see:
When bright processions took their airy march
Beneath the curvéd moon's triumphal arch. 30

But might I now each passing moment give
To the coy muse, with me she would not live
In this dark city, nor would condescend
'Mid contradictions her delights to lend,
Should e'er the fine-ey'd maid to me be kind,
Ah! surely it must be whene'er I find
Some flowery spot, sequester'd, wild, romantic,
That often must have seen a poet frantic;
Where oaks, that erst the Druid knew, are
        growing,
And flowers, the glory of one day, are blow-
        ing;   40

Where the dark-leav'd laburnum's drooping
  clusters
Reflect athwart the stream their yellow lustres,
And interwin'd the cassia's arms unite,
With its own drooping buds, but very white.
Where on one side are covert branches hung,
'Mong which the nightingales have always
  sung
In leafy quiet: where to pry, aloof,
Atween the pillars of the sylvan roof,
Would be to find where violet beds were nest-
  ling,
And where the bee with cowslip bells was
  wrestling.   50
There must be too a ruin dark, and gloomy,
To say "joy not too much in all that's
  bloomy."

Yet this is vain— O Mathew lend thy aid
To find a place where I may greet the maid—
Where we may soft humanity put on,
And sit, and rhyme, and think on Chatterton;
And that warm-hearted Shakespeare sent to
  meet him
Four laurell'd spirits, heaven-ward to intreat
  him.
With reverence would we speak of all the
  sages
Who have left streaks of light athwart their
  ages: 60
And thou shouldst moralize on Milton's
  blindness,
And mourn the fearful dearth of human kind-
  ness
To those who strove with the bright golden
  wing
Of genius, to flap away each sting
Thrown by the pitiless world. We next could
  tell
Of those who in the cause of freedom fell;
Of our own Alfred, of Helvetian Tell;
Of him whose name to ev'ry heart's a solace,
High-minded and unbending William Wallace.
While to the rugged north our musing turns 70
We well might drop a tear for him, and Burns.

Felton! without incitements such as these,
How vain for me the niggard Muse to tease:
For thee, she will thy every dwelling grace,
And make a 'sun-shine in a shady place':
For thou wast once a floweret blooming wild,
Close to the source, bright, pure, and undefil'd,
Whence gush the streams of song: in happy
  hour

Came chaste Diana from her shady bower,
Just as the sun was from the east uprising; 80
And, as for him some gift she was devising,
Beheld thee, pluck'd thee, cast thee in the
  stream
To meet her glorious brother's greeting beam.
I marvel much that thou hast never told
How, from a flower, into a fish of gold
Apollo chang'd thee; how thou next didst
  seem
A black-ey'd swan upon the widening stream;
And when thou first didst in that mirror
  trace
The placid features of a human face:
That thou hast never told thy travels strange,
And all the wonders of the mazy range   91
O'er pebbly crystal, and o'er golden sands;
Kissing thy daily food from Naiad's pearly
  hands.

           November, 1815.

TO MY BROTHER GEORGE

Full many a dreary hour have I past,
My brain bewilder'd, and my mind o'ercast
With heaviness; in seasons when I've thought
No spherey strains by me could e'er be
  caught
From the blue dome, though I to dimness
  gaze
On the far depth where sheeted lightning
  plays;
Or, on the wavy grass outstretch'd supinely,
Pry 'mong the stars, to strive to think di-
  vinely:
That I should never hear Apollo's song,
Though feathery clouds were floating all
  along   10
The purple west, and, two bright streaks be-
  tween,
The golden lyre itself were dimly seen:
That the still murmur of the honey bee
Would never teach a rural song to me:
That the bright glance from beauty's eyelids
  slanting
Would never make a lay of mine enchanting,
Or warm my breast with ardour to unfold
Some tale of love and arms in time of old.

But there are times, when those that love the
  bay,
Fly from all sorrowing far, far away;   20
A sudden glow comes on them, nought they
  see

In water, earth, or air, but poesy.
It has been said, dear George, and true I
  hold it,
(For knightly Spenser to Libertas told it,)
That when a Poet is in such a trance,
In air he sees white coursers paw, and prance,
Bestridden of gay knights, in gay apparel,
Who at each other tilt in playful quarrel,
And what we, ignorantly, sheet-lightning call,
Is the swift opening of their wide portal,   30
When the bright warder blows his trumpet
  clear,
Whose tones reach nought on earth but Poet's
  ear.
When these enchanted portals open wide,
And through the light the horsemen swiftly
  glide,
The Poet's eye can reach those golden halls,
And view the glory of their festivals:
Their ladies fair, that in the distance seem
Fit for the silv'ring of a seraph's dream;
Their rich brimm'd goblets, that incessant run
Like the bright spots that move about the
  sun;   40
And, when upheld, the wine from each bright
  jar
Pours with the lustre of a falling star.
Yet further off, are dimly seen their bowers,
Of which, no mortal eye can reach the flowers;
And 'tis right just, for well Apollo knows
'Twould make the Poet quarrel with the rose.
All that's reveal'd from that far seat of
  blisses,
Is, the clear fountains' interchanging kisses,
As gracefully descending, light and thin,
Like silver streaks across a dolphin's fin,   50
When he upswimmeth from the coral caves,
And sports with half his tail above the waves.

These wonders strange he sees, and many
  more,
Whose head is pregnant with poetic lore.
Should he upon an evening ramble fare,
With forehead to the soothing breezes bare,
Would he naught see but the dark, silent blue
With all its diamonds trembling through and
  through?
Or the coy moon, when in the waviness
Of whitest clouds she does her beauty dress,   60
And staidly paces higher up, and higher,
Like a sweet nun in holy-day attire?
Ah, yes! much more would start into his
  sight—
The revelries, and mysteries of night:

And should I ever see them, I will tell you
Such tales as needs must with amazement
  spell you.

These are the living measures of the bard:
But richer far posterity's award.
What does he murmur with his latest breath,
While his proud eye looks through the film of
  death?   70
"What though I leave this dull, and earthly
  mould,
"Yet shall my spirit lofty converse hold
"With after times.—The patriot shall feel
"My stern alarum, and unsheath his steel;
"Or, in the senate thunder out my numbers
"To startle princes from their easy slum-
  bers.
"The sage will mingle with each moral theme
"My happy thoughts sententious; he will teem
"With lofty periods when my verses fire him,
"And then I'll stoop from heaven to inspire
  him.   80
"Lays have I left of such a dear delight
"That maids will sing them on their bridal
  night.
"Gay villagers, upon a morn of May,
"When they have tir'd their gentle limbs with
  play,
"And form'd a snowy circle on the grass,
"And plac'd in midst of all that lovely lass
"Who chosen is their queen,—with her fine
  head
"Crowned with flowers purple, white, and red:
"For there the lily, and the musk-rose, sigh-
  ing,
"Are emblems true of hapless lovers dying: 90
"Between her breasts, that never yet felt
  trouble,
"A bunch of violets full blown, and double,
"Serenely sleep:—she from a casket takes
"A little book,—and then a joy awakes
"About each youthful heart,—with stifled
  cries,
"And rubbing of white hands, and sparkling
  eyes:
"For she's to read a tale of hopes, and fears;
"One that I foster'd in my youthful years:
"The pearls, that on each glist'ning circle
  sleep,
"Gush ever and anon with silent creep,   100
"Lur'd by the innocent dimples. To sweet rest
"Shall the dear babe, upon its mother's breast,
"Be lull'd with songs of mine. Fair world,
  adieu!

"Thy dales, and hills, are fading from my
  view
"Swiftly I mount, upon wide-spreading pin-
  ions,
"Far from the narrow bounds of thy do-
  minions,
"Full joy I feel, while thus I cleave the air,
"That my soft verse will charm thy daughters
  fair,
"And warm thy sons!" Ah, my dear friend
  and brother,   109
Could I, at once, my mad ambition smother,
For tasting joys like these, sure I should be
Happier and dearer to society.
At times, 'tis true, I've felt relief from pain
When some bright thought has darted through
  my brain:
Through all that day I've felt a greater pleas-
  ure
Than if I'd brought to light a hidden treasure.
As to my sonnets, though none else should
  heed them,
I feel delighted, still, that you should read
  them.
Of late, too, I have had much calm enjoy-
  ment,
Stretch'd on the grass at my best lov'd em-
  ployment   120
Of scribbling lines for you. These things I
  thought
While, in my face, the freshest breeze I
  caught.
E'en now I'm pillow'd on a bed of flowers
That crowns a lofty clift, which proudly
  towers
Above the ocean-waves. The stalks, and
  blades,
Chequer my tablet with their quivering
  shades.
On one side is a field of drooping oats,
Through which the poppies show their scarlet
  coats;
So pert and useless, that they bring to mind
The scarlet coats that pester human-kind. 130
And on the other side, outspread, is seen
Ocean's blue mantle streak'd with purple,
  and green.
Now 'tis I see a canvass'd ship, and now
Mark the bright silver curling round her
  prow.
I see the lark down-dropping to his nest,
And the broad winged sea-gull never at rest;
For when no more he spreads his feathers free,
His breast is dancing on the restless sea.

Now I direct my eyes into the west,   139
Which at this moment is in sunbeams drest:
Why westward turn? 'Twas but to say adieu!
'Twas but to kiss my hand, dear George, to
  you!
                             August, 1816.

TO CHARLES COWDEN CLARKE

Oft have you seen a swan superbly frowning,
And with proud breast his own white shadow
  crowning;
He slants his neck beneath the waters bright
So silently, it seems a beam of light
Come from the galaxy: anon he sports,—
With outspread wings the Naiad Zephyr
  courts,
Or ruffles all the surface of the lake
In striving from its crystal face to take
Some diamond water drops, and them to
  treasure
In milky nest, and sip them off at leisure. 10
But not a moment can he there insure them,
Nor to such downy rest can he allure them;
For down they rush as though they would be
  free,
And drop like hours into eternity.
Just like that bird am I in loss of time,
Whene'er I venture on the stream of rhyme;
With shatter'd boat, oar snapt, and canvas
  rent,
I slowly sail, scarce knowing my intent;
Still scooping up the water with my fingers,
In which a trembling diamond never lingers.
By this, friend Charles, you may full plainly
  see   21
Why I have never penn'd a line to thee:
Because my thoughts were never free, and
  clear,
And little fit to please a classic ear;
Because my wine was of too poor a savour
For one whose palate gladdens in the flavour
Of sparkling Helicon:—small good it were
To take him to a desert rude, and bare,
Who had on Baiæ's shore reclin'd at ease,
While Tasso's page was floating in a breeze 30
That gave soft music from Armida's bowers,
Mingled with fragrance from her rarest flow-
  ers:
Small good to one who had by Mulla's stream
Fondled the maidens with the breasts of
  cream;
Who had beheld Belphœbe in a brook,
And lovely Una in a leafy nook.

And Archimago leaning o'er his book:
Who had of all that's sweet tasted, and seen,
From silv'ry ripple, up to beauty's queen;
From the sequester'd haunts of gay Titania, 40
To the blue dwelling of divine Urania:
One, who, of late, had ta'en sweet forest walks
With him who elegantly chats, and talks—
The wrong'd Libertas,—who has told you stories
Of laurel chaplets, and Apollo's glories;
Of troops chivalrous prancing through a city,
And tearful ladies made for love, and pity:
With many else which I have never known.
Thus have I thought; and days on days have flown
Slowly, or rapidly—unwilling still   50
For you to try my dull, unlearned quill.
Nor should I now, but that I've known you long;
That you first taught me all the sweets of song:
The grand, the sweet, the terse, the free, the fine;
What swell'd with pathos, and what right divine:
Spenserian vowels that elope with ease,
And float along like birds o'er summer seas;
Miltonian storms, and more, Miltonian tenderness,
Michael in arms, and more, meek Eve's fair slenderness.
Who read for me the sonnet swelling loudly 60
Up to its climax and then dying proudly?
Who found for me the grandeur of the ode,
Growing, like Atlas, stronger from its load?
Who let me taste that more than cordial dram,
The sharp, the rapier-pointed epigram?
Show'd me that epic was of all the king,
Round, vast, and spanning all like Saturn's ring?
You too upheld the veil from Clio's beauty,
And pointed out the patriot's stern duty;
The might of Alfred, and the shaft of Tell; 70
The hand of Brutus, that so grandly fell
Upon a Tyrant's head. Ah! had I never seen,
Or known your kindness, what might I have been?
What my enjoyments in my youthful years,
Bereft of all that now my life endears?
And can I e'er these benefits forget?
And can I e'er repay the friendly debt?

No, doubly no;—yet should these rhymings please,
I shall roll on the grass with twofold ease:
For I have long time been my fancy feeding
                                              80
With hopes that you would one day think the reading
Of my rough verses not an hour misspent;
Should it e'er be so, what a rich content!
Some weeks have pass'd since last I saw the spires
In lucent Thames reflected:—warm desires
To see the sun o'erpeep the eastern dimness,
And morning shadows streaking into slimness
Across the lawny fields, and pebbly water;
To mark the time as they grow broad, and shorter;
To feel the air that plays about the hills, 90
And sips its freshness from the little rills;
To see high, golden corn wave in the light
When Cynthia smiles upon a summer's night,
And peers among the cloudlets jet and white,
As though she were reclining in a bed
Of bean blossoms, in heaven freshly shed.
No sooner had I stepp'd into these pleasures
Than I began to think of rhymes and measures:
The air that floated by me seem'd to say
"Write! thou wilt never have a better day." 100
And so I did. When many lines I'd written,
Though with their grace I was not over-smitten,
Yet, as my hand was warm, I thought I'd better
Trust to my feelings, and write you a letter.
Such an attempt requir'd an inspiration
Of a peculiar sort,—a consummation;—
Which, had I felt, these scribblings might have been
Verses from which the soul would never wean:
But many days have passed since last my heart
Was warm'd luxuriously by divine Mozart; 110
By Arne delighted, or by Handel madden'd;
Or by the song of Erin pierc'd and sadden'd:
What time you were before the music sitting,
And the rich notes of each sensation fitting.
Since I have walk'd with you through shady lanes
That freshly terminate in open plains,
And revell'd in a chat that ceased not
When at nightfall among your books we got:
No, nor when supper came, nor after that,—
Nor when reluctantly I took my hat; 120

No, nor till cordially you shook my hand
Mid-way between our homes:—your accents
    bland
Still sounded in my ears, when I no more
Could hear your footsteps touch the grav'ly
    floor.
Sometimes I lost them, and then found again;
You chang'd the footpath for the grassy plain.
In those still moments I have wish'd you
    joys
That well you know to honor:—"Life's very
    toys
"With him," said I, "will take a pleasant
    charm;
"It cannot be that ought will work him
    harm." 130
These thoughts now come o'er me with all
    their might:—
Again I shake your hand,—friend Charles,
    good night.

                SEPTEMBER, 1816.

SONNETS

I

WRITTEN ON THE DAY THAT MR. LEIGH HUNT
LEFT PRISON

WHAT though, for showing truth to flatter'd
    state,
  Kind Hunt was shut in prison, yet has he,
  In his immortal spirit, been as free
As the sky-searching lark, and as elate.
Minion of grandeur! think you he did wait?
  Think you he nought but prison walls did
    see,
  Till, so unwilling, thou unturn'dst the key?
Ah, no! far happier, nobler was his fate!
In Spenser's halls he stray'd, and bowers fair,
  Culling enchanted flowers; and he flew   10
With daring Milton through the fields of air:
  To regions of his own genius true
Took happy flights. Who shall his fame im-
    pair
  When thou art dead, and all thy wretched
    crew?

II

How many bards gild the lapses of time!
  A few of them have ever been the food
  Of my delighted fancy,—I could brood
Over their beauties, earthly, or sublime:

And often, when I sit me down to rhyme,
  These will in throngs before my mind in-
    trude:
But no confusion, no disturbance rude
Do they occasion; 't is a pleasing chime.
So the unnumber'd sounds that evening store:
  The songs of birds—the whisp'ring of the
    leaves—   10
  The voice of waters—the great bell that
    heaves
With solemn sound,—and thousand others
    more,
  That distance of recognizance bereaves,
Make pleasing music, and not wild uproar.

III

TO A FRIEND WHO SENT ME SOME ROSES

As late I rambled in the happy fields,
  What time the sky-lark shakes the tremu-
    lous dew
  From his lush clover covert;—when anew
Adventurous knights take up their dinted
    shields:
I saw the sweetest flower wild nature yields,
  A fresh-blown musk-rose: 't was the first
    that threw
  Its sweets upon the summer: graceful it
    grew
As is the wand that queen Titania wields.
And, as I feasted on its fragrancy,
  I thought the garden-rose it far excell'd: 10
But when, O Wells! thy roses came to me
  My sense with their deliciousness was
    spell'd:
Soft voices had they, that with tender plea
  Whisper'd of peace, and truth, and friend-
    liness unquell'd.

IV

O Solitude! if I must with thee dwell,
  Let it not be among the jumbled heap
  Of murky buildings; climb with me to the
    steep,—
Nature's observatory—whence the dell,
Its flowery slopes, its river's crystal swell,
  May seem a span; let me thy vigils keep
  'Mongst boughs pavilion'd, where the deer's
    swift leap
Startles the wild bee from the fox-glove bell.
But though I'll gladly trace these scenes with
    thee,
                                9

Yet the sweet converse of an innocent mind
Whose words are images of thoughts re-
fin'd,
Is my soul's pleasure; and it sure must be
Almost the highest bliss of human-kind,
When to thy haunts two kindred spirits flee.

V

KEEN, fitful gusts are whisp'ring here and
there
Among the bushes half leafless, and dry;
The stars look very cold about the sky,
And I have many miles on foot to fare.
Yet feel I little of the cool bleak air,
Or of the dead leaves rustling drearily,
Or of those silver lamps that burn on high,
Or of the distance from home's pleasant lair:
For I am brimful of the friendliness
That in a little cottage I have found;   10
Of fair-hair'd Milton's eloquent distress,
And all his love for gentle Lycid drown'd:
Of lovely Laura in her light green dress,
And faithful Petrarch gloriously crown'd.

VI

To one who has been long in city pent,
'Tis very sweet to look into the fair
And open face of heaven,—to breathe a
prayer
Full in the smile of the blue firmament.
Who is more happy, when, with heart's con-
tent,
Fatigued he sinks into some pleasant lair
Of wavy grass, and reads a debonair
And gentle tale of love and languishment?
Returning home at evening, with an ear
Catching the notes of Philomel,—an eye 10
Watching the sailing cloudlet's bright career,
He mourns that day so soon has glided by:
E'en like the passage of an angel's tear
That falls through the clear ether silently.

VII

ON FIRST LOOKING INTO CHAPMAN'S HOMER

MUCH have I travell'd in the realms of gold,
And many goodly states and kingdoms seen;
Round many western islands have I been
Which bards in fealty to Apollo hold.
Oft of one wide expanse had I been told

That deep-brow'd Homer rul'd as his
demesne;
Yet did I never breathe its pure serene
Till I heard Chapman speak out loud and
bold:
Then felt I like some watcher of the skies
When a new planet swims into his ken; 10
Or like stout Cortez when with eagle eyes
He star'd at the Pacific—and all his men
Look'd at each other with a wild surmise—
Silent, upon a peak in Darien.

VIII

ADDRESSED TO HAYDON

GREAT spirits now on earth are sojourning;
He of the cloud, the cataract, the lake,
Who of Helvellyn's summit, wide awake,
Catches his freshness from Archangel's wing:
He of the rose, the violet, the spring,
The social smile, the chain for Freedom's
sake:
And lo!—whose steadfastness would never
take
A meaner sound than Raphael's whispering.
And other spirits there are standing apart
Upon the forehead of the age to come; 10
These, these will give the world another heart
And other pulses. Hear ye not the hum
Of mighty workings?—
Listen awhile ye nations, and be dumb.

IX

ON THE GRASSHOPPER AND CRICKET

THE poetry of earth is never dead:
When all the birds are faint with the hot
sun,
And hide in cooling trees, a voice will run
From hedge to hedge about the new-mown
mead;
That is the Grasshopper's—he takes the lead
In summer luxury,—he has never done
With his delights; for when tired out with
fun,
He rests at ease beneath some pleasant weed.
The poetry of earth is ceasing never:
On a lone winter evening, when the frost 10
Has wrought a silence, from the stove
there shrills
The Cricket's song, in warmth increasing ever,
And seems to one in drowsiness half lost,

The Grasshopper's among some grassy hills.

SLEEP AND POETRY

"As I lay in my bed slepe full unmete
Was unto me, but why that I ne might
Rest I ne wist, for there n'as erthly wight
[As I suppose] had more of hertis ese
Than I, for I n'ad sicknesse nor disese."
CHAUCER.

WHAT is more gentle than a wind in summer?
What is more soothing than the pretty hummer
That stays one moment in an open flower,
And buzzes cheerily from bower to bower?
What is more tranquil than a musk-rose blowing
In a green island, far from all men's knowing?
More healthful than the leafiness of dales?
More secret than a nest of nightingales?
More serene than Cordelia's countenance?
More full of visions than a high romance? 10
What, but thee, Sleep? Soft closer of our eyes!
Low murmurer of tender lullabies!
Light hoverer around our happy pillows!
Wreather of poppy buds, and weeping willows!
Silent entangler of a beauty's tresses!
Most happy listener! when the morning blesses
Thee for enlivening all the cheerful eyes
That glance so brightly at the new sun-rise.

But what is higher beyond thought than thee?
Fresher than berries of a mountain tree? 20
More strange, more beautiful, more smooth, more regal,
Than wings of swans, than doves, than dim-seen eagle?
What is it? And to what shall I compare it?
It has a glory, and nought else can share it:
The thought thereof is awful, sweet, and holy,
Chasing away all worldliness and folly;
Coming sometimes like fearful claps of thunder,
Or the low rumblings earth's regions under;
And sometimes like a gentle whispering
Of all the secrets of some wond'rous thing 30
That breathes about us in the vacant air;
So that we look around with prying stare,
Perhaps to see shapes of light, aerial lymning;
And catch soft floatings from a faint-heard hymning;

To see the laurel wreath, on high suspended,
That is to crown our name when life is ended.
Sometimes it gives a glory to the voice,
And from the heart up-springs, rejoice! rejoice!
Sounds which will reach the Framer of all things,
And die away in ardent mutterings. 40

No one who once the glorious sun has seen,
And all the clouds, and felt his bosom clean
For his great Maker's presence, but must know
What 't is I mean, and feel his being glow:
Therefore no insult will I give his spirit,
By telling what he sees from native merit.

O Poesy! for thee I hold my pen
That am not yet a glorious denizen
Of thy wide heaven—Should I rather kneel
Upon some mountain-top until I feel 50
A glowing splendour round about me hung,
And echo back the voice of thine own tongue?
O Poesy! for thee I grasp my pen
That am not yet a glorious denizen
Of thy wide heaven; yet, to my ardent prayer,
Yield from thy sanctuary some clear air,
Smooth'd for intoxication by the breath
Of flowering bays, that I may die a death
Of luxury, and my young spirit follow
The morning sun-beams to the great Apollo
Like a fresh sacrifice; or, if I can bear 61
The o'erwhelming sweets, 'twill bring to me the fair
Visions of all places: a bowery nook
Will be elysium—an eternal book
Whence I may copy many a lovely saying
About the leaves, and flowers—about the playing
Of nymphs in woods, and fountains; and the shade
Keeping a silence round a sleeping maid;
And many a verse from so strange influence
That we must ever wonder how, and whence
It came. Also imaginings will hover 71
Round my fire-side, and haply there discover
Vistas of solemn beauty, where I'd wander
In happy silence, like the clear Meander
Through its lone vales; and where I found a spot
Of awfuller shade, or an enchanted grot,
Or a green hill o'erspread with checker'd dress
Of flowers, and fearful from its loveliness,
Write on my tablets all that was permitted.

All that was for our human senses fitted.　80
Then the events of this wide world I'd seize
Like a strong giant, and my spirit tease
Till at its shoulders it should proudly see
Wings to find out an immortality.
Stop and consider! life is but a day;
A fragile dewdrop on its perilous way
From a tree's summit; a poor Indian's sleep
While his boat hastens to the monstrous steep
Of Montmorenci. Why so sad a moan?
Life is the rose's hope while yet unblown;　90
The reading of an ever-changing tale;
The light uplifting of a maiden's veil;
A pigeon tumbling in clear summer air;
A laughing school-boy, without grief or care,
Riding the springy branches of an elm.

O for ten years, that I may overwhelm
Myself in poesy; so I may do the deed
That my own soul has to itself decreed.
Then will I pass the countries that I see
In long perspective, and continually.　100
Taste their pure fountains. First the realm I'll
　pass
Of Flora, and old Pan: sleep in the grass,
Feed upon apples red, and strawberries,
And choose each pleasure that my fancy sees;
Catch the white-handed nymphs in shady
　places,
To woo sweet kisses from averted faces,—
Play with their fingers, touch their shoulders
　white
Into a pretty shrinking with a bite
As hard as lips can make it: till agreed,
A lovely tale of human life we'll read.　110
And one will teach a tame dove how it best
May fan the cool air gently o'er my rest;
Another, bending o'er her nimble tread,
Will set a green robe floating round her head,
And still will dance with ever varied ease,
Smiling upon the flowers and the trees:
Another will entice me on, and on
Through almond blossoms and rich cinnamon;
Till in the bosom of a leafy world
We rest in silence, like two gems upcurl'd　120
In the recesses of a pearly shell.

And can I ever bid these joys farewell?
Yes, I must pass them for a nobler life,
Where I may find the agonies, the strife
Of human hearts: for lo! I see afar,
O'ersailing the blue cragginess, a car
And steeds with streamy manes—the chariot-
　eer
Looks out upon the winds with glorious fear:

And now the numerous tramplings quiver
　lightly
Along a huge cloud's ridge; and now with
　sprightly　130
Wheel downward come they into fresher skies,
Tipt round with silver from the sun's bright
　eyes.
Still downward with capacious whirl they
　glide;
And now I see them on a green-hill's side
In breezy rest among the nodding stalks.
The charioteer with wond'rous gesture talks
To the trees and mountains; and there soon
　appear
Shapes of delight, of mystery, and fear,
Passing along before a dusky space
Made by some mighty oaks: as they would
　chase　140
Some ever-fleeting music on they sweep.
Lo! how they murmur, laugh, and smile, and
　weep:
Some with upholden hand and mouth severe;
Some with their faces muffled to the ear
Between their arms; some, clear in youthful
　bloom,
Go glad and smilingly athwart the gloom;
Some looking back, and some with upward
　gaze;
Yes, thousands in a thousand different ways
Flit onward—now a lovely wreath of girls
Dancing their sleek hair into tangled curls;
And now broad wings. Most awfully intent　151
The driver of those steeds is forward bent,
And seems to listen: O that I might know
All that he writes with such a hurrying glow!

The visions all are fled—the car is fled
Into the light of heaven, and in their stead
A sense of real things comes doubly strong,
And, like a muddy stream, would bear along
My soul to nothingness: but I will strive
Against all doubtings, and will keep alive　160
The thought of that same chariot, and the
　strange
Journey it went.

　　　　　　Is there so small a range
In the present strength of manhood, that the
　high
Imagination cannot freely fly
As she was wont of old? prepare her steeds,
Paw up against the light, and do strange deeds
Upon the clouds? Has she not shown us all?
From the clear space of ether, to the small

Breath of new buds unfolding? From the
    meaning
Of Jove's large eyebrow, to the tender green-
    ing   170
Of April meadows? Here her altar shone,
E'en in this isle; and who could paragon
The fervid choir that lifted up a noise
Of harmony, to where it aye will poise
Its mighty self of convoluting sound,
Huge as a planet, and like that roll round,
Eternally around a dizzy void?
Ay, in those days the Muses were nigh cloy'd
With honors; nor had any other care   179
Than to sing out and soothe their wavy hair.

Could all this be forgotten? Yes, a schism
Nurtured by foppery and barbarism,
Made great Apollo blush for this his land.
Men were thought wise who could not under-
    stand
His glories: with a puling infant's force
They sway'd about upon a rocking horse,
And thought it Pegasus. Ah dismal soul'd!
The winds of heaven blew, the ocean roll'd
Its gathering waves—ye felt it not. The blue
Bared its eternal bosom, and the dew   190
Of summer nights collected still to make
The morning precious: beauty was awake!
Why were ye not awake? But ye were dead
To things ye knew not of,—were closely wed
To musty laws lined out with wretched rule
And compass vile: so that ye taught a school
Of dolts to smooth, inlay, and clip, and fit,
Till, like the certain wands of Jacob's wit,
Their verses tallied. Easy was the task:
A thousand handicraftsmen wore the mask 200
Of Poesy. Ill-fated, impious race!
That blasphem'd the bright Lyrist to his face,
And did not know it,—no, they went about,
Holding a poor, decrepid standard out
Mark'd with most flimsy mottos, and in large
The name of one Boileau!

                  O ye whose charge
It is to hover round our pleasant hills!
Whose congregated majesty so fills
My boundly reverence, that I cannot trace
Your hallowed names, in this unholy place, 210
So near those common folk; did not their
    shames
Affright you? Did our old lamenting Thames
Delight you? Did ye never cluster round
Delicious Avon, with a mournful sound,
And weep? Or did ye wholly bid adieu

To regions where no more the laurel grew?
Or did ye stay to give a welcoming
To some lone spirits who could proudly sing
Their youth away, and die? 'T was even so:
But let me think away those times of woe: 220
Now 't is a fairer season; ye have breathed
Rich benedictions o'er us; ye have wreathed
Fresh garlands: for sweet music has been
    heard
In many places;—some has been upstirr'd
From out its crystal dwelling in a lake,
By a swan's ebon bill; from a thick brake,
Nested and quiet in a valley mild,
Bubbles a pipe; fine sounds are floating wild
About the earth: happy are ye and glad.

These things are doubtless; yet in truth we've
    had   230
Strange thunders from the potency of song;
Mingled indeed with what is sweet and strong,
From majesty: but in clear truth the themes
Are ugly clubs, the Poets Polyphemes
Disturbing the grand sea. A drainless shower
Of light is poesy; 't is the supreme of power;
'T is might half slumb'ring on its own right
    arm.
The very archings of her eyelids charm
A thousand willing agents to obey,   239
And still she governs with the mildest sway:
But strength alone though of the Muses born
Is like a fallen angel: trees uptorn,
Darkness, and worms, and shrouds, and sepul-
    chres
Delight it; for it feeds upon the burrs,
And thorns of life; forgetting the great end
Of poesy, that it should be a friend,
To soothe the cares, and lift the thoughts of
    man.

    Yet I rejoice: a myrtle fairer than
E'er grew in Paphos, from the bitter weeds
Lifts its sweet head into the air, and feeds 250
A silent space with ever sprouting green.
All tenderest birds there find a pleasant screen,
Creep through the shade with jaunty flutter-
    ing,
Nibble the little cupped flowers and sing.
Then let us clear away the choking thorns
From round its gentle stem; let the young
    fawns,
Yeaned in after times, when we are flown,
Find a fresh sward beneath it, overgrown
With simple flowers: let there nothing be
More boisterous than a lover's bended knee;

Nought more ungentle than the placid look 261
Of one who leans upon a closéd book;
Nought more untranquil than the grassy
    slopes
Between two hills. All hail delightful hopes!
As she was wont, th' imagination
Into most lovely labyrinths will be gone,
And they shall be accounted poet kings
Who simply tell the most heart-easing things.
O may these joys be ripe before I die.

Will not some say that I presumptuously 270
Have spoken? that from hastening disgrace
'T were better far to hide my foolish face?
That whining boyhood should with reverence
    bow
Ere the dread thunderbolt could reach? How!
If I do hide myself, it sure shall be
In the very fane, the light of Poesy:
If I do fall, at least I will be laid
Beneath the silence of a poplar shade;
And over me the grass shall be smooth
    shaven;
And there shall be a kind memorial graven. 280
But off Despondence! miserable bane!
They should not know thee, who athirst to
    gain
A noble end, are thirsty every hour.
What though I am not wealthy in the dower
Of spanning wisdom; though I do not know
The shiftings of the mighty winds that blow
Hither and thither all the changing thoughts
Of man: though no great minist'ring reason
    sorts
Out the dark mysteries of human souls
To clear conceiving: yet there ever rolls 290
A vast idea before me, and I glean
Therefrom my liberty; thence too I've seen
The end and aim of Poesy. 'T is clear
As anything most true; as that the year
Is made of the four seasons—manifest
As a large cross, some old cathedral's crest,
Lifted to the white clouds. Therefore should I
Be but the essence of deformity,
A coward, did my very eye-lids wink
At speaking out what I have dar'd to think. 300
Ah! rather let me like a madman run
Over some precipice; let the hot sun
Melt my Dedalian wings, and drive me down
Convuls'd and headlong! Stay! an inward
    frown
Of conscience bids me be more calm awhile.
An ocean dim, sprinkled with many an isle,
Spreads awfully before me. How much toil!

How many days! what desperate turmoil!
Ere I can have explored its widenesses.
Ah, what a task! upon my bended knees, 310
I could unsay those—no, impossible!
Impossible!

                For sweet relief I'll dwell
On humbler thoughts, and let this strange
    assay
Begun in gentleness die so away.
E'en now all tumult from my bosom fades:
I turn full hearted to the friendly aids
That smooth the path of honor; brotherhood,
And friendliness the nurse of mutual good.
The hearty grasp that sends a pleasant sonnet
Into the brain ere one can think upon it; 320
The silence when some rhymes are coming
    out;
And when they're come, the very pleasant
    rout:
The message certain to be done to-morrow.
'Tis perhaps as well that it should be to bor-
    row
Some precious book from out its snug retreat,
To cluster round it when we next shall meet.
Scarce can I scribble on; for lovely airs
Are fluttering round the room like doves in
    pairs;
Many delights of that glad day recalling,
When first my senses caught their tender fall-
    ing.   330
And with these airs come forms of elegance
Stooping their shoulders o'er a horse's prance,
Careless, and grand—fingers soft and round
Parting luxuriant curls;—and the swift bound
Of Bacchus from his chariot, when his eye
Made Ariadne's cheek look blushingly.
Thus I remember all the pleasant flow
Of words at opening a portfolio.

Things such as these are ever harbingers
To trains of peaceful images: the stirs 340
Of a swan's neck unseen among the rushes:
A linnet starting all about the bushes:
A butterfly, with golden wings broad parted,
Nestling a rose, convuls'd as though it smarted
With over pleasure—many, many more,
Might I indulge at large in all my store
Of luxuries: yet I must not forget
Sleep, quiet with his poppy coronet:
For what there may be worthy in these
    rhymes
I partly owe to him: and thus, the chimes 350
Of friendly voices had just given place

To as sweet a silence, when I 'gan retrace
The pleasant day, upon a couch at ease.
It was a poet's house who keeps the keys
Of pleasure's temple. Round about were hung
The glorious features of the bards who sung
In other ages—cold and sacred busts
Smiled at each other. Happy he who trusts
To clear Futurity his darling fame!
Then there were fauns and satyrs taking aim
At swelling apples with a frisky leap   361
And reaching fingers, 'mid a luscious heap
Of vine-leaves. Then there rose to view a fane
Of liny marble, and thereto a train
Of nymphs approaching fairly o'er the sward:
One, loveliest, holding her white hand toward
The dazzling sun-rise: two sisters sweet
Bending their graceful figures till they meet
Over the trippings of a little child:
And some are hearing, eagerly, the wild
Thrilling liquidity of dewy piping.   370
See, in another picture, nymphs are wiping
Cherishingly Diana's timorous limbs;—
A fold of lawny mantle dabbling swims
At the bath's edge, and keeps a gentle mo-
       tion
With the subsiding crystal: as when ocean
Heaves calmly its broad swelling smoothness
       o'er
Its rocky marge, and balances once more
The patient weeds; that now unshent by foam
Feel all about their undulating home.   380

Sappho's meek head was there half smiling
       down
At nothing; just as though the earnest frown
Of over thinking had that moment gone
From off her brow, and left her all alone.

Great Alfred's too, with anxious, pitying eyes,
As if he always listened to the sighs
Of the goaded world; and Kosciusko's worn
By horrid suffrance—mightily forlorn.

Petrarch, outstepping from the shady green,
Starts at the sight of Laura; nor can wean   390
His eyes from her sweet face. Most happy
       they!
For over them was seen a free display
Of outspread wings, and from between them
       shone
The face of Poesy: from off her throne
She overlook'd things that I scarce could tell.
The very sense of where I was might well

Keep Sleep aloof: but more than that there
       came
Thought after thought to nourish up the flame
Within my breast; so that the morning light
Surprised me even from a sleepless night;   400
And up I rose refresh'd, and glad, and gay,
Resolving to begin that very day
These lines; and howsoever they be done,
I leave them as a father does his son.

ENDYMION

BOOK I

A THING of beauty is a joy for ever:
Its loveliness increases; it will never
Pass into nothingness; but still will keep
A bower quiet for us, and a sleep
Full of sweet dreams, and health, and quiet
       breathing.
Therefore, on every morrow, are we wreathing
A flowery band to bind us to the earth,
Spite of despondence, of the inhuman dearth
Of noble natures, of the gloomy days,
Of all the unhealthy and o'er-darkened ways
Made for our searching: yes, in spite of all,   11
Some shape of beauty moves away the pall
From our dark spirits. Such the sun, the
       moon,
Trees old, and young, sprouting a shady boon
For simple sheep; and such are daffodils
With the green world they live in; and clear
       rills
That for themselves a cooling covert make
'Gainst the hot season; the mid forest brake,
Rich with a sprinkling of fair musk-rose
       blooms:
And such too is the grandeur of the dooms   20
We have imagined for the mighty dead;
All lovely tales that we have heard or read:
An endless fountain of immortal drink,
Pouring unto us from the heaven's brink.

   Nor do we merely feel these essences
For one short hour; no, even as the trees
That whisper round a temple become soon
Dear as the temple's self, so does the moon,
The passion poesy, glories infinite,
Haunt us till they become a cheering light   30
Unto our souls, and bound to us so fast,
That, whether there be shine, or gloom o'er-
       cast,
They alway must be with us, or we die.

Therefore, 'tis with full happiness that I
Will trace the story of Endymion.
The very music of the name has gone
Into my being, and each pleasant scene
Is growing fresh before me as the green
Of our own vallies: so I will begin
Now while I cannot hear the city's din;   40
Now while the early budders are just new,
And run in mazes of the youngest hue
About old forests; while the willow trails
Its delicate amber; and the dairy pails
Bring home increase of milk. And, as the
    year
Grows lush in juicy stalks, I'll smoothly steer
My little boat, for many quiet hours,
With streams that deepen freshly into bowers.
Many and many a verse I hope to write,
Before the daisies, vermeil rimm'd and white,
Hide in deep herbage; and ere yet the bees 51
Hum about globes of clover and sweet peas,
I must be near the middle of my story.
O may no wintry season, bare and hoary,
See it half finish'd: but let Autumn bold,
With universal tinge of sober gold,
Be all about me when I make an end.
And now at once, adventuresome, I send
My herald thought into a wilderness:
There let its trumpet blow, and quickly dress
My uncertain path with green, that I may
    speed   61
Easily onward, through flowers and weed.

Upon the sides of Latmus was outspread
A mighty forest; for the moist earth fed
So plenteously all weed-hidden roots
Into o'er-hanging boughs, and precious fruits.
And it had gloomy shades, sequestered deep,
Where no man went; and if from shepherd's
    keep
A lamb stray'd far a-down those inmost glens,
Never again saw he the happy pens   70
Whither his brethren, bleating with content,
Over the hills at every nightfall went.
Among the shepherds, 't was believed ever,
That not one fleecy lamb which thus did sever
From the white flock, but pass'd unworried
By angry wolf, or pard with prying head,
Until it came to some unfooted plains
Where fed the herds of Pan: aye great his
    gains
Who thus one lamb did lose. Paths there were
    many,
Winding through palmy fern, and rushes
    fenny,   80

And ivy banks; all leading pleasantly
To a wide lawn, whence one could only see
Stems thronging all around between the swell
Of turf and slanting branches: who could
    tell
The freshness of the space of heaven above,
Edg'd round with dark tree tops? through
    which a dove
Would often beat its wings, and often too
A little cloud would move across the blue.

Full in the middle of this pleasantness
There stood a marble altar, with a tress   90
Of flowers budded newly; and the dew
Had taken fairy phantasies to strew
Daisies upon the sacred sward last eve,
And so the dawnéd light in pomp receive.
For 'twas the morn: Apollo's upward fire
Made every eastern cloud a silvery pyre
Of brightness so unsully'd, that therein
A melancholy spirit well might win
Oblivion, and melt out his essence fine
Into the winds: rain-scented eglantine   100
Gave temperate sweets to that well-wooing
    sun;
The lark was lost in him; cold springs had
    run
To warm their chilliest bubbles in the grass;
Man's voice was on the mountains; and the
    mass
Of nature's lives and wonders puls'd tenfold,
To feel this sunrise and its glories old.

Now while the silent workings of the dawn
Were busiest, into that self-same lawn
All suddenly, with joyful cries, there sped
A troop of little children garlanded;   110
Who gathering round the altar, seem'd to pry
Earnestly round as wishing to espy
Some folk of holiday: nor had they waited
For many moments, ere their ears were sated
With a faint breath of music, which ev'n then
Fill'd out its voice, and died away again.
Within a little space again it gave
Its airy swellings, with a gentle wave,
To light-hung leaves, in smoothest echoes
    breaking
Through copse-clad vallies,—ere their death,
    o'ertaking   120
The surgy murmurs of the lonely sea.

And now, as deep into the wood as we
Might mark a lynx's eye, there glimmered
    light

Fair faces and a rush of garments white,
Plainer and plainer showing, till at last
Into the widest alley they all past,
Making directly for the woodland altar.
O kindly muse! let not my weak tongue falter
In telling of this goodly company,
Of their old piety, and of their glee: 130
But let a portion of ethereal dew
Fall on my head, and presently unmew
My soul; that I may dare, in wayfaring,
To stammer where old Chaucer used to sing.

Leading the way, young damsels danced
    along,
Bearing the burden of a shepherd song;
Each having a white wicker over brimm'd
With April's tender younglings: next, well
    trimm'd,
A crowd of shepherds with as sunburnt looks
As may be read of in Arcadian books; 140
Such as sat listening round Apollo's pipe,
When the great deity, for earth too ripe,
Let his divinity o'er-flowing die
In music, through the vales of Thessaly:
Some idly trail'd their sheep-hooks on the
    ground,
And some kept up a shrilly mellow sound
With ebon-tipped flutes: close after these,
Now coming from beneath the forest trees,
A venerable priest full soberly,
Begirt with ministring looks: always his eye 150
Stedfast upon the matted turf he kept,
And after him his sacred vestments swept.
From his right hand there swung a vase, milk-
    white,
Of mingled wine, out-sparkling generous light;
And in his left he held a basket full
Of all sweet herbs that searching eye could
    cull:
Wild thyme, and valley-lilies whiter still
Than Leda's love, and cresses from the rill.
His aged head, crowned with beechen wreath,
Seem'd like a poll of ivy in the teeth 160
Of winter hoar. Then came another crowd
Of shepherds, lifting in due time aloud
Their share of the ditty. After them appear'd,
Up-followed by a multitude that rear'd
Their voices to the clouds, a fair wrought car,
Easily rolling so as scarce to mar
The freedom of three steeds of dapple brown:
Who stood therein did seem of great renown
Among the throng. His youth was fully blown,
Showing like Ganymede to manhood grown;
And, for those simple times, his garments were

A chieftain king's: beneath his breast, half
    bare, 172
Was hung a silver bugle, and between
His nervy knees there lay a boar-spear keen.
A smile was on his countenance; he seem'd,
To common lookers on, like one who dream'd
Of idleness in groves Elysian:
But there were some who feelingly could scan
A lurking trouble in his nether lip,
And see that oftentimes the reins would slip
Through his forgotten hands: then would they
    sigh, 181
And think of yellow leaves, of owlets' cry,
Of logs pil'd solemnly.—Ah, well-a-day,
Why should our young Endymion pine away!

Soon the assembly, in a circle rang'd,
Stood silent round the shrine: each look was
    chang'd
To sudden veneration: women meek
Beckon'd their sons to silence; while each
    cheek
Of virgin bloom pal'd gently for slight fear.
Endymion too, without a forest peer, 190
Stood, wan, and pale, and with an awed face,
Among his brothers of the mountain chace.
In midst of all, the venerable priest
Eyed them with joy from greatest to the least,
And, after lifting up his aged hands,
Thus spake he: "Men of Latmos! shepherd
    bands!
Whose care it is to guard a thousand flocks:
Whether descended from beneath the rocks
That overtop your mountains; whether come
From vallies where the pipe is never dumb;
Or from your swelling downs, where sweet
    air stirs 201
Blue hare-bells lightly, and where prickly
    furze
Buds lavish gold; or ye, whose precious
    charge
Nibble their fill at ocean's very marge,
Whose mellow reeds are touch'd with sounds
    forlorn
By the dim echoes of old Triton's horn:
Mothers and wives! who day by day prepare
The scrip, with needments, for the mountain
    air;
And all ye gentle girls who foster up
Udderless lambs, and in a little cup 210
Will put choice honey for a favored youth:
Yea, every one attend! for in good truth
Our vows are wanting to our great god Pan.
Are not our lowing heifers sleeker than

Night-swollen mushrooms? Are not our wide
    plains
Speckled with countless fleeces? Have not
    rains
Green'd over April's lap? No howling sad
Sickens our fearful ewes; and we have had
Great bounty from Endymion our lord.
The earth is glad: the merry lark has pour'd
His early song against yon breezy sky,   221
That spreads so clear o'er our solemnity."

    Thus ending, on the shrine he heap'd a
    spire
Of teeming sweets, enkindling sacred fire;
Anon he stain'd the thick and spongy sod
With wine, in honor of the shepherd-god.
Now while the earth was drinking it, and while
Bay leaves were crackling in the fragrant pile,
And gummy frankincense was sparkling bright
'Neath smothering parsley, and a hazy light
Spread gayly eastward, thus a chorus sang: 231

    "O THOU, whose mighty palace roof doth
    hang
From jagged trunks, and overshadoweth
Eternal whispers, glooms, the birth, life, death
Of unseen flowers in heavy peacefulness;
Who lov'st to see the hamadryads dress
Their ruffled locks where meeting hazels
    darken;
And through whole solemn hours dost sit,
    and hearken
The dreary melody of bedded reeds—
In desolate places, where dank moisture
    breeds   240
In pipy hemlock to strange overgrowth;
Bethinking thee, how melancholy loth
Thou wast to lose fair Syrinx—do thou now,
By thy love's milky brow!
By all the trembling mazes that she ran,
Hear us, great Pan!

    "O thou, for whose soul-soothing quiet,
    turtles
Passion their voices cooingly 'mong myrtles,
What time thou wanderest at eventide
Through sunny meadows, that outskirt the
    side   250
Of thine enmossed realms: O thou, to whom
Broad leaved fig trees even now foredoom
Their ripen'd fruitage; yellow girted bees
Their golden honeycombs; our village leas
Their fairest blossom'd beans and poppied
    corn;

The chuckling linnet its five young unborn,
To sing for thee; low creeping strawberries
Their summer coolness; pent up butterflies
Their freckled wings; yea, the fresh budding
    year
All its completions—be quickly near,   260
By every wind that nods the mountain pine,
O forester divine!

    "Thou, to whom every faun and satyr flies
For willing service; whether to surprise
The squatted hare while in half sleeping fit;
Or upward ragged precipices flit
To save poor lambkins from the eagle's maw;
Or by mysterious enticement draw
Bewildered shepherds to their path again;
Or to tread breathless round the frothy main,
And gather up all fancifullest shells   271
For thee to tumble into Naiads' cells,
And, being hidden, laugh at their out-peeping;
Or to delight thee with fantastic leaping,
The while they pelt each other on the crown
With silvery oak apples, and fir cones brown—
By all the echoes that about thee ring,
Hear us, O satyr king!

    "O Hearkener to the loud clapping shears,
While ever and anon to his shorn peers   280
A ram goes bleating: Winder of the horn,
When snouted wild boars routing tender corn
Anger our huntsmen: Breather round our
    farms,
To keep off mildews, and all weather harms:
Strange ministrant of undescribéd sounds,
That come a swooning over hollow grounds,
And wither drearily on barren moors:
Dread opener of the mysterious doors
Leading to universal knowledge—see,
Great son of Dryope,   290
The many that are come to pay their vows
With leaves about their brows!

    "Be still the unimaginable lodge
For solitary thinkings; such as dodge
Conception to the very bourne of heaven,
Then leave the naked brain: be still the
    leaven,
That spreading in this dull and clodded earth
Gives it a touch ethereal—a new birth:
Be still a symbol of immensity;
A firmament reflected in a sea;   300
An element filling the space between;
An unknown—but no more: we humbly
    screen

With uplift hands our foreheads, lowly bend-
ing,
And giving out a shout most heaven rending,
Conjure thee to receive our humble Pæan,
Upon thy Mount Lycean!"

Even while they brought the burden to a
close,
A shout from the whole multitude arose,
That lingered in the air like dying rolls
Of abrupt thunder, when Ionian shoals   310
Of dolphins bob their noses through the
brine.
Meantime, on shady levels, mossy fine,
Young companions nimbly began dancing
To the swift treble pipe, and humming string.
Aye, those fair living forms swam heavenly
To tunes forgotten—out of memory:
Fair creatures! whose young children's chil-
dren bred
Thermopylæ its heroes—not yet dead,
But in old marbles ever beautiful.
High genitors, unconscious did they cull   320
Time's sweet first-fruits—they danc'd to
weariness,
And then in quiet circles did they press
The hillock turf, and caught the latter end
Of some strange history, potent to send
A young mind from its bodily tenement
Or they might watch the quoit-pitchers, in-
tent
On either side; pitying the sad death
Of Hyacinthus, when the cruel breath
Of Zephyr slew him,—Zephyr penitent,
Who now, ere Phœbus mounts the firmament,
Fondles the flower amid the sobbing rain. 331
The archers too, upon a wider plain,
Beside the feathery whizzing of the shaft,
And the dull twanging bowstring, and the raft
Branch down sweeping from a tall ash top,
Call'd up a thousand thoughts to envelope
Those who would watch. Perhaps, the trem-
bling knee
And frantic gape of lonely Niobe,
Poor, lonely Niobe! when her lovely young
Were dead and gone, and her caressing
tongue   340
Lay a lost thing upon her pale lip,
And very, very deadliness did nip
Her motherly cheeks. Arous'd from this sad
mood
By one, who at a distance loud halloo'd,
Uplifting his strong bow into the air,
Many might after brighter visions stare:

After the Argonauts, in blind amaze
Tossing about on Neptune's restless ways,
Until, from the horizon's vaulted side,
There shot a golden splendour far and wide, 350
Spangling those million poutings of the brine
With quivering ore: 'twas even an awful shine
From the exaltation of Apollo's bow;
A heavenly beacon in their dreary woe.
Who thus were ripe for high contemplating,
Might turn their steps towards the sober ring
Where sat Endymion and the aged priest
'Mong shepherds gone in eld, whose looks in-
creas'd
The silvery setting of their mortal star.
There they discours'd upon the fragile bar 360
That keeps us from our homes ethereal;
And what our duties there: to nightly call
Vesper, the beauty-crest of summer weather;
To summon all the downiest clouds together
For the sun's purple couch; to emulate
In ministring the potent rule of fate
With speed of fire-tail'd exhalations;
To tint her pallid cheek with bloom, who cons
Sweet poesy by moonlight: besides these,
A world of other unguess'd offices.   370
Anon they wander'd, by divine converse,
Into Elysium; vieing to rehearse
Each one his own anticipated bliss.
One felt heart-certain that he could not miss
His quick gone love, among fair blossom'd
boughs,
Where every zephyr-sigh pouts, and endows
Her lips with music for the welcoming.
Another wish'd, mid that eternal spring,
To meet his rosy child, with feathery sails,
Sweeping,   eye-earnestly,   through   almond
vales: 380
Who, suddenly, should stoop through the
smooth wind,
And with the balmiest leaves his temples
bind;
And, ever after, through those regions be
His messenger, his little Mercury.
Some were athirst in soul to see again
Their fellow huntsmen o'er the wide cham-
paign
In times long past; to sit with them, and
talk
Of all the chances in their earthly walk;
Comparing, joyfully, their plenteous stores
Of happiness, to when upon the moors,   390
Benighted, close they huddled from the cold,
And shar'd their famish'd scrips. Thus all
out-told

Their fond imaginations,—saving him
Whose eyelids curtain'd up their jewels dim,
Endymion: yet hourly had he striven
To hide the cankering venom, that had riven
His fainting recollections. Now indeed
His senses had swoon'd off: he did not heed
The sudden silence, or the whispers low,
Or the old eyes dissolving at his woe,   400
Or anxious calls, or close of trembling palms,
Or maiden's sigh, that grief itself embalms:
But in the self-same fixed trance he kept,
Like one who on the earth had never stept.
Aye, even as dead-still as a marble man,
Frozen in that old tale Arabian.

Who whispers him so pantingly and close?
Peona, his sweet sister: of all those,
His friends, the dearest. Hushing signs she
      made,
And breath'd a sister's sorrow to persuade   410
A yielding up, a cradling on her care.
Her eloquence did breathe away the curse:
She led him, like some midnight spirit nurse
Of happy changes in emphatic dreams,
Along a path between two little streams,—
Guarding his forehead, with her round elbow,
From low-grown branches, and his footsteps
      slow
From stumbling over stumps and hillocks
      small;
Until they came to where these streamlets
      fall,
With mingled bubblings and a gentle rush,   420
Into a river, clear, brimful, and flush
With crystal mocking of the trees and sky.
A little shallop, floating there hard by,
Pointed its beak over the fringed bank;
And soon it lightly dipt, and rose, and sank,
And dipt again, with the young couple's
      weight,—
Peona guiding, through the water straight,
Towards a bowery island opposite;
Which gaining presently, she steered light
Into a shady, fresh, and ripply cove,   430
Where nested was an arbor, overwove
By many a summer's silent fingering;
To whose cool bosom she was used to bring
Her playmates, with their needle broidery,
And minstrel memories of times gone by.

So she was gently glad to see him laid
Under her favorite bower's quiet shade,
On her own couch, new made of flower leaves,
Dry'd carefully on the cooler side of sheaves

When last the sun his autumn tresses shook,
And the tann'd harvesters rich armfuls took.
Soon was he quieted to slumbrous rest: 442
But, ere it crept upon him, he had prest
Peona's busy hand against his lips,
And still, a sleeping, held her finger-tips
In tender pressure. And as a willow keeps
A patient watch over the stream that creeps
Windingly by it, so the quiet maid
Held her in peace: so that a whispering blade
Of grass, a wailful gnat, a bee bustling   450
Down in the blue-bells, or a wren light rus-
      tling
Among sere leaves and twigs, might all be
      heard.

O magic sleep! O comfortable bird,
That broodest o'er the troubled sea of the
      mind
Till it is hush'd and smooth! O unconfin'd
Restraint! imprisoned liberty! great key
To golden palaces, strange minstrelsy,
Fountains grotesque, new trees, bespangled
      caves,
Echoing grottos, full of tumbling waves
And moonlight; aye, to all the mazy world   460
Of silvery enchantment!—who, upfurl'd
Beneath thy drowsy wing a triple hour,
But renovates and lives?—Thus, in the bower,
Endymion was calm'd to life again.
Opening his eyelids with a healthier brain,
He said: "I feel this thine endearing love
All through my bosom: thou art as a dove
Trembling its closed eyes and sleeked wings
About me; and the pearliest dew not brings
Such morning incense from the fields of May,
As do those brighter drops that twinkling
      stray   471
From those kind eyes,—the very home and
      haunt
Of sisterly affection. Can I want
Aught else, aught nearer heaven, than such
      tears?
Yet dry them up, in bidding hence all fears
That, any longer, I will pass my days
Alone and sad. No, I will once more raise
My voice upon the mountain-heights; once
      more
Make my horn parley from their foreheads
      hoar:
Again my trooping hounds their tongues shall
      loll   480
Around the breathed boar: again I'll poll
The fair-grown yew tree, for a chosen bow:

And, when the pleasant sun is getting low,
Again I'll linger in a sloping mead
To hear the speckled thrushes, and see feed
Our idle sheep. So be thou cheered sweet,
And, if thy lute is here, softly intreat
My soul to keep in its resolved course."

Hereat Peona, in their silver source,
Shut her poor sorrow drops with glad exclaim,
And took a lute, from which there pulsing
    came   491
A lively prelude, fashioning the way
In which her voice should wander. 'Twas a
    lay
More subtle cadenced, more forest wild
Than Dryope's lone lulling of her child;
And nothing since has floated in the air
So mournful strange. Surely some influence
    rare
Went, spiritual, through the damsel's hand;
For still, with Delphic emphasis, she spann'd
The quick invisible strings, even though she
    saw   500
Endymion's spirit melt away and thaw
Before the deep intoxication.
But soon she came, with sudden burst, upon
Her self-possession—swung the lute aside,
And earnestly said: "Brother, 'tis vain to hide
That thou dost know of things mysterious,
Immortal, starry; such alone could thus
Weigh down thy nature. Hast thou sinn'd in
    aught
Offensive to the heavenly powers? Caught
A Paphian dove upon a message sent?   510
Thy deathful bow against some deer-herd
    bent,
Sacred to Dian? Haply, thou hast seen
Her naked limbs among the alders green;
And that, alas! is death. No I can trace
Something more high perplexing in thy face!"
Endymion look'd at her, and press'd her
    hand,
And said, "Art thou so pale, who wast so
    bland
And merry in our meadows? How is this?
Tell me thine ailment: tell me all amiss!—
Ah! thou hast been unhappy at the change 520
Wrought suddenly in me. What indeed more
    strange?
Or more complete to overwhelm surmise?
Ambition is no sluggard: 't is no prize,
That toiling years would put within my grasp,
That I have sigh'd for: with so deadly gasp
No man e'er panted for a mortal love.

So all have set my heavier grief above
These things which happen. Rightly have they
    done:
I, who still saw the horizontal sun
Heave his broad shoulder o'er the edge of the
    world,   530
Out-facing Lucifer, and then had hurl'd
My spear aloft, as signal for the chace—
I, who, for very sport of heart, would race
With my own steed from Araby; pluck down
A vulture from his towery perching; frown
A lion into growling, loth retire—
To lose, at once, all my toil breeding fire,
And sink thus low! but I will ease my breast
Of secret grief, here in this bowery nest.

"This river does not see the naked sky, 540
Till it begins to progress silverly
Around the western border of the wood,
Whence, from a certain spot, its winding flood
Seems at the distance like a crescent moon:
And in that nook, the very pride of June,
Had I been used to pass my weary eyes;
The rather for the sun unwillingly leaves
So dear a picture of his sovereign power,
And I could witness his most kingly hour,
When he doth tighten up the golden reins, 550
And paces leisurely down amber plains
His snorting four. Now when his chariot last
Its beams against the zodiac-lion cast,
There blossom'd suddenly a magic bed,
Of sacred ditamy, and poppies red:
At which I wondered greatly, knowing well
That but one night had wrought this flowery
    spell;
And, sitting down close by, began to muse
What it might mean. Perhaps, thought I,
    Morpheus,
In passing here, his owlet pinions shook; 560
Or, it may be, ere matron Night uptook
Her ebon urn, young Mercury, by stealth,
Had dipt his rod in it: such garland wealth
Came not by common growth. Thus on I
    thought
Until my head was dizzy and distraught.
Moreover, through the dancing poppies stole
A breeze, most softly lulling to my soul;
And shaping visions all about my sight
Of colors, wings, and bursts of spangly light;
The which became more strange, and strange,
    and dim,   570
And then were gulph'd in a tumultuous swim:
And then I fell asleep. Ah! can I tell
The enchantment that afterwards befel?

Yet it was but a dream: yet such a dream
That never tongue, although it overteem
With mellow utterance, like a craven spring,
Could figure out and to conception bring
All I beheld and felt. Methought I lay
Watching the zenith, where the milky way
Among the stars in virgin splendour pours; 580
And travelling my eye, until the doors
Of heaven appear'd to open for my flight,
I became loth and fearful to alight
From such high soaring by a downward
    glance:
So kept me steadfast in that airy trance,
Spreading imaginary pinions wide.
When, presently, the stars began to glide,
And faint away, before my eager view:
At which I sigh'd that I could not pursue,
And dropt my vision to the horizon's verge;
And lo! from opening clouds, I saw emerge 591
The loveliest moon, that ever silver'd o'er
A shell for Neptune's goblet: she did soar
So passionately bright, my dazzled soul
Commingling with her argent spheres did roll
Through clear and cloudy, even when she
    went
At last into a dark and vapoury tent—
Whereat, methought, the lidless-eyed train
Of planets all were in the blue again.
To commune with those orbs, once more I
    rais'd   600
My sight right upward: but it was quite daz'd
By a bright something, sailing down apace,
Making me quickly veil my eyes and face:
Again I look'd, and, O ye deities,
Who from Olympus watch our destinies!
Whence that completed form of all com-
    pleteness?
Whence came that high perfection of all
    sweetness?
Speak, stubborn earth, and tell me where, O
    where
Hast thou a symbol of her golden hair?   609
Not oat-sheaves drooping in the western
    sun;
Not—thy soft hand, fair sister! let me shun
Such follying before thee—yet she had,
Indeed, locks bright enough to make me mad;
And they were simply gordian'd up and
    braided,
Leaving, in naked comeliness, unshaded,
Her pearl round ears, white neck, and orbed
    brow;
The which were blended in, I know not how,
With such a paradise of lips and eyes,

Blush tinted cheeks, half smiles, and faintest
    sighs,   611
That, when I think thereon, my spirit clings
And plays about its fancy, till the stings
Of human neighbourhood envenom all.
Unto what awful power shall I call?
To what high fane?—Ah! see her hovering
    feet,
More bluely vein'd, more soft, more whitely
    sweet
Than those of sea-born Venus, when she rose
From out her cradle shell. The wind out-
    blows
Her scarf into a fluttering pavilion;
'T is blue, and over-spangled with a million
Of little eyes, as though thou wert to shed, 630
Over the darkest, lushest blue-bell bed,
Handfuls of daisies."—"Endymion, how
    strange!
Dream within dream!"—"She took an airy
    range,
And then, towards me, like a very maid,
Came blushing, waning, willing, and afraid,
And press'd me by the hand: Ah! 'twas too
    much;
Methought I fainted at the charmed touch,
Yet held my recollection, even as one
Who dives three fathoms where the waters run
Gurgling in beds of coral: for anon,   640
I felt upmounted in that region
Where falling stars dart their artillery forth,
And eagles struggle with the buffeting north
That balances the heavy meteor-stone;—
Felt too, I was not fearful, nor alone,
But lapp'd and lull'd along the dangerous
    sky.
Soon, as it seem'd, we left our journeying
    high,
And straightway into frightful eddies swoop'd;
Such as aye muster where grey time has
    scoop'd   649
Huge dens and caverns in a mountain's side:
There hollow sounds arous'd me, and I sigh'd
To faint once more by looking on my bliss—
I was distracted; madly did I kiss
The wooing arms which held me, and did give
My eyes at once to death: but 'twas to live,
To take in draughts of life from the gold
    fount
Of kind and passionate looks; to count, and
    count
The moments, by some greedy help that
    seem'd
A second self, that each might be redeem'd

And plunder'd of its load of blessedness. 660
Ah! desperate mortal! I e'en dar'd to press
Her very cheek against my crowned lip,
And, at that moment, felt my body dip
Into a warmer air; a moment more
Our feet were soft in flowers. There was store
Of newest joys upon that alp. Sometimes
A scent of violets, and blossoming limes,
Loiter'd around us; then of honey cells,
Made delicate from all white-flower bells;
And once, above the edges of our nest,   670
An arch face peep'd,—an Oread as I guess'd.

"Why did I dream that sleep o'er-power'd
    me
In midst of all this heaven? Why not see,
Far off, the shadows of his pinions dark,
And stare them from me? But no, like a spark
That needs must die, although its little beam
Reflects upon a diamond, my sweet dream
Fell into nothing—into stupid sleep.
And so it was, until a gentle creep,
A careful moving caught my waking ears, 680
And up I started: Ah! my sighs, my tears,
My clenched hands;—for lo! the poppies
    hung
Dew-dabbled on their stalks, the ouzel sung
A heavy ditty, and the sullen day
Had chidden herald Hesperus away,
With leaden looks: the solitary breeze
Bluster'd, and slept, and its wild self did teaze
With wayward melancholy; and I thought,
Mark me, Peona! that sometimes it brought
Faint   fare-thee-wells,   and   sigh-shrilled
    adieus!—   690
Away I wander'd—all the pleasant hues
Of heaven and earth had faded: deepest
    shades
Were deepest dungeons; heaths and sunny
    glades
Were full of pestilent light; our taintless rills
Seem'd sooty, and o'er-spread with upturn'd
    gills
Of dying fish; the vermeil rose had blown
In frightful scarlet, and its thorns out-grown
Like spiked aloe. If an innocent bird
Before my heedless footsteps stirr'd, and
    stirr'd
In little journeys, I beheld in it   700
A disguis'd demon, missioned to knit
My soul with under darkness; to entice
My stumblings down some monstrous preci-
    pice:
Therefore I eager followed, and did curse

The disappointment. Time, that aged nurse,
Rock'd me to patience. Now, thank gentle
    heaven!
These things, with all their comfortings, are
    given
To my down-sunken hours, and with thee,
Sweet sister, help to stem the ebbing sea
Of weary life."

                    Thus ended he, and both 710
Sat silent: for the maid was very loth
To answer; feeling well that breathed words
Would all be lost, unheard, and vain as swords
Against the enchased crocodile, or leaps
Of grasshoppers against the sun. She weeps,
And wonders; struggles to devise some blame;
To put on such a look as would say, *Shame
On this poor weakness!* but, for all her strife,
She could as soon have crush'd away the life
And crushed out lives, by secret barbarous
    ways.
From a sick dove. At length, to break the
    pause,   720
She said with trembling chance: "Is this the
    cause?
This all? Yet it is strange, and sad, alas!
That one who through this middle earth
    should pass
Most like a sojourning demi-god, and leave
His name upon the harp-string, should achieve
No higher bard than simple maidenhood,
Singing alone, and fearfully,—how the blood
Left his young cheek; and how he used to
    stray
He knew not where; and how he would say,
    nay,   729
If any said 'twas love: and yet 'twas love;
What could it be but love? How a ring-dove
Let fall a sprig of yew tree in his path;
And how he died: and then, that love doth
    scathe,
The gentle heart, as northern blasts do roses;
And then the ballad of his sad life closes
With sighs, and an alas!—Endymion!
Be rather in the trumpet's mouth,—anon
Among the winds at large—that all may
    hearken!
Although, before the crystal heavens darken,
I watch and dote upon the silver lakes   740
Pictur'd in western cloudiness, that takes
The semblance of gold rocks and bright gold
    sands,
Islands, and creeks, and amber-fretted strands
With horses prancing o'er them, palaces

And towers of amethyst,—would I so tease
My pleasant days, because I could not mount
Into those regions? The Morphean fount
Of that fine element that visions, dreams,
And fitful whims of sleep are made of, streams
Into its airy channels with so subtle,   750
So thin a breathing, not the spider's shuttle,
Circled a million times within the space
Of a swallow's nest door, could lay a trace,
A tinting of its quality: how light
Must dreams themselves be; seeing they're
        more slight
Than the mere nothing that engenders them!
Then wherefore sully the entrusted gem
Of high and noble life with thoughts so sick?
Why pierce high-fronted honor to the quick
For nothing but a dream?" Hereat the youth
Look'd up: a conflicting of shame and ruth 761
Was in his plaited brow: yet, his eyelids
Widened a little, as when Zephyr bids
A little breeze to creep between the fans
Of careless butterflies: amid his pains
He seem'd to taste a drop of manna-dew,
Full palatable; and a colour grew
Upon his cheek, while thus he lifeful spake:

"Peona! ever have I long'd to slake
My thirst for the world's praises: nothing
        base,   770
No merely slumberous phantasm, could unlace
The stubborn canvas for my voyage pre-
        par'd—
Though now 't is tatter'd; leaving my bark
        bar'd
And sullenly drifting; yet my higher hope
Is of too wide, too rainbow-large a scope,
To fret at myriads of earthly wrecks.
Wherein lies happiness? In that which becks
Our ready minds to fellowship divine,
A fellowship with essence; till we shine,
Full alchemiz'd, and free of space. Behold 780
The clear religion of heaven! Fold
A rose leaf round thy finger's taperness,
And soothe thy lips: hist, when the airy stress
Of music's kiss impregnates the free winds,
And with a sympathetic touch unbinds
Æolian magic from their lucid wombs:
Then old songs waken from enclouded tombs;
Old ditties sigh above their father's grave;
Ghosts of melodious prophesyings rave
Round every spot where trod Apollo's foot;
Bronze clarions awake, and faintly bruit, 791
Where long ago a giant battle was;
And, from the turf, a lullaby doth pass

In every place where infant Orpheus slept.
Feel we these things?—that moment have we
        stept
Into a sort of oneness, and our state
Is like a floating spirit's. But there are
Richer entanglements, enthralments far
More self-destroying, leading, by degrees,
To the chief intensity: the crown of these 800
Is made of love and friendship, and sits high
Upon the forehead of humanity.
All its more ponderous and bulky worth
Is friendship, whence there ever issues forth
A steady splendor; but at the tip-top,
There hangs by unseen film, an orbed drop
Of light, and that is love: its influence,
Thrown in our eyes, genders a novel sense,
At which we start and fret; till in the end,
Melting into its radiance, we blend,   810
Mingle, and so become a part of it,—
Nor with aught else can our souls interknit
So wingedly: when we combine therewith,
Life's self is nourish'd by its proper pith,
And we are nurtured like a pelican brood.
Aye, so delicious is the unsating food,
That men, who might have tower'd in the van
Of all the congregated world, to fan
And winnow from the coming step of time
All chaff of custom, wipe away all slime 820
Left by men-slugs and human serpentry,
Have been content to let occasion die,
Whilst they did sleep in love's elysium.
And, truly, I would rather be struck dumb,
Than speak against this ardent listlessness:
For I have ever thought that it might bless
The world with benefits unknowingly;
As does the nightingale, upperched high,
And cloister'd among cool and bunched
        leaves—
She sings but to her love, nor e'er conceives 830
How tiptoe Night holds back her dark-grey
        hood.
Just so may love, although 't is understood
The mere commingling of passionate breath,
Produce more than our searching witnesseth:
What I know not: but who, of men, can tell
That flowers would bloom, or that green fruit
        would swell
To melting pulp, that fish would have bright
        mail,
The earth its dower of river, wood, and vale,
The meadows runnels, runnels pebble-stones,
The seed its harvest, or the lute its tones, 840
Tones ravishment, or ravishment its sweet
If human souls did never kiss and greet?

"Now, if this earthly love has power to
  make
Men's being mortal, immortal; to shake
Ambition from their memories, and brim
Their measure of content; what merest whim,
Seems all this poor endeavor after fame,
To one, who keeps within his stedfast aim
A love immortal, an immortal too.
Look not so wilder'd; for these things are
  true,   850
And never can be born of atomies
That buzz about our slumbers, like brain-flies,
Leaving us fancy-sick. No, no, I'm sure,
My restless spirit never could endure
To brood so long upon one luxury,
Unless it did, though fearfully, espy
A hope beyond the shadow of a dream.
My sayings will the less obscured seem,
When I have told thee how my waking sight
Has made me scruple whether that same night
Was pass'd in dreaming. Hearken, sweet
  Peona!   861
Beyond the matron-temple of Latona,
Which we should see but for these darkening
  boughs,
Lies a deep hollow, from whose ragged brows
Bushes and trees do lean all round athwart,
And meet so nearly, that with wings out-
  raught,
And spreaded tail, a vulture could not glide
Past them, but he must brush on every side.
Some moulder'd steps lead into this cool cell,
Far as the slabbed margin of a well,   870
Whose patient level peeps its crystal eye
Right upward, through the bushes, to the sky.
Oft have I brought thee flowers, on their stalks
  set
Like vestal primroses, but dark velvet
Edges them round, and they have golden pits:
'Twas there I got them, from the gaps and
  slits
In a mossy stone, that sometimes was my
  seat,
When all above was faint with mid-day heat.
And there in strife no burning thoughts to
  heed,
I'd bubble up the water through a reed;   880
So reaching back to boyhood: make me ships
Of moulted feathers, touchwood, alder chips,
With leaves stuck in them; and the Neptune
  be
Of their petty ocean. Oftener, heavily,
When love-lorn hours had left me less a child,
I sat contemplating the figures wild

Of o'er-head clouds melting the mirror
  through.
Upon a day, while thus I watch'd, by flew
A cloudy Cupid, with his bow and quiver;
So plainly character'd, no breeze would shiver
The happy chance: so happy, I was fain   891
To follow it upon the open plain,
And, therefore, was just going; when, behold!
A wonder, fair as any I have told—
The same bright face I tasted in my sleep,
Smiling in the clear well. My heart did leap
Through the cool depth.—It mov'd as if to
  flee—
I started up, when lo! refreshfully,
There came upon my face, in plenteous show-
  ers,
Dew-drops, and dewy buds, and leaves, and
  flowers,   900
Wrapping all objects from my smothered
  sight,
Bathing my spirit in a new delight.
Aye, such a breathless honey-feel of bliss
Alone preserv'd me from the dread abyss
Of death, for the fair form had gone again.
Pleasure is oft a visitant; but pain
Clings cruelly to us, like the gnawing sloth
On the deer's tender haunches: late, and loth,
'T is scar'd away by slow returning pleasure.
How sickening, how dark the dreadful leisure
Of weary days, made deeper exquisite,   911
By a fore-knowledge of unslumbrous night!
Like sorrow came upon me, heavier still,
Than when I wander'd from the poppy hill:
And a whole age of lingering moments crept
Sluggishly by, ere more contentment swept
Away at once the deadly yellow spleen.
Yes, thrice have I this fair enchantment seen;
Once more been tortured with renewed life.
When last the wintry gusts gave over strife 920
With the conquering sun of spring, and left
  the skies
Warm and serene, but yet with moistened
  eyes
In pity of the shatter'd infant buds,—
That time thou didst adorn, with amber studs,
My hunting cap, because I laugh'd and smil'd,
Chatted with thee, and many days exil'd
All torment from my breast;—'t was even
  then,
Straying about, yet, coop'd up in the den
Of helpless discontent,—hurling my lance
From place to place, and following at chance,
At last, by hap, through some young trees it
  struck,   931

And, plashing among bedded pebbles, stuck
In the middle of a brook,—whose silver ramble
Down twenty little falls, through reeds and
     bramble,
Tracing along, it brought me to a cave,
Whence it ran brightly forth, and white did
     lave
The nether sides of mossy stones and rock,—
'Mong which it gurgled blythe adieus, to mock
Its own sweet grief at parting. Overhead,
Hung a lush screen of drooping weeds, and
     spread   940
Thick, as to curtain up some wood-nymph's
     home.
"Ah! impious mortal, whither do I roam?"
Said I, low voic'd: "Ah, whither! 'Tis the
     grot
"Of Proserine, when Hell, obscure and hot,
"Doth her resign; and where her tender hands
"She dabbles, on the cool and sluicy sands:
"Or 'tis the cell of Echo, where she sits,
"And babbles thorough silence, till her wits
"Are gone in tender madness, and anon,
"Faints into sleep, with many a dying tone   950
"Of sadness. O that she would take my vows,
"And breathe them sighingly among the
     boughs,
"To sue her gentle ears for whose fair head,
"Daily, I pluck sweet flowerets from their bed,
"And weave them dyingly—send honey-
     whispers
"Round every leaf, that all those gentle lispers
"May sigh my love unto her pitying!
"Oh charitable echo! hear, and sing
"This ditty to her!—tell her"—so I stay'd
My foolish tongue, and listening, half afraid,
Stood stupefied with my own empty folly,   961
And blushing for the freaks of melancholy.
Salt tears were coming, when I heard my
     name
Most fondly lipp'd, and then these accents
     came:
"Endymion! the cave is secreter
"Than the isle of Delos. Echo hence shall stir
"No sighs but sigh-warm kisses, or light noise
"Of thy combing hand, the while it travelling
     cloys
"And trembles through my labyrinthine hair."
At that oppress'd I hurried in.—Ah! where   970
Are those swift moments? Whither are they
     fled:
I'll smile no more, Peona; nor will wed
Sorrow the way to death; but patiently
Bear up against it: so farewell, sad sigh;

And come instead demurest meditation,
To occupy me wholly, and to fashion
My pilgrimage for the world's dusky brink.
No more will I count over, link by link,
My chain of grief: no longer strive to find
A half-forgetfulness in mountain wind   980
Blustering about my ears: aye, thou shalt see,
Dearest of sisters, what my life shall be;
What a calm round of hours shall make my
     days.
There is a paly flame of hope that plays
Where'er I look: but yet, I'll say 't is naught—
And here I bid it die. Have not I caught,
Already, a more healthy countenance?
By this the sun is setting; we may chance
Meet some of our near-dwellers with my car."

     This said, he rose, faint-smiling like a star
Through autumn mists, and took Peona's
     hand: 991
They stept into the boat, and launch'd from
     land.

LAMIA

PART I

UPON a time, before the faery broods
Drove Nymph, and Satyr from the prosperous
     woods,
Before King Oberon's bright diadem,
Sceptre, and mantle, clasp'd with dewy gem,
Frighted away the Dryads and the Fauns
From rushes green, and brakes, and cowslip'd
     lawns,
The ever-smitten Hermes empty left
His golden throne, bent warm on amorous
     theft:
From high Olympus had he stolen light,
On this side of Jove's clouds, to escape the
     sight   10
Of his great summoner, and made retreat
Into a forest on the shores of Crete.
For somewhere in that sacred island dwelt
A nymph, to whom all hoofed Satyrs knelt;
At whose white feet the languid Tritons
     poured
Pearls, while on land they wither'd and adored.
Fast by the springs where she to bathe was
     wont,
And in those meads where sometime she might
     haunt,
Were strewn rich gifts, unknown to any Muse,

Though Fancy's casket were unlock'd to
  choose.   20
Ah, what a world of love was at her feet!
So Hermes thought, and a celestial heat
Burnt from his winged heels to either ear,
That from a whiteness, as the lily clear,
Blush'd into roses 'mid his golden hair,
Fallen in jealous curls about his shoulders
  bare.

From vale to vale, from wood to wood, he
  flew,
Breathing upon the flowers his passion new,
And wound with many a river to its head,
To find where this sweet nymph prepar'd her
  secret bed: 30
In vain; the sweet nymph might nowhere be
  found,
And so he rested, on the lonely ground,
Pensive, and full of painful jealousies
Of the Wood-Gods, and even the very trees.
There as he stood, he heard a mournful voice,
Such as once heard, in gentle heart, destroys
All pain but pity: thus the lone voice spake:
"When from this wreathed tomb shall I
  awake!
"When move in a sweet body fit for life,
"And love, and pleasure, and the ruddy strife
"Of hearts and lips! Ah, miserable me!"   41
The God, dovefooted, glided silently
Round bush and tree, soft-brushing, in his
  speed,
The taller grasses and full-flowering weed,
Until he found a palpitating snake,
Bright, and cirque-couchant in a dusky brake.

She was a gordian shape of dazzling hue,
Vermilion-spotted, golden, green, and blue;
Strip'd like a zebra, freckled like a pard,
Ey'd like a peacock, and all crimson barr'd;   50
And full of silver moons, that, as she breathed,
Dissolv'd, or brighter shone, or interwreathed
Their lustres with the gloomier tapestries—
So rainbow-sided, touch'd with miseries,
She seem'd at once, some penanc'd lady elf,
Some demon's mistress, or the demon's self.
Upon her crest she wore a wannish fire
Sprinkled with stars, like Ariadne's tiar:
Her head was serpent, but ah, bitter-sweet!
She had a woman's mouth with all its pearls
  complete: 60
And for her eyes: what could such eyes do
  there

But weep, and weep, that they were born so
  fair?
As Proserpine still weeps for her Sicilian air.
Her throat was serpent, but the words she
  spake
Came, as through bubbling honey, for Love's
  sake,
And thus; while Hermes on his pinions lay,
Like a stoop'd falcon ere he takes his prey.

"Fair Hermes, crown'd with feathers, flut-
  tering light,
"I had a splendid dream of thee last night:
"I saw thee sitting, on a throne of gold,   70
"Among the Gods, upon Olympus old,
"The only sad one; for thou didst not hear
"The soft, lute-finger'd Muses chaunting clear,
"Nor even Apollo when he sang alone,
"Deaf to his throbbing throat's long, long
  melodious moan.
"I dreamt I saw thee, rob'd in purple flakes,
"Break amorous through the clouds, as morn-
  ing breaks,
"And, swiftly as a bright Phœbean dart,
"Strike for the Cretan isle; and here thou
  art!
"Too gentle Hermes, hast thou found the
  maid?"   80
Whereat the star of Lethe not delay'd
His rosy eloquence, and thus inquired:
"Thou smooth-lipped serpent, surely high in-
  spired!
"Thou beauteous wreath, with melancholy
  eyes,
"Possess whatever bliss thou canst devise,
"Telling me only where my nymph is fled.—
"Where she doth breathe!" "Bright planet,
  thou hast said,"
Returned the snake, "but seal with oaths,
  fair God!"
"I swear," said Hermes, "by my serpent rod,
"And by thine eyes, and by thy starry crown!"
Light flew his earnest words, among the blos-
  soms blown.   91
Then thus again the brilliance feminine:
"Too frail of heart! for this lost nymph of
  thine,
"Free as the air, invisibly, she strays
"About these thornless wilds; her pleasant
  days
"She tastes unseen; unseen her nimble feet
"Leave traces in the grass and flowers sweet;
"From weary tendrils, and bow'd branches
  green,

"She plucks the fruit unseen, she bathes unseen:
"And by my power is her beauty veil'd 100
"To keep it unaffronted, unassail'd
"By the love-glances of unlovely eyes,
"Of satyrs, Fauns, and blear'd Silenus' sighs.
"Pale grew her immortality, for woe
"Of all these lovers, and she grieved so
"I took compassion on her, bade her steep
"Her hair in weird syrops, that would keep
"Her loveliness invisible, yet free
"To wander as she loves, in liberty.
"Thou shalt behold her, Hermes, thou alone,
"If thou wilt, as thou swearest, grant my
    boon." 111
Then, once again, the charméd God began
An oath, and through the serpent's ears it ran
Warm, tremulous, devout, psalterian.
Ravish'd, she lifted her Circean head,
Blush'd a live damask, and swift-lisping said,
"I was a woman, let me have once more
"A woman's shape, and charming as before.
"I love a youth of Corinth— O the bliss!
"Give me my woman's form, and place me
    where he is. 120
"Stoop, Hermes, let me breathe upon thy
    brow,
"And thou shalt see thy sweet nymph even
    now."
The God on half-shut feathers sank serene,
She breath'd upon his eyes, and swift was
    seen
Of both the guarded nymph near-smiling on
    the green.
It was no dream; or say a dream it was,
Real are the dreams of Gods, and smoothly
    pass
Their pleasures in a long immortal dream,
One warm, flush'd moment, hovering, it might
    seem
Dash'd by the wood-nymph's beauty, so he
    burn'd; 130
Then, lighting on the printless verdure, turn'd
To the swoon'd serpent, and with languid arm,
Delicate, put to proof the lythe Caducean
    charm.
So done, upon the nymph his eyes he bent
Full of adoring tears and blandishment,
And towards her stept: she, like a moon in
    wane,
Faded before him, cower'd, nor could restrain
Her fearful sobs, self-folding like a flower
That faints into itself at evening hour:
But the God fostering her chilled hand 140

She felt the warmth, her eyelids open'd bland,
And, like new flowers at morning song of bees,
Bloom'd, and gave up her honey to the lees.
Into the green-recessed woods they flew;
Nor grew they pale, as mortal lovers do.

Left to herself, the serpent now began
To change; her elfin blood in madness ran,
Her mouth foam'd, and the grass, therewith
    besprent,
Wither'd at dew so sweet and virulent; 149
Her eyes in torture fix'd, and anguish drear,
Hot, glaz'd, and wide, with lid-lashes all sear,
Flash'd phosphor and sharp sparks, without
    one cooling tear.
The colours all inflam'd throughout her train,
She writh'd about, convuls'd with scarlet pain:
A deep volcanian yellow took the place
Of all her milder-moonéd body's grace;
And, as the lava ravishes the mead,
Spoilt all her silver mail, and golden brede;
Made gloom of all her frecklings, streaks and
    bars,
Eclips'd her crescents, and lick'd up her
    stars: 160
So that, in moments few, she was undrest
Of all her sapphires, greens, and amethyst,
And rubious-argent: of all these bereft,
Nothing but pain and ugliness were left.
Still shone her crown; that vanish'd, also she
Melted and disappear'd as suddenly;
And in the air, her new voice luting soft,
Cry'd, "Lycius! gentle Lycius!"—Borne aloft
With the bright mists about the mountains
    hoar
These words dissolv'd:Crete's forests heard
    no more. 170

Whither fled Lamia, now a lady bright,
A full-born beauty new and exquisite?
She fled into that valley they pass o'er
Who go to Corinth from Cenchreas' shore;
And rested at the foot of those wild hills,
The rugged founts of the Peræan rills,
And of that other ridge whose barren back
Stretches, with all its mist and cloudy rack,
South-westward to Cleone. There she stood
About a young bird's flutter from a wood, 180
Fair, on a sloping green of mossy tread,
By a clear pool, wherein she passioned
To see herself escap'd from so sore ills,
While her robes flaunted with the daffodils.

Ah, happy Lycius!—for she was a maid

More beautiful than ever twisted braid,
Or sigh'd, or blush'd, or on spring-flowered
    lea
Spread a green kirtle to the minstrelsy:
A virgin purest-lipp'd, yet in the lore   189
Of love deep learned to the red heart's core:
Not one hour old, yet of sciential brain
To unperplex bliss from its neighbor pain:
Define their pettish limits, and estrange
Their points of contact, and swift counter-
    change;
Intrigue with the specious chaos, and dispart
Its most ambiguous atoms with sure art;
As though in Cupid's college she had spent
Sweet days a lovely graduate, still unshent,
And kept his rosy terms in idle languishment.

Why this fair creature chose so faerily   200
By the wayside to linger, we shall see;
But first 'tis fit to tell how she could muse
And dream, when in the serpent prison-house,
Of all she list, strange or magnificent:
However, where she will'd, her spirit went;
Whether to faint Elysium, or where
Down through tress-lifting waves the Nereids
    fair
Wind into Thetis' bower by many a pearly
    stair;
Or where God Bacchus drains his cups divine,
Stretch'd out, at ease, beneath a glutinous
    pine;   210
Or where in Pluto's gardens palatine
Mulciber's columns gleam in far piazzian line.
And sometimes into cities she would send
Her dream, with feast and rioting to blend;
And once, while among mortals dreaming thus,
She saw the young Corinthian Lycius
Charioting foremost in the envious race,
Like a young Jove with calm uneager face,
And fell into a swooning love of him.
Now on the moth-time of that evening dim 220
He would return that way, as well she knew,
To Corinth from the shore; for freshly blew
The eastern soft wind, and his galley now
Grated the quaystones with her brazen prow
In port Cenchreas, from Egina isle
Fresh anchor'd; whither he had been awhile
To sacrifice to Jove, whose temple there
Waits with high marble doors for blood and
    incense rare.
Jove heard his vows, and better'd his desire;
For by some freakful chance he made retire 230
From his companions, and set forth to walk,
Perhaps grown wearied of their Corinth talk:

Over the solitary hills he fared,
Thoughtless at first, but ere eve's star ap-
    peared
His phantasy was lost, where reason fades,
In the calm'd twilight of Platonic shades.
Lamia beheld him coming, near, more near—
Close to her passing, in indifference drear,
His silent sandals swept the mossy green;
So neighbour'd to him, as yet so unseen   240
She stood: he pass'd shut up in mysteries,
His mind wrapp'd like his mantle, while her
    eyes
Follow'd his steps, and her neck regal white
Turn'd—syllabling thus, "Ah, Lycius bright,
"And will you leave me on the hills alone?
Lycius, look back! and be some pity shown."
He did; not with cold wonder fearingly,
But Orpheus-like at an Eurydice;
For so delicious were the words she sung,
It seem'd he had lov'd them a whole summer
    long;   250
And soon his eyes had drunk her beauty up,
Leaving no drop in the bewildering cup,
And still the cup was full,—while he, afraid
Lest she should vanish ere his lips had paid
Due adoration, thus began to adore;
Her soft look growing coy, she saw his chain
    so sure:
"Leave thee alone! Look back! Oh, Goddess,
    see
"Whether my eyes can ever turn from thee!
"For pity do not this sad heart belie—
"Even as thou vanishest so I shall die.   260
"Stay! though a Naiad of the rivers, stay!
"To thy far wishes will thy streams obey:
"Stay! though the greenest woods be thy
    domain,
"Alone they can drink up the morning rain:
"Though a descended Pleiad, will not one
"Of thine harmonious sisters keep in tune
"Thy spheres, and as thy silver proxy shine?
"So sweetly to these ravish'd ears of mine
"Came thy sweet greeting, that if thou
    shouldst fade
"Thy memory will waste me to a shade:— 270
"For pity do not melt!"—"If I should stay,"
Said Lamia, "here, upon this floor of clay,
"And pain my steps upon these flowers too
    rough,
"What canst thou say or do of charm enough
"To dull the nice remembrance of my home?
"Thou canst not ask me with thee here to
    roam
"Over these hills, and vales, where no joy is,—

"Empty of immortality and bliss!
"Thou art a scholar, Lycius, and must know
"That finer spirits cannot breathe below   280
"In human climes, and live: Alas! poor youth,
"What taste of purer air hast thou to soothe
"My essence? What serener palaces,
"Where I may all my many senses please,
"And by mysterious sleights a hundred thirsts
     appease?
"It cannot be— Adieu!" So said, she rose
Tiptoe with white arms spread. He, sick to
     lose
The amorous promise of her lone complain,
Swoon'd, murmuring of love, and pale with
     pain.
The cruel lady, without any show   290
Of sorrow for her tender favourite's woe,
But rather, if her eyes could brighter be,
With brighter eyes and slow amenity,
Put her new lips to his, and gave afresh
The life she had so tangled in her mesh:
And as he from one trance was wakening
Into another, she began to sing,
Happy in beauty, life, and love, and every
     thing,
A song of love, too sweet for earthly lyres,
While, like held breath, the stars drew in
     their panting fires.   300
And then she whisper'd in such trembling tone,
As those who, safe together met alone
For the first time through many anguish'd
     days,
Use other speech than looks; bidding him
     raise
His drooping head, and clear his soul of doubt,
For that she was a woman, and without
Any more subtle fluid in her veins
Than throbbing blood, and that the self-same
     pains
Inhabited her frail-strung heart as his.
And next she wonder'd how his eyes could
     miss   310
Her face so long in Corinth, where, she said,
She dwelt but half retir'd, and there had led
Days happy as the gold coin could invent
Without the aid of love; yet in content
Till she saw him, as once she pass'd him
     by,
Where 'gainst a column he leant thoughtfully
At Venus' temple porch, 'mid baskets heap'd
Of amorous herbs and flowers, newly reap'd
Late on that eve, as 'twas the night before
The Adonian feast; whereof she saw no
     more,   320

But wept alone those days, for why should she
     adore?
Lycius from death awoke into amaze,
To see her still, and singing so sweet lays;
Then from amaze into delight he fell
To hear her whisper woman's lore so well;
And every word she spake enticed him on
To unperplex'd delights and pleasure known.
Let the mad poets say whate'er they please,
There is not such a treat among them all,
Haunters of cavern, lake, and waterfall,   330
As a real woman, lineal indeed
From Pyrrha's pebbles or old Adam's seed.
Thus gentle Lamia judg'd, and judg'd aright,
That Lycius could not love in half a fright,
So threw the goddess off, and won his heart
More pleasantly by playing woman's part,
With no more awe than what her beauty gave,
That, while it smote, still guaranteed to save.
Lycius to all made eloquent reply,   340
Marrying to every word a twinborn sigh;
And last, pointing to Corinth, asked her sweet,
If 'twas too far that night for her soft feet.
The way was short, for Lamia's eagerness
Made, by a spell, the triple league decrease
To a few paces; not at all surmised
By blinded Lycius, so in her comprized.
They pass'd the city gates, he knew not how,
So noiseless, and he never thought to know.

As men talk in a dream, so Corinth all,   350
Throughout her palaces imperial,
And all her populous streets and temples
     lewd,
Mutter'd, like tempest in the distance brew'd,
To the wide-spreaded night above her towers.
Men, women, rich and poor, in the cool hours,
Shuffled their sandals o'er the pavement white,
Companion'd or alone; while many a light
Flar'd, here and there, from wealthy festivals,
And threw their moving shadows on the walls,
Or found them cluster'd in the cornic'd shade
Of some arch'd temple door, or dusky
     colonnade.   361

Muffling his face, of greeting friends in fear,
Her fingers he press'd hard, as one came near
With curl'd grey beard, sharp eyes, and
     smooth bald crown,
Slow-stepp'd, and rob'd in philosophic gown:
Lycius shrank closer, as they met and past,
Into his mantle, adding wings to haste,
While hurried Lamia trembled: "Ah," said he,
"Why do you shudder, love, so ruefully?

"Why does your tender palm dissolve in
 dew?"—   370
"I'm wearied," said fair Lamia: "tell me who
"Is that old man? I cannot bring to mind
"His features:—Lycius! wherefore did you
 blind
"Yourself from his quick eyes?" Lycius
 reply'd,
" 'Tis Apollonius sage, my trusty guide
"And good instructor; but to-night he seems
"The ghost of folly haunting my sweet
 dreams."

While yet he spake they had arriv'd before
A pillar'd porch, with lofty portal door,
Where hung a silver lamp, whose phosphor
 glow
Reflected in the slabbed steps below, 381
Mild as a star in water; for so new,
And so unsully'd was the marble's hue,
So through the crystal polish, liquid fine,
Ran the dark veins, that none but feet divine
Could e'er have touch'd there. Sounds Æolian
Breath'd from the hinges, as the ample span
Of the wide doors disclos'd a place unknown
Some time to any but those two alone.
And a few Persian mutes, who that same
 year   390
Were seen about the markets: none knew
 where
They could inhabit; the most curious
Were foil'd, who watch'd to trace them to
 their house:
And but the flitter-winged verse must tell,
For truth's sake, what woe afterwards befell,
'Twould humour many a heart to leave them
 thus,
Shut from the busy world of more incredulous.

PART II

LOVE in a hut, with water and a crust,
Is—Love, forgive us!—cinders, ashes, dust;
Love in a palace is perhaps at last
More grievous torment than a hermit's fast:—
That is a doubtful tale from faery land,
Hard for the non-elect to understand.
Had Lycius liv'd to hand his story down,
He might have given the moral a fresh frown,
Or clench'd it quite: but too short was their
 bliss
To breed distrust and hate, that make the
 soft voice hiss.   10
Besides, there, nightly, with terrific glare,

Love, jealous grown of so complete a pair,
Hover'd and buzz'd his wings, with fearful
 roar,
Above the lintel of their chamber door,
And down the passage cast a glow upon the
 floor.

For all this came a ruin: side by side
They were enthroned, in the even tide,
Upon a couch, near to a curtaining
Whose airy texture, from a golden string,
Floated into the room, and let appear 20
Unveil'd the summer heaven, blue and clear,
Betwixt two marble shafts:—there they re-
 posed,
Where use had made it sweet, with eyelids
 closed,
Saving a tythe which love still open kept,
That they might see each other while they al-
 most slept;
When from the slope side of a suburb hill,
Deafening the swallow's twitter, came a thrill
Of trumpets—Lycius started—the sounds fled,
But left a thought, a buzzing in his head.
For the first time, since first he harbour'd in
That purple-lined palace of sweet sin, 31
His spirits pass'd beyond its golden bourn
Into the noisy world almost forsworn.
The lady, ever watchful, penetrant,
Saw this with pain, so arguing a want
Of something more, more than her empery
Of joys; and she began to moan and sigh
Because he mused beyond her, knowing well
That but a moment's thought is passion's
 passing bell.
"Why do you sigh, fair creature?" whisper'd
 he: 40
"Why do you think?" return'd she tenderly:
"You have deserted me;—where am I now?
"Not in your heart while care weighs on your
 brow:
"No, no, you have dismiss'd me; and I go
"From your breast houseless: aye, it must be
 so."
He answer'd, bending to her open eyes,
Where he was mirror'd small in paradise,
"My silver planet, both of eve and morn!
"Why will you plead yourself so sad forlorn,
"While I am striving how to fill my heart 50
"With deeper crimson, and a double smart?
"How to entangle, trammel up and snare
"Your soul in mine, and labyrinth you there
"Like the hid scent in an unbudded rose?
"Aye, a sweet kiss—you see your mighty woes.

"My thoughts! shall I unveil them? Listen
    then!
"What mortal hath a prize, that other men
"May be confounded and abash'd withal,
"But lets it sometimes pace a broad majestical,
"And triumph, as in thee I should rejoice   60
"Amid the hoarse alarm of Corinth's voice.
"Let my foes choke, and my friends shout
    afar,
"While through the thronged streets your
    bridal car
"Wheels round its dazzling spokes."—The
    lady's cheek
Trembled; she nothing said, but, pale and
    meek,
Arose and knelt before him, wept a rain
Of sorrows at his words; at last with pain
Beseeching him, the while his hand she wrung,
To change his purpose. He thereat was stung,
Perverse, with stronger fancy to reclaim   70
Her wild and timid nature to his aim:
Besides, for all his love, in self-despite,
Against his better self, he took delight
Luxurious in her sorrows, soft and new.
His passion, cruel grown, took on a hue
Fierce and sanguineous as 'twas possible
In one whose brow had no dark veins to swell.
Fine was the mitigated fury, like
Apollo's presence when in act to strike
The serpent— Ha, the serpent! certes, she   80
Was none. She burnt, she lov'd the tyranny,
And, all subdu'd, consented to the hour
When to the bridal he should lead his para-
    mour.
Whispering in midnight silence, said the youth,
"Sure, some sweet name thou hast, though, by
    my truth,
"I have not ask'd it, ever thinking thee
"Not mortal, but of heavenly progeny,
"As still I do. Hast any mortal name,
"Fit appellation for this dazzling frame?
"Or friends or kinsfolk on the citied earth, 90
"To share our marriage feast and nuptial
    mirth?"
"I have no friends," said Lamia, "No, not
    one;
"My presence in wide Corinth hardly known:
"My parents' bones are in their dusty urns
"Sepulchred, where no kindled incense burns,
"Seeing all their luckless race are dead, save
    me,
"And I neglect the holy rite for thee.
"Even as you list invite your many guests;
"But if, as now it seems, your vision rests

"With any pleasure on me, do not bid   100
"Old Apollonius—from him keep me hid."
Lycius, perplex'd at words so blind and blank,
Made close inquiry; from whose touch she
    shrank,
Feigning a sleep; and he to the dull shade
Of deep sleep in a moment was betray'd.

    It was the custom then to bring away
The bride from home at blushing shut of day,
Veil'd, in a chariot, heralded along
By strewn flowers, torches, and a marriage
    song,
With other pageants: but this fair unknown
Had not a friend. So being left alone,   110
(Lycius was gone to summon all his kin)
And knowing surely she could never win
His foolish heart from its mad pompousness,
She set herself, high-thoughted, how to dress
The misery in fit magnificence.
She did so, but 'tis doubtful how and whence
Came, and who were her subtle servitors.
About the halls, and to and from the doors,
There was a noise of wings, till in short
    space   120
The glowing banquet-room shone with wide-
    arched grace.
A haunting music, sole perhaps and lone
Supportress of the faery-roof, made moan
Throughout, as fearful the whole charm
    might fade.
Fresh carved cedar, mimicking a glade
Of palm and plantain, met from either side,
High in the midst, in honor of the bride:
Two palms and then two plantains, and so on,
From either side their stems branch'd one
    to one
All down the aisled place; and beneath all   130
There ran a stream of lamps straight on from
    wall to wall.
So canopy'd, lay an untasted feast
Teeming with odours. Lamia, regal drest,
Silently paced about, and as she went,
In pale contented sort of discontent,
Mission'd her viewless servants to enrich
The fretted splendour of each nook and niche.
Between the tree-stems, marbled plain at
    first,
Came jasper panels; then, anon, there burst
Forth creeping imagery of slighter trees, 140
And with the larger wove in small intricacies.
Approving all, she faded at self-will,
And shut the chamber up, close, hush'd and
    still,

Complete and ready for the revels rude,
When dreadful guests would come to spoil
    her solitude.

The day appear'd, and all the gossip rout.
O senseless Lycius! Madman! wherefore flout
The silent-blessing fate, warm cloister'd hours,
And show to common eyes these secret
    bowers?
The herd approach'd; each guest, with busy
    brain,   150
Arriving at the portal, gaz'd amain,
And enter'd marveling: for they knew the
    street,
Remember'd it from childhood all complete
Without a gap, yet ne'er before had seen
That royal porch, that high-built fair demesne;
So in they hurried all, maz'd, curious and
    keen:
Save one, who look'd thereon with eye severe,
And with calm-planted steps walk'd in aus-
    tere;
'Twas Apollonius: something too he laugh'd,
As though some knotty problem, that had
    daft   160
His patient thought, had now begun to thaw,
And solve and melt:—'twas just as he foresaw.

He met within the murmurous vestibule
His young disciple. " 'Tis no common rule,
"Lycius," said he, "for uninvited guest
"To force himself upon you, and infest
"With an unbidden presence the bright throng
"Of younger friends; yet must I do this
    wrong,
"And you forgive me." Lycius blush'd, and led
The old man through the inner doors broad-
    spread;   170
With reconciling words and courteous mien
Turning into sweet milk the sophist's spleen.

Of wealthy lustre was the banquet-room,
Fill'd with pervading brilliance and perfume:
Before each lucid panel fuming stood
A censer fed with myrrh and spiced wood,
Each by a sacred tripod held aloft,
Whose slender feet wide-swerv'd upon the soft
Wool-woofed carpets: Fifty wreaths of smoke
From fifty censers their light voyage took 180
To the high roof, still mimick'd as they rose
Along the mirror'd walls by twin-clouds odor-
    ous.
Twelve sphered tables, by silk seats in-
    spher'd,

High as the level of a man's breast rear'd
On libbard's paws, upheld the heavy gold
Of cups and goblets, and the store thrice told
Of Cere's horn, and, in huge vessels, wine
Come from the gloomy tun with merry shine.
Thus loaded with a feast the tables stood,
Each shrining in the midst the image of a
    God.   190

When in an antechamber every guest
Had felt the cold full sponge to pleasure
    press'd,
By minist'ring slaves, upon his hands and feet,
And fragrant oils with ceremony meet
Pour'd on his hair, they all mov'd to the
    feast
In white robes, and themselves in order
    placed
Around the silken couches, wondering
Whence all this mighty cost and blaze of
    wealth could spring.

Soft went the music the soft air along,
While fluent Greek a vowel'd undersong 200
Kept up among the guests, discoursing low
At first, for scarcely was the wine at flow;
But when the happy vintage touch'd their
    brains,
Louder they talk, and louder come the strains
Of powerful instruments:—the gorgeous dyes,
The space, the splendor of the draperies,
The roof of awful richness, nectarous cheer,
Beautiful slaves, and Lamia's self, appear,
Now, when the wine has done its rosy deed,
And every soul from human trammels freed,
No more so strange; for merry wine, sweet
    wine,   211
Will make Elysian shades not too fair, too
    divine.
Soon was God Bacchus at meridian height;
Flush'd were their cheeks, and bright eyes
    double bright:
Garlands of every green, and every scent
From vales deflower'd, or forest-trees branch-
    rent,
In baskets of bright osier'd gold were bought
High as the handles heap'd, to suit the thought
Of every guest; that each, as he did please,
Might fancy-fit his brows, silk-pillow'd at his
    ease.   220

What wreath for Lamia? What for Lycius?
What for the sage, old Apollonius?
Upon her aching forehead be there hung

The leaves of willow and of adder's tongue;
And for the youth, quick, let us strip for him
The thyrsus, that his watching eyes may
　　swim
Into forgetfulness; and, for the sage,
Let spear-grass and the spiteful thistle wage
War on his temples. Do not all charms fly
At the mere touch of cold philosophy?　　230
There was an awful rainbow once in heaven:
We know her woof, her texture; she is given
In the dull catalogue of common things.
Philosophy will clip an Angel's wings,
Conquer all mysteries by rule and line,
Empty the haunted air, and gnomed mine—
Unweave a rainbow, as it erewhile made
The tender-person'd Lamia melt into a shade.

By her glad Lycius sitting, in chief place,
Scarce saw in all the room another face,　240
Till, checking his love trance, a cup he took
Full brimm'd, and opposite sent forth a look
'Cross the broad table, to beseech a glance
From his old teacher's wrinkled countenance,
And pledge him. The bald-head philosopher
Had fix'd his eye, without a twinkle or stir
Full on the alarmed beauty of the bride,
Brow-beating her fair form, and troubling her
　　sweet pride.
Lycius then press'd her hand, with devout
　　touch,
As pale it lay upon the rosy couch:　　250
'Twas icy, and the cold ran through his veins;
Then sudden it grew hot, and all the pains
Of an unnatural heat shot to his heart.
"Lamia, what means this? Wherefore dost
　　thou start?
"Know'st thou that man?" Poor Lamia an-
　　swer'd not.
He gaz'd into her eyes, and not a jot
Own'd they the lovelorn piteous appeal:
More, more he gaz'd: his human senses reel:
Some hungry spell that loveliness absorbs;
There was no recognition in those orbs.　260
"Lamia!" he cry'd—and no soft-ton'd reply.
The many heard, and the loud revelry
Grew hush; the stately music no more
　　breathes;
The myrtle sicken'd in a thousand wreaths.
By faint degrees, voice, lute, and pleasure
　　ceased;
A deadly silence step by step increased,
Until it seem'd a horrid presence there,
And not a man but felt the terror in his hair.

"Lamia!" he shriek'd; and nothing but the
　　shriek
With its sad echo did the silence break.　270
"Begone, foul dream!" he cry'd, gazing again
In the bride's face, where now no azure vein
Wander'd on fair-spac'd temples; no soft
　　bloom
Misted the cheek; no passion to illume
The deep-recessed vision:—all was blight;
Lamia, no longer fair, there sat a deadly
　　white.
"Shut, shut those juggling eyes, thou ruthless
　　man!
"Turn them aside, wretch! or the righteous
　　ban
"Of all the Gods, whose dreadful images
"Here represent their shadowy presences,　280
"May pierce them on the sudden with the
　　thorn
"Of painful blindness; leaving thee forlorn,
"In trembling dotage to the feeblest fright
"Of conscience, for their long offended might,
"For all thine impious proud-heart soph-
　　istries,
"Unlawful magic, and enticing lies.
"Corinthians! look upon that grey-beard
　　wretch!
"Mark how, possess'd, his lashless eyelids
　　stretch
"Around his demon eyes! Corinthians, see!
"My sweet bride withers at their potency."　290
"Fool!" said the sophist, in an under-tone
Gruff with contempt; with a death-nighing
　　moan
From Lycius answer'd, as heart-struck and
　　lost,
He sank supine beside the aching ghost.
"Fool! Fool!" repeated he, while his eyes
　　still
Relented not, nor mov'd; "from every ill
"Of life have I preserv'd thee to this day,
"And shall I see thee made a serpent's prey?"
Then Lamia breath'd death breath; the soph-
　　ist's eye,　　299
Like a sharp spear, went through her utterly,
Keen, cruel, perceant, stinging: she, as well
As her weak hand could any meaning tell,
Motion'd him to be silent; vainly so,
He look'd and look'd again a level— No!
"A serpent!" echoed he; no sooner said,
Than with a frightful scream she vanishéd:
And Lycius' arms were empty of delight,
As were his limbs of life, from that same
　　night.

On the high couch he lay!—his friends came
    round—
Supported him—no pulse, or breath he found,
And, in its marriage robe, the heavy body
    wound.   311

ISABELLA; OR, THE POT OF BASIL

I

FAIR Isabel, poor simple Isabel!
    Lorenzo, a young palmer in Love's eye!
They could not in the self-same mansion dwell
    Without some stir of heart, some malady;
They could not sit at meals but feel how well
    It soothed each to be the other by;
They could not, sure, beneath the same roof
    sleep
But to each other dream, and nightly weep.

II

With every morn their love grew tenderer,
    With every eve deeper and tenderer still; 10
He might not in house, field, or garden stir,
    But her full shape would all his seeing fill;
And his continual voice was pleasanter
    To her, than noise of trees or hidden rill;
Her lute-string gave an echo of his name,
She spoilt her half-done broidery with the
    same.

III

He knew whose gentle hand was at the latch,
    Before the door had given her to his eyes;
And from her chamber-window he would catch
    Her beauty farther than the falcon spies; 20
And constant as her vespers would he watch,
    Because her face was turn'd to the same
    skies;
And with sick longing all the night outwear,
To hear her morning-step upon the stair.

IV

A whole long month of May in this sad plight
    Made their cheeks paler by the break of
    June:
"To-morrow will I bow to my delight,
    "To-morrow will I ask my lady's boon."—
"O may I never see another night,
    "Lorenzo, if thy lips breathe not love's
    tune."—   30

So spake they to their pillows; but, alas,
Honeyless days and days did he let pass;

V

Until sweet Isabella's untouch'd cheek
    Fell sick within the rose's just domain,
Fell thin as a young mother's, who doth seek
    By every lull to cool her infant's pain:
"How ill she is," said he, "I may not speak,
    "And yet I will, and tell my love all plain:
"If looks speak love-laws, I will drink her
    tears,
"And at the least 'twill startle off her cares." 40

VI

So said he one fair morning, and all day
    His heart beat awfully against his side;
And to his heart he inwardly did pray
    For power to speak; but still the ruddy tide
Stifled his voice, and puls'd resolve away—
    Fever'd his high conceit of such a bride,
Yet brought him to the meekness of a child:
Alas! when passion is both meek and wild!

VII

So once more he had wak'd and anguished
    A dreary night of love and misery,   50
If Isabel's quick eye had not been wed
    To every symbol on his forehead high;
She saw it waxing very pale and dead,
    And straight all flush'd; so, lisped tenderly,
"Lorenzo!"—here she ceas'd her timid quest,
But in her tone and look he read the rest.

VIII

"O Isabella, I can half perceive
    "That I may speak my grief into thine ear;
"If thou didst ever any thing believe,   59
    "Believe how I love thee, believe how near
"My soul is to its doom: I would not grieve
    "Thy hand by unwelcome pressing, would
    not fear
"Thine eyes by gazing; but I cannot live
"Another night, and not my passion shrive.

IX

"Love! thou art leading me from wintry cold,
    "Lady! thou leadest me to summer clime,
"And I must taste the blossoms that unfold

"In its ripe warmth this gracious morning
   time."
So said, his erewhile timid lips grew bold,
   And poesied with hers in dewy rhyme: 70
Great bliss was with them, and great happiness
Grew, like a lusty flower in June's caress.

X

Parting they seem'd to tread upon the air,
   Twin roses by the zephyr blown apart
Only to meet again more close, and share
   The inward fragrance of each other's heart.
She, to her chamber gone, a ditty fair
   Sang, of delicious love and honey'd dart;
He with light steps went up a western hill,
And bade the sun farewell, and joy'd his fill. 80

XI

All close they met again, before the dusk
   Had taken from the stars its pleasant veil,
All close they met, all eves, before the dusk
   Had taken from the stars its pleasant veil,
Close in a bower of hyacinth and musk,
   Unknown of any, free from whispering tale.
Ah! better had it been for ever so,
Than idle ears should pleasure in their woe.

XII

Were they unhappy then?—It cannot be—
   Too many tears for lovers have been shed, 90
Too many sighs give we to them in fee,
   Too much of pity after they are dead,
Too many doleful stories do we see,
   Whose matter in bright gold were best be
   read;
Except in such a page where Theseus' spouse
Over the pathless waves towards him bows.

XIII

But, for the general award of love,
   The little sweet doth kill much bitterness;
Though Dido silent is in under-grove,
   And Isabella's was a great distress, 100
Though young Lorenzo in warm Indian clove
   Was not embalm'd, this truth is not the less
Even bees, the little almsmen of spring-bowers,
Know there is richest juice in poison-flowers.

XIV

With her two brothers this fair lady dwelt,
   Enriched from ancestral merchandise,
And for them many a weary hand did swelt
   In torched mines and noisy factories,
And many once proud-quiver'd loins did melt
   In blood from stinging whip;—with hollow
   eyes 110
Many all day in dazzling river stood,
To take the rich-ored drifting of the flood.

XV

For them the Ceylon diver held his breath,
   And went all naked to the hungry shark;
For them his ears gush'd blood; for them in
   death
The seal on the cold ice with piteous bark
Lay full of darts; for them alone did seethe
   A thousand men in troubles wide and dark·
Half-ignorant, they turn'd an easy wheel,
That set sharp racks at work, to pinch and
   peel. 120

XVI

Why were they proud? Because their marble
   founts
   Gush'd with more pride than do a wretch's
   tears?—
Why were they proud? Because fair orange-
   mounts
   Were of more soft accent than lazar
   stairs?—
Why were they proud? Because red-lin'd
   accounts
Were richer than the songs of Grecian
   years?—
Why were they proud? again we ask aloud,
Why in the name of Glory were they proud?

XVII

Yet were these Florentines as self-retired
   In hungry pride and gainful cowardice, 130
As two close Hebrews in that land inspired,
   Pal'd in and vineyarded from beggar-spies;
The hawks of ship-mast forests—the untired
   And pannier'd mules for ducats and old
   lies—
Quick cat's-paws on the generous stray-
   away,—
Great wits in Spanish, Tuscan, and Malay.

XVIII

How was it these same ledger-men could spy
  Fair Isabella in her downy nest?
How could they find out in Lorenzo's eye
  A straying from his toil? Hot Egypt's pest
Into their vision covetous and sly!   141
  How could these money-bags see east and
    west?—
Yet so they did—and every dealer fair
Must see behind, as doth the hunted hare.

XIX

O eloquent and famed Boccaccio!
  Of thee we now should ask forgiving boon,
And of thy spicy myrtles as they blow,
  And of thy roses amorous of the moon,
And of thy lillies, that do paler grow
  Now they can no more hear thy ghittern's
    tune,   150
For venturing syllables that ill beseem
The quiet glooms of such a piteous theme.

XX

Grant thou a pardon here, and then the tale
  Shall move on soberly, as it is meet;
There is no other crime, no mad assail
  To make old prose in modern rhyme more
    sweet:
But it is done—succeed the verse or fail—
  To honour thee, and thy gone spirit greet;
To stead thee as a verse in English tongue,
And echo of thee in the north-wind sung.   160

XXI

These brethren having found by many signs
  What love Lorenzo for their sister had,
And how she lov'd him too, each unconfines
  His bitter thoughts to other, well nigh mad
That he, the servant of their trade designs,
  Should in their sister's love be blithe and
    glad,
When 'twas their plan to coax her by degrees
To some high noble and his olive-trees.

XXII

And many a jealous conference had they,
  And many times they bit their lips alone,   170
Before they fixed upon a surest way.
  To make the youngster for his crime atone;

And at the last, these men of cruel clay
  Cut Mercy with a sharp knife to the bone;
For they resolved in some forest dim
To kill Lorenzo and there bury him.

XXIII

So on a pleasant morning, as he leant
  Into the sun-rise, o'er the balustrade
Of the garden-terrace, towards him they bent
  Their footing through the dews; and to him
    said,   180
"You seem there in the quiet of content,
  "Lorenzo, and we are most loath to invade
"Calm speculation; but if you are wise,
"Bestride your steed while cold is in the skies.

XXIV

"To-day we purpose, aye, this hour we mount
  "To spur three leagues toward the Apennine;
"Come down, we pray thee, ere the hot sun
    count
  "His dewy rosary on the eglantine."
Lorenzo, courteously as he was wont,
  Bow'd a fair greeting to these serpents'
    whine;   190
And went in haste, to get in readiness,
With belt, and spur, and bracing huntsman's
    dress.

XXV

And as he to the court-yard pass'd along,
  Each third step did he pause, and listen'd
    oft
If he could hear his lady's matin-song,
  Or the light whisper of her footstep soft;
And as he thus over his passion hung,
  He heard a laugh full musical aloft;
When, looking up, he saw her features bright
Smile through an in-door lattice, all delight. 200

XXVI

"Love, Isabel!" said he, "I was in pain
  "Lest I should miss to bid thee a good
    morrow:
"Ah! what if I should lose thee, when so fain
  "I am to stifle all the heavy sorrow
"Of a poor three hours' absence? but we'll
    gain
  "Out of the amorous dark what day doth
    borrow.

"Good bye! I'll soon be back."—"Good bye!"
   said she:
And as he went she chanted merrily.

XXVII

So the two brothers and their murder'd man
   Rode past fair Florence, to where Arno's
      stream   210
Gurgles through straiten'd banks, and still
      doth fan
Itself with dancing bulrush, and the bream
Keeps head against the freshets. Sick and wan
   The brothers' faces in the ford did seem,
Lorenzo's flush with love.—They pass'd the
      water
Into a forest quiet for the slaughter.

XXVIII

There was Lorenzo slain and buried in,
   There in that forest did his great love cease;
Ah! when a soul doth thus its freedom win,
   It aches in loneliness—is ill at peace   220
As the break-covert blood-hounds of such sin;
   They dipp'd their swords in the water, and
      did tease
Their horses homeward, with convulsed spur,
Each richer by his being a murderer.

XXIX

They told their sister how, with sudden speed,
   Lorenzo had ta'en ship for foreign lands,
Because of some great urgency and need
   In their affairs' requiring trusty hands.
Poor Girl! put on thy stifling widow's weed,
   And 'scape at once from Hope's accursed
      bands;   230
To-day thou wilt not see him, nor to-morrow,
And the next day will be a day of sorrow.

XXX

She weeps alone for pleasures not to be;
   Sorely she wept until the night came on,
And then, instead of love, O misery!
   She brooded o'er the luxury alone:
His image in the dusk she seem'd to see,
   And to the silence made a gentle moan,
Spreading her perfect arms upon the air,
And on her couch low murmuring "Where? O
   where?"   240

XXXI

But Selfishness, Love's cousin, held not long
   Its fiery vigil in her single breast;
She fretted for the golden hour, and hung
   Upon the time with feverish unrest—
Not long—for soon into her heart a throng
   Of higher occupants, a richer zest,
Came tragic; passion not to be subdu'd,
And sorrow for her love in travels rude.

XXXII

In the mid days of autumn, on their eves
   The breath of Winter comes from far away,
And the sick west continually bereaves   250
   Of some gold tinge, and plays a roundelay
Of death among the bushes and the leaves,
   To make all bare before he dares to stray
From his north cavern. So sweet Isabel
By gradual decay from beauty fell,

XXXIII

Because Lorenzo came not. Oftentimes
   She ask'd her brothers, with an eye all pale,
Striving to be itself, what dungeon climes
   Could keep him off so long? They spake a
      tale   260
Time after time, to quiet her. Their crimes
   Came on them, like a smoke from Hinnom's
      vale;
And every night in dreams they groan'd aloud,
To see their sister in her snowy shroud.

XXXIV

And she had died in drowsy ignorance,
   But for a thing more deadly dark than all;
It came like a fierce potion, drunk by chance,
   Which saves a sick man from the feather'd
      pall
For some few gasping moments; like a lance
   Waking an Indian from his cloudy hall   270
With cruel pierce, and bringing him again
Sense of the gnawing fire at heart and brain.

XXXV

It was a vision.—In the drowsy gloom,
   The dull of midnight, at her couch's foot
Lorenzo stood, and wept: the forest tomb
   Had marr'd his glossy hair which once
      could shoot

Lustre into the sun, and put cold doom
  Upon his lips, and take the soft lute
From his lorn voice, and past his loamed ears
Had made a miry channel for his tears. 280

XXXVI

Strange sound it was, when the pale shadow
    spake;
  For there was striving, in its piteous tongue,
To speak as when on earth it was awake,
  And Isabella on its music hung:
Languor there was in it, and tremulous shake,
  As in a palsied Druid's harp unstrung;
And through it moan'd a ghostly under-song,
Like hoarse night-gusts sepulchral briars
    among.

XXXVII

Its eyes, though wild, were still all dewy bright
  With love, and kept all phantom fear aloof
From the poor girl by magic of their light, 291
  The while it did unthread the horrid woof
Of the late darken'd time,—the murderous
    spite
  Of pride and avarice,—the dark pine roof
In the forest,—and the sodden turfed dell,
Where, without any word, from stabs he fell.

XXXVIII

Saying moreover, "Isabel, my sweet!
  "Red whortle-berries droop above my head,
"And a large flint-stone weighs upon my feet;
  "Around me beeches and high chestnuts
    shed   300
"Their leaves and prickly nuts; a sheep-fold
    bleat
  "Comes from beyond the river to my bed:
"Go, shed one tear upon my heather-bloom,
"And it shall comfort me within the tomb.

XXXIX

"I am a shadow now, alas! alas!
  "Upon the skirts of human-nature dwelling
"Alone: I chant alone the holy mass,
  "While little sounds of life are round me
    knelling,
"And glossy bees at noon do fieldward pass,
  "And many a chapel bell the hour is telling,
"Paining me through: those sounds grow
    strange to me,   311
"And thou art distant in Humanity.

XL

"I know what was, I feel full well what is,
  "And I should rage, if spirits could go mad;
"Though I forgot the taste of earthly bliss,
  "That paleness warms my grave, as though
    I had
"A Seraph chosen from the bright abyss
  "To be my spouse: thy paleness makes me
    glad;
"Thy beauty grows upon me, and I feel 319
"A greater love through all my essence steal."

XLI

The Spirit mourn'd "Adieu!"—dissolv'd, and
    left
  The atom darkness in a slow turmoil;
As when of healthful midnight sleep bereft,
  Thinking on rugged hours and fruitless toil,
We put our eyes into a pillowy cleft,
  And see the spangly gloom froth up and
    boil:
It made sad Isabella's eyelids ache,
And in the dawn she started up awake;

XLII

"Ha! ha!" said she, "I knew not this hard
    life,
  "I thought the worst was simple misery; 330
"I thought some Fate with pleasure or with
    strife
  "Portion'd us—happy days, or else to die;
"But there is crime—a brother's bloody knife!
  "Sweet Spirit, thou hast school'd my in-
    fancy:
"I'll visit thee for this, and kiss thine eyes,
"And greet thee morn and even in the skies."

XLIII

When the full morning came, she had de-
    vised
  How she might secret to the forest hie;
How she might find the clay, so dearly prized,
  And sing to it one latest lullaby;   340
How her short absence might be unsurmised,
  While she the inmost of the dream would
    try.
Resolv'd, she took with her an aged nurse,
And went into that dismal forest-hearse.

XLIV

See, as they creep along the river side,
  How she doth whisper to that aged Dame,
And, after looking round the champaign wide,
  Shows her a knife.—"What feverous hectic
      flame
"Burns in thee, child?—What good can thee
      betide,
  "That thou should'st smile again?"—The
      evening came,   350
And they had found Lorenzo's earthy bed;
The flint was there, the berries at his head.

XLV

Who hath not loiter'd in a green church-yard,
  And let his spirit, like a demon-mole,
Work through the clayey soil and gravel
      hard,
  To see scull, coffin'd bones, and funeral
      stole;
Pitying each form that hungry Death hath
      marr'd,
  And filling it once more with human soul?
Ah! this is holiday to what was felt
When Isabella by Lorenzo knelt.   360

XLVI

She gazed into the fresh-thrown mould, as
      though
  One glance did fully all its secrets tell;
Clearly she saw, as other eyes would know
  Pale limbs at bottom of a crystal well;
Upon the murderous spot she seem'd to grow,
  Like to a native lily of the dell:
Then with her knife, all sudden, she began
To dig more fervently than misers can.

XLVII

Soon she turn'd up a soiled glove, whereon
  Her silk had play'd in purple phantasies, 370
She kiss'd it with a lip more chill than stone,
  And put it in her bosom, where it dries
And freezes utterly unto the bone
  Those dainties made to still an infant's
      cries:
Then 'gan she work again; nor stay'd her care,
But to throw back at times her veiling hair.

XLVIII

That old nurse stood beside her wondering,
  Until her heart felt pity to the core
At sight of such a dismal laboring,
  And so she kneeled, with her locks all hoar,
And put her lean hands to the horrid thing: 381
  Three hours they labour'd at this travail
      sore;
At last they felt the kernel of the grave,
And Isabella did not stamp and rave.

XLIX

Ah! wherefore all this wormy circumstance?
  Why linger at the yawning tomb so long?
O for the gentleness of old Romance,
  The simple plaining of a minstrel's song!
Fair reader, at the old tale take a glance,
  For here, in truth, it doth not well belong 390
To speak:—O turn thee to the very tale,
And taste the music of that vision pale.

LI

With duller steel than the Perséan sword
  They cut away no formless monster's head,
But one, whose gentleness did well accord
  With death, as life. The ancient harps have
      said,
Love never dies, but lives, immortal Lord:
  If Love impersonate was ever dead,
Pale Isabella kiss'd it, and low moan'd.
  'Twas love; cold,—dead indeed, but not de-
      thron'd.   400

LI

In anxious secrecy they took it home,
  And then the prize was all for Isabel:
She calm'd its wild hair with a golden comb,
  And all around each eye's sepulchral cell
Pointed each fringéd lash; the smearéd loam
  With tears, as chilly as a dripping well,
She drench'd away:—and still she comb'd, and
      kept
Sighing all day—and still she kiss'd, and wept.

LII

Then in a silken scarf,—sweet with the dews
  Of precious flowers pluck'd in Araby,   410
And divine liquids come with odorous ooze

Through the cold serpent-pipe refresh-
    fully,—
She wrapp'd it up; and for its tomb did choose
    A garden-pot, wherein she laid it by,
And cover'd it with mould, and o'er it set
    Sweet Basil, which her tears kept ever wet.

LIII

And she forgot the stars, the moon, and sun,
    And she forgot the blue above the trees,
And she forgot the dells where waters run,
    And she forgot the chilly autumn breeze; 420
She had no knowledge when the day was done,
    And the new morn she saw not: but in
        peace
Hung over her sweet Basil evermore,
And moisten'd it with tears unto the core.

LIV

And so she ever fed it with thin tears,
    Whence thick, and green, and beautiful it
        grew,
So that it smelt more balmy than its peers
    Of Basil-tufts in Florence; for it drew
Nurture besides, and life, from human fears,
    From the fast mouldering head there shut
        from view: 430
So that the jewel, safely casketed,
Came forth, and in perfumed leafits spread.

LV

O Melancholy, linger here awhile!
    O Music, Music, breathe despondingly!
O Echo, Echo, from some sombre isle,
    Unknown, Lethean, sigh to us— O sigh!
Spirits in grief, lift up your heads, and smile;
    Lift up your heads, sweet Spirits, heavily,
And make a pale light in your cypress glooms,
Tinting with silver wan your marble tombs. 440

LVI

Moan hither, all ye syllables of woe,
    From the deep throat of sad Melpomene.
Through bronzed lyre in tragic order go,
    And touch the strings into a mystery;
Sound mournfully upon the winds and low;
    For simple Isabel is soon to be
Among the dead: She withers, like a palm
Cut by an Indian for its juicy balm.

LVII

O leave the palm to wither by itself;
    Let not quick Winter chill its dying hour!—
It may not be—those Baälites of pelf, 451
    Her brethren, noted the continual shower
From her dead eyes; and many a curious elf,
    Among her kindred, wonder'd that such
        dower
Of youth and beauty should be thrown aside
By one mark'd out to be a Noble's bride.

LVIII

And, furthermore, her brethren wonder'd
    much
    Why she sat drooping by the Basil green,
And why it flourish'd, as by magic touch;
    Greatly they wonder'd what the thing might
        mean: 460
They could not surely give belief, that such
    A very nothing would have power to wean
Her from her own fair youth, and pleasures
    gay,
And even remembrance of her love's delay.

LIX

Therefore they watch'd a time when they
    might sift
    This hidden whim; and long they watch'd
        in vain;
For seldom did she go to chapel-shrift,
    And seldom felt she any hunger-pain;
And when she left, she hurried back, as swift
    As bird on wing to breast its eggs again; 470
And, patient as a hen-bird, sat her there
Beside her Basil, weeping through her hair.

LX

Yet they contriv'd to steal the Basil-pot,
    And to examine it in secret place:
The thing was vile with green and livid spot,
    And yet they knew it was Lorenzo's face:
The guerdon of their murder they had got,
    And so left Florence in a moment's space,
Never to turn again.—Away they went,
With blood upon their heads, to banishment.

LXI

O Melancholy, turn thine eyes away! 481
    O Music, Music, breathe despondingly!

O Echo, Echo, on some other day,
　From isles Lethean, sigh to us— O sigh!
Spirits of grief, sing not your "Well-a-way!"
　For Isabel, sweet Isabel, will die;
Will die a death too lone and incomplete,
Now they have ta'en away her Basil sweet.

LXII

Piteous she look'd on dead and senseless
　　things,
　Asking for her lost Basil amorously;　490
And with melodious chuckle in the strings
　Of her lorn voice, she oftentimes would cry
After the Pilgrim in his wanderings,
　To ask him where her Basil was; and why
'Twas hid from her: "For cruel 'tis," said she,
"To steal my Basil-pot away from me."

LXIII

And so she pined, and so she died forlorn,
　Imploring for her Basil to the last.
No heart was there in Florence but did mourn
　In pity of her love, so overcast.　500
And a sad ditty of this story born
　From mouth to mouth through all the coun-
　　try pass'd:
Still is the burthen sung— "O cruelty,
"To steal my Basil-pot away from me!"

THE EVE OF ST. AGNES

I

St. Agnes' Eve— Ah, bitter chill it was!
　The owl, for all his feathers, was a-cold;
　The hare limp'd trembling through the
　　frozen grass,
And silent was the flock in woolly fold:
　Numb were the Beadsman's fingers, while
　　he told
His rosary, and while his frosted breath,
Like pious incense from a censer old,
　Seem'd taking flight for heaven, without a
　　death,
Past the sweet Virgin's picture, while his
　prayer he saith.

II

His prayer he saith, this patient, holy man;
　Then takes his lamp, and riseth from his
　　knees,　　11

And back returneth, meagre, barefoot, wan,
　Along the chapel aisle by slow degrees:
　The sculptur'd dead, on each side, seem to
　　freeze,
Emprison'd in black, purgatorial rails:
Knights, ladies, praying in dumb orat'ries,
　He passeth by; and his weak spirit fails
To think how they may ache in icy hoods and
　mails.

III

Northward he turneth through a little door,
　And scarce three steps, ere Music's golden
　　tongue　　20
Flatter'd to tears this aged man and poor;
　But no—already had his deathbell rung;
　The joys of all his life were said and sung:
His was harsh penance on St. Agnes' Eve:
Another way he went, and soon among
　Rough ashes sat he for his soul's reprieve,
And all night kept awake, for sinners' sake to
　grieve.

IV

That ancient Beadsman heard the prelude
　　soft;
　And so it chanc'd, for many a door was
　　wide,
From hurry to and fro. Soon, up aloft,　　30
　The silver, snarling trumpets 'gan to chide:
　The level chambers, ready with their pride,
Were glowing to receive a thousand guests:
　The carved angels, ever eager-eyed,
Stared, where upon their heads the cornice
　rests,
With hair blown back, and wings put cross-
　wise on their breasts.

V

At length burst in the argent revelry,
　With plume, tiara, and all rich array,
Numerous as shadows haunting faerily
　The brain, new stuff'd, in youth, with triumphs
　　gay　　40
Of old romance. These let us wish away,
　And turn, sole-thoughted, to one Lady there,
Whose heart had brooded, all that wintry
　day,
On love, and wing'd St. Agnes' saintly care,
As she had heard old dames full many times
　declare.

VI

They told her how, upon St. Agnes' Eve,
Young virgins might have visions of delight,
And soft adorings from their loves receive
Upon the honey'd middle of the night,
If ceremonies due they did aright;   50
As, supperless to bed they must retire,
And couch supine their beauties, lily white;
Nor look behind, nor sideways, but require
Of Heaven with upward eyes for all that they
    desire.

VII

Full of this whim was thoughtful Madeline:
The music, yearning like a God in pain,
She scarcely heard: her maiden eyes divine,
Fix'd on the floor, saw many a sweeping
    train
Pass by—she heeded not at all: in vain
Came many a tiptoe, amorous cavalier,   60
And back retir'd; not cool'd by high dis-
    dain,
But she saw not; her heart was otherwhere:
She sigh'd for Agnes' dreams, the sweetest of
    the year.

VIII

She danc'd along with vague, regardless
    eyes,
Anxious her lips, her breathing quick and
    short:
The hallow'd hour was near at hand: she
    sighs
Amid the timbrels, and the throng'd resort
Of whisperers in anger, or in sport;
'Mid looks of love, defiance, hate, and scorn,
Hoodwink'd with faery fancy; all amort, 70
Save to St. Agnes and her lambs unshorn,
And all the bliss to be before to-morrow morn.

IX

So, purposing each moment to retire,
She linger'd still. Meantime, across the
    moors,
Had come young Porphyro, with heart on
    fire
For Madeline. Beside the portal doors,
Buttress'd from the moonlight, stands he,
    and implores
All saints to give him sight of Madeline,

But for one moment in the tedious hours,
That he might gaze and worship all unseen
Perchance speak, kneel, touch, kiss—in sooth
    such things have been.   81

X

He ventures in: let no buzz'd whisper tell:
All eyes be muffled, or a hundred swords
Will storm his heart, Love's fev'rous cita-
    del:
For him, those chambers held barbarian
    hordes,
Hyena foemen, and hot-blooded lords,
Whose very dogs would execrations howl
Against his lineage: not one breast affords
Him any mercy, in that mansion foul,
Save one old beldame, weak in body and in
    soul.   90

XI

Ah, happy chance! the aged creature came,
Shuffling along with ivory-headed wand,
To where he stood, hid from the torch's
    flame,
Behind a broad hall-pillar, far beyond
The sound of merriment and chorus bland:
He startled her; but soon she knew his face,
And grasp'd his fingers in her palsied hand,
Saying, "Mercy, Porphyro! hie thee from
    this place;
"They are all here to-night, the whole blood-
    thirsty race!

XII

"Get hence! get hence! there's dwarfish
    Hildebrand;   100
"He had a fever late, and in the fit
"He cursed thee and thine, both house and
    land:
"Then there's that old Lord Maurice, not a
    whit
"More tame for his grey hairs— Alas me!
    flit!
"Flit like a ghost away."—"Ah, Gossip
    dear,
"We're safe enough; here in this arm-chair
    sit,
"And tell me how"—"Good Saints! not
    here, not here;
"Follow me, child, or else these stones will be
    thy bier."

XIII

He follow'd through a lowly arched way, 109
Brushing the cobwebs with his lofty plume,
And as she mutter'd "Well-a—well-a-day!"
He found him in a little moonlight room,
Pale, lattic'd, chill, and silent as a tomb.
"Now tell me where is Madeline," said he,
"O tell me, Angela, by the holy loom
"Which none but secret sisterhood may see,
"When they St. Agnes' wool are weaving
        piously."

XIV

"St. Agnes! Ah! it is St. Agnes' Eve—
"Yet men will murder upon holy days:
"Thou must hold water in a witch's sieve, 120
"And be liege-lord of all the Elves and Fays,
"To venture so: it fills me with amaze
"To see thee, Porphyro!—St. Agnes' Eve!
"God's help! my lady fair the conjuror
        plays
"This very night: good angels her deceive!
"But let me laugh awhile, I've mickle time
        to grieve."

XV

Feebly she laugheth in the languid moon,
While Porphyro upon her face doth look,
Like puzzled urchin on an aged crone
Who keepeth clos'd a wond'rous riddle-
        book, 130
As spectacled she sits in chimney nook.
But soon his eyes grew brilliant, when she
        told
His lady's purpose; and he scarce could
        brook
Tears, at the thought of those enchantments
        cold,
And Madeline asleep in lap of legends old.

XVI

Sudden a thought came like a full-blown
        rose,
Flushing his brow, and in his pained heart
Made purple riot: then doth he propose
A stratagem, that makes the beldame start:
"A cruel man and impious thou art: 140
"Sweet lady, let her pray, and sleep, and
        dream
"Alone with her good angels, far apart

"From wicked men like thee. Go, go!—I
        deem
"Thou canst not surely be the same that thou
        didst seem."

XVII

"I will not harm her, by all saints I swear,"
Quoth Porphyro: "O may I ne'er find grace
"When my weak voice shall whisper its last
        prayer,
"If one of her soft ringlets I displace,
"Or look with ruffian passion in her face:
"Good Angela, believe me by these tears; 150
"Or I will, even in a moment's space,
"Awake, with horrid shout, my foemen's
        ears,
"And beard them, though they be more fang'd
        than wolves and bears."

XVIII

"Ah! why wilt thou affright a feeble soul?
"A poor, weak, palsy-stricken, churchyard
        thing
"Whose passing-bell may ere the midnight
        toll;
"Whose prayers for thee, each morn and
        evening,
"Were never miss'd."—Thus plaining, doth
        she bring
A gentler speech from burning Porphyro;
So woful, and of such deep sorrowing,   160
That Angela gives promise she will do
Whatever he shall wish, betide her weal or
        woe.

XIX

Which was, to lead him, in close secrecy,
Even to Madeline's chamber, and there hide
Him in a closet, of such privacy
That he might see her beauty unespy'd,
And win perhaps that night a peerless bride,
While legion'd faeries pac'd the coverlet,
And pale enchantment held her sleepy-ey'd.
Never on such a night have lovers met,   170
Since Merlin paid his Demon all the mon-
        strous debt.

XX

"It shall be as thou wishest," said the dame:
"All cates and dainties shall be stored there

"Quickly on this feast-night: by the tambour frame
"Her own lute thou wilt see: no time to spare,
"For I am slow and feeble, and scarce dare
"On such a catering trust my dizzy head.
"Wait here, my child, with patience; kneel in prayer
"The while: Ah! thou must needs the lady wed,
"Or may I never leave my grave among the dead." 180

XXI

So saying, she hobbled off with busy fear.
The lover's endless minutes slowly pass'd;
The dame return'd, and whisper'd in his ear
To follow her; with aged eyes aghast
From fright of dim espial. Safe at last,
Through many a dusky gallery, they gain
The maiden's chamber, silken, hush'd, and chaste;
Where Porphyro took covert, pleas'd amain.
His poor guide hurried back with agues in her brain.

XXII

Her falt'ring hand upon the balustrade, 190
Old Angela was feeling for the stair,
When Madeline, St. Agnes' charmed maid,
Rose, like a mission'd spirit, unaware:
With silver taper's light, and pious care,
She turn'd, and down the aged gossip led
To a safe level matting. Now prepare,
Young Porphyro, for gazing on that bed;
She comes, she comes again, like ring-dove fray'd and fled.

XXIII

Out went the taper as she hurried in;
Its little smoke, in pallid moonshine, died:
She clos'd the door, she panted, all akin 201
To spirits of the air, and visions wide:
No uttered syllable, or, woe betide!
But to her heart, her heart was voluble,
Paining with eloquence her balmy side;
As though a tongueless nightingale should swell
Her throat in vain, and die, heart-stifled, in her dell.

XXIV

A casement high and triple-arch'd there was,
All garlanded with carven imag'ries
Of fruits, and flowers, and bunches of knotgrass, 210
And diamonded with panes of quaint device,
Innumerable of stains and splendid dyes,
As are the tiger-moth's deep-damask'd wings;
And in the midst, 'mong thousand heraldries,
And twilight saints, and dim emblazonings,
A shielded scutcheon blush'd with blood of queens and kings.

XXV

Full on this casement shone the wintry moon,
And threw warm gules on Madeline's fair breast,
As down she knelt for heaven's grace and boon;
Rose-bloom fell on her hands, together prest, 220
And on her silver cross soft amethyst,
And on her hair a glory, like a saint:
She seem'd a splendid angel, newly drest,
Save wings, for heaven:—Porphyro grew faint:
She knelt, so pure a thing, so free from mortal taint.

XXVI

Anon his heart revives: her vespers done,
Of all its wreathed pearls her hair she frees;
Unclasps her warmed jewels one by one;
Loosens her fragrant bodice; by degrees
Her rich attire creeps rustling to her knees:
Half-hidden, like a mermaid in sea-weed, 231
Pensive awhile she dreams awake, and sees,
In fancy, fair St. Agnes in her bed,
But dares not look behind, or all the charm is fled.

XXVII

Soon, trembling in her soft and chilly nest,
In sort of wakeful swoon, perplex'd she lay,
Until the poppied warmth of sleep oppress'd
Her soothed limbs, and soul fatigued away;

Flown, like a thought, until the morrow-
    day;   239
Blissfully haven'd both from joy and pain;
Clasp'd like a missal where swart Paynims
    pray;
Blinded alike from sunshine and from rain,
As though a rose should shut, and be a bud
    again.

XXVIII

Stol'n to this paradise, and so entranced,
Porphyro gaz'd upon her empty dress,
And listen'd to her breathing, if it chanced
To wake into a slumberous tenderness;
Which when he heard, that minute did he
    bless,
And breath'd himself: then from the closet
    crept,
Noiseless as fear in a wide wilderness,   250
And over the hush'd carpet, silent, stept,
And 'tween the curtains peep'd, where, lo!—
    how fast she slept.

XXIX

Then by the bed-side, where the faded moon
Made a dim, silver twilight, soft he set
A table, and, half anguish'd, threw thereon
A cloth of woven crimson, gold, and jet.—
O for some drowsy Morphean amulet!
The boisterous, midnight, festive clarion,
The kettle-drum, and far-heard clarinet,
Affray his ears, though but in dying tone:—
The hall door shuts again, and all the noise is
    gone.   261

XXX

And still she slept an azure-lidded sleep,
In blanched linen, smooth, and lavender'd,
While he from forth the closet brought a
    heap
Of candied apple, quince, and plum, and
    gourd;
With jellies soother than the creamy curd,
And lucent syrops, tinct with cinnamon;
Manna and dates, in argosy transferr'd
From Fez; and spiced dainties, every one,
From silken Samarcand to cedar'd Lebanon. 270

XXXI

These delicates he heap'd with glowing hand

On golden dishes and in baskets bright
Of wreathed silver: sumptuous they stand
In the retired quiet of the night,
Filling the chilly room with perfume light.—
"And now, my love, my seraph fair, awake!
"Thou art my heaven, and I thine eremite:
"Open thine eyes, for meek St. Agnes' sake,
"Or I shall drowse beside thee, so my soul
    doth ache."   279

XXXII

Thus whispering, his warm, unnerved arm
Sank in her pillow. Shaded was her dream
By the dusk curtains:—'twas a midnight
    charm
Impossible to melt as iced stream:
The lustrous salvers in the moonlight gleam;
Broad golden fringe upon the carpet lies:
It seem'd he never, never could redeem
From such a steadfast spell his lady's eyes;
So mus'd awhile, entoil'd in woofed phantasies.

XXXIII

Awakening up, he took her hollow lute,—
Tumultuous,—and, in chords that tenderest
    be,   290
He play'd an ancient ditty, long since mute,
In Provence call'd, "La belle dame sans
    mercy":
Close to her ear touching the melody;—
Wherewith disturb'd, she utter'd a soft
    moan.
He ceas'd—she panted quick—and suddenly
Her blue affrayed eyes wide open shone:
Upon his knees he sank, pale as smooth-
    sculptured stone

XXXIV

Her eyes were open, but she still beheld,
Now wide awake, the vision of her sleep:
There was a painful change, that nigh ex-
    pell'd   300
The blisses of her dream so pure and deep
At which fair Madeline began to weep,
And moan forth witless words with many a
    sigh;
While still her gaze on Porphyro would
    keep;
Who knelt, with joined hands and piteous
    eye,

Fearing to move or speak, she look'd so dreamingly.

XXXV

"Ah, Porphyro!" said she, "but even now
"Thy voice was at sweet tremble in mine ear,
"Made tuneable with every sweetest vow;
"And those sad eyes were spiritual and clear: 310
"How chang'd thou art! how pallid, chill, and drear!
"Give me that voice again, my Porphyro,
"Those looks immortal, those complainings dear!
"Oh leave me not in this eternal woe,
"For if thou diest, my Love, I know not where to go."

XXXVI

Beyond a mortal man impassion'd far
At these voluptuous accents, he arose,
Ethereal, flush'd, and like a throbbing star
Seen midst the sapphire heaven's deep repose;
Into her dream he melted, as the rose 320
Blendeth its odour with the violet,—
Solution sweet: meantime the frost-wind blows
Like Love's alarum pattering the sharp sleet
Against the window-panes; St. Agnes' moon hath set.

XXXVII

'Tis dark: quick pattereth the flaw-blown sleet:
"This is no dream, my bride, my Madeline!"
" 'Tis dark: the iced gusts still rave and beat:
"No dream, alas! alas! and woe is mine!
"Porphyro will leave me here to fade and pine.—
"Cruel! what traitor could thee hither bring? 330
"I curse not, for my heart is lost in thine,
"Though thou forsakest a deceived thing;—
"A dove forlorn and lost with sick unpruned wing."

XXXVIII

"My Madeline! sweet dreamer! lovely bride!

"Say, may I be for aye thy vassal blest?
"Thy beauty's shield, heart-shap'd and vermeil dy'd?
"Ah, silver shrine, here will I take my rest
"After so many hours of toil and quest,
"A famish'd pilgrim,—sav'd by miracle.
"Though I have found, I will not rob thy nest 340
"Saving of thy sweet self; if thou think'st well
"To trust, fair Madeline, to no rude infidel.

XXXIX

"Hark! 'tis an elfin-storm from faery land,
"Of haggard seeming, but a boon indeed:
"Arise—arise! the morning is at hand;—
"The bloated wassaillers will never heed:—
"Let us away, my love, with happy speed;
"There are no ears to hear, or eyes to see,—
"Drown'd all in Rhenish and the sleepy mead:
"Awake! arise! my love, and fearless be, 350
"For o'er the southern moors I have a home for thee."

XL

She hurried at his words, beset with fear,
For there were sleeping dragons all around,
At glaring watch, perhaps, with ready spears—
Down the wide stairs a darkling way they found.—
In all the house was heard no human sound.
A chain-droop'd lamp was flickering by each door;
The arras, rich with horseman, hawk, and hound,
Flutter'd in the besieging wind's uproar;
And the long carpets rose along the gusty floor. 360

XLI

They glide, like phantoms, into the wide hall,
Like phantoms, to the iron porch, they glide;
Where lay the Porter, in uneasy sprawl,
With a huge empty flagon by his side:
The wakeful bloodhound rose, and shook his hide,
But his sagacious eye an inmate owns:

By one, and one, the bolts full easy slide:—
The chains lie silent on the footworn
    stones;—
The key turns, and the door upon its hinges
    groans.

XLII

And they are gone: aye, ages long ago   370
These lovers fled away into the storm.
That night the Baron dreamt of many a
    woe,
And all his warrior-guests, with shade and
    form
Of witch, and demon, and large coffin-worm,
Were long be-nightmar'd. Angela the old
Died palsy-twitch'd, with meagre face de-
    form;
The Beadsman, after thousand aves told,
For aye unsought for slept among his ashes
    cold.

ODE TO A NIGHTINGALE

1

My heart aches, and a drowsy numbness pains
  My sense, as though of hemlock I had
    drunk,
    Or emptied some dull opiate to the drains
One minute past, and Lethe-wards had
    sunk:
'Tis not through envy of thy happy lot,
  But being too happy in thine happiness,—
    That thou, light-winged Dryad of the
    trees,
      In some melodious plot
Of beechen green, and shadows numberless,
Singest of summer in full-throated ease.   10

2

O, for a draught of vintage! that hath been
  Cool'd a long age in the deep-delved earth,
Tasting of Flora and the country green,
  Dance, and Provençal song, and sunburnt
    mirth!
O for a beaker full of the warm South,
  Full of the true, the blushful Hippocrene,
    With beaded bubbles winking at the brim,
      And purple-stained mouth;
That I might drink, and leave the world un-
    seen,

And with thee fade away into the forest
    dim: 20

3

Fade far away, dissolve, and quite forget
  What thou among the leaves hast never
    known,
The weariness, the fever, and the fret
  Here, where men sit and hear each other
    groan;
Where palsy shakes a few, sad, last grey hairs,
  Where youth grows pale, and spectre-thin,
    and dies;
    Where but to think is to be full of sorrow
      And leaden-ey'd despairs,
    Where Beauty cannot keep her lustrous
    eyes,
      Or new Love pine at them beyond to-
    morrow.   30

4

Away! away! for I will fly to thee,
  Not charioted by Bacchus and his pards,
But on the viewless wings of Poesy,
  Though the dull brain perplexes and re-
    tards:
Already with thee! tender is the night,
  And haply the Queen-Moon is on her
    throne,
    Cluster'd around by all her starry Fays;
      But here there is no light,
Save what from heaven is with the breezes
    blown
    Through verdurous glooms and winding
    mossy ways.   40

5

I cannot see what flowers are at my feet,
  Nor what soft incense hangs upon the
    boughs,
But, in embalmed darkness, guess each sweet
Wherewith the seasonable month endows
The grass, the thicket, and the fruit-tree wild;
  White hawthorn, and the pastoral eglantine;
    Fast fading violets cover'd up in leaves;
      And mid-May's eldest child,
The coming musk-rose, full of dewy wine,
    The murmurous haunt of flies on summer
    eves.   50

6

Darkling I listen; and, for many a time
    I have been half in love with easeful Death,
Call'd him soft names in many a mused
    rhyme,
    To take into the air my quiet breath;
      Now more than ever seems it rich to die,
To cease upon the midnight with no pain,
    While thou art pouring forth thy soul
      abroad
        In such an ecstasy!
Still wouldst thou sing, and I have ears in
      vain—
    To thy high requiem become a sod.   60

7

Thou wast not born for death, immortal Bird!
    No hungry generations tread thee down;
The voice I hear this passing night was heard
    In ancient days by emperor and clown:
Perhaps the self-same song that found a
    path
Through the sad heart of Ruth, when, sick
    for home,
    She stood in tears amid the alien corn;
      The same that oft-times hath
Charm'd magic casements, opening on the
    foam
Of perilous seas, in faery lands forlorn. 70

8

Forlorn! the very word is like a bell
    To toll me back from thee to my sole self!
Adieu! the fancy cannot cheat so well
    As she is famed to do, deceiving elf.
Adieu! adieu! thy plaintive anthem fades
    Past the near meadows, over the still
      stream,
    Up the hill-side; and now 'tis buried deep
      In the next valley-glades:
    Was it a vision, or a waking dream?   79
      Fled is that music:—Do I wake or sleep?

ODE ON A GRECIAN URN

1

THOU still unravish'd bride of quietness,
    Thou foster-child of silence and slow time,
Sylvan historian, who canst thus express

A flowery tale more sweetly than our
    rhyme:
What leaf-fring'd legend haunts about thy
    shape
Of deities or mortals, or of both,
    In Tempe or the dales of Arcady?
What men or gods are these? What maidens
    loth?
What mad pursuit? What struggle to escape?
    What pipes and timbrels? What wild ec-
      stasy?   10

2

Heard melodies are sweet, but those unheard
    Are sweeter; therefore, ye soft pipes, play
    on;
Not to the sensual ear, but, more endear'd,
    Pipe to the spirit ditties of no tone:
Fair youth, beneath the trees, thou canst not
    leave
    Thy song, nor ever can those trees be bare;
      Bold Lover, never, never canst thou kiss,
Though winning near the goal—yet, do not
    grieve;
    She cannot fade, though thou hast not thy
      bliss,   19
    For ever wilt thou love, and she be fair!

3

Ah, happy, happy boughs! that cannot shed
    Your leaves, nor ever bid the Spring adieu;
And, happy melodist, unwearied,
    For ever piping songs for ever new;
More happy love! more happy, happy love!
    For ever warm and still to be enjoy'd,
      For ever panting, and for ever young;
All breathing human passion far above,
    That leaves a heart high-sorrowful and
      cloy'd,   29
A burning forehead, and a parching tongue.

4

Who are these coming to the sacrifice?
    To what green altar, O mysterious priest,
Lead'st thou that heifer lowing at the skies,
    And all her silken flanks with garlands
      drest?
What little town by river or sea shore,
    Or mountain-built with peaceful citadel,
    Is emptied of this folk, this pious morn?
And, little town, thy streets for evermore

Will silent be; and not a soul to tell
Why thou art desolate, can e'er return. 40

5

O Attic shape! Fair attitude! with brede
Of marble men and maidens overwrought,
With forest branches and the trodden weed;
   Thou, silent form, dost tease us out of
      thought
As doth eternity: Cold Pastoral!
  When old age shall this generation waste,
    Thou shalt remain, in midst of other woe
Than ours, a friend to man, to whom thou
    say'st,
  "Beauty is truth, truth beauty,"—that is all
    Ye know on earth, and all ye need to
      know. 50

ODE TO PSYCHE

O GODDESS! hear these tuneless numbers, wrung
  By sweet enforcement and remembrance
    dear,
And pardon that thy secrets should be sung
Even into thine own soft-conched ear:
Surely I dreamt to-day, or did I see
  The winged Psyche with awaken'd eyes?
I wander'd in a forest thoughtlessly,
  And, on the sudden, fainting with surprise,
Saw two fair creatures, couched side by side
  In deepest grass, beneath the whisp'ring
    roof 10
  Of leaves and trembled blossoms, where
    there ran
    A brooklet, scarce espied:

'Mid hush'd, cool-rooted flowers, fragrant-
    eyed,
  Blue, silver-white, and budded Tyrian,
They lay calm-breathing, on the bedded grass;
  Their arms embraced, and their pinions too;
  Their lips touch'd not, but had not bade
    adieu,
As if disjoined by soft-handed slumber,
And ready still past kisses to outnumber
  At tender eye-dawn of aurorean love: 20
    The winged boy I knew;
  But who wast thou, O happy, happy dove?
    His Psyche true!

O latest born and loveliest vision far
  Of all Olympus' faded hierarchy!
Fairer than Phœbe's sapphire-region'd star,
  Or Vesper, amorous glow-worm of the sky;

Fairer than these, though temple thou hast
    none,
    Nor altar heap'd with flowers;
Nor virgin-choir to make delicious moan 30
    Upon the midnight hours;
No voice, no lute, no pipe, no incense sweet
  From chain-swung censer teeming;
  No shrine, no grove, no oracle, no heat
    Of pale-mouth'd prophet dreaming.

O brightest! though too late for antique vows,
  Too, too late for the fond believing lyre,
When holy were the haunted forest boughs,
  Holy the air, the water, and the fire;
Yet even in these days so far retir'd 40
  From happy pieties, thy lucent fans,
  Fluttering among the faint Olympians,
I see, and sing, by my own eyes inspir'd.
So let me be thy choir, and make a moan
    Upon the midnight hours;
Thy voice, thy lute, thy pipe, thy incense
    sweet
  From swinged censer teeming;
Thy shrine, thy grove, thy oracle, thy heat
  Of pale-mouth'd prophet dreaming.

Yes, I will be thy priest, and build a fane 50
  In some untrodden region of my mind,
Where branched thoughts, new grown with
    pleasant pain,
  Instead of pines shall murmur in the wind:
Far, far around shall those dark-cluster'd trees
  Fledge the wild-ridged mountains steep by
    steep;
And there by zephyrs, streams, and birds, and
    bees,
  The moss-lain Dryads shall be lull'd to
    sleep;
And in the midst of this wide quietness
A rosy sanctuary will I dress
With the wreath'd trellis of a working brain, 60
  With buds, and bells, and stars without a
    name,
With all the gardener Fancy e'er could feign,
  Who breeding flowers, will never breed the
    same:
And there shall be for thee all soft delight
  That shadowy thought can win,
A bright torch, and a casement ope at night,
  To let the warm Love in!

FANCY

EVER let the fancy roam,
Pleasure never is at home:

At a touch sweet pleasure melteth,
Like to bubbles when rain pelteth;
Then let winged Fancy wander
Through the thought still spread beyond her:
Open wide the mind's cage-door,
She'll dart forth, and cloudward soar.
O sweet Fancy! let her loose;   10
Summer's joys are spoilt by use,
And the enjoying of the Spring
Fades as does its blossoming;
Autumn's red-lipp'd fruitage too,
Blushing through the mist and dew,
Cloys with tasting: What do then?
Sit thee by the ingle, when
The sear fagot blazes bright,
Spirit of a winter's night;
When the soundless earth is muffled,
And the caked snow is shuffled   20
From the ploughboy's heavy shoon;
When the Night doth meet the Noon
In a dark conspiracy
To banish Even from her sky.
Sit thee there, and send abroad,
With a mind self-overaw'd,
Fancy, high commission'd:—send her!
She has vassals to attend her:
She will bring, in spite of frost,
Beauties that the earth hath lost;   30
She will bring thee, altogether,
All delights of summer weather;
All the buds and bells of May,
From dewy sward or thorny spray;
All the heaped Autumn's wealth,
With a still, mysterious stealth:
She will mix these pleasures up
Like three fit wines in a cup,
And thou shalt quaff it:—thou shalt hear
Distant harvest-carols clear;   40
Rustle of the reaped corn;
Sweet birds antheming the morn:
And, in the same moment—hark!
'Tis the early April lark,
Or the rooks, with busy caw,
Foraging for sticks and straw.
Thou shalt, at one glance, behold
The daisy and the marigold;
White-plum'd lilies, and the first
Hedge-grown primrose that hath burst;   50
Shaded hyacinth, alway
Sapphire queen of the mid-May;
And every leaf, and every flower
Pearled with the self-same shower.
Thou shalt see the field-mouse peep
Meagre from its celled sleep;

And the snake all winter-thin
Cast on sunny bank its skin;
Freckled nest-eggs thou shalt see
Hatching in the hawthorn-tree,   60
When the hen-bird's wing doth rest
Quiet on her mossy nest;
Then the hurry and alarm
When the bee-hive casts its swarm;
Acorns ripe down-pattering,
While the autumn breezes sing.

Oh, sweet Fancy! let her loose;
Every thing is spoilt by use:
Where's the cheek that doth not fade,
Too much gaz'd at? Where's the maid   70
Whose lip mature is ever new?
Where's the eye, however blue,
Doth not weary? Where's the face
One would meet in every place?
Where's the voice, however soft,
One would hear so very oft?
At a touch sweet Pleasure melteth
Like to bubbles when rain pelteth.
Let, then, winged Fancy find
Thee a mistress to thy mind: 80
Dulcet-eyed as Ceres' daughter,
Ere the God of Torment taught her
How to frown and how to chide;
With a waist and with a side
White as Hebe's, when her zone
Slipt its golden clasp, and down
Fell her kirtle to her feet,
While she held the goblet sweet,
And Jove grew languid.—Break the mesh
Of the Fancy's silken leash;   90
Quickly break her prison-string
And such joys as these she'll bring.—
Let the winged Fancy roam,
Pleasure never is at home.

ODE

[WRITTEN ON THE BLANK PAGE BEFORE BEAU-
MONT AND FLETCHER'S TRAGI-COMEDY "THE
FAIR MAID OF THE INN."]

BARDS of Passion and of Mirth!
Ye have left your souls on earth!
Have ye souls in heaven too,
Double-liv'd in regions new?
Yes, and those of heaven commune
With the spheres of sun and moon;
With the noise of fountains wond'rous,
And the parle of voices thund'rous;

With the whisper of heaven's trees
And one another, in soft ease   10
Seated on Elysian lawns
Browsed by none but Dian's fawns;
Underneath large blue-bells tented,
Where the daisies are rose-scented,
And the rose herself has got
Perfume which on earth is not;
Where the nightingale doth sing
Not a senseless, tranced thing,
But divine melodious truth;
Philosophic numbers smooth;   20
Tales and golden histories
Of heaven and its mysteries.

Thus ye live on high, and then
On the earth ye live again;
And the souls ye left behind you
Teach us, here, the way to find you,
Where your other souls are joying,
Never slumber'd, never cloying.
Here, your earth-born souls still speak
To mortals, of their little week;   30
Of their sorrows and delights;
Of their passions and their spites;
Of their glory and their shame;
What doth strengthen and what maim.
Thus ye teach us, every day,
Wisdom, though fled far away.

Bards of Passion and of Mirth,
Ye have left your souls on earth!
Ye have souls in heaven too,
Double-liv'd in regions new!   40

LINES ON THE MERMAID TAVERN

SOULS of Poets dead and gone,
What Elysium have ye known,
Happy field or mossy cavern,
Choicer than the Mermaid Tavern?
Have ye tippled drink more fine
Than mine host's Canary wine?
Or are fruits of Paradise
Sweeter than those dainty pies
Of venison? O generous food!
Drest as though bold Robin Hood   10
Would, with his maid Marian,
Sup and bowse from horn and can.

I have heard that on a day
Mine host's sign-board flew away,
Nobody knew whither, till
An astrologer's old quill

To a sheepskin gave the story,
Said he saw you in your glory,
Underneath a new old-sign
Sipping beverage divine,   20
And pledging with contented smack
The Mermaid in the Zodiac.
Souls of Poets dead and gone,
What Elysium have ye known,
Happy field or mossy cavern,
Choicer than the Mermaid Tavern?

ROBIN HOOD

TO A FRIEND

No! those days are gone away,
And their hours are old and grey,
And their minutes buried all
Under the down-trodden pall
Of the leaves of many years:
Many times have winter's shears,
Frozen North, and chilling East,
Sounded tempests to the feast
Of the forest's whispering fleeces,
Since men knew nor rent nor leases.   10

No, the bugle sounds no more;
And the twanging bow no more;
Silent is the ivory shrill
Past the heath and up the hill;
There is no mid-forest laugh,
Where lone Echo gives the half
To some wight, amaz'd to hear
Jesting, deep in forest drear.

On the fairest time of June
You may go, with sun or moon,   20
Or the seven stars to light you;
Or the polar ray to right you;
But you never may behold
Little John, or Robin bold;
Never one, of all the clan,
Thrumming on an empty can
Some old hunting ditty, while
He doth his green way beguile
To fair hostess Merriment,
Down beside the pasture Trent;   30
For he left the merry tale
Messenger for spicy ale.

Gone, the merry morris din;
Gone, the song of Gamelyn;
Gone, the tough-belted outlaw
Idling in the "grenè shawe";

All are gone away and past!
And if Robin should be cast
Sudden from his turfed grave,
And if Marian should have   40
Once again her forest days,
She would weep, and he would craze:
He would swear, for all his oaks,
Fall'n beneath the dockyard strokes,
Have rotted on the briny sea;
She would weep that her wild bees
Sang not to her—strange! that honey
Can't be got without hard money!

So it is: yet let us sing,
Honor to the old bow-string!   50
Honor to the bugle-horn!
Honor to the woods unshorn!
Honor to the Lincoln green!
Honor to the archer keen!
Honor to tight little John,
And the horse he rode upon!
Honor to bold Robin Hood,
Sleeping in the underwood!
Honor to maid Marian,
And to all the Sherwood-clan!   60
Though their days have hurried by
Let us too a burden try.

TO AUTUMN

1

SEASON of mists and mellow fruitfulness,
    Close bosom-friend of the maturing sun;
Conspiring with him how to load and bless
    With fruit the vines that round the thatch-
        eves run;
To bend with apples the moss'd cottage-trees,
    And fill all fruit with ripeness to the core;
        To swell the gourd, and plump the hazel
            shells
    With a sweet kernel; to set budding more,
And still more, later flowers for the bees,
Until they think warm days will never cease,
    For Summer has o'er-brimm'd their
        clammy cells.   11

2

Who hath not seen thee oft amid thy store?
    Sometimes whoever seeks abroad may find
Thee sitting careless on a granary floor,
    Thy hair soft-lifted by the winnowing wind;
Or on a half-reap'd furrow sound asleep,

Drows'd with the fume of poppies, while
    thy hook
    Spares the next swath and all its twined
        flowers:
And sometimes like a gleaner thou dost keep
    Steady thy laden head across a brook;   20
    Or by a cyder-press, with patient look,
        Thou watchest the last oozings hours by
            hours.

3

Where are the songs of Spring? Ay, where
    are they?
    Think not of them, thou hast thy music
        too,—
While barred clouds bloom the soft-dying day,
    And touch the stubble-plains with rosy hue;
Then in a wailful choir the small gnats mourn
    Among the river sallows, borne aloft
        Or sinking as the light wind lives or
            dies;
And full-grown lambs loud bleat from hilly
    bourn;   30
    Hedge-crickets sing; and now with treble
        soft
    The red-breast whistles from a garden-
        croft;
        And gathering swallows twitter in the
            skies.

ODE ON MELANCHOLY

1

No, no, go not to Lethe, neither twist
    Wolf's-bane, tight-rooted, for its poisonous
        wine;
Nor suffer thy pale forehead to be kiss'd
    By nightshade, ruby grape of Proserpine;
Make not your rosary of yew-berries,
    Nor let the beetle, nor the death-moth be
        Your mournful Psyche, nor the downy
            owl
A partner in your sorrow's mysteries:
    For shade to shade will come too drowsily,
        And drown the wakeful anguish of the
            soul.   10

2

But when the melancholy fit shall fall
    Sudden from heaven like a weeping cloud,
That fosters the droop-headed flowers all,

And hides the green hill in an April shroud;
Then glut thy sorrow on a morning rose,
　Or on the rainbow of the salt sand-wave,
　Or on the wealth of globed peonies;
Or if thy mistress some rich anger shows,
　Emprison her soft hand, and let her rave,
　　And feed deep, deep upon her peerless
　　　eyes.　　20

3

She dwells with Beauty—Beauty that must
　die;
　And joy, whose hand is ever at his lips
Bidding adieu; and aching Pleasure nigh,
　Turning to poison while the bee-mouth sips:
Ay, in the very temple of Delight
　Veil'd Melancholy has her sovran shrine,
　　Though seen of none save him whose
　　　strenuous tongue
　Can burst Joy's grape against his palate
　　fine;
His soul shall taste the sadness of her might,
　And be among her cloudy trophies hung.　30

HYPERION

Book I

DEEP in the shady sadness of a vale
Far sunken from the healthy breath of morn,
Far from the fiery noon, and eve's one star,
Sat grey-hair'd Saturn, quiet as a stone,
Still as the silence round about his lair;
Forest on forest hung about his head
Like cloud on cloud. No stir of air was there
Not so much life as on a summer's day
Robs not one light seed from the feather'd
　grass,
But where the dead leaf fell, there did it rest.
A stream went voiceless by, still deadened
　more　　11
By reason of his fallen divinity
Spreading a shade: the Naiad 'mid her reeds
Press'd her cold finger closer to her lips.

　Along the margin-sand large foot-marks
　　went,
No further than to where his feet had stray'd,
And slept there since. Upon the sodden ground
His old right hand lay nerveless, listless, dead,
Unsceptred; and his realmless eyes were
　closed;

While his bow'd head seem'd list'ning to the
　Earth,　　20
His ancient mother, for some comfort yet.

　It seem'd no force could wake him from his
　　place;
But there came one, who with a kindred hand
Touch'd his wide shoulders, after bending low
With reverence, though to one who knew it
　not,
She was a Goddess of the infant world;
By her in stature the tall Amazon
Had stood a pigmy's height; she would have
　ta'en
Achilles by the hair and bent his neck;
Or with a finger stay'd Ixion's wheel.　　30
Her face was large as that of Memphian sphinx,
Pedestal'd haply in a palace court,
When sages look'd to Egypt for their lore.
But oh! how unlike marble was that face:
How beautiful, if sorrow had not made
Sorrow more beautiful than Beauty's self.
There was a listening fear in her regard,
As if calamity had but begun;
As if the vanward clouds of evil days
Had spent their malice, and the sullen rear　40
Was with its stored thunder labouring up.
One hand she press'd upon that aching spot
Where beats the human heart, as if just there,
Though an immortal, she felt cruel pain:
The other upon Saturn's bended neck
She laid, and to the level of his ear
Leaning with parted lips, some words she
　spake
In solemn tenor and deep organ tone:
Some mourning words, which in our feeble
　tongue
Would come in these like accents; O how frail
To that large utterance of the early Gods!　51
"Saturn, look up!—though wherefore, poor old
　King?
"I have no comfort for thee, no not one:
"I cannot say 'O wherefore sleepest thou?'
"For heaven is parted from thee, and the
　earth
"Knows thee not, thus afflicted, for a God;
"And ocean too, with all its solemn noise,
"Has from thy sceptre pass'd; and all the air
"Is emptied of thine hoary majesty.
"Thy thunder, conscious of the new command,
"Rumbles reluctant o'er our fallen house;　61
"And thy sharp lightning in unpractis'd hands
"Scorches and burns our once serene domain.
"O aching time! O moments big as years!

"All as ye pass swell out the monstrous truth,
"And press it so upon our weary griefs
"That unbelief has not a space to breathe.
"Saturn, sleep on:—O thoughtless, why did I
"Thus violate thy slumbrous solitude?
"Why should I ope thy melancholy eyes? 70
"Saturn, sleep on! while at thy feet I weep."

As when, upon a tranced summer-night,
Those green-rob'd senators of mighty woods,
Tall oaks, branch-charmed by the earnest stars,
Dream, and so dream all night without a stir,
Save from one gradual solitary gust
Which comes upon the silence, and dies off,
As if the ebbing air had but one wave;
So came these words and went; the while in tears,
She touch'd her fair large forehead to the ground, 80
Just where her falling hair might be outspread
A soft and silken mat for Saturn's feet.
One moon, with alteration slow, had shed
Her silver seasons four upon the night,
And still these two were postured motionless,
Like natural sculpture in cathedral cavern;
The frozen God still couchant on the earth,
And the sad Goddess weeping at his feet:
Until at length old Saturn lifted up
His faded eyes, and saw his kingdom gone, 90
And all the gloom and sorrow of the place,
And that fair kneeling Goddess; and then spake,
As with a palsied tongue, and while his beard
Shook horrid with such aspen-malady:
"O tender spouse of gold Hyperion,
"Thea, I feel thee ere I see thy face;
"Look up, and let me see our doom in it;
"Look up, and tell me if this feeble shape
"Is Saturn's; tell me, if thou hear'st the voice
"Of Saturn; tell me, if this wrinkling brow
"Naked and bare of its great diadem, 101
"Peers like the front of Saturn. Who had power
"To make me desolate? whence came the strength?
"How was it nurtur'd to such bursting forth,
"While Fate seem'd strangled in my nervous grasp?
"But it is so; and I am smother'd up,
"And buried from all godlike exercise
"Of influence benign on planets pale,
"Of admonitions to the winds and seas,
"Of peaceful sway above man's harvesting, 110

"And all those acts which Deity supreme
"Doth ease its heart of love in.—I am gone
"Away from my own bosom: I have left
"My strong identity, my real self,
"Somewhere between the throne, and where I sit
"Here on this spot of earth. Search, Thea, search!
"Open thine eyes eterne, and sphere them round
"Upon all space: space starr'd, and lorn of light;
"Space region'd with life-air; and barren void;
"Spaces of fire, and all the yawn of hell.— 120
"Search, Thea, search! and tell me, if thou seest
"A certain shape or shadow, making way
"With wings or chariot fierce to repossess
"A heaven he lost erewhile: it must—it must
"Be of ripe progress—Saturn must be king
"Yes, there must be a golden victory;
"There must be Gods thrown down, and trumpets
"Of triumph calm, and hymns of festival
"Upon the gold clouds metropolitan,
"Voices of soft proclaim, and silver stir 130
"Of strings in hollow shells; and there shall be
"Beautiful things made new, for the surprise
"Of the sky-children; I will give command:
"Thea! Thea! Thea! where is Saturn?"

This passion lifted him upon his feet,
And made his hands to struggle in the air,
His Druid locks to shake and ooze with sweat,
His eyes to fever out, his voice to cease.
He stood, and heard not Thea's sobbing deep;
A little time, and then again he snatch'd, 140
Utterance thus.—"But cannot I create?
"Cannot I form? Cannot I fashion forth
"Another world, another universe,
"To overbear and crumble this to nought?
"Where is another chaos? Where?"—That word
Found way unto Olympus, and made quake
The rebel three.—Thea was startled up
And in her bearing was a sort of hope,
As thus she quick-voiced spake, yet full of awe.

"This cheers our fallen house: come to our friends, 150
"O Saturn! come away, and give them heart;
"I know the covert, for thence came I hither."

Thus brief; then with beseeching eyes she
 went
With backward footing through the shade a
 space:
He follow'd, and she turn'd to lead the way
Through aged boughs, that yielded like the
 mist
Which eagles cleave upmounting from their
 nest.

Meanwhile in other realms big tears were
 shed,
More sorrow like to this, and such like woe,
Too huge for mortal tongue or pen of scribe:
The Titans fierce, self-hid, or prison-bound, 161
Groan'd for the old allegiance once more,
And listen'd in sharp pain for Saturn's voice.
But one of the whole mammoth-brood still
 kept
His sov'reignty, and rule, and majesty;—
Blazing Hyperion on his orbed fire
Still sat, still snuff'd the incense, teeming up
From man to the sun's God; yet unsecure:
For as among us mortals omens drear
Fright and perplex, so also shuddered he— 170
Not at dog's howl, or gloom-bird's hated
 screech,
Or the familiar visiting of one
Upon the first toll of his passing-bell,
Or prophesyings of the midnight lamp;
But horrors, portion'd to a giant nerve,
Oft made Hyperion ache. His palace bright
Bastion'd with pyramids of glowing gold,
And touch'd with shade of bronzed obelisks,
Glar'd a blood-red through all its thousand
 courts,
Arches, and domes, and fiery galleries; 180
And all its curtains of Aurorian clouds
Flush'd angerly: while sometimes eagle's
 wings,
Unseen before by Gods or wondering men,
Darken'd the place; and neighing steeds were
 heard,
Not heard before by Gods or wondering men.
Also, when he would taste the spicy wreaths
Of incense, breath'd aloft from sacred hills,
Instead of sweets, his ample palate took
Savour of poisonous brass and metal sick:
And so, when harbour'd in the sleepy west, 190
After the full completion of fair day,—
For rest divine upon exalted couch
And slumber in the arms of melody,
He pac'd away the pleasant hours of ease
With stride colossal, on from hall to hall;

While far within each aisle and deep recess,
His winged minions in close clusters stood,
Amaz'd and full of fear; like anxious men
Who on wide plains gather in panting troops,
When earthquakes jar their battlements and
 towers. 200
Even now, while Saturn, rous'd from icy
 trance,
Went step for step with Thea through the
 woods,
Hyperion, leaving twilight in the rear,
Came slope upon the threshold of the west;
Then, as was wont, his palace-door flew ope
In smoothest silence, save what solemn tubes,
Blown by the serious Zephyrs, gave of sweet
And wandering sounds, slow-breathed mel-
 odies;
And like a rose in vermeil tint and shape,
In fragrance soft, and coolness to the eye, 210
That inlet to severe magnificence
Stood full blown, for the God to enter in.

He enter'd, but he enter'd full of wrath;
His flaming robes stream'd out beyond his
 heels,
And gave a roar, as if of earthly fire,
That scar'd away the meek ethereal Hours
And made their dove-wings tremble. On he
 flared,
From stately nave to nave, from vault to
 vault,
Through bowers of fragrant and enwreathed
 light,
And diamond-paved lustrous long arcades, 220
Until he reach'd the great main cupola;
There standing fierce beneath, he stampt his
 foot,
And from the basements deep to the high
 towers
Jarr'd his own golden region; and before
The quavering thunder thereupon had ceas'd,
His voice leapt out, despite of godlike curb,
To this result: "O dreams of day and night!
"O monstrous forms! O effigies of pain!
"O spectres busy in a cold, cold gloom!
"O lank-ear'd Phantoms of black-weeded
 pools! 230
"Why do I know ye? why have I seen ye?
 why
"Is my eternal essence thus distraught
"To see and to behold these horrors new?
"Saturn is fallen, am I too to fall?
"Am I to leave this haven of my rest,
"This cradle of my glory, this soft clime,

"This calm luxuriance of blissful light,
"These crystalline pavilions, and pure fanes,
"Of all my lucent empire? It is left
"Deserted, void, nor any haunt of mine. 240
"The blaze, the splendour, and the symmetry,
"I cannot see—but darkness, death and darkness.
"Even here, into my centre of repose,
"The shady visions come to domineer,
"Insult, and blind, and stifle up my pomp.—
"Fall!—No, by Tellus and her briny robes!
"Over the fiery frontier of my realms
"I will advance a terrible right arm
"Shall scare that infant thunderer, rebel Jove,
"And bid old Saturn take his throne again."—
He spake, and ceas'd, the while a heavier threat 251
Held struggle with his throat but came not forth;
For as in theatres of crowded men
Hubbub increases more they call out "Hush!"
So at Hyperion's words the Phantoms pale
Bestirr'd themselves, thrice horrible and cold;
And from the mirror'd level where he stood
A mist arose, as from a scummy marsh.
At this, through all his bulk an agony
Crept gradual, from the feet unto the crown,
Like a lithe serpent vast and muscular 261
Making slow way, with head and neck convuls'd
From over-strained might. Releas'd, he fled
To the eastern gates, and full six dewy hours
Before the dawn in season due should blush,
He breath'd fierce breath against the sleepy portals,
Clear'd them of heavy vapours, burst them wide
Suddenly on the ocean's chilly streams.
The planet orb of fire, whereon he rode
Each day from east to west the heavens through, 270
Spun round in sable curtaining of clouds;
Not therefore veiled quite, blindfold, and hid,
But ever and anon the glancing spheres,
Circles, and arcs, and broad-belting colure,
Glow'd through, and wrought upon the muffling dark
Sweet-shaped lightnings from the nadir deep
Up to the zenith,—hieroglyphics old,
Which sages and keen-ey'd astrologers
Then living on the earth, with labouring thought
Won from the gaze of many centuries: 280
Now lost, save what we find on remnants huge

Of stone, or marble swart; their import gone,
Their wisdom long since fled.—Two wings this orb
Possess'd for glory, two fair argent wings,
Ever exalted at the God's approach:
And now, from forth the gloom their plumes immense
Rose, one by one, till all outspreaded were;
While still the dazzling globe maintain'd eclipse,
Awaiting for Hyperion's command.
Fain would he have commanded, fain took throne 290
And bid the day begin, if but for change.
He might not:—No, though a primeval God:
The sacred seasons might not be disturb'd.
Therefore the operations of the dawn
Stay'd in their birth, even as here 'tis told.
Those silver wings expanded sisterly,
Eager to sail their orb; the porches wide
Open'd upon the dusk demesnes of night;
And the bright Titan, phrenzied with new woes,
Unused to bend, by hard compulsion bent 300
His spirit to the sorrow of the time;
And all along a dismal rack of clouds,
Upon the boundaries of day and night,
He stretch'd himself in grief and radiance faint.
There as he lay, the Heaven with its stars
Look'd down on him with pity, and the voice
Of Cœlus, from the universal space,
Thus whisper'd low and solemn in his ear.
"O brightest of my children dear, earth-born
"And sky-engendered, Son of Mysteries 310
"All unrevealed even to the powers
"Which met at thy creating; at whose joys
"And palpitations sweet, and pleasures soft,
"I, Cœlus, wonder, how they came and whence;
"And at the fruits thereof what shapes they be,
"Distinct, and visible; symbols divine,
"Manifestations of that beauteous life
"Diffus'd unseen throughout eternal space:
"Of these new-form'd art thou, oh brightest child!
"Of these, thy brethren and the Goddesses! 320
"There is sad feud among ye, and rebellion
"Of son against his sire. I saw him fall,
"I saw my first-born tumbled from his throne!
"To me his arms were spread, to me his voice
"Found way from forth the thunders round his head!

"Pale wox I, and in vapours hid my face.
"Art thou, too, near such doom? vague fear
    there is:
"For I have seen my sons most unlike Gods.
"Divine ye were created, and divine
"In sad demeanour, solemn, undisturb'd,   330
"Unruffled, like high Gods, ye liv'd and ruled:
"Now I behold in you fear, hope, and wrath;
"Actions of rage and passion; even as
"I see them, on the mortal world beneath,
"In men who die.—This is the grief, O Son!
"Sad sign of ruin, sudden dismay, and fall!
"Yet do thou strive; as thou art capable,
"As thou canst move about, an evident God;
"And canst oppose to each malignant hour
"Ethereal presence:—I am but a voice;   340
"My life is but the life of winds and tides,
"No more than winds and tides can I avail:—
"But thou canst.—Be thou therefore in the
    van
"Of circumstance; yea, seize the arrow's barb
"Before the tense string murmur.—To the
    earth!
"For there thou wilt find Saturn, and his woes.
"Meantime I will keep watch on thy bright
    sun,
"And of thy seasons be a careful nurse."—
Ere half this region-whisper had come down,
Hyperion arose, and on the stars   350
Lifted his curved lids, and kept them wide
Until it ceas'd; and still he kept them wide:
And still they were the same bright, patient
    stars.
Then with a slow incline of his broad breast,
Like to a diver in the pearly seas,
Forward he stoop'd over the airy shore,
And plung'd all noiseless into the deep night.

BOOK II

JUST at the self-same beat of Time's wide
    wings
Hyperion slid into the rustled air,
And Saturn gain'd with Thea that sad place
Where Cybele and the bruised Titans mourn'd.
It was a den where no insulting light
Could glimmer on their tears; where their own
    groans
They felt, but heard not, for the solid roar
Of thunderous waterfalls and torrents hoarse,
Pouring a constant bulk, uncertain where.
Crag jutting forth to crag, and rocks that
    seem'd   10
Ever as if just rising from a sleep,

Forehead to forehead held their monstrous
    horns;
And thus in thousand hugest phantasies
Made a fit roofing to this nest of woe.
Instead of thrones, hard flint they sat upon,
Couches of rugged stone, and slaty ridge
Stubborn'd with iron. All were not assembled:
Some chain'd in torture, and some wandering.
Cœus, and Gyges, and Briareüs,
Typhon, and Dolour, and Porphyrion,   20
With many more, the brawniest in assault,
Were pent in regions of laborious breath;
Dungeon'd in opaque element, to keep
Their clench'd teeth still clench'd, and all
    their limbs
Lock'd up like veins of metal, crampt and
    screw'd;
Without a motion, save of their big hearts
Heaving in pain, and horribly convuls'd
With sanguine feverous boiling gurge of pulse.
Mnemosyne was straying in the world;
Far from her moon had Phœbe wandered;   30
And many else were free to roam abroad,
But for the main, here found they covert
    drear.
Scarce images of life, one here, one there,
Lay vast and edgeways; like a dismal cirque
Of Druid stones, upon a forlorn moor,
When the chill rain begins at shut of eve,
In dull November, and their chancel vault,
The Heaven itself, is blinded throughout night.
Each one kept shroud, nor to his neighbor
    gave
Or word, or look, or action of despair.   40
Creüs was one; his ponderous iron mace
Lay by him, and a shatter'd rib of rock
Told of his rage, ere he thus sank and pined.
Iäpetus another; in his grasp,
A serpent's plashy neck; its barbed tongue
Squeez'd from the gorge, and all its uncurled
    length
Dead; and because the creature could not spit
Its poison in the eyes of conquering Jove.
Next Cottus: prone he lay, chin uppermost,
As though in pain; for still upon the flint   50
He ground severe his skull, with open mouth
And eyes at horrid working. Nearest him
Asia, born of most enormous Caf,
Who cost her mother Tellus keener pangs,
Though feminine, than any of her sons:
More thought than woe was in her dusky face,
For she was prophesying of her glory:
And in her wide imaginations stood
Palm-shaded temples, and high rival fanes,

By Oxus or in Ganges' sacred isles.   60
Even as Hope upon her anchor leans,
So leant she, not so fair, upon a tusk
Shed from the broadest of her elephants.
Above her, on a crag's uneasy shelve,
Upon his elbow rais'd, all prostrate else,
Shadow'd Enceladus; once tame and mild
As grazing ox unworried in the meads;
Now tiger-passion'd, lion-thoughted, wroth,
He meditated, plotted, and even now
Was hurling mountains in that second war, 70
Not long delay'd, that scared the younger
    Gods
To hide themselves in forms of beast and bird.
Not far hence Atlas; and beside him prone
Phorcus, the sire of Gorgons. Neighbor'd close
Oceanus, and Tethys, in whose lap
Sobb'd Clymene among her tangled hair.
In midst of all lay Themis, at the feet
Of Ops the queen all clouded round from
    sight;
No shape distinguishable, more than when
Thick night confounds the pine-tops with the
    clouds: 80
And many else whose names may not be told.
For when the Muse's wings are air-ward
    spread,
Who shall delay her flight? And she must
    chaunt
Of Saturn, and his guide, who now had climb'd
With damp and slippery footing from a depth
More horrid still. Above a sombre cliff
Their heads appear'd, and up their statue
    grew
Till on the level height their steps found ease;
Then Thea spread abroad her trembling arms
Upon the precincts of this nest of pain,   90
And sidelong fix'd her eye on Saturn's face:
There saw she direst strife; the supreme God
At war with all the frailty of grief,
Of rage, of fear, anxiety, revenge,
Remorse, spleen, hope, but most of all despair.
Against these plagues he strove in vain; for
    Fate
Had pour'd a mortal oil upon his head,
A disanointing poison: so that Thea,
Affrighted, kept her still, and let him pass
First onwards in, among the fallen tribe.   100

As with us mortal men, the laden heart
Is persecuted more, and fever'd more,
When it is nighing to the mournful house
Where other hearts are sick of the same
    bruise;

So Saturn, as he walk'd into the midst,
Felt faint, and would have sunk among the
    rest,
But that he met Enceladus's eye,
Whose mightiness, and awe of him, at once
Came like an inspiration; and he shouted,
"Titans, behold your God!" at which some
    groan'd: 110
Some started on their feet; some also shouted;
Some wept, some wail'd, all bow'd with rever-
    ence;
And Ops, uplifting her black folded veil,
Show'd her pale cheeks, and all her forehead
    wan,
Her eye-brows thin and jet, and hollow eyes.
There is a roaring in the bleak-grown pines
When Winter lifts his voice; there is a noise
Among immortals when a God gives sign,
With hushing finger, how he means to load
His tongue with the full weight of utterless
    thought,   120
With thunder, and with music, and with
    pomp:
Such noise is like the roar of bleak-grown
    pines;
Which, when it ceases in this mountain'd
    world,
No other sound succeeds; but ceasing here,
Among these fallen, Saturn's voice therefrom
Grew up like organ, that begins anew
Its strain, when other harmonies, stopt short,
Leave the dinn'd air vibrating silverly.
Thus grew it up—"Not in my own sad breast,
"Which is its own great judge and searcher
    out,   130
"Can I find reason why ye should be thus:
"Not in the legends of the first of days,
"Studied from that old spirit-leaved book
"Which starry Uranus with finger bright
"Sav'd from the shores of darkness, when the
    waves
"Low-ebb'd still hid it up in shallow gloom;—
"And the which book ye know I ever kept
"For my firm-based footstool:—Ah, infirm!
"Not there, nor in sign, symbol, or portent
"Of element, earth, water, air, and fire,— 140
"At war, at peace, or inter-quarreling
"One against one, or two, or three, or all
"Each several one, against the other three,
"As fire with air loud warring when rain-floods
"Drown both, and press them both against
    earth's face,
"Where, finding sulphur, a quadruple wrath
"Unhinges the poor world;—not in that strife,

"Wherefrom I take strange lore, and read it
　　deep,
"Can I find reason why ye should be thus:
"No, no-where can unriddle, though I search,
"And pore on Nature's universal scroll 　　150
"Even to swooning, why ye Divinities,
"The first-born of all shap'd and palpable
　　Gods,
"Should cower beneath what, in comparison,
"Is untremendous might. Yet ye are here,
"O'erwhelm'd, and spurn'd, and batter'd, ye
　　are here!
"O Titans, shall I say, 'Arise!'—Ye groan:
"Shall I say 'Crouch!'—Ye groan. What can
　　I then?
"O Heaven wide! O unseen parent dear!
"What can I? Tell me, all ye brethren Gods,
"How we can war, how engine our great
　　wrath! 　　161
"O speak your counsel now, for Satu n's ear
"Is all a-hunger'd. Thou, Oceanus,
"Ponderest high and deep; and in thy face
"I see, astonied, that severe content
"Which comes of thought and musing: give
　　us help!"

So ended Saturn; and the God of the Sea,
Sophist and sage, from no Athenian grove,
But cogitation in his watery shades,
Arose, with locks not oozy, and began, 　　170
In murmurs, which his first-endeavouring
　　tongue
Caught infant-like from the far-foamed sands.
"O ye, whom wrath consumes! who, passion-
　　stung,
"Writhe at defeat, and nurse your agonies!
"Shut up your senses, stifle up your ears,
"My voice is not a bellows unto ire.
"Yet listen, ye who will, whilst I bring proof
"How ye, perforce, must be content to stoop;
"And in the proof much comfort will I give,
"If we will take that comfort in its truth 　180
"We fall by course of Nature's law, not force
"Of thunder, or of Jove. Great Saturn, thou
"Has sifted well the atom-universe;
"But for this reason, that thou art the King,
"And only blind from sheer supremacy,
"One avenue was shaded from thine eyes,
"Through which I wandered to eternal truth.
"And first, as thou wast not the first of powers,
"So art thou not the last; it cannot be:
"Thou art not the beginning nor the end. 　190
"From chaos and parental darkness came
"Light, the first fruits of that intestine broil.

"That sullen ferment, which for wondrous
　　ends
"Was ripening in itself. The ripe hour came,
"And with it light, and light, engendering
"Upon its own producer, forthwith touch'd
"The whole enormous matter into life.
"Upon that very hour, our parentage,
"The Heavens and the Earth, were manifest:
"Then thou first-born, and we the giant-race,
"Found ourselves ruling new and beauteous
　　realms. 　　201
"Now comes the pain of truth, to whom 'tis
　　pain;
"O folly! for to bear all naked truths,
"And to envisage circumstance, all calm,
"That is the top of sovereignty. Mark well!
"As Heaven and Earth are fairer, fairer far
"Than Chaos and blank Darkness, though once
　　chiefs:
"And as we show beyond that Heaven and
　　Earth
"In form and shape compact and beautiful,
"In will, in action free, companionship, 　　210
"And thousand other signs of purer life;
"So on our heel a fresh perfection treads,
"A power more strong in beauty, born of us
"And fated to excel us, as we pass
"In glory that old Darkness: nor are we
"Thereby more conquer'd, than by us the rule
"Of shapeless Chaos. Say, doth the dull soil
"Quarrel with the proud forests it hath fed,
"And feedeth still, more comely than itself?
"Can it deny the chiefdom of green groves? 220
"Or shall the tree be envious of the dove
"Because it cooeth, and hath snowy wings
"To wander wherewithal and find its joys?
"We are such forest-trees, and our fair boughs
"Have bred forth, not pale solitary doves,
"But eagles golden-feather'd, who do tower
"Above us in their beauty, and must reign
"In right thereof; for 'tis the eternal law
"That first in beauty should be first in might:
"Yea, by that law, another race may drive 230
"Our conquerors to mourn as we do now.
"Have ye beheld the young God of the Seas,
"My dispossessor? Have ye seen his face?
"Have ye beheld his chariot, foam'd along
"By noble winged creatures he hath made?
"I saw him on the calmed waters scud,
"With such a glow of beauty in his eyes,
"That it enforc'd me to bid sad farewell
"To all my empire: farewell sad I took,
"And hither came, to see how dolorous fate 240
"Had wrought upon ye; and how I might best

"Give consolation in this woe extreme.
"Receive the truth and let it be your balm."

Whether through poz'd conviction, or dis-
　　dain,
They guarded silence, when Oceanus
Left murmuring, what deepest thought can
　　tell?
But so it was, none answer'd for a space,
Save one whom none regarded, Clymene;
And yet she answer'd not, only complain'd,
With hectic lips, and eyes up-looking mild, 250
Thus wording timidly among the fierce:
"O Father, I am here the simplest voice,
"And all my knowledge is that joy is gone,
"And this thing woe crept in among our
　　hearts,
"There to remain forever, as I fear:
"I would not bode of evil, if I thought
"So weak a creature could turn off the help
"Which by just right should come of mighty
　　Gods;
"Yet let me tell my sorrow, let me tell　259
"Of what I heard, and how it made me weep,
"And know that we had parted from all hope.
"I stood upon a shore, a pleasant shore,
"Where a sweet clime was breathed from a
　　land
"Of fragrance, quietness, and trees, and
　　flowers.
"Full of calm joy it was, as I of grief;
"Too full of joy and soft delicious warmth;
"So that I felt a movement in my heart
"To chide, and to reproach that solitude
"With songs of misery, music of our woes; 269
"And sat me down, and took a mouthed shell
"And murmur'd into it, and made melody—
"O melody no more! for while I sang,
"And with poor skill let pass into the breeze
"The dull shell's echo, from a bowery strand
"Just opposite, an island of the sea,
"There came enchantment with the shifting
　　wind,
"That did both drown and keep alive my ears.
"I threw my shell away upon the sand,
"And a wave fill'd it, as my sense was fill'd
"With that new blissful golden melody.　280
"A living death was in each gush of sounds,
"Each family of rapturous hurried notes,
"That fell, one after one, yet all at once,
"Like pearl beads dropping sudden from their
　　string:
"And then another, then another strain,
"Each like a dove leaving its olive perch,

"With music wing'd instead of silent plumes,
"To hover round my head, and make me sick
"Of joy and grief at once. Grief overcame,
"And I was stopping up my frantic ears,　290
"When, past all hindrance of my trembling
　　hands,
"A voice came sweeter, sweeter than all tune,
"And still it cry'd, 'Apollo! young Apollo!
" 'The morning-bright Apollo! young Apollo!'
"I fled, it follow'd me, and cry'd 'Apollo!'
"O Father, and O Brethren, had ye felt
"Those pains of mine; O Saturn, hadst thou
　　felt,
"Ye would not call this too indulged tongue
"Presumptuous, in thus venturing to be
　　heard."

So far her voice flow'd on, like timorous
　　brook　　　　　　　　　　　　　　300
That, lingering along a pebbled coast,
Doth fear to meet the sea: but sea it met,
And shudder'd; for the overwhelming voice
Of huge Enceladus swallow'd it in wrath:
The ponderous syllables, like sullen waves
In the half-glutted hollows of reef-rocks,
Came booming thus, while still upon his arm
He lean'd; not rising, from supreme contempt,
"Or shall we listen to the over-wise,
"Or to the over-foolish giant, Gods?　310
"Not thunderbolt on thunderbolt, till all
"That rebel Jove's whole armory were spent,
"Not world on world upon these shoulders
　　piled,
"Could agonize me more than baby-words
"In midst of this dethronement horrible.
"Speak! roar! shout! yell! ye sleepy Titans
　　all.
"Do ye forget the blows, the buffets vile?
"Are ye not smitten by a youngling arm?
"Dost thou forget, sham Monarch of the
　　Waves,
"Thy scalding in the seas? What, have I
　　rous'd　　　　　　　　　　　　　　320
"Your spleens with so few simple words as
　　these?
"O joy! for now I see ye are not lost:
"O joy! for now I see a thousand eyes
"Wide glaring for revenge!"—As this he said,
He lifted up his stature vast, and stood,
Still without intermission speaking thus:
"Now ye are flames, I'll tell you how to burn,
"And purge the ether of our enemies;
"How to feed fierce the crooked stings of fire,
"And singe away the swollen clouds of Jove,

"Stifling that puny essence in its tent.   331
"O let him feel the evil he hath done;
"For though I scorn Oceanus's lore,
"Much pain have I for more than loss of
    realms:
"The days of peace and slumberous calm are
    fled;
"Those days, all innocent of scathing war,
"When all the fair Existences of heaven
"Came open-eyed to guess what we would
    speak:—
"That was before our brows were taught to
    frown,
"Before our lips knew else but solemn sounds;
"That was before we knew the winged thing,
"Victory, might be lost, or might be won. 341
"And be ye mindful that Hyperion,
"Our brightest brother, still is undisgraced—
"Hyperion, lo! his radiance is here!"

    All eyes were on Enceladus's face,
And they beheld, while still Hyperion's name
Flew from his lips up to the vaulted rocks,
A pallid gleam across his features stern:
Not savage, for he saw full many a God   350
Wroth as himself. He look'd upon them all,
And in each face he saw a gleam of light,
But splendider in Saturn's, whose hoar locks
Shone like the bubbling foam about a keel
When the prow sweeps into a midnight cove.
In pale and silver silence they remain'd,
Till suddenly a splendour, like the morn,
Pervaded all the beetling gloomy steeps,
All the sad spaces of oblivion,
And every gulf, and every chasm old,   360
And every height, and every sullen depth,
Voiceless, or hoarse with loud tormented
    streams:
And all the everlasting cataracts,
And all the headlong torrents far and near,
Mantled before in darkness and huge shade,
Now saw the light and made it terrible
It was Hyperion:—a granite peak
His bright feet touch'd, and there he stay'd to
    view
The misery his brilliance had betray'd
To the most hateful seeing of itself.   370
Golden his hair of short Numidian curl,
Regal his shape majestic, a vast shade
In midst of his own brightness, like the bulk
Of Memnon's image at the set of sun
To one who travels from the dusking East:
Sighs, too, as mournful as that Memnon's harp
He utter'd, while his hands contemplative

He press'd together, and in silence stood.
Despondence seiz'd again the fallen Gods:
At sight of the dejected King of Day,   380
And many hid their faces from the light:
But fierce Enceladus sent forth his eyes
Among the brotherhood; and, at their glare,
Uprose Iäpetus, and Creüs too,
And Phorcus, sea-born, and together strode
To where he towered on his eminence
There those four shouted forth old Saturn's
    name;
Hyperion from the peak loud answered, "Sat-
    urn!"
Saturn sat near the Mother of the Gods,
In whose face was no joy, though all the
    Gods   390
Gave from their hollow throats the name of
    "Saturn!"

Book III

THUS in alternate uproar and sad peace,
Amazed were those Titans utterly.
O leave them, Muse! O leave them to their
    woes;
For thou art weak to sing such tumults dire:
A solitary sorrow best befits
Thy lips, and antheming a lonely grief.
Leave them, O Muse! for thou anon wilt find
Many a fallen old Divinity
Wandering in vain about bewildered shores.
Meantime touch piously the Delphic harp,   10
And not a wind of heaven but will breathe
In aid soft warble from the Dorian flute;
For lo! 'tis for the Father of all verse.
Flush everything that hath a vermeil hue,
Let the rose glow intense and warm the air,
And let the clouds of even and of morn
Float in voluptuous fleeces o'er the hills;
Let the red wine within the goblet boil,
Cold as a bubbling well; let faint-lipp'd shells,
On sands, or in great deeps, vermilion turn 20
Through all their labyrinths; and let the maid
Blush keenly, as with some warm kiss sur-
    pris'd.
Chief isle of the embowered Cyclades,
Rejoice, O Delos, with thine olive green,
And poplars, and lawn-shading palms, and
    beech,
In which the Zephyr breathes the loudest song,
And hazels thick, dark-stemm'd beneath the
    shade:
Apollo is once more the golden theme!
Where was he, when the Giant of the Sun

Stood bright, amid the sorrow of his peers? 30
Together had he left his mother fair
And his twin-sister sleeping in their bower,
And in the morning twilight wandered forth
Beside the osiers of a rivulet,
Full ankle-deep in lilies of the vale.
The nightingale had ceas'd, and a few stars
Were lingering in the heavens, while the
thrush
Began calm-throated. Throughout all the isle
There was no covert, no retired cave 39
Unhaunted by the murmurous noise of waves,
Though scarcely heard in many a green re-
cess.
He listen'd, and he wept, and his bright tears
Went trickling down the golden bow he held.
Thus with half-shut suffused eyes he stood,
While from beneath some cumbrous boughs
hard by
With solemn step an awful Goddess came,
And there was purport in her looks for him,
Which he with eager guess began to read
Perplex'd, the while melodiously he said:
"How cam'st thou over the unfooted sea? 50
"Or hath that antique mien and robed form
"Mov'd in these vales invisible till now?
"Sure I have heard those vestments sweeping
o'er
"The fallen leaves, when I have sat alone
"In cool mid-forest. Surely I have traced
"The rustle of those ample skirts about
"The grassy solitudes, and seen the flowers
"Lift up their heads, as still the whisper
pass'd.
"Goddess! I have beheld those eyes before,
"And their eternal calm, and all that face, 60
"Or I have dream'd."—"Yes," said the su-
preme shape,
"Thou hast dream'd of me, and awaking up
"Didst find a lyre all golden by thy side,
"Whose strings touch'd by thy fingers, all the
vast
"Unwearied ear of the whole universe
"Listen'd in pain and pleasure at the birth
"Of such new tuneful wonder. Is't not strange
"That thou shouldst weep, so gifted? Tell me,
youth,
"What sorrow thou canst feel; for I am sad
"When thou dost shed a tear: explain thy
griefs 70
"To one who in this lonely isle hath been
"The watcher of thy sleep and hours of life,
"From the young day when first thy infant
hand

"Pluck'd witless the weak flowers, till thine
arm
"Could bend that bow heroic to all times.
"Show thy heart's secret to an ancient Power
"Who hath forsaken old and sacred thrones
"For prophecies of thee, and for the sake
"Of loveliness new born."—Apollo then,
With sudden scrutiny and gloomless eyes, 80
Thus answer'd, while his white melodious
throat
Throbb'd with the syllables.—"Mnemosyne!
"Thy name is on my tongue, I know not how;
"Why should I tell thee what thou so well
seest?
"Why should I strive to show what from thy
lips
"Would come no mystery? For me, dark, dark,
"And painful vile oblivion seals my eyes:
"I strive to search wherefore I am so sad,
"Until a melancholy numbs my limbs;
"And then upon the grass I sit, and moan, 90
"Like one who once had wings.—O why
should I
"Feel cured and thwarted, when the liegeless
air
"Yields to my step aspirant? why should I
"Spurn the green turf as hateful to my feet?
"Goddess benign, point forth some unknown
thing:
"Are there not other regions than this isle?
"What are the stars? There is the sun, the
sun!
"And the most patient brilliance of the moon!
"And stars by thousands! Point me out the
way
"To any one particular beauteous star, 100
"And I will flit into it with my lyre,
"And make its silvery splendour pant with
bliss.
"I have heard the cloudy thunder: Where is
power?
"Whose hand, whose essence, what divinity
"Makes this alarm in the elements,
"While I here idle listen on the shores
"In fearless yet in aching ignorance?
"O tell me, lonely Goddess, by thy harp,
"That waileth every morn and eventide.
"Tell me why thus I rave, about these
groves! 110
"Mute thou remainest— Mute! yet I can read
"A wondrous lesson in thy silent face:
"Knowledge enormous makes a God of me.
"Names, deeds, grey-legends, dire events, re-
bellions,

"Majesties, sovran voices, agonies,
"Creations and destroyings, all at once
"Pour into the wide hollows of my brain,
"And defy me, as if some blithe wine
"Or bright elixir peerless I had drunk,
"And so become immortal."—Thus the God,
While his enkindled eyes, with level glance 121
Beneath his white soft temples, steadfast kept
Trembling with light upon Mnemosyne.
Soon wild commotions shook him, and made
      flush
All the immortal fairness of his limbs;
Most like the struggle at the gate of death;
Or liker still to one who should take leave
Of pale immortal death, and with a pang
As hot as death's is chill, with fierce convulse
Die into life: so young Apollo anguish'd: 130
His very hair, his golden tresses famed
Kept undulation round his eager neck.
During the pain Mnemosyne upheld
Her arms as one who prophesied.—At length
Apollo shriek'd;—and lo! from all his limbs
Celestial   *   *   *   *   *
*   *   *   *   *   *   *

SONNET

ON SEEING THE ELGIN MARBLES

My spirit is too weak—mortality
    Weighs heavily on me like unwilling sleep,
    And each imagin'd pinnacle and steep
Of godlike hardship, tells me I must die
Like a sick Eagle looking at the sky.
    Yet 'tis a gentle luxury to weep
    That I have not the cloudy winds to keep,
Fresh for the opening of the morning's eye.
Such dim-conceived glories of the brain
    Bring round the heart an undescribable
        feud;   10
So do these wonders a most dizzy pain,
    That mingles Grecian grandeur with the
        rude
Wasting of old Time—with a billowy main—
A sun—a shadow of a magnitude.

SONNET

ON A PICTURE OF LEANDER

COME hither all sweet maidens soberly,
    Down-looking aye, and with a chasten'd
        light,
    Hid in the fringes of your eyelids white,
And meekly let your fair hands joined be,
As if so gentle that ye could not see,
    Untouch'd, a victim of your beauty bright,
    Sinking away to his young spirit's night,—
Sinking bewilder'd 'mid the dreary sea:
'Tis young Leander toiling to his death;
    Nigh swooning, he doth purse his weary
        lips   10
    For Hero's cheek, and smiles against her
        smile.
O horrid dream! see how his body dips
    Dead-heavy; arms and shoulders gleam
        awhile:
He's gone; up bubbles all his amorous breath!

SONNET

ON THE SEA

IT keeps eternal whisperings around
    Desolate shores, and with its mighty swell
    Gluts twice ten thousand caverns, till the
        spell
Of Hecate leaves them their old shadowy
        sound.
Often 'tis in such gentle temper found,
    That scarcely will the very smallest shell
    Be mov'd for days from whence it some-
        time fell,
When last the winds of heaven were unbound.
Oh ye! who have your eyeballs vex'd and
        tir'd,
    Feast them upon the wideness of the Sea; 10
    Oh ye! whose ears are dinn'd with up-
        roar rude,
Or fed too much with cloying melody,—
    Sit ye near some old cavern's mouth, and
        brood
Until ye start, as if the sea-nymphs quir'd!

SONNET

WHEN I have fears that I may cease to be
    Before my pen has glean'd my teeming
        brain,
Before high piléd books, in charactry,
    Hold like rich garners the full ripen'd grain;
When I behold, upon the night's starr'd face,
    Huge cloudy symbols of a high romance,
And think that I may never live to trace
    Their shadows, with the magic hand of
        chance;
And when I feel, fair creature of an hour,
    That I shall never look upon thee more, 10

Never have relish in the faery power
  Of unreflecting love;—then on the shore
Of the wide world I stand alone, and think
Till love and fame to nothingness do sink.

THE EVE OF SAINT MARK

A FRAGMENT

UPON a Sabbath-day it fell;
Twice holy was the Sabbath-bell,
That call'd the folk to evening prayer;
The city streets were clean and fair
From wholesome drench of April rains;
And, on the western window panes
The chilly sunset faintly told
Of unmatur'd green vallies cold,
Of the green thorny bloomless hedge,
Of rivers new with spring-tide sedge,   10
Of primroses by shelter'd rills,
And daisies on the aguish hills.
Twice holy was the Sabbath-bell:
The silent streets were crowded well
With staid and pious companies,
Warm from their fire-side orat'ries;
And moving, with demurest air,
To even-song, and vesper prayer.
Each arched porch, and entry low,
Was fill'd with patient folk and slow,   20
With whispers hush, and shuffling feet,
While play'd the organ loud and sweet.

The bells had ceas'd, the prayers began,
And Bertha had not yet half done
A curious volume, patch'd and torn,
That all day long, from earliest morn,
Had taken captive her two eyes,
Among its golden broideries;
Perplex'd her with a thousand things,—
The stars of Heaven, and angels' wings,   30
Martyrs in a fiery blaze,
Azure saints and silver rays,
Moses' breastplate, and the seven
Candlesticks John saw in Heaven,
The winged Lion of Saint Mark,
And the Covenantal Ark,
With its many mysteries,
Cherubim and golden mice.

Bertha was a maiden fair,
Dwelling in th' old Minster-square;   40
From her fire-side she could see,
Sidelong, its rich antiquity,
Far as the Bishop's garden-wall;

Where sycamores and elm-trees tall,
Full-leav'd, the forest had outstript,
By no sharp north-wind ever nipt,
So shelter'd by the mighty pile,
Bertha arose, and read awhile,
With forehead 'gainst the window-pane.
Again she try'd, and then again,   50
Until the dusk eve left her dark
Upon the legend of St. Mark.
From plaited lawn-frill, fine and thin,
She lifted up her soft warm chin,
With aching neck and swimming eyes,
And daz'd with saintly imageries.

All was gloom, and silent all,
Save now and then the still foot-fall
Of one returning homewards late,
Past the echoing minster-gate.   60
The clamorous daws, that all the day
Above tree-tops and towers play,
Pair by pair had gone to rest,
Each in its ancient belfry-nest,
Where asleep they fall betimes,
To music and the drowsy chimes.

All was silent, all was gloom,
Abroad and in the homely room:
Down she sat, poor cheated soul!
And struck a lamp from the dismal coal;   70
Lean'd forward, with bright drooping hair
And slant book, full against the glare.
Her shadow, in uneasy guise,
Hover'd about, a giant size,
On ceiling-beam and old oak chair,
The parrot's cage, and panel square;
And the warm angled winter-screen,
On which were many monsters seen,
Call'd doves of Siam, Lima mice,
And legless birds of Paradise,   80
Macaw, and tender Avadavat,
And silken-furr'd Angora cat.
Untir'd she read, her shadow still
Glower'd about, as it would fill
The room with wildest forms and shades,
As though some ghostly queen of spades
Had come to mock behind her back,
And dance, and ruffle her garments black.
Untir'd she read the legend page,
Of holy Mark, from youth to age,   90
On land, on sea, in pagan chains,
Rejoicing for his many pains,
Sometimes the learned eremite,
With golden star, or dagger bright,
Referr'd to pious poesies

Written in smallest crow-quill size
Beneath the text; and thus the rhyme
Was parcell'd out from time to time:
——"Als writith he of swevenis,
Men han beforne they wake in bliss,   100
Whanne than hir friendes thinke him bound
In crimped shroude farre under grounde;
And how a litling child mote be
A saint er its nativitie,
Gif that the modre (God her blesse!)
Kepen in solitarinesse,
And kissen devoute the holy croce,
Of Goddes love, and Sathan's force,—
He writith; and thinges many mo
Of swiche things I may not show.   110
Bot I must tellen verile
Somdel of Saintè Cicilie,
And chieflie what he auctorethe
Of Saintè Markis life and dethe":

At length her constant eyelids come
Upon the fervent martyrdom;
Then lastly to his holy shrine,
Exalt amid the tapers' shrine
At Venice,—

ODE TO INDOLENCE

"They toil not, neither do they spin."

1

ONE morn before me were three figures seen,
    With bowed necks, and joined hands, side-
        faced;
    And one behind the other stepp'd serene,
In placid sandals, and in white robes graced;
They pass'd, like figures on a marble urn,
    When shifted round to see the other side;
    They came again; as when the urn once
        more
Is shifted round, the first seen shades return;
And they were strange to me, as may be-
        tide
    With vases, to one deep in Phidian lore. 10

2

How is it, Shadows! that I knew ye not?
    How came ye muffled in so hush a mask?
Was it a silent deep-disguised plot
    To steal away, and leave without a task
My idle days? Ripe was the drowsy hour;
    The blissful cloud of summer-indolence

Benumb'd my eyes; my pulse grew less
        and less;
Pain had no sting, and pleasure's wreath no
        flower: 18
    O, why did ye not melt, and leave my sense
Unhaunted quite of all but—nothingness?

3

A third time pass'd they by, and, passing,
        turn'd
    Each one the face a moment whiles to me;
Then faded, and to follow them I burn'd
    And ach'd for wings, because I knew the
        three;
The first was a fair Maid, and Love her name;
    The second was Ambition, pale of cheek,
        And ever watchful, with fatigued eye;
The last, whom I love more, the more of
        blame
    Is heap'd upon her, maiden most unmeek,—
    I knew to be my demon Poesy.   30

4

They faded, and, forsooth! I wanted wings:
    O folly! What is love? and where is it?
And for that poor Ambition! it springs
    From a man's little heart's short fever-fit;
For Poesy!—no, she has not a joy,—
    At least for me,—so sweet as drowsy noons,
        And evenings steep'd in honied indolence;
O, for an age so shelter'd from annoy,
    That I may never know how change the
        moons,   39
        Or hear the voice of busy common-sense!

5

And once more came they by;—alas! where-
        fore?
    My sleep had been embroider'd with dim
        dreams;
My soul had been a lawn besprinkled o'er
    With flowers, and stirring shades, and
        baffled beams:
The morn was clouded, but no shower fell,
    Tho' in her lids hung the sweet tears of
        May;
        The open casement press'd a new-leav'd
        vine,
    Let in the budding warmth and throstle's
        lay;
O Shadows! 'twas a time to bid farewell!

Upon your skirts had fallen no tears of
    mine.   50

6

So, ye three Ghosts, adieu! Ye cannot raise
  My head cool-bedded in the flowery grass;
For I would not be dieted with praise,
  A pet-lamb in a sentimental farce!
Fade softly from my eyes, and be once more
  In masque-like figures on the dreamy urn;
    Farewell! I yet have visions for the night,
And for the day faint visions there is store;
    Vanish, ye Phantoms! from my idle
      spright,
Into the clouds, and never more return!   60

LA BELLE DAME SANS MERCI

1

"Ah, what can ail thee, knight-at-arms,
  Alone and palely loitering;
The sedge is wither'd from the lake,
  And no birds sing.

2

"Ah, what can ail thee, knight-at-arms,
  So haggard and so woe-begone?
The squirrel's granary is full,
  And the harvest's done.

3

"I see a lily on thy brow,
  With anguish moist and fever dew;   10
And on thy cheek a fading rose
  Fast withereth too."

4

"I met a lady in the meads
  Full beautiful, a faery's child;
Her hair was long, her foot was light,
  And her eyes were wild.

5

"I made a garland for her head,
  And bracelets too, and fragrant zone;
She look'd at me as she did love,
  And made sweet moan.   20

6

"I set her on my pacing steed,
  And nothing else saw all day long;
For sideways would she lean, and sing
  A faery's song.

7

"She found me roots of relish sweet,
  And honey wild, and manna dew;
And sure in language strange she said,
  I love thee true.

8

"She took me to her elfin grot,
  And there she wept and sighed full sore, 30
And there I shut her wild, wild eyes—
  With kisses four.

9

"And there she lullèd me asleep,
  And there I dream'd, ah woe betide,
The latest dream I ever dream'd
  On the cold hill's side.

10

"I saw pale kings, and princes too,
  Pale warriors, death-pale were they all;
Who cry'd—'La belle Dame sans merci
  Hath thee in thrall!'   40

11

"I saw their starv'd lips in the gloom
  With horrid warning gaped wide,
And I awoke, and found me here
  On the cold hill's side.

12

"And this is why I sojourn here
  Alone and palely loitering,
Though the sedge is wither'd from the lake,
  And no birds sing."

SONNET

WRITTEN ON A BLANK PAGE IN SHAKESPEARE'S
POEMS, FACING "A LOVER'S COMPLAINT."

Bright star, would I were stedfast as thou
  art—

Not in lone splendour hung aloft the
    night
And watching, with eternal lids apart,
    Like nature's patient, sleepless Eremite,
The moving waters at their priestlike task
    Of pure ablution round earth's human
      shores,
Or gazing on the new soft-fallen mask

Of snow upon the mountains and the
    moors—
No—yet still stedfast, still unchangeable,
    Pillow'd upon my fair love's ripening breast,
To feel for ever its soft fall and swell,
    Awake for ever in a sweet unrest,
Still, still to hear her tender-taken breath,
And so live ever—or else swoon to death.

SELECTIONS FROM THE LETTERS OF JOHN KEATS

I

TO JOHN HAMILTON REYNOLDS

Carisbrooke, April 17th [1817].
. . . I find I cannot exist without Poetry—
without eternal Poetry—half the day will not
do—the whole of it—I began with a little, but
habit has made me a Leviathan. I had become
all in a Tremble from not having written anything of late—the Sonnet overleaf did me
good. I slept the better last night for it—this
Morning, however, I am nearly as bad
again. . . .

II

TO LEIGH HUNT

Margate, May 10, 1817.
MY DEAR HUNT—The little gentleman that
sometimes lurks in a gossip's bowl, ought to
have come in the very likeness of a *roasted*
crab, and choaked me outright for not answering your letter ere this: however, you must not
suppose that I was in town to receive it: no,
it followed me to the Isle of Wight, and I got it
just as I was going to pack up for Margate. . . .
The last Examiner was a battering-ram against
Christianity, blasphemy, Tertullian, Erasmus,
Sir Philip Sidney; and then the dreadful Petzelians and their expiation by blood; and do
Christians shudder at the same thing in a newspaper which they attribute to their God in its
most aggravated form? What is to be the end
of this? I must mention Hazlitt's Southey.
O that he had left out the grey hairs; or that
they had been in any other paper not concluding with such a thunder-clap! That sentence
about making a page of the feeling of a whole
life, appears to me like a whale's back in the

sea of prose. I ought to have said a word on
Shakspeare's Christianity. There are two which
I have not looked over with you, touching the
thing: the one for, the other against: that in
favour is in Measure for Measure, Act II.
Scene ii.—

Isab. Alas, alas!
Why, all the souls that were, were forfeit once;
And He that might the 'vantage best have took,
Found out the remedy.

That against is in Twelfth Night, Act III.
Scene ii.—

Maria. For there is no Christian that means to
be saved by believing rightly, can ever believe
such impossible passages of grossness.

Before I come to the Nymphs, I must get
through all disagreeables. I went to the Isle
of Wight, thought so much about poetry, so
long together, that I could not get to sleep
at night; and, moreover, I know not how it
was, I could not get wholesome food. By this
means, in a week or so, I became not over
capable in my upper stories, and set off pell-
mell for Margate, at least a hundred and fifty
miles, because, forsooth, I fancied that I should
like my old lodging here, and could contrive
to do without trees. Another thing, I was too
much in solitude, and consequently was
obliged to be in continual burning of thought,
as an only resource. However, Tom is with me
at present, and we are very comfortable. We
intend, though, to get among some trees. . . .
I vow that I have been down in the mouth
lately at this work. These last two days, however, I have felt more confident—I have asked
myself so often why I should be a poet more
than other men, seeing how great a thing it is,
—how great things are to be gained by it, what

a thing to be in the mouth of Fame,—that at last the idea has grown so monstrously beyond my seeming power of attainment, that the other day I nearly consented with myself to drop into a Phaethon. Yet 'tis a disgrace to fail, even in a huge attempt; and at this moment I drive the thought from me. I began my poem about a fortnight since, and have done some every day, except travelling ones. Perhaps I may have done a good deal for the time, but it appears such a pin's point to me, that I will not copy any out. When I consider that so many of these pin-points go to form a bodkin-point (God send I end not my life with a bare bodkin, in its modern sense!), and that it requires a thousand bodkins to make a spear bright enough to throw any light to posterity, I see nothing but continual uphill journeying. Now is there anything more unpleasant (it may come among the thousand and one) than to be so journeying and to miss the goal at last? But I intend to whistle all these cogitations into the sea, where I hope they will breed storms violent enough to block up all exit from Russia. Does Shelley go on telling strange stories of the deaths of kings? Tell him, there are strange stories of the deaths of poets. Some have died before they were conceived. "How do you make that out, Master Vellum?" Does Mrs. S. cut bread and butter as neatly as ever? Tell her to procure some fatal scissors, and cut the thread of life of all to-be-disappointed poets. Does Mrs. Hunt tear linen as straight as ever? Tell her to tear from the book of life all blank leaves. Remember me to them all; to Miss Kent and the little ones all.

Your sincere Friend

John Keats *alias* Junkets.

You shall hear where we move.

III

TO BENJAMIN ROBERT HAYDON

Margate, Saturday Eve [May 10, 1817].

My Dear Haydon,

"Let Fame, that all pant after in their lives,
Live register'd upon our brazen tombs,
And so grace us in the disgrace of death:
When spite of cormorant devouring Time
The endeavour of this present breath may buy
That Honour which shall bate his Scythe's keen
    edge
And make us heirs of all eternity."

Love's Labour's Lost, I. i. 1–7.

To think that I have no right to couple myself with you in this speech would be death to me, so I have e'en written it, and I pray God that our "brazen tombs" be nigh neighbours. It cannot be long first; the "endeavour of this present breath" will soon be over, and yet it is as well to breathe freely during our sojourn—it is as well as if you have not been teased with that Money affair, that bill-pestilence. However, I must think that difficulties nerve the Spirit of a Man—they make our Prime Objects a Refuge as well as a Passion. The Trumpet of Fame is as a tower of Strength, the ambitious bloweth it and is safe. I suppose, by your telling me not to give way to forebodings, George has mentioned to you what I have lately said in my Letters to him —truth is I have been in such a state of Mind as to read over my Lines and hate them. I am one that "gathers Samphire, dreadful trade"— the Cliff of Poesy towers above me—yet when Tom who meets with some of Pope's Homer in Plutarch's Lives reads some of those to me they seem like Mice to mine. I read and write about eight hours a day. There is an old saying "well begun is half done"—'t is a bad one. I would use instead, "Not begun at all till half done;" so according to that I have not begun my Poem and consequently (à priori) can say nothing about it. Thank God! I do begin arduously where I leave off, notwithstanding occasional depressions; and I hope for the support of a High Power while I climb this little eminence, and especially in my Years of more momentous Labour. I remember your saying that you had notions of a good Genius presiding over you. I have of late had the same thought, for things which I do half at Random are afterwards confirmed by my judgment in a dozen features of Propriety. Is it too daring to fancy Shakspeare this Presider? When in the Isle of Wight I met with a Shakspeare in the Passage of the House at which I lodged— it comes nearer to my idea of him than any I have seen—I was but there a Week, yet the old woman made me take it with me though I went off in a hurry. Do you not think this is ominous of good? I am glad you say every man of great views is at times tormented as I am.

. . . I am extremely glad that a time must come when everything will leave not a wrack behind. You tell me never to despair—I wish it was as easy for me to observe the saying— truth is I have a horrid Morbidity of Tempera-

ment which has shown itself at intervals—it is
I have no doubt the greatest Enemy and
stumbling-block I have to fear—I may even
say that it is likely to be the cause of my disappointment. However every ill has its share
of good—this very bane would at any time
enable me to look with an obstinate eye on
the Devil Himself—aye to be as proud of being the lowest of the human race as Alfred
could be in being of the highest. I feel confident
I should have been a rebel angel had the opportunity been mine. I am very sure that you
do love me as your very Brother—I have seen
it in your continual anxiety for me—and I assure you that your welfare and fame is and will
be a chief pleasure to me all my Life. I know
no one but you who can be fully sensible of the
turmoil and anxiety, the sacrifice of all what
is called comfort, the readiness to measure time
by what is done and to die in six hours could
plans be brought to conclusions—the looking
upon the Sun, the Moon, the Stars, the Earth
and its contents, as materials to form greater
things—that is to say ethereal things—but here
I am talking like a Madman,—greater things
than our Creator himself made!!

I wrote to Hunt yesterday—scarcely know
what I said in it. I could not talk about Poetry
in the way I should have liked for I was not
in humor with either his or mine. His self-
delusions are very lamentable—they have enticed him into a Situation which I should be
less eager after than that of a galley Slave—
what you observe thereon is very true must be
in time.

Perhaps it is a self-delusion to say so—but
I think I could not be deceived in the manner
that Hunt is—may I die to-morrow if I am to
be. There is no greater Sin after the seven
deadly than to flatter oneself into an idea of
being a great Poet—or one of those beings who
are privileged to wear out their Lives in the
pursuit of Honor—how comfortable a feel it
is to feel that such a Crime must bring its
heavy Penalty? That if one be a Self-deluder
accounts must be balanced? I am glad you are
hard at Work—'t will now soon be done—I
long to see Wordsworth's as well as to have
mine in: but I would rather not show my face
in Town till the end of the Year—if that will
be time enough—if not I shall be disappointed
if you do not write for me even when you think
best. I never quite despair and I read Shakspeare—indeed I shall I think never read any

other Book much. Now this might lead me into
a long Confab but I desist. I am very near
agreeing with Hazlitt that Shakspeare is enough
for us. . . .

Your everlasting Friend JOHN KEATS.

IV

TO BENJAMIN BAILEY

Hampstead, Wednesday [October 8, 1817].

MY DEAR BAILEY—After a tolerable journey,
I went from Coach to Coach as far as Hamp-
stead where I found my Brothers—the next
Morning finding myself tolerably well I went to
Lamb's Conduit Street and delivered your parcel. Jane and Marianne were greatly improved.
Marianne especially, she has no unhealthy
plumpness in the face, but she comes me
healthy and angular to the chin—I did not see
John—I was extremely sorry to hear that poor
Rice, after having had capital health during
his tour, was very ill. I daresay you have heard
from him. From No. 19 I went to Hunt's and
Haydon's who live now neighbours.—Shelley
was there—I know nothing about anything in
this part of the world—every Body seems at
Loggerheads. There's Hunt infatuated—there's
Haydon's picture in statu quo—There's Hunt
walks up and down his painting room criticising
every head most unmercifully. There's Horace
Smith tired of Hunt. "The web of our life is
of mingled yarn." Haydon having removed
entirely from Marlborough Street, Cripps must
direct his letter to Lisson Grove, North Pad-
dington. Yesterday Morning while I was at
Brown's, in came Reynolds, he was pretty
bobbish, we had a pleasant day—he would walk
home at night that cursed cold distance. Mrs.
Bentley's children are making a horrid row—
whereby I regret I cannot be transported to
your Room to write to you. I am quite disgusted with literary men and will never know
another except Wordsworth—no not even
Byron. Here is an instance of the friendship of
such. Haydon and Hunt have known each
other many years—now they live, pour ainsi
dire, jealous neighbours—Haydon says to me,
Keats, don't show your lines to Hunt on any
Account, or he will have done half for you—so
it appears Hunt wishes it to be thought. When
he met Reynolds in the Theatre, John told him
that I was getting on to the completion of 4000
lines—Ah! says Hunt, had it not been for me

they would have been 7000! If he will say this to Reynolds, what would he to other people? Haydon received a Letter a little while back on this subject from some Lady—which contains a caution to me, through him, on the subject— now is not all this a most paltry thing to think about? You may see the whole of the case by the following Extract from a Letter I wrote to George in the Spring—"As to what you say about my being a Poet, I can return no Answer but by saying that the high Idea I have of poetical fame makes me think I see it towering too high above me. At any rate, I have no right to talk until Endymion is finished—it will be a test, a trial of my Powers of Imagination, and chiefly of my invention, which is a rare thing indeed—by which I must make 4000 lines of one bare circumstance, and fill them with poetry: and when I consider that this is a great task, and that when done it will take me but a dozen paces towards the temple of fame—it makes me say—God forbid that I should be without such a task! I have heard Hunt say, and I may be asked—*why endeavour after a long Poem?* To which I should answer, Do not the Lovers of Poetry like to have a little Region to wander in, where they may pick and choose, and in which the images are so numerous that many are forgotten and found new in a second Reading: which may be food for a Week's stroll in the Summer? Do not they like this better than what they can read through before Mrs. Williams comes down stairs? a Morning work at most.

"Besides, a long poem is a test of invention, which I take to be the Polar star of Poetry, as Fancy is the Sails—and Imagination the rudder. Did our great Poets ever write short Pieces? I mean in the shape of Tales—this same invention seems indeed of late years to have been forgotten as a Poetical excellence— But enough of this, I put on no Laurels till I shall have finished Endymion, and I hope Apollo is not angered at my having made a Mockery at him at Hunt's"—

You see, Bailey, how independent my Writing has been. Hunt's dissuasion was of no avail —I refused to visit Shelley that I might have my own unfettered scope;—and after all, I shall have the Reputation of Hunt's élève. His corrections and amputations will by the knowing ones be traced in the Poem. This is, to be sure, the vexation of a day, nor would I say so many words about it to any but those whom

I know to have my welfare and reputation at heart. Haydon promised to give directions for those Casts, and you may expect to see them soon, with as many Letters— You will soon hear the dinning of Bells—never mind! you and Gleig will defy the foul fiend—But do not sacrifice your health to Books: do take it kindly and not so voraciously. I am certain if you are your own Physician, your Stomach will resume its proper strength and then what great benefits will follow.—My sister wrote a Letter to me, which I think must be at the post-office—Ax Will to see. My Brother's kindest remembrances to you—we are going to dine at Brown's where I have some hopes of meeting Reynolds. The little Mercury I have taken has corrected the poison and improved my health— though I feel from my employment that I shall never be again secure in Robustness. Would that you were as well as

Your Sincere friend and brother

JOHN KEATS.

V

TO BENJAMIN BAILEY

[London, November 5, 1817].

. . . There has been a flaming attack upon Hunt in the E*n*dinburgh Magazine. I never read anything so virulent—accusing him of the greatest Crimes, depreciating his Wife, his Poetry, his Habits, his Company, his Conversation. These Philippics are to come out in numbers—called "the Cockney School of Poetry." There has been but one number published—that on Hunt—to which they have prefixed a motto from one Cornelius Webb Poetaster—who unfortunately was of our party occasionally at Hampstead and took it into his head to write the following,—something about "we'll talk on Wordsworth, Byron, a theme we never tire on;" and so forth till he comes to Hunt and Keats. In the Motto they have put Hunt and Keats in large letters—I have no doubt that the second number was intended for me: but have hopes of its non-appearance, from the following Advertisement in last Sunday's Examiner: "To Z.—The writer of the Article signed Z., in Blackwood's Edinburgh Magazine for October 1817 is invited to send his address to the printer of the Examiner, in order that Justice may be Executed on the proper person." I don't mind the thing much—

but if he should go to such lengths with me as he has done with Hunt, I must infallibly call him to an Account if he be a human being, and appears in Squares and Theatres, where we might possibly meet—I don't relish his abuse. . . .

VI

TO BENJAMIN BAILEY

[Burford Bridge, November 22, 1817].

MY DEAR BAILEY—I will get over the first part of this (*un*paid) Letter as soon as possible, for it relates to the affairs of poor Cripps.—To a Man of your nature such a Letter as Haydon's must have been extremely cutting—What occasions the greater part of the World's Quarrels?—simply this—two Minds meet, and do not understand each other time enough to prevent any shock or surprise at the conduct of either party—As soon as I had known Haydon three days, I had got enough of his Character not to have been surprised at such a Letter as he has hurt you with. Nor, when I knew it, was it a principle with me to drop his acquaintance; although with you it would have been an imperious feeling. I wish you knew all that I think about Genius and the Heart—and yet I think that you are thoroughly acquainted with my innermost breast in that respect, or you could not have known me even thus long, and still hold me worthy to be your dear Friend. In passing, however, I must say one thing that has pressed upon me lately, and increased my Humility and capability of submission—and that is this truth—Men of Genius are great as certain ethereal Chemicals operating on the Mass of neutral intellect—but they have not any individuality, any determined Character—I would call the top and head of those who have a proper self Men of Power.

But I am running my head into a subject which I am certain I could not do justice to under five Years' study, and 3 vols. octavo—and, moreover, I long to be talking about the Imagination—so my dear Bailey, do not think of this unpleasant affair, if possible do not—I defy any harm to come of it—I defy. I shall write to Cripps this week, and request him to tell me all his goings-on from time to time by Letter wherever I may be. It will go on well—so don't because you have suddenly discovered a Coldness in Haydon suffer yourself to be teased—Do not my dear fellow—O! I wish I was as certain of the end of all your troubles as that of your momentary start about the authenticity of the Imagination. I am certain of nothing but of the holiness of the Heart's affections, and the truth of Imagination. What the Imagination seizes as Beauty must be truth—whether it existed before or not,—for I have the same idea of all our passions as of Love: they are all, in their sublime, creative of essential Beauty. In a Word, you may know my favourite speculation by my first Book, and the little Song I sent in my last, which is a representation from the fancy of the probable mode of operating in these Matters. The Imagination may be compared to Adam's dream,—he awoke and found it truth:—I am more zealous in this affair, because I have never yet been able to perceive how anything can be known for truth by consecutive reasoning—and yet it must be. Can it be that even the greatest Philosopher ever arrived at his Goal without putting aside numerous objections? However it may be, O for a life of Sensations rather than of Thoughts! It is "a Vision in the form of Youth," a shadow of reality to come—And this consideration has further convinced me,—for it has come as auxiliary to another favourite speculation of mine,—that we shall enjoy ourselves hereafter by having what we called happiness on Earth repeated in a finer tone—And yet such a fate can only befall those who delight in Sensation, rather than hunger as you do after Truth. Adam's dream will do here, and seems to be a Conviction that Imagination and its empyreal reflection, is the same as human life and its spiritual repetition. But, as I was saying, the Simple imaginative Mind may have its rewards in the repetition of its own silent Working coming continually on the Spirit with a fine Suddenness—to compare great things with small, have you never by being surprised with an old Melody, in a delicious place by a delicious voice, *felt* over again your very speculations and surmises at the time it first operated on your soul?—do you not remember forming to yourself the Singer's face—more beautiful than it was possible, and yet with the elevation of the Moment you did not think so? Even then you were mounted on the Wings of Imagination, so high that the prototype must be hereafter—that delicious face you will see. What a time! I am continually running away from the subject.

Sure this cannot be exactly the Case with a complex mind—one that is imaginative, and at the same time careful of its fruits,—who would exist partly on Sensation, partly on thought —to whom it is necessary that years should bring the philosophic Mind? Such a one I consider yours, and therefore it is necessary to your eternal happiness that you not only drink this old Wine of Heaven, which I shall call the redigestion of our most ethereal Musings upon Earth, but also increase in knowledge and know all things. I am glad to hear that you are in a fair way for Easter. You will soon get through your unpleasant reading, and then!—but the world is full of troubles, and I have not much reason to think myself pestered with many.

I think Jane or Marianne has a better opinion of me than I deserve: for, really and truly, I do not think my Brother's illness connected with mine—you know more of the real Cause than they do; nor have I any chance of being rack'd as you have been. You perhaps at one time thought there was such a thing as worldly happiness to be arrived at, at certain periods of time marked out,—you have of necessity from your disposition been thus led away—I scarcely remember counting upon any Happiness—I look not for it if it be not in the present hour,—nothing startles me beyond the moment. The Setting Sun will always set me to rights, or if a Sparrow come before my Window, I take part in its existence and pick about the gravel. The first thing that strikes me on hearing a Misfortune having befallen another is this—"Well, it cannot be helped: he will have the pleasure of trying the resources of his Spirit"—and I beg now, my dear Bailey, that hereafter should you observe anything cold in me not to put it to the account of heartlessness, but abstraction—for I assure you I sometimes feel not the influence of a passion or affection during a whole Week—and so long this sometimes continues, I begin to suspect myself, and the genuineness of my feelings at other times— thinking them a few barren Tragedy Tears.

My brother Tom is much improved—he is going to Devonshire—whither I shall follow him. At present, I am just arrived at Dorking —to change the Scene—change the Air, and give me a spur to wind up my Poem, of which there are wanting 500 lines. I should have been here a day sooner, but the Reynoldses persuaded me to stop in Town to meet your friend Christie. There were Rice and Martin—we talked about Ghosts. I will have some Talk with Taylor and let you know,—when please God I come down at Christmas. I will find that Examiner if possible. My best regards to Gleig, my Brothers' to you and Mrs. Bentley.

Your affectionate Friend JOHN KEATS.

I want to say much more to you—a few hints will set me going. Direct Burford Bridge near Dorking.

VII

TO GEORGE AND THOMAS KEATS

Hampstead, December 22, 1817.

MY DEAR BROTHERS—I must crave your pardon for not having written ere this. . . . I saw Kean return to the public in Richard III., and finally he did it, and, at the request of Reynolds, I went to criticise his *Duke* in Rich^d.—the critique is in to-day's Champion, which I send you with the Examiner, in which you will find very proper lamentation on the obsoletion of Christmas Gambols and pastimes: but it was mixed up with so much egotism of that drivelling nature that pleasure is entirely lost. Hone the publisher's trial, you must find very amusing, and as Englishmen very encouraging: his *Not Guilty* is a thing, which not to have been, would have dulled still more Liberty's Emblazoning—Lord Ellenborough has been paid in his own coin—Wooler and Hone have done us an essential service. I have had two very pleasant evenings with Dilke yesterday and to-day, and am at this moment just come from him, and feel in the humour to go on with this, begun in the morning, and from which he came to fetch me. I spent Friday evening with Wells and went next morning to see *Death on the Pale horse*. It is a wonderful picture, when West's age is considered; but there is nothing to be intense upon, no women one feels mad to kiss, no face swelling into reality. The excellence of every art is its intensity, capable of making all disagreeables evaporate from their being in close relationship with Beauty and Truth—Examine King Lear, and you will find this exemplified throughout; but in this picture we have unpleasantness without any momentous depth of speculation excited, in which to bury its repulsiveness—The picture is larger than Christ rejected.

I dined with Haydon the Sunday after you left, and had a very pleasant day. I dined too (for I have been out too much lately) with Horace Smith and met his two Brothers with Hill and Kingston and one Du Bois, they only served to convince me how superior humour is to wit, in respect to enjoyment—These men say things which make one start, without making one feel, they are all alike; their manners are alike; they all know fashionables; they have all a mannerism in their very eating and drinking, in their mere handling a Decanter. They talked of Kean and his low company—would I were with that company instead of yours said I to myself! I know such like acquaintance will never do for me and yet I am going to Reynolds, on Wednesday. Brown and Dilke walked with me and back from the Christmas pantomime. I had not a dispute, but a disquisition, with Dilke upon various subjects; several things dove-tailed in my mind, and at once it struck me what quality went to form a Man of Achievement, especially in Literature, and which Shakspeare possessed so enormously—I mean *Negative Capability*, that is, when a man is capable of being in uncertainties, mysteries, doubts, without any irritable reaching after fact and reason. Coleridge, for instance, would let go by a fine isolated verisimilitude caught from the Penetralium of mystery, from being incapable of remaining content with half-knowledge. This pursued through volumes would perhaps take us no further than this, that with a great poet the sense of Beauty overcomes every other consideration, or rather obliterates all consideration.

Shelley's poem is out and there are words about its being objected to, as much as Queen Mab was. Poor Shelley I think he has his Quota of good qualities, in sooth la! Write soon to your most sincere friend and affectionate Brother

JOHN.

VIII

TO GEORGE AND THOMAS KEATS

[Hampstead,] Friday 23d January [1818].

MY DEAR BROTHERS—I was thinking what hindered me from writing so long, for I have so many things to say to you, and know not where to begin. It shall be upon a thing most interesting to you, my Poem. Well! I have given the first Book to Taylor; he seemed more than

satisfied with it, and to my surprise proposed publishing it in Quarto if Haydon would make a drawing of some event therein, for a Frontispiece. I called on Haydon, he said he would do anything I liked, but said he would rather paint a finished picture, from it, which he seems eager to do; this in a year or two will be a glorious thing for us; and it will be, for Haydon is struck with the 1st Book. I left Haydon and the next day received a letter from him, proposing to make, as he says, with all his might, a finished chalk sketch of my head, to be engraved in the first style and put at the head of my Poem, saying at the same time he had never done the thing for any human being, and that it must have considerable effect as he will put his name to it—I begin to-day to copy my 2nd Book—"thus far into the bowels of the land"—You shall hear whether it will be Quarto or non Quarto, picture or non picture. Leigh Hunt I showed my 1st Book to——he allows it not much merit as a whole; says it is unnatural and made ten objections to it in the mere skimming over. He says the conversation is unnatural and too high-flown for Brother and Sister—says it should be simple forgetting do ye mind that they are both overshadowed by a supernatural Power, and of force could not speak like Francesca in the Rimini. He must first prove that Caliban's poetry is unnatural—This with me completely overturns his objections—the ʹact is he and Shelley are hurt, and perhaps justly, at my not having showed them the affair officiously and from several hints I have had they appear much disposed to dissect and anatomise any trip or slip I may have made.—But who's afraid? Ay! Tom! Demme if I am. I went last Tuesday, an hour too late, to Hazlitt's Lecture on poetry, got there just as they were coming out, when all these pounced upon me. Hazlitt, John Hunt and Son, Wells, Bewick, all the Landseers, Bob Harris, aye and more—the Landseers enquired after you particularly—I know not whether Wordsworth has left town—But Sunday I dined with Hazlitt and Haydon, also that I took Haslam with me—I dined with Brown lately. Dilke having taken the Champion Theatricals was obliged to be in town—Fanny has returned to Walthamstow.—Mr. Abbey appeared very glum, the last time I went to see her, and said in an indirect way, that I had no business there—Rice has been ill, but has been mending much lately—

I think a little change has taken place in my intellect lately—I cannot bear to be uninterested or unemployed, I, who for so long a time have been addicted to passiveness. Nothing is finer for the purposes of great productions than a very gradual ripening of the intellectual powers. . . . I hope I have not tired you by this filling up of the dash in my last. Constable the bookseller has offered Reynolds ten guineas a sheet to write for his Magazine —it is an Edinburgh one, which Blackwood's started up in opposition to. Hunt said he was nearly sure that the "Cockney School" was written by Scott so you are right Tom!—There are no more little bits of news I can remember at present.

I remain, My dear Brothers, Your very affectionate Brother JOHN.

IX

TO JOHN TAYLOR

[Hampstead, January 30, 1818].

MY DEAR TAYLOR—These lines as they now stand about "happiness," having rung in my ears like "a chime a mending"—See here,

"Behold
Wherein lies happiness, Peona? fold, etc."

It appears to me the very contrary of blessed. I hope this will appear to you more eligible.

"Wherein lies Happiness? In that which becks
Our ready minds to fellowship divine,
A fellowship with Essence till we shine
Full alchemised, and free of space—Behold
The clear religion of Heaven—fold, etc."

You must indulge me by putting this in, for setting aside the badness of the other, such a preface is necessary to the subject. The whole thing must, I think, have appeared to you, who are a consecutive man, as a thing almost of mere words, but I assure you that, when I wrote it, it was a regular stepping of the Imagination towards a truth. My having written that argument will perhaps be of the greatest service to me of anything I ever did. It set before me the gradations of happiness, even like a kind of pleasure thermometer, and is my first step towards the chief attempt in the drama. The playing of different natures with joy and Sorrow—

Do me this favour, and believe me
Your sincere friend   J. KEATS.

I hope your next work will be of a more general Interest. I suppose you cogitate a little about it, now and then.

X

TO JOHN HAMILTON REYNOLDS

Hampstead, Tuesday [February 3, 1818].

MY DEAR REYNOLDS—I thank you for your dish of Filberts—would I could get a basket of them by way of dessert every day for the sum of twopence. Would we were a sort of ethereal Pigs, and turned loose to feed upon spiritual Mast and Acorns—which would be merely being a squirrel and feeding upon filberts, for what is a squirrel but an airy pig, or a filbert but a sort of archangelical acorn? About the nuts being worth cracking, all I can say is, that where there are a throng of delightful Images ready drawn, simplicity is the only thing. The first is the best on account of the first line, and the "arrow, foil'd of its antler'd food," and moreover (and this is the only word or two I find fault with, the more because I have had so much reason to shun it as a quicksand) the last has "tender and true." We must cut this, and not be rattlesnaked into any more of the like. It may be said that we ought to read our contemporaries, that Wordsworth, etc. should have their due from us. But, for the sake of a few fine imaginative or domestic passages, are we to be bullied into a certain Philosophy engendered in the whims of an Egotist? Every man has his speculations, but every man does not brood and peacock over them till he makes a false coinage and deceives himself. Many a man can travel to the very bourne of Heaven, and yet want confidence to put down his half-seeing. Sancho will invent a Journey heavenward as well as anybody. We hate poetry that has a palpable design upon us, and, if we do not agree, seems to put its hand into its breeches pocket. Poetry should be great and unobtrusive, a thing which enters into one's soul, and does not startle it or amaze it with itself—but with its subject. How beautiful are the retired flowers!—how would they lose their beauty were they to throng into the highway, crying out, "Admire me, I am a violet! Dote upon me, I am a primrose!" Modern poets differ from the Elizabethans in this: each of the moderns like an Elector of Hanover governs his petty state and knows how many straws are swept daily from the Causeways in all his dominions, and has a continual itching that all the Housewives should have their coppers well scoured: The ancients were Emperors of vast Provinces, they had only heard of the remote ones and scarcely cared to visit them. I will cut all this—I will have no more of Wordsworth or Hunt in particular—Why should we be of the tribe of Manasseh, when we can wander with Esau? Why should we kick against the Pricks, when we can walk on Roses? Why should we be owls, when we can be eagles? Why be teased with "nice-eyed wagtails," when we have in sight "the Cherub Contemplation"? Why with Wordsworth's "Matthew with a bough of wilding in his hand," when we can have Jacques "under an oak," etc? The secret of the Bough of Wilding will run through your head faster than I can write it. Old Matthew spoke to him some years ago on some nothing, and because he happens in an Evening Walk to imagine the figure of the old Man, he must stamp it down in black and white, and it is henceforth sacred. I don't mean to deny Wordsworth's grandeur and Hunt's merit, but I mean to say we need not be teased with grandeur and merit when we can have them uncontaminated and unobtrusive. Let us have the old Poets and Robin Hood. Your letter and its sonnets gave me more pleasure than will the Fourth Book of Childe Harold and the whole of anybody's life and opinions. In return for your Dish of Filberts, I have gathered a few Catkins, I hope they'll look pretty.

[To J. H. R. in answer to his Robin Hood Sonnets. See p. 41.]

I hope you will like them—they are at least written in the Spirit of Outlawry. Here are the Mermaid lines,

[See p. 40.]

I will call on you at 4 tomorrow, and we will trudge together, for it is not the thing to be a stranger in the Land of Harpsicols. I hope also to bring you my 2nd Book. In the hope that these Scribblings will be some amusement for you this Evening, I remain, copying on the Hill,

Your sincere friend and Co-scribbler
JOHN KEATS.

XI

TO JOHN TAYLOR

Hampstead, February 27 [1818].

MY DEAR TAYLOR—Your alteration strikes me as being a great Improvement—And now I will attend to the punctuations you speak of— The comma should be at *soberly,* and in the other passage, the Comma should follow *quiet.* I am extremely indebted to you for this alteration, and also for your after admonitions. It is a sorry thing for me that any one should have to overcome prejudices in reading my verses—that affects me more than any hypercriticism on any particular passage—In Endymion, I have most likely but moved into the go-cart from the leading-strings—In poetry I have a few axioms, and you will see how far I am from their centre.

1st. I think poetry should surprise by a fine excess, and not by singularity; It should strike the reader as a wording of his own highest thoughts, and appear almost a remembrance.

2d. Its touches of beauty should never be half-way, thereby making the reader breathless, instead of content. The rise, the progress, the setting of Imagery should, like the sun, come natural to him, shine over him, and set soberly, although in magnificence, leaving him in the luxury of twilight. But it is easier to think what poetry should be, than to write it—And this leads me to

Another axiom—That if poetry comes not as naturally as the leaves to a tree, it had better not come at all.—However it may be with me, I cannot help looking into new countries with "O for a Muse of Fire to ascend!" If Endymion serves me as a pioneer, perhaps I ought to be content—I have great reason to be content, for thank God I can read, and perhaps understand Shakspeare to his depths; and I have I am sure many friends, who, if I fail, will attribute any change in my life and temper to humbleness rather than pride—to a cowering under the wings of great poets, rather than to a bitterness that I am not appreciated. I am anxious to get Endymion printed that I may forget it and proceed. I have copied the 3rd Book and begun the 4th. On running my eye over the proofs, I saw one mistake—I will notice it presently, and also any others, if there be any. There should be no comma in "the raft branch down sweeping from a tall ash-top." I have besides made one or two alterations, and also altered the thirteenth line p. 32 to make sense of it, as you will see. I will take care the printer shall not trip up my heels. There should be no dash after Dryope in the line "Dryope's lone lulling of her child."

Remember me to Percy Street.

Your sincere and obliged friend

JOHN KEATS.

XII

TO BENJAMIN ROBERT HAYDON

Wednesday, [Teignmouth, April 8, 1818].

MY DEAR HAYDON—I am glad you were pleased with my nonsense, and if it so happen that the humour takes me when I have set down to prose to you I will not gainsay it. I should be (God forgive me) ready to swear because I cannot make use of your assistance in going through Devon if I was not in my own Mind determined to visit it thoroughly at some more favourable time of the year. But now Tom (who is getting greatly better) is anxious to be in Town—therefore I put off my threading the County. I purpose within a month to put my knapsack at my back and make a pedestrian tour through the North of England, and part of Scotland—to make a sort of Prologue to the Life I intend to pursue—that is to write, to study and to see all Europe at the lowest expence. I will clamber through the Clouds and exist. I will get such an accumulation of stupendous recollections that as I walk through the suburbs of London I may not see them— I will stand upon Mount Blanc and remember this coming Summer when I intend to straddle Ben Lomond—with my soul!—galligaskins are out of the Question. I am nearer myself to hear your "Christ" is being tinted into immortality. Believe me Haydon your picture is part of myself—I have ever been too sensible of the labyrinthian path to eminence in Art (judging from Poetry) ever to think I understood the emphasis of painting. The innumerable compositions and decompositions which take place between the intellect and its thousand materials before it arrives at that trembling delicate and snail-horn perception of beauty. I know not your many havens of intenseness—nor ever can know them: but for this I hope not [sic nought?] you achieve is lost upon me: for when a Schoolboy the abstract Idea I had of an heroic painting—was what I cannot describe. I saw it somewhat sideways, large, prominent, round, and colour'd with magnificence—somewhat like the feel I have of Anthony and Cleopatra. Or of Alcibiades leaning on his Crimson Couch in his Galley, his broad shoulders imperceptibly heaving with the Sea. That passage in Shakspeare is finer than this—

See how the surly Warwick mans the Wall.

I like your consignment of Corneille—that's the humour of it—they shall be called your Posthumous Works. I don't understand your bit of Italian. I hope she will awake from her dream and flourish fair—my respects to her. The Hedges by this time are beginning to leaf— Cats are becoming more vociferous—young Ladies who wear Watches are always looking at them. Women about forty-five think the Season very backward—Ladies' Mares have but half an allowance of food. It rains here again, has been doing so for three days—however as I told you I'll take a trial in June, July, or August next year.

I am afraid Wordsworth went rather huffd out of Town—I am sorry for it—he cannot expect his fireside Divan to be infallible—he cannot expect but that every man of worth is as proud as himself. O that he had not fit with a Warrener—that is dined at Kingston's. I shall be in town in about a fortnight and then we will have a day or so now and then before I set out on my northern expedition— we will have no more abominable Rows—for they leave one in a fearful silence—having settled the Methodists let us be rational—not upon compulsion—no—if it will out let it— but I will not play the Bassoon any more deliberately. Remember me to Hazlitt, and Bewick—

Your affectionate friend, JOHN KEATS.

XIII

TO JOHN HAMILTON REYNOLDS

Thy. morng., [Teignmouth, April 9, 1818].

MY DEAR REYNOLDS—Since you all agree that the thing [the first preface to *Endymion*] is bad, it must be so—though I am not aware there is anything like Hunt in it (and if there is, it is my natural way, and I have something in common with Hunt). Look it over again, and examine into the motives, the seeds, from which any one sentence sprung—I have not the slightest feel of humility towards the public—or to anything in existence,—but the eternal Being, the Principle of Beauty, and the Memory of great Men. When I am writing for myself for the mere sake of the moment's enjoyment, perhaps nature has its course with me—but a Preface is written to the Public; a thing I cannot help looking upon as an Enemy, and which I cannot address without feelings of Hostility. If I write a Preface in a supple or subdued style, it will not be in character with me as a public speaker—I would be subdued before my friends, and thank them for subduing me—but among Multitudes of Men—I have no feel of stooping, I hate the idea of humility to them.

I never wrote one single Line of Poetry with the least Shadow of public thought.

Forgive me for vexing you and making a Trojan horse of such a Trifle, both with respect to the matter in Question, and myself—but it eases me to tell you—I could not live without the love of my friends—I would jump down Ætna for any great Public good—but I hate a Mawkish Popularity. I cannot be subdued before them—My glory would be to daunt and dazzle the thousand jabberers about Pictures and Books—I see swarms of Porcupines with their Quills erect "like lime-twigs set to catch my Wingèd Book," and I would fright them away with a torch. You will say my Preface is not much of a Torch. It would have been too insulting "to begin from Jove," and I could not set a golden head upon a thing of clay. If there is any fault in the Preface it is not affectation, but an undersong of disrespect to the Public—if I write another Preface it must be done without a thought of those people—I will think about it. If it should not reach you in four or five days, tell Taylor to publish it without a Preface, and let the Dedication simply stand—"inscribed to the Memory of Thomas Chatterton." . . .

Your affectionate Friend JOHN KEATS.

XIV

TO JOHN TAYLOR

Teignmouth, Friday [April 24, 1818].
MY DEAR TAYLOR—I think I did wrong to leave to you all the trouble of Endymion—But I could not help it then—another time I shall be more bent to all sorts of troubles and disagreeables. Young men for some time have an idea that such a thing as happiness is to be had, and therefore are extremely impatient under any unpleasant restraining. In time however, of such stuff is the world about them, they know better, and instead of striving from uneasiness, greet it as an habitual sensation, a pannier which is to weigh upon them through life—And in proportion to my disgust at the task is my sense of your kindness and anxiety. The book pleased me much. It is very free from faults: and, although there are one or two words I should wish replaced, I see in many places an improvement greatly to the purpose.

I think those speeches which are related —those parts where the speaker repeats a speech, such as Glaucus's repetition of Circe's words, should have inverted commas to every line. In this there is a little confusion.—If we divide the speeches into *indentical* and *related;* and to the former put merely one inverted Comma at the beginning and another at the end; and to the latter inverted Commas before every line, the book will be better understood at the 1st glance. Look at pages 126, 127, you will find in the 3d line the beginning of a related speech marked thus "Ah! art awake—" while, at the same time, in the next page the continuation of the *indentical* speech is marked in the same manner, "Young man of Latmos—" You will find on the other side all the parts which should have inverted commas to every line.

I was proposing to travel over the North this summer. There is but one thing to prevent me.—I know nothing—I have read nothing—and I mean to follow Solomon's directions, "Get learning—get understanding." I find earlier days are gone by—I find that I can have no enjoyment in the world but continual drinking of knowledge. I find there is no worthy pursuit but the idea of doing some good for the world—Some do it with their Society—some with their wit—some with their benevolence—some with a sort of power of conferring pleasure and good-humour on all they meet—and in a thousand ways, all dutiful to the command of great Nature—there is but one way for me. The road lies through application, study, and thought.—I will pursue it;

and for that end, purpose retiring for some years. I have been hovering for some time between an exquisite sense of the luxurious, and a love for philosophy,—were I calculated for the former, I should be glad. But as I am not, I shall turn all my soul to the latter.—My brother Tom is getting better, and I hope I shall see both him and Reynolds better before I retire from the world. I shall see you soon, and have some talk about what Books I shall take with me.

Your very sincere friend JOHN KEATS.

Pray remember me to Hessey Woodhouse and Percy Street.

XV

TO JOHN HAMILTON REYNOLDS

Teignmouth, May 3d [1818].

MY DEAR REYNOLDS—

. . . Every department of Knowledge we see excellent and calculated towards a great whole—I am so convinced of this that I am glad at not having given away my medical Books, which I shall again look over to keep alive the little I know thitherwards; and moreover intend through you and Rice to become a sort of pip-civilian. An extensive knowledge is needful to thinking people—it takes away the heat and fever; and helps, by widening speculation, to ease the Burden of the Mystery, a thing which I begin to understand a little, and which weighed upon you in the most gloomy and true sentence in your Letter. The difference of high Sensations with and without knowledge appears to me this: in the latter case we are falling continually ten thousand fathoms deep and being blown up again, without wings, and with all horror of a bare-shouldered Creature—in the former case, our shoulders are fledged, and we go through the same air and space without fear. . . .

My Branchings out therefrom have been numerous: one of them is the consideration of Wordsworth's genius and as a help, in the manner of gold being the meridian Line of worldly wealth, how he differs from Milton. And here I have nothing but surmises, from an uncertainty whether Milton's apparently less anxiety for Humanity proceeds from his seeing further or not than Wordsworth: And whether Wordsworth has in truth epic passion, and martyrs himself to the human heart, the main region of his song. In regard to his genius alone—we find what he says true as far as we have experienced, and we can judge no further but by larger experience—for axioms in philosophy are not axioms until they are proved upon our pulses. We read fine things, but never feel them to the full until we have gone the same steps as the author.— I know this is not plain; you will know exactly my meaning when I say that now I shall relish Hamlet more than I ever have done— Or, better—you are sensible no man can set down Venery as a bestial or joyless thing until he is sick of it, and therefore all philosophising on it would be mere wording. Until we are sick, we understand not; in fine, as Byron says, "Knowledge is sorrow"; and I go on to say that "Sorrow is wisdom"—and further for aught we can know for certainty "Wisdom is folly."

. . . I will return to Wordsworth—whether or no he has an extended vision or a circumscribed grandeur—whether he is an eagle in his nest or on the wing—And to be more explicit and to show you how tall I stand by the giant, I will put down a simile of human life as far as I now perceive it: that is, to the point to which I say we both have arrived at— Well—I compare human life to a large Mansion of Many apartments, two of which I can only describe, the doors of the rest being as yet shut upon me— The first we step into we call the infant or thoughtless Chamber, in which we remain as long as we do not think—We remain there a long while, and notwithstanding the doors of the second Chamber remain wide open, showing a bright appearance, we care not to hasten to it; but are at length imperceptibly impelled by the awakening of the thinking principle within us—we no sooner get into the second Chamber, which I shall call the Chamber of Maiden-Thought, than we become intoxicated with the light and the atmosphere, we see nothing but pleasant wonders, and think of delaying there for ever in delight: However among the effects this breathing is father of is that tremendous one of sharpening one's vision into the heart and nature of Man—of convincing one's nerves that the world is full of Misery and Heartbreak, Pain, Sickness, and oppression— whereby this Chamber of Maiden-Thought becomes gradually darkened, and at the same time, on all sides of it, many doors are set open

—but all dark—all leading to dark passages—
We see not the balance of good and evil—we
are in a mist—*we* are now in that state—We
feel the "burden of the Mystery." To this
point was Wordsworth come, as far as I can 5
conceive, when he wrote "Tintern Abbey," and
it seems to me that his Genius is explorative
of those dark Passages. Now if we live, and go
on thinking, we too shall explore them—He is
a genius and superior to us, in so far as he 10
can, more than we, make discoveries and shed
a light in them—Here I must think Wordsworth is deeper than Milton, though I think it
has depended more upon the general and gre-
garious advance of intellect, than individual 15
greatness of Mind—From the Paradise Lost
and the other Works of Milton, I hope it is
not too presuming, even between ourselves, to
say, that his philosophy, human and divine, may
be tolerably understood by one not much ad- 20
vanced in years. In his time, Englishmen were
just emancipated from a great superstition,
and Men had got hold of certain points and
resting-places in reasoning which were too
newly born to be doubted, and too much op- 25
posed by the Mass of Europe not to be thought
ethereal and authentically divine—Who could
gainsay his ideas on virtue, vice, and Chastity
in Comus, just at the time of the dismissal of
a hundred disgraces? who would not rest satis- 30
fied with his hintings at good and evil in the
Paradise Lost, when just free from the Inquisition and burning in Smithfield? The Reformation produced such immediate and great
benefits, that Protestantism was considered un- 35
der the immediate eye of heaven, and its own
remaining Dogmas and superstitions then, as
it were, regenerated, constituted those resting-
places and seeming sure points of Reasoning—
from that I have mentioned, Milton, whatever 40
he may have thought in the sequel, appears to
have been content with these by his writings—
He did not think into the human heart as
Wordsworth has done—Yet Milton as a Philosopher had sure as great powers as Words- 45
worth—What is then to be inferred? O many
things—It proves there is really a grand
march of intellect,—It proves that a mighty
providence subdues the mightiest Minds to
the service of the time being, whether it be in 50
human Knowledge or Religion. I have often
pitied a tutor who has to hear "Nom. Musa"
so often dinn'd into his ears—I hope you may
not have the same pain in this scribbling—I

may have read these things before, but I
never had even a thus dim perception of them;
and moreover I like to say my lesson to one
who will endure my tediousness for my own
sake—After all there is certainly something
real in the world—Moore's present to Hazlitt
is real—I like that Moore, and am glad I saw
him at the Theatre just before I left Town.
Tom has spit a *leetle* blood this afternoon, and
that is rather a damper—but I know—the 10
truth is there is something real in the World.
Your third Chamber of Life shall be a lucky
and a gentle one—stored with the wine of
love—and the Bread of Friendship—When 15
you see George if he should not have received
a letter from me tell him he will find one at
home most likely—tell Bailey I hope soon to
see him—Remember me to all. The leaves
have been out here for *mony* a day—I have 20
written to George for the first stanzas of my
Isabel—I shall have them soon, and will copy
the whole out for you.

　　Your affectionate Friend JOHN KEATS.

XVI

TO JAMES AUGUSTUS HESSEY

[Hampstead, October 9, 1818].

MY DEAR HESSEY—You are very good in
sending me the letters from the Chronicle—
and I am very bad in not acknowledging such
a kindness sooner—pray forgive me. It has so 35
chanced that I have had that paper every day
—I have seen to-day's. I cannot but feel indebted to those Gentlemen who have taken my
part—As for the rest, I begin to get a little
acquainted with my own strength and weak- 40
ness.—Praise or blame has but a momentary
effect on the man whose love of beauty in the
abstract makes him a severe critic on his own
Works. My own domestic criticism has given
me pain without comparison beyond what 45
Blackwood or the Quarterly could possibly inflict—and also when I feel I am right, no external praise can give me such a glow as my
own solitary reperception and ratification of
what is fine. J. S. is perfectly right in regard 50
to the slip-shod Endymion. That it is so is
no fault of mine. No!—though it may sound a
little paradoxical. It is as good as I had power
to make it—by myself—Had I been nervous
about its being a perfect piece, and with that

view asked advice, and trembled over every page, it would not have been written; for it is not in my nature to fumble—I will write independently.—I have written independently *without Judgment*. I may write independently, and *with Judgment* hereafter. The Genius of Poetry must work out its own salvation in a man: It cannot be matured by law and precept, but by sensation and watchfulness in itself—That which is creative must create itself—In Endymion, I leaped headlong into the sea, and thereby have become better acquainted with the Soundings, the quicksands, and the rocks, than if I had stayed upon the green shore, and piped a silly pipe, and took tea and comfortable advice. I was never afraid of failure; for I would sooner fail than not be among the greatest—But I am nigh getting into a rant. So, with remembrances to Taylor and Woodhouse etc. I am

Yours very sincerely   JOHN KEATS.

XVII

TO RICHARD WOODHOUSE

[Hampstead, October 27, 1818].
MY DEAR WOODHOUSE—Your letter gave me great satisfaction, more on account of its friendliness than any relish of that matter in it which is accounted so acceptable to the "genus irritabile." The best answer I can give you is in a clerklike manner to make some observations on two principal points which seem to point like indices into the midst of the whole pro and con about genius, and views, and achievements, and ambition, et cætera. 1st. As to the poetical Character itself (I mean that sort, of which, if I am anything, I am a member; that sort distinguished from the Wordsworthian, or egotistical Sublime; which is a thing per se, and stands alone,) it is not itself—it has no self—It is everything and nothing—It has no character—it enjoys light and shade; it lives in gusto, be it foul or fair, high or low, rich or poor, mean or elevated—It has as much delight in conceiving an Iago as an Imogen. What shocks the virtuous philosopher delights the chameleon poet. It does no harm from its relish of the dark side of things, any more than from its taste for the bright one, because they both end in speculation. A poet is the most unpoetical of anything in existence, because he has no Identity—he is continually in for and filling some other body. The Sun,—the Moon,—the Sea, and men and women, who are creatures of impulse, are poetical, and have about them an unchangeable attribute; the poet has none, no identity—he is certainly the most unpoetical of all God's creatures.—If then he has no self, and if I am a poet, where is the wonder that I should say I would write no more? Might I not at that very instant have been cogitating on the Characters of Saturn and Ops? It is a wretched thing to confess; but it is a very fact, that not one word I ever utter can be taken for granted as an opinion growing out of my identical Nature—how can it, when I have no Nature? When I am in a room with people, if I ever am free from speculating on creations of my own brain, then, not myself goes home to myself, but the identity of every one in the room begins to press upon me, so that I am in a very little time annihilated—not only among men; it would be the same in a nursery of Children. I know not whether I make myself wholly understood: I hope enough so to let you see that no dependence is to be placed on what I said that day.

In the 2d place, I will speak of my views, and of the life I purpose to myself. I am ambitious of doing the world some good: if I should be spared, that may be the work of maturer years —in the interval I will assay to reach to as high a summit in poetry as the nerve bestowed upon me will suffer. The faint conceptions I have of poems to come bring the blood frequently into my forehead—All I hope is, that I may not lose all interest in human affairs— that the solitary Indifference I feel for applause, even from the finest spirits, will not blunt any acuteness of vision I may have. I do not think it will. I feel assured I should write from the mere yearning and fondness I have for the beautiful, even if my night's labours should be burnt every Morning, and no eye ever shine upon them. But even now I am perhaps not speaking from myself, but from some Character in whose soul I now live.

I am sure however that this next sentence is from myself—I feel your anxiety, good opinion, and friendship, in the highest degree, and am

Yours most sincerely   JOHN KEATS.

XVIII

TO GEORGE AND GEORGIANA KEATS

Sunday Morn^g February 14, [1818].

MY DEAR BROTHER AND SISTER—

. . . I have not seen Mr. Lewis lately, for I have shrunk from going up the hill. Mr. Lewis went a few mornings ago to town with Mrs. Brawne. They talked about me, and I heard that Mr. L. said a thing I am not at all contented with. Says he, "O, he is quite the little poet." Now this is abominable—You might as well say Buonaparte is quite the little soldier. You see what it is to be under six foot and not a lord. . . .

I was surprised to hear from Taylor the amount of money of the bookseller's last sale. What think you of £25,000? He sold 4000 copies of Lord Byron. I am sitting opposite the Shakspeare I brought from the Isle of Wight— and I never look at him but the silk tassels on it give me as much pleasure as the face of the poet itself.

In my next packet, as this is one by the way, I shall send you the Pot of Basil, St. Agnes Eve, and if I should have finished it, a little thing called the Eve of St. Mark. You see what fine Mother Radcliff names I have—it is not my fault—I do not search for them. I have not gone on with Hyperion—for to tell the truth I have not been in great cue for writing lately—I must wait for the spring to rouse me up a little. The only time I went out from Bedhampton was to see a chapel consecrated— . . .

The chapel is built in Mr. Way's park. The consecration was not amusing. There were numbers of carriages—and his house crammed with clergy—They sanctified the Chapel, and it being a wet day, consecrated the burial-ground through the vestry window. I begin to hate parsons; they did not make me love them that day when I saw them in their proper colours. A parson is a Lamb in a drawing-room, and a Lion in a vestry. The notions of Society will not permit a parson to give way to his temper in any shape—So he festers in himself—his features get a peculiar, diabolical, self sufficient, iron stupid expression. He is continually acting—his mind is against every man, and every man's mind is against him—He is a hypocrite to the Believer and a coward to the unbeliever—He must be either a knave or an idiot—and there is no man so much to be pitied as an idiot parson. The soldier who is cheated into an Esprit du Corps by a red coat, a band, and colours, for the purpose of nothing, is not half so pitiable as the parson who is led by the nose by the Bench of Bishops and is smothered in absurdities—a poor necessary subaltern of the Church.

Friday, Feby. 18.

. . . I never drink now above three glasses of wine—and never any spirits and water. Though by the bye, the other day Woodhouse took me to his coffee house and ordered a Bottle of Claret—now I like Claret, whenever I can have Claret I must drink it,—'t is the only palate affair that I am at all sensual in. Would it not be a good speck to send you some vine roots—could it be done? I'll enquire—If you could make some wine like Claret to drink on summer evenings in an arbour! For really 't is so fine—it fills one's mouth with a gushing freshness—then goes down cool and feverless —then you do not feel it quarrelling with your liver—no, it is rather a Peacemaker, and lies as quiet as it did in the grape; then it is as fragrant as the Queen Bee, and the more ethereal Part of it mounts into the brain, not assaulting the cerebral apartments like a bully in a bad-house looking for his trull and hurrying from door to door bouncing against the wainscoat, but rather walks like Aladdin about his own enchanted palace so gently that you do not feel his step. Other wines of a heavy and spirituous nature transform a Man to a Silenus. . . . I have not said in any Letter yet a word about my affairs—in a word I am in no despair about them—my poem has not at all succeeded; in the course of a year or so I think I shall try the public again—in a selfish point of view I should suffer my pride and my contempt of public opinion to hold me silent—but for yours and Fanny's sake I will pluck up a spirit and try again. I have no doubt of success in a course of years if I persevere—but it must be patience, for the Reviews have enervated and made indolent men's minds—few think for themselves. These Reviews too are getting more and more powerful, especially the Quarterly—they are like a superstition which the more it prostrates the Crowd and the longer it continues the more powerful it becomes just in proportion to their increasing weakness. I was in hopes that when people saw, as they must do now, all the trickery and iniquity of these Plagues they would scout them, but no, they are like the spectators at the Westminster cock-pit—they like the battle and do not care who wins or who loses. . . .

A Man's life of any worth is a continual allegory, and very few eyes can see the Mystery of his life—a life like the scriptures, figurative—which such people can no more make out than they can the Hebrew Bible. Lord Byron cuts a figure but he is not figurative— Shakspeare led a life of Allegory: his works are the comments on it— . . .

I have by me at present Hazlitt's Letter to Gifford—perhaps you would like an extract or two from the high-seasoned parts. It begins thus:

Sir, you have an ugly trick of saying what is not true of any one you do not like; and it will be the object of this Letter to cure you of it. You say what you please of others; it is time you were told what you are. In doing this give me leave to borrow the familiarity of your style: —for the fidelity of the picture I shall be answerable. You are a little person but a considerable cat's paw; and so far worthy of notice. Your clandestine connection with persons high in office constantly influences your opinions and alone gives importance to them. You are the government critic, a character nicely differing from that of a government spy—the invisible link which connects literature with the Police.

Again:

Your employers, Mr. Gifford, do not pay their hirelings for nothing—for condescending to notice weak and wicked sophistry; for pointing out to contempt what excites no admiration; for cautiously selecting a few specimens of bad taste and bad grammar where nothing else is to be found. They want your invisible pertness, your mercenary malice, your impenetrable dulness, your bare-faced impudence, your pragmatical self-sufficiency, your hypocritical zeal, your pious frauds to stand in the gap of their Prejudices and pretensions to fly-blow and taint public opinion, to defeat independent efforts, to apply not the touch of the scorpion but the touch of the Torpedo to youthful hopes, to crawl and leave the slimy track of sophistry and lies over every work that does not dedicate its sweet leaves to some Luminary of the treasury bench, or is not fostered in the hotbed of corruption. This is your office: "this is what is look'd for at your hands, and this you do not baulk"—to sacrifice what little honesty and prostitute what little intellect you possess to any dirty job you are commission'd to execute. "They keep you as an ape does an apple in the corner of his jaw, first mouth'd to be at last swallow'd." You are by appointment literary toadeater to greatness and taster to the

court. You have a natural aversion to whatever differs from your own pretensions, and an acquired one for what gives offence to your superiors. Your vanity panders to your interest, and your malice truckles only to your love of Power. If your instructive or premeditated abuse of your enviable trust were found wanting in a single instance; if you were to make a single slip in getting up your select committee of enquiry and green bag report of the state of Letters, your occupation would be gone. You would never after obtain a squeeze of the hand from acquaintance, or a smile from a Punk of quality. The great and powerful whom you call wise and good do not like to have the privacy of their self-love startled by the obtrusive and unmanageable claims of Literature and Philosophy, except through the intervention of people like you, whom, if they have common penetration, they soon find out to be without any superiority of intellect; or if they do not, whom they can despise for their meanness of soul. You "have the office opposite to Saint Peter." You keep a corner in the public mind for foul prejudice and corrupt power to knot and gender in; you volunteer your services to people of quality to ease scruples of mind and qualms of conscience; you lay the flattering unction of venal prose and laurell'd verse to their souls. You persuade them that there is neither purity of morals, nor depth of understanding except in themselves and their hangers-on; and would prevent the unhallow'd names of Liberty and humanity from ever being whispered in ears polite! You, sir, do you not all this? I cry you mercy then: I took you for the Editor of the Quarterly Review.

This is the sort of feu de joie he keeps up. There is another extract or two—one especially which I will copy to-morrow—for the candles are burnt down and I am using the wax taper—which has a long snuff on it—the fire is at its last click—I am sitting with my back to it with one foot rather askew upon the rug and the other with the heel a little elevated from the carpet—I am writing this on the Maid's Tragedy, which I have read since tea with great pleasure—Besides this volume of Beaumont and Fletcher, there are on the table two volumes of Chaucer and a new work of Tom Moore's, called Tom Cribb's Memorial to Congress—nothing in it. These are trifles— but I require nothing so much of you but that you will give one a like description of yourselves, however it may be when you are writing to me. Could I see the same thing done of any great Man long since dead it would be a great delight: as to know in what position Shakspeare sat when he began "To be or not to be"—such things become interesting from distance of time or place. . . .

I know not why Poetry and I have been so distant lately; I must make some advances soon or she will cut me entirely. Hazlitt has this fine Passage in his Letter: Gifford in his Review of Hazlitt's characters of Shakspeare's plays attacks the Coriolanus critique. He says that Hazlitt has slandered Shakspeare in saying that he had a leaning to the arbitrary side of the question. Hazlitt thus defends himself,

My words are, "Coriolanus is a storehouse of political common-places. The Arguments for and against aristocracy and democracy on the Privileges of the few and the claims of the many, on Liberty and slavery, power and the abuse of it, peace and war, are here very ably handled, with the spirit of a Poet and the acuteness of a Philosopher. Shakspeare himself seems to have had a leaning to the arbitrary side of the question, perhaps from some feeling of contempt for his own origin, and to have spared no occasion of bating the rabble. What he says of them is very true; what he says of their betters is also very true, though he dwells less upon it." I then proceed to account for this by showing how it is that "the cause of the people is but little calculated for a subject for poetry; or that the language of Poetry naturally falls in with the language of power." I affirm, Sir, that Poetry, that the imagination generally speaking, delights in power, in strong excitement, as well as in truth, in good, in right, whereas pure reason and the moral sense approve only of the true and good. I proceed to show that this general love or tendency to immediate excitement or theatrical effect, no matter how produced, gives a Bias to the imagination often consistent with the greatest good, that in Poetry it triumphs over principle, and bribes the passions to make a sacrifice of common humanity. You say that it does not, that there is no such original Sin in Poetry, that it makes no such sacrifice or unworthy compromise between poetical effect and the still small voice of reason. And how do you prove that there is no such principle giving a bias to the imagination and a false colouring to poetry? Why, by asking in reply to the instances where this principle operates, and where no other can with much modesty and simplicity—"But are these the only topics that afford delight in Poetry, etc.?" No; but these objects do afford delight in poetry, and they afford it in proportion to their strong and often tragical effect, and not in proportion to the good produced, or their desireableness in a moral point of view. Do we read with more pleasure of the ravages of a beast of prey than of the Shepherd's pipe upon the Mountain? No; but we do read with pleasure of the ravages of a beast of prey, and we do so on the principle I have stated, namely, from the sense of power abstracted from the sense of good; and it is the same principle that makes us read with admiration and reconciles us in fact to the triumphant progress of the conquerors and mighty Hunters of mankind, who come to stop the Shepherd's Pipe upon the Mountains and sweep away his listening flock. Do you mean to deny that there is anything imposing to the imagination in power, in grandeur, in outward show, in the accumulation of individual wealth and luxury, at the expense of equal justice and the common weal? Do you deny that there is anything in the "Pride, Pomp, and Circumstances of glorious war, that makes ambition virtue" in the eyes of admiring multitudes? Is this a new theory of the pleasures of the imagination, which says that the pleasures of the imagination do not take rise solely in the calculation of the understanding? Is it a paradox of my creating that "one murder makes a villain, millions a Hero"? or is it not true that here, as in other cases, the enormity of the evil overpowers and makes a convert of the imagination by its very magnitude? You contradict my reasoning because you know nothing of the question, and you think that no one has a right to understand what you do not. My offence against purity in the passage alluded to, "which contains the concentrated venom of my malignity," is that I have admitted that there are tyrants and slaves abroad in the world; and you would hush the matter up and pretend that there is no such thing in order that there may be nothing else. Further, I have explained the cause, the subtle sophistry of the human mind, that tolerates and pampers the evil in order to guard against its approaches; you would conceal the cause in order to prevent the cure, and to leave the proud flesh about the heart to harden and ossify into one impenetrable mass of selfishness and hypocrisy, that we may not "sympathise in the distresses of suffering virtue" in any case in which they come in competition with the fictitious wants and "imputed weaknesses of the great." You ask, "Are we gratified by the cruelties of Domitian or Nero?" No, not we—they were too petty and cowardly to strike the imagination at a distance; but the Roman senate tolerated them, addressed their perpetrators, exalted them into gods, the fathers of the people, they had pimps and scribblers of all sorts in their pay, their Senecas, etc., till a turbulent rabble, thinking there were no injuries to Society greater than the endurance of unlimited and wanton oppression, put an end to the farce and abated the sin as well as they could. Had you and I lived in those times we should have been what we are now, I "a sour malcontent," and you "a sweet courtier."

The manner in which this is managed: the force and innate power with which it yeasts and works up itself—the feeling for the costume of society; is in a style of genius. He hath a demon, as he himself says of Lord Byron. . . .

Don't think I am writing a petition to the Governors of St. Luke—no, that would be in another style. May it please your Worships; forasmuch as the undersigned has committed, transferred, given up, made over, consigned, and aberrated himself, to the art and mystery of poetry; forasmuch as he hath cut, rebuffed, affronted, huffed, and shirked, and taken stint at, all other employments, arts, mysteries, and occupations, honest, middling, and dishonest; forasmuch as he hath at sundry times and in divers places, told truth unto the men of this generation, and eke to the women; moreover, forasmuch as he hath kept a pair of boots that did not fit, and doth not admire Sheil's play, Leigh Hunt, Tom Moore, Bob Southey, and Mr. Rogers; and does admire Wm. Hazlitt; moreoverer for as more as he liketh half of Wordsworth, and none of Crabbe; moreover-est for as most as he hath written this page of penmanship—he prayeth your Worships to give him a lodging—Witnessed by Rd. Abbey and Co., cum familiaribus et consanguineis (signed) Count de Cockaigne. . . .

I have been at different times turning it in my head whether I should go to Edinburgh and study for a physician; I am afraid I should not take kindly to it; I am sure I could not take fees—and yet I should like to do so; it's not worse than writing poems, and hanging them up to be fly-blown on the Review shambles. . . .

Friday 19th March.

This morning I have been reading "the False One." Shameful to say, I was in bed at ten— I mean this morning. The Blackwood Review-ers have committed themselves in a scandalous heresy—they have been putting up Hogg, the Ettrick Shepherd, against Burns: the senseless villains! The Scotch cannot manage them-selves at all, they want imagination, and that is why they are so fond of Hogg, who has a little of it. This morning I am in a sort of temper, indolent and supremely careless—I long after a Stanza or two of Thomson's Castle of Indolence—my passions are all asleep, from my having slumbered till nearly eleven, and weakened the animal fibre all over me, to a delightful sensation, about three degrees on this side of faintness. If I had teeth of pearl and the breath of lilies I should call it languor, but as I am set * I must call it laziness. In this state of effeminacy the fibres of the brain are relaxed in common with the rest of the body, and to such a happy degree that pleasure has no show of enticement and pain no unbearable power. Neither Poetry, nor Ambition, nor Love have any alertness of countenance as they pass by me; they seem rather like figures on a

* Especially as I have a black eye.

Greek vase—a Man and two women whom no one but myself could distinguish in their dis-guisement. This is the only happiness, and is a rare instance of the advantage of the body overpowering the Mind. I have this moment received a note from Haslam, in which he ex-pects the death of his Father, who has been for some time in a state of insensibility; his mother bears up he says very well—I shall go to town to-morrow to see him. This is the world—thus we cannot expect to give way many hours to pleasure. Circumstances are like Clouds continually gathering and bursting— While we are laughing, the seed of some trouble is put into the wide arable land of events— while we are laughing it sprouts it grows and suddenly bears a poison fruit which we must pluck. Even so we have leisure to reason on the misfortunes of our friends; our own touch us too nearly for words. Very few men have ever arrived at a complete disinterestedness of Mind: very few have been influenced by a pure desire of the benefit of others,—in the greater part of the Benefactors to Humanity some meretricious motive has sullied their greatness —some melodramatic scenery has fascinated them. From the manner in which I feel Has-lam's misfortune I perceive how far I am from any humble standard of disinterestedness. Yet this feeling ought to be carried to its highest pitch, as there is no fear of its ever injuring society—which it would do, I fear, pushed to an extremity. For in wild nature the Hawk would lose his Breakfast of Robins and the Robin his of Worms—The Lion must starve as well as the swallow. The greater part of Men make their way with the same instinctive-ness, the same unwandering eye from their pur-poses, the same animal eagerness as the Hawk. The Hawk wants a Mate, so does the Man— look at them both, they set about it and procure one in the same manner. They want both a nest and they both set about one in the same manner —they get their food in the same manner. The noble animal Man for his amusement smokes his pipe—the Hawk balances about the Clouds —that is the only difference of their leisures. This it is that makes the Amusement of Life —to a speculative Mind—I go among the Fields and catch a glimpse of a Stoat or a fieldmouse peeping out of the withered grass— the creature hath a purpose, and its eyes are bright with it. I go amongst the buildings of a city and I see a Man hurrying along—to what? The Creature has a purpose and his eyes are bright with it. But then, as Wordsworth says, "we have all one human heart——" There is an electric fire in human nature tending to purify—so that among these human creatures there is continually some birth of new heroism. The pity is that we must wonder at it, as we should at finding a pearl in rubbish. I have no doubt that thousands of people never heard of have had hearts completely disinterested: I can remember but two —Socrates and Jesus—Their histories evince it. What I heard a little time ago, Taylor observe with respect to Socrates, may be said of Jesus—That he was so great a man that though he transmitted no writing of his own to posterity, we have his Mind and his sayings and his greatness handed to us by others. It is to be lamented that the history of the latter was written and revised by Men interested in the pious frauds of Religion. Yet through all this I see his splendour. Even here, though I myself am pursuing the same instinctive course as the veriest human animal you can think of, I am, however young, writing at random, straining at particles of light in the midst of a great darkness, without knowing the bearing of any one assertion, of any one opinion. Yet may I not in this be free from sin? May there not be superior beings amused with any graceful, though instinctive, attitude my mind may fall into as I am entertained with the alertness of a Stoat or the anxiety of a Deer? Though a quarrel in the Streets is a thing to be hated, the energies displayed in it are fine; the commonest Man shows a grace in his quarrel. By a superior Being our reasonings may take the same tone—though erroneous they may be fine. This is the very thing in which consists Poetry, and if so it is not so fine a thing as philosophy— For the same reason that an eagle is not so fine a thing as a truth. Give me this credit— Do you not think I strive—to know myself? Give me this credit, and you will not think that on my own account I repeat Milton's lines—

How charming is divine Philosophy,
Not harsh and crabbed, as dull fools suppose,
But musical as is Apollo's lute.

No—not for myself—feeling grateful as I do to have got into a state of mind to relish them properly. Nothing ever becomes real till it is experienced—Even a Proverb is no proverb to you till your Life has illustrated it. I am ever afraid that your anxiety for me will lead you to fear for the violence of my temperament continually smothered down: for that reason I did not intend to have sent you the following sonnet—but look over the two last pages and ask yourselves whether I have not that in me which will bear the buffets of the world. It will be the best comment on my sonnet; it will show you that it was written with no Agony but that of ignorance; with no thirst of anything but Knowledge when pushed to the point though the first steps to it were through my human passions—they went away and I wrote with my Mind—and perhaps I must confess a little bit of my heart—

[Why did I laugh to-night? No voice will tell.]

I went to bed and enjoyed an uninterrupted sleep. Sane I went to bed and sane I arose. . . .

Wordsworth is going to publish a Poem called Peter Bell—what a perverse fellow it is! Why will he talk about Peter Bells—I was told not to tell—but to you it will not be telling— Reynolds hearing that said Peter Bell was coming out, took it into his head to write a skit upon it called Peter Bell. He did it as soon as thought on, it is to be published this morning, and comes out before the real Peter Bell, with this admirable motto from the "Bold Stroke for a Wife" "I am the real Simon Pure." It would be just as well to trounce Lord Byron in the same manner. I am still at a stand in versifying—I cannot do it yet with any pleasure—I mean, however, to look round on my resources and means, and see what I can do without poetry— . . .

Last Sunday I took a Walk towards Highgate and in the lane that winds by the side of Lord Mansfield's park I met Mr. Green our Demonstrator at Guy's in conversation with Coleridge—I joined them, after enquiring by a look whether it would be agreeable—I walked with him at his alderman-after-dinner pace for near two miles I suppose. In those two Miles he broached a thousand things—let me see if I can give you a list—Nightingales—Poetry —on Poetical Sensation—Metaphysics—Different genera and species of Dreams—Nightmare—a dream accompanied by a sense of touch—single and double touch—a dream related—First and second consciousness—the difference explained between will and Volition —so say metaphysicians from a want of smok·

ing the second consciousness—Monsters—the Kraken—Mermaids—Southey believes in them —Southey's belief too much diluted—a Ghost story—Good morning—I heard his voice as he came towards me—I heard it as he moved away —I had heard it all the interval—if it may be called so. He was civil enough to ask me to call on him at Highgate. Good-night! . . .

[Later, April 18 or 19.]

The fifth canto of Dante pleases me more and more—it is that one in which he meets with Paolo and Francesca. I had passed many days in rather a low state of mind, and in the midst of them I dreamt of being in that region of Hell. The dream was one of the most delightful enjoyments I ever had in my life. I floated about the whirling atmosphere, as it is described, with a beautiful figure, to whose lips mine were joined as it seemed for an age—and in the midst of all this cold and darkness I was warm—even flowery tree-tops sprung up, and we rested on them, sometimes with the lightness of a cloud, till the wind blew us away again. I tried a sonnet upon it—there are fourteen lines, but nothing of what I felt in it— O that I could dream it every night— . . .

[As Hermes once took to his feathers light.]

When Reynolds was here on Monday he asked me to give Hunt a hint to take notice of his Peter Bell in the Examiner—the best thing I can do is to write a little notice of it myself, which I will do here, and copy out if it should suit my Purpose—

Peter Bell. There have been lately advertised two Books both Peter Bell by name; what stuff the one was made of might be seen by the motto—"I am the real Simon Pure." This false Florimel has hurried from the press and obtruded herself into public notice, while for aught we know the real one may be still wandering about the woods and mountains. Let us hope she may soon appear and make good her right to the magic girdle. The Pamphleteering Archimage, we can perceive, has rather a splenetic love than a downright hatred to real Florimels—if indeed they had been so christened—or had even a pretention to play at bob cherry with Barbara Lewthwaite: but he has a fixed aversion to those three rhyming Graces Alice Fell, Susan Gale and Betty Foy; and now at length especially to Peter Bell— fit Apollo. It may be seen from one or two

Passages in this little skit, that the writer of it has felt the finer parts of Mr. Wordsworth, and perhaps expatiated with his more remote and sublimer muse. This as far as it relates to Peter Bell is unlucky. The more he may love the sad embroidery of the Excursion, the more he will hate the coarse Samplers of Betty Foy and Alice Fell; and as they come from the same hand, the better will he be able to imitate that which can be imitated, to wit Peter Bell—as far as can be imagined from the obstinate Name. We repeat, it is very unlucky —this real Simon Pure is in parts the very Man—there is a pernicious likeness in the scenery, a "pestilent humour" in the rhymes, and an inveterate cadence in some of the Stanzas, that must be lamented. If we are one part amused with this we are three parts sorry that an appreciator of Wordsworth should show so much temper at this really provoking name of Peter Bell—!

This will do well enough—I have copied it and enclosed it to Hunt. You will call it a little politic—seeing I keep clear of all parties. I say something for and against both parties— and suit it to the tune of the Examiner—I meant to say I do not unsuit it—and I believe I think what I say, nay I am sure I do—I and my conscience are in luck to-day—which is an excellent thing. . . .

I have been reading lately two very different books, Robertson's America and Voltaire's Siècle de Louis XIV. It is like walking arm and arm between Pizarro and the great-little Monarch. In how lamentable a case do we see the great body of the people in both instances; in the first, where Men might seem to inherit quiet of Mind from unsophisticated senses; from uncontamination of civilisation, and especially from their being, as it were, estranged from the mutual helps of Society and its mutual injuries—and thereby more immediately under the Protection of Providence—even there they had mortal pains to bear as bad, or even worse than Bailiffs, Debts, and Poverties of civilised Life. The whole appears to resolve into this— that Man is originally a poor forked creature subject to the same mischances as the beasts of the forest, destined to hardships and disquietude of some kind or other. If he improves by degrees his bodily accommodations and comforts—at each stage, at each ascent there are waiting for him a fresh set of annoyances— he is mortal, and there is still a heaven with its Stars above his head. The most interesting question that can come before us is, How far by the persevering endeavours of a seldom appearing Socrates Mankind may be made happy—I can imagine such happiness carried to an extreme, but what must it end in?—Death—and who could in such a case bear with death? The whole troubles of life, which are now frittered away in a series of years, would then be accumulated for the last days of a being who instead of hailing its approach would leave this world as Eve left Paradise. But in truth I do not at all believe in this sort of perfectibility—the nature of the world will not admit of it—the inhabitants of the world will correspond to itself. Let the fish Philosophise the ice away from the Rivers in winter time, and they shall be at continual play in the tepid delight of summer. Look at the Poles and at the Sands of Africa, whirlpools and volcanoes—Let men exterminate them and I will say that they may arrive at earthly Happiness. The point at which Man may arrive is as far as the parallel state in inanimate nature, and no further. For instance suppose a rose to have sensation, it blooms on a beautiful morning, it enjoys itself, but then comes a cold wind, a hot sun—it cannot escape it, it cannot destroy its annoyances—they are as native to the world as itself: no more can man be happy in spite, the worldly elements will prey upon his nature. The common cognomen of this world among the misguided and superstitious is "a vale of tears," from which we are to be redeemed by a certain arbitrary interposition of God and taken to Heaven—What a little circumscribed straightened notion! Call the world if you please "The vale of Soul-making." Then you will find out the use of the world (I am speaking now in the highest terms for human nature admitting it to be immortal which I will here take for granted for the purpose of showing a thought which has struck me concerning it) I say "Soul-making"—Soul as distinguished from an Intelligence. There may be intelligences or sparks of the divinity in millions—but they are not Souls till they acquire identities, till each one is personally itself. Intelligences are atoms of perception—they know and they see and they are pure, in short they are God—how then are Souls to be made? How then are these sparks which are God to have identity given them—so as ever to possess a bliss peculiar to each one's individual existence? How, but by the medium of a world like this? This point I sincerely wish to consider because I think it a grander system of salvation than the Christian religion—or rather it is a system of Spirit-creation—This is effected by three grand materials acting the one upon the other for a series of years—These three Materials are the *Intelligence*—the *human heart* (as distinguished from intelligence or Mind), and the *World* or *Elemental space* suited for the proper action of *Mind and Heart* on each other for the purpose of forming the *Soul* or *Intelligence destined to possess the sense of Identity*. I can scarcely express what I but dimly perceive—and yet I think I perceive it—that you may judge the more clearly I will put it in the most homely form possible. I will call the *world* a School instituted for the purpose of teaching little children to read—I will call the *human heart* the *horn Book* used in that School—and I will call the *Child able to read, the Soul* made from that *School* and its *horn book*. Do you not see how necessary a World of Pains and troubles is to school an Intelligence and make it a soul? A Place where the heart must feel and suffer in a thousand diverse ways. Not merely is the Heart a Hornbook, It is the Mind's Bible, it is the Mind's experience, it is the text from which the Mind or Intelligence sucks its identity. As various as the Lives of Men are—so various become their souls, and thus does God make individual beings, Souls, Identical Souls of the sparks of his own essence. This appears to me a faint sketch of a system of Salvation which does not offend our reason and humanity—I am convinced that many difficulties which Christians labour under would vanish before it—there is one which even now strikes me—the salvation of Children. In them the spark or intelligence returns to God without any identity—it having had no time to learn of and be altered by the heart—or seat of the human Passions. It is pretty generally suspected that the Christian scheme has been copied from the ancient Persian and Greek Philosophers. Why may they not have made this simple thing even more simple for common apprehension by introducing Mediators and Personages, in the same manner as in the heathen mythology abstractions are personified? Seriously I think it probable that this system of Soul-making may have been the Parent of all the more palpable and personal schemes of Redemption among the Zoroastrians the Christians and the

Hindoos. For as one part of the human species must have their carved Jupiter; so another part must have the palpable and named Mediator and Saviour, their Christ, their Oromanes, and their Vishnu. If what I have said should not be plain enough, as I fear it may not be, I will put you in the place where I began in this series of thoughts—I mean I began by seeing how man was formed by circumstances—and what are circumstances but touchstones of his heart? and what are touchstones but provings of his heart, but fortifiers or alterers of his nature? and what is his altered nature but his Soul?—and what was his Soul before it came into the world and had these provings and alterations and perfectionings?—An intelligence without Identity—and how is this Identity to be made? Through the medium of the Heart? and how is the heart to become this Medium but in a world of Circumstances? . . .

The following Poem—the last I have written—is the first and the only one with which I have taken even moderate pains. I have for the most part dash'd off my lines in a hurry. This I have done leisurely—I think it reads the more richly for it, and will I hope encourage me to write other things in even a more peaceable and healthy spirit. You must recollect that Psyche was not embodied as a goddess before the time of Apuleius the Platonist who lived after the Augustan age, and consequently the Goddess was never worshipped or sacrificed to with any of the ancient fervour—and perhaps never thought of in the old religion—I am more orthodox than to let a heathen Goddess be so neglected—

[The Ode to Psyche,]

Here endethe ye Ode to Psyche.

Incipit altera Sonneta

I have been endeavouring to discover a better Sonnet Stanza than we have. The legitimate does not suit the language over well from the pouncing rhymes—the other kind appears too elegiac—and the couplet at the end of it has seldom a pleasing effect—I do not pretend to have succeeded—it will explain itself.

[May 3.]
This is the third of May, and everything is in delightful forwardness; the violets are not withered before the peeping of the first rose. You must let me know everything—how parcels go and come, what papers you have, and what newspapers you want, and other things. God bless you, my dear brother and sister.

Your ever affectionate Brother
JOHN KEATS.

XIX

TO BENJAMIN ROBERT HAYDON

Wentworth Place,
[Postmark, March 8, 1819].

MY DEAR HAYDON,—You must be wondering where I am and what I am about! I am mostly at Hampstead, and about nothing; being in a sort of qui bono temper, not exactly on the road to an epic poem. Nor must you think I have forgotten you. No, I have about every three days been to Abbey's and to the Law[y]ers. Do let me know how you have been getting on, and in what spirits you are.

You got out gloriously in yesterday's Examiner. What a set of little people we live amongst! I went the other day into an ironmonger's shop—without any change in my sensations—men and tin kettles are much the same in these days—they do not study like children at five and thirty—but they talk like men of twenty. Conversation is not a search after knowledge, but an endeavour at effect.

In this respect two most opposite men, Wordsworth and Hunt, are the same. A friend of mine observed the other day that if Lord Bacon were to make any remark in a party of the present day, the conversation would stop on the sudden. I am convinced of this, and from this I have come to this resolution—never to write for the sake of writing or making a poem, but from running over with any little knowledge or experience which many years of reflection may perhaps give me; otherwise I will be dumb. What imagination I have I shall enjoy, and greatly, for I have experienced the satisfaction of having great conceptions without the trouble of sonnetteering. I will not spoil my love of gloom by writing an Ode to Darkness!

With respect to my livelihood, I will not write for it,—for I will not run with that most vulgar of all crowds, the literary. Such things I ratify by looking upon myself, and trying myself at lifting mental weights, as it were. I am three and twenty with little knowledge and middling intellect. It is true that in the height of enthusiasm I have been cheated into some fine passages; but that is not the thing.

I have not been to see you because all my going out has been to town, and that has been a great deal. Write soon.

Yours constantly,   JOHN KEATS.

XX

TO BENJAMIN BAILEY

[Winchester, August 15, 1819].

.   .   .   .

We removed to Winchester for the convenience of a library, and find it an exceeding pleasant town, enriched with a beautiful Cathedral and surrounded by a fresh-looking country. We are in tolerably good and cheap lodgings—Within these two months I have written 1500 lines, most of which, besides many more of prior composition, you will probably see by next winter. I have written 2 tales, one from Boccaccio, called the Pot of Basil, and another called St. Agnes's Eve, on a popular Superstition, and a 3rd called Lamia (half finished). I have also been writing parts of my "Hyperion," and completed 4 Acts of a tragedy. It was the opinion of most of my friends that I should never be able to write a scene. I will endeavour to wipe away the prejudice—I sincerely hope you will be pleased when my labours, since we last saw each other, shall reach you. One of my Ambitions is to make as great a revolution in modern dramatic writing as Kean has done in acting. Another to upset the drawling of the blue-stocking literary world —if in the Course of a few years I do these two things, I ought to die content, and my friends should drink a dozen of claret on my tomb. I am convinced more and more every day that (excepting the human friend philosopher), a fine writer is the most genuine being in the world. Shakspeare and the Paradise lost every day become greater wonders to me. I look upon fine phrases like a lover. I was glad to see by a passage of one of Brown's letters, some time ago, from the North that you were in such good spirits. Since that you have been married, and in congratulating you I wish you every continuance of them. Present my respects to Mrs. Bailey. This sounds oddly to me, and I daresay I do it awkwardly enough: but I

suppose by this time it is nothing new to you. Brown's remembrances to you. As far as I know, we shall remain at Winchester for a goodish while.

Ever your sincere friend   JOHN KEATS.

XXI

TO JOHN TAYLOR

Winchester, Monday morn [August 23, 1819].

MY DEAR TAYLOR—

. . . Brown and I have together been engaged (this I should wish to remain secret) on a Tragedy which I have just finished and from which we hope to share moderate profits. . . . I feel every confidence that, if I choose, I may be a popular writer. That I will never be; but for all that I will get a livelihood. I equally dislike the favour of the public with the love of a woman. They are both a cloying treacle to the wings of Independence. I shall ever consider them (People) as debtors to me for verses, not myself to them for admiration—which I can do without. I have of late been indulging my spleen by composing a preface AT them: after all resolving never to write a preface at all. "There are so many verses," would I have said to them, "give so much means for me to buy pleasure with, as a relief to my hours of labour"—You will observe at the end of this if you put down the letter, "How a solitary life engenders pride and egotism!" True—I know it does: but this pride and egotism will enable me to write finer things than anything else could—so I will indulge it. Just so much as I am humbled by the genius above my grasp am I exalted and look with hate and contempt upon the literary world.— A drummer-boy who holds out his hand familiarly to a field Marshal,—that drummer-boy with me is the good word and favour of the public. Who could wish to be among the common-place crowd of the little famous—who are each individually lost in a throng made up of themselves? Is this worth louting or playing the hypocrite for? To beg suffrages for a seat on the benches of a myriad-aristocracy in letters? This is not wise.—I am not a wise man—'T is pride—I will give you a definition of a proud man—He is a man who has neither Vanity nor Wisdom—One filled with hatreds cannot be vain, neither can he be wise. Pardon me for hammering instead of writing. Remember me to Woodhouse Hessey and all in Percy Street.

Ever yours sincerely   JOHN KEATS.

XXII

TO GEORGE AND GEORGIANA KEATS

Winchester, Saturday [September 18].

MY DEAR GEORGE—With my inconstant disposition it is no wonder that this morning, amid all our bad times and misfortunes, I should feel so alert and well-spirited. At this moment you are perhaps in a very different state of mind. It is because my hopes are ever paramount to my despair. I have been reading over a part of a short poem I have composed lately, called Lamia, and I am certain there is that sort of fire in it that must take hold of people some way. Give them either pleasant or unpleasant sensation—what they want is a sensation of some sort. I wish I could pitch the key of your spirits as high as mine is; but your organ-loft is beyond the reach of my voice. . . .

When I left Mr. Abbey on Monday evening, I walked up Cheapside, but returned to put some letters in the post, and met him again in Bucklesbury. We walked together through the Poultry as far as the baker's shop he has some concern in—He spoke of it in such a way to me, I thought he wanted me to make an offer to assist him in it. I do believe if I could be a hatter I might be one. He seems anxious about me. He began blowing up Lord Byron while I was sitting with him: "However, may be the fellow says true now and then," at which he picked up a magazine, and read some extracts from Don Juan (Lord Byron's last flash poem), and particularly one against literary ambition. I do think I must be well spoken of among sets, for Hodgkinson is more than polite, and the coffee German endeavoured to be very close to me the other night at Covent Garden, where I went at half price before I tumbled into bed. Every one, however distant an acquaintance, behaves in the most conciliating manner to me. You will see I speak of this as a matter of interest. On the next sheet I will give you a little politics.

In every age there has been in England, for two or three centuries, subjects of great popular interest on the carpet, so that however great the uproar, one can scarcely prophecy any material change in the Government, for as loud disturbances have agitated the country many times. All civilized countries become gradually more enlightened, and there should be a continual change for the better. Look at this country at present, and remember it when it was even thought impious to doubt the justice of a trial by combat. From that time there has been a gradual change. Three great changes have been in progress: first for the better, next for the worse, and a third for the better once more. The first was the gradual annihilation of the tyranny of the nobles, when kings found it their interest to conciliate the common people, elevate them, and be just to them. Just when baronial power ceased, and before standing armies were so dangerous, taxes were few, kings were lifted by the people over the heads of their nobles, and those people held a rod over kings. The change for the worse in Europe was again this: the obligation of kings to the multitude began to be forgotten. Custom had made noblemen the humble servants of kings. Then kings turned to the nobles as the adorners of their power, the slaves of it, and from the people as creatures continually endeavouring to check them. Then in every kingdom there was a long struggle of kings to destroy all popular privileges. The English were the only people in Europe who made a grand kick at this. They were slaves to Henry VIII, but were freemen under William III at the time the French were abject slaves under Louis XIV. The example of England, and the liberal writers of France and England, sowed the seed of opposition to this tyranny, and it was swelling in the ground till it burst out in the French Revolution. That has had an unlucky termination. It put a stop to the rapid progress of free sentiments in England, and gave our Court hopes of turning back to the despotism of the eighteenth century. They have made a handle of this event in every way to undermine our freedom. They spread a horrid superstition against all innovation and improvement. The present struggle in England of the people is to destroy this superstition. What has roused them to do it is their distresses. Perhaps, on this account, the present distresses of this nation are a fortunate thing though so horrid in their experience. You will see I mean that the French Revolution put a temporary stop to this third change—the change for the better—Now it is in progress again, and I think it is an effectual one. This is no contest between Whig and Tory, but between right and wrong. There is scarcely a grain of party spirit now in England. Right and wrong considered by each man abstractedly, is the fashion. I know very little of these things. I am convinced, however, that apparently small causes make great alterations. There are little signs whereby we may know how matters are going on. This makes the business of Carlisle the bookseller of great amount in my mind. He has been selling deistical pamphlets, republished Tom Paine, and many other works held in superstitious horror. He even has been selling, for some time, immense numbers of a work called The Deist, which comes out in weekly numbers. For this conduct he, I think, has had about a dozen indictments issued against him, for which he has found bail to the amount of many thousand pounds. After all, they are afraid to prosecute. They are afraid of his defence; it would be published in all the papers all over the empire. They shudder at this. The trials would light a flame they could not extinguish. Do you not think this of great import? You will hear by the papers of the proceedings at Manchester, and Hunt's triumphal entry into London. It would take me a whole day and a quire of paper to give you anything like detail. I will merely mention that it is calculated that 30,000 people were in the streets waiting for him. The whole distance from the Angel at Islington to the Crown and Anchor was lined with multitudes. . . .

You speak of Lord Byron and me. There is this great difference between us: he describes what he sees—I describe what I imagine. Mine is the hardest task; now see the immense difference. The Edinburgh Reviewers are afraid to touch upon my poem. They do not know what to make of it; they do not like to condemn it, and they will not praise it for fear. They are as shy of it as I should be of wearing a Quaker's hat. The fact is, they have no real taste. They dare not compromise their judgments on so puzzling a question. If on my next publication they should praise me, and so lug in Endymion, I will address them in a manner they will not at all relish. The cowardliness of the Edinburgh is more than the abuse of the Quarterly. . . .

Believe me, my dear brother and sister, your affectionate and anxious Brother

JOHN KEATS.

XXIII

TO JOHN HAMILTON REYNOLDS

Winchester, September 22, 1819.

MY DEAR REYNOLDS—

. . . I hope you are better employed than in gaping after weather. I have been at different times so happy as not to know what weather it was—No I will not copy a parcel of verses. I always somehow associate Chatterton with autumn. He is the purest writer in the English Language. He has no French idiom or particles, like Chaucer—'t is genuine English Idiom in English words. I have given up Hyperion—there were too many Miltonic inversions in it—Miltonic verse cannot be written but in an artful, or, rather, artist's humour. I wish to give myself up to other sensations. English ought to be kept up. It may be interesting to you to pick out some lines from Hyperion, and put a mark ✕ to the false beauty proceeding from art, and one ‖ to the true voice of feeling. Upon my soul 't was imagination—I cannot make the distinction—Every now and then there is a Miltonic intonation—But I cannot make the division properly.

Ever your affectionate friend

JOHN KEATS.

XXIV

TO FANNY BRAWNE

MY DEAR FANNY,—Do not let your mother suppose that you hurt me by writing at night. For some reason or other your last night's note was not so treasureable as former ones. I would fain that you call me *Love* still. To see you happy and in high spirits is a great consolation to me—still let me believe that you are not half so happy as my restoration would make you. I am nervous, I own, and may think myself worse than I really am; if so you must indulge me, and pamper with that sort of tenderness you have manifested towards me in different Letters. My sweet creature when I look back upon the pains and torments I have suffer'd for you from the day I left you to go to the Isle of Wight; the ecstasies in which I have pass'd some days and the miseries in their turn, I wonder the more at the Beauty which has kept up the spell so fervently. When I send this round I shall be in the front parlour watching to see you show yourself for a minute in the garden. How illness stands as a barrier betwixt me and you! Even if I was well—I must make myself as good a Philosopher as possible. Now I have had opportunities of passing nights anxious and awake I have found other thoughts intrude upon me. "If I should die," said I to myself, "I have left no immortal work behind me—nothing to make my friends proud of my memory—but I have lov'd the principle of beauty in all things, and if I had had time I would have made myself remember'd." Thoughts like these came very feebly whilst I was in health and every pulse beat for you —now you divide with this (may *I* say it?) "last infirmity of noble minds" all my reflection.

God bless you, Love.   J. KEATS.

XXV

TO PERCY BYSSHE SHELLEY

[Wentworth Place, Hampstead, August, 1820].

MY DEAR SHELLEY—I am very much gratified that you, in a foreign country, and with a mind almost over-occupied, should write to me in the strain of the letter beside me. If I do not take advantage of your invitation, it will be prevented by a circumstance I have very much at heart to prophesy. There is no doubt that an English winter would put an end to me, and do so in a lingering hateful manner. Therefore, I must either voyage or journey to Italy, as a soldier marches up to a battery. My nerves at present are the worst part of me, yet they feel soothed that, come what extreme may, I shall not be destined to remain in one spot long enough to take a hatred of any four particular bedposts. I am glad you take any pleasure in my poor poem, which I would willingly take the trouble to unwrite, if possible, did I care so much as I have done about reputation. I received a copy of the Cenci, as from yourself, from Hunt. There is only one part of it I am judge of—the poetry and dramatic effect, which by many spirits nowadays is considered the Mammon. A modern work, it is said, must have a purpose, which may be the God. An artist must serve Mammon; he must have "self-concentration"—selfishness, perhaps. You, I am sure, will forgive me for sincerely remarking that you might curb your magnanimity, and be more of an artist, and load every rift of your subject with ore. The thought of such discipline must fall like cold chains upon you, who perhaps never sat with your wings furled for six months together. And is this not extraordinary talk for the writer of Endymion, whose mind was like a pack of scattered cards? I am picked up and sorted to a pip. My imagination is a monastery, and I am its monk. I am in expectation of Prometheus every day. Could I have my own wish effected, you would have it still in manuscript, or be but now putting an end to the second act. I remember you advising me not to publish my first blights, on Hampstead Heath. I am returning advice upon your hands. Most of the poems in the volume I send you have been written above two years, and would never have been published but for hope of gain; so you see I am inclined enough to take your advice now. I must express once more my deep sense of your kindness, adding my sincere thanks and respects for Mrs. Shelley.

In the hope of soon seeing you, I remain most sincerely yours   JOHN KEATS.

MAJOR CRITICS
OF THE
ROMANTIC MOVEMENT

MAJOR CRITICS OF THE ROMANTIC MOVEMENT

WILLIAM HAZLITT

1778–1830

The literature of power in the early nineteenth century is deeply rooted in the literature of knowledge of the latter eighteenth century. The one grows out of the other naturally. The writers of the earlier years in putting to full test the rules of common sense and reason perform a vital service for those who later are to try the laws of imagination and passion. As we calendar the new century we must remember that we are but dating superficially an organic evolution.

Pope may have been a "pyrotechnic artist," preëminent in "the sportive and aërial graces of the mock heroic and satiric muse"; but we must suspect De Quincey of a greater delight in nice phrases than in profound philosophy when he says of the *Essay on Criticism* that it is merely "a metrical multiplication table, of commonplaces the most mouldy with which criticism has baited its rat-traps." If in literary criticism we owe nothing else to Pope and to Dryden, we owe them an understanding of the fact that they proved the values of common sense and reason finally. Where they set the limits it was not necessary for men to go further. Their service was a primary service.

Because of the success of the classicists in the regions where they worked, other men were left free to explore new continents. The Wartons understood this truth half a century before our period begins. By permission of this truth both Gray and Cowper embedded in their letters critical observations of the purest worth, and Young crossed "all public roads into fresh untrodden ground." When, therefore, in 1818 Hazlitt, speaking on *Poetry in General,* said, "Nothing—can be more absurd than the outcry which has been sometimes raised by frigid and pedantic critics, for reducing the language of poetry to the standard of common sense and reason: for the end and use of poetry, 'both at the first and now, was and is to hold the mirror up to nature,' seen through the medium of passion and imagination," he ungraciously failed in the acknowledgment of a debt, hoping that by establishing an antithesis he might make more secure the enormous claim of his romantic nature.

Nevertheless, Hazlitt had in his hand the new end of truth. There was a tide moving in the hearts of men, leading on to other fortunes in literature. Wordsworth, as we have seen, had given that tide fullness and direction; and Shelley was to follow him. Between the two Hazlitt rose as the great critic of the Romantic Movement.

Perhaps the significance of Hazlitt is associated with the fact that he welcomed antithesis, so that with his hand against neo-classicism he shoved himself face-forward into romanticism. Then, too, he was by nature subject to "the enthusiasm of fancy and feeling." He was one who instinctively and sensitively sought to "conform the show of things to the desire of the soul." In his mind "poetry and philosophy met together," although he chose to listen largely to the "language of the imagination and the passions," and to believe in the creed of beauty. In fact, he was persuaded that "the moral and intellectual in us" are but emanations of our emotions, and that the truth of life is to be felt with the heart and not known by the brain. Nowhere is he better announced as a critic of romanticism than in the words he wrote to describe his experience after he had walked with Coleridge and turned away home: "I had a sound in my ears, it was the voice of Fancy: I had a light before me, it was the face of Poetry."

The outer affairs of Hazlitt's life are of little consequence when compared with this inner set of his mind. In the essay *My First Acquaintance with Poets* he tells us of such events in his youth as seem to him important. At fifteen years of age he entered a dissenting theological school, only to rebel against the thought of becoming a clergyman. Upon his return home, three years later, the rationalism with which he had charged his mind was warmly touched by the emotionalism of Rousseau and the genius of Coleridge. While these conflicting qualities, the rationalistic and the emotional, still locked all his powers in static balance, he followed the lead of his brother John and turned to painting. In this art he wasted the years from 1798 to 1808, and crowned the period by an unfortunate marriage with Sarah Stoddart. However, even while he handled his brushes awkwardly, he began to use his pen with skill. In 1805, he wrote the *Principles of Human Action;* in 1813, the first of his dramatic criticisms; and in a short time those more personal and familiar essays which Leigh Hunt welcomed into *The Examiner.* Already Hazlitt had come to know not only Coleridge and Hunt, but Southey, Wordsworth, and those staunch friends, the Lambs, in the comfort of whose hearth he was at his best. The years were now few before, at the Surrey Institution in 1818, his *Lectures on the English Poets* made it manifest that there was in England what Thackeray called "one of the keenest and brightest critics that ever lived." His subsequent lectures on the *English Comic Writers* (1819), and the *Dramatic Literature of the Age of Elizabeth* (1820), confirmed his claims to genius. In the *Spirit of the Age* (1825) and the *Plain Speaker* (1826) his natural force did not abate. His mind had mastered those wide reaches of literature which lay between the time of Elizabeth and his own. The quality of his work had its final and happy attestation in the remark of Robert Louis Stevenson: "We are fine fellows, but we can't write like William Hazlitt." And although his domestic and private relationships seemed too often given to the pleasure of hating, the friend who stood beside his death bed was Charles Lamb, and the last words of the critic were, "Well, I have had a happy life."

Whether or not it is true that, as Baudelaire says, "It would be impossible for a critic to become a poet, and it is impossible for a poet not to contain a critic," the resurgence in the nineteenth century of the perennial stuff of our nature which we call romantic contained in itself William Hazlitt. The critic within the poet is not more naturally born there than was William Hazlitt born within the Romantic Movement. However, it does not follow that he always entered sympathetically into the creative mood of his great contemporaries or shared happily their purposes. "He is your only good damner," wrote Keats, "'and if ever I am damn'd—damn me if I shouldn't like him to damn me." But, as if the effect of this merry prayer had gone awry, it was not Keats whom Hazlitt damned, but Byron and Shelley and Scott and even his beloved Coleridge. We do not mean that he turned entirely against them or that he was always justified when he did. A part of the opportunity which this volume affords to the student is that of determining for himself when the prejudice of Hazlitt led him to be uncritical, or when he could not rise to a full appreciation of the man with whom he dealt. Whatever errors of tact or of judgment the student may recognize, he will nevertheless find in Hazlitt a nature sensitive to the best appeals of the literature of his time and a mind acute and subtle in the appraisal of elements both good and bad. Writing to Haydon Keats said, "There are three things to rejoice at in this Age—The Excursion, Your Pictures, and Hazlitt's depth of taste."

If Hazlitt at times, as in his criticism of *Christabel* or of the posthumous poems of Shelley, failed to appreciate some of the magic and the beauty, he nevertheless had a fuller conception than any other contemporary critic of the subject-matter of poetry and of the forms and the harmonies to which that subject-matter should give being. He saw indeed that poetry is "the stuff of which our life is made." All else, history itself, is but a cumbrous mass of shadows strutting and fretting upon their way to nothingness. Believing these things profoundly, and believing as did a later critic that in poetry mankind would come to find a surer and a surer stay, and having, as he said, a light before him, he rose at his best to prose of passionate force. In this prose there is no trick, no artifice. It is idiomatic, colloquial, rapid, spontaneous, and sincere. He passed through the libraries of three centuries, but there is no smell of a book upon him. His rhythms are

sinewy and rugged, like those of nature. "He handles his subject with great *gusto*," an early commentator says of him. From the depth of his comprehension of that which literature is and from his zest for those qualities in literature which are good his prose drew ever refreshed vitality. It is a proud thing which he says of himself, but a true: "I have written no commonplace, nor a line that licks the dust."

LEIGH HUNT

1784–1859

It is the peculiar distinction of Leigh Hunt that through his discernment "Keats and Shelley were first made known to lovers of the beautiful." His also remains the honor of drafting the *credo* of the romantic poets. It matters little that he himself wrote no authentic poetry or that he did write long volumes of wraith-like prose which have already drifted away to limbo. He first made Keats and Shelley known; and for his age he wrote the answer to the question, *What Is Poetry?* That should be sufficient.

Since in this volume the significant things which Hunt did lie open to the hand of the student; and since it is the purpose of the book rather to stimulate students in working out critical opinions of their own than to furnish them with conclusions, we shall restrict our comments to those matters which may make the position of Hunt more understandable. In his birth, like Hazlitt, he found himself on the side of rebellion and contradiction; for his father was an attorney who left the colonies because he was a loyalist only to become a Unitarian minister in England; and his mother was a woman who, however patient with her own pain, defied injustice to others as though it were the foul fiend. Leigh, having in his school time regaled himself with Spenser and other unworldly poets, at the age of twenty-four undertook the editorship of *The Examiner*, setting within his purpose such pretty problems as the reform of Parliament, Catholic emancipation, the abolition of capital punishment, child labor, the slave trade, the correction of social injustice, economic injustice, political injustice, the stamping out of cruelty to prisoners, animals, and frogs, or—as he put it—"to assist liberality of opinion in general, and a fusion of literary taste into all subjects whatsoever."

This program did not want ambition; but, although it attracted to him Hazlitt, the young Keats and Shelley, it set against him the government and those powerful Tory organs some of whose attacks we have included. In other words, there was in Hunt just that youthful presumption and rebellion which among conservatives aroused contempt and wrath, and unfortunately aroused these emotions in such a measure that there was left over enough for those who associated with him. In brief, Hunt was soon spending two years in prison for speaking of the Prince Regent with brilliant exactness, and Keats and Shelley were rushing forward to gather approbrium with both hands diligently by giving him the sympathy due a martyr. The more pugnacious Keats snapped his fingers at the general enemy, asking,

Who shall his fame impair
When thou art dead, and all thy wretched crew?

Between Hunt's release from prison in 1815, and his death in 1859, lay a life of journalistic warfare and various toil. He nearly killed himself with writing essays and articles of such profusion that the mind aches at it. Time and tide have found their faults, and few indeed of all his works have "lasted sound and true." Further, his overmastering improvidence ate up the financial rewards of his labor. He might perceive more swiftly than any other man the quintessence of genius in *The Cenci;* but a column of plain figures remained to him always an inexplicable mystery. Into his life one after another came almost all the great literary figures of half a century; and his work reaches from the beginning of the Romantic period into the establishment of the Victorian. At the last he wrote his *Autobiography* (1850) where the student may find in mellow beauty the full record of his life.

As a critic, it is in his "delicate snail-horn perception" of that which is right and inevitable that he excels. He loved books and trusted his intuition in dealing with them. Taste he held to be "the very maker of judgment." He proved poetry upon his pulses. Whether the method for him was right or wrong the student may assure himself by paying careful attention to the quotations in the essay *What Is Poetry*. To us it seems that he knew the ways of the poetic fancy and of the shaping imagination, of the gentle subtleties of harmony and of the sweetness that lives in all real poetry from Chaucer to Tennyson. Because as a critic he was given the gift of rightness and because as a man he was given the courage to trust his taste, he recognized Keats as a "great poet and noble-hearted man," and he asked no man's permission when he said of Shelley, "If there ever was a man upon earth, of more spiritual nature than ordinary, partaking of the errors and perturbations of his species, but seeing and working through them with a seraphical purpose of good, such a man was Percy Bysshe Shelley."

Of Hunt's faults let his friend Keats speak informally to his brother and sister: "Hunt . . . is certainly a pleasant fellow in the main when you are with him—but in reality he is vain, egotistical, and disgusting in matters of taste and in morals. He understands many a beautiful thing; but then, instead of giving other minds credit for the same degree of perception as he himself possesses—he begins an explanation in such a curious manner that our taste and self-love is offended continually. Hunt does one harm by making fine things pretty, and beautiful things hateful.—This distorts one's mind—makes one's thoughts bizarre—perplexes one in the standard of Beauty."

Of Hunt's virtues let his dearer friend Shelley speak as he dedicates *The Cenci:* "Had I known a person more highly endowed than yourself with all that it becomes a man to possess, I had solicited for this work the ornament of his name. One more gentle, honourable, innocent and brave; one of more exalted toleration for all who do and think evil, and yet himself more free from evil; one who knows better how to confer a benefit, though he must ever confer far more than he can receive . . . In that patient and irreconcilable enmity with domestic and political tyranny and imposture, which the tenour of your life has illustrated, and which, had I the health and talents, should illustrate mine, let us, comforting each other in our task, live and die."

THOMAS DE QUINCEY

1785–1859

When De Quincey tells us that poetry is "the science of human passion in all its fluxes and refluxes—in its wondrous depths below depths, and its starry altitudes that ascend to the heavens," we know that if we walk with him at all we must tread on shadowy ground or ascend aloft to where the heaven of heavens is but a veil. We must do more; we must wander eternally in amazement, suffering preternatural paroxysms as we glimpse about us the incarnations of the eternal paradox. For De Quincey, with his inward-turning eye, does not see that human passions do not move in fluxes and refluxes, and that, moreover, were there a science of them that science could not be poetry. His is the eternal fallacy which, were it true of the great romanticists, would have wrecked them by now; namely, that there is a separation between power and knowledge. Precisely at the place where that dispartment does exist, so-called romanticism becomes unworthy of respect. De Quincey's ingenious but frail attempt to unite his own critical definition with a poor paraphrase of Wordsworth's sublime poetical record reveals a characteristic of his criticism: lacking the steady intellectual power of the great poet, he stumbles into over-subtlety and falls on the other side of his own thought.

His volumes are stricken with over-subtlety. There is in his pages more magic than meaning. As did Coleridge, he too talks like an angel; but when the heavenly message has been delivered, we rouse to wonder at just what has been said; and finding nothing substantive, accuse ourselves for neglecting so great salvation. "What wouldn't one give," said Jane Carlyle, "to have that little man in a box and take him out now and then to talk?" All who knew De Quincey marvelled at his limpid conversation; no one of them remembered what he said. The thing itself had been subtilized away. The style of the speech was charming; but it was not the buckram style which could make men sure that there was something in it.

This lack of substance in the thought of De Quincey—unless it were, as indeed it sometimes was the substance of pure genius—left his mind without method. His thoughts lacked the tangibility necessary to the mind if it is to take hold of them, order them, set them in system. They were, like the dagger of Macbeth, air-drawn; he had them not and yet he saw them still. While following one, he would see another moving near it; and while following that, still another, until he seemed bewitched into an endless sequacity. As one of his guardians said of him, "He followed his own devil." And as he struggled to relate all thoughts to some principle of life, his involvement became most heavy and he complained of the difficulty in "attempting to hold things steadily together, and to bring them under a comprehensive or unifying act of the judging faculty." There is, then, in De Quincey more of promise than of fulfillment. Even in those essays which we have somewhat unified by the omission of pages, the student will observe that the thoughts, however inspired, are often loosely darting hither and thither. They appear like excited butterflies beneath a dome of many-colored glass.

However, De Quincey had the strength of his weaknesses. By the penetrative power of his intelligence he earned a place among the romantic critics. He was from his birth "an intellectual creature"; and he strove to examine literature "under the light of philosophic principles." That those principles were formed in part of substances presented to his mind by his dreaming faculty, does not necessarily impair their validity. Whether he saw in vision or not, he saw more clearly than his fellow romantics that "the object of the fine arts [poetry being one] is not pleasure, but the sense of power and the illimitable incarnated as it were in pleasure." In this statement he lifted the best work of his contemporaries to a position of unassailable dignity. De Quincey thought of himself as a philosopher; and we are safe in dealing with him only when we remember that he was one.

When the critic was fourteen years of age he read the Lyrical Ballads. He called that reading an event, "the greatest event in the unfolding of my mind." His admiration for Coleridge and his reverence for Wordsworth, however they may have become touched by disappointment and bitterness, remained among the formative influences which determined his critical philosophy. From Wordsworth he learned the value of knowledge, the worth of joy and of pain, and the dignity of striving after the infinite. The best of what he wrote about his acknowledged master and about the other great poets of the time we have brought together for the student, and we need not anticipate his conclusions by our comment. Impossible as it is to evaluate the worth of De Quincey

as a critic, we may be sure that his best is excellent; for he was one "pleased with his own passions and volitions," and one "endowed with more lively sensibility" than other men.

SELECTED BIBLIOGRAPHY

TEXTS

HAZLITT:
Collected Works, ed. by A. R. Waller and A. Glover, 12 Vols., 1902–6. Introduction by W. E. Henley.
Hazlitt on English Literature, ed. with a critical introduction by J. Zeitlin, 1913.

HUNT:
The Autobiography of Leigh Hunt, ed. by Roger Ingpen, 2 Vols., 1903.
Essays, ed. by A. Symons, 1887, 1903.
Poetical Works, ed. by Thornton Hunt, 1860.
Poetical Works, ed. by H. S. Milford, 1923.

DE QUINCEY:
A Diary of Thomas De Quincey, 1803, in replica, ed. by Horace A. Eaton, 1927.
Collected Writings, ed. by D. Masson, 14 Vols., 1889, 1896.
Literary Criticism, ed. by H. Darbishire, 1909.
Uncollected Writings, ed. by J. Hogg, 2 Vols., 1890.

CRITICAL WORKS

HAZLITT:
Birrell, A., William Hazlitt, 1902.
Douady, J., Vie de William Hazlitt, l'Essayiste, 1907. Note also Douady's Liste Chronologique des œuvres de William Hazlitt, 1906.
Hazlitt, W. C., Memoirs of William Hazlitt, 2 Vols., 1867.

HUNT:
Blunden, E., Leigh Hunt, a Biography, 1930. See also Blunden's Leigh Hunt's "Examiner" Examined, 1928.
Ireland, A., List of the Writings of William Hazlitt and Leigh Hunt, 1868.
Johnson, R. B., Leigh Hunt, 1896. See also Johnson's Shelley—Leigh Hunt: How Friendship Made History, 1928.
Trelawny, E. J., Records of Shelley and Byron, 1858.

DE QUINCEY:
Japp, A. H., Thomas De Quincey: His Life and Writings, With Unpublished Correspondence, 1877, 1890.
Masson, D., Thomas De Quincey, 1881.
Salt, H. S., De Quincey, 1904.

WILLIAM HAZLITT

MY FIRST ACQUAINTANCE WITH POETS [1]

MY FATHER was a Dissenting Minister at

[1] The Liberal, Vol. II, pp. 23–46. London, 1823; Printed for John Hunt.

W——m in Shropshire; and in the year 1798 (the figures that compose that date are to me like the "dreaded name of Demogorgon") Mr. Coleridge came to Shrewsbury, to succeed Mr. Rowe in the spiritual charge of a Unitarian congregation there. He did not come till late on the Saturday afternoon before he was to preach; and Mr. Rowe, who himself went down to the coach in a state of anxiety and expectation, to look for the arrival of his successor, could find no one at all answering the description but a round-faced man in a short black coat (like a shooting-jacket) which hardly seemed to have been made for him, but who seemed to be talking at a great rate to his fellow-passengers. Mr. Rowe had scarce returned to give an account of his disappointment, when the round-faced man in black entered, and dissipated all doubts on the subject, by beginning to talk. He did not cease while he staid; nor has he since, that I know of. He held the good town of Shrewsbury in delightful suspense for three weeks that he remained there, "fluttering the *proud Salopians* like an eagle in a dove-cote;" and the Welch mountains that skirt the horizon with their tempestuous confusion, agree to have heard no such mystic sounds since the days of

High-born Hoel's harp or soft Llewellyn's lay!

As we passed along between W——m and Shrewsbury, and I eyed their blue tops seen through the wintry branches, or the red rustling leaves of the sturdy oak-trees by the road-side, a sound was in my ears as of a Siren's song; I was stunned, startled with it, as from deep sleep; but I had no notion then that I should ever be able to express my admiration to others in motley imagery or quaint allusion, till the light of his genius shone into my soul, like the sun's rays glittering in the puddles of the road. I was at that time dumb, inarticulate, helpless, like a worm by the way-side, crushed, bleeding, lifeless; but now, bursting from the deadly bands that "bound them,

With Styx nine times round them,

my ideas float on winged words, and as they expand their plumes, catch the golden light of other years. My soul had indeed remained in its original bondage, dark, obscure, with longings infinite and unsatisfied; my heart, shut up in the prison-house of this rude clay, has never found, nor will it ever find, a heart to speak to; but that my understanding also did not remain dumb and brutish, or at length found a language to express itself, I owe to Coleridge. But this is not to my purpose.

My father lived ten miles from Shrewsbury, and was in the habit of exchanging visits with Mr. Rowe, and with Mr. Jenkins of Whit-church (nine miles farther on) according to the custom of Dissenting Ministers in each other's neighbourhood. A line of communication is thus established, by which the flame of civil and religious liberty is kept alive, and nourishes its smouldering fire unquenchable, like the fires in the Agamemnon of Æschylus, placed at different stations, that waited for ten long years to announce with their blazing pyra-mids the destruction of Troy. Coleridge had agreed to come over to see my father, accord-ing to the courtesy of the country, as Mr. Rowe's probable successor; but in the mean-time I had gone to hear him preach the Sun-day after his arrival. A poet and philosopher getting up into a Unitarian pulpit to preach the Gospel, was a romance in these degenerate days, a sort of revival of the primitive spirit of Christianity, which was not to be resisted.

It was in January, 1798, that I rose one morning before day-light, to walk ten miles in the mud, and went to hear this celebrated person preach. Never, the longest day I have to live, shall I have such another walk as this cold, raw, comfortless one, in the winter of the year 1798.—*Il y a des impressions que ni le temps ni les circonstances peuvent effacer. Dusse-je vivre des siècles entiers, le doux temps de ma jeunesse ne put renaitre pour moi, ni s'effacer jamais dans ma mémoire.* When I got there, the organ was playing the 100th psalm, and, when it was done, Mr. Coleridge rose and gave out his text, "And he went up into the mountain to pray, HIMSELF, ALONE." As he gave out this text, his voice "rose like a steam of rich distilled perfumes," and when he came to the two last words, which he pronounced loud, deep, and distinct, it seemed to me, who was then young, as if the sounds had echoed from the bottom of the hu-man heart, and as if that prayer might have floated in solemn silence through the universe. The idea of St. John came into mind, "of one crying in the wilderness, who had his loins girt about, and whose food was locusts and wild honey." The preacher then launched into his subject, like an eagle dallying with the wind. The sermon was upon peace and war; upon church and state—not their alliance, but their separation—on the spirit of the world and the spirit of Christianity, not as the same, but as opposed to one another. He talked of those who had "inscribed the cross of Christ on banners dripping with human gore." He made a poetical and pastoral excursion,—and to shew the fatal effects of war, drew a striking contrast between the simple shepherd boy, driving his team afield, or sitting under the hawthorn, piping to his flock, "as though he should never be old," and the same poor country-lad, crimped, kidnapped, brought into town, made drunk at an alehouse, turned into a wretched drummer-boy, with his hair sticking on end with powder and pomatum, a long cue at his back, and tricked out in the loathsome finery of the profession of blood.

Such were the notes our once-lov'd poet sung.

And for myself, I could not have been more delighted if I had heard the music of the spheres. Poetry and Philosophy had met together, Truth and Genius had embraced, under the eye and with the sanction of Religion. This was even beyond my hopes. I returned home well satisfied. The sun that was still labouring pale and wan through the sky, obscured by thick mists, seemed an emblem of the *good cause;* and the cold dank drops of dew that hung half melted on the beard of the thistle, had something genial and refreshing in them; for there was a spirit of hope and youth in all nature, that turned every thing into good. The face of nature had not then the brand of Jus Divinum on it:

Like to that sanguine flower inscrib'd with woe.

On the Tuesday following, the half-inspired speaker came. I was called down into the room where he was, and went half-hoping, half-afraid. He received me very graciously, and I listened for a long time without uttering a word. I did not suffer in his opinion by my silence. "For those two hours," he afterwards was pleased to say, "he was conversing with W. H.'s forehead!" His appearance was different from what I had anticipated from seeing him before. At a distance, and in the dim light of the chapel, there was to me a strange wildness in his aspect, a dusky obscurity, and I thought him pitted with the small-pox. His complexion was at that time clear, and even bright—

As are the children of yon azure sheen.

His forehead was broad and high, light as i[f] built of ivory, with large projecting eyebrows and his eyes rolling beneath them like a se[a] with darkened lustre. "A certain tender bloom his face o'erspread," a purple tinge as we se[e] it in the pale thoughtful complexions of th[e] Spanish portrait-painters, Murillo and Velasquez. His mouth was gross, voluptuous, open, eloquent; his chin good-humoured and round, but his nose, the rudder of the face, the inde[x] of the will, was small, feeble, nothing—lik[e] what he has done. It might seem that the geniu[s] of his face as from a height surveyed and projected him (with sufficient capacity and hug[e] aspiration) into the world unknown of though[t] and imagination, with nothing to support o[r] guide his veering purpose, as if Columbus ha[d] launched his adventurous course for the New World in a scallop, without oars or compass[.] So at least I comment on it after the event[.] Coleridge in his person was rather above th[e] common size, inclining to the corpulent, or lik[e] Lord Hamlet, "somewhat fat and pursy." His hair (now, alas! grey) was then black an[d] glossy as the raven's, and fell in smooth masses over his forehead. This long pendulous hair i[s] peculiar to enthusiasts, to those whose minds tend heavenward; and is traditionally inseparable (though of a different colour) from th[e] pictures of Christ. It ought to belong, as a character, to all who preach *Christ crucified* and Coleridge was at that time one o[f] those!

It was curious to observe the contrast between him and my father, who was a veteran in the cause, and then declining into the vale of years. He had been a poor Irish lad, carefully brought up by his parents, and sent to the University of Glasgow (where he studied under Adam Smith) to prepare him for his future destination. It was his mother's proudest wish to see her son a Dissenting Minister. So if we look back to past generations (as far as eye can reach) we see the same hopes, fears, wishes, followed by the same disappointments, throbbing in the human heart; and so we may see them (if we look forward) rising up for ever, and disappearing, like vapourish bubbles, in the human breast! After being tossed about from congregation to congregation in the heats of the Unitarian controversy, and squabbles about the American War, he had been relegated to an obscure village, where he was to spend the last thirty years of his life, far from the

only converse that he loved, the talk about disputed texts of Scripture and the cause of civil
and religious liberty. Here he passed his days,
repining but resigned, in the study of the Bible,
and the perusal of the Commentators,—huge
folios, not easily got through, one of which
would outlast a winter! Why did he pore on
these from morn to night (with the exception
of a walk in the fields or a turn in the garden
to gather brocoli-plants or kidney-beans of
his own rearing, with no small degree of pride
and pleasure)?—Here were "no figures nor no
fastasies,"—neither poetry nor philosophy—
nothing to dazzle, nothing to excite modern
curiosity; but to his lack-lustre eyes there appeared, within the pages of the ponderous, unwieldy, neglected tomes, the sacred name of
JEHOVAH in Hebrew capitals: pressed down
by the weight of the style, worn to the last
fading thinness of the understanding, there
were glimpses, glimmering notions of the patriarchal wanderings, with palm-trees hovering in
the horizon, and processions of camels at the
distance of three thousand years; there was
Moses with the Burning Bush, the number of
the Twelve Tribes, types, shadows, glosses on
the law and the prophets; there were discussions (dull enough) on the age of Methuselah,
a mighty speculation! there were outlines, rude
guesses at the shape of Noah's Ark and of the
riches of Solomon's Temple; questions as to
the date of the creation, predictions of the end
of all things; the great lapses of time, the
strange mutations of the globe were unfolded
with the voluminous leaf, as it turned over;
and though the soul might slumber with an
hieroglyphic veil of inscrutable mysteries drawn
over it, yet it was in a slumber ill-exchanged
for all the sharpened realities of sense, wit,
fancy, or reason. My father's life was comparatively a dream; but it was a dream of infinity and eternity, of death, the resurrection,
and a judgment to come!

No two individuals were ever more unlike
than were the host and his guest. A poet was
to my father a sort of nondescript: yet whatever added grace to the Unitarian cause was
to him welcome. He could hardly have been
more surprised or pleased, if our visitor had
worn wings. Indeed, his thoughts had wings;
and as the silken sounds rustled round our little wainscoted parlor, my father threw back
his spectacles over his forehead, his white hairs
mixing with its sanguine hue; and a smile of
delight beamed across his rugged cordial face,
to think that Truth had found a new ally in
Fancy. Besides, Coleridge seemed to take considerable notice of me, and that of itself was
enough. He talked very familiarly, but agreeably, and glanced over a variety of subjects.
At dinner-time he grew more animated, and
dilated in a very edifying manner on Mary
Wolstonecraft and Mackintosh. The last, he
said, he considered (on my father's speaking of
his *Vindiciæ Gallicæ* as a capital performance) as a clever scholastic man—a master of
the topics,—or as the ready warehouseman of
letters, who knew exactly where to lay his hand
on what he wanted, though the goods were not
his own. He thought him no match for Burke,
either in style or matter. Burke was a metaphysician, Mackintosh a mere logician. Burke
was an orator (almost a poet) who reasoned in
figures, because he had an eye for nature:
Mackintosh, on the other hand, was a rhetorician, who had only an eye to common-places.
On this I ventured to say that I had always
entertained a great opinion of Burke, and that
(as far as I could find) the speaking of him
with contempt might be made the test of a
vulgar democratical mind. This was the first
observation I ever made to Coleridge, and he
said it was a very just and striking one. I
remember the leg of Welsh mutton and the
turnips on the table that day had the finest
flavour imaginable. Coleridge added that Mackintosh and Tom. Wedgwood (of whom, however, he spoke highly) had expressed a very
indifferent opinion of his friend Mr. Wordsworth, on which he remarked to them—"He
strides on so far before you, that he dwindles
in the distance!" Godwin had once boasted to
him of having carried on an argument with
Mackintosh for three hours with dubious success; Coleridge told him—"If there had been a
man of genius in the room, he would have
settled the question in five minutes." He asked
me if I had ever seen Mary Wolstonecraft, and
I said, I had once for a few moments, and that
she seemed to me to turn off Godwin's objections to something she advanced with quite a
playful, easy air. He replied, that "this was
only one instance of the ascendancy which people of imagination exercised over those of mere
intellect." He did not rate Godwin very high
(this was caprice or prejudice, real or affected)
but he had a great idea of Mrs. Wolstonecraft's
powers of conversation, none at all of her tal-

ent for book-making. We talked a little about Holcroft. He had been asked if he was not much struck *with* him, and he said, he thought himself in more danger of being struck *by* him. I complained that he would not let me get on at all, for he required a definition of every [*sic*] the commonest word, explaining, "What do you mean by a *sensation*, Sir? What do you mean by an *idea?*" This, Coleridge said, was barricadoing the road to truth:—it was setting up a turnpike-gate at every step we took. I forget a great number of things, many more than I remember; but the day passed off pleasantly, and the next morning Mr. Coleridge was to return to Shrewsbury. When I came down to breakfast, I found that he had just received a letter from his friend, T. Wedgwood, making him an offer of £150. a-year if he chose to waive his present pursuit, and devote himself entirely to the study of poetry and philosophy. Coleridge seemed to make up his mind to close with this proposal in the act of trying on one of his shoes. It threw an additional damp on his departure. It took the wayward enthusiast quite from us to cast him into Deva's winding vales, or by the shores of old romance. Instead of living at ten miles distance, of being the pastor of a Dissenting congregation at Shrewsbury, he was henceforth to inhabit the Hill of Parnassus, to be a Shepherd on the Delectable Mountains. Alas! I knew not the way thither, and felt very little gratitude for Mr. Wedgwood's bounty. I was presently relieved from this dilemma; for Mr. Coleridge, asking for a pen and ink, and going to a table to write something on a bit of card, advanced towards me with undulating step, and giving me the precious document, said that that was his address, *Mr. Coleridge, Nether-Stowey, Somersetshire;* and that he should be glad to see me there in a few weeks' time, and, if I chose, would come half-way to meet me. I was not less surprised than the shepherd-boy (this simile is to be found in Cassandra) when he sees a thunder-bolt fall close at his feet. I stammered out my acknowledgments and acceptance of this offer (I thought Mr. Wedgwood's annuity a trifle to it) as well as I could; and this mighty business being settled, the poet-preacher took leave, and I accompanied him six miles on the road. It was a fine morning in the middle of winter, and he talked the whole way. The scholar in Chaucer is described as going

——Sounding on his way.

So Coleridge went on his. In digressing, in dilating, in passing from subject to subject, he appeared to me to float in air, to slide on ice. He told me in confidence (going along) that he should have preached two sermons before he accepted the situation at Shrewsbury, one on Infant Baptism, the other on the Lord's Supper, shewing that he could not administer either, which would have effectually disqualified him for the object in view. I observed that he continually crossed me on the way by shifting from one side of the foot-path to the other. This struck me as an odd movement; but I did not at that time connect it with any instability of purpose or involuntary change of principle as I have done since. He seemed unable to keep on in a straight line. He spoke slightingly of Hume (whose Essay on Miracles he said was stolen from an objection started in one of South's Sermons—*Credat Judæus Apella!*). I was not very much pleased at this account of Hume, for I had just been reading, with infinite relish, that completest of all metaphysical *choke-pears*, his *Treatise on Human Nature,* to which the *Essays,* in point of scholastic subtlety and close reasoning, are mere elegant trifling, light summer-reading. Coleridge even denied the excellence of Hume's general style which I think betrayed a want of taste or candour. He however made me amends by the manner in which he spoke of Berkeley. He dwelt particularly on his *Essay on Vision* as a masterpiece of analytical reasoning. So it undoubtedly is. He was exceedingly angry with Dr. Johnson for striking the stone with his foot, in allusion to this author's Theory of Matter and Spirit, and saying, "Thus I confute him, Sir." Coleridge drew a parallel (I don't know how he brought about the connection) between Bishop Berkeley and Tom Paine. He said the one was an instance of a subtle, the other of an acute mind, than which no two things could be more distinct. The one was a shop-boy's quality, the other the characteristic of a philosopher. He considered Bishop Butler as a true philosopher, a profound and conscientious thinker, a genuine reader of nature and of his own mind. He did not speak of his *Analogy,* but of his *Sermons at the Rolls Chapel,* of which I had never heard. Coleridge somehow always contrived to prefer the *unknown* to the *known.* In this instance he was right. The *Analogy* is a tissue of sophistry, of wire-drawn, theological special-pleadings; the *Sermons* (with the Preface to them) are in a fine vein of deep, matured reflection, a candid appeal to our observation of human nature, without pedantry and without bias. I told Coleridge I had written a few remarks, and was sometimes foolish enough to believe that I had made a discovery on the same subject (the *Natural Disinterestedness of the Human Mind*)—and I tried to explain my view of it to Coleridge, who listened with great willingness, but I did not succeed in making myself understood. I sat down to the task shortly afterwards for the twentieth time, got new pens and paper, determined to make clear work of it, wrote a few meagre sentences in the skeleton-style of a mathematical demonstration, stopped half-way down the second page; and, after trying in vain to pump up any words, images, notions, apprehensions, facts, or observations, from that gulph of abstraction in which I had plunged myself for four or five years preceding, gave up the attempt as labour in vain, and shed tears of helpless despondency on the blank unfinished paper. I can write fast enough now. Am I better than I was then? Oh no! One truth discovered, one pang of regret at not being able to express it, is better than all the fluency and flippancy in the world. Would that I could go back to what I then was! Why can we not revive past times as we can revisit old places? If I had the quaint Muse of Sir Philip Sidney to assist me, I would write a *Sonnet to the Road between W—m and Shrewsbury,* and immortalise every step of it by some fond enigmatical conceit. I would swear that the very milestones had ears, and that Harmer-hill stooped with all its pines, to listen to a poet, as he passed! I remember but one other topic of discourse in this walk. He mentioned Paley, praised the naturalness and clearness of his style, but condemned his sentiments, thought him a mere time-serving casuist, and said that "the fact of his work on Moral and Political Philosophy being made a text-book in our Universities was a disgrace to the national character." We parted at the six-mile stone; and I returned homeward, pensive but much pleased. I had met with unexpected notice from a person, whom I believed to have been prejudiced against me. "Kind and affable to me had been his con-descension, and should be honoured ever with suitable regard." He was the first poet I had known, and he certainly answered to that inspired name. I had heard a great deal of his powers of conversation, and was not disappointed. In fact, I never met with anything at all like them, either before or since. I could easily credit the accounts which were circulated of his holding forth to a large party of ladies and gentlemen, an evening or two before, on the Berkeleian Theory, when he made the whole material universe look like a transparency of fine words; and another story (which I believed he has somewhere told himself) of his being asked to a party at Birmingham, of his smoking tobacco and going to sleep after dinner on a sofa, where the company found him to their no small surprise, which was increased to wonder when he started up of a sudden, and rubbing his eyes, looked about him, and launched into a three-hours' description of the third heaven, of which he had had a dream, very different from Mr. Southey's Vision of Judgment, and also from that other Vision of Judgment, which Mr. Murray, the Secretary of the Bridge-street Junto, has taken into his especial keeping!

On my way back, I had a sound in my ears, it was the voice of Fancy: I had a light before me, it was the face of Poetry. The one still lingers there, the other has not quitted my side! Coleridge in truth met me half-way on the ground of philosophy, or I should not have been won over to his imaginative creed. I had an uneasy, pleasurable sensation all the time, till I was to visit him. During those months the chill breath of winter gave me a welcoming; the vernal air was balm and inspiration to me. The golden sun-sets, the silver star of evening, lighted me on my way to new hopes and prospects. *I was to visit Coleridge in the Spring.* This circumstance was never absent from my thoughts, and mingled with all my feelings. I wrote to him at the time proposed, and received an answer postponing my intended visit for a week or two, but very cordially urging me to complete my promise then. This delay did not damp, but rather increased my ardour. In the meantime, I went to Llangollen Vale, by way of initiating myself in the mysteries of natural scenery; and I must say I was enchanted with it. I had been reading Coleridge's description of England, in his fine *Ode on the Departing Year,* and I applied it, *con amore,* to the objects before me. That valley was to me (in a manner) the cradle of a new existence: in the river that winds through it, my spirit was baptised in the waters of Helicon!

I returned home, and soon after set out on my journey with unworn heart and untired feet. My way lay through Worcester and Gloucester, and by Upton, where I thought of Tom Jones and the adventure of the muff. I remember getting completely wet through one day, and stopping at an inn (I think it was at Tewkesbury) where I sat up all night to read Paul and Virginia. Sweet were the showers in early youth that drenched my body, and sweet the drops of pity that fell upon the books I read! I recollect a remark of Coleridge's upon this very book, that nothing could shew the gross indelicacy of French manners and the entire corruption of their imagination more strongly than the behaviour of the heroine in the last fatal scene, who turns away from a person on board the sinking vessel, that offers to save her life, because he has thrown off his clothes to assist him in swimming. Was this a time to think of such a circumstance? I once hinted to Wordsworth, as we were sailing in his boat on Grasmere lake, that I thought he had borrowed the ideas of his *Poems on the Naming of Places* from the local inscriptions of the same kind in Paul and Virginia. He did not own the obligation, and stated some distinction without a difference, in defence of his claim to originality. Any the slightest variation would be sufficient for this purpose in his mind; for whatever *he* added or omitted would inevitably be worth all that any one else had done, and contain the marrow of the sentiment.—I was still two days before the time fixed for my arrival, for I had taken care to set out early enough. I stopped these two days at Bridgewater, and when I was tired of sauntering on the banks of its muddy river, returned to the inn, and read Camilla. So have I loitered my life away, reading books, looking at pictures, going to plays, hearing, thinking, writing on what pleased me best. I have wanted only one thing to make me happy; but wanting that, have wanted every thing!

I arrived, and was well received. The country about Nether Stowey is beautiful, green and hilly, and near the sea-shore. I saw it but the other day, after an interval of twenty years, from a hill near Taunton. How was the map of my life spread out before me, as the map of the country lay at my feet! In the afternoon, Coleridge took me over to All-Foxden, a romantic old family-mansion of the St. Aubins, where Wordsworth lived. It was then in the possession of a friend of the poet's, who gave him the free use of it. Somehow that period (the time just after the French Revolution) was not a time when *nothing was given for nothing.* The mind opened, and a softness might be perceived coming over the heart of individuals, beneath "the scales that fence" our self-interest. Wordsworth himself was from home, but his sister kept house, and set before us a frugal repast; and we had free access to her brother's poems, the *Lyrical Ballads,* which were still in manuscript, or in the form of *Sybilline Leaves.* I dipped into a few of these with great satisfaction, and with the faith of a novice. I slept that night in an old room with blue hangings, and covered with the round-faced family-portraits of the age of George I. and II. and from the wooded declivity of the adjoining park that overlooked my window, at the dawn of day, could

——hear the loud stag speak.

In the outset of life (and particularly at this time I felt it so) our imagination has a body to it. We are in a state between sleeping and waking, and have indistinct but glorious glimpses of strange shapes, and there is always something to come better than what we see. As in our dreams the fulness of the blood gives warmth and reality to the coinage of the brain, so in youth our ideas are clothed, and fed, and pampered with our good spirits; we breathe thick with thoughtless happiness, the weight of future years presses on the strong pulses of the heart, and we repose with undisturbed faith in truth and good. As we advance, we exhaust our fund of enjoyment and of hope. We are no longer wrapped in *lamb's-wool,* lulled in Elysium. As we taste the pleasures of life, their spirit evaporates, the sense palls; and nothing is left but the phantoms, the lifeless shadows of what *has been!*

That morning, as soon as breakfast was over, we strolled out into the park, and seatng ourselves on the trunk of an old ash-tree that stretched along the ground, Coleridge read aloud with a sonorous and musical voice, the ballad of *Betty Foy*. I was not critically or sceptically inclined. I saw touches of truth and nature, and took the rest for granted. But in the *Thorn*, the *Mad Mother*, and the *Complaint of a Poor Indian Woman*, I felt that deeper power and pathos which have been since acknowledged,

In spite of pride, in erring reason's spite,

as the characteristic of this author; and the sense of a new style and a new spirit in poetry came over me. It had to me something of the effect that arises from the turning up of the fresh soil, or of the first welcome breath of Spring,

While yet the trembling year is unconfirmed.

Coleridge and myself walked back to Stowey that evening, and his voice sounded high

Of Providence, foreknowledge, will, and fate, Fix'd fate, free-will, foreknowledge absolute,

as we passed through echoing grove, by fairy stream or waterfall, gleaming in the summer moonlight! He lamented that Wordsworth was not prone enough to believe in the traditional superstitions of the place, and that there was something corporeal, a *matter-of-factness*, a clinging of the palpable, or often to the petty, in his poetry, in consequence. His genius was not a spirit that descended to him through the air; it sprung out of the ground like a flower, or unfolded itself from a green spray, on which the gold-finch sang. He said, however (if I remember right) that this objection must be confined to his descriptive pieces, that his philosophic poetry had a grand and comprehensive spirit in it, so that his soul seemed to inhabit the universe like a palace, and to discover truth by intiution, rather than by deduction. The next day Wordsworth arrived from Bristol at Coleridge's cottage. I think I see him now. He answered in some degree to his friend's description of him, but was more gaunt and Don Quixote-like. He was quaintly dressed (according to the *costume* of that unconstrained period) in a brown fustian jacket and striped pantaloons. There was something of a

roll, a lounge in his gait, not unlike his own Peter Bell. There was a severe, worn pressure of thought about his temples, a fire in his eye (as if he saw something in objects more than the outward appearance) an intense high narrow forehead, a Roman nose, cheeks furrowed by strong purpose and feeling, and a convulsive inclination to laughter about the mouth, a good deal at variance with the solemn, stately expression of the rest of his face. Chantry's bust wants the marking traits; but he was teazed into making it regular and heavy: Haydon's head of him, introduced into the *Entrance of Christ into Jerusalem*, is the most like his drooping weight of thought and expression. He sat down and talked very naturally and freely, with a mixture of clear gushing accents in his voice, a deep guttural intonation, and a strong tincture of the northern *burr*, like the crust on wine. He instantly began to make havoc of the half of a Cheshire cheese on the table, and said triumphantly that "his marriage with experience had not been so unproductive as Mr. Southey's in teaching him knowledge of the good things of this life." He had been to see the *Castle Spectre* by Monk Lewis, while at Bristol, and described it very well. He said "it fitted the taste of the audience like a glove." This *ad captandum* merit was however by no means a recommendation of it, according to the severe principles of the new school, which reject rather than court popular effect. Wordsworth, looking out of the low, latticed window, said, "How beautifully the sun sets on that yellow bank!" I thought within myself, "With what eyes these poets see nature!" and ever after, when I saw the sunset stream upon the objects facing it, conceived I had made a discovery, or thanked Mr. Wordsworth for having made one for me! We went over to All-Foxden again the day following, and Wordsworth read us the story of Peter Bell in the open air; and the comment made upon it by his face and voice was very different from that of some later critics! Whatever might be thought of the poem, "his face was as a book where men might read strange matters," and he announced the fate of his hero in prophetic tones. There is a *chaunt* in the recitation both of Coleridge and Wordsworth, which acts as a spell upon the hearer, and disarms the judgment. Perhaps they have deceived themselves by making habitual use of this ambiguous accompaniment. Coleridge's manner is more full, animated, and varied; Wordsworth's more equable, sustained, and internal. The one might be termed more *dramatic,* the other more *lyrical.* Coleridge has told me that he himself liked to compose in walking over uneven ground, or breaking through the straggling branches of a copsewood; whereas Wordsworth always wrote (if he could) walking up and down a straight gravel-walk, or in some spot where the continuity of his verse met with no collateral interruption. Returning that same evening, I got into a metaphysical argument with Wordsworth, while Coleridge was explaining the different notes of the nightingale to his sister, in which we neither of us succeeded in making ourselves perfectly clear and intelligible. Thus I passed three weeks at Nether Stowey and in the neighbourhood, generally devoting the afternoons to a delightful chat in an arbour made of bark by the poet's friend Tom Poole, sitting under two fine elm-trees, and listening to the bees humming round us, while we quaffed our *flip.* It was agreed, among other things, that we should make a jaunt down the Bristol-Channel, as far as Linton. We set off together on foot, Coleridge, John Chester, and I. This Chester was a native of Nether Stowey, one of those who were attracted to Coleridge's discourse as flies are to honey, or bees in swarming-time to the sound of a brass pan. He "followed in the chase, like a dog who hunts, not like one that made up the cry." He had on a brown cloth coat, boots, and corduroy breeches, was low in stature, bow-legged, had a drag in his walk like a drover, which he assisted by a hazel switch, and kept on a sort of trot by the side of Coleridge, like a running footman by a state coach, that he might not lose a syllable or sound, that fell from Coleridge's lips. He told me his private opinion, that Coleridge was a wonderful man. He scarcely opened his lips, much less offered an opinion the whole way: yet of the three, had I to chuse during that journey, I would be John Chester. He afterwards followed Coleridge into Germany, where the Kantean philosophers were puzzled how to bring him under any of their categories. When he sat down at table with his idol, John's felicity was complete; Sir Walter Scott's, or Mr. Blackwood's, when they sat down at the same table with the King, wa not more so. We passed Dunster on ou right, a small town between the brow of hill and the sea. I remember eying it wist fully as it lay below us: contrasted with th woody scene around, it looked as clear, a pure, as *embrowned* and ideal as any land scape I have seen since, of Gasper Poussin' or Domenichino's. We had a long day's march —(our feet kept time to the echoes of Cole ridge's tongue)—through Minehead and by the Blue Anchor, and on to Linton, which we did not reach till near midnight, and where we had some difficulty in making a lodgment. We however knocked the people of the house up at last, and we were repaid for our apprehensions and fatigue by some excellent rashers of fried bacon and eggs. The view in coming along had been splendid. We walked for miles and miles on dark brown heaths overlooking the channel, with the Welsh hills beyond, and at times descended into little sheltered valleys close by the sea-side, with a smuggler's face scowling by us, and then had to ascend conical hills with a path winding up through a coppice to a barren top, like a monk's shaven crown, from one of which I pointed out to Coleridge's notice the bare masts of a vessel on the very edge of the horizon and within the red-orbed disk of the setting sun, like his own spectre-ship in the *Ancient Mariner.* At Linton the character of the sea-coast becomes more marked and rugged. There is a place called the *Valley of Rocks* (I suspect this was only the poetical name for it) bedded among precipices overhanging the sea, with rocky caverns beneath, into which the waves dash, and where the sea-gull for ever wheels its screaming flight. On the tops of these are huge stones thrown transverse, as if an earthquake had tossed them there, and behind these is a fretwork of perpendicular rocks, something like the *Giant's Causeway.* A thunder-storm came on while we were at the inn, and Coleridge was running out bareheaded to enjoy the commotion of the elements in the *Valley of Rocks,* but as if in spite, the clouds only muttered a few angry sounds, and let fall a few refreshing drops. Coleridge told me that he and Wordsworth were to have made this place the scene of a prose-tale, which was to have been in the manner of, but far superior to, the *Death of Abel,* but they had relinquished the design. In the morning of the second day, we breakfasted luxuriously in an old-fashioned parlour, on tea, toast, eggs, and honey, in the very sight of the bee-hives from which it had been taken, and a garden full of thyme and wild flowers that had produced it. On this occasion Coleridge spoke of Virgil's *Georgics,* but not well. I do not think he had much feeling for the classical or elegant. It was in this room that we found a little worn-out copy of the *Seasons,* lying in a window-seat, on which Coleridge exclaimed, *"That* is true fame!" He said Thomson was a great poet, rather than a good one; his style was as meretricious as his thoughts were natural. He spoke of Cowper as the best modern poet. He said the *Lyrical Ballads* were an experiment about to be tried by him and Wordsworth, to see how far the public taste would endure poetry written in a more natural and simple style than had hitherto been attempted; totally discarding the artifices of poetical diction, and making use only of such words as had probably been common in the most ordinary language since the days of Henry II. Some comparison was introduced between Shakespear and Milton. He said "he hardly knew which to prefer. Shakespear appeared to him a mere stripling in the art; he was as tall and as strong, with infinitely more activity than Milton, but he never appeared to have come to man's estate; or if he had, he would not have been a man, but a monster." He spoke with contempt of Gray, and with intolerance of Pope. He did not like the versification of the latter. He observed that "the ears of these couplet-writers might be charged with having short memories, that could not retain the harmony of whole passages." He thought little of Junius as a writer; he had a dislike of Dr. Johnson; and a much higher opinion of Burke as an orator and politician, than of Fox or Pitt. He however thought him very inferior in richness of style and imagery to some of our elder prose-writers, particularly Jeremy Taylor. He liked Richardson, but not Fielding; nor could I get him to enter into the merits of *Caleb Williams.* In short, he was profound and discriminating with respect to those authors whom he liked, and where he gave his judgment fair play; capricious, perverse, and prejudiced in his antipathies and distastes.

We loitered on the "ribbed sea-sands," in such talk as this, a whole morning, and I recollect met with a curious sea-weed, of which John Chester told us the country name! A fisherman gave Coleridge an account of a boy that had been drowned the day before, and that they had tried to save him at the risk of their own lives. He said "he did not know how it was that they ventured, but, Sir, we have a *nature* towards one another." This expression, Coleridge remarked to me, was a fine illustration of that theory of disinterestedness which I (in common with Butler) had adopted. I broached to him an argument of mine to prove that *likeness* was not mere association of ideas. I said that the mark in the sand put one in mind of a man's foot, not because it was part of a former impression of a man's foot (for it was quite new) but because it was like the shape of a man's foot. He assented to the justness of this distinction (which I have explained at length elsewhere, for the benefit of the curious) and John Chester listened; not from any interest in the subject, but because he was astonished that I should be able to suggest any thing to Coleridge that he did not already know. We returned on the third morning, and Coleridge remarked the silent cottage-smoke curling up the valleys where, a few evenings before, we had seen the lights gleaming through the dark.

In a day or two after we arrived at Stowey, we set out, I on my return home, and he for Germany. It was a Sunday morning, and he was to preach that day for Dr. Toulmin of Taunton. I asked him if he had prepared anything for the occasion? He said he had not even thought of the text, but should as soon as we parted. I did not go to hear him,—this was a fault,—but we met in the evening at Bridgewater. The next day we had a long day's walk to Bristol, and sat down, I recollect, by a well-side on the road, to cool ourselves and satisfy our thirst, when Coleridge repeated to me some descriptive lines from his tragedy of Remorse; which I must say became his mouth and that occasion better than they, some years after, did Mr. Elliston's and the Drury-lane boards,—

Oh memory! shield me from the world's poor strife,
And give those scenes thine everlasting life.

I saw no more of him for a year or two,

during which period he had been wandering in the Hartz Forest in Germany; and his return was cometary, meteorous, unlike his setting out. It was not till some time after that I knew his friends Lamb and Southey. The last always appears to me (as I first saw him) with a common-place book under his arm, and the first with a *bon-mot* in his mouth. It was at Godwin's that I met him with Holcroft and Coleridge, where they were disputing fiercely which was the best—*Man as he was, or man as he is to be.* "Give me," says Lamb, "man as he is *not* to be." This saying was the beginning of a friendship between us, which I believe still continues. Enough of this for the present.

> But there is matter for another rhyme,
> And I to this may add a second tale.

ON POETRY IN GENERAL [1]

THE best general notion which I can give of poetry is, that it is the natural impression of any object or event, by its vividness exciting an involuntary movement of imagination and passion, and producing, by sympathy, a certain modulation of the voice, or sounds, expressing it.

In treating of poetry, I shall speak first of the subject-matter of it, next of the forms of expression to which it gives birth, and afterwards of its connection with harmony of sound.

Poetry is the language of the imagination and the passions. It relates to whatever gives immediate pleasure or pain to the human mind. It comes home to the bosoms and businesses of men; for nothing but what so comes home to them in the most general and intelligible shape, can be a subject for poetry. Poetry is the universal language which the heart holds with nature and itself. He who has a contempt for poetry, cannot have much respect for himself, or for any thing else. It is not a mere frivolous accomplishment, (as some persons have been led to imagine) the trifling amusement of a few idle readers or leisure hours— it has been the study and delight of mankind in all ages. Many people suppose that poetry is something to be found only in books, contained in lines of ten syllables, with like

[1] This essay and the following one are from the *Lectures on the English Poets,* 1818.

endings: but wherever there is a sense of beauty, or power, or harmony, as in the motion of a wave of the sea, in the growth of a flower that "spreads its sweet leaves to the air, and dedicates its beauty to the sun,"— *there* is poetry, in its birth. If history is a grave study, poetry may be said to be a graver: its materials lie deeper, and are spread wider. History treats, for the most part, of the cumbrous and unwieldly masses of things, the empty cases in which the affairs of the world are packed, under the heads of intrigue or war, in different states, and from century to century: but there is no thought or feeling that can have entered into the mind of man, which he would be eager to communicate to others, or which they would listen to with delight, that is not a fit subject for poetry. It is not a branch of authorship: it is "the stuff of which our life is made." The rest is "mere oblivion," a dead letter: for all that is worth remembering in life, is the poetry of it. Fear is poetry, hope is poetry, love is poetry, hatred is poetry; contempt, jealousy, remorse, admiration, wonder, pity, despair, or madness, are all poetry. Poetry is that fine particle within us, that expands, rarefies, refines, raises our whole being: without it "man's life is poor as beast's." Man is a poetical animal: and those of us who do not study the principles of poetry, act upon them all our lives, like Molière's *Bourgeois Gentilhomme,* who had always spoken prose without knowing it. The child is a poet in fact, when he first plays at hide-and-seek, or repeats the story of Jack the Giant-killer; the shepherd-boy is a poet, when he first crowns his mistress with a garland of flowers; the countryman, when he stops to look at the rainbow; the city-apprentice, when he gazes after the Lord-Mayor's show; the miser, when he hugs his gold; the courtier, who builds his hopes upon a smile; the savage, who paints his idol with blood; the slave, who worships a tyrant, or the tyrant, who fancies himself a god;—the vain, the ambitious, the proud, the choleric man, the hero and the coward, the beggar and the king, the rich and the poor, the young and the old, all live in a world of their own making; and the poet does no more than describe what all the others think and act. If his art is folly and madness, it is folly and madness at second hand. "There is warrant for it." Poets alone have not "such seething brains, such shaping fantasies, that apprehend more than cooler reason" can.

The lunatic, the lover, and the poet
Are of imagination all compact.
One sees more devils than vast hell can hold;
The madman. While the lover, all as frantic,
Sees Helen's beauty in a brow of Egypt.
The poet's eye in a fine frenzy rolling,
Doth glance from heav'n to earth, from earth to
    heav'n;
And as imagination bodies forth
The forms of things unknown, the poet's pen
Turns them to shape, and gives to airy nothing
A local habitation and a name.
Such tricks hath strong imagination.

If poetry is a dream, the business of life is much the same. If it is a fiction, made up of what we wish things to be, and fancy that they are, because we wish them so, there is no other nor better reality. Ariosto has described the loves of Angelica and Medoro: but was not Medoro, who carved the name of his mistress on the barks of trees, as much enamoured of her charms as he? Homer has celebrated the anger of Achilles: but was not the hero as mad as the poet? Plato banished the poets from his Commonwealth, lest their descriptions of the natural man should spoil his mathematical man, who was to be without passions and affections, who was neither to laugh nor weep, to feel sorrow nor anger, to be cast down nor elated by any thing. This was a chimera, however, which never existed but in the brain of the inventor; and Homer's poetical world has outlived Plato's philosophical Republic.

Poetry then is an imitation of nature, but the imagination and the passions are a part of man's nature. We shape things according to our wishes and fancies, without poetry; but poetry is the most emphatical language that can be found for those creations of the mind "which ecstacy is very cunning in." Neither a mere description of natural objects, nor a mere delineation of natural feelings, however distinct or forcible, constitutes the ultimate end and aim of poetry, without the heightenings of the imagination. The light of poetry is not only a direct but also a reflected light, that while it shews us the object, throws a sparkling radiance on all around it: the flame of the passions, communicated to the imagination, reveals to us, as with a flash of lightning, the inmost recesses of thought, and penetrates our whole being. Poetry represents forms chiefly as they suggest other forms; feelings, as they suggest forms or other feelings. Poetry puts a spirit of life and motion into the universe. It describes the flowing, not the fixed. It does not define the limits of sense, or analyze the distinctions of the understanding, but signifies the excess of the imagination beyond the actual or ordinary impression of any object or feeling. The poetical impression of any object is that uneasy, exquisite sense of beauty or power that cannot be contained within itself; that is impatient of all limit; that (as flame bends to flame) strives to link itself to some other image of kindred beauty or grandeur; to enshrine itself, as it were, in the highest forms of fancy, and to relieve the aching sense of pleasure by expressing it in the boldest manner, and by the most striking examples of the same quality in other instances. Poetry, according to Lord Bacon, for this reason, "has something divine in it, because it raises the mind and hurries it into sublimity, by conforming the shows of things to the desires of the soul, instead of subjecting the soul to external things, as reason and history do." It is strictly the language of the imagination; and the imagination is that faculty which represents objects, not as they are in themselves, but as they are moulded by other thoughts and feelings, into an infinite variety of shapes and combinations of power. This language is not the less true to nature, because it is false in point of fact; but so much the more true and natural, if it conveys the impression which the object under the influence of passion makes on the mind. Let an object, for instance, be presented to the senses in a state of agitation or fear—and the imagination will distort or magnify the object, and convert it into the likeness of whatever is most proper to encourage the fear. "Our eyes are made the fools" of our other faculties. This is the universal law of the imagination,

That if it would but apprehend some joy,
It comprehends some bringer of that joy:
Or in the night imagining some fear,
How easy is each bush suppos'd a bear!

When Iachimo says of Imogen,

——The flame o' th' taper
Bows toward her, and would under-peep her lids
To see the enclosed lights—

this passionate interpretation of the motion of the flame to accord with the speaker's own feelings, is true poetry. The lover, equally with the poet, speaks of the auburn tresses of his mistress as locks of shining gold, because the least tinge of yellow in the hair has, from novelty and a sense of personal beauty, a more lustrous effect to the imagination than the purest gold. We compare a man of gigantic stature to a tower: not that he is any thing like so large, but because the excess of his size beyond what we are accustomed to expect, or the usual size of things of the same class, produces by contrast a greater feeling of magnitude and ponderous strength than another object of ten times the same dimensions. The intensity of the feeling makes up for the disproportion of the objects. Things are equal to the imagination, which have the power of affecting the mind with an equal degree of terror, admiration, delight, or love. When Lear calls upon the heavens to avenge his cause, "for they are old like him," there is nothing extravagant or impious in this sublime identification of his age with theirs; for there is no other image which could do justice to the agonising sense of his wrongs and his despair!

Poetry is the high-wrought enthusiasm of fancy and feeling. As in describing natural objects, it impregnates sensible impressions with the forms of fancy, so it describes the feelings of pleasure or pain, by blending them with the strongest movements of passion, and the most striking forms of nature. Tragic poetry, which is the most impassioned species of it, strives to carry on the feeling to the utmost point of sublimity or pathos, by all the force of comparison or contrast; loses the sense of present suffering in the imaginary exaggeration of it; exhausts the terror or pity by an unlimited indulgence of it; grapples with impossibilities in its desperate impatience of restraints; throws us back upon the past, forward into the future; brings every moment of our being or object of nature in startling review before us; and in the rapid whirl of events, lifts us from the depths of woe to the highest contemplations on human life. When Lear says of Edgar, "Nothing but his unkind daughters could have brought him to this;" what a bewildered amazement, what a wrench of the imagination, that cannot be brought to conceive of any other cause of misery than that which has bowed it down, and absorbs

all other sorrow in its own! His sorrow, like a flood, supplies the sources of all other sorrow. Again, when he exclaims in the mad scene, "The little dogs and all, Tray, Blanche, and Sweetheart, see, they bark at me!" it is passion lending occasion to imagination to make every creature in league against him, conjuring up ingratitude and insult in their least looked-for and most galling shapes, searching every thread and fibre of his heart, and finding out the last remaining image of respect or attachment in the bottom of his breast, only to torture and kill it! In like manner, the "So I am" of Cordelia gushes from her heart like a torrent of tears, relieving it of a weight of love and of supposed ingratitude, which had pressed upon it for years. What a fine return of the passion upon itself is that in Othello—with what a mingled agony of regret and despair he clings to the last traces of departed happiness—when he exclaims,

——Oh now, for ever
Farewel the tranquil mind. Farewel content;
Farewel the plumed troops and the big war,
That make ambition virtue! Oh farewel!
Farewel the neighing steed, and the shrill trump,
The spirit-stirring drum, th' ear-piercing fife,
The royal banner, and all quality,
Pride, pomp, and circumstance of glorious war:
And O you mortal engines, whose rude throats
Th' immortal Jove's dread clamours counterfeit,
Farewel! Othello's occupation's gone!

How his passion lashes itself up and swells and rages like a tide in its sounding course, when in answer to the doubts expressed of his returning love, he says,

Never, Iago. Like to the Pontic sea,
Whose icy current and compulsive course
Ne'er feels retiring ebb, but keeps due on
To the Propontic and the Hellespont:
Even so my bloody thoughts, with violent pace,
Shall ne'er look back, ne'er ebb to humble love,
Till that a capable and wide revenge
Swallow them up.—

The climax of his expostulation afterwards with Desdemona is at that line,

But there where I had garner'd up my heart,
To be discarded thence!

One mode in which the dramatic exhibition of passion excites our sympathy without raising our disgust is, that in proportion as it sharpens the edge of calamity and disappointment, it strengthens the desire of good. It enhances our consciousness of the blessing, by making us sensible of the magnitude of the loss. The storm of passion lays bare and shews us the rich depths of the human soul: the whole of our existence, the sum total of our passions and pursuits, of that which we desire and that which we dread, is brought before us by contrast; the action and re-action are equal; the keenness of immediate suffering only gives us a more intense aspiration after, and a more intimate participation with the antagonist world of good; makes us drink deeper of the cup of human life; tugs at the heart-strings; loosens the pressure about them; and calls the springs of thought and feeling into play with tenfold force.

Impassioned poetry is an emanation of the moral and intellectual part of our nature, as well as of the sensitive—of the desire to know, the will to act, and the power to feel; and ought to appeal to these different parts of our constitution, in order to be perfect. The domestic or prose tragedy, which is thought to be the most natural, is in this sense the least so, because it appeals almost exclusively to one of these faculties, our sensibility. The tragedies of Moore and Lillo, for this reason, however affecting at the time, oppress and lie like a dead weight upon the mind, a load of misery which it is unable to throw off: the tragedy of Shakspeare, which is true poetry, stirs our inmost affections; abstracts evil from itself by combining it with all the forms of imagination, and with the deepest workings of the heart, and rouses the whole man within us.

The pleasure, however, derived from tragic poetry, is not any thing peculiar to it as poetry, as a fictitious and fanciful thing. It is not an anomaly of the imagination. It has its source and ground-work in the common love of strong excitement. As Mr. Burke observes, people flock to see a tragedy; but if there were a public execution in the next street, the theatre would very soon be empty. It is not then the difference between fiction and reality that solves the difficulty. Children are satisfied with the stories of ghosts and witches in plain prose: nor do the hawkers of full, true, and particular accounts of murders and executions about the streets, find it necessary to have them turned into penny ballads, before they can dispose of these interesting and authentic documents. The grave politician drives a thriving trade of abuse and calumnies poured out against those whom he makes his enemies for no other end than that he may live by them. The popular preacher makes less frequent mention of heaven than of hell. Oaths and nicknames are only a more vulgar sort of poetry or rhetoric. We are as fond of indulging our violent passions as of reading a description of those of others. We are as prone to make a torment of our fears, as to luxuriate in our hopes of good. If it be asked, Why we do so? the best answer will be, Because we cannot help it. The sense of power is as strong a principle in the mind as the love of pleasure. Objects of terror and pity exercise the same despotic control over it as those of love or beauty. It is as natural to hate as to love, to despise as to admire, to express our hatred or contempt, as our love or admiration.

Masterless passion sways us to the mood
Of what it likes or loathes.

Not that we like what we loathe; but we like to indulge our hatred and scorn of it; to dwell upon it, to exasperate our idea of it by every refinement of ingenuity and extravagance of illustration; to make it a bugbear to ourselves, to point it out to others in all the splendour of deformity, to embody it to the senses, to stigmatise it by name, to grapple with it in thought, in action, to sharpen our intellect, to arm our will against it, to know the worst we have to contend with, and to contend with it to the utmost. Poetry is only the highest eloquence of passion, the most vivid form of expression that can be given to our conception of any thing, whether pleasurable or painful, mean or dignified, delightful or distressing. It is the perfect coincidence of the image and the words with the feeling we have, and of which we cannot get rid in any other way, that gives an instant "satisfaction to the thought." This is equally the origin of wit and fancy, of comedy and tragedy, of the sublime and pathetic. When Pope says of the Lord Mayor's shew,—

Now night descending, the proud scene is o'er,
But lives in Settle's numbers one day more!

—when Collins makes Danger, "with limbs of giant mould,"

——Throw him on the steep
Of some loose hanging rock asleep:

when Lear calls out in extreme anguish,

Ingratitude, thou marble-hearted fiend,
How much more hideous shew'st in a child
Than the sea-monster!

—the passion of contempt in the one case, of
terror in the other, and of indignation in the
last, is perfectly satisfied. We see the thing
ourselves, and shew it to others as we feel it
to exist, and as, in spite of ourselves, we are
compelled to think of it. The imagination, by
thus embodying and turning them to shape,
gives an obvious relief to the indistinct and
importunate cravings of the will.—We do not
wish the thing to be so; but we wish it to appear such as it is. For knowledge is conscious
power; and the mind is no longer, in this case,
the dupe, though it may be the victim of vice
or folly.

Poetry is in all its shapes the language of the
imagination and the passions, of fancy and
will. Nothing, therefore, can be more absurd
than the outcry which has been sometimes
raised by frigid and pedantic critics, for reducing the language of poetry to the standard
of common sense and reason: for the end and
use of poetry, "both at the first and now, was
and is to hold the mirror up to nature," seen
through the medium of passion and imagination, not divested of that medium by means of
literal truth or abstract reason. The painter
of history might as well be required to represent the face of a person who has just trod
upon a serpent with the still-life expression of
a common portrait, as the poet to describe the
most striking and vivid impressions which
things can be supposed to make upon the mind,
in the language of common conversation. Let
who will strip nature of the colours and the
shapes of fancy, the poet is not bound to do
so; the impressions of common sense and
strong imagination, that is, of passion and indifference, cannot be the same, and they must
have a separate language to do justice to
either. Objects must strike differently upon
the mind, independently of what they are in
themselves, as long as we have a different interest in them, as we see them in a different
point of view, nearer or at a greater distance
(morally or physically speaking) from novelty,
from old acquaintance, from our ignorance of
them, from our fear of their consequences,
from contrast, from unexpected likeness. We
can no more take away the faculty of the imagination, than we can see all objects without
light or shade. Some things must dazzle us
by their preternatural light; others must hold
us in suspense, and tempt our curiosity to explore their obscurity. Those who dispel
these various illusions, to give us their drab-
coloured creation in their stead, are not very
wise. Let the naturalist, if he will, catch the
glow-worm, carry it home with him in a box,
and find it next morning nothing but a little
grey worm; let the poet or the lover of poetry
visit it at evening, when beneath the scented
hawthorn and the crescent moon it has built
itself a palace of emerald light. This is also
one part of nature, one appearance which the
glow-worm presents, and that not the least
interesting; so poetry is one part of the history
of the human mind, though it is neither science nor philosophy. It cannot be concealed,
however, that the progress of knowledge and
refinement has a tendency to circumscribe the
limits of the imagination, and to clip the wings
of poetry. The province of the imagination is
principally visionary, the unknown and undefined: the understanding restores things to
their natural boundaries, and strips them of
their fanciful pretensions. Hence the history of
religious and poetical enthusiasm is much the
same; and both have received a sensible shock
from the progress of experimental philosophy.
It is the undefined and uncommon that gives
birth and scope to the imagination; we can
only fancy what we do not know. As in looking into the mazes of a tangled wood we fill
them with what shapes we please, with ravenous beasts, with caverns vast, and drear enchantments, so in our ignorance of the world
about us, we make gods or devils of the first
object we see, and set no bounds to the wilful
suggestions of our hopes and fears.

And visions, as poetic eyes avow,
Hang on each leaf and cling to every bough.

There can never be another Jacob's dream.
Since that time, the heavens have gone farther
off, and grown astronomical. They have become averse to the imagination, nor will they
return to us on the squares of the distances,
or on Doctor Chalmers's Discourses. Rembrandt's picture brings the matter nearer to
us.—It is not only the progress of mechanical
knowledge, but the necessary advances of civilization that are unfavourable to the spirit of

poetry. We not only stand in less awe of the the preternatural world, but we can calculate more surely, and look with more indifference, upon the regular routine of this. The heroes of the fabulous ages rid the world of monsters and giants. At present we are less exposed to the vicissitudes of good or evil, to the incursions of wild beasts or "bandit fierce," or to the unmitigated fury of the elements. The time has been that "our fell of hair would at a dismal treatise rouse and stir as life were in it." But the police spoils all; and we now hardly so much as dream of a midnight murder. Macbeth is only tolerated in this country for the sake of the music; and in the United States of America, where the philosophical principles of government are carried still farther in theory and practice, we find that the Beggar's Opera is hooted from the stage. Society, by degrees, is constructed into a machine that carries us safely and insipidly from one end of life to the other, in a very comfortable prose style.

> Obscurity her curtain round them drew,
> And siren Sloth a dull quietus sung.

The remarks which have been here made, would, in some measure, lead to a solution of the question of the comparative merits of painting and poetry. I do not mean to give any preference, but it should seem that the argument which has been sometimes set up, that painting must affect the imagination more strongly, because it represents the image more distinctly, is not well founded. We may assume without much temerity, that poetry is more poetical than painting. When artists or connoisseurs talk on stilts about the poetry of painting, they shew that they know little about poetry, and have little love for the art. Painting gives the object itself; poetry what it implies. Painting embodies what a thing contains in itself: poetry suggests what exists out of it, in any manner connected with it. But this last is the proper province of the imagination. Again, as it relates to passion, painting gives the event, poetry the progress of events: but it is during the progress, in the interval of expectation and suspense, while our hopes and fears are strained to the highest pitch of breathless agony, that the pinch of the interest lies.

> Between the acting of a dreadful thing
> And the first motion, all the interim is

> Like a phantasma or a hideous dream.
> The mortal instruments are then in council;
> And the state of man, like to a little kingdom,
> Suffers then the nature of an insurrection.

But by the time that the picture is painted, all is over. Faces are the best part of a picture; but even faces are not what we chiefly remember in what interests us most.—But it may be asked then, Is there anything better than Claude Lorraine's landscapes, than Titian's portraits, than Raphael's cartoons, or the Greek statues? Of the two first I shall say nothing, as they are evidently picturesque, rather than imaginative. Raphael's cartoons are certainly the finest comments that ever were made on the Scriptures. Would their effect be the same, if we were not acquainted with the text? But the New Testament existed before the cartoons. There is one subject of which there is no cartoon, Christ washing the feet of the disciples the night before his death. But that chapter does not need a commentary! It is for want of some such resting place for the imagination that the Greek statues are little else than specious forms. They are marble to the touch and to the heart. They have not an informing principle within them. In their faultless excellence they appear sufficient to themselves. By their beauty they are raised above the frailities of passion or suffering. By their beauty they are deified. But they are not objects of religious faith to us, and their forms are a reproach to common humanity. They seem to have no sympathy with us, and not to want our admiration.

Poetry in its matter and form is natural imagery or feeling, combined with passion and fancy. In its mode of conveyance, it combines the ordinary use of language with musical expression. There is a question of long standing, in what the essence of poetry consists; or what it is that determines why one set of ideas should be expressed in prose, another in verse. Milton has told us his idea of poetry in a single line—

> Thoughts that voluntary move
> Harmonious numbers.

As there are certain sounds that excite certain movements, and the song and dance go together, so there are, no doubt, certain thoughts that lead to certain tones of voice, or modulations of sound and change "the words of Mercury into the songs of Apollo."

There is a striking instance of this adaptation of the movement of sound and rhythm to the subject, in Spenser's description of the Satyrs accompanying Una to the cave of Sylvanus.

So from the ground she fearless doth arise
   And walketh forth without suspect of crime.
They, all as glad as birds of joyous prime,
   Thence lead her forth, about her dancing round,
Shouting and singing all a shepherd's rhyme;
   And with green branches strewing all the
      ground,
Do worship her as queen with olive garland
   crown'd.

And all the way their merry pipes they sound,
   That all the woods and doubled echoes ring;
And with their horned feet do wear the ground,
   Leaping like wanton kids in pleasant spring;
So towards old Sylvanus they her bring,
   Who with the noise awaked, cometh out.
                              Faery Queen, b. i. c. vi.

On the contrary, there is nothing either musical or natural in the ordinary construction of language. It is a thing altogether arbitrary and conventional. Neither in the sounds themselves, which are the voluntary signs of certain ideas, nor in their grammatical arrangements in common speech, is there any principle of natural imitation, or correspondence to the individual ideas, or to the tone of feeling with which they are conveyed to others. The jerks, the breaks, the inequalities, and harshnesses of prose, are fatal to the flow of a poetical imagination, as a jolting road or a stumbling horse disturbs the reverie of an absent man. But poetry makes these odds all even. It is the music of language, answering to the music of the mind, untying as it were "the secret soul of harmony." Wherever any object takes such a hold of the mind as to make us dwell upon it, and brood over it, melting the heart in tenderness, or kindling it to a sentiment of enthusiasm;—wherever a movement of imagination or passion is impressed on the mind, by which it seeks to prolong and repeat the emotion, to bring all other objects into accord with it, and to give the same movement of harmony, sustained and continuous, or gradually varied according to the occasion, to the sounds that express it—this is poetry. The musical in sound is the sustained and continuous; the musical in thought is the sustained and continuous also. There is a near connection between music and deep-rooted passion. Mad people sing. As often as articulation passes naturally into intonation, there poetry begins. Where one idea gives a tone and colour to others, where one feeling melts others into it, there can be no reason why the same principle should not be extended to the sounds by which the voice utters these emotions of the soul, and blends syllables and lines into each other. It is to supply the inherent defect of harmony in the customary mechanism of language, to make the sound an echo to the sense, when the sense becomes a sort of echo to itself—to mingle the tide of verse, "the golden cadences of poetry," with the tide of feeling, flowing and murmuring as it flows—in short, to take the language of the imagination from off the ground, and enable it to spread its wings where it may indulge its own impulses—

Sailing with supreme dominion
Through the azure deep of air—

without being stopped, or fretted, or diverted with the abruptnesses and petty obstacles, and discordant flats and sharps of prose, that poetry was invented. It is to common language, what springs are to a carriage, or wings to feet. In ordinary speech we arrive at a certain harmony by the modulations of the voice: in poetry the same thing is done systematically by a regular collocation of syllables. It has been well observed, that every one who declaims warmly, or grows intent upon a subject, rises into a sort of blank verse or measured prose. The merchant, as described in Chaucer, went on his way "sounding always the increase of his winning." Every prose-writer has more or less of rhythmical adaptation, except poets, who, when deprived of the regular mechanism of verse, seem to have no principle of modulation left in their writings.

An excuse might be made for rhyme in the same manner. It is but fair that the ear should linger on the sounds that delight it, or avail itself of the same brilliant coincidence and unexpected recurrence of syllables, that have been displayed in the invention and collocation of images. It is allowed that rhyme assists the memory; and a man of wit and shrewdness has been heard to say, that the only four good lines of poetry are the well-known ones which tell the number of days in the months of the year.

Thirty days hath September, &c.

But if the jingle of names assists the memory, may it not also quicken the fancy? and there are other things worth having at our fingers' ends, besides the contents of the almanac.—Pope's versification is tiresome, from its excessive sweetness and uniformity. Shakspeare's blank verse is the perfection of dramatic dialogue.

All is not poetry that passes for such: nor does verse make the whole difference between poetry and prose. The Iliad does not cease to be poetry in a literal translation; and Addison's Campaign has been very properly denominated a Gazette in rhyme. Common prose differs from poetry, as treating for the most part either of such trite, familiar, and irksome matters of fact, as convey no extraordinary impulse to the imagination, or else of such difficult and laborious processes of the understanding, as do not admit of the wayward or violent movements either of the imagination or the passions.

I will mention three works which come as near to poetry as possible without absolutely being so, namely, the Pilgrim's Progress, Robinson Crusoe, and the Tales of Boccaccio. Chaucer and Dryden have translated some of the last into English rhyme, but the essence and the power of poetry was there before. That which lifts the spirit above the earth, which draws the soul out of itself with indescribable longings, is poetry in kind, and generally fit to become so in name, by being "married to immortal verse." If it is of the essence of poetry to strike and fix the imagination, whether we will or no, to make the eye of childhood glisten with the starting tear, to be never thought of afterwards with indifference, John Bunyan and Daniel Defoe may be permitted to pass for poets in their way. The mixture of fancy and reality in the Pilgrim's Progress was never equalled in any allegory. His pilgrims walk above the earth, and yet are on it. What zeal, what beauty, what truth of fiction! What deep feeling in the description of Christian's swimming across the water at last, and in the picture of the Shining Ones within the gates, with wings at their backs and garlands on their heads, who are to wipe all tears from his eyes! The writer's genius, though not "dipped in dews of Castalie," was baptised with the Holy Spirit and with fire. The prints in this book are no small part of it. If the confinement of Philoctetes in the island of Lemnos was a subject for the most beautiful of all the Greek tragedies, what shall we say to Robinson Crusoe in his? Take the speech of the Greek hero on leaving his cave, beautiful as it is, and compare it with the reflections of the English adventurer in his solitary place of confinement. The thoughts of home, and of all from which he is for ever cut off, swell and press against his bosom, as the heaving ocean rolls its ceaseless tide against the rocky shore, and the very beatings of his heart become audible in the eternal silence that surrounds him. Thus he says,

As I walked about, either in my hunting, or for viewing the country, the anguish of my soul at my condition would break out upon me on a sudden, and my very heart would die within me to think of the woods, the mountains, the deserts I was in; and how I was a prisoner, locked up with the eternal bars and bolts of the ocean, in an uninhabited wilderness, without redemption. In the midst of the greatest composures of my mind, this would break out upon me like a storm, and make me wring my hands, and weep like a child. Sometimes it would take me in the middle of my work, and I would immediately sit down and sigh, and look upon the ground for an hour or two together, and this was still worse to me, for if I could burst into tears or vent myself in words, it would go off, and the grief having exhausted itself would abate. P. 50.

The story of his adventures would not make a poem like the Odyssey, it is true; but the relator had the true genius of a poet. It has been made a question whether Richardson's romances are poetry; and the answer perhaps is, that they are not poetry, because they are not romance. The interest is worked up to an inconceivable height; but it is by an infinite number of little things, by incessant labour and calls upon the attention, by a repetition of blows that have no rebound in them. The sympathy excited is not a voluntary contribution, but a tax. Nothing is unforced and spontaneous. There is a want of elasticity and motion. The story does not "give an echo to the seat where love is throned." The heart does not answer of itself like a chord in music. The fancy does not run on before the writer with breathless expectation, but is dragged along with an infinite number of pins and wheels, like those with which the Lilliputians dragged Gulliver pinioned to the royal palace.—Sir Charles Grandison is a coxcomb. What sort of a figure would he cut, translated into an epic poem, by the side of Achilles? Clarissa, the divine Clarissa, is too interesting by half. She is interesting in her ruffles, in her gloves, her samplers, her aunts and uncles—she is interesting in all that is uninteresting. Such things, however intensely they may be brought home to us, are not conductors to the imagination. There is infinite truth and feeling in Richardson; but it is extracted from a *caput mortuum* of circumstances: it does not evaporate of itself. His poetical genius is like Ariel confined in a pine-tree, and requires an artificial process to let it out. Shakspeare says—

> Our poesy is as a gum
> Which issues whence 'tis nourished, our gentle flame
> Provokes itself, and like the current flies
> Each bound it chafes.[1]

I shall conclude this general account with some remarks on four of the principal works of poetry in the world, at different periods of history—Homer, the Bible, Dante, and let me add, Ossian. In Homer, the principle of action or life is predominant; in the Bible, the principle of faith and the idea of Providence; Dante is a personification of blind will; and in Ossian we see the decay of life, and the lag end of the world. Homer's poetry is the heroic: it is full of life and action: it is bright as the day, strong as a river. In the vigour of his intellect, he grapples with all the objects of nature, and enters into all the relations of social life. He saw many countries, and the manners of many men; and he has brought them all together in his poem. He describes his heroes going to battle with a prodigality of life, arising from an exuberance of animal spirits: we see them before us, their number, and their order of battle, poured out upon the plain "all plumed like estriches, like eagles newly bathed, wanton as goats, wild as young bulls, youthful as May, and gorgeous as the sun at midsummer," covered with glittering armour, with dust and blood; while the Gods quaff their nectar in golden cups, or mingle in the fray; and the old men assembled on the walls of Troy rise up with reverence as Helen passes by them. The multitude of things in Homer is wonderful; their splendour, their truth, their force, and variety. His poetry is, like his religion, the poetry of number and form: he describes the bodies as well as the souls of men.

The poetry of the Bible is that of imagination and of faith: it is abstract and disembodied: it is not the poetry of form, but of power; not of multitude, but of immensity. It does not divide into many, but aggrandises into one. Its ideas of nature are like its ideas of God. It is not the poetry of social life, but of solitude: each man seems alone in the world, with the original forms of nature, the rocks, the earth, and the sky. It is not the poetry of action or heroic enterprise, but of faith in a supreme Providence, and resignation to the power that governs the universe. As the idea of God was removed farther from humanity, and a scattered polytheism, it became more profound and intense, as it became more universal, for the Infinite is present to every thing: "If we fly into the uttermost parts of the earth, it is there also; if we turn to the east or the west, we cannot escape from it." Man is thus aggrandised in the image of his Maker. The history of the patriarchs is of this kind; they are founders of a chosen race of people, the inheritors of the earth; they exist in the generations which are to come after them. Their poetry, like their religious creed, is vast, unformed, obscure, and infinite; a vision is upon it—an invisible hand is suspended over it. The spirit of the Christian religion consists in the glory hereafter to be revealed; but in the Hebrew dispensation, Providence took an immediate share in the affairs of this life. Jacob's dream arose out of this intimate communion between heaven and earth: it was this that let down, in the sight of the youthful patriarch, a golden ladder from the sky to the earth, with angels ascending and descending upon it, and shed a light upon the lonely place, which can never pass away. The story of Ruth, again, is as if all the depth

[1] Burke's writings are not poetry, notwithstanding the vividness of the fancy, because the subject matter is abstruse and dry, not natural, but artificial. The difference between poetry and eloquence is, that the one is the eloquence of the imagination, and the other of the understanding. Eloquence tries to persuade the will, and convince the reason: poetry produces its effect by instantaneous sympathy. Nothing is a subject for poetry that admits of a dispute. Poets are in general bad prose-writers, because their images, though fine in themselves, are not to the purpose, and do not carry on the argument. The French poetry wants the forms of the imagination. It is didactic more than dramatic. And some of our own poetry which has been most admired, is only poetry in the rhyme, and in the studied use of poetic diction.

of natural affection in the human race was involved in her breast. There are descriptions in the book of Job more prodigal of imagery, more intense in passion, than any thing in Homer, as that of the state of his prosperity, and of the vision that came upon him by night. The metaphors in the Old Testament are more boldly figurative. Things were collected more into masses, and gave a greater *momentum* to the imagination.

Dante was the father of modern poetry, and he may therefore claim a place in this connection. His poem is the first great step from Gothic darkness and barbarism; and the struggle of thought in it to burst the thraldom in which the human mind had been so long held, is felt in every page. He stood bewildered, not appalled, on that dark shore which separates the ancient and the modern world; and saw the glories of antiquity dawning through the abyss of time, while revelation opened its passage to the other world. He was lost in wonder at what had been done before him, and he dared to emulate it. Dante seems to have been indebted to the Bible for the gloomy tone of his mind, as well as for the prophetic fury which exalts and kindles his poetry; but he is utterly unlike Homer. His genius is not a sparkling flame, but the sullen heat of a furnace. He is power, passion, self-will personified. In all that relates to the descriptive or fanciful part of poetry, he bears no comparison to many who had gone before, or who have come after him; but there is a gloomy abstraction in his conceptions, which lies like a dead weight upon the mind; a benumbing stupor, a breathless awe, from the intensity of the impression; a terrible obscurity, like that which oppresses us in dreams; an identity of interest, which moulds every object to its own purposes, and clothes all things with the passions and imaginations of the human soul, —that make amends for all other deficiencies. The immediate objects he presents to the mind are not much in themselves, they want grandeur, beauty, and order; but they become every thing by the force of the character he impresses upon them. His mind lends its own power to the objects which it contemplates, instead of borrowing it from them. He takes advantage even of the nakedness and dreary vacuity of his subject. His imagination peoples the shades of death, and broods over the silent air. He is the severest of all writers, the most hard and impenetrable, the most opposite to the flowery and glittering; who relies most on his own power, and the sense of it in others, and who leaves most room to the imagination of his readers. Dante's only endeavour is to interest; and he interests by exciting our sympathy with the emotion by which he is himself possessed. He does not place before us the objects by which that emotion has been created; but he seizes on the attention, by shewing us the effect they produce on his feelings; and his poetry accordingly gives the same thrilling and overwhelming sensation, which is caught by gazing on the face of a person who has seen some object of horror. The improbability of the events, the abruptness and monotony in the Inferno, are excessive: but the interest never flags, from the continued earnestness of the author's mind. Dante's great power is in combining internal feelings with external objects. Thus the gate of hell, on which that withering inscription is written, seems to be endowed with speech and consciousness, and to utter its dread warning, not without a sense of mortal woes. This author habitually unites the absolutely local and individual with the greatest wildness and mysticism. In the midst of the obscure and shadowy regions of the lower world, a tomb suddenly rises up with the inscription, "I am the tomb of Pope Anastasius the Sixth": and half the personages whom he has crowded into the Inferno are his own acquaintance. All this, perhaps, tends to heighten the effect by the bold intermixture of realities, and by an appeal, as it were, to the individual knowledge and experience of the reader. He affords few subjects for picture. There is, indeed, one gigantic one, that of Count Ugolino, of which Michael Angelo made a bas-relief, and which Sir Joshua Reynolds ought not to have painted.

Another writer whom I shall mention last, and whom I cannot persuade myself to think a mere modern in the groundwork, is Ossian. He is a feeling and a name that can never be destroyed in the minds of his readers. As Homer is the first vigour and lustihed, Ossian is the decay and old age of poetry. He lives only in the recollection and regret of the past. There is one impression which he conveys more entirely than all other poets, namely, the sense of privation, the loss of all things, of friends, of good name, of country—he is even without God in the world. He converses only with the spirits of the departed; with the motionless and silent clouds. The cold moonlight sheds its faint lustre on his head; the fox peeps out of the ruined tower; the thistle waves its beard to the wandering gale; and the strings of his harp seem, as the hand of age, as the tale of other times, passes over them, to sigh and rustle like the dry reeds in the winter's wind! The feeling of cheerless desolation, of the loss of the pith and sap of existence, of the annihilation of the substance, and the clinging to the shadow of all things as in a mock-embrace, is here perfect. In this way, the lamentation of Selma for the loss of Salgar is the finest of all. If it were indeed possible to shew that this writer was nothing, it would only be another instance of mutability, another blank made, another void left in the heart, another confirmation of that feeling which makes him so often complain, "Roll on, ye dark brown years, ye bring no joy on your wing to Ossian!"

ON THE LIVING POETS [1]

No more of talk where God or Angel guest
With man, as with his friend, familiar us'd
To sit indulgent. ——

GENIUS is the heir of fame; but the hard condition on which the bright reversion must be earned is the loss of life. Fame is the recompense not of the living, but of the dead. The temple of fame stands upon the grave: the flame that burns upon its altars is kindled from the ashes of great men. Fame itself is immortal, but it is not begot till the breath of genius is extinguished. For fame is not popularity, the shout of the multitude, the idle buzz of fashion, the venal puff, the soothing flattery of favour or of friendship; but it is the spirit of a man surviving himself in the minds and thoughts of other men, undying and imperishable. It is the power which the intellect exercises over the intellect, and the lasting homage which is paid to it, as such, independently of time and circumstances, purified from partiality and evil-speaking. Fame is the sound which the stream of high thoughts, carried down to future ages, makes as it flows—deep, distant, murmuring evermore like the waters of the mighty ocean. He who has ears truly touched to this music, is in a manner deaf to the voice of popularity.—The love of fame differs from mere vanity in this, that the one is

[1] In this and other essays by Hazlitt, italics may not be used to indicate titles.

immediate and personal, the other ideal and abstracted. It is not the direct and gross homage paid to himself, that the lover of true fame seeks or is proud of; but the indirect and pure homage paid to the eternal forms of truth and beauty as they are reflected in his mind, that gives him confidence and hope. The love of nature is the first thing in the mind of the true poet: the admiration of himself the last. A man of genius cannot well be a coxcomb; for his mind is too full of other things to be much occupied with his own person. He who is conscious of great powers in himself, has also a high standard of excellence with which to compare his efforts: he appeals also to a test and judge of merit, which is the highest, but which is too remote, grave, and impartial, to flatter his self-love extravagantly, or puff him up with intolerable and vain conceit. This, indeed, is one test of genius and of real greatness of mind, whether a man can wait patiently and calmly for the award of posterity, satisfied with the unwearied exercise of his faculties, retired within the sanctuary of his own thoughts; or whether he is eager to forestal his own immortality, and mortgage it for a newspaper puff. He who thinks much of himself, will be in danger of being forgotten by the rest of the world: he who is always trying to lay violent hands on reputation, will not secure the best and most lasting. If the restless candidate for praise takes no pleasure, no sincere and heartfelt delight in his works, but as they are admired and applauded by others, what should others see in them to admire or applaud? They cannot be expected to admire them because they are *his;* but for the truth and nature contained in them, which must first be inly felt and copied with severe delight, from the love of truth and nature, before it can ever appear there. Was Raphael, think you, when he painted his pictures of the Virgin and Child in all their inconceivable truth and beauty of expression, thinking most of his subject or of himself? Do you suppose that Titian, when he painted a landscape, was pluming himself on being thought the finest colourist in the world, or making himself so by looking at nature? Do you imagine that Shakspeare, when he wrote Lear or Othello, was thinking of any thing but Lear and Othello? Or that Mr. Kean, when he plays these characters, is thinking of the audience?—No: he who would be great in the eyes of others, must first learn to be nothing in his own. The love of fame, as it enters at times into his mind, is only another name for the love of excellence; or it is the ambition to attain the highest excellence, sanctioned by the highest authority—that of time.

Those minds, then, which are the most entitled to expect it, can best put up with the postponement of their claims to lasting fame. They can afford to wait. They are not afraid that truth and nature will ever wear out; will lose their gloss with novelty, or their effect with fashion. If their works have the seeds of immortality in them, they will live; if they have not, they care little about them as theirs. They do not complain of the start which others have got of them in the race of everlasting renown, or of the impossibility of attaining the honours which time alone can give, during the term of their natural lives. They know that no applause, however loud and violent, can anticipate or over-rule the judgment of posterity; that the opinion of no one individual, nor of any one generation, can have the weight, authority (to say nothing of the force of sympathy and prejudice), which must belong to that of successive generations. The brightest living reputation cannot be equally imposing to the imagination, with that which is covered and rendered venerable with the hoar of innumerable ages. No modern production can have the same atmosphere of sentiment around it, as the remains of classical antiquity. But then our moderns may console themselves with the reflection, that they will be old in their turn, and will either be remembered with still increasing honours, or quite forgotten!

I would speak of the living poets as I have spoken of the dead (for I think highly of many of them); but I cannot speak of them with the same reverence, because I do not feel it; with the same confidence, because I cannot have the same authority to sanction my opinion. I cannot be absolutely certain that any body, twenty years hence, will think any thing about any of them; but we may be pretty sure that Milton and Shakspeare will be remembered twenty years hence. We are, therefore, not without excuse if we husband our enthusiasm a little, and do not prematurely lay out our whole stock in untried ventures, and what may turn out to be false bottoms. I have myself out-lived one generation of favourite poets, the Darwins, the Hayleys, the Sewards. Who reads them now?—If, however, I have not the verdict of posterity to bear me out in bestowing the most unqualified praises on their immediate successors, it is also to be remembered, that neither does it warrant me in condemning them. Indeed, it was not my wish to go into this ungrateful part of the subject; but something of the sort is expected from me, and I must run the gauntlet as well as I can. Another circumstance that adds to the difficulty of doing justice to all parties is, that I happen to have had a personal acquaintance with some of these jealous votaries of the Muses; and that is not the likeliest way to imbibe a high opinion of the rest. Poets do not praise one another in the language of hyperbole. I am afraid, therefore, that I labour under a degree of prejudice against some of the most popular poets of the day, from an early habit of deference to the critical opinions of some of the least popular. I cannot say that I ever learnt much about Shakspeare or Milton, Spenser or Chaucer, from these professed guides; for I never heard them say much about them. They were always talking of themselves and one another. Nor am I certain that this sort of personal intercourse with living authors, while it takes away all real relish or freedom of opinion with regard to their contemporaries, greatly enhances our respect for themselves. Poets are not ideal beings; but have their prose-sides, like the commonest of the people. We often hear persons say, What they would have given to have seen Shakspeare! For my part, I would give a great deal not to have seen him; at least, if he was at all like any body else that I have ever seen. But why should he; for his works are not! This is, doubtless, one great advantage which the dead have over the living. It is always fortunate for ourselves and others, when we are prevented from exchanging admiration for knowledge. The splendid vision that in youth haunts our idea of the poetical character, fades, upon acquaintance, into the light of common day; as the azure tints that deck the mountain's brow are lost on a nearer approach to them. It is well, according to the moral of one of the Lyrical Ballads,—"To leave Yarrow unvisited." But to leave this "face-making," and begin.—

I am a great admirer of the female writers of the present day; they appear to me like so many modern Muses. I could be in love with Mrs. Inchbald, romantic with Mrs. Radcliffe, and sarcastic with Madame D'Arblay: but they are novel-writers, and, like Audrey, may "thank the Gods for not having made them poetical." Did any one here ever read Mrs. Leicester's School? If they have not, I wish they would; there will be just time before the next three volumes of the Tales of My Landlord come out. That is not a school of affectation, but of humanity. No one can think too highly of the work, or highly enough of the author.

The first poetess I can recollect is Mrs. Barbauld, with whose works I became acquainted before those of any other author, male or female, when I was learning to spell words of one syllable in her story-books for children. I became acquainted with her poetical works long after in Enfield's Speaker; and remember being much divided in my opinion at that time, between her Ode to Spring and Collins's Ode to Evening. I wish I could repay my childish debt of gratitude in terms of appropriate praise. She is a very pretty poetess; and, to my fancy, strews the flowers of poetry most agreeably round the borders of religious controversy. She is a neat and pointed prose-writer. Her "Thoughts on the Inconsistency of Human Expectations," is one of the most ingenious and sensible essays in the language. There is the same idea in one of Barrow's Sermons.

Mrs. Hannah More is another celebrated modern poetess, and I believe still living. She has written a great deal which I have never read.

Miss Baillie must make up this trio of female poets. Her tragedies and comedies, one of each to illustrate each of the passions, separately from the rest, are heresies in the dramatic art. She is a Unitarian in poetry. With her the passions are, like the French republic, one and indivisible: they are not so in nature, or in Shakspeare. Mr. Southey has, I believe, somewhere expressed an opinion, that the Basil of Miss Baillie is superior to Romeo and Juliet. I shall not stay to contradict him. On the other hand, I prefer her De Montfort, which was condemned on the stage, to some later tragedies, which have been more fortunate—to the Remorse, Bertram, and lastly, Fazio. There is in the chief character of that play a nerve, a continued unity of interest, a setness of purpose and precision of outline which John Kemble alone was capable of giving; and there is all the grace which women have in writing. In saying that De Montfort was a character which just suited Mr. Kemble, I mean to pay a compliment to both. He was not "a man of no mark or likelihood": and what he could be supposed to do particularly well, must have a meaning in it. As to the other tragedies just mentioned, there is no reason why any common actor should not "make mouths in them at the invisible event,"—one as well as another. Having thus expressed my sense of the merits of the authoress, I must add, that her comedy of the Election, performed last summer at the Lyceum with indifferent success, appears to me the perfection of baby-house theatricals. Every thing in it has such a *do-me-good* air, is so insipid and amiable. Virtue seems such a pretty playing at make-believe, and vice is such a naughty word. It is a theory of some French author, that little girls ought not to be suffered to have dolls to play with, to call them *pretty dears,* to admire their black eyes and cherry cheeks, to lament and bewail over them if they fall down and hurt their faces, to praise them when they are good, and scold them when they are naughty. It is a school of affectation: Miss Baillie has profited of it. She treats her grown men and women as little girls treat their dolls—makes moral puppets of them, pulls the wires, and they talk virtue and act vice, according to their cue and the title prefixed to each comedy or tragedy, not from any real passions of their own, or love either of virtue or vice.

The transition from these to Mr. Rogers's Pleasures of Memory, is not far: he is a very lady-like poet. He is an elegant, but feeble writer. He wraps up obvious thoughts in a glittering cover of fine words; is full of enigmas with no meaning to them; is studiously inverted, and scrupulously far-fetched; and his verses are poetry, chiefly because no particle, line, or syllable of them reads like prose. He differs from Milton in this respect, who is accused of having inserted a number of prosaic lines in Paradise Lost. This kind of poetry, which is a more minute and inoffensive species of the Della Cruscan, is like the game of asking what one's thoughts are like. It is a tortuous, tottering, wriggling, fidgetty translation of every thing from the vulgar tongue, into all the tantalizing, teasing, tripping, lisping *mimminee-pimminee* of the highest brilliancy and fashion of poetical diction. You have nothing like truth of nature or simplicity of expression. The fastidious and languid reader is never shocked by meeting, from the rarest chance in the world, with a single homely phrase or intelligible idea. You cannot see the thought for the ambiguity of the language, the figure for the finery, the picture for the varnish. The whole is refined, and frittered away into an appearance of the most evanescent brilliancy and tremulous imbecility.—There is no other fault to be found with the Pleasures of Memory, than a want of taste and genius. The sentiments are amiable, and the notes at the end highly interesting, particularly the one relating to the Countess Pillar (as it is called) between Appleby and Penrith, erected (as the inscription tells the thoughtful traveller) by Anne Countess of Pembroke, in the year 1648, in memory of her last parting with her good and pious mother in the same place in the year 1616.

> To shew that power of love, how great
> Beyond all human estimate.

This story is also told in the poem, but with so many artful innuendos and tinsel words, that it is hardly intelligible; and still less does it reach the heart.

Campbell's Pleasures of Hope is of the same school, in which a painful attention is paid to the expression in proportion as there is little to express, and the decomposition of prose is substituted for the composition of poetry. How much the sense and keeping in the ideas are sacrificed to a jingle of word and epigrammatic turn of expression, may be seen in such lines as the following:—one of the characters, an old invalid, wishes to end his days under

> Some hamlet shade, to yield his sickly form
> Health in the breeze, and shelter in the storm.

Now the antithesis here totally fails: for it is the breeze, and not the tree, or as it is quaintly expressed, *hamlet shade,* that affords health, though it is the tree that affords shelter in or from the storm. Instances of the same sort of *curiosa infelicitas* are not rare in this author. His verses on the Battle of Hohenlinden have considerable spirit and animation. His Gertrude of Wyoming is his principal performance. It is a kind of historical paraphrase of Mr. Wordsworth's poem of Ruth. It shews little power, or power enervated by extreme fastidiousness. It is

> ———— Of outward show
> Elaborate; of inward less exact.

There are painters who trust more to the setting of their pictures than to the truth of the likeness. Mr. Campbell always seems to me to be thinking how his poetry will look when it comes to be hot-pressed on superfine wove paper, to have a disproportionate eye to points and commas, and dread of errors of the press. He is so afraid of doing wrong, of making the smallest mistake, that he does little or nothing. Lest he should wander irretrievably from the right path, he stands still. He writes according to established etiquette. He offers the Muses no violence. If he lights upon a good thought, he immediately drops it for fear of spoiling a good thing. When he launches a sentiment that you think will float him triumphantly for once to the bottom of the stanza, he stops short at the end of the first or second line, and stands shivering on the brink of beauty, afraid to trust himself to the fathomless abyss. *Tutus nimium, timidusque procellarum.* His very circumspection betrays him. The poet, as well as the woman, that deliberates, is undone. He is much like a man whose heart fails him just as he is going up in a balloon, and who breaks his neck by flinging himself out of it when it is too late. Mr. Campbell too often maims and mangles his ideas before they are full formed, to fit them to the Procustes' bed of criticism; or strangles his intellectual offspring in the birth, lest they should come to an untimely end in the Edinburgh Review. He plays the hypercritic on himself, and starves his genius to death from a needless apprehension of a plethora. No writer who thinks habitually of the critics, either to tremble at their censures or set them at defiance, can write well. It is the business of reviewers to watch poets, not of poets to watch reviewers.—There is one admirable simile in this poem, of the European child brought by the sooty Indian in his hand, "like morning brought by night." The love-scenes in Gertrude of Wyoming breathe a balmy voluptuousness of sentiment; but they are generally broken off in the middle; they are like the scent of a bank of violets, faint and rich, which the gale suddenly conveys in a different direction. Mr. Campbell is careful of his own reputation, and economical of the pleasures of his readers. He treats them as the fox in the fable treated his guest the stork; or, to use his own expression, his fine things are

Like angel's visits, few, and far between.[1]

There is another fault in this poem, which is the mechanical structure of the fable. The most striking events occur in the shape of antitheses. The story is cut into the form of a parallelogram. There is the same systematic alternation of good and evil, of violence and repose, that there is of light and shade in a picture. The Indian, who is the chief agent in the interest of the poem, vanishes, and returns after long intervals, like the periodical revolutions of the planets. He unexpectedly appears just in the nick of time, after years of absence, and without any known reason but the convenience of the author and the astonishment of the reader; as if nature were a machine constructed on a principle of complete contrast, to produce a theatrical effect. *Nec Deus intersit, nisi dignus vindice nodus.* Mr. Campbell's savage never appears but upon great occasions, and then his punctuality is preternatural and alarming. He is the most wonderful instance on record of poetical *reliability*. The most dreadful mischiefs happen at the most mortifying moments; and when your expectations are wound up to the highest pitch, you are sure to have them knocked on the head by a premeditated and remorseless stroke of the poet's pen. This is done so often for the convenience of the author, that in the end it ceases to be for the satisfaction of the reader.

Tom Moore is a poet of a quite different stamp. He is as heedless, gay, and prodigal of his poetical wealth, as the other is careful, reserved, and parsimonious. The genius of both is national. Mr. Moore's Muse is another Ariel, as light, as tricksy, as indefatigable, and as humane a spirit. His fancy is for ever on the wing, flutters in the gale, glitters in the sun. Every thing lives, moves, and sparkles in his poetry, while over all love waves his purple light. His thoughts are as restless, as many, and as bright as the insects that people the sun's beam. "So work the honey-bees," extracting liquid sweets from opening buds; so the butterfly expands its wings to the idle air; so the thistle's silver down is wafted over summer seas. An airy voyager on life's stream, his mind inhales the fragrance of a thousand shores, and drinks of endless pleasures under halcyon skies. Wherever his footsteps tend over the enamelled ground of fairy fiction—

Around him the bees in play flutter and cluster,
And gaudy butterflies frolic around.

The fault of Mr. Moore is an exuberance of involuntary power. His facility of production lessens the effect of, and hangs as a dead weight upon, what he produces. His levity at last oppresses. The infinite delight he takes in such an infinite number of things, creates indifference in minds less susceptible of pleasure than his own. He exhausts attention by being inexhaustible. His variety cloys; his rapidity dazzles and distracts the sight. The graceful ease with which he lends himself to every subject, the genial spirit with which he indulges in every sentiment, prevents him from giving their full force to the masses of things, from connecting them into a whole. He wants intensity, strength, and grandeur. His mind does not brood over the great and permanent; it glances over the surfaces, the first impressions of things, instead of grappling with the deep-rooted prejudices of the mind, its inveterate habits, and that "perilous stuff that weighs upon the heart." His pen, as it is rapid and fanciful, wants momentum and passion. It requires the same principle to make us thoroughly like poetry, that makes us like ourselves so well, the feeling of continued identity. The impressions of Mr. Moore's poetry are detached, desultory, and physical. Its gorgeous colours brighten and fade like the rainbow's. Its sweetness evaporates like the effluvia exhaled from beds of flowers! His gay laughing style, which relates to the immediate pleasures of love or wine, is better than his sentimental and romantic vein. His Irish melodies are not free from affectation and a certain sickliness of pretension. His serious descriptions are apt to run into flowery tenderness. His pathos sometimes melts into a mawkish sensibility, or crystallizes into all the prettinesses of allegorical language, and glittering hardness of external imagery. But he has wit at will, and of the first quality. His satirical and burlesque poetry is his best: it is first-rate. His Twopenny Post-Bag is a perfect "nest of spicery"; where the Cayenne is not spared. The politician there sharpens the

---

[1] There is the same idea in Blair's Grave.

——————Its visits,
Like those of angels, short, and far between.

Mr. Campbell in altering the expression has spoiled it. "Few," and "far between," are the same thing.

poet's pen. In this too, our bard resembles the bee—he has its honey and its sting.

Mr. Moore ought not to have written Lalla Rookh, even for three thousand guineas. His fame is worth more than that. He should have minded the advice of Fadladeen. It is not, however, a failure, so much as an evasion and a consequent disappointment of public expectation. He should have left it to others to break conventions with nations, and faith with the world. He should, at any rate, have kept his with the public. Lalla Rookh is not what people wanted to see whether Mr. Moore could do; namely, whether he could write a long epic poem. It is four short tales. The interest, however, is often high-wrought and tragic, but the execution still turns to the effeminate and voluptuous side. Fortitude of mind is the first requisite of a tragic or epic writer. Happiness of nature and felicity of genius are the pre-eminent characteristics of the bard of Erin. If he is not perfectly contented with what he is, all the world beside is. He had no temptation to risk any thing in adding to the love and admiration of his age, and more than one country

> Therefore to be possessed with double pomp,
> To guard a title that was rich before,
> To gild refined gold, to paint the lily,
> To throw a perfume on the violet,
> To smooth the ice, or add another hue
> Unto the rainbow, or with taper light
> To seek the beauteous eye of heav'n to garnish,
> Is wasteful and ridiculous excess.

The same might be said of Mr. Moore's seeking to bind an epic crown, or the shadow of one, round his other laurels.

If Mr. Moore has not suffered enough personally, Lord Byron (judging from the tone of his writings) might be thought to have suffered too much to be a truly great poet. If Mr. Moore lays himself too open to all the various impulses of things, the outward shews of earth and sky, to every breath that blows, to every stray sentiment that crosses his fancy; Lord Byron shuts himself up too much in the impenetrable gloom of his own thoughts, and buries the natural light of things in "nook monastic." The Giaour, the Corsair, Childe Harold, are all the same person, and they are apparently all himself. The everlasting repetition of one subject, the same dark ground of fiction, with the darker colours of the poet's mind spread over it, the unceasing accumulation of horrors on horror's head, steels the mind against the sense of pain, as inevitably as the unwearied Siren sounds and luxurious monotony of Mr. Moore's poetry make it inaccessible to pleasure. Lord Byron's poetry is as morbid as Mr. Moore's is careless and dissipated. He has more depth of passion, more force and impetuosity, but the passion is always of the same unaccountable character, at once violent and sullen, fierce and gloomy. It is not the passion of a mind struggling with misfortune, or the hopelessness of its desires, but of a mind preying upon itself, and disgusted with, or indifferent to all other things. There is nothing less poetical than this sort of unaccommodating selfishness. There is nothing more repulsive than this sort of ideal absorption of all the interests of others, of the good and ills of life, in the ruling passion and moody abstraction of a single mind, as if it would make itself the centre of the universe, and there was nothing worth cherishing but its intellectual diseases. It is like a cancer, eating into the heart of poetry. But still there is power; and power rivets attention and forces admiration. "He hath a demon:" and that is the next thing to being full of the God. His brow collects the scattered gloom: his eye flashes livid fire that withers and consumes. But still we watch the progress of the scathing bolt with interest, and mark the ruin it leaves behind with awe. Within the contracted range of his imagination, he has great unity and truth of keeping. He chooses elements and agents congenial to his mind, the dark and glittering ocean, the frail bark hurrying before the storm, pirates and men that "house on the wild sea with wild usages." He gives the tumultuous eagerness of action, and the fixed despair of thought. In vigour of style and force of conception, he in one sense surpasses every writer of the present day. His indignant apothegms are like oracles of misanthropy. He who wishes for "a curse to kill with," may find it in Lord Byron's writings. Yet he has beauty lurking underneath his strength, tenderness sometimes joined with the phrenzy of despair. A flash of golden light sometimes follows from a stroke of his pencil, like a falling meteor. The flowers that adorn his poetry bloom over charnel-houses and the grave!

There is one subject on which Lord Byron is fond of writing, on which I wish he would not write—Buonaparte. Not that I quarrel with his writing for him, or against him, but with his writing both for him and against him. What right has he to do this? Buonaparte's character, be it what else it may, does not change every hour according to his Lordship's varying humour. He is not a pipe for Fortune's finger, or for his Lordship's Muse, to play what stop she pleases on. Why should Lord Byron now laud him to the skies in the hour of his success, and then peevishly wreak his disappointment on the God of his idolatry? The man he writes of does not rise or fall with circumstances: but "looks on tempests and is never shaken." Besides, his is a subject for history, and not for poetry.

Great princes' favourites their fair leaves spread,
  But as the marigold at the sun's eye,
And in themselves their pride lies buried;
  For at a frown they in their glory die.
The painful warrior, famoused for fight,
  After a thousand victories once foil'd,
Is from the book of honour razed quite,
  And all the rest forgot for which he toil'd.

If Lord Byron will write any thing more on this hazardous theme, let him take these lines of Shakspeare for his guide, and finish them in the spirit of the original—they will then be worthy of the subject.

Walter Scott is the most popular of all the poets of the present day, and deservedly so. He describes that which is most easily and generally understood with more vivacity and effect than any body else. He has no excellences, either of a lofty or recondite kind, which lie beyond the reach of the most ordinary capacity to find out; but he has all the good qualities which all the world agree to understand. His style is clear, flowing, and transparent: his sentiments, of which his style is an easy and natural medium, are common to him with his readers. He has none of Mr. Wordsworth's *idiosyncracy*. He differs from his readers only in a greater range of knowledge and facility of expression. His poetry belongs to the class of *improvisatori* poetry. It has neither depth, height, nor breadth in it; neither uncommon strength, nor uncommon refinement of thought, sentiment, or language. It has no originality. But if this author has no research, no moving power in his own breast, he relies with the greater safety and success on the force of his subject. He selects a story such as is sure

to please, full of incidents, characters, peculiar manners, costume, and scenery; and he tells it in a way that can offend no one. He never wearies or disappoints you. He is communicative and garrulous; but he is not his own hero. He never obtrudes himself on your notice to prevent your seeing the subject. What passes in the poem, passes much as it would have done in reality. The author has little or nothing to do with it. Mr. Scott has great intuitive power of fancy, great vividness of pencil in placing external objects and events before the eye. The force of his mind is picturesque, rather than *moral.* He gives more of the features of nature than the soul of passion. He conveys the distinct outlines and visible changes in outward objects, rather than "their mortal consequences." He is very inferior to Lord Byron in intense passion, to Moore in delightful fancy, to Mr. Wordsworth in profound sentiment: but he has more picturesque power than any of them; that is, he places the objects themselves, about which *they* might feel and think, in a much more striking point of view, with greater variety of dress and attitude, and with more local truth of colouring. His imagery is Gothic and grotesque. The manners and actions have the interest and curiosity belonging to a wild country and a distant period of time. Few descriptions have a more complete reality, a more striking appearance of life and motion, than that of the warriors in the Lady of the Lake, who start up at the command of Rhoderic Dhu, from their concealment under the fern, and disappear again in an instant. The Lay of the Last Minstrel and Marmion are the first and perhaps the best of his works. The Goblin Page, in the first of these, is a very interesting and inscrutable little personage. In reading these poems, I confess I am a little disconcerted, in turning over the page, to find Mr. Westall's pictures, which always seem *facsimiles* of the persons represented, with ancient costume and a theatrical air. This may be a compliment to Mr. Westall, but it is not one to Walter Scott. The truth is, there is a modern air in the midst of the antiquarian research of Mr. Scott's poetry. It is history or tradition in masquerade. Not only the crust of old words and images is worn off with time,—the substance is grown comparatively light and worthless. The forms are old and uncouth; but the spirit is effeminate and frivolous. This is a deduction from the praise I have given to his pencil for extreme fidelity, though it has been no obstacle to its drawing-room success. He has just hit the town between the romantic and the fashionable; and between the two, secured all classes of readers on his side. In a word, I conceive that he is to the great poet, what an excellent mimic is to a great actor. There is no determinate impression left on the mind by reading his poetry. It has no results. The reader rises up from the perusal with new images and associations, but he remains the same man that he was before. A great mind is one that moulds the minds of others. Mr. Scott has put the Border Minstrelsy and scattered traditions of the country into easy, animated verse. But the Notes to his poems are just as entertaining as the poems themselves, and his poems are only entertaining.

Mr. Wordsworth is the most original poet now living. He is the reverse of Walter Scott in his defects and excellences. He has nearly all that the other wants, and wants all that the other possesses. His poetry is not external, but internal; it does not depend upon tradition, or story, or old song; he furnishes it from his own mind, and is his own subject. He is the poet of mere sentiment. Of many of the Lyrical Ballads, it is not possible to speak in terms of too high praise, such as Hart-leap Well, the Banks of the Wye, Poor Susan, parts of the Leech-gatherer, the lines to a Cuckoo, to a Daisy, the Complaint, several of the Sonnets, and a hundred others of inconceivable beauty, of perfect originality and pathos. They open a finer and deeper vein of thought and feeling than any poet in modern times has done, or attempted. He has produced a deeper impression, and on a smaller circle, than any other of his contemporaries. His powers have been mistaken by the age, nor does he exactly understand them himself. He cannot form a whole. He has not the constructive faculty. He can give only the fine tones of thought, drawn from his mind by accident or nature, like the sounds drawn from the Æolian harp by the wandering gale.—He is totally deficient in all the machinery of poetry. His *Excursion*, taken as a whole, notwithstanding the noble materials thrown away in it, is a proof of this. The line labours, the sentiment moves slow, but the poem stands stock-still. The reader makes no way from the first line to the last. It is more than any thing in the world like Robinson Crusoe's boat, which would have been an excellent good boat, and would have carried him to the other side of the globe, but that he could not get it out of the sand where it stuck fast. I did what little I could to help to launch it at the time, but it would not do. I am not, however, one of those who laugh at the attempts or failures of men of genius. It is not my way to cry "Long life to the conqueror." Success and desert are not with me synonymous terms; and the less Mr. Wordsworth's general merits have been understood, the more necessary is it to insist upon them. This is not the place to repeat what I have already said on the subject. The reader may turn to it in the Round Table. I do not think, however, there is any thing in the larger poem equal to many of the detached pieces in the Lyrical Ballads. . . .

Mr. Wordsworth is at the head of that which has been denominated the Lake school of poetry; a school which, with all my respect for it, I do not think sacred from criticism or exempt from faults, of some of which faults I shall speak with becoming frankness; for I do not see that the liberty of the press ought to be shackled, or freedom of speech curtailed, to screen either its revolutionary or renegado extravagances. This school of poetry had its origin in the French revolution, or rather in those sentiments and opinions which produced that revolution; and which sentiments and opinions were indirectly imported into this country in translations from the German about that period. Our poetical literature had, towards the close of the last century, degenerated into the most trite, insipid, and mechanical of all things, in the hands of the followers of Pope and the old French school of poetry. It wanted something to stir it up, and it found that something in the principles and events of the French revolution. From the impulse it thus received, it rose at once from the most servile imitation and tamest common-place, to the utmost pitch of singularity and paradox. The change in the belles-lettres was as complete, and to many persons as startling, as the change in politics, with which it went hand in hand. There was a mighty ferment in the heads of statesmen and poets, kings and people. According to the prevailing notions, all was to be natural and new. Nothing that was established was to be tolerated. All the common-place figures of poetry, tropes, allegories, personifications, with the whole heathen mythology, were instantly discarded; a classical allusion was considered as a piece of antiquated foppery; capital letters were no more allowed in print, than letters-patent of nobility were permitted in real life; kings and queens were dethroned from their rank and station in legitimate tragedy or epic poetry, as they were decapitated elsewhere; rhyme was looked upon as a relic of the feudal system, and regular metre was abolished along with regular government. Authority and fashion, elegance or arrangement, were hooted out of countenance, as pedantry and prejudice. Every one did that which was good in his own eyes. The object was to reduce all things to an absolute level; and a singularly affected and outrageous simplicity prevailed in dress and manners, in style and sentiment. A striking effect produced where it was least expected, something new and original, no matter whether good, bad, or indifferent, whether mean or lofty, extravagant or childish, was all that was aimed at, or considered as compatible with sound philosophy and an age of reason. The licentiousness grew extreme: Coryate's Crudities were nothing to it. The world was to be turned topsy-turvy; and poetry, by the good will of our Adamwits, was to share its fate and begin *de novo*. It was a time of promise, a renewal of the world and of letters; and the Deucalions, who were to perform this feat of regeneration, were the present poet-laureat and the two authors of the Lyrical Ballads. The Germans, who made heroes of robbers, and honest women of cast-off mistresses, had already exhausted the extravagant and marvellous in sentiment and situation: our native writers adopted a wonderful simplicity of style and matter. The paradox they set out with was, that all things are by nature equally fit subjects for poetry; or that if there is any preference to be given, those that are the meanest and most unpromising are the best, as they leave the greatest scope for the unbounded stores of thought and fancy in the writer's own mind. Poetry had with them "neither buttress nor coigne of vantage to make its pendant bed and procreant cradle." It was not "born so high: its aiery buildeth in the cedar's top, and dallies with the wind, and scorns the sun." It grew like a mushroom out of the ground; or was hidden in it like a truffle, which it required a particular sagacity and industry to find out and dig up. They founded the new school on a principle of sheer humanity, on pure nature void of art.

It could not be said of these sweeping reformers and dictators in the republic of letters, that "in their train walked crowns and crownets; that realms and islands, like plates, dropt from their pockets": but they were surrounded, in company with the Muses, by a mixed rabble of idle apprentices and Botany Bay convicts, female vagrants, gipsies, meek daughters in the family of Christ, of ideot boys and mad mothers, and after them "owls and night-ravens flew." They scorned "degrees, priority, and place, insisture, course, proportion, season, form, office, and custom in all line of order": —the distinctions of birth, the vicissitudes of fortune, did not enter into their abstracted, lofty, and levelling calculations of human nature. He who was more than man, with them was none. They claimed kindred only with the commonest of the people: peasants, pedlars, and village-barbers were their oracles and bosom friends. Their poetry, in the extreme to which it professedly tended, and was in effect carried, levels all distinctions of nature and society; has "no figures nor no fantasies," which the prejudices of superstition or the customs of the world draw in the brains of men; "no trivial fond records" of all that has existed in the history of past ages; it has no adventitious pride, pomp, or circumstance, to set it off; "the marshal's truncheon, nor the judge's robe"; neither tradition, reverence, nor ceremony, "that to great ones 'longs": it breaks in pieces the golden images of poetry, and defaces its armorial bearings, to melt them down in the mould of common humanity or of its own upstart self-sufficiency. They took the same method in their new-fangled "metre ballad-mongering" scheme, which Rousseau did in his prose paradoxes—of exciting attention by reversing the established standards of opinion and estimation in the world. They were for bringing poetry back to its primitive simplicity and state of nature, as he was for bringing society back to the savage state: so that the only thing remarkable left in the world by this change, would be the persons who had produced it. A thorough adept in this school of poetry and philanthropy is jealous of all excellence but his own. He does not even like to share his reputation with his subject; for he would have it all proceed from his own power and originality of mind. Such a one is slow to admire any thing that is admirable; feels no interest in what is most interesting to others, no grandeur in any thing grand, no beauty in any thing beautiful. He tolerates only what he himself creates; he sympathizes only with what can enter into no competition with him, with "the bare trees and mountains bare, and grass in the green field." He sees nothing but himself and the universe. He hates all greatness and all pretensions to it, whether well or ill-founded. His egotism is in some respects a madness; for he scorns even the admiration of himself, thinking it a presumption in any one to suppose that he has taste or sense enough to understand him. He hates all science and all art; he hates chemistry, he hates con-chology; he hates Voltaire; he hates Sir Isaac Newton; he hates wisdom; he hates wit; he hates metaphysics, which he says are unintel-ligible, and yet he would be thought to under-stand them; he hates prose; he hates all poetry but his own; he hates the dialogues in Shake-speare; he hates music, dancing, and painting; he hates Rubens, he hates Rembrandt; he hates Raphael, he hates Titian; he hates Vandyke; he hates the antique; he hates the Apollo Bel-videre; he hates the Venus of Medicis. This is the reason that so few people take an interest in his writings, because he takes an interest in nothing that others do!—The effect has been perceived as something odd; but the cause or principle has never been distinctly traced to its source before, as far as I know. The proofs are to be found every where—in Mr. Southey's Botany Bay Eclogues, in his book of Songs and Sonnets, his Odes and Inscriptions, so well parodied in the Anti-Jacobin Review, in his Joan of Arc, and last, though not least, in his Wat Tyler:

> When Adam delved, and Eve span,
> Where was then the gentleman?

(—or the poet laureate either, we may ask?)— In Mr. Coleridge's Ode to an Ass's Foal, in his Lines to Sarah, his Religious Musings; and in his and Mr. Wordsworth's Lyrical Bal-lads, *passim*.

Of Mr. Southey's larger epics, I have but a faint recollection at this distance of time, but all that I remember of them is mechanical and extravagant, heavy and superficial. His af-fected, disjointed style is well imitated in the Rejected Addresses. The difference between him and Sir Richard Blackmore seems to be, that the one is heavy and the other light, the one solemn and the other pragmatical, the one phlegmatic and the other flippant; and that there is no Gay in the present time to give a Catalogue Raisonné of the performances of the living undertaker of epics. Kehama is a loose sprawling figure, such as we see cut out of wood or paper, and pulled or jerked with wire or thread, to make sudden and surprising motions, without meaning, grace, or nature in them. By far the best of his works are some of his shorter personal compositions, in which there is an ironical mixture of the quaint and serious, such as his lines on a picture of Gaspar Poussin, the fine tale of Gualberto, his Descrip-tion of a Pig, and the Holly-tree, which is an affecting, beautiful, and modest retrospect on his own character. May the aspiration with which it concludes be fulfilled!—But the little he has done of true and sterling excellence, is overloaded by the quantity of indifferent mat-ter which he turns out every year, "prosing or versing," with equally mechanical and irresist-ible facility. His Essays, or political and moral disquisitions, are not so full of original mat-ter as Montaigne's. They are second or third rate compositions in that class.

It remains that I should say a few words of Mr. Coleridge; and there is no one who has a better right to say what he thinks of him than I have. "Is there here any dear friend of Cæsar? To him I say, that Brutus's love to Cæsar was no less than his." But no matter.— His Ancient Mariner is his most remarkable performance, and the only one that I could point out to any one as giving an adequate idea of his great natural powers. It is high German, however, and in it he seems to "conceive of poetry but as a drunken dream, reckless, care-less, and heedless, of past, present, and to come." His tragedies (for he has written two) are not answerable to it; they are, except a few poetical passages, drawling sentiment and metaphysical jargon. He has no genuine dra-matic talent. There is one fine passage in his Christabel, that which contains the descrip-tion of the quarrel between Sir Leoline and Sir Roland de Vaux of Tryermaine, who had been friends in youth.

> Alas! they had been friends in youth,
> But whispering tongues can poison truth;
> And constancy lives in realms above;
> And life is thorny; and youth is vain;
> And to be wroth with one we love,
> Doth work like madness in the brain:

And thus it chanc'd as I divine,
With Roland and Sir Leoline.
Each spake words of high disdain
And insult to his heart's best brother,
And parted ne'er to meet again!
But neither ever found another
To free the hollow heart from paining—

They stood aloof, the scars remaining,
Like cliffs which had been rent asunder:
A dreary sea now flows between,
But neither heat, nor frost, nor thunder,
Shall wholly do away I ween
The marks of that which once hath been.

Sir Leoline a moment's space
Stood gazing on the damsel's face;
And the youthful lord of Tryermaine
Came back upon his heart again.

It might seem insidious if I were to praise his ode entitled Fire, Famine, and Slaughter, as an effusion of high poetical enthusiasm, and strong political feeling. His Sonnet to Schiller conveys a fine compliment to the author of the Robbers, and an equally fine idea of the state of youthful enthusiasm in which he composed it.

Schiller! that hour I would have wish'd to die,
    If through the shudd'ring midnight I had sent
    From the dark dungeon of the tower time-rent,
That fearful voice, a famish'd father's cry—

That in no after moment aught less vast
    Might stamp me mortal! A triumphant shout
    Black Horror scream'd, and all her goblin rout
From the more with'ring scene diminish'd pass'd.

Ah! Bard tremendous in sublimity!
    Could I behold thee in thy loftier mood,
Wand'ring at eve, with finely frenzied eye,
    Beneath some vast old tempest-swinging wood!
Awhile, with mute awe gazing, I would brood,
Then weep aloud in a wild ecstasy!—

His *Conciones ad Populum*, Watchman, &c. are dreary trash. Of his Friend, I have spoken the truth elsewhere. But I may say of him here, that he is the only person I ever knew who answered to the idea of a man of genius. He is the only person from whom I ever learnt any thing. There is only one thing he could learn from me in return, but *that* he has not. He was the first poet I ever knew. His genius at that time had angelic wings, and fed on manna. He talked on for ever; and you wished him to talk on for ever. His thoughts did not seem to come with labour and effort; but as if borne on the gusts of genius, and as if the wings of his imagination lifted him from off his feet.

His voice rolled on the ear like the pealing organ, and its sound alone was the music of thought. His mind was clothed with wings; and raised on them, he lifted philosophy to heaven. In his descriptions, you then saw the progress of human happiness and liberty in bright and never-ending succession, like the steps of Jacob's ladder, with airy shapes ascending and descending, and with the voice of God at the top of the ladder. And shall I, who heard him then, listen to him now? Not I! . . . That spell is broke; that time is gone for ever; that voice is heard no more: but still the recollection comes rushing by with thoughts of long-past years, and rings in my ears with never-dying sound.

What though the radiance which was once so bright,
Be now for ever taken from my sight,
Though nothing can bring back the hour
Of glory in the grass, of splendour in the flow'r;
    I do not grieve, but rather find
    Strength in what remains behind;
    In the primal sympathy,
    Which having been, must ever be;
    In the soothing thoughts that spring
    Out of human suffering;
In years that bring the philosophic mind!—

I have thus gone through the task I intended, and have come at last to the level ground. I have felt my subject gradually sinking from under me as I advanced, and have been afraid of ending in nothing. The interest has unavoidably decreased at almost every successive step of the progress, like a play that has its catastrophe in the first or second act. This, however, I could not help. I have done as well as I could.

MR. COLERIDGE [1]

THE present is an age of talkers, and not of doers; and the reason is, that the world is growing old. We are so far advanced in the Arts and Sciences, that we live in retrospect, and doat on past achievements. The accumulation of knowledge has been so great, that we are lost in wonder at the height it has reached, instead of attempting to climb or add to it; while the variety of objects distracts and dazzles the looker-on. What *niche* remains unoc-

[1] The remaining essays, with the exception of that on Shelley, are from *The Spirit of the Age*, 1825.

cupied? What path untried? What is the use of doing anything, unless we could do better than all those who have gone before us? What hope is there of this? We are like those who have been to see some noble monument of art, who are content to admire without thinking of rivalling it; or like guests after a feast, who praise the hospitality of the donor "and thank the bounteous Pan"—perhaps carrying away some trifling fragments; or like the spectators of a mighty battle, who still hear its sound afar off, and the clashing of armour and the neighing of the war-horse and the shout of victory is in their ears, like the rushing of innumerable waters!

Mr. Coleridge has "a mind reflecting ages past"; his voice is like the echo of the congregated roar of the "dark rearward and abyss" of thought. He who has seen a mouldering tower by the side of a chrystal lake, hid by the mist, but glittering in the wave below, may conceive the dim, gleaming, uncertain intelligence of his eye: he who has marked the evening clouds uprolled (a world of vapours), has seen the picture of his mind, unearthly, unsubstantial, with gorgeous tints and ever-varying forms—

That which was now a horse, even with a thought
The rack dislimns, and makes it indistinct
As water is in water.

Our author's mind is (as he himself might express it) *tangential*. There is no subject on which he has not touched, none on which he has rested. With an understanding fertile, subtle, expansive, "quick, forgetive, apprehensive," beyond all living precedent, few traces of it will perhaps remain. He lends himself to all impressions alike; he gives up his mind and liberty of thought to none. He is a general lover of art and science, and wedded to no one in particular. He pursues knowledge as a mistress, with outstretched hands and winged speed; but as he is about to embrace her, his Daphne turns—alas! not to a laurel! Hardly a speculation has been left on record from the earliest time, but it is loosely folded up in Mr. Coleridge's memory, like a rich, but somewhat tattered piece of tapestry: we might add (with more seeming than real extravagance), that scarce a thought can pass through the mind of man, but its sound has at some time or other passed over his head with rustling pinions. On whatever question or author you speak, he is prepared to take up the theme with advantage—from Peter Abelard down to Thomas Moore, from the subtlest metaphysics to the politics of the *Courier*. There is no man of genius, in whose praise he descants, but the critic seems to stand above the author, and "what in him is weak, to strengthen, what is low, to raise and support": nor is there any work of genius that does not come out of his hands like an illuminated Missal, sparkling even in its defects. If Mr. Coleridge had not been the most impressive talker of his age, he would probably have been the finest writer; but he lays down his pen to make sure of an auditor, and mortgages the admiration of posterity for the stare of an idler. If he had not been a poet, he would have been a powerful logician; if he had not dipped his wing in the Unitarian controversy, he might have soared to the very summit of fancy. But in writing verse, he is trying to subject the Muse to *transcendental* theories: in his abstract reasoning, he misses his way by strewing it with flowers. All that he has done of moment, he had done twenty years ago: since then, he may be said to have lived on the sound of his own voice. Mr. Coleridge is too rich in intellectual wealth, to need to task himself to any drudgery: he has only to draw the sliders of his imagination, and a thousand subjects expand before him, startling him with their brilliancy, or losing themselves in endless obscurity—

And by the force of blear illusion,
They draw him on to his confusion.

What is the little he could add to the stock, compared with the countless stores that lie about him, that he should stoop to pick up a name, or to polish an idle fancy? He walks abroad in the majesty of an universal understanding, eyeing the "rich strond," or golden sky above him, and "goes sounding on his way," in eloquent accents, uncompelled and free!

Persons of the greatest capacity are often those, who for this reason do the least; for surveying themselves from the highest point of view, amidst the infinite variety of the universe, their own share in it seems trifling, and scarce worth a thought, and they prefer the contemplation of all that is, or has been, or can be, to the making a coil about doing what, when done, is no better than vanity. It is hard to concentrate all our attention and efforts on one pursuit, except from ignorance of others; and without this concentration of our faculties, no great progress can be made in any one thing. It is not merely that the mind is not capable of the effort; it does not think the effort worth making. Action is one; but thought is manifold. He whose restless eye glances through the wide compass of nature and art, will not consent to have "his own nothings monstered": but he must do this before he can give his whole soul to them. The mind, after "letting contemplation have its fill," or

> Sailing with supreme dominion
> Through the azure deep of air,

sinks down on the ground, breathless, exhausted, powerless, inactive; or if it must have some vent to its feelings, seeks the most easy and obvious; is soothed by friendly flattery, lulled by the murmur of immediate applause, thinks as it were aloud, and babbles in its dreams! A scholar (so to speak) is a more disinterested and abstracted character than a mere author. The first looks at the numberless volumes of a library, and says, "All these are mine": the other points to a single volume (perhaps it may be an immortal one) and says, "My name is written on the back of it." This is a puny and groveling ambition, beneath the lofty amplitude of Mr. Coleridge's mind. No, he revolves in his wayward soul, or utters to the passing wind, or discourses to his own shadow, things mightier and more various!— Let us draw the curtain, and unlock the shrine.

Learning rocked him in his cradle, and while yet a child,

> He lisped in numbers, for the numbers came.

At sixteen he wrote his *Ode on Chatterton*, and he still reverts to that period with delight, not so much as it relates to himself (for that string of his own early promise of fame rather jars than otherwise) but as exemplifying the youth of a poet. Mr. Coleridge talks of himself, without being an egotist, for in him the individual is always merged in the abstract and general. He distinguished himself at school and at the University by his knowledge of the classics, and gained several prizes for Greek epigrams. How many men are there (great scholars, celebrated names in literature) who having done the same thing in their youth, have no other idea all the rest of their lives but of this achievement, of a fellowship and dinner, and who, installed in academic honours, would look down on our author as a mere strolling bard! At Christ's Hospital, where he was brought up, he was the idol of those among his schoolfellows, who mingled with their bookish studies the music of thought and of humanity; and he was usually attended round the cloisters by a group of these (inspiring and inspired) whose hearts, even then, burnt within them as he talked, and where the sounds yet linger to mock ELIA on his way, still turning pensive to the past! One of the finest and rarest parts of Mr. Coleridge's conversation, is when he expatiates on the Greek tragedians (not that he is not well acquainted, when he pleases, with the epic poets, or the philosophers, or orators, or historians of antiquity)—on the subtle reasonings and melting pathos of Euripides, on the harmonious gracefulness of Sophocles, tuning his love-laboured song, like sweetest warblings from a sacred grove; on the high-wrought trumpet-tongued eloquence of Æschylus, whose Prometheus, above all, is like an Ode to Fate, and a pleading with Providence, his thoughts being let loose as his body is chained on his solitary rock, and his afflicted will (the emblem of mortality)

> Struggling in vain with ruthless destiny.

As the impassioned critic speaks and rises in his theme, you would think you heard the voice of the Man hated by the Gods, contending with the wild winds as they roar, and his eye glitters with the spirit of Antiquity!

Next, he was engaged with Hartley's tribes of mind, "etherial braid, thought-woven,"— and he busied himself for a year or two with vibrations and vibratiuncles and the great law of association that binds all things in its mystic chain, and the doctrine of Necessity (the mild teacher of Charity) and the Millennium, anticipative of a life to come—and he plunged deep into the controversy on Matter and Spirit, and, as an escape from Dr. Priestley's Materialism, where he felt himself imprisoned by the logician's spell, like Ariel in the cloven pine-tree, he became suddenly enamoured of Bishop Berkeley's fairy-world,[1] and used in

[1] Mr. Coleridge named his eldest son (the writer of some beautiful Sonnets) after Hartley, and the second after Berkeley. The third was called Derwent, after the river of that name. Nothing can be more characteristic of his mind than this cir-

all companies to build the universe, like a brave poetical fiction, of fine words—and he was deep-read in Malebranche, and in Cudworth's Intellectual System (a huge pile of learning, unwieldly, enormous) and in Lord Brook's hieroglyphic theories, and in Bishop Butler's Sermons, and in the Duchess of Newcastle's fantastic folios, and in Clarke and South and Tillotson, and all the fine thinkers and masculine reasoners of that age—and Leibnitz's *Pre-Established Harmony* reared its arch above his head, like the rainbow in the cloud, convenanting with the hopes of man—and then he fell plump, ten thousand fathoms down (but his wings saved him harmless) into the *hortus siccus* of Dissent, where he pared religion down to the standard of reason, and stripped faith of mystery, and preached Christ crucified and the Unity of the Godhead, and so dwelt for a while in the spirit with John Huss and Jerome of Prague and Socinus and old John Zisca, and ran through Neal's History of the Puritans, and Calamy's Non-Conformists' Memorial, having like thoughts and passions with them —but then Spinoza became his God, and he took up the vast chain of being in his hand, and the round world became the centre and the soul of all things in some shadowy sense, forlorn of meaning, and around him he beheld the living traces and the sky-pointing proportions of the mighty Pan—but poetry redeemed him from this spectral philosophy, and he bathed his heart in beauty, and gazed at the golden light of heaven, and drank of the spirit of the universe, and wandered at eve by fairy-stream or fountain,

——When he saw nought but beauty,
When he heard the voice of that Almighty One
In every breeze that blew, or wave that murmured—

and wedded with truth in Plato's shade, and in the writings of Proclus and Plotinus saw the ideas of things in the eternal mind, and unfolded all mysteries with the Schoolmen and fathomed the depths of Duns Scotus and Thomas Aquinas, and entered the third heaven with Jacob Behmen, and walked hand in hand with Swedenborg through the pavilions of the

cumstance. All his ideas indeed are like a river, flowing on for ever, and still murmuring as it flows, discharging its waters and still replenished—

And so by many winding nooks it strays,
With willing sport to the wild ocean!

New Jerusalem, and sung his faith in the promise and in the word in his *Religious Musings*—and lowering himself from that dizzy height, poised himself on Milton's wings, and spread out his thoughts in charity with the glad prose of Jeremy Taylor, and wept over Bowles's Sonnets, and studied Cowper's blank verse, and betook himself to Thomson's Castle of Indolence, and sported with the wits of Charles the Second's days and of Queen Anne, and relished Swift's style and that of the John Bull (Arbuthnot's we mean, not Mr. Croker's), and dallied with the British Essayists and Novelists, and knew all qualities of more modern writers with a learned spirit, Johnson, and Goldsmith, and Junius, and Burke, and Godwin, and the Sorrows of Werter, and Jean Jacques Rousseau, and Voltaire, and Marivaux, and Crebillon, and thousands more—now "laughed with Rabelais in his easy chair" or pointed to Hogarth, or afterwards dwelt on Claude's classic scenes, or spoke with rapture of Raphael, and compared the women at Rome to figures that had walked out of his pictures, or visited the Oratory of Pisa, and described the works of Giotto and Ghirlandaio and Massaccio, and gave the moral of the picture of the Triumph of Death, where the beggars and the wretched invoke his dreadful dart, but the rich and mighty of the earth quail and shrink before it; and in that land of siren sights and sounds, saw a dance of peasant girls, and was charmed with lutes and gondolas,—or wandered into Germany and lost himself in the labyrinths of the Hartz Forest and of the Kantean philosophy, and amongst the cabalistic names of Fichté and Schelling and Lessing, and God knows who—this was long after, but all the former while, he had nerved his heart and filled his eyes with tears, as he hailed the rising orb of liberty, since quenched in darkness and in blood, and had kindled his affections at the blaze of the French Revolution, and sang for joy when the towers of the Bastile and the proud places of the insolent and the oppressor fell, and would have floated his bark, freighted with fondest fancies, across the Atlantic wave with Southey and others to seek for peace and freedom—

In Philarmonia's undivided dale!

Alas! "Frailty, thy name is *Genius!*"—What is become of all this mighty heap of hope, of thought, of learning, and humanity? It has ended in swallowing doses of oblivion and in writing paragraphs in the *Courier.*—Such and so little is the mind of man!

It was not to be supposed that Mr. Coleridge could keep on at the rate he set off; he could not realize all he knew or thought, and less could not fix his desultory ambition; other stimulants supplied the place, and kept up the intoxicating dream, the fever and the madness of his early impressions. Liberty (the philosopher's and the poet's bride) had fallen a victim, meanwhile, to the murderous practices of the hag, Legitimacy. Proscribed by court-hirelings, too romantic for the herd of vulgar politicians, our enthusiast stood at bay, and at last turned on the pivot of a subtle casuistry to the *unclean side:* but his discursive reason would not let him trammel himself into a poet-laureate or stamp-distributor, and he stopped, ere he had quite passed that well-known "bourne from whence no traveller returns"— and so has sunk into torpid, uneasy repose, tantalized by useless resources, haunted by vain imaginings, his lips idly moving, but his heart for ever still, or, as the shattered chords vibrate of themselves, making melancholy music to the ear of memory! Such is the fate of genius in an age, when in the unequal contest with sovereign wrong, every man is ground to powder who is not either a born slave, or who does not willingly and at once offer up the yearnings of humanity and the dictates of reason as a welcome sacrifice to besotted prejudice and loathsome power.

Of all Mr. Coleridge's productions, the *Ancient Mariner* is the only one that we could with confidence put into any person's hands, on whom we wished to impress a favourable idea of his extraordinary powers. Let whatever other objections be made to it, it is unquestionably a work of genius—of wild, irregular, overwhelming imagination, and has that rich, varied movement in the verse, which gives a distant idea of the lofty or changeful tones of Mr. Coleridge's voice. In the *Christabel,* there is one splendid passage on divided friendship. The *Translation of Schiller's Wallenstein* is also a masterly production in its kind, faithful and spirited. Among his smaller pieces there are occasional bursts of pathos and fancy, equal to what we might expect from him; but these form the exception, and not the rule. Such, for instance, is his affecting Sonnet to the author of the Robbers.

Schiller! that hour I would have wish'd to die,
  If through the shudd'ring midnight I had sent
  From the dark dungeon of the tower time-rent,
That fearful voice, a famish'd father's cry—
That in no after-moment aught less vast
  Might stamp me mortal! A triumphant shout
  Black horror scream'd, and all her goblin rout
From the more with'ring scene diminish'd pass'd.
Ah! Bard tremendous in sublimity!
  Could I behold thee in thy loftier mood,
Wand'ring at eve, with finely frenzied eye,
  Beneath some vast old tempest-swinging wood!
  Awhile, with mute awe gazing, I would brood,
Then weep aloud in a wild ecstasy.

His Tragedy, entitled *Remorse,* is full of beautiful and striking passages, but it does not place the author in the first rank of dramatic writers. But if Mr. Coleridge's works do not place him in that rank, they injure instead of conveying a just idea of the man, for he himself is certainly in the first class of general intellect.

If our author's poetry is inferior to his conversation, his prose is utterly abortive. Hardly a gleam is to be found in it of the brilliancy and richness of those stores of thought and language that he pours out incessantly, when they are lost like drops of water in the ground. The principal work, in which he has attempted to embody his general views of things, is the FRIEND, of which, though it contains some noble passages and fine trains of thought, prolixity and obscurity are the most frequent characteristics.

No two persons can be conceived more opposite in character or genius than the subject of the present and of the preceding sketch. Mr. Godwin, with less natural capacity, and with fewer acquired advantages, by concentrating his mind on some given object, and doing what he had to do with all his might, has accomplished much, and will leave more than one monument of a powerful intellect behind him; Mr. Coleridge, by dissipating his, and dallying with every subject by turns, has done little or nothing to justify to the world or to posterity, the high opinion which all who have ever heard him converse, or known him intimately, with one accord entertain of him. Mr. Godwin's faculties have kept at home, and plied their task in the workshop of the brain, diligently and effectually: Mr. Coleridge's have gossiped away their time, and gadded about from house to house, as if life's business were to melt the hours in listless talk. Mr. Godwin is intent on a subject, only as it concerns himself and his reputation; he works it out as a matter of duty, and discards from his mind whatever does not forward his main object as impertinent and vain. Mr. Coleridge, on the other hand, delights in nothing but episodes and digressions, neglects whatever he undertakes to perform, and can act only on spontaneous impulses, without object or method. "He cannot be constrained by mastery." While he should be occupied with a given pursuit, he is thinking of a thousand other things; a thousand tastes, a thousand objects tempt him, and distract his mind, which keeps open house, and entertains all comers; and after being fatigued and amused with morning calls from idle visitors, finds the day consumed and its business unconcluded. Mr. Godwin, on the contrary, is somewhat exclusive and unsocial in his habits of mind, entertains no company but what he gives his whole time and attention to, and wisely writes over the doors of his understanding, his fancy, and his senses—"No admittance except on business." He has none of that fastidious refinement and false delicacy, which might lead him to balance between the endless variety of modern attainments. He does not throw away his life (nor a single half-hour of it) in adjusting the claims of different accomplishments, and in choosing between them or making himself master of them all. He sets about his task, (whatever it may be) and goes through it with spirit and fortitude. He has the happiness to think an author the greatest character in the world, and himself the greatest author in it. Mr. Coleridge, in writing an harmonious stanza, would stop to consider whether there was not more grace and beauty in a *Pas de trois*, and would not proceed till he had resolved this question by a chain of metaphysical reasoning without end. Not so Mr. Godwin. That is best to him, which he can do best. He does not waste himself in vain aspirations and effeminate sympathies. He is blind, deaf, insensible to all but the trump of Fame. Plays, operas, painting, music, ball-rooms, wealth, fashion, titles, lords, ladies, touch him not—all these are no more to him than to the magician in his cell, and he writes on to the end of the chapter, through good report and evil report. *Pingo in eternitatem*—is his motto. He neither envies nor admires what others are, but is contented to be what he is, and strives to do the utmost he can. Mr. Coleridge has flirted with the Muses as with a set of mistresses: Mr. Godwin has been married twice,

to Reason and to Fancy, and has to boast no short-lived progeny by each. So to speak, he has *valves* belonging to his mind, to regulate the quantity of gas admitted into it, so that like the bare, unsightly, but well-compacted steam-vessel, it cuts its liquid way, and arrives at its promised end: while Mr. Coleridge's bark, "taught with the little nautilus to sail," the sport of every breath, dancing to every wave,

Youth at its prow, and Pleasure at its helm,

flutters its gaudy pennons in the air, glitters in the sun, but we wait in vain to hear of its arrival in the destined harbour. Mr. Godwin, with less variety and vividness, with less subtlety and susceptibility both of thought and feeling, has had firmer nerves, a more determined purpose, a more comprehensive grasp of his subject, and the results are as we find them. Each has met with his reward: for justice has, after all, been done to the pretensions of each; and we must, in all cases, use means to ends!

It was a misfortune to any man of talent to be born in the latter end of the last century. Genius stopped the way of Legitimacy, and therefore it was to be abated, crushed, or set aside as a nuisance. The spirit of the monarchy was at variance with the spirit of the age. The flame of liberty, the light of intellect, was to be extinguished with the sword—or with slander, whose edge is sharper than the sword. The war between power and reason was carried on by the first of these abroad—by the last at home. No quarter was given (then or now) by the Government-critics, the authorised censors of the press, to those who followed the dictates of independence, who listened to the voice of the tempter, Fancy. Instead of gathering fruits and flowers, immortal fruits and amaranthine flowers, they soon found themselves beset not only by a host of prejudices, but assailed with all the engines of power, by nicknames, by lies, by all the arts of malice, interest and hypocrisy, without the possibility of their defending themselves "from the pelting of the pitiless storm," that poured down upon them from the strong-holds of corruption and authority. The philosophers, the dry abstract reasoners, submitted to this reverse pretty well, and armed themselves with patience "as with triple steel," to bear discomfiture, persecution, and disgrace. But the poets, the creatures of sympathy, could not stand the frowns both of king and people. They did not like to be shut out when places and pensions, when the critic's praises, and the laurel-wreath were about to be distributed. They did not stomach being *sent to Coventry*, and Mr. Coleridge sounded a rerteat for them by the help of casuistry, and a musical voice.— "His words were hollow, but they pleased the ear" of his friends of the Lake School, who turned back disgusted and panic-struck from the dry desert of unpopularity, like Hassan the camel-driver,

And curs'd the hour, and curs'd the luckless day,
When first from Shiraz' walls they bent their way.

They are safely inclosed there, but Mr. Coleridge did not enter with them; pitching his tent upon the barren waste without, and having no abiding place nor city of refuge!

MR. WORDSWORTH

MR. WORDSWORTH'S genius is a pure emanation of the Spirit of the Age. Had he lived in any other period of the world, he would never have been heard of. As it is, he has some difficulty to contend with the hebetude of his intellect, and the meanness of his subject. With him "lowliness is young ambition's ladder": but he finds it a toil to climb in this way the steep of Fame. His homely Muse can hardly raise her wing from the ground, nor spread her hidden glories to the sun. He has "no figures nor no fantasies, which busy *passion* draws in the brains of men:" neither the gorgeous machinery of mythologic lore, nor the splendid colours of poetic diction. His style is vernacular: he delivers household truths. He sees nothing loftier than human hopes; nothing deeper than the human heart. This he probes, this he tampers with, this he poises, with all its incalculable weight of thought and feeling, in his hands; and at the same time calms the throbbing pulses of his own heart, by keeping his eye ever fixed on the face of nature. If he can make the life-blood flow from the wounded breast, this is the living colouring with which he paints his verse: if he can assuage the pain or close up the wound with the balm of solitary musing, or the healing power of plants and herbs and "skyey influences," this is the sole

triumph of his art. He takes the simplest elements of nature and of the human mind, the mere abstract conditions inseparable from our being, and tries to compound a new system of poetry from them; and has perhaps succeeded as well as any one could. *"Nihil humani a me alienum puto"*—is the motto of his works. He thinks nothing low or indifferent of which this can be affirmed: every thing that professes to be more than this, that is not an absolute essence of truth and feeling, he holds to be vitiated, false, and spurious. In a word, his poetry is founded on setting up an opposition (and pushing it to the utmost length) between the natural and the artificial; between the spirit of humanity, and the spirit of fashion and of the world!

It is one of the innovations of the time. It partakes of, and is carried along with, the revolutionary movement of our age: the political changes of the day were the model on which he formed and conducted his poetical experiments. His Muse (it cannot be denied, and without this we cannot explain its character at all) is a levelling one. It proceeds on a principle of equality, and strives to reduce all things to the same standard. It is distinguished by a proud humility. It relies upon its own resources, and disdains external show and relief. It takes the commonest events and objects, as a test to prove that nature is always interesting from its inherent truth and beauty, without any of the ornaments of dress or pomp of circumstances to set it off. Hence the unaccountable mixture of seeming simplicity and real abstruseness in the *Lyrical Ballads*. Fools have laughed at, wise men scarcely understand them. He takes a subject or a story merely as pegs or loops to hang thought and feeling on; the incidents are trifling, in proportion to his contempt for imposing appearances; the reflections are profound, according to the gravity and the aspiring pretensions of his mind.

His popular, inartificial style gets rid (at a blow) of all the trappings of verse, of all the high places of poetry: "the cloud-capt towers, the solemn temples, the gorgeous palaces," are swept to the ground, and "like the baseless fabric of a vision, leave not a wreck [*sic*] behind." All the traditions of learning, all the superstitions of age, are obliterated and effaced. We begin *de novo*, on a *tabula rasa* of poetry. The purple pall, the nodding plume of tragedy are exploded as mere pantomime and trick, to return to the simplicity of truth and nature. Kings, queens, priests, nobles, the altar and the throne, the distinctions of rank, birth, wealth, power, "the judge's robe, the marshal's truncheon, the ceremony that to great ones 'longs," are not to be found here. The author tramples on the pride of art with greater pride. The Ode and Epode, the Strophe and the Antistrophe, he laughs to scorn. The harp of Homer, the trump of Pindar and of Alcæus are still. The decencies of costume, the decorations of vanity are stripped off without mercy as barbarous, idle, and Gothic. The jewels in the crisped hair, the diadem on the polished brow are thought meretricious, theatrical, vulgar; and nothing contents his fastidious taste beyond a simple garland of flowers. Neither does he avail himself of the advantages which nature or accident holds out to him. He chooses to have his subject a foil to his invention, to owe nothing but to himself. He gathers manna in the wilderness, he strikes the barren rock for the gushing moisture. He elevates the mean by the strength of his own aspirations; he clothes the naked with beauty and grandeur from the stores of his own recollections. No cypress grove loads his verse with funeral pomp: but his imagination lends "a sense of joy

> To the bare trees and mountains bare,
> And grass in the green field."

No storm, no shipwreck startles us by its horrors: but the rainbow lifts its head in the cloud, and the breeze sighs through the withered fern. No sad vicissitude of fate, no overwhelming catastrophe in nature deforms his page: but the dew-drop glitters on the bending flower, the tear collects in the glistening eye.

Beneath the hills, along the flowery vales,
The generations are prepared; the pangs,
The internal pangs are ready; the dread strife
Of poor humanity's afflicted will,
Struggling in vain with ruthless destiny.

As the lark ascends from its low bed on fluttering wing, and salutes the morning skies; so Mr. Wordsworth's unpretending Muse, in russet guise, scales the summits of reflection, while it makes the round earth its footstool, and its home!

Possibly a good deal of this may be regarded as the effect of disappointed views and an inverted ambition. Prevented by native pride and indolence from climbing the ascent of learning or greatness, taught by political opinions to say to the vain pomp and glory of the world, "I hate ye," seeing the path of classical and artificial poetry blocked up by the cumbrous ornaments of style and turgid *commonplaces*, so that nothing more could be achieved in that direction but by the most ridiculous bombast or the tamest servility; he has turned back partly from the bias of his mind, partly perhaps from a judicious policy—has struck into the sequestered vale of humble life, sought out the Muse among sheep-cotes and hamlets and the peasant's mountain-haunts, has discarded all the tinsel pageantry of verse, and endeavoured (not in vain) to aggrandise the trivial and add the charm of novelty to the familiar. No one has shown the same imagination in raising trifles into importance: no one has displayed the same pathos in treating of the simplest feelings of the heart. Reserved, yet haughty, having no unruly or violent passions, (or those passions having been early suppressed,) Mr. Wordsworth has passed his life in solitary musing, or in daily converse with the face of nature. He exemplifies in an eminent degree the power of *association;* for his poetry has no other source or character. He has dwelt among pastoral scenes, till each object has become connected with a thousand feelings, a link in the chain of thought, a fibre of his own heart. Every one is by habit and familiarity strongly attached to the place of his birth, or to objects that recall the most pleasing and eventful circumstances of his life. But to the author of the *Lyrical Ballads,* nature is a kind of home; and he may be said to take a personal interest in the universe. There is no image so insignificant that it has not in some mood or other found the way into his heart: no sound that does not awaken the memory of other years.—

To him the meanest flower that blows can give
Thoughts that do often lie too deep for tears.

The daisy looks up to him with sparkling eye as an old acquaintance: the cuckoo haunts him with sounds of early youth not to be expressed: a linnet's nest startles him with boyish delight: an old withered thorn is weighed down with a heap of recollections: a grey cloak, seen on some wild moor, torn by the wind, or drenched in the rain, afterwards becomes an object of imagination to him: even the lichens on the rock have a life and being in his thoughts. He has described all these objects in a way and with an intensity of feeling that no one else had done before him, and has given a new view or aspect of nature. He is in this sense the most original poet now living, and the one whose writings could the least be spared: for they have no substitute elsewhere. The vulgar do not read them, the learned, who see all things through books, do not understand them, the great despise, the fashionable may ridicule them: but the author has created himself an interest in the heart of the retired and lonely student of nature, which can never die. Persons of this class will still continue to feel what he has felt: he has expressed what they might in vain wish to express, except with glistening eye and faultering tongue! There is a lofty philosophic tone, a thoughtful humanity, infused into his pastoral vein. Remote from the passions and events of the great world, he has communicated interest and dignity to the primal movements of the heart of man, and ingrafted his own conscious reactions on the casual thoughts of hinds and shepherds. Nursed amidst the grandeur of mountain scenery, he has stooped to have a nearer view of the daisy under his feet, or plucked a branch of white-thorn from the spray: but in describing it, his mind seems imbued with the majesty and solemnity of the objects around him—the tall rock lifts its head in the erectness of his spirit; the cataract roars in the sound of his verse; and in its dim and mysterious meaning, the mists seem to gather in the hollows of Helvellyn, and the forked Skiddaw hovers in the distance. There is little mention of mountainous scenery in Mr. Wordsworth's poetry; but by internal evidence one might be almost sure that it was written in a mountainous country, from its bareness, its simplicity, its loftiness and its depth!

His later philosophic productions have a somewhat different character. They are a departure from, a dereliction of his first principles. They are classical and courtly. They are polished in style, without being gaudy; dignified in subject, without affectation. They seem to have been composed not in a cottage at Grasmere, but among the half-inspired groves and stately recollections of Cole-Orton. We might allude in particular, for examples of what we mean, to the lines on a Picture by Claude Lorraine, and to the exquisite poem, entitled *Laodamia*. The last of these breathes

the pure spirit of the finest fragments of antiquity—the sweetness, the gravity, the strength, the beauty and the languor of death—

Calm contemplation and majestic pains.

Its glossy brilliancy arises from the perfection of the finishing, like that of careful sculpture, not from gaudy colouring—the texture of the thoughts has the smoothness and solidity of marble. It is a poem that might be read aloud in Elysium, and the spirits of departed heroes and sages would gather round to listen to it! Mr. Wordsworth's philosophic poetry, with a less glowing aspect and less tumult in the veins than Lord Byron's on similar occasions, bends a calmer and keener eye on mortality; the impression, if less vivid, is more pleasing and permanent; and we confess it (perhaps it is a want of taste and proper feeling) that there are lines and poems of our author's, that we think of ten times for once that we recur to any of Lord Byron's. Or if there are any of the latter's writings, that we can dwell upon in the same way, that is, as lasting and heart-felt sentiments, it is when laying aside his usual pomp and pretension, he descends with Mr. Wordsworth to the common ground of a disinterested humanity. It may be considered as characteristic of our poet's writings, that they either make no impression on the mind at all, seem mere *nonsense-verses*, or that they leave a mark behind them that never wears out. They either

Fall blunted from the indurated breast—

without any perceptible result, or they absorb it like a passion. To one class of readers he appears sublime, to another (and we fear the largest) ridiculous. He has probably realised Milton's wish,—"and fit audience found, though few"; but we suspect he is not reconciled to the alternative. There are delightful passages in the Excursion, both of natural description and of inspired reflection (passages of the latter kind that in the sound of the thoughts and of the swelling language resemble heavenly symphonies, mournful *requiems* over the grave of human hopes); but we must add, in justice and in sincerity, that we think it impossible that this work should ever become popular, even in the same degree as the *Lyrical Ballads*. It affects a system without having any intelligible clue to one; and instead of unfolding a principle in various and striking lights, repeats the same conclusions till they become flat and insipid. Mr. Wordsworth's mind is obtuse, except as it is the organ and the receptacle of accumulated feelings: it is not analytic, but synthetic; it is reflecting, rather than theoretical. The Excursion, we believe, fell still-born from the press. There was something abortive, and clumsy, and ill-judged in the attempt. It was long and laboured. The personages, for the most part, were low, the fare rustic: the plan raised expectations which were not fulfilled, and the effect was like being ushered into a stately hall and invited to sit down to a splendid banquet in the company of clowns, and with nothing but successive courses of apple-dumplings served up. It was not even *toujours perdrix!*

Mr. Wordsworth, in his person, is above the middle size, with marked features, and an air somewhat stately and Quixotic. He reminds one of some of Holbein's heads, grave, saturnine, with a slight indication of sly humour, kept under by the manners of the age or by the pretensions of the person. He has a peculiar sweetness in his smile, and great depth and manliness and a rugged harmony, in the tones of his voice. His manner of reading his own poetry is particularly imposing; and in his favourite passages his eye beams with preternatural lustre, and the meaning labours slowly up from his swelling breast. No one who has seen him at these moments could go away with an impression that he was a "man of no mark or likelihood." Perhaps the comment of his face and voice is necessary to convey a full idea of his poetry. His language may not be intelligible, but his manner is not to be mistaken. It is clear that he is either mad or inspired. In company, even in a *tête-à-tête*, Mr. Wordsworth is often silent, indolent, and reserved. If he is become verbose and oracular of late years, he was not so in his better days. He threw out a bold or an indifferent remark without either effort or pretension, and relapsed into musing again. He shone most (because he seemed most roused and animated) in reciting his own poetry, or in talking about it. He sometimes gave striking views of his feelings and trains of association in composing certain passages; or if one did not always understand his distinctions, still there was no want of interest—there was a latent meaning worth inquiring into, like a vein of ore that one cannot exactly hit upon at the moment,

but of which there are sure indications. His standard of poetry is high and severe, almost to exclusiveness. He admits of nothing below, scarcely of any thing above himself. It is fine to hear him talk of the way in which certain subjects should have been treated by eminent poets, according to his notions of the art. Thus he finds fault with Dryden's description of Bacchus in the *Alexander's Feast,* as if he were a mere good-looking youth, or boon companion—

> Flushed with a purple grace,
> He shows his honest face—

instead of representing the God returning from the conquest of India, crowned with vine-leaves, and drawn by panthers, and followed by troops of satyrs, of wild men and animals that he had tamed. You would think, in hearing him speak on this subject, that you saw Titian's picture of the meeting of *Bacchus and Ariadne* —so classic were his conceptions, so glowing his style. Milton is his great idol, and he sometimes dares to compare himself with him. His Sonnets, indeed, have something of the same high-raised tone and prophetic spirit. Chaucer is another prime favourite of his, and he has been at the pains to modernize some of the Canterbury Tales. Those persons who look upon Mr. Wordsworth as a merely puerile writer, must be rather at a loss to account for his strong predilection for such geniuses as Dante and Michael Angelo. We do not think our author has any very cordial sympathy with Shakespear. How should he? Shakespear was the least of an egotist of anybody in the world. He does not much relish the variety and scope of dramatic composition. "He hates those interlocutions between Lucius and Caius." Yet Mr. Wordsworth himself wrote a tragedy when he was young; and we have heard the following energetic lines quoted from it, as put into the mouth of a person smit with remorse for some rash crime:

> ———Action is momentary,
> The motion of a muscle this way or that;
> Suffering is long, obscure, and infinite!

Perhaps for want of light and shade, and the unshackled spirit of the drama, this performance was never brought forward. Our critic has a great dislike to Gray, and a fondness for Thomson and Collins. It is mortifying to hear him speak of Pope and Dryden, whom, because they have been supposed to have all the possible excellences of poetry, he will allow to have none. Nothing, however, can be fairer, or more amusing, than the way in which he sometimes exposes the unmeaning verbiage of modern poetry. Thus, in the beginning of Dr. Johnson's *Vanity of Human Wishes*—

> Let observation with extensive view
> Survey mankind from China to Peru—

he says there is a total want of imagination accompanying the words, the same idea is repeated three times under the disguise of a different phraseology: it comes to this—"let *observation,* with extensive *observation, observe* mankind"; or take away the first line, and the second,

> Survey mankind from China to Peru,

literally conveys the whole. Mr. Wordsworth is, we must say, a perfect Drawcansir as to prose writers. He complains of the dry reasoners and matter-of-fact people for their want of *passion;* and he is jealous of the rhetorical declaimers and rhapsodists as trenching on the province of poetry. He condemns all French writers (as well of poetry as prose) in the lump. His list in this way is indeed small. He approves of Walton's Angler, Paley, and some other writers of an inoffensive modesty of pretension. He also likes books of voyages and travels, and Robinson Crusoe. In art, he greatly esteems Bewick's woodcuts, and Waterloo's sylvan etchings. But he sometimes takes a higher tone, and gives his mind fair play. We have known him enlarge with a noble intelligence and enthusiasm on Nicolas Poussin's fine landscape-compositions, pointing out the unity of design that pervades them, the superintending mind, the imaginative principle that brings all to bear on the same end; and declaring he would not give a rush for any landscape that did not express the time of day, the climate, the period of the world it was meant to illustrate, or had not this character of *wholeness* in it. His eye also does justice to Rembrandt's fine and masterly effects. In the way in which that artist works something out of nothing, and transforms the stump of a tree, a common figure into an *ideal* object by the gorgeous light and shade thrown upon it, he perceives an analogy to his own mode of investing the minute details of nature with an atmosphere of sentiment; and in pronouncing Rembrandt to be a man of genius, feels that he strength-

ens his own claim to the title. It has been said of Mr. Wordsworth, that "he hates conchology, that he hates the Venus of Medicis." But these, we hope, are mere epigrams and *jeux-d'esprit,* as far from truth as they are free from malice; a sort of running satire or critical clenches—

> Where one for sense and one for rhyme
> Is quite sufficient at one time.

We think, however, that if Mr. Wordsworth had been a more liberal and candid critic, he would have been a more sterling writer. If a greater number of sources of pleasure had been open to him, he would have communicated pleasure to the world more frequently. Had he been less fastidious in pronouncing sentence on the works of others, his own would have been received more favourably, and treated more leniently. The current of his feelings is deep, but narrow; the range of his understanding is lofty and aspiring rather than discursive. The force, the originality, the absolute truth and identity with which he feels some things, makes him indifferent to so many others. The simplicity and enthusiasm of his feelings, with respect to nature, renders him bigotted and intolerant in his judgments of men and things. But it happens to him, as to others, that his strength lies in his weakness; and perhaps we have no right to complain. We might get rid of the cynic and the egotist, and find in his stead a common-place man. We should "take the good the Gods provide us": a fine and original vein of poetry is not one of their most contemptible gifts, and the rest is scarcely worth thinking of, except as it may be a mortification to those who expect perfection from human nature; or who have been idle enough at some period of their lives, to deify men of genius as possessing claims above it. But this is a chord that jars, and we shall not dwell upon it.

Lord Byron we have called, according to the old proverb, "the spoiled child of fortune": Mr. Wordsworth might plead, in mitigation of some peculiarities, that he is "the spoiled child of disappointment." We are convinced, if he had been early a popular poet, he would have borne his honours meekly, and would have been a person of great *bonhommie* and frankness of disposition. But the sense of injustice and of undeserved ridicule sours the temper and narrows the views. To have produced works of genius, and to find them neglected or treated with scorn, is one of the heaviest trials of human patience. We exaggerate our own merits when they are denied by others, and are apt to grudge and cavil at every particle of praise bestowed on those to whom we feel a conscious superiority. In mere self-defence we turn against the world, when it turns against us; brood over the undeserved slights we receive; and thus the genial current of the soul is stopped, or vents itself in effusions of petulance and self-conceit. Mr. Wordsworth has thought too much of contemporary critics and criticism; and less than he ought of the award of posterity, and of the opinion, we do not say of private friends, but of those who were made so by their admiration of his genius. He did not court popularity by a conformity to established models, and he ought not to have been surprised that his originality was not understood as a matter of course. He has *gnawed too much on the bridle;* and has often thrown out crusts to the critics, in mere defiance or as a point of honour when he was challenged, which otherwise his own good sense would have withheld. We suspect that Mr. Wordsworth's feelings are a little morbid in this respect, or that he resents censure more than he is gratified by praise. Otherwise, the tide has turned much in his favour of late years—he has a large body of determined partisans—and is at present sufficiently in request with the public to save or relieve him from the last necessity to which a man of genius can be reduced—that of becoming the God of his own idolatry!

SIR WALTER SCOTT

SIR WALTER SCOTT is undoubtedly the most popular writer of the age—the "lord of the ascendant" for the time being. He is just half what the human intellect is capable of being: if you take the universe, and divide it into two parts, he knows all that it *has been;* and all that it *is to be* is nothing to him. His is a mind brooding over antiquity—scorning "the present ignorant time." He is "laudator temporis acti"—a *"prophesier* of things past." The old world is to him a crowded map; the new one a dull, hateful blank. He dotes on all well-authenticated superstitions; he shudders at the shadow of innovation. His retentiveness of memory, his accumulated weight of interested prejudice or romantic association have overlaid his other faculties. The cells of his memory are vast, various, full even to bursting with life and motion; his speculative understanding is empty, flaccid, poor, and dead. His mind receives and treasures up every thing brought to it by tradition or custom—it does not project itself beyond this into the world unknown, but mechanically shrinks back as from the edge of a precipice. The land of pure reason is to his apprehension like *Van Dieman's Land;*—barren, miserable, distant, a place of exile, the dreary abode of savages, convicts, and adventurers. Sir Walter would make a bad hand of a description of the *Millennium,* unless he could lay the scene in Scotland five hundred years ago, and then he would want facts and worm-eaten parchments to support his drooping style. Our historical novelist firmly thinks that nothing *is* but what *has been*—that the moral world stands still, as the material one was supposed to do of old—and that we can never get beyond the point where we actually are without utter destruction, though every thing changes and will change from what it was three hundred years ago to what it is now, —from what it is now to all that the bigoted admirer of the good old times most dreads and hates!

It is long since we read, and long since we thought of our author's poetry. It would probably have gone out of date with the immediate occasion, even if he himself had not contrived to banish it from our recollection. It is not to be denied that it had great merit, both of an obvious and intrinsic kind. It abounded in vivid descriptions, in spirited action, in smooth and flowing versification. But it wanted *character.* It was "poetry of no mark or likelihood." It slid out of the mind as soon as read, like a river; and would have been forgotten, but that the public curiosity was fed with ever new supplies from the same teeming liquid source. It is not every man that can write six quarto volumes in verse, that are caught up with avidity, even by fastidious judges. But what a difference between *their* popularity and that of the Scotch Novels! It is true, the public read and admired the *Lay of the Last Minstrel, Marmion,* and so on, and each individual was contented to read and admire because the public did so: but with regard to the prose-works of the same (supposed) author, it is quite *another-guess* sort of thing. Here every one stands forward to applaud on his own ground, would be thought to go before the public opinion, is eager to extol his favourite characters louder, to understand them better than every body else, and has his own scale of comparative excellence for each work, supported by nothing but his own enthusiastic and fearless convictions. It must be amusing to the *Author of Waverley* to hear his readers and admirers (and are not these the same thing? [1]) quarrelling which of his novels is the best, opposing character to character, quoting passage against passage, striving to surpass each other in the extravagance of their encomiums, and yet unable to settle the precedence, or to do the author's writings justice—so various, so equal, so transcendent are their merits! His volumes of poetry were received as fashionable and well-dressed acquaintances: we are ready to tear the others in pieces as old friends. There was something meretricious in Sir Walter's ballad-rhymes; and like those who keep opera *figurantes,* we were willing to have our admiration shared, and our taste confirmed by the town: but the Novels are like the betrothed of our hearts, bone of our bone, and flesh of our flesh, and we are jealous that any one should be as much delighted or as thoroughly acquainted with their beauties as ourselves. For which of his poetical heroines would the reader break a lance so soon as for Jeanie Deans? What *Lady of the Lake* can compare with the beautiful Rebecca? We believe the late Mr. John Scott went to his death-bed (though a painful and premature one) with some degree of satisfaction, inasmuch as he had penned the most elaborate panegyric on the *Scotch Novels* that had as yet appeared!—The *Epics* are not poems, so much as metrical romances. There is a glittering veil of verse thrown over the features of nature and of old romance. The deep incisions into character are "skinned and filmed over"—the details are lost or shaped into flimsy and insipid decorum; and the truth of feeling and of circumstance is trans-

lated into a tinkling sound, a tinsel *commonplace.* It must be owned, there is a power in true poetry that lifts the mind from the ground of reality to a higher sphere, that penetrates the inert, scattered, incoherent materials presented to it, and by a force and inspiration of its own, melts and moulds them into sublimity and beauty. But Sir Walter (we contend, under correction) has not this creative impulse, this plastic power, this capacity of reacting on his first impressions. He is a learned, a literal, *a matter-of-fact* expounder of truth or fable: [2] he does not soar above and look down upon his subject, imparting his own lofty views and feelings to his descriptions of nature—he relies upon it, is raised by it, is one with it, or he is nothing. A poet is essentially a *maker;* that is, he must atone for what he loses in individuality and local resemblance by the energies and resources of his own mind. The writer of whom we speak is deficient in these last. He has either not the faculty or not the will to impregnate his subject by an effort of pure invention. The execution also is much upon a par with the more ephemeral effusions of the press. It is light, agreeable, effeminate, diffuse. Sir Walter's Muse is a *Modern Antique.* The smooth, glossy texture of his verse contrasts happily with the quaint, uncouth, rugged materials of which it is composed; and takes away any appearance of heaviness or harshness from the body of local traditions and obsolete costume. We see grim knights and iron armour; but then they are woven in silk with a careless, delicate hand, and have the softness of flowers. The poet's figures might be compared to old tapestries copied on the finest velvet:—they are not like Raphael's *Cartoons,* but they are very like Mr. Westall's drawings, which accompany, and are intended to illustrate them. This facility and grace of execution is the more remarkable, as a story goes that not long before the appearance of the *Lay of the Last Minstrel* Sir Walter (then Mr.) Scott, having, in the company of a friend, to cross the Frith of Forth in a ferry-boat, they proposed to beguile the time by writing a number of verses on a given subject, and that at the end of an hour's hard study, they found they had produced only six lines between them. "It is plain," said the unconscious author to his fellow-labourer, "that you and I need never think of getting our living by writ-

[1] No! For we met with a young lady who kept a circulating library and a milliner's shop, in a watering-place in the country, who, when we inquired for the *Scotch Novels,* spoke indifferently about them, said they were "so dry she could hardly get through them," and recommended us to read *Agnes.* We never thought of it before; but we would venture to lay a wager that there are many other young ladies in the same situation, and who think "Old Mortality" "dry."

[2] Just as Cobbett is a matter-of-fact reasoner.

ing poetry!" In a year or so after this, he set to work, and poured out quarto upon quarto, as if they had been drops of water. As to the rest, and compared with true and great poets, our Scottish Minstrel is but "a metre ballad-monger." We would rather have written one song of Burns, or a single passage in Lord Byron's *Heaven and Earth,* or one of Wordsworth's "fancies and good-nights," than all his epics. What is he to Spenser, over whose immortal, ever-amiable verse beauty hovers and trembles, and who has shed the purple light of Fancy, from his ambrosial wings, over all nature? What is there of the might of Milton, whose head is canopied in the blue serene, and who takes us to sit with him there? What is there (in his ambling rhymes) of the deep pathos of Chaucer? Or of the o'er-informing power of Shakespeare, whose eye, watching alike the minutest traces of characters and the strongest movements of passion, "glances from heaven to earth, from earth to heaven," and with the lambent flame of genius, playing round each object, lights up the universe in a robe of its own radiance? Sir Walter has no voluntary power of combination: all his associations (as we said before) are those of habit or of tradition. He is a mere narrative and descriptive poet, garrulous of the old time. The definition of his poetry is a pleasing superficiality.

Not so of his Novels and Romances. There we turn over a new leaf—another and the same—the same in matter, but in form, in power how different! The author of Waverley has got rid of the tagging of rhymes, the eking out of syllables, the supplying of epithets, the colours of style, the grouping of his characters, and the regular march of events, and comes to the point at once, and strikes at the heart of his subject, without dismay and without disguise. His poetry was a lady's waiting-maid, dressed out in cast-off finery: his prose is a beautiful, rustic nymph, that, like Dorothea in Don Quixote, when she is surprised with dishevelled tresses bathing her naked feet in the brook, looks round her, abashed at the admiration her charms have excited! The grand secret of the author's success in these latter productions is that he has completely got rid of the trammels of authorship; and torn off at one rent (as Lord Peter got rid of so many yards of lace in the *Tale of a Tub*) all the ornaments of fine writing and worn-out sentimentality. All is fresh, as from the hand

of nature: by going a century or two back and laying the scene in a remote and uncultivated district, all becomes new and startling in the present advanced period.—Highland manners, characters, scenery, superstitions, Northern dialect and costume, the wars, the religion, and politics of the sixteenth and seventeenth centuries, give a charming and wholesome relief to the fastidious refinement and "over-laboured lassitude" of modern readers, like the effect of plunging a nervous valetudinarian into a cold-bath. The *Scotch Novels,* for this reason, are not so much admired in Scotland as in England. The contrast, the transition is less striking. From the top of the Calton Hill, the inhabitants of "Auld Reekie" can descry, or fancy they descry the peaks of Ben Lomond and the waving outline of Rob Roy's country: we who live at the southern extremity of the island can only catch a glimpse of the billowy scene in the descriptions of the Author of Waverley. The mountain air is most bracing to our languid nerves, and it is brought us in ship-loads from the neighbourhood of Abbot's-Ford. There is another circumstance to be taken into the account. In Edinburgh there is a little opposition and something of the spirit of cabal between the partisans of works proceeding from Mr. Constable's and Mr. Blackwood's shops. Mr. Constable gives the highest prices; but being the Whig bookseller, it is grudged that he should do so. An attempt is therefore made to transfer a certain share of popularity to the second-rate Scotch novels, "the embryo fry, the little airy of *ricketty* children" issuing through Mr. Blackwood's shop-door. This operates a diversion, which does not affect us here. The Author of Waverley wears the palm of legendary lore alone. Sir Walter may, indeed, surfeit us: his imitators make us sick! It may be asked, it has been asked, "Have we no materials for romance in England? Must we look to Scotland for a supply of whatever is original and striking in this kind?" And we answer—"Yes!" Every foot of soil is with us worked up: nearly every movement of the social machine is calculable. We have no room left for violent catastrophes; for grotesque quaintnesses; for wizard spells. The last skirts of ignorance and barbarism are seen hovering (in Sir Walter's pages) over the Border. We have, it is true, gipsies in this country as well as at the Cairn of Derncleugh: but they live under clipped hedges, and repose in camp-beds, and do not perch on crags, like eagles, or take shelter, like sea-mews, in basaltic subterranean caverns. We have heaths with rude heaps of stones upon them: but no existing superstition converts them into the Geese of Micklestane-Moor, or sees a Black Dwarf groping among them. We have sects in religion: but the only thing sublime or ridiculous in that way is Mr. Irving, the Caledonian preacher, who "comes like a satyr staring from the woods, and yet speaks like an orator!" We had a Parson Adams not quite a hundred years ago—a Sir Roger de Coverley rather more than a hundred! Even Sir Walter is ordinarily obliged to pitch his angle (strong as the hook is) a hundred miles to the North of the "Modern Athens" or a century back. His last work,[1] indeed, is mystical, is romantic in nothing but the title-page. Instead of "a holy-water sprinkle dipped in dew," he has given us a fashionable watering-place—and we see what he had made of it. He must not come down from his fastnesses in traditional barbarism and native rusticity; the level, the littleness, the frippery of modern civilization will undo him as it has undone us!

Sir Walter has found out (oh, rare discovery) that facts are better than fiction; that there is no romance like the romance of real life; and that if we can but arrive at what men feel, do, and say in striking and singular situations, the result will be "more lively, audible, and full of vent," than the fine-spun cobwebs of the brain. With reverence be it spoken, he is like the man who having to imitate the squeaking of a pig upon the stage, brought the animal under his coat with him. Our author has conjured up the actual people he has to deal with, or as much as he could get of them, in "their habits as they lived." He has ransacked old chronicles, and poured the contents upon his page; he has squeezed out musty records; he has consulted wayfaring pilgrims, bed-rid sibyls; he has invoked the spirits of the air; he has conversed with the living and the dead, and let them tell their story their own way; and by borrowing of others, has enriched his own genius with everlasting variety, truth, and freedom. He has taken his materials from the original, authentic sources, in large concrete masses, and not tampered with or too much frittered them away. He is only the amanuensis of truth and

[1] St. Ronan's Well.

history. It is impossible to say how fine his writings in consequence are, unless we could describe how fine nature is. All that portion of the history of his country that he has touched upon (wide as the scope is) the manners, the personages, the events, the scenery, lives over again in his volumes. Nothing is wanting—the illusion is complete. There is a hurtling in the air, a trampling of feet upon the ground, as these perfect representations of human character or fanciful belief come thronging back upon our imaginations. We will merely recall a few of the subjects of his pencil to the reader's recollection; for nothing we could add, by way of note or commendation, could make the impression more vivid.

There is (first and foremost, because the earliest of our acquaintance) the Baron of Bradwardine, stately, kind-hearted, whimsical, pedantic; and Flora MacIvor (whom even we forgive for her Jacobitism), the fierce Vich Ian Vohr, and Evan Dhu, constant in death, and Davie Gellatly roasting his eggs or turning his rhymes with restless volubility, and the two stag-hounds that met Waverley, as fine as ever Titian painted, or Paul Veronese:—then there is old Balfour of Burley, brandishing his sword and his Bible with fire-eyed fury, trying a fall with the insolent, gigantic Bothwell at the 'Changehouse, and vanquishing him at the noble battle of Loudon-hill; there is Bothwell himself, drawn to the life, proud, cruel, selfish, profligate, but with the love-letters of the gentle Alice (written thirty years before), and his verses to her memory, found in his pocket after his death: in the same volume of *Old Mortality* is that lone figure, like a figure in Scripture, of the woman sitting on the stone at the turning to the mountain, to warn Burley that there is a lion in his path; and the fawning Claverhouse, beautiful as a panther, smooth-looking, blood-spotted; and the fanatics, Macbriar and Mucklewrath, crazed with zeal and sufferings; and the inflexible Morton and the faithful Edith, who refused to "give her hand to another while her heart was with her lover in the deep and dead sea." And in *The Heart of Mid Lothian* we have Effie Deans (that sweet, faded flower) and Jeanie her more than sister, and old David Deans, the patriarch of St. Leonard's Crags, and Butler, and Dumbiedikes, eloquent in his silence, and Mr. Bartoline Saddle-tree and his prudent helpmate, and Porteous swinging in the wind, and Madge Wildfire, full of finery and madness, and her ghastly mother.—Again, there is Meg Merrilies, standing on her rock, stretched on her bier with "her head to the east," and Dirk Hatterick (equal to Shakespear's Master Barnardine), and Glossin, the soul of an attorney, and Dandy Dinmont, with his terrier-pack and his pony Dumple, and the fiery Colonel Mannering, and the modish old counsellor Pleydell, and Dominie Sampson,[1] and Rob Roy (like the eagle in his eyry), and Baillie Nicol Jarvie, and the inimitable Major Galbraith, and Rashleigh Osbaldistone, and Die Vernon, the best of secret-keepers; and in the *Antiquary*, the ingenious and abstruse Mr. Jonathan Oldbuck, and the old beadsman Edie Ochiltree, and that preternatural figure of old Edith Elspeith, a living shadow, in whom the lamp of life had been long extinguished, had it not been fed by remorse and "thick-coming" recollections; and that striking picture of the effects of feudal tyranny and fiendish pride, the unhappy Earl of Glenallan; and the Black Dwarf, and his friend Habby of the Heughfoot (the cheerful hunter), and his cousin Grace Armstrong, fresh and laughing like the morning; and the *Children of the Mist*, and the baying of the blood-hound that tracks their steps at a distance (the hollow echoes are in our ears now), and Amy and her hapless love, and the villain Varney, and the deep voice of George of Douglas—and the immoveable Balafre, and Master Oliver the Barber in Quentin Durward—and the quaint humour of the Fortunes of Nigel, and the comic spirit of Peveril of the Peak—and the fine old English romance of Ivanhoe. What a list of names! What a host of associations! What a thing is human life! What a power is that of genius! What a world of thought and feelings is thus rescued from oblivion! How many hours of heartfelt satisfaction has our author given to the gay and thoughtless! How many sad hearts has he soothed in pain and solitude! It is no wonder that the public repay with lengthened applause and gratitude the pleasure they receive. He writes as fast as they can read, and he does not write himself down. He is always in the public eye, and we do not tire of him. His worst is better than any other person's best. His *back-grounds* (and his later works

[1] Perhaps the finest scene in all these novels, is that where the Dominie meets his pupil, Miss Lucy, the morning after her brother's arrival.

are little else but back-grounds capitally made out) are more attractive than the principal figures and most complicated actions of other writers. His works (taken together) are almost like a new edition of human nature. This is indeed to be an author!

The political bearing of the *Scotch Novels* has been a considerable recommendation to them. They are a relief to the mind, rarefied as it has been with modern philosophy, and heated with ultra-radicalism. At a time also, when we bid fair to revive the principles of the Stuarts, it is interesting to bring us acquainted with their persons and misfortunes. The candour of Sir Walter's historic pen levels our bristling prejudices on this score, and sees fair play between Roundheads and Cavaliers, between Protestant and Papist. He is a writer reconciling all the diversities of human nature to the reader. He does not enter into the distinctions of hostile sects or parties, but treats of the strength or the infirmity of the human mind, of the virtues or vices of the human breast, as they are to be found blended in the whole race of mankind. Nothing can show more handsomely or be more gallantly executed. There was a talk at one time that our author was about to take Guy Faux for the subject of one of his novels, in order to put a more liberal and human construction on the Gunpowder Plot than our "No Popery" prejudices have hitherto permitted. Sir Walter is a professed *clarifier* of the age from the vulgar and still lurking old-English antipathy to Popery and Slavery. Through some odd process of *servile* logic, it should seem, that in restoring the claims of the Stuarts by the courtesy of romance, the House of Brunswick are more firmly seated in point of fact, and the Bourbons, by collateral reasoning, become legitimate! In any other point of view, we cannot possibly conceive how Sir Walter imagines "he has done something to revive the declining spirit of loyalty" by these novels. His loyalty is founded on *would-be* treason: he props the actual throne by the shadow of rebellion. Does he really think of making us enamoured of the "good old times" by the faithful and harrowing portraits he has drawn of them? Would he carry us back to the early stages of barbarism, of clanship, of the feudal system as "a consummation devoutly to be wished"? Is he infatuated enough, or does he so dote and drivel over his own slothful and self-willed prejudices,

as to believe that he will make a single convert to the beauty of Legitimacy, that is, of
lawless power and savage bigotry, when he himself is obliged to apologise for the horrors he
describes, and even render his descriptions cred- 5
ible to the modern reader by referring to the
authentic history of these delectable times? [1]
He is indeed so besotted as to the moral of his
own story, that he has even the blindness to
go out of his way to have a fling at *flints* and 10
dungs (the contemptible ingredients, as he
would have us believe, of a modern rabble) at
the very time when he is describing a mob of
the twelfth century—a mob (one should think)
after the writer's own heart, without one par- 15
ticle of modern philosophy or revolutionary
politics in their composition, who were to a
man, to a hair, just what priests, and kings, and
nobles *let* them be, and who were collected to
witness (a spectacle proper to the times) the 20
burning of the lovely Rebecca at a stake for
a sorceress, because she was a Jewess, beautiful and innocent, and the consequent victim

[1] "And here we cannot but think it necessary
to offer some better proof than the incidents of
an idle tale, to vindicate the melancholy representation of manners which has been just laid
before the reader. It is grievous to think that
those valiant Barons, to whose stand against the
crown the liberties of England were indebted for
their existence, should themselves have been such
dreadful oppressors, and capable of excesses, contrary not only to the laws of England, but to
those of nature and humanity. But alas! we have
only to extract from the industrious Henry one
of those numerous passages which he has collected from contemporary historians, to prove
that fiction itself can hardly reach the dark reality
of the horrors of the period.
"The description given by the author of the
Saxon Chronicle of the cruelties exercised in the
reign of King Stephen by the great barons and
lords of castles, who were all Normans, affords a
strong proof of the excesses of which they were
capable when their passions were inflamed. 'They
grievously oppressed the poor people by building
castles; and when they were built, they filled
them with wicked men or rather devils, who
seized both men and women who they imagined
had any money, threw them into prison, and put
them to more cruel tortures than the martyrs
ever endured. They suffocated some in mud, and
suspended others by the feet, or the head, or the
thumbs, kindling fires below them. They squeezed
the heads of some with knotted cords till they
pierced their brains, while they threw others into
dungeons swarming with serpents, snakes, and
toads.' But it would be cruel to put the reader to
the pain of perusing the remainder of the description."—*Henry's Hist.* edit. 1805, **vol. vii.** p.
346.

of insane bigotry and unbridled profligacy.
And it is at this moment (when the heart is
kindled and bursting with indignation at the
revolting abuses of self-constituted power)
that Sir Walter *stops the press* to have a sneer
at the people, and to put a spoke (as he thinks)
in the wheel of upstart innovation! This is
what he "calls backing his friends"—it is thus
he administers charms and philtres to our love
of Legitimacy, makes us conceive a horror of
all reform, civil, political, or religious, and
would fain put down the *Spirit of the Age.*
The author of Waverley might just as well get
up and make a speech at a dinner at Edinburgh, abusing Mr. Mac-Adam for his improvements in the roads, on the ground that
they were nearly *impassable* in many places
"sixty years since"; or object to Mr. Peel's
Police-Bill, by insisting that Hounslow-Heath
was formerly a scene of greater interest and
terror to highwaymen and travellers, and cut
a greater figure in the Newgate Calendar than
it does at present.—Oh! Wickliff, Luther,
Hampden, Sidney, Somers, mistaken Whigs,
and thoughtless Reformers in religion and
politics, and all ye, whether poets or philosophers, heroes or sages, inventors of arts or
sciences, patriots, benefactors of the human
race, enlighteners and civilisers of the world,
who have (so far) reduced opinion to reason,
and power to law, who are the cause that we
no longer burn witches and heretics at slow
fires, that the thumb-screws are no longer applied by ghastly, smiling judges, to extort confession of imputed crimes from sufferers for
conscience sake; that men are no longer strung
up like acorns on trees without judge or jury,
or hunted like wild beasts through thickets
and glens, who have abated the cruelty of
priests, the pride of nobles, the divinity of
kings in former times; to whom we owe it,
that we no longer wear round our necks the
collar of Gurth the swineherd, and of Wamba
the jester; that the castles of great lords are
no longer the dens of banditti, from whence
they issue with fire and sword, to lay waste
the land; that we no longer expire in loathsome
dungeons without knowing the cause, or have
our right hands struck off for raising them in
self-defence against wanton insult; that we can
sleep without fear of being burnt in our beds,
or travel without making our wills; that no
Amy Robsarts are thrown down trap-doors by
Richard Varneys with impunity; that no Red

Reiver of Westburn-Flat sets fire to peaceful cottages; that no Claverhouse signs cold-blooded death-warrants in sport; that we have no Tristan the Hermit, or Petit-André, crawling near us, like spiders, and making our flesh creep, and our hearts sicken within us at every moment of our lives—ye who have produced this change in the face of nature and society, return to earth once more, and beg pardon of Sir Walter and his patrons, who sigh at not being able to undo all that you have done! Leaving this question, there are two other remarks which we wished to make on the Novels. The one was, to express our admiration of the good-nature of the mottos, in which the author has taken occasion to remember and quote almost every living author (whether illustrious or obscure) but himself—an indirect argument in favour of the general opinion as to the source from which they spring—and the other was, to hint our astonishment at the innumerable and incessant instances of bad and slovenly English in them, more, we believe, than in any other works now printed. We should think the writer could not possibly read the manuscript after he has once written it, or overlook the press.

If there were a writer, who "born for the universe"—

——Narrow'd his mind,
And to party gave up what was meant for mankind—

who, from the height of his genius looking abroad into nature, and scanning the recesses of the human heart, "winked and shut his apprehension up" to every thought or purpose that tended to the future good of mankind—who, raised by affluence, the reward of successful industry, and by the voice of fame above the want of any but the most honourable patronage, stooped to the unworthy arts of adulation, and abetted the views of the great with the pettifogging feelings of the meanest dependant on office—who, having secured the admiration of the public (with the probable reversion of immortality), showed no respect for himself, for that genius that had raised him to distinction, for that nature which he trampled under foot—who, amiable, frank, friendly, manly in private life, was seized with the dotage of age and the fury of a woman, the instant politics were concerned—who reserved all his candour and comprehensiveness of view for history, and vented his littleness, pique,

resentment, bigotry, and intolerance on his contemporaries—who took the wrong side, and defended it by unfair means—who, the moment his own interest or the prejudices of others interfered, seemed to forget all that was due to the pride of intellect, to the sense of manhood—who, praised, admired by men of all parties alike, repaid the public liberality by striking a secret and envenomed blow at the reputation of every one who was not the ready tool of power—who strewed the slime of rankling malice and mercenary scorn over the bud and promise of genius, because it was not fostered in the hot-bed of corruption, or warped by the trammels of servility—who supported the worst abuses of authority in the worst spirit—who joined a gang of desperadoes to spread calumny, contempt, infamy, wherever they were merited by honesty or talent on a different side—who officiously undertook to decide public questions by private insinuations, to prop the throne by nicknames, and the altar by lies—who being (by common consent), the finest, the most humane and accomplished writer of his age, associated himself with and encouraged the lowest panders of a venal press; deluging, nauseating the public mind with the offal and garbage of Billingsgate abuse and vulgar *slang;* showing no remorse, no relent-ing or compassion towards the victims of this nefarious and organized system of party-proscription, carried on under the mask of literary criticism and fair discussion, insulting the misfortunes of some, and trampling on the early grave of others—

Who would not grieve if such a man there be?
Who would not weep if Atticus were he?

But we believe there is no other age or country of the world (but ours), in which such genius could have been so degraded!

LORD BYRON

LORD BYRON and Sir Walter Scott are among writers now living [1] the two, who would carry away a majority of suffrages as the greatest geniuses of the age. The former would, perhaps, obtain the preference with the fine gentlemen and ladies (squeamishness apart)—the latter with the critics and the vulgar. We shall treat of them in the same connection, partly

[1] This Essay was written just before Lord Byron's death.

on account of their distinguished pre-eminence, and partly because they afford a complete contrast to each other. In their poetry, in their prose, in their politics, and in their tempers, no two men can be more unlike.

If Sir Walter Scott may be thought by some to have been

> Born universal heir to all humanity,

it is plain Lord Byron can set up no such pretension. He is, in a striking degree, the creature of his own will. He holds no communion with his kind; but stands alone, without mate or fellow—

> As if a man were author of himself,
> And owned no other kin.

He is like a solitary peak, all access to which is cut off not more by elevation than distance. He is seated on a lofty eminence, "cloud-capt," or reflecting the last rays of setting suns; and in his poetical moods, reminds us of the fabled Titans, retired to a ridgy steep, playing on their Pan's-pipes, and taking up ordinary men and things in their hands with haughty indifference. He raises his subject to himself, or tramples on it; he neither stoops to, no loses himself in it. He exists not by sympathy, but by antipathy. He scorns all things, even himself. Nature must come to him to sit for her picture—he does not go to her. She must consult his time, his convenience, and his humour; and wear a *sombre* or a fantastic garb, or his Lordship turns his back upon her. There is no ease, no unaffected simplicity of manner, no "golden mean." All is strained, or petulant in the extreme. His thoughts are sphered and crystalline; his style "prouder than when blue Iris bends"; his spirit fiery, impatient, wayward, indefatigable. Instead of taking his impressions from without, in entire and almost unimpaired masses, he moulds them according to his own temperament, and heats the materials of his imagination in the furnace of his passions.—Lord Byron's verse glows like a flame, consuming every thing in its way; Sir Walter Scott's glides like a river, clear, gentle, harmless. The poetry of the first scorches, that of the last scarcely warms. The light of the one proceeds from an internal source, ensanguined, sullen, fixed; the other's reflects the hues of Heaven, or the face of nature, glancing vivid and various. The productions of the Northern Bard have the rust and the fresh-ness of antiquity about them; those of the Noble Poet cease to startle from their extreme ambition of novelty, both in style and matter. Sir Walter's rhymes are "silly sooth"—

> And dally with the innocence of thought,
> Like the old age—

his Lordship's Muse spurns *the olden time,* and affects all the supercilious airs of a modern fine lady and an upstart. The object of the one writer is to restore us to truth and nature: the other chiefly thinks how he shall display his own power, or vent his spleen, or astonish the reader either by starting new subjects and trains of speculation, or by expressing old ones in a more striking and emphatic manner than they have been expressed before. He cares little what it is he says, so that he can say it differently from others. This may account for the charges of plagiarism which have been repeatedly brought against the Noble Poet—if he can borrow an image or sentiment from another, and heighten it by an epithet or an allusion of greater force and beauty than is to be found in the original passage, he thinks he shows his superiority of execution in this in a more marked manner than if the first suggestion had been his own. It is not the value of the observation itself he is solicitous about; but he wishes to shine by contrast—even nature only serves as a foil to set off his style. He therefore takes the thoughts of others (whether contemporaries or not) out of their mouths, and is content to make them his own, to set his stamp upon them, by imparting to them a more meretricious gloss, a higher relief, a greater loftiness of tone, and a characteristic inveteracy of purpose. Even in those collateral ornaments of modern style, slovenliness, abruptness, and eccentricity (as well as in terseness and significance), Lord Byron, when he pleases, defies competition and surpasses all his contemporaries. Whatever he does, he must do in a more decided and daring manner than any one else—he lounges with extravagance, and yawns so as to alarm the reader! Self-will, passion, the love of singularity, a disdain of himself and of others (with a conscious sense that this is among the ways and means of procuring admiration) are the proper categories of his mind: he is a lordly writer, is above his own reputation, and condescends to the Muses with a scornful grace!

Lord Byron, who in his politics is a *liberal,*

in his genius is haughty and aristocratic: Walter Scott, who is an aristocrat in principle, is popular in his writings, and is (as it were) equally *servile* to nature and to opinion. The genius of Sir Walter is essentially imitative, or "denotes a foregone conclusion": that of Lord Byron is self-dependent; or at least requires no aid, is governed by no law, but the impulses of its own will. We confess, however much we may admire independence of feeling and erectness of spirit in general or practical questions, yet in works of genius we prefer him who bows to the authority of nature, who appeals to actual objects, to mouldering superstitions, to history, observation, and tradition, before him who only consults the pragmatical and restless workings of his own breast, and gives them out as oracles to the world. We like a writer (whether poet or prose-writer) who takes in (or is willing to take in) the range of half the universe in feeling, character, description, much better than we do one who obstinately and invariably shuts himself up in the Bastile of his own ruling passions. In short, we had rather be Sir Walter Scott (meaning thereby the Author of Waverley) than Lord Byron, a hundred times over. And for the reason just given, namely, that he casts his descriptions in the mould of nature, ever-varying, never tiresome, always interesting and always instructive, instead of casting them constantly in the mould of his own individual impressions. He gives us man as he is, or as he was, in almost every variety of situation, action, and feeling. Lord Byron makes man after his own image, woman after his own heart; the one is a capricious tyrant, the other a yielding slave; he gives us the misanthrope and the voluptuary by turns; and with these two characters, burning or melting in their own fires, he makes out everlasting centos of himself. He hangs the cloud, the film of his existence over all outward things —sits in the centre of his thoughts, and enjoys dark night, bright day, the glitter and the gloom "in cell monastic"—we see the mournful pall, the crucifix, the death's heads, the faded chaplet of flowers, the gleaming tapers, the agonized brow of genius, the wasted form of beauty—but we are still imprisoned in a dungeon, a curtain intercepts our view, we do not breathe freely the air of nature or of our own thoughts—the other admired author draws aside the curtain, and the veil of egotism is rent, and he shows us the crowd of living men and women, the endless groups, the landscape back-ground, the cloud and the rainbow, and enriches our imaginations and relieves one passion by another, and expands and lightens reflection, and takes away that tightness at the breast which arises from thinking or wishing to think that there is nothing in the world out of a man's self!—In this point of view, the Author of Waverley is one of the greatest teachers of morality that ever lived, by emancipating the mind from petty, narrow, and bigotted prejudices: Lord Byron is the greatest pamperer of those prejudices, by seeming to think there is nothing else worth encouraging but the seeds or the full luxuriant growth of dogmatism and self-conceit. In reading the *Scotch Novels,* we never think about the author, except from a feeling of curiosity respecting our unknown benefactor: in reading Lord Byron's works, he himself is never absent from our minds. The colouring of Lord Byron's style, however rich and dipped in Tyrian dyes, is nevertheless opaque, is in itself an object of delight and wonder: Sir Walter Scott's is perfectly transparent. In studying the one, you seem to gaze at the figures cut in stained glass, which exclude the view beyond, and where the pure light of Heaven is only a means of setting off the gorgeousness of art: in reading the other, you look through a noble window at the clear and varied landscape without. Or to sum up the distinction in one word, Sir Walter Scott is the most *dramatic* writer now living; and Lord Byron is the least so. It would be difficult to imagine that the Author of Waverley is in the smallest degree a pedant; as it would be hard to persuade ourselves that the author of Childe Harold and Don Juan is not a coxcomb, though a provoking and sublime one. In this decided preference given to Sir Walter Scott over Lord Byron, we distinctly include the prose-works of the former; for we do not think his poetry alone by any means entitles him to that precedence. Sir Walter in his poetry, though pleasing and natural, is a comparative trifler: it is in his anonymous productions that he has shown himself for what he is!—

Intensity is the great and prominent distinction of Lord Byron's writings. He seldom gets beyond force of style, nor has he produced any regular work or masterly whole. He does not prepare any plan beforehand, nor revise and retouch what he has written with polished accuracy. His only object seems to be to stimulate himself and his readers for the moment—to keep both alive, to drive away *ennui*, to substitute a feverish and irritable state of excitement for listless indolence or even calm enjoyment. For this purpose he pitches on any subject at random without much thought or delicacy—he is only impatient to begin—and takes care to adorn and enrich it as he proceeds with "thoughts that breathe and words that burn." He composes (as he himself has said) whether he is in the bath, in his study, or on horseback—he writes as habitually as others talk or think—and whether we have the inspiration of the Muse or not, we always find the spirit of the man of genius breathing from his verse. He grapples with his subject, and moves, penetrates, and animates it by the electric force of his own feelings. He is often monotonous, extravagant, offensive; but he is never dull, or tedious, but when he writes prose. Lord Byron does not exhibit a new view of nature, or raise insignificant objects into importance by the romantic associations with which he surrounds them; but generally (at least) takes commonplace thoughts and events and endeavours to express them in stronger and statelier language than others. His poetry stands like a Martello tower by the side of his subject. He does not, like Mr. Wordsworth, lift poetry from the ground, or create a sentiment out of nothing. He does not describe a daisy or a periwinkle, but the cedar or the cypress: not "poor men's cottages, but princes' palaces." His *Childe Harold* contains a lofty and impassioned review of the great events of history, of the mighty objects left as wrecks of time, but he dwells chiefly on what is familiar to the mind of every schoolboy; has brought out few new traits of feeling or thought; and has done no more than justice to the reader's preconceptions by the sustained force and brilliancy of his style and imagery.

Lord Byron's earlier productions, *Lara*, the *Corsair*, &c. were wild and gloomy romances, put into rapid and shining verse. They discover the madness of poetry, together with the inspiration: sullen, moody, capricious, fierce, inexorable, gloating on beauty, thirsting for revenge, hurrying from the extremes of pleasure to pain, but with nothing permanent, nothing healthy or natural. The gaudy decorations and the morbid sentiments remind one of flowers strewed over the face of death! In his *Childe Harold* (as has been just observed) he assumes a lofty and philosophic tone, and "reasons high of providence, fore-knowledge, will, and fate." He takes the highest points in the history of the world, and comments on them from a more commanding eminence: he shows us the crumbling monuments of time, he invokes the great names, the mighty spirit of antiquity. The universe is changed into a stately mausoleum:—in solemn measures he chaunts a hymn to fame. Lord Byron has strength and elevation enough to fill up the moulds of our classical and time-hallowed recollections, and to rekindle the earliest aspirations of the mind after greatness and true glory with a pen of fire. The names of Tasso, of Ariosto, of Dante, of Cincinnatus, of Cæsar, of Scipio lose nothing of their pomp or their lustre in his hands, and when he begins and continues a strain of panegyric on such subjects, we indeed sit down with him to a banquet of rich praise, brooding over imperishable glories,

Till Contemplation has her fill.

Lord Byron seems to cast himself indignantly from "this bank and shoal of time," or the frail tottering bark that bears up modern reputation, into the huge sea of ancient renown, and to revel there with untired, outspread plume. Even this in him is spleen—his contempt of his contemporaries makes him turn back to the lustrous past, or project himself forward to the dim future!—Lord Byron's tragedies, Faliero,[1] Sardanapalus, &c. are not equal to his other works. They want the essence of the drama. They abound in speeches and descriptions, such as he himself might make either to himself or others, lolling on his couch of a morning, but do not carry the reader out of the poet's mind to the scenes and events recorded. They have neither action, character, nor interest, but are a sort of *gossamer* tragedies, spun out, and glittering, and spreading a flimsy veil over the face of nature. Yet he spins them on. Of all that he has done in this way the *Heaven and Earth* (the same subject as Mr. Moore's *Loves of the Angels*) is the best. We prefer it even to *Manfred*. *Manfred* is merely himself, with a fancy-drapery on: but in the dramatic fragment published in the *Liberal*, the space between Heaven and Earth, the stage on which

[1] "Don Juan was my Moscow, and Faliero
My Leipsic, and my Mont St. Jean seems Cain."
Don Juan, Canto XI.

his characters have to pass to and fro, seems to fill his Lordship's imagination; and the Deluge, which he has so finely described, may be said to have drowned all his own idle humours.

We must say we think little of our author's turn for satire. His "English Bards and Scotch Reviewers" is dogmatical and insolent, but without refinement or point. He calls people names, and tries to transfix a character with an epithet, which does not stick, because it has no other foundation than his own petulance and spite; or he endeavours to degrade by alluding to some circumstance of external situation. He says of Mr. Wordsworth's poetry, that "it is his aversion." That may be: but whose fault is it? This is the satire of a lord, who is accustomed to have all his whims or dislikes taken for gospel, and who cannot be at the pains to do more than signify his contempt or displeasure. If a great man meets with a rebuff which he does not like, he turns on his heel, and this passes for a repartee. The Noble Author says of a celebrated barrister and critic, that he was "born in a garret sixteen stories high." The insinuation is not true; or if it were, it is low. The allusion degrades the person who makes, not him to whom it is applied. This is also the satire of a person of birth and quality, who measures all merit by external rank, that is, by his own standard. So his Lordship, in a "Letter to the Editor of My Grandmother's Review," addresses him fifty times as *"my dear Robarts"*; nor is there any other wit in the article. This is surely a mere assumption of superiority from his Lordship's rank, and is the sort of *quizzing* he might use to a person who came to hire himself as a valet to him at *Long's*—the waiters might laugh, the public will not. In like manner, in the controversy about Pope, he claps Mr. Bowles on the back with a coarse facetious familiarity, as if he were his chaplain whom he had invited to dine with him, or was about to present to a benefice. The reverend divine might submit to the obligation, but he has no occasion to subscribe to the jest. If it is a jest that Mr. Bowles should be a parson, and Lord Byron a peer, the world knew this before; there was no need to write a pamphlet to prove it.

The *Don Juan* indeed has great power; but its power is owing to the force of the serious writing, and to the oddity of the contrast between that and the flashy passages with which it is interlarded. From the sublime to the ridiculous there is but one step. You laugh and are surprised that any one should turn round and *travestie* himself: the drollery is in the utter discontinuity of ideas and feelings. He makes virtue serve as a foil to vice; *dandyism* is (for want of any other) a variety of genius. A classical intoxication is followed by the splashing of soda-water, by frothy effusions of ordinary bile. After the lightning and the hurricane, we are introduced to the interior of the cabin and the contents of wash-hand basins. The solemn hero of tragedy plays *Scrub* in the farce. This is "very tolerable and not to be endured." The Noble Lord is almost the only writer who has prostituted his talents in this way. He hallows in order to desecrate; takes a pleasure in defacing the images of beauty his hands have wrought; and raises our hopes and our belief in goodness to Heaven only to dash them to the earth again, and break them in pieces the more effectually from the very height they have fallen. Our enthusiasm for genius or virtue is thus turned into a jest by the very person who has kindled it, and who thus fatally quenches the sparks of both. It is not that Lord Byron is sometimes serious and sometimes trifling, sometimes profligate, and sometimes moral—but when he is most serious and most moral, he is only preparing to mortify the unsuspecting reader by putting a pitiful *hoax* upon him. This is a most unaccountable anomaly. It is as if the eagle were to build its eyry in a common sewer, or the owl were seen soaring to the mid-day sun. Such a sight might make one laugh, but one would not wish or expect it to occur more than once.[1]

In fact, Lord Byron is the spoiled child of fame as well as fortune. He has taken a surfeit of popularity, and is not contented to delight, unless he can shock the public. He would force them to admire in spite of decency and common sense—he would have them read what they would read in no one but himself, or he would not give a rush for their applause. He is to be "a chartered libertine," from whom insults are favours, whose contempt is to be a new incentive to admiration. His Lordship is hard to please: he is equally averse to notice or neglect, enraged at censure and scorning praise.

[1] This censure applies to the first Cantos of DON JUAN much more than to the last. It has been called a TRISTRAM SHANDY in rhyme: it is rather a poem written about itself.

He tries the patience of the town to the very utmost, and when they show signs of weariness or disgust, threatens to *discard* them. He says he will write on, whether he is read or not. He would never write another page, if it were not to court popular applause, or to affect a superiority over it. In this respect also, Lord Byron presents a striking contrast to Sir Walter Scott. The latter takes what part of the public favour falls to his share, without grumbling (to be sure he has no reason to complain); the former is always quarrelling with the world about his *modicum* of applause, the *spolia opima* of vanity, and ungraciously throwing the offerings of incense heaped on his shrine back in the faces of his admirers. Again, there is no taint in the writings of the Author of *Waverley*, all is fair and natural and *aboveboard:* he never outrages the public mind. He introduces no anomalous character: broaches no staggering opinion. If he goes back to old prejudices and superstitions as a relief to the modern reader, while Lord Byron floats on swelling paradoxes—

> Like proud seas under him;

if the one defers too much to the spirit of antiquity, the other panders to the spirit of the age, goes to the very edge of extreme and licentious speculation, and breaks his neck over it. Grossness and levity are the playthings of his pen. It is a ludicrous circumstance that he should have dedicated his *Cain* to the worthy Baronet! Did the latter ever acknowledge the obligation? We are not nice, not very nice; but we do not particularly approve those subjects that shine chiefly from their rottenness: nor do we wish to see the Muses drest out in the flounces of a false or questionable philosophy, like *Portia* and *Nerissa* in the garb of Doctors of Law. We like metaphysics as well as Lord Byron; but not to see them making flowery speeches, nor dancing a measure in the fetters of verse. We have as good as hinted, that his Lordship's poetry consists mostly of a tissue of superb common-places; even his paradoxes are *common-place*. They are familiar in the schools: they are only new and striking in his dramas and stanzas, by being out of place. In a word, we think that poetry moves best within the circle of nature and received opinion: speculative theory and subtle casuistry are forbidden ground to it. But Lord Byron often wanders into this ground wantonly, wilfully, and unwarrantably. The only apology we can conceive for the spirit of some of Lord Byron's writings, is the spirit of some of those opposed to him. They would provoke a man to write anything. "Farthest from them is best." The extravagance and license of the one seems a proper antidote to the bigotry and narrowness of the other. The first *Vision of Judgment* was a set-off to the second, though

> None but itself could be its parallel.

Perhaps the chief cause of most of Lord Byron's errors is, that he is that anomaly in letters and in society, a Noble Poet. It is a double privilege, almost too much for humanity. He has all the pride of birth and genius. The strength of his imagination leads him to indulge in fantastic opinions; the elevation of his rank sets censure at defiance. He becomes a pampered egotist. He has a seat in the House of Lords, a niche in the Temple of Fame. Every-day mortals, opinions, things are not good enough for him to touch or think of. A mere nobleman is, in his estimation, but "the tenth transmitter of a foolish face": a mere man of genius is no better than a worm. His Muse is also a lady of quality. The people are not polite enough for him: the Court not sufficiently intellectual. He hates the one and despises the other. By hating and despising others, he does not learn to be satisfied with himself. A fastidious man soon grows querulous and splenetic. If there is nobody but ourselves to come up to our idea of fancied perfection, we easily get tired of our idol. When a man is tired of what he is, by a natural perversity he sets up for what he is not. If he is a poet, he pretends to be a metaphysician: if he is a patrician in rank and feeling, he would fain be one of the people. His ruling motive is not the love of the people, but of distinction; not of truth, but of singularity. He patronizes men of letters out of vanity, and deserts them from caprice, or from the advice of friends. He embarks in an obnoxious publication to provoke censure, and leaves it to shift for itself for fear of scandal. We do not like Sir Walter's gratuitous servility: we like Lord Byron's preposterous *liberalism* little better. He may affect the principles of equality, but he resumes his privilege of peerage, upon occasion. His Lordship has made great offers of service to the

Greeks—money and horses. He is at present in Cephalonia, waiting the event!

．　．　．　．　．　．　．

We had written thus far when news came of the death of Lord Byron, and put an end at once to a strain of somewhat peevish invective, which was intended to meet his eye, not to insult his memory. Had we known that we were writing his epitaph, we must have done it with a different feeling. As it is, we think it better and more like himself, to let what we had written stand, than to take up our leaden shafts, and try to melt them into "tears of sensibility," or mould them into dull praise, and an affected show of candour. We were not silent during the author's life-time, either for his reproof or encouragement (such as we could give, and *he* did not disdain to accept) nor can we now turn undertakers' men to fix the glittering plate upon his coffin, or fall into the procession of popular woe.—Death cancels every thing but truth; and strips a man of every thing but genius and virtue. It is a sort of natural canonization. It makes the meanest of us sacred—it installs the poet in his immortality, and lifts him to the skies. Death is the great assayer of the sterling ore of talent. At his touch the drossy particles fall off, the irritable, the personal, the gross, and mingle with the dust—the finer and more ethereal part mounts with the winged spirit to watch over our latest memory, and protect our bones from insult. We consign the least worthy qualities to oblivion, and cherish the nobler and imperishable nature with double pride and fondness. Nothing could show the real superiority of genius in a more striking point of view than the idle contests and the public indifference about the place of Lord Byron's interment, whether in Westminster Abbey or his own family-vault. A king must have a coronation—a nobleman a funeral-procession.—The man is nothing without the pageant. The poet's cemetery is the human mind, in which he sows the seeds of never-ending thought—his monument is to be found in his works:

Nothing can cover his high fame but Heaven;
No pyramids set off his memory,
But the eternal substance of his greatness.

Lord Byron is dead: he also died a martyr to his zeal in the cause of freedom, for the last, best hopes of man. Let that be his excuse and his epitaph!

PERCY BYSSHE SHELLEY [1]

Mr Shelley's style is to poetry what astrology is to natural science—a passionate dream, a straining after impossibilities, a record of fine conjectures, a confused embodying of vague abstractions,—a fever of the soul, thirsting and craving after what it cannot have, indulging its love of power and novelty at the expense of truth and nature, associating ideas by contraries, and wasting great powers by their application to unattainable objects.

Poetry, we grant, creates a world of its own; but it creates it out of existing materials. Mr Shelley is the maker of his own poetry—out of nothing. Not that he is deficient in the true sources of strength and beauty, if he had given himself fair play (the volume before us, as well as his other productions, contains many proofs to the contrary): But, in him, fancy, will, caprice, predominated over and absorbed the natural influences of things; and he had no respect for any poetry that did not strain the intellect as well as fire the imagination—and was not sublimed into a high spirit of metaphysical philosophy. Instead of giving a language to thought, or lending the heart a tongue, he utters dark sayings, and deals in allegories and riddles. His Muse offers her services to clothe shadowy doubts and inscrutable difficulties in a robe of glittering words, and to turn nature into a brilliant paradox. We thank him—but we must be excused. Where we see the dazzling beacon-lights streaming over the darkness of the abyss, we dread the quicksands and the rocks below. Mr Shelley's mind was of "too fiery a quality" to repose (for any continuance) on the probable or the true—it soared "beyond the visible diurnal sphere" to the strange, the improbable, and the impossible. He mistook the nature of the poet's calling, which should be guided by involuntary, not by voluntary impulses. He shook off, as an heroic and praiseworthy act, the trammels of sense, custom, and sympathy, and became the creature of his own will. He was "all air," disdaining the bars and ties of mortal mould. He ransacked his brain for incongruities, and believed in what-

[1] *The Edinburgh Review.* Vol. XL, No. LXXX, pp. 494–514. July, 1824. *Posthumous Poems of Percy Bysshe Shelley.* 8 vo. pp. 400. London, 1824. J. & H. L. Hunt.

ever was incredible. Almost all is effort, almost all is extravagant, almost all is quaint, incomprehensible, and abortive, from aiming to be more than it is. Epithets are applied, because they do not fit: subjects are chosen, because they are repulsive: the colours of his style, for their gaudy, changeful, startling effect, resemble the display of fire-works in the dark, and, like them, have neither durability, nor keeping, nor discriminate form. Yet Mr Shelley, with all his faults, was a man of genius; and we lament that uncontrollable violence of temperament which gave it a forced and false direction. He has single thoughts of great depth and force, single images of rare beauty, detached passages of extreme tenderness; and, in his smaller pieces, where he has attempted little, he has done most. If some casual and interesting idea touched his feelings or struck his fancy, he expressed it in pleasing and unaffected verse: but give him a larger subject, and time to reflect, and he was sure to get entangled in a system. The fumes of vanity rolled volumes of smoke, mixed with sparkles of fire, from the cloudy tabernacle of his thought. The success of his writings is therefore in general in the inverse ratio of the extent of his undertakings; inasmuch as his desire to teach, his ambition to excel, as soon as it was brought into play, encroached upon, and outstripped his powers of execution.

Mr Shelley was a remarkable man. His person was a type and shadow of his genius. His complexion, fair, golden, freckled, seemed transparent with an inward light, and his spirit within him

——so divinely wrought,
That you might almost say his body thought.

He reminded those who saw him of some of Ovid's fables. His form, graceful and slender, drooped like a flower in the breeze. But he was crushed beneath the weight of thought which he aspired to bear, and was withered in the lightning-glare of a ruthless philosophy! He mistook the nature of his own faculties and feelings—the lowly children of the valley, by which the skylark makes its bed, and the bee murmurs, for the proud cedar or the mountain-pine, in which the eagle builds its eyry, "and dallies with the wind, and scorns the sun."—He wished to make of idle verse and idler prose the frame-work of the universe, and to bind all possible existence in the visionary chain of intellectual beauty—

More subtle web Arachne cannot spin,
Nor the fine nets, which oft we woven see
Of scorched dew, do not in th' air more lightly flee.

Perhaps some lurking sense of his own deficiencies in the lofty walk which he attempted, irritated his impatience and his desires; and urged him on, with winged hopes, to atone for past failures, by more arduous efforts, and more unavailing struggles.

With all his faults, Mr Shelley was an honest man. His unbelief and his presumption were parts of a disease, which was not combined in him either with indifference to human happiness, or contempt for human infirmities. There was neither selfishness nor malice at the bottom of his illusions. He was sincere in all his professions; and he practised what he preached—to his own sufficient cost. He followed up the letter and the spirit of his theoretical principles in his own person, and was ready to share both the benefit and the penalty with others. He thought and acted logically, and was what he professed to be, a sincere lover of truth, of nature, and of human kind. To all the rage of paradox, he united an unaccountable candour and severity of reasoning: in spite of an aristocratic education, he retained in his manners the simplicity of a primitive apostle. An Epicurean in his sentiments, he lived with the frugality and abstemiousness of an ascetick [sic]. His fault was, that he had no deference for the opinions of others, too little sympathy with their feelings (which he thought he had a right to sacrifice, as well as his own, to a grand ethical experiment)—and trusted too implicitly to the light of his own mind, and to the warmth of his own impulses. He was indeed the most striking example we remember of the two extremes described by Lord Bacon as the great impediments to human improvement, the love of Novelty, and the love of Antiquity. "The first of these (impediments) is an extreme affection of two extremities, the one Antiquity, the other Novelty; wherein it seemeth the children of time do take after the nature and malice of the father. For as he devoureth his children, so one of them seeketh to devour and suppress the other; while Antiquity envieth there should be new additions, and Novelty cannot be content to add, but it may deface. Surely the advice of the Prophet is the true direction in this matter: *Stand upon the old ways, and see which is the right and good way, and walk therein.* Antiquity deserveth that reverence, that men should make a stand thereupon, and discover what is the best way; but when the discovery is well taken, then to take progression. And to speak truly, *Antiquitas seculi Juventas mundi.* These times are the ancient times, when the world is ancient, and not those which we count ancient, *ordine retrogrado,* by a computation backwards from ourselves." (ADVANCEMENT OF LEARNING, Book I. p. 46.)—Such is the text: and Mr Shelley's writings are a splendid commentary on one half of it. Considered in this point of view, his career may not be uninstructive even to those whom it most offended; and might be held up as a beacon and warning no less to the bigot than the sciolist. We wish to speak of the errors of a man of genius with tenderness. His nature was kind, and his sentiments noble; but in him the rage of free inquiry and private judgment amounted to a species of madness. Whatever was new, untried, unheard of, unauthorized, exerted a kind of fascination over his mind. The examples of the world, the opinion of others, instead of acting as a check upon him, served but to impel him forward with double velocity in his wild and hazardous career. Spurning the world of realities, he rushed into the world of nonentities and contingencies, like air into a *vacuum.* If a thing was old and established, this was with him a certain proof of its having no solid foundation to rest upon: if it was new, it was good and right. Every paradox was to him a self-evident truth; every prejudice an undoubted absurdity. The weight of authority, the sanction of ages, the common consent of mankind, were vouchers only for ignorance, error, and imposture. Whatever shocked the feelings of others, conciliated his regard; whatever was light, extravagant, and vain, was to him a proportionable relief from the dulness and stupidity of established opinions. The worst of it however was, that he thus gave great encouragement to those who believe in all received absurdities, and are wedded to all existing abuses; his extravagance seeming to sanction their grossness and selfishness, as theirs were a full justification of his folly and eccentricity. The two extremes in this way often meet, jostle,—and confirm one another. The infirmities of age are a foil to the presumption of youth; and "there the antics sit," mocking one another—the ape Sophistry pointing with reckless scorn at "palsied eld," and the bed-rid hag, Legitimacy, rattling her chains, counting her beads, dipping her hands in blood, and blessing herself from all change and from every appeal to common sense and reason! Opinion thus alternates in a round of contradictions: the impatience or obstinacy of the human mind takes part with, and flies off to one or other of the two extremes "of affection" and leaves a horrid gap, a blank sense and feeling in the middle, which seems never likely to be filled up, without a total change in our mode of proceeding. The martello-towers with which we are to repress, if we cannot destroy, the systems of fraud and oppression should not be castles in the air, or clouds in the verge of the horizon, but the enormous and accumulated pile of abuses which have arisen out of their own continuance. The principles of sound morality, liberty and humanity, are not to be found only in a few recent writers, who have discovered the secret of the greatest happiness to the greatest numbers, but are truths as old as the creation. To be convinced of the existence of wrong, we should read history rather than poetry: the levers with which we must work out our regeneration are not the cobwebs of the brain, but the warm, palpitating fibres of the human heart. It is the collision of passions and interests, the petulance of party-spirit, and the perversities of self-will and self-opinion that have been the great obstacles to social improvement—not stupidity or ignorance; and the caricaturing one side of the question and shocking the most pardonable prejudices on the other, is not the way to allay heats or produce unanimity. By flying to the extremes of scepticism, we make others shrink back, and shut themselves up in the strongholds of bigotry and superstition—by mixing up doubtful or offensive matters with salutary and demonstrable truths, we bring the whole into question, fly-blow the cause, risk the principle, and give a handle and a pretext to the enemy to treat all philosophy and all reform as a compost of crude, chaotic, and monstrous absurdities. We thus arm the virtues as well as the vices of the community against us; we trifle with their understandings, and exasperate their self-love; we give to superstition and injustice all their old security and sanctity, as if they were the only alternatives of impiety and profligacy, and league the natural with the selfish prejudices of mankind in hostile array against us. To this consummation, it must be confessed that too many of Mr Shelley's productions pointedly tend. He makes no account of the opinions of others, or the consequences of any of his own; but proceeds—tasking his reason to the utmost to account for every thing, and discarding every thing as mystery and error for which he cannot account by an effort of mere intelligence—measuring man, providence, nature, and even his own heart, by the limits of the understanding—now hallowing high mysteries, now desecrating pure sentiments, according as they fall in with or exceed those limits; and exalting and purifying, with Promethean heat, whatever he does not confound and debase.

Mr Shelly [sic] died, it seems, with a volume of Mr Keats's poetry grasped with one hand in his bosom! These are two out of four poets, patriots and friends, who have visited Italy within a few years, both of whom have been soon hurried to a more distant shore. Keats died young; and "yet his infelicity had years too many." A canker had blighted the tender bloom that o'erspread a face in which youth and genius strove with beauty. The shaft was sped—venal, vulgar, venomous, that drove him from his country, with sickness and penury for companions, and followed him to his grave. And yet there are those who could trample on the faded flower —men to whom breaking hearts are a subject of merriment—who laugh loud over the silent urn of Genius, and play out their game of venality and infamy with the crumbling bones of their victims! To this band of immortals a third has since been added!—a mightier genius, a haughtier spirit, whose stubborn impatience and Achilles-like pride only Death could quell. Greece, Italy, the world, have lost their poet-hero; and his death has spread a wider gloom, and been recorded with a deeper awe, than has waited on the obsequies of any of the many great who have died in our remembrance. Even detraction has been silent at his tomb; and the more generous of his enemies have fallen into the rank of his mourners. But he set like the sun in his glory; and his orb was greatest and brightest at the last; for his memory is now consecrated no less by free-

dom than genius. He probably fell a martyr to his zeal against tyrants. He attached himself to the cause of Greece, and dying, clung to it with a convulsive grasp, and has thus gained a niche in her history; for whatever *she* claims as hers is immortal, even in decay, as the marble sculptures on the columns of her fallen temples! . . .

The march of these lines [*Julian and Maddalo*] is, it must be confessed, slow, solemn, sad: there is a sluggishness of feeling, a dearth of imagery, an unpleasant glare of lurid light. It appears to us, that in some poets, as well as in some painters, the organ of colour (to speak in the language of the adepts) predominates over that of form; and Mr Shelley is of the number. We have every where a profusion of dazzling hues, of glancing splendours, of floating shadows, but the objects on which they fall are bare, indistinct, and wild. There is something in the preceding extract that reminds us of the arid style and matter of Crabbe's versification, or that apes the labour and throes of parturition of Wordsworth's blank-verse. It is the preface to a story of Love and Madness—of mental anguish and philosophic remedies—not very intelligibly told, and left with most of its mysteries unexplained, in the true spirit of the modern metaphysical style—in which we suspect there is a due mixture of affectation and meagreness of invention.

This poem is, however, in Mr Shelley's best *and least mannered* manner. If it has less brilliancy, it has less extravagance and confusion. It is in his stanza-poetry, that his Muse chiefly runs riot, and baffles all pursuit of common comprehension or critical acumen. The *Witch of Atlas,* the *Triumph of Life,* and *Marianne's Dream,* are rhapsodies or allegories of this description; full of fancy and of fire, with glowing allusions and wild machinery, but which it is difficult to read through, from the disjointedness of the materials, the incongruous metaphors and violent transitions, and of which, after reading them through, it is impossible, in most instances, to guess the drift or the moral. They abound in horrible imaginings, like records of a ghastly dream;— life, death, genius, beauty, victory, earth, air, ocean, the trophies of the past, the shadows of the world to come, are huddled together in a strange and hurried dance of words and all that appears clear, is the passion and paroxysm of thought of the poet's spirit. The poem entitled the *Triumph of Life,* is in fact a new and terrific *Dance of Death;* but it is thus Mr Shelley transposes the appelations of the commonest things, and subsists only in the violence of contrast. How little this poem is deserving of its title, how worthy it is of its author, what an example of the waste of power, and of genius "made as flax," and devoured by its own elementary ardours, let the reader judge from the concluding stanzas. . . . Any thing more filmy, enigmatical, discontinuous, unsubstantial than this, we have not seen; nor yet more full of morbid genius and vivifying soul. We cannot help preferring *The Witch of Atlas* to *Alastor, or the Spirit of Solitude;* for, though the purport of each is equally perplexing and undefined, (both being a sort of mental voyage through the unexplored regions of space and time), the execution of the one is much less dreary and lamentable than that of the other. In the "Witch," he has indulged his fancy more than his melancholy, and wantoned in the felicity of embryo and crude conceits even to excess. . . .

This we conceive to be the very height of wilful extravagance and mysticism. Indeed it is curious to remark every where the proneness to the marvellous and supernatural, in one who so resolutely set his face against every received mystery, and all traditional faith. Mr Shelley must have possessed, in spite of all his obnoxious and indiscreet scepticism, a large share of credulity and wondering curiosity in his composition, which he reserved from common use, and bestowed upon his own inventions and picturesque caricatures. To every other species of imposture or disguise he was inexorable; and indeed it is his only antipathy to established creeds and legitimate crowns that ever tears the veil from his *ideal* idolatries, and renders him clear and explicit. Indignation makes him pointed and intelligible enough, and breathes into his verse a spirit very different from his own boasted spirit of Love.

The *Letter to a Friend in London* shows the author in a pleasing and familiar, but somewhat prosaic light; and his *Prince Athanase, a Fragment,* is, we suspect, intended as a portrait of the writer. It is amiable, thoughtful, and not much over-charged. We had designed to give an extract, but from the apparently personal and doubtful interest attached to it, perhaps it had better be read altogether, or not at all. We rather choose to quote a part of the *Ode to Naples,* during her brief revolution,—in which immediate and strong local feelings have at once raised and pointed Mr Shelley's style, and "made of light-winged toys of feathered cupid," the flaming ministers of Wrath and Justice. . . .

This Ode for Liberty, though somewhat turbid and overloaded in the diction, we regard as a fair specimen of Mr Shelley's highest powers—whose eager animation wanted only a greater sternness [*sic*] and solidity to be sublime. . . .

MR. JEFFREY

THE *Quarterly Review* arose out of the *Edinburgh,* not as a corollary, but in contradiction to it. An article had appeared in the latter on Don Pedro Cevallos, which stung the Tories to the quick by the free way in which it spoke of men and things, and something must be done to check these *escapades* of the *Edinburgh.* It was not to be endured that the truth should *out* in this manner, even occasionally and half in jest. A startling shock was thus given to established prejudices, the mask was taken off from grave hypocrisy, and the most serious consequences were to be apprehended. The persons who wrote in this Review seemed "to have their hands full of truths," and now and then, in a fit of spleen or gaiety, let some of them fly; and while this practice continued, it was impossible to say that the Monarchy or the Hierarchy was safe. Some of the arrows glanced, others might stick, and in the end prove fatal. It was not the principles of the *Edinburgh Review,* but the spirit that was looked at with jealousy and alarm. The principles were by no means decidedly hostile to existing institutions: but the spirit was that of fair and free discussion; a field was open to argument and wit; every question was tried upon its own ostensible merits, and there was no foul play. The tone was that of a studied impartiality (which many called *trimming*) or of a sceptical indifference. This tone of impartiality and indifference, however, did not at all suit those who profited or existed by abuses, who breathed the very air of corruption. They know well enough, that "those who are not *for* them are *against* them." They wanted a publication impervious alike to truth and candour; that, hood-winked itself, should lead public opinion blindfold; that should stick at nothing to serve the turn of a party; that should be the exclusive organ of prejudice, the sordid tool of power; that should go the whole length of want of principle in palliating every dishonest measure, of want of decency in defaming every honest man; that should prejudge every question, traduce every opponent; that should give no quarter to fair inquiry or liberal sentiment; that should be "ugly all over with hypocrisy," and present one foul blotch of servility, intolerance, falsehood, spite, and ill manners. The *Quarterly Review* was accordingly set up.

> Sithence no fairy lights, no quickning ray,
> Nor stir of pulse, nor object to entice
> Abroad the spirits; but the cloister'd heart
> Sits squat at home, like Pagod in a niche
> Obscure!

This event was accordingly hailed (and the omen has been fulfilled!) as a great relief to all those of his Majesty's subjects who are firmly convinced that the only way to have things remain exactly as they are is to put a stop to all inquiries whether they are right or wrong, and that if you cannot answer a man's arguments, you may at least try to take away his character.

We do not implicitly bow to the political opinions, nor to the critical decisions of the *Edinburgh Review;* but we must do justice to the talent with which they are supported, and to the tone of manly explicitness in which they are delivered.[1] They are eminently characteristic of the Spirit of the Age; as it is the express object of the *Quarterly Review* to discountenance and extinguish that spirit, both in theory and practice. The *Edinburgh Review* stands upon the ground of opinion; it asserts the supremacy of intellect: the pre-eminence it claims is from an acknowledged superiority of talent and information and literary attainment, and it does not build one tittle of its influence on ignorance, or prejudice, or authority, or personal malevolence. It takes up a question, and argues it *pro* and *con* with great knowledge and boldness and skill; it points out an absurdity, and runs it down, fairly, and according to the evidence adduced. In the former case, its conclusions may be wrong, there may be a bias in the mind of the writer, but he states the arguments and circumstances on both sides, from which a judgment is to be formed—it is not his cue, he has neither the effrontery nor the meanness to falsify facts or to suppress objections. In the latter case, or where a vein of sarcasm or irony is resorted to, the ridicule is not barbed by some allusion (false or true) to private history; the object of it has brought the infliction on himself by some literary folly or political delinquency which is referred to as the understood and justifiable provocation, instead of being held up to scorn as a knave for not being a tool, or as a blockhead for thinking for himself. In the *Edinburgh Review* the talents of those on the opposite side are always extolled *pleno ore*—in the *Quarterly Review* they are denied altogether, and the justice that is in this way withheld from them is compensated by a proportionable supply of personal abuse. A man of genius who is a lord, and who publishes with Mr. Murray, may now and then stand as good a chance as a lord who is not a man of genius and who publishes with Messrs. Longman: but that is the utmost extent of the impartiality of the *Quarterly*. From its account you would take Lord Byron and Mr. Stuart Rose for two very pretty poets; but Mr. Moore's Magdalen Muse is sent to Bridewell without mercy, to beat hemp in silk-stockings. In the *Quarterly* nothing is regarded but the political creed or external circumstances of a writer; in the *Edinburgh* nothing is ever adverted to but his literary merits. Or if there is a bias of any kind, it arises from an affectation of magnanimity and candour in giving heaped measure to those on the aristocratic side in politics, and in being critically severe on others. Thus Sir Walter Scott is lauded to the skies for his romantic powers, without any allusion to his political demerits (as if this would be compromising the dignity of genius and of criticism by the introduction of party-spirit)—while Lord Byron is called to a grave moral reckoning. There is, however, little of the cant of morality in the *Edinburgh Review* —and it is quite free from that of religion. It keeps to its province, which is that of criticism —or to the discussion of debateable topics,

---

[1] The style of philosophical criticism, which has been the boast of the *Edinburgh Review,* was first introduced into the Monthly Review about the year 1796, in a series of articles by Mr. William Taylor, of Norwich.

and acquits itself in both with force and spirit. This is the natural consequence of the composition of the two Reviews. The one appeals with confidence to its own intellectual resources, to the variety of its topics, to its very character and existence as a literary journal, which depend on its setting up no pretensions but those which it can make good by the talent and ingenuity it can bring to bear upon them—it therefore meets every question, whether of a lighter or a graver cast, on its own grounds; the other *blinks* every question, for it has no confidence but in the *powers that be*—shuts itself up in the impregnable fastnesses of authority, or makes some paltry cowardly attack (under cover of anonymous criticism) on individuals, or dispenses its award of merit entirely according to the rank or party of the writer. The faults of the *Edinburgh Review* arise out of the very consciousness of critical and logical power. In political questions it relies too little on the broad basis of liberty and humanity, enters too much into mere dry formalities, deals too often in *mootpoints,* and descends too readily to a sort of special-pleading in defence of *home* truths and natural feelings: in matters of taste and criticism, its tone is sometimes apt to be supercilious and *cavalier* from its habitual faculty of analysing defects and beauties according to given principles, from its quickness in deciding, from its facility in illustrating its views. In this latter department it has been guilty of some capital oversights. The chief was in its treatment of the *Lyrical Ballads* at their first appearance—not in its riccidule of their puerilities, but in its denial of their beauties, because they were included in no school, because they were reducible to no previous standard or theory of poetical excellence. For this, however, considerable reparation has been made by the prompt and liberal spirit that has been shown in bringing forward other examples of poetical genius. Its capital sin, in a doctrinal point of view, has been (we shrewdly suspect) in the uniform and unqualified encouragement it has bestowed on Mr. Malthus's system. We do not mean that the *Edinburgh Review* was to join in the general *hue and cry* that was raised against this writer; but while it asserted the soundness of many of his arguments, and yielded its assent to the truths he has divulged, it need not have screened his errors. On this subject alone we think the *Quarterly* has the

advantage of it. But as the *Quarterly Review* is a mere mass and tissue of prejudices on all subjects, it is the foible of the *Edinburgh Review* to affect a somewhat fastidious air of superiority over prejudices of all kinds, and a determination not to indulge in any of the amiable weaknesses of our nature, except as it can give a reason for the faith that is in it. Luckily, it is seldom reduced to this alternative: "reasons" are with it "as plenty as blackberries!"

Mr. Jeffrey is the Editor of the *Edinburgh Review,* and is understood to have contributed nearly a fourth part of the articles from its commencement. No man is better qualified for this situation; nor indeed so much so. He is certainly a person in advance of the age, and yet perfectly fitted both from knowledge and habits of mind to put a curb upon its rash and headlong spirit. He is thoroughly acquainted with the progress and pretensions of modern literature and philosophy; and to this he adds the natural acuteness and discrimination of the logician with the habitual caution and coolness of his profession. If the *Edinburgh Review* may be considered as the organ of or at all pledged to a party, that party is at least a respectable one, and is placed in the middle between two extremes. The Editor is bound to lend a patient hearing to the most paradoxical opinions and extravagant theories which have resulted in our times from the "infinite agitation of wit," but he is disposed to qualify them by a number of practical objections, of speculative doubts, of checks and drawbacks, arising out of actual circumstances and prevailing opinions, or the frailties of human nature. He has a great range of knowledge, an incessant activity of mind; but the suspension of his judgment, the well-balanced moderation of his sentiments, is the consequence of the very discursiveness of his reason. What may be considered as a *common-place* conclusion is often the result of a comprehensive view of all the circumstances of a case. Paradox, violence, nay even originality of conception is not seldom owing to our dwelling long and pertinaciously on some one part of a subject, instead of attending to the whole. Mr. Jeffrey is neither a bigot nor an enthusiast. He is not the dupe of the prejudices of others, nor of his own. He is not wedded to any dogma, he is not long the sport of any whim; before he can settle in any fond or fantastic opinion, another starts up to match it, like beads on sparkling wine. A too restless display of talent, a too undisguised statement of all that can be said for and against a question, is perhaps the great fault that is to be attributed to him. Where there is so much power and prejudice to contend with in the opposite scale, it may be thought that the balance of truth can hardly be held with a slack or an even hand; and that the infusion of a little more visionary speculation, of a little more popular indignation into the great Whig Review would be an advantage both to itself and to the cause of freedom. Much of this effect is chargeable less on an Epicurean levity of feeling or on party-trammels, than on real sanguineness of disposition, and a certain fineness of professional tact. Our sprightly Scotchman is not of a desponding and gloomy turn of mind. He argues well for the future hopes of mankind from the smallest beginnings, watches the slow, gradual, reluctant growth of liberal views, and smiling sees the aloe of Reform blossom at the end of a hundred years; while the habitual subtlety of his mind makes him perceive decided advantages where vulgar ignorance or passion sees only doubts and difficulty; and a flaw in an adversary's argument stands him instead of the shout of a mob, the votes of a majority, or the fate of a pitched battle. The Editor is satisfied with his own conclusions, and does not make himself uneasy about the fate of mankind. The issue, he thinks, will verify his moderate and well-founded expectations.— We believe also that late events have given a more decided turn to Mr. Jeffery's mind, and that he feels that as in the struggle between liberty and slavery, the views of the one party have been laid bare with their success, so the exertions on the other side should become more strenuous, and a more positive stand be made against the avowed and appalling encroachments of priestcraft and arbitrary power.

The characteristics of Mr. Jeffrey's general style as a writer correspond, we think, with what we have here stated as the characteristics of his mind. He is a master of the foils; he makes an exulting display of the dazzling fence of wit and argument. His strength consists in great range of knowledge, an equal familiarity with the principles and the details of a subject, and in a glancing brilliancy and rapidity of style. Indeed, we doubt whether the brilliancy of his manner does not resolve itself into the rapidity, the variety and aptness of his illustrations. His pen is never at a loss, never stands still; and would dazzle for this reason alone, like an eye that is ever in motion. Mr. Jeffrey is far from a flowery or affected writer; he has few tropes or figures, still less any odd startling thoughts or quaint innovations in expression: —but he has a constant supply of ingenious solutions and pertinent examples; he never proses, never grows dull, never wears an argument to tatters; and by the number, the liveliness and facility of his transitions, keeps up that appearance of vivacity, of novel and sparkling effect, for which others are too often indebted to singularity of combination or tinsel ornaments.

It may be discovered, by a nice observer, that Mr. Jeffrey's style of composition is that of a person accustomed to public speaking. There is no pause, no meagreness, no inanimateness, but a flow, a redundance and volubility like that of a stream or of a rolling-stone. The language is more copious than select, and sometimes two or three words perform the office of one. This copiousness and facility is perhaps an advantage in *extempore* speaking, where no stop or break is allowed in the discourse, and where any word or any number of words almost is better than coming to a dead stand; but in written compositions it gives an air of either too much carelessness or too much labour. Mr. Jeffrey's excellence, as a public speaker, has betrayed him into this peculiarity. He makes fewer *blots* in addressing an audience than any one we remember to have heard. There is not a hair-breadth space between any two of his words, nor is there a single expression either ill-chosen or out of its place. He speaks without stopping to take breath, with ease, with point, with elegance, and without "spinning the thread of his verbosity finer than the staple of his argument." He may be said to weave words into any shapes he pleases for use or ornament, as the glass-blower moulds the vitreous fluid with his breath; and his sentences shine like glass from their polished smoothness, and are equally transparent. His style of eloquence, indeed, is remarkable for neatness, for correctness, and epigrammatic point; and he has applied this as a standard to his written compositions, where the very same degree of correctness and precision produces, from the contrast between writing and speaking, an agreeable diffuseness, freedom and animation. Whenever the Scotch advocate has appeared at the bar of the English House of Lords, he has been admired by those who were in the habit of attending to speeches there, as having the greatest fluency of language and the greatest subtlety of distinction of any one of the profession. The law-reporters were as little able to follow him from the extreme rapidity of his utterance as from the tenuity and evanescent nature of his reasoning.

Mr. Jeffrey's conversation is equally lively, various, and instructive. There is no subject on which he is not *au fait:* no company in which he is not ready to scatter his pearls for sport. Whether it be politics, or poetry, or science, or anecdote, or wit, or raillery, he takes up his cue without effort, without preparation, and appears equally incapable of tiring himself or his hearers. His only difficulty seems to be, not to speak, but to be silent. There is a constitutional buoyancy and elasticity of mind about him that cannot subside into repose, much less sink into dulness. There may be more original talkers, persons who occasionally surprise or interest you more; few, if any, with a more uninterrupted flow of cheerfulness and animal spirits, with a greater fund of information, and with fewer specimens of the *bathos* in their conversation. He is never absurd, nor has he any favourite points which he is always bringing forward. It cannot be denied that there is something bordering on petulance of manner, but it is of that least offensive kind which may be accounted for from merit and from success, and implies no exclusive pretensions nor the least particle of ill-will to others. On the contrary, Mr. Jeffrey is profuse of his encomiums and admiration of others, but still with a certain reservation of a right to differ or to blame. He cannot rest on one side of a question: he is obliged to a mercurial habit and disposition to vary his point of view. If he is ever tedious, it is from an excess of liveliness: he oppresses from a sense of airy lightness. He is always setting out on a fresh scent: there are always *relays* of topics; the harness is put to, and he rattles away as delightfully and as briskly as ever. New causes are called; he holds a brief in his hand for every possible question. This is a fault. Mr. Jeffrey is not obtrusive, is not impatient of opposition, is not unwilling to be interrupted; but what is said by another, seems to make no impression on him; he is bound to dispute, to answer it, as if he was in Court, or as if it were in a paltry Debating Society, where young beginners were trying their hands. This is not to maintain a character, or for want of good-nature—it is a thoughtless habit. He cannot help cross-examining a witness, or stating the adverse view of the question. He listens not to judge, but to reply. In consequence of this, you can as little tell the impression your observations make on him as what weight to assign to his. Mr. Jeffrey shines in mixed company; he is not good in a *tête-à-tête.* You can only show your wisdom or your wit in general society: but in private your follies or your weaknesses are not the least interesting topics; and our critic has neither any of his own to confess, nor does he take delight in hearing those of others. Indeed in Scotland generally, the display of personal character, the indulging your whims and humours in the presence of a friend, is not much encouraged—every one there is looked upon in the light of a machine or a collection of topics. They turn you round like a cylinder to see what use they can make of you, and drag you into a dispute with as little ceremony as they would drag out an article from an Encyclopedia. They criticise every thing, analyse every thing, argue upon every thing, dogmatise upon every thing; and the bundle of your habits, feelings, humours, follies and pursuits is regarded by them no more than a bundle of old clothes. They stop you in a sentiment by a question or a stare, and cut you short in a narrative by the time of night. The accomplished and ingenious person of whom we speak, has been a little infected by the tone of his countrymen—he is too didactic, too pugnacious, too full of electrical shocks, too much like a voltaic battery, and reposes too little on his own excellent good sense, his own love of ease, his cordial frankness of temper and unaffected candour. He ought to have belonged to us!

The severest of critics (as he has been sometimes termed) is the best-natured of men. Whatever there may be of wavering or indecision in Mr. Jeffrey's reasoning, or of harshness in his critical decisions, in his disposition there is nothing but simplicity and kindness. He is a person that no one knows without esteeming, and who both in his public connections and private friendships, shows the same manly uprightness and unbiassed independence of spirit. At a distance, in his writings, or even in his manner, there may be something to excite a little uneasiness and apprehension: in his conduct there is nothing to except against. He is a person of strict integrity himself, without pretence or affectation; and knows how to respect this quality in others, without prudery or intolerance. He can censure a friend or a stranger, and serve him effectually at the same time. He expresses his disapprobation, but not as an excuse for closing up the avenues of his liberality. He is a Scotchman without one particle of hypocrisy, of cant, of servility, or selfishness in his composition. He has not been spoiled by fortune—has not been tempted by power—is firm without violence, friendly without weakness—a critic and even-tempered, a casuist and an honest man—and amidst the toils of his profession and the distractions of the world, retains the gaiety, the unpretending carelessness and simplicity of youth. Mr. Jeffrey in his person is slight, with a countenance of much expression, and a voice of great flexibility and acuteness of tone.

LEIGH HUNT

AN ANSWER TO THE QUESTION

WHAT IS POETRY?

INCLUDING

REMARKS ON VERSIFICATION [1]

POETRY, strictly and artistically so called, that is to say, considered not merely as poetic feeling, which is more or less shared by all the world, but as the operation of that feeling, such as we see it in the poet's book, is the utterance of a passion for truth, beauty, and power, embodying and illustrating its conceptions by imagination and fancy, and modulating its language on the principle of variety in uniformity. Its means are whatever the universe contains; and its ends, pleasure and exaltation. Poetry stands between nature and convention, keeping alive among us the enjoyment of the external and the spiritual world; it has constituted the most enduring fame of nations; and, next to Love and Beauty, which are its parents, is the greatest proof to man of the pleasure to be found in all things, and of the probable riches of infinitude.

Poetry is a passion,* because it seeks the deepest impressions; and because it must undergo, in order to convey, them.

It is a passion for truth, because without truth the impression would be false or defective.

It is a passion for beauty, because its office is to exalt and refine by means of pleasure, and because beauty is nothing but the loveliest form of pleasure.

It is a passion for power, because power is impression triumphant, whether over the poet, as desired by himself, or over the reader, as affected by the poet.

It embodies and illustrates its impressions by imagination, or images of the objects of which it treats, and other images brought in to throw light on those objects, in order that it may enjoy and impart the feeling of their truth in its utmost conviction and affluence.

It illustrates them by fancy, which is a lighter play of imagination, or the feeling of analogy coming short of seriousness, in order that it may laugh with what it loves, and show how it can decorate it with fairy ornament.

It modulates what it utters, because in running the whole round of beauty it must needs include beauty of sound; and because, in the height of its enjoyment, it must show the perfection of its triumph, and make difficulty itself become part of its facility and joy.

And lastly, Poetry shapes this modulation into uniformity for its outline, and variety for its parts, because it thus realizes the last idea of beauty itself, which includes the charm of diversity within the flowing round of habit and ease.

Poetry is imaginative passion. The quickest and subtlest test of the possession of its essence is in expression; the variety of things to be expressed shows the amount of its

[1] We are printing this essay as it appeared in Leigh Hunt's volume entitled *Imagination and Fancy* (London, 1844). For the allocation of references and the correction of quotations, see the edition by Albert S. Cook (Boston, 1893).

* *Passio,* suffering in a good sense,—ardent subjection of one's-self to emotion.

resources; and the continuity of the song completes the evidence of its strength and greatness. He who has thought, feeling, expression, imagination, action, character, and continuity, all in the largest amount and highest degree, is the greatest poet.

Poetry includes whatsoever of painting can be made visible to the mind's eye, and whatsoever of music can be conveyed by sound and proportion without singing or instrumentation. But it far surpasses those divine arts in suggestiveness, range, and intellectual wealth;— the first, in expression of thought, combination of images, and the triumph over space and time; the second, in all that can be done by speech, apart from the tones and modulations of pure sound. Painting and music, however, include all those portions of the gift of poetry that can be expressed and heightened by the visible and melodious. Painting, in a certain apparent manner, is things themselves; music, in a certain audible manner, is their very emotion and grace. Music and painting are proud to be related to poetry, and poetry loves and is proud of them.

Poetry begins where matter of fact or of science ceases to be merely such, and to exhibit a further truth, that is to say, the connection it has with the world of emotion, and its power to produce imaginative pleasure. Inquiring of a gardener, for instance, what flower it is we see yonder, he answers, "a lily." This is matter of fact. The botanist pronounces it to be of the order of "Hexandria Monogynia." This is matter of science. It is the "lady" of the garden, says Spenser; and here we begin to have a poetical sense of its fairness and grace. It is

> The plant and flower of *light*,

says Ben Jonson; and poetry then shows us the beauty of the flower in all its mystery and splendour.

If it be asked, how we know perceptions like these to be true, the answer is, by the fact of their existence—by the consent and delight of poetic readers. And as feeling is the earliest teacher, and perception the only final proof of things the most demonstrable by science, so the remotest imaginations of the poets may often be found to have the closest connection with matter of fact; perhaps might always be so, if the subtlety of our perceptions were a match for the causes of them. Consider this image of Ben Jonson's—of a lily being the flower of light. Light, undecomposed, is white; and as the lily is white, and light is white, and whiteness itself is nothing *but* light, the two things, so far, are not merely similar, but identical. A poet might add, by an analogy drawn from the connection of light and colour, that there is a "golden dawn" issuing out of the white lily, in the rich yellow of the stamens. I have no desire to push this similarity farther than it may be worth. Enough has been stated to show that, in poetical as well as in other analogies, "the same feet of Nature," as Bacon says, may be seen "treading in different paths;" and that the most scornful, that is to say, dullest disciple of fact, should be cautious how he betrays the shallowness of his philosophy by discerning no poetry in its depths.

But the poet is far from dealing only with these subtle and analogical truths. Truth of every kind belongs to him, provided it can bud into any kind of beauty, or is capable of being illustrated and impressed by the poetic faculty. Nay, the simplest truth is often so beautiful and impressive of itself, that one of the greatest proofs of his genius consists in his leaving it to stand alone, illustrated by nothing but the light of its own tears or smiles, its own wonder, might, or playfulness. Hence the complete effect of many a simple passage in our old English ballads and romances, and of the passionate sincerity in general of the greatest early poets, such as Homer and Chaucer, who flourished before the existence of a "literary world," and were not perplexed by a heap of notions and opinions, or by doubts how emotion ought to be expressed. The greatest of their successors never write equally to the purpose, except when they can dismiss everything from their minds but the like simple truth. In the beautiful poem of "Sir Eger, Sir Graham, and Sir Gray-Steel" (see it in Ellis's Specimens, or Laing's Early Metrical Tales), a knight thinks himself disgraced in the eyes of his mistress:—

> Sir Eger said "If it be so,
> Then wot I well I must forgo
> Love-liking, and manhood, all clean."
> *The water rush'd out of his een!*

Sir Gray-Steel is killed:—

> Gray-Steel into his death thus thrawes
> [throes?]

He *walters* [welters,—throws himself about] *and
the grass up drawes;*

.   .   .   .   .

> *A little while then lay he still
> (Friends that him saw, liked full ill)
> And bled into his armour bright.*

The abode of Chaucer's *Reve,* or Steward, in
the Canterbury Tales, is painted in two lines
which nobody ever wished longer:—

His wonning [dwelling] was ful fair upon an
    heath,
With greeny trees yshadowed was his place.

Every one knows the words of Lear, "most
matter-of-fact, most melancholy."

>   Pray do not mock me;
> I am a very foolish fond old man
> Fourscore and upwards:
> Not an hour more, nor less; and to deal plainly
> I fear I am not in my perfect mind.

It is thus, by exquisite pertinence, melody,
and the implied power of writing with exuberance, if need be, that beauty and truth become
identical in poetry, and that pleasure, or at
the very worst, a balm in our tears, is drawn
out of pain.

It is a great and rare thing, and shows a
lovely imagination, when the poet can write a
commentary, as it were, of his own, on such
sufficing passages of nature, and be thanked
for the addition. There is an instance of this
kind in Warner, an old Elizabethan poet, than
which I know nothing sweeter in the world.
He is speaking of Fair Rosamond, and of a
blow given her by Queen Eleanor.

> With that she dash'd her on the lips,
>   *So dyèd double red:*
> *Hard was the heart that gave the blow,*
>   *Soft were those lips that bled.*

There are different kinds and degrees of imagination, some of them necessary to the formation of every true poet, and all of them possessed by the greatest. Perhaps they may be
enumerated as follows:—First, that which presents to the mind any object or circumstance
in every-day life; as when we imagine a man
holding a sword, or looking out of a window;
—Second, that which presents real, but not
every-day circumstances; as King Alfred tending the loaves, or Sir Philip Sidney giving up
the water to the dying soldier;—Third, that

which combines character and events directly
imitated from real life, with imitative realities
of its own invention; as the probable parts of
the histories of Priam and Macbeth, or what
may be called natural fiction as distinguished
from supernatural;—Fourth, that which con-
jures up things and events not to be found
in nature; as Homer's gods, and Shakespeare's
witches, enchanted horses and spears, Ariosto's
hippogriff, &c.;—Fifth, that which, in order
to illustrate or aggravate one image, introduces another; sometimes in simile, as when
Homer compares Apollo descending in his
wrath at noon-day to the coming of night-
time: sometimes in metaphor, or simile comprised in a word, as in Milton's "motes that
people the sunbeams;" sometimes in concentrating into a word the main history of any
person or thing, past or even future, as in the
"starry Galileo" of Byron, and that ghastly
foregone conclusion of the epithet "murdered"
applied to the yet living victim in Keats's story
from Boccaccio,—

> So the two brothers and their *murder'd* man
> Rode towards fair Florence;—

sometimes in the attribution of a certain representative quality which makes one circumstance stand for others; as in Milton's grey-fly
winding its *"sultry* horn," which epithet contains the heat of a summer's day;—Sixth, that
which reverses this process, and makes a variety of circumstances take colour from one, like
nature seen with jaundiced or glad eyes, or under the influence of storm or sunshine; as when
in Lycidas, or the Greek pastoral poets, the
flowers and the flocks are made to sympathize
with a man's death; or, in the Italian poet, the
river flowing by the sleeping Angelica seems
talking of love—

> Parea che l' erba le fiorisse intorno,
>   E d' amor ragionasse quella rival—

or in the voluptuous homage paid to the sleeping Imogen by the very light in the chamber
and the reaction of her own beauty upon itself; or in the "witch element" of the tragedy
of Macbeth and the May-day night of Faust;
—Seventh, and last, that which by a single expression, apparently of the vaguest kind, not
only meets but surpasses in its effect the extremest force of the most particular description; as in that exquisite passage of Coleridge's
Christabel, where the unsuspecting object of
the witch's malignity is bidden to go to bed:—

Quoth Christabel, So let it be!
And as the lady bade, did she.
Her gentle limbs did she undress
And lay down in her loveliness;—

a perfect verse surely, both for feeling and music. The very smoothness and gentleness of the limbs is in the series of the letter *l's*.

I am aware of nothing of the kind surpassing that most lovely inclusion of physical beauty in moral, neither can I call to mind any instances of the imagination that turns accompaniments into accessories, superior to those I have alluded to. Of the class of comparison, one of the most touching (many a tear must it have drawn from parents and lovers) is in a stanza which has been copied into the "Friar of Orders Gray" out of Beaumont and Fletcher:—

Weep no more, lady, weep no more,
   Thy sorrow is in vain;
For violets pluck'd the sweetest showers
Will ne'er make grow again.

And Shakespeare and Milton abound in the very grandest; such as Antony's likening his changing fortunes to the cloud-rack; Lear's appeal to the old age of the heavens; Satan's appearance in the horizon, like a fleet "hanging in the clouds;" and the comparisons of him with the comet and the eclipse. Nor unworthy of this glorious company, for its extraordinary combination of delicacy and vastness, is that enchanting one of Shelley's in the Adonais:—

Life, like a dome of many-coloured glass,
Stains the white radiance of eternity.

I multiply these particulars in order to impress upon the reader's mind the great importance of imagination in all its phases, as a constituent part of the highest poetic faculty.

The happiest instance I remember of imaginative metaphor, is Shakespeare's moonlight "sleeping" on a bank; but half his poetry may be said to be made up of it, metaphor indeed being the common coin of discourse. Of imaginary creatures, none out of the pale of mythology and the East, are equal, perhaps, in point of invention, to Shakespeare's Ariel and Caliban; though poetry may grudge to prose the discovery of a Winged Woman, especially such as she has been described by her inventor in the story of Peter Wilkins; and in point of treatment, the Mammon and Jealousy of Spenser, some of the monsters in Dante, particularly his Nimrod, his interchangements of

creatures into one another, and (if I am not presumptuous in anticipating what I think will be the verdict of posterity) the Witch in Coleridge's Christabel, may rank even with the creations of Shakespeare. It may be doubted, indeed, whether Shakespeare had bile and nightmare enough in him to have thought of such detestable horrors as those of the interchanging adversaries (now serpent, now man), or even of the huge, half-blockish enormity of Nimrod,—in Scripture, the "mighty hunter" and builder of the tower of Babel,—in Dante, a tower of man in his own person, standing with some of his brother giants up to the middle in a pit in hell, blowing a horn to which a thunderclap is a whisper, and hallooing after Dante and his guide in the jargon of a lost tongue! The transformations are too odious to quote: but of the towering giant we cannot refuse ourselves the "fearful joy" of a specimen. It was twilight, Dante tells us, and he and his guide Virgil were silently pacing through one of the dreariest regions of hell, when the sound of a tremendous horn made him turn all his attention to the spot from which it came. He there discovered through the dusk, what seemed to be the towers of a city. Those are no towers, said his guide; they are giants, standing up to the middle in one of these circular pits.[1]

Assuredly it could not have been easy to find a fiction so uncouthly terrible as this in the hypochondria of Hamlet. Even his father had evidently seen no such ghost in the other world. All his phantoms were in the world he had left. Timon, Lear, Richard, Brutus, Prospero, Macbeth himself, none of Shakespeare's men had, in fact, any thought but of the earth they lived on whatever supernatural fancy crossed them. The thing fancied was still a thing of this world, "in its habit as it lived," or no remoter acquaintance than a witch or a fairy. Its lowest depths (unless Dante suggested them) were the cellars under the stage. Caliban himself is a cross-breed between a witch and a clown. No offence to Shakespeare; who was not bound to be the greatest of healthy poets, and to have every morbid inspiration besides. What he might have done, had he set his wits to compete with Dante, I know not: all I know is, that in the infernal line he did nothing like him; and it is not to be wished he had. It is far better that, as a higher, more universal, and more beneficent variety of

[1] *Inferno* 31, 34-81.

the genus Poet, he should have been the happier man he was, and left us the plump cheeks on his monument, instead of the carking visage of the great, but over-serious, and comparatively one-sided Florentine. Even the imagination of Spenser, whom we take to have been a "nervous gentleman" compared with Shakespeare, was visited with no such dreams as Dante. Or, if it was, he did not choose to make himself thinner (as Dante says *he* did) with dwelling upon them. He had twenty visions of nymphs and bowers, to one of the mud of Tartarus. Chaucer, for all he was "a man of this world" as well as the poets' world, and as great, perhaps a greater enemy of oppression than Dante, besides being one of the profoundest masters of pathos that ever lived, had not the heart to conclude the story of the famished father and his children, as finished by the inexorable anti-Pisan. But enough of Dante in this place. Hobbes, in order to daunt the reader from objecting to his friend Davenant's want of invention, says of these fabulous creations in general, in his letter prefixed to the poem of Gondibert, that "impenetrable armours, enchanted castles, invulnerable bodies, iron men, flying horses, and a thousand other such things, are easily feigned by them that dare." These are girds at Spenser and Ariosto. But, with leave of Hobbes (who translated Homer as if on purpose to show what execrable verses could be written by a philosopher), enchanted castles and flying horses are not easily feigned, as Ariosto and Spenser feigned them; and that just makes all the difference. For proof, see the accounts of Spenser's enchanted castle in Book the Third, Canto Twelfth, of the Fairy Queen; and let the reader of Italian open the Orlando Furioso at its first introduction of the Hippogriff, where Bradamante, coming to an inn, hears a great noise, and sees all the people looking up at something in the air; upon which, looking up herself, she sees a knight in shining armour riding towards the sunset upon a creature with variegated wings, and then dipping and disappearing among the hills. Chaucer's steed of brass, that was

> So horsly and so quick of eye,

is copied from the life. You might pat him and feel his brazen muscles. Hobbes, in objecting to what he thought childish, made a childish mistake. His criticism is just such as a boy might pique himself upon, who was educated on mechanical principles, and thought he had outgrown his Goody Two-shoes. With a wonderful dimness of discernment in poetic matters, considering his acuteness in others, he fancies he has settled the question by pronouncing such creations "impossible!" To the brazier they are impossible, no doubt; but not to the poet. Their possibility, if the poet wills it, is to be conceded; the problem is, the creature being given, how to square its actions with probability, according to the nature assumed of it. Hobbes did not see that the skill and beauty of these fictions lay in bringing them within those very regions of truth and likelihood in which he thought they could not exist. Hence the serpent Python of Chaucer,

> *Sleeping against the sun upon a day,*

when Apollo slew him. Hence the chariot-drawing dolphins of Spenser, softly swimming along the shore lest they should hurt themselves against the stones and gravel. Hence Shakespeare's Ariel, living under blossoms, and riding at evening on the bat; and his domestic namesake in the "Rape of the Lock" (the imagination of the drawing-room) saving a lady's petticoat from the coffee with his plumes, and directing atoms of snuff into a coxcomb's nose. In the "Orlando Furioso" is a wild story of a cannibal necromancer, who laughs at being cut to pieces, coming together again like quicksilver, and picking up his head when it is cut off, sometimes by the hair, sometimes by the nose! This, which would be purely childish and ridiculous in the hands of an inferior poet, becomes interesting, nay grand, in Ariosto's, from the beauties of his style, and its conditional truth to nature. The monster has a fated hair on his head,—a single hair,—which must be taken from it before he can be killed. Decapitation itself is of no consequence, without that proviso. The Paladin Astolfo, who has fought this phenomenon on horseback, and succeeded in getting the head and galloping off with it, is therefore still at a loss what to be at. How is he to discover such a needle in such a bottle of hay? The trunk is spurring after him to recover it, and he seeks for some evidence of the hair in vain. At length he bethinks him of scalping the head. He does so; and the moment the operation arrives at the place of the hair, *the face of the head becomes pale, the eyes turn in their sockets,* and the lifeless pursuer tumbles from his horse. . . . It is thus, and thus only, by making Nature his companion wherever he goes, even in the most supernatural region, that the poet, in the words of a very instructive phrase, takes the world along with him. It is true, he must not (as the Platonists would say) humanize weakly or mistakenly in that region; otherwise he runs the chance of forgetting to be true to the supernatural itself, and so betraying a want of imagination from that quarter. His nymphs will have no taste of their woods and waters; his gods and goddesses be only so many fair or frowning ladies and gentlemen, such as we see in ordinary paintings; he will be in no danger of having his angels likened to a sort of wild-fowl, as Rembrandt has made them in his Jacob's Dream. His Bacchuses will never remind us, like Titian's, of the force and fury, as well as of the graces of wine. His Jupiter will reduce no females to ashes; his fairies be nothing fantastical; his gnomes, not "of the earth, earthy." And this again will be wanting to Nature; for it will be wanting to the supernatural, as Nature would have made it, working in a supernatural direction. Nevertheless, the poet, even for imagination's sake, must not become a bigot to imaginative truth, dragging it down into the region of the mechanical and the limited, and losing sight of its paramount privilege, which is to make beauty, in a human sense, the lady and queen of the universe. He would gain nothing by making his ocean-nymphs mere fishy creatures, upon the plea that such only could live in the water: his wood-nymphs with faces of knotted oak; his angels without breath and song, because no lungs could exist between the earth's atmosphere and the empyrean. The Grecian tendency in this respect is safer than the Gothic; nay, more imaginative; for it enables us to imagine *beyond* imagination, and to bring all things healthily round to their only present final ground of sympathy,—the human. When we go to heaven, we may idealize in a superhuman mode, and have altogether different notions of the beautiful; but till then we must be content with the loveliest capabilities of earth. The sea-nymphs of Greece were still beautiful women, though they lived in the water. The gills and fins of the ocean's natural inhabitants were confined to their lowest semi-human attendants; or if Triton himself was not quite human, it was because he represented the fiercer part of the vitality of the seas, as they did the fairer. . . .

To come now to Fancy,—she is a younger sister of Imagination, without the other's weight of thought and feeling. Imagination indeed, purely so called, is all feeling; the feeling of the subtlest and most affecting analogies; the perception of sympathies in the nature of things, or in their popular attributes. Fancy is a sporting with their resemblance, real or supposed, and with airy and fantastical creations.

—Rouse yourself; and the weak wanton Cupid
Shall from your neck unloose his amorous fold,
And, like a dew-drop from the lion's mane,
Be shook to air.
                    Troilus and Cressida, Act. iii. sc. 3.

That is imagination;—the strong mind sympathizing with the strong beast, and the weak love identified with the weak dew-drop.

Oh!—and I forsooth
In love! I, that have been love's whip!
A very beadle to a humorous sigh!—
A domineering pedant o'er the boy,—
This whimpled, whining, purblind, wayward boy,
This senior-junior, giant-dwarf, Dan Cupid,
Regent of love-rhymes, lord of folded arms,
The anointed sovereign of sighs and groans, &c.
                    Love's Labour Lost, Act. iii. sc. 1.

That is fancy;—a combination of images not in their nature connected, or brought together by the feeling, but by the will and pleasure; and having just enough hold of analogy to betray it into the hands of its smiling subjector.

Silent icicles
Quietly shining to the quiet moon.
                    Coleridge's *Frost at Midnight.*

That, again, is imagination;—analogical sympathy; and exquisite of its kind it is.

"You are now sailed *into the north of my lady's opinion; where you will hang like an icicle on a Dutchman's beard,* unless you do redeem it by some laudable attempt.
                    Twelfth Night, Act. iii. sc. 2.

And that is fancy;—one image capriciously suggested by another, and but half connected with the subject of discourse; nay, half opposed to it; for in the gaiety of the speaker's animal spirits, the "Dutchman's beard" is made to represent the lady!

Imagination belongs to Tragedy, or the serious muse; Fancy to the comic. Macbeth, Lear,

Paradise Lost, the poem of Dante, are full of imagination: the Midsummer Night's Dream and the Rape of the Lock, of fancy: Romeo and Juliet, the Tempest, the Fairy Queen, and the Orlando Furioso, of both. The terms were formerly identical, or used as such; and neither is the best that might be found. The term Imagination is too confined: often too material. It presents too invariably the idea of a solid body;—of "images" in the sense of the plaster-cast cry about the streets. Fancy, on the other hand, while it means nothing but a spiritual image or apparition (φαντασμα, appearance, *phantom*), has rarely that freedom from visibility which is one of the highest privileges of imagination. Viola, in Twelfth Night, speaking of some beautiful music, says:—

> It gives a very echo to the seat,
> Where Love is throned.

In this charming thought, fancy and imagination are combined; yet the fancy, the assumption of Love's sitting on a throne, is the image of a solid body; while the imagination, the sense of sympathy between the passion of love and impassioned music, presents us no image at all. Some new term is wanting to express the more spiritual sympathies of what is called Imagination.

One of the teachers of Imagination is Melancholy; and like Melancholy, as Albert Durer has painted her, she looks out among the stars, and is busied with spiritual affinities and the mysteries of the universe. Fancy turns her sister's wizard instruments into toys. She takes a telescope in her hand, and puts a mimic star on her forehead, and sallies forth as an emblem of astronomy. Her tendency is to the child-like and sportive. She chases butterflies, while her sister takes flight with angels. She is the genius of fairies, of gallantries, of fashions; of whatever is quaint and light, showy and capricious; of the poetical part of wit. She adds wings and feelings to the images of wit; and delights as much to people nature with smiling ideal sympathies, as wit does to bring antipathies together, and make them strike light on absurdity. Fancy, however, is not incapable of sympathy with Imagination. She is often found in her company; always, in the case of the greatest poets; often in that of less, though with them she is the greater favourite. Spenser has great imagination and

fancy too, but more of the latter; Milton both also, the very greatest, but with imagination predominant; Chaucer the strongest imagination of real life, beyond any writers but Homer, Dante, and Shakespeare, and in comic painting inferior to none; Pope has hardly any imagination, but he has a great deal of fancy; Coleridge little fancy, but imagination exquisite; Shakespeare alone, of all poets that ever lived, enjoyed the regard of both in equal perfection. A whole fairy poem of his writing will be found in the present volume. See also his famous description of Queen Mab and her equipage, in Romeo and Juliet:—

> Her wagon-spokes made of long spinners' legs;
> The cover, of the wings of grasshoppers:
> Her traces of the smallest spider's web;
> Her collars of the moonshine's watery beams, &c

That is Fancy, in its playful creativeness. As a small but pretty rival specimen, less known, take the description of a fairy palace from Drayton's "Nymphidia":—

> This palace standeth in the air,
> By necromancy placèd there,
> That it no tempest needs to fear,
>   Which way soe'er it blow it:
> And somewhat southward tow'rd the noon,
> Whence lies a way up to the moon,
> And thence the Fairy can as soon
>   Pass to the earth below it.
> The walls of spiders' legs are made,
> Well mortisèd and finely laid;
> He was the master of his trade,
>   It curiously that builded:
> *The windows of the eyes of cats:*

(because they see best at night)

> And for the roof instead of slats,
> Is cover'd with the skins of bats
> *With moonshine that are gilded.*

Here also is a fairy bed, very delicate, from the same poet's Muse's Elysium.

> Of leaves of roses, *white and red,*
> Shall be the covering of her bed;
> The curtains, vallens, tester all,
> Shall be the flower imperial;
> And for the fringe it all along
> *With azure hare-bells shall be hung.*
> *Of lilies shall the pillows be*
> *With down stuft of the butterfly.*

Of fancy, so full of gusto as to border on imagination, Sir John Suckling, in his "Ballad on a Wedding," has given some of the most playful and charming specimens in the language. They glance like twinkles of the eye, or cherries bedewed:

> *Her feet beneath her petticoat,*
> *Like little mice stole in and out*
> *As if they fear'd the light:*
> But oh! she dances such a way!
> *No sun upon an Easter day*
> Is half so fine a sight.

It is very daring, and has a sort of playful grandeur, to compare a lady's dancing with the sun. But as the sun has it all to himself in the heavens, so she, in the blaze of her beauty, on earth. This is imagination fairly displacing fancy. The following has enchanted every body:—

> Her lips were red, *and one was thin*
> *Compared with that was next her chin,*
> *Some bee had stung it newly.*

Every reader has stolen a kiss at that lip, gay or grave.

With regard to the principle of Variety in Uniformity by which verse ought to be modulated, and one-ness of impression diversely produced, it has been contended by some, that Poetry need not be written in verse at all; that prose is as good a medium, provided poetry be conveyed through it; and that to think otherwise is to confound letter with spirit, or form with essence. But the opinion is a prosaical mistake. Fitness and unfitness for *song*, or metrical excitement, just make all the difference between a poetical and prosaical subject; and the reason why verse is necessary to the form of poetry, is, that the perfection of poetical spirit demands it;—that the circle of its enthusiasm, beauty and power, is incomplete without it. I do not mean to say that a poet can never show himself a poet in prose; but that, being one, his desire and necessity will be to write in verse; and that, if he were unable to do so, he would not, and could not, deserve his title. Verse to the true poet is no clog. It is idly called a trammel and a difficulty. It is a help. It springs from the same enthusiasm as the rest of his impulses, and is necessary to their satisfaction and effect. Verse is no more a clog than the condition of rushing upward is a clog to fire, or than the roundness and order of the globe we live on is a clog to the freedom and variety that abound within its sphere. Verse is no dominator over the poet, except inasmuch as the bond is reciprocal, and the poet dominates over the

verse. They are lovers, playfully challenging each other's rule, and delighted equally to rule and to obey. Verse is the final proof to the poet that his mastery over his art is complete. It is the shutting up of his powers in *"measureful* content;" the answer of form to his spirit; of strength and ease to his guidance. It is the willing action, the proud and fiery happiness, of the winged steed on whose back he has vaulted,

To witch the world with wondrous horsemanship.

Verse, in short, is that finishing, and rounding, and "tuneful planetting" of the poet's creations, which is produced of necessity by the smooth tendencies of their energy or inward working, and the harmonious dance into which they are attracted round the orb of the beautiful. Poetry, in its complete sympathy with beauty, must, of necessity, leave no sense of the beautiful, and no power over its forms, unmanifested; and verse flows as inevitably from this condition of its integrity, as other laws of proportion do from any other kind of embodiment of beauty (say that of the human figure), however free and various the movements may be that play within their limits. What great poet ever wrote his poems in prose? or where is a good prose poem, of any length, to be found? The poetry of the Bible is understood to be in verse, in the original. Mr. Hazlitt has said a good word for those prose enlargements of some fine old song, which are known by the name of Ossian; and in passages they deserve what he said; but he judiciously abstained from saying anything about the form. Is Gesner's Death of Abel a poem? or Hervey's Meditations? The Pilgrim's Progress has been called one; and, undoubtedly, Bunyan had a genius which tended to make him a poet, and one of no mean order: and yet it was of as ungenerous and low a sort as was compatible with so lofty an affinity; and this is the reason why it stopped where it did. He had a craving after the beautiful, but not enough of it in himself to echo to its music. On the other hand, the possession of the beautiful will not be sufficient without force to utter it. The author of Telemachus had a soul full of beauty and tenderness. He was not a man who, if he had had a wife and children, would have run away from them, as Bunyan's hero did, to get a place by himself in heaven. He was "a little lower than the angels," like our own Bishop Jewells and Berkeleys; and yet he was no poet. He was too delicately, not to say feebly, absorbed in his devotions, to join in the energies of the seraphic choir.

Every poet, then, is a versifier; every poet an excellent one; and he is the best whose verse exhibits the greatest amount of strength, sweetness, straightforwardness, unsuperfluousness, *variety*, and *one-ness;*—one-ness, that is to say, consistency, in the general impression, metrical and moral; and variety, or every pertinent diversity of tone and rhythm, in the process. *Strength* is the muscle of verse, and shows itself in the number and force of the marked syllables; as,

Sonòrous mètal blòwing màrtial sòunds.
　　　　　　　　　　　Paradise Lost.

Behèmoth, biggest born of eàrth, ùphèav'd
His vàstness.　　　　　　　　　*Id.*

Blòw wìnds and cràck your chèeks! ràge! blòw!
You càtàràcts and hurricànoes, spòut,
Till you have drènch'd our stèeples, dròwn'd the còcks!
You sùlphurous and thòught-èxecuting fìres,
Vàunt coùriers to òak clèaving thùnderbòlts,
Sìnge my whìte hèad! and thòu, àll-shàking thùnder,
Strìke flàt the thìck rotùndity o' the wòrld!

Unexpected locations of the accent double this force, and render it characteristic of passion and abruptness. And here comes into play the reader's corresponding fineness of ear, and his retardations and accelerations in accordance with those of the poet:—

Then in the keyhole turns
The ìntrĭcăte wards, and every bolt and bar
Unfastens.—On ă sŭddĕn òpen fly
With ìmpètuous recoil and jarring sound
The infernal doors, and on their hinges grate
Harsh thunder.　　　　*Par. Lost,* Book II.

Abòmĭnăblĕ—unùttĕrăblĕ—and worse
Than fables yet have feigned.　　　　*Id.*

Wàllŏwĭng ŭnwìĕldy—ènòrmous in their gait. *Id.*

Of unusual passionate accent, there is an exquisite specimen in the Fairy Queen, where Una is lamenting her desertion by the Red-Cross Knight:—

But he, my lion, and my noble lord,
How does he find in cruel heart to hate
Her that him lov'd, and ever most ador'd
As *the gòd of my lìfe?*　Why hath he me abhorr'd?

See the whole stanza, with a note upon it, in the present volume.

The abuse of strength is harshness and heaviness; the reverse of it is weakness. There is a noble sentiment—it appears both in Daniel's and Sir John Beaumont's works, but is most probably the latter's,—which is a perfect outrage of strength in the sound of the words:—

Only the firmest and the *constant'st* hearts
God sets to act the *stout'st* and hardest parts.

Stout'st and *constant'st* for "stoutest" and "most constant!" It is as bad as the intentional crabbedness of the line in Hudibras;

He that hangs or *beats out's* brains,
The devil's in him if *he* feigns.

Beats out's brains, for "beats out his brains." Of heaviness, Davenant's "Gondibert" is a formidable specimen, almost throughout:—

With sìlence (òrder's help, and màrk of càre)
They chìde thàt nòise which hèedless yòuth affèct;
Still coùrse for ùse, for hèalth thèy clèanness wèar
And sàve in well-fìx'd àrms, all nìceness chèck'd.
Thèy thòught, thòse that, unàrm'd, expòs'd fràil lìfe,
But nàked nàture vàliantly betràyed;
Whò wàs, thòugh nàked, sàfe, till prìde màde strìfe,
But màde defènse must ùse, nòw dànger's màde.

And so he goes digging and lumbering on, like a heavy preacher thumping the pulpit in italics, and spoiling many ingenious reflections.

Weakness in versification is want of accent and emphasis. It generally accompanies prosaicalness, and is the consequence of weak thoughts, and of the affectation of a certain well-bred enthusiasm. The writings of the late Mr. Hayley were remarkable for it; and it abounds among the lyrical imitators of Cowley, and the whole of what is called our French school of poetry, when it aspired above its wit and "sense." It sometimes breaks down in a horrible, hopeless manner, as if giving way at the first step. The following ludicrous passage in Congreve, intended to be particularly fine, contains an instance:—

And lo! Silence himself is here;
Methinks I see the midnight god appear.
In all his downy pomp array'd,

Behold the reverend shade.
An ancient sigh he sits upon!!!
Whose memory of sound is long since gone,
And purposely annihilated for his throne!!!
Ode on the singing of Mrs. Arabella Hunt.

See also the would-be enthusiasm of Addison about music:—

    For ever consecrate the *day*
      To music and *Cecilia;*
Music, the greatest good that mortals know,
    And all of heaven we have below,
    Music can noble HINTS *impart!!!*

It is observable that the unpoetic masters of ridicule are apt to make the most ridiculous mistakes, when they come to affect a strain higher than the one they are accustomed to. But no wonder. Their habits neutralize the enthusiasm it requires.

Sweetness, though not identical with smoothness, any more than feeling is with sound, always includes it; and smoothness is a thing so little to be regarded for its own sake, and indeed so worthless in poetry, but for some taste of sweetness, that I have not thought necessary to mention it by itself; though such an all-in-all in versification was it regarded not a hundred years back, that Thomas Warton himself, an idolater of Spenser, ventured to wish the following line in the *Fairy Queen,*

And was admirèd much of fooles, *wòmen,* and
    boys—

altered to

And was admirèd much of women, fools, and
    boys—

thus destroying the fine scornful emphasis on the first syllable of "women!" (an ungallant intimation, by the way, against the fair sex, very startling in this no less woman-loving than great poet). Any poetaster can be smooth. Smoothness abounds in all small poets, as sweetness does in the greater. Sweetness is the smoothness of grace and delicacy,—of the sympathy with the pleasing and lovely. Spenser is full of it,—Shakespeare—Beaumont and Fletcher—Coleridge. Of Spenser's and Coleridge's versification it is the prevailing characteristic. Its main secrets are a smooth progression between variety and sameness, and a voluptuous sense of the continuous,—"linked sweetness long drawn out." Observe the first and last lines of the stanza in the Fairy Queen,

describing a shepherd brushing away the gnats;
—the open and the close *e's* in the one,

    As gèntle shèpherd in swēēt ēventide—

and the repetition of the word *oft,* and the fall from the vowel *a,* into the two *u's* in the other,—

She brusheth *oft,* and *oft* doth màr their mùrmŭrings.

So in his description of two substances in the handling, both equally smooth;—

Each smoother seems than each, and each than
    each seems smoother.

An abundance of examples from his poetry will be found in the volume before us. His beauty revolves on itself with conscious loveliness. And Coleridge is worthy to be named with him, as the reader will see also, and has seen already. Let him take a sample meanwhile from the poem called the Day-Dream! Observe both the variety and sameness of the vowels, and the repetition of the soft consonants:—

My eyes make pictures when they're shut:—
    I see a fountain, large and fair,
A willow and a ruin'd hut,
    And *thee* and *me* and Mary there.
O Mary! make thy gentle lap our pillow;
    Bend o'er us, like a bower, my beautiful green
      willow.

By *Straightforwardness* is meant the flow of words in their natural order, free alike from mere prose, and from those inversions to which bad poets recur in order to escape the charge of prose, but chiefly to accommodate their rhymes. In Shadwell's play of Psyche, Venus gives the sisters of the heroine an answer, of which the following is the *entire* substance, literally, in so many words. The author had nothing better for her to say:—

I receive your prayers with kindness, and will give success to your hopes. I have seen, with anger, mankind adore your sister's beauty and deplore her scorn: which they shall do no more. For I'll so resent their idolatry, as shall content your wishes to the full.

Now in default of all imagination, fancy, and expression, how was the writer to turn these words in poetry or rhyme? Simply by diverting them from their natural order, and twisting the halves of the sentences each before the other.

With kindness I your prayers receive,
And to your hopes success will give.
I have, with anger, seen mankind adore
Your sister's beauty and her scorn deplore;
Which they shall do no more.
For their idolatry I'll so resent,
As shall your wishes to the full content!!

This is just as if a man were to allow that
there was no poetry in the words, "How do you
find yourself?" "Very well, I thank you;" but
to hold them inspired, if altered into

Yourself how do you find?
Very well, you I thank.

It is true, the best writers in Shadwell's age
were addicted to these inversions, partly for
their own reasons, as far as rhyme was concerned, and partly because they held it to be
writing in the classical and Virgilian manner.
What has since been called Artificial Poetry
was then flourishing, in contradistinction to
Natural; or Poetry seen chiefly through art
and books, and not in its first sources. But
when the artificial poet partook of the natural,
or, in other words, was a true poet after his
kind, his best was always written in his most
natural and straightforward manner. Hear
Shadwell's antagonist Dryden. Not a particle of
inversion, beyond what is used for the sake of
emphasis in common discourse, and this only in
one line (the last but three), is to be found in
his immortal character of the Duke of Buck-
ingham:—

A man so various, that he seemed to be
Not one, but all mankind's epitome:
Stiff in opinions, *always in the wrong*,
Was everything by starts, and nothing long;
But in the course of one revolving moon
Was chemist, fiddler, statesman, and buffoon:
Then all for women, rhyming, dancing, drinking,
Besides ten thousand freaks that died in thinking.
Blest madman! who could every hour employ
With something new to wish or to enjoy!
Railing and praising were his usual themes;
And both, to show his judgment, in extremes:
So over violent, or over civil,
That every man with him was god or devil.
In squandering wealth was his peculiar art;
Nothing went unrewarded, but desert.
Beggar'd by fools, whom still he found too late,
He had his jest, and they had his estate.

Inversion itself was often turned into a
grace in these poets, and may be in others, by
the power of being superior to it; using it only
with a classical air, and as a help lying next to
them, instead of a salvation which they are
obliged to seek. In jesting passages also i
sometimes gave the rhyme a turn agreeabl
wilful, or an appearance of choosing what la
in its way; as if a man should pick up a stone t
throw at another's head, where a less confiden
foot would have stumbled over it. Such i
Dryden's use of the word *might*—the mer
sign of a tense—in his pretended ridicule of th
monkish practice of rising to sing psalms in th
night.

And much they griev'd to see so nigh their ha
The bird that warn'd St. Peter of his fall;
That he should raise his mitred crest on high,
And clap his wings and call his family
To sacred rites; and vex th' ethereal powers
With midnight matins at uncivil hours;
Nay more, his quiet neighbors should molest
Just in the sweetness of their morning rest.

(What a line full of "another doze" is that!)

Beast of a bird! supinely, when he *might*
Lie snug and sleep, to rise before the light
What if his dull forefathers used that cry?
Could he not let a bad example die?

I the more gladly quote instances like those
of Dryden, to illustrate the points in question,
because they are specimens of the very highest kind of writing in the heroic couplet upon
subjects not heroical. As to prosaicalness in
general, it is sometimes indulged in by young
writers on the plea of its being natural; but
this is a mere confusion of triviality with propriety, and is usually the result of indolence.

Unsuperfluousness is rather a matter of style
in general, than of the sound and order of
words: and yet versification is so much
strengthened by it, and so much weakened by
its opposite, that it could not but come within
the category of its requisites. When superflu-
ousness of words is not occasioned by overflowing animal spirits, as in Beaumont and Fletcher,
or by the very genius of luxury, as in Spenser
(in which cases it is enrichment as well as
overflow), there is no worse sign for a poet altogether, except pure barrenness. Every word
that could be taken away from a poem, unre-
ferable to either of the above reasons for it, is
a damage; and many such are death; for there
is nothing that posterity seems so determined
to resent as this want of respect for its time
and trouble. The world is too rich in books to
endure it. Even true poets have died of this
Writer's Evil. Trifling ones have survived, with
scarcely any pretensions but the terseness of

their trifles. What hope can remain for wordy mediocrity? Let the discerning reader take up any poem, pen in hand, for the purpose of discovering how many words he can strike out of it that give him no requisite ideas, no relevant ones that he cares for, and no reasons for the rhyme beyond its necessity, and he will see what blot and havoc he will make in many an admired production of its day,—what marks of its inevitable fate. Bulky authors in particular, however safe they may think themselves, would do well to consider what parts of their cargo they might dispense with in their proposed voyage down the gulfs of time; for many a gallant vessel, thought indestructible in its age, has perished;—many a load of words, expected to be in eternal demand, gone to join the wrecks of self-love, or rotted in the warehouses of change and vicissitude. I have said the more on this point, because in an age when the true inspiration has undoubtedly been re-awakened by Coleridge and his fellows, and we have so many new poets coming forward, it may be as well to give a general warning against that tendency to an accumulation and ostentation of *thoughts,* which is meant to be a refutation in full of the pretensions of all poetry less cogitabund, whatever may be the requirements of its class. Young writers should bear in mind, that even some of the very best materials for poetry are not poetry built; and that the smallest marble shrine, of exquisite workmanship, outvalues all that architect ever chipped away. Whatever can be so dispensed with is rubbish.

Variety in versification consists in whatsoever can be done for the prevention of monotony, by diversity of stops and cadences, distribution of emphasis, and retardation and acceleration of time; for the whole real secret of versification is a musical secret, and is not attainable to any vital effect, save by the ear of genius. All the mere knowledge of feet and numbers, of accent and quantity, will no more impart it, than a knowledge of the "Guide to Music" will make a Beethoven or a Paisiello. It is a matter of sensibility and imagination; of the beautiful in poetical passion, accompanied by musical; of the imperative necessity for a pause here, and a cadence there, and a quicker or slower utterance in this or that place, created by analogies of sound with sense, by the fluctuations of feeling, by the demands of the gods and graces that visit the poet's

harp, as the winds visit that of Æolus. The same time and quantity which are occasioned by the spiritual part of this secret, thus become its formal ones,—not feet and syllables, long and short, iambics or trochees; which are the reduction of it to its *less* than dry bones. You might get, for instance, not only ten and eleven, but thirteen or fourteen syllables into a rhyming, as well as blank, heroical verse, if time and the feeling permitted; and in irregular measure this is often done; just as musicians put twenty notes in a bar instead of two, quavers instead of minims, according as the feeling they are expressing impels them to fill up the time with short and hurried notes, or with long; or as the choristers in a cathedral retard or precipitate the words of the chaunt, according as the quantity of its notes, and the colon which divides the verse of the psalm, conspire to demand it. Had the moderns borne this principle in mind when they settled the prevailing systems of verse, instead of learning them, as they appear to have done, from the first drawling and one-syllabled notation of the church hymns, we should have retained all the advantages of the more numerous versification of the ancients, without being compelled to fancy that there was no alternative for us between our syllabical uniformity and the hexameters or other special forms unsuited to our tongues. But to leave this question alone, we will present the reader with a few sufficing specimens of the difference between monotony and variety in versification, first from Pope, Dryden, and Milton, and next from Gay and Coleridge. The following is the boasted melody of the nevertheless exquisite poet of the "Rape of the Lock,"—exquisite in his wit and fancy, though not in his numbers. The reader will observe that it is literally *see-saw,* like the rising and falling of a plank, with a light person at one end who is jerked up in the briefer time, and a heavier one who is set down more leisurely at the other. It is in the otherwise charming description of the heroine of that poem:—

On her white breast—a sparkling cross she wore,
Which Jews might kiss—and infidels adore;
Her lively looks—a sprightly mind disclose,
Quick as her eyes—and as unfix'd as those;
Favours to none—to all she smiles extends,
Oft she rejects—but never once offends;
Bright as the sun—her eyes the gazers strike,
And like the sun—they shine on all alike;
Yet graceful ease—and sweetness void of pride,

Might hide her faults—if belles had faults to hide;
If to her share—some female errors fall,
Look on her face—and you'll forget them all.

Compare with this the description of Iphigenia in one of Dryden's stories from Boccaccio:—

It happen'd—on a summer's holiday,
That to the greenwood shade—he took his way,
For Cymon shunn'd the church—and used not
　　much to pray.
His quarter-staff—which he could ne'er forsake,
Hung half before—and half behind his back:
He trudg'd along—not knowing what he sought,
And whistled as he went—for want of thought.

By chance conducted—or by thirst constrain'd,
The deep recesses of a grove he gain'd:—
Where—in a plain defended by a wood,
Crept through the matted grass—a crystal
　　flood,
By which—an alabaster fountain stood;
And on the margent of the fount was laid—
Attended by her slaves—a sleeping maid;
Like Dian and her nymphs—when, tir'd with
　　sport,
To rest by cool Eurotas they resort.—
The dame herself—the goddess well express'd,
Not more distinguished by her purple vest—
Than by the charming features of the face—
And e'en in slumber—a superior grace:
Her comely limbs—compos'd with decent care,
Her body shaded—with a light cymarr,
Her bosom to the view—was only bare;
Where two beginning paps were scarcely spied—
For yet their places were but signified.—
The fanning wind upon her bosom blows—
To meet the fanning wind—the bosom rose;
The fanning wind—and purling stream—continue her repose.

For a further variety take, from the same author's Theodore and Honoria, a passage in which the couplets are run one into the other, and all of it modulated, like the former, according to the feeling demanded by the occasion:—

Whilst listening to the murmuring leaves he
　　stood—
More than a mile immers'd within the wood—
At once the wind was laid.|—The whispering
　　sound
Was dumb.|—A rising earthquake rock'd the
　　ground.
With deeper brown the grove was overspread—
A sudden horror seiz'd his giddy head—
And his ears tinkled—and his colour fled.

Nature was in alarm.—Some danger nigh
Seem'd threaten'd—though unseen to mortal eye.
Unused to fear—he summon'd all his soul,
And stood collected in himself—and whole:
Not long.—

But for a crowning specimen of variety of pause and accent, apart from emotion, nothing can surpass the account, in Paradise Lost, of the Devil's search for an accomplice:—

　　　　　　　　　　There was a plàce,
Nòw nòt—though Sìn—not Tìme—first wroùght
　　the chànge,
Where Tìgris—at the foot of Pàradise,
Into a gùlf—shòt under ground—till pàrt
Ròse up a foùntain by the Trèe of Lìfe.
In with the river sunk—and *with* it *ròse*
Sàtan—invòlved in rìsing mìst—then soùght
Whère to lie hìd.—Sèa he had searched—and
　　lànd
From Eden over Pòntus—and the Pòol
Mæòtis—*ùp* beyond the river *Ob;*
Dòwnward as fàr antàrctic;—and in lèngth
West from Oròntes—to the òcean bàrr'd
At Dàriën—thènce to the lànd whère flòws
Gànges and Indus.—Thùs the òrb he ròamed
With nàrrow sèarch;—and with inspèction deep
Consìdered èvery crèature—whìch of àll
Mòst opportùne mìght sèrve his wìles—and foùnd
The sèrpent—sùbtlest bèast of all the fièld.

If the reader cast his eye again over this passage, he will not find a verse in it which is not varied and harmonized in the most remarkable manner. Let him notice in particular that curious balancing of the lines in the sixth and tenth verses:—

　　In with the river sunk, &c.

and

　　Up beyond the river *Ob.*

It might, indeed, be objected to the versification of Milton, that it exhibits too constant a perfection of this kind. It sometimes forces upon us too great a sense of consciousness on the part of the composer. We miss the first sprightly runnings of verse,—the ease and sweetness of spontaneity. Milton, I think, also too often condenses weight into heaviness.

Thus much concerning the chief of our two most popular measures. The other, called octosyllabic, or the measure of eight syllables, offered such facilities for *namby-pamby,* that it had become a jest as early as the time of Shakespeare, who makes Touchstone call it the "butterwoman's rate to market," and the "very false gallop of verses." It has been advocated, in opposition to the heroic measure, upon the ground that ten syllables lead a man into epithets and other superfluities, while eight syllables compress him into a sensible and pithy gentleman. But the heroic measure laughs at it.

So far from compressing, it converts one line into two, and sacrifices everything to the quick and importunate return of the rhyme. With Dryden, compare Gay, even in the strength of Gay,—

The wind was high, the window shakes;
With sudden start the miser wakes;
Along the silent room he stalks,

(A miser never "stalks;" but a rhyme was desired for 'walks')

Looks back, and trembles as he walks:
Each lock and every bolt he tries,
In every creek and corner pries;
Then opes the chest with treasure stor'd,
And stands in rapture o'er his hoard;

("Hoard" and "treasure stor'd" are just made for one another,)

But now, with sudden qualms possess'd,
He wrings his hands, he beats his breast;
By conscience stung, he wildly stares,
And thus his guilty soul declares.

And so he denounces his gold, as miser never denounced it; and sighs, because

Virtue resides on earth no more!

Coleridge saw the mistake which had been made with regard to this measure, and restored it to the beautiful freedom of which it was capable, by calling to mind the liberties allowed its old musical professors the minstrels, and dividing it by *time* instead of *syllables;*— by the *beat of four* into which you might get as many syllables as you could, instead of allotting eight syllables to the poor time, whatever it might have to say. He varied it further with alternate rhymes and stanzas, with rests and omissions precisely analogous to those in music and rendered it altogether worthy to utter the manifold thoughts and feelings of himself and his lady Christabel. He even ventures, with an exquisite sense of solemn strangeness and license (for there is witchcraft going forward), to introduce a couplet of blank verse, itself as mystically and beautifully modulated as anything in the music of Gluck or Weber.

'Tis the middle of night by the castle clock,
And the owls have awaken'd the crowing cock;
Tu—whit!——Tu—whoo!
And hark, again! the crowing cock,
How drowsily he crew.
Sir Leoline, the baron rich,

Hath a toothless mastiff bitch;
From her kennel beneath the rock
She maketh answer to the clock,
Fòur fŏr thĕ quàrtĕrs ănd twèlve fŏr thĕ hòur;
Ever and aye, by shine and shower,
Sixteen short howls, not over loud:
Some say, she sees my lady's shroud.

Is the nìght chìlly and dàrk?
The nìght is chìlly, but nòt dàrk.
The thin grey cloud is spread on high,
It covers, but not hides, the sky.
The moon is behind, and at the full,
And yet she looks both small and dull.
The night is chilly, the cloud is grey;

(These are not superfluities, but mysterious returns of importunate feeling)

'Tis a month before the month of May,
And the spring comes slowly up this way.
The lovely lady, Christabel,
Whom her father loves so well,
What makes her in the wood so late,
A furlong from the castle-gate?
She had dreams all yesternight
Of her own betrothèd knight;
And shè ĭn thĕ midnight wood will pray
For the wèal ŏf hĕr lover that's far away.

She stole along, she nothing spoke,
The sighs she heaved were soft and low.
And nought was green upon the oak,
But moss and rarest mistletoe;
She kneels beneath the huge oak tree,
And in silence prayeth she.

The lady sprang up suddenly,
The lovely lady, Christabel!
It moan'd as near as near can be,
But what it is, she cannot tell.
On the other side it seems to be
Of thĕ hùge, broàd-breàsted, òld oàk trèe.

The night is chill; the forest bare;
Is it the wind that moaneth bleak?

(This "bleak moaning" is a witch's)

There is not wind enough in the air
To move away the ringlet curl
From the lovely lady's cheek—
There is not wind enough to twirl
The òne rèd lèaf, the làst ŏf ĭts clàn,
That dàncĕs ăs òftĕn ăs dànce ĭt càn,
Hàngĭng sŏ lìght and hàngĭng sŏ hìgh,
On thĕ tòpmost twìg thăt lŏoks ùp ăt thĕ sky.

Hush, beating heart of Christabel!
Jesu Maria, shield her well!
She folded her arms beneath her cloak,
And stole to the other side of the oak.
What sees she there?

There she sees a damsel bright,
Dressed in a robe of silken white.

That shadowy in the moonlight shone:
The neck that made that white robe wan,
Her stately neck and arms were bare:
Her blue-veined feet unsandaled were;
And wildly glitter'd, here and there,
The gems entangled in her hair.
I guess 'twas *frightful* there to see
A lady so richly clad as she—
Beautiful exceedingly.

The principle of Variety in Uniformity is
here worked out in a style "beyond the reach
of art." Everything is diversified according to
the demand of the moment, of the sounds, the
sights, the emotions; the very uniformity of
the outline is gently varied; and yet we feel
that *the whole is one and of the same char-*
acter, the single and sweet unconsciousness of
the heroine making all the rest seem more conscious, and ghastly, and expectant. It is thus
that *versification itself becomes part of the*
sentiment of a poem, and vindicates the pains
that have been taken to show its importance. I
know of no very fine versification unaccompanied with fine poetry; no poetry of a mean
order accompanied with verse of the highest.

As to Rhyme, which might be thought too
insignificant to mention, it is not at all so. The
universal consent of modern Europe, and of the
East in all ages, has made it one of the musical beauties of verse for all poetry but epic
and dramatic, and even for the former with
Southern Europe,—a sustainment for the
enthusiasm, and a demand to enjoy. The mastery of it consists in never writing it for its
own sake, or at least never appearing to do
so; in knowing how to vary it, to give it
novelty, to render it more or less strong, to
divide it (when not in couplets) at the proper
intervals, to repeat it many times where luxury
or animal spirits demand it (see an instance in
Titania's speech to the Fairies), to impress an
affecting or startling remark with it, and to
make it, in comic poetry, a new and surprising
addition to the jest.

Large was his bounty and his soul sincere,
  Heav'n did a recompense as largely send;
He gave to misery all he had, *a tear;*
  He gained from heav'n ('twas all he wish'd)
    a friend.   Gray's *Elegy.*

The fops are proud of scandal; for they cry
At every lewd, low character,—"That's *I.*"
    Dryden's *Prologue to the Pilgrim.*

What makes all doctrines plain and clear?
About two hundred pounds a-year.

And that which was proved true before,
Prove false again? *Two hundred more.*
                  Hudibras.

Compound for sins they are *inclin'd to,*
By damning those they have *no mind to.*   *Id.*

——Stor'd with deletery *med'cines,*
Which whosoever took is *dead since.*   *Id.*

Sometimes it is a grace in a master like
Butler to force his rhyme, thus showing a
laughing wilful power over the most stubborn
materials:—

                             Win
The women, and make them draw in
The men, as Indians with a *fèmale*
Tame elephant inveigle *the* male.
                    Hudibras.

  He made an instrument to know
  If the moon shines at full or no;
  That would, as soon as e'er she *shone,*
    straight,
  Whether 'twere day or night *demonstrate;*
  Tell what her diameter to an *inch is,*
  And prove that she's not made of *green*
    cheese.

Pronounce it, by all means, *grinches,* to make
the joke more wilful. The happiest triple
rhyme, perhaps, that ever was written, is in
Don Juan:—

But oh! ye lords of ladies *intellectual,*
Inform us truly,—haven't they *hen-peck'd you*
  all?

The sweepingness of the assumption completes
the flowing breadth of effect.

Dryden confessed that a rhyme often gave
him a thought. Probably the happy word
"sprung" in the following passage from Ben
Jonson was suggested by it; but then the poet
must have had the feeling in him.

  —Let our trumpets sound,
  And cleave both air and ground
    With beating of our drums.
  Let every lyre be strung,
  Harp, lute, theorbo, *sprung*
    With touch of dainty thumbs.

Boileau's trick for appearing to rhyme naturally was to compose the second line of his
couplet first! which gives one the crowning
idea of the "artificial school of poetry." Perhaps the most perfect master of rhyme, the
easiest and most abundant, was the greatest
writer of comedy that the world has seen,—
Molière.

If a young reader should ask, after all,

What is the quickest way of knowing bad poets from good, the best poets from the next best, and so on? the answer is, the only and two-fold way; first, the perusal of the best poets with the greatest attention; and, second, the cultivation of that love of truth and beauty which made them what they are. Every true reader of poetry partakes a more than ordinary portion of the poetic nature; and no one can be completely such, who does not love, or take an interest in, everything that interests the poet, from the firmament to the daisy,—from the highest heart of man to the most pitiable of the low. It is a good practice to read with pen in hand, marking what is liked or doubted. It rivets the attention, realizes the greatest amount of enjoyment, and facilitates reference. It enables the reader also, from time to time, to see what progress he makes with his own mind, and how it grows up towards the stature of its exalter.

If the same person should ask, What class of poetry is the highest? I should say, undoubtedly, the Epic; for it includes the drama, with narration besides; or the speaking and action of the characters, with the speaking of the poet himself, whose utmost address is taxed to relate all well for so long a time, particularly in the passages least sustained by enthusiasm. Whether this class has included the greatest poet, is another question still under trial; for Shakespeare perplexes all such verdicts, even when the claimant is Homer; though, if a judgment may be drawn from his early narratives (Venus and Adonis, and the Rape of Lucrece), it is to be doubted whether even Shakespeare could have told a story like Homer, owing to that incessant activity and superfœtation of thought, a little less of which might be occasionally desired even in his plays;—if it were possible, once possessing anything of his, to wish it away. Next to Homer and Shakespeare come such narrators as the less universal, but still intenser Dante; Milton, with his dignified imagination; the universal, profoundly simple Chaucer; and luxuriant, remote Spenser—immortal child in poetry's most poetic solitudes: then the great second-rate dramatists; unless those who are better acquainted with Greek tragedy than I am, demand a place for them before Chaucer: then the airy yet robust universality of Ariosto; the hearty, out-of-door nature of Theocritus, also a universalist; the finest lyrical poets (who only take short flights, compared with the narrators); the purely contemplative poets who have more thought than feeling; the descriptive, satirical, didactic, epigrammatic. It is to be borne in mind, however, that the first poet of an inferior class may be superior to followers in the train of a higher one, though the superiority is by no means to be taken for granted; otherwise Pope would be superior to Fletcher, and Butler to Pope. Imagination, teeming with action and character, makes the greatest poets; feeling and thought the next; fancy (by itself) the next; wit the last. Thought by itself makes no poet at all; for the mere conclusions of the understanding can at best be only so many intellectual matters of fact. Feeling, even destitute of conscious thought, stands a far better poetical chance; feeling being a sort of thought without the process of thinking,—a grasper of the truth without seeing it. And what is very remarkable, feeling seldom makes the blunders that thought does. An idle distinction has been made between taste and judgment. Taste is the very maker of judgment. Put an artificial fruit in your mouth, or only handle it, and you will soon perceive the difference between judging from taste or tact, and judging from the abstract figment called judgment. The latter does but throw you into guesses and doubts. Hence the conceits that astonish us in the gravest, and even subtlest thinkers, whose taste is not proportionate to their mental perceptions; men like Donne, for instance; who, apart from accidental personal impressions, seem to look at nothing as it really is, but only as to what may be thought of it. Hence, on the other hand, the delightfulness of those poets who never violate truth of feeling, whether in things real or imaginary; who are always consistent with their object and its requirements; and who run the great round of nature, not to perplex and be perplexed, but to make themselves and us happy. And luckily, delightfulness is not incompatible with greatness, willing soever as men may be in their present imperfect state to set the power to subjugate above the power to please. Truth, of any great kind whatsoever, makes great writing. This is the reason why such poets as Ariosto, though not writing with a constant detail of thought and feeling like Dante, are justly considered great as well as delightful. Their greatness proves itself by the same truth of nature, and sustained power, though in a different way. Their action is not so crowded and weighty; their sphere has more territories less fertile; but it has enchantments of its own, which excess of thought would spoil, —luxuries, laughing graces, animal spirits; and not to recognize the beauty and greatness of these, treated as they treat them, is simply to be defective in sympathy. Every planet is not Mars or Saturn. There is also Venus and Mercury. There is one genius of the south, and another of the north, and others uniting both. The reader who is too thoughtless or too sensitive to like intensity of any sort, and he who is too thoughtful or too dull to like anything but the greatest possible stimulus of reflection or passion, are equally wanting in complexional fitness for a thorough enjoyment of books. Ariosto occasionally says as fine things as Dante, and Spenser as Shakespeare; but the business of both is to enjoy; and in order to partake their enjoyment to its full extent, you must feel what poetry is in the general as well as the particular, must be aware that there are different songs of the spheres, some fuller of notes, and others of a sustained delight; and as the former keep you perpetually alive to thought or passion, so from the latter you receive a constant harmonious sense of truth and beauty, more agreeable perhaps on the whole, though less exciting. Ariosto, for instance, does not *tell a story* with the brevity and concentrated passion of Dante; every sentence is not so full of matter, nor the style so removed from the indifference of prose; yet you are charmed with a truth of another sort, equally characteristic of the writer, equally drawn from nature and substituting a healthy sense of enjoyment for intenser emotion. Exclusiveness of liking for this or that mode of truth, only shows, either that a reader's perceptions are limited, or that he would sacrifice truth itself to his favorite form of it. Sir Walter Raleigh, who was as trenchant with his pen as his sword, hailed the Faery Queen of his friend Spenser in verses in which he said that "Petrarch" was thenceforward to be no more heard of; and that in all English poetry there was nothing he counted "of any price" but the effusions of the new author. Yet Petrarch is still living; Chaucer was not abolished by Sir Walter; and Shakespeare is thought somewhat valuable. A botanist might as well have said, that myrtles and oaks were to disappear, because acacias had come up. It is with the poet's creations as with nature's, great or small.

Wherever truth and beauty, whatever their amount, can be worthily shaped into verse, and answer to some demand for it in our hearts, there poetry is to be found; whether in productions grand and beautiful as some great event, or some mighty, leafy solitude, or no bigger and more pretending than a sweet face or a bunch of violets; whether in Homer's epic or Gray's Elegy, in the enchanted gardens of Ariosto and Spenser, or the very pot-herbs of the Schoolmistress of Shenstone, the balms of the simplicity of a cottage. Not to know and feel this is to be deficient in the universality of Nature herself, who is a poetess on the smallest as well as the largest scale, and who calls upon us to admire all her productions; not indeed with the same degree of admiration, but with no refusal of it, except to defect.

I cannot draw this essay towards its conclusion better than with three memorable words of Milton; who has said, that poetry, in comparison with science, is "simple, sensuous, and passionate." By simple, he means unperplexed and self-evident; by sensuous, genial and full of imagery; by passionate, excited and enthusiastic. I am aware that different constructions have been put on some of these words; but the context seems to me to necessitate those before us. I quote, however, not from the original, but from an extract in the Remarks on Paradise Lost by Richardson.

What the poet has to cultivate above all things is love and truth;—what he has to avoid, like poison, is the fleeting and the false. He will get no good by proposing to be "in earnest at the moment." His earnestness must be innate and habitual; born with him, and felt to be his most precious inheritance. "I expect neither profit nor general fame by my writings," says Coleridge, in the Preface to his Poems; "and I consider myself as having been amply repaid without either. Poetry has been to me its *'own exceeding great reward;'* it has soothed my afflictions; it has multiplied and refined my enjoyments; it has endeared solitude; and it has given me the habit of wishing to discover the good and the beautiful in all that meets and surrounds me."

"Poetry," says Shelley, "lifts the veil from the hidden beauty of the world, *and makes familiar objects be as if they were not familiar.* It reproduces all that it represents; and the impersonations clothed in its Elysian light stand thenceforward in the minds of those who have once contemplated them, as memorials of that gentle and exalted content which extends itself over all thoughts and actions with which it co-exists. The great secret of morals is love, or a going out of our own nature, and an identification of ourselves with the beautiful which exists in thought, action, or person, not our own. A man, to be greatly good, must imagine intensely and comprehensively; he must put himself in the place of another, and of many others: the pains and pleasures of his species must become his own. The great instrument of moral good is the imagination; and poetry administers to the effect by acting upon the cause."

I would not willingly say anything after perorations like these; but as treatises on poetry may chance to have auditors who think themselves called upon to vindicate the superiority of what is termed useful knowledge, it may be as well to add, that if the poet may be allowed to pique himself on any one thing more than another, compared with those who undervalue him, it is on that power of undervaluing nobody, and no attainments different from his own, which is given him by the very faculty of imagination they despise. The greater includes the less. They do not see that their inability to comprehend him argues the smaller capacity. No man recognizes the worth of utility more than the poet: he only desires that the meaning of the term may not come short of its greatness, and exclude the noblest necessities of his fellow-creatures. He is quite as much pleased, for instance, with the facilities for rapid conveyance afforded him by the railroad, as the dullest confiner of its advantages to that single idea, or as the greatest two-idead man who varies that single idea with hugging himself on his "buttons" or his good dinner. But he sees also the beauty of the country through which he passes, of the towns, of the heavens, of the steam-engine itself, thundering and fuming along like a magic horse, of the affections that are carrying, perhaps, half the passengers on their journey, nay, of those of the great two-idead man; and, beyond all this, he discerns the incalculable amount of good, and knowledge, and refinement, and mutual consideration, which this wonderful invention is fitted to circulate over the globe, perhaps to the displacement of war itself, and certainly to the diffusion of millions of enjoyments.

"And a button-maker, after all, invented it!" cries our friend.

Pardon me—it was a nobleman. A button-maker may be a very excellent, and a very poetical man too, and yet not have been the first man visited by a sense of the gigantic powers of the combination of water and fire. It was a nobleman who first thought of this most poetical bit of science. It was a nobleman who first thought of it,—a captain who first tried it,—and a button-maker who perfected it. And he who put the nobleman on such thoughts, was the great philosopher, Bacon, who said that poetry had "something divine in it," and was necessary to the satisfaction of the human mind.

YOUNG POETS

The Examiner. No. 466, pp. 761–2. Sunday, Dec. 1, 1816.

In sitting down to this subject, we happen to be restricted by time to a much shorter notice than we could wish: but we mean to take it up again shortly. Many of our readers however have perhaps observed for themselves, that there has been a new school of poetry rising of late, which promises to extinguish the French one that has prevailed among us since the time of Charles the 2d. It began with something excessive, like most revolutions, but this gradually wore away; and an evident aspiration after real nature and original fancy remained, which called to mind the finer times of the English Muse. In fact it is wrong to call it a new school, and still more so to represent it is as one of innovation, it's [1] only object being to restore the same love of Nature, and of *thinking* instead of mere *talking*, which formerly rendered us real poets, and not merely versifying wits, and bead-rollers of couplets.

We were delighted to see the departure of the old school acknowledged in the number of the *Edinburgh Review* just published,—a candour the more generous and spirited, inasmuch as that work has hitherto been the greatest surviving ornament of the same school in prose and criticism, as it is now destined, we trust, to be still the leader in the new.

[1] Having taken our copy directly from *The Examiner* and *The Indicator*, we have preferred to present the text as it is there printed. We have, however, made uniform the spelling of *it's* and *Keat's*.

We also felt the same delight at the third canto of Lord Byron's *Child Harolde,* in which, to our conceptions at least, he has fairly renounced a certain leaven of the French style, and taken his place where we always said he would be found,—among the poets who have a real feeling for numbers, and who go directly to Nature for inspiration. But more of this poem in our next.

The object of the present article is merely to notice three young writers, who appear to us to promise a considerable addition of strength to the new school. Of the first who came before us, we have, it is true, yet seen only one or two specimens, and these were no sooner sent us than we unfortunately mislaid them; but we shall procure what he has published, and if the rest answer to what we have seen, we shall have no hesitation in announcing him for a very striking and original thinker. His name is Percy Bysshe Shelley, and he is the author of a poetical work entitled *Alastor, or the Spirit of Solitude.*

The next with whose name we became acquainted, was John Henry Reynolds, author of a tale called Safie, written, we believe, in imitation of Lord Byron, and more lately of a small set of poems published by Taylor and Hessey, the principal of which is called the *Naiad.* . . . [Quotes first twenty-seven lines.]

We shall give another extract or two in a future number. The author's style is too artificial, though he is evidently an admirer of Mr. Wordsworth. Like all young poets too, properly so called, his love of detail is too overwrought and indiscriminate; but still he is a young poet, and only wants a still closer attention to things as opposed to the seduction of words, to realize all that he promises. His nature seems very true and amiable.

The last of these young aspirants whom we have met with, and who promise to help the new school to revive Nature and

To put a spirit of youth in everything,—

is, we believe, the youngest of them all, and just of age. His name is JOHN KEATS. He has not yet published anything except in a newspaper; but a set of his manuscripts was handed us the other day, and fairly surprised us with the truth of their ambition, and ardent grappling with Nature. In the following Sonnet there is one incorrect rhyme, which might be easily altered, but which shall serve in the

meantime as a peace-offering to the rhyming critics. The rest of the composition, with the exception of a little vagueness in calling the regions of poetry "the realms of gold," we do not hesitate to pronounce excellent, especially the last six lines. The word *swims* is complete; and the whole conclusion is equally powerful and quiet: . . . ["On First Looking into Chapman's Homer" follows.]

We have spoken with the less scruple of these poetical promises, because we really are not in the habit of lavishing praises and announcements, and because we have no fear of any pettier vanity on the part of young men, who promise to understand human nature so well.

POEMS BY JOHN KEATS

12mo.—C. and J. Ollier.—

The Examiner. No. 492, p. 345. Sunday, June 1, 1817.

THIS is the production of the young writer, whom we had the pleasure of announcing to the public a short time since, and several of whose Sonnets have appeared meanwhile in the *Examiner* with the signature of J. K. From these and stronger evidences in the book itself, the readers will conclude that the author and his critic are personal friends; and they are so,—made however, in the first instance, by nothing but his poetry, and at no greater distance of time than the announcement above-mentioned. We had published one of his Sonnets in our paper, without knowing more of him than any other anonymous correspondent; but at the period in question, a friend brought us one morning some copies of verses, which he said were from the pen of a youth. We had not been led, generally speaking, by a good deal of experience in these matters, to expect pleasure from introductions of the kind, so much as pain; but we had not read more than a dozen lines, when we recognized "a young poet indeed."

It is no longer a new observation, that poetry has of late years undergone a very great change, or rather, to speak properly, poetry has undergone no change, but something which was not poetry has made way for the return of something which is. The school which existed till lately since the restoration of Charles the 2d, was rather a school of wit and ethics in verse, than anything else; nor was the verse, with the exception of Dryden's, of the best order. The authors, it is true, are to be held in great honour. Great wit there certainly was, excellent satire, excellent sense, pithy sayings; and Pope distilled as much real poetry as could be got from the drawing-room world in which the art then lived,—from the flowers and luxuries of artificial life,—into that exquisite little toilet-bottle of essence, the *Rape of the Lock*. But there was little imagination, of a higher order, no intense feeling of nature, no sentiment, no real music or variety. Even the writers who gave evidences meanwhile of a truer poetical faculty, Gray, Thomson, Akenside, and Collins himself, were content with a great deal of second-hand workmanship, and with false styles made up of other languages and a certain kind of inverted cant. It has been thought that Cowper was the first poet who re-opened the true way to nature and a natural style; but we hold this to be a mistake, arising merely from certain negations on the part of that amiable but by no means powerful writer. Cowper's style is for the most part as inverted and artificial as that of the others; and we look upon him to have been by nature not so great a poet as Pope: but Pope, from certain infirmities on his part, was thrown into the society of the world, and thus had to get what he could out of an artificial sphere:— Cowper, from other and more distressing infirmities, (which by the way the wretched superstition that undertook to heal, only burnt in upon him) was confined to a still smaller though more natural sphere, and in truth did not much with it, though quite as much perhaps as was to be expected from an organization too sore almost to come in contact with any thing.

It was the Lake Poets in our opinion (however grudgingly we say it, on some accounts) that were the first to revive a true taste for nature; and like most Revolutionists, especially of the cast which they have since turned out to be, they went to an extreme, calculated rather at first to make the readers of poetry disgusted with originality and adhere with contempt and resentment to their magazine common-places. This had a bad effect also in the way of re-action; and none of those writers have ever since been able to free themselves from certain stubborn affectations, which hav-ing been ignorantly confounded by others with the better part of them, have been retained by their self-love with a still less pardonable want of wisdom. The greater part indeed of the poetry of Mr. Southey, a weak man in all respects, is really made up of little else. Mr. Coleridge still trifles with his poetical as he has done with his metaphysical talent. Mr. Lamb, in our opinion, has a more real tact of humanity, a modester, Shakespearean wisdom, than any of them; and had he written more, might have delivered the school victoriously from all it's defects. But it is Mr. Wordsworth who has advanced it the most, and who in spite of some morbidities as well as mistaken theories in other respects, has opened upon us a fund of thinking and imagination, that ranks him as the successor of the true and abundant poets of the older time. Poetry, like Plenty, should be represented with a cornucopia, but it should be a real one; not swelled out and insidiously *optimized* at the top, like Mr. Southey's stale strawberry baskets, but fine and full to the depth, like a heap from the vintage. Yet from the time of Milton till lately, scarcely a tree had been planted that could be called a poet's own. People got shoots from France, that ended in nothing but a little barren wood, from which they made flutes for young gentlemen and fan-sticks for ladies. The rich and enchanted ground of real poetry, fertile with all that English succulance could produce, bright with all that Italian sunshine could lend, and haunted with exquisite humanities, had become invisible to mortal eyes like the garden of Eden:—

And from that time those Graces were not found.

No. 497, pp. 428–9. Sunday, July 6, 1817.

These Graces, however, are re-appearing; and one of the greatest evidences is the little volume before us; for the work is not one of mere imitation, or a compilation of ingenious and promising things that merely announce better, and that after all might only help to keep up a bad system; but here is a young poet giving himself up to his own impressions, and revelling in real poetry for it's own sake. He has had his advantages, because others have cleared the way into those happy bowers; but it shews the strength of his natural tendency, that he has not been turned aside by the lingering enticements of a former system, and by the self-love which interests others in enforcing them. We do not, of course, mean to say that Mr. Keats has as much talent as he will have ten years hence, or that there are no imitations in his book, or that he does not make mistakes common to inexperience;—the reverse is inevitable at his time of life. In proportion to our ideas, or impressions of the images of things, must be our acquaintance with the things themselves. But our author has all the sensitiveness of temperament requisite to receive these impressions; and wherever he has turned hitherto, he has evidently felt them deeply.

The very faults indeed of Mr. Keats arise from a passion for beauties, and a young impatience to vindicate them; and as we have mentioned these, we shall refer to them at once. They may be comprised in two;—first, a tendency to notice every thing too indiscriminately and without an eye to natural proportion and effect; and second, a sense of the proper variety of versification without a due consideration of it's principles.

The former error is visible in several parts of the book, but chiefly though mixed with great beauties in the Epistles, and more between pages 28 and 47, where are collected the author's earliest pieces, some of which, we think, might have been omitted, especially the string of magistrate-interrogatories about a shell and a copy of verses. See also (p. 61) a comparison of wine poured out in heaven to the appearance of a falling star, and (p. 62) the sight of far-seen fountains in the same region to "silver streaks across a dolphin's fin." It was by thus giving way to every idea that came across him, that Marino, a man of real poetical fancy, but no judgment, corrupted the poetry of Italy; a castastrophe, which however we by no means anticipate in our author, who with regard to this point is much more deficient in age than in good taste. We shall presently have to notice passages of a reverse nature, and these are by far the most numerous. But we warn him against a fault, which is the more tempting to a young writer of genius, inasmuch as it involves something so opposite to the contented common-place and vague generalities of the late school of poetry. There is a super-abundance of detail, which, though not so wanting, of course, in power of perception, is as faulty and unseasonable sometimes as common-place. It depends upon circumstances,

whether we are to consider ourselves near enough, as it were, to the subject we are describing to grow microscopical upon it. A person basking in a landscape, for instance, and a person riding through it, are in two very different situations for the exercise of their eyesight; and even where the license is most allowable, care must be taken not to give to small things and great, to nice detail and to general feeling, the same proportion of effect. Errors of this kind in poetry answer to a want of perspective in painting, and of a due distribution of light and shade. To give an excessive instance in the former art, there was Denner, who copied faces to a nicety amounting to a horrible want of it, like Brobdignagian visages encountered by Gulliver; and who, according to the facetious Peter Pindar,

Made a bird's beak appear at twenty mile.

And the same kind of specimen is afforded in poetry by Darwin, a writer now almost forgotten and deservedly, but who did good in his time by making unconscious caricatures of all the poetical faults in vogue, and flattering himself that the sum total went to the account of his original genius. Darwin would describe a dragon-fly and a lion in the same terms of proportion. You did not know which he would have scrambled from the sooner. His pictures were like the two-penny sheets which the little boys buy, and in which you see J Jackdaw and K King, both of the same dimensions.

Mr. Keats's other fault, the one in his versification, arises from a similar cause,—that of contradicting over-zealously the fault on the opposite side. It is this which provokes him now and then into mere roughnesses and discords for their own sake, not for that of variety and contrasted harmony. We can manage, by substituting a greater feeling for a smaller, a line like the following:—

I shall roll on the grass with two-fold ease;—

but by no contrivance of any sort can we prevent this from jumping out of the heroic measure into mere rhythmicality,

How many bards gild the lapses of time!

We come now however to the beauties; and the reader will easily perceive that they not only outnumber the faults a hundred fold, but that they are of a nature decidedly opposed to what is false and inharmonious. Their characteristics indeed are a fine ear, a fancy and imagination at will, and an intense feeling of external beauty in it's most natural and least expressible simplicity.

We shall give some specimens of the least beauty first, and conclude with a noble extract or two that will shew the second, as well as the powers of our young poet in general. The harmony of his verses will appear throughout.

The first poem consists of a piece of luxury in a rural spot, ending with an allusion to the story of Endymion and to the origin of other lovely tales of mythology, on the ground suggested by Mr. Wordsworth in a beautiful passage of his *Excursion.* Here, and in the other largest poem, which closes the book, Mr. Keats is seen to his best advantage, and displays all that fertile power of association and imagery which constitutes the abstract poetical faculty as distinguished from every other. He wants age for a greater knowledge of humanity, but evidences of this also bud forth here and there. —To come however to our specimens:—

The first page of the book presents us with a fancy, founded, as all beautiful fancies are, on a strong sense of what really exists or occurs. He is speaking of

A gentle Air in Solitude

There crept
A little noiseless noise among the leaves,
Born of the very sigh that silence heaves.

Young Trees

There too should be
The frequent chequer of a youngling tree,
That with a score of light green brethren shoots
From the quaint mossiness of aged roots;
Round which is heard a spring-head of clear
waters.

Anybody who has seen a throng of young beeches, furnishing those natural clumpy seats at the root, must recognize the truth and grace of this description. The remainder of this part of the poem, especially from—

Open afresh your round of starry folds,
Ye ardent marigolds!—

down to the bottom of page 5, affords an exquisite proof of close observation of nature as well as the most luxuriant fancy.

The Moon.

Lifting her silver rim
Above a cloud, and with a gradual swim
Coming into the blue with all her light.

Fir Trees.

Fir trees grow around,
Aye dropping their hard fruit upon the ground.

This last line is in the taste of the Greek simplicity.

A starry Sky.

The dark silent blue
With all it's diamonds trembling through and
through.

Sound of a Pipe.

And some are hearing eagerly the wild
Thrilling liquidity of dewy piping.

The *Specimen of an Induction to a Poem,* and the fragment of the Poem itself entitled *Calidore,* contain some very natural touches on the human side of things; as when speaking of a lady who is anxiously looking out on the top of a tower for her defender, he describes her as one

Who cannot feel for cold her tender feet;

and when Calidore has fallen into a fit of amorous abstraction, he says that

—The kind voice of good Sir Clerimond
Came to his ear, as something from beyond
His present being.

No. 498, pp. 443–4. Sunday, July 13, 1817.

The Epistles, the Sonnets, and indeed the whole of the book, contain strong evidences of warm and social feelings, but particularly the Epistle to Charles Cowden Clarke, and the Sonnet to his own Brothers, in which the "faint cracklings" of the coal-fire are said to be

Like whispers of the household gods that keep
A gentle empire o'er fraternal souls.

The Epistle to Mr. Clarke is very amiable as well as poetical, and equally honourable to both parties,—to the young writer who can be so grateful towards his teacher, and to the teacher who had the sense to perceive his genius, and the qualities to call forth his affection. It consists chiefly of recollections of what his friend had pointed out to him in poetry and in general taste; and the lover of Spenser will readily judge of his preceptor's qualifications, even from a single triplet, in which he is described, with a deep feeling of simplicity, as one

Who had beheld Belphœbe in a brook,
And lovely Una in a leafy nook,
And Archimago leaning o'er his book.

The Epistle thus concludes:—

Picture of Companionship.

But many days have past—
Since I have walked with you through shady 5
   lanes,
That freshly terminate in open plains,
And revell'd in a chat that ceased not,
When at night-fall among your books we got;
No, nor when supper came,—nor after that,—
Nor when reluctantly I took my hat;
No, nor till cordially you shook my hand   10
Midway between our homes:—your accents bland
Still sounded in my ears, when I no more
Could hear your footsteps touch the gravelly
   floor.
Sometimes I lost them, and then found again,
You changed the footpath for the grassy plain. 15
In those still moments I have wished you joys
That well you know to honour:—"Life's very
   toys
With him," said I, "will take a pleasant charm;
It cannot be that ought will work him harm."
                                              20

And we can only add, without any disrespect
to the graver warmth of our young poet, that
if Ought attempted it, Ought would find he had
stout work to do with more than one person.

The following passage in one of the Sonnets 25
passes, with great happiness, from the mention
of physical associations to mental; and concludes with a feeling which must have struck
many a contemplative mind, that has found
the sea-shore like a border, as it were, of ex- 30
istence. He is speaking of

THE OCEAN

The Ocean with it's vastness, it's blue green,
It's ships, it's rocks, it's caves,—it's hopes, it's 35
   fears,—
It's voice mysterious, which whoso hears
Must think on what will be, and what has been.

We have read somewhere the remark of a 40
traveller, who said that when he was walking
alone at night-time on the sea-shore, he felt
conscious of the earth, not as the common
everyday sphere it seems, but as one of the
planets, rolling round with him in the mighti- 45
ness of space. The same feeling is common to
imaginations that are not in need of similar
local excitements.

The best poem is certainly the last and
longest, entitled *Sleep and Poetry*. It orig- 50
inated in sleeping in a room adorned with
busts and pictures, and is a striking specimen
of the restlessness of the young poetical appetite, obtaining its food by the very desire

of it, and glancing for fit subjects of creation
"from earth to heaven." Nor do we like it the
less for an impatient, and as it may be thought
by some irreverend assault upon the late French
school of criticism and monotony, which has
held poetry chained long enough to render it
somewhat indignant when it has got free.

The following ardent passage is highly imaginative:—

An Aspiration after Poetry.

[Quotation, beginning "O Poesy! for thee I grasp
my pen," and ending, "Wings to find out an immortality."]

Mr. Keats takes an opportunity, though with
very different feelings toward the school than
he has exhibited towards the one above-
mentioned, to object to the morbidity that
taints the productions of the Lake Poets. They
might answer perhaps, generally, that they
chuse to grapple with what is unavoidable,
rather than pretend to be blind to it; but the
more smiling Muse may reply, that half of the
evils alluded to are produced by brooding over
them; and that it is much better to strike at
as many *causes* of the rest as possible, than
to pretend to be satisfied with them in the
midst of the most evident dissatisfaction.

Happy Poetry Preferred.

These things are doubtless: yet in truth we've had
Strange thunders from the potency of song;
Mingled indeed with what is sweet and strong,
From majesty: but in clear truth the themes
Are ugly clubs, the Poets Polyphemes
Disturbing the grand sea. A drainless shower
Of light is poesy; 'tis the supreme of power;
'Tis might half slumb'ring on it's own right arm
The very archings of her eye-lids charm
A thousand willing agents to obey.
And still she governs with the mildest sway:
But strength alone though of the Muses born
Is like a fallen angel: trees uptorn,
Darkness, and worms, and shrouds, and sepulchres
Delight it; for it feeds upon the burrs
And thorns of life; forgetting the great end
Of poesy, that it should be a friend
To soothe the cares, and lift the thoughts of man.

We conclude with the beginning of the paragraph which follows this passage, and which
contains an idea of as lovely and powerful a
nature in embodying an abstraction, as we ever
remember to have seen put into words:—

Yet I rejoice: a myrtle fairer than
E'er grew in Paphos, from the bitter weeds
Lifts it's sweet head into the air, *and feeds
A silent space with ever sprouting green.*

Upon the whole, Mr. Keats's book cannot be better described than in a couplet written by Milton when he too was young, and in which he evidently alludes to himself. It is a little luxuriant heap of

> Such sights as youthful poets dream
> On summer eves by haunted stream.

The Indicator. No. XLIV, pp. 351–52. Wednesday, August 9th, 1820.

The Stories of Lamia, The Pot of Basil, The Eve of St. Agnes, &c. as Told by Mr. Keats.

. . . We have now to conclude the surprise of the reader, who has seen what solid stuff these poems are made of, with informing him of what the book has not mentioned,—that they were almost all written four years ago, when the author was but twenty. Ay, indeed! cries a critic, rubbing his hands delighted (if indeed even criticism can do so, any longer); "then that accounts for the lines you speak of, written in the taste of Marino."—It does so; but, sage Sir, after settling the merits of those one or two lines you speak of, what accounts, pray, for a small matter which you leave unnoticed, namely, all the rest?—The truth is, we rather mention this circumstance as a matter of ordinary curiosity, than anything else; for great faculties have great privileges, and leap over time as well as other obstacles. Time itself, and its continents, are things yet to be discovered. There is no knowing even how much duration one man may crowd into a few years, while others drag out their slender lines. There are circular roads full of hurry and scenery, and straight roads full of listlessness and barrenness; and travellers may arrive by both, at the same hour. The Miltons, who begin intellectually old, and still intellectual, end physically old, are indeed Methusalems; and may such be our author, their son.

Mr. Keats's versification sometimes reminds us of Milton in his blank verse, and sometimes of Chapman both in his blank verse and rhyme; but his faculties, essentially speaking, though partaking of the unearthly aspirations and abstract yearnings of both these poets, are altogether his own. They are ambitious, but less directly so. They are more social, and in the finer sense of the word, sensual, than either. They are more coloured by the modern philosophy of sympathy and natural justice. Endymion, with all it's extraordinary powers, partook of the faults of youth, though the best ones; but the reader of Hyperion and these other stories would never guess that they were written at twenty. The author's versification is now perfected, the exuberances of his imagination restrained, and a calm power, the surest and loftiest of all power, takes place of the impatient workings of the younger god within him. The character of his genius is that of energy and voluptuousness, each able at will to take leave of the other, and possessing, in their union, a high feeling of humanity not common to the best authors who can less combine them. Mr. Keats undoubtedly takes his seat with the oldest and best of our living poets. . . .

The Indicator. No. L, pp. 399–400. Wednesday, September 20, 1820.

[No Title.]

Ah, dear friend, as valued a one as thou art a poet,—John Keats,—we cannot, after all, find it in our hearts to be glad, now thou art gone away with the swallows to seek a kindlier clime. The rains began to fall heavily, the moment thou wast to go;—we do not say, poet-like, for thy departure. One tear in an honest eye is more precious to thy sight, than all the metaphorical weepings in the universe; and thou didst leave many starting to think how many months it would be till they saw thee again. And yet thou didst love metaphorical tears too, in their way; and couldst always liken every thing in nature to something great or small; and the rains that beat against thy cabin window will set, we fear, thy overworking wits upon many comparisons that ought to be much more painful to others than thyself;—Heaven mend their envious and ignorant numskulls. But thou hast "a mighty soul in a little body;" and the kind cares of the former for all about thee shall no longer subject the latter to the chance of impressions which it scorns; and the soft skies of Italy shall breathe balm upon it; and thou shalt return with thy friend the nightingale, and make all thy other friends as happy with thy voice as they are sorrowful to miss it. The little cage thou didst sometime share with us, looks as deficient without thee, as thy present one may do without us; but—farewell for awhile: thy heart is in our fields: and thou wilt soon be back to rejoin it.

THE REVOLT OF ISLAM,—A POEM,—

BY PERCY BYSHE SHELLEY.—LONDON: C. AND
J. OLLIER.

The Examiner. No. 527, pp. 75–6. Sunday, Feb. 1, 1818.

THIS is an extraordinary production. The ignorant will not understand it; the idle will not take the pains to get acquainted with it; even the intelligent will be startled at first with its air of mysticism and wildness; the livelier man of the world will shake his head at it good naturedly; the sulkier one will cry out against it; the bigot will be shocked, terrified, and enraged, and fall to proving all that is said against himself; the negatively virtuous will resent the little quarter that is given to mere custom; the slaves of bad customs or bad passions of any sort will either seize their weapons against it, trembling with rage or conscious worthlessness, or hope to let it quietly pass by, as an enthusiasm that must end in air; finally, the hopeless, if they are ill-tempered, will envy it's hopefulness,—if good tempered, will sorrowfully anticipate it's disappointment; both from self-love, though of two different sorts;—but we will venture to say, that the intelligent and the good, who are yet healthy-minded, and who have not been so far blinded by fear and self-love as to confound superstition with desert, anger and hatred with firmness, or despondency with knowledge, will find themselves amply repaid by breaking through the outer shell of this production, even if it be with the single reflection, that so much ardour for the happy virtues, and so much power to recommend them, have united in the same person. To will them with hope indeed is to create them; and to extend that will is the object of the writer before us.

The story of the "Revolt of Islam" is this. The poet, rising from "visions of despair" occasioned by the late triumphs over the progress of mankind, goes meditating by the sea-shore, and after an awful and prophetic tempest, suddenly sees in the air the extraordinary spectacle of a combat between a serpent and an eagle:—

The Serpent's mailed and many-coloured skin
Shone through the plumes it's coils were twined
  within
By many a swollen and knotted fold; and high
And far, the neck, receding light and thin,
Sustained a crested head, which warily
Shifted and glanced before the Eagle's stedfast eye.

The Serpent is defeated, and falls into the sea, from whence he is received into the bosom of a beautiful woman who sits lamenting upon the shore. She invites the poet to go somewhere across the sea with them in a boat. He consents, more in fear for her than for himself; and in the course of the voyage she tells him that the Serpent and the Eagle are the Powers of Good and Evil, who combat with each other at intervals, that the Serpent, Power of Good, has again been defeated; and that she herself is his selected companion, whom in his more radiant shape he appeared to once at night, and announced his having fallen in love with. The Serpent all this while lies still, recovering from the effects of the combat; and at last the voyagers come to a magnificent temple beyond the polar ocean, in which

—There sat on many a sapphire throne
The Great, who had departed from mankind,
A mighty Senate;—some, whose white hair shone
Like mountain snow, mild, beautiful, and blind;
Some female forms, whose gestures beamed with
  mind;
And ardent youths,—and children bright and fair;
And some had lyres, whose strings were inter-
  twined
With pale and clinging flames, which ever there
Waked faint yet thrilling sounds that pierced the
  chrystal air.

A magic and obscure circumstance then takes place, the result of which is, that the woman and serpent are seen no more, but that a cloud opens asunder, and a bright and beautiful shape, which seems compounded of both, is beheld sitting on a throne,—a circumstance apparently imitated from Milton:

Wonder and joy a passing faintness threw
Over my brow—a hand supported me,
Whose touch was magic strength: *an eye of blue
Looked into mine like moonlight, soothingly;*
And a voice said—Thou must a listener be
This day—two mighty Spirits now return,
Like birds of calm from the world's raging sea;
They pour fresh light from Hope's immortal urn,
A tale of human power—despair not—list and
  learn!

I looked, and lo! one stood forth eloquently;
His eyes were dark and deep, and the clear brow
Which shadowed them was like the morning sky,
The cloudless Heaven of Spring, when in their
    flow
Through the bright air, the soft winds as they 5
    blow,
Wake the green world.

Beneath the darkness of his outspread hair
He stood thus beautiful: but there was one
Who sate beside him like his shadow there,
And held his hand—far lovelier—*she was known*
To be thus fair by the few lines alone,
Which through her floating locks and gathered
    cloak,
Glances of soul-dissolving glory, shone.

This is a fine Grecian feeling of what may be
called the sentiment of shape. The two
strangers are the hero and heroine of the
poem: and here the more human part of the
story commences. *Laon,* the hero, relates it. 20
He was an ardent and speculative youth, born
in modern Greece; and grew up with great admiration of the beauties and kindness of external nature, and a great horror of the superstitions and other oppressions with which his 25
country and mankind in general were afflicted.
A beautiful female orphan under the care of
his parents shared these feelings with him; and
mutual love was the consequences. She even
speculated upon taking some extraordinary 30
though gentle step to deliver the world from
it's thraldom; when she was torn away from
him by some slaves of the Grand Turk's
Seraglio; and he himself, for endeavouring to
rescue her, and for taking that opportunity of 35
proclaiming freedom, was shut up in a prison in
a rock, where his senses forsook him. The effect
of the circumstance however is not lost. He is
delivered from his dungeon by an old man,
and after a second but milder insanity, is in- 40
formed by his preserver, that the people had
been awakened to new ideas, and that there
was a maiden who went about exciting them to
a bloodless freedom. It was his love *Cythna,*
after having been made a victim of the ty- 45
rant's lust, and having been likewise imprisoned, and robbed of her senses. A considerable interval elapses while *Laon* recovers his
reason, but on so doing, and hearing of the
exploits of her whom he justly supposed to be 50
his lovely friend, he takes leave of the old
man, and journeys for Constantinople or the
Golden City, where he finds the people risen,
the tyrant fallen, and *Cythna* the predominant

spirit of the change. He goes with others to
the palace, and sees the "sceptered wretch"
sitting silent and sullen on the footstool of his
throne,—

Alone, but for one child, who led before him
A graceful dance:—*weeping and murmuring*
'Mid her sad task of unregarded love,
That to no smiles it might his speechless sadness
    move.

She clasps the tyrant's feet, and then stands
up when the strangers come nigh;—

Her lips and cheeks seemed very pale and wan,
But on her forehead, and within her eye
Lay beauty, which makes hearts that feed thereon
Sick with excess of sweetness; on the throne
She leaned; the King, with gathered brow and
    lips
Wreathed by long scorn, did inly sneer and frown
With hue like that when some great painter dips
His pencil in the gloom of earthquake and eclipse.

Laon saves his life from the fury of the
crowd; a festival is held at which *Cythna* presides like a visible angel, and every thing
seems happiness and security. The Revolters
however are suddenly assailed by the allies of
the tyrant; and the fortune of the contest is
changed. *Cythna* reaches *Laon* through the
lost battle on a huge black Tartarian horse,
"whose path makes a solitude;" and they fly
to a distance through a desolate village, in the
dwellings of which the flames and human beings were now dead;

           But the wide sky,
Flooded with lightning, *was ribbed overhead*
By the black rafters; and around did lie
Women, and babes, and men, slaughtered con-
    fusedly.

The only survivor is a female, who has gone
mad, and fancies herself the Plague. The description of her desperate laughter and actions
is appalling, though not without a tendency,
we think, to something overwrought and artificial. When the travellers arrive at a place of
rest, *Cythna* tells *Laon* her adventures. They
have been briefly alluded to, and include a
finely-fancied and pathetic account of a child
which she had in her dungeon, and which was
taken from her. *Laon* goes out from the retreat occasionally to get food and intelligence,
and finds that Revenge, and subsequently Pestilence and Famine, have been making terrible
havoc in the city. The tyrant and his slaves, in
their terror, make frightened addresses to

heaven, and a priest advises them to expiate it's "vengeance" by sacrificing *Laon* and *Cythna*. He accordingly dispatches numbers to hunt them out; upon which *Laon* comes forward disguised, and offers to give up the man provided the woman be spared. They take an oath to do so, and he declares himself; but it is then declared impious to have made the oath; and at last, *Cythna* comes voluntarily forward, and shares the funeral pyre with her beloved friend, from which they find themselves suddenly sailing on a beautiful sea to the Paradise in which the Spirit of Good resides, where *Cythna* meets with her child who had died of the plague; and the poem concludes.

No. 530, pp. 121–2. Sunday, Feb. 22, 1818.

We have given the story of this extraordinary book, and some extracts by which the reader can easily judge of it's general merits. We have some remarks however to make on the particular qualities of it's poetry, and on the deep social interests upon which it speculates; but as we are much pressed for room now the Parliament are sitting, and yet do not wish to pass over the work lightly, we had better occupy our present article at once with some extracts we intended to make from the author's preface. He explains in them the general object of his poem, and touches in a masterly manner upon the great political point of it, and indeed of the age in which we live.

"The poem," says he, "which I now present to the world is an attempt from which I scarcely dare to expect success, and in which a writer of established fame might fail without disgrace. It is an experiment on the temper of the public mind, as to *how far a thirst for a happier condition of moral and political society survives, among the enlightened and refined, the tempests which have shaken the age in which we live.* I have sought to enlist the harmony of metrical language, the ethereal combinations of the fancy, the rapid and subtle transitions of human passion, all those elements which essentially compose a Poem, in the cause of a liberal and comprehensive morality, and in the view of kindling, within the bosoms of my readers, a virtuous enthusiasm, for those doctrines of liberty and justice, *that faith and hope in something good,* which

neither violence, nor misrepresentation, nor prejudice, can ever totally extinguish among mankind."

After dilating a little more on the subjects of his poem, Mr. Shelley, with the feeling that ever seems to be at the bottom of his warmth, gives the following placid and easy solution of a difficulty, which the world, we believe, is also instinctively solving, but which, as he says, has been the "moral ruin" of some eminent spirits among us. If the Lake School, as they are called, were not as dogmatic in their despair as they used to be in their hope, we should earnestly recommend the passage to their attention. They might see in it, at any rate, how it becomes an antagonist to talk; and how charitable and consistent the mind can be, that really inquires into the philosophical causes of things. Mr. Shelley does not say that Mr. Southey is "no better than a housebreaker;" nor does he exclaim with Mr. Wordsworth, in the ill-concealed melancholy of a strange piety, which would be still stranger if it were really cheerful, that "Carnage is God's daughter." He is not in the habit, evidently, of begging the question against the low and uneducated; nor has he the least respect for that very sweeping lady, Miss Theodosia Carnage:—but stop; we must not be violating the charity of his philosophy.

"The panic," says our author, "which, like an epidemic transport, seized upon all classes of men during the excesses consequent upon the French Revolution, is gradually giving place to sanity. It has ceased to be believed, that whole generations of mankind ought to consign themselves to a hopeless inheritance of ignorance and misery, *because* a nation of men who had been dupes and slaves for centuries were incapable of conducting themselves with the wisdom and tranquillity of freemen, as soon as some of their fetters were partially loosened. That their conduct could not have been marked by any other characters than ferocity and thoughtlessness, is *the historical fact from which liberty derives all it's deformity.* There is a reflux in the tide of human things, which bears the shipwrecked hopes of men into a secure haven after the storms are past. Methinks, those who now live have survived an age of despair."

"The French Revolution may be considered as one of those manifestations of a general state of feeling among civilized mankind, produced by a defect of correspondence between the knowledge existing in society and the improvement, or gradual abolition of political institions. The year 1788 may be assumed as the epoch of one of the most important crisis [sic] produced by this feeling. The sympathies connected with that event extended to every bosom. The most generous and amiable natures were those which participated the most extensively in these sympathies. *But such a degree of unmingled good was expected, as it was impossible to realize. If the Revolution had been in every respect prosperous, then misrule and superstition would lose half their claims to our abhorrence, as fetters which the captive can unlock with the slightest motion of his fingers, and which do not eat with poisonous rust into the soul.* The revulsion occasioned by the atrocities of the demagogues, and the re-establishment of successive tyrannies in France, was terrible, and felt in the remotest corner of the civilized world. Could they listen to the plea of reason, who had groaned under the calamities of a social state, according to the provisions of which, one man riots in luxury, while another famishes for want of bread? *Can he who the day before was a trampled slave, SUDDENLY become liberal-minded, forbearing and independent? This is the consequence of the habits of a state of society to be produced by resolute perseverance and indefatigable hope, and long suffering and long believing courage, and the systematic efforts of generations of men of intellect and virtue.* Such is the lesson which experience teaches now. But on the first reverses of hope in the progress of French liberty, the sanguine eagerness for good overleaped the solution of those questions, and for a time extinguished itself in the unexpectedness of their result. Thus many of the most ardent and tender-hearted of the worshippers of public good have been *morally ruined,* by what a partial glimpse of the events they deplored appeared to shew as the melancholy desolation of all their cherished hopes. Hence gloom and misanthropy have become the characteristics of the age in which we live, the solace of a disappointment that unconsciously finds relief only in the wilful exaggeration of it's own despair. This influence has tainted the literature of the age with the hopelessness of the minds from which it flows. Metaphysics, and inquiries into moral and political science, have become little else than vain attempts to revive exploded superstitions, or sophisms like those of Mr. Malthus, calculated to lull the oppressors of mankind into a security of everlasting triumph. Our works of fiction and poetry have been overshadowed by the same infectious gloom. But mankind appear to me to be emerging from their trance. I am aware, methinks, of a slow, gradual, silent change. In that belief I have composed the following Poem."

No. 531, pp. 139–141. Sunday, March 1, 1818.

The reader has seen the fable as well as some passages of this poem, and heard the author's own account of his intentions in extracts from the preface. It remains for me to give a general criticism upon it, interspersed with a few more specimens; and as the object of the work is decidedly philosophical, we shall begin with the philosophy.

Mr. Shelley is of opinion with many others that the world is a very beautiful one externally, but wants a good deal of mending with respect to it's mind and habits; and for this purpose he would quash as many cold and selfish passions as possible, and rouse up the gentle element of Love, till it set our earth rolling more harmoniously. The answer made to a writer, who sets out with endeavours like these, is that he is idly aiming at perfection; but Mr. Shelley has no such aim, neither have nine hundred and ninety-nine out of a thousand of the persons, who have ever been taunted with it. Such a charge, in truth, is only the first answer which egotism makes to any one who thinks he can go beyond it's own ideas of the possible. If this however be done away, the next answer is, that you are attempting something wild and romantic,—that you will get disliked for it as well as lose your trouble, and that you had better coquet, or rather play the prude, with things as they are. The worldly sceptic smiles, and says "Hah!"—the dull rogues wonder, or laugh out;—the disappointed egotist gives you a sneering admonition, having made up his mind about all these things because he and his friends could not alter them; the hypocrite affects to be shocked; the bigot anticipates the punishment that awaits you for daring to say that God's creation is not a vile world, nor his creatures bound to be miserable;—and even the more amiable compromiser with superstition expresses alarm for you,—does not know what you may be hazarding, though he believes nevertheless that God is all good and just,—refers you to the fate of Adam, to shew you that because he introduced the knowledge of evil, you must not attempt to do it away again,—and finally, advises you to comfort yourself with *faith*, and to secure a life in the next world because *this* is a bad business, and *that*, of course, you may find a worse. It seems forgotten all this while, that Jesus Christ himself recommended Love as the great law that was to supersede others; and recommended it too to an extreme, which has been held impracticable. How far it has been found impracticable, in consequence of his doctrines having been mixed up with contradictions and threatening dogmas, and with a system of after-life which contradicts all its principles, may be left to the consideration. Will theologians never discover, that men, in order to be good and just to each other, must either think well of a Divine Being, really and not pretendingly, or not think of him at all? That they must worship Goodness and a total absence of the revengeful and malignant passions, if not Omnipotence? or else that they must act upon this quality for themselves, and agree with a devout and amiable Pagan, that "it were better men should say there was no such being as Plutarch, than that there was one Plutarch who eat his own children?" Instead of the alarms abcut searches after happiness being wise and salutary, when the world is confessedly discordant, they would seem, if we believed in such things, the most fatal and ingenious invention of an enemy of mankind. But it is only so much begging of the question, fatal indeed as far as it goes, and refusing in the strangest manner to look after good, because there is a necessity for it. And as to the Eastern apologue of Adam and Eve (for so many Christians as well as others have thought it), it would be merely shocking to humanity and to a sense of justice in any other light; but it is, in fact, a very deep though not wisely managed allegory, deprecating the folly of mankind in losing their simplicity and enjoyment, and in taking to those very mistakes about vice and virtue, which it is the object of such authors as the one before us to do away again. Faith! It is the very object they have in view; not indeed faiths in endless terrors and contradictions, but "a faith and hope," as Mr. Shelley says, "in something good,"—that faith in the power of men to be kinder and happier, which other faiths take so much pains, and professed pains, to render unbelievable even while they recommend it! "Have faith," says the theologian, "and bear your wretchedness, and escape the wrath to come." "*Have* faith," says the philosopher, "and begin to be happier now, and do not attribute odious qualities to any one."

People get into more inconsistencies in opposing the hopes and efforts of a philosophical enthusiasm than on any other subject. They say, "use your reason, instead of your expectations;" and yet this is the reverse of what they do in their own beliefs. They say, take care how you contradict custom;—yet Milton, whom they admire, set about ridiculing it, and paying his addresses to another woman in his wife's life-time, till the latter treated him better. They say it is impossible the world should alter; and yet it has often altered. They say it is impossible, at any rate it should mend; yet people are no longer burnt at the stake. They say, but it is too old to alter to any great purpose of happiness,—that all it's experience goes to the contrary; and yet they talk at other times of the brief life and shortsighted knowledge of man, and of the nothingness of "a thousand years." The experience of a man and an ephemeris are in fact just on a par in all that regards the impossibility of change. But one man,—they say —what can one man do? Let a glorious living person answer,—let Clarkson answer; who sitting down in his youth by a roadside, thought upon the horrors of the Slave Trade, and vowed he would dedicate his life to endeavour at overthrowing it. He was laughed at; he was violently opposed; he was called presumptuous and even irreligious; he was thought out of his senses; he made a noble sacrifice of his own health and strength, and he has *lived* to see the Slave Trade, aye, even the slavery of the descendants of the "cursed" Ham, made a Felony.

We have taken up so much room in noticing these objections, that we have left ourselves none for entering into a further account of Mr. Shelley's views than he himself has given; and we have missed any more quotations at last. But we are sure that he will be much better pleased to see obstructions cleared away from the progress of such opinions as his, than the most minute account given of them in particular. It may be briefly repeated, that they are at war with injustice, violence, and selfishness of every species, however disguised;—that they represent, in a very striking light, the folly and misery of systems, either practical or theoretical, which go upon penal and resentful grounds, and add "pain to pain;" and that they would have men, instead of worshipping tyrannies and terrors of any sort, worship goodness and gladness, diminish the vices and sorrows made by custom only, encourage the virtues and enjoyments which mutual benevolence may realize; and in short, make the best and utmost of this world, as well as hope for another.

The beauties of the poem consist in depth of sentiment, in grandeur of imagery, and a versification remarkably sweet, various, and noble, like the placid playing of a great organ. If the author's genius reminds us of any other poets, it is of two very opposite ones, Lucretius and Dante. The former he resembles in the Dædalian part of it, in the boldness of his speculations, and in his love of virtue, of external nature, and of love itself. It is his gloomier or more imaginative passages that sometimes remind us of Dante. The sort of supernatural architecture in which he delights has in particular the grandeur as well as obscurity of that great genius, to whom however he presents this remarkable and instructive contrast, that superstition and pain and injustice go hand in hand even in the pleasantest parts of Dante, like the three Furies, while philosophy, pleasure, and justice, smile through the most painful passages of our author, like the three Graces.

Mr. Shelley's defects as a poet are obscurity, inartificial and yet no natural economy, violation of costume, and too great a sameness and gratuitousness of image and metaphor, and of image and metaphor too drawn from the elements, particularly the sea. The book is full of humanity; and yet it certainly does not go the best way to work for appealing to it, because it does not appeal to it through the medium of it's common knowledges. It is for this reason that we must say something, which we would willingly leave unsaid, both from admiration of Mr. Shelley's genius and love of his benevolence; and this is, that the work cannot possibly become popular. It may set others thinking and writing, and we have no doubt will do so; and those who can understand and relish it, will relish it exceedingly; but the author must forget his metaphysics and sea-sides a little more in his future works, and give full effect to that nice knowledge of men and things which he otherwise really possesses to an extraordinary degree. We have no doubt he is destined to be one of the leading spirits of his age, and indeed has already fallen into his place as such; but however resolute as to his object, he will only be doing it justice to take the most effectual means in his power to forward it.

We have only to observe in conclusion, as another hint to the hopeless, that although the art of printing is not new, yet the Press in any great and true sense of the word is a modern engine in the comparison, and the changeful times of society have never yet been accompanied with so mighty a one. *Books* did what was done before; they have now a million times the range and power; and the Press, which has got hold of Superstition, and given it some irrecoverable wounds already, will, we hope and believe, finally draw it in altogether, and crush it as a steam-engine would a great serpent.

ROSALIND AND HELEN, A MODERN ECLOGUE; WITH OTHER POEMS,

BY PERCY BYSSHE SHELLEY, 1819.

The Examiner. No. 593, pp. 302–3. Sunday, May 9, 1819.

THIS is another poem in behalf of liberality of sentiment and the deification of love, by the author of the *Revolt of Islam.* It is "not an attempt," says the writer, "in the highest style of poetry. It is in no degree calculated to excite profound meditation; and if, by interesting the affections and amusing the imagination, it awaken a certain ideal melancholy favourable to the reception of the more important impressions, it will produce in the reader all that the writer experienced in the composition. I resigned myself, as I wrote, to the impulse of the feelings which moulded the conception of the story; and this impulse determined the pauses of a measure, which only pretends to be regular inasmuch as it corresponds with, and expresses, the irregularity of the imaginations which inspired it."

Mr. Shelley has eminently succeeded in all that he thus wished to do. The speakers, who tell each other their stories, are two fine-hearted women, who have been unhappy in their loves,—the one having seen her partner in life die of a disappointed sympathy with mankind in consequence of the late great political changes; and the other, having for the sake of her reduced family accepted a hard, cold-blooded man for her husband, after she had been on the eve of marrying a beloved friend, who turned out at the altar to be her brother. The father

> —Came from a distant land
> And with a loud and fearful cry
> Rushed between us suddenly.
> *I saw the stream of his thin grey hair,*
> *I saw his lean and lifted hand,*
> And heard his words,—and live! Oh God!
> Wherefore do I live?—"Hold, hold!"
> He cried,—"I tell thee 'tis her brother!"

The couplet marked in Italics, especially the first line, is very striking and fearful. He comes between them like a spirit grown old.—There is something very beautiful in the way in which the two heroines meet. It is in Italy, whither they have both gone, like solitary birds of passage, from a climate every way colder; and *Rosalind,* who it seems is a legitimate widow, turns away from her old friend, who had adopted Mary Woolstonecraft's opinion in those matters. This fortune however, coming in aid of her former tenderness, melted her heart; and it again ran into that of *Helen* with tears. They unite their fortunes, and have the pleasure of seeing their children, a girl and boy, grow up in love with each other, till in their union they saw,

The shadow of the peace denied to them.

This little publication, in form and appearance resembling the one we criticised last week, presents a curious contrast with it in every other respect. It is in as finer a moral taste, as *Rosalind* and *Helen* are pleasanter names than *Peter Bell.* The object of Mr. Wordsworth's administrations of melancholy is to make men timid, servile, and (considering his religion) selfish;—that of Mr. Shelley's, to render them fearless, independent, affectionate, infinitely social. You might be made to worship a devil by the process of Mr. Wordsworth's philosophy; by that of Mr. Shelley, you might re-seat a dethroned goodness. The Poet of the Lakes always carries his egotism and "saving knowledge" about with him, and unless he has the settlement of the matter, will go in a pet and plant himself by the side of the oldest tyrannies and slaveries;—our Cosmopolite-Poet would evidently die with pleasure to all personal identity, could he but see his fellow-creatures reasonable and happy. He has no sort of respect, real or sullen, for mere power and success. It does not affect him in it's most powerful shapes; and he is inclined to come to no compromise with it; he wants others happy, not himself privileged.—But comparisons are never so odious, as when they serve to contrast two spirits who ought to have agreed. Mr. Wordsworth has become hopeless of this world, and therefore would make everybody else so;—Mr. Shelley is superior to hopelessness itself, and does not see why all happiness and all strength is to be bounded by what he himself can feel or can effect.

But we shall again be tempted to transgress the limits of our Literary Notices. We must give some further specimens of the poetry. The following is a passage which will go to every true woman's heart:—

> When flowers were dead, and grass was green
> Upon my mother's grave,—that mother
> Whom to outlive, and cheer, and make
> My wan eyes glitter for her sake,
> Was my vowed task, the single care
> Which once gave life to my despair,—
> When she was a thing that did not stir,
> And the crawling worms were cradling her
> To a sleep more deep and so more sweet
> Than a baby's rocked on it's nurse's knee,
> I lived: a living pulse then beat
> Beneath my heart that awakened me.
> What was this pulse so warm and free?
> Alas! I knew it could not be
> My own dull blood: 'twas like a thought
> Of liquid love, that spread and wrought
> Under my bosom and in my brain,
> And crept with the blood through every vein?
> And hour by hour, day after day,
> The wonder could not charm away,
> But laid in sleep my wakeful pain,
> Until I knew it was a child,
> And then I wept. For long, long years
> These frozen eyes had shed no tears:
> But now—'twas the season fair and mild
> When April has wept itself to May:
> I sate through the sweet sunny day
> By my window bowered round with leaves,

And down my cheeks the quiet tears ran
Like twinkling rain-drops from the eaves,
When warm spring showers are passing o'er:
O Helen, none can ever tell
The joy it was to weep once more!

Of *Helen's* lover *Lionel*, in his happier times,
it is said that

> A winged band
> Of bright persuasions, which had fed
> On his sweet lips and liquid eyes,
> *Kept their swift pinions half outspread*
> To do on men his least command.

The gentle noise arising from the earth during a still summer evening is thus delightfully
described:—but we must go back, and make a
larger extract than we intended. *Lionel* comes
out of a prison, into which he had been cast
for his opinions; and so, says his fond survivor,

> We travelled on
> By woods, and fields of yellow flowers,
> And towns, and villages, and towers,
> Day after day of happy hours.
> It was the azure time of June,
> When the skies are deep in the stainless noon,
> And the warm and fitful breezes shake
> The fresh green leaves of the hedge-row briar,
> And there were odours then to make
> The very breath we did respire
> A liquid element, whereon
> Our spirits, like delighted things
> That walk the air on subtle wings,
> Floated and mingled far away,
> 'Mid the warm winds of the sunny day.
> And when the evening star came forth
> Above the curve of the new bent moon,
> And light and sound ebbed from the earth,
> Like the tide of the full and weary sea
> To the depths of it's tranquillity,
> Our natures to it's own repose
> Did the earths' breathless sleep attune:
> Like flowers, which on each other close
> Their languid leaves when day-light's gone.

A picture follows, which we were going to
say would be appreciated by none but the
most delicate minded; but Mr. Shelley can
make his infinite earnestness and sincerity understood even by critics of a very different
cast, who happen to have no personal pique
with him; though we understand also that
they take care to abuse him enough, in order
to shew the time-serving bigotry of their opinions in general.

To the chief poem succeeds a smaller one
entitled "Lines written among the Euganean
Hills." Some of them are among the grandest

if not the deepest that Mr. Shelley has produced, with a stately stepping in the measure.
But we have not space to quote any, not even
a noble compliment which he introduces to
his friend Lord Byron. We must also abstain
from many other passages which tempt us in
the poem we have criticised.

Upon the whole, with all our admiration of
the *Revolt of Islam*, we think that *Rosalind and
Helen* contains, for the size, a still finer and
more various, as well as a more popular style
of poetry. The humanity is brought nearer to
us, while the abstractions remain as lofty and
noble. Mr. Shelley seems to look at Nature
with such an earnest and intense love, that at
last if she does not break her ancient silence,
she returns him look for look. She seems to
say to him, "You know me, if others do not."
For him, if for any poet that ever lived, the
beauty of the external world has an answering heart, and the very whispers of the wind
a meaning. Things, with mankind in general,
are mere words: they have only a few paltry
common-places about them, and see only the
surface of those. To Mr. Shelley, all that exists, exists indeed,—colour, sound, motion,
thought, sentiment, the lofty and the humble,
great and small, detail and generality,—from
the beauties of a blade of grass or the most
evanescent tint of a cloud, to the heart of
man which he would elevate, and the mysterious spirit of the universe which he would seat
above worship itself.

THE QUARTERLY REVIEW, AND REVOLT OF ISLAM.

The Examiner. No. 613, pp. 620–1. Sunday,
Sept. 26, 1819.

SINCE our last paper, we have met with the
Quarterly Review; and we shall beg our reader's disgust at that publication to be patient
a little, while we say something upon it's
present number.—The *Quarterly Review itself*
(for there are one or two deeper articles in
it, this time, than usual) ought to be ashamed
of the one it has written upon Mr. Shelley.
Heavy, and swelling, and soft with venom, it
creeps through the middle of it like a skulking
toad. The Editor, and the other more malignant writers in this Review, (for we know too
much of such publications to confound all the
writers together), have grown a little more

cunning in their mode of attack. They only missed their aim, and pitched themselves headlong, with their blind fury, in such articles as that on the *Story of Rimini*. They have since undertaken to be more candid and ac- knowledging; and accordingly, by a ludicrous effort of virtue, they now make a point of praising some *one* thing, or rather giving some *one* extract, which they find rather praise-worthy than otherwise; and then they set to, sharper than ever, and reward their new morals with a double draught of malignity.

They are always too impatient however, not to betray themselves at the outset. They begin their article on Mr. Shelley's *Revolt of Islam* by referring to the same book under another title, which that gentleman suppressed. He suppressed it by the advice of his friends, because in the ardour of his sincerity he had carried one of his theories to an excess which they thought would injure the perusal of it. Perhaps but two or three copies of that first impression were sold. The public at large certainly knew nothing of it. And yet the Quarterly Reviewers, who think these theories so pernicious, drag forth the impression, in order to abuse what he has not used. If on the other hand, he had not suppressed it, then the cry would have been—Surely he ought at least to have suppressed this;—and he would have been reproached for what he did use.

We are not going to nauseate the reader with all the half-sighted and whole-clawed meanness of the article in question. It is, in truth, a dull as well as a malicious endeavour; and to any body acquainted with the speculations which it undertakes to handle, talks quite as much against itself as for. We will content ourselves with a short specimen or two. Mr. Shelley, in endeavouring to shew the perniciousness of superstition in general, from which the perniciousness of it's family members is to be deduced, lays the scene of his philosophical poem among the Mahometans: —upon which the Reviewer after blessing himself upon our present happy government, and expressing his own infinite content with it (which we have no doubt is great) calls upon the author to witness his triumph in the following manner:—

"The laws and government on which Mr. Shelley's reasoning proceeds, are the Turkish, administered by a lawless despot; his religion is the Mohammedan, maintained by servile hypocrites; and his scene for their joint operation Greece, the land full beyond all others of recollections of former glory and independence, now covered with shame and sunk in slavery. We are Englishmen, Christians, free, and independent: we ask Mr. Shelley how his case applies to *us?* Or what *we* learn from it to the prejudice of our own constitution?" The Reviewer might as well ask what we learnt from any other fiction, which was to apply without being literal. Mr. Shelley is not bound to answer for his critic's stupidity. The reader of Gulliver's Travels might as well ask how the big or little men applied to *him*, he being neither as tall as a church nor as short as a mole-hill. The Editor of the Review himself, for instance, might as well ask how Mr. Hazlitt's appellation of *Grildrig* applied to him,—his name being not *Grildrig*, but *Giffard;* and he never having stood in the hand of an enormous prince, though he has licked the feet of petty ones, and thrown stones at their discarded mistresses' crutches.

Another,—and we have done with specimens. Mr. Shelley, says the Reviewer, "speaks of his school as 'a world of woes,' of his masters as 'tyrants,' of his school-fellows as 'enemies:'—Alas! what is this but to bear evidence against himself? Every one who knows what a public school ordinarily must be, can only trace in these lines the language of an insubordinate, a vain, a mortified spirit."

Now, Reader, take the following lines:—

—Public schools 'tis public folly feeds.
The slaves of custom and establish'd mode,
With pack-horse constancy we keep the road,
Crooked or strait, through quags or thorny dells,
True to the jingling of our leader's bells.
To follow foolish precedents, and wink
With both our eyes, is easier than to think.

Speaking of the worldly views with which even future priests are sent to these schools, the Poet says,

Egregious purpose worthily begun,
In barb'rous prostitution of your son;
Press'd on *his* part by means, that would disgrace
A scriv'ner's clerk, or footman out of place;
And ending, if at last it's end be gain'd,
In sacrilege, in God's own house profan'd.

*   *   *

The *royal letters* are a thing of course;
A King, that would, might recommend his horse;
And Deans, no doubt, and Chapters with one voice,
As bound in duty, would confirm the choice.

And lastly:—

> Would you your son should be a sot, or dunce,
> Lascivious, headstrong, or all these at once;
> That in good time the stripling's finished taste
> For loose expense, and fashionable waste,
> Should prove your ruin, and his own at last,
> Train him in public with a mob of boys.

Reader, these are not the profane Mr. Shelley's verses, but the pious Cowper's;—Cowper, the all-applauded as well as the deserving, who in these lines, according to the Quarterly Reviewer, "bears evidence against himself," and proves that there is nothing to be traced in them but the "language of an insubordinate, a vain, a mortified spirit;"—Cowper, in short, the independent, the good, and the sensitive,—who, because he had not callousness enough to reconcile his faith in the dreadful dogmas of the Church to his notions of the Supreme Goodness, like these reviewing worshippers of power,—nor courage enough to wage war with them, like Mr. Shelley,—finally lost his senses; and withered away in the very imagination of "blasts from hell," like a child on the altar of Moloch.

No. 614, pp. 635–6. Sunday, Oct. 3, 1819.

Our reviewing Scribes and Pharisees beg the question against Mr. Shelley's theories because he does not believe in their own creed. As if they had any creed but that which is established; and the better spirit of which they, and men like them, have ever prevented from appearing! They cannot affect meekness itself, but out of hostility. In the course of an article, full of anger, scandal, and bigotry, they put on little pale-lipped airs of serenity like a vixenish woman; and during one of these they say they would recommend Mr. Shelley to read the Bible, only it is "a sealed book to a proud spirit." We will undertake to say that Mr. Shelley knows more of the Bible, than all the priests who have any thing to do with the Review or its writers. He does not abjure "the pomps and vanities of this wicked world," only to put them on with the greater relish. To them, undoubtedly, the Bible is not a sealed book, in one sense. They open it to good profit enough. But in the sense which the Reviewer means, they contrive to have it sealed wherever the doctrines are inconvenient. What do they say to the injunctions against "judging

others that ye be not judged,"—against revenge,—against tale-bearing,—against lying, hypocrisy, "partiality," riches, pomps and vanities, swearing, perjury (videlicet, Nolo-Episcopation), Pharisaical scorn, and every species of worldliness and malignity? Was Mr. Canning (the parodist) a worthy follower of him that condoled with the lame and blind, when he joked upon a man's diseases? Was Mr. Croker, (emphatically called "the Admiralty Scribe") a worthy follower of him who denounced Scribes, Pharisees, and "devourers of widows' houses," when he swallowed up all those widows' pensions? Was Mr. Giffard a worthy follower of him who was the forgiver and friend of Mary Magdalen, when he ridiculed the very lameness and crutches of a Prince's discarded mistress! Men of this description are incapable of their own religion. If Christianity is compatible with all that they do and write, it is a precious thing. But if it means something much better—which we really believe it does mean, in spite both of such men and of much more reverenced and ancient authorities, then is the spirit of it to be found in the aspiration of the very philosophies which they are most likely to ill treat. The Reviewer for instance quotes, with horrified Italics, such lines as these—

> Nor hate another's crime, nor loathe thine own.
> And love of joy can make the foulest breast
> A paradise of flowers, where peace might build
> her nest.

What is this first passage but the story of the woman taken in adultery? And what the second, but the story of Mary Magdalen, "out of whom went seven devils," and who was forgiven because "she loved much?" Mr. Shelley may think that the sexual intercourse might be altered much for the better, so as to diminish the dreadful evils to which it is now subject. His opinions on that matter, however denounced or misrepresented, he shares in common with some of the best and wisest names in philosophy, from Plato down to Condorcet. It has been doubted by Doctors of the Church, whether Christ himself thought on these matters as the Jews did. But be this as it may, it does not hurt the parallel spirit of the passages. The Jews were told "not to hate another's crime." The woman was not told to loathe her sin, but simply not to repeat it; and was dismissed gently with these remarkable words, "Has any man condemned thee? No, Lord. Neither do I condemn thee." Meaning, on the most impartial construction, that if no man had brought her before a judge to be condemned, neither would he be the judge to condemn her. She sinned, because she violated the conventional ideas of virtue, and thus hazarded unhappiness to others, who had not been educated in a different opinion; but the goodness of the opinion itself is left doubtful. It is to the spirit of Christ's actions and theories that we look, and not to the comments or contradictions even of apostles. It was a very general spirit, if it was any thing, going upon the sympathetic excess, instead of the anti-pathetic—notoriously opposed to existing establishments, and reviled with every term of opprobrium by the Scribes and Pharisees then flourishing. If Mr. Shelley's theological notions run counter to those which have been built upon the supposed notions of Christ, we have no hesitation in saying that the moral spirit of his philosophy approaches infinitely nearer to that Christian benevolence, so much preached and so little practised, than any the most orthodox dogmas ever published. The Reviewers with their usual anti-christian falsehood say that he recommends people to "hate no crime" and "abstain from no gratification." In the Christian sense he *does* tell them to "hate no crime"; and in a sense as benevolent, he does tell them to "abstain from no gratification." But a world of gratification is shut out from his code, which the Reviewer would hate to be debarred from; and which he instinctively hates him for denouncing already. Hear the end of the Preface to the *Revolt of Islam*. "I have avoided all *flattery* to those violent and malignant passions of our nature, which are ever on the watch to mingle with and to alloy the most beneficial innovations. *There is no quarter given to Revenge, Envy, or Prejudice.* Love is celebrated every where as the sole law which should govern the moral world." Now, if Envy is rather tormenting to ye, Messieurs Reviewers, there is some little gratification, is there not, in Revenge? and some little gratifying profit or so in Prejudice? "Speak, Grildrig."

No. 615, pp. 652–3. Sunday, Oct. 10, 1819.

Failing in the attempt to refute Mr. Shelley's philosophy, the Reviewers attack his private life. What is the argument of this? or what right have they to know any thing of the private life of an author? or how would they like to have the same argument used against themselves? Mr. Shelley is now seven and twenty years of age. He entered life about 17; and every body knows, and every candid person will allow, that a young man at that time of life, upon the very strength of a warm and trusting nature, especially with theories to which the world are not accustomed, may render himself liable to the misrepresentations of the worldly. But what have the Quarterly Reviewers to do with this? What is Mr. Shelley's private life to the *Quarterly Review*, any more than Mr. Gifford's, or Mr. Croker's, or any other Quarterly Reviewer's private life is to the *Examiner*, or the *Morning Chronicle*, or to the *Edinburgh Review*,—a work, by the bye, as superior to the *Quarterly*, in all the humanities of social intercourse, as in the liberality of it's opinions in general. The Reviewer talks of what he *"now"* knows of Mr. Shelley. What does this pretended *judge* and actual male-gossip, this willing listener to scandal, this minister to the petty wants of excitement, now know more than he ever knew, of an absent man, whose own side of whatever stories have been told him he has never heard? Suppose the opponents of the *Quarterly Review* were to listen to all the scandals that have been reported of writers in it, and to proclaim this man by name as a pimp, another as a scamp, and another as a place or pulpit hunting slave made out of a school-boy tyrant? If the use of private matters in public criticism is not to be incompatible with the decencies and charities of life, let it be proved so; and we know who would be the sufferers. We have experienced, in our own persons, what monstrous misrepresentations can be given of a man, even with regard to the most difficult and unselfish actions of his life, and solely because others just knew enough of delicacy, to avail themselves of the inflexible love of it in others.

We shall therefore respect the silence hitherto observed publicly by Mr. Shelley respecting such matters, leaving him when he returns to England to take such notice or otherwise of his calumniators as may seem best to him. But we cannot resist the impulse to speak of one particular calumny of this Reviewer, the falsehood of which is doubly impressed upon us in consequence of our own personal and repeated knowledge of the reverse. He says Mr. Shelley "is shamefully dissolute in his conduct." We laugh the scandalmonger to scorn. Mr. Shelley has theories, as we have said before, with regard to the regulation of society, very different certainly from those of the Quarterly Reviewers, and very like opinions which have been held by some of the greatest and best men, ancient and modern. And be it observed that all the greatest and best men who have ever attempted to alter the condition of sexual intercourse at *all* have been calumniated as profligates, the devout Milton not excepted. A man should undoubtedly carry these theories into practice with caution, as well as any other new ones, however good, which tend to hurt the artificial notions of virtue, before reasoning and education have prepared them. We differ with Mr. Shelley in some particulars of his theory, but we agree in all the spirit of it; and the consequence has partly been to us, what it has been to him:—those who have only a belief, or an acquiescence, and no real principle at all;— or who prefer being rigid theorists and lax practisers, with the zest of hypocrisy first and penitence afterwards;—or who love to confound conventional agreements and reputations with all that is to be wished for in human nature, and hate, and persecute, and delight to scandalize any body, who, with the kindest intentions, would win them out of the hard crust of their egotism, however wretched, —or lastly, those who, having acted with the most abominable selfishness and unfeelingness themselves, rejoice in the least opportunity of making a case out to the world against those they have injured,—these, and such persons as these, have chosen to assume from our theories all which they think the world would least like in point of practice; and because we disdained to notice them, or chose to spare not only the best feelings of others, whom they should have been the last to wound, but even their own bad, false, and malignant ones, would have continued to turn that merciful silence against us, had they not unfortunately run beyond their mark, and shown their own fear and horror at being called upon to come forward. But to return to Mr. Shelley. The Reviewer asserts that he "is shamefully dissolute in his conduct." We heard of similar assertions, when we resided in the same house

with Mr. Shelley for nearly three months; and how was he living all that time? As much like Plato himself, as any of his theories resemble Plato,—or rather still more like a Pythagorean. This was the round of his daily life:—He was up early; breakfasted sparingly; wrote this *Revolt of Islam* all the morning; went out in his boat or into the woods with some Greek author or the *Bible* in his hands; came home to a dinner of vegetables (for he took neither meat nor wine); visited (if necessary) *"the sick and the fatherless,"* whom others gave Bibles to and no help; wrote or studied again, or read to his wife and friends the whole evening; took a crust of bread or a glass of whey for his supper; and went early to bed. This is literally the whole of the life he led, or that we believe he now leads in Italy; nor have we ever known him, in spite of the malignant and ludicrous exaggerations on this point, deviate, notwithstanding his theories, even into a single action which those who differ with him might think blameable. We do not say, that he would always square his conduct by their opinions as a matter of principle: we only say, that he acted just as if he did so square them. We forbear, out of regard for the very bloom of their beauty, to touch upon numberless other charities and generosities which we have known him exercise; but this we must say is general, that we never lived with a man who gave so complete an idea of an ardent and principled aspirant in philosophy as Percy Shelley; and that we believe him, from the bottom of our hearts, to be one of the noblest hearts as well as heads which the world has seen for a long time. We never met in short with a being who came nearer, perhaps so near, to that height of humanity mentioned in the conclusion of an essay of Lord Bacon's, where he speaks of excess of Charity and of it's not being in the power of "man or angel to come in danger by it."

"If a man be gracious and courteous to strangers," continues this wise man of the world, in opening the final organ-stop of his high worship of a greater and diviner wisdom, —"If a man be gracious towards strangers, it shews he is a citizen of the world, and that his heart is no island cut off from other lands, but a continent that joins to them. If he be compassionate towards the afflictions of others, it shews that his heart is like the noble tree that is wounded itself when it gives the balm. If he easily pardons and remits offences, it shews that his mind is planted above injuries, so that he cannot be shot. If he be thankful for small benefits, it shews that he weighs men's minds, and not their trash. But, above all, if he have St. Paul's perfection, that he would wish to be an anathema from Christ, for the salvation of his brethren, it shews much of a divine nature, and a kind of conformity with Christ himself."

We could talk, after this, of the manner in which natures of this kind are ever destined to be treated by the Scribes, Pharisees, and Hypocrites of all times and nations; but what room can we have for further indignation, when the ideas of benevolence and wisdom unite to fill one's imagination? Blessings be upon thee, friend; and a part of the spirit which ye profess to serve, upon ye, enemies.

PROMETHEUS UNBOUND

The Examiner. No. 752, pp. 389–390. Sunday, June 23, 1822.

As a conclusive proof of Mr. Shelley's nonsense, the Reviewer selects one of his passages which most require attention, separates it from its proper context, and turns it into prose: after which he triumphantly informs the reader that this prose is not prose, but "the conclusion of the third act of *Prometheus verbatim et literatim.*" Now poetry has often a language as well as music of its own, so distinct from prose, and so universally allowed a right to the distinction (which none are better aware of than the versifiers in the *Quarterly Review*), that secretly to decompose a poetical passage into prose, and then call for a criticism of a reader upon it, is like depriving a body of its distinguishing properties, or confounding their rights and necessities, and then asking where they are. Again, to take a passage abruptly from its context, especially when a context is more than usually necessary to its illustration, is like cutting out a piece of shade from a picture, and reproaching it for want of light. And finally, to select an obscure passage or two from an author, or even to shew that he is often obscure, and then to pretend from these specimens, that he is nothing but obscurity and nonsense, is mere dishonesty.

For instance, Dante is a great genius who is often obscure; but suppose a critic were to pick out one of his obscurest passages, and assert that Dante was a mere writer of jargon. Suppose he were to select one of the metaphysical odes from his *Amoroso Convivio;* or to take a passage from Mr. Cary's translation of his great poem, and turn it into prose for the better mystification of the reader. Here is a specimen:—

"Every orb, corporeal, doth proportion its extent unto the virtue through its parts diffused. The greater blessedness preserves the more. The greater is the body (if all parts share equally) the more is to preserve. Therefore the circle, whose swift course enwheels the universal frame, answers to that, which is supreme in knowledge and in love. Thus by the virtue, not the seeming breadth of substance, measuring, thou shalt see the heavens, each to the intelligence that ruleth it, greater to more, and smaller unto less, suited in strict and wondrous harmony."—*Paradise,* Canto 28.

The lines in question from Mr. Shelley's poem are as follow. A spirit is describing a mighty change that has just taken place on earth. It is the consummation of a state of things, for which all the preceding part of the poem has been yearning:

The painted veil, by those who were, called life,
Which mimicked, as with colours idly spread,
All men believed and hoped, is torn aside;
The loathsome mask is fallen, the man remains
Sceptreless, free, uncircumscribed, but man
Equal, unclassed, tribeless, and nationless,
Exempt from awe, worship, degree, the king
Over himself; just, gentle, wise: but man
Passionless; no, yet free from guilt or pain,
Which were, for his will made or suffered them;
Nor yet exempt, tho' ruling them like slaves,
From chance, and death, and mutability,
The clogs of that which else might oversoar
The loftiest star of unascended heaven,
Pinnacled dim in the intense inane.

That is to say,—The veil, or superficial state of things, which was called life by those who lived before us, and which had nothing but an idle resemblance to that proper state of things, which we would fain have thought it, is no longer existing. The loathsome mask is fallen; and the being who was compelled to wear it, is now what he ought to be, one of a great family who are their own rulers, just, gentle, wise and passionless; no, not passionless, though free from guilt or pain, which were only the consequences of their former wilful mistakes; nor are they exempt, though they turn them to the best and most philosophical account, from chance, and death, and mutability; things, which are the clogs of that lofty spirit of humanity, which else might rise beyond all that we can conceive of the highest and happiest star of heaven, pinnacled, like an almost viewless atom, in the space of the universe.—*The intense inane* implies excess of emptiness, and is a phrase of Miltonian construction, like "the palpable obscure" and "the vast abrupt." Where is the unintelligible nonsense of all this? and where is the want of "grammar," with which the "pride" of the Reviewer, as *Mr. Looney M'Twoulter* says, would "come over" him?

Mr. Shelley has written a great deal of poetry equally unmetaphysical and beautiful. The whole of the tragedy of the *Cenci*, which the Reviewers do not think it to their interest to notice, is written in a style equally plain and noble. But we need not go farther than the volume before us, though, according to the Reviewer, the "whole" of it does not contain *"one* original image of nature, *one* simple expression of human feeling, or *one* new association of the appearances of the moral with those of the material world." We really must apologize to all intelligent readers who know anything of Mr. Shelley's genius, for appearing to give more notice to these absurdities than they are worth; but there are good reasons why they ought to be exposed. The *Prometheus* has already spoken for itself. Now take the following *Ode* to a *Skylark,* of which I will venture to say, that there is not in the whole circle of lyric poetry a piece more *full* of "original images of nature, of simple expressions of human feeling, and of the associations of the appearances of the moral with those of the material world." You shall have it entire, for it is as fitting for the season, as it is true to the musical and etherial beauty of its subject.

. . . . . .

I know of nothing more beautiful than this,— more choice of tones, more natural in words, more abundant in exquisite, cordial, and most poetical associations. One gets the stanzas by heart unawares, and repeats them like "snatches of old tunes." To say that nobody

who writes in the *Quarterly Review* could produce anything half as good (unless Mr. Wordsworth writes in it, which I do not believe he does) would be sorry praise. When Mr. Gifford "sings" as the phrase is, one is reminded of nothing but snarling. Mr. Southey, though the gods have made him more poetical than Mr. Gifford, is always affecting something original, and tiring one to death with common-place. "Croker," as Goldsmith says, "rhymes to joker;" and as to the chorus of priests and virgins,—of scribes and pharisees,—which make up the poetical undersong of the Review, it is worthy of the discordant mixture of worldliness and religion, of faith and bad practice, of Christianity and malignity, which finds in it something ordinary enough to merit its approbation.

One passage more from this immoral and anti-christian volume, that contains, "not one simple expression of human feeling," and I will close my letter. It is part of *"An Ode, written October* 1819, *before the Spaniards had recovered their liberty:"*—

Glory, glory, glory,
To those who have greatly suffered and done!
  Never name in story
Was greater than that which ye shall have won.
Conquerors have conquered their foes alone,
Whose revenge, pride, and power they have overthrown:
Ride ye, more victorious, over your own.

Hear that, ye reverend and pugnacious Christians of the Quarterly!

  Bind, bind every brow
With crownals of violet, ivy, and pine:
  Hide the blood-stains now
With hues which sweet nature has made divine;
Green strength, azure hope, and eternity;
But let not the pansy among them be;
Ye were injured, and that means memory.

How well the Spaniards have acted up to this infidel injunction is well known to the whole of wondering Christendom, and affords one of the happiest presages to the growth of true freedom and philosophy. Why did not the Reviewer quote such passages as these by way of specimens of the author's powers and moral feeling? Why did his boasted Christianity lead him to conceal these, as well as to omit what was necessary to the one quoted in my last? You pretty well understand why by this time; but I have still further elucidations to give, which are more curious than any we have had yet, and which you shall see. (—I shake your hands.)

ON MR. SHELLEY'S NEW POEM, ENTITLED *ADONAIS*

The Examiner. No. 754, pp. 419–421. Sunday, July 7, 1822.

SINCE I left London, Mr. Shelley's *Adonais, or Elegy on the Death of Mr. Keats,* has, I find, made it's appearance. I have not seen the London edition; but I have an Italian one printed at Pisa, with which I must content myself at present. The other was to have had notes. It is not a poem calculated to be popular, any more than the *Prometheus Unbound;* it is of too abstract and subtle a nature for that purpose; but it will delight the few, to whom Mr. Shelley is accustomed to address himself. Spenser would be pleased with it if he were living. A mere town reader and a Quarterly Reviewer will find it *caviare. Adonais,* in short, is such an elegy as poet might be expected to write upon poet. The author has had before him his recollections of Lycidas, of Moschus and Bion, and of the doctrines of Plato; and in the stanza of the most poetical of poets, Spenser, has brought his own genius, in all its etherial beauty, to lead a pomp of Loves, Graces, and Intelligences, in honour of the departed.

Nor is the Elegy to be considered less sincere, because it is full of poetical abstractions. Dr. Johnson would have us believe, that *Lycidas* is not "the effusion of real passion." —"Passion," says he, in his usual conclusive tone, (as if the force of critic could no further go) "plucks no berries from the myrtle and ivy; nor calls upon Arethuse and Mincius, nor tells of rough Satyrs and Fauns with cloven heel. Where there is leisure for fiction, there is little grief." This is only a more genteel common-place, brought in to put down a vulgar one. Dr. Johnson, like most critics, had no imagination; and because he found nothing natural to his own impulses in the associations of poetry, and saw them so often abused by the practice of versifiers inferior to himself, he was willing to conclude, that on natural occasions they were always improper. But a

poet's world is as real to him as the more palpable one to people in general. He spends his time in it as truly as Dr. Johnson did his in Fleet-street or at the club. Milton felt that the happiest hours he had passed with his friend had been passed in the regions of poetry. He had been accustomed to be transported with him "beyond the visible diurnal sphere" of his fire-side and supper-table, things which he could record nevertheless with a due relish. (See the *Epitaphium Damonis.*) The next step was to fancy himself again among them, missing the dear companion of his walks; and then it is that the rivers murmur complainingly, and the flowers hang their heads,—which to a truly poetical habit of mind, though to no other, they may literally be said to do, because such is the aspect which they present to an afflicted imagination. "I see nothing in the world but melancholy," is a common phrase with persons who are suffering under a great loss. With ordinary minds in this condition the phrase implies a vague feeling, but still an actual one. The poet, as in other instances, gives it a life and particularity. The practice has doubtless been abused; so much so, that even some imaginative minds may find it difficult at first to fall in with it, however beautifully managed. But the very abuse shews that it is founded in a principle in nature. And a great deal depends upon the character of the poet. What is mere frigidity and affectation in common magazine rhymers, or men of wit and fashion about town, becomes another thing in minds accustomed to live in the sphere I spoke of. It was as unreasonable in Dr. Johnson to sneer at Milton's grief in *Lycidas,* as it was reasonable in him to laugh at Prior and Congreve for comparing Chloe to Venus and Diana, and *pastoralizing* about Queen Mary. Neither the turn of their genius, nor their habits of life, included this sort of ground. We feel that Prior should have stuck to his tuckers and boddices, and Congreve appeared in his proper Court-mourning.

Milton perhaps overdid the matter a little when he personified the poetical enjoyments of his friend and himself under the character of actual shepherds. Mr. Shelley is the more natural in this respect, inasmuch as he is entirely abstract and imaginative, and recalls his lamented acquaintance to mind in no other shape than one strictly poetical. I say acquaintance, because such Mr. Keats was; and it happens, singularly enough, that the few hours which he and Mr. Shelley passed together were almost entirely of a poetical character. I recollect one evening in particular, which they spent with the writer of these letters in composing verses on a given subject. But it is not as a mere acquaintance, however poetical, that Mr. Shelley records him. It is as the intimate acquaintance of all lovely and lofty thoughts, as the nursling of the Muse, the hope of her coming days, the creator of additional Beauties and Intelligences for the adornment and the inhabitation of the material world. The poet commences with calling upon Urania to weep for her favourite; and in a most beautiful stanza, the termination of which is in the depths of the human heart, informs us where he is lying. You are aware that Mr. Keats died at Rome:—

To that high Capital, where kingly Death
Keeps his pale court in beauty and decay,
He came;—and bought, with price of purest breath,
A grave among the eternal—Come away!
Haste, while the vault of blue Italian day
Is yet his fitting charnel-roof! while still
He lies, as if in dewy sleep he lay;
Awake him not! surely he takes his fill
Of deep and liquid rest, forgetful of all ill.

"The forms of things unseen," which Mr. Keats's imagination had turned into shape,— the "airy nothings" to which it is the high prerogative of the poet to give "a local habitation and a name," are then represented, in a most fanciful manner, as crowding about his lips and body, and lamenting him who called them into being:—

And others came . . . Desires and Adorations,
Winged Persuasions and veiled Destinies,
Splendours, and glooms, and glimmering Incarnations
Of hopes and fears, and twilight Phantasies;
And Sorrow, with her family of sighs;
And Pleasure, blind with tears, led by the gleam
Of her own dying smile instead of eyes.
All he had loved, and moulded into thought,
From shape, and hue, and odour, and sweet sound,
Lamented Adonais.

A phrase in the first line of the following passage would make an admirable motto for that part of the *Literary Pocket Book*, in which the usual lists of kings and other passing domina-tions are superseded by a list of Eminent Men:—

And he is gathered to *the kings of thought*,
Who waged contention with their time's decay,
And of the past are all that cannot pass away.

The spot in which Mr. Keats lies buried is thus finely pointed out. The two similes at the close are among the happiest we recollect, especially the second:—

Go thou to Rome,—at once the Paradise,
The grave, the city, and the wilderness;
And where its wrecks like shattered mountains rise,
And flowering weeds, and fragrant copses dress
The bones of Desolation's nakedness,
Pass, till the Spirit of the spot shall lead
Thy footsteps to a slope of green access,
Where, like an infant's smile, over the dead,
A light of laughing flowers along the grass is spread.

And gray walls moulder round, on which dull Time
Feeds, like slow fire upon a hoary brand.

In the course of the poem some living writers are introduced, among whom Lord Byron is designated as

The Pilgrim of Eternity, whose fame
Over his living head like Heaven is bent
An early but enduring monument!

The poet of Ireland is called, with equal brevity and felicity,

The sweetest lyrist of her saddest wrong:

And among "others of less note," is modestly put one, the description of whom is strikingly calculated to excite a mixture of sympathy and admiration. The use of the Pagan mythology is supposed to have been worn out; but in fact, they who say so, or are supposed to have worn it out, never wore it at all. See to what a natural and noble purpose a true scholar can turn it:—

He, as I guess,
Had gazed on Nature's naked loveliness,
Actæon-like, and now he fled astray
With feeble steps o'er the world's wilderness,
And his own thoughts, along that rugged way,
Pursued, like raging hounds, their father and their prey.

A pard-like Spirit, beautiful and swift—
A Love in desolation masked;—a Power

Girt round with weakness;—it can scarce uplift
The weight of the superincumbent hour;
It is a dying lamp, a falling shower,
A breaking billow;—even while we speak
Is it not broken? On the withering flower   5
The killing sun smiles brightly: on a cheek
The life can burn in blood, even while the heart
    may break.

    Ah! te meæ si partem animæ rapit
     Maturior vis!—

But the poet is here, I trust, as little of a
prophet, as affection and a beautiful climate,
and the extraordinary and most vital energy
of his spirit, can make him. The singular termination of this description, and the useful re-   15
flections it is calculated to excite, I shall
reserve for another subject in my next. But
how is it, that even that termination could not
tempt the malignant common-place of the
Quarterly Reviewers to become blind to the
obvious beauty of this poem, and venture
upon laying some of its noble stanzas before
their readers? How is it that in their late
specimens of Mr. Shelley's powers they said
nothing of the style and versification of the   25
majestic tragedy of the *Cenci*, which would
have been equally intelligible to the lowest,
and instructive to the highest, of their readers? How is it that they have not even hinted
at the existence of this *Elegy on the death of*   30
Mr. Keats, though immediately after the arrival of copies of it from Italy they thought
proper to give a pretended review of a poem
which appeared to them the least calculated
for their readers' understandings? And finally,   35
how happens it, that Mr. Gifford has never
taken any notice of Mr. Keats's *last* publication,—the beautiful volume containing *Lamia*,
the Story from Boccaccio, and that magnificent
fragment *Hyperion?* Perhaps the following   40
passage of the Elegy will explain:—

Our Adonais has drunk poison!—Oh,
What deaf and viperous murderer could crown
Life's early cup with such a draught of woe?
The nameless worm would now itself disown:
It felt, yet could escape the magic tone   45
Whose prelude held all envy, hate, and wrong,
But what was howling in one breast alone
Silent with expectation, of the song,
Whose master's hand is cold, whose silver lyre
    unstrung.   50

Live thou, whose infamy is not thy fame!
Live! fear no heavier chastisement from me,
Thou noteless blot on a remembered name!
But be thyself, and know thyself to be!
And ever at thy season be thou free

To spill the venom when thy fangs o'erflow:
Remorse and Self-Contempt shall cling to thee;
Hot shame shall burn upon thy secret brow,
And like a beaten hound tremble thou shalt—as
    now.

This, one would think, would not have been
"unintelligible" to the dullest *Quarterly*
peruser, who had read the review of Mr.
Keats's *Endymion.* Nor would the following   10
perhaps have been quite obscure:—

Nor let us weep that our delight is fled
Far from these carrion kites that scream below;
He wakes or sleeps with the enduring dead;   15
Thou canst not soar where he is sitting now.
Dust to the dust! but the pure spirit shall flow
Back to the burning fountain whence it came,
A portion of the Eternal, which must glow
Through time and change, unquenchably the
    same,   20
While thy cold embers choke the sordid hearth of
    shame.

However, if further explanation had been
wanted, the Preface to the Elegy furnishes it
in an abundance, which even the meanest admirers of Mr. Gifford could have no excuse
for not understanding? Why then did he not
quote this? Why could he not venture, once in
his life, to try and look a little fair and handsome; and instead of making all sorts of misrepresentations of his opponents, lay before
his readers something of what his opponents
say of him? He only ventures to allude, in
convulsive fits and starts, and then not by   35
name, to the *Feast of the Poets.* He dares not
even allude to Mr. Hazlitt's epistolary dissection of him. And now he, or some worthy co-
adjutor for him, would pretend that he knows
nothing of Mr. Shelley's denouncement of   40
him, but criticises his other works out of pure
zeal for religion and morality! Oh these
modern "Scribes, Pharisees, and Hypocrites!"
How exactly do they resemble their prototypes of old!
"It may well be said," observes Mr. Shelley's Preface, "that these wretched men know
not what they do. They scatter their insults
and their slanders without heed as to whether
the poisoned shaft lights on a heart made cal-   50
lous by many blows, or one, like Keats's, composed of more penetrable stuff. One of their
associates is, to my knowledge, a most base
and unprincipled calumniator. As to 'Endymion,' was it a poem, whatever might be it's

defects, to be treated contemptuously by those who had celebrated with various degrees of complacency and panegyric, 'Paris,' and 'Woman,' and a 'Syrian Tale,' and Mrs. Lefanu, and Mr. Barrett, and Mr. Howard Payne, and a long list of the illustrious obscure? Are these the men, who in their venal good-nature, presumed to draw a parallel between the Rev. Mr. Milman and Lord Byron? What gnat did they strain at here, after having swallowed all those camels? Against what woman taken in adultery, dares the foremost of these literary prostitutes to cast his opprobrious stone? Miserable man! you, one of the meanest, have wantonly defaced one of the noblest specimens of the workmanship of God. Nor shall it be your excuse, that murderer as you are, you have spoken daggers but used none."

Let us take the taste of the Gifford out of one's mouth with the remainder of the Preface, which is like a sweet nut after one with a worm in it.

"The circumstances of the closing scene of poor Keats's life were not made known to me until the Elegy was ready for the press. I am given to understand that the wound which his sensitive spirit had received from the criticism of 'Endymion,' was exasperated by the bitter sense of unrequited benefits; the poor fellow seems to have been hooted from the stage of life, no less by those on whom he had wasted the promise of his genius, than those on whom he had lavished his fortune and his care. He was accompanied to Rome, and attended in his last illness by Mr. Severn, a young artist of the highest promise, who, I have been informed, 'almost risked his own life, and sacrificed every prospect to unwearied attendance upon his dying friend.' Had I known these circumstances before the completion of my poem, I should have been tempted to add my feeble tribute of applause to the more solid recompense which the virtuous man finds in the recollection of his own motives. Mr. Severn can dispense with a reward from 'such stuff as dreams are made of.' His conduct is a golden augury of the success of his future career—may the unextinguished Spirit of his illustrious friend animate the creations of his pencil, and plead against oblivion for his name!"

Amen! says one who knew the poet, and who knows the painter.

ON *DON JUAN. CANTOS 1ST AND 2ND*

The Examiner. No. 618, pp. 700–702. Sunday, Oct. 31, 1819.

SOME persons consider this the finest work of Lord Byron,—or at least that in which he displays most power. It is at all events the most extraordinary that he has yet published. His other poems, with the exception of that amusing satire—*Beppo,* are written for the most part with one sustained serious feeling throughout,—either of pathos, or grandeur, or passion, or all united. But *Don Juan* contains specimens of all the author's modes of writing, which are mingled together and push one another about in a strange way. The groundwork (if we may so speak of a stile [*sic*]) is the satirical and humourous; but you are sometimes surprised and moved by a touching piece of human nature, and again startled and pained by the sudden transition from loveliness or grandeur to ridicule or the mock-heroic. The delicious and deep descriptions of love, and youth, and hope, came upon us like the "young beams" of the sun breaking through the morning dew, and the terrific pictures of the misery of man and his most appalling sensations, like awful flashes of lightning; —but when the author reverses this change, he trifles too much with our feelings, and occasionally goes on, turning to ridicule or hopelessness all the fine ideas he has excited, with a recklessness that becomes extremely unpleasant and mortifying. What, for instance, can be more beautiful and at the same time true to nature than where,—just after a very anti-pathetic description of the confusion of *Julia* at her husband's sudden appearance, and her contrivances and lovers' falsehoods to elude his search for the beloved youth, he says (speaking of their alarm at the unexpected return of the old gentleman)—

> Julia did not speak,
> But pressed her bloodless lip to Juan's cheek.

> He turn'd his lip to hers, and with his hand
> Call'd back the tangles of her wandering hair;
> Even then their love they could not all command,
> And half forgot their danger and despair.

What more calculated to "harrow up one's soul" than the following stanzas, which come in the very midst of some careless jests on the abstract ludicrousness of the wretched shifts of starving sailors in a becalmed boat, surrounded by a boundless prospect of the ocean? The Italics are our own.

The seventh day, and no wind—the burning sun 5
  Blister'd and scorch'd; and, stagnant on the sea,
They lay like carcases! and hope was none,
  Save in the breeze which came not: *savagely
They glared upon each other*—all was done,
  Water, and wine, and food,—and you might see
The *longings of the cannibal arise*, 10
(Although they spoke not) in their *wolfish* eyes.

At length one whispered his companion, who
  Whispered another, and thus it went round,
And then into a *hoarser murmur* grew,
  An ominous and wild and desperate sound; 15
And when his comrade's thought each sufferer
    knew,
  'Twas but his own, suppress'd till now, he
    found:
And *out they spoke* of lots for flesh and blood,
And who should die to be his fellow's food. 20

Then immediately following this awful passage, comes an affected delicacy at the tearing up of *Julia's* letter to *Juan* to make the lots ("materials which must shock the muse"), and a *sang froid* account of the division of the 25 body: shortly after follow some terrific lines relating the dreadful consequences of this gorging of human flesh; and a little farther on there is a laughable description of Juan's dislike to feed on "poor Pedrillo" and his prefer- 30 ence for "chewing a piece of bamboo and some lead, the stanza ending with the irresistible fact, that

At length they caught two boobies and a noddy, 35
And then they left off eating the dead body.

It is not difficult to account for this heterogeneous mixture,—for the bard has furnished us with the key to his own mind. His early 40 hopes were blighted, and his disappointment vents itself in satirizing absurdities which rouse his indignation; and indeed a good deal of bitterness may be found at the bottom of much of his satire. But his genius is not natu- 45 rally satirical; he breaks out therefore into those frequent veins of passion and true feeling of which we have just given specimens, and goes on with them till his memory is no longer able to bear the images conjured up by 50 his fine genius; and it is to get rid of such painful and "thick-coming" recollections, that he dashes away and relieves himself by getting into another train of ideas however incon-

gruous or violently contrasted with the former. This solution will, we think, be borne out by the following affecting description of the poet's feelings. Observe in particular the remarkable parenthesis after the first line, whose pregnant meaning seems to have compelled him to take refuge in a lighter and more humourous idea:—

But now at thirty years my hair is grey— 10
  (I wonder what it will be like at forty?
I thought of a peruke the other day)—
  My heart is not much greener; and, in short, I
Have squandered my whole summer while 'twas
    May,
  And feel no more the spirit to retort; I 15
Have spent my life, both interest and principal,
And deem not, what I deem'd, my soul invincible.

No more—no more—Oh! never more on me
  The freshness of the heart can fall like dew,
Which out of all the lovely things we see
  Extracts emotions beautiful and new, 20
Hived in our bosoms like the bag o' the bee:
  Think'st thou the honey with those objects
    grew?
Alas! 'twas not in them, but in thy power
To double even the sweetness of a flower.

No more—no more—Oh! never more, my heart, 25
  Canst thou be my sole world—my universe!
Once all in all, but now a thing apart
  Thou canst not be my blessing or my curse.

Here is some evidence that the poet is not without the milk of human kindness, and to our minds there is much more in the rest of the volume. His bent is not, as we have said, satirical, nor is he naturally disposed to be ill-natured with respect to the faults and vices of his fellow-creatures. There is an evident struggle throughout these two cantos in the feelings of the writer, and it is very fine to see him, as he gets on, growing more interested in his fiction, and pouring out at the conclusion in a much less interrupted strain of rich and deep beauty. . . .

Don Juan is accused of being an "immoral" work, which we cannot at all discover. We suppose that this charge more particularly alludes to the first canto. Let us see then on what foundation it rests. The son of a Spanish patrician, educated in the most prudish manner by a licentious, yet affectedly virtuous mother, falls in love with the young wife of an old man. She returns his affection, and their passion being favoured by opportunity, she gives way to her natural feelings, and is unfaithful to her marriage vows, the example (observe) being set her by this very husband's intrigues with *Juan's* mother. Now Lord Byron speaks lightly of the effect of any scruples of conscience upon her, and of her infidelity; and this, it is said, has tendency to corrupt the minds of "us youth," and to make us *think* lightly of breaking the matrimonial contract. But if to do this be immoral, we can only say that Nature is immoral. Lord Byron does no more than relate the consequences of certain absurdities. If he speaks slightingly of the ties between a girl and a husband old enough for her father, it is because the ties themselves *are* slight. He does not ridicule the bonds of marriage generally, or where they are formed as they should be: he merely shows the folly and wickedness of setting forms and opinions against nature. If stupid and selfish parents will make up matches between persons whom difference of age or disposition disqualifies for mutual affection, they must take the consequences:—but we do not think it fair that a poet should be exclaimed against as a promoter of nuptial infidelity because he tells them what those consequences are. In this particular case, too, the author does not omit some painful consequences to those who have sinned according to "nature's law." *Julia*, the victim of selfishness and "damned custom," is shut up in a convent, where no consolation remains to her but the remembrance of her entire and hapless love; but even that was perhaps pleasanter to her than living in the constant irksomeness of feigning an affection she could not feel.

There are a set of prudish and very suspicious moralists who endeavour to make vice appear to inexperienced eyes much more hateful than it really is. They would correct Nature;—and they always over-reach themselves. Nature has made vice to a certain degree pleasurable, though its painful consequences outweigh its present gratification. Now the said prudes, in their lectures and sermons and moral discourses (for they are chiefly priests) are constantly declaiming on the *deformity* of vice, and its almost total want of attraction. The consequence is, that when they are found to have deceived (as they always are) and immoral indulgence is discovered to be not without its charms,—the minds of young persons are apt to confound their true with their false maxims, and to think the threats of future pain and repentance mere fables invented to deter them from their rightful enjoyments. Which then, we would ask, are the immoral writings,—those which, by misrepresenting the laws of nature, lead to false views of morality and consequent licentiousness?—or those, which ridicule and point out the effects of absurd contradictions of human feelings and passions, and help to bring about a reformation of such practises.

Of the story in the second canto it is unnecessary to say much, for these remarks will apply to both. We suppose there has been some sermonizing on the description of the delight arising from the "illicit intercourse" of *Juan* and *Haidee*. People who talk in this way can perceive no distinctions. It certainly is not to be inculcated, that every handsome young man and woman will find their account in giving way to all their impulses, because the very violent breaking through the habits and forms of society would create a great deal of unhappiness, both to the individuals, and to others. But what is there to blame in a beautiful and affectionate girl who gives way to a passion for a young shipwrecked human creature, bound to her by gratitude as well as love? She exacts no promises, says the bard, because she fears no inconstancy. Her father had exposed her to the first temptation that comes across her, because he had not provided against it by allowing her to know more of mankind. And does she not receive, as well as bestow, more real pleasure (for that is the question) in the enjoyment of a first and deep passion, than in becoming the wife of some brother in iniquity to whom her pirating father would have trucked her for lucre?

The fact is, at the bottom of all these questions, that many things are made vicious, which are not so by nature; and many things made virtuous, which are only so by calling and agreement: and it is on the horns of this self-created dilemma, that society is continually writhing and getting desperate.

We must not conclude without informing our readers of the Poet's intention of continuing the story of *Don Juan* through twelve or (perhaps) twenty-four cantos, of which these two are the first. The following is the poetical table of contents:—

My poem's epic, and is meant to be
  Divided in twelve books; each book containing
With love and war, a heavy gale at sea,
  A list of ships and captains, and kings reigning;

New characters; the episodes are three;
  A panorama view of hell's in training,
After the stile [*sic*] of Virgil and of Homer,
So that my name of epic's no misnomer.

And he adds, with a hit at the "moral" conclusion of hell-fire,—that "comfortable creed" (as he elsewhere stiles it) of some Christians—

I've got new mythological machinery,
And very handsome supernatural scenery.

COLERIDGE [1]

COLERIDGE lived in the most extraordinary and agitated period of modern history; and to a certain extent he was so mixed up with its controversies, that he was at one time taken for nothing but an apostate republican, and at another for a dreaming theosophist. The truth is, that both his politics and theosophy were at the mercy of a discursive genius, intellectually bold but educationally timid, which, anxious, or rather willing, to bring conviction and speculation together, mooting all points as it went, and throwing the subtlest glancing lights on many, ended in satisfying nobody, and concluding nothing. Charles Lamb said of him, that he had "the art of making the unintelligible appear intelligible." He was the finest dreamer, the most eloquent talker, and the most original thinker of the day; but for want of complexional energy, did nothing with all the vast *prose* part of his mind but help the Germans to give a subtler tone to criticism, and sow a few valuable seeds of thought in minds worthy to receive them. Nine-tenths of his theology would apply equally well to their own creeds in the mouths of a Brahmin or a Mussulman.

His poetry is another matter. It is so beautiful, and was so quietly content with its beauty, making no call on the critics, and receiving hardly any notice, that people are but now beginning to awake to a full sense of its merits. Of pure poetry, strictly so called, that is to say, consisting of nothing but its essential self, without conventional and perishing helps, he was the greatest master of his

[1] Leigh Hunt: *Selections from the English Poets*, 1859.

time. If you would see it in a phial, like a distillation of roses (taking it, I mean, at its best), it would be found without a speck. The poet is happy with so good a gift, and the reader is "happy in his happiness." Yet so little, sometimes, are a man's contemporaries and personal acquaintances able or disposed to estimate him properly, that while Coleridge, unlike Shakspeare, lavished praises on his poetic friends, he had all the merit of the generosity to himself; and even Hazlitt, owing perhaps to causes of political alienation, could see nothing to admire in the exquisite poem of Christabel, but the description of the quarrel between the friends! After speaking, too, of the Ancient Mariner as the only one of his poems that he could point out to any one as giving an adequate idea of his great natural powers, he adds, "It is high German, however, and in it he seems to conceive of poetry but as a drunken dream, reckless, careless, and heedless of past, present, and to come." This is said of a poem, with which fault has been found for the exceeding conscientiousness of its moral! O, ye critics, the best of ye, what havoc does personal difference play with your judgments! It was Mr. Hazlitt's only or most unwarrantable censure, or one which friendship found hardest to forgive. But peace, and honor too, be with his memory! If he was a splenetic and sometimes jealous man, he was a disinterested politician and an admirable critic: and lucky were those whose natures gave them the right and the power to pardon him.

Coleridge, though a born poet, was in his style and general musical feeling the disciple partly of Spenser, and partly of the fine old English ballad-writers in the collection of Bishop Percy. But if he could not improve on them in some things, how he did in others, especially in the art of being thoroughly musical! Of all our writers of the briefer narrative poetry, Coleridge is the finest since Chaucer; and assuredly he is the sweetest of all our poets. Waller's music is but a court-flourish in comparison; and though Beaumont and Fletcher, Collins, Gray, Keats, Shelley, and others, have several as sweet passages, and Spenser is in a certain sense musical throughout, yet no man has written whole poems, of equal length, so perfect in the sentiment of music, so varied with it, and yet leaving on the ear so unbroken and single an effect. . . .

THOMAS DE QUINCEY

SAMUEL TAYLOR COLERIDGE [1]

It was, I think, in the month of August, but certainly in the summer season, and certainly in the year 1807, that I first saw this illustrious man. My knowledge of him as a man of most original genius began about the year 1799. A little before that time Wordsworth had published the first edition (in a single volume) of the "Lyrical Ballads," and into this had been introduced Mr. Coleridge's poem of the "Ancient Mariner," as the contribution of an anonymous friend. It would be directing the reader's attention too much to myself if I were to linger upon this, the greatest event in the unfolding of my own mind. Let me say, in one word, that, at a period when neither the one nor the other writer was valued by the public—both having a long warfare to accomplish of contumely and ridicule before they could rise into their present estimation—I found in these poems "the ray of a new morning," and an absolute revelation of untrodden worlds teeming with power and beauty as yet unsuspected amongst men. I may here mention that, precisely at the same time, Professor Wilson, entirely unconnected with myself, and not even known to me until ten years later, received the same startling and profound impressions from the same volume. . . .

Two or three days had slipped away in waiting for Coleridge's re-appearance at Nether Stowey, when suddenly Lord Egmont called upon Mr. Poole, with a present for Coleridge: it was a canister of peculiarly fine snuff, which Coleridge now took profusely. Lord Egmont, on this occasion, spoke of Coleridge in the terms of excessive admiration, and urged Mr. Poole to put him upon undertaking some great monumental work, that might furnish a sufficient arena for the display of his various and rare accomplishments; for his multiform erudition on the one hand, for his splendid power of theorizing and combining large and remote notices of facts on the other. And he suggested, judiciously enough, as one theme which offered a field at once large enough and indefinite enough to suit a mind that could not show its full compass of power unless upon very plastic materials—

[1] From *Reminiscences of the English Lake Poets*, 1834.

a History of Christianity, in its progress and in its chief divarications into Church and Sect, with a continual reference to the relations subsisting between Christianity and the current philosophy; their occasional connections or approaches, and their constant mutual repulsions. "But, at any rate, let him do something," said Lord Egmont; "for at present he talks very much like an angel, and does nothing at all." Lord Egmont I understood from everybody to be a truly good and benevolent man; and on this occasion he spoke with an earnestness which agreed with my previous impression. Coleridge, he said, was now in the prime of his powers—uniting something of youthful vigour with sufficient experience of life; having the benefit, beside, of vast meditation, and of reading unusually discursive. No man had ever been better qualified to revive the heroic period of literature in England, and to give a character of weight to the philosophic erudition of the country upon the Continent. "And what a pity," he added, "if this man were, after all, to vanish like an apparition, and you, I, and a few others, who have witnessed his grand *bravuras* of display, were to have the usual fortune of ghost-seers, in meeting no credit for any statements that we might vouch on his behalf!"

On this occasion we learned, for the first time, that Lord Egmont's carriage had, some days before, conveyed Coleridge to Bridgewater, with a purpose of staying one single day at that place, and then returning to Mr. Poole's. From the sort of laugh with which Lord Egmont taxed his own simplicity, in having confided at all in the stability of any Coleridgian plan, I now gathered that procrastination in excess was, or had become, a marking feature in Coleridge's daily life. Nobody who knew him ever thought of depending on any appointment he might make: spite of his uniformly honourable intentions, nobody attached any weight to his assurances *in re futura:* those who asked him to dinner or any other party, as a matter of course, sent a carriage for him, and went personally or by proxy to fetch him; and, as to letters, unless the address were in some female hand that commanded his affectionate esteem, he tossed them all into one general *dead-letter bureau,* and rarely, I believe, opened them at all. . . .

But, on that same day, all this, which I heard now for the first time, and with much concern, was fully explained; for already he was under the full dominion of opium, as he himself revealed to me, and with a deep expression of horror at the hideous bondage, in a private walk of some length which I took with him about sunset.

Lord Egmont's information, and the knowledge now gained of Coleridge's habits, making it very uncertain when I might see him in my present hospitable quarters, I immediately took my leave of Mr. Poole, and went over to Bridgewater. I had received directions for finding out the house where Coleridge was visiting; and, in riding down a main street of Bridgewater, I noticed a gateway corresponding to the description given me. Under this was standing, and gazing about him, a man whom I will describe. In height he might seem to be about five feet eight (he was, in reality, about an inch and a half taller, but his figure was of an order which drowns the height); his person was broad and full, and tended even to corpulence; his complexion was fair, though not what painters technically style fair, because it was associated with black hair; his eyes were large, and soft in their expression; and it was from the peculiar appearance of haze or dreaminess which mixed with their light that I recognized my object. This was Coleridge. I examined him steadfastly for a minute or more; and it struck me that he saw neither myself nor any other object in the street. He was in a deep reverie; for I had dismounted, made two or three trifling arrangements at an inn-door, and advanced close to him, before he had apparently become conscious of my presence. The sound of my voice, announcing my own name, first awoke him; he started, and for a moment seemed at a loss to understand my purpose or his own situation; for he repeated rapidly a number of words which had no relation to either of us. There was no *mauvaise honte* in his manner, but simple perplexity, and an apparent difficulty in recovering his position amongst daylight realities. This little scene over, he received me with a kindness of manner so marked that it might be called gracious. The hospitable family with whom he was domesticated were distinguished for their amiable manners and enlightened understandings: they were descendants from Chubb, the philosophic writer, and bore the same name. For Coleridge they all testified deep affection and esteem—sentiments in which the whole town of Bridgewater seemed to share; for in the evening, when the heat of the day had declined, I walked out with him; and rarely, perhaps never, have I seen a person so much interrupted in one hour's space as Coleridge, on this occasion, by the courteous attentions of young and old. . . .

In the autumn of 1810, Coleridge left the Lakes; and, so far as I am aware, for ever. I once, indeed, heard a rumour of his having passed through with some party of tourists—some reason struck me at the time for believing it untrue—but, at all events, he never returned to them as a resident. What might be his reason for this eternal self-banishment from scenes which he so well understood in all their shifting forms of beauty, I can only guess. Perhaps it was the very opposite reason to that which is most obvious: not, possibly, because he had become indifferent to their attractions, but because his undecaying sensibility to their commanding power had become associated with too afflicting remembrances, and flashes of personal recollections, suddenly restored and illuminated—recollections which will

Sometimes leap
From hiding-places ten years deep,

and bring into collision the present with some long-forgotten past, in a form too trying and too painful for endurance. . . . Phantoms of lost power, sudden intuitions, and shadowy restorations of forgotten feelings, sometimes dim and perplexing, sometimes by bright but furtive glimpses, sometimes by a full and steady revelation, overcharged with light— throw us back in a moment upon scenes and remembrances that we have left full thirty years behind us. In solitude, and chiefly in the solitudes of nature, and, above all, amongst the great and *enduring* features of nature, such as mountains, and quiet dells, and the lawny recesses of forests, and the silent shores of lakes, features with which (as being themselves less liable to change) our feelings have a more abiding association—under these circumstances it is that such evanescent hauntings of our past and forgotten selves are most apt to startle and to waylay us. These are *positive* torments from which the agitated mind shrinks in fear; but there are others *negative* in their nature—that is, blank mementoes of powers extinct, and of faculties burnt out within us. And from both forms of anguish—from this twofold scourge—poor Coleridge fled, perhaps, in flying from the beauty of external nature. In alluding to this latter, or negative form of suffering—that form, I mean, which presents not the too fugitive glimpses of past power, but its blank annihilation—Coleridge himself most beautifully insists upon and illustrates the truth that all which we find in Nature must be created by ourselves; and that alike whether Nature is so gorgeous in her beauty as to seem apparelled in her wedding-garment or so powerless and extinct as to seem palled in her shroud. In either case,

O, Lady, we receive but what we give,
And in *our* life alone does nature live;
Ours is her wedding-garment, ours her shroud.

It were a vain endeavour,
    Though I should gaze for ever
On that green light that lingers in the west:
I may not hope from *outward* forms to win
The passion and the life whose fountains are
    within.

This was one, and the most common, shape of extinguished power from which Coleridge fled to the great city. But sometimes the same decay came back upon his heart in the more poignant shape of intimations and vanishing glimpses, recovered for one moment from the paradise of youth, and from fields of joy and power, over which, for him, too certainly, he felt that the cloud of night was settling for ever. Both modes of the same torment exiled him from Nature; and for the same reasons he fled from poetry and all commerce with his own soul; burying himself in the profoundest abstractions from life and human sensibilities.

For not to think of what I needs must feel,
    But to be still and patient all I can;
And haply *by abstruse research to steal,*
    From my own nature, all the natural man;
This was my sole resource, my only plan;
Till *that,* which suits a part, infects the whole,
And now is almost grown the habit of my
    soul. . . .

WILLIAM WORDSWORTH [1]

. . . Passing from the diction of Wordsworth's poetry to its matter, the least plausible

[1] *Tait's Magazine,* September, 1845.

objection ever brought against it was that of Mr. Hazlitt: "One would suppose," he said, "from the tenor of his subjects, that on this earth there was neither marrying nor giving in marriage." But as well might it be said of Aristophanes: "One would suppose that in Athens no such thing had been known as sorrow and weeping." Or Wordsworth himself might say reproachfully to some of Mr. Hazlitt's more favoured poets: "Judging by *your* themes, a man must believe that there is no such thing on our planet as fighting and kicking." Wordsworth has written many memorable poems (for instance, *On the Tyrolean and the Spanish Insurrections, On the Retreat from Moscow, On the Feast of Brougham Castle*), all sympathizing powerfully with the martial spirit. Other poets, favourites of Mr. Hazlitt, have never struck a solitary note from this Tyrtaean lyre; and who blames them? Surely, if every man breathing finds his powers limited, every man would do well to respect this silent admonition of nature, by not travelling out of his appointed walk, through any coxcombry of sporting a spurious versatility. And in this view, what Mr. Hazlitt made the reproach of the poet, is amongst the first of his praises. But there is another reason why Wordsworth could not meddle with festal raptures like the glory of a wedding-day. These raptures are not only too brief, but (which is worse) they tend downwards: even for as long as they last, they do not move upon an ascending scale. And even *that* is not their worst fault: they do not diffuse or communicate themselves: the wretches chiefly interested in a marriage are so selfish, that they keep all the rapture to themselves. Mere joy, that does not linger and reproduce itself in reverberations and endless mirrors, is not fitted for poetry. What would the sun be itself, if it were a mere blank orb of fire that did not multiply its splendours through millions of rays refracted and reflected; or if its glory were not endlessly caught, splintered, and thrown back by atmospheric repercussions?

There is, besides, a still subtler reason (and one that ought not to have escaped the acuteness of Mr. Hazlitt) why the muse of Wordsworth could not glorify a wedding festival. Poems no longer than a sonnet he *might* derive from such an impulse: and one such poem of his there really is. But whosoever looks searchingly into the characteristic **genius** of Wordsworth, will see that he does not willingly deal with a passion in its direct aspect, or presenting an unmodified contour, but in forms more complex and oblique, and when passing under the shadow of some secondary passion. Joy, for instance, that wells up from constitutional sources, joy that is ebullient from youth to age, and cannot cease to sparkle, he yet exhibits in the person of Matthew,[1] the village schoolmaster, as touched and overgloomed by memories of sorrow. In the poem of *We are Seven,* which brings into day for the first time a profound fact in the abysses of human nature—viz. that the mind of an infant cannot admit the idea of death, cannot comprehend it, any more than the fountain of light can comprehend the aboriginal darkness (a truth on which Mr. Ferrier has since commented beautifully in his *Philosophy of Consciousness*)—the little mountaineer, who furnishes the text for this lovely strain, she whose fullness of life could not brook the gloomy faith in a grave, is yet (for the effect upon the reader) brought into connexion with the reflex shadows of the grave: and if she herself has *not,* the reader *has,* and through this very child, the gloom of that contemplation obliquely irradiated, as raised in relief upon his imagination, even by *her.* That same infant, which subjectively could not tolerate death, being by the reader contemplated objectivity, flashes upon us the tenderest images of death. Death and its sunny antipole are forced into connexion. I remember, again, to have heard a man complain, that in a little poem of Wordsworth's, having for its very subject the universal diffusion (and the gratuitous diffusion) of joy—

> Pleasure is spread through the earth,
> In stray gifts to be claim'd by whoever shall find,

a picture occurs which overpowered him with melancholy: it was this—

> In sight of the spires
> All alive with the fires
> Of the sun going down to his rest,
> In the broad open eye of the solitary sky

[1] See the exquisite poems, so little understood by the commonplace reader, of the *Two April Mornings,* and the *Fountain.*

> They dance—there are three, as jocund as free,
> While they dance on the calm river's breast.[2]

Undeniably there is (and without ground for complaint there is) even here, where the spirit of gaiety is professedly invoked, an oblique though evanescent image flashed upon us of a sadness that lies deep behind the laughing figures, and of a solitude that is the real possessor in fee of all things, but is waiting an hour or so for the dispossession of the dancing men and maidens who for that transitory hour are the true, but, alas! the fugitive tenants.

An inverse case, as regards the three just cited, is found in the poem of *Hart-leap-well,* over which the mysterious spirit of the noonday Pan seems to brood. Out of suffering there is evoked the image of peace. Out of the cruel leap, and the agonizing race through thirteen hours—out of the anguish in the perishing brute, and the headlong courage of his final despair,

> Not unobserved by sympathy divine—

out of the ruined lodge and the forgotten mansion, bowers that are trodden under foot, and pleasure-houses that are dust—the poet calls up a vision of *palingenesis* (or restorative resurrection); he interposes his solemn images of suffering, of decay, and ruin, only as a visionary haze through which gleams transpire of a trembling dawn far off, but surely even now on the road.

> The pleasure-house is dust: behind, before,
> This is no common waste, no common gloom;
> But Nature in due course of time once more
> Shall here put on her beauty and her bloom.
>
> She leaves these objects to a slow decay,
> That what we are, and have been, may be known;
> But, at the coming of the milder day,
> These monuments shall all be overgrown.

[2] Coleridge had a grievous infirmity of mind as regarded pain. He could not contemplate the shadows of fear, of sorrow, of suffering, with any steadiness of gaze. He was, in relation to that subject, what in Lancashire they call *nesh*—i. e. soft, or effeminate. This frailty claimed indulgence, had he not erected it at times into a ground of superiority. Accordingly, I remember that he also complained of this passage in Wordsworth, and on the same ground, as being too overpoweringly depressing in the fourth line, when modified by the other five.

This influx of the joyous into the sad, and of the sad into the joyous—this reciprocal entanglement of darkness in light, and of light in darkness—offers a subject too occult for popular criticism; but merely to have suggested it, may be sufficient to account for Wordsworth not having chosen a theme of pure garish sunshine, such as the hurry of a wedding-day, so long as others, more picturesque or more plastic to a subtle purpose of creation, were to be had. A wedding-day is, in many a life, the sunniest of its days. But, unless it is overcast with some event more tragic than could be wished, its uniformity of blaze, without shade or relief, makes it insipid to the mere bystander. It must not be forgotten, that a wedding is pre-eminently that sort of festival which swamps all individuality of sentiment or character. The *epithalamia* of Edmund Spenser are the most impassioned that exist; but nobody reads them.

But far beyond these causes of repulsiveness to ordinary readers was the class of subjects selected, and the mode of treating them. The earliest line of readers, the van in point of time, always includes a majority of the young, the commonplace, and the unimpassioned. Subsequently these are sifted and winnowed, as the rear ranks come forward in succession. But at first it was sure to ruin any poems, if the situations treated are not those which reproduce to the fancy of readers their own hopes and prospects. The meditative are interested by all that has an interest for human nature; but what cares a young lady, dreaming of lovers kneeling at her feet, for the agitations of a mother forced into resigning her child? or for the sorrow of a shepherd at eighty parting for ever amongst mountain solitudes with an only son of seventeen, innocent and hopeful, whom soon afterwards the guilty town seduces into ruin irreparable? Romances and novels in verse constitute the poetry which is *immediately* successful; and that is a poetry, it may be added, which, being successful through one generation, afterwards is unsuccessful for ever. . . .

[Here follows a discussion of *The Excursion*.]

Not, therefore, in the *Excursion* must we look for that reversionary influence which awaits Wordsworth with posterity. It is the vulgar superstition in behalf of big books and sounding pretensions, that must have prevailed upon Coleridge and others to undervalue, by comparison with the direct philosophic poetry of Wordsworth, those earlier poems which are short, but generally scintillating with gems of far profounder truth. I speak of that truth which strengthens into solemnity an impression very feebly acknowledged previously, or truth which suddenly unveils a connexion between objects hitherto regarded as irrelate and independent. In astronomy, to gain the rank of discoverer, it is not required that you should reveal a star absolutely new: find out with respect to an old star some new affection—as, for instance, that it has an ascertainable parallax—and immediately you bring it within the verge of a human interest; or with respect to some old familiar planet, that its satellites suffer periodical eclipses, and immediately you bring it within the verge of terrestrial uses. Gleams of steadier vision, that brighten into certainty appearances else doubtful, or that unfold relations else unsuspected, are not less discoveries of truth than the downright revelations of the telescope, or the absolute conquests of the diving-bell. It is astonishing how large a harvest of new truths would be reaped, simply through the accident of a man's feeling, or being made to feel, more *deeply* than other men. He sees the same objects, neither more nor fewer, but he sees them engraved in lines far stronger and more determinate: and the difference in the strength makes the whole difference between consciousness and sub-consciousness. And in questions of the mere understanding, we see the same fact illustrated: the author who wins notice the most, is not he that perplexes men by truths drawn from fountains of absolute novelty—truths as yet unsunned, and from that cause obscure; but he that awakens into illuminated consciousness ancient lineaments of truth long slumbering in the mind, although too faint to have extorted attention. Wordsworth has brought many a truth into life both for the eye and for the understanding, which previously had slumbered indistinctly for all men.

For instance, as respects the eye, who does not acknowledge instantaneously the magical strength of truth in his saying of a cataract seen from a station two miles off, that it was "frozen by distance"? In all nature, there is not an object so essentially at war with the stiffening of frost, as the headlong and desperate life of a cataract; and yet notoriously the effect of distance is to lock up this frenzy of motion into the most petrific column of stillness. This effect is perceived at once when pointed out; but how few are the eyes that ever *would* have perceived it for themselves! Twilight, again—who before Wordsworth ever distinctly noticed its *abstracting* power?— that power of removing, softening, harmonizing, by which a mode of obscurity executes for the eye the same mysterious office which the mind so often, within its own shadowy realms, executes for itself. In the dim interspace between day and night, all disappears from our earthly scenery, as if touched by an enchanter's rod, which is either mean or inharmonious or unquiet, or expressive of temporary things. Leaning against a column of rock, looking down upon a lake or river, and at intervals carrying your eyes forward through a vista of mountains, you become aware that your sight rests upon the very same spectacle, unaltered in a single feature, which once at the same hour was beheld by the legionary Roman from his embattled camp, or by the roving Briton in his "wolf-skin vest," lying down to sleep, and looking

Through some leafy bower,
Before his eyes were closed.

How magnificent is the summary or abstraction of the elementary features in such a scene, as executed by the poet himself, in illustration of this abstraction daily executed by nature, through her handmaid Twilight! Listen, reader, to the closing strain, solemn as twilight is solemn, and grand as the spectacle which it describes:—

By him [i. e. the roving Briton] was seen,
The self-same vision which *we* now behold,
At thy meek bidding, shadowy Power, brought
forth,
These mighty barriers, and the gulf between;
The floods, the stars—a spectacle as old
As the beginning of the heavens and earth.

Another great field there is amongst the pomps of nature, which, if Wordsworth did not first notice, he certainly has noticed most circumstantially. I speak of cloud-scenery, or those pageants of sky-built architecture, which sometimes in summer, at noonday, and in all seasons about sunset, arrest or appal the meditative; "perplexing monarchs" with the spectacle of armies manœuvring, or deepening the solemnity of evening by towering edifices, that mimic—but which also in mimicking mock—the transitory grandeurs of man. It is singular that these gorgeous phenomena, not less than those of the *aurora borealis,* have been so little noticed by poets. The *aurora* was naturally neglected by the southern poets of Greece and Rome, as not much seen in their latitudes. But the cloud-architecture of the daylight belongs alike to north and south. Accordingly, I remember one notice of it in Hesiod, a case where the clouds exhibited

The beauteous semblance of a flock at rest.

Another there is, a thousand years later, in Lucan: amongst the portents which that poet notices as prefiguring the dreadful convulsions destined to shake the earth at Pharsalia, I remember some fiery coruscation of arms in the heavens; but, so far as I recollect the appearances might have belonged equally to the workmanship of the clouds or the *aurora.* Up and down the next eight hundred years, are scattered evanescent allusions to these vapoury appearances; in *Hamlet* and elsewhere occur gleams of such allusions; but I remember no distinct sketch of such an appearance before that in the *Antony and Cleopatra* of Shakespeare, beginning,

Sometimes we see a cloud that's dragonish.

Subsequently to Shakespeare, these notices, as of all phenomena whatsoever that demanded a familiarity with nature in the spirit of love, became rarer and rarer. At length, as the eighteenth century was winding up its accounts, forth stepped William Wordsworth, of whom, as a reader of all pages in nature, it may be said that, if we except Dampier, the admirable buccaneer, the gentle *flibustier,* and some few professional naturalists, he first and he last looked at natural objects with the eye that neither will be dazzled from without nor cheated by preconceptions from within. Most men look at nature in the hurry of a confusion that distinguishes nothing; *their* error is from without. Pope, again, and many who live in towns,[1] make such blunders as

---

[1] It was not, however, that all poets then lived in towns; neither had Pope himself generally lived in towns. But it is perfectly useless to be familiar with nature unless there is a public trained to

that of supposing the moon to tip with silver the hills *behind* which she is rising, not by erroneous use of their eyes (for they use them not at all), but by inveterate preconceptions. Scarcely has there been a poet with what could be called a learned eye, or an eye *extensively* learned, before Wordsworth. Much affectation there has been of that sort since *his* rise, and at all times much counterfeit enthusiasm; but the sum of the matter is this, that Wordsworth had his passion for nature fixed in his blood; it was a necessity, like that of the mulberry-leaf to the silkworm; and through his commerce with nature did he live and breathe. Hence it was—viz. from the *truth* of his love—that his knowledge grew; whilst most others, being merely hypocrites in their love, have turned out merely sciolists in their knowledge. This chapter, therefore, of *sky*-scenery may be said to have been re-vivified amongst the resources of poetry by Wordsworth—rekindled, if not absolutely kindled. The sublime scene indorsed upon the draperies of the storm in the fourth book of the *Excursion*—that scene again witnessed upon the passage of the Hamilton Hills in Yorkshire—the solemn "sky prospect" from the fields of France, are unrivalled in that order of composition; and in one of these records Wordsworth has given first of all the true key-note of the sentiment belonging to these grand pageants. They are, says the poet, speaking in a case where the appearance had occurred towards night,

Meek nature's evening comment on the shows
And all the fuming vanities of earth.

Yes, that is the secret moral whispered to the mind. These mimicries express the laughter which is in heaven at earthly pomps. Frail and vapoury are the glories of man, even as the visionary parodies of those glories are frail, even as the scenical copies of these glories are frail, which nature weaves in clouds.

As another of those natural appearances which must have haunted men's eyes since

the Flood, but yet had never forced itself into *conscious* notice until arrested by Wordsworth, I may notice an effect of *iteration* daily exhibited in the habits of cattle:—

The cattle are grazing,
Their heads never raising,
There are forty feeding like one.

Now, merely as a *fact*, and if it were nothing more, this characteristic appearance in the habits of cows, when all repeat the action of each, ought not to have been overlooked by those who profess themselves engaged in holding up a mirror to nature. But the fact has also a profound meaning as a hieroglyphic. In all animals which live under the protection of man a life of peace and quietness, but do not share in his labours or his pleasures, what we regard is the species, and not the individual. Nobody but a grazier ever looks at one cow amongst a field of cows, or at one sheep in a flock. But as to those animals which are more closely connected with man, not passively connected, but actively, being partners in his toils, and perils, and recreations—such as horses, dogs, falcons—they are regarded as individuals, and are allowed the benefit of an individual interest. It is not that cows have not a differential character, each for herself; and sheep, it is well known, have all a separate physiognomy for the shepherd who has cultivated their acquaintance. But men generally have no opportunity or motive for studying the individualities of creatures, however otherwise respectable, that are too much regarded by all of us in the reversionary light of milk, and beef, and mutton. Far otherwise it is with horses, who share in man's martial risks, who sympathize with man's frenzy in hunting, who divide with man the burdens of noonday. Far otherwise it is with dogs, that share the hearths of man, and adore the footsteps of his children. These man loves; of these he makes dear, though humble friends. These often fight for *him*; and for *them* he reciprocally will sometimes fight. Of necessity, therefore, every horse and every dog is an individual—has a sort of personality that makes him *separately* interesting—has a beauty and a character of his own. Go to Melton, therefore, on some crimson morning, and what will you see? Every man, every horse, every dog, glorying in the plenitude of life, is in a different attitude, motion, gesture, action.

love and value nature. It is not what the individual sees that will fix itself as beautiful in his recollections, but what he sees under a consciousness that others will sympathize with his feelings. Under any other circumstances familiarity does but realize the adage, and "breeds contempt." The great despisers of rural scenery, its fixed and permanent undervaluers, are rustics.

It is not there the sublime unity which you must seek, where forty are like one; but the sublime infinity, like that of ocean, like that of Flora, like that of nature, where no repetitions are endured, no leaf is the copy of another leaf, no absolute identity, and no painful tautologies. This subject might be pursued into profounder recesses; but in a popular discussion it is necessary to forbear.

A volume might be filled with such glimpses of novelty as Wordsworth has first laid bare, even to the apprehension of the *senses.* For the *understanding,* when moving in the same track of human sensibilities, he has done only not so much. How often (to give an instance or two) must the human heart have felt the case, and yearned for an expression of the case, when there are sorrows which descend far below the region in which tears gather; and yet who has ever given utterance to this feeling until Wordsworth came with his immortal line:—

Thoughts that do often lie too deep for tears?

This sentiment, and others that might be adduced (such as "The child is father of the man"), have even passed into the popular heart, and are often quoted by those who know not *whom* they are quoting. Magnificent, again, is the sentiment, and yet an echo to one which lurks amongst all hearts, in relation to the frailty of merely human schemes for working good, which so often droop and collapse through the unsteadiness of human energies—

> Foundations must be laid
> In heaven.

How? Foundations laid in realms that are *above?* But *that* is impossible; *that* is at war with elementary physics; foundations must be laid *below.* Yes; and even so the poet throws the mind yet more forcibly on the hyperphysical character—on the grandeur transcending all physics—of those spiritual and shadowy foundations which alone are enduring.

But the great distinction of Wordsworth, and the pledge of his increasing popularity, is the extent of his sympathy with what is *really* permanent in human feelings, and also the depth of this sympathy. Young and Cowper, the two earlier leaders in the province of meditative poetry, are too circumscribed in the range of their sympathies, too narrow, too illiberal, and too exclusive. Both these poets manifested the quality of their strength in the quality of their public reception. Popular in some degree from the first, they entered upon the inheritance of their fame almost at once. Far different was the fate of Wordsworth; for in poetry of this class, which appeals to what lies deepest in man, in proportion to the native power of the poet, and his fitness for permanent life, is the strength of resistance in the public taste. Whatever is too original will be hated at the first. It must slowly mould a public for itself; and the resistance of the early thoughtless judgements must be overcome by a counter resistance to itself, in a better audience slowly mustering against the first. Forty and seven years it is since William Wordsworth first appeared as an author. Twenty of those years he was the scoff of the world, and his poetry a by-word of scorn. Since then, and more than once, senates have rung with acclamations to the echo of his name. Now at this moment, whilst we are talking about him, he has entered upon his seventy-sixth year. For himself, according to the course of nature, he cannot be far from his setting; but his poetry is only now clearing the clouds that gathered about its rising. Meditative poetry is perhaps that province of literature which will ultimately maintain most power amongst the generations which are coming; but in this department, at least, there is little competition to be apprehended by Wordsworth from anything that has appeared since the death of Shakespeare.

PERCY BYSSHE SHELLEY [1]

THERE is no writer named amongst men, of whom, so much as of Percy Bysshe Shelley, it is difficult for a conscientious critic to speak with the truth and the respect due to his exalted powers, and yet without offence to feelings the most sacred, which too memorably he outraged. The indignation which this powerful young writer provoked, had its root in no personal feelings—those might have been conciliated; in no worldly feelings—those might have proved transitory; but in feelings the holiest which brood over human

[1] The following three articles are taken from *Essays on the Poets,* 1853.

life, and which guard the sanctuary of religious truth. Consequently, which is a melancholy thought for any friend of Shelley's, the indignation is likely to be co-extensive and co-enduring with the writings that provoked it. That bitterness of scorn and defiance which still burns against his name in the most extensively meditative section of English society, viz. the religious section, is not of a nature to be propitiated: selfish interests, being wounded, might be compensated; merely human interests might be soothed; but interests that transcend all human valuation, being *so* insulted, must upon principle reject all human ransom or conditions of human compromise. Less than penitential recantation could not be accepted: and *that* is now impossible. "Will ye *transact* with God?" is the indignant language of Milton in a case of that nature. And in this case the language of many pious men said aloud,—"It is for God to forgive: but we, his servants, are bound to recollect, that this young man offered to Christ and to Christianity the deepest insult which ear has heard, or which it has entered into the heart of man to conceive." Others, as in Germany, had charged Christ with committing suicide, on the principle that he who tempts or solicits death by doctrines fitted to provoke that result, is virtually the causer of his own destruction. . . .

These were affronts to the Founder of Christianity, offered too much in the temper of malignity. But Shelley's was worse; more bitter, and with less of countenance, even in show or shadow, from any fact, or insinuation of a fact, that Scripture suggests. In his "Queen Mab," he gives a dreadful portrait of God; and that no question may arise, of *what* God? he names him; it is Jehovah. He asserts his existence; he affirms him to be "an almighty God, and vengeful as almighty," He goes on to describe him as the "omnipotent fiend," who found "none but slaves" [Israel in Egypt, no doubt] to be "his tools," and none but "a murderer" [Moses, I presume] "to be his accomplice in crime." He introduces this dreadful Almighty as speaking, and as speaking thus,—

From an eternity of idleness
I, God, awoke; in seven days' toil made earth
From nothing; rested; and created man.

But man he hates; and he goes on to curse him; till at the intercession of "the murderer," who is electrified into pity for the human race by the very horror of the divine curses, God promises to send his son—only, however, for the benefit of a few. This son appears; the poet tells us that—

——the Incarnate came; humbly he came,
Veiling his horrible Godhead in the shape
Of man, scorn'd by the world, his name unheard
Save by the rabble of his native town.

The poet pursues this incarnate God as a teacher of men; teaching, "in semblance," justice, truth, and peace; but underneath all this, kindling "quenchless flames," which eventually were destined

—to satiate, with the blood
Of truth and freedom, his malignant soul.

He follows him to his crucifixion; and describes him, whilst hanging on the cross, as shedding malice upon a reviler,—*malice on the cross!*

A smile of godlike malice reillumined
His fading lineaments:

and his parting breath is uttered in a memorable curse.

This atrocious picture of the Deity, in his dealings with man, both pre-Christian and post-Christian, is certainly placed in the mouth of the wandering Jew. But the internal evidence, as well as collateral evidence from without, make it clear that the Jew, (whose version of scriptural records nobody in the poem disputes,) here represents the person of the poet. Shelley had opened his career as an atheist; and as a proselytizing atheist. But he was then a boy. At the date of "Queen Mab" he was a young man. And we now find him advanced from the station of an atheist to the more intellectual one of a believer in God and in the mission of Christ; but of one who fancied himself called upon to defy and to hate both, in so far as they had revealed their relations to man.

Mr. Gilfillan thinks that "Shelley was far too harshly treated in his speculative boyhood;" and it strikes him "that, had pity and kind-hearted expostulation been tried, instead of reproach and abrupt expulsion, they might have weaned him from the dry dugs of Atheism to the milky breast of the faith and 'worship of sorrow;' and the touching spectacle had been renewed, of the demoniac sitting, 'clothed, and in his right mind,' at the feet of Jesus." I am not of that opinion: it is an opinion which seems to question the *sincerity* of Shelley,—that quality which in him was deepest, so as to form the basis of his nature, if we allow ourselves to think that, by personal irritation, he had been piqued into infidelity, or that by flattering conciliation he could have been bribed back into a profession of Christianity. Like a wild horse of the Pampas, he would have thrown up his heels and *whinnied* his disdain of any man coming to catch *him* with a bribe of oats. He had a constant vision of a manger and a halter in the rear of all such caressing tempters, once having scented the gales of what he thought perfect freedom, from the lawless desert. His feud with Christianity was a craze derived from some early wrench of his understanding, and made obstinate to the degree in which we find it, from having rooted itself in certain combinations of ideas that, once coalescing, could not be shaken loose; such as, that Christianity underpropped the corruptions of the earth, in the shape of wicked governments that might else have been overthrown, or of wicked priesthoods that, but for the shelter of shadowy and spiritual terrors, must have trembled before those whom they overawed. Kings that were clothed in bloody robes; dark hierarchies that scowled upon the poor children of the soil; these objects took up a permanent station in the background of Shelley's imagination, not to be dispossessed more than the phantom of Banquo from the festival of Macbeth, and composed a towering Babylon of mystery that, to *his* belief, could not have flourished, under any umbrage less vast than that of Christianity. Such was the inextricable association of images that domineered over Shelley's mind: such was the hatred which he built upon that association,—an association casual and capricious, yet fixed and petrified as if by frost. Can we imagine the case of an angel touched by lunacy? Have we ever seen the spectacle of a human intellect, exquisite by its functions of creation, yet in one chamber of its shadowy house already ruined before the light of manhood had cleansed its darkness? Such an angel, such a man,—if ever such there were,—such a lunatic angel, such a

ruined man, was Shelley, whilst yet standing on the earliest threshold of life.

Mr. Gilfillan, whose eye is quick to seize the lurking and the stealthy aspect of things, does not overlook the absolute midsummer madness which possessed Shelley upon the subject of Christianity. Shelley's total nature was altered and darkened when that theme arose: transfiguration fell upon him. He that was so gentle, became savage; he that breathed by the very lungs of Christianity—that was so merciful, so full of tenderness and pity, of humility, of love and forgiveness, then raved and screamed like an idiot whom once I personally knew, when offended by a strain of heavenly music at the full of the moon. In both cases, it was the sense of perfect beauty revealed under the sense of morbid estrangement. This it is, as I presume, which Mr. Gilfillan alludes to in the following passage, (p. 104): "On all *other* subjects the wisest of the wise, the gentlest of the gentle, the bravest of the brave, yet, when *one* topic was introduced, he became straightway insane; his eyes glared, his voice screamed, his hand vibrated frenzy." But Mr. Gilfillan is entirely in the wrong when he countenances the notion that harsh treatment had any concern in riveting the fanaticism of Shelley. On the contrary, he met with an indulgence to the first manifestation of his anti-Christian madness, better suited to the goodness of the lunatic than to the pestilence of his lunacy. It was at Oxford that this earliest explosion of Shelleyism occurred; and though, with respect to secrets of prison-houses, and to discussions that proceed "with closed doors," there is always a danger of being misinformed, I believe, from the uniformity of such accounts as have reached myself, that the following *brief* of the matter may be relied on. Shelley, being a venerable sage of sixteen, or rather less, came to a resolution that he would convert, and that it was his solemn duty to convert, the universal Christian church to Atheism or to Pantheism, no great matter *which*. But, as such large undertakings require time, twenty months, suppose, or even two years,—for you know, reader, that a railway requires on an average little less,—Shelley was determined to obey no impulse of youthful rashness. Oh no! Down with presumption, down with levity, down with boyish precipitation! Changes of religion are awful things: people must have time to think. He would move slowly and discreetly. So first he wrote a pamphlet, clearly and satisfactorily explaining the necessity of being an atheist; and, with his usual exemplary courage, (for, seriously, he was the least *false* of human creatures,) Shelley put his name to the pamphlet, and the name of his college. His ultimate object was to accomplish a general apostasy in the Christian church of whatever name. But for one six months, it was quite enough if he caused a revolt in the Church of England. And as, before a great naval action, when the enemy is approaching, you throw a long shot or two by way of trying his range,— on that principle Shelley had thrown out his tract in Oxford. Oxford formed the advanced squadron of the English Church; and, by way of a *coup d'essai*, though in itself a bagatelle, what if he should begin with converting Oxford? To make any beginning at all is one half the battle; or, as a writer in this magazine [June 1845] suggests, a good deal more. To speak seriously, there is something even thus far in the boyish presumption of Shelley, not altogether without nobility. He affronted the armies of Christendom. Had it been possible for *him* to be jesting, it would *not* have been noble. But here, even in the most monstrous of his undertakings, here, as always, he was perfectly sincere and single-minded. Satisfied that Atheism was the sheet anchor of the world, he was not the person to speak by halves. Being a boy, he attacked those [upon a point the most sure to irritate] who were gray; having no station in society, he flew at the throats of none but those who *had;* weaker than an infant for the purpose before him, he planted his fist in the face of a giant, saying, "Take *that,* you devil, and *that,* and *that.*" . . .

The life of Shelley, according to the remark of Mr. Gilfillan, was "among the most romantic in literary story." Everything was romantic in his short career; everything wore a tragic interest. From his childhood he moved through a succession of afflictions. Always craving for love, loving and seeking to be loved, always he was destined to reap hatred from those with whom life had connected him. If in the darkness he raised up images of his departed hours, he would behold his family disowning him, and the home of his infancy knowing him no more; he would behold his magnificent university, that under happier circumstances would have gloried in his genius, rejecting him for ever; he would behold his first wife, whom once he had loved passionately, through calamities arising from himself, called away to an early and a tragic death. The peace after which his heart panted for ever, in what dreadful contrast it stood to the eternal contention upon which his restless intellect or accidents of position threw him like a passive victim! It seemed as if not any choice of his, but some sad doom of opposition from without, forced out, as by a magnet, struggles of frantic resistance from *him,* which as gladly he would have evaded, as ever victim of epilepsy yearned to evade his convulsions! Gladly he would have slept in eternal seclusion, whilst eternally the trumpet summoned him to battle. In storms unwillingly created by himself, he lived; in a storm, cited by the finger of God, he died.

It is affecting,—at least it is so for any one who believes in the profound sincerity of Shelley, a man (however erring) whom neither fear, nor hope, nor vanity, nor hatred, ever seduced into falsehood, or even into dissimulation,—to read the account which he gives of a revolution occurring in his own mind at school: so early did his struggles begin! It is in verse, and forms part of those beautiful stanzas addressed to his second wife, which he prefixed to "The Revolt of Islam." Five or six of these stanzas may be quoted with a certainty of pleasing many readers, whilst they throw light on the early condition of Shelley's feelings, and of his early anticipations with regard to the promises and the menaces of life.

Thoughts of great deeds were mine, dear friend, when first
The clouds which wrap this world, from youth did pass
I do remember well the hour which burst
My spirit's sleep; a fresh May-dawn it was,
When I walk'd forth upon the glittering grass,
And wept—I knew not why; until there rose,
From the near school-room, voices that, alas!
Were but one echo from a world of woes—
The harsh and grating strife of tyrants and of foes.

And then I clasp'd my hands, and look'd around—
(But none was near to mock my streaming eyes,
Which pour'd their warm drops on the sunny ground,)
So without shame I spake—I will be wise,
And just, and free, and mild, if in me lies

Such power: for I grow weary to behold
The selfish and the strong still tyrannize
Without reproach or check. I then controll'd
My tears; my heart grew calm; and I was meek
    and bold.

And from that hour did I with earnest thought
Heap knowledge from forbidden mines of lore:
Yet nothing, that my tyrants knew or taught,
I cared to learn; but from that secret store
Wrought linked armor for my soul, before
It might walk forth to war among mankind:
Thus power and hope were strengthen'd more
    and more
Within me, till there came upon my mind
A sense of loneliness, a thirst with which I pined.

Alas, that love should be a blight and snare
To those who seek all sympathies in one!—
Such once I sought in vain; then black despair,
The shadow of a starless night, was thrown
Over the world in which I moved alone:—
Yet never found I one not false to me,
Hard hearts and cold, like weights of icy stone
Which crush'd and wither'd mine, that could
    not be
Aught but a lifeless clog, until revived by thee.

Thou, friend, whose presence on my wintry
    heart
Fell, like bright spring upon some herbless
    plain;
How beautiful and calm and free thou wert
In thy mortal wisdom, when the mortal chain
Of Custom thou didst burst and rend in twain,
And walk'd as free as light the clouds among,
Which many an envious slave then breathed in
    vain
From his dim dungeon, and my spirit sprung
To meet thee from the woes which had begirt it
    long.

No more alone through the world's wilderness,
Although I trod the paths of high intent,
I journey'd now: no more companionless,
Where solitude is like despair, I went.

.   .   .   .

Now has descended a serener hour;
And, with inconstant fortune, friends return:
Though suffering leaves the knowledge and the
    power
Which says—Let scorn be not repaid with
    scorn.
And from thy side two gentle babes are born
To fill our home with smiles; and thus are we
Most fortunate beneath life's beaming morn;
And these delights and thou have been to me
The parents of the song I consecrate to thee. . . .

However shocked at Shelley's obstinate
revolt from all religious sympathies with his
fellow-men, no man is entitled to deny the
admirable qualities of his moral nature, which
were as striking as his genius. Many people remarked something seraphic in the expression
of his features; and something seraphic there
was in his nature. No man was better qualified
to have loved Christianity; and to no man,
resting under the shadow of that one darkness,
would Christianity have said more gladly—
talis cum sis, utinam noster esses! Shelley
would, from his earliest manhood, have sacrificed all that he possessed to any comprehensive purpose of good for the race of man. He
dismissed all injuries and insults from his
memory. He was the sincerest and the most
truthful of human creatures. He was also the
purest. If he denounced marriage as a vicious
institution, *that* was but another phasis of the
partial lunacy which affected him: for to no
man were purity and fidelity more essential
elements in his idea of real love. I agree,
therefore, heartily with Mr. Gilfillan, in protesting against the thoughtless assertion of
some writer in *The Edinburgh Review*—that
Shelley at all selected the story of his "Cenci"
on account of its horrors, or that he has found
pleasure in dwelling on those horrors. So far
from it, he has retreated so entirely from the
most shocking feature of the story, viz., the
incestuous violence of Cenci the father, as
actually to leave it doubtful whether the murder were in punishment of the last outrage
committed, or in repulsion of a menace continually repeated. The true motive of the
selection of such a story was—not its darkness, but (as Mr. Gilfillan, with so much penetration, perceives,) the light which fights with
the darkness: Shelley found the whole attraction of this dreadful tale in the angelic nature
of Beatrice, as revealed in the portrait of her
by Guido. Everybody who has read with
understanding the *Wallenstein* of Schiller, is
aware of the repose and the divine relief arising upon a background of so much darkness,
such a tumult of ruffians, bloody intriguers,
and assassins, from the situation of the two
lovers, Max. Piccolomini and the princess
Thekla, both yearning so profoundly after
peace, both so noble, both so young, and both
destined to be so unhappy. The same fine relief, the same light shining in darkness, arises
here from the touching beauty of Beatrice,
from her noble aspirations after deliverance,
from the remorse which reaches her in the
midst of real innocence, from her meekness,
and from the agitation of her inexpressible
affliction. Even the murder, even the parricide, though proceeding from herself, do but

deepen that background of darkness, which throws into fuller revelation the glory of that suffering face immortalized by Guido.

Something of a similar effect arises to myself when reviewing the general abstract of Shelley's life,—so brief, so full of agitation, so full of strife. When one thinks of the early misery which he suffered, and of the insolent infidelity which, being yet so young, he wooed with a lover's passion, then the darkness of midnight begins to form a deep, impenetrable background, upon which the phantasmagoria of all that is to come may arrange itself in troubled phosphoric streams, and in sweeping processions of wo [sic]. Yet, again, when one recurs to his gracious nature, his fearlessness, his truth, his purity from all fleshliness of appetite, his freedom from vanity, his diffusive love and tenderness,—suddenly out of the darkness reveals itself a morning of May, forests and thickets of roses advance to the foreground, from the midst of them looks out "the eternal child," cleansed from his sorrow, radiant with joy, having power given him to forget the misery which he suffered, power given him to forget the misery which he caused, and leaning with his heart upon that dove-like faith against which his erring intellect had rebelled.

JOHN KEATS

MR. GILFILLAN introduces this section with a discussion upon the constitutional peculiarities ascribed to men of genius; such as nervousness of temperament, idleness, vanity, irritability, and other disagreeable tendencies ending in *ty* or in *ness;* one of the *ties* being "poverty"; which disease is at least not amongst those morbidly cherished by the patients. All that can be asked from the most penitent man of genius is, that he should humbly confess his own besetting infirmities, and endeavor to hate them, and, as respects this one infirmity at least, I never heard of any man (however eccentric in genius) who did otherwise. But what special relation has such a preface to Keats? . . .

His biography, stripped of its false coloring, offers little to win attention: for he was not the victim of any systematic malignity, as has been represented. He met, as I have understood, with unusual kindness from his liberal publishers, Messrs. Taylor and Hessey. He met with unusual severity from a cynical reviewer, the late Mr. Gifford, then editor of *The Quarterly Review.* The story ran, that this article of Mr. G.'s had killed Keats; upon which, with natural astonishment, Lord Byron thus commented, in the 11th canto of Don Juan:—

John Keats who was kill'd off by one critique,
    Just as he really promised something great,
If not intelligible,—without Greek,
    Contrived to talk about the gods of late,
Much as they might have been supposed to speak.
    Poor fellow! his was an untoward fate:
'Tis strange the mind, that very fiery particle,
Should let itself be snuff'd out by an Article.

Strange, indeed! and the friends, who honor Keats's memory, should not lend themselves to a story so degrading. He died, I believe, of pulmonary consumption; and would have died of it, probably, under any circumstances of prosperity as a poet. Doubtless, in a condition of languishing decay, slight causes of irritation act powerfully. But it is hardly conceivable that one ebullition of splenetic bad feeling, in a case so proverbially open to revision as the pretensions of a poet, could have overthrown any masculine life, unless where that life had already been *irrecoverably* undermined by sickness. As a man, and viewed in relation to social objects, Keats was nothing. It was as mere an affectation when he talked with apparent zeal of liberty, or human rights, or human prospects, as is the hollow enthusiasm which many people profess for music, or most poets for external nature. For these things Keats fancied that he cared; but in reality he cared not at all. Upon them, or any of their aspects, he had thought too little, and too indeterminately, to feel for them as personal concerns. Whereas Shelley, from his earliest days, was mastered and shaken by the great moving realities of life, as a prophet is by the burden of wrath or of promise which he has been commissioned to reveal. Had there been no such thing as literature, Keats would have dwindled into a cipher. Shelley, in the same event, would hardly have lost one plume from his crest. It is in relation to literature, and to the boundless questions as to the true and the false arising out of literature and poetry, that Keats challenges a fluctuating interest; sometimes an interest of strong disgust, sometimes of deep admiration. There is not, I believe, a case on record throughout European literature, where feelings so repulsive of each other have centred in the same individual. The very midsummer madness of affectation, of false vapory sentiment, and of fantastic effeminacy, seemed to me combined in Keats's *Endymion*, when I first saw it near the close of 1821. The Italian poet, Marino, had been reputed the greatest master of gossamery affectation in Europe. But *his* conceits showed the palest of rosy blushes by the side of Keats's bloody crimson. Naturally, I was discouraged from looking further. But about a week later, by pure accident, my eye fell upon his *Hyperion*. The first feeling was that of incredulity that the two poems could, under change of circumstances or lapse of time, have emanated from the same mind. The *Endymion* displays absolutely the most shocking revolt against good sense and just feeling, that all literature does now, or ever *can,* furnish. The *Hyperion,* as Mr. Gilfillan truly says, "is the greatest of poetical torsos." The first belongs essentially to the vilest collections of wax-work filagree, or gilt gingerbread. The other presents the majesty, the austere beauty, and the simplicity of Grecian temples enriched with Grecian sculpture. . . .

But there is another fault in Keats, of the first magnitude, which youth does not palliate, which youth even aggravates. This lies in the most shocking abuse of his mother-tongue. If there is one thing in this world that, next after the flag of his country and its spotless honor, should be wholly [*sic*] in the eyes of a young poet,—it is the *language* of his country. He should spend the third part of his life in studying this language, and cultivating its total resources. He should be willing to pluck out his right eye, or to circumnavigate the globe, if by such a sacrifice, if by such an exertion, he could attain to greater purity, precision, compass, or idiomatic energy of diction. This if he were even a Kalmuck Tartar, who by the way *has* the good feeling and patriotism to pride himself upon his beastly language. But Keats was an Englishman; Keats had the honor to speak the language of Chaucer, Shakspeare, Bacon, Milton, Newton. The more awful was the obligation of his allegiance. And yet upon this mother tongue, upon this English language, has Keats trampled as with the hoofs of a buffalo. With its syntax, with its prosody, with its idiom, he

has played such fantastic tricks as could enter only into the heart of a barbarian, and for which only the anarchy of Chaos could furnish a forgiving audience. Verily it required the *Hyperion* to weigh against the deep treason of these unparalleled offences.

WILLIAM HAZLITT

THIS man, who would have drawn in the scales against a select vestry of Fosters, is for the present deeper in the world's oblivion than the man with whom I here connect his name. *That* seems puzzling. For, if Hazlitt were misanthropic, so was Foster: both as writers were splenetic and more than peevish; but Hazlitt requited his reader for the pain of travelling through so gloomy an atmosphere, by the rich vegetation which his teeming intellect threw up as it moved along. The soil in *his* brain was of a volcanic fertility; whereas, in Foster, as in some tenacious clay, if the life were deep, it was slow and sullen in its throes. The reason for at all speaking of them in connection is, that both were essayists; neither in fact writing anything of note *except* essays, moral or critical; and both were bred at the feet of Dissenters. But how different were the results from that connection! Foster turned it to a blessing, winning the jewel that is most of all to be coveted, peace and the *fallentis semita vitae.* Hazlitt, on the other hand, sailed wilfully away from this sheltering harbor of his father's profession,—for sheltering it might have proved to *him,* and *did* prove to his youth,—only to toss ever afterwards as a drifting wreck at the mercy of storms. Hazlitt was not one of those who *could* have illusstrated the benefits of a connection with a sect, i. e. with a small confederation hostile by position to a larger; for the hostility from without, in order to react, presumes a concord from within. Nor does *his* case impeach the correctness of what I have said on that subject in speaking of Foster. He owed no introduction to the Dissenters; but it was because he *would* owe none. The Ishmaelite, whose hand is against every man, yet smiles at the approach of a brother, and gives the salutation of "Peace be with you!" to the tribe of his father. But Hazlitt smiled upon no man, nor exchanged tokens of peace with the nearest of fraternities. Wieland in his "Oberon," says of a benign patriarch—

His eye a smile on all creation beam'd.

Travestied as to one word, the line would have described Hazlitt,—

"*His* eye a scowl on all creation beam'd."

This inveterate misanthropy was constitutional; exasperated it certainly had been by accidents of life, by disappointments, by mortifications, by insults, and still more by having wilfully placed himself in collision from the first with all the interests that were in the sunshine of this world, and with all the persons that were then powerful in England. . . .

Whatever is—so much I conceive to have been a fundamental lemma for Hazlitt—*is wrong*. So much he thought it safe to postulate. *How* it was wrong, might require an impracticable investigation; you might fail for a century to discover: but *that* it was wrong, he nailed down as a point of faith, that could stand out against all counter-presumptions from argument, or counter-evidences from experience. A friend of his it was, a friend wishing to love him, and admiring him almost to extravagance, who told me, in illustration of the dark sinister gloom which sat for ever upon Hazlitt's countenance and gestures, that involuntarily when Hazlitt put his hand within his waistcoat, (as a mere unconscious trick of habit,) he himself felt a sudden recoil of fear, as from one who was searching for a hidden dagger. Like "a Moor of Malabar," as described in the Faery Queen, at intervals Hazlitt threw up his angry eyes, and dark locks, as if wishing to affront the sun, or to search the air for hostility. And the same friend, on another occasion, described the sort of feudal fidelity to his belligerent duties, which in company seemed to animate Hazlitt, as though he were mounting guard on all the citadels of malignity, under some *sacramentum militare*, by the following trait,—that, if it had happened to Hazlitt to be called out of the room, or to be withdrawn for a moment from the current of the general conversation, by a fit of abstraction, or by a private whisper to himself from some person sitting at his elbow, always on resuming his place as a party to what might be called the public business of the company, he looked round him with a mixed air of suspicion and defiance, such as seemed to challenge everybody by some stern adjuration into revealing whether, during his own absence or inattention, anything had been said demanding condign punishment at his hands. "Has any man uttered or presumed to insinuate," he seemed to insist upon knowing, "during this *interregnum*, things that I ought to proceed against as treasonable to the interests which I defend?" He had the unresting irritability of Rousseau, but in a nobler shape; for Rousseau transfigured every possible act or design of his acquaintances into some personal relation to himself. The vile act was obviously meant, as a child could understand, to injure the person of Rousseau, or his interests, or his reputation. It was meant to wound his feelings, or to misrepresent his acts calumniously, or secretly to supplant his footing. But, on the contrary, Hazlitt viewed all personal affronts or casual slights towards himself, as tending to something more general, and masquing under a pretended horror of Hazlitt, the author, a real hatred, deeper than it was always safe to avow, for those social interests which he was reputed to defend. "It was not Hazlitt whom the wretches struck at; no, no—it was democracy, or it was freedom, or it was Napoleon, whose shadow they saw in the rear of Hazlitt; and Napoleon, not for anything in him that might be really bad, but in revenge of that consuming wrath against the thrones of Christendom, for which (said Hazlitt) let us glorify his name eternally."

Yet Hazlitt, like other men, and perhaps with more bitterness than other men, sought for love and for intervals of rest, in which all anger might sleep, and enmity might be laid aside like a travelling dress, after tumultuous journeys. . . .

But Hazlitt, restless as the sea-horse, as the raven, as the chamois, found not their respites from storm; he sought, but sought in vain. . . . Domicile he had not, round whose hearth his affections might gather: rest he had not, for the sole of his burning foot. . . .

I prefer closing this section with the words of Mr. Gilfillan:

"Well says Bulwer, that of all the mental wrecks which have occurred in our era, this was the most melancholy. Others may have been as unhappy in their domestic circumstances, and gone down steeper places of dissipation than he; but they had meanwhile the breath of popularity, if not of wealth and station, to give them a certain solace." What had Hazlitt of this nature? Mr. Gilfillan answers,

—"Absolutely nothing to support and cheer him. With no hope, no fortune, no *status* in society; no certain popularity as a writer, no domestic peace, little sympathy from kindred spirits, little support from his political party, no moral management, no definite belief; with great powers, and great passions within, and with a host of powerful enemies without, it was his to enact one of the saddest tragedies on which the sun ever shone. Such is a faithful portraiture of an extraordinary man, whose restless intellect and stormy passions have now, for fifteen years, found that repose in the grave which was denied them above it." Mr. Gilfillan concludes with expressing his conviction, in which I desire to concur, that both enemies and friends will *now* join in admiration for the man; "both will readily concede *now,* that a subtle thinker, an eloquent writer, a lover of beauty **and** poetry, and man and truth, one of the best of critics, and not the worst of men, expired in William Hazlitt." *Requiescat in pace!*

CRITICAL REVIEWS
OF THE
EARLY NINETEENTH
CENTURY

CRITICAL REVIEWS OF THE EARLY NINETEENTH CENTURY

To treat of the history of the English Review is not within our purpose. Were we to do so we should have to begin with John Florio's translation of the *Essais* of Montaigne (1583), or with the *Journal des Sçavans* begun in Paris by Denis de Sallo (1665), imitations of which were prevalent in England down to the time of Addison. It is enough if we remember that in 1749 Ralph Griffiths established the *Monthly Review,* a Whig and Non-Conformist publication which undertook to print "Proper Abstracts of, and Extracts from, the New Books"; and that in 1756 Archibald Hamilton began the *Critical Review,* a rival publication, Tory in spirit and champion of the Established Church. Oliver Goldsmith toiled for the first, Tobias Smollett edited the second. The student should observe that these periodicals were founded upon partisanship and that they began to publish book notices, not yet reviews.

Passing over half a century during which time, although there were several additional publications established, there were few developments in the art of writing book reviews, we come to October 10, 1802. On that date the first number of the *Edinburgh Review* appeared. The publication was significant not only because it contained among twenty-nine articles six which were written by Francis Jeffrey, not only because it voiced the liberal opinions of young men in conflict with conservatism, but also because it gave much more space and serious attention to literary discussion than had ever before been given. The magazine instantly became a success; but as it grew in power it did not forget its predominant political purpose. In October, 1808, it triumphed over the Tories with a Whiggish critique of Don Pedro Cevallo's *French Usurpation of Spain.* Such lively liberalism caused Tory contributors to revolt, and among them significantly was Sir Walter Scott. At the time he not only refused further to read the periodical, but he also set about establishing a rival publication. That publication was the famous *Quarterly Review,* born of party difference and in its turn conservative. The first number, appearing in February, 1809, contained three articles by Scott. William Gifford, formerly successful in conducting the *Anti-Jacobin* (1797–98), was made the editor. With him were associated, among others, George Ellis, Robert Southey, John Gibson Lockhart, and the somewhat infamous John Wilson Croker. Upon Gifford's resignation in 1824, John Taylor Coleridge conducted the publication until 1825, when Lockhart, the son-in-law of Scott, began an editorship which lasted until 1853.

The warfare against the liberal *Edinburgh* was carried into the northern capital in 1817. At that time William Blackwood established the *Edinburgh Monthly Magazine,* which after six issues was renamed *Blackwood's Edinburgh Magazine.* Among the men whose services were enlisted in the new venture was the son-in-law of Scott; so that between the *Quarterly* and *Blackwood's* there was established an interlocking contributorship. However, the new organ of Toryism was fiercer than the old; and, consequently, in dealing with literary figures it seemed on the whole to prefer vituperation to criticism. The genius which determined its astonishing success was that of John Wilson, supported by the meaner and sharper abilities of John Gibson Lockhart. The first could deliver a swashing blow, the second was the master of the *coup de grâce.* When we remember the political alignment of these men and their associates, as well as the imperious presumption of their temper, it will be easy for us to appreciate their admiration for Scott, their early praise of Lord Byron, and their sympathy for the older Wordsworth. We can understand, furthermore, their irritation with Coleridge, their suspicion of Shelley, and their brutal antipathy not only for the liberal Leigh Hunt but also for John Keats and the entire Cockney School. In fact, we have given these details in order that the student, while working with the following materials, may remember one very important thing; namely, that the reviews printed in these three major publications are seldom purely literary in interest, but are often intended either to exalt or to damn authors according to their political preferences or their social purposes. This truth in turn goes far to explain its correlate, which is that we now study these reviews not because we expect to find in them literary criticism of high and uniform worth, but because, regardless of their quality, we do find in them attitudes and comments vital to our understanding of the Romantic Movement.

There is, indeed, a significance in the praise or the censure of a reviewer other than he could have anticipated in his own time; for although he did lead the unthinking, he was nevertheless predisposed to follow public opinion. In an undeterminable measure he expressed the conclusions of his age. Few reviewers, like Jeffrey, kept crying out their early mistakes until the gathering winds of opinion blew their words back into their own mouths. Usually, they condemned that which it was safe for them to condemn, and they praised that which it was well for them to praise. Out of their very pusillanimity, then, as well as out of their deftness and their skill, grew an historical significance quite apart from other aspects of their work.

Even while we rejoice in the repetitious adulation with which the critics came to receive the work of Scott, we must remember that he had won almost at a stroke the continuous applause of the people. It is necessary for us to include only one review of his work, because, on the whole, there was only one contemporary opinion of it. The more stormy public life of Byron reflects itself in the reviews about him. Of no poet is it so difficult to gather critiques. It is as if the writers could not be sure of a public which now would exhaust itself in praise of a man, and now vent its very life in spleen against him. Then, too, Byron was a lord, and that made a difference. Jeffrey never quite rose above the fact; and up until the time when the best people were being too much shocked by *Don Juan*, the anonymous Tory critics of *Blackwood's* said magnificent things of the noble bard. In the *Quarterly* we find three innocuous reviews by George Ellis, after which Scott rose to do justice to a compeer. Coleridge, in his turn, was not treated with great respect and surely not with sympathetic understanding until his own relatives had taken charge of the *Quarterly;* and Wordsworth, except for the support which he received from his friend John Wilson of *Blackwood's,* had largely to make his own way in so far as the three dominant periodicals were concerned. Should the student ask, What were the *Edinburgh* and the *Quarterly* writing of Wordsworth between 1815 and 1837, the only answer would be nothing. Shelley, while he received three bitter lashings from the *Quarterly* and as many patronizing recognitions from *Blackwood's,* was granted, by the cautious *Edinburgh,* the benediction of silence. This benediction the *Edinburgh* extended to Keats also, while the *Quarterly* gained lasting disgrace through Croker's review of *Endymion* and the *Blackwood's* something more bitter than disgrace by its smart buffoonery.

However, in spite of the obvious personal and political interests which seem to keep periodical reviews from the higher levels of criticism, we must not form the opinion that they are in all instances splenetic and low. Far from it. In the following pages the student will find critical opinions that transfix truth. He will find paragraphs swept with gusto, strong in health, and worthy

of the acclaim which once they had. Such men as Lord Jeffrey and Professor Wilson were regarded not only as the greatest critics of their age, but also as men of universal genius; and the student will find them to be thinkers of genuine significance. Carlyle, in speaking of Jeffrey, asserted that "there has no critic appeared among us since who was worth naming beside him." Macaulay said of him, "Take him all in all, I think him more nearly an universal genius than any man of our time." Maugre his wayward belief that Wordsworth, Shelley, and Keats were moving into oblivion, while Rogers and Campbell remained in unfading elegance, Jeffrey was and he still is a man to reckon with. John Wilson, in turn, was regarded as "a good man of his inches." To the quality of his work Leigh Hunt paid high tribute in the *London Journal* of May 20, 1835: "Wilson's prose (and we could not express our admiration of it more highly) might stretch forth its thick and rich territory by the side of Keats's poetry." We may be piqued by his gay self-delight, we may resent the noisiness of his laugh which is at times greater than the bellowing of "ten thousand beeves at pasture," but we shall find in him, nevertheless, both sanity and health.

More particularly, we may be persuaded that Lockhart was right in pronouncing Jeffrey's review of *The Lady of the Lake* the best contemporary criticism of Scott's poetry. Surely Walter Scott's article on *Childe Harold* is a noble and generous work. Although "so mercilessly mangled by Gifford, that *he* entreated Wordsworth not to read it," Lamb's article on the *Excursion* has in it some absolute truth. That which H. N. Coleridge wrote of his uncle was not made unjust but more just by a relationship which was partly of the mind itself. Even among the worked-up prejudices of these reviewers the careful student will find observations that are right. Croker himself, lower than whom we find only Lockhart and a few hidden men, found a real weakness in Keats. Certain it is that a comparative study of all those criticisms right or wrong, when brought to supplement the student's analysis of the poems themselves, will give him an understanding of the Romantic Movement which otherwise he could not have gained.

SELECTED BIBLIOGRAPHY

Cockburn, H., *Life of Lord Jeffrey, with a Selection from his Correspondence,* 2 Vols., 1852, 1874.
Croker Papers, The, ed. by L. J. Jennings, 1884.
Douglas, G. P. S., *The "Blackwood" Group,* 1897.
Gordon, M. W., *Christopher North, a Memoir,* 2 Vols., 1862.
Graham, W. J., *English Literary Periodicals,* 1930. This work contains a valuable bibliography.
Graham, W. J., *Tory Criticism in the Quarterly Review,* 1921. This work gives a list of reviews. Cf. the *Gentleman's Magazine,* 1844,–45,–47.

Graham, W. J., *Contemporary Critics of Coleridge, the Poet,* P M L A 38: 278–289, 1923.
Haney, T. L., *Early Reviews of English Poets,* 1904. This work contains valuable notes.
Jeffrey's Contributions to the Edinburgh Review, 1852.
Jeffrey's Literary Criticism, ed. by D. N. Smith, 1910.
Marsh, G. L., *The Early Reviews of Shelley,* Mod Phil 27: 73–95, 1929.
Walpole, S., *Essays, Political and Biographical,* 1908.
Wilson's Works, ed. by J. F. Ferrier, 1865–68.
Winchester, C. T., *A Group of English Essayists,* 1910.

A WORD OF EXPLANATION FOR THE STUDENT

The number and variety of reviews published between 1793 (see Wordsworth I, note) and 1834 (see Coleridge VI) necessitated a careful selection for this text. Many valuable articles have perforce been omitted; some of those which have been included are of worth only when studied in conjunction with others. Our object was in no way to present an anthology of reviews, but rather to bring to the student materials which would aid him in understanding the literature of the period. With a view to making our selection as useful as possible to him, we are offering a word of explanation.

1. All reviews included in this text are of works published during the lives of their authors.
2. In making the selection we have tried to involve as many different poems as possible, giving the preference to those included in this volume. The student will find exceptions to this rule, especially in such a case as the review of *The Lady of the Lake*. In certain instances the treatment of poems outside our text was distinctly of more significance than the treatment of poems in our text.
3. We have, in all cases, taken material verbatim from first publications. This has necessitated the retention of certain inaccuracies. Where the error is obviously the printer's, or where we wish to call particular attention to spelling, we have used the designation *sic*.
4. The average review of the period is not only verbose and overstocked with quotations, but it tends also to incoherent digressions. We have, therefore, deleted much material, when the deletion did not distort the meaning of the writer. Our purpose in doing this was to save space in order that we might present as many points of view as possible.
5. Many reviews are made up of three standardized parts: a generalizing introduction; a section of quoted matter touched with brief comments; an admonitory or generalizing conclusion. We have retained largely sections one and three, its being to a degree purposeless to include the quoted matter.
6. We have not selected articles with a view to their representing the standards of various periodicals, or primarily because of the worth of the articles themselves. Our belief has been that a review such as that on Shelley's *Queen Mab* may be as valuable for the scholar as Scott's tribute to Byron or Jeffrey's comment on the *Excursion*.
7. Where we have been able to indicate the name of the reviewer with certainty we have done so; but since most articles were anonymous, we have not, in some cases, been able to assure ourselves of the author.
8. Our effort and primary object throughout has been to present materials useful to the student in making a comparative study of the criticism of the period and of its relationship to Romantic literature.

SAMUEL TAYLOR COLERIDGE

REVIEWS OF HIS WORK

I

The British Critic. Vol. VII, p. 549. May, 1796.

Poems on various Subjects. By S. T. Coleridge, late of Jesus College, Cambridge. 12mo. 188 pp. 4s. Robinsons. 1796.

Reviewer: Unknown.

THIS collection is marked by tenderness of sentiment, and elegance of expression, neither however sufficiently chastened by experience of mankind, or habitude of writing. The following will be no unacceptable specimen of its merit. [There follows *The Sigh*.]

Mr. C. does not, in this volume, betray much of his politics, except in his violent rant to Lord Stanhope. [Entire review.]

II

The Monthly Magazine. Vol. VI, p. 514. December, 1798.

[The following comment was inserted under the general head, *Poetry*.]

Reviewer: Unknown.

THE author of *"Lyrical Ballads,"* has attempted to imitate the style of our old English versifiers, with unusual success; *"The Auncient Mariners,"* [*sic*] however, on which he particularly prides himself, is in our opinion, a particular exception; some of his pieces are beautiful, but others are stiff and laboured. [Entire notice. Observe that Coleridge was thought to be the author of all of the poems.]

III

The British Critic. Vol. XIV, pp. 364–369.
October, 1799.

> *Lyrical Ballads, with a few other Poems.*
> 12mo. 210 pp. 5s. Arch, Gracechurch-
> Street. 1798.

Reviewer: Probably Francis Wrangham.

THE attempt made in this little volume is one
that meets our cordial approbation; and it is
an attempt by no means unsuccessful. The endeavour of the author is to recall our poetry,
from the fantastical excess of refinement, to
simplicity and nature. The account of this design, and its probable effects upon modern
readers, is so very sensibly given in the Introduction, that we shall insert the passage at
large. [Passage from P. iv inserted.]

We fully agree with the author, that the true
notion of poetry must be sought among the
poets, rather than the critics; and we will add
that, unless a critic is a poet also, he will generally make but indifferent work in judging
of the effusions of Genius. In the collection of
poems subjoined to this introduction, we do
not often find expressions that we esteem too
familiar, or deficient in dignity; on the contrary, we think that in general the author has
succeeded in attaining that judicious degree of
simplicity, which accommodates itself with
ease even to the sublime. It is not by pomp of
words, but by energy of thought, that sublimity is most successfully achieved; and we infinitely prefer the simplicity, even of the most
unadorned tale in this volume, to all the
meretricious frippery of the *Darwinian* taste.

The Poem of "the Ancyent Marinere," with
which the collection opens, has many excellencies, and many faults; the beginning and
the end are striking and well-conducted; but
the intermediate part is too long, and has, in
some places, a kind of confusion of images,
which loses all effect, from not being quite intelligible. The author, who is confidently said
to be Mr. Coleridge, is not correctly versed
in the old language, which he undertakes to
employ. "Noises of a *swound*," p. 9, and
"broad as a *weft*," p. 11, are both nonsensical;
but the ancient style is so well imitated, while
the antiquated words are so very few, that the
latter might with advantage be entirely removed without any detriment to the effect of
the Poem. The opening of the Poem is admi-

rably calculated to arrest the reader's attention, by the well-imagined idea of the Wedding Guest, who is held to hear the tale, in
spite of his efforts to escape. The beginning of
the second canto, or fit, has much merit, if we
except the very unwarrantable comparison of
the Sun to that which no man can conceive:—
"like God's own head," a simile which makes
a reader shudder; not with poetic feeling, but
with religious disapprobation. . . .

The conclusion, as we remarked before, is
very good, particularly the idea that the Marinere has periodical fits of agony, which oblige
him to relate his marvellous adventure; and
this,

> I pass, like night, from land to land,
> I have strange power of speech;
> The moment that his face I see,
> I know the man that must hear me;
> To him my tale I teach. P. 49.

Whether the remaining poems of the volume are by Mr. Coleridge, we have not been
informed; but they seem to proceed from the
same mind; and in the Advertisement, the
writer speaks of himself as of a single person
accountable for the whole. It is therefore
reasonable to conclude, that this is the fact.
They all have merit, and many among them a
very high rank of merit, which our feelings
respecting some parts of the supposed author's
character do not authorize or incline us to
deny. The Poem on the Nightingale, which is
there styled *a conversational Poem,* is very
good; but we do not perceive it to be more
conversational than Cowper's Task, which is
the best poem in that style that our language
possesses. "The Female Vagrant," is a composition of exquisite beauty, nor is the combination of events, related in it, out of the compass of possibility; yet we perceive, with regret, the drift of the author in composing it;
which is to show the worst side of civilized
society, and thus to form a satire against it.
But let fanciful men rail as they will at the
evils which no care can always prevent, they
can have no dream more wild than the supposition, that any human wisdom can possibly
exclude all evils from a state which divine
Providence has decreed, for reasons the most
wise, to be a state of suffering and of trial.
The sufferers may be changed, by infinite
revolutions, but sufferers there will be, till
Heaven shall interfere to change the nature of
our tenure upon earth. From this beautiful

Poem, partly on account of its apparent design, and partly because the loss of the connection would destroy much of its effect, we shall make no extract.

The story of "Goody Blake and Harry Gill," is founded, the Introduction tells us, "on a well-authenticated fact which happened in Warwickshire." Yet it is a miracle; and modern miracles can seldom be admitted, without some degree of credulity, or a very uncommon weight of evidence. One of the simplest stories in the book, is that entitled "We are Seven;" yet he must be a very fastidious reader who will deny that it has great beauty and feeling.

The tale of "the Thorn" has many beauties; nor can we pass without notice "the Mad Mother," or the long and familiar tale of "the Idiot Boy," which, though it descends quite to common life, is animated by much interest, and told with singular felicity. One more Poem we shall particularly notice for its pathos, and shall indeed insert the whole. The imagery of it is in many instances new, and is introduced with admirable effect.[1] [Here is quoted *The Complaint of a Forsaken Indian Woman.*]

The purchasers of this little volume will find that, after all we have said, there are poems, and passages of poems, which we have been obliged to pass over, that well deserve attention and commendation; nor does there appear any offensive mixture of enmity to present institutions, except in one or two instances, which are so unobtrusive as hardly to deserve notice.

IV

The Edinburgh Review. Vol. XXVII, No. LIII, pp. 58–67. September, 1816.

   Christabel: Kubla Khan, a Vision. The Pains of Sleep. By S. T. Coleridge Esq. London. Murray, 1816.

   Reviewer: William Hazlitt.

THE advertisement by which this work was announced to the publick, carried in its front a recommendation from Lord Byron,—who, it seems, has somewhere praised Christabel, as "a wild and singularly original and beautiful poem." Great as the noble bard's merits undoubtedly are in poetry, some of his latest *publications* dispose us to distrust his authority, where the question is what ought to meet the public eye; and the works before us afford an additional proof, that his judgment on such matters is not absolutely to be relied on. Moreover, we are a little inclined to doubt the value of the praise which one poet lends another. It seems now-a-days to be the practice of that once irritable race to laud each other without bounds; and one can hardly avoid suspecting, that what is thus lavishly advanced may be laid out with a view to being repaid with interest. Mr Coleridge, however, must be judged by his own merits.

It is remarked, by the writers upon the Bathos, that the true *profound* is surely known by one quality—its being wholly bottomless; insomuch, that when you think you have attained its utmost depth in the work of some of its great masters, another, or peradventure the same, astonishes you, immediately after, by a plunge so far more vigorous, as to outdo all his former outdoings. So it seems to be with the new school, or, as they may be termed, the wild or lawless poets. After we had been admiring their extravagance for many years, and marvelling at the ease and rapidity with which one exceeded another in the unmeaning or infantine, until not an idea was left in the rhyme—or in the insane, until we had reached something that seemed the untamed effusion of an author whose thoughts were rather more free than his actions—forth steps Mr Coleridge, like a giant refreshed with sleep, and as if to redeem his character after so long a silence, ("his poetic powers having been, he says, from 1808 till very lately, in a state of suspended animation," p. v.) breaks out in these precise words—

[1] Robert Southey, writing in the *Critical Review*, XXIV, pp. 197–204, Oct., 1798, offered the following comment on *The Idiot Boy* and other poems: "No tale less deserved the labour that appears to have been bestowed upon this. . . . The other ballads of this kind are in narration. With that which is entitled the Thorn we were altogether displeased. The advertisement says, it is not in the person of the author, but in that of some loquacious narrator. The author should have recollected that he who personates tiresome loquacity, becomes tiresome himself. . . . In a very different style of poetry, is the Rime of the Ancyent Marinere. . . . Many of the stanzas are laboriously beautiful; but in connection they are absurd."—Other reviews appeared in the *Analytical Review*, XXVIII, pp. 583–587, December, 1798, and the *Monthly Review*, XXIX, pp. 202–210, May, 1799.

'Tis the middle of night by the castle clock,
And the owls have awaken'd the crowing cock;
Tu-whit!———Tu-whoo!
And hark, again! the crowing cock,
How drowsily it crew.—
Sir Leoline, the Baron rich,
Hath a toothless mastiff bitch; [1]
From her kennel beneath the rock
She makes answer to the clock,
Four for the quarters, and twelve for the hour;
Ever and aye, moonshine or shower,
Sixteen short howls, not over loud;
Some say she sees my lady's shroud.—
Is the night chilly and dark?
The night is chilly, but not dark. p. 3, 4.

It is probable that Lord Byron may have had this passage in his eye, when he called the poem "wild" and "original;" but how he discovered it to be "beautiful," is not quite so easy for us to imagine.

Much of the art of the wild writers consists in sudden transitions—opening eagerly upon some topic, and then flying from it immediately. This indeed is known to the medical men, who not unfrequently have the care of them, as an unerring symptom. Accordingly, here we take leave of the Mastiff Bitch, and lose sight of her entirely, upon the entrance of another personage of higher degree,

> The lovely Lady Christabel,
> Whom her father loves so well—

And who, it seems, has been rambling about all night, having, the night before, had dreams about her lover, which "made her moan and *leap.*" While kneeling, in the course of her rambles, at an old oak, she hears a noise on the other side of the stump, and going round, finds, to her great surprise, another fair damsel in white silk, but with her dress and hair in some disorder; at the mention of whom, the poet takes fright, not, as might be imagined, because of her disorder, but on account of her beauty and her fair attire—

> I guess 'twas frightful there to see
> A lady so richly clad as she—
> Beautiful exceedingly!

Christabel naturally asks who she is, and is answered, at some length, that her name is Geraldine; that she was, on the morning before, seized by five warriors, who tied her on a white horse, and drove her on, they themselves following, also on white horses; and that they had rode all night. Her narrative now gets to be a little contradictory, which gives rise to

[1] Cf. Hunt's *What Is Poetry, supra.*

unpleasant suspicions. She protests vehemently, and with oaths, that she had no idea who the men were; only that one of them, the tallest of the five, took her and placed her under the tree, and that they all went away, she knew not whither; but how long she had remained there she cannot tell—

> Nor do I know how long it is,
> For I have lain in fits, I *wis;*

—although she had previously kept a pretty exact account of the time. The two ladies then go home together. . . .

The ladies pass forward, and take off their shoes, and tread softly all the way up stairs, as Christabel observes that her father is a bad sleeper. At last, however, they do arrive at the bed room, and comfort themselves with a dram of some home-made liquor, which proves to be very old; for it was made by Lady C.'s mother; and when her new friend asks if she thinks the old lady will take her part, she answers, that this is out of the question, in as much as she happened to die in childbed of her. The mention of the old lady, however, gives occasion to the following pathetic couplet.—Christabel says,

> O mother dear, that thou wert here!
> I would, said Geraldine, she were!

A very mysterious conversation next takes place between Lady Geraldine and the old gentlewoman's ghost, which proving extremely fatiguing to her, she again has recourse to the bottle—and with effect, as appears by these lines.

> Again the wild-flower wine she drank;
> Her fair large eyes 'gan glitter bright,
> And from the floor whereon she sank,
> The lofty Lady stood upright: . . .[1]

One word on the metre of Christabel, or, as Mr Coleridge terms it, *"the* Christabel"— happily enough; for indeed we doubt if the peculiar force of the definite article was ever more strongly exemplified. He says, that though the reader may fancy there prevails a great *irregularity* in the metre, some lines being of four, others of twelve syllables, yet in reality it is quite regular; only that it is "founded on a new principle, namely, that of counting in each line the accents, not the syllables." We say nothing of the monstrous assurance of any man coming forward coolly at

[1] To the end of the Second Part Hazlitt continues in this vein.

this time of day, and telling the readers of English poetry, whose ear has been tuned to the lays of Spenser, Milton, Dryden, and Pope, that he makes his metre "on a new principle!" but we utterly deny the truth of the assertion, and defy him to show us *any* principle upon which his lines can be conceived to tally. We give two or three specimens, to confound at once this miserable piece of coxcombry and shuffling. Let our "wild, and singularly original and beautiful" author, show us how these lines agree either in number of accents or of feet.

Ah wel-a-day!—
For this is alone in—
And didst bring her home with thee in love and
   in charity—
I pray you drink this cordial wine—
Sir Leoline—
And found a bright lady surpassingly fair—
Tu-whit!——Tu-whoo!

Kubla Khan is given to the public, it seems, "at the request of a poet of great and deserved celebrity;"—but whether Lord Byron the praiser of "the Christabel," or the Laureate, the praiser of "Princes, we are not informed. As far as Mr Coleridge's "own opinions are concerned," it is published, "not upon the ground of any *poetic* merits," but "as a PSYCHOLOGICAL CURIOSITY!" In these opinions of the candid author, we entirely concur; but for this reason we hardly think it was necessary to give the minute detail which the Preface contains. . . . It was in the year 1797, and in the summer season. Mr Coleridge was in bad health;—the particular disease is not given; but the careful reader will form his own conjectures. He had retired very prudently to a lonely farm-house; and whoever would see the place which gave birth to the "psychological curiosity," may find his way thither without a guide; for it is situated on the confines of Somerset and Devonshire, and on the Exmoor part of the boundary; and it is, moreover, between Porlock and Linton. In that farm-house, he had a slight indisposition, and had taken an anodyne, which threw him into deep sleep in his chair, (whether after dinner or not he omits to state), "at the moment that he was reading a sentence in Purchas's Pilgrims," relative to a palace of Kubla Khan. The effects of the anodyne, and the sentence together, were prodigious: They

produced the "curiosity" now before us; for, during his three-hours sleep, Mr Coleridge "has the most vivid confidence that he could not have composed less than from two to three hundred lines." On awaking, he "instantly and eagerly" wrote down the verses here published; when he was (he says *"unfortunately"*) called out by a "person on business from Porlock, and detained by him above an hour;" and when he returned, the vision was gone. . . .

Upon the whole, we look upon this publication as one of the most notable pieces of impertinence of which the press has lately been guilty; and one of the boldest experiments that has yet been made on the patience or understanding of the public. . . .

V

Blackwoods Edinburgh Magazine. Vol. II, No. VII, pp. 3–18. October, 1817.

Some Observations on the "Biographia Literaria" of S.T. Coleridge, Esq.—1817.

Reviewer: E. H. Coleridge in *Christabel* (1907) ascribes this review to William Hazlitt.

. . . CONSIDERED merely in a literary point of view, the work is most execrable. He rambles from one subject to another in the most wayward and capricious manner; either from indolence, or ignorance, or weakness, he has never in one single instance finished a discussion; and while he darkens what was dark before into tenfold obscurity, he so treats the most ordinary common-places as to give them the air of mysteries, till we no longer know the faces of our old acquaintances beneath their cowl and hood, but witness plain flesh and blood matters of fact miraculously converted into a troop of phantoms. That he is a man of genius is certain; but he is not a man of a strong intellect nor of powerful talents. He has a great deal of fancy and imagination, but little or no real feeling, and certainly no judgment. He cannot form to himself any harmonious landscape such as it exists in nature, but beautified by the serene light of imagination. He cannot conceive simple and majestic groupes of human figures and characters acting on the theatre of real existence. But his pictures of nature are fine only as imaging the dreaminess, and obscurity, and confusion of distempered sleep; while all his agents pass before our eyes like shadows, and only impress and affect us with phantasmagorial splendour.

It is impossible to read many pages of this work without thinking that Mr Coleridge conceives himself to be a far greater man than the Public is likely to admit; and we wish to waken him from what seems to us a most ludicrous delusion. He seems to believe that every tongue is wagging in his praise,—that every ear is open to imbibe the oracular breathings of his inspiration. Even when he would fain convince us that his soul is wholly occupied with some other illustrious character, he breaks out into laudatory exclamations concerning himself; no sound is so sweet to him as that of his own voice: the ground is hallowed on which his footsteps tread; and there seems to him something more than human in his very shadow. He will read no books that other people read; his scorn is as misplaced and extravagant as his admiration; opinions that seem to tally with his own wild ravings are holy and inspired; and, unless agreeable to his creed, the wisdom of ages is folly; and wits, whom the world worship, dwarfed when they approach his venerable side. His admiration of nature or of man,—we had almost said his religious feeling towards his God,—are all narrowed, weakened, and corrupted and poisoned by inveterate and diseased egotism; and instead of his mind reflecting the beauty and glory of nature, he seems to consider the mighty universe itself as nothing better than a mirror, in which, with a grinning and idiot self-complacency, he may contemplate the Physiognomy of Samuel Taylor Coleridge. Though he has yet done nothing in any one department of human knowledge, yet he speaks of his theories, and plans, and views, and discoveries, as if he had produced some memorable revolution in Science. He at all times connects his own name in Poetry with Shakespeare, and Spenser, and Milton; in politics with Burke, and Fox, and Pitt; in metaphysics with Locke, and Hartley, and Berkley, and Kant;—feeling himself not only to be the worthy compeer of those illustrious Spirits, but to unite, in his own mighty intellect, all the glorious powers and faculties by which they are separately distinguished, as if his soul were endowed with all human power, and was the depository of the aggregate, or rather the essence, of all human knowledge. So deplorable a delusion as this has only been equalled by that of Joanna Southcote, who mistook a complaint of the bowels for the divine afflatus; and believed herself about to give birth to the regenerator of the world, when sick unto death of an incurable and loathsome disease.

The truth is, that Mr Coleridge is but an obscure name in English literature. In London he is well known in literary society, and justly admired for his extraordinary loquacity: he has his own little circle of devoted worshippers, and he mistakes their foolish babbling for the voice of the world. His name, too, has been often foisted into Reviews, and accordingly is known to many who never saw any of his works. In Scotland few know or care anything about him; and perhaps no man who has spoken and written so much, and occasionally with so much genius and ability, ever made so little impression on the public mind. Few people know how to spell or pronounce his name; and were he to drop from the clouds among any given number of well informed and intelligent men north of the Tweed, he would find it impossible to make any intelligible communication respecting himself; for of him and his writings there would prevail only a perplexing dream, or the most untroubled ignorance. We cannot see in what the state of literature would have been different had he been cut off in childhood, or had he never been born. . . .

This absurd self-elevation forms a striking contrast with the dignified deportment of all the other great living Poets. Throughout all the works of Scott, the most original-minded man of this generation of Poets, scarcely a single allusion is made to himself; and then it is with a truly delightful simplicity, as if he were not aware of his immeasurable superiority to the ordinary run of mankind. From the rude songs of our forefathers he has created a kind of Poetry, which at once brought over the dull scenes of this our unimaginative life all the pomp, and glory, and magnificence of a chivalrous age. He speaks to us like some ancient Bard awakened from his tomb, and singing of visions not revealed in dreams, but contemplated in all the freshness and splendour of reality. Since he sung his bold, and wild, and romantic lays, a more religious solemnity breathes from our mouldering abbeys, and a sterner grandeur frowns over our time-shattered castles. He has peopled our hills with heroes, even as Ossian peopled them; and, like a presiding spirit, his Image haunts the magnificent cliffs of our Lakes and Seas. . . .

We have done. We have felt it our duty to speak with severity of this book and its author. . . . We have not been speaking in the cause of Literature only, but, we conceive, in the cause of Morality and Religion. For it is not fitting that He should be held up as an example to the rising generation (but, on the contrary, it is most fitting that he should be exposed as a most dangerous model), who has alternately embraced, defended, and thrown aside all systems of Philosophy, and all creeds of Religion;—who seems to have no power of retaining an opinion,—no trust in the principles which he defends,—but who fluctuates from theory to theory, according as he is impelled by vanity, envy, or diseased desire of change,—and who, while he would subvert and scatter into dust those structures of knowledge, reared by the wise men of this and other generations, has nothing to erect in their room but the baseless and air-built fabrics of a dreaming imagination.

VI

The Quarterly Review. Vol. LII, No. CIII, pp. 1–38. August, 1834.

The Poetical Works of S. T. Coleridge. 3 vols. 12mo. London. 1834.

Reviewer: H. N. Coleridge.

. . . THE precise Miltonic movement in blank verse has never, to our knowledge, been caught by any later poet. It is Mr. Coleridge's own strong remark, that you might as well think of pushing a brick out of a wall with your forefinger as attempt to remove a word out of the finished passages in Shakspeare or Milton. The amotion or transposition will alter the thought, or the feeling, or at least the tone. They are as pieces of Mosaic work, from which you cannot strike the smallest block without making a hole in the picture.

And so it is—in due proportion—with Coleridge's best poems. They are distinguished in a remarkable degree by the perfection of their rhythm and metrical arrangement. The labour bestowed upon this point must have been very great; the tone and quantity of words seem weighed in scales of gold. It will, no doubt, he considered ridiculous by the Fannii and Fanniæ of our day to talk of varying the trochee with the iambus, or of resolving either into the tribrach. Yet it is evident to us that these, and even minuter points of accentual scansion, have been regarded by Mr. Coleridge as worthy of study and observation. We do not, of course, mean that rules of this kind were always in his mind while composing, any more than that an expert disputant is always thinking of the distinctions of mood and figure, whilst arguing; but we certainly believe that Mr. Coleridge has almost from the commencement of his poetic life looked upon versification as constituting in and by itself a much more important branch of the art poetic than most of his eminent contemporaries appear to have done. And this more careful study shows itself in him in no technical peculiarities or fantastic whims, against which the genius of our language revolts; but in a more exact adaptation of the movement to the feeling, and in a finer selection of particular words with reference to their local fitness for sense and sound. Some of his poems are complete models of versification, exquisitely easy to all appearance, and subservient to the meaning, and yet so subtle in the links and transitions of the parts as to make it impossible to produce the same effect merely by imitating the syllabic metre as it stands on the surface. The secret of the sweetness lies within, and is involved in the feeling. It is this remarkable power of making his verse musical that gives a peculiar character to Mr. Coleridge's lyric poems. In some of the smaller pieces, as the conclusion of the "Kubla Khan," for example, not only the lines by themselves are musical, but the whole passage sounds all at once as an outburst or crash of harps in the still air of autumn. The verses seem as if *played* to the ear upon some unseen instrument. . . .

The minute study of the laws and properties of metre is observable in almost every piece in these volumes. Every kind of lyric measure, rhymed and unrhymed, is attempted with success; and we doubt whether, upon the whole, there are many specimens of the heroic couplet or blank verse superior in construction to what Mr. Coleridge has given us. We mention this the rather, because it was at one time, although that time is past, the fashion to say that the Lake school—as two or three poets, essentially unlike to each other, were foolishly called—had abandoned the old and established measures of the English poetry for new conceits of their own. There was no truth in that charge. . . .

We should not have dwelt so long upon this point of versification, unless we had conceived it to be one distinguishing excellence of Mr. Coleridge's poetry, and very closely connected with another, namely, fulness and individuality of thought. It seems to be a fact, although we do not pretend to explain it, that condensation of meaning is generally found in poetry of a high import in proportion to perfection in metrical harmony. Petrarch, Spenser, Shakspeare, and Milton are obvious instances. Goethe and Coleridge are almost equally so. Indeed, whether in verse, or prose, or conversation, Mr. Coleridge's mind may be fitly characterized as an energetic mind—a mind always at work, always in a course of reasoning. He cares little for anything, merely because it was or is; it must be referred, or be capable of being referred, to some law or principle, in order to attract his attention. This is not from ignorance of the facts of natural history or science. His written and published works alone sufficiently show how constantly and accurately he has been in the habit of noting all the phenomena of the material world around us; and the great philosophical system now at length in preparation for the press demonstrates, we are told, his masterly acquaintance with almost all the sciences, and with not a few of the higher and more genial of the arts. Yet his vast acquirements of this sort are never put forward by or for themselves; it is in his apt and novel illustrations, his indications of analogies, his explanation of anomalies, that he enables the hearer or reader to get a glimpse of the extent of his practical knowledge. He is always reasoning out from an inner point, and it is the inner point, the principle, the law which he labours to bring forward into light. If he can convince you or himself of the principle à priori, he generally leaves the facts to take care of themselves. He leads us into the laboratories of art or nature as a showman guides you through a cavern crusted with spar and stalactites, all cold, and dim, and motionless, till he lifts his torch aloft, and on a sudden you gaze in admiration on walls and roof of flaming crystals and stars of eternal diamond.

All this, whether for praise or for blame, is perceptible enough in Mr. Coleridge's verse, but perceptible, of course, in such degree and mode as the law of poetry in general, and the nature of the specific poem in particular, may require. But the main result from this frame and habit of his mind is very distinctly traceable in the uniform subjectivity of almost all his works. He does not belong to that grand division of poetry and poets which corresponds with painting and painters; of which Pindar and Dante are the chief;—those masters of the picturesque, who, by a felicity inborn, view and present everything in the completeness of actual objectivity—and who have a class derived from and congenial with them, presenting few pictures indeed, but always full of picturesque matter; of which secondary class Spenser and Southey may be mentioned as eminent instances. To neither of these does Mr. Coleridge belong; in his "Christabel," there certainly are several *distinct pictures* of great beauty; but he, as a poet, clearly comes within the other division which answers to music and the musician, in which you have a magnificent mirage of words with the subjective associations of the poet curling, and twisting, and creeping round, and through, and above every part of it. This is the class to which Milton belongs, in whose poems we have heard Mr. Coleridge say that he remembered but two proper pictures—Adam bending over the sleeping Eve at the beginning of the fifth book of the "Paradise Lost," and Dalilah approaching Samson towards the end of the "Agonistes." But when we point out the intense personal feeling, the self-projection, as it were, which characterizes Mr. Coleridge's poems, we mean that such feeling is the soul and spirit, not the whole body and form, of his poetry. For surely no one has ever more earnestly and constantly borne in mind the maxim of Milton, that poetry ought to be *simple, sensuous, and impassioned*. The poems in these volumes are no authority for that dreamy, half-swooning style of verse which was criticized by Lord Byron (in language too strong for print) as the fatal sin of Mr. John Keats, and which, unless abjured betimes, must prove fatal to several younger aspirants— male and female—who for the moment enjoy some popularity. The poetry before us is distinct and clear, and accurate in its imagery; but the imagery is rarely or never exhibited for description's sake alone; it is rarely or never exclusively objective; that is to say, put forward as a spectacle, a picture on which the mind's eye is to rest and terminate. You may if your sight is short, or your imagination cold, regard the imagery in itself and go no farther; but the poet's intention is that you should feel and imagine a great deal more than you see. His aim is to awaken in the reader the same mood of mind, the same cast of imagination and fancy whence issued the associations which animate and enlighten his pictures. You must think with him, must sympathize with him, must suffer yourself to be lifted out of your own school of opinion or faith, and fall back upon your own consciousness, an unsophisticated man. If you decline this, *non tibi spirat.* From his earliest youth to this day, Mr. Coleridge's poetry has been a faithful mirror reflecting the images of his mind. Hence he is so original, so individual. With a little trouble, the zealous reader of the "Biographia Literaria" may trace in these volumes the whole course of mental struggle and self-evolvement narrated in that odd but interesting work; but he will see the track marked in light; the notions become images, the images glorified, and not unfrequently the abstruse position stamped clearer by the poet than by the psychologist. No student of Coleridge's philosophy can fully understand it without a perusal of the illumining, and if we may so say, *popularizing* commentary of his poetry. . . .

We have not yet referred to the "Ancient Mariner," "Christabel," the "Odes on France," and the "Departing Year," or the "Love Poems." All these are well known by those who know no other parts of Coleridge's poetry, and the length of our preceding remarks compels us to be brief in our notice. Mrs. Barbauld, meaning to be complimentary, told our poet, that she thought the "Ancient Mariner" very beautiful, but that it had the fault of containing no moral. "Nay, madam," replied the poet, "if I may be permitted to say so, the only fault in the poem is that there is *too much!* In a work of such pure imagination I ought not to have stopped to give reasons for things, or inculcate humanity to beasts. 'The

Arabian Nights' might have taught me better." They might—the tale of the merchant's son who puts out the eyes of a genii by flinging his date-shells down a well, and is therefore ordered to prepare for death—might have taught this law of imagination; but the fault is small indeed; and the "Ancient Mariner" is, and will ever be, one of the most perfect pieces of imaginative poetry, not only in our language, but in the literature of all Europe. We have, certainly, sometimes doubted whether the miraculous destruction of the vessel in the presence of the pilot and hermit, was not an error, in respect of its bringing the purely preternatural into too close contact with the actual framework of the poem. The only link between those scenes of out-of-the-world wonders, and the wedding guest, should, we rather suspect, have been the blasted unknown being himself who described them. There should have been no other witnesses of the truth of any part of the tale, but the "Ancient Mariner" himself. This by the way: but take the work altogether, there is nothing else like it; it is a poem by itself, between it and other compositions, in *pari materia,* there is a chasm which you cannot overpass; the sensitive reader feels himself insulated, and a sea of wonder and mystery flows round him as round the spell-stricken ship itself. It was a sad mistake in the able artist—Mr. Scott, we believe—who in his engravings has made the ancient mariner an old decrepit man. That is not the true image; no! he should have been a growthless, decayless being, impassive to time or season, a silent cloud—the wandering Jew. The curse of the dead men's eyes should not have passed away. But this was, perhaps, too much for any pencil, even if the artist had fully entered into the poet's idea. Indeed, it is no subject for painting. The "Ancient Mariner" displays Mr. Coleridge's peculiar mastery over the wild and preternatural in a brilliant manner; but in his next poem, "Christabel," the exercise of his power in this line is still more skilful and singular. The thing attempted in "Christabel" is the most difficult of execution in the whole field of romance—witchery by daylight; and the success is complete. . . .

We are not amongst those who wish to have "Christabel" finished. It cannot be finished. The poet has spun all he could without snapping. The theme is too fine and subtle to bear much extension. It is better as it is, imperfect as a story, but complete as an exquisite production of the imagination, differing in form and colour from the "Ancient Mariner," yet differing in effect from it only so as the same powerful faculty is directed to the feudal or the mundane phases of the preternatural.

From these remarkable works we turn to the love poems scattered through the volumes before us. There is something very peculiar in Mr. Coleridge's exhibition of the most lovely of the passions. His love is not gloomy as Byron's, nor gay as Moore's, nor intellectual as Wordsworth's. It is a clear unclouded passion, made up of an exquisite respect and gentleness, a knightly tenderness and courtesy,—pure yet ardent, impatient yet contemplative. It is Petrarch and Shakspeare incorporate—it is the midsummer moonlight of all love poetry. . . .

It would be strange, indeed, if we concluded a notice of Mr. Coleridge's poetry without particularly adverting to his Odes. We learn from Captain Medwin, that Mr. Shelley pronounced the "France" to be the finest English ode of modern times. We think it the most complete—the most finished as a whole; but we do not agree that it is equal in imagination —in depth—in fancy—to "The Departing Year," or "Dejection," although these latter are less perfect in composition. It is rather passionate than imaginative: it has more of eloquence than of fancy. We may be wrong in setting up the imaginative before the passionate in an ode, and especially in an ode on such a subject; but we think the majestic strophe with which it concludes will, when compared with any part of the other two odes, prove the accuracy of the distinction taken as a matter of fact. . . .

It has been impossible to express, in the few pages to which we are necessarily limited, even a brief opinion upon all those pieces which might seem to call for notice in an estimate of this author's poetical genius. We know no writer of modern times whom it would not be easier to characterize in one page than Coleridge in two. The volumes before us contain so many integral efforts of imagination, that a distinct notice of each is indispensable, if we would form a just conclusion upon the total powers of the man. Wordsworth, Scott, Moore, Byron, Southey, are incomparably more uniform in the direction of their poetic mind. But

if you look over these volumes for indications of their author's poetic powers, you find him appearing in at least half a dozen shapes, so different from each other, that it is in vain to attempt to mass them together. It cannot indeed he said, that he has ever composed what is popularly termed a *great* poem; but he is great in several lines, and the union of such powers is an essential term in a fair estimate of his genius. The romantic witchery of the "Christabel," and "Ancient Mariner," the subtle passion of the love-strains, the lyrical splendour of the three great odes, the affectionate dignity, thoughtfulness, and delicacy of the blank verse poems—especially the "Lover's Resolution," "Frost at Midnight," and that most noble and interesting "Address to Mr. Wordsworth"—the dramas, the satires, the epigrams—these are so distinct and so whole in themselves, that they might seem to proceed from different authors, were it not for that same individualizing power, that "shaping spirit of imagination" which more or less sensibly runs through them all. It is the *predominance* of this power, which, in our judgment, constitutes the essential difference between Coleridge and any other of his great contemporaries. . . .

WILLIAM WORDSWORTH

REVIEWS OF HIS WORKS

I

The Gentleman's Magazine. Vol. LXIV, pp. 252–53. March, 1794.[1]

> *An Evening Walk, an Epistle to a Young Lady, from the Lakes of the North of England.* By W. Wordsworth, *A.B. of St.* John's *College,* Cambridge.
>
> *Reviewed by a Travelling Correspondent.*

Mr. Urban,

Penrith, Sept. 6.

On my arrival at this place, after having just compleated a tour of the Lakes, I chanced yesterday to meet with Mr. Wordsworth's poem. I have read it through carefully more than

[1] Wordsworth's first publications appeared in 1793. One bore the title *An Evening Walk,* the other *Descriptive Sketches.* We include this review because of its interest, not because of its

once; and, finding myself much pleased with it, not only as a poem in the abstract, but more particularly as a companion of the traveller who knows how to feel and estimate the real beauties of Nature, and, at the same time, is not averse to the children of the Muse; I know not how I can better repay to these delightful vales the very large debt of pleasure I owe them, than by attempting farther to extend the prevalence of their charms, by recommending this poem to the attention of their several visitants.

Of the author of this poem the only knowledge I can boast is that of having seen him once or twice while I was his contemporary at Cambridge. The only time, indeed, that I have a clear recollection of having met him, I remember his speaking very highly in praise of the beauties of the North; with a warmth indeed which, at that time, appeared to me hardly short of enthusiasm. He mentioned too, which appears also from the present poem, that he had received the whole of his education

priority over the more negative comment in the *Monthy Review*, XII, pp. 216–18, October, 1793. A still earlier critique has been pointed out by James R. McGillivray in *Modern Language Notes*, Vol. XLV, pp. 387–88, June, 1930. This article appeared in the *Analytical Review* for March, 1793, and may well be the first review of Wordsworth's poetry. Of the *Descriptive Sketches* it said, "The diversified pictures of nature which are sketched in this poem, could only have been produced by a lively imagination, furnished by actual and attentive observation with an abundant store of materials. The majestic grandeur of mountains, the rich and varied scenery of lakes and vallies, the solemn gloom of ruined monasteries and abbeys, and the different aspect of Alpine scenes in the morning and evening, during a storm, and in other atmospherical changes, are described with studied variety of imagery; the piece is occasionally enlivened with human figures, and the whole is rendered instructive by the frequent introduction of moral reflections. At the same time we must own, that this poem is on the whole less interesting than the subject led us to expect; owing in part, we believe, to the want of a general thread of narrative to connect the several descriptions, or of some episodical tale, to vary the impression; and in part also to a certain laboured and artificial cast of expression, which often involves the poet's meaning in obscurity. . . .

"This descriptive poem is so nearly of the same character with the preceding, that it is only necessary to remark in general, that it affords distinct and circumstantial views of nature, both inanimate and animate, which discover the eye of a diligent observer, and the hand of an able copyist of nature." . . .

in the very bosom of the Lakes, at a small seminary, which has produced of late years in our University several names which have done it very considerable credit.

After giving a short characteristic sketch of the principal Lakes, he concludes the enumeration with that of Esthwaite, the name of the one which adorns the sweet vale,

> where *he* taught, a happy child,
> The echoes of the rocks *his* carols wild.

After some beautiful and pathetic lines which contrast his present with his former wanderings,

> When link'd with thoughtless mirth *he* cours'd
> the plain,
> And hope itself was all *he* knew of pain,

he checks his complaints, and proceeds thus,

> Say, will my friend, with soft affection's ear,
> The hist'ry of a poet's evening hear?

Afterwards succeeds a very accurate and well-marked description of a sultry summer's noon, and a waterfall, which, as a note informs us, is meant to convey the features of that delicious little scene, the lower cascade at Rydal, where he hides himself

> Till eve's mild hour invites his steps abroad.

Among the several particulars of his Walk your readers will admire the following description of a slate quarry: [Lines 7–18, page 5 of Everyman's edition are quoted.]

I am unwilling to trouble you much with quotations, otherwise I should be tempted to transcribe Mr. Wordsworth's spirited description of the cock, or his very elegant one of the swan, and the tale of the beggar which succeeds it. You will excuse me, however, if, farther to justify the good opinion I have conceived of this poem, I request your insertion of the following description of the Northern lights, and that of night which succeeds it: [Lines 7–40, page 10, and lines 1–16 of page 11 of Everyman's edition are quoted.]

Of this poem I have yet seen no review. I wish the pleasure, which I myself have received from it, to be imparted to others who shall have to make, or who have already made, the same tour. Lest, however, any one should be tempted to look into this poem by my recommendation and find himself disappointed, I much forewarn your readers that no description of particular spots is here aimed at; such an attempt in poetry could have been productive of little but vague, uninteresting, description, and tiresome repetition: they will find, however, the general imagery of the country enumerated and described with a spirit and elegance which prove that the author has viewed nature with the attentive and warm regard of a true poet. Feeling for the credit of my own University, I think we have reason to expect much from this, I suppose, first production (though by no means a faultless one) of Mr. W's muse; I trust he will restore to us that laurel to which, since Gray laid down "his head upon the lap of earth," and Mason "declined into the vale of years," we have had so slight pretensions. From the concluding page of this poem I am glad to find it not the only offspring of Mr. Wordsworth's pen; he there advertises "Descriptive Sketches taken during a pedestrian Tour in the Alps."

PEREGRINATOR.

II

The Edinburgh Review. Vol. 1, No. 1, pp. 63–83. October, 1802.

Thalaba, the Destroyer: A Metrical Romance. By Robert Southey. 2 vols. 12mo. London.

Reviewer: Francis Jeffrey.

POETRY has this much, at least, in common with religion, that its standards were fixed long ago, by certain inspired writers, whose authority it is no longer lawful to call in question; and that many profess to be entirely devoted to it, who have no *good works* to produce in support of their pretensions. The catholic poetical church, too, has worked but few miracles since the first ages of its establishment; and has been more prolific, for a long time, of Doctors, than of Saints: it has had its corruptions and reformation also, and has given birth to an infinite variety of heresies and errors, the followers of which have hated and persecuted each other as cordially as other bigots.

The author who is now before us, belongs to a *sect* of poets, that has established itself in this country within these ten or twelve years, and is looked upon, we believe, as one of its chief champions and apostles. The peculiar doctrines of this sect, it would not, perhaps, be very easy to explain; but, that they are *dissenters* from the established systems in poetry and criticism, is admittted, and proved indeed, by the whole tenor of their compositions. Though they lay claim, we believe, to a creed and a revelation of their own, there can be little doubt, that their doctrines are of *German* origin, and have been derived from some of the great modern reformers in that country. Some of their leading principles, indeed, are probably of an earlier date, and seem to have been borrowed from the great apostle of Geneva. . . .

The disciples of this school boast much of its originality, and seem to value themselves very highly, for having broken loose from the bondage of ancient authority, and re-asserted the independence of genius. Originality, however, we are persuaded, is rarer than mere alteration; and a man may change a good master for a bad one, without finding himself at all nearer to independence. That our new poets have abandoned the old models, may certainly be admitted; but we have not been able to discover that they have yet created any models of their own; and are very much inclined to call in question the worthiness of those to which they have transferred their admiration. The productions of this school, we conceive, are so far from being entitled to the praise of originality, that they cannot be better characterised, than by an enumeration of the sources from which their materials have been derived. The greater part of them, we apprehend, will be found to be composed of the following elements: 1. The antisocial principles, and distempered sensibility of Rousseau—his discontent with the present constitution of society—his paradoxical morality, and his perpetual hankerings after some unattainable state of voluptuous virtue and perfection. 2. The simplicity and energy (*horresco referens*) of Kotzebue and Schiller. 3. The homeliness and harshness of some of Cowper's language and versification, interchanged occasionally with the *innocence* of Ambrose Philips, or the quaintness of Quarles and Dr. Donne. From the diligent study of these few originals, we have no doubt that an entire art of poetry may be collected, by the assistance of which, the very *gentlest* of our readers may soon be qualified to compose a poem as correctly versified as Thalaba, and to deal out sentiment and description, with all the sweetness of Lambe, and all the magnificence of Coleridge.

The authors, of whom we are now speaking, have, among them, unquestionably, a very considerable portion of poetical talent, and have, consequently, been enabled to seduce many into an admiration of the false taste (as it appears to us) in which most of their productions are composed. They constitute, at present, the most formidable conspiracy that has lately been formed against sound judgment in matters poetical; and are entitled to a larger share of our censorial notice, than could be spared for an individual delinquent. We shall hope for the indulgence of our readers, therefore, in taking this opportunity to inquire a little more particularly into their merits, and to make a few remarks upon those peculiarities which seem to be regarded by their admirers as the surest proofs of their excellence.

Their most distinguishing symbol, is undoubtedly an affectation of great simplicity and familiarity of language. They disdain to make use of the common poetical phraseology, or to ennoble their diction by a selection of fine or dignified expressions. There would be too much *art* in this, for that great love of nature with which they are all of them inspired; and their sentiments, they are determined shall be indebted, for their effect, to nothing but their intrinsic tenderness or elevation. There is something very noble and conscientious, we will confess, in this plan of composition; but the misfortune is, that there are passages in all poems, that can neither be pathetic nor sublime; and that, on these occasions, a neglect of the embellishments of language is very apt to produce absolute meanness and insipidity. The language of passion, indeed, can scarcely be deficient in elevation and when an author is wanting in that particular, he may commonly be presumed to have failed in the truth, as well as in the dignity of his expression. The case, however, is extremely different with the subordinate parts of a composition; with the narrative and description, that are necessary to preserve its connection; and the explanation, that must frequently prepare us for the great scenes and splendid passage. In these, all the requisite ideas may be conveyed, with sufficient clearness, by the meanest and most negligent expressions; and if magnificence or beauty is ever to be observed in them, it must have been introduced from some other motive than that of adapting the style to the subject. It is in such passages, accordingly, that we are most frequently offended with low and inelegant expressions; and that the language, which was intended to be simple and natural, is found oftenest to degenerate into mere slovenliness and vulgarity. It is in vain, too, to expect that the meanness of those parts may be redeemed by the excellence of others. A poet, who aims at all at sublimity or pathos, is like an actor in a high tragic character, and must sustain his dignity throughout, or become altogether ridiculous. We are apt enough to laugh at the mock-majesty of those whom we know to be but common mortals in private; and cannot permit Hamlet to make use of a single provincial intonation, although it should only be in his conversation with the grave-diggers.

The followers of simplicity are, therefore, at all times in danger of occasional degradation; but the simplicity of this new school seems intended to ensure it. *Their* simplicity does not consist, by any means, in the rejection of glaring or superfluous ornament,—in the substitution of elegance to splendour, or in that refinement of art which seeks concealment in its own perfection. It consists, on the contrary, in a very great degree, in the positive and *bona fide* rejection of art altogether, and in the bold use of those rude and negligent expressions, which would be banished by a little discrimination. One of their own authors, indeed, has very ingeniously set forth, (in a kind of manifesto that preceded one of their most flagrant acts of hostility), that it was their capital object "to adapt to the uses of poetry, the ordinary language of conversation among the middling and lower orders of the people." What advantages are to be gained by the success of this project, we confess ourselves unable to conjecture. The language of the higher and more cultivated orders may fairly be presumed to be better than that of their inferiors: at any rate, it has all those associations in its favour, by means of which, a style can never [sic] appear beautiful or exalted, and is adapted to the purposes of poetry, by having been long consecrated to its use. The language of the vulgar, on the other hand, has all the opposite associations to contend with; and must seem unfit for poetry, (if there were no other reason), merely because it has scarcely even been employed in it. A great genius may indeed overcome these disadvantages; but we can scarcely conceive that he should court them. We may excuse a certain homeliness of language in the productions of a ploughman or a milkwoman; but we cannot bring ourselves to admire it in an author, who has had occasion to indite odes to his college bell, and inscribe hymns to the Penates.

But the mischief of this new system is not confined to the depravation of language only; it extends to the sentiments and emotions, and leads to the debasement of all those feelings which poetry is designed to communicate. It is absurd to suppose, that an author should make use of the language of the vulgar, to express the sentiments of the refined. His professed object, in employing that language, is to bring his compositions nearer to the true standard of nature; and his intention to copy the sentiments of the lower orders, is implied in his resolution to make use of their style. Now, the different classes of society have each of them a distinct character, as well as a separate idiom; and the names of the various passions to which they are subject respectively, have a signification that varies essentially according to the condition of the persons to whom they are applied. The love, or grief, or indignation of an enlightened and refined character, is not only expressed in a different language, but is in itself a different emotion from the love, or grief, or anger, of a clown, a tradesman, or a market-wench. The things themselves are radically and obviously distinct; and the representation of them is calculated to convey a very different train of sympathies and sensations to the mind. The question, therefore, comes simply to be—which of them is the most proper object for poetical imitation? It is needless for us to answer a question, which the practice of all the world has long ago decided irrevocably. The poor and vulgar may interest us, in poetry, by their *situation;* but never, we apprehend, by any sentiments that are peculiar to their condition, and still less by any language that is characteristic of it. The truth is, that it is impossible to copy their diction or their sentiments correctly, in a serious composition; and this, not merely because poverty makes men ridiculous, but because just taste and refined sentiment are rarely to be met with among the uncultivated part of mankind; and a language, fitted for their expression, can still more rarely form any part of their "ordinary conversation." . . .

The *style* of our modern poets, is that, no doubt, by which they are most easily distinguished: but their genius has also an internal character; and the peculiarities of their taste may be discovered, without the assistance of their diction. Next after great familiarity of language, there is nothing that appears to them so meritorious as perpetual exaggeration of thought. There must be nothing moderate, natural, or easy, about their sentiments. There must be a "qu'il mourut," and a "let there be light," in every line; and all their characters must be in agonies and ecstasies, from their entrance to their exit. To those who are acquainted with their productions, it is needless to speak of the fatigue that is produced by this unceasing summons to admiration, or of the compassion which is excited by the spectacle of these eternal strainings and distortions. Those authors appear to forget, that a whole poem cannot be made up of striking passages; and that the sensations produced by sublimity, are never so powerful and entire, as when they are allowed to subside and revive, in a slow and spontaneous succession. It is delightful, now and then, to meet with a rugged mountain, or a roaring stream; but where there is no sunny slope, nor shaded plain, to relieve them—where all is beetling cliff and yawning abyss, and the landscape presents nothing on every side but prodigies and terrors—the head is apt to grow giddy, and the heart to languish for the repose and security of a less elevated region. . . .

The qualities of style and imagery, however, form but a small part of the characteristics by which a literary faction is to be distinguished. The subject and object of their compositions, and the principles and opinions they are calculated to support, constitute a far more imporant criterion, and one to which it is usually altogether as easy to refer. Some poets are sufficiently described as the flatterers of greatness and power, and others as the champions of independence. One set of writers is known by its antipathy to decency and religion; another, by its methodistical cant and intolerance. Our new school of poetry has a moral character also; though it may not be possible, perhaps, to delineate it quite so concisely.

A splenetic and idle discontent with the existing institutions of society, seems to be at the bottom of all their serious and peculiar sentiments. Instead of contemplating the wonders and the pleasures which civilization has created for mankind, they are perpetually brooding over the disorders by which its progress has been attended. They are filled with horror and compassion at the sight of poor men spending their blood in the quarrels of princes, and brutifying their sublime capabilities in the drudgery of unremitting labour. For all sorts of vice and profligacy in the lower orders of society, they have the same virtuous horror, and the same tender compassion. While the existence of these offences overpowers them with grief and confusion, they never permit themselves to feel the smallest indignation or dislike towards the offenders. The present vicious constitution of society alone is responsible for all these enormities: the poor sinners are but the helpless victims or instruments of its disorders, and could not possibly have avoided the errors into which they have been betrayed. Though they can bear with crimes, therefore, they cannot reconcile themselves to punishments; and have an unconquerable antipathy to prisons, gibbets, and house of correction, as engines of oppression, and instruments of attrocious injustice. While the plea of moral necessity is thus artfully brought forward to convert all the excesses of the poor into innocent misfortunes, no sort of indulgence is shown to the offences of the powerful and rich. Their oppressions, and seductions, and debaucheries, are the theme of many an angry verse; and the indignation and abhorrence of the reader is relentlessly conjured up against those perturbators of society, and scourges of mankind.

It is not easy to say, whether the fundamental absurdity of this doctrine, or the partiality of its application, be entitled to the severest reprehension. If men are driven to commit crimes, through a certain moral necessity; other men are compelled, by a similar necessity, to hate and despise them for their commission. The indignation of the sufferer is at least as natural as the guilt of him who makes him suffer; and the good order of society would probably be as well preserved, if our sympathies were sometimes called forth in behalf of the former. At all events, the same apology ought certainly to be admitted for the wealthy, as for the needy offender. They are subject alike to the overruling influence of necessity, and equally affected by the miserable condition of society. If it be natural for a poor man to murder and rob, in order to make himself comfortable, it is no less natural for a rich man to gormandize and domineer, in order to have the full use of his riches. Wealth is just as valid an excuse for the one class of vices, as indigence is for the other. . . .

III

The Edinburgh Review. Vol. XI, No. XXI, pp. 214–231. October, 1807.

Poems, in Two Volumes. By William Wordsworth, *Author of the Lyrical Ballads.* 8vo. pp. 320. London, 1807.

Reviewer: Francis Jeffrey.

THIS author is known to belong to a certain brotherhood of poets, who have haunted for some years about the Lakes of Cumberland; and is generally looked upon, we believe, as the purest model of the excellences and peculiarities of the school which they have been labouring to establish. Of the general merits of that school, we have had occasion to express our opinion pretty fully, in more places than one, and even to make some allusion to the former publications of the writer now before us. We are glad, however, to have found an opportunity of attending somewhat more particularly to his pretensions.

The Lyrical Ballads were unquestionably popular; and, we have no hesitation in saying, deservedly popular; for in spite of their occasional vulgarity, affectation, and silliness, they were undoubtedly characterised by a strong spirit of originality, of pathos, and natural feeling; and recommended to all good minds by the clear impression which they bore of the amiable dispositions and virtuous principles of the author. By the help of these qualities, they were enabled, not only to recommend themselves to the indulgence of many judicious readers, but even to beget among a pretty numerous class of persons, a sort of admiration of the very defects by which they were attended. It was upon this account chiefly, that we thought it necessary to set ourselves against this alarming innovation. Childishness, conceit, and affectation, are not of themselves very popular or attractive; and though mere novelty has sometimes been found sufficient to give them a temporary currency, we should have had no fear of their prevailing to any dangerous extent, if they had been graced with no more seductive accompaniments. It was precisely because the perverseness and bad taste of this new school was combined with a great deal of genius and of laudable feeling, that we were afraid of their spreading and gaining ground among us, and that we entered into the discussion with a degree of zeal and animosity which some might think unreasonable towards authors, to whom so much merit had been conceded. There are times and moods indeed, in which we were led to suspect ourselves of unjustifiable severity, and to doubt, whether a sense of public duty had not carried us rather too far in reprobation of errors, that seemed to be atoned for, by excellences of no vulgar description. At other times, the magnitude of these errors—the disgusting absurdities into which they led their feebler admirers, and the derision and contempt which they drew from the more fastidious, even upon the merits with which they were associated, made us wonder more than ever at the perversity by which they were retained, and regret that we had not declared ourselves against them with still more formidable and decided hostility. . . .

Mr Wordsworth, we think, has now brought the question, as to the merit of his new school of poetry, to a very fair and decisive issue. The volumes before us are much more strongly marked by all its peculiarities than any former publication of the fraternity. In our apprehension, they are, on this very account, infinitely less interesting or meritorious; but it belongs to the public, and not to us, to decide upon their merit, and we will confess, that so strong is our conviction of their obvious inferiority, and the grounds of it, that we are willing for once to wave our right of appealing to posterity, and to take the judgment of the present generation of readers, and even of Mr Wordsworth's former admirers, as conclusive on this occasion. If these volumes, which have all the benefit of the author's former popularity, turn out to be nearly as popular as the lyrical ballads—if they sell nearly to the same extent —or are quoted and imitated among half as many individuals, we shall admit that Mr Wordsworth has come much nearer the truth in his judgment of what constitutes the charm of poetry, than we had previously imagined— and shall institute a more serious and respectful inquiry into his principles of composition than we have yet thought necessary. On the other hand,—if this little work, selected from the compositions of five maturer years, and written avowedly for the purpose of exalting a system, which has already excited a good deal of attention, should be generally rejected by those whose prepossessions were in its favour, there is room to hope, not only that the system itself will meet with no more encouragement, but even that the author will be persuaded to abandon a plan of writing, which defrauds his industry and talents of their natural reward. . . .

We shall not resume any of the particular discussions by which we formerly attempted to ascertain the value of the improvements which this new school has effected in poetry; but shall lay the grounds of our opposition, for this time, a little more broadly. The end of poetry, we take it, is to please—and the name, we think, is strictly applicable to every metrical composition from which we receive pleasure, without any laborious exercise of the understanding. This pleasure, may, in general, be analyzed into three parts—that which we receive from the excitement of Passion or emotion—that which is derived from the play of Imagination, or the easy exercise of Reason —and that which depends on the character and qualities of the Diction. The two first are the vital and primary springs of poetical delight, and can scarcely require explanation to any one. The last has been alternately overrated and undervalued by the professors of the poetical art, and is in such low estimation with the author now before us and his associates, that it is necessary to say a few words in explanation of it. . . .

From this great source of pleasure, we think the readers of Mr Wordsworth are in a great measure cut off. His diction has no where any pretensions to elegance or dignity; and he has scarcely ever condescended to give the grace of correctness or melody to his versification. If it were merely slovenly and neglected, however, all this might be endured. Strong sense and powerful feeling will ennoble any expressions; or, at least, no one who is capable of estimating those higher merits, will be disposed to mark these little defects. But, in good truth, no man, now-a-days, composes verses for publication with a slovenly neglect of their language. It is a fine and laborious manufacture, which can scarcely ever be made in a hurry; and the faults which it has, may, for the most part, be set down to bad taste or incapacity, rather than to carelessness or oversight. With Mr Wordsworth and his friends, it is plain that their peculiarities of diction are things of choice, and not of accident. They write as they do, upon principle and system; and it evidently costs them much pains to keep *down* to the standard which they have proposed to themselves. They are, to the full, as much mannerists, too, as the poetasters who ring changes on the common-places of magazine versification; and all the difference between them is, that they borrow their phrases from a different and a scantier *gradus ad Parnassum*. If they were, indeed, to discard all imitation and set phraseology, and to bring in no words merely for show or for metre,—as much, perhaps, might be gained in freedom and originality, as would infallibly be lost in allusion and authority; but, in point of fact, the new poets are just as great borrowers as the old; only that, instead of borrowing from the more popular passages of their illustrious predecessors, they have preferred furnishing themselves from vulgar ballads and plebeian nurseries.

Their peculiarities of diction alone, are enough, perhaps, to render them ridiculous; but the author before us really seems anxious to court this literary martyrdom by a device still more infallible,—we mean, that of connecting his most lofty, tender, or impassioned conceptions, with objects and incidents, which the greater part of his readers will probably persist in thinking low, silly, or uninteresting. Whether this is done from affectation and conceit alone, or whether it may not arise, in some measure, from the self-illusion of a mind of extraordinary sensibility, habituated to solitary meditation, we cannot undertake to determine. It is possible enough, we allow, that the sight of a friend's garden-spade, or a sparrow's nest, or a man gathering leeches, might really have suggested to such a mind a train of powerful impressions and interesting reflections; but it is certain, that, to most minds, such associations will always appear forced, strained, and unnatural; and that the composition in which it is attempted to exhibit them, will always have the air of parody, or ludicrous and affected singularity. All the world laughs at Elegiac stanzas to a sucking-pig—a Hymn on Washing-day——Sonnets to one's grandmother—or Pindarics on gooseberry-pye; and yet, we are afraid, it will not be quite easy to convince Mr Wordsworth, that the same ridicule must infallibly attach to most of the pathetic pieces in these volumes. . . .

IV

The Edinburgh Review, Vol. XXIV, No. XLVII, pp. 1–31. November, 1814.

The Excursion, being a portion of the Recluse, a Poem. By William Wordsworth. 4to. pp. 447. London, 1814.

Reviewer: Francis Jeffrey.

THIS will never do. It bears no doubt the stamp of the author's heart and fancy; but unfortunately not half so visibly as that of his peculiar system. His former poems were intended to recommend that system, and to bespeak favour for it by their individual merit;—but this, we suspect, must be recommended by the system—and can only expect to succeed where it has been previously established. It is longer, weaker, and tamer, than any of Mr Wordsworth's other productions; with less boldness of originality, and less even of that extreme simplicity and lowliness of tone which wavered so prettily, in the Lyrical Ballads, between silliness and pathos. We have imitations of Cowper, and even of Milton here, engrafted on the natural drawl of the Lakers—and all diluted into harmony by that profuse and irrepressible wordiness which deluges all the blank verse of this school of poetry, and lubricates and weakens the whole structure of their style.

Though it fairly fills four hundred and twenty good quarto pages, without note, vignette, or any sort of extraneous assistance, it is stated in the title—with something of an imprudent candour—to be but "a portion" of a larger work; and in the preface, where an attempt is rather unsuccessfully made to explain the whole design, it is still more rashly disclosed, that it is but "a part of the second part of a *long* and laborious work"—which is to consist of three parts.

What Mr Wordsworth's ideas of length are, we have no means of accurately judging; but we cannot help suspecting that they are liberal, to a degree that will alarm the weakness of most modern readers. As far as we can gather from the preface, the entire poem—or one of them, for we really are not sure whether there is to be one or two—is of a biographical nature; and is to contain the history of the author's mind, and of the origin and progress of his poetical powers, up to the period when they were sufficiently matured to qualify him for the great work on which he has been so long employed. Now, the quarto before us contains an account of one of his youthful rambles in the vales of Cumberland, and occupies precisely the period of three days; so that, by the use of a very powerful *calculus*, some estimate may be formed of the probable extent of the entire biography.

This small specimen, however, and the statements with which it is prefaced, have been sufficient to set our minds at rest in one particular. The case of Mr Wordsworth, we perceive, is now manifestly hopeless; and we give him up as altogether incurable, and beyond the power of criticism. We cannot indeed altogether omit taking precautions now and then against the spreading of the malady;—but for himself, though we shall watch the progress of his symptoms as a matter of professional curiosity and instruction, we really think it right not to harass him any longer with nauseous remedies,—but rather to throw in cordials and lenitives, and wait in patience for the natural termination of the disorder. In order to justify this desertion of our patient, however, it is proper to state why we despair of the success of a more active practice.

A man who has been for twenty years at work on such matter as is now before us, and who comes complacently forward with a whole quarto of it after all the admonitions he has received, cannot reasonably be expected to "change his hand, or check his pride," upon the suggestion of far weightier monitors than we can pretend to be. Inveterate habit must now have given a kind of sanctity to the errors of early taste; and the very powers of which we lament the perversion, have probably become incapable of any other application. The

very quantity, too, that he has written, and is at this moment working up for publication upon the old pattern, makes it almost hopeless to look for any change of it. All this is so much capital already sunk in the concern; which must be sacrificed if it be abandoned: and no man likes to give up for lost the time and talent and labour which he has embodied in any permanent production. We were not previously aware of these obstacles to Mr Wordsworth's conversion; and, considering the peculiarities of his former writings merely as the result of certain wanton and capricious experiments on public taste and indulgence, conceived it to be our duty to discourage their repetition by all the means in our power. We now see clearly, however, how the case stands; —and, making up our minds, though with the most sincere pain and reluctance, to consider him as finally lost to the good cause of poetry, shall endeavour to be thankful for the occasional gleams of tenderness and beauty which the natural force of his imagination and affections must still shed over all his productions, —and to which we shall ever turn with delight, in spite of the affectation and mysticism and prolixity, with which they are so abundantly contrasted.

Long habits of seclusion, and an excessive ambition of originality, can alone account for the disproportion which seems to exist between this author's taste and his genius; or for the devotion with which he has sacrificed so many precious gifts at the shrine of those paltry idols which he has set up for himself among his lakes and his mountains. Solitary musings, amidst such scenes, might no doubt be expected to nurse up the mind to the majesty of poetical conception,—(though it is remarkable, that all the greater poets lived, or had lived, in the full current of society):—But the collision of equal minds,—the admonition of prevailing impressions—seems necessary to reduce its redundancies, and repress that tendency to extravagance or puerility, into which the self-indulgence and self-admiration of genius is so apt to be betrayed, when it is allowed to wanton, without awe or restraint, in the triumph and delight of its own intoxication. That its flights should be graceful and glorious in the eyes of men, it seems almost to be necessary that they should be made in the consciousness that mens' eyes are to behold them,—and that the inward transport and vigour by which they are inspired, should be tempered by an occassional [*sic*] reference to what will be thought of them by those ultimate dispensers of glory. An habitual and general knowledge of the few settled and permanent maxims, which form the canon of general taste in all large and polished societies—a certain tact, which informs us at once that many things, which we still love and are moved by in secret, must necessarily be despised as childish, or derided as absurd, in all such societies—though it will not stand in the place of genius, seems necessary to the success of its exertions; and though it will never enable any one to produce the higher beauties of art, can alone secure the talent which does produce them, from errors that must render it useless. Those who have most of the talent, however, commonly acquire this knowledge with the greatest facility;—and if Mr Wordsworth, instead of confining himself almost entirely to the society of the dalesmen and cottagers, and little children, who form the subjects of his book, had condescended to mingle a little more with the people that were to read and judge of it, we cannot help thinking, that its texture would have been considerably improved: At least it appears to us to be absolutely impossible, that any one who had lived or mixed familiarly with men of literature and ordinary judgment in poetry, (of course we exclude the coadjustors and disciples of his own school), could ever have fallen into such gross faults, or so long mistaken them for beauties. His first essays we looked upon in a good degree as poetical paradoxes,—maintained experimentally, in order to display talent, and court notoriety;—and so maintained, with no more serious belief in their truth, than is usually generated by an ingenious and animated defence of other paradoxes. But when we find, that he has been for twenty years exclusively employed upon articles of this very fabric, and that he has still enough of raw material on hand to keep him so employed for twenty years to come, we cannot refuse him the justice of believing that he is a sincere convert to his own system, and must ascribe the peculiarities of his composition, not to any transient affectation, or accidental caprice of imagination, but to a settled perversity of taste or understanding, which has been fostered, if not altogether created, by the circumstances to which we have already alluded.

The volume before us, if we were to describe it very shortly, we should characterize as a tissue of moral and devotional ravings, in which innumerable changes are rung upon a few very simple and familiar ideas:—but with such an accompaniment of long words, long sentences, and unwieldly phrases—and such a hubbub of strained raptures and fantastical sublimities, that it is often extremely difficult for the most skilful and attentive student to obtain a glimpse of the author's meaning—and altogether impossible for an ordinary reader to conjecture what he is about. Moral and religious enthusiasm, though undoubtedly poetical emotions, are at the same time but dangerous inspirers of poetry; nothing being so apt to run into interminable dulness or mellifluous extravagance, without giving the unfortunate author the slightest intimation of his danger. His laudable zeal for the efficacy of his preachments, he very naturally mistakes for the ardour of poetical inspiration;—and, while dealing out the high words and glowing phrases which are so readily supplied by themes of this description, can scarcely avoid believing that he is eminently original and impressive:—All sorts of commonplace notions and expressions are sanctified in his eyes, by the sublime ends for which they are employed; and the mystical verbiage of the methodist pulpit is repeated, till the speaker entertains no doubt that he is the elected organ of divine truth and persuasion. But if such be the common hazards of seeking inspiration from those potent fountains, it may easily be conceived what chance Mr Wordsworth had of escaping their enchantment,—with his natural propensities to wordiness, and his unlucky habit of debasing pathos with vulgarity. The fact accordingly is, that in this production he is more obscure than a Pindaric poet of the seventeenth century; and more verbose "than even himself of yore;" while the wilfulness with which he persists in choosing his examples of intellectual dignity and tenderness exclusively from the lowest ranks of society, will be sufficiently apparent, from the circumstance of his having thought fit to make his chief prolocutor in this poetical dialogue, and chief advocate of Providence and Virtue, *an old Scotch Pedlar*—retired indeed from business—but still rambling about in his former haunts, and gossiping among his old customers, without his pack on his shoulders. The other persons of the drama are, a retired military chaplain, who has grown half an atheist and half a misanthrope—the wife of an unprosperous weaver—a servant girl with her infant—a parish pauper, and one or two other personages of equal rank and dignity.

The character of the work is decidedly di- 5 dactic; and more than nine tenths of it are occupied with a species of dialogue, or rather a series of long sermons or harangues which pass between the pedlar, the author, the old chaplain, and a worthy vicar, who entertains 10 the whole party at dinner on the last day of their excursion. The incidents which occur in the course of it are as few and trifling as can be imagined;—and those which the different speakers narrate in the course of their dis- 15 courses, are introduced rather to illustrate their arguments or opinions, than for any interest they are supposed to possess of their own.— The doctrine which the work is intended to enforce, we are by no means certain that we have 20 discovered. In so far as we can collect, however, it seems to be neither more nor less than the old familiar one, that a firm belief in the providence of a wise and beneficent Being must be our great stay and support under all afflic- 25 tions and perplexities upon earth—and that there are indications of his power and goodness in all the aspects of the visible universe, whether living or inanimate—every part of which should therefore be regarded with love 30 and reverence, as exponents of those great attributes. We can testify, at least, that these salutary and important truths are inculcated at far greater length, and with more repetitions, than in any ten volumes of sermons that we 35 ever perused. It is also maintained, with equal conciseness and originality, that there is frequently much good sense, as well as much enjoyment, in the humbler conditions of life; and that, in spite of great vices and abuses, there is 40 a reasonable allowance both of happiness and goodness in society at large. If there be any deeper or more recondite doctrines in Mr Wordsworth's book, we must confess that they have escaped us;—and, convinced as we are 45 of the truth and soundness of those to which we have alluded, we cannot help thinking that they might have been better enforced with less parade and prolixity. His effusions on what may be called the physiognomy of external 50 nature, or its moral and theological expression, are eminently fantastic, obscure, and affected. . . .

Nobody can be more disposed to do justice to the great powers of Mr Wordsworth than we are; and from the first time that he came before us, down to the present moment, we have uniformly testified in their favour, and assigned indeed our high sense of their value as the chief ground of the bitterness with which we resented their perversion. That perversion, however, is now far more visible than their original dignity; and while we collect the fragments it is impossible not to lament the ruins from which we are condemned to pick them. If any one should doubt of the existence of such a perversion, or be disposed to dispute about the instances we have hastily brought forward, we would just beg leave to refer him to the general plan and the characters of the poem now before us.—Why should Mr Wordsworth have made his hero a superannuated Pedlar? What but the most wretched and provoking perversity of taste and judgment, could induce any one to place his chosen advocate of wisdom and virtue in so absurd and fantastic a condition? Did Mr Wordsworth really imagine, that his favourite doctrines were likely to gain any thing in point of effect or authority by being put into the mouth of a person accustomed to higgle about tape, or brass sleeve-buttons? Or is it not plain that, independent of the ridicule and disgust which such a personification must give to many of his readers, its adoption exposes his work throughout to the charge of revolting incongruity, and utter disregard of probability or nature? For, after he has thus wilfully debased his moral teacher by a low occupation, is there one word that he puts into his mouth, or one sentiment of which he makes him the organ, that has the most remote reference to that occupation? Is there any thing in his learned, abstracted, and logical harangues, that savours of the calling that is ascribed to him? Are any of their materials such as a pedlar could possibly have dealt in? Are the manners, the diction, the sentiments, in any, the very smallest degree, accommodated to a person in that condition? or are they not eminently and conspicuously such as could not by possibility belong to it? A man who went about selling flannel and pocket-handkerchiefs in this lofty diction, would soon frighten away all his customers; and would infallibly pass either for a madman, or for some learned and affected gentleman who, in a frolic, had taken up a character which he was peculiarly ill qualified for supporting.

The absurdity in this case, we think, is palpable and glaring; but it is exactly of the same nature with that which infects the whole substance of the work—a puerile ambition of singularity engrafted on an unlucky predilection for truisms; and an affected passion for simplicity and humble life, most awkwardly combined with a taste for mystical refinements, and all the georgeousness of obscure phraseology. His taste for simplicity is evinced, by sprinkling up and down his interminable declamations, a few descriptions of baby-houses, and of old hats with wet brims; and his amiable partiality for humble life, by assuring us, that a wordy rhetorician, who talks about Thebes, and allegorizes all the heathen mythology, was once a pedlar—and making him break in upon his magnificent orations with two or three awkward notices of something that he had seen when selling winter raiment about the country—or of the changes in the state of society, which had almost annihilated his former calling.

V

The Quarterly Review. Vol. XII, No. XXIII, pp. 100–111. October, 1814.

The Excursion; a Poem. By William Wordsworth. London. 4to. pp. 447.

Reviewer: Charles Lamb.

. . . THE causes which have prevented the poetry of Mr. Wordsworth from attaining its full share of popularity are to be found in the boldness and originality of his genius. The times are past when a poet could securely follow the direction of his own mind into whatever tracts it might lead. A writer, who would be popular, must timidly coast the shore of prescribed sentiment and sympathy. He must have just as much more of the imaginative faculty than his readers, as will serve to keep their apprehensions from stagnating, but not so much as to alarm their jealousy. He must not think or feel too deeply.

If he had the fortune to be bred in the midst of the most magnificent objects of creation, he must not have given away his heart to them; or if he have, he must conceal his love, or not carry his expressions of it beyond that point of rapture, which the occasional tourist thinks it not overstepping decorum to betray, or the limit which that gentlemanly spy upon Nature, the picturesque traveller, has vouchsafed to countenance. He must do this, or be content to be thought an enthusiast.

If from living among simple mountaineers, from a daily intercourse with them, not upon the footing of a patron, but in the character of an equal, he has detected, or imagines that he has detected, through the cloudy medium of their unlettered discourse, thoughts and apprehensions not vulgar; traits of patience and constancy, love unwearied, and heroic endurance, not unfit (as he may judge) to be made the subject of verse, he will be deemed a man of perverted genius by the philanthropist who, conceiving of the peasantry of his country only as objects of a pecuniary sympathy, starts at finding them elevated to a level of humanity with himself, having their own loves, enmities, cravings, aspirations, &c., as much beyond his faculty to believe, as his beneficence to supply.

If from a familiar observation of the ways of children, and much more from a retrospect of his own mind when a child, he has gathered more reverential notions of that state than fall to the lot of ordinary observers, and, escaping from the dissonant wranglings of men, has tuned his lyre, though but for occasional harmonies, to the milder utterance of that soft age,—his verses shall be censured as infantile by critics who confound poetry "having children for its subject" with poetry that is "childish," and who, having themselves perhaps never been *children*, never having possessed the tenderness and docility of that age, know not what the soul of a child is—how apprehensive! how imaginative! how religious!

We have touched upon some of the causes which we conceive to have been unfriendly to the author's former poems. We think they do not apply in the same force to the one before us. There is in it more of uniform elevation, a wider scope of subject, less of manner, and it contains none of those starts and imperfect shapings which in some of this author's smaller pieces offend the weak, and gave scandal to the perverse. It must indeed be approached with seriousness. It has in it much of that quality which "draws the devout, deterring the profane." Those who hate the Paradise Lost will not love this poem. The steps of the great master are discernible in it; not in direct imitation or injurious parody, but in the followmg of the spirit, in free homage and generous subjection.

One objection it is impossible not to foresee. It will be asked, why put such eloquent discourse in the mouth of a pedlar? It might be answered that Mr. Wordsworth's plan required a character in humble life to be the organ of his philosophy. It was in harmony with the system and scenery of his poem. We read Pier's Plowman's Creed, and the lowness of the teacher seems to add a simple dignity to the doctrine. Besides, the poet has bestowed an unusual share of education upon him. Is it too much to suppose that the author, at some early period of his life, may himself have known such a person, a man endowed with sentiments above his situation, another Burns; and that the dignified strains which he has attributed to the Wanderer may be no more than recollections of his conversation, heightened only by the amplification natural to poetry, or the lustre which imagination flings back upon the objects and companions of our youth? After all, if there should be found readers willing to admire the poem, who yet feel scandalized at a *name*, we would advise them, wherever it occurs, to substitute silently the word *Palmer*, or *Pilgrim*, or any less offensive designation, which shall connect the notion of sobriety in heart and manners with the experience and privileges which a wayfaring life confers.

VI

The Quarterly Review. Vol. XIV, No. XXVII, pp. 201–225. October, 1815.

    1. *Poems by* William Wordsworth; *including Lyrical Ballads, and the Miscellaneous Pieces of the Author, with additional Poems, a New Preface, and a Supplementary Essay.* In two vols. London. 1815.
    2. *The White Doe of Rylstone; or, the Fate of the Nortons. A Poem. By* William Wordsworth. London. 1815.

Reviewer. William Rowe Lyall.—Ascribed to William Gifford by *Gent. Mag.*, Vol. XXI, p. 140, 1844.

    . . . AMONG those who are really qualified to judge for themselves in matters of taste, we think that one opinion only is entertained respecting the productions of Mr. Wordsworth, —that they exhibit a mind richly stored with all the materials from which poetry is formed; —elevation of sentiment—tenderness of heart —the truest sensibility for the beauties of nature—combined with extraordinary fervour of imagination, and a most praiseworthy love of simplicity both in thought and language. It would appear, however, upon a first view of the fact, that he has by no means turned these valuable endowments to their greatest advantage. If the business of the poet be to please, Mr. Wordsworth's endeavours have hitherto not met with the most flattering success. . . .

With regard to the style in which Mr. Wordsworth writes, we doubt whether it can be greatly praised. There is indeed a raciness about his language, and an occasional eloquence in his manner, which serve to keep the reader's attention alive. But these advantages are more than counteracted by that same intellectual straining after something beyond plain good sense, which is so unpleasant in much of his poetry. In other respects the comparison is in favour of the latter. Instead of that graceful softness of manner which forms so principal a charm in his poetic effusions, his prose is distinguished by a tone which, in any other person, we should feel ourselves called upon to treat with some little severity. For a writer to protest that he *prides* himself upon the disapprobation of his contemporaries, and considers it as an evidence of the originality of his genius, and an earnest of the esteem in which he will be held by succeeding generations, is whimsical enough, to say the least of it; but Mr. Wordsworth ought, at all events, to be consistent with himself; and since he derives so many auspicious assurances from the opposition which his opinions have met with, he should speak with a little more moderation of those by whom they happen to be opposed. He should remember, moreover, that the public, and those who profess to be the organs of the public voice in these matters, have at least as much right to dislike *his* poetical taste, as he has to dislike *theirs*. If he voluntarily steps forward to make an attack upon the latter, the burthen of proof rests clearly upon him: to be in an ill temper merely because his opponents will not at once surrender at discretion, is surely most unreasonable.

It appears to us, that whatever difference of opinion may be entertained respecting the peculiarities of Mr. Wordsworth's poetical compositions, we might admit, in nearly all their extent, the poetical doctrines which he wishes to introduce, without materially touching upon the questions about which the public are really at issue with him. For example, it is a prominent tenet with him that the *language and incidents of low and rustic life* are better fitted for the purposes of his art, than the language and incidents which we have hitherto been accustomed to meet with in poetry; [Quotes from vol. ii. p. 366.]

Now all this may be true, for aught that we know to the contrary; it may be very wrong, in a metaphysical point of view, for a person to have a predilection for other subjects; but the fact obviously is, that people do not resort to poetry for metaphysical instruction; and the question about which Mr. Wordsworth's readers are interested is, whether other subjects do not afford equal or superior pleasure, not whether they throw greater or less light upon the "elementary feelings," and "essential passions," and "primary laws of our nature." Let us suppose a person were to express a distaste for the subject of the poem, at vol. i. p. 328, upon a bed of daffodils; it would probably not at all alter his opinion to say that "the subject is an elementary feeling and simple impression (approaching to the nature of an ocular spectrum) upon the imaginative faculty;" nor will the pleasure which most readers will probably receive from the lines at vol. i. p. 297, with which the "Poems of the Imagination" are introduced, be at all augmented, by being told—what few would otherwise have guessed—that the poet was describing "a commutation, or transfer of internal feelings, cooperating with internal accidents, to plant for immortality images of sound and sight in the celestial soil of the imagination." How far poetry, upon the principles of Mr. Wordsworth, is capable of being made subservient to a metaphysical analysis of the human mind, is an inquiry which we apprehend to be quite foreign to our present purpose; the question about which the public are at issue with him is, whether the doctrines which he wishes to establish are likely to open purer or more copious sources of poetical delight than those at which his readers hitherto have drunk. . . .

But Mr. Wordsworth is an advocate, not only for the "incidents" of "low and rustic life," as better suited than any other for poetry, but also for its "language," which, on several accounts, he considers as being "a far more philosophical language than that which is frequently substituted for it by poets." Now, to talk of one language as being more *philosophical* than another, is, perhaps, not a very philosophical way of speaking; but be it as he supposes; still, we think, he will not deny, that the most convenient language, either for a poet or any other man to make use of, is that by which he can with most precision make himself understood by those to whom he addresses himself. Does our author then write for people in low and rustic life, or for people in high and educated life? If for the former, good; but if for the latter, surely to select a language in which, as he himself partly confesses, vol. ii. p. 390, he necessarily exposes himself to the danger of raising opposite ideas to those which he intended to convey, is paying to mere sounds (be they ever so philosophical) an homage which we can never be brought to believe that they deserve. . . .

But although we cannot bring ourselves to approve of Mr. Wordsworth's project for substituting the language of "low and rustic life" in place of that which we are accustomed to meet with in poetry; yet, in many respects, we feel pretty much disposed to coincide with him in disapproving of the latter. We think, with him, that the language of poetry ought to be language really used by men, and constructed upon the same principles as the language of prose. That this cannot be affirmed of that peculiar sort of diction technically called *poetical*, a slight inspection of the poetry which has prevailed in this country since the Restoration will, we think, sufficiently prove. How far Mr. Wordsworth's account of the origin and distinctive character of this artificial phraseology is just and satisfactory, we are, perhaps, not competent to decide; as far, however, as we were able to enter into his meaning, his observations upon the subject seemed in general well-grounded. . . .

It is impossible to take up the works of Mr. Wordsworth without remarking that, instead of employing his pen upon subjects of durable and general interest, he devotes himself almost exclusively to the delineation of himself and his own peculiar feelings, as called forth by objects incidental to the particular kind of life he leads. Now, although this be a plan apparently contrived to gratify the pleasure which poets, as our author tells us, take in their "own passions and volitions," rather than any curiosity which the reader, generally speaking, can be supposed to feel upon the subject, yet, in common cases, it is productive of no very *positive* inconvenience. Poets, as well as other people, feel, for the most part, pretty much alike; so that what is true with respect to any individual, will commonly be true with respect to mankind at large, under the same circumstances. As long as the feelings of the poet are founded on such occasions as ordinarily give rise to them, although the subjects of his effusions may be particular, yet the interest and the application of them will be, to a great degree, general. But the fact is, that the habits of Mr. Wordsworth's life are not more different from those of people in general, than are the habits of his mind; so that not only the incidents which form the subjects of his poetry are such as the greater part of his readers take much less interest in, than he imagines, but the feelings, moreover, with which he usually contemplates them are often such as hardly any person whatever can participate. . . .

All we can say is, that whenever Mr. Wordsworth's own flights are through "the region" of truth and nature, and sober sense, we accompany him with pleasure; but when he penetrates into the *terra Australis* beyond, then, indeed, our inclination to continue of the party, as well as our ability, leaves us. . . .

VII

The Edinburgh Review. Vol. XXV, No. L, pp. 355–363. October, 1815.

The White Doe of Rylstone; or the Fate of the Nortons: a Poem. By William Wordsworth. 4to. pp. 162. London, 1815.

Reviewer: Francis Jeffrey.

THIS, we think, has the merit of being the very worst poem we ever saw imprinted in a quarto volume; and though it was scarcely to be expected, we confess, that Mr Wordsworth, with all his ambition, should so soon have attained to that distinction, the wonder may perhaps be diminished, when we state, that is seems to us to consist of a happy union of all the faults, without any of the beauties, which belong to his school of poetry. It is just such a work, in short, as some wicked enemy of that school might be supposed to have devised, on purpose to make it ridiculous; and when we first took it up, we could not help fancying that some ill-natured critic had taken this harsh method of instructing Mr Wordsworth, by example, in the nature of those errors, against which our precepts had been so often directed in vain. We had not gone far, however, till we felt intimately, that nothing in the nature of a joke could be so insupportably dull;—and that this must be the work of one who honestly believed it to be a pattern of pathetic simplicity, and gave it out as such to the admiration of all intelligent readers. In this point of view, the work may be regarded as curious at least, if not in some degree interesting; and, at all events, it must be instructive to be made aware of the excesses into which superior understandings may be betrayed, by long self-indulgence, and the strange extravagances into which they may run, when under the influence of that intoxication which is produced by unrestrained admiration of themselves. This poetical intoxication, indeed, to pursue the figure a little farther, seems capable of assuming as many forms as the vulgar one which arises from wine; and it appears to require as delicate a management to make a man a good poet by the help of the one, as to make him a good companion by means of the other. In both cases, a little mistake as to the dose or the quality of the inspiring fluid may make him absolutely outrageous, or lull him over into the most profound stupidity, instead of brightening up the hidden stores of his genius: And truly we are concerned to say, that Mr Wordsworth seems hitherto to have been unlucky in the choice of his liquor—or of his bottle holder. In some of his odes and ethic exhortations, he was exposed to the public in a state of incoherent rapture and glorious delirium, to which we think we have seen a parallel among the humbler lovers of jollity. In the Lyrical Ballads, he was exhibited, on the whole, in a vein of very pretty deliration; but in the poem before us, he appears in a state of low and maudlin imbecility, which would not have misbecome Master Silence himself, in the close of a social day. Whether this unhappy result is to be ascribed to any adulteration of his Castalian cups, or to the unlucky choice of his company over them, we cannot presume to say. It may be, that he has dashed his Hippocrene with too large an infusion of lake water, or assisted its operation too exclusively by the study of the ancient historical ballads of "the north countrie." That there are palpable imitations of the style and manner of those venerable compositions in the work before us, is indeed undeniable; but it unfortunately happens, that while the hobbling versification, the mean diction, and flat stupidity of these models are very exactly copied, and even improved upon, in this imitation, their rude energy, manly simplicity, and occasional felicity of expression, have totally disappeared; and, instead of them, a large allowance of the author's own metaphysical sensibility, and mystical wordiness, is forced into an unnatural combination with the borrowed beauties which have just been mentioned. . . .

VIII

Blackwood's Edinburgh Magazine. Vol. III, No. XVI, pp. 369–381. July, 1818.

Essays on the Lake School of Poetry. No. I. Wordsworth's *White Doe of Rylstone.*

Reviewer: John Wilson.

THE three great master-spirits of our day, in the poetical world, are Scott, Wordsworth, and Byron. But there never were minds more unlike to each other than theirs are, either in original conformation or in the course of life. It is great and enduring glory to this age, to have produced three Poets,—of perfectly original genius,—unallied to each other,—drinking inspiration from fountains far apart,—who have built up superb structures of imagination, of distinct orders of architecture,—and who may indeed be said to rule, each by a legitimate sovereignty, over separate and powerful provinces in the kingdom of Mind. If we except the Elizabethan age, in which the poetical genius of the country was turned passionately to the drama, and which produced an unequalled constellation of great spirits, we believe that no other period of English literature could exhibit three such poets as these, standing in conspicuous elevation among a crowd of less potent, but enlightened and congenial Worthies. There is unquestionably an etherial flush of poetry over the face of this land. Poets think and feel for themselves, fearlessly and enthusiastically. There is something like inspiration in the works of them all. They are far superior indeed to the mere clever versewriters of our Augustan age. It is easy to see in what feelings, and in what faculties, our living Poets excell their duller prose brethren; and the world is not now so easily duped, as to bestow the "hallowed name" upon such writers as the Sprats, and Yaldens, and Dukes, and Pomfrets, "et hoc genus omne," whom the courtesy and ignorance of a former age admitted into the poetical brotherhood. Unless a Poet be now a Poet indeed,—unless he possess something of "the vision and the faculty divine,"—he dies at once, and is heard of no more. . . .

Though greatly inferior in many things to his illustrious brethren, Scott is perhaps, after all, the most unequivocally original. We do not know of any model after which the form of his principal Poems has been moulded. . . . He has given a most intensely real representation of the living spirit of the chivalrous age of his country. He has not shrouded the figures or the characters of his heroes in high poetical lustre, so as to dazzle us by resplendent fictitious beings, shining through the scenes and events of a half-imaginary world. They are as much real men in his poetry, as the "mighty Earls" of old are in our histories and annals. The incidents, too, and events, are all wonderfully like those of real life; and when we add to this, that all the most interesting and impressive superstitions and fancies of the times are in his poetry incorporated and intertwined with the ordinary tissue of mere human existence, we feel ourselves hurried from this our civilized age, back into the troubled bosom of semibarbarous life, and made keen partakers in all its impassioned and poetical credulities. His Poems are historical narrations, true in all things to the spirit of history, but everywhere overspread with those bright and breathing colours which only genius can bestow on reality; and when it is recollected, that the times in which his scenes are laid

and his heroes act were distinguished by many
of the most energetic virtues that can grace or
dignify the character of a free people, and
marked by the operation of great passions and
important events, every one must feel that
the poetry of Walter Scott is, in the noblest
sense of the word, national; that it breathes
upon us the bold and heroic spirit of perturbed
but magnificent ages, and connects us, in the
midst of philosophy, science, and refinement,
with our turbulent but high-minded ancestors,
of whom we have no cause to be ashamed,
whether looked on in the fields of war or in
the halls of peace. He is a true knight in all
things,—free, courteous, and brave. War, as he
describes it, is a noble game, a kingly pastime.
He is the greatest of the War-Poets. His
Poetry might make a very coward fearless.
. . . We glory in him as the great modern National Poet of Scotland. . . .

Byron is in all respects the very opposite of
Scott. He never dreams of wholly giving up
his mind to the influence of the actions of men,
or the events of history. He lets the world roll
on, and eyes its wide-weltering and tumultuous
waves—even the calamitous shipwrecks that
strew its darkness—with a stern, and sometimes even a pitiless misanthropy. He cannot
sympathise with the ordinary joys or sorrows
of humanity, even though intense and overpowering. They must live and work in intellect
and by intellect, before they seem worthy of
the sympathy of his impenetrable soul. His idea
of man, in the abstract, is boundless and magnificent; but of men, as individuals, he thinks
with derision and contempt. Hence he is in
one stanza a sublime moralist, elevated and
transported by the dignity of human nature;
in the next a paltry satirist, sneering at its
meanness. Hence he is unwilling to yield love
or reverence to any thing that has yet life;
for life seems to sink the little that is noble
into the degradation of the much that is vile.
The dead, and the dead only, are the objects
of his reverence or his love; for death separates the dead from all connexion, all intimacy
with the living; and the memories of the great
or good alone live in the past, which is a
world of ashes. Byron looks back to the tombs
of those great men "that stand in assured
rest;" and gazing, as it were, on the bones of
a more gigantic race, his imagination then teems
with corresponding births, and he holds converse with the mighty in language worthy to
be heard by the spirits of the mighty. It is
[in] this contrast between his august conceptions of man, and his contemptuous opinion
of men, that much of the almost incomprehensible charm, and power, and enchantment
of his Poetry exists. We feel ourselves alternately sunk and elevated, as if the hand of
an invisible being had command over us. At
one time we are a little lower than the angels;
in another, but little higher than the worms.
We feel that our elevation and our disgrace are
alike the lot of our nature; and hence the
Poetry of Byron, as we before remarked, is
read as a dark, but still a divine revelation.

If Byron be altogether unlike Scott, Wordsworth is yet more unlike Byron. With all the
great and essential faculties of the Poet, he
possesses the calm and self-commanding powers of the Philosopher. He looks over human
life with a steady and serene eye; he listens
with a fine ear "to the still sad music of humanity." His faith is unshaken in the prevalence of virtue over vice, and of happiness over
misery; and in the existence of a heavenly
law operating on earth, and, in spite of transitory defeats, always visibly triumphant in the
grand field of human warfare. Hence he looks
over the world of life, and man, with a sublime
benignity; and hence, delighting in all the
gracious dispensations of God, his great mind
can wholly deliver itself up to the love of a
flower budding in the field, or of a child asleep
in its cradle; nor, in doing so, feels that
Poetry can be said to stoop or to descend, much
less to be degraded, when she embodies, in
words of music, the purest and most delightful fancies and affections of the human heart.
This love of the nature to which he belongs,
and which is in him the fruit of wisdom and
experience, gives to all his poetry a very peculiar, a very endearing, and, at the same time,
a very lofty character. His Poetry is little
coloured by the artificial distinctions of society.
In his delineations of passion or character, he
is not so much guided by the varieties produced
by customs, institutions, professions, or modes
of life, as by those great elementary laws of
our nature which are unchangeable and the
same; and therefore the pathos and the truth
of his most felicitous Poetry are more profound than any other, not unlike the most
touching and beautiful passages in the Sacred
Page. The same spirit of love, and benignity,
and etherial purity, which breathes over all

his pictures of the virtues and the happiness of man, pervades those too of external nature. Indeed, all the Poets of the age,—and none can dispute that they must likewise be the best Critics,—have given up to him the palm in that Poetry which commerces with the forms, and hues, and odours, and sounds, of the material world. He has brightened the earth we inhabit to our eyes; he has made it more musical to our ears; he has rendered it more creative to our imaginations. . . .

IX

Blackwood's Edinburgh Review. Vol. XII, No. LXVII, pp. 175–191. August, 1822.

Wordsworth's Sonnets and Memorials.

Reviewer: John Wilson.

WORDSWORTH never comes forth before the public, from his solitude among the mountains, without deeply delighting all true lovers of poetry.—"His soul is like a star, and dwells apart." He is the same man in all things now, that he was twenty years ago, when the "Lyrical Ballads" produced such a wonderful sensation, and told that another great poet had been given to England. All the other first-rate writers of the age have, more or less, written directly and expressly for the age; have followed as often as guided the prevalent taste; and have varied their moods and measures according to the fluctuations of popular feeling, sentiment, and opinion. We do not say that they have been at all to blame in this; for it suited their genius so to do, and they naturally wished to feel their expanded wings borne up on the air of popular favour. The highest, best, and most powerful of them all, has uniformly written upon such principles, and has, we observe, avowed them, in the very lively preface to his last admirable Work. But Wordsworth buries his spirit in the solitary haunts and recesses of nature, and suffers no living thing to intrude there, to disturb the dreams of his own imagination. He is to himself all in all.—He holds communings with the great spirit of human life, and feels a sanctity in all the revelations that are made to him in his solitude. Profoundly versed in the knowledge of all sentiments, feelings, and passions, that ever dignified, adorned, or purified man's

heart, Wordsworth broods over them incessantly, and they are to him his own exceeding great reward. He knows that his poetry is good, and he is calmly satisfied. Indeed, his poetry is to him religion; and we venture to say, that it has been felt to be so by thousands. It would be absolute profanation to speak one word against many of his finest breathings; and as the author and promulgator of such divine thoughts, Wordsworth, beyond all poets, living or dead, is felt to be the object of the soul's purest reverence, gratitude, and love.

For our own parts, we believe that Wordsworth's genius has had a greater influence on the spirit of poetry in Britain, than was ever before exercised by any individual mind. He was the first man who impregnated all his descriptions of external nature with sentiment or passion. In this he has been followed—often successfully—by other true poets. He was the first man that vindicated the native dignity of human nature, by shewing that all her elementary feelings were capable of poetry —and in that too he has been followed by other true Poets, although here he stands, and probably ever will stand, unapproached. He was the first man that stripped thought and passion of all vain or foolish disguises, and shewed them in their just proportions and unencumbered power. He was the first man who in poetry knew the real province of language, and suffered it not to veil the meanings of the spirit. In all these things,—and in many more,—Wordsworth is indisputably the most ORIGINAL POET OF THE AGE; and it is impossible, in the very nature of things, that he ever can be eclipsed. From his golden urn other orbs may draw light; but still it will be said of him—

———Then shone the firmament
With living sapphires. HESPERUS, WHO LED
THE STARRY HOST, SHONE BRIGHTEST.

Accordingly, what living poet is not indebted to Wordsworth? No two minds can be imagined, for example, more unlike each other, than his and Sir Walter Scott's; and yet many of the most beautiful passages of the Mighty Minstrel, wherein he speaks not of knights, squires, and steeds, but of himself perhaps, or of other men, living or dying in a peaceful world, are manifestly coloured and inspirited by the light and soul of the Genius of the Lakes. And not a few of the most touching and pathetic conceptions in his glorious Novels, we owe to the same source. A few beautiful Wordsworthian verses, quoted at the heads of chapters, shew to the skilful eye how the genius of one man may kindle that of another, though cast by prodigal Nature in very different moulds, and animated, in general, by a very different spirit. The two last cantos of Childe Harold, although sufficiently original to place Lord Byron in the first rank of genius, are, in many places, absolutely written, it may be said, by Wordsworth. He it was that taught Byron how to look on a mountain, and how to listen to a cataract or the sea. . . .

These are the other two great Poets of the Trio; but every other living poet of any eminence, without one single exception, owes much of his power or inspiration to Wordsworth. Coleridge—Southey—even Campbell—lately Crabbe—Bowles, who by nature has much of Wordsworth's pure sentiment—nay Moore, with all his false feeling and meretricious ornament—Rogers, with his puny elegance—Wilson —Hunt—Milman—Montgomery— &c. &c. &c. &c. &c. all are indebted to Wordsworth, to a prodigious extent, indeed far more than any can ever repay. But such debts are honourable to them—at least as long as they are gratefully acknowledged and proclaimed; and we mention them now not to their disparagement, but simply as a fact regarding the poetical character of the age.

Wordsworth's Miscellaneous Poems were lately published by Longman in four octavo volumes, and the Excursion makes another. Were we desirous of bestowing a gift of inestimable value on a young mind of power, beginning to contemplate human nature with a thoughtful eye, it would be these five volumes. There is no deception there—no dim or glaring views—nothing false or hollow— nothing tottering or unstable—but truth in her simplicity, and her magnificence—lessons for the lowly and the lofty—steps leading up safely from the earth's loveliest and most innocent haunts, to the gorgeous clouds and the "blue depths serene" of heaven. . . .

The sentiments and feelings that embalm all these fine Compositions, are peculiarly important at the present day. It is thus that Christianity, and great Establishments for the preservation of its doctrines pure and unsullied, ought to be thought of in the meditative mind of genius. In those beautiful sketches, we see the power of religion—true or false—working to effect the elevation or the overthrow of the human soul. We see, in short but impressive glimpses, the history of our forefathers remembering or forgetting God, and how their empire was great on earth, as their spirit aspired to heaven. The ecclesiastical picture reveals political truth; and never was the alliance between church and state so philosophically illustrated as by this prevailing poet. Contrast those benign, solemn, and pious breathings of one of the noblest spirits of the age, with the heartless, arrogant, and blasphemous ravings of those disturbers of the clear waters of the well of life, whose cause, when they were suffering under the just infliction of the law misnamed persecution, too many who might have known better have been found to espouse; and with what a divine lustre shines forth the countenance and the figure of Faith! Here we see the highest intellect bowing down in reverence and adoration before the spirit of Christianity—the most splendid imagination overpowered by its sanctities, whether sleeping silently in the dark depths of bosoms agitated by mortal hope and fear, or embodied, to outward eyes, in beautiful and magnificent rites. Here we see that genius can conceive no image so august, no emotion so affecting, as those that rise up at the feet of the altar. . . .

But beautiful and majestic as these Ecclesiastical Sketches must be felt to be by all capable of feeling poetry, their full power can be known only by those who are familiar with Mr Wordsworth's Sonnets dedicated to Liberty. In these he unfolds the true principles of national greatness in the kingdoms of Christendom. He shews how thrones are supported, and by what fatalities they are laid prostrate. His mind is not darkened by the veil of the present; but it penetrates through gloom and glitter, into the vital spirit of human power; and if there be a speck of decay or disease there, his eye discerns it, and he gives warning of dissolution. He shews how virtue, religion, independence, and freedom, are the ministers of mortality, and that the science of politics is simple to the wise and good. He sees final abasement in the temporary triumphs of the wicked, and when all is wrapt in mist and sleet, and howling darkness, he beholds the reappearing of the mountain-tops. Nor does he deal in that splendid series of sonnets, with mere stately generalities—but he grasps the truth as it has been shewn on the stage of real life, either in joyful events, or terrible catastrophies, in the sunshine of smiles or in showers of blood. The poet of the peaceful vale has not feared to walk among moral earthquakes; revolution and anarchy have been food for his meditations, and in his boldest language he has called "Carnage the Daughter of the Lord." We never read these compositions without thinking of these fine verses of Cowper,—

A terrible sagacity informs
The poet's heart; he looks to distant storms,
He hears the thunder ere the tempest roar,
The billow ere it breaks upon the shore.

These sonnets of Wordsworth have been compared with those of Milton; and Mr Jeffrey has said, that Milton's are as far superior to them as they themselves are superior to all other English sonnets. The critic could have said this only with the vain hope of mortifying the poet—for he cannot think so. But it is easy to overshadow living merit by some mighty name from the dead.—Milton's sonnets furnished a model to Wordsworth; but he has far surpassed his model both in thought and expression. A few of Milton's sonnets are exceedingly fine; but even these owe much of their power over our minds to ideas and feelings associated with his personal character and high and happy destiny. In future times, Wordsworth's will be read with somewhat similar emotions; for although his own existence has been tranquil, aloof from all agitating public affairs, and unconnected with the goings-on of governments, yet his spirit has been often among them as vividly and energetically as Milton's own; and the whole heart and soul of his poetry has been poured over human life, to ameliorate and dignify it, to expose error and delusion stript of all their pretences, and to shew the foundations of all true national greatness. Independently of all such personal associations, Wordsworth's sonnets, we repeat it, are infinitely superior to Milton's. They embrace a wide and various range—and of themselves constitute a great Work. Considered as to composition merely, they are perfect;—the music flows on like a stream, or rolls like a river, or expands like the sea, according as the thought is beautiful, or majestic, or sublime; and often as the soul listens to the harmony, swelling and deepening to a close, it is as if

Through the long-drawn aisle and fretted vault,
The pealing anthem swell'd the note of praise. . . .

SIR WALTER SCOTT

REVIEW OF HIS WORK

The Edinburgh Review. Vol. XVI, No. XXXII, pp. 263–293. August, 1810.[1]

The Lady of the Lake: A Poem. By Walter Scott. Second Edition. 8vo. pp. 434. 1810.

Reviewer: Francis Jeffrey.

MR SCOTT, though living in an age usually prolific of original poetry, has manifestly outstripped all his competitors in the race of popularity; and stands already upon a height to which no other writer has attained in the memory of any one now alive. We doubt, indeed, whether any English poet *ever* had so many of his books sold, or so many of his verses read and admired by such a multitude of persons, in so short a time. We are credibly informed, that nearly thirty thousand copies of "The Lay" have been already disposed of in this country; and that the demand for Marmion, and the poem now before us, has been still more considerable,—a circulation, we believe, altogether without example, in the case of a bulky work, not addressed to the bigotry of the mere mob, either religious or political. . . .

The great secret of his popularity, however, and the leading characteristic of his poetry, appear to us to consist evidently in this, that he has made more use of common topics, images and expressions, than any original poet of later times; and, at the same time, displayed more genius and originality than any recent author who has worked in the same materials. By the latter peculiarity, he has entitled himself to the admiration of every description of readers;—by the former, he is recommended in an especial manner to the inexperienced, at the hazard of some little offence to the more cultivated and fastidious.

In the choice of his subjects, for example, he does not attempt to interest merely by fine observation or pathetic sentiment, but takes the assistance of a story, and enlists the reader's curiosity among his motives for attention. Then his characters are all selected from the

[1] Since there is little variety among the reviews of Scott's poems, we include only this one which has been regarded as the best.

most common *dramatis personæ* of poetry;
—Kings, warriors, knights, outlaws, nuns,
minstrels, secluded damsels, wizards, and true
lovers. He never ventures to carry us into the
cottage of the peasant, like Crabbe or Cowper; 5
nor into the bosom of domestic privacy, like
Campbell; nor among creatures of the imagination, like Southey or Darwin. Such personages,
we readily admit, are not in themselves so
interesting or striking as those to whom Mr 10
Scott has devoted himself; but they are far
less familiar in poetry—and are therefore more
likely, perhaps, to engage the attention of
those to whom poetry is familiar. In the management of the passions, again, Mr Scott 15
appears to us to have pursued the same popular, and comparatively easy course. He has
raised all the most familiar and poetical emotions, by the most obvious aggravations, and
in the most compendious and judicious way. 20
He has dazzled the reader with the splendour,
and even warmed him with the transient beat
of various affections; but he has nowhere
fairly kindled him with enthusiasm, or melted
him into tenderness. Writing for the world at 25
large, he has wisely abstained from attempting
to raise any passion to a height to which
worldly people could not be transported; and
contented himself with giving his reader the
chance of feeling, as a brave, kind and affection- 30
ate gentleman should often feel in the ordinary
course of his existence, without trying to
breathe into him either that lofty enthusiasm
which disdains the ordinary business and
amusements of life, or that quiet and deep 35
sensibility which unfits for all its pursuits.
With regard to diction and imagery, too, it is
quite obvious that Mr Scott has not aimed at
writing either in a pure or a very consistent
style. He seems to have been anxious only to 40
strike, and to be easily and universally understood; and, for this purpose, to have culled
the most glittering and conspicuous expressions
of the most popular authors, and to have interwoven them in splendid confusion with his own 45
nervous diction and irregular versification. Indifferent whether he coins or borrows, and
drawing with equal freedom on his memory and
his imagination, he goes boldly forward, in
full reliance on a neverfailing abundance; 50
and dazzles, with his richness and variety,
and even those who are most apt to be offended with his glare and irregularity. There
is nothing, in Mr Scott, of the severe and

majestic style of Milton—or of the terse and
fine composition of Pope—or of the elaborate
elegance and melody of Campbell—or even
of the flowing and redundant diction of
Southey.—But there is a medley of bright images and glowing words, set carelessly and
loosely together—a diction, tinged successively
with the careless richness of Shakespeare, the
harshness and antique simplicity of the old
romances, the homeliness of vulgar ballads and
anecdotes, and the sentimental glitter of the
most modern poetry,—passing from the borders of the ludicrous to those of the sublime
—alternately minute and energetic—sometimes
artificial, and frequently negligent—but always full of spirit and vivacity,—abounding
in images, that are striking, at first sight, to
minds of every contexture—and never expressing a sentiment which it can cost the most
ordinary reader any exertion to comprehend.

Such seem to be the leading qualities that
have contributed to Mr Scott's popularity;
and, as some of them are obviously of a kind
to diminish his merit in the eyes of more
fastidious judges, it is but fair to complete
this view of his peculiarities by a hasty notice
of such of them as entitle him to unqualified
admiration;—and here it is impossible not to
be struck with that vivifying spirit of strength
and animation which pervades all the inequalities of his composition, and keeps constantly
on the mind of the reader the impression of
great power, spirit and intrepidity. There is
nothing cold, creeping or feeble, in all Mr
Scott's poetry;—no laborious littleness, or
puling classical affectation. He has his failures,
indeed, like other people; but he always attempts vigorously; and never fails in his immediate object, without accomplishing something far beyond the reach of an ordinary
writer. Even when he wanders from the paths
of pure taste, he leaves behind him the footsteps of a powerful genius; and moulds the
most humble of his materials into a form
worthy of a nobler substance. Allied to this
inherent vigour and animation, and in a great
degree derived from it, is that air of facility
and freedom which adds so peculiar a grace to
most of Mr Scott's compositions. There is
certainly no living poet whose works seem to
come from him with so much ease, or who so
seldom appears to labour, even in the most
burdensome parts of his performance. He
seems, indeed, never to think, either of himself

or his reader, but to be completely identified and lost in the personages with whom he is occupied; and the attention of the reader is consequently either transferred, unbroken, to their adventures, or, if it glance back for a moment to the author, it is only to think how much more might be done, by putting forth that strength at full, which has, without effort, accomplished so many wonders. It is owing partly to these qualities, and partly to the great variety of his style, that Mr Scott is much less frequently tedious than any other bulky poet with whom we are acquainted. His store of images is so copious, that he never dwells upon one long enough to produce weariness in the reader; and, even where he deals in borrowed or in tawdry wares, the rapidity of his transitions, and the transient glance with which he is satisfied as to each, leave the critic no time to be offended, and hurry him forward along with the multitude, enchanted with the brilliancy of the exhibition. Thus, the very frequency of his deviations from pure taste, comes, in some sort, to constitute their apology; and the profusion and variety of his faults to afford a new proof of his genius.

LORD BYRON

REVIEWS OF HIS WORKS

I

The Edinburgh Review. Vol. XI, No. XXII, pp. 285–289. January, 1808.

> *Hours of Idleness: A Series of Poems, Original and Translated.* By George Gordon, Lord Byron, a Minor. 8 vo. pp. 200. Newark. 1807.

Reviewer: Henry Brougham.

THE poesy of this young lord belongs to the class which neither gods nor men are said to permit. Indeed, we do not recollect to have seen a quantity of verse with so few deviations in either direction from that exact standard. His effusions are spread over a dead flat, and can no more get above or below the level, than if they were so much stagnant water. As an extenuation of this offence, the noble author is peculiarly forward in pleading minority. We have it in the title-page, and on the very back of the volume; it follows his name like a favourite part of his *style.* Much stress is

laid upon it in the preface, and the poems are connected with this general statement of his case, by particular dates, substantiating the age at which each was written. Now, the law upon the point of minority, we hold to be perfectly clear. It is a plea available only to the defendant; no plaintiff can offer it as a supplementary ground of action. Thus, if any suit could be brought against Lord Byron, for the purpose of compelling him to put into court a certain quantity of poetry; and if judgement [*sic*] were given against him; it is highly probably that an exception would be taken, were he to deliver *for poetry,* the contents of this volume. To this he might plead *minority;* but as he now makes voluntary tender of the article, he hath no right to sue, on that ground, for the price in good current praise, should the goods be unmarketable. This is our view of the law on the point, and we dare to say, so will it be ruled. Perhaps however, in reality, all that he tells us about his youth, is rather with a view to increase our wonder, than to soften our censures. He possibly means to say, "See how a minor can write! This poem was actually composed by a young man of eighteen and this by one of only sixteen!"— But, alas, we all remember the poetry of Cowley at ten, and Pope at twelve; and so far from hearing, with any degree of surprise, that very poor verses were written by a youth from his leaving school to his leaving college, inclusive, we really believe this to be the most common of all occurrences; that it happens in the life of nine men in ten who are educated in England; and that the tenth man writes better verse than Lord Byron.

His other plea of privilege, our author rather brings forward in order to wave it. He certainly, however, does allude frequently to his family and ancestors—sometimes in poetry, sometimes in notes; and while giving up his claim on the score of rank, he takes care to remember us of Dr. Johnson's saying, that when a nobleman appears as an author, his merit should be handsomely acknowledged. In truth, it is this consideration only, that induces us to give Lord Byron's poems a place in our review, beside our desire to counsel him, that he do forthwith abandon poetry, and turn his talents, which are considerable, and his opportunities, which are great, to better account.

With this view, we must beg leave seriously

to assure him, that the mere rhyming of the final syllable, even when accompanied by the presence of a certain number of feet; nay, although (which does not always happen) those feet should scan regularly, and have been all counted accurately upon the fingers,—is not the whole art of poetry. We would entreat him to believe, that a certain portion of liveliness, somewhat of fancy, is necessary to constitute a poem; and that a poem in the present day, to be read, must contain at least one thought, either in a little degree different from the ideas of former writers, or differently expressed. . . .

But whatever judgment may be passed on the poems of this noble minor, it seems we must take them as we find them, and be content; for they are the last we shall ever have from him. He is at best, he says, but an intruder into the groves of Parnassus; he never lived in a garret, like thorough-bred poets; and "though he once roved a careless mountaineer in the Highlands of Scotland," he has not of late enjoyed this advantage. Moreover, he expects no profit from his publication; and whether it succeeds or not, "it is highly improbable, from his situation and pursuits hereafter," that he should again condescend to become an author. Therefore, let us take what we get and be thankful. What right have we poor devils to be nice? We are well off to have got so much from a man of this Lord's station, who does not live in a garret, but "has the sway" of Newstead Abbey. Again, we say, let us be thankful; and, with honest Sancho, bid God bless the giver, nor look the gift horse in the mouth.

II

The Edinburgh Review. Vol. XXIII, No. XLV, pp. 198–229. April, 1814.

> *The Corsair: a Tale.* By Lord Byron. Fifth Edition. 8vo. pp. 100. London. 1814.
> *The Bride of Abydos: a Turkish Tale.* by Lord Byron. Sixth Edition. 8vo. pp. 72. London. 1813.

Reviewer: Francis Jeffrey.

LORD BYRON has clear titles to applause, in the spirit and beauty of his diction and versification, and the splendour of many of his descriptions: But it is to his pictures of the stronger passions, that he is indebted for the fulness of his fame. He has delineated, with unequalled force and fidelity, the workings of those deep and powerful emotions which alternately enchant and agonize the minds that are exposed to their inroads; and represented, with a terrible energy, those struggles and sufferings and exaltations, by which the spirit is at once torn and transported, and traits of divine inspiration, or demoniacal possession, thrown across the tamer features of humanity. It is by this spell, chiefly, we think, that he has fixed the admiration of the public; and while other poets delight by their vivacity, or enchant by their sweetness, he alone has been able to *command* the sympathy, even of reluctant readers, by the natural magic of his moral sublimity, and the terrors and attractions of those overpowering feelings, the depths and heights of which he seems to have so successfully explored. All the considerable poets of the present age have, indeed, possessed this gift in a greater or lesser degree; but there is no man, since the time of Shakespeare himself, in whom it has been made manifest with greater fulness and splendour, than in the noble author before us. . . .

The other merits of his composition are such as his previous publications had already made familiar to the public,—an unparalleled rapidity of narrative, and condensation of thoughts and images—a style always vigorous and original, though sometimes quaint and affected, and more frequently strained, harsh, and abrupt— a diction and versification invariably spirited, and almost always harmonious and emphatic: Nothing diluted in short, or diffused into weakness, but full of life, and nerve, and activity— expanding only in the eloquent expression of strong and favourite affections, and everywhere else concise, energetic, and impetuous—hurrying on with a disdain of little ornaments and accuracies, and not always very solicitous about being comprehended by readers of inferior capacity.

III

The Quarterly Review. Vol. XVI, No. XXXI, pp. 172–208. October, 1816.

> *Childe Harold's Pilgrimage, Canto III.* 8vo. *The Prisoner of Chillon, a Dream; and other Poems.* By Lord Byron. 8vo. John Murray: London.

Reviewer: Sir Walter Scott.

We have felt ourselves very much affected by the perusal of these poems, nor can we suppose that we are singular in our feelings. Other poets have given us their literary productions as the subject of criticism, impersonally as it were, and generally speaking, abstracted from their ordinary habits and feelings; and all, or almost all, might apply to their poetical effusions, though in somewhat a different sense, the *l'envoy* of Ovid. . . .

It has been, however, reserved for our own time to produce one distinguished example of the Muse having descended upon a bard of a wounded spirit, and lent her lyre to tell, and we trust to soothe, afflictions of no ordinary description, afflictions originating probably in that singular combination of feeling which has been called the poetical temperament, and which has so often saddened the days of those on whom it has been conferred. If ever a man could lay claim to that character in all its strength and all its weakness, with its unbounded range of enjoyment, and its exquisite sensibility of pleasure and of pain, it must certainly be granted to Lord Byron. Nor does it require much time or a deep acquaintance with human nature to discover why these extraordinary powers should in many cases have contributed more to the wretchedness than to the happiness of their possessor.

The "imagination all compact," which the greatest poet who ever lived has assigned as the distinguishing badge of his brethren, is in every case a dangerous gift. It exaggerates, indeed, our expectations, and can often bid its possessor hope, where hope is lost to reason: but the delusive pleasure arising from these visions of imagination, resembles that of a child whose notice is attracted by a fragment of glass to which a sun-beam has given momentary splendour. He hastens to the spot with breathless impatience, and finds the object of his curiosity and expectation is equally vulgar and worthless. Such is the man of quick and exalted powers of imagination. His fancy over-estimates the object of his wishes, and pleasure, fame, dictinction, [*sic*] are alternately pursued, attained, and despised when in his power. Like the enchanted fruit in the palace of a sorcerer, the objects of his admiration lose their attraction and value as soon as they are grasped by the adventurer's hand, and all that remains is regret for the time lost in the chase, and astonishment at the hallucina-

tion under the influence of which it was undertaken. The disproportion between hope and possession which is felt by all men, is thus doubled to those whom nature has endowed with the power of gilding a distant prospect by the rays of imagination. These reflections, though trite and obvious, are in a manner forced from us by the poetry of Lord Byron, by the sentiments of weariness of life and enmity with the world which they so frequently express—and by the singular analogy which such sentiments hold with incidents of his life so recently before the public. The works before us contain so many direct allusions to the author's personal feelings and private history, that it becomes impossible for us to divide Lord Byron from his poetry, or to offer our criticism upon the continuation of Childe Harold, without reverting to the circumstances in which the commencement of that singular and original work first appeared.

Distinguished by title and descent from an illustrious line of ancestry, Lord Byron shewed, even in his earliest years, that nature had added to those advantages the richest gifts of genius and fancy. His own tale is partly told in two lines of Lara:

Left by his Sire, too young such loss to know, Lord of himself, that heritage of woe.

His first literary adventure and its fate are well remembered. The poems which he published in his minority had, indeed, those faults of conception and diction which are inseparable from juvenile attempts, and in particular might rather be considered as imitations of what had caught the ear and fancy of the youthful author, than as exhibiting originality of conception and expression. It was like the first essay of the singing bird catching at and imitating the notes of its parent, ere habit and time have given the fullness of tone, confidence, and self-possession which renders assistance unnecessary. Yet though there were many, and those not the worst judges, who discerned in these juvenile productions, a depth of thought and felicity of expression which promised much at a more mature age, the errors did not escape the critical lash; and certain brethren of ours yielded to the opportunity of pouncing upon a titled author, and to that which most readily besets our fraternity, and to which we dare not pronounce ourselves wholly inaccessible, the temptation, namely, of shewing our own wit, and entertaining our readers with a lively article without much respect to the feelings of the author, or even to the indications of merit which the work may exhibit. The review was read and raised mirth; the poems were neglected, the author was irritated, and took his revenge in keen iambics, not only on the offending critic, but on many others, in whose conduct or writings the juvenile bard had found, or imagined he had found, some cause of offence. The satire which has been since suppressed, as containing opinions hastily expressed, contained a spirit at least sufficiently poignant for all the purposes of reprisal; and although the verses might, in many respects, be deemed the offspring of hasty and indiscriminating resentment, they bore a strong testimony to the ripening talents of the author. Having thus vented his indignation against the critics and their readers, and put many, if not all the laughers upon his side, Lord Byron went abroad, and the controversy was forgotten for some years.

It was in 1812, when Lord Byron returned to England, that Childe Harold's Pilgrimage made its first appearance, producing an effect upon the public, at least equal to any work which has appeared within this or the last century. Reading is indeed so general among all ranks and classes, that the impulse received by the public mind on such occasions is instantaneous through all but the very lowest classes of society, instead of being slowly communicated from one set of readers to another, as was the case in the days of our fathers. "The Pilgrimage," acting on such an extensive medium, was calculated to rouse and arrest the attention in a peculiar degree. The fictitious personage, whose sentiments, however, no one could help identifying with those of the author himself, presented himself with an avowed disdain of all the attributes which most men would be gladly supposed to possess. Childe Harold is represented as one satiated by indulgence in pleasure, and seeking in change of place and clime a relief from the tedium of a life which glided on without an object. The assuming of such a character as the medium of communicating his poetry and his sentiments indicated a feeling towards the public, which, if it fell short of contemning their favour, disdained, at least, all attempt to propitiate them. Yet the very audacity of this repulsive personification, joined to the energy with which it was supported, and

to the indications of a bold, powerful, and original mind which glanced through every line of the poem, electrified the mass of readers, and placed at once upon Lord Byron's head the garland for which other men of genius have toiled long, and which they have gained late. He was placed pre-eminent among the literary men of his country by general acclamation. Those who had so rigorously censured his juvenile essays, and perhaps "dreaded such another field," were the first to pay warm and, we believe, sincere homage to his matured efforts; while others, who saw in the sentiments of Childe Harold much to regret and to censure, did not withhold their tribute of applause to the depth of thought, the power and force of expression, the beauty of description, and the energy of sentiment which animated the "Pilgrimage." If the volume was laid aside for a moment, under the melancholy and unpleasing impression that it seemed calculated to chase hope from the side of man, and to dim his prospects both of this life and of futurity, it was immediately and almost involuntarily assumed again, as our feeling of the author's genius predominated over our dislike to contemplate the gloomy views of human nature which it was his pleasure to place before us. Something was set down to the angry recollection of his first failure, which might fairly authorize so high a mind to hold the world's opinion in contempt; something was allowed for the recent family losses to which the poem alluded, and under the feeling of which it had been partly written: and it seemed to most readers as if gentler and more kindly features were, at times, seen to glance from under the cloud of misanthropy, which the author had flung around his hero. Thus, as all admired the Pilgrimage of Childe Harold, all were prepared to greet the author with that fame which is the poet's best reward, and which is chiefly and most justly due to one who, in these exhausted days, strikes out a new and original line of composition.

It was amidst such feelings of admiration that Lord Byron entered, we may almost say for the first time, the public stage on which he has, for four years, made so distinguished a figure. Every thing in his manner, person, and conversation, tended to maintain the charm which his genius had flung around him; and those admitted to his conversation, far from finding that the inspired poet sunk into ordi-

nary mortality, felt themselves attached to
him, not only by many noble qualities, but by
the interest of a mysterious, undefined, and
almost painful curiosity.

It is well known how wide the doors of so- 5
ciety are opened in London to literary merit
even of a degree far inferior to Lord Byron's,
and that it is only necessary to be honourably
distinguished by the public voice to move as a
denizen in the first circles. This passport was 10
not necessary to Lord Byron who possessed the
hereditary claims of birth and rank. But the
interest which his genius attached to his presence, and to his conversation, was of a nature
far beyond what these hereditary claims could 15
of themselves have conferred, and his reception was enthusiastic beyond any thing we
have ever witnessed, or even heard reported.
We have already noticed that Lord Byron is
not one of those literary men of whom it may 20
be truly said, *Minuit praesentia famam*. A
countenance, exquisitely modeled to the expression of feeling and passion, and exhibiting
the remarkable contrast of very dark hair and
eye-brows, with light and expressive eyes, pre- 25
sented to the physiognomist the most interesting subject for the exercise of his art. The
predominating expression was that of deep and
habitual thought, which gave way to the most
rapid play of features when he engaged in in- 30
teresting discussion; so that a brother poet
compared them to the sculpture of a beautiful
alabaster vase, only seen to perfection when
lighted up from within. The flashes of mirth,
gaiety, indignation, or satirical dislike which 35
frequently animated Lord Byron's countenance,
might, during an evening's conversation, be
mistaken by a stranger, for the habitual expression, so easily and so happily was it
formed for them all; but those who had an 40
opportunity of studying his features for a
length of time, and upon various occasions,
both of rest and emotion, will agree with us
that their proper language was that of melancholy. Sometimes shades of this gloom in- 45
terrupted even his gayest and most happy moments, and the following verses are said to
have dropped from his pen to excuse a transient expression of melancholy which over-
clouded the general gaiety. 50

When from the heart where Sorrow sits,
　Her dusky shadow mounts too high,
And o'er the changing aspect flits,
　And clouds the brow, or fills the eye—

Heed not the gloom that soon shall sink:
　My thoughts their dungeon know too well;
Back to my breast the captives shrink,
　And bleed within their silent cell.

It was impossible to behold this interesting
countenance, expressive of a dejection belonging neither to the rank, the age, nor the success
of this young nobleman, without feeling an
indefinable curiosity to ascertain whether it
had a deeper cause than habit or constitutional
temperament. It was obviously of a degree
incalculably more serious than that alluded to
by Prince Arthur—

————I remember when I was in France,
Young gentlemen would be as sad as night
Only for wantonness————

But howsoever derived, this, joined to Lord
Byron's air of mingling in amusements and
sports as if he contemned them, and felt, that
his sphere was far above the frivolous crowd
which surrounded him, gave a strong effect of
colouring to a character whose tints were
otherwise romantic. Noble and far descended,
his mind fraught with ancient learning and
modern accomplishment, the pilgrim of distant
and savage countries, eminent as a poet among
the first whom Britain has produced, and having besides cast around him a mysterious charm
arising from the sombre tone of his poetry,
and the occasional melancholy of his deportment, Lord Byron occupied the eyes, and interested the feelings of all. The enthusiastic
looked on him to admire, the serious with a
wish to admonish, and the soft with a desire
to console. Even literary envy, a base sensation, from which, perhaps, this age is more free
than any other, forgave the man whose splendour dimmed the fame of his competitors. The
generosity of Lord Byron's disposition, his
readiness to assist merit in distress, and to
bring it forward where unknown, deserved and
obtained the general regard of those who partook of such merit, while his poetical effusions,
poured forth with equal force and fertility,
shewed at once a daring confidence in his own
powers, and a determination to maintain, by
continued effort, the high place he had attained in British literature. This rapidity of
composition and publication we have heard
blamed as endangering the fame of the author,
while it gave such proofs of talent. We are inclined to dispute the proposition, at least in
the present instance. . . .

It is certain, to return to the subject from which we have gone somewhat astray, that the rapidity with which Lord Byron's poems succeeded each other, during four years, served to arrest as well as to dazzle and delight the public; nor did there appear room to apply to him, in the height of his fame and the flower of his age, the caution which we might whisper to other bards of popular celebrity. The Giaour, the Bride of Abydos, the Corsair, Lara, the Siege of Corinth, followed each other with a celerity, which was only rivalled by their success; and if at times the author seemed to pause in his poetic career, with the threat of forbearing further adventure for a time, the public eagerly pardoned the breach of a promise by keeping which they must have been sufferers. Exquisitely beautiful in themselves, these tales received a new charm from the romantic climes into which they introduced us, and from the oriental costume so strictly preserved and so picturesquely exhibited. Greece, the cradle of the poetry with which our earliest studies are familiar, was presented to us among her ruins and her sorrows. Her delightful scenery, once dedicated to those deities who, though dethroned from their own Olympus, still preserve a poetical empire, was spread before us in Lord Byron's poetry, varied by all the moral effect derived from what Greece is and what she has been, while it was doubled by comparisons, perpetually excited, between the philosophers and heroes who formerly inhabited that romantic country, and their descendants, who either stoop to their Scythian conquerors, or maintain, among the recesses of their classical mountains, an independence as wild and savage as it is precarious. The oriental manners also and diction, so peculiar in their picturesque effect that they can cast a charm even over the absurdities of an eastern tale, had here the more honourable occupation of decorating that which in itself was beautiful, and enhancing by novelty what would have been captivating without its aid. The powerful impression produced by this peculiar species of poetry confirmed us in a principle, which, though it will hardly be challenged when stated as an axiom, is very rarely complied with in practice. It is, that every author should, like Lord Byron, form to himself, and communicate to the reader, a precise, defined and distinct view of the landscape, sentiment, or action which he intends to de-

scribe to the reader. This simple proposition has been so often neglected that we feel warranted in giving it a little more consideration and illustration than plain men may at first sight think necessary. . . .

It is another remarkable property of the poetry of Lord Byron, that although his manner is frequently varied—although he appears to have assumed for an occasion the characteristic stanza and style of several contemporaries, yet not only is his poetry marked in every instance by the strongest cast of originality, but in some leading particulars, and especially in the character of his heroes, each story so closely resembled the other, that managed by a writer of less power, the effect would have been an unpleasing monotony. All, or almost all, his heroes, have somewhat the attributes of Childe Harold:—all, or almost all, have minds which seem at variance with their fortunes, and exhibit high and poignant feelings of pain and pleasure; a keen sense of what is noble and honourable, and an equally keen susceptibility of injustice or injury, under the garb of stoicism or contempt of mankind. The strength of early passion, and the glow of youthful feeling, are uniformly painted as chilled or subdued by a train of early imprudences or of darker guilt, and the sense of enjoyment tarnished, by too intimate and experienced an acquaintance with the vanity of human wishes. These general attributes mark the stern features of all Lord Byron's heroes, from those which are shaded by the scalloped hat of the illustrious Pilgrim, to those which lurk under the turban of Alp, the Renegade. The public, ever anxious in curiosity or malignity to attach to fictitious characters real prototypes, were obstinate in declaring that in these leading traits of character Lord Byron copied from the individual features reflected in his own mirror. . . .

We are not writing Lord Byron's private history, though from the connection already stated between his poetry and his character, we feel ourselves forced upon considering his literary life, his deportment, and even his personal appearance. But we know enough even of his private story to give our warrant that, though his youth may have shared somewhat too largely in the indiscretions of those left too early masters of their own actions and fortunes, falsehood and malice alone can impute to him any real cause for hopeless remorse or gloomy misanthropy. To what, then, are we to ascribe the singular peculiarity which induced an author of such talent, and so well skilled in tracing the darker impressions which guilt and remorse leave on the human character, so frequently to affix features peculiar to himself to the robbers and and [sic] corsairs which he sketched with a pencil as forcible as that of Salvator?—More than one answer may be returned to this question; nor do we pretend to say which is best warranted by the facts. The practice may arise from a temperament which radical and constitutional melancholy has, as in the case of Hamlet, predisposed to identify its *owner* with scenes of that deep and arouzing [sic] interest which arises from the stings of conscience contending with the stubborn energy of pride, and delighting to be placed in supposed situations of guilt and danger, as some men love instinctively to tread the giddy edge of a precipice, or, holding by some frail twig, to stoop forward over the abyss into which the dark torrent discharges itself. Or it may be that these disguises were assumed capriciously as a man might chuse [sic] the cloak, poniard, and dark-lantern of a bravo, for his disguise at a masquerade. Or feeling his own powers in painting the sombre and the horrible, Lord Byron assumed in his fervour the very semblance of the characters he describes, like an actor who presents on the stage at once his own person and the tragic character with which for the time he is invested. Nor is it altogether incompatible with his character to believe that, in contempt of the criticisms which on this account had attended Childe Harold, he was determined to shew to the public how little he was affected by them, and how effectually it was in his power to compel attention and respect, even when imparting a portion of his own likeness and his own peculiarities to pirates, and outlaws.

But although we do not pretend to ascertain the motive on which Lord Byron acted in bringing the peculiarities of his own sentiments and feeling so frequently before his readers, it is with no little admiration that we regard these extraordinary powers, which, amidst this seeming uniformity, could continue to rivet the public attention, and secure general and continued applause. The versatility of authors who have been able to draw and support characters as different from each other as from their own,

has given to their productions the inexpressible charm of variety, and has often secured them against that neglect which in general attends what is technically called mannerism. But it was reserved to Lord Byron to present the same character on the public stage again and again, varied only by the exertions of that powerful genius, which searching the springs of passion and of feeling in their innermost recesses, knew how to combine their operations, so that the interest was eternally varying, and never abated, although the most important personage of the drama retained the same lineaments. It will one day be considered as not the least remarkable literary phenomenon of this age, that during a period of four years, notwithstanding the quantity of distinguished poetical talent of which we may be permitted to boast, a single author, and he managing his pen with the careless and negligent ease of a man of quality, and chusing [sic] for his theme subjects so very similar, and personages bearing so close a resemblance to each other,—did, in despite of these circumstances, of the unamiable attributes with which he usually invested his heroes, and of the proverbial fickleness of the public, maintain the ascendency in their favour, which he had acquired by his first matured production. So however it indisputably has been; and those comparatively small circles of admirers excepted, which assemble naturally around individual poets of eminence, Lord Byron has been for that time, and may for some time continue to be, the Champion of the English Parnassus. . . .

We have said that Lord Byron occasionally, though without concealing his own original features, assumes the manner and style of his contemporaries. Of these we have more than one instance in the present collection. It is impossible to read the Prisoner of Chillon without finding several passages—that last quoted, for example,—which strongly remind us of Wordsworth. There is another, called "Churchill's Grave," for which Southey seems to afford the model, not in his epic strains, but in his English eclogues, in which moral truths are expressed, to use the poet's own language in "an almost colloquial plainness of language," and an air of quaint and original expression, assumed to render the sentiment at once impressive and *piquant*. The grave of Churchill, however, might have called from Lord Byron a deeper commemoration; for though they generally differed in character and genius, there was a resemblance between their history and character. The satire of Churchill flowed with a more profuse, though not a more embittered stream; while, on the other hand, he cannot be compared to Lord Byron in point of tenderness or imagination. But both these poets held themselves above the opinion of the world, and both were followed by the fame and popularity which they seemed to despise. The writings of both exhibit an inborn, though sometimes ill regulated generosity of mind, and a spirit of proud independence, frequently pushed to extremes. Both carried their hatred of hypocrisy beyond the verge of prudence, and indulged their vein of satire to the borders of licentiousness. In the flower of his age Churchill died in a foreign land,—here we trust the parallel will cease, and that the subject of our criticism will long survive to honour his own.

Two other pieces in this miscellany recal [sic] to our mind the wild, unbridled, and fiery imagination of Coleridge. To this poet's high poetical genius we have always paid deference; though not uniformly perhaps, he has, too frequently for his own popularity, wandered into the wild and mystic, and left the reader at a loss accurately to determine his meaning. Perhaps in that called the "Spell" the resemblance may be fanciful, but we cannot allow it to be so in the singular poem called "Darkness," well entitled

A dream which is not all a dream.

In this case our author has abandoned the art, so peculiarly his own, of shewing the reader where his purpose tends, and has contended himself with presenting a mass of powerful ideas unarranged, and the meaning of which we certainly confess ourselves not always able to attain. A succession of terrible images is placed before us flitting and mixing, and disengaging themselves as in the dream of a feverish man—Chimeras dire, to whose existence the mind refuses credit, which confound and weary the ordinary reader, and baffle the comprehension even of those more accustomed to the flights of a poetic muse. The subject is the progress of utter darkness, until it becomes, in Shakspeare's [sic] phrase, the "burier of the dead," and the assemblage of terrific ideas which the poet has placed before us only fail in exciting our terror from the extravagance of the plan. These mystical prolusions do indeed produce upon us the effect described in Henry Mur's lines quoted in Southey's Omniana—

A lecture strange he seem'd to read to me;
And though I did not rightly understand
His meaning, yet I deemed it to be
Some goodly thing. . . .

There is no royal and no poetical path to contentment and heart's-ease: that by which they are attained is open to all classes of mankind, and lies within the most limited range of intellect. To narrow our wishes and desires within the scope of our powers of attainment; to consider our misfortunes, however peculiar in their character, as our inevitable share in the patrimony of Adam; to bridle those irritable feelings, which ungoverned are sure to become governors; to shun that intensity of galling and self-wounding reflection which our poet has so forcibly described in his own burning language:

————I have thought
Too long and darkly, till my brain became,
In its own eddy, boiling and o'erwrought,
A whirling gulf of phantasy and flame—

—to stoop, in short, to the realities of life; repent if we have offended, and pardon if we have been trespassed against; to look on the world less as our foe than as a doubtful and capricious friend, whose applause we ought as far as possible to deserve, but neither to court nor contemn—such seem the most obvious and certain means of keeping or regaining mental tranquillity. . . .

We are compelled to dwell upon this subject: for future ages, while our language is remembered, will demand of this why Lord Byron was unhappy? We retort this query on the noble poet himself while it is called "today." He does injustice to the world, if he imagines he has left it exclusively filled with those who rejoice in his sufferings. If the voice of consolation be in cases like his less loudly heard than that of reproach or upbraiding, it is because those who long to conciliate, to advise, to mediate, to console, are timid in thrusting forward their sentiments, and fear to exasperate where they most seek to soothe; while the busy and officious intrude, without shame or sympathy, and embitter the privacy of affliction by their rude gaze and importunate clamour. But the pain which such insects can give only lasts while the wound is raw. Let the patient submit to the discipline of the soul enjoined by religion, and recommended by philosophy, and the scar will become speedily insensible to their stings. Lord Byron may not have loved the world, but the world has loved him, not perhaps with a wise or discriminating affection, but as well as it is capable of loving any one. And many who do not belong to the world, as the word is generally understood, have their thoughts fixed on Lord Byron, with the anxious wish and eager hope that he will bring his powerful understanding to combat with his irritated feelings, and that his next efforts will shew that he has acquired the peace of mind necessary for the free and useful exercise of his splendid talents.

IV

The Edinburgh Review. Vol. XXVII, No. LIV, pp. 277–310. December, 1816.

> *Childe Harold's Pilgrimage, Canto the Third*. By Lord Byron. 8vo. pp. 79. London. 1816.
> *The Prisoner of Chillon, and other Poems.* By Lord Byron. 8vo. pp. 60. London. 1816.

Reviewer: Francis Jeffrey.

IF the finest poetry be that which leaves the deepest impression on the minds of its readers —and this is not the worst test of its excellence—Lord Byron, we think, must be allowed to take precedence of all his distinguished contemporaries. He has not the variety of Scott— nor the delicacy of Campbell—nor the absolute truth of Crabbe—nor the polished sparkling of Moore; but in force of diction, and inextinguishable energy of sentiment, he clearly surpasses them all. "Words that breathe, and thoughts that burn," are not merely the ornaments, but the common staple of his poetry; and he is not inspired or impressive only in some happy passages, but through the whole body and tissue of his composition. It was an unavoidable condition, perhaps, of this higher excellence, that his scene should be narrow, and his persons few. To compass such ends as he had in view, it was necessary to reject all ordinary agents, and all trivial combinations. He could not possibly be amusing, or ingenious, or playful; or hope to maintain the requisite pitch of interest by the recitation of sprightly adventures, or the opposition of common characters. To produce great effects, he felt that it was necessary to deal only with the greater passions—with the exaltations of a daring fancy, and the errors of a lofty intellect—with the pride, the terrors, and the agonies of strong emotion—the fire and air alone of our human elements.

In this respect, and in his general notion of the end and the elements of poetry, we have sometimes thought that his views fell more in with those of the Lake poets, than of any other party in the poetical commonwealth; and, in some of his later productions especially, it is impossible not to be struck with his occasional approaches to the style and manner of this class of writers. Lord Byron, however, it should be observed, like all other persons of a quick sense of beauty, and sure enough of their own oiginality to be in no fear of paltry imputations, is a great mimic of styles and manners, and a great borrower of external character. He and Mr Scott are full of imitations of all the writers from whom they have ever derived gratification; and the two most original writers of the age might appear, to superficial observers, to be the most deeply indebted to their predecessors. In this particular instance, we have no fault to find with Lord Byron: for undoubtedly the finer passages of Wordsworth and Southey have in them wherewithal to give an impulse to the utmost ambition of rival genius; and their diction and manner of writing is frequently both striking and original. But we must say, that it would afford us still greater pleasure to find these tuneful gentlemen returning the compliment which Lord Byron has here paid to their talents, and forming themselves on the model rather of his imitations, than of their own originals. In these imitations they will find that, though he is sometimes abundantly mystical, he never, or at least very rarely, indulges in absolute nonsense—never takes his lofty flights upon mean or ridiculous occasions—and, above all, never dilutes his strong conceptions and magnificent imaginations with a flood of oppressive verbosity. On the contrary, he is, of all living writers, the most concise and condensed; and, we would fain hope, may go far, by his example, to redeem the great reproach of our modern literature—its intolerable prolixity and redundance.

In his nervous and manly lines, we find no elaborate amplification of common sentiments —no ostentatious polishing of pretty expressions; and we really think that the brilliant success which has rewarded his disdain of these paltry artifices, should put to shame for ever that puling and self-admiring race, who can live through half a volume on the stock of a single thought, and expatiate over diverse fair quarto pages with the details of one tedious description.—In Lord Byron, on the contrary, we have a perpetual stream of thick-coming fancies—an eternal spring of fresh-blown images, which seem called into existence by the sudden flash of those glowing thoughts and overwhelming emotions, that struggle for expression through the whole flow of his poetry— and impart to a diction that is often abrupt and irregular, a force and a charm which seem frequently to realize all that is said of inspiration.

With all these undoubted claims to our admiration, however, it is impossible to deny that the Noble author before us has still something to learn, and a good deal to correct. He is frequently abrupt and careless, and sometimes obscure. There are marks, occasionally, of effort and straining after an emphasis which is generally spontaneous;—and, above all, there is far too great a monotony in the moral colouring of his pictures, and too much repetition of the same sentiments and maxims. He delights too exclusively in the delineation of a certain morbid exaltation of character and of feeling,—a sort of demoniacal sublimity, not without some traits of the ruined Archangel. He is haunted almost perpetually with the image of a being feeding and fed upon by violent passions, and the recollections of the catastrophes they have occasioned: And, though worn out by their past indulgence, unable to sustain the burden of an existence which they do not continue to animate—full of pride and revenge and obduracy—disdaining life and death, and mankind and himself—and trampling, in his scorn, not only upon the falsehood and formality of polished life, but upon its tame virtues and slavish devotion: Yet envying, by fits, the selfish beings he despises, and melting into mere softness and compassion when the helplessness of childhood or the frailty of woman make an appeal to his generosity. Such is the person with whom we are called upon almost exclusively to sympathize in all the greater productions of this distin-

guished writer:—In Childe Harold—in the Corsair—in Lara—in the Siege of Corinth— in Parisina, and in most of the smaller pieces.

It is impossible to represent such a character better than Lord Byron has done in all these productions,—or indeed to represent anything more terrible in its anger, or more attractive in its relenting. In point of effect, we readily admit, that no one character can be more poetical or impressive:—But it is really too much to find the scene perpetually filled by one character—not only in all the acts, but in all the different pieces;—and, grand and impressive as it is, we feel at last that these very qualities make some relief more indispensable, and oppress the spirits of ordinary mortals with too deep an impression of awe and repulsion. There is too much guilt in short, and too much gloom, in the leading character;— and though it be a fine thing to gaze, now and then, on stormy seas, and thunder-shaken mountains, we should prefer passing our days in sheltered vallies, and by the murmur of calmer waters. . . .

V

Blackwood's Edinburgh Magazine. Vol. I, No. III, pp. 289–295. June, 1817.

Manfred. A Dramatic Poem. By Lord Byron. 8vo. Murray, London, 1817.

Reviewer: Unknown.

LORD BYRON has been elected by acclamation to the throne of poetical supremacy; nor are we disposed to question his title to the crown. There breathes over all his genius an air of kingly dignity; strength, vigour, energy, are his attributes; and he wields his faculties with a proud consciousness of their power, and a confident anticipation of their effect. Living poets perhaps there are, who have taken a wider range, but none who have achieved such complete, such perfect triumphs. In no great attempt has he ever failed; and, soon as he begins his flight, we feel that he is to soar upon unflagging wings—that when he has reached the black and tempestuous elevation of his favourite atmosphere, he will, eagle-like, sail on undisturbed through the heart of clouds, storms, and darkness.

To no poet was there ever given so awful a revelation of the passions of the human soul.

He surveys, with a stern delight, the tumult and conflict of terrible thoughts from which other gifted and powerful minds have involuntarily recoiled; he calmly and fearlessly stands upon the brink of that abyss from which the soul would seem to shrink with horror; and he looks down upon, and listens to, the everlasting agitation of the howling waters. There are in his poetry feelings, thoughts, sentiments, and passions, that we at once recognise to be human, though we know not whence they come: they break upon us like the sudden flash of a returning dream,—like some wild cry from another world. And even those whose lives have had little experience of the wilder passions, for a moment feel that an unknown region of their own souls has been revealed to them, and that there are indeed fearful mysteries in our human nature.

When this dark and powerful spirit for a while withdraws from the contemplation of his own wild world, and condescends to look upon the ordinary shews and spectacles of life, he often seems unexpectedly to participate in the feelings and emotions of beings with whom it might be thought he could claim no kindred; and thus many passages are to be found in his poetry, of the most irresistible and overpowering pathos, in which the depth of his sympathy with common sorrows and common sufferers, seems as profound as if his nature knew nothing more mournful than sighs and tears.

We have no intention of drawing Lord Byron's poetical character, and have been led, we know not how, into these very general and imperfect observations. But perhaps the little we have said may in some degree shew, why hitherto this great poet has dealt so seldom with the forms of the external world. He has so deeply looked into the soul of man, and so intensely sympathized with all the struggles there—that he has had no feelings or passions to fling away on the mere earth he inhabits. But it is evident that the same powers, which he has so gloriously exerted upon man as their subject, would kindle up and enlighten, or darken and disturb, the features of external nature; and that, if he so willed it, his poetry, instead of being rife with wrath, despair, remorse, and all other agitating passions, might present an equally sublime assemblage of woods, glens, and mountains,—of lakes and rivers, cataracts and oceans. In the third canto of Childe Harold, accordingly, he has delivered up his soul to the impulses of Nature, and we have seen how that high communion has elevated and sublimed it. He instantly penetrated into her heart, as he had before into the heart of Man; and, in a few months of solitary wandering among the Alps, his soul became as deeply embued with her glory and magnificence, as if, from youth, he had dedicated himself to no other power, and had for ever devoutly worshipped at her altar. He leapt at once into the first rank of descriptive poets. He came into competition with Wordsworth upon his own ground, and with his own weapons; and in the first encounter he vanquished and overthrew him. His description of the stormy night among the Alps—of the blending —the mingling—the fusion of his own soul, with the raging elements around him,—is alone worth all the dull metaphysics of the Excursion, and shews that he might enlarge the limits of human consciousness regarding the operations of matter upon mind, as widely as he has enlarged them regarding the operations of mind upon itself. . . .

VI

Blackwood's Edinburgh Magazine. Vol. III, No. XIV, pp. 216–226. May, 1818.

Fourth Canto of Childe Harold.

Reviewer: Unknown.

IT would be worse than idle to endeavour to shadow out the lineaments of that Mind, which, exhibiting itself in dark and perturbed grandeur, has established a stronger and wider sway over the passions of men, than any other poetical Intellect of modern times. We feel as if there were a kind of absurdity in criticising the power that hurries us along with it like a whirlwind. When standing within the magic circle, and in the immediate presence of the magician, we think not upon his art itself, but yield ourselves up to its wonder-working influence. We have no wish to speculate on the causes which awoke and stirred up all the profoundest feelings and energies of our souls,— the deep pathos, the stormy passion, has been enjoyed or suffered,—and, in the exaltation or prostration of our nature, we own the power of the poet to be divine,—and, with a satisfied and unquestioning delight, deliver ourselves up to his gentle fascination, or his irresistible dominion.

We do not say that Lord Byron stands above criticism—but that criticism seems to be altogether foreign to the nature and to the purposes of his genius. It is impossible to speak of his poetry without also speaking of himself, morally, as a man; and this, who shall dare to do, who has had even a feeble glimpse into the haunted darkness of the human soul? In his poetry, more than any other man's, there is felt a continual presence of himself—there is everlasting self-representation and self-reference; and perhaps that, which to cold and unimpassioned judgment might seem the essential fault of his poetry, constitutes its real excellence, and gives it power, sovereign and despotical.

Strictly speaking, and according to the rules by which great poems have been builded, it cannot be said that Byron has ever created a great Poem. He has celebrated no mighty exploit, or event, or revolution in the destinies of mankind; nor brought before us one majestic portion of the history of our species, in which, as in a course perfect and complete, the mind of man has been seen to run a career of power and glory. He has brought forward from the darkness of past times, no shining spectres—no immortal ghosts. One Figure alone is seen stalking through the city and through the solitude—over the earth and over the sea: and that Figure, stern, melancholy, and majestic, is still no other than Himself, on the same dark, mournful, solitary, and perplexing Pilgrimage. . . .

We have no hesitation in saying, that Byron's creations are not so much poems, as they are glorious manifestations of a poet's mind, all irresistibly tending towards poetry. Having in himself deep sense of beauty—deeper passions than probably any other great poet ever had—and aspiring conceptions of power, the poetry in which he expresses himself must be full of vivid portraiture of beauty, deep spirit of passion, and daring suggestions of power. It is obvious that he has never yet soared to his utmost pitch. He is the poet of the age from whom most is to be expected. For there are things in his poetry—strong and irregular bursts of power, beyond the strength of the strongest. At times he seems possessed and over-mastered by an inspiration. A spirit is then in him that works at will, and it is a

spirit that in its perfect grandeur seems to have visited none other of the children of men.

The popular belief, that his heroes are himself, is a true belief; and the world has at last convinced the poet of that which he had at first but indistinctly understood, and imperfectly believed. His heroes are himself—that is, either what he is, or has been, or what he would wish or fear to be. Whatever may have been his intention, there is in his mind a predominant consciousness of himself, which determines the character he draws. This appears most in the first two Cantos of Childe Harold, where his mind seems so enslaved in itself, that it cannot escape even from a direct journal of his own travels. But much more than his characters are drawn from himself. Almost every feeling, passion, thought, or image, or represented object in his poetry, has magnitude or interest assigned to it, not in proportion to its plan in the poem, but to its direct interest to his own mind,—and not to his imagination, but to his passions, and his life of passion. He thus seems seldom to go back to the early periods even of his own mind, and then but by fits and starts—but to be continually living in the last, almost the present years of his life. He is indeed a mind under the dominion of its passions, and which cannot escape from them even in imagination. This may, indeed must, make a sameness in his writings. But in proportion to their sameness is their variety. It is almost incredible, that a man producing continually the same passions and the same feelings, should produce them, as he has done, in such continual change of shape, that we never complain of repetition. This can only be owing to the unequalled intenseness of passion, which, like the power of life, is endlessly unfolding itself in new forms. It can only be the simple, natural, human force of the vivid utterance of intense passion, that produces in minds of every description so strong a sympathy with Byron in all his different moods, and too often, in spite of reluctance and repugnance, of moral and intellectual condemnation.

But does not the question naturally arise, Is this the best, the noblest poetry? Is it fitting, is it truly great, that a highly-gifted spirit, potent by nature, and enriched by the highest studies, should voluntarily circumscribe the sphere of its dominion that its power may be more despotical? Or if it be not a free agent, is there not something degrading to the soul of man in the idea, that inward disease or outward affliction can subjugate under its yoke him, who, nevertheless, would seem to despise subjugation, and who vainly imagines that he can display the spirit of freedom in the majestic air with which he drags his chains?

We must all feel that Byron, with all his mighty faculties, is at times only shielded from contempt, by the conviction that many of his miseries are self-inflicted. They are often imaginary; and therefore is it that our imagination redeems him who awakens it. He exasperates his soul into agony. He sinks it down into despair. But genius breathes forth the profoundest sighs that disturb us, and often converts them, in an instant, into an exulting hymn. And often the long majestic sweep of sorrow, that winds up a subduing stanza, is suddenly succeeded by airy music, as if in derision of the melancholy close; and Byron's soul bounds exultingly forward, escaping from the dim cell into which it had retired in voluntary imprisonment.

Many awful lessons may certainly be learned from the poetry of Lord Byron. Yet, undoubtedly, there are many things there barren and unavailing. The good, the happy, and the innocent, can draw no instruction from what they cannot imagine even in dreams; while the erring or passion-stricken spirit contemplates, too often, the ruins as it were of its own nature, without hope of the temple being rebuilt, or if so, ever again being animated with the spirit that is fled.

Of the danger resulting from such poetry to souls of fine aspirations, but unsteadfast wills,—to souls where passion is the only or chief impulse, and where there is a tendency to hold cheap, and in derision, the dull duties of ordinary life, and at the same time not strength sufficient to grasp and master the objects of a more ambitious existence,—to such souls (and they are numerous among the youth of Britain,) that poetry is most fatal which flings aside the antiquated bonds consecrated by mere every-day associations,—which renders reason itself subservient to the senses (ennobled as they are by the imagination), and admits no other laws of life but the tyrannic passions cherished in the conscious pride of that power, which, in turn, uses those passions as its most abject slaves.

If such may be the effect of Byron's poetry on good natures, it is to be feared that it may exert a lamentable influence over those prone to evil. There must appear in the splendour, and power, and majesty, wherein his genius enshrouds feelings and passions intrinsically worthless or pernicious, a fatal justification of that evil, from which, in its native nakedness, even the fallen spirit would turn with aversion. When virtue is dead, pride often remains in full life. It firmly fastens on representations like these, by which a veil is thrown over its own meanness,—and a false but dazzling world is thus created for it, wherein it may move, and act as bold and fearless a part as virtue herself walking in her untroubled beauty. To Byron, and to great though erring spirits like his, we mournfully allow the privilege of his pride. It is a shirt of mail wherewith he would seek to guard his bosom from the shafts of sorrow. And it may be, that its folds sometimes indeed repel those "unkindest blows of all," against whose infliction the soul hath no other shield in its solitude. But with them whose passions tend only towards mere earthly objects— unsanctified by genius or by grief—reckless, importunate, and selfish—sacrificing to their indulgence, without compunction, the happiness of other hearts—how pernicious must that philosophy be (and the poetry of Byron is but too full of it), that lends robes of royalty, and a seeming sceptre to passions that are in themselves base, odious, and contemptible, or, haply, such as conduct to ruin, agony, and death.

There is one school of poetry (we use the word somewhat unwillingly) from which this great Poet has already learned much, and from which his noble nature may yet learn more— the poetry of the Lakes. Byron need not be ashamed—nay, he must exult to be instructed by the wisdom of Wordsworth. Nothing can impair the originality of his genius; little need be added to its power. But a warning voice may arise from the untroubled magnificence of the mountain solitude, and the wandering "Childe" may pause in the darkest track of his pilgrimage, to hear the calm, pure, lofty anthem that the poet sings to nature in the sinless happiness which she has created, sanctified, and blest against violence or decay. Lord Byron seems to have roamed through the Alps with the spirit of Wordsworth often at his side;—and his soul was elevated by the communion. It is cold and unmeaning to say, that in the third canto of

Childe Harold, he imitated or competed with the author of the Excursion. He followed him— he was led by him—to the same eternal fountain of all beauty and all grandeur. Different as are the souls of these two illustrious men, nature bowed them down or elevated them up into similitude; so that in Byron's glorious songs among the Alps, we see the same soul at work that had before sublimed the mountains of England,—and are delighted to behold how the calm wisdom of contemplative age and recluse philosophy can purify, and sustain, and strengthen, the impetuous energy of a wilder spirit, revelling deliriously among the maddening magnificence of nature. . . .

Byron . . . knows, that the great poet to whom we have alluded, though accused of bigotry, infatuation, and narrowness of view, has taken ampler and nobler prospects of the soul of man than any other living mind. He knows the depths of the calm of that wisdom, which the storms of the world cannot disturb. He knows that poetry is a divine art—that its influences are divine. And all may see scattered throughout the darkest scenery of his own soul, lights that seem as if they would fain break through the gloom, and that wait but for his will to shine on him and his spirit for evermore, and make him, what every great poet should be, the glad, exulting, hoping, undismayed, friend and vindicator of the immortal destinies of man. . . .

VII

The Edinburgh Review. Vol. XXX, No. LIX, pp. 87–120. June, 1818.

> *Childe Harold's Pilgrimage. Canto the Fourth.* By Lord Byron. 8vo. pp. 257. London, 1818.

Reviewer: John Wilson.[1]

THERE are two writers, in modern literature, whose extraordinary power over the minds of men, it may be truly said, has existed less in their works than in themselves,—Rousseau and Lord Byron. They have other points of resemblance. Both are distinguished by the most ardent and vivid delineations of intense conception, and by an intense sensibility of passion, rather than of affection.

[1] This is the only review which John Wilson is known to have contributed to the *Edinburgh.*

Both, too, by this double power, have held a dominion over the sympathy of their readers, far beyond the range of those ordinary feelings which are usually excited by the mere efforts of genius. The impression of this interest still accompanies the perusal of their writings: But there is another interest of more lasting, and far stronger power, which the one has possessed, and the other now possesses,—which lies in the continual embodying of the individual character,—it might almost be said, of the very person of the writer. When we speak or think of Rousseau or Byron, we are not conscious of speaking or thinking of an author. We have a vague but impassioned remembrance of men of surpassing genius, eloquence and power,—of prodigious capacity both of misery and happiness. We feel as if we had transiently met such beings in real life, or had known them in the dim and dark communion of a dream. Each of their works presents, in succession, a fresh idea of themselves; and, while the productions of other great men stand out from them, like something they have created, theirs, on the contrary, are images, pictures, busts of their living selves,—clothed, no doubt, at different times in different drapery, and prominent from a different background,—but uniformly impressed with the same form, and mien, and lineaments, and not to be mistaken for the representations of any other of the children of men.

But this view of the subject, though universally felt to be a true one, requires perhaps a little explanation. The personal character of which we have spoken, it should be understood, is not, altogether, that on which the seal of life has been set,—and to which, therefore, moral approval or condemnation is necessarily annexed, as to the language or conduct of actual existence. It is the character, so to speak, which is prior to conduct, and yet open to good and to ill,—the constitution of the being, in body and in soul. Each of those illustrious writers has, in this light, filled his works with expressions of his own character,—has unveiled to the world the secrets of his own being,—the mysteries of the framing of man. They have gone down into those depths which every man may sound for himself, though not for another; and they have made disclosures to the world of what they beheld and knew there—disclosures that have commanded and enforced a profound and universal sympathy, by proving that all mankind, the troubled and the untroubled, the lofty and the low, the strongest and the frailest, are linked together by the bonds of a common but inscrutable nature.

Thus, each of these wayward and richly-gifted spirits has made himself the object of profound interest to the world,—and that too, during periods of society when ample food was everywhere spread abroad for the meditations and passions of men. What love and desire,—what longing and passionate expectation hung upon the voice of Rousseau, the idol of his day!—That spell is broken. We now can regard his works in themselves, in great measure free from all the delusions and illusions that, like the glories of a bright and vapoury atmosphere, were for ever rising up and encircling the image of their wonderful creator. Still is the impression of his works vivid and strong. . . . But that which made the spirits of men, from one end of Europe to the other, turn to the name of Rousseau,—that idolizing enthusiasm which we can now hardly conceive, was the illusion of one generation, and has not survived to another. And what was the spell of that illusion? Was it merely that bewitching strain of dreaming melancholy which lent to moral declamation the tenderness of romance? Or that fiery impress of burning sensibility which threw over abstract and subtle disquisitions all the colours of a lover's tale? These undoubtedly—but not these alone. It was that continual impersonation of himself in his writings, by which he was for ever kept brightly present before the eyes of men. There was in him a strange and unsated desire of depicturing himself, throughout all the changes of his being. His wild temper only found ease in tracing out, in laying bare to the universal gaze, . . . the darkest coverts of one of the most wayward and unimaginable minds ever framed by nature. . . . Shy, and shunning the faces of men in his daily walks, yet searching and rending up the inmost recesses of his heart for the inspection of that race which he feared or hated. As a man, turning from the light, as from something unsupportably loathsome, and plunging into the thickest shades. Yet, in that other existence which he held from imagination, living only in the presence of men, . . . and eagerly, impetuously, passionately, unsparingly seizing on all his own most hidden thoughts—his loneliest moods—his most sacred feelings—

. . . and flinging them out into the open air, that they might feed the curiosity of that eager, idle, frivolous world from which he had fled in misanthropical disgust. . . .

When death removes such a writer from our sight, the magical influence of which we have spoken gradually fades away; and a new generation . . . may perhaps be wearied with that perpetual self-reference which to them seems merely the querulousness or the folly of unhappy or diseased egotism. . . .

It would, indeed, be in most violent contradiction to all we have formerly written of Lord Byron, were we to say that he stands in this predicament. Yet, there is a certain applicability of our observations even to him. . . . Posterity may make fewer allowances for much in himself and his writings, than his contemporaries are willing to do; nor will they, with the same passionate and impetuous zeal, follow the wild voice that too often leads into a haunted wilderness of doubt and darkness. To them, as to us, there will always be something majestic in his misery—something sublime in his despair. But they will not, like us, be withheld from sterner and severer feelings, and from the more frequent visitings of moral condemnation. . . .

There are three only even among the great poets of modern times, who have chosen to depict, in their full shape and vigour, those agonies to which great and meditative intellects are, in the present progress of human history, exposed by the eternal recurrence of a deep and discontented scepticism. But there is only one who has dared to represent himself as the victim of these nameless and undefinable sufferings. Goëthe chose for his doubts and his darkness the terrible disguise of the mysterious Faustus. Schiller, with still greater boldness, planted the same anguish in the restless, haughty and heroic bosom of Wallenstein. But Byron has sought no external symbol in which to embody the inquietudes of his soul. He takes the world and all that it inherit for his arena and his spectators; and he displays himself before their gaze, wrestling unceasingly and ineffectually with the demon that torments him. At times there is something mournful and depressing in his scepticism; but oftener, it is of a high and solemn character, approachng to the very verge of a confiding faith. Whatever the poet may believe, we his readers always feel ourselves too much ennobled and elevated even by his melancholy, not to be confirmed in our own belief by the very doubts so majestically conceived and uttered. His scepticism, if it ever approaches to a creed, carries with it its refutation in its grandeur. Their [*sic*] is neither philosophy nor religion in those bitter and savage taunts which have been cruelly thrown out, from many quarters, against those moods of mind which are involuntary, and will not pass away;—the shadows and spectres which still haunt his imagination, may once have disturbed our own;—through his gloom there are frequent flashes of illumination;—and the sublime sadness which, to him, is breathed from the mysteries of mortal existence, is always joined with a longing after immortality, and expressed in language that is itself divine.

VIII

Blackwood's Edinburgh Magazine. Vol. V, No. XXIX, pp. 512–518. August, 1819.

Remarks on Don Juan.

Reviewer: Unknown.

IT has not been without much reflection and overcoming many reluctancies, that we have at last resolved to say a few words more to our readers concerning this very extraordinary poem. The nature and causes of our difficulties will be easily understood by those of them who have read any part of Don Juan—but we despair of standing justified as to the conclusion at which we have arrived, in the opinion of any but those who have read and understood the whole of a work, in the composition of which there is unquestionably a more thorough and intense infusion of genius and vice—power and profligacy—than in any poem which had ever before been written in the English, or indeed in any other modern language. Had the wickedness been less inextricably mingled with beauty and the grace, and the strength of a most inimitable and incomprehensible muse, our task would have been easy: But silence would be a very poor and a very useless chastisement to be inflicted by us, or by any one, on a production, whose corruptions have been so effectually embalmed—which, in spite of all that critics can do or refrain from doing, nothing can possibly prevent from taking a high place in the literature of our country, and remaining to all ages a perpetual monument

of the exalted intellect, and the depraved heart, of one of the most remarkable men to whom that country has had the honour and disgrace of giving birth. . . .

The moral strain of the whole poem is pitched in the lowest key—and if the genius of the author lifts him now and then out of his pollution, it seems as if he regretted the elevation, and made all haste to descend again. To particularize the offences committed in its pages would be worse than vain—because the great genius of the man seems to have been throughout exerted to its utmost strength, in devising every possible method of pouring scorn upon every element of good or noble nature in the hearts of his readers. Love—honour—patriotism—religion, are mentioned only to be scoffed at and derided, as if their sole resting-place were or ought to be, in the bosoms of fools. It appears, in short, as if this miserable man, having exhausted every species of sensual gratification—having drained the cup of sin even to its bitterest dregs, were resolved to shew us that he is no longer a human being, even in his frailties;—but a cool unconcerned fiend. . . .

The same proud hardness of heart which makes the author of Don Juan a despiser of the Faith for which his fathers bled, has rendered him a scorner of the better part of woman; and therefore it is that his love poetry is a continual insult to the beauty that inspires it. The earthly part of the passion is all that has found a resting place within his breast—His idol is all of clay—and he dashes her to pieces almost in the moment of his worship. Impiously railing against his God—madly and meanly disloyal to his Sovereign and his country,—and brutally outraging all the best feelings of female honour, affection, and confidence—How small a part of chivalry is that which remains to the descendant of the Byrons—a gloomy vizor, and a deadly weapon! . . .

Those who are acquainted with the main incidents in the private life of Lord Byron;—and who have not seen this production,—will scarcely believe, that the odious malignity of this man's bosom should have carried him so far, as to make him commence a filthy and impious poem, with an elaborate satire on the character and manners of his wife—from whom, even by his own confession, he has been separated only in consequence of his own cruel and heartless misconduct. It is in vain for Lord Byron to attempt to justify his own behaviour in that affair; and, now that he has so openly and audaciously invited inquiry and reproach, we do not see any good reason why he should not be plainly told so by the general voice of his countrymen. . . . For impurities there might be some possibility of pardon, were they supposed to spring only from the reckless buoyancy of young blood and fiery passions,— for impiety there might at least be pity, were it visible that the misery of the impious soul were as great as its darkness;—but for offences such as this, which cannot proceed either from the madness of sudden impulse, or the bewildered agonies of self-perplexing and self-despairing doubt—but which speak the wilful and determined spite of an unrepenting, unsoftened, smiling, sarcastic, joyous sinner— for such diabolical, such slavish vice, there can be neither pity nor pardon. . . .

But the best and the worst part of the whole is without doubt the description of the shipwreck. As a piece of terrible painting, it is as much superior as can be to every description of the kind—not even accepting that in the Æneid—that ever was created. In comparison with the fearful and intense realities of its horrors, every thing that any former poet has thrown together to depict the agonies of that awful scene, appears chill and tame. . . .

But even here the demon of his depravity does not desert him. We dare not stain our pages with quoting any specimens of the disgusting merriment with which he has interspersed his picture of human suffering. He paints it well, only to shew that he scorns it the more effectually; and of all the fearful sounds which ring in the ears of the dying, the most horrible is the demoniacal laugh with which this unpitying brother exults over the contemplation of their despair. Will our readers believe that the most innocent of all his odious sarcasms is contained in these two lines?

They grieved for those that perished in the cutter,
And also for the biscuit, casks, and butter.

IX

The Edinburgh Review. Vol. XXXVI, No. LXXII, pp. 413–452. February, 1822.

    Sardanapalus, a Tragedy. The Two Foscari, a Tragedy. Cain, a Mystery. By Lord Byron. 8vo. pp. 440. Murray, London, 1822.

    Reviewer: Francis Jeffrey.

. . . But it is not with him, or the merits of the treatment he has either given or received, that we have now any concern. We have a word or two to say on the griefs of Lord Byron himself. He complains bitterly of the detraction by which he has been assailed—and intimates that his works have been received by the public with far less cordiality and favour than he was entitled to expect. We are constrained to say that this appears to us a very extraordinary mistake. In the whole course of our experience, we cannot recollect a single author who has had so little reason to complain of his reception—to whose genius the public has been so early and so constantly just—to whose faults they have been so long and so signally indulgent. From the very first, he must have been aware that he offended the principles and shocked the prejudices of the majority, by his sentiments, as much as he delighted them by his talents. Yet there never was an author so universally and warmly applauded, so gently admonished—so kindly entreated to look more heedfully to his opinions. He took the praise, as usual, and rejected the advice. As he grew in fame and authority, he aggravated all his offences—clung more fondly to all he had been reproached with—and only took leave of Childe Harold to ally himself to Don Juan! That he has since been talked of, in public and in private, with less unmingled admiration—that his name is now mentioned as often for censure as for praise—and that the exultation with which his countrymen once hailed the greatest of our living poets, is now alloyed by the recollection of the tendency of his writings—is matter of notoriety to all the world; but matter of surprise, we should imagine, to nobody but Lord B. himself. . . .

He has no priestlike cant or priestlike reviling to apprehend from us. We do not charge him with being either a disciple or an apostle of Satan; nor do we describe his poetry as a mere compound of blasphemy and obscenity. On the contrary, we are inclined to believe that he wishes well to the happiness of mankind—and are glad to testify, that his poems abound with sentiments of great dignity and tenderness, as well as passages of infinite sublimity and beauty. But their general tendency we believe to be in the highest degree pernicious; and we even think that it is chiefly by means of the fine and lofty sentiments they contain, that they acquire their most fatal power of corruption. This may sound at first, perhaps, like a paradox; but we are mistaken if we shall not make it intelligible enough in the end.

We think there are indecencies and indelicacies, seductive descriptions and profligate representations, which are extremely reprehensible; and also audacious speculations, and erroneous and uncharitable assertions, equally indefensible. But if these had stood alone, and if the whole body of his works had been made up of gaudy ribaldry and flashy scepticism, the mischief, we think, would have been much less than it is. He is not more obscene, perhaps, than Dryden or Prior, and other classical and pardoned writers; nor is there any passage in the history even of Don Juan, so degrading as Tom Jones's affair with Lady Bellaston. It is no doubt a wretched apology for the indecencies of a man of genius, that equal indecencies have been forgiven to his predecessors: But the precedent of lenity might have been followed; and we might have passed both the levity and the voluptuousness—the dangerous warmth of his romantic situations, and the scandal of his cold-blooded dissipation. It might not have been so easy to get over his dogmatic scepticism—his hard-hearted maxims of misanthropy—his cold-blooded and eager expositions of the non-existence of virtue and honour. Even this, however, might have been comparatively harmless, if it had not been accompanied by that which may look, at first sight, as a palliation—the frequent presentment of the most touching pictures of tenderness, generosity, and faith. . . .

This is the charge which we bring against Lord Byron. We say that, under some strange misapprehension as to the truth, and the duty of proclaiming it, he has exerted all the powers of his powerful mind to convince his readers, both directly and indirectly, that all ennobling pursuits, and disinterested virtues, are mere deceits or illusions—hollow and despicable mockeries for the most part, and, at best, but laborious follies. Love, patriotism, valour, devotion, constancy, ambition—all are to be laughed at, disbelieved in, and despised!—and nothing is really good, so far as we can gather, but a succession of dangers to stir the blood, and of banquets and intrigues to sooth it again! If this doctrine stood alone, with its examples, it would revolt, we believe, more than it would

seduce:—but the author of it has the unlucky gift of personating all those sweet and lofty illusions, and that with such grace and force and truth to nature, that it is impossible not to suppose, for the time, that he is among the most devoted of their votaries—till he casts off the character with a jerk—and, the moment after he has moved and exalted us to the very height of our conception, resumes his mockery at all things serious or sublime—and lets us down at once on some coarse joke, hard-hearted sarcasm, or fierce and relentless personality— as if on purpose to show

Whoe'er was edified, himself was not—

or to demonstrate practically as it were, and by example, how possible it is to have all fine and noble feelings, or their appearance, for a moment, and yet retain no particle of respect for them—or of belief in their intrinsic worth or permanent reality. Thus, we have an indelicate but very clever scene of the young Juan's concealment in the bed of an amorous matron, and of the torrent of "rattling and audacious eloquence" with which she repels the too just suspicions of her jealous lord. All this is merely comic, and a little coarse:—But then the poet chuses to make this shameless and abandoned woman address to her young gallant, an epistle breathing the very spirit of warm, devoted, pure and unalterable love—thus profaning the holiest language of the heart, and indirectly associating it with the most hateful and degrading sensuality. In like manner, the sublime and terrific description of the Shipwreck is strangely and disgustingly broken by traits of low humour and buffoonery;—and we pass immediately from the moans of an agonizing father fainting over his famished son, to facetious stories of Juan's begging a paw of his father's dog—and refusing a slice of his tutor!—as if it were a fine thing to be hard-hearted—and pity and compassion were fit only to be laughed at. In the same spirit, the glorious Ode on the aspirations of Greece after Liberty, is instantly followed up by a strain of dull and cold-blooded ribaldry;—and we are hurried on from the distraction and death of Haidee to merry scenes of intrigue and masquerading in the seraglio. Thus all good feelings are excited only to accustom us to their speedy and complete extinction; and we are brought back, from their transient and theatrical exhibition, to the staple and substantial doctrine of the work—the non-existence of constancy in women or honour in men, and the folly of expecting to meet with any such virtues, or of cultivating them for an undeserving world;—and all this mixed up with so much wit and cleverness, and knowledge of human nature, as to make it irresistibly pleasant and plausible—while there is not only no antidote supplied, but every thing that might have operated in that way has been anticipated, and presented already in as strong and engaging a form as possible—but under such associations as to rob it of all efficacy, or even turn it into an auxiliary of the poison. . . .

PERCY BYSSHE SHELLEY

REVIEWS OF HIS WORK

I

The London Literary Gazette. Vol. V, No. 226, pp. 305–308. May 19, 1821.

Queen Mab. By Percy Bysshe Shelley. London, 1821. 8vo. pp. 182.

Reviewer: Unknown.

THE mixture of sorrow, indignation, and loathing, with which this volume has overwhelmed us, will, we fear, deprive us of the power of expressing our sentiments upon it, in the manner best suited to the subject itself, and to the effect which we wish our criticism to have upon society. Our desire is to do justice *to* the writer's genius, and *upon* his principles: not to deny his powers, while we deplore their perversion; and above all, when we lay before our readers the examples of his poetry, to warn them against the abominable and infamous contagion with which in the sequel he poisons these splendid effusions. We have doubted whether we ought to notice this book at all; and if our silence could have prevented its being disseminated, no allusion to it should ever have stained the Literary Gazette. But the activity of the vile portion of the press, is too great to permit this hope.[1] [*sic*] and on weighing every considera-

tion presented to our minds, we have come to the conclusion to lay, as far as we are able, the bane and the antidote before the public. Queen Mab has long been in limited and private circulation, as a duodecimo; and the first two or three cantos, under the title of The Demon of the World, were reprinted at the end of a poem called Alastor; as was also the principal note against Christianity in a detached pamphlet. Though the hellish ingredients, therefore, are now for the first time brought together into one cauldron, they have, like those of the evil beings in Macbeth, previously disgusted the world in forms of separate obsceneness.

We have spoken of Shelley's genius, and it is doubtless of a high order; but when we look at the purposes to which it is directed, and contemplate the infernal character of all its efforts, our souls revolt with tenfold horror at the energy it exhibits, and we feel as if one of the darkest of the fiends had been clothed with a human body, to enable him to gratify his enmity against the human race, and as if the supernatural atrocity of his hate were only heightened by his power to do injury. So strongly has this impression dwelt upon our minds, that we absolutely asked a friend who had seen this individual, to describe him to us—as if a cloven foot, or horn, or flames from the mouth, must have marked the external appearance of so bitter an enemy to mankind. We were almost disappointed to learn that the author was only a tall, boyish looking man, with eyes of unearthly brightness, and a countenance of the wildest cast: that he strode about with a hurried and impatient gait, and that a perturbed spirit seemed to preside over all his movements. It is not then in his outer semblance but in his inner man, that the explicit demon is seen; and it is a frightful supposition, that his own life may have been a fearful commentary upon his principles [2]— principles, which in the balance of law and

[1] As this is a book of so blasphemous a nature, as to have no claim to the protection of copyright; it may be published by Scoundrels at all prices, to destroy the moral feeling of every class of the community. In the present instance the author has not, we imagine, been consulted. [See Shelley's letter to the *Examiner,* June 22, 1821.]

[2] We are aware, that the ordinary criticism has little or nothing to do with the personal conduct of authors; but when the most horrible doctrines are promulgated with appalling force, it is the duty of every man to expose, in every way, the abominations to which they irresistibly drive their odious professors. We declare against receiving our social impulses from a destroyer of every social virtue; our moral creed, from an incestuous wretch; or our religion, from an atheist, who denied God, and reviled the purest institutes of human philosophy and divine ordination, did such a demon exist.

justice, happily deprived him of the superintendance of his infants, while they plunged an unfortunate wife and mother into ruin, guilt, and suicide.

Such, alas! are the inevitable consequences of the fatal precepts enforced in this publication, which spares not one grace, one good, one ornament, nor one blessing, that can ameliorate our lot on earth; which wages exterminating war against all that can refine, delight or improve human kind; which ridicules every thing that can contribute to our happiness here, and boldly tries to crush every hope that could point to our happiness hereafter. . . .

The utter annihilation of every enjoyment which man can have on earth—the black catalogue of woes, to which so dreadful a creed as this must tend—the blank and dismaying prospect which it opens to the revolting sense—all the idiotcy of its conception, and all the villany of its avowal—deprive us of words to speak our detestation of its author. But the blaster of his race stops not here: in the very next page—we tremble while we transcribe it —he desperately, insanely asserts—"There is no God."

Miserable worm! Pity pleads for thee; and contempt, disgust, and horror, are tempered by compassion for thy wretched infirmity of mind. But an overwhelming passion rises when we gaze on the hideous blasphemy of thy more prolix commentary on this detestable text. We hardly dare copy it; but it is our duty to show to what monstrous extent the author carries his impious profanation. . . .

We cannot proceed: pages of raving atheism . . . follow; and the blasphemer revels in all the pruriency of his disordered and diabolical fancy. For men like the writer, when they are known to exist, there are no terms of infamy sufficiently strong. We may therefore say, in the mild language of Bentley, that as "no atheist, as such, can be a true friend, an affectionate relation, or a loyal subject," we leave to his conscience . . . this demoniac proscriber of his species, and insolent insulter of his Maker. . . .

It is hardly worth while to ask how a theorist of Mr. Shelley's class would act in relations between man and man. It can hardly be doubted but his practice would square with his principles, and be calculated to disturb all the harmonies of nature. A disciple following his tenets, would not hesitate to debauch, or, after

debauching, to abandon any woman: to such, it would be a matter of perfect indifference to rob a confiding father of his daughters, and incestuously to live with all the branches of a family whose morals were ruined by the damned sophistry of the seducer; to such would be sport to tell a deserted wife to obtain with her pretty face support by prostitution; and, when the unhappy maniac sought refuge in self-destruction, to laugh at the fool while in the arms of associate strumpets. For what are the ties of nature, what are the pangs of humanity, to them? They are above the idle inventions of tyrants and priests—the worthless restrictions of "morals, law, and custom,"—the delusions of virtue, and the ordinances of deity. . . .

We will not stain our pages with another line; and we trust to Heaven, that in discharging as painful and difficult a duty as ever fell upon a Review, we may be pardoned if we have acted unwisely, since we are sure we have acted conscientiously.

II

The Quarterly Review. Vol. XXI, No. XLII, pp. 460–471. April, 1819.

> 1. *Laon and Cythna, or the Revolution of the Golden City. A Vision of the Nineteenth Century, in the Stanza of Spenser.* By Percy B. Shelley. London. 1818.
> 2. *The Revolt of Islam. A Poem, in Twelve Cantos.* By Percy Bysshe Shelley. London. 1818.

Reviewer: John Taylor Coleridge.

THIS is one of that industrious knot of authors, the tendency of whose works we have in our late Numbers exposed to the caution of our readers—novel, poem, romance, letters, tours, critique, lecture and essay follow one another, framed to the same measure, and in subjection to the same key-note, while the sweet undersong of the weekly journal, filling up all pauses, strengthening all weaknesses, smoothing all abruptness, harmonizes the whole strain. Of all his brethren Mr. Shelley carries to the greatest length the doctrines of the sect. He is, for this and other reasons, by far the least pernicious of them; indeed there is a naiveté and openness in his manner of laying down the most extravagant positions, which in some measure deprives them of their venom; and when he enlarges on what certainly are but necessary results of opinions more guardedly delivered by others, he might almost be mistaken for some artful advocate of civil order and religious institutions. This benefit indeed may be drawn from his book, for there is scarcely any more persuasive argument for truth than to carry out to all their legitimate consequences the doctrines of error. But this is not Mr. Shelley's intention; he is, we are sorry to say, in sober earnest:—with perfect deliberation, and the steadiest perseverance he perverts all the gifts of his nature, and does all the injury, both public and private, which his faculties enable him to perpetrate. . . .

Mr. Shelley is a philosopher by the courtesy of the age, and has a theory of course respecting the government of the world; we will state in as few words as we can the general outlines of that theory, the manner in which he demonstrates it, and the practical consequences, which he proposes to deduce from it. It is to the second of these divisions that we would beg his attention; we despair of convincing him directly that he has taken up false and pernicious notions; but if he pays any deference to the common laws of reasoning, we hope to shew him that, let the goodness of his cause be what it may, his manner of advocating it is false and unsound. This may be mortifying to a teacher of mankind; but a philosopher seeks the truth, and has no vanity to be mortified.

The existence of evil, physical and moral, is the grand problem of all philosophy; the humble find it a trial, the proud make it a stumbling-block; Mr. Shelley refers it to the faults of those civil institutions and religious creeds which are designed to regulate the conduct of man here, and his hopes in a hereafter. In these he seems to make no distinction, but considers them all as bottomed upon principles pernicious to man and unworthy of God, carried into details the most cruel, and upheld only by the stupidity of the many on the one hand, and the selfish conspiracy of the few on the other. According to him the earth is a boon garden needing little care or cultivation, but pouring forth spontaneously and inexhaustibly all innocent delights and luxuries to her innumerable children; the seasons have no inclemencies, the air no pestilences for man in his proper state of wisdom and liberty; his business here is to en-

joy himself, to abstain from no gratification, to repent of no sin, hate no crime, but be wise, happy and free, with plenty of "lawless love." This is man's natural state, the state to which Mr. Shelley will bring us, if we will but break up the "crust of our outworn opinions," as he calls them, and put them into his magic cauldron. But kings have introduced war, legislators crime, priests sin; the dreadful consequences have been that the earth has lost her fertility, the seasons their mildness, the air its salubrity, man his freedom and happiness. We have become a foul-feeding carnivorous race, are foolish enough to feel uncomfortable after the commission of sin; some of us even go so far as to consider vice odious; and we all groan under a multiplied burthen of crimes *merely conventional;* among which Mr. Shelley specifies with great *sang froid* the commission of *incest!*

We said that our philosopher makes no distinction in his condemnation of creeds; we should rather have said, that he makes no exception; distinction he does make, and it is to the prejudice of that which we hold. In one place indeed he assembles a number of names of the founders of religions, to treat them all with equal disrespect.

And through the host contention wild befell,
As each of his own God the wondrous works did tell;
And Oromaze and Christ and Mahomet,
Moses and Buddh, Zerdusht, and Brahm and Foh,
A tumult of strange names, &.—p. 227.

But in many other places he manifests a dislike to Christianity which is frantic, and would be, if in such a case any thing could be, ridiculous. When the votaries of all religions are assembled with one accord (this unanimity by the bye is in a vision of the *nineteenth* century) to stifle the first breathings of liberty, and execute the revenge of a ruthless tyrant, he selects a Christian priest to be the organ of sentiments outrageously and pre-eminently cruel. The two characteristic principles upon which Christianity may be said to be built are repentance and faith. Of repentance he speaks thus:—

Reproach not thine own soul, but know thyself;
Nor hate another's crime, nor loathe thine own.
It is the dark idolatry of self
Which, when our thoughts and actions once are gone,

Demands that we should weep and bleed and
    groan;
O vacant expiation! be at rest—
The past is death's—the future is thine own;
And love and joy can make the *foulest* breast
A paradise of flowers where peace might build
    her nest. p. 188.

Repentance then is selfishness in an extreme
which amounts to idolatry! but what is Faith?
our readers can hardly be prepared for the odious accumulation of sin and sorrow which Mr.
Shelley conceives under this word. "Faith is
the Python, the Ogress, the Evil Genius, the
Wicked Fairy, the Giantess of our children's
tales;" whenever any thing bad is to be accounted for, any hard name to be used, this
convenient monosyllable fills up the blank. . . .

Such is Mr. Shelley's victory, such its security, and such the means of obtaining it! These
last, we confess, are calculated to throw a damp
upon our spirits, for if the hopes of mankind
must depend upon the exertion of super-eminent
eloquence, we have the authority of one who
had well considered the subject, for believing
that they could scarcely depend upon any thing
of more rare occurrence. Plures in omnibus
rebus, quam in dicendo admirabiles, was the
remark of Cicero a great many ages ago, and
the experience of all those ages has served but
to confirm the truth of it.

Mr. Shelley, however, is not a man to propose a difficult remedy without suggesting the
means of procuring it. If we mistake not, Laon
and Cythna, and even the sage, (for there is a
sort of good stupid Archimago in the poem),
are already provided, and intent to begin their
mission if we will but give them hearing. In
short, Mr. Shelley is his own Laon: this is
clear from many passages of the preface and
dedication. The lady to whom the poem is addressed is certainly the original of Cythna: we
have more consideration for her than she has
had for herself, and will either mortify her
vanity, or spare her feelings, by not producing
her before the public; it is enough for the philanthropist to know that when the season arrives, she will be forth-coming. Mr. Shelley
says of himself and her, in a simile picturesque
in itself, but laughable in its application,—

                    thou and I.
Sweet friend, can look from our tranquillity,
Like lamps, into the world's tempestuous night—
Two tranquil stars, while clouds are passing by
Which wrap them from the foundering seaman's
    sight,

That burn from year to year with unextinguished
    light.—p. xxxii.

Neither will the reader be much at a loss to
discover what sapient personage is dimly
shadowed out in Archimago; but a clue is afforded even to the uninitiate by a note in the
preface, in which we are told that Mr. Malthus
by his last edition has reduced the Essay on
Population to a commentary illustrative of the
unanswerableness of *Political Justice*.

With such instruments doubtless the glorious
task will be speedily accomplished—and what
will be the issue? this indeed is a serious question; but, as in most schemes of reform, it is
easier to say what is to be removed, and destroyed, than what is to be put in its place.
Mr. Shelley would abrogate our laws—this
would put an end to felonies and misdemean-
ours at a blow; he would abolish the rights of
property, of course there could thenceforward
be no violations of them, no heart-burnings between the poor and the rich, no disputed wills,
no litigated inheritances, no food in short for
sophistical judges, or hireling lawyers; he would
overthrow the constitution, and then we should
have no expensive court, no pensions or
sinecures, no silken lords or corrupt common-
ers, no slavish and enslaving army or navy; he
would pull down our churches, level our Establishment, and burn our bibles—then we
should pay no tithes, be enslaved by no superstitions, abused by no priestly artifices: marriage he cannot endure, and there would at
once be a stop put to the lamented increase of
adulterous connections amongst us, whilst by
repealing the canon of heaven against incest,
he would add to the purity, and heighten the
ardour of those feelings with which brother and
sister now regard each other; finally, as the
basis of the whole scheme, he would have us
renounce our belief in our religion, extinguish,
if we can, the light of conscience within us,
which embitters our joys here, and drown in
oblivion the hopes and fears that hang over
our hereafter. This is at least intelligible; but
it is not so easy to describe the structure, which
Mr. Shelley would build upon this vast heap
of ruins. "Love," he says, "is to be the sole law
which shall govern the moral world;" but Love
is a wide word with many significations, and
we are at a loss as to which of them he would
have it now bear. We are loath to understand it
in its lowest sense, though we believe that as
to the issue this would be the correctest mode

of interpreting it; but this at least is clear, that Mr. Shelley does not mean it in its highest sense: he does not mean that love, which is the fulfilling of the law, and which walks after the commandments, for he would erase the Decalogue, and every other code of laws; not the love which is said to be of God, and which is beautifully coupled with "joy, peace, long suffering, gentleness, goodness, faith, meekness, temperance," for he preeminently abhors that religion, which is built on that love and inculcates it as the essence of all duties, and its own fulfilment.

It is time to draw to an end.—We have examined Mr. Shelley's system slightly, but, we hope, dispassionately; there will be those, who will say that we have done so coldly. He has indeed, to the best of his ability, wounded us in the tenderest part.—As far as in him lay, he has loosened the hold of our protecting laws, and sapped the principles of our venerable polity; he has invaded the purity and chilled the unsuspecting ardour of our fireside intimacies; he has slandered, ridiculed and blasphemed our holy religion; yet these are all too sacred objects to be defended bitterly or unfairly. We have learned too, though not in Mr. Shelley's school, to discriminate between a man and his opinions, and while we shew no mercy to the sin, we can regard the sinner with allowance and pity. It is in this spirit, that we conclude with a few lines, which may serve for a warning to others, and for reproof, admonition, and even if he so pleases of encouragement to himself. We have already said what we think of his powers as a poet, and doubtless, with those powers, he might have risen to respectability in any honourable path, which he had chosen to pursue, if to his talents he had added industry, subordination, and good principles. But of Mr. Shelley much may be said with truth, which we not long since said of his friend and leader Mr. Hunt: he has not, indeed, all that is odious and contemptible in the character of that person; so far as we have seen he has never exhibited the bustling vulgarity, the ludicrous affectation, the factious flippancy, or the selfish heartlessness, which it is hard for our feelings to treat with the mere contempt they merit. Like him, however, Mr. Shelley is a very vain man; and like most very vain men, he is but half instructed in knowledge, and less than half-disciplined in his reasoning powers; his vanity, wanting the controul of the faith which he de-

rides, has been his ruin; it has made him too impatient of applause and distinction to earn them in the fair course of labour; like a speculator in trade, he would be rich without capital and without delay, and, as might have been anticipated, his speculations have ended only in disappointments. They both began, his speculations and his disappointments, in early childhood, and even from that period he has carried about with him a soured and discontented spirit—unteachable in boyhood, unamiable in youth, querulous and unmanly in manhood,—singularly unhappy in all three. He speaks of his school—as "a world of woes," of his masters "as tyrants," of his school-fellows as "enemies,"—alas! what is this, but to bear evidence against himself? every one who knows what a public school ordinarily must be, will only trace in these lines the language of an insubordinate, a vain, a mortified spirit.

We would venture to hope that the past may suffice for the speculations in which Mr. Shelley has hitherto engaged; they have brought him neither honour abroad nor peace at home, and after so fair a trial it seems but common prudence to change them for some new venture. He is still a young man, and though his account be assuredly black and heavy, he may yet hope to redeem his time, and wipe it out. He may and he should retain all the love for his fellow-creatures, all the zeal for their improvement in virtue and happiness which he now professes, but let that zeal be armed with knowledge and regulated by judgment. Let him not be offended at our freedom, but he is really too young, too ignorant, too inexperienced, and too vicious to undertake the task of reforming any world, but the little world within his own breast; that task will be a good preparation, for the difficulties which he is more anxious at once to encounter. There is a book which will help him to this preparation, which has more poetry in it than Lucretius, more interest than Godwin, and far more philosophy than both. But it is a sealed book to a proud spirit; if he would read it with effect, he must be humble where he is now vain, he must examine and doubt himself where now he boldly condemns others, and instead of relying on his own powers, he must feel and acknowledge his weakness, and pray for strength from above. . . .

Scarcely any man ever set himself in array against the cause of social order and religion, but from a proud and rebel mind, or a corrupt and undisciplined heart: where these are, true knowledge cannot grow. In the enthusiasm of youth, indeed, a man like Mr. Shelley may cheat himself with the imagined loftiness and independence of his theory, and it is easy to invent a thousand sophisms, to reconcile his conscience to the impurity of his practice: but this lasts only enough to lead him on beyond the power of return; he ceases to be the dupe, but with desperate malignity he becomes the deceiver of others. Like the Egyptian of old, the wheels of his chariot are broken, the path of "mighty waters" closes in upon him behind, and a still deepening ocean is before him:—for a short time, are seen his impotent struggles against a resistless power, his blasphemous execrations are heard, his despair but poorly assumes the tone to triumph and defiance, and he calls ineffectually on others to follow him to the same ruin—finally, he sinks "like lead" to the bottom, and is forgotten. So it is now in part, so shortly will it be entirely with Mr. Shelley:— if we might withdraw the veil of private life, and tell what we *now* know about him, it would be indeed a disgusting picture that we should exhibit, but it would be an unanswerable comment on our text; it is not easy for those who *read only*, to conceive how much low pride, how much cold selfishness, how much unmanly cruelty are consistent with the laws of the "universal" and "lawless love." But we must only use our knowledge to check the groundless hopes which we were once prone to entertain of him.

III

Blackwood's Edinburgh Magazine. Vol. VI, No. XXXII, pp. 148–154. November, 1819.

Alastor; or, the Spirit of Solitude: and Other Poems.

Reviewer: Probably John Wilson.[1]

WE believe this little volume to be Mr Shelley's first publication; and such of our readers as have been struck by the power and splendour of genius displayed in the Revolt of Islam, and by the frequent tenderness and pathos of "Rosalind and Helen," will be glad to observe some

of the earliest efforts of a mind destined, in our opinion, under due discipline and self-management, to achieve great things in poetry. It must be encouraging to those who, like us, cherish high hopes of this gifted but wayward young man, to see what advances his intellect has made within these five years, and to compare its powerful, though still imperfect display, in his principal poem with its first gleamings and irradiations throughout this production almost of his boyhood. . . .

We beg leave, in conclusion, to say a few words about the treatment which Mr Shelley has, in his poetical character, received from the public. By our periodical critics he has either been entirely overlooked, or slightly noticed, or grossly abused.[2] There is not so much to find fault with in the mere silence of critics; but we do not hesitate to say, with all due respect for the general character of that journal, that Mr Shelley has been infamously and stupidly treated in the Quarterly Review. His Reviewer there, whoever he is, does not shew himself a man of such lofty principles as to entitle him to ride the high horse in company with the author of the Revolt of Islam. And when one compares the vis inertiae of his motionless prose with the "eagle-winged raptures" of Mr Shelley's poetry, one does not think indeed of Satan reproving Sin, but one does think, we will say it in plain words and without a figure, of a dunce rating a man of genius. If that critic does not know that Mr Shelley is a poet, almost in the very highest sense of that mysterious word, then, we appeal to all those whom we have enabled to judge for themselves, if he be not unfit to speak of poetry before the people of England. If he does not know that Mr Shelley is a great poet, what manner of man is he who, with such conviction, brings himself, with the utmost difficulty, to admit that there is any beauty at all in Mr Shelley's writings, and is happy to pass that admission off with an accidental and niggardly phrase of vague and valueless commendation. This is manifest and mean—glaring and gross injustice on the part of a man who comes forward as the champion of morality, truth, faith, and religion. This is being guilty of one of the very worst charges of which he accuses another; nor will any man who loves and honours genius,

---

[1] See Alan Lang Strout, "*Maga,* Champion of Shelley," *Studies in Philology* 29:95–119, 1932.

[2] It would be well for the student to read G. L. Marsh, "The Early Reviews of Shelley," *Modern Philology* 27:73–95, 1929.

even though that genius may have occasionally suffered itself to be both stained and led astray, think but with contempt and indignation and scorn of a critic who, while he pretends to wield the weapons of honour, virtue, and truth, yet clothes himself in the armour of deceit, hypocrisy, and falsehood. He *exults* to calumniate Mr Shelly's [*sic*] moral character, but he *fears* to acknowledge his genius. And therefore do we, as the sincere though sometimes sorrowing friends of Mr Shelley, scruple not to say, even though it may expose us to the charge of personality from those from whom alone such a charge could at all affect our minds, that the critic shews himself by such conduct as far inferior to Mr Shelley as a man of worth, as the language in which he utters his falsehood and uncharitableness shews him to be inferior as a man of intellect.

In the present state of public feeling, with regard to poets and poetry, a critic cannot attempt to defraud a poet of his fame, without paying the penalty either of his ignorance or his injustice. So long as he confines the expression of his envy or stupidity to works of moderate or doubtful merit, he may escape punishment; but if he dare to insult the spirit of England by contumelious and scornful treatment of any one of her gifted sons, that contumely and that scorn will most certainly be flung back upon himself, till he be made to shrink and to shiver beneath the load. It is not in the power of all the critics alive to blind one true lover of poetry to the splendour of Mr Shelley's genius—and the reader who, from mere curiosity, should turn to the Revolt of Islam to see what sort of trash it was that so moved the wrath and the spleen and the scorn of the Reviewer, would soon feel, that to understand the greatness of the poet, and the littleness of his traducer, nothing more was necessary than to recite to his delighted sense any six successive stanzas of that poem, so full of music, imagination, intellect, and passion. We care comparatively little for injustice offered to one moving majestically in the broad day of fame—it is the injustice done to the great, while their greatness is unknown or misunderstood that a generous nature most abhors, in as much as it seems more basely wicked to wish that genius might never lift its head, than to envy the glory with which it is encircled.

There is, we firmly believe, a strong love of genius in the people of this country, and they are willing to pardon to its possessor much extravagance and error—nay, even more serious transgressions. Let both Mr Shelley and his critic think of that—let it encourage the one to walk onwards to his bright destiny, without turning into dark or doubtful or wicked ways—let it teach the other to feel a proper sense of his own insignificance, and to be ashamed, in the midst of his own weakness and deficiencies and meannesses, to aggravate the faults of the highly-gifted, and to gloat with a sinful satisfaction on the real or imaginary debasement of genius and intellect.

And here we ought, perhaps, to stop. But the Reviewer has dealt out a number of dark and oracular denunciations against the Poet, which the public can know nothing about, except that they imply a charge of immorality and wickedness. Let him speak out plainly, or let him hold his tongue. There are many wicked and foolish things in Mr Shelley's creed, and we have not hitherto scrupled, nor shall we henceforth scruple to expose that wickedness and that folly. But we do not think that he believes his own creed—at least, that he believes it fully and to utter conviction—and we doubt not but the scales will yet all fall from his eyes. The Reviewer, however, with a face of most laughable horror, accuses Mr Shelly [*sic*] in the same breath of some nameless act of atrocity, and of having been rusticated, or expelled, or warned to go away from the University of Oxford! He seems to shudder with the same holy fear at the violation of the laws of morality and the breaking of college rules. He forgets that in the world men do not wear caps and gowns as at Oriel or Exeter. He preaches not like Paul—but like a Proctor.

Once more, then we bid Mr Shelley farewell. Let him come forth from the eternal city, where, we understand, he has been sojourning, —in his strength, conquering and to conquer. Let his soul watch his soul, and listen to the voice of its own noble nature—and there is no doubt that the future will make amends for the past, whatever its errors may have been— and that the Poet may yet be good, great, and happy.

IV

Blackwood's Edinburgh Magazine. Vol. V, No. XXVII, pp. 268-274. June, 1819.

Rosalind and Helen, A Modern Eclogue.

Reviewer: Probably John Wilson.[1]

WE have already expressed our belief that Mr Shelley is a true poet, and that it will be his own fault if his name does not hold a conspicuous place in the literature of his country. With our high hopes of him are mingled, however, many disheartening fears, which, we lament to say, are far from being weakened by the spirit of his new poem. For, while this modern eclogue breathes throughout strong feeling, and strong passion, and strong imagination, it exhibits at the same time a strange perversion of moral principle—a wilful misrepresentation of the influence of the laws of human society on human virtue and happiness—and a fierce and contemptuous scorn of those sacred institutions which nature protects and guards for the sake of her own worth and dignity. Indeed, Mr Shelley does not write like a conscientious man, sinking into fatal error through the imbecility of his intellect—nor like an enthusiastic man hurried away into fatal error by the violence of his passions—but he often writes like a man angry and dissatisfied with the world, because he is angry and dissatisfied with himself—impotently striving to break those bonds which he yet feels are rivetted by a higher power—and because his own headstrong and unhappy will frets and fevers within the salutary confinement of nature's gracious laws, impiously scheming to bring these laws into disrepute, by representing them as the inventions and juggleries of tyranny and priestcraft. We are willing to attribute this monstrous perversity in a man of genius and talents like Mr Shelley, to causes that are external, and that, therefore, will pass away. We leave it to others to speak of him in the bitterness of anger and scorn—to others again to speak of him in the

exultation of sympathy and praise. We claim no kindred with either set of critics—seeing in this highly-gifted man much to desire—nay much to love—but much also to move to pity and to sorrow. For what can be more mournful than the degredation of youthful genius involving in its fall virtue, respectability and happiness? . . .

But we cannot leave Mr Shelley without expressing ourselves in terms of the most decided reprobation of many of his principles, if, indeed, such vague indefinite and crude vagaries can, by any latitude of language, be so designated. And, first of all, because priests have been bloody and intolerant, is it worthy of a man of liberal education and endowments, to talk with uniform scorn and contempt of the ministers of religion? Can any thing be more puerile in taste, more vulgar in feeling, more unfounded in fact, or more false in philosophy? Mr Shelley goes out of his way—out of the way of the leading passion of his poetry to indulge in the gratification of this low and senseless abuse—and independently of all higher considerations, such ribaldry utterly destroys all impassioned emotion in the hearts of his readers, and too frequently converts Mr Shelley from a poet into a satirist, from a being who ought, in his own pure atmosphere, to be above all mean prejudices, into a slave, basely walking in voluntary trammels.

From his hatred and contempt of priests, the step is but a short one to something like hatred and contempt of all religion—and accordingly superstition is a word eternally upon his lips. How many fine, pure, and noble spirits does he thus exclude from his audience? And how many sympathies does he dry up in his own heart? If the christian faith be all fable and delusion, what does this infatuated young man wish to substitute in its stead? One seeks, in vain, through his poetry, fine as it often is, for any principles of action in the characters who move before us. They are at all times fighting against the law of the world, the law of nature, and the law of God—there is nothing satisfactory in their happiness, and always something wilful in their misery. Nor could Mr Shelley's best friend and most warm admirer do otherwise than confess that he is ever an obscure and cheerless moralist, even when his sentiments are most lofty, and when he declaims with greatest eloquence against the delusions of religious faith. That a poet should be blind, deaf, and insensible to the divine beauty of Christianity, is wonderful and deplorable, when, at the same time, he is so alive to the beauty of the external world, and, in many instances, to that of the human soul. If Mr Shelley were a settled—a confirmed disbeliever, we should give him up as a man of whom no high hopes could rationally be held—but we think him only an inconsiderate and thoughtless scoffer, who will not open his eyes to a sense of his wickedness and folly —and therefore it is that we express ourselves thus strongly, not out of anger or scorn, but real sorrow, and sincere affection.

It is also but too evident, from Mr Shelley's poetry, that he looks with an evil eye on many of the most venerable institutions of civil polity. His creed seems to be the same, in many points, as that once held by a celebrated political writer and novelist, who has lived to abjure it. But in all that Godwin wrote, one felt the perfect sincerity of the man—whereas, Mr Shelley seems to have adopted such opinions, not from any deep conviction of their truth, but from waywardness and caprice, from the love of singularity, and, perhaps, as a vain defence against the reproaches of his own conscience. His opinions, therefore, carry no authority along with them to others—nay, they seem not to carry any authority with them to himself. The finer essence of his poetry never penetrates them—the hues of his imagination never clothes them with attractive beauty. The cold, bald, clumsy, and lifeless parts of this poem are those in which he obtrudes upon us his contemptible and long-exploded dogmas. Then his inspiration deserts him. He never stops nor stumbles in his career, except when he himself seems previously to have laid blocks before the wheels of his chariot.

Accordingly there is no great moral flow in his poetry. Thus, for example, what lesson are we taught by this eclogue, Rosalind and Helen? Does Mr Shelley mean to prove that marriage is an evil institution, because by it youth and beauty may be condemned to the palsied grasp of age, avarice and cruelty? Does he mean to shew the injustice of law, because a man may by it bequeath his property to strangers, and leave his wife and children beggars? Does he mean to shew the wickedness of that law by which illegitimate children do not succeed to the paternal and hereditary estates of their father? The wickedness lay with Lionel and Helen, who, aware of them all, indulged their own passion, in violation of such awful restraints—and gave life to innocent creatures for whom this world was in all probability to be a world of poverty, sorrow, and humiliation.

But we have stronger charges still—even than these—against this poet. What is it that he can propose to himself by his everlasting allusions to the unnatural loves of brothers and sisters? In this poem there are two stories of this sort—altogether gratuitous—and, as far as we can discover, illustrative of nothing. Why then introduce such thoughts, merely to dash, confound, and horrify? Such monstrosities betoken a diseased mind;—but be this as it may—it is most certain that such revolting passages coming suddenly upon us, in the midst of so much exquisite beauty, startle us out of our dream of real human life, and not only break in upon, but put to flight all the emotions of pleasure and of pathos with which we were following its disturbed courses. God knows there is enough of evil and of guilt in this world, without our seeking to raise up such hideous and unnatural phantasms of wickedness—but thus to mix them up for no earthly purpose with the ordinary events of human calamity and crime, is the last employment which a man of genius would desire—for there seems to be really no inducement to it, but a diseased desire of degrading and brutifying humanity.

We hope ere long to see the day when Mr Shelley, having shaken himself free from these faults—faults so devoid of any essential or fundamental alliance with his masterly genius —will take his place as he ought to do, not far from the first poets of his time. It is impossible to read a page of his Revolt of Islam, without perceiving that in nerve and pith of conception he approaches more nearly to Scott and Byron than any other of their contemporaries—while in this last little eclogue, he touches with equal mastery the same softer strings of pathos and tenderness which had before responded so delightfully to the more gentle inspirations of Wordsworth, Coleridge, and Wilson. His fame will yet be a glorious plant if he do not blast its expanding leaves by the suicidal chillings of immorality—a poison that cannot be resisted long by any product of the soil of England.

V

The London Literary Gazette. Vol. IV, No. 167, pp. 209–210. April 1, 1820.[1]

The Cenci. A Tragedy, in Five Acts. By Percy B. Shelley. Italy: Printed for Olliers. London, 1819. pp. 104.

Reviewer: Unknown.

OF all the abominations which intellectual perversion, and poetical atheism, have produced in our times, this tragedy appears to us to be the most abominable. We have much doubted whether we ought to notice it; but, as watchmen place a light over the common sewer which has been opened in a way dangerous to passengers, so have we concluded it to be our duty to set up a beacon on this noisome and noxious publication. We have heard of Mr. Shelley's genius; and were it exercised upon any subject not utterly revolting to human nature, we might acknowledge it. But there are topics so disgusting—and this is one of them; there are themes so vile—as this is; there are descriptions so abhorrent to mankind—and this drama is full of them; there are crimes so beastly and demoniac—in which The Cenci riots and luxuriates, that no feelings can be excited by their obtrusion but those of detestation at the choice, and horror at the elaboration. We protest most solemnly, that when we reached the last page of this play, our minds were so impressed with its odious and infernal character, that we could not believe it to be written by a mortal being for the gratification of his fellow-creatures on earth: it seemed to be the production of a fiend, and calculated for the entertainment of devils in hell.

That monsters of wickedness have been seen in the world, it is true; but not to speak of the diseased appetite which would delight to revel in their deeds, we will affirm that depravity so damnable as that of Count Cenci, in the minute portraiture of which Mr. S. takes so much pains, and guilt so atrocious as that which he paints in every one of his dramatic personages, never had either individual or aggregate existence. No; the whole design, and every part of it, is a libel upon humanity;

[1] Compare the *Monthly Review* XCIV, pp. 161–168; the *London Magazine* I, pp. 401–405; the *New Monthly Magazine* XIII, pp. 550–553.

the conception of a brain not only distempered, but familiar with infamous images, and accursed contemplations. What adds to the shocking effect is the perpetual use of the sacred name of God, and incessant appeals to the Saviour of the universe. The foul mixture of religion and blasphemy, and the dreadful association of virtuous principles with incest, parricide, and every deadly sin, form a picture which, "To look upon we dare not." . . .

VI

The London Literary Gazette. Vol. V, No. 255, pp. 772–773. December 8, 1821.

Adonais. An Elegy, on the Death of Mr. John Keats. By P. B. Shelley.

Reviewer: Unknown.

WE have already given some of our columns to this writer's merits, and we will not now repeat our convictions of his incurable absurdity. . . . Adonais is an elegy after *the manner of Moschus,* on a foolish young man, who, after writing some volumes of very weak, and, in the greater part, of very indecent poetry, died some time since of a consumption: the breaking down of an infirm constitution having, in all probability, been accelerated by the discarding his neckcloth, a practice of the cockney poets, who look upon it as essential to genius, inasmuch as neither Michael Angelo, Raphael nor Tasso are supposed to have worn those antispiritual incumberances. In short, as the vigor of Sampson lay in his hair, the secret of talent with these persons lies in the neck; and what aspirations can be expected from a mind enveloped in muslin. Keats caught cold in training for a genius, and, after a lingering illness, died, to the great loss of the Independents of South America, whom he had intended to visit with an English epic poem, for the purpose of exciting them to liberty. But death, even the death of a radically presumptuous profligate, is a serious thing; and as we believe that Keats was made presumptuous chiefly by the treacherous puffing of his cockney fellow gossips, and profligate in his poems merely to make them saleable, we regret that he did not live long enough to acquire common sense, and abjure the pestilent and perfidious gang who betrayed his weakness to the grave, and are now panegyrising his memory into contempt. For what is the praise of the cockneys but disgrace, or what honourable inscription can be placed over the dead by the hands of notorious libellers, exiled adulterers, and avowed atheists.

Adonais, an Elegy, is the form in which Mr Shelley puts forth his woes. We give a verse at random. . . .

A pardlike spirit, beautiful and swift—
  A love in *desolation mask'd,*—a Power
Girt *round with weakness;*—it can scarce *uplift*
  The *weight* of the *superincumbent hour!*

We have some idea that this fragment of character is intended for Mr. Shelley himself. It closes with a passage of memorable and ferocious blasphemy:—

————He with a sudden hand
Made bare his branded and ensanguin'd brow,
Which was like Cain's or CHRIST'S !!!

What can be said to the wretched person capable of this daring profanation. The name of the first murderer—the accurst of God— brought into the same aspect image with that of the Saviour of the World! We are scarcely satisfied that even to quote such passages may not be criminal. The subject is too repulsive for us to proceed even in expressing our disgust for the general folly that makes the Poem as miserable in point of authorship, as in point of principle. We know that among a certain class this outrage and this inanity meet with some attempt at palliation, under the idea that frenzy holds the pen. That any man who insults the common order of society, and denies the being of God, is essentially mad we never doubted. But for the madness, that retains enough of rationality to be wilfully mischievous, we can have no more lenity than for the appetites of a wild beast. The poetry of the work is *contemptible*—a mere collection of bloated words heaped on each other without order, harmony, or meaning; the refuse of a school-boy's common-place book, full of the vulgarisms of pastoral poetry, yellow gems and blue stars, bright Phoebus and rosy-fingered Aurora; and of this stuff is Keats's wretched Elegy compiled. . . .

Solemn as the subject is, it is hardly possible to help laughing at the mock solemnity with which Shelley charges the Quarterly Review for having murdered his friend with—a critique! If Criticism killed the disciples of that school, Shelley would not have been alive to write an Elegy on another. . . .

VII

Blackwood's Edinburgh Magazine. Vol. X, No. LIX, pp. 696–700. December, 1821.

Remarks on Shelley's Adonais.

Reviewer: William Maginn.

. . . THE present story is thus:—A *Mr John Keats,* a young man who had left a decent calling for the melancholy trade of Cockney-poetry, has lately died of a consumption, after having written two or three little books of verses, much neglected by the public. His vanity was probably wrung not less than his purse; for he had it upon the authority of the Cockney Homers and Virgils, that he might become a light to their region at a future time. But all this is not necessary to help a consumption to the death of a poor sedentary man, with an unhealthy aspect, and a mind harassed by the first troubles of verse-making. The New School, however, will have it that he was slaughtered by a criticism of the Quarterly Review.—"O flesh, how art thou fishified!"—There is even an aggravation in this cruelty of the Review—for it had taken three or four years to slay its victim, the deadly blow having been inflicted at least as long since. We are not now to defend a publication so well able to defend itself. But the fact is, that the Quarterly finding before it a work at once silly and presumptuous, full of the servile *slang* that Cockaigne dictates to its servitors, and the vulgar indecorums which that Grub Street Empire rejoiceth to applaud, told the truth of the volume, and recommended a change of manners and of masters to the scribbler. Keats wrote on; but he wrote *indecently,* probably in the indulgence of his social propensities. He selected from Boccacio, and, at the feet of the Italian Priapus, supplicated for fame and farthings.

Both halves the winds dispersed in empty air.

Mr P. B. Shelly [*sic*] having been the person appointed by the *Pisan* triumvirate to canonize the name of this apprentice, "nipt in the bud," as he fondly tells us, has accordingly produced an Elegy, in which he weeps "after the manner of Moschus for Bion." The canonizer is worthy of the saint.—Locke says, that the most resolute liar cannot lie more than once in every three sentences. Folly is more engrossing; for we could prove, from the present Elegy, that it is possible to write two sentences of pure nonsense out of every three. A more faithful calculation would bring us to ninety-nine out of every hundred, or,—as the present consists of only fifty-five stanzas,—leaving about five readable lines in the entire. . . .

As this wild waste of words is altogether beyond our comprehension, we will proceed to the more gratifying office of giving a whole, unbroken specimen of the Poet's powers, exercised on a subject rather more within their sphere. The following Poem has been sent to us as written by Percy Byshe [sic], and we think it contains all the essence of his odoriferous, colorific, and daisy-enamoured style. . . .

Weep for my Tomcat! all ye Tabbies weep,
  For he has gone at last! Not dead alone,
In flowery beauty sleepeth he no sleep;
  Like that bewitching youth Endymion!
My love is dead, alas, as any stone,
  That by some violet-sided smiling river
Weepeth too fondly! He is dead and gone,
  And fair Aurora, o'er her young believer,
With fingers gloved with roses, doth make moan,
And every bud its petal green doth sever,
  And Phoebus sets in night for ever, and for
    ever!
And others come! ye Splendours! and ye
    Beauties!
  Ye Raptures! with your robes of pearl and
    blue;
Ye blushing Wonders! with your scarlet shoe-
    ties;
  Ye Horrors bold! with breasts of lily hue;
Ye Hope's stern flatterers! He would trust to you,
  Whene'er he saw you with your chestnut hair,
Dropping sad daffodils; and rosepinks true!
  Ye Passions proud! with lips of bright despair;
Ye Sympathies! with eyes like evening star,
When on the glowing east she rolls her crimson
    car.

Oh, bard-like spirit! beautiful and swift!
  Sweet lover of pale night; when Luna's lamp
Shakes sapphire dew-drops through a cloudy rift;
  Purple as woman's mouth, o'er ocean damp;
Thy quivering rose-tinged tongue—thy stealing
    tramp;
  The dazzling glory of thy gold-tinged tail;
Thy whisker-waving lips, as o'er the swamp
  Rises the meteor, when the year doth fail,
Like beauty in decay, all, all are flat and stale.

This poem strikes us as an evidence of the improvement that an appropriate subject makes in a writer's style. It is incomparably less nonsensical, verbose, and inflated, than Adonais; while it retains all its knowledge of nature, vigour of colouring, and felicity of language. Adonais has been published by the author in Italy, the fitting soil for the poem, sent over to his honoured correspondents throughout the realm of Cockaigne, with a delightful mysteriousness worthy of the dignity of the subject and the writer.

VIII

The Quarterly Review. Vol. XXVI, No. LI, pp. 168–180. October, 1822.

Prometheus Unbound, a Lyrical Drama, in Four Acts; with other Poems. By Percy Bysshe Shelley. 8vo. 1821.

Reviewer: W. S. Walker.

A GREAT lawyer of the present day is said to boast of practising three different modes of writing: one which anybody can read; another which only himself can read; and a third, which neither he nor anybody else can read. So Mr. Shelley may plume himself upon writing in three different styles: one which can be generally understood; another which can be understood only by the author; and a third which is absolutely and intrinsically unintelligible. Whatever his command may be of the first and second of these styles, this volume is a most satisfactory testimonial of his proficiency in the last.

If we might venture to express a general opinion of what far surpasses our comprehension, we should compare the poems contained in this volume to the visions of gay colours mingled with darkness, which often in childhood, when we shut our eyes, seem to revolve at an immense distance around us. In Mr. Shelley's poetry all is brilliance, vacuity, and confusion. We are dazzled by the multitude of words which sound as if they denoted something very grand or splendid: fragments of images pass in crowds before us; but when the procession has gone by, and the tumult of it is over, not a trace of it remains upon the memory. The mind, fatigued and perplexed, is mortified by the consciousness that its labour has not been rewarded by the acquisition of a single distinct conception; the ear, too, is dissatisfied: for the rhythm of the verse is often harsh and unmusical; and both the ear and the understanding are disgusted by new and uncouth words, and by the awkward, and intricate construction of the sentences.

The predominating characteristic of Mr. Shelley's poetry, however, is its frequent and total want of meaning. . . . Upon a question of mere beauty, there may be a difference of taste. . . . But the question of meaning, or no meaning, is a matter of fact on which common sense, with common attention, is adequate to decide. . . . If, however, we should completely establish this charge, we look upon the question of Mr. Shelley's poetical merits as at an end; for he who has the trick of writing very showy verses without ideas, or without coherent ideas, can contribute to the instruction of none, and can please only those who have learned to read without having ever learned to think. . . .

Sometimes Mr. Shelley's love of the unintelligible yields to his preference for the disgusting and the impious. Thus the bodies of the dead sailors are thrown out of the ship:

And the sharks and the dog-fish their grave-
    cloths unbound,
And were glutted, like Jews, with this manna
    rained down
From God on their wilderness.—p. 177. . . .

Sometimes to the charms of nonsense those of doggrel are added. This is the conclusion of a song of certain beings, who are called "Spirits of the human mind:"

And Earth, Air, and Light,
    And the Spirit of Might,
Which drives round the stars in their fiery flight;
    And Love, Thought, and Breath,
    The powers that quell Death,
Wherever we soar shall assemble beneath.
    And our singing shall build
    In the void's loose field
A world for the Spirit of Wisdom to wield;
    We will take our plan
    From the new world of man,
And our work shall be called the Promethean.—
    p. 130.

Another characteristic trait of Mr. Shelley's poetry is, that in his descriptions he never describes the thing directly, but transfers it to the properties of something which he conceives to resemble it by language which is to be taken partly in a metaphorical meaning, and partly in no meaning at all. The whole of a long poem, in three parts, called "the Sensitive Plant," the object of which we cannot discover, is an instance of this. The first part is devoted to the description of the plants. The sensitive plant takes the lead:

No flower ever trembled and panted with bliss,
In the garden, the field, or the wilderness,
Like a doe in the noon-tide with love's sweet
    want,
As the companionless sensitive plant.—p. 157.

Next come the snow-drop and the violet:

And their breath was mixed with fresh odour,
    sent
From the turf, *like the voice and the instrument*.

The rose, too,

—Unveiled the depth of her glowing breast,
Till, fold after fold, *to the fainting air*
The soul of her beauty and love lay bare.

The hyacinth is described in terms still more quaint and affected:

The hyacinth, purple, and white, and blue,
Which flung from *its bells a sweet peal anew*,
Of music so delicate, soft, and intense,
It was felt like an odour within the sense.

It is worth while to observe the train of thought in this stanza. The bells of the flower occur to the poet's mind; but ought not bells to ring a peal? Accordingly, by a metamorphosis of the odour, the bells of the hyacinth are supposed to do so: the fragrance of the flower is first converted into a peal of music, and then the peal of music is in the last line transformed back into an odour. These are the tricks of a mere poetical harlequin, amusing himself with

The clock-work tintinnabulum of rhyme.

In short, it is not too much to affirm, that in the whole volume there is not one original image of nature, one simple expression of human feeling, or one new association of the appearances of the moral with those of the material world.

As Mr. Shelley disdains to draw his materials from nature, it is not wonderful that his subjects should in general be widely remote from every thing that is level with the comprehension, or interesting to the heart of man. He has been pleased to call "Prometheus Unbound" a lyrical drama, though it has neither action nor dramatic dialogue. The subject of it is the transition of Prometheus from a state of suffering to a state of happiness; together with a corresponding change in the situation of mankind. But no distinct account is given of either of these states, nor of the means by which Prometheus and the world pass from the one to the other. The Prometheus of Mr. Shelley is not the Prometheus of ancient mythology. He is a being who is neither a God nor a man, who has conferred supreme power on Jupiter. Jupiter torments him; and Demogorgon, by annihilating Jupiter's power, restores him to happiness. Asia, Panthea, and Ione, are female beings of a nature similar to that of Prometheus. Apollo, Mercury, the Furies, and a faun, make their appearance; but have not much to do in the piece. To fill up the *personae dramatis*, we have voices of the mountains, voices of the air, voices of the springs, voices of the whirlwinds, together with several echoes. Then come spirits without end: spirits of the moon, spirits of the earth, spirits of the human mind, spirits of the hours; who all attest their super-human nature by singing and saying things which no human being can comprehend. We do not find fault with this poem, because it is built on notions which no longer possess any influence over the human mind, but because its basis and its materials are mere dreaming, shadowy, incoherent abstractions. It would have been quite as absurd and extravagant in the time of Æschylus, as it is now.

It may seem strange that such a volume should find readers, and still more strange that it should meet with admirers. We were ourselves surprised by the phenomenon: nothing similar to it occurred to us, till we recollected the numerous congregations which the incoherencies of an itinerant Methodist preacher attract. These preachers, without any connected train of thought, and without attempting to reason, or to attach any definite meaning to the terms which they use, pour out a deluge of sonorous words that relate to sacred objects and devout feelings. These words, connected as they are with all that is most venerable in the eyes of man, excite a multitude of pious associations in the hearer, and produce in him a species of mental intoxication.

His feelings are awakened, and his heart touched, while his imagination and understanding are bewildered; and he receives temporary pleasure, sometimes even temporary improvement, at the expense of the essential and even permanent depravation of his character. In the same way, poetry like that of Mr. Shelley presents every where glittering constellations of words, which taken separately have a meaning, and either communicate some activity to the imagination, or dazzle it by their brilliance. Many of them relate to beautiful or interesting objects, and are therefore capable of imparting pleasure to us by the associations attached to them. The reader is conscious that his mind is raised from a state of stagnation, and he is willing to believe, that he is astounded and bewildered, not by the absurdity, but by the originality and sublimity of the author. . . .

But it is often said, that though the poems are bad, they at least show poetical power. Poetical power can be shown only by writing good poetry, and this Mr. Shelley has not done. The proofs of Mr. Shelley's genius, which his admirers allege, are the very exaggeration, copiousness of verbiage, and incoherence of ideas which we complain of as intolerable. They argue in criticism, as those men do in morals, who think debauchery and dissipation an excellent proof of a good heart. The want of meaning is called sublimity, absurdity becomes venerable under the name of originality, the jumble of metaphor is the richness of imagination, and even the rough, clumsy, confused structure of the style, with not unfrequent violations of the rules of grammar, is, forsooth, the sign and effect of a bold overflowing genius, that disdains to walk in common trammels. If the poet is one who whirls round his reader's brain, till it becomes dizzy and confused; if it is his office to envelop he knows not what in huge folds of a clumsy drapery of splendid words and showy metaphors, then, without doubt, may Mr. Shelley place the Delphic laurel on his head. But take away from him the unintelligible, the confused, the incoherent, the bombastic, the affected, the extravagant, the hideously gorgeous, and "Prometheus," and the poems which accompany it, will sink at once into nothing.

But great as are Mr. Shelley's sins against sense and taste, would that we had nothing more to complain of! Unfortunately, to his long list of demerits he has added the most flagrant offences against morality and religion. We should abstain from quoting instances, were it not that we think his language too gross and too disgusting to be dangerous to any but those who are corrupted beyond the hope of amendment. After a revolting description of the death of our Saviour, introduced merely for the sake of intimating, that *the religion he preached is the great source of human misery and vice,* he adds,

—Thy name I will not speak,
It hath become a curse.

Will Mr. Shelley, to excuse this blasphemy against the name *"in which all the nations of the earth shall be made blessed,"* pretend, that these are the words of Prometheus, not of the poet? . . .

The real cause of his aversion to Christianity is easily discovered. Christianity is the great prop of the social order of the civilized world; this social order is the subject of Mr. Shelley's hatred; and, therefore, the pillar must be demolished, that the building may tumble down. His views of the nature of men and of society are expressed, we dare not say explained, in some of those *"beautiful idealisms of moral excellence,"* (we use his own words,) in which the "Prometheus" abounds.

The painted veil, by those who were, called life, which mimicked, as with colours idly spread, all men believed and hoped, is torn aside; the loathsome mask has fallen, the man remains sceptreless, free, uncircumscribed, but man equal, unclassed, tribeless, and nationless, exempt from awe, worship, degree, the king over himself; just, gentle, wise: but man passionless; no, yet free from guilt or pain, which were for his will made or suffered them, nor yet exempt, tho' ruling them like slaves, from chance and death, and mutability, the clogs of that which else might oversoar the loftiest star of unascended heaven, pinnacled dim in the intense inane.—p. 120.

Our readers may be puzzled to find out the meaning of this paragraph; we must, therefore, inform them that it is not prose, but the conclusion of the third act of Prometheus verbatim et literatim. With this information they will cease to wonder at the absence of sense and grammar; and will probably perceive, that Mr. Shelley's poetry is, in sober sadness, *drivelling prose run mad.*

With the prophetic voice of a misgiving conscience, Mr. Shelley objects to criticism. "If

my attempt be ineffectual, (he says) let the punishment of an unaccomplished purpose have been sufficient; let none trouble themselves to heap the dust of oblivion upon my efforts." Is there no respect due to common sense, to sound taste, to morality, to religion? Are evil spirits to be allowed to work mischief with impunity, because, forsooth, the instruments with which they work are contemptible? Mr. Shelley says, that his intentions are pure. Pure! They may be so in his vocabulary; for (to say nothing of having unfortunately mistaken nonsense for poetry, and blasphemy for an imperious duty,) vice and irreligion, and the subversion of society are, according to his system, pure and holy things; Christianity, and moral virtue, and social order, are alone impure. But we care not about his intentions, or by what epithet he may choose to characterize them, so long as his works exhale contagious mischief. On his own principles he must admit, that, in exposing to the public what we believe to be the character and tendency of his writings, we discharge a sacred duty. He professes to write in order to reform the world. The essence of the proposed reformation is the destruction of religion and government. Such a reformation is not to our taste; and he must, therefore, applaud us for scrutinizing the merits of works which are intended to promote so detestable a purpose. Of Mr. Shelley himself we know nothing, and desire to know nothing. Be his private qualities what they may, his poems (and it is only with his poems that we have any concern) are at war with reason, with taste, with virtue, in short, with all that dignifies man, or that man reveres.

JOHN KEATS

REVIEWS OF HIS WORK

I

The Champion. March 9, 1817.[1]

Poems: By John Keats, Price 6s. London. Ollier, Welbeck-Street.

Reviewer: Probably Benjamin Haydon.

HERE is a little volume filled throughout with very graceful and genuine poetry. The author

[1] For our extracts from this review we are indebted to Roberta D. Cornelius' *Two Early Reviews of Keats's First Volume,* PMLA 40: 193–

is a very young man, and one, as we augur from the present work, that is likely to make a great addition to those who would overthrow that artificial taste which French criticism has long planted amongst us. At a time when nothing is talked of but the power and the passion of Lord Byron, and the playful and elegant fancy of Moore, and the correctness of Rogers, and the sublimity and pathos of Campbell (these terms we should conceive are kept ready composed in the Edinburgh Review-shop) a young man starts suddenly before us, with a genius that is likely to eclipse them all. He comes fresh from nature,—and the originals of his images are to be found in her keeping. Young writers are in general in their early productions imitators of their favorite poet; like young birds that in their first songs, mock the notes of those warblers, they hear the most, and love the best: but this youthful poet appears to have tuned his voice in solitudes,—to have sung from the pure inspiration of nature. In the simple meadows he has proved that he can

——See shapes of light, aerial lymning,
And catch soft floating from a faint heard hymning.

We find in his poetry the glorious effect of summer days and leafy spots on rich feelings, which are in themselves a summer. He relies directly and wholly on nature. He marries poesy to genuine simplicity. He makes her artless,—yet abstains carefully from giving her an uncomely homeliness:—that is, he shows one can be familiar with nature, yet perfectly strange to the habits of common life. Mr. Keats is fated, or "we have no judgment in an honest face;" to look at natural objects with his mind, as Shakespeare and Chaucer did,—and not merely with his eye as nearly all modern poets do;—to clothe his poetry with a grand intellectual light,—and to lay his name in the lap of immortality. Our readers will think

210, March, 1925. Miss Cornelius accepts "this as the very earliest review of Keats's book," noting that Hunt's articles in the *Examiner* were for June 1, July 6, and July 13, 1817, while that in the *Eclectic Review* was for September, 1817, and that in the *Scots and Edinburgh Magazine* was for October, 1817.—The second review quoted by Miss Cornelius, that in the *European Magazine* for May, 1817, was probably written by George Felton Mathews. We omit it as it is too laden with quotation and preachment to be of great value in our study.

that we are speaking too highly of this young poet,—but luckily we have the power of making good the ground on which we prophesy so hardily. We shall extract largely from his volume:—It will be seen how familiar he is with all that is green, light, and beautiful in nature;—and with what an originality his mind dwells on all great or graceful objects. His imagination is very powerful,—and one thing we have observed with pleasure, that it never attempts to soar on undue occasions. The imagination, like the eagle on the rock, should keep its eye constantly on the sun,—and should never be started heavenward, unless something magnificent marred its solitude. Again, though Mr. Keats' poetry is remarkably abstracted, it is never out of reach of the mind; there are one or two established writers of this day who think that mystery is the soul of poetry—that artlessness is a vice—and that nothing can be graceful that is not metaphysical;—and even young writers have sunk into this error, and endeavoured to puzzle the world with a confused sensibility. We must however hasten to the consideration of the little volume before us, and not fill up our columns with observations, which extracts will render unnecessary. . . .

We conclude with earnestly recommending the work to all our readers. It is not without defects, which may be easily mentioned, and as easily rectified. The author, from his natural freedom of versification, at times passes to an absolute faultiness of measure:—This he should avoid. He should also abstain from the use of compound epithets as much as possible. He has a few faults which youth must have;—he is apt occasionally to make his descriptions over-wrought,—but on the whole we never saw a book which had so little reason to plead youth as its excuse. The best poets of the day might not blush to own it. . . .

II

Blackwood's Edinburgh Magazine. Vol. II, No. VII, pp. 38–41. October, 1817.

On the Cockney School of Poetry.

Reviewer: Possibly John Gibson Lockhart.

WHILE the whole critical world is occupied with balancing the merits, whether in theory or in execution, of what is commonly called THE LAKE SCHOOL, it is strange that no one seems to think it at all necessary to say a single word about another new school of poetry which has of late sprung up among us. This school has not, I believe, as yet received any name; but if I may be permitted to have the honour of christening it, it may henceforth be referred to by the designation of THE COCKNEY SCHOOL. Its chief Doctor and Professor is Mr Leigh Hunt, a man certainly of some talents, of extravagant pretensions both in wit, poetry, and politics, and withal of exquisitely bad taste, and extremely vulgar modes of thinking and manners in all respects. He is a man of little education. He knows absolutely nothing of Greek, almost nothing of Latin, and his knowledge of Italian literature is confined to a few of the most popular of Petrarch's sonnets, and an imperfect acquaintance with Ariosto, through the medium of Mr Hoole. As to the French poets, he dismisses them in the mass as a set of prim, precise, unnatural pretenders. . . . Of all the great critical writers, either of ancient or of modern times, he is utterly ignorant, excepting only Mr Jeffrey among ourselves. . . .

All the great poets of our country have been men of some rank in society, and there is no vulgarity in any of their writings; but Mr Hunt cannot utter a dedication, or even a note, without betraying the *Shibboleth* of low birth and low habits. He is the ideal of a Cockney Poet. He raves perpetually about "green fields," "jaunty streams," and "o'er-arching leafiness," exactly as a Cheapside shop-keeper does about the beauties of his box on the Camberwell road. Mr Hunt is altogether unacquainted with the face of nature in her magnificent scenes; he has never seen any mountain higher than Highgate-hill, nor reclined by any stream more pastoral than the Serpentine River. But he is determined to be a poet eminently rural, and he rings the changes—till one is sick of him, on the beauties of the different "high views" which he has taken of God and nature, in the course of some Sunday dinner parties, at which he has assisted in the neighborhood of London. His books are indeed not known in the country; his fame as a poet (and I might almost say, as a politician too,) is . . . confined to the young attorneys and embryo-barristers about town. In the opinion of these competent judges, London is the world—and Hunt is a Homer.

Mr Hunt is not disqualified by his ignorance and vulgarity alone, for being the founder of a respectable sect in poetry. He labours under the burden of a sin more deadly than either of these. The two great elements of all dignified poetry, religious feeling, and patriotic feeling, have no place in his writings. His religion is a poor tame dilution of the blasphemies of the *Encyclopædie*—his patriotism a crude, vague ineffectual, and sour Jacobinism. His works exhibit no reverence either for God or man; neither altar nor throne have any dignity in his eyes. He speaks well of nobody but two or three great dead poets. . . . Mr Leigh Hunt's ideas concerning the sublime, and concerning his own powers, bear a considerable resemblance of those of his friend Bottom, the weaver, on the same subjects; "I will roar, that it shall do any man's heart good to hear me."—"I will roar you an 'twere any nightingale."

The poetry of Mr Hunt is such as might be expected from the personal character and habits of its author. As a vulgar man is perpetually labouring to be genteel—in like manner, the poetry of this man is always on the stretch to be grand. He has been allowed to look for a moment from the antichamber into the saloon, and mistaken the waving of feathers and the painted floor for the *sine qua non's* of elegant society. He would fain be always tripping and waltzing, and is sorry that he cannot be allowed to walk about in the morning with yellow breeches and flesh-coloured silk-stockings. He sticks an artificial rose-bud into his button hole in the midst of winter. He wears no neckcloth, and cuts his hair in imitation of the Prints of Petrarch. In his verses he is always desirous of being airy, graceful, easy, courtly, and ITALIAN. . . . He has gone into a strange delusion about himself, and is just as absurd in supposing that he resembles the Italian Poets, as a greater Quack still (Mr Coleridge) is, in imagining that he is a philosopher after the manner of Kant or Mendelshon—and that "the eye of Lessing bears a remarkable likeness to MINE," i. e. the eye of Mr Samuel Coleridge.

The extreme moral depravity of the Cockney School is another thing which is forever thrusting itself upon the public attention, and convincing every man of sense who looks into their productions, that they who sport such sentiments can never be great poets. How could any man of high original genius ever stoop publicly, at the present day, to dip his fingers in the least of those glittering and rancid obscenities which float on the surface of Mr Hunt's Hippocrene? His poetry resembles that of a man who has kept company with kept-mistresses. His muse talks indelicately like a tea-sipping milliner girl. Some excuse for her there might have been, had she been hurried away by imagination or passion; but with her, indecency seems a disease, she appears to speak unclean things from perfect inanition. . . .

The shallow and impotent pretensions, tenets, and attempts, of this man,—and the success with which his influence seems to be extending itself among a pretty numerous, though certainly a very paltry and pitiful, set of readers,—have for the last two or three years been considered by us with the most sickening aversion. The very culpable manner in which his chief poem was reviewed in the Edinburgh Review (we believe it is no secret, at his own impatient and feverish request, by his partner in the Round Table), was matter of concern to more readers than ourselves. The masterly pen which inflicted such signal chastisement on the early licentiousness of Moore, should not have been idle on that occasion. Mr Jeffrey does ill, when he delegates his important functions into such hands as those of Mr Hazlitt. It was chiefly in consequence of that gentleman's allowing Leigh Hunt to pass unpunished through a scene of slaughter, which his execution might so highly have graced, that we came to the resolution of laying before our readers a series of essays of *the Cockney School*—of which here terminates the first.

III

Blackwood's Edinburgh Magazine. Vol. III, No. XVII, pp. 519–524. August, 1818.

Cockney School of Poetry: No. IV.

Reviewer: Possibly John Gibson Lockhart.

——— of Keats,
The Muses' son of Promise, and what feats
He yet may do, &.

                              CORNELIUS WEBB

OF all the manias of this mad age, the most incurable, as well as the most common, seems to be no other than *Metromanie*. . . . To witness the disease of any human understanding, however feeble, is distressing; but the spectacle of an able mind reduced to a state of insanity is of course ten times more afflicting. It is with such sorrow as this that we have contemplated the case of Mr John Keats. This young man appears to have received from nature talents of an excellent, perhaps even of a superior order—talents which devoted to the purposes of any useful profession, must have rendered him a respectable, if not an eminent citizen. His friends, we understand, destined him to the career of medicine, and he was bound apprentice some years ago to a worthy apothecary in town. But all has been undone by a sudden attack of the malady to which we have alluded. . . . For some time we were in hopes, that he might get off with a violent fit or two; but of late the symptoms are terrible. The phrenzy of the "Poems" was bad enough in its way; but it did not alarm us half so seriously as the calm, settled, imperturbable drivelling idiocy of "Endymion." . . .

The old story of the moon falling in love with a shepherd . . . has been seized upon by Mr John Keats, to be done with as might seem good unto the sickly fancy of one who never read a single line either of Ovid or of Wieland. If the quantity, not the quality, of the verses dedicated to the story is to be taken into account, there can be no doubt that Mr John Keats may now claim Endymion entirely to himself. To say the truth, we do not suppose either the Latin or the German poet would be very anxious to dispute about the property of the hero of the "Poetic Romance." Mr Keats has thoroughly appropriated the character, if not the name. His Endymion is not a Greek shepherd, loved by a Grecian goddess; he is merely a young Cockney rhymester. . . . Before giving any extracts, we must inform our readers, that this romance is meant to be written in English heroic rhyme. To those who have read any of Hunt's poems, this hint might indeed be needless. Mr Keats has adopted the loose, nerveless versification, and Cockney rhymes of the poet of Rimini; but in fairness to that gentleman, we must add, that the defects of the system are tenfold more conspicuous in his disciple's work than in his own. Mr Hunt is a small poet, but he is a clever man. Mr Keats is a still smaller poet, and he is only a boy of pretty abilities, which he has done every thing in his power to spoil. . . .

And now, good-morrow to "the Muses' son

of Promise;" as for "the feats he yet may do," as we do not pretend to say, like himself, "Muse of my native land am I inspired," we shall adhere to the safe old rule of *pauca verba*. We venture to make one small prophecy, that his bookseller will not a second time venture £50 upon anything he can write. It is a better and a wiser thing to be a starved apothecary than a starved poet; so back to the shop Mr John, back to "plasters, pills, and ointment boxes," &. But, for Heaven's sake, young Sangrado, be a little more sparing of extenuatives and soporifics in your practice than you have been in your poetry.

IV

The Quarterly Review. Vol. XIX, No. XXXVII, pp. 204–208. April, 1818.

Endymion: A Poetic Romance. By John Keats. London. 1818. pp. 207.

Reviewer: John Wilson Croker.—By Byron, Shelley, and others, this article was mistakenly thought to have "killed John Keats."

REVIEWERS have been sometimes accused of not reading the works which they affected to criticise. On the present occasion we shall anticipate the author's complaint, and honestly confess that we have not read his work. Not that we have been wanting in our duty—far from it—indeed, we have made efforts almost as superhuman as the story itself appears to be, to get through it; but with the fullest stretch of our perseverance, we are forced to confess that we have not been able to struggle beyond the first of the four books of which this Poetic Romance consists. We should extremely lament this want of energy, or whatever it may be, on our parts, were it not for one consolation—namely, that we are no better acquainted with the meaning of the book through which we have so painfully toiled, than we are with that of the three which we have not looked into.

It is not that Mr. Keats, (if that be his real name, for we almost doubt that any man in his senses would put his real name to such a rhapsody,) it is not, we say, that the author has not powers of language, rays of fancy, and gleams of genius—he has all these; but he is unhappily a disciple of the new school of what has been somewhere called Cockney poetry; which may be defined to consist of the most incongruous ideas in the most uncouth language.

Of this school, Mr. Leigh Hunt, as we observed in a former Number,[1] aspires to be the hierophant. Our readers will recollect the pleasant recipes for harmonious and sublime poetry which he gave us in his preface to "Rimini," and the still more facetious instances of his harmony and sublimity in the verses themselves; and they will recollect above all the contempt of Pope, Johnson, and such like poetasters and pseudo-critics, which so forcibly contrasted itself with Mr. Leigh Hunt's self-complacent approbation of

—all the things itself had wrote,
Of special merit though of little note.

This author is a copyist of Mr. Hunt; but he is more unintelligible, almost as rugged, twice as diffuse, and ten times more tiresome and absurd than his prototype, who, though he impudently presumed to seat himself in the chair of criticism, and to measure his own poetry by his own standard, yet generally had a meaning. But Mr. Keats had advanced no dogmas which he was bound to support by examples; his nonsense therefore is quite gratuitous; he writes it for its own sake, and being bitten by Mr. Leigh Hunt's insane criticism, more than rivals the insanity of his poetry.

Mr. Keats's preface hints that his poem was produced under peculiar circumstances.

Knowing within myself (he says) the manner in which this Poem has been produced, it is not without a feeling of regret that I make it public. What manner I mean, will be *quite clear* to the reader, who must soon perceive great inexperience, immaturity, and every error denoting a feverish attempt, rather than a deed accomplished.—*Preface*, p. vii.

We humbly beg his pardon, but this does not appear to us to be *quite so clear*—we really do not know what he means—but the next passage is more intelligible.

The two first books, and indeed the two last, I feel sensible are not of such completion as to warrant their passing the press.—*Preface*, p. vii.

Thus "the two first books" are, even in his own judgment, unfit to appear, and "the two

[1] Vol. XIV, No. XXVIII, pp. 473–481. January, 1816.

last" are, it seems, in the same condition—and as two and two make four, and as that is the whole number of books, we have a clear and, we believe, a very just estimate of the entire work.

Mr. Keats, however, deprecates criticism on this "immature and feverish work" in terms which are themselves sufficiently feverish; and we confess that we should have abstained from inflicting upon him any of the tortures of the "*fierce hell*" of criticism, which terrify his imagination, if he had not begged to be spared in order that he might write more; if we had not observed in him a certain degree of talent which deserves to be put in the right way, or which, at least, ought to be warned of the wrong; and if, finally, he had not told us that he is of an age and temper which imperiously require mental discipline.

Of the story we have been able to make out but little; it seems to be mythological, and probably relates to the loves of Diana and Endymion; but of this, as the scope of the work has altogether escaped us, we cannot speak with any degree of certainty; and must therefore content ourselves with giving some instances of its diction and versification:—and here again we are perplexed and puzzled.—At first it appeared to us, that Mr. Keats had been amusing himself and wearying his readers with an immeasurable game at *boutsrimés;* but, if we recollect rightly, it is an indispensable condition at this play, that the rhymes when filled up shall have a meaning; and our author, as we have already hinted, has no meaning. He seems to us to write a line at random, and then he follows not the thought excited by this line, but that suggested by the *rhyme* with which it concludes. There is hardly a complete couplet inclosing a complete idea in the whole book. He wanders from one subject to another, from the association, not of ideas but of sounds, and the work is composed of hemistichs which, it is quite evident, have forced themselves upon the author by the mere force of the catchwords on which they turn.

We shall select, not as the most striking instance, but as that least liable to suspicion, a passage from the opening of the poem.

> —Such the sun, the moon,
> Trees old and young, sprouting a shady boon
> For simple sheep; and such are daffodils
> With the green world they live in; and clear rills
> That for themselves a cooling covert make

> 'Gainst the hot season; the mid forest brake,
> Rich with a sprinkling of fair musk-rose blooms:
> And such too is the grandeur of the dooms
> We have imagined for the mighty dead; &. &.—
> pp. 3, 4.

Here it is clear that the word, and not the idea, *moon* produces the simple sheep and their shady *boon,* and that "the *dooms* of the mighty dead" would never have intruded themselves but for the "*fair musk-rose blooms.*"

Again.

> For 'twas the morn: Apollo's upward fire
> Made every eastern cloud a silvery pyre
> Of brightness so unsullied, that therein
> A melancholy spirit well might win
> Oblivion, and melt out his essence fine
> Into the winds: rain-scented eglantine
> Gave temperate sweets to that well-wooing sun;
> The lark was lost in him; cold springs had run
> To warm their chilliest bubbles in the grass;
> Man's voice was on the mountains; and the mass
> Of nature's lives and wonders puls'd tenfold,
> To feel this sun-rise and its glories old.—p. 8.

Here Apollo's *fire* produces a *pyre,* a silvery pyre of clouds, *wherein* a spirit might *win* oblivion and melt his essence *fine,* and scented *eglantine* gives sweets to the *sun,* and cold springs had *run* into the *grass,* and then the pulse of the *mass* pulsed *tenfold* to feel the glories *old* of the new-born day, &.

One example more.

> Be still the unimaginable lodge
> For solitary thinkings; such as dodge
> Conception to the very bourne of heaven,
> Then leave the naked brain: be still the leaven,
> That spreading in this dull and clodded earth
> Gives it a touch ethereal—a new birth.—p. 17.

Lodge, dodge—heaven, leaven—earth, birth; such, in six words, is the sum and substance of six lines.

We come now to the author's taste in versification. He cannot indeed write a sentence, but perhaps he may be able to spin a line. Let us see. The following are specimens of his prosodial notions of our English heroic metre.

> Dear as the temple's self, so does the moon,
> The passion poesy, glories infinite.—p. 4.

> So plenteously all weed-hidden roots.—p. 6.

> Of some strange history, potent to send.—p. 18.

> Before the deep intoxication.—p. 27.

> Her scarf into a fluttering pavilion.—p. 33.

> The stubborn canvass for my voyage prepared—.
> —p. 39.

"Endymion! the cave is secreter
Than the isle of Delos. Echo hence shall stir
No sighs but sigh-warm kisses, or light noise
Of thy combing hand, the while it travelling cloys
And trembles through my labyrinthine hair."—p.
48.

By this time our readers must be pretty well satisfied as to the meaning of his sentences and the structure of his lines: we now present them with some of the new words with which, in imitation of Mr. Leigh Hunt, he adorns our language.

We are told that "turtles *passion* their voices," (p. 15); that "an arbour was *nested*," (p. 23); and a lady's locks *"gordian'd* up," (p. 32); and to supply the place of the nouns thus verbalized Mr. Keats, with great fecundity, spawns new ones; such as "men-slugs and human *serpentry*," (p. 41); the *"honey-feel* of bliss," (p. 45); "wives prepare *needments*," (p. 13)—and so forth.

Then he has formed new verbs by the process of cutting off their natural tails, the adverbs, and affixing them to their foreheads; thus, "the wine out-sparkled," (p. 10); the "multitude up-followed," (p. 11); and "night up-took," (p. 29). "The wind up-blows," (p. 32); and the "hours are down-sunken," (p. 36).

But if he sinks some adverbs in the verbs he compensates the language with adverbs and adjectives which he separates from the parent stock. Thus, a lady "whispers *pantingly* and and close," makes *"hushing* signs," and steers her skiff into a *"ripply* cove," (p. 23); a shower falls *"refreshfully,"* (45); and a vulture has a *"spreaded* tail," (44).

But enough of Mr. Leigh Hunt and his simple neophyte.—If any one should be bold enough to purchase this "Poetic Romance," and so much more patient, than ourselves, as to get beyond the first book, and so much more fortunate as to find a meaning, we entreat him to make us acquainted with his success; we shall then return to the task which we now abandon in despair, and endeavour to make all due amends to Mr. Keats and to our readers.

V

The Examiner. No. 563, pp. 648–649. Sunday, October 11, 1818.

The Quarterly Review—Mr. Keats.

Reviewer: John Hamilton Reynolds.[1]

[1] "There have been two Letters in my defence

WE have met with a singular instance, in the last number of the *Quarterly Review,* of that unfeeling arrogance, and cold ignorance, which so strangely marked the minds and hearts of Government sycophants and Government writers. The Poem of a young man of genius, which evinces more natural power than any other work of this day, is abused and cried down, in terms which would disgrace any other pens than those used in the defence [*sic*] of an *Oliver* or a *Castles.* We have read the poetic romance of *Endymion* (the book in question) with no little delight; and could hardly believe that it was written by so young a man as the preface infers. Mr. Keats, the author of it, is a genius of the highest order; and no one but a Lottery Commissioner and a Government Pensioner, (both of which, Mr. William Gifford, the Editor of the *Quarterly Review,* is) could, with a false and remorseless pen, have striven to frustrate hopes and aims, so youthful and so high as this young Poet nurses. The Monthly Reviewers, it will be remembered, endeavoured, some few years back, to crush the rising heart of Kirk White; and indeed they in part generated that melancholy which ultimately destroyed him; but the world saw the cruelty, and, with one voice, hailed the genius which malignity would have repressed, and lifted it to fame. Reviewers are creatures that "stab men in the dark:"—young and enthusiastic spirits are their dearest prey. Our readers will not easily forget the brutality with which the Quarterly Reviewers, in a late number of their ministerial book, commented on the work of an intelligent and patriotic woman, whose ardour and independence happened to be high enough to make them her enemies. The language used by these Government critics, was lower than man would dare to utter to female ears; but Party knows no distinctions,—no proprieties,—and a woman is the best prey for its malignity, because it is the gentlest and most undefended. We certainly think that criticism might vent its petty passions on other subjects; that it might chuse its objects from

in the Chronicle and one in the Examiner, copied from the Alfred Exeter Paper, and written by Reynolds. I do not know who wrote those in the Chronicle. This is mere matter of the moment— I think I shall be among the English Poets after my death. Even as a Matter of present interest the attempt to crush me in the Quarterly has only brought me more into notice."
John Keats to George and Georgiana Keats, October 14 or 15, 1818.

the vain, the dangerous, and the powerful, and not from the young and the unprotected.

> It should strike hearts of age and care,
> And spare the youthful and the fair.

The cause of the unmerciful condemnation which has been passed on Mr. Keats, is pretty apparent to all who have watched the intrigues of literature, and the wily and unsparing contrivances of political parties. This young and powerful writer was noticed some little time back in the *Examiner,* and pointed out, by its Editor, as one who was likely to revive the early vigour of English poetry. Such a prediction was a fine but dangerous compliment to Mr. Keats: it exposed him instantly to the malice of the *Quarterly Review.* Certain it is, that hundreds of fashionable and flippant readers will henceforth set down this young poet as a pitiable and nonsensical writer, merely on the assertions of some single heartless critic, who has just energy enough to despise what is good, because it would militate against his pleasantry, if he were to praise it.

The genius of Mr. Keats is peculiarly classical; and, with the exception of a few faults, which are the natural followers of youth, his imaginations and his language have a spirit and an intensity which we should in vain look for in half the popular poets of the day. Lord Byron is a splendid and noble egotist: he visits classical shores; roams over romantic lands, and wanders through magnificent forests; courses the dark and restless waves of the sea, and rocks his spirit on the midnight lakes; but no spot is conveyed to our minds that is not peopled by the gloomy and ghastly feelings of one proud and solitary man. It is as if he and the world were the only two things which the air clothed. His lines are majestic vanities;— his poetry always is marked with a haughty selfishness;—he writes loftily, because he is the spirit of an ancient family;—he is liked by most of his readers, because he is a Lord. If a common man were to dare to be as moody, as contemptuous, and as misanthropical, the world would laugh at him. There must be a coronet marked on all his little pieces of poetical insolence, or the world would not countenance them. Mr. Keats has none of this egotism—this daring selfishness, which is a stain on the robe of poesy. His feelings are full, earnest, and original, as those of the olden writers were and are; they are made for all time, not for the drawing-room and the moment. Mr. Keats always speaks of, and describes nature, with an awe and a humility, but with a deep and almost breathless affection.—He knows that Nature is better and older than he is, and he does not put himself on an equality with her. You do not see him when you see her. The moon, and the mountainous foliage of the woods, and the azure sky, and the ruined and magic temple; the rock, the desart [*sic*], and the sea; the leaf of the forest, and the embossed foam of the most living ocean, are the spirits of his poetry; but he does not bring them in his own hand, or obtrude his person before you, when you are looking at them. Poetry is a thing of generalities—a wanderer amid persons and things—not a pauser over one thing, or with one person. The mind of Mr. Keats, like the minds of our older poets, goes round the universe in its speculations and its dreams. It does not set itself a task. The manners of the world, the fictions and the wonders of other worlds, are its subjects; not the pleasures of hope, or the pleasures of memory. The true poet confines his imagination to no one thing—his soul is an invisible ode to the passions.—He does not make a home for his mind in one land—its productions are an universal story, not an eastern tale. The fancies of Moore are exquisitely beautiful, as fancies, but they are always of one colour;—his feelings are pathetic, but they are "still harping on my daughter." The true pathetic is to be found in the reflections on things, not in the moods and miseries of one person. There is not one poet of the present day, that enjoys any popularity that will live; each writes for his booksellers and the ladies of fashion, and not for the voice of centuries. Time is a lover of old books, and he suffers few new ones to become old. Posterity is a difficult mark to hit; and few minds can send the arrow full home. Wordsworth might have safely cleared the rapids in the stream of time, but he lost himself by looking at his own image in the waters. Coleridge stands bewildered in the cross-road of fame;—his genius will commit suicide, and be buried in it. Southey is Poet Laureate, "so there is no heed to be taken of him." Campbell has relied on two stools, *"The Pleasures of Hope,"* and *"Gertrude of Wyoming;"* but he will come to the ground, after the fashion of the old proverb. The journey of fame is an endless one; and does Mr. Rogers think that pumps and silk stockings (which his genius wears) will last him the whole way? Poetry is the coyest creature that ever was wooed by man: she has something of the coquet in her; for she flirts with many, and seldom loves one.

Mr. Keats has certainly not perfected any thing yet; but he has the power, we think, within him, and it is in consequence of such an opinion that we have written these few hasty observations. If he should ever see this, he will not regret to find that all the country is not made up of Quarterly Reviewers. All that we wish is, that our readers would read the Poem, as we have done, before they assent to its condemnation—they will find passages of singular feeling, force, and pathos. We have the highest hopes of this young Poet. We are obscure men, it is true, and not gifted with that perilous power of mind, and truth of judgment, which are possessed by Mr. Croker, Mr. Canning, Mr. Barrow, or Mr. Gifford, (all "honourable men," and writers in the *Quarterly Review*). We live far from the world of letters,—out of the pale of fashionable criticism,—aloof from the atmosphere of a Court; but we are surrounded by a beautiful country, and love Poetry, which we read out of doors, as well as in. We think we see glimpses of a high mind in this young man, and surely the feeling is better that urges us to nourish its strength, than that which prompts the Quarterly Reviewer to crush it in its youth, and for ever. If however the mind of Mr. Keats be of the quality we think it to be of, it will not be cast down by this wanton and empty attack. Malice is a thing of the scorpion kind—it drives the sting into its own heart. The very passages which the *Quarterly Review* quotes as ridiculous, have in them the beauty that sent us to the Poem itself. . . .

Does the author of such poetry as this deserve to be made the sport of so servile a dolt as a Quarterly Reviewer?—No. Two things have struck us on the perusal of this singular poem. The first is, that Mr. Keats excels, in what Milton excelled—the power of putting a spirit of life and novelty into the Heathen Mythology. The second is, that in the structure of his verse, and the *sinewy* quality of his thoughts, Mr. Keats greatly resembles old Chapman, the nervous translator of Homer. His mind has "thews and limbs like to its ancestors." Mr. Gifford, who knows something of the old dramatists, ought to have paused before he sanctioned the abuse of a spirit kindred

with them. If he could not feel, he ought to know better.

VI

The Edinburgh Review. Vol. XXXIV, No. LXVII, pp. 203–213. August, 1820.

> 1. *Endymion: A Poetic Romance.* By John Keats. 8vo. pp. 207. London, 1818.
> 2. *Lamia, Isabella, The Eve of St. Agnes, and other Poems.* By John Keats, Author of Endymion. 12mo. pp. 200. London, 1820.

Reviewer: Francis Jeffrey.

WE had never happened to see either of these volumes till very lately—and have been exceedingly struck with the genius they display, and the spirit of poetry which breathes through all their extravagance. That imitation of our older writers, and especially of our older dramatists, to which we cannot help flattering ourselves that we have somewhat contributed, has brought on, as it were, a second spring in our poetry;—and few of its blossoms are either more profuse of sweetness or richer in promise, than this which is now before us. Mr Keats, we understand, is still a very young man; and his whole works, indeed, bear evidence enough of the fact. They are full of extravagance and irregularity, rash attempts at originality, interminable wanderings, and excessive obscurity. They manifestly require, therefore, all the indulgence that can be claimed for a first attempt:—but we think it no less plain that they deserve it; for they are flushed all over with the rich lights of fancy, and so coloured and bestrewn with the flowers of poetry, that even while perplexed and bewildered in their labyrinths, it is impossible to resist the intoxication of their sweetness, or to shut our hearts to the enchantments they so lavishly present. The models upon which he has formed himself, in the Endymion, the earliest and by much the most considerable of his poems, are obviously the Faithful Shepherdess of Fletcher, and the Sad Shepherd of Ben Johnson;—the exquisite metres and inspired diction of which he has copied with great boldness and fidelity—and, like his great originals, has also contrived to impart to the whole piece that true rural and poetical air which breathes only in them and in Theocritus—which is at once homely and majestic, luxurious and rude, and sets before us the genuine sights and sounds and smells of the country, with all the magic and grace of Elysium. His subject has the disadvantage of being mythological; and in this respect, as well as on account of the raised and rapturous tone it consequently assumes, his poetry may be better compared perhaps to the Comus and the Arcades of Milton, of which, also, there are many traces of imitation. The great distinction, however, between him and these divine authors, is, that imagination in them is subordinate to reason and judgment, while, with him, it is paramount and supreme—that their ornaments and images are employed to embellish and recommend just sentiments, engaging incidents, and natural characters, while his are poured out without measure or restraint, and with no apparent design but to unburden the breast of the author, and give vent to the overflowing vein of his fancy. The thin and scanty tissue of his story is merely the light frame work on which his florid wreaths are suspended; and while his imaginations go rambling and entangling themselves everywhere, like wild honeysuckles, all idea of sober reason, and plan, and consistency, is utterly forgotten, and are "strangled in their waste fertility." A great part of the work indeed, is written in the strangest and most fantastical manner that can be imagined. It seems as if the author had ventured everything that occurred to him in the shape of a glittering image or striking expression—taken the first word that presented itself to make up a rhyme, and then made that word the germ of a new cluster of images—a hint for a new excursion of the fancy—and so wandered on, equally forgetful whence he came, and heedless whither he was going, till he had covered his pages with an interminable arabesque of connected and incongruous figures, that multiplied as they extended, and were only harmonized by the brightness of their tints, and the graces of their forms. In this rash and headlong career he has of course many lapses and failures. There is no work, accordingly, from which a malicious critic could cull more matter for ridicule, or select more obscure, unnatural, or absurd passages. But we do not take *that* to be our office;—and just beg leave, on the contrary, to say, that any one who, on this account, would represent the whole poem as despicable, must either have no notion of poetry, or no regard to truth.

It is, in truth, at least as full of genius as of absurdity; and he who does not find a great deal in it to admire and to give delight, cannot in his heart see much beauty in the two exquisite dramas to which we have already alluded, or find any great pleasure in some of the finest creations of Milton and Shakespeare. There are very many such persons, we verily believe, even among the reading and judicious part of the community—correct scholars we have no doubt many of them, and, it may be very classical composers in prose and in verse—but utterly ignorant of the true genius of English poetry, and incapable of estimating its appropriate and most exquisite beauties. With that spirit we have no hesitation in saying that Mr K. is deeply imbued—and of those beauties he has presented us with many striking examples. We are very much inclined indeed to add, that we do not know any book which we would sooner employ as a test to ascertain whether any one had in him a native relish for poetry, and a genuine sensibility to its intrinsic charm. . . .

Mr Keats has unquestionably a very beautiful imagination, and a great familiarity with the finest diction of English poetry; but he must learn not to misuse or misapply these advantages; and neither to waste the good gifts of nature and study on intractable themes, nor to luxuriate too recklessly on such as are more suitable.

VII

The London Magazine. Vol. II, No. IX, pp. 315–321. September, 1820.[1]

Lamia, Isabella, the Eve of Saint Agnes, and other Poems. By John Keats, Author of Endymion, London, Taylor and Hessey, 12mo. pp. 199.

Reviewer: Unknown.

WE opened this volume with very considerable anxiety:—an anxiety partly occasioned by the unqualified praises of which the author has been the object,—but more owing to the abuse

[1] Vol. 1, No. IV, pp. 380–89, April, 1820, carries an article in appreciation of *Endymion*. The reviewer sharply attacks the impertinence of John Wilson Croker (*supra*).

by which he has been assailed. Perhaps from the whole history of criticism, real and pretended, nothing more truly unprincipled than that abuse can be quoted; nothing more heartless, more vindictive,—more nefarious in design, more pitiful and paltry in spirit. We consider it one of the worst signs of these, the worst times which England, we are afraid, has ever seen, that the miserable selfishness of political party has erected itself into a literary authority, and established, by means of popular channels, the most direct and easy access to the public ear on literary questions. The provocation, we allow, is reciprocal: the vanity of the Examiner manifests just as great a deficiency in real candour as is apparent in the bitter spite of the Quarterly, or the merry ruffianism of Blackwood. But the distinct consciousness of depravity in the two latter, which must accompany them in many of their lubrications, gives a blacker feature to their conduct. . . .

Mr. Keats, though not a political writer, plunged at once, with what we shall take the liberty of calling a boyish petulance, and with an air of rather insulting bravado, into some very delicate subjects;—subjects on which, we have no hesitation to say, those very qualities of his mind which confer on his poetry its most characteristic beauties, incapacitate him fairly to pronounce. . . .

There are some stanzas introduced into his delicious tale of "Isabel—poor simple Isabel," . . . which, we think, dreadfully mar the musical tenderness of its general strain. They are no better than extravagant school-boy vituperation of trade and traders; just as if lovers did not trade,—and that, often in stolen goods—or had in general any higher object than a barter of enjoyment! These stanzas in Mr. Keats's poem, when contrasted with the larger philosophy of Boccacio, and his more genial spirit, as exemplified with reference to the very circumstances in question, are additionally offensive. Instead of tirading against the brothers as "money-bags," "Baalites of pelf," "ledger-men,"—and asking, "why, in the name of glory, were they proud?" Boccacio describes the honor of the family as actually injured by Lorenzo, whom they employed—he shows us the elder brother, on discovering his sister's dishonour, afflicted with grief and perplexity, and passing a sleepless night on his bed—he even compliments the discretion of this member of the family—and it is thus naturally, and faithfully, and feelingly introduced, that he leads up the dreadful catastrophe to its consummation in Italian revenge, and the broken-heartedness of widowed love. . . . Mr. Keats, we are sure, has a sensibility sufficiently delicate to feel this beauty in Boccacio: why then has he substituted for it, in his own composition, a boisterous rhapsody, which interrupts the harmony of the sorrowful tale,—repels sympathy by the introduction of caricature,—and suggests all sorts of dissenting, and altercating prejudices and opinions? His device is a clumsy one: Boccacios delicate and true. . . .

We mention these things, not because we desire to see Mr. Keats playing the hypocrite, or enlisted as a florid declaimer on the profitable side of things; but because, with our admiration of his powers, we are loath to see him irrecoverably committed to a flippant and false system of reasoning on human nature;—because to his picturesque imagination, we wish that he would add a more pliable, and, at the same time, a more magnanimous sensibility. Nor need his philosophy be a whit more condescending to what is grovelling and base. Let him write, as much as he pleases, in the bold indignant style of Wordsworth's glorious Sonnet!

The world is too much with us! . . .

The injustice which has been done to our author's works, in estimating their poetical merit, rendered us doubly anxious, on opening his last volume, to find it likely to seize fast hold of general sympathy, and thus turn an overwhelming power against the paltry traducers of a talent, more eminently promising in many respects, than any that the present age has been called upon to encourage. We have not found it to be quite all that we wished in this respect—and it would have been very extraordinary if we had, for our wishes went far beyond reasonable expectations. But we have found it of a nature to present to common understandings the poetical power with which the author's mind is gifted, in a more tangible and intelligible shape than that in which it has appeared in any of his former compositions. It is, therefore, calculated to throw shame on the lying, vulgar spirit, in which this young worshipper in the temple of the Muses has been cried-down. . . .

Will not readers feel it as a disgrace attaching to the character of the period, that a dastardly attempt should have been made to assassinate a poet of power: . . . that one should come like a thief to steal his "precious diadem";—a murder and a robbery "most foul and horrible?" Cold-blooded conscious dishonesty, we have no hesitation to say, must have directed the pen of the critic of Endymion in the Quarterly Review: making every allowance for the callousness of a worldly spirit, it is impossible to conceive a total insensibility to the vast beauties scattered profusely over that disordered, ill-digested work. The author provokes opposition, as we have already fully said: not unfrequently he even suggests angry censure. We cannot help applying the word *insolent,* in a literary sense, to some instances of his neglectfulness, to the random swagger of occasional expressions, to the bravado style of many of his sentiments. But, coupling these great faults with his still greater poetical merits, what a fine, what an interesting subject did he offer for perspicacious, honourable criticism! But he was beset by a very dog-kennel; and he must be more than human if he has not had his erroneous tendencies hardened in him in consequence.

What strikes us as the principal faults of his poetry, impeding his popularity, we would venture thus to specify.

1. His frequent obscurity and confusion of language. As an instance of the latter, we may mention, that he attaches the epithet of *"leaden-eyed,"* to despair, considered as a quality or sentiment. Were it a personification of despair, the compound would be as finely applied, as, under the actual circumstances, it is erroneously so. There are many, many passages too, in his last volume, as well as in his earlier ones, from which we are not able, after taking some pains to understand them, to derive any distinct notion or meaning whatever.

2. He is too fond of running out glimmerings of thoughts, and indicating distant shadowy fancies: he shows, also, a fondness for dwelling on features which are not naturally the most important or prominent. His imagination coquets with, and mocks the reader in this respect; and plain earnest minds turn away from such tricks with disgust. The greatest poets have always chiefly availed themselves of the plainest and most palpable materials.

3. He affects, in bad taste, a quaint strangeness of phrase; as some folks affect an odd manner of arranging their neckcloths, &c. This "shows a most pitiful ambition." We wish Mr. Keats would not talk of *cutting mercy with a sharp knife to the bone;* we cannot contemplate the *skeleton* of mercy. Nor can we familiarize ourselves pleasantly with the *dainties made to still an infant's cries:*—the latter is indeed a very round-about way of expression,—and not very complimentary either, we think. Young ladies, who know, of course, little or nothing of the economy of the nursery, will be apt, we imagine, to pout at this periphrasis, which puts their charms on a level with babycorals!

But we are by this time tired of criticism; as we hope our readers are:—let us then all turn together to the book itself. We have said here what we have deemed it our duty to say: we shall there find what it will be our delight to enjoy.

A SELECTIVE BIOGRAPHICAL DICTIONARY OF AUTHORS FREQUENTLY OR SIGNIFICANTLY MENTIONED BY THE WRITERS OF THE ROMANTIC MOVEMENT

Following the names of English writers are given titles of pertinent or representative works. Special references not concerned in this selective record are given in the notes. For the sake of clarity, references are sometimes repeated.

e. = English, f. = French, gn. = German, g. = Greek
i. = Italian, r. = Roman, s. = Spanish.

Addison, Joseph (1672–1719) e. *The Campaign* (1704); *Contributions to the Spectator* (1711–1714).

Æschylus (525–456 B. C.) g. dramatist and poet.

Anacreon (563?–478 B. C.) g. lyric poet.

Ariosto, Ludovico (1474–1533) i. poet.

Aristotle (384–322 B. C.) g. philos.

Aurelius, Marcus (121–180) r. philos.

Bacon, Francis (1561–1626) e. *Advancement of Learning* (1605), *New Atlantis* (1627).

Baillie, Joanna (1762–1851) e. *Plays on the Passions* (1798–1802), *De Montfort* (1800).

Barbauld, Anna Letitia (1743–1825) e. *Miscellaneous Poems* (1773).

Beaumont, Frances (1584?–1616) e. *The Maid's Tragedy* (1609?).

Berkeley, George (1685–1753) e. *Principles of Human Knowledge* (1710), *Siris* (1744).

Boccaccio, Giovanni (1313–1345) i. story teller.

Boileau, Nicolas (1636–1711) f. critic and versifier.

Bolingbroke (Henry St. John—1678–1751) e. *Idea of a Patriot King* (1735), *Philosophical Writings* (1754).

Bowles, William Lisle (1762–1850) e. *Sonnets* (1789).

Bunyan, John (1628–1688) e. *The Pilgrim's Progress* (1678–1684).

Burke, Edmund (1729–1797) e. *Speech on American Taxation* (1774), *Reflections on the Revolution in France* (1790).

Burns, Robert (1759–1796) e. *Poems* (1786, 1793).

Butler, Samuel (1612–1680) e. *Hudibras* (1663, 1664, 1678).

Calderon, Pedro (1600–1681) s. dramatic poet.

Campbell, Thomas (1777–1844) e. *Pleasures of Hope* (1799), *Gertrude of Wyoming* (1809).

Catullus—Caius Valerius (87–54 B. C.) r. poet.

Cervantes, Miguel (1547–1616) s. author.

Chapman, George (1559?–1634) e. *Bussy d'Ambois* (1607), *Translation of the Iliad* (1610, 1611).

Chaucer, Geoffrey (1340?–1400) e. *The Canterbury Tales* (1373, 1393).

Churchill, Charles (1731–1764) e. *Night* (1761), *The Ghost* (1762).

Cicero—Marcus Tullius (106–43 B. C.) r. statesman and philos.

Collins, William (1721–1759) e. *Odes on Several Subjects* (1746).

Congreve, William (1670–1729) e. *The Way of the World* (1700).

Cowley, Abraham (1618–1667) e. *Poems* (1656), *Pindaric Odes* (1656).

Cowper, William (1731–1800) e. *Olney Hymns* (1779), *The Task* (1785).

Crabbe, George (1754–1832) e. *The Village* (1783).

Cumberland, Richard (1732–1811) e. *Calvary* (1792).

Daniel, Samuel (1562–1619) e. *The Civil Wars* (1595, 1599, 1609), *Musophilus* (1599).

Dante, Alighieri (1265–1321) i. poet.

D'Arblay, Frances (1752–1840) e. *Evelina* (1778), *Camilla* (1796).

Darwin, Erasmus (1731–1802) e. *The Loves of the Plants* (1789), *The Botanic Garden* (1791).

Davenant, Sir William (1606–1668) e. *Gondibert* (1651), *The Unfortunate Lovers* (1638).

Defoe, Daniel (1661?–1731) e. *Robinson Crusoe* (1719).

Descartes, René (1596–1650) f. philos.

Diogenes (412?–323? B. C.) g. philos.

Donne, John (1573–1631) e. *Sermons* (1640), *Poems* (1633).

Drayton, Michael (1563–1631) e. *The Shepherd's Garland* (1593), *Nymphidia* (1627).

Dryden, John (1631–1700) e. *All for Love* (1678), *Mac Flecknoe* (1782).

Epictetus (60?–120?) r. philos.

Euripides (480–406 B. C.) g. tragic poet.

Fielding, Henry (1707–1754) e. *The Adventures of Joseph Andrews* (1742), *The History of Tom Jones* (1749).

Fletcher, John (1579–1625) e. *The Faithful Shepherdess* (1610).

Gay, John (1685–1732) e. *Trivia* (1715), *The Beggar's Opera* (1728).

Gibbon, Edward (1737–1794) e. *The History of the Decline and Fall of the Roman Empire* (1776, 1781, 1788).

Godwin, William (1756–1836) e. *Inquiry Concerning Political Justice* (1793), *Caleb Williams* (1794).

Goethe, Johann Wolfgang (1749–1832) gn. poet and philos.

Gray, Thomas (1716–1771) e. *Elegy in a Country Churchyard* (1751), *Poems* (1768).

Hartley, David (1705–1757) e. *Observations on Man* (1749).

Herodotus (484?–425? B. C.) g. historian.

Hervey, James (1714–1758) e. *Meditations and Contemplations* (1746).

Hesiod (8th c. B. C.) g. poet.

Holcroft, Thomas (1744–1809) e. *The Road to Ruin* (1792).

Homer, (circ. 9th B. C.) g. epic poet.

Horace—Quintus Horatius Flaccus (65–8 B. C.) r. poet.

Hume, David (1711–1776) e. *Essay on Miracles* (1748), *Inquiry Concerning Human Understanding* (1748).

Inchbald, Elizabeth (1753–1821) e. *A Simple Story* (1791).

Jonson, Benjamin (1573–1637) e. *Everyman in His Humour* (1596), *Masques at Court* (1603–1633).

Kant, Immanuel (1724–1804) gn. philos.

Klopstock, Friedrich Gottlieb (1724–1803) gn. poet.

Kotzebue, August F. F. (1761–1819) gn. dramatist.

Lamb, Charles (1775–1834) e. *Essays of Elia* (1820–1825).

Lessing, Gotthold Ephraim (1729–1781) gn. dramatist and critic.

Lewis, Matthew Gregory (1775–1818) e. *The Monk* (1795), *The Castle Spectre* (1797).

Lillo, George (1693–1739) e. *The London Merchant* (1731).

Livy—Titus Livius (59 B. C.–17 A. D.) r. historian.

Locke, John (1632–1704) e. *Essay Concerning Human Understanding* (1690).

Lucan—Marcus Annaeus Lucanus (39–65) r. poet.

Lucretius—Titus Lucretius Carus (96?–55 B. C.) r. poet.

Machiavelli, Niccolo (1469–1527) e. political writer.

Mackintosh, Sir James (1765–1832) e. *Vindiciae Gallicae* (1791), *History of England* (1830–1832).

Macpherson, James (1738–1796) e. *Fragments of Ancient Poetry* (1760), *Fingal* (1762).

Malthus, Thomas Robert (1766–1834) e. *Essay on the Principle of Population* (1798).

Marini, Giambattista (1569–1625) i. poet.

Milman, Henry Hart (1791–1868) e. *Fazio* (1815).

Milton, John (1608–1674) e. *Paradise Lost* (1667, 1674).

Molière (Jean Baptiste Poquelin—1622–1673) f. dramatist.

Montaigne, Michel Eyquem (1533–1592) f. essayist.

Montesquieu, Charles de Secondat (1689–1755) f. philos.

Montgomery, James (1771–1854) e. *Pelican Island* (1827).

Moore, Edward (1712–1757) e. *The Gamester* (1753).

Moore, Thomas (1779–1852) e. *Irish Melodies* (1807–1834), *Life of Byron* (1830).

More, Hannah (1745–1833) e. *Essays for Young Ladies* (1789), *Practical Piety* (1811).

Otway, Thomas (1652–1685) e. *Venice Preserved* (1682).

Ovid—Publius Ovidius Naso (43 B. C.–17 A. D.) r. poet.

Paine, Thomas (1737–1809) e. *Common Sense* (1776), *The Rights of Man* (1791–1792).

Paley, William (1743–1805) e. *Natural Theology* (1802).

Percy, Thomas (1729–1811) e. *Reliques of Ancient English Poetry* (1765).

Petrarca, Francesco (1304–1374) i. poet.

Philips, Ambrose (1671–1749) e. *Poems* (1748).

Pindar (522–448? B. C.) g. lyric poet.

Plato (427–347 B. C.) g. philos.

Plotinus (205?–270?) Egyptian philos.

Plutarch (46?–120?) g. biographer.

Priestley, Joseph (1733–1804) e. *Disquisitions Relating to Matter and Spirit* (1777).

Prior, Matthew (1664–1721) e. *Poems on Several Occasions* (1709–1718).

Pythagoras (582–507? B. C.) g. philos.

Quarles, Francis (1592–1644) e. *Divine Poems* (1630).

Radcliffe, Ann (1764–1823) e. *The Mysteries of Udolpho* (1794).

Raleigh, Sir Walter (1552–1618) e. *A History of the World* (1614).

Rogers, Samuel (1763–1855) e. *The Pleasures of Memory* (1792).

Rousseau, Jean Jacques (1712–1778) f. philos.

Schiller, Johann C. F. (1759–1905) gn. poet.

Shadwell, Thomas (1640–1692) e. *The Sullen Lovers* (1669).

Shenstone, William (1714–1763) e. *The Schoolmistress* (1737).

Sidney, Sir Philip (1554–1586) e. *The Countess of Pembroke's Arcadia* (1590), *An Apology for Poetry* (1595).

Smith, Adam (1723–1790) e. *An Inquiry into the Nature and Causes of the Wealth of Nations* (1776).

Sophocles (496?–406 B. C.) g. tragic poet.

Southey, Robert (1774–1843) e. *Wat Tyler* (1794), *Thalaba the Destroyer* (1801).

Spenser, Edmund (1552–1599) e. *The Faerie Queene* (1590, 1596).

Spinoza, Baruch (1632–1677) Jewish philos.

Sterne, Lawrence (1713–1768) e. *Sentimental Journey* (1768), *The Life and Opinions of Tristram Shandy* (1759, 1767).

Suckling, Sir John (1609–1641) e. *Fragmenta Aurea* (1646).

Swift, Jonathan (1667–1745) e. *The Tale of a Tub* (1698), *Travels of Lemuel Gulliver* (1726).

Tacitus—Publius Cornelius (55?–117?) r. historian.

Tasso, Torquato (1544–1595) i. poet.

Taylor, Jeremy (1613–1667) e. *Holy Living* (1650), *Holy Dying* (1651).

Theocritus (3d c. B. C.) g. pastoral poet.

Thomson, James (1700–1748) e. *The Seasons* (1726, 1727, 1728, 1730).

Thucydides (471–400 B. C.) g. historian.

Virgil—Publius Vergilius Maro (70–19 B. C.) r. poet.

Voltaire (François Marie Arouet—1694–1778) f. philos.

Waller, Edmund (1606–1687) e. *Poems* (1645, 1664).

Warner, William (1558?–1606) e. *Albion's England* (1586, 1602).

White, Henry Kirke (1785–1806) e. *Poems* (1804), *Remains* (1807).

Wieland, Christoph Martin (1733–1813) gn. poet and novelist.

Wollstonecraft, Mary (1759–1797) e. *Vindication of the Rights of Woman* (1792).

NOTES

Legend: a. = left column; b. = right column. For poetry the number of the line of the poem is given; for prose the number of the line on the page.

SAMUEL TAYLOR COLERIDGE

TO THE AUTHOR OF "THE ROBBERS"

7. a. 4. "a famish'd Father's cry": Coleridge's note in the 1803 ed.—"The Father of Moor in the Play of the Robbers." By Schiller.

TO A YOUNG ASS

7. b. 10. "Dell of Peace": In 1794 Coleridge, Southey, and ten other "gentlemen of good education . . . with twelve ladies" were to establish an ideal colony in some "delightful part of the new back settlements" of America. This was to be the Pantisocracy. The scheme never materialized.

THE EOLIAN HARP

7. b. 1. "My pensive Sara": His bride, Sara Fricker, was to become one of the "twelve ladies" of the Pantisocracy.
8. a. 12. "that simplest Lute": A box with strings drawn across it was set in a window where the wind might touch the strings to music.

REFLECTIONS

8. b. "Sermoni propriora": Lamb's trans.: "Properer for a sermon."
8. b. 9. "The Valley of Seclusion": For their honeymoon Coleridge and his bride took a cottage at Clevedon. See text, p. 5.
9. a. 49. "Howard": John Howard, Sheriff of Bedford, published *The State of the Prisons* in 1777. His work was instrumental in bringing about prison reform.

ODE TO THE DEPARTING YEAR

9. b. The Greek lines, which are from the distraught speeches of Cassandra, may be translated as follows: "Ah! Ah! Woe! Woe! Again the dreadful pangs of prevision assail me, whirling my soul with a confused beginning. What is to be will come to pass. Nay, thy very self wilt say compassionately that the prophet is only too true."
10. a. 32. "the dread Name": Coleridge's note: "The Name of Liberty, which at the commencement of the French Revolution was both the occasion and the pretext of unnumbered crimes."

10. a. 40. "the Northern Conquerors": Coleridge's note: "I rejoice, as at the extinction of the evil Principle impersonated! This very day, six years ago, the massacre of Ismail was perpetrated. Thirty thousand human beings, men, women, and children, murdered in cold blood." See *Don Juan* VIII.
10. b. 76. "the Lampards seven": See *Revelation* 4: 7.
10. b. 88. "Afric's wrongs": It was not until 1833 that parliament passed the *Emancipation Act*, freeing all slaves in the British Empire.
10. b. 91. "gifts": in the Scriptural sense of corruption.

THIS LIME-TREE BOWER MY PRISON

12. a. 17. "long lank weeds": Coleridge's note: "The Asplenium scolopendrium, called in some countries the Adder's Tongue."
12. a. 28. "My gentle-hearted Charles": Charles Lamb.
12. b. 74. "Flew creaking": Coleridge quotes Bartram's observations on the Savanna Crane: "When these birds move their wings in flight . . . their shafts and webs upon one another creek."

THE RIME OF THE ANCIENT MARINER

13. a. The Latin motto may be translated thus: "Easily do I believe that there are more invisible things in the universe than visible. But of all these things who shall explain to us the kind and the rank and the kinship and the distinguishing features and the functions of each? What do they do? What places do they inhabit? Ever the human mind has circled about this knowledge, but never attained it. Yet I do not doubt that it is good sometimes to contemplate in the mind, as in a picture, the image of a greater and a better world: lest the mind accustomed to the petty details of daily life should become narrow, and settle down completely into paltry thoughts. But meanwhile we must be watchful of truth and we must keep proportion, in order that we may distinguish the certain from the uncertain, day from night."

CHRISTABEL

20. b. The title of the poem may have been suggested to Coleridge by the ballad *Sir Cauline*.

The conclusion to Part II, sent separately in a letter to Southey, may never have been intended as part of the work. See Note 116 in *The Works of Coleridge* ed. by James Dykes Campbell (1909).

FROST AT MIDNIGHT

27. b. 7. "My cradled infant": Hartley. See Earl L. Griggs: *Hartley Coleridge: His Life and Work* (1929).
28. a. 37. "the stern preceptor": Boyer, the master of Christ's Hospital, knocked Coleridge down and flogged him when the boy, believing himself an infidel, expressed a desire to become a shoemaker and not a clergyman.
28. a. 43. "My play-mate": His beloved sister Ann.
28. a. 53. "the sky and stars": The boy, while at Christ's Hospital, used to lie upon the roof in order to watch the clouds and the stars. When in 1800 Coleridge moved to Keswick his son was in reality taken into the region of mountains.

FRANCE: AN ODE

29. a. 42. "And hung my head": Cf. *The Prelude* X and XI, text, pp. 146–147.
29. b. 67. "Helvetia": Switzerland. In 1798 the French invaded the Swiss Cantons.

THE NIGHTINGALE

33. b. The setting of this poem is about Nether Stowey and Alfoxden. The Friend and Sister (34. a. 40.) are William and Dorothy Wordsworth. Dorothy is also the "gentle Maid" of 34. b. 69.

KUBLA KHAN

35. b. The passage which Coleridge read in *Purchas his Pilgrimage* before he fell asleep (see text, p. 775) was the following: "In Xanadu did Cublai Can build a stately palace, encompassing sixteen miles of plaine ground with a wall wherein are fertile Meddowes, pleasant Springs, delightful Streames and all sorts of beasts of chase and game, and in the middest thereof a sumptuous house of pleasure."

THE DEVIL'S THOUGHTS

37. a. 17. "a white horse": See *Revelation* 5: 8. Cf. Shelley's *The Devil's Walk* (1812), Byron's *The Devil's Drive* (1813), and Southey's later version of fifty-seven stanzas.
37. a. 33. "England's commercial prosperity": Robert Walpole, between 1712 and 1742, had made "prosperity" the aim of England's statesmanship. See Norris A. Brisco: *The Economic Policy of Robert Walpole* (1907).
37. b. 37. "his prisons": See 9. a. 49.
37. b. 44. "the Slave-trade": See 10. b. 88. In England Thomas Clarkson (1760–1846) led the fight for abolition.

DEJECTION: AN ODE

39. a. This poem was originally addressed to Wordsworth, the name "William" appearing throughout in the place of "Lady" (lines 25 and 47) and of "Otway" (line 120). It was first printed in the *Morning Post* on October 4, 1802, Wordsworth's wedding day. Due to an estrangement between the two poets the names were changed. Cf. Wordsworth's *Ode*, text, p. 158.

HYMN BEFORE SUNRISE

41. a. Chamouni is a valley in the Savoy Alps. Above it rises "sovran Blanc." Coleridge, who had never been there, "created the dry bones" of a work by the German poetess Frederike Brun "into the fulness of life." Similarly the poem *On a Cataract* (p. 36) was "created" out of the German of Stolberg.

THE PAINS OF SLEEP

42. a. In a letter to the Beaumonts (Sept. 22, 1803) and in a letter to Thomas Poole (Oct. 3, 1803), Coleridge asserted that this poem did not exaggerate his actual experiences. He had been suffering from gout and had sought relief through drugs.

A TOMBLESS EPITAPH

44. a. 1. "Idoloclastes Satyrane": Coleridge himself. The poem is a self-study.

THE BIOGRAPHIA LITERARIA

45. a. 13. "Mr. Southey's writings—a new school": Robert Southey (1774–1843), brother-in-law of Coleridge, was commonly classed among the "Lake Poets"—the "new school." See Review II, text, p. 782.
46. b. 29. "albo lapide notatae": With a white stone marked. The Romans used white stones to mark fortunate days.
47. a. 16. "the dulcia vitia": Trans.: "seductive faults." The poets named employed just those sweet artifices which Wordsworth condemned.
47. b. 27. "The poetic Psyche—the butterfly": Among the Greeks, the butterfly became associated with Psyche as a symbol of immortality.
48. a. 21. "Spenser's own style": Edmund Spenser (1552–1599), author of *The Faerie Queene* (1590, 1596), developed the stanza which bears the name Spenserian.
48. b. 42. "Milton": John Milton (1608–1674) was profoundly admired by the poets of the Romantic Movement.
49. a. 37. "Mr. W. Taylor's recent volume of synonyms": See *British Synonyms discriminated*, by W. Taylor, quoted by Wordsworth, text, p. 223.

49. b. 16. "Ecclesiastical Polity of—Hooker": Richard Hooker (1553–1600) wrote *Laws of Ecclesiastical Polity* (1594, 1597, 1618).

50. a. 24. "vis theoretica et scientifica": Power theoretical and scientific.

50. b. 16. "Archimedes": A Greek mathematician (287?–212 B.C.). See his famous saying at the opening of *Queen Mab*, text, p. 394.

50. b. 33. "sage of Koenigsberg": Koenigsberg is a city in Pomerania where lived the philosopher Immanuel Kant (1724–1804). His famous works are *Critique of Pure Reason* and *Critique of Practical Reason*.

51. a. 2. "mutatis mutandis": Necessary changes being made.

51. a. 13. "Nihil negativum irrepraesentabile": Nothing negative can be represented.

51. a. 15. "Aliquid cogitabile": Something that can be pondered by the reasoning power.

51. b. 12. "Non omnia possumus omnes": Not all can have all power; not all things are possible to all people.

51. b. 25. "tertium aliquid": A third something.

51. b. 32. "letter from a friend": Coleridge himself wrote the letter.

52. b. 1. "Trophonius": A legendary hero of architecture who, after the murder of his brother Agamedes, was swallowed up by the earth. By decree of Apollo an oracle was dedicated to him at Lebadea in Boetia; hence the "dark cave."

52. b. 49. "omne scibile": Everything that can be known.

56. a. 5. "Praecipitandus est liber spiritus, says Petronius": Trans.: Headlong must be the free spirit.—Petronius was a Roman satirist of the first century.

56. a. 13. "Burnet's theory of the Earth": This is the Thomas Burnet (1635–1715) quoted on p. 13 of our text. For his theory of the earth, see *Telluris Theoria Sacra*.

56. b. 5. "laxis effertur habenis": It is driven with reins relaxed.

56. b. 20. "Sir John Davies (1569–1626)": Author of *Nosce Teipsum* (1599) and *Hymns of Astrea* (1599).

58. a. 52. "Dr. Henry More (1614–1687)": Author of *Antidote against Atheism* (1653).

58. b. 20. "Poor Laws": In England laws providing for public relief of the poor began with the Poor Relief Act of 1601. At the time of Coleridge poor rates were greatly increased.

61. a. 35. "Bacon to Tom Brown or Sir Roger L'Estrange": Francis Bacon (1561–1626), author of *Advancement of Learning* (1605); Thomas Brown (1778–1820), author of *The Relation of Cause and Effect* (1804); L'Estrange (1616–1704), author of *A Brief History of the Times* (1687).

61. b. 17. "Algernon Sidney (1622–1683)": Author of *Discourse Concerning Government* (1698).

61. b. 28. "lingua communis": Common speech.

61. b. 48. "pro bono publico": For the public good.

65. b. 14. "poor Smart's distich": Christopher Smart (1722–1770), author of *Poems* (1752) and *Song to David* (1763), was periodically insane.

65. b. 26. "The Children in the Wood": See text, 202. a. 32.

65. b. 39. "Pierce Plouman": William Langland (c. 1332–c. 1400) wrote the *Vision of Piers Plowman*, A text, 1362; B text, 1378; C text, 1393(?). Langland used "alliterative metre."

66. a. 5. "Θαυματα Θαυμαστότατα": Wonder of wonders.

68. b. 42. "The Civil Wars of Daniel": Samuel Daniel (1562–1619), author of *The Civil Wars* (1595, 1599, 1609).

69. a. 37. "Lamb's Dramatic Specimens": Charles Lamb (1775–1834), author of *Specimens from the Dramatic Poets* (1807).

70. b. 30. "Μόρφωσις-ποίησις": Form or semblance—finished creation.

71. a. 16. "Dodsley's collection": Robert Dodsley (1703–1764), English poet and bookseller.

73. a. 19. "Cotton": Charles Cotton (1630–1687), author of *Scarronides, the First Book of Virgil Travesty* (1664).

74. b. 51. "Consolation of Boetius—Argensis of Barclay": Boetius (475–524) was known for his *De Consolatione Philosophiae,* which was first translated into English by King Alfred. John Barclay (1582–1621) wrote the *Argensis* (Latin, 1621; English, 1625).

75. a. 14. "Metastasio": Pietro A. D. B. Metastasio (1698–1782), Italian poet and dramatist.

76. b. 1. "Aristotle pronounces to be σπουδαιότατον καὶ φιλοσοφώτατον γένος": Aristotle (384–322 B.C.) developed critical theories which greatly influenced English writers.—Trans.: The most intense and philosophical kind.

76. b. 5. "Davenant's—letter to Hobbes": The letter pertains to Davenant's play *Gondibert* (1651). See 710. a. 21.

77. a. 24. "vestigia communia": Common traces.

77. a. 27. "penna duplex": Double wing; that is, vision in sound, sound in vision.

78. a. 12. "Antonine": Marcus Aurelius (121–180), a Roman philosopher, famous for his *Meditations.*

79. b. 53. "Hercules with the distaff of Omphale": For three years Hercules, dressed as a maid and spinning with the maids, was forced to serve Omphale, queen of Lydia.

81. a. 2. "ruines of Golconda and Mexico": The mines of Golconda, India, were rich in diamonds; the mines of Mexico produced gold.

81. a. 25. "ΕΝ ΚΑΙ ΠΑΝ": One and all.

81. a. 32. "Jacobi": Probably Friedrich Heinrich Jacobi (1743–1819), a German metaphysician.

81. a. 35. "Gleim, (the Tyrtaeus)": Johann Wilhelm Ludwig Gleim (1719–1803) was a German poet whom Coleridge here compares to Tyrtaeus, a Spartan poet of the 7th c. B.C.

82. a. 39. "Sidonius Apollinaris": Roman patrician, bishop, and poet (430?–482?).

84. b. 8. The quotation is from Pindar's

Olympian II. 84–88. We quote the translation by Lewis Richard Faruell.

"I have many a winged song-shaft in the quiver beneath my arm,
Fraught with speech that hath meaning for the wise,
But for the general they need interpreters.
Wise is he who hath rich lore by the light of nature:

But those two men who have only learned by rote,
Violent-mouthed with reckless speech, waste their breath in chattering,
Like crows screaming against the holy bird of Zeus."

85. a. 32. "spectator, haud particeps": Spectator, by no means a participant.

WILLIAM WORDSWORTH

THE REVERIE OF POOR SUSAN

90. b. 8. "Cheapside": The central thoroughfare of the official "City" of London.

SIMON LEE

91. b. 1. "Cardigan": A shire in Wales.

RUTH

105. b. 246. "Quantock": The name given to a range of hills in Somerset.

RESOLUTION AND INDEPENDENCE

108. a. 43. "Chatterton": Thomas Chatterton (1752–1770) a precocious boy poet who wrote a collection of poems in what he thought was middle English. The work he attributed to Thomas Rowly, a priest of the 15th century associated with the Church of St. Mary Redcliffe in Bristol. He committed suicide in London at the age of eighteen.

LINES COMPOSED A FEW MILES ABOVE TINTERN ABBEY

109. "Tintern Abbey": A picturesque ruined mediæval abbey situated in Monmouthshire on the river Wye.
124. "To H. C.": Hartley Coleridge (1796–1849), the oldest son of the poet Samuel Taylor Coleridge. A poet himself, he possessed many of the idiosyncrasies of genius.

IT IS A BEAUTEOUS EVENING

126. a. 9. "Dear Child": His natural daughter, Caroline, whose mother was a French woman Annette Vallon. The girl, in 1802, was about ten years old.

TO TOUSSAINT L'OUVERTURE

126. b. "Toussaint": Surnamed L'Ouverture in 1793, because he broke through the Spanish fortifications. A Haitian revolutionist (1743–1803), a negro, by 1799 undisputed ruler of the island nominally under France. In 1801 he threw off this allegiance, because Napoleon had re-established slavery in Haiti, and proclaimed himself President for life.

Napoleon sent a force which subdued the island, arrested Toussaint and sent him to France, where he died in prison.

GREAT MEN HAVE BEEN AMONG US

127. a. 3. "The later Sidney": Algernon Sidney (1622–1683) was a prominent officer in the Parliamentary army and later an official of the Commonwealth.—"Marvel, Harrington, young Vane": These three were all associated with the Commonwealth. To Wordsworth each was a type of self-abasing hero.

THE PRELUDE

127. b. 21. "Derwent": A river in Cumberland.
127. b. 41. "Skiddaw": A mountain in Cumberland near Keswick,—a little over 3000 feet in height and so one of the highest in England.
128. a. 50. "That beloved Vale": Hawkshead, where at the age of eight, he went to school.
130. b. 289. "Bothnic Main": That part of the Baltic Sea between Finland and Sweden.
132. b. 55. "Plain of Windermere": The surface of Lake Windermere, situated on the boundary of Lancashire and Westmoreland.
133. a. 102. "The Druids worshipped": Druids were the priests among the ancient Celts of Britain. Their places of worship were oakgroves.

BOOK THIRD

137. a. 1. "The Evangelist St. John": Wordsworth was a student at St. John's College, Cambridge University.
137. a. 8. "Trinity": i. e., Trinity College.

BOOK ELEVENTH

147. b. 37. "Timoleon": A Greek general and statesman, who in 343 B. C. delivered Syracuse from the tyrant Dionysus the younger and reorganized the entire Greek power in Sicily.

BOOK FOURTEENTH

150. a. 6. "Snowdon": A mountain in Wales, 3590 feet high, the highest in either England or Wales.

THE RECLUSE

153. b. 75. "The Bard": Milton.
153. b. 76. "Urania": The Muse of astronomy and celestial powers.
154. a. 87. "Erebus": In Greek mythology a place of nether darkness through which souls passed on their way to Hades.

ODE TO DUTY

154. b. "Jam non consilio": Good not by design, but guided by custom to the point where I can not so much act well as that I can not act at all unless well.

ELEGIAC STANZAS

155. b. Sir George Beaumont, the landscape painter, painted two pictures of Peele Castle. There are two castles of this name, the subject of the picture being the one in Lancashire. While in college Wordsworth visited for four weeks a cousin who lived in a village near the castle.
156. a. 42. "Of Him whom I deplore": Wordsworth's brother, John, who went down with his ship, an East Indianian, on February 5, 1805.

PERSONAL TALK

157. b. 41. "The gentle lady": Desdemona.
157. b. 42. "Una": a character in the first book of Spenser's The Faerie Queene.

THOUGHT OF A BRITON

160 b. Wordsworth may refer to the invasion of Switzerland by France in 1797, but more likely he refers to Napoleon's Act of Mediation of 1803, by which the Swiss Confederation was re-instituted and Bonaparte's influence in Switzerland made predominant.

SONG AT THE FEAST OF BROUGHAM CASTLE

160. b. Henry Lord Clifford, whose family was antagonistic to the house of York, after the triumph of this family at the Battle of Towton in 1461, was deprived of his estates and honors. During this time he lived as a shepherd in Cumberland, where the domain of his father-in-law lay. He was restored to his estate and honors when Henry VII of Lancaster came to the throne in 1485.
161. a. 2. "Emont's murmur": The ruins of Brougham Castle are near the junction of the Emont and Lowther rivers.
161. a. 7. "Thirty years": The duration of the wars of the Roses: 1455–1585.
161. a. 25. "Bosworth-field": The battle in which Richard III was slain in 1485.
161. a. 36. "Skipton": A market-town in Yorkshire, the castle of which was deserted while Clifford was in hiding.

161. a. 40. "Pendragon": Another fortress in the hands of the Cliffords. It is named from Uther Pendragon, the father of King Arthur, its fabled founder.
161. a. 46. "And she": The reference is to Appleby Castle near which runs the river Eden.
161. b. 95. Sir Lancelot Threlkeld": Lord Clifford's father-in-law.
162. a. 122. "The undying fish": Superstition had it that two immortal fish lived in this tarn.

YARROW UNVISITED

165. a. 6. "Winsome Marrow": Marrow means companion: it is perhaps a corruption of the French mare.
165. a. 17. "Leader Haughs": The holms or low lands of the river Leader or Lander.
165. a. 20. "Lintwhites": linnets.
165. a. 35. "Apple": The red berry of the mountain-ash.
165. a. 37. "Strath": A valley through which a river flows.
165. b. 43. "St. Mary Lake": The source of the Yarrow.

YARROW VISITED

166. a. 25. "The famous Flower": In Logan's poem The Braes of Yarrow the lady laments a slaughtered youth, her lover, whom she calls "the flower of Yarrow."
166. a. 31. "The Water-wraith": Another reference to Logan's poem.
166. a. 55. "Newark's Tower": The castle in which Scott has the minstrel sing his Last Lay.

SURPRISED BY JOY

166. b. 3. "But thee": His daughter Catherine, who died June 4, 1812, in her fourth year.
166. b. 11. "When I stood forlorn": Wordsworth was away from home when the little girl died.

DION

166. b. "Dion (408 B.C.–353 B.C.): A follower of Plato when the latter visited Syracuse. Banished from Syracuse, he went to Athens and lived in close association with his philosophical master. He later returned to Sicily, became ruler of Syracuse in 355 B.C., and put to death his chief political opponent Heracleides. One of his followers conspired against Dion and secured his assassination in 353 B.C.
    The first stanza was rejected in 1837 on the ground that it kept the reader too long from the actual subject of the poem.
167. a. 10. "Grove of Academe": The place in the suburbs of Athens where Plato taught. It was named after Academus, to whom it originally belonged.
167. b. 43. "Ilissus": One of the chief rivers of Attica.
168. a. 67. "A shape": In Plutarch the apparition

took the form of a majestic woman, in dress and face like a Fury, an omen of coming evil.

168. a. 71. "Auster": The south wind.
168. a. 75. "Mænalus": A mountain in Arcadia.
168. b. 110. "The marble city": Syracuse. Marble from a neighboring quarry was used to make the city magnificent.

INSIDE OF KING'S COLLEGE CHAPEL, CAMBRIDGE

178. a. 1. "the royal Saint": King Henry VI.
178. b. 8. "that younger Pile": St. Paul's Cathedral, London.

A LETTER TO THE BISHOP OF LANDAFF

179 b. The Bishop of Landaff was Richard Watson. In 1791 he had written in favor of the French Constitution as being the only one to assert and support natural human rights. Early in 1793 he published a sermon delivered some time before, to which he added a political appendix. In this he shows himself so shocked at the execution of King Louis XVI, that he rigorously attacks the republican form of government and argues in favor of a monarchy.

179. a. 7. "Addison in a sublime allegory": The Vision of Mirza, published in Paper No. 159 of the Spectator. In it human life is represented by a bridge in the midst of the Tide of Eternity.

179. b. 33. "the late royal martyr": Louis XVI of France, guillotined at Paris, January 21, 1793.

179. b. 52. "the tenth of August": On August 10, 1792, a crowd assailed the palace of the Tuilleries and caused Louis XVI to take refuge in the Assembly.

180. a. 44. "I refer to a striking passage of Racine": The reference is to Athalie I. II. 114–118. The high priest Joad, speaking of the young King Joas, says:

Il faut sur le thrône un roy soit élevé
Qui se souvienne un jour—qu'au rang de ses anecestres
Dieu l'a fait remonter par la main de ses prestres
L'a tiré par leur main d'l'oubli du tombeau
Et de David éteint rallumé le flambeau.

181. b. 15. "Mr. Burke in a philosophical lamentation": Reflections on the Revolution in France, 1790.

182. b. 30. "The philosophic Priestley": Joseph Priestley (1733–1804) was an English clergyman, a chemist, the discoverer of oxygen and a sympathizer with the French Revolution. For this last crime, he was attacked by a mob, his house set on fire and his scientific instruments destroyed. In 1794 he moved to America.

183. a. 40. "hoary Machiavelism": Niccolo Machiavelli (1469–1527) wrote in Il Principe (The Prince) a manual of practical statesmanship. His theory that the end justified the means led him to recommend so many forms of ruthless and deceitful policy that his name stands for this sort of evil statesmanship.

189. a. 9. "Maury": Jean Siffrein Maury (1746–1817) was a French Cardinal and politician distinguished as a Royalist orator in the French Constituent Assembly, 1789–1791.

189. a. 9. "Cazalès": Jacques Antoine Marie (1758–1804) was a lawyer, also a royalist advocate in the Constituent Assembly.

189. a. 10. "Lafayette": The Marquis de Lafayette's (1757–1834) services to the American Revolution are well known. He was also a member of the States-General, Commander-in-Chief of the National Guard in 1789–1791, Commander of an army against the Austrians in 1792, and in the same year left France because of the enmity of the Jacobins.

189. a. 11. "Mirabeau": Comte de Mirabeau (1749–1791), a representative of the "third estate" in the Assembly, he became its President in 1791. He is commonly regarded as the greatest orator of the French Revolution. He futilely sought to have the King establish a constitutional Monarchy like that of England. Wordsworth's contempt for him and for Lafayette was caused by their refusal to accept the radical doctrines of the extremists.

A LETTER TO JOHN WILSON

189. b. John Wilson (1785–1854), whose pseudonym was Christopher North. For four years he lived on an estate on Windermere called Elleray, and became intimate with Wordsworth, Coleridge, Southey, and DeQuincey. After the founding of Blackwood's Magazine (1817) he was for years its principal contributor. In 1820 he was elected to the chair of moral philosophy in Edinburgh University.

193. a. 5. "Catullus, Terence, and Lucretius": Catullus (87 B.C.–54 B.C.), a Latin lyric and elegiac poet; Terence (185–159 B.C.), a Roman writer of comedy; and Lucretius (96–55 B.C.), a philosophical poet, author of De rerum natura, are not strict contemporaries, but are poets of Republican Rome.

193. a. 6. "Statius or Claudian": Statius (45 A.D.–96 A.D.), a Latin poet, author of the epic poem Thebais, and Claudian (365 A.D.–408 A.D.), the author of De raptu Proserpinae, are in no sense contemporaries; they are, however, both poets of Rome's decline.

194. b. 24. "sickly and stupid German tragedies": The melodramas, particularly of Kotzebue, translations of which flooded the English stage at this time (1802).

200. b. 29. "Clarissa Harlowe": The long sentimental and very popular novel of Samuel Richardson (1689–1761) published in 1748. The Gamester: A sentimental tragedy by

Edward Moore (1712-1757) first produced in 1753.

202. b. 40. "Sir Joshua Reynolds (1723–1792)": A celebrated English portrait painter. The reference in the text is to his *Discourses,* or annual addresses to the Royal Academy.

LETTER TO LADY BEAUMONT

205. b. 54. "Mr. Paul or Sir Francis Burdett": Sir Francis was a member of Parliament from Westminster (1807–1837).

ESSAY, SUPPLEMENTARY TO THE PREFACE

211. b. 15. "Dubartas": A French poet (1544–1590), the author of *La Première semaine* or *La Création* which went through thirty editions in a few years.

211. b. 21. "Ariosto (1474–1533)": An Italian poet whose most famous work was the epic *Orlando Furioso.* He was also the author of comedies.

211. b. 52. "Settle and Shadwell": Settle (1648–1723) and Shadwell (1640–1692), two minor dramatists of the Restoration, both literary enemies of Dryden.

212. a. 38. "Baron Grimm": Friedrich Melchior Grimm (1723–1807), a diplomat, long a resident at Paris, a friend of Diderot, wrote his critical essays in French.

212. b. 20. "George Steevens (1736–1800)": A Shakesperean editor, the definite results of whose scholarship were embodied in an edition of the plays in 15 volumes, published in 1793. He excluded the sonnets and the poems, averring that "the strongest act of Parliament that could be framed would fail to compel readers into their service."

213. a. 4. "Voss": Johann Voss (1751–1826), a German poet, noted principally as a translator of the *Odyssey* and of Shakespere's plays.

212. a. 19. "Metaphysical poets": A curiously inept descriptive term applied by Dr. Johnson to Donne and some of his contemporaries of the 17th century whose work was characterized by strained and fantastic figurative language.

213. b. 2. "Flatman's Poems": Thomas Flatman (1637–1688) was a minor court poet of King Charles II's time. His *Poems and Songs* appeared in 1674.

213. b. 3. "Waller": Edmund Waller (1605–1687) was a favorite court poet of the Restoration. He was noted for the ease and polish of his verse.

213. b. 4. "Norris of Bemerton": John Norris 1657–1717), whose minor poetry is now quite forgotten. He is remembered for some of his neo-Platonic essays.

214. a. 13. "Lord Rochester": John Wilmot (1647–1680), a poet, courtier and profligate of the Restoration.

214. a. 14. "Denham": Sir John Denham (1615–1669), a poet who during the Revolution

took up arms for the King. His best-known poem is *Cooper's Hill,* 1642.

214. a. 15. "Shaftesbury": Anthony Ashley Cooper (1671–1713), son of the anti-Court, anti-Catholic politician of Charles II's time, was an influential writer on philosophy and ethics. His principal work was *Characteristics of Men, Manners, Opinions, and Times* (1711).

214. a. 37. "Gay": John Gay (1685–1732) published in 1714 *The Shepherd's Week,* a series of eclogues depicting rustic life "with the gilt off."

214. a. 53. "Thomson's Winter": The first part of James Thomson's (1700–1748) long descriptive poem was "Winter," published in 1726.

214. b. 39. "Lady Winchilsea": "The Nocturnal Reverie" was one of Anne Finch's poems appearing in *Miscellany Poems* (1713).

215. b. 23. "The elder Warton": Joseph Warton's (1722–1800) essay on *The Genius and Writings of Pope* (1757) was revolutionary in that it ranked Shakespere, Spenser, and Milton above Pope.

215. b. 33. "Collins": William Collins (1721–1759), shared with Gray the distinction of being the greatest lyric poet of the 18th century. His *Elegy on Thomson* appeared in 1749.

216. a. 6. "Reliques": Bishop Thomas Percy's (1729–1811) *Reliques of Ancient English Poetry* (1765) contained 176 poems and ballads. It was based on an old manuscript collection of poetry in which ballads predominated.

216. b. 1. "Bürger": Gottfried August Bürger (1747–1794), a German poet noted particularly for his ballads, of which *Leonore* and *Der wilde Jäger* (The Wild Huntsman) are the most famous.

216. b. 2. "Klopstock": Friedrich Gottlieb Klopstock (1724–1803), noted for his religious epic *Messias* (1773), consisting of twenty cantos written in hexameters. Wordsworth and Coleridge called upon him in Hamburg in the fall of 1798.

216. b. 32. "Macpherson": James Macpherson (1736–1796) published *Poems of Ossian* (1762–1763) purporting to be translations of Gallic verse of a semi-historical Gaelic bard *Oisin.* The real author of the work was Macpherson himself.

217. a. 37. "Mr. Malcolm Laing": A Scottish historian (1762–1818) who in 1805 brought out an edition of Ossian's poems in two volumes, in which appears the criticism referred to in the text.

217. a. 54. "Madame de Staël (1766–1817)": A French novelist and essayist, the daughter of the famous financier Necker. She was regarded by her contemporaries as the greatest woman in literary history.

217. b. 5. "Lucien Buonaparte (1775–1840)": The most volatile of Napoleon I's brothers, at odds with him almost constantly throughout his career.

217. b. 10. "Dunbar": William Dunbar (1460–

1525), a Scottish poet whose most famous work is the *Dance of the Seven Deadly Sins.*

217. b. 11. "Buchanan": George Buchanan (1506–1582), one of Scotland's greatest scholars and humanists. He wrote in Latin two tragedies: *Baptistes* and *Jephthes,* a prose satire and many poems.

218. a. 29. "Roscommon . . . Broome": Writers of the later seventeenth and of the eighteenth

centuries, most of them obscure, except William Congreve (1670–1729), who wrote *The Way of the World* (1700), the most brilliant comedy of the Restoration.

223. b. 47–48. "Non ego . . . videbo": "In the future I shall not, stretched out in the green cave, behold you in the distance hanging from a bushy cliff."

225. a. 50. "Modo—Athenis": "At one moment he places me in Thebes; at another, in Athens."

SIR WALTER SCOTT

THE SUN UPON THE WEIRDLAW HILL

245. a. 12. "Melrose": Melrose Abbey is the finest ruin in Scotland.

BORDER BALLAD

245. b. 4. "Blue Bonnets": Scotchmen.
245. b. 11. "hirsels": cattle.

THE EVE OF ST. JOHN

246. a. 1. "Smaylho'me": Smaylholm or Smallholm Tower is on the northern boundary of Roxburghshire.
246. a. 11. "Sperthe": A battle-axe.
246. a. 17. "Ancram Moor": At this place in 1545 the Scottish forces of the Earl of Augus defeated the English marauders under Lord Evers decisively, slaying eight hundred men and taking a thousand prisoners.
246. b. 38. "Watchfold": One of the crags which surround Smallholm.
247. a. 79. "black-wood-stone": A crucifix of black marble belonging to the abbey and supposed to be of great sanctity.
247. b. 108. "Eildon tree": Eildon is a high hill above the town of Melrose. Under Eildon tree Thomas the Rhymer, the Scottish poet (1225–1300), uttered his prophecies and beneath it ran the path to the halls of the Queen of Fairy.
247. b. 123. "Dryburgh": Another abbey, now a ruin.
247. b. 127. "bartizan-seat": A bartizan is a small overhanging turret.

CADYOW CASTLE

248. b. The ruins of Cadyow, dismantled during the wars of Queen Mary's reign, are on the banks of the river Evan a few miles above the point where it joins the Clyde. It was the seat of the Hamilton family.
249. a. 60. "The Mountain Bull": In the district was long preserved a very ferocious breed of wild cattle. Except for their muzzles, horns and hoofs, which were black, they were milk-white.
249. b. 93. "False Murray's ruthless spoilers": On a cold night Sir James Bellenden, one of the favorites of Regent Murray, seized Bothwellhaugh's house and turned his wife naked

into the fields, where she went mad before daybreak.

249. b. 117. "selle": Saddle.
250. a. 137. "With hackbut bent": With gun cocked.
250. a. 142. "Murder's foul minion": Morton had been an accomplice in the murder of David Rizzio, a favorite of Mary Queen of Scots, who entered her service as a musician and became her adviser. He was killed (1566) by a group of lords led by Darnley, Mary's second husband. Morton was later privy to Darnley's murder with gunpowder by the Earl of Bothwell, 1567.
250. a. 147. "haggard Lindesay": Lord Lindesay was the most cruel of the Regent's faction. He was delegated to force Queen May to sign the deed of resignation.

ELSPETH'S BALLAD

251. a. 9. "cronach": A coronach was a dirge.
251. a. 23. "pibrochs": A pibroch is a Highland air played on a bagpipe.

THE LAY OF THE LAST MINSTREL

251. b. 27. "Newark's stately tower": A square tower now ruined, on the banks of the Yarrow. The castle was one of the seats of the family of Buccleuch of which Sir Walter Scott himself was a descendant.
251. b. 37. "The Duchess": The Duchess of Buccleuch and Monmouth, the widow of James, Duke of Monmouth, beheaded in 1685.
252. a. 49. "Earl Francis": Francis Scott, the Earl of Buccleuch and the father of the Duchess.
252. a. 50. "Earl Walter": The grandfather of the Duchess.
252. a. 81. "Holyrood": An ancient royal palace in Edinburgh.

CANTO FIRST

252. b. 1. "Branksome tower": The principal seat of the Buccleuch family, situated on the Teviot.
253. a. 39. "Jedwood-axe": A sort of pike or partisan used by horsemen.
253. a. 58. "Lord Walter fell": Sir Walter Scott, who succeeded to the title in 1492, fell in one of the battles of a feud between the Scotts and the Kerrs (or Carrs).

253. b. 114. "Art that none may name": Necromancy.

254. a. 120. "No darkening shadow traced": A necromancer's shadow does not depend on the sun.

254. a. 131. "Scaur": Precipice.

254. a. 137. "ban-dogs": Watch dogs.

255. a. 198. "Moss-trooper": A name given to the Border marauders.

255. a. 208. "Unicorn's pride": The arms of the Kerrs contained the heads of three unicorns.

255. a. 209. "Crescent and the Star": A reference to the arms of the Scotts.

255. a. 233. "Wighest": Most active.

255. b. 259. "My neck-verse at Hairibee": Hairibee was the place where the Border marauders were executed, neck-verse being the verse read as a test of learning by a criminal claiming benefit of the clergy. It was usually the first verse of the 51st Psalm, beginning "Misereri mei."

255. b. 262. "barbican": Fortification at a castle's gate or bridge.

255. b. 265. "basnet": Helmet.

255. b. 267. "Moat-hill's mound": A mound so-called because there anciently a "Mott" (the Anglo-Saxon word for council) of the surrounding tribes used to assemble.

256. a. 312. "barded": Armored.

256. a. 322. "Halidon": The seat of the Kerrs (or Carrs) of Cessford. Near it lay the field of battle alluded to in the stanza.

256. b. 335. "Old Melros": This ancient monastery was founded by David I of Scotland (1124–1153). It is now a picturesque ruin. See note 245. a. 12.

CANTO SECOND

257. a. 39. "Aventayle": Visor of the helmet.

257. b. 60. "drie": Endure.

258. a. 90. "jeunet": A small Spanish horse.

258. a. 109. "Chief of Otterburne": James, Earl of Douglas, killed at the battle of Otterburne, August 15, 1388. In spite of his death, the Scots won the day over Henry Percy, called Hotspur, who was himself taken prisoner.

258. a. 110. "Knight of Liddesdale": William Douglas, who flourished during the reign of David II (1324–1370). For the valor displayed in his exploits he was called "The Flower of Chivalry."

258. a. 138. "Michael Scott": Sir Michael Scott (more often Scot) of Bolivearie flourished during the 13th century. He was a writer on astrology and alchemy. Hence he has acquired a posthumous reputation as a magician.

258. a. 140. "Salamanca's cave": In Spain there were, in the Middle Ages, public schools of science which were supposed to involve magic. In Salamanca the school was held in a deep cavern, which was walled up by Queen Isabella (1504).

259. b. 214. "Amice": A fur-lined cape with hood.

261. b. 377. "litherlie": Mischievous.

261. b. 411. "cushat-dove": Wood-pigeon.

CANTO THIRD

262. b. 33. "Crane on the Baron's crest": The crest of the Craustorius was a crane holding a stone in his foot.

263. a. 103. "glamour": The magic power of imposing on the eyesight of a spectator, so that an object would appear quite different from reality.

263. b. 140. "gramarye": Magic.

264. a. 152. "lurcher": A cross-bred dog, properly between the collie and the greyhound.

264. b. 216. "barret-cap": Cloth-cap.

265. a. 272. "bandelier": Belt in which ammunition was carried.

265. a. 273. "hackbuteer": Soldier armed with a hackbut or heavy musket.

CANTO FOURTH

267. b. 40. "Watt Tuilinn": A retainer of the Buccleuch family, famous as an archer.

267. b. 64. "Morion": Helmet.

268. a. 74. "Belted Will Howard," Warden of the Western Marches.

268. a. 76. "German hackbut men": In the wars with Scotland Henry VIII and his successors employed German mercenaries.

268. a. 106. "Thirlestane brave": Sir John Scott of Thirlestane flourished in the reign of James V (1513–1542). When this monarch assembled his nobility at Fala, with the intention of invading England, Sir John was the only knight ready to follow his king. In return he was allowed to bear on his arms a border of fleur-de-lis similar to that in the royal arms.

268. b. 159. "a heriot": Tribute due to a feudal lord from his vassal.

270. b. 321. "Morsing-horns": Powder flasks.

271. b. 407. "flemens firth": Harbor for outlaws.

271. b. 418. "warrison": Note of assault.

272. b. 443. "Ancram's ford": The battle of Ancram fought in 1545, at which the English were routed.

272. a. 453. "lyke-wake": Watching of the corpse before burial.

272. a. 458. "pensils": Small pennons.

272. b. 505. "blanche lion": A cognizance of the house of Howard.

CANTO FIFTH

274. b. 51. "The bloody heart": The cognizance of the House of Douglas, because to one of the family Robert Bruce had given his heart to be carried to the Holy Land.

274. b. 55. "Seven Spears": Refers to the seven sons of Sir David Home of Wedderburn.

274. b. 56. "Swinton": Sir John Swin unhorsed the Duke of Clarence, brother to Henry V (1413–1422), at the Battle of Beauge in France.

275. a. 121. "Whingers": Poinards.

277. b. 334. "Claymore": A large sword.

279. b. 494. "Blood-hound": The man injured by Border marauders had the right to follow

them with bloodhounds. If the dogs traced the scent, he might pursue the enemy across the border.

CANTO SIXTH

280. b. 79. "Merlin": A sparrow-hawk often carried by ladies as a falcon.
281. b. 154. "Buccleuch": A cleuch is a glen or morass. The story referred to tells how a certain John seized by the horns a buck whom the King of Scotland and his followers had driven into a glen, lifted him onto his back and then carried him a mile or more and placed him at the king's feet.
282. a. 184. "Land Debateable": So called because it was claimed by both England and Scotland.
282. b. 229. "The gentle Surrey": Henry Howard

(1517–1547), noted for his *Songs and Sonetes* printed in 1557 with those of Sir Thomas Wyatt in *Tottel's Miscellany*.
283. a. 272. "almagest": Astrological treatise.
284. a. 336. "Sea Snake": The Serpent, which according to Norse mythology, encircles the world.
284. a. 338. "Dread Maids": The Valkyries, who at Odin's command rode through the air with the heroes brought from fields of battle to Valhalla.
285. a. 455. "Spectre-hound in Man": According to Manx folk-lore a spectre in the shape of a black spaniel is supposed to haunt Peel Castle on the Isle of Man.
286. a. 36. "Dies Irae, dies illa, etc.": A sequence to be sung according to the Roman missal in masses for the dead. Its subject is the day of judgment.

LORD BYRON

SONNET ON CHILLON

293. a. "Chillon": The Castle of Chillon, with its towers, massive walls, and dungeon, is situated on an isolated rock near the west end of the Lake of Geneva, between Clarens and Villeneuve.
293. b. 1. "Bonnivard": Francis Bonivard (1496–1570) fought on the side of the Republic of Geneva against the Duke of Savoy. He was captured and confined in the castle from 1530 to 1536. He is, of course, not to be identified with the Prisoner of Chillon.

THE PRISONER OF CHILLON

297. a. 341. "a little isle": Île de Peilz, a tiny islet planted with three elm trees over a hundred years ago.

EPISTLE TO AUGUSTA

297. b. Augusta was his half-sister, then Mrs. Leigh, with whom he was in love.
298. a. 16. "Our grandsire": See p. 290.
298. b. 63. "a lake": Lake Geneva.
298. b. 64. "our own of old": The Lake at Newstead Abbey.
300. a. 27. "two beings in the hues of youth": Mary Chaworth and Byron. She was a distant cousin, older than he, with whom he fell in love during one of his vacations from Eton.
300. b. 71. "She loved another": John Musters, her future husband.
302. a. 191. "Pontic Monarch of Old Days": Mithradates VI, King of Pontus (B.C. 120–63), called the Great. He waged violent and partially successful wars against the Romans under Sulla and Lucullus but was finally defeated by Pompey.

CHILDE HAROLD'S PILGRIMAGE

302. a. "D'Alembert": Jean Baptiste le-Rond D'Alembert (1717–1783), a noted French

mathematician, philosopher and editor of the famous *Encyclopédie*, lost in May, 1776, his friend Mlle L'Espinasse.
302. a. 2. "Ada": His daughter Augusta Ada (1815–1852) married in 1835 William King Noel, afterward Earl of Lovelace.
305. b. 180. "Harmodius": He and his friend Aristogeiton slew Hipparchus the younger brother of Hippias, the Athenian tyrant, in 514 B.C. They thus took revenge for a public affront to the sister of Harmodius.
305. b. 181. "a sound of revelry by night": The now famous ball given by the Duchess of Rchmond on June 15, 1815, on the eve of the battle.
305. b. 200. "Brunswick's fated chieftain". Frederick William, Duke of Brunswick (1771–1815), a nephew of George III, was killed early in the battle.
306. a. 205. "his father": Charles William Ferdinand was killed at Auerbach, October 14, 1806.
306. b. 226. "Camerons gathering": The regiment of Highlanders drawn from the clan Cameron of Lochiel.
306. b. 234. "Evan's, Donald's": Evan (1629–1719) fought in behalf of Charles II and the Royalist cause. Donald joined the young pretender, Charles Edward, in 1745, was wounded during his service and escaped to France, dying there 1748.
307. a. 261. "young gallant Howard": The Hon. Frederick Howard (1785–1815), the third son of the fifth Earl of Carlisle.
308. a. 323. "re-assume the imperial mien": Napoleon at St. Helena received imperial honors from his suite and protested when the British authorities failed to grant him similar homage.
310. a. 435. "Love, which lent a blazon to their shields": The blazon was usually a bleeding heart.
311. b. 541. "Marcean": François Sévern Marcean-Desgravier (1769–1796), a famous French officer, who began his career by joining in

the attack on the Bastille and ended it while covering the retreat of the armies of Jourdan and Moreau over the Rhine after their invasion of Germany in 1796. His body was placed under a pyramid designed by his friend, General Kleber.

312. b. 601. "Morat": A small Swiss town which, in 1476, held out gallantly against Charles the Bold, Duke of Burgundy, until the Swiss army arrived and defeated the besiegers.

312. b. 606. "The Stygian Coast": According to Greek superstition, shades of unburied dead could not cross the river Styx, which bounded Hades.

312. b. 608. "Cannae": A town in ancient Apulia, near which in 216 B. C. Hannibal almost completely destroyed a Roman army of about 80,000 men.

313. a. 609. "Marathon": The plain in Attica upon which in 490 B. C. eleven thousand Greeks under Miltiades won a great victory over 100,000 Persians in one of the decisive battles of history.

313. a. 616. "Draconic clause": Draco was an Athenian legislator who made, about 620 B. C., the first written code for the city. The penalty for a great number of offenses was death.

313. a. 625. "Adventicum": The Roman name for Avenche, capital of Helvetia (Ancient Switzerland).

313. a. 627. "Julia": This reference is based on an epitaph of the Priestess of the goddess Aventia, now known to be a modern forgery.

315. a. 743. "Julie": The heroine of Rousseau's novel, *Nouvelle Héloise,* the mistress of Saint-Preux.

315. b. 762. "Pythian's mystic cave": The sanctuary of Pythian Apollo at Delphi whence came his famous oracles.

316. b. 848. "Cytherea": A surname of Aphrodite from the island of Cythera.

318. a. 923 "Clarens": A village on Lake Geneva immortalized as the scene of the love of Julie and Saint-Preux in *La Nouvelle Héloise.*

320. a. 1022. "fierce Carthaginian": Hannibal (247–183 B. C.).

326. a. 99. "Mount Rosenberg": On September 2, 1826, a huge mass of rock 1000 feet broad and 100 feet thick detached itself from Mount Rosenberg not far from Lucerne and slipped into the valley below, destroying nearly five hundred human beings.

329. a. 91. "The Magi": The priests of ancient Persia, who professed to practice magic.

329. a. 93. "Eros and Anteros": Two spirits in the form of youths conjured up from the depths of a fountain in Gadara, Syria, by Jamblicus the neo-plantonic philosopher, who died about 330 B. C. The names of the spirits signified Love and Love's contrary.

330. a. 181–182. "the hag of Endor": The witch of Endor, whom Saul visited and who summoned up for him the spirit of Samuel. (Cf. *I Kings* 28:7–25).

330. a. 182. "the Spartan Monarch": Pausanias

(c. 466 B. C.) slew by mistake his unwilling Byzantine mistress Cleonice. Thereafter her menacing image appeared to him every night and finally it enigmatically foretold his death.

330. b. c16. "a Voice without, singing": This voice prophesies that Napoleon will escape from St. Helena, as he did from Elba, and shed more blood.

330. b. 32. "a traitor on land": Perhaps this was Thomas, Lord Cochrane (1775–1860), an effective commander in the British Navy.

331. a. c60. "Nemesis": A Goddess in Greek mythology whose duty it was to distribute to every man his share of fortune, either good or bad.

331. b. c72. "Arimanes": The spirit of evil or the counter-creator in the Persian religion of Zoroaster or Zarathustra.

332. b. 81. "Astarte": The Greek goddess of love and of fecundity, derived ultimately from the Babylonians. She here clearly represents his half-sister, Augusta, whom he had loved guiltily.

334. a. 19. "The Abbot of St. Maurice": The Augustinian abbey of St. Maurice was in the valley of the Rhone.

335. a. 88. "Rome's sixth emperor": Nero (37–68).

336. a. 6. "The giant sons of the embrace of Angels": See *Genesis* 6:4.

DON JUAN

CANTO THE SECOND

340. a. 56. "Fazzioli": Small veils.

355. b. 984. "Achilles ordered dinner": The wine and meat which Achilles ordered Patroclus to prepare for his guests, Ajax, Odysseus and Phœnix (*Illiad* IX. 193).

356. b. 1037. "vous": Mind.

357. a. 1096. "My grand-dad's narrative": "A narrative of the Honorable John Byron" (1723–1786) in which he describes the hardships suffered by him and his companions on the coast of Patagonia, while accompanying Anson in his voyage of discovery round the world.

360. a. 1288. "Romaic": The Greeks at the time of the capture of Constantinople were proud of being called Romans; hence the name Romaic was given to their popular language.

360. b. 1317. "Barrow, South, Tillotson": Isaac Barrow (1630–1677), Robert South (1633–1716), and John Tillotson (1630–1694) were all English theological writers.

360. b. 1318. "Also Blair": Hugh Blair (1718–1800), a lecturer in Rhetoric and Belles Lettres at the University of Edinburgh, wrote an important work, *Lectures on Rhetoric,* 1783.

362. a. 1391. "to carry off an Io": Io in Greek mythology was the daughter of Inachus, King of Argus. According to one legend she was carried off by Phœnician traders.

362. a. 1392. "Scio": An island in the Ægean Sea,

belonging to Turkey. In classical Greek times it was called Chias.

362. b. 1435. "Xerxes": Xerxes I (519–464 B.C.), the King of Persia.

365. b. 1624. "Castlereagh": Robert Stewart, Viscount Castlereagh (1764–1822), a British statesman, foreign secretary 1812–1822, one of the "elder statesmen" who, at the Congress of Vienna (1814–1815), reformed the world after the fall of Napoleon.

366. a. 1634. "Titus": Titus Flavius Vespasianus, Roman Emperor (70–79), and capturer of Jerusalem, fell in love with Berenice the daughter of Agrippa I [Herod], King of Judæa. Though she followed him to Rome, he gave her up because of the Roman prejudice against marriage with an alien. Racine's play *Berenice* is the most famous version of the story.

366. a. 1636. "Sappho": The Greek lyric poetess, who flourished about 600 B.C. Tradition has it that she hurled herself from the promontory of Leucas, one of the Ionian Islands, into the sea because of unrequited love for a youth Phaon.

366. a. 1643. "Cæsar and Pompey, Mahomet, Belisarius": Cæsar's third wife Pompeia was suspected of infidelity with Clodius; Pompey's third wife, Mucia, was over-friendly with Cæsar; Mahomet's favorite wife, Ayesha, on one occasion was suspected, and Antonina, the wife of Belisarius (505–565), the great Byzantine general, was notoriously immoral.

366. a. 1650. "Aristippus (c. 380 B.C.)": He was, like Epicurus, a hedonistic philosopher. He was a pupil of Socrates and founded the so-called Cyrenaic School of Philosophy.

366. a. 1656. "Sardanapalus": The name the Greeks gave to the Assyrian king Ashurbanipal (668–626 B.C.). His court was a place of artistic achievement, splendor, extravagance and profligacy.

368. a. 10. "Cheops": A king of the 4th dynasty (c. 2900 B.C.).

368. b. 7. "Longinus o'er a Bottle": Longinus (210–273) was a Greek critic and philosopher to whom is attributed the essay *On Sublimity*, one of the most famous critical documents of antiquity.

368. b. "Mr. Sotheby's Muse": William Sotheby (1757–1833), a minor man of letters who became prominent in London literary society through his patronage of struggling authors. His best work was a verse translation of Virgil's *Georgics*.

369. b. 27. "Ravenna's immemorial wood": The famous *pineto* or pinewoods lies five miles south of the city. It was in existence in the time of Odoacer (434–493).

369. b. 28. "Once the Adrian wave": The *pineto* was once on a peninsula; now it is about six miles from the sea.

369. b. 30. "Boccaccio's lore": The reference is to the eighth tale of the fifth day of *The Decameron*.

369. b. 31. "Dryden's lay": *Theodore and Honoria*

is an adaptation of the above-mentioned tale.

369. b. 37. "Spectre huntsman of Onesti's line": In Dryden's poem the ghost of Guido Cavalcanti hunts and slays every day a woman who had scorned his love.

370. b. 30. "Cato (95 B.C.–46 B.C.)": A stoic philosopher and Roman general.

370. b. 31. "Diogenes (412 B.C.–323 B.C.)": An eccentric Greek cynic philosopher who, while a student at Athens, lived in a tub.

CANTO IX, I–IV

371. a. 1. "Villainton": Two lines of an epigram composed when the allies occupied Paris in 1815–1816 are:

"These French *petit-maitres* who the spectacle throng
Say of Wellington's dress *qu'il fait vilainton."*

371. a. 9. "Kinnaird": Lord Kinnaird was informed on January 30, 1818, by a fraudulent Belgian official named Marmet, of a plot to assassinate the Duke of Wellington. Kinnaird, refusing to tell the name of the informant, was promised safe conduct to Paris. He took Marmet with him and while Kinnaird was the Duke's guest, Marmet was arrested,—a breach of faith on the Duke's part.

THE VISION OF JUDGMENT

372. b. 5. "The Gallic era eighty-eight": 1788, the date at which Byron conceives the French Revolution to have begun.

373. b. 55. "Saint John's foretold beast": The beast described in Chapter XIII of the book of *Revelation*.

373. b. 57. "first year of freedom's second dawn": George III died in January, 1820, a year in which the revolutionary spirit was manifest in south Europe.

375. a. 145. "King of France": King Louis XVI was guillotined on January 21, 1793.

375. a. 157. "St. Bartholomew": According to tradition he was flayed alive.

376. a. 216. "Captain Parry's Crew": Sir William Parry (1790–1855), an arctic explorer, in 1819 explored Barrow Strait and adjacent waters and reached Melville's Island in September, 1819. By crossing longitude 110° W., he won a £5,000 prize offered by Parliament.

376. a. 224. "Johanna Southcote": A religious fanatic living from 1750 to 1814. Pretending to have supernatural gifts, she dictated prophecies in rhyme.

378. a. 340. "How to a minion": John Stuart, third Earl of Bute (1713–1792). He was prime minister from May, 1762, to April, 1763, and a very unpopular one.

380. a. 475. "Otaheite's isle": The old name for Tahite.

380. b. 520. "Jack Wilkes": John Wilkes, the political agitator (1727–1797). He was im-

prisoned for attacking George III in his paper *The North Briton.* A caricature by Hogarth shows him as squinting.

381. a. 557. "I beat him hollow at the last": After being elected to Parliament several times and being declared ineligible, in October, 1774, he was finally allowed to take his seat without opposition.

381. b. 564. "Grafton": Augustus Henry Fitzroy, third Duke of Grafton (1735–1811), was prime minister from September, 1767, to January, 1770.

381. b. 570. "You turn'd to half a courtier": In 1774 Wilkes became Lord-Mayor. In 1790 he voted against the Whigs.

381. b. 581. "With Fox's lard was basting William Pitt": Charles James Fox (1749–1806), a liberal English Whig, defended the French Revolution as essentially just when William Pitt (1759–1806), as prime minister, along with most of England, became violently anti-Jacobin.

381. b. 585. "Call Junius": The pseudonym used by the unknown author of a series of letters appearing in *The London Advertiser* from November, 1768, to January, 1772, which attacked the British ministry and others.

382. b. 3. "Iron Mask": The man with the Iron Mask was a French Prisoner confined in the Bastille in 1703. His name was never mentioned and he always wore a mask of iron covered with black velvet.

383. a. 667. "Nominis Umbra": The ghost of a name.

383. a. 670. "John Horne Tooke": Horne Tooke was the assumed name of John Horne (1736–1812), a liberal politician who vigorously opposed the American war. He was also a writer on philology.

383. a. 675. "Asmodeus": In Jewish demonology, a destructive devil. His escapades are narrated in the Apocryphal work of Tobit.

383. a. 685. "Skiddaw": A mountain near Keswick, where Southey lived.

384. a. 728. "Non Di, non hominis": Neither gods nor men.

384. a. 736. "Pye come again": Henry James Pye (1745–1813) was Southey's predecessor in the office of Poet Laureate.

384. b. 768. "Rhymes on Blenheim": This is *The Battle of Blenheim* published in the *Annual Anthology* of 1800.—"Waterloo": This refers to *The Poet's Pilgrimage to Waterloo* published in 1816.

385. a. 785. "Wesley's life": *The Life of Wesley and Rise and Progress of Methodism* was published in 1820.

385. a. 807. "King Alfonso": Alfonso X, King of Castile (1221–1284), is said to have remarked of the Ptolemaic system of the Universe that if he had been consulted at the creation of the world, he would have saved the Almighty from some absurdities.

THE ISLES OF GREECE

386. a. 4. "Delos": The ancient Ortygia, the smallest of the Cyclades, in the Ægean Sea. According to Greek legend, it was originally a floating island, the birthplace of Apollo (Phœbus) and Artemus.

386. a. 7. "Scian muse": The island of Chios (now Scio) was noted for its school of epic poets. It was one of the places which claimed to be the birthplace of Homer.

386. a. 7. "Teian muse": A name given to the Greek lyric poet Anacreon (563 B.C.–478 B.C.), because he was born in Teas, in Asia Minor.

386. a. 20. "Salamis": An island of ancient Greece south of Attica near which a Greek fleet gained a great victory over the Persian fleet on September 20, 480 B.C.

386. b. 55. "Pyrrhic dance": An ancient Greek martial dance, executed in fast time to the accompaniment of the flute.

386. b. 59. "Cadmus": The reputed founder of Thebes and the man who introduced the letters of the Greek alphabet.

386. b. 64. "Polycrates": Died 522 B.C. He was the tyrant of the island of Samos and the patron of poets and artists, of Anacreon in particular.

386. b. 67. "Chersonese": The Greek word for peninsula. Here the reference is to the Thracian Chersonese, or the modern Gallipoli.

386. b. 69. "Miltiades (6th c. B.C.)": An Athenian who led a colony to the Chersonese and later became tyrant of the place.

387. a. 74. "Suli": A mountainous district in Albania.

387. a. 74. "Parga": A sea-port in Albania.

387. a. 91. "Sunium's-steep": The ancient name of the promontory at the south-eastern extremity of Attica, now called Cape Colonna. It is marbled because it contains the ruins of a temple of Athena.

PERCY BYSSHE SHELLEY

QUEEN MAB

394. a. The Mottoes: (1) *Voltaire:* Crush the vile wretch;—an expression referring to superstition, intolerance, oppression. (2) *Lucretius:* I wander among the far haunts of the Pierides, never before trodden by the foot of man. I rejoice to approach fresh springs, and to drink my fill; and I rejoice to pluck fresh flowers . . . whence never before the Muses have wreathed the brow of any man. First because I teach concerning great things; and I hasten to free minds from the close bonds of religion. (3) *Archimedes:* Give me a place on which to stand and I will move the world.

Mary Shelley, in her note on the poem, adds: "He was animated . . . by compassion for his fellow-creatures. His sympathy was excited by the misery with which the world is burning." On June 22, 1821, Shelley wrote to Leigh Hunt: "A poem entitled *Queen Mab* was written by me at the age of eighteen [sic], I daresay in a sufficiently intemperate spirit. . . . I doubt not but that it is perfectly worthless in point of literary composition; and that, in all that concerns moral and political speculation, as well as in the subtler discriminations of metaphysical and religious doctrine, it is still more crude and immature."

"To Harriet": Harriet Westbrook, his first wife.

395. b. 59. "Behold the chariot": Cf. the apparition in *The Ruins of Empire* by Constantin François de Volney (1757–1820).

396. a. 125. "resolute will": Cf. 400. a. 12, 407. b. 132. and 419. a. 189. "He was," writes Mary Shelley in her note on *Prometheus Unbound*, "attached to [this opinion] with fervent enthusiasm."

397. a. 242. "The sun's unclouded orb": See Shelley's *Notes on Queen Mab* in *Complete Poetical Works* ed. by Thomas Hutchinson (1929), p. 791.

398. b. 110. "Palmyra": A city of ancient Syria.

399. a. 137. "Salem": Jerusalem. Cf. passages from the Old Testament repudiated by Shelley in *A Refutation of Deism*: Ex. 32:26, Nu. 3 entire, Deut. 3:6, I Sam. 5:8, II Sam. 12:29, Josh. 10 entire, Ezek. 4, 16, and 23 entire.

400. b. 22. "Behold a gorgeous palace": See F. J. Foakes Jackson, *Social Life in England*, pp. 184–187. Cf. *The Rights of Man* by Thomas Paine, and *A Letter to the Bishop of Landaff*, text, p. 179.

405. a. 168. "War": Shelley, in Note 3, quotes from William Godwin's *Enquirer*, Essay V.

407. a. 80. "the wealth of nations": See Adam Smith's *Wealth of Nations* and cf. *A Philosophical View of Reform*, text, p. 528.

410. b. 171. "No atom of this turbulence": "Dans les convulsions terribles qui agitent quelquefois les sociétés politiques, et qui produisent souvent le renversement d'un empire, il n'y a pas une seule action, une seule parole, une seule pensée, une seule volonté, une seule passion dans les agens qui concourent à la révolution comme destructeurs ou comme victimes, qui ne soit nécessaire, qui n'agisse comme elle doit agir."—In his Note 11 Shelley quotes this from D'Holbach's *Système de la Nature*, vol. i, p. 44, and here we find the germ of his early conception of Necessity. See also his Note 12 and William Godwin's *Political Justice*.

411. b. 13. "There is no God": Cf. Ps. 14:1.—Shelley here returns to the thesis of his Oxford tract *The Necessity of Atheism* (1811).

412. a. 67. "Ahasuerus": The Jewish cobbler who would not permit Jesus to rest when passing his house on the way to Calvary. According to legend Jesus pronounced this curse upon him: "Thou shalt wander on the earth till I return."—See *The Wandering Jew* (1810), pub. by Bertram Dobell, 1887.

ALASTOR

419. b. Thomas Love Peacock, who suggested this title to Shelley after the poem was written, says: "The Greek word Ἀλάστωρ is an evil genius. . . . The poem treated the spirit of solitude as a spirit of evil."—(*Memoirs*, p. 55.)

The motto: "Not yet I loved, and I loved to love; I sought what I should love, loving to love."

In his Preface to the poem Shelley writes: "The poem . . . represents a youth of uncorrupted feelings and adventurous genius led forth by an imagination inflamed and purified through familiarity with all that is excellent and majestic, to the contemplation of the universe. . . . His mind is at length suddenly awakened and thirsts for intercourse with an intelligence similar to itself. . . . Conversant with speculations of the sublimest and most perfect natures, the vision in which he embodies his own imaginations unites all of wonderful, or wise, or beautiful. . . . He seeks in vain for a prototype of his conception. Blasted by his disappointment, he descends to an untimely grave. . . .

"The Poet's self-centered seclusion was avenged by the furies of an irresistible passion pursuing him to speedy ruin. But that Power which strikes the luminaries of the world with sudden darkness and extinction, by awakening them to too exquisite a perception of its influences, dooms to a slow and poisonous decay those meaner spirits that dare abjure its dominion."

PROMETHEUS UNBOUND

428. b. The motto: "Hear you not these things, Amphiaraus, hidden under the earth?"

In his Preface Shelley writes: "*The Prometheus Unbound* of Aeschylus supposed the reconciliation of Jupiter with his victim as the price of the disclosure of the danger threatened to his empire by the consummation of his marriage with Thetis. . . . I was averse from a catastrophe so feeble as that of reconciling the Champion with the Oppressor of mankind. . . . The only imaginary being resembling in any degree Prometheus, is Satan; and Prometheus is, in my judgement, a more poetical character than Satan, because, in addition to courage, and majesty, and firm and patient opposition to omnipotent force, he is susceptible of being described as exempt from the taints of ambition, envy, revenge, and a desire for personal aggrandisement. . . . But Prometheus is, as it were, the type of the highest perfection of moral and intellectual nature, impelled by the purest and the truest motives to the best and noblest ends."

Mary Shelley, in her note, explains the difficult legend of the drama: "He followed certain classical authorities in figuring Saturn as the good principle, Jupiter the usurping evil one, and Prometheus as the regenerator, who, unable to bring mankind back to primitive innocence, used knowledge as a weapon to defeat evil, by leading mankind, beyond the state wherein they are sinless through ignorance, to that in which they are virtuous through wisdom. Jupiter punished the temerity of the Titan by chaining him to a rock of Caucasus, and causing a vulture to devour his still-renewed heart. There was a prophecy afloat in heaven portending the fall of Jove, the secret of which was known only to Prometheus; and the god offered freedom from torture on condition of its being communicated to him. According to the mythological story, this referred to the offspring of Thetis, who was destined to be greater than his father. Prometheus at last bought pardon for his crime of enriching mankind with his gifts, by revealing the prophecy. Hercules killed the vulture, and set him free; and Thetis was married to Peleus, the father of Achilles.

"Shelley adapted the catastrophe of this story to his peculiar views. The son greater than his father, born of the nuptials of Jupiter and Thetis, was to dethrone Evil, and bring back a happier reign than that of Saturn. Prometheus defies the power of his enemy, and endures centuries of torture; till the hour arrives when Jove, blind to the real event, but darkly guessing that some great good to himself will flow, espouses Thetis. At the moment, the Primal Power of the world drives him from his usurped throne, and Strength, in the person of Hercules, liberates Humanity, typified in Prometheus. . . . Asia, one of the Oceanides, is the wife of Prometheus—she was, according to other mythological interpretations, the same as Venus or Nature. When the benefactor of mankind is liberated, Nature resumes the beauty of her prime, and is united to her husband, the emblem of the human race, in perfect and happy union."

428. b. 34. "Heaven's wingèd hound". The vulture which tore up his heart.

429. a. 48. "The wingless, crawling hours": The hour that marks Jove's espousal of Thetis will be fatal to him. See III. i. 34–36, and note I. i. 297, 406, 644; II. iv. 128, 140; III. i. 20, 51.

429. a. 53. "I pity thee": In Prometheus the moral ideal has been perfected through pain. This, says George Edward Woodberry, "is the true cause of the end of the reign of evil." Cf. lines 303–305 and the Gospel of Matthew 5:44.

430. b. 192. "Magus Zoroaster": According to Shelley, the wise Zarathustra, founder of the ancient Persian religion (c. 650–583 B.C.), met his own image because there is a real world of life and a phantom world of shadows. Hence (line 221) the Phantasm of Jupiter is called up, although the living Jupiter is on his throne in Heaven (III. i).

431. a. 228. "O thou of many wounds": Cf. I. i. 426, 474, 546, 564, 585, 816–817. The student should note the Messianic elements in the characterization of Prometheus.

431. b. 266. "Rain then thy plagues": Mary Shelley writes: "He meditated three subjects as the groundwork for lyrical dramas . . . one founded on the *Book of Job*."

432. a. 274. "And my own will": See 396. a. 125.

432. a. 289. "A robe of envenomed agony": Hercules, poisoned by the shirt which Deianira had steeped in the blood of the Centaur, Nessus, killed himself.

432. a. 308. "That Jove . . . should vanquish thee": Earth, true to her nature, mistakes the triumph of love for defeat.

432. b. 342. "Son of Maia": According to Roman mythology Maia was the mother of Mercury..

433. a. 347. "Geryon — Gorgon — Chimera — Sphinx": Geryon, a monster having three bodies; Gorgon, a creature with snaky hair, possessing the power of turning its beholder to stone; Chimera, a monster which vomited flame; Sphinx, another monster having a lion's body, wings, and the head of a woman.

433. a. 371. "there is a secret known": See note 429. a. 48.

435. b. 546. "One came forth of gentle worth": Jesus. See note 431. a. 228.—Let the student observe carefully the fearful sophistry of the Furies in this Chorus, in the following Semichorus, in the speeches of the Furies beginning with lines 594 and 618. The torturing of Prometheus by exhibiting to him the crucifixion is of a piece with this sophistry and belongs exclusively to the mind of the Furies. The triumphant repudiation of the sophistry is suggested in the Chorus of Good Spirits (lines 780–788) and established by the entire drama.

439. b. 30. "The shadow of that soul": In the first dream of Panthea (line 61) Prometheus has become transfigured. Imbued with his spirit (love) she goes to Asia. She seems to serve as a medium between the two. Note II. i. 71. and II. i. 113. The second dream (lines 127–130) becomes a shape which urges Asia and Panthea "to the realm of Demogorgon," the place of increate being.

443. a. 90. "thwart Silenus": Silenus, a Satyr, foster-father of Bacchus, is in this case referred to as stubborn and perverse.

443. b. 9. "Maenads—Evoe": Maenads were drunken nymphs attendant upon Dionysus; hence the cry of the bacchanals, Evoe!

444. b. 2. "The veil has fallen": According to Shelley there is a veil which obscures from us alike "the scene of things," the essential beauty of the world, "the wonder of our being," and Infinitude (517. a. 34–53.). "The white radiance of eternity," or Truth, is hidden by this veil. The veil, then, he often

regards as evil or error "not inherent in the system of creation, but an accident that might be expelled" by the will of man. See Mary Shelley's note *supra* and cf. II. iii. 59; iv. 17–21; III. iii. 62, 113; iv. 70–77, 190.

445. a. 61. "Nepenthe, Moly, Amaranth": Nepenthe—to remove sorrow; Moly—to counteract the spells of Circe; Amaranth—to keep life fadeless.

446. a. 119. "Fate, Time, Occasion, Chance, and Change"; These are the masters of Jove, but not of Prometheus. Shelley agreed with Dante in regarding love as the Inviolable Ultimate. See 505. a. 49. and note 512. b. 45.

449. a. 65. "That thou wouldst make mine enemy my judge": Jupiter's final tribute to Prometheus.

449. a. 72. "a vulture and a snake": Cf. *The Revolt of Islam* I. viii *et seq.* The vulture, for Shelley, was the symbol of power or evil; the snake was the symbol of good.

449. b. 24. "Blue Proteus": Blue, because he was a sea god. Proteus, who served Neptune, had the power of assuming various shapes. Cf. Wordsworth's Sonnet, 171. a. 13.

450. a. 15. "the mountain's frozen tears": Stalactites. Cf. *Alastor* 420. b. 93.

450. a. 23. "Where we will sit and talk": Cf. *King Lear* V. iii.

450. b. 42. "aëreal Enna—Himera": Cities of ancient Sicily.

452. a. 65. "Praxitelean shapes": Praxiteles was a Greek sculptor, c. 340 B.C.—Phidias (line 112) was of the 5th c. B.C.

452. b. 19. "dipsas": A serpent whose bite was fabled to cause deadly thirst. The "amphisbaenic snake" of 453. b. 119. was a fabulous serpent with a head at either end.

454. b. Of Act IV Mary Shelley writes: "At first he completed the drama in three acts. It was not till several months after, when at Florence, that he conceived that a fourth act, a sort of hymn of rejoicing in the fulfillment of the prophecies in regard to Prometheus, ought to be added to complete the composition."

461. a. 74. "Agave—Cadmaean": Agave, daughter of Cadmus and mother of Pentheus, joined the Bacchic women who slew her son when he resisted the introduction of Bacchic worship into Thebes.

462. b. 561. "And folds over the world its healing wings": Cf. Matt. 23:37; Luke 13:34.

THE MASK OF ANARCHY

462. b. On August 16, 1819, seven thousand unarmed people were holding a mass meeting at Manchester. To disperse them local government officials ordered a charge of three hundred hussars. Six of the people were killed, eighty were wounded. Shelley was residing near Leghorn, Italy, at the time. News of the event, says Mary Shelley, "roused in him violent emotions of indignation and compassion."—Compare this poem carefully with *A Philosophical View of Re-form, infra,* p. 519, especially stanzas LXV-XCI of the poem and pages 539–541 of the prose document.—Among the authorities who approved of the massacre were Castlereagh, Foreign Secretary; Eldon, Lord High Chancellor; and Sidmouth, Home Secretary.

463. a. 30. "Last came Anarchy": Shelley regarded Anarchy as an evil retort to Tyranny. Cf. 401. a. 95–106. True liberty arises from the self-immolation of Hope. See line 110.

464. b. 160. " 'Tis to work": Notice the realistic contrast of Slavery (XL–LI) with Freedom (LII–LXIV).

ADONAIS

467. b. The name Adonais distinguishes John Keats, the son of the "mighty Mother" Urania, from the Adonis of Bion's *Lament,* who was the lover of the Pandemian Aphrodite. The distinction is between the heavenly and the earthly.

In addition to the Hebrew writings and the works of Plato, Shelley drew from Bion's *Lament for Adonis,* Moschus's *Lament for Bion,* Theocritus's *Song of Thyrsis,* Virgil's *Eclogues* V and X, and Milton's *Lycidas.*

468. a. 30. "the Sire of an immortal strain": Milton. Moschus makes a similar reference to Homer.

468. a. 36. "the third among the sons of light": See 513. b. 42. and 514. a. 4.

468. a. 48. "a pale flower by some sad maiden cherished": See 585. a. 414.

468. b. 55. "To that high Capital": Cf. stanza XLIX: "Go thou to Rome."

469. b. 140. "Phœbus — Hyacinth — Narcissus": Phœbus loved the beautiful Hyacinthus and accidentally slew him. Narcissus died of love for his own image reflected in a fountain.

470. a. 145. "the lorn nightingale": See text, p. 592. For a reference to the eagle, see sonnet *On Seeing the Elgin Marbles,* p. 608.

470. a. 151. "the curse of Cain": The first of the references to the reviewers. See also stanzas XXVII, XXVIII, XXXVI, and XXXVII, and see Keats's Letters V, XVI, and XXII, *inf.*

470. a. 191. "Wake thou": Shelley is here following closely his own translation of Bion: "Wake . . . 'tis Misery calls."

471. a. 211. "wounded the invisible palms of her tender feet": Cf. Plato's *Symposium* 195, and Bion's *Lament* 21, 22, 65.

471. b. 240. "Wisdom the mirrored shield, or scorn the spear": When he slew Medusa, Perseus used the polished shield of Athene as a mirror.

471. b. 250. "The Pythian": Lord Byron. See his *English Bards and Scotch Reviewers.* For the fawning of these reviewers, see text, p. 801 ff. The "Pilgrim of Eternity" of XXX is also Byron. The "sweetest lyrist" is Thomas Moore, from Irene (Ireland).

472. a. 271. "one frail form": Stanzas XXXI-XXXIV are about Shelley himself. Acteon, because he had looked upon Diana in her

bath, was changed into a stag and killed by his own hounds.

472. b. 306. "like Cain's or Christ's": This is Shelley's boldest association of himself with the Galilean poet.

472. b. 312. "gentlest of the wise": Leigh Hunt.

472. b. 316. "Our Adonais has drunk poison": Shelley originally prefaced the poem with lines 111–114 from Moschus: "Poison came, Bion, to thy mouth—thou didst know poison. To such lips as thine did it come and was not sweetened? What mortal was so cruel that could mix poison for thee, or who could give thee the venom that heard thy voice? Surely, he had no music in his soul." —Lang's trans.

474. a. 399. "Chatterton—Sidney—Lucan": Chatterton and Lucan both took poison at an early age; Sidney was killed in battle.

474. b. 439. "a slope of green access": The Protestant cemetery in Rome where Shelley's son William was already buried (LI). Here Keats and Severn were buried; and here, ultimately, to the right of the "one keen pyramid" were deposited the ashes of Shelley.

HYMN TO INTELLECTUAL BEAUTY

476. b. 61. "I vowed that I would dedicate my powers": Cf. Wordsworth's dedication, 140. b. 157., and further declarations by Shelley: 761. b. 53., 483. a. 61., 484. b. 36., 485. a. 105., 518. b. 45., 526. b. 22.

OZYMANDIAS

477. a. Ozymandias is Rameses II. Diodorus Siculus gives a prose description of the statue and translates the inscription rendered in lines 10 and 11.

LINES—EUGANEAN HILLS

477 b. Shelley's infant daughter Clara had just died. He himself was in poor health.

478. b. 97. "Amphitrite": Wife of Poseidon and goddess of the sea.

479. a. 152. "Celtic Anarch": Here and in line 223 Shelley refers to the Austrian exploitation of Italy.

479. a. 174. "a tempest-cleaving swan": Lord Byron.

479. b. 195. "Scamander": A river near Troy.

480. a. 239. "Ezzelin": The tyrant Ezzelino da Romano (1194–1259). Cf. 524. b. 19.

480. a. 257. "Padua": The University of Padua was established in 1222. It was the third of the Italian universities, one having been established at Salerno in 1050, one at Bologna in 1125.

ODE TO LIBERTY

485. b. The best approach to this poem is *A Philosophical View of Reform*, p. 519.

486. b. 92. "Cadmean Maenad": See 461. a. 473.

486. b. 98. "Camillus—Atilius": Camillus (*ante* 403–365 B.C.) was a Roman patrician and patriot. Atilius (c. 100 B.C.) was a Roman jurist. Cf. also 511. a. 53.

487. a. 103. "Palatinus": A personification of the Palatine Hill. Roman poets and philosophers in part imitated the Greeks. See 511. a. 39.

487. a. 115. "Scald—Druid": Scald was a Scandinavian name for poet; Druid was a Celtic name for one of a religious order.

487. a. 119. "The Galilean serpent": Woodberry notes that the reference is to "Christianity in its mediaeval forms."

488. a. 175. "The Anarch": Napoleon. Note Shelley's repudiation of the French Revolution.

488. a. 194. "In the dim West": America. Cf. 521. b. 52.

488. a. 196. "Tomb of Arminius": Arminius was a German hero (18 B.C.–21 A.D.)

FROM HELLAS

489. b. The references are these: Peneus, a river in Thessaly; Tempe, a valley in Thessaly; Cyclads, islands in the Ægean Sea; Argo, the vessel of Jason; Orpheus, a musician, son of Apollo and Calliope; Calypso, an island visited by Ulysses; Laian, Laius, a despot king of Thebes.

490. a. 3. "One who rose": Cf. 435. b. 546.

ESSAY ON CHRISTIANITY

491. a. An invaluable study of this document is that by Stopford A. Brooke: "Shelley's interpretation of Christ and His Teachings," *The Hibbert Journal* 16:366. The student should also read intensively the Gospel of Matthew 6–8.

492. a. 52. "Job": Cf. note 431. b. 266.

493. b. 9. "they are the passive slaves": Cf. 495. a. 25., 503. b. 51 ff., and note 396. a. 125.

493. b. 39. "Quocunque vides, quodcunque moveris,
Et caelum et virtus": Whithersoever you look, whatsoever you move, there is heaven and virtue (God).

494. a. 6. "impostors": Cf. 409. b. 64 ff. and observe that Shelley distinguishes between the real teachings of Christ and the perversion of those teachings.

494. b. 30. "holy patriots": This is one of the few instances in which Shelley condones the use of violence. Cf. 539. b. 24 ff.

500. b. 45. "Rousseau": Shelley does not everywhere place a high value upon Rousseau. On May 15, 1811, he wrote Thomas Jefferson Hogg: "The 'Confessions of Rousseau' . . . are either a disgrace to the confessor, or a string of falsehoods, probably the latter." In his *Proposals for an Association*, pp. 13, 14 of the 1812 ed. we read: "Rousseau gave licence by his writings, to passions that only incapacitate and contract the human heart." Cf. 514. b. 43. and 523. b. 12.

502. a. 45. "Saturnian period": Cf. *sup*. Mary Shelley's note to *Prometheus Unbound*. Happiness is not to be found by reverting to a state of noble savagery but by facing the future wisely.

A DEFENCE OF POETRY

505. a. 24. "Janus": A Roman deity presiding over gates and doors; hence represented with two faces.

505. a. 49. "choruses of Aeschylus": Shelley points to these choruses in the dramas of Aeschylus because of their high lyric quality. To the *Paradiso* of Dante Shelley was attracted because, as he tells us, it is the story of "how all things are transfigured except Love."

505. b. 50. "the popular division": Cf. 56. a. 15., 67. b. 6., 195. b. 16., 713. a. 31. Throughout this Essay observe similarities to Wordsworth's *Preface*, p. 192.

506. a. 17. "the curse of Babel": See Genesis 14:9.

507. a. 20. "the jury—composed of his peers": See *Paradise Lost* VII. 31. Cf. also 208. a. 41. and 218. b. 29.

509. a. 3. "The Oedipus Tyrannus or the Agamemnon": Plays by Sophocles and Aeschylus.

509. a. 15. "Calderon—Autos": Calderon (1600–1681), Spanish dramatist. His *Autos sacramentales* (1653) were allegorical pieces dealing with the mystery of the Eucharist.

509. b. 38. "Addison's Cato": The tragedy, acted in 1713, was a cold imitation of "classical" forms. For a "moral" play, see *The London Merchant* (1731).

510. b. 40. "Astraea": The Goddess of Justice was the last of the divinities to leave the earth at the end of the Golden Age.

511. a. 53. "Regulus": Marcus Atilius Regulus (c. 250 B.C.) was a Roman general tortured to death by the Carthaginians; hence he became the type of heroic endurance. See Horace *Odes* iii. 5 and cf. 486. b. 98.—When the Goths entered the senate chamber the senators remained quietly in their places.— At Cannae (Aug. 2, 216 B.C.) Hannibal destroyed 80,000 Romans with a loss on his own part of 6,000.

511. b. 12. "quia carent vate sacro": Since they are without the divine poet.

512. b. 33. "Galeotto fù il libro, e chi lo scrisse": Galeotto was the book, and he who wrote it.

512. b. 34. "Provençal Trouveurs": For Trouveurs Shelley meant to indicate the Troubadours, poets who flourished in the south of France between the 11th and the 13th centuries.

512. b. 45. "Dante—His Vita Nuova": Beatrice, whom Dante loved, died in June, 1290. Between 1292 and 1294 the poet gathered lyrics written in her honor and connected them with a prose narrative, composing thus the *Vita Nuova—New Life*.

513. a. 41. "Riphaeus, whom Virgil calls justissimus unus": Riphaeus the Trojan was described by Virgil (*Aen*. ii. 426) as "above all others the most just among the Trojans." Virgil, it will be remembered, was Dante's guide through Hell. See *Paradiso* XX.

513. b. 7. "Milton's Devil": See Shelley's Preface to *Prometheus Unbound, supra*.

514. a. 1. "Apollonius Rhodius, etc.": These are lesser Roman poets.

514. a. 6. *Aeneid*: by Virgil; *Orlando Furioso*: by Ariosto; *Gerusalemme Liberata*: by Tasso; *Lusiad*: by Camoens; *Fairy Queen*: by Spenser.

515. a. 3. "Scylla and Charybdis": Scylla was a rock on the Italian coast opposite Charybdis, a whirlpool off the coast of Sicily.

517. b. 5. "Non merita nome di creatore, se non Iddio ed il Poeta": No one deserves the name of creator, except God and the poet.

517. b. 39. "Their errors": Observe that this sentence is a fusion of materials from Dan. 5:27; Is. 1:18; Rev. 1:5; Rev. 5:9; Mt. 7:13.

518. a. 43. "Theseids of the hoarse Codri": Although Virgil ridicules one Codrus, the name was probably applied to dull versifiers who annoyed people by reading their productions to them.—Bavius was a stupid poet who with Maevius attacked Virgil and Horace. See *The Baviad* (1794) and *The Maeviad* (1795) of William Gifford (1756–1826)— 666. b. 45.

A PHILOSOPHICAL VIEW OF REFORM

519. a. This document, like the *Essay on Christianity*, remained in rough draft and was never prepared for publication by Shelley.

519. a. 42. "Lombard League": A federation of the cities of northern Italy against the tyranny of Frederick Barbarossa, c. 1163.

519. a. 45. "Medici": Cosimo (1389–1464); Lorenzo (1448–1492).

519. b. 23. "Reformation": Martin Luther (1483–1546) nailed his Ninety-five Theses to the door of the castle church at Wittenberg in 1517.

519. b. 30. "oppressed peasantry": In southern Germany 100,000 people were killed in the Peasants' War (1524–1525).

519. b. 45. "Republic of Holland": Established in 1609, Holland became the asylum of the persecuted and the home of philosophers.

519. b. 52. "Republics of Switzerland": In 1291 the Swiss cantons united against the Hapsburgs in the *Everlasting Compact*.

520. a. 7. "Elizabeth and James I": Elizabeth (1558–1603); James I (1603–1625).

520. a. 15. "one of those chiefs": On Jan. 30, 1649, Charles I was sentenced as "a tyrant, traitor, murderer."—Charles II (1660–1685).

520. a. 28. "Revolution": In 1688 James II was forced to flee to France. William and Mary ascended the throne, accepting constitutional restrictions of their power.

521. a. 14. "A crowd of writers in France": Shelley may have had in mind such men as Diderot, D'Holbach, Voltaire, Rousseau.

523. b. 44. "Restoration of the Bourbons": After Napoleon had fallen, Louis XVIII reigned from 1815 to 1824.

524. b. 16. "sanguinary tyrant": Ferdinand VII.
525. a. 20. "Epicharis": Implicated in a conspiracy against the life of Nero (A. D.), Epicharis remained silent under torture.
525. a. 44. "Moloch of oppression": Moloch was a Semitic deity whose worship was accompanied by human sacrifice.
525. a. 53. "Indian": In 1613 the East India Company established its first factory at Surat.
526. a. 11. "West Indian islands": Cf. Words-worth's *Toussaint L'Ouverture*, p. 126.
527. a. 2. "some change": In 1832 the Reform Act disfranchised boroughs of less than 2,000, and extended the franchise to the middle classes. Cf. 182. a. 30.
537. a. 20. "with patience": Cf. 538. b. 29. and 541. b. 12.
539. b. 29. "Manchester": Cf. *The Mask of Anarchy*, p. 462 ff.
542. a. 31. "Robespierre": Maximilien Marie Isadore (1758–1794), a French revolutionist.

JOHN KEATS

POETRY

Editors' Note: The work of Keats is so filled with references to mythological figures and places that we are offering here an abridged glossary of names. The student may refer to this glossary as he comes upon the several references.

Æolus: God of the winds. See *Ody.* X.
Adonis: A beautiful youth loved by Venus. He was slain by a wild boer.
Apollo: God of youth and beauty, gifted in music and poetry.
Arcadia: A mountainous region of Greece, where people lived a simple, happy, pastoral life.
Argonauts: Those heroes, including Jason, who sailed in the "Argo" to Colchis, at the eastern end of the Euxine Sea.
Ariadne: Daughter of Minos of Crete. After her marriage to Bacchus, she was translated into a constellation of seven stars. She was painted by Titian as wearing a tiar of stars. Keats knew the picture.
Asia: Daughter of Oceanus and Tethys, and by Iäpetus the mother of Prometheus. See Clymene.
Atlas: A Titan, forced to bear the earth. In myth, the son of Iäpetus and Asia.
Aurora: The rosy-fingered goddess of the dawn.
Bacchus: God of wine. See Ariadne and 558. b. 335.
Briareüs: A hundred-handed giant. See Cottus and Gyges.
Caduceus: The magic rod of Hermes, by the charm of which he controlled the Stygian monsters.
Caf: A fabulous mountain of Mohammedan legend. Keats gives imaginative personification to Caf, ascribing to it the parentage of Asia.
Cenchreæ: The port or harbor of Corinth.
Ceres: Daughter of Saturn and Ops, and goddess of growing things, identified with Demeter.
Chaos: God of primordial matter.
Circe: A sorceress having power to change men into animals. See *Ody.* X.
Cleone: There were two cities of this name, one in Argolis, one in Chalcidice.
Clio: The muse of history.
Clymene: An ocean nymph, wife of Iäpetus.
Cœlus: Another name for Uranus.
Cœus: A Titan. See Uranus.
Corinth: A city in southern Greece.
Cottus: A giant, son of Uranus and Ge. See Briareüs and Gyges.
Crete: An island in the Mediterranean Sea.
Creüs: A Titan, son of Uranus and Ge. See Cœus.
Cupid: Child of Venus and god of love.
Cybele: Wife of Saturn and Queen of the Titans. See Ops.
Cyclades: Islands in the Ægean Sea.
Cynthia: Moon goddess. See Diana and Phœbe.
Dedalus: Inventor of wings, father of Icarus. See note 558. a. 303.
Delos: One of Cyclades.
Delphi: A town in Phocis, ancient Greece, containing the famous oracle of Apollo.
Diana: Goddess of the moon. See Cynthia and Phœbe.
Dido: Queen of Tyre and Carthage, hostess of Æneas.
Dolour: Although Keats conceived Dolour as one of the Titans or giants, there is in reality no such figure in ancient myth.
Dryope: Wife of Andraemon. While nursing her child and gathering flowers, she broke off some lotus. The lotus had grown from the changed body of the nymph Lotis, and Dryope was transformed into a tree.
Echo: A nymph, daughter of Air and Earth, who, for love of Narcissus, pined away until nothing was left of her but her voice.
Egina: Geographically, an island with a city of the same name, situated in the Saronic Gulf. In myth, a daughter of Asopus and mother of Æacus by Jupiter.
Elysium: The dwelling place of happy souls.
Enceladus: Mightiest of the giants, by Ovid associated with Typhon.
Endymion: A beautiful youth loved by the moon goddess and cast into a sleepy swoon that she might caress him. He sometimes is fabled as a shepherd or hunter on Mount Latmus.
Eurydice: Wife of Orpheus, who, fleeing an admirer, was killed by a snake and taken back to earth provided Orpheus would

not look around at her. But he did, and she returned to the shades.

Faun: A cheerful sylvan deity, represented in human form, with small horns, pointed ears, and a goat's tail. See Pan.

Flora: Goddess of flowers and spring.

Ganymede: The cupbearer of Jove, loved of the god. See Ovid, *Met.* X.

Gorgon: A monstrous female, with huge teeth, brazen claws, and snakes for hair. She had the power of turning beholders to stone.

Gyges: A Titan. See Briarëus and Cottus.

Hebe: Daughter of Juno, and cupbearer to the gods.

Hecate: A goddess of the moon and the underworld, later associated with dark magic.

Helicon: A mountain in Greece, residence of Apollo and the muses. See note 592.a. 16.

Hermes: The messenger of the gods, called "star of Lethe" because it was his duty to escort the souls of the dead to Hades. See *Ody.* XXIV.

Hero: Priestess of Venus, loved by Leander.

Hesperus: The evening star. See Vesper.

Hippocrene: A fountain on Mount Helicon. See note 592.a. 16.

Hyacinthus: A Spartan youth loved of Apollo and accidentally slain by him. The god turned the youth into a flower. See Ovid, *Met.* X.

Hyperion: A Titan, son of Uranus and Ge, and father of Atlas and Prometheus. See Asia.

Ionia: The coast of Asia Minor, inhabited by Greeks.

Ixion: Once sovereign of Thessaly, sentenced in Tartarus to be lashed with serpents to a wheel which a strong wind drove continuously around.

Jove: Chief of the gods, sometimes called Zeus.

Lamia: In classical myth, a creature with the head and breast of a woman and the body of a serpent. Later the reference was to a vampire or sorceress.

Latmus: A mountain where the moon goddess fell in love with Endymion.

Latona: In Greek myth, the mother of Apollo and Artemus by Zeus. She gives birth to her children in Delos.

Leander: A youth of Abydos, who, while swimming the Hellespont to see Hero, his love, was drowned.

Leda: Queen of Sparta, wooed by Jupiter in the form of a swan. See Ovid, *Met.* VI.

Lethe: A river of Hades, the water of which, when drunk, caused forgetfulness.

Love: The same as Eros. Love issued from an egg of Night, and with torch and arrows produced life and joy.

Lucifer: The bright fore-runner of Aurora, the morning star, Venus. See Ovid, *Met.* II. 114.

Melpomene: The muse of tragedy.

Memnon: Son of Tithonus and Aurora, slain by Achilles.

Mercury: A Latin name for Hermes, the messenger of the gods.

Mnemosyne: By Jupiter the mother of the Muses.

Morpheus: The son of Sleep and the god of dreams.

Mulciber: The Latin name for Vulcan, the god of fire. Used both by Milton (*Par. Lost* I. 740) and Spenser (*The Faerie Queene* III. ii. 26).

Muse: There are nine sister goddesses of poetry and song, the arts and the sciences.

Naiad: A nymph of river, lake, or stream.

Narcissus: A youth who died of desire for his own image seen in water. See Ovid, *Met.* III.

Neptune: Son of Saturn and Ops, and god of the sea.

Niobe: Daughter of Tantalus, Queen of Thebes, and wife of Amphion. After Apollo and Diana slew her seven sons and seven daughters, her husband died, and Niobe wept until she was turned to stone.

Nymph: A beautiful maiden, a lesser divinity of nature:—Dryad: tree-nymph; Naiad: water-nymph; Nereid: sea-nymph; Oread: mountain-nymph.

Oberon: See note 570.b. 3.

Oceanus: The wise Titan who alone did not join in war against the Olympians. See 604. b. 228.

Olympus: A mountain in Greece, the dwelling-place of the gods:

Ops: A female Titan, wife of Saturn, and mother of the gods. See Tellus.

Oread: A mountain nymph.

Orpheus: Son of Apollo and Calliope, famous as a musician. See Eurydice.

Oxus: A river of central Asia, now called Amu Darya.

Pan: God of flocks, pastures, and forests; patron of shepherds, hunters, and fishermen. Represented as having the legs, ears, and horns of a goat.

Paphos: Daughter of the sculptor Pygmalion and the beautiful statue to which Venus gave life.—The city, Paphos, where the daughter was born, is sacred to Venus.

Pegasus: A winged horse sprung from the blood of Medusa. With a blow of his hoof he caused Hippocrene, the fountain of the Muses, to spring from Mount Helicon.

Peona: Probably a combination of Lemprière's Paeon, son of Endymion, and Spenser's Pæana; or a name suggested by Ovid's Pæon. See *Met.* XV.

Peræa: A part of Palestine, between the river Jordan and the mountains of Arnon.

Perseus: The son of Zeus and Danaë, who slew the Gorgon Medusa.

Phidias: Sculptor and builder of the Parthenon, killed by the people of Athens. Some of his work may be extant in the Elgin Marbles.

Phœbe: The moon goddess. See Cynthia and Diana.

Phœbus: See Apollo.

Phorcus: A sea deity, son of Pontus and Terra.

Pleiad: The Pleiades were seven of Diana's nymphs changed into stars. One was lost.

Pluto: God of the Infernal Region, the same as Hades and Dis.

Polyphemus: A one-eyed giant, son of Neptune. See note 557. b. 234.

Porphyrion: Son of Cœlus and Terra, a formidable giant overcome by Jupiter and Hercules.

Proserpine: The daughter of Zeus and Demeter, abducted by Hades (Pluto), but allowed to spend two thirds of the year with her mother.

Psyche: A beautiful maiden loved by Cupid. Sometimes the personification of the human soul and the symbol of immortality. Cf. *The Faerie Queene* III. vi. 50.

Pyrrha: The wife of Deucalion who, together with her husband, repeopled the world by casting stones behind them. The stones became men.—See Ovid, *Met.* I.

Saturn: An ancient god of the golden age, deposed by the younger gods. See note 599. b. 147.

Satyr: A sylvan deity, part man and part horse, given to merriment and lechery.

Silenus: A tipsy companion of Bacchus, a stout old satyr. The son of Hermes or of Pan.

Syrinx: A nymph of Arcadia, who, having fled from Pan to the river Ladon, was changed into a reed from which Pan made his pipe. See Ovid, *Met.* I.

Tellus: Goddess of the earth, identified with Ops or Rhea.

Tempe: A beautiful valley in Thessaly.

Tethys: Wife of Oceanus and goddess of the sea.

Thea: Sister of Saturn.

Themis: A Titan, law-counsellor of Jove.

Theseus: Son of Ægeus and Æthra, and king of Athens.

Thessaly: A beautiful region of north-eastern Greece.

Thetis: Mother of Achilles.

Titan: The children of Uranus and Ge were Titans. They were primeval deities who in their war with the Olympian gods were overthrown. They are sometimes confused with the giants.

Titania: Wife of Oberon and Queen of the fairies. See note 570. b. 3.

Triton: Son of Poseidon and Amphitrite, a demigod of the sea. His trumpet was a conch-shell.

Typhon: Son of Tellus and Tantarus, whom Keats regarded as one of the Titans. See Briareüs.

Urania: The Muse of astronomy.

Uranus: The most ancient of the gods, husband of Tithea (Earth) and father of the Titans. See Ops.

Venus: The sea-born goddess of Love.

Vesper: The evening star. See Hesper.

Zephyrus: God of the south wind.

I STOOD TIP-TOE

546. a. 64. "ring-doves' cooings": Cf. 107. b. 5. and compare Keats and Wordsworth in their treatment of nature.

547. a. 151. "So did he feel": The reference may be to Ovid who, in *Met.* I, told the story as Keats knew it. Professor Clarence D. Thorpe, however, feels that the reference may be more general.

547. b. 181. "Where had he been": Again Professor Thorpe suggests that the reference is a general reference to "a bard of old."

548. a. 219. "Apollo on the pedestal": The Apollo of the Belvedere.

TO GEORGE FELTON MATHEW

548. b. 18. "Lydian airs": Lydia was a country of ancient Asia Minor. There in the 6th c. B. C. Greek and Oriental peoples united to form a rich culture. See Milton's *L'Allegro* 136.

549. a. 67. "Alfred—Helvetian Tell—Wallace": Alfred the Great (871–901), king of the West Saxons, not only defended his people from invasion, but educated them.—As ancient Switzerland was called Helvetia, William Tell, the legendary hero, is styled Helvetian. —William Wallace (1270–1305) surpassed even Robert Bruce in heroic achievements for Scotland.

549. a. 75. "sun-shine in a shady place": The quotation is from *The Faerie Queene* I. iii. 4.

TO MY BROTHER GEORGE

550. a. 24. "Spenser to Libertas told it": Libertas is Leigh Hunt.

TO CHARLES COWDEN CLARKE

551. b. 29. "Baiae": An ancient watering place ten miles west of Naples.—Armida is a sorceress, in Tasso's *Jerusalem Delivered* (1581). —Mulla was the stream that ran near Spenser's home at Kilcolman.—Belphœbe, in Spenser's *The Faerie Queene*, personifies the beauty of virtue; Una personifies the beauty of truth; Archimago personifies hypocrisy. Cf. *The Faerie Queene* II.

552. a. 44. "The wrong'd Libertas": Cf. note 550. a. 24. Hunt was persecuted for his liberalism.

V

554. a. 13. "Laura": It was to Laura, his beloved, that Petrarch addressed his sonnets.

VII

554. b. 8. "Chapman": George Chapman began his translation of Homer in 1610.—The reference to Cortez, in line 11, is an error. It was Balboa who discovered the Pacific.

VIII

554. b. 1. "Great spirits": Wordsworth, Hunt, and Haydon.

SLEEP AND POETRY

555. b. 74. "Meander": A river in Phrygia, proverbial for its windings. Cf. *Comus* 232.

556. a. 89. "Montmorenci": A noted falls in the St. Lawrence River.

557. a. 181. "a schism": After Milton came the Neo-Classicists, whom, in the person of Boileau with his rules of poetry, Keats rejects.

557. a. 198. "Jacob's wit": See Gen. 30: 37–42.

557. b. 218. "lone spirits": These verses indicate Chatterton, just as those immediately following indicate Wordsworth and Hunt.

557. b. 234. "ugly clubs, the Poets Polyphemes": The Cyclops, Polyphemus, carried a huge club of olive wood. It was with this club, sharpened and heated, that Odysseus put out the eye of the drunk monster. Polyphemus did not, however, use his club to "disturb the sea" in a blind effort to wreck the fleeing Odysseus, but rather hurled great stones into the sea. See *Ody.* IX.

557. b. 237. "might half slumb'ring": Probably a recollection of the Elgin Marbles.

558. a. 303. "Dedalian wings": See Ovid's *Met.* VIII. Dædalus, weary of his exile in Crete, made wings of wax and feathers. His son Icarus, having put them on, flew so near the sun that the wax melted. Icarus fell into the sea and was drowned.

559. a. 381. "Sappho": A bed for Keats had been set up in Hunt's study. The young poet is here describing some of the pictures he saw there.—Sappho was a Greek lyric poetess who lived on the island Lesbos c. 600 B.C.— Thaddeus Kosciusko (1746–1817) was a Polish patriot. Cf. the sonnet "Good Kosciusko." For references to Alfred, Petrarch, and Laura see notes 549. a. 67. and 554. a. 13.

ENDYMION

563. a. 18. "Thermopylae": A pass in Eastern Greece where, in 480 B.C., three hundred Spartans were slain by the Persians.—The "old marbles" seems to be another reference to the Elgin Marbles.

564. a. 406. "old tale Arabian": H. Buxton Forman marks this passage as an "allusion to the Eldest Lady's story in *The Porter and the Three Ladies of Bagdad.*"

568. b. 815. "a pelican brood": Here Keats may have had in mind Shakespere's "kind, life-rendering pelican" which fed its young with its own blood.

LAMIA

570. b. 3. "King Oberon": King of the fairies, and husband of Titania. Since the fairies are the creation of mediæval myth, they are referred to as having driven away the creatures of ancient legend.

572. a. 115. "Circean head": Circe, the sorceress, had the power to change men into creature forms. Hence the word "Circean" may refer to Lamia's head as having been changed to that of a snake.

572. a. 133. "Caducean charm". Here, as in line 89 and in *Endymion* I. 562, we have reference to the magic charm of the Caduceus, or the "serpent rod" which Hermes bears.

ISABELLA

581. a. 140. "Hot Egypt's pest": See Ex., Chapters 8–12.

582. b. 262. "Hinnom's vale": A valley south of Jerusalem, the scene of Moloch worship, and the place into which the Jews cast refuse and dead bodies. Fires were kept burning there to prevent infection. See Neh. 11: 30; Jos. 15: 8; Mt. 5: 22.

585. b. 451. "Baalites of pelf": The word baal is an Amoritish word meaning owner, and came to refer to those among the corrupted Hebrew race who were interested in material possessions.

THE EVE OF ST. AGNES

586. b. De Sélincourt, in his excellent notes to *The Poems of John Keats* (1905), p. 465, quotes Burton's *Anatomy of Melancholie* (pt. iii. sect. ii. mem. iii. subs. i) as the probable source of Keats's inspiration for this poem. " 'Tis their only desire if it may be done by Art, to see their husband's picture in a glass, they'll give anything to know when they shall be married, how many husbands they shall have, by *Crommyomantia*, a kind of divination with Omons laid on the Altar on Christmas Eve, or by fasting on St. Agnes' Eve or Night, to know who shall be their first husband."—Cf. Ben Jonson's *The Satyr* (50–53).

587. b. 5. "Gossip": Although Angela may have been Porphyro's godmother, he probably means only to call her by a familiar and endearing name.

590. a. 241. "swart Paynims": Paynims were "heathens," especially Mohammedans.

ODE TO A NIGHTINGALE

592. a. 14. "Provençal song": In the Middle Ages the people of Provence distinguished themselves by dance and song. From among them came the troubadours.

592. a. 16. "Hippocrene": A fountain on Mount Helicon, whose waters are supposed to impart poetic inspiration.

ODE TO PSYCHE

594. a. 14. "budded Tyrian": The buds were of a purple color. Tyrian purple was famous among the Greeks and Romans.

ROBIN HOOD

596. b. 34. "Gamelyn": The tale of Gamelyn, used by Chaucer in *The Cooks' Tale of Gamelyn* and by Shakespere in *As You Like It*, is originally of East Midland origin, c. 1350.

HYPERION

599. b. 147. "The rebel three": Jupiter, Neptune, and Pluto.

606. a. 374. "Memnon's image": Tradition has it that near Thebes there is a statue of this dusky son of Tithonus and Aurora. The statue, touched by the rising sun, emits harplike sounds.

607. a. 31. "his mother fair": Jupiter and Latona were the parents of Apollo and his twin sister Artemis (Diana).

ON A PICTURE OF LEANDER

608. b. What picture inspired this sonnet is not known. The reference is to Leander's being drowned in the Hellespont while swimming to his beloved, Hero, a priestess of Venus.

THE EVE OF SAINT MARK

609. a. 33. "Moses' breastplate": See Ex. 28:15; 39:8. For "the seven Candlesticks" see Rev. 1:12. For the "Covenantal Ark" see Ex. 25:17. The "Lion of St. Mark" is the famous lion of Venice.

THE LETTERS OF JOHN KEATS

612. b. We are not undertaking to note the many literary allusions in the letters of Keats. The influence of Shakespere alone upon the images and the diction of the earlier letters would make the task impracticable.

612. a. 39. "dreadful Petzelians": Leigh Hunt in *The Examiner* of May 4, 1817, refers to this sect, named from its founder, Petzel, a priest of Branau, in upper Austria. Human sacrifice was practiced by the sect.

612. a. 44. "Hazlitt's Southey": In reviewing Southey's *Letter to William Smith Esq.*, *M.P.*, Hazlitt had been not only severe but personal. See *The Examiner* for May 4, 1817.

613. a. 4. "drop into a Phaethon": Over the grave of Phaethon, who attempted to drive the horses of Helios and who was struck down

by Zeus, was placed this epitaph: "Great was the attempt in which he failed."

613. a. 31. "fatal scissors": See *The Three Fates*, by Michael Angelo; now in the Pitti Gallery, Florence.

614. a. 47. "hard at work": Haydon was painting his famous picture, *Christ's Entry into Jerusalem*, in which he introduced likenesses of Wordsworth, Keats, and others of his friends.

614. b. 47. "pour ainsi dire": So to say.

618. a. 36. "Shelley's poem": The poem appeared under the title *Laon and Cythna*, Oct., 1817. Chiefly because of certain unpopular references to the Deity and to priests, the work was suppressed and republished on Jan. 10, 1818, under the title *The Revolt of Islam*. Certain minor changes had been made.

618. b. 29. "Francesca—Rimini": Leigh Hunt published *The Story of Rimini* in 1816. Francesca was the daughter of Duke Guido, betrothed to Giovanni, Lord of Rimini, but loved by and in love with Paulo, the brother of Giovanni.

618. b. 50. "Mr. Abbey": Mr. Richard Abbey, one of the guardians of the Keats family. See 635. a. 26.

619. a. 13. "Cockney School": See 834. b. 45, and the refutation in Andrew Lang's *The Life and Letters of John Gibson Lockhart*, I. 150–155.

620. a. 12. "tribe of Manasseh": Manasseh received the direct blessing of Jacob (Gen. 48), and carried forward the formal traditions of Israel. Formerly Jacob had cheated Esau, who wrought out his own destiny. Keats, at any rate, preferred to do his own work free of influence.

620. a. 48. "Harpsicols": An obsolete or corrupt form of *harpsichord*, probably after *virginal*.

622. a. 22. "Trojan horse": Meaning, a great matter out of a little.

624. a. 52. "Nom. Musa": The reference is to the declension of the Latin noun *Musa*.

624. b. 49. "J. S. is perfectly right": In *The Morning Chronicle* of Oct. 3, 1818, John Scott pointed to evidences of "haste and carelessness" in the poem.

627. b. 31. "feu de joie": A firing of guns in token of joy.

631. a. 40. "Florimel": The character in *The Faerie Queene* represents womanly sweetness, the name signifying "honey-flower." Archimage: See note 551. b. 29.

631. b. 34. "Pizarro": Francisco Pizarro (1471–1541) was the conqueror of Peru.

633. b. 18. "Qui bono": What's the use.

636. a. 26. "Hunt's triumphal entry": As H. Buxton Forman points out, this is "Henry Hunt, of Manchester Massacre fame." It was on Nov. 11, 1822, that he entered London.

WILLIAM HAZLITT

MY FIRST ACQUAINTANCE WITH POETS

645. a. 19. "proud Salopians": The Latin name for Shropshire, in which Shrewsbury is sit-

uated, was Salopia. Cf. *Coriolanus* V. vi. 115.

645. b. 10. "the fires in the Agamemnon of Æschylus": See ll. 281–316.

645. b. 29. "Il y a des impressions": Trans.: There are impressions which neither time nor circumstances can efface. Were I enabled to live whole ages, the sweet days of my youth could not revive for me, nor ever be effaced from my memory."—Rousseau's *Confessions*.

647. b. 9. "Mary Wolstonecraft and Mackintosh": Mary Woolstonecraft (1759–1797), author of *Vindication of the Rights of Woman* (1792), was the second wife of William Godwin and the mother of Shelley's second wife Mary Godwin. Her teachings were liberal.—Sir James Mackintosh (1765–1832), historian and philosopher, wrote *Vindiciae Gallicae* (1791).

647. b. 33. "Tom. Wedgwood": He is remembered as a benefactor of S. T. Coleridge. See R. B. Litchfield's *Life* (1903).

648. a. 44. "Cassandra": *Cassandre*, by Gautier de Costes de la Calprenède (1610–1663), French novelist and dramatist.

648. b. 20. "Hume": David Hume (1711–1776) was a Scotch philosopher whose *Essay on Miracles* (1748) shook orthodox theology. Still more important was his *Inquiry Concerning Human Understanding* (1748).

648. b. 22. "South's Sermons": Robert South (1633–1716). His sermons were printed variously between 1678 and 1744.—*Credat Judaeus Apella!*—Let the Jew Apella believe!

648. b. 42. "Bishop Berkley and Tom Paine": George Berkeley (1685–1753), author of *Principles of Human Knowledge* (1710), taught that the external world is not material, but an idea of God manifest to the human mind. He is significant in our period as one denying materialism.—Thomas Paine (1737–1809), author of *Common Sense* (1776) and *The Rights of Man* (1791, 1792), was a patriot of humanity. It is said that his words were as instrumental to the success of the American Revolution as were the guns of Washington.

649. b. 14. "he has somewhere told himself": Cf. *Biographia Literaria* X.

649. b. 25. "that other Vision of Judgment": Byron's satire on Southey was published in Leigh Hunt's *Liberal*, No. 1. (See text, p. 372.) The ironic reference to "the Bridgestreet Junto" is to an association for the suppression of seditious publications.

650. a. 11. "Tom Jones and the adventure of the muff": See X. v of *The History of Tom Jones* (1749) by Henry Fielding (1707–1754).

650. a. 33. "Paul and Virginia": *Paul et Virginie* (1788), by Jaques Henri Bernardin St. Pierre (1737–1814).

650. a. 46. "Camilla": The third novel by Madam D'Arblay (née Frances Burney, 1752–1840), published in 1796.

651. a. 4. "the ballad of Betty Foy": These and the other titles mentioned are among the *Lyrical Ballads* (1798).

651. b. 27. "Monk Lewis": Matthew Gregory Lewis (1775–1818), called Monk Lewis because of his novel *The Monk* (1795). His play, *The Castle Spectre*, was produced at Drury Lane on Dec. 14, 1797.

652. b. 54. "Death of Abel": *Tod Abels* (1758) by Solomon Gessner (1730–1788), Swiss poet.

653. a. 41. "Junius": The "nobody at all" (stat nominis umbra) whose satirical *Letters* appeared in *The Public Advertiser* from Jan. 21, 1769 to Jan. 21, 1772. See 381. b. 585.

653. a. 50. "Caleb Williams": The first novel by William Godwin (1756–1836), author of *Political Justice* (1793).

653. b. 48. "Mr. Elliston": Robert William Elliston (1774–1831), an actor.

ON POETRY IN GENERAL

655. a. 21. "Angelica and Medoro": Characters in the *Orlando Furioso* (1516) of Ludovico Ariosto (1474–1533).

655. a. 35. "Plato's philosophical Republic": It is in Book X of *The Republic* that Plato suggests banishing the poets.

655. b. 21. "according to Lord Bacon": See *The Advancement of Learning* (1605) II. xiii.

657. a. 42. "as Mr. Burke observes": Edmund Burke (1729–1797), in *Our Ideas of the Sublime and the Beautiful* (1756).

658. b. 50. "Doctor Chalmers's Discourses": Thomas Chalmers (1780–1847) wrote *A Series of Discourses on the Christian Revelation, viewed in connection with Modern Astronomy* (1817).

659. a. 14. "Macbeth—for the sake of the music": Henry Purcell (1658?–1695) wrote the music for D'Avenant's version of *Macbeth* produced in 1672.

659. a. 19. "Beggar's Opera": A popular songplay written by John Gay (1685–1752) in 1728.

661. a. 10. "Addison's Campaign": Joseph Addison (1672–1719) wrote *The Campaign* in 1704 to celebrate Marlborough's victory at Blenheim.

662. a. 8. "caput mortuum": A death's head.

662. a. 23. "Ossian": In 1760 James Macpherson (1738–1796) published *Fragments of Ancient Poetry collected in the Highlands."*

ON THE LIVING POETS

665. a. 53. "Darwins—Hayleys—Sewards": Erasmus Darwin (1731–1802), author of *The Loves of the Plants* (1789) and *The Botanic Garden* (1791), the latter poem having been suggested by lines written by Anna Seward (1747–1809). See Carl Henry Grabo's *A Newton Among Poets* (1930) iii, iv.— William Hayley (1745–1820) wrote *The Triumphs of Temper* (1781).

666. a. 3. "Mrs. Leicester's School": Narratives by Charles and Mary Lamb, 1806.

666. a. 28. "Barrow's Sermons": Isaac Barrow (1630–1677). His sermons were published after his death, from 1683 to 1687.

666. a. 47. "Remorse, Bertram,—Fazio": Plays respectively by S. T. Coleridge (1813), C. R Maturin (1816), and Dean Milman (1815)

666. b. 45. "Della Cruscan": An affected style satirized by William Gifford (1756–1826) in *The Baviad* (1794) and *The Maeviad* (1795).—See note 518. a. 43.

667. a. 28. "Campbell's Pleasures of Hope": Thomas Campbell (1777–1844), author of *Pleasures of Hope* (1799).

667. a. 47. "curiosa infelicitas": Infelicity of expression arising from care. Petronius had applied to Horace the expression *curiosa felicitas*. In other words, Campbell, unlike Horace, is an incapable artist.

667. b. 24. "Tutus nimium, timidusque procellarum": Too timid, he fears the storms. See Horace, *De Arte Poetica* 28.

668. a. 19. "Nec Deus intersit, nisi dignus vindice nodus": Let no god be present, unless there be a knot worthy of one to untie it. Horace is speaking against the over-use of the Deus ex Machina. See *De Arte Poetica* 191.

670. b. 42. "Westall's pictures": Richard Westall (1765–1836) was an illustrator of the works of the poets.

672. a. 24. "Coryate's Crudities": Thomas Coryate (1577–1617) wrote *Coryate's Crudities* (1611) and *Coryate Crambe* (1611).

673. a. 35. "Anti-Jacobin Review": The reference should be to *The Anti-Jacobin*. At the time of writing *Wat Tyler* (1794) Robert Southey (1774–1843) was a radical. He later became a conservative.

673. a. 52. "Rejected Addresses": These were written by Horace and James Smith in 1812. Shelley, who had given up his early admiration for Southey, ordered a copy from Thomas Hookham on Jan. 31, 1813.

673. a. 53. "Sir Richard Blackmore": He was the court physician to William and Anne, and the author of sixty volumes of epic verse.

674. a. 40. "His Conciones ad Populum, watchman, &—Friend": These are respectively two Addresses, a weekly Miscellany, and a weekly Paper.

MR. COLERIDGE

676. b. 13. "Elia": See the *Essays of Elia* (1820, 1825) by Charles Lamb (1775–1834). Note text, p. 642.

676. b. 36. "Hartley's tribes": The reference is to the associationism of David Hartley (1705–1757). Both Coleridge and Wordsworth as young men were influenced by Hartley's *Observations on Man* (1749). See *Presiding Ideas in Wordsworth's Poetry* (1931), by Melvin M. Rader.

676. b. 46. "Dr. Priestley": Joseph Priestley (1733–1804), author of *Disquisitions Relating to Matter and Spirit* (1777).

677. a. 3. "Malebranche": Nicolas Malebranche (1638–1715), author of *De la Vérité* (1674). —The congeries of names continued in this paragraph, intended to show the variety of Coleridge's reading, cannot be dealt with in limited notes.

677. a. 15. "hortus siccus": A dry garden.

679. a. 36. "Pas de trois": A dance movement executed by three people.

679. a. 49. "Pingo in eternitatem": I paint in the eternal.

MR. WORDSWORTH

680. b. 7. "Nihil humani a me alienum puto": I think nothing human alien to me. See Terence, *Heautontimorumenos* I. i.

682. b. 40. "Milton's wish": See *Paradise Lost* VII. 31.

683. a. 17. "toujours perdrix": Always partridge; too much of a good thing.

684. a. 20. "Drawcansir": A character in George Villier's (1627–1688) *The Rehearsal,* a play produced at the Theatre Royal on Dec. 7, 1671. Drawcansir burlesques Almanzor in Dryden's *The Conquest of Granada* (1670), threatening to slay "both friend and foe."

SIR WALTER SCOTT

685. a. 48. "laudator temporis acti": A praiser of time past. See Horace, *De Arte Poetica* 173.

686. a. 34. "Mr. John Scott": Scott, born in 1783, became the able editor of *The London Magazine*. In 1821 he was killed in a duel with one Christie, representative of John Lockhart, son-in-law of Sir Walter Scott.

687. a. 52. "Tale of a Tub": A satire written by Jonathan Swift (1667–1745) in 1698. It was Martin, not Peter, who "at one twitch brought off a large handful of points." See Section VI.

687. b. 16. "Auld Reekie": Edinburgh.

687. b. 29. "Mr. Constable": Archibald Constable (1774–1827), in whose failure Sir Walter Scott was involved. See text, p. 243.

688. a. 12. "Parson Adams": A character in Henry Fielding's *History of the Adventures of Joseph Andrews and His Friend Mr. Abraham Adams* (1742). The eccentric William Young was the original.

690. b. 15. "Mr. Mac-Adam": John Loudon McAdam (1756–1836), a Scottish engineer after whom macadam roads are named.

690. b. 18. "Mr. Peel's Police—Bill": Through Peel's efforts the London Metropolitan Police were established in 1829.—Newgate is a prison.

LORD BYRON

694. b. 49. "the Liberal": Only four numbers of this quarterly, established in Italy by Byron, Shelley, and Hunt, were issued (1822, 1823).

695. a. 41. "Mr. Bowles": William Lisle Bowles (1762–1850) through his *Sonnets* (1748) influenced not only Keats but other young writers of the early nineteenth century.

695. b. 13. "Scrub in the farce": A minor character in *The Beaux' Stratagem* (1707), by George Farquhar (1678–1707).

696. b. 9. "The first Vision of Judgment": Robert Southey's *Vision of Judgment* was mocked by Byron's of 1822. See note 649. b. 25.

PERCY BYSSHE SHELLEY

697. b. 48. "he was all air": Cf. text, pp. 519–542.
—In this review, as well as in his review of the *Biographia Literaria* (see text, p. 775), Hazlitt does himself little credit. P. G. Patmore suggests in *My Friends and Acquaintance* III. 136 that Hazlitt was not familiar with Shelley's poetry.

699. a. 9. "Antiquitas seculi Juventas mundi": What we call antiquity was the youth of the world.

700. a. 21. "Mr. Shelly [*sic*] died": He was drowned off Via Reggio on July 18, 1822. In one pocket of his coat was found a volume of Sophocles, in another "a volume of Mr. Keats's poetry."

700. a. 40. "a third": Byron died at Mesolonghi on April 19, 1824.

MR. JEFFREY

701. b. 21. "An article—on Don Pedro Cevallos": See Vol. XIII. 15. Four months later, in February, 1809, the first number of the *Quarterly* appeared.

702. b. 22. "pleno ore": With a full mouth; that is, liberally.

702. b. 33. "Mr. Stuart Rose": William Stuart Rose (1775–1843) translated Ariosto between 1823 and 1831.

703. a. 47. "Mr. Malthus System": Malthus taught that there was a correlation between population and means of subsistence. See Hazlitt's *A Reply to the Essay on Population by the Rev. T. R. Malthus* (1807).

705. a. 13. "au fait": Expert, well instructed.

LEIGH HUNT

WHAT IS POETRY

708. b. 39. "sleeping Angelica": See *Orlando Innamorato* I. iii. 69.

708. b. 41. "Parea che l'erba le [a lei] fiorisse intorno, E d'amor ragionasse quella riva!"—The grass seemed to flourish about her, and the river to speak of love.

709. a. 51. "the story of Peter Wilkins": Written in 1750 by Robert Paltock (1699–1767).

710. a. 21. "Hobbes—in his letter": Cf. 76. b. 5.

710. a. 39. "Orlando Furioso": Cf. 514. a. 6.

710. b. 25. "his domestic namesake": A reference to the parlor poetry of Pope.

713. b. 34. "Ossian": See note 662. a. 23.

713. b. 37. "Gesner's Death of Abel": See note 652. b. 54.

713. b. 49. "The author of Telemachus": François de Salignac de la Mothe Fénelon (1651–1715).

722. a. 41. "Sir Walter Raleigh": The verses were these from *A Vision upon this conceipt of the Faery Queene*, 6–8.
"All suddenly I saw the Faery Queene;
At whose approach the soul of *Petrarke* wept,
And from thenceforth those graces were not seene."

POEMS BY JOHN KEATS

725. a. 21. "Cowper": William Cowper (1731–1800), due to mental infirmity, withdrew from the world. Since it was not his practice to read his contemporaries, his work bore unusual evidences of independence.

726. b. 18. "Peter Pindar": John Wolcot, who assaulted William Gifford.

729. b. 43. "a mighty soul": John Keats was small in stature. Cf. the lines of Noodle in Henry Fielding's *Tom Thumb the Great* I. i. 27, 29:
"Tho' small his body be, so very small . . .
Yet is his soul like any mountain big."
The "envious and ignorant numskulls" may

well be John Gibson Lockhart and John Wilson Croker. See text, pp. 836 ff.

THE REVOLT OF ISLAM,—A POEM

732. b. 24. "Carnage is God's daughter": See Wordsworth's *Thanksgiving Ode*, Jan. 18, 1816, satirized by Byron in *Don Juan* VIII. ix. 6–8. Wordsworth omitted the obnoxious verse in late editions of his poems.

735. a. 24. "Dante": Leigh Hunt was a careful student of Dante, as his marginalia in the copy now owned by Mr. Luther A. Brewer of Cedar Rapids, Iowa, will attest.

ROSALIND AND HELEN

736. a. 34. "Mary Woolstonecraft's opinion": The point is that Helen had not married the man whom she loved. See note 647. b. 9.

THE QUARTERLY REVIEW

738. a. 4. "Story of Rimini": A poem (1816) by Leigh Hunt, supposed to have a deleterious effect upon the style of his friends Keats and Shelley.

738. b. 18. "Grildrig": Glumdalclitch's pet name for Gulliver. See *Gulliver's Travels* (1726) II. ii, by Jonathan Swift (1667–1745). Giffard was the infamous William Gifford, editor of the *Quarterly Review* and for a long time supposed to be the author of the article written by John Wilson Croker (see text, p. 837). For a taste of Hazlitt's attack, see text, p. 627; for Shelley's, see lines 238 and 316 of *Adonais*, text, p. 467. Cf. note 470. a. 151.

739. a. 42. "a sealed book": Cf. 823. b. 44. See also Bennett Weaver: *Toward the Understanding of Shelley* (1931).

ON MR. SHELLEY'S NEW POEM

744. a. 26. "caviare": Pickled sturgeon roe. See *Hamlet* II. 457.
745. a. 16. "Urania": Urania Aphrodite of Plato's *Banquet* 180.
746. b. 42. "Scribes, Pharisees, and Hypocrites": See *Matthew* 23.
747. a. 9. "Rev. Mr. Milman": Henry Hart Milman (1791–1868), author of *Fazio* (1815).

ON DON JUAN

748. a. 30. "poor Pedrillo": Don Juan's tutor; hence Juan's nice preference for bamboo.

COLERIDGE

750. b. 40. "Bishop Percy": Thomas Percy (1729–1811), compiler of *Reliques of Ancient English Poetry* (1765).

THOMAS DE QUINCEY

SAMUEL TAYLOR COLERIDGE

751. a. 26. "Professor Wilson": John Wilson (1785–1854), friend of Wordsworth, professor at the University of Edinburgh, and the "Christopher North" of *Blackwood's*. See text, p. 770.
752. a. 45. "mauvaise honte": bashfulness.

WILLIAM WORDSWORTH

754. a. 19. "Mr. Ferrier": Probably James Frederick Ferrier (1808–1864).
755. a. 20. "epithalamia": See the Four Hymns (1596).
756. b. 42. "Dampier": William Dampier (1652–1715).

PERCY BYSSHE SHELLEY

759. b. 49. "Mr. Gilfillan": Robert Gilfillan (1798–1850), Scottish poet.

761. a. 18. "coup d'essai": A first attempt.
761. b. 2. "rejecting him forever": The University of Oxford has attested its appreciation of Shelley by a monument erected in University College, of which the poet was a member.
762. b. 6. "talis cum sis, utinam noster esses": Since you are such a man, would you were one of ours.

JOHN KEATS

763. b. 3. "Mr. Gifford": Cf. 738. b. 18 and note 470. a. 151.

WILLIAM HAZLITT

764. b. 15. "Foster": John Foster (1770–1843), essayist.
764. b. 31. "fallentis semita vitae": The way of the hidden life.

THE CRITICAL REVIEWS

SAMUEL TAYLOR COLERIDGE

771. b. 2. "Lord Stanhope": See the sonnet *To Lord Stanhope*, printed in the *Morning Chronicle* of Jan. 31, 1795, and Coleridge's letter *anent* to Miss Cruikshanks (1807).
772. a. 37. "Darwinian taste": See 665. a. 53 and "dulcia vitia" of 47. a. 16.
772. b. 35. "Cowper's Task": See 725. a. 21.—*The Task* (1785).
775. a. 52. "Purchas's Pilgrims": Samuel Purchas (1577–1626), author of *Purchas: His Pilgrimage* (1613). Both Coleridge and Wordsworth were given to reading books on travel.
776. b. 3. "Joanna Southcote": An aged lunatic who died in 1815. See *The Vision of Judgment* 376. a. 224.
777. a. 2. "Ossian": See 662. a. 23.
777. b. 3. "Fannii and Fanniae": John Hervey (1696–1743), an English writer, was called "Lord Fanny" because of his effeminacy.
779. a. 21. "non tibi spirat": It does not exist for you.
779. b. 26. "pari materia": Equal or like matter.
780. a. 24. "Captain Medwin": Thomas Medwin, a cousin of Shelley. His *Life of Shelley* appeared in 1847.

WILLIAM WORDSWORTH

782. a. 16. "Gray—Mason": The reference is to verse 1 of *The Epitaph* concluding the *Elegy* (1751) by Thomas Gray (1716–1771).—William Mason (1725–1797) was a poet and the author of a Life of Gray (1774).
782. b. 14. "great apostle of Geneva": Jean Jacques Rousseau (1712–1778).
782. b. 44. "horesco referens": I shudder to bring their names forward,—that is, in comparison.
783. a. 1. "Thalaba": A poem by Robert Southey, written in 1801.
783. a. 40. "to adapt to the uses": Let the student note carefully just what Wordsworth does say on this matter. See *Preface*, p. 192.
784. b. 16. "qu'il mourut": That he die.
785. b. 4. "influence of necessity": See *Political Justice* (1793) by William Godwin (1756–1836). Cf. 653. a. 50.
787. a. 23. "gradus ad Parnassum": A step to Parnassus.
792. a. 10. "read Pier's Plowman's Creed": See 65. b. 39.
794. a. 34. "terra Australis": Southern land.
795. b. 18. "et hoc genus omne": And all that tribe. The writers mentioned are of no worth,

such as John Pomfret (1667–1703), author of *The Choice* (1699).

799. a. 7. "Carnage the Daughter": See note 732. b. 24.

LORD BYRON

802. a. 19. "an intruder into the groves of Parnassus; he never lived in a garret": See Samuel Johnson's Essay No. 117 in *The Rambler* of Tuesday, April 30, 1751.

802. a. 33. "Newstead Abbey": The ancestral home of the Byrons. See text, p. 293.

802. a. 35. "Sancho": The squire in Cervantes's *Don Quixote*.

803. a. 10. "l'envoy of Ovid": Publius Ovidius Nasso (43 B.C.–17 A.D.) was a Roman poet banished for alleged misconduct. The reference may be to the *Tristium Liber Primus* of his *Tristia*.

804. a. 7. "his revenge": *English Bards and Scotch Reviewers* (1809).

805. a. 21. "Minuit praesentia famam": His presence diminished his reputation.

807. a. 9. "Salvator": Rosa Salvator (1615–1673), Italian painter.

807. b. 53. "the grave of Churchill": Charles Churchill (1731–1764), author of *Night* (1761) and *The Ghost* (1762).

817. b. 42. "an apostle of Satan": The reference is to Southey's appelative "Satanic." See Southey's Preface to *A Vision of Judgment:* "The school which they have set up may properly be called the Satanic school." See also Byron's rejoinder in his Preface to *The Vision of Judgment.*

818. a. 18. "Tom Jones' affair": See Book XIII of *Tom Jones* by Henry Fielding.

PERCY BYSSHE SHELLEY

820. a. 3. "unfortunate wife": See text, p. 392, and Mark Twain: *How to Tell a Story, and Other Essays* (1905).

820. a. 42. "Bentley": Richard Bentley (1662–1742), author of *Remarks on a Latin Discourse on Freethinking* (1743).

820. b. 40. "industrious knot of authors": The attack here is really against Leigh Hunt. Cf. 823. a. 43. The remark is as untrue as it is mean.

822. a. 26. "Plures in omnibus rebus, quam in dicendo admirabiles": More men are worthy of admiration in all pursuits, than in oratory.

822. a. 35. "Archimago": A character in Edmund Spenser's *The Faerie Queene* (1590–1596).

822. b. 7. "Mr. Malthus": Thomas Robert Malthus (1766–1834), author of the *Essay on the Principle of Population* (1798). Cf. 703. a. 47.

822. b. 10. "Political Justice": See 653. a. 50 and 785. b. 4.

823. b. 43. "Lucretius": Titus Lucretius Carus (96?–55 B.C.), a Roman poet whose *De Rerum Natura* was much read between 1750 and 1825.

824. b. 30. "Satan reproving Sin": *Paradise Lost* II 650.

828. b. 25. "Moschus": See Moschus's *Lament for Bion*. Cf. 830. a. 2.

829. b. 40. "Cockaigne": An imaginary land of idle luxury. The appellation was satirically used to describe London and its suburbs. See text, p. 834, Keats II.

829. b. 43. "Grub Street Empire": A London street "much inhabited by writers." It is now called Milton Street.

829. b. 48. "Boccacio—the Italian Priapus": Giovanni Boccaccio (1313–1345) was an Italian story writer. He is associated with Priapus, the son of Dionysus and Aphrodite, because Maginn wishes to impute indecency to Boccaccio and to Keats.

832. a. 11. "Prometheus of Mr. Shelley": See Shelley's Preface and Mary Shelley's Notes.

832. b. 45. "Delphic laurel": The reference is to the prophets of Delphi who pronounced upon the meaning of the inspired words of the priestess Pythia.

JOHN KEATS

835. a. 9. "Cockney School": See 829. b. 40.

835. a. 20. "Ariosto, through the medium of Mr. Hoole": Ludovico Ariosto (1474–1533), an Italian poet, was translated by John Hoole in 1773–1783.

835. a. 41. "Highgate-hill — Serpentine River": These are within the environs of London.

835. b. 8. "the blasphemies of the Encyclopaedie": See *Encyclopédie ou Dictionnaire raisonné des Sciences, des Arts, et des Métiers* (1751–1772). This work essentially undermined orthodox dogma.

835. b. 45. "Lessing": Gotthold Ephraim Lessing (1729–1781), German critic and dramatist.

836. b. 45. "poet of Rimini": Leigh Hunt. See 738. a. 4.

837. a. 4. "pauca verba": Few words.

837. a. 9. "back to the shop Mr John": Keats was a trained physician.

838. a. 31. "boutsrimés": Riming words proposed to fill out verses.

839. b. 11. "Oliver—Castles": Conservatives supported by the writers of *The Quarterly Review*.

839. b. 25. "Kirk White": Henry Kirke White (1785–1806), a young Cambridge poet who died of epilepsy.

POETRY

INDEX TO FIRST LINES

PROSE

INDEX